2021
STATE TAX
Handbook

Wolters Kluwer Editorial Staff Publication

Wolters Kluwer

Wolters Kluwer Editorial Staff Publication

Editors .... Timothy Bjur, J.D., Brian Nudelman, J.D.
Production .... Ravikishore. M, Shashikant. G

ISBN: 978-0-8080-5509-9

2700 Lake Cook Road
Riverwoods, IL 60015
800 344 3734
CCHCPELink.com

Printed in the United States of America

FSC www.fsc.org MIX From responsible sources FSC® C099992

Preface

The CCH *State Tax Handbook* provides readers an overview of the taxation scheme of each state and the District of Columbia, as well as multistate charts on income tax, sales and use taxes, property tax, and practice and procedure. The book is set out in five parts that together give an overall picture of the states' levies, bases and rates, principal payment and return dates, and other important tax information on major taxes.

In the first portion, the book details the taxing authorities for each jurisdiction and taxes governed by each office. Also included are uniform outlines of each jurisdiction's overall taxation system. The CCH STATE TAX GUIDEBOOK series should be consulted for additional details.

The second and third portions of the book are comprised of multistate charts relating to income tax (corporate and personal) and sales and use tax. The charts cover discrete issues for income tax, such as filing extensions and depreciation, and for sales and use tax, such as manufacturing exemptions and sales for resales.

The fourth portion of the book contains multistate charts addressing property tax issues, including personal property rendition filing requirements and administrative appeals.

Finally, the fifith portion features multistate charts concerning practice and procedure issues, such as electronic filing options and requirements and estimated taxes. Parts of this publication are compiled from the CCH STATE TAX GUIDE, MULTISTATE CORPORATE INCOME TAX GUIDE, MULTISTATE PROPERTY TAX GUIDE, and MULTISTATE SALES TAX GUIDE. All material in the *State Tax Handbook* is current as of December 3, 2020, unless otherwise noted.

December 2020

Table of Contents

Page

Information by State

Information by State—Introduction 11
Taxes by State 13

Alabama 13
Alaska 17
Arizona 20
Arkansas 24
California 30
Colorado 36
Connecticut 39
Delaware 44
District of Columbia 48
Florida 50
Georgia 55
Hawaii 58
Idaho 62
Illinois 66
Indiana 71
Iowa 74
Kansas 77
Kentucky 80
Louisiana 83
Maine 86
Maryland 89
Massachusetts 92
Michigan 95
Minnesota 99
Mississippi 102
Missouri 106
Montana 109
Nebraska 113
Nevada 115
New Hampshire 117
New Jersey 120
New Mexico 124
New York 128
North Carolina 134
North Dakota 138
Ohio 141
Oklahoma 146
Oregon 149
Pennsylvania 153
Rhode Island 157
South Carolina 159
South Dakota 161
Tennessee 165
Texas 168
Utah 171
Vermont 174
Virginia 178
Washington 181
West Virginia 184
Wisconsin 188
Wyoming 191

Income Taxes

Income Taxes—Introduction 193
Table of 2020 Corporate Income Tax Rates 195
Personal Income Table of 2020 Rates 203
Alternative Minimum Tax 220
Amended Return Deadline for Reporting Federal Changes—C Corporations 225
Amended Return Deadline for Reporting Federal Changes—Partnerships, LLPs, and LLCs 230
Amended Return Deadline for Reporting Federal Changes—S Corporations 235
Amended Return Forms—C Corporations 240
Amended Return Forms—Partnerships, LLPs, and LLCs 244
Amended Return Forms—S Corporations 247
Apportionment Formulas 251
Apportionment—Airlines 256
Apportionment—Athletics 260

Apportionment—Construction 263
Apportionment—Financial Corporations 266
Apportionment—Motor Carriers 269
Apportionment—Others 273
Apportionment—Pipelines 279
Apportionment—Railroads 282
Apportionment—Ship Transport 286
Asset Expense Election—IRC § 179 289
Bad Debt Deduction 296
Banks and Financial Institutions 298
Business Interest Expenses—IRC § 163(j) 301
Capital Loss Carryovers 305
Combined Reporting Requirements—Elective Combination 309
Combined Reporting Requirements—Mandatory Combinations 312
Composite Returns—Partnerships, LLPs, and LLCs 318
Composite Returns—S Corporations 332
Consolidated Returns 346
Credit for Taxes Paid to Another State—Resident 351
Credit for Taxes Paid to Another State—Nonresident 354
Deadline for Reporting Federal Changes 357
Depletion Deduction 360
Depreciation Rules—IRC § 167, IRC § 168 364
Determining Business and Nonbusiness Income 375
Dividends Received Deduction 380
Due Date for Annual Return 387
E-Filing: Application and Acknowledgement Process—Acknowledgement Process 395
E-Filing: Application and Acknowledgement Process—Application Process 398
E-Filing: Mandates/Options for C and S Corporations 401
E-Filing: Mandates/Options for Individuals 406
E-Filing: Mandates/Options for Partnerships, LLPs, and LLCs 411
E-Filing: PIN Signatures 415
E-Filing: Signature Forms 418
E-Filing: Supported/Accepted Programs—Fed/State E-File Program 422
E-Filing: Supported/Accepted Programs—State Direct E-Filing Program 424
E-Filing: Supported/Accepted Programs—State Online E-Filing 427
E-Filing: Supported/Accepted Programs—State Only Returns 432
E-Filing: Tax Authority Contact Information 434
EFT Requirements and Options (Corporate Income) 439
EFT Requirements and Options (Personal Income) 447
Estimated Tax—S Corporations 450
Estimated Tax for Nonresident Owners—Partnerships, LLCs, and LLPs 455
Estimated Tax Requirements—AIM/ASIM 460
Estimated Tax Requirements—Installments/Forms 462
Estimated Tax Requirements—Safe Harbor Calculation 472
Estimated Tax Requirements—Threshold 480
Estimated Tax Requirements—Underpayment Penalties 483

FDII and GILTI Deduction—IRC § 250	490
Federal Form Attachment Requirements (Corporate Income)	494
Federal Form Attachment Requirements (Personal Income)	502
Federal Income Taxes Paid	513
Federal Return Attachment—Partnerships, LLPs, and LLCs	516
Federal Return Attachment—S Corporations	520
Global Intangible Low-Taxed Income (GILTI)—IRC § 951A	524
Information Returns—Annuities	528
Information Returns—Dividends	530
Information Returns—Due Date	532
Information Returns—Interest	535
Information Returns—Nonemployee Compensation	537
Information Returns—Premiums	539
Information Returns—Rents/Royalties	541
Insurance Companies—Corporation Income Tax	543
Insurance Companies—Premiums Tax	545
IRC Conformity and Taxable Income Starting Point—IRC Conformity	555
IRC Conformity and Taxable Income Starting Point—Starting Point	561
Limitation Periods for Assessment and Refund—Refunds	564
Limitation Periods for Assessment and Refund—Standard Limitation Periods	567
Limitation Periods for Assessment and Refund—Understatements, Fraud, or Failure to File	570
Limited Liability Companies: Recognition of Federal Election	574
Limited Liability Companies: Taxation	576
Lump Sum Distributions	580
Mortgage Interest—IRC § 163(h)	584
Net Operating Loss (Corporate Income)	587
Net Operating Loss (Personal Income)	592
Payment by Credit Card	602
Payroll Factor Rules	605
Property Factor Rules—Owned Property	611
Property Factor Rules—Rented Property	617
Public Utilities	622
Qualified Business Income—IRC § 199A	625
Reciprocal Personal Income Tax Agreements	628
Related Party Expense Addback Requirements	630
Repatriation or Transition Income—IRC § 965	642
Return Due Dates	648
Return Filing Extensions (Corporate Income)	653
Return Filing Extensions (Personal Income)	662
S Corporations: Recognition of Federal Election	668
S Corporations: Taxation	671
Sales Factor Rules—Destination Test	676
Sales Factor Rules—Income-Producing Activity and Cost of Performance Sourcing	679
Sales Factor Rules—Throwback or Throwout Rules	683
Social Security Benefits	689
Standard Deduction	693
Starting Point	705

Start-Up and Organizational Expenditures—IRC § 195, IRC § 248, and IRC § 709 707
State, Local, and Foreign Taxes—IRC Sec. 164 710
Taxability of Bond Interest (Corporate Income)—Other States' Bonds 716
Taxability of Bond Interest (Corporate Income)—State's Own Bonds 719
Taxability of Bond Interest (Corporate Income)—U.S. Bonds 722
Taxability of Bond Interest (Personal Income)—Other States' Bonds 725
Taxability of Bond Interest (Personal Income)—State's Own Bonds . 727
Taxability of Bond Interest (Personal Income)—U.S. Bonds 729
Taxes Paid Deduction—Federal Income Taxes 731
Taxes Paid Deduction—Foreign Taxes Paid 733
Taxes Paid Deduction—State and Local Income Taxes 736
UDITPA Conformity 741
Withholding—Partnerships, LLPs, and LLCs 744
Withholding—S Corporations 750
Withholding Returns and Deposits—Annual Reconciliation 755
Withholding Returns and Deposits—Monthly Deposits 758
Withholding Returns and Deposits—Quarterly Returns 762

Sales and Use Taxes

Sales and Use Taxes—Introduction 767
Sales and Use Tax Rates 769
Administrative Appeals 772
Affiliate Nexus 775
Clothing 781
Collection Discounts Allowed Seller 784
Components of Basis—Bad Debts 788
Components of Basis—Coupons and Cash Discounts 790
Components of Basis—Excise Taxes 794
Components of Basis—Finance Charges 799
Components of Basis—Installation Charges 801
Components of Basis—Installment Sales 803
Components of Basis—Returns and Repossessions 806
Computers: Canned Software—Delivered on Tangible Personal Property 810
Computers: Canned Software—Downloaded 812
Computers: Custom Software—Delivered on Tangible Personal Property 815
Computers: Custom Software—Downloaded 818
Computers: Customization of Canned Software 820
Department Appeals 824
Digital Products 827
Direct Pay Permits 831
Drop Shipments 835
Economic Nexus 838
Electronic Filing of Sales Tax Returns 845
Electronic Payment of Sales Tax 848
Exemption Certificate Validity Periods 853
Food and Meals—Caterers 857
Food and Meals—Grocery Food 860
General Nexus Rules and Internet Sales—General Rules 863

General Nexus Rules and Internet Sales—Internet Sales 873
Judicial Appeals 886
Leases and Rentals—Motor Vehicles 890
Leases and Rentals—Tangible Personal Property 893
Manufacturing and Machinery—Machinery 895
Manufacturing and Machinery—Raw Materials 898
Manufacturing and Machinery—Utilities/Fuel 900
Medical Devices 903
Medical Services 906
Medicines 908
Newspapers 910
Occasional Sales 912
Occasional Sales of Motor Vehicles 915
Optional Maintenance Contracts 918
Parts Purchased for Use in Performing Service Under Optional Maintenance Contracts 921
Periodicals 924
Pollution Control Equipment 927
Resale Certificate Validity Periods 932
Return Due Dates 936
Sales for Resale 939
Sales Tax Holiday 942
Services—Generally 947
Services—Janitorial 949
Services—Repair (Labor) 951
Services—Transportation 954
Shipping 957
Statutes of Limitations 962
Trade-Ins 965
Vending Machine Sales—Food 967
Vending Machine Sales—Merchandise 970

Property Tax

Property Tax—Introduction 973
Administrative Appeals 975
Assessment/Valuation Date 982
Construction Work In Progress 984
Freeport Exemptions 989
Intangible Property 995
Legal Basis for Assessment 998
Personal Property Renditions 1001
Real Property Delinquency Date 1004
Real Property Lien Date 1007
Real Property Payment Date 1009
Real Property Tax Year 1012
Tangible Personal Property 1014
Taxation of Inventories 1018

Practice and Procedure

Practice and Procedure—Introduction 1021
Abatement of Penalties and Interest 1023

Installment Payments 1027
Interest Rates on Overpayments—2020 1031
Interest Rates on Underpayments—2020 1034
Interest Rates on Overpayments—2019 1037
Interest Rates on Underpayments—2019 1040
Interest Rates on Overpayments—2018 1043
Interest Rates on Underpayments—2018 1046
Mailing Rules—Delivery Rules 1049
Mailing Rules—Postmark 1051
Managed Audits 1053
Record Retention 1055
State Contacts 1061
Taxpayer Representation 1067
Whole Dollar Reporting 1071

INFORMATION BY STATE

The following pages contain general information regarding the taxes imposed in each state, as well as the relevant tax administration bodies. Topics include a state-by-state listing of taxing authorities and charts summarizing which taxes are imposed by each state, including information on rates and filing/payment dates.

TAXES BY STATE
Alabama

Tax System.—A general property tax for state and local purposes in Alabama is imposed upon real and personal property at uniform rates in the taxing districts where such property is located. The property tax is supplemented by (1) state taxes on franchises, incomes, privileges and occupations, (2) county taxes on privileges and occupations, and (3) municipal licenses and inspection fees. An outline of the Alabama tax system follows:

Tax	Basis—Rates	Due Dates
Business privilege tax.	Business privilege tax imposed on Alabama net worth: taxable income of the taxpayer is less than $1, $0.25 per $1,000; taxable income of the taxpayer is at least $1 but less than $200,000, $1.00 per $1,000; taxable income of the taxpayer is at least $200,000 but less than $500,000, $1.25 per $1,000; taxable income of the taxpayer is at least $500,000 but less than $2.5 million, $1.50 per $1,000; taxable income of the taxpayer is at least $2.5 million, $1.75 per $1,000.	Returns are generally due by the same date as the corresponding federal income tax return. Financial institutions—tax returns are due by the corresponding Alabama financial institution excise tax return. An initial business privilege tax return is due within 2 1/2 months after incorporation, registration, organization, qualification, or beginning doing business in Alabama.
	Minimum tax—$100. Minimum aggregate business privilege tax and corporate shares tax for a financial institution—$0.125 per $1,000 of deposits for a financial institution group with total deposits in Alabama of less than $1 billion; $0.17 per $1,000 of deposits for a group with total deposits in Alabama of $1 billion to $6 billion; and $0.225 per $1,000 of deposits for a group with total deposits in Alabama exceeding $6 billion.	
	Maximum tax for corporations and limited liability entities other than financial institutions, insurance companies subject to insurance premiums tax, electing family limited liability entities, and certain nonprofit corporations—$15,000. Maximum tax for financial institutions and for insurance companies subject to insurance premiums tax—$3 million. Maximum tax for electing family limited liability entities—$500. Maximum tax for certain nonprofit corporations—$100.	
	Short taxable years—Taxpayers having an Alabama taxable year of less than 12 months are subject to a prorated business privilege tax, with a minimum tax of $100.	

Tax	Basis—Rates	Due Dates
General income tax.	Individuals: married filing jointly, 2% of first $1,000 of taxable income, 4% of next $5,000, and 5% of excess over $6,000; all others, 2% of first $500 of taxable income, 4% of next $2,500, and 5% of excess over $3,000. General withholding required.	Individuals—reports and payments due by the same date as the corresponding federal return.
	Corporations: 6.5% of taxable net income.	Corporations—reports and payments due by the same date as the corresponding federal return.
	Financial institutions: 6.5% of taxable net income.	Financial institutions—reports and payments due April 15.
	Certain multistate businesses with gross sales volumes not over $100,000: 0.25% of gross sales receipts.	
General property tax (state tax only).	State rate 0.65% annually.	Returns and payments—individuals and corporations, October 1 (delinquent after December 31). Public utilities, March 1.
Occupancy taxes.	Occupancy tax—5% in mountain lakes areas (Blount, Cherokee, Colbert, Cullman, DeKalb, Etowah, Franklin, Jackson, Lauderdale, Lawrence, Limestone, Madison, Marion, Marshall, Morgan and Winston counties); 4% in all other counties on renting or furnishing of a room, lodging or accommodations.	Reports and payments—20th of each month for preceding month. An annual report is due on or before 30 days after the end of the tax year.
Alcoholic beverages tax.	Beer 5¢ for each 12 ounces or fraction thereof; liquors & fortified wines, 56% of cost marked up price; vinous liquors, 58% of selling price; table wine, 45¢ per liter on wine containing not more than 16.5% alcohol by volume; fortified wine, $2.42 per liter on wine containing more than 16.5% alcohol by volume	
Gasoline, diesel fuel, lubricating oils taxes.	Gasoline—26¢ per gallon (24¢ prior to October 1, 2020). Diesel fuel—27¢ per gallon (25¢ prior to October 1, 2020). Rates for fuel used to propel aircraft are $0.035 per gallon for jet or turbine fuel and $0.095 per gallon for aviation gasoline.	Reports and payments—suppliers, importers, blenders, permissive suppliers, exporters, entities other than importers: 22th of each month.
	Motor carrier fuel tax—same as gasoline and diesel fuel taxes.	Motor carrier fuel tax—last day of April, July, October, and January.
Severance tax.	Uniform severance—10¢ per ton of sand, gravel, sandstone, granite, shale, clay. Coal severance is also imposed.	Reports—20th of each month.
	Oil and gas—8%[1, 2] (plus 2% conservation tax) of gross value at point of production of oil or gas; 4%[2] for incremental oil or gas production resulting from a qualified enhanced recovery project; 4%[2] for wells producing 25 barrels or less of oil per day or producing 200,000 cubic feet or less of gas per day; 6%[1, 2] for oil or gas produced offshore at depths greater than 18,000 feet below mean sea level.	Oil and gas—15th day of the 2nd month following month of production.

Tax	Basis—Rates	Due Dates
Tobacco stamp and use tax.	Cigarettes—67.5¢ per pack of 20.	Reports—20th of each month; use tax, 10th of each month.
	Cigars, cheroots, and stogies—4.05¢ each; 4¢ per 10 little cigars/filtered cigars; 1.5¢ each filtered cigar.	Payment and returns—wholesalers and retailers, by affixing stamps immediately upon receipt of merchandise; tobacco products—20th of each month.
	Smoking tobacco—4¢ to 21¢ on packages weighing up to 4 ozs. plus 6¢ per oz. over 4.	
	Chewing tobacco—1.5¢ per oz.	
Document filing tax.	Document—Deeds—50¢ for each $500 of property conveyed; mortgages—15¢ for each $100 of indebtedness.	Payment—at time of recording.
Sales and use tax; rental tax.	Sales—general rate, 4%; agricultural, mining, and manufacturing machinery and equipment, 1.5%; food sold through vending machines, 3%; and sales of motor vehicles, mobile homes, and motorboats, 2%. Rentals and leases of tangible personal property are taxed at 4% of gross proceeds, except the tax is 1.5% on vehicle and trailer rentals and 2% on linen and garment rentals. Street and highway contracts are taxed at 5% of gross receipts from public road, highway, and bridge contracts.	Reports and payments—sales, rentals or leases, 20th of each month; 20th day of the month following each calendar quarter for taxpayers owing not more than $200 per month (annually, if total tax does not exceed $10 per month). Taxpayers whose average state sales tax liability was $2,500 or more must make estimated payments on or before the 20th day of each month.
	Use—same as sales tax rates. Basis is sales price of tangible personal property used, consumed, or stored in Alabama.	Reports and payments—use, 20th day of each month.
Public utilities taxes.	Electric or hydroelectric utilities, 2.2% per $1 of gross receipts. Hydroelectric sellers and manufacturers, 2/5 mill per kilowatt hour.	Reports and payments—same as the gross receipts and use tax.
	Express, 2.5% of gross receipts; alternative tax, flat fee based on intrastate miles of transit line used or $4,000, whichever is greater.	
	Freight lines, 3.5% of 30% of value of average number of cars within state for the previous 12 months.	
	All utilities, except electric, telephone, telegraph, railroad, sleeping car and express companies, 2.2% per $1 of gross receipts.	
	Telecommunication services and providers, 6%.	

Tax	Basis—Rates	Due Dates
Insurance companies tax.	Domestic and foreign life insurers are taxed at 2.3%. Individual life insurance policies in a face amount greater than $5,000 and up to $25,000, excluding group policies, 1%. Individual life insurance policies in a face amount of $5,000 or less, excluding group policies, 0.5%. For health insurance, and accident and health insurance for which a separate premium is charged, 1.6%. Health care benefits provided by an employer-sponsored plan for groups with fewer than 50 insured participants, 0.5%. Other insurance premiums or policies other than life, health, or accident health, 3.6%. Property and multi-peril insurance written in fire protection Classes 9 and 10 and mobile homes, mobile homeowners, homeowners and low-value dwelling policies in a face amount of $40,000 or less, 1%. Medical liability insurance, 1.6%. Surplus line brokers, 6%. Independently procured insurance from surplus line insurers, 4%. Foreign companies subject to retaliatory taxes.	Reports—March 1. Payments May 15, August 15, November 15, and March 1.

[1] The rate is reduced by 2% for any well for which the initial permit issued by the Oil and Gas Board is dated on or after July 1, 1988, except for replacement wells if the permit for the original well was dated before July 1, 1988.

[2] The applicable rate is reduced by 50% for a 5-year period from the date production begins for any well for which the initial permit issued by the Oil and Gas Board is dated on or after July 1, 1996, and before July 1, 2002, except for replacement wells if the permit for the original well was dated before July 1, 1996. Thereafter, the tax rates in footnote 1 apply.

Alaska

Tax System.—The Alaska tax system is based primarily on severance, income, and license taxes. In addition to a direct tax on corporate income, many license fees measured by income are imposed. Municipalities and boroughs are the only localities authorized to levy taxes on real and personal property. The personal income tax was repealed on January 1, 1979. The state levies no general property tax. Although Alaska does not impose a statewide sales and use tax, some boroughs and municipalities impose local sales and use taxes. An outline of the tax system follows:

Tax	Basis—Rates	Due Dates
Corporation net income tax.	**Corporation net income tax.**— Taxable income of less than $25,000: 0%; $25,000–$48,999: 2%; $49,000-$73,999, $480 plus 3%; $74,000-$98,999, $1,230 plus 4%; $99,000-$123,999, $2,230 plus 5%; $124,000-$147,999, $3,480 plus 6%; $148,000-$172,999, $4,920 plus 7%; $173,000-$197,999, $6,670 plus 8%; $198,000-$221,999, $8,670 plus 9%; $222,000 or more, $10,830 plus 9.4%. **Personal holding company tax.**—12.6% of apportioned income. **Accumulated earnings tax.**—4.95% of first $100,000 and 6.93% of excess. **Alternative tax on capital gains.**—4.5% for tax years before 2018. **Alternative minimum tax.**—18% of taxpayer's federal alternative minimum tax for tax years before 2018. **Base erosion and anti-abuse tax.**—Taxpayers must pay the base erosion and anti-abuse tax (BEAT) under IRC Sec. 59A for tax years after 2017 if they paid the tax for federal income tax purposes.	**Payment.**—April 15 or 15th day of fourth month after close of fiscal tax year **Return.**—May 15 or within 30 days after federal due date.
Mining license tax.	Net income of taxpayer reported to federal government and royalties from Alaska mining property at following rates: Over $40,000 to $50,000, $1,200 plus 3% of the excess over $40,000; $50,001 to $100,000, $1,500 plus 5% of excess over $50,000; $100,001 or over, $4,000 plus 7% of excess over $100,000.	Reports and payments—April 30 or last day of 4th month following close of fiscal year.
Property tax.	Property is assessed at full and true value. Rates fixed locally to meet budget, maximum of 3% for cities and 2% for second class cities.	Fixed locally.
Oil and gas property tax.	Property used or committed for use in exploration, production, and pipeline transportation of unrefined oil or gas, 20 mills of full and true value. Municipal taxes may be levied on such property.	Returns—may be required. Payment—June 30.
Alcoholic beverages tax.	Excise—Beer, including malt beverages, $1.07 per gal.; wine and liquor, $2.50 per gal. if 21% alcohol or less; and $12.80 per gal. if more than 21% alcohol; cider, $1.07 per gal. if 0.5%-7% alcohol by volume; beer (small breweries), $0.35 per gal. on first 60,000 barrels per year with qualifications.	

Tax	Basis—Rates	Due Dates
Motor fuel tax.	8¢ per gal. of motor fuel sold or otherwise transferred in Alaska. Aviation gasoline, 4.7¢ per gallon; aviation fuel other than gasoline, 3.2¢ per gallon; fuel for watercraft, 5¢ per gallon. Effective July 1, 2015, a surcharge of .95¢/gallon is imposed on refined fuel.	Reports and payments—last day of month for preceding month.
Oil and gas production tax.	For oil and gas produced after December 31, 2013, the annual "production tax value" of the taxable oil and gas as calculated under AS 43.55.160(a)(1) multiplied by 35%. Gross revenue exclusion and per-barrel credit may apply.	Reports and payments—annually, by March 31. Monthly information reports—last day of the month following the month in which the activity occurred.
Fisheries taxes.	Fishery business taxes—Salmon canned at a shore-based cannery, 4.5%; other salmon and all other fisheries resources processed by a shore-based fisheries business, 3%. Fisheries resources processed by floating fisheries business, 5%. Developing commercial fish species processed at shore-based fisheries business, 1%. Developing commercial fish species processed at floating fisheries business, 3%.	Report and payment—March 31.
	Dive fishery management assessment—1%, 2%, 3%, 4%, 5%, 6%, or 7% of the value of fishery resources taken in dive gear, as determined by certain elections.	Payment—Depending on business, due last day of month following end of calendar quarter or March 31 after close of calendar year.
	Fishery resource landing tax—For a developing commercial fish species, 1% of the value of the fishery resource at the place of landing. For an established fish species, 3% of value of fishery resource at place of landing.	Report and payment—Estimated payments due by last day of quarter; final payment due March 31 of following year.
	Regional seafood development tax—Levied on certain species acquired by certain gear types within designated regions, 1% of value.	Report and payment—Commercial fishermen and others file annually, due March 31 of following year; licensed buyers file monthly, due by last day of following month.
	Salmon enhancement tax—Based on region where purchased or exported, 2% or 3% of value.	Report and payment—Commercial fishermen and others file annually, due March 31 of following year; licensed buyers file monthly, due by last day of following month.
	Seafood marketing assessment—0.5% of value of seafood products exported from, processed, or first landed in Alaska if processors/fishermen produce at least $50,000 worth of seafood products during calendar year.	Report and payment—April 1.
Cigarette and tobacco products taxes.	$2 per pack of 20 cigarettes. Cigarettes manufactured by a nonparticipating manufacturer, $2.25 per pack of 20 cigarettes. Tobacco products, other than cigarettes, 75% of the wholesale sales price.	Reports and payments—last day of each month.

Tax	Basis—Rates	Due Dates
Insurance companies tax.	**Domestic and foreign insurers.**—2.7% **Individual life insurers.**—2.7% on premiums up to $100,000, plus .08% (.1% before 2016) on premiums in excess of $100,000. **Hospital and medical service corporations.**—6% on gross premiums less claims paid. **Title insurers.**—1% **Wet marine and transportation insurers.**—0.75% **Surplus lines brokers.**—2.7% on property and casualty premiums, 0.75% on wet marine and transportation premiums, and 1% filing fee on premiums. **Unauthorized insurers.**—3.7%, except 0.75% on wet marine and transportation insurers. **Independently procured insurance.**—3.7%, except 0.75% on wet marine and transportation insurers. Foreign companies subject to retaliatory taxes.	March 1
Vehicle rental tax.	Passenger vehicle tax—10% of the total fees and costs for the lease or rental of passenger vehicles. Recreational vehicle tax—3% of the total fees and costs for the lease or rental of recreational vehicles.	Return and payment—April 30, July 31, October 31, and January 31
Tire fees.	Tire fee—$2.50 per tire on sales of new tires for motor vehicles designed for use on a highway. Studded tires—additional $5 per tire for tires studded with metal studs or spikes sold or installed on a motor vehicle designed for use on a highway (total $7.50 for new studded tires).	Return and payment—April 30, July 30, October 30, January 30.

Arizona

Tax System.—The revenue system of Arizona is based on a general property tax at uniform rates in the taxing district in which the property is located. The property tax is supplemented by taxes on income, occupations, and privileges. An outline of the Arizona tax system follows:

Tax	Basis—Rates	Due Dates
General income tax.	**Tax year 2020:** *Married taxpayers filing jointly and heads of household:* $0 to $54,544 x 2.59% minus $0; $54,545 to $109,088 x 3.34% minus $409.00; $109,089 to $327,263 x 4.17% minus $1,315.00; $327,264 and over x 4.54% minus $2,394.00. *Single filers and married filing separately:* $0 to $27,272 x 2.59% minus $0; $27,273 to $54,544 x 3.34% minus $205.00; $54,545 to $163,632 x 4.17% minus $657.00; $163,633 and over x 4.50% minus $1,197.00. **Tax year 2019:** *Married taxpayers filing jointly and heads of household:* $0 to $53,000 x 2.59% minus $0; $53,001 to $106,000 x 3.34% minus $397.50; $106,001 to $318,000 x 4.17% minus $1,277.30; $318,001 and over x 4.50% minus $2,326.70. *Single filers and married filing separately:* $0 to $26,500 x 2.59% minus $0; $26,501 to $53,000 x 3.34% minus $198.75; $53,001 to $159,000 x 4.17% minus $638.65; $159.001 and over x 4.50% minus $1,163.35.	Returns—April 15 or 15th day of 4th month after close of income year. Payment—Corporations, tax due with return; corporations having a tax liability in excess of credits that is at least $1,000 must make estimated payments by the 15th day of the fourth, sixth, ninth, and 12th months of the tax year. Individuals, tax due with return; estimated tax payments due April 15, June 15, September 15, and January 15 if gross income for preceding year exceeded or gross income for current year is expected to exceed $75,000 ($150,000 if married filing a joint return).
	Withholding required. Corporations and financial institutions—4.9%. Minimum tax: $50.	
General property tax and private car companies tax.	Property tax—sum of state, county and municipal rates fixed to meet budget. If not statutorily prescribed, measured by market value of real and personal property; property is divided into 9 classes and assessed at percentage, depending upon classification.	Property tax—Annual Statements—general business report statement, April 1; railroads and utilities, April 1. Payment—December 31; or 50% by October 1, the remaining 50% by March 1.
	Private car companies tax—levied at a rate that equals the sum of the average rates for primary and secondary property taxes in the taxing jurisdictions for the current year.	Private car companies tax—Report—April 1. Payment—November 1.
	Lease excise tax on government property—based on space and use. Rates adjusted annually by 12/1, posted by 12/15 by Department of Revenue.	Report and payment—December 1.
Alcoholic beverage tax.	Excise—sold at wholesale: spirituous liquor, $3 per gal.; vinous liquor to and including 24% alcohol, 84¢ per gal.; over 24% alcohol, 25¢ per 8 ozs.; malt liquor and hard cider, 16¢ per gal.	

Tax	Basis—Rates	Due Dates
Motor vehicle fuel tax, use fuel tax.	Motor vehicle fuel—18¢ per gallon of motor fuel imported, manufactured, processed or possessed (plus additional 1¢ per gallon LUST tax). Aviation fuel distributors pay an additional 5¢ per gallon tax.	Gasoline and aviation fuel—Reports and payment—on or before 27th day of each month for preceding month.
	Use fuel tax—18¢ per gallon of motor fuel used by a light motor vehicle; 26¢ per gallon for road tractors, truck tractors, and vehicles exceeding 26,000 pounds gross weight, except no use tax on alternative fuels, and 18¢ per gallon on vehicles exempt from gross weight fees. 9¢ per gallon for motor vehicles transporting forest products, no use fuel tax on alternative fuels (eff. 9/1/2012 through 12/31/2024).	Use fuel—collected and remitted by suppliers as advance payments and added to the price of use fuel and to be recovered from the consumer; tax imposed when fuel is imported into state or is removed from terminal or bulk plant for delivery within state.
	Jet fuel excise and use tax—3.05¢ per gallon for the first 10 million gallons; amounts over 10 million gallons are not subject to tax.	Jet fuel taxes—Reports and payments—on or before 20th day of each month.
	Underground storage tank tax—1¢ per gallon of regulated substance placed in a tank.	Returns and payments—March 31.
Severance tax.	Mining—2.5% of net severance base or, if less, of the gross value of production minus production costs.	Returns and payments—same as provided under transaction privilege (sales) tax.
Cigarette, cigar, and tobacco products tax.	Cigarettes—$2.00 per pack of 20.	Reports—cigarettes, 20th day of each month. Distributors of cigars and tobacco products other than cigarettes, 20th day of month following accrual.
	Tobacco products—snuff, smoking tobacco, 22.3¢ per oz.; cavendish, plug or twist, 5.5¢ per oz.; small cigars, 44.1¢ each 20; cigars 5¢ each or less, 21.8¢ each 3; cigars over 5¢, 21.8¢ each.	
Realty transfer fee.	$2 per deed or contract required to be recorded.	Payment—prior to recording the deed or contract.

Tax	Basis—Rates	Due Dates
Transaction privilege (sales) tax and use tax.	Transaction privilege (sales) tax rate: 5.6% of gross income on retail sales, motor carriers, public utilities, telephone and telegraph, railroads and aircraft, oil and gas pipelines, private car lines, newspapers and periodicals, printing, contracting, retailing, restaurants, amusements, personal property rentals; 3.13% of gross income on non-metal mining; 2.5% of gross income on metalliferous mining; 5.5% of gross income on transient lodgings.	Returns and payment—for all taxpayers not filing electronically, returns must received by the Department on or before the second to last business day of the month. Electronic filers must file by the last day of the month by 5:00 PM. Quarterly payments are authorized for taxpayers with annual transaction privilege tax liabilities between \$2,000 and \$8,000. Annual tax payments are authorized for taxpayers whose estimated tax is less than \$2,000. A taxpayer with liability of \$1,000,000 or more in the preceding year for transaction privilege, telecommunication services excise and country excise taxes, or such anticipated liability in the current year must make an annual estimated payment of 50% of total liability for May or for the first 15 days of June, to be paid on June 20. All taxpayers with \$20,000 total annual tax liability are required to make electronic payments.
	Use tax—same rate as sales tax for the same type of transaction or business activity on sales price of tangible personal property purchased from a retailer.	
Telecommunication service excise tax.	Telecommunication service excise tax—20¢ per month. On every public service corporation's gross proceeds of sales or gross income derived from the business of providing exchange access services, 1.1%.	Reports and payments—monthly. Large taxpayers (tax liability of \$100,000 or more) report and pay estimated tax equal to either 1/2 of the tax due for May or the tax due for the first 15 days of June. Payment is due on or before June 20.
Prepaid wireless telecommunications E911 tax.	Prepaid wireless telecommunications E911 tax—0.8% of the gross proceeds of sales or gross income.	Reports and payments—same as provided under transaction privilege (sales) tax.
Water use tax.	Tax on water use—0.65¢ per 1,000 gallons of water.	Reports and payments—same as transaction privilege (sales) tax.

Tax	Basis—Rates	Due Dates
Insurance premiums tax.	1.75% for net general insurance and prepaid legal insurance premiums received for 2020 (1.70% for 2021 and subsequent years); 2.2% for fire insurance premiums (except 0.66% for fire insurance premiums on located in an unincorporated city or town that procures the services of a private fire company); 3% for surplus line brokers, domestic surplus lines insurers, and industrial insureds contracting with unauthorized insurers; 2% for disability insurance, hospital and medical service corporations, prepaid dental plan organizations, health care service organizations, and health care providers of Medicaid services; additional 0.4312% of net premiums from insurance carried on or for vehicles. Foreign companies subject to retaliatory taxes.	Returns and payment—March 1. Insurers owing $50,000 or more for the preceding year must file a report on or before the 15th day of each month from March through August and pay installments for each of those months equal to 15% of the amount required to be paid during the preceding calendar year. Medicaid service providers tax returns and payment—Estimated tax payable quarterly by September 15, December 15, March 15, and June 15. Surplus lines tax returns and payment—semiannually February 15 and August 15, except taxes on surplus lines insurance business covering multistate risks transacted by a broker on behalf of insureds whose home state is Arizona must be remitted with required quarterly statements to the clearinghouse responsible for administering the compact or multistate agreement entered into by the Director.

Arkansas

Tax System.—The revenue system of Arkansas is based on a gross receipts tax, which is supplemented by (1) state taxes, part of the revenue from which in some cases is shared by local governments, on occupations, franchises and privileges, and (2) municipal license taxes and inspection fees that the General Assembly permits the local governments to exact. An outline of the Arkansas tax system follows:

Tax	Basis—Rates	Due Dates
Corporation franchise tax.	Mutual assessment corporations and nonstock corporations are subject to a flat tax of $300.	Reports and payments—May 1. Effective May 1, 2021, payments be remitted with the franchise tax report and submitted to the department with the corporation's income tax return. For corporations not required to file income tax returns, the franchise tax must be remitted with the report on or before May 1 of the reporting year.
	Mortgage loan corporations—0.3% of the corporation's outstanding capital stock apportioned to Arkansas. Minimum, $300. Legal reserve mutual insurance corporations—Assets of less than $100 million, $300. Assets of $100 million or more, $400. Insurance companies—Outstanding capital stock of less than $500,000, $300. Outstanding capital stock of more than $500,000, $400. Other corporations—0.3% of the corporation's outstanding capital stock that is apportioned to Arkansas. Minimum, $150.	

Tax	Basis—Rates	Due Dates
Income tax.	**Tax Year 2019**—Individuals with net income $22,600 up to $80,800: $4,599 or less of net taxable income, the tax rate is 0.75%; at least $4,600, but not more than $9,099, the tax rate is 2.5% minus $80.49; at least $9,100, but not more than $13,699, the tax rate is 3.5% minus $171.48; at least $13,700, but not more than $22,1599, the tax rate is 4.5% minus $308.47; at least $22,600, but not more than $37,899, the tax rate is 5.0% minus $421.46; and $37,900, but not more than $80,799, the tax rate is 6.0% minus $800.45. Individuals with net income over $80,800: $4,599 or less of net taxable income, the tax rate is 0.9%; at least $4,600, but not more than $9,099, the tax rate is 2.5% minus $73.59; at least $9,100, but not more than $13,699, the tax rate is 3.5% minus $164.58; at least $13,700, but not more than $22,599, the tax rate is 4.5% minus $301.57; at least $22,600, but not more than $37,899, the tax rate is 6.0% minus $640.55; and $37,900 and above, the tax rate is 6.9% minus $981.64. Individuals with net income from $79,301 up to $84,600 reduce income tax due by deducting a bracket adjustment amount of: $440 reduction for $79,301 up to $80,300; $340 reduction for $80,301 up to $81,300; $240 reduction for $81,301 up to $82,500; $140 reduction for $82,501 up to $83,600; $40 reduction for $83,601 up to $84,600; or $0 reduction for $84,601 and over. Brackets indexed for inflation annually. **Tax years beginning on and after 2020**—Indexed brackets for 2020 not yet released. For net income under $22,200, rates range from 0% to 3.4%. For net income from $22,200 to $79,300, rates range from 0.75% to 5.9%. For net income over $79,300, rates range from 2% to 6.6%. For tax years beginning on and after 2021, the top rate of 6.6% is reduced to 5.9%.	Returns and payments—Personal income tax returns for the preceding calendar year are due on or before April 15. Corporate income tax returns for the preceding calendar year must be filed before April 15. A corporate income tax return for a fiscal year must be filed on or before the expiration of 3½ months after the end of the period covered. Returns for cooperative associations for the preceding calendar year must be filed before September 15, or on or before the expiration of 8½ months after the end of the period covered if the return is for a fiscal year. If corporation has federal extension, corporation has until federal extension date to file Arkansas returns. Declaration of estimated tax—Corporations or individuals expecting a tax liability of more than $1,000 must file a declaration on Form AR1100ESCT before the 15th day of the 4th month of the taxpayer's income year. The estimated tax may be paid in full at the time the declaration is filed or, if the estimated tax is greater than $1,000, the taxpayer may elect to pay it in four equal installments. Taxpayers must file the declaration and make the first or full estimated tax payment by the 15th day of the 4th month of the income year. Subsequent installment payments for corporate income taxpayers are due by the 15th day of the 6th, 9th, and 12th months of the income year. Subsequent payments for personal income taxpayers are due by the 15th day of the 6th and 9th months of the income year and the 15th day of the first month of the following year.

Tax	Basis—Rates	Due Dates
	Corporations—Through 2020, graduated corporate tax rates are imposed at the following levels on net income not exceeding $100,000: $0 to $3,000—1%; $3,001 to $6,000—2%; $6,001 to $11,000—3%; $11,001 to $25,000—5%; $25,001 to $100,000—6%; $100,001 and above—6.5%. Effective for the tax year beginning on January 1, 2021, the top rate is reduced from 6.5% to 6.2% for income of $100,001 and above. Effective for tax years beginning on or after January 1, 2022, the top rate is further reduced to 5.9% for income of $25,001 and above. Nonresidents and foreign corporations—same except that tax is imposed only on net income earned in Arkansas.	
General property tax.	Sum of county, municipal and school rates fixed to meet budgets. Measured by 20% of true or actual market value of real and tangible personal property. No state levy. Intercounty public transportation carriers—average of levies throughout state.	Returns—Tangible personal property, May 31; utilities, March 1; motor carriers, March 31; private car companies, April 1. Payments—utilities and carriers: 25% 3rd Monday in April, 25% 2nd Monday in June, 50% October 15; others: October 15; optional installment payments for taxpayers besides utilities: 25% 3rd Monday in April, 25% 3rd Monday in July, 50% October 15
Tourism tax.	2% on the gross proceeds or gross receipts derived from (1) the service of furnishing condominiums, townhouses, rental houses, guest rooms, suites, or other accommodations by hotels, motels, lodging houses, tourist camps or courts, property management companies, and any other provider of accommodations to transient guests, (2) camping fees at a public or privately owned campground (except federal campgrounds), and (3) the admission price to tourist attractions. Tourism tax is also imposed on rentals of watercraft, boat motors and related motor equipment, life jackets and cushions, water skis, and oars or paddles by businesses engaged in the rental of watercraft.	Reports and payments—same as other gross receipts taxes.
Alcoholic beverages tax.	Excise—Combined rates (including any gallonage tax and enforcement/inspection tax) for beer and malt beverages are as follows: Beer produced/distributed by a native brewery is taxed at $7.50 per barrel. Malt beverage produced/distributed by a native brewery is taxed at $7.50 per barrel. Malt beverage purchased/distributed by a distributor/ wholesaler (non-native brewery) is taxed at $6.20 per barrel. Wine and Liquor Rates are as follows: $2.50 per gallon of spirituous liquor; $1.00 per gallon of premixed spirituous liquor; 50¢ per gallon of light spirituous liquor; 75¢ per gallon of vinous liquor except native wines; 25¢ per gallon of light wine except native light wine.	

Tax	Basis—Rates	Due Dates
Fuel taxes.	24.5¢ per gallon of motor fuels sold or used, or purchased for sale or use in the state; 28.5¢ per gallon of distillate special fuel sold, used, or consumed in the state; 16.5¢ per gallon of liquefied gas.	Reports and payments—25th day of the month following the reporting month. Reports must be filed, even if no tax is due, until the taxpayer notifies the Director in writing that he or she is no longer liable for the reports. 25th day following each calendar quarter for liquefied gas special fuel interstate users and interstate users of alternative fuels. Last day of the month following each calendar quarter for interstate users of distillate special fuel.
Severance or production tax; oil and gas conservation tax.	Severance—coal, lignite and iron ore: 2¢ per ton (8¢ per ton additional tax on coal). New-discovery gas: 1.5% of market value, applicable to first 24 consecutive months beginning on date of first production from new-discovery gas well, regardless of whether production commenced prior to 2009 (all production attributable to period prior to 2009, will be taxed at rate in effect prior to January 1, 2009) High-cost gas: 1.5% of market value, applicable to first 36 consecutive months beginning on date of first production from high-cost gas well, regardless of whether production commenced prior to 2009 (all production attributable to period prior to 2009, will be taxed at rate in effect prior to January 1, 2009) Marginal gas: 1.25% of market value Other natural gas: 5% Oil - wells producing more than 10 barrels per day: 5% plus a combined additional 25 mills per barrel and an additional 2¢ per barrel Oil - wells producing 10 or fewer barrels per day (includes wells that are used for pressure maintenance or secondary recovery purposes): 4%, plus a combined additional 25 mills per barrel and an additional 2¢ per barrel Pine timber: $0.178 per ton; All other timber: $0.125 per ton. Others: 5% of market value at time and point of severance.	Severance—reports and payment: within 25 days after end of month.
Tobacco products tax.	Cigarettes—total rate of $57.50 per 1,000 cigarettes ($1.15 per pack of 20). The tax may be lower for cities adjoining state lines. Tobacco products—total rate of 68% of manufacturer's selling price. Premium cigars—sum of (1) $0.50 per premium cigar and (2) 2% of manufacturer's invoiced selling price prior to any discount. Cigarette papers—75¢ per package of approximately 32 sheets.	Reports and payments—15th of each month.

Tax	Basis—Rates	Due Dates
Realty transfer tax.	$3.30 per $1,000 of actual consideration on transactions in excess of $100.	Payment—at time of transfer, evidenced by tax stamps.
Gross receipts tax and use tax; utilities' compensating tax.	Gross receipts (sales) tax—6.5% of gross proceeds of retail sales of tangible personal property, utility services, telecommunications services, lodging, cleaning services, cable television services, printing services, photography, other selected services, admissions to places of amusement, and specified digital products or a digital code. Food and food ingredients, 0.125%. Natural gas and electricity sales to a manufacturer for use or consumption directly in the actual manufacturing process: 0.625%. Natural gas and electricity sales to an electric power generator that operates facility using combined-cycle gas turbine technology: 1.625%. Additional local rate may apply to above state rates.	Gross receipts—reports and payments: 20th of each month for preceding month; but if monthly average net sales for preceding calendar year exceed $200,000, 40% of tax on monthly average net sales is due by the 12th and 24th of each month, or 80% by the 24th of each month, with remaining 20% due with the regular report on the 20th day of the following month. If taxpayer's average tax due for the previous fiscal year does not exceed $100 per month, Director may allow quarterly reports and payments due on the 20th day of July, October, January and April. If taxpayer's average tax due for the previous fiscal year does not exceed $25 per month, Director may allow annual reports and payments due on January 20.
	Use tax—6.5% of sales price of tangible personal property, taxable services, and specified digital products or a digital code purchased from outside the state for storage, use, distribution, or consumption within the state.	Use—reports and payments: 20th of each month for preceding month.
Public utilities tax.	Not in excess of 0.4% of gross earnings of public utilities from properties in the state.	Reports—Public utilities, statements due March 31; payment due August 31.
	Natural gas pipeline (greater than 50 miles) transporters, owners, and operators—in proportion to the total pipeline safety program's cost that each transporter's, owner's, or operator's miles of natural gas pipeline in Arkansas, excluding service lines in distribution systems, bears to the total number of miles of pipeline in the state. Each natural gas transporter, owner, or operator of pipeline facilities of fewer than 50 miles must pay a fee equal to the product of 0.0015 multiplied by the total cost of operating the pipeline safety program for the assessment year.	Natural gas pipeline transporters, owners, and operators do not have to submit a certified statement of their gross earnings on or before March 31; instead, they must pay the annual assessment fee on or before June 30.

Tax	Basis—Rates	Due Dates
Insurance companies tax.	Foreign and domestic life and disability, 2.5% of net premiums; other insurers, except wet marine or foreign trade insurers, 2.5% of net premiums. Wet marine and foreign trade insurers, 0.75% of gross underwriting profits. Non-profit hospital and medical service corporations, 2.5% of gross receipts. Surplus lines brokers, 4% of direct premiums written; health maintenance organizations, 2.5%. Legal insurers, 2.5% of gross premiums; Worker's Compensation, up to 3%. Captive insurance companies: 0.25% on first $20 million; 0.15% on the next $20 million; and 0.05% on each dollar above, subject to minimum tax of $5,000, maximum tax of $100,000. Effective October 1, 2019, travel insurance companies: 2.5% of net premiums.	Reports—Annual report, March 1.
	Foreign companies are subject to retaliatory taxation if rates in home state are higher than those in Arkansas, except companies more than 15% of whose stock is owned by an Arkansas corporation.	Payments—Life and disability insurers, wet marine and foreign trade insurance, legal insurance premiums, health maintenance organizations, and workers' compensation carriers, made on a quarterly estimated basis and reconciled annually when the report is filed. Self-insurers tax on workers' compensation, April 1. Unauthorized insurers, within 30 days after the insurance was procured, continued, or renewed. Surplus lines brokers, within 60 days following the end of the calendar quarter during which the insurance was procured. Hospital and medical service corporations, on or before March 1.

California

Tax System.—The California revenue system is based on (1) state taxes on franchises, personal incomes, privileges and occupations, and (2) municipal taxes and inspection fees that the legislature permits the local government to exact. An outline of the California tax system follows:

Tax	Basis—Rates	Due Dates
Corporation franchise tax.	Corporations and LLCs electing to be treated as a corporation, 8.84% of net income derived from business transacted in California. S corporations, 1.5%. Minimum tax, $800. Corporations subject to the corporate income tax are not subject to the minimum franchise tax. A 6.65% alternative minimum tax is imposed.	Corporation franchise tax returns—15th day of 4th month following income year for C corporations; 15th day of 3rd month following income year for S corporations; 15th day of 9th month following income year for agricultural cooperatives. Estimated payment due 15th day of 4th, 6th, 9th, and 12th months (due 15th day of 4th month if estimated tax does not exceed minimum tax).
Corporation income tax.	Direct tax on net income, derived from sources within the state, of corporations not taxable under Bank and Corporation Franchise Tax Act, at same rate as franchise tax (8.84%). A 6.65% alternative minimum tax is imposed.	Corporation income tax returns—15th day of 4th month following income year for C corporations; 15th day of 3rd month following income year for S corporations; 15th day of 9th month following income year for agricultural cooperatives. Estimated payment due 15th day of 4th, 6th, 9th, and 12th months (due 15th day of 4th month if estimated tax does not exceed minimum tax).
Bank and financial corporations tax.	Equal to corporate franchise tax rate plus 2% (10.84%). Minimum tax, $800. For a bank or financial corporation that is an S corporation, 3.5%. An alternative minimum tax is imposed equal to the corporate rate plus 2% (8.65%).	Bank and financial corporations tax returns and payments—15th day of 4th month following income year. Estimated payment due 15th day of 4th, 6th, 9th, and 12th months (due 15th day of 4th month if estimated tax does not exceed minimum tax).
LLC tax.	$800 minimum franchise tax for an LLC doing business in California or that has articles of organization accepted or a certificate of registration issued by the Secretary of State. Annual LLC fees are determined as follows: for California-source income of $250,000 or more but less than $500,000, $900; $500,000 or more but less than $1 million, $2,500; $1 million or more but less than $5 million, $6,000; $5 million or more, $11,790.	LLC tax—15th day of 3rd month following close of taxable year (fiscal year) or March 15 (calendar year)

Tax	Basis—Rates	Due Dates
Personal income tax.	**2020 rates:** For single taxpayers, married filing separately, and fiduciaries: $0 to $8,932, 1%; over $8,932 to $21,175, $89.32 plus 2% of the amount over $8,932; over $21,175 to $33,421, $334.18 plus 4% of the amount over $21,175; over $33,421 to $46,394, $824.02 plus 6% of the amount over $33,421; over $46,394 to $58,634, $1,602.40 plus 8% of the amount over $46,394; over $58,634 to $299,508, $2,581.60 plus 9.3% of the amount over $58,634; over $299,508 to $359,407, $24,982.88 plus 10.3% of the amount over $299,508; over $359,407 to $599,012, $31,152.48 plus 11.3% of the amount over $359,407; and over $599,012, $58,227.85 plus 12.3% of the amount over $599,012. For married couples or registered domestic partners filing jointly and qualifying widow(er): $0 to $17,864 1%; over $17,864 to $42,350, $178.64 plus 2% of the amount over $17,864; over $42,350 to $66,842, $668.36 plus 4% of the amount over $42,350; over $66,842 to $92,788, $1,648.04 plus 6% of the amount over $66,842; over $92,788 to $117,268, $3,204.80 plus 8% of the amount over $92,788; over $117,268 to $599,016, $5,163.20 plus 9.3% of the amount over $117,268; over $599,016 to $718,814, $49,965.76 plus 10.3% of the amount over $599,016; over $718,814 to $1,198,024, $62,304.95 plus 11.3% of the amount over $718,814; and over $1,198,024, $116,455.68 plus 12.3% of the amount over $1,198,024. For heads of households: $0 to $17,876, 1%; over $17,876 to $42,353, $178.76 plus 2% of the amount over $17,876; over $42,353 to $54,597, $668.30 plus 4% of the amount over $42,353; over $54,597 to $67,569, $1,158.06 plus 6% of the amount over $54,597; over $67,569 to $79,812, $1,936.38 plus 8% of the amount over $67,569; $79,812 to $407,329, $2,915.82 plus 9.3% of the amount over $79,812; over $407,329 to $488,796, $33,374.90 plus 10.3% of the amount over $407,329; over $488,796 to $814,658, $41,766.00 plus 11.3% of the amount over $488,796; and over $814,658, $78,588.41 plus 12.3% of the amount over $814,658. Additional 1% tax on income in excess of $1 million.	Returns and payment—April 15 following the close of the calendar year. Taxpayers with a fiscal year different from the calendar year, 15th day of 4th month after close of fiscal year. Partnerships—15th day of 3rd month following close of taxable year (fiscal year) or March 15 (calendar year)

Tax	Basis—Rates	Due Dates
	2019 rates: For single taxpayers, married filing separately, and fiduciaries: $0 to $8,809, 1%; over $8,809 to $20,883, $88.09 plus 2% of the amount over $8,809; over $20,883 to $32,960, $329.57 plus 4% of the amount over $20,883; over $32,960 to $45,753, $812.65 plus 6% of the amount over $32,960; over $45,753 to $57,824, $1,580.23 plus 8% of the amount over $45,753; over $57,824 to $295,373, $2,545.91 plus 9.3% of the amount over $57,824; over $295,373 to $354,445, $24,637.97 plus 10.3% of the amount over $295,373; over $354,445 to $590,742, $30,722.39 plus 11.3% of the amount over $354,445; and over $590,742, $57,423.95 plus 12.3% of the amount over $590,742. For married couples or registered domestic partners filing jointly and qualifying widow(er): $0 to $17,618 1%; over $17,618 to $41,766, $176.18 plus 2% of the amount over $17,618; over $41,766 to $65,920, $659.14 plus 4% of the amount over $41,766; over $65,920 to $91,506, $1,625.30 plus 6% of the amount over $65,920; over $91,506 to $115,648, $3,160.46 plus 8% of the amount over $91,506; over $115,648 to $590,746, $5,091.82 plus 9.3% of the amount over $115,648; over $590,746 to $708,890, $49,275.93 plus 10.3% of the amount over $590,746; over $708,890 to $1,181,484, $61,444.76 plus 11.3% of the amount over $708,890; and over $1,181,484, $114,847.88 plus 12.3% of the amount over $1,181,484. For heads of households: $0 to $17,629, 1%; over 17,629 to $41,768, $176.29 plus 2% of the amount over $17,629; over $41,768 to $53,843, $659.07 plus 4% of the amount over $41,768; over $53,843 to $66,636, $1,142.07 plus 6% of the amount over $53,843; over $66,636 to $78,710, $1,909.65 plus 8% of the amount over $66,636; $78,710 to $401,705, $2,875.57 plus 9.3% of the amount over $78,710; over $401,705 to $482,047, $32,914.11 plus 10.3% of the amount over $401,705; over $482,047 to $803,410, $41,189.34 plus 11.3% of the amount over $482,047; and over $803,410, $77,503.36 plus 12.3% of the amount over $803,410. Additional 1% tax on income in excess of $1 million.	
General property tax.	Rates fixed locally to meet budget. Property is assessed at 100% of full cash value. Intangible property is excluded from the value. The maximum amount of property tax on realty is limited to 1% of full cash value of the property (the 1975-76 assessed value of property is the base value, unless property is newly constructed or has changed ownership) plus taxes or assessments to pay interest and debt on acquisition or improvement of property approved by voters.	Property statements—between January 1 and April 1. Payment—on secured personalty, Nov. 1; on unsecured personalty, January 1; on realty, 1/2 by Nov. 1 and 1/2 by Feb. 1.
Alcoholic beverage tax.	Excise—beer, wine, and sparkling hard cider, $0.20 per gallon; champagne and sparkling wines, 30¢ per gallon; distilled spirits, 100 proof strength or less, $3.30 per gallon; distilled spirits more than 100 proof, $6.60 per gallon.	

Tax	Basis—Rates	Due Dates
Fuel taxes.	Motor vehicle fuel (gasoline) excise tax—July 1, 2020 through June 30, 2021: $0.505 per gallon (excludes AV gas).	Returns and payment—last day of each month following the calendar month the tax liability accrues.
	Diesel fuel excise tax—July 1, 2020 through June 30, 2021: $0.385 per gallon.	Returns and payment—last day of each month following the calendar month the tax liability accrues (quarterly for interstate truckers).
	Aircraft jet fuel excise tax—July 1, 2020 through June 30, 2021: $0.02 per gallon.	Same as motor fuels tax.
	Use fuel—$0.18 per gallon; liquefied petroleum gas (LPG), $0.06 per gallon; compressed natural gas (CNG), $0.0887 per gasoline gallon equivalent of 126.67 cubic feet or 5.66 pounds; liquefied natural gas (LNG), $0.1017 per diesel gallon equivalent of 6.06 pounds; ethanol or methanol, $0.09 per gallon.	Reports and payments—last day of month following each calendar quarter.
	Annual flat rate fuel tax—in lieu of taxes on liquefied petroleum gas, liquid natural gas or compressed natural gas, owners or operators of vehicles using such fuels exclusively in California may pay a tax ranging from $36 for vehicles 4,000 lbs. or less to $168 for vehicles 12,000 lbs. or more.	Annual flat rate—payment due annually.
	Lubricating oil fee—oil manufacturers pay 6¢ for each quart, or 24¢ for each gallon, of lubricating oil (or 3¢ for each quart, or 12¢ for each gallon of 70% re-refined base lubricant) sold or transferred in, or imported into, California.	Reports and payment—due on or before the last day of the month following the end of each quarter.
Severance (oil and gas) tax.	For 2019-2020 fiscal year, $0.565336900 per barrel of oil produced or per 10,000 cubic feet of natural gas produced (rate determined annually based upon estimate of annual conservation costs). As of press time, the 2020-2021 fiscal year assessment rate had not yet been posted by the California Department of Conservation.	Reports—monthly reports due on or before the last day of each month; annual reports for operators that produce oil by unconventional techniques due by March 1. Payment—assessments $10 but less than $500 due July 1 (delinquent after August 15); assessments $500 or more due July 1 (1/2 delinquent after August 15; remaining 1/2 delinquent after February 1).
Timber yield tax.	2.9%	Returns—filed with the CDTFA on or before the last day of the month following each calendar quarter.
Cigarette and tobacco products tax.	Effective July 1, 2020 through June 30, 2021, the cigarette tax rate is $2.87 per 20-pack of cigarettes ($0.1435 per cigarette or 143.5 mills per cigarette) and the tobacco tax rate for all tobacco products other than cigarettes is 56.93% of wholesale cost.	Reports, returns, payments—filing and payment is due by the 25th day of each month.

Tax	Basis—Rates	Due Dates
Sales and use taxes.	Sales—7.25% (total statewide base) of gross receipts from retail sales of tangible personal property. A 1% assessment is imposed, in addition to any sales or use tax imposed, on a person who purchases a lumber product or an engineered wood product. Effective July 1, 2018, through June 30, 2021, the sales and use tax rates for fuels are: 2.25% for motor vehicle fuel (gasoline); 7.25% for aircraft jet fuel; and 13% for diesel fuel.	Returns and payments—quarterly by last day of month following each quarterly period. Prepayments required of taxpayers whose average monthly estimated measure of tax liability is $17,000 or more.
	Use—7.25% (total statewide base) of sales price of tangible personal property purchased for storage, use or consumption.	The qualified use tax of an eligible purchaser is due and payable on or before April 15 following the close of the calendar year in which the liability for use tax was incurred.
	Returns and payments—quarterly returns due by last day of month following each quarterly period. Persons whose estimated taxable receipts average $17,000 or more per month must file a quarterly prepayment report and prepay the tax.	
Energy resources surcharge (electrical).	The surcharge rate is $.00030 per kilowatt-hour. Emergency telephone users surcharge amount for each access line a service user subscribes for use in California, and for each retail transaction of prepaid mobile telephony services purchased in California is $0.30.	Returns and payments from electric utilities are due by the last day of the month following each calendar quarter; telephone surcharge—on or before the last day of the 2nd month of each calendar quarter covering the preceding quarter.
Insurance companies tax.	General insurers—2.35% of gross premiums less return premiums and excluding reinsurance; 0.5% for certain federally exempt pension and profit-sharing plans.	Returns—April 1, except June 15 for ocean marine insurers and March 1 for surplus line brokers.
		Payment—with return April 1 except ocean marine insurers (June 15) and surplus line brokers (March 1). Quarterly prepayments due 4/1, 6/1, 9/1, and 12/1 from insurers whose annual tax for the preceding calendar year was $20,000 or more. Surplus line brokers whose annual tax for the preceding calendar year was $20,000 or more must make monthly installment payments on or before the 1st day of the 3rd calendar month following the month in which business was conducted.

Tax	Basis—Rates	Due Dates
	Surplus line brokers and nonadmitted insurance—3% of gross premiums less return premiums. Ocean marine—5% of portion of underwriting profit apportioned to California on basis of gross premiums. Foreign companies subject to retaliatory taxes.	

Colorado

Tax System.—The revenue system of Colorado is based on a general property tax, assessed uniformly on all property for state, county, city and town, and district purposes. The property tax is supplemented by an income tax and by taxes on privileges and occupants. An outline of the Colorado tax system follows:

Tax	Basis—Rates	Due Dates
General income tax.	Individuals—4.55% of federal taxable income plus alternative minimum tax for tax years commencing on or after January 1, 2020 (excess of 3.47% of Colorado alternative minimum taxable income over flat state income tax rate). For tax years commencing prior to January 1, 2020, rate was 4.63%. Temporary income tax rate reduction to 4.5% for 2019 tax year.	Returns and payments—15th day of 4th month after end of income year. Estimated declaration of tax due on or before the 15th day of the 4th month of the tax year; estimated payments due on or before the 15th day of the 4th, 6th, 9th and 13th (12th for corporations) months of the tax year. Employers with annual withholding liabilities of more than $50,000 are required to pay through electronic funds transfer (EFT).
	Withholding required.	
	Corporations, banks, trust, finance, savings and loan companies and cooperatives—4.55% for tax years commencing on or after January 1, 2020. For tax years commencing prior to January 1, 2020, rate was 4.63%. Temporary income tax rate reduction to 4.5% for 2019 tax year.	
	In lieu of either the corporate income tax or the personal income tax, a qualified taxpayer may pay an alternative tax of 0.5% of gross receipts if required to file a return, the taxpayer's only activity in Colorado is making sales, the taxpayer has Colorado sales of less than $100,000, and the taxpayer does not own or rent real estate in Colorado.	
General property tax.	Sum of state and local rates fixed to meet budget. Based on actual value of real property and tangible personal property. Residential realty is assessed at 7.15% of actual value; all other property is assessed at 29% of actual value.	Returns—Personal property, April 15; industries classified as utilities, by April 1.
		Payment—If $25 or less, April 30; if $25 or more, 1/2 last day of Feb. and 1/2 June 15.
Alcoholic beverage taxes.	Excise tax—malt beverages, 3.2% beer, hard cider, 8¢ per gallon; vinous liquors except hard cider, 7.33¢ per liter (plus 1¢ per liter wine development fee on all wines) (plus additional surcharge on Colorado wines of 5¢ per liter for the first 9,000 liters, 3¢ per liter for the next 36,000 liters, and 1¢ per liter for all additional amounts); spirituous liquors, 60.26¢ per liter.	
	Tax on grapes—$10 per ton.	

Tax	Basis—Rates	Due Dates
Gasoline and special fuel taxes.	Gasoline—22¢ per gallon of motor fuel sold, distributed or used, except 6¢ per gallon on gasoline used in nonturbo-propeller or nonjet engine aircraft and 4¢ per gallon on gasoline used in turbo-propeller or jet engine aircraft (does not apply to air carriers). LNG—12¢ per gallon; LPG/Propane—13.5¢ per gallon; CNG—18.3¢ per gallon.	Gasoline—reports and payments—26th of each month.
	Special fuel tax—20.5¢ per gallon.	Special fuel—26th day of each month.
Severance tax.	Metallic minerals—2.25% of income over $19 million. Molybdenum ore—first 625,000 tons produced by an individual in each quarter of a taxable year not taxed, 5¢ per ton thereafter. Oil and gas—under $25,000 of gross income: 2%; $25,000 to $99,999: $500 plus 3% of excess over $24,999; $100,000 to $299,999: $2,750 plus 4% of excess over $99,999; $300,000 and over, $10,750 plus 5% of excess over $299,999. Oil shale—after the first 180 days of operation; the greater of 15,000 tons per day or 10,000 barrels per day are exempt; 1st year 1% of gross proceeds, 2nd year 2% of gross proceeds, 3rd year 3% of gross proceeds, 4th year and after 4% of gross proceeds.	Returns and payment—molybdenum ore, 15th day of the month following each quarter; all others, 15th day of 4th month after end of year. Oil and gas estimated payments due monthly by electronic filing; all others estimated payments due on the 15th day of April, June, September, and December if annual estimated tax is more than $1,000.
Coal severance tax.	First 300,000 tons produced each quarter are exempt. Over 300,000 at a rate published monthly by the Department of Revenue at https://www.colorado.gov/pacific/tax/severance-tax-legal-research. Credits: 50% credit for coal from underground mines; additional 50% credit for production of lignitic coal.	Reports and payments—annual return 15th day of 4th month following end of tax year; estimated payments due the 15th day of the 4th, 6th, 9th, and 12th month of the taxable year.
Oil and gas conservation tax.	Not to exceed 1.7 mills per $1 of the market value at the well.	Reports and payments—quarterly returns due March 1, June 1, September 1, and December 1.
Cigarette tax; tobacco products tax.	4.2¢ per cigarette (84¢ per pack of 20).	Reports—10th of each month following the month of purchase. Payment—evidenced by affixing stamps.
	Tobacco products—40% of manufacturer's list price.	Reports and payments—20th day of month following the month reported. Payment must accompany return.
Realty conveyance tax.	2¢ per $100 of consideration in excess of $500.	Payment—prior to recording.

Tax	Basis—Rates	Due Dates
Sales and use tax.	2.9% of gross receipts from retail sale of personalty, telephone, telegraph, gas and electric services, meals furnished the public, cover charges and room rentals, or of sales price of personalty purchased for storage, use or consumption. 15% retail (recreational) marijuana sales tax on all sales of retail marijuana and retail marijuana-infused products; however those items are exempt from general state sales tax.	Reports and payments—sales tax, by 20th of each month; use tax, by 20th day of month following month in which cumulative tax due at end of month exceeds $300. If total tax due in a month is less than $300, but more than $15, a quarterly return and payment is due by the 20th day of the month following the reporting period. If total tax due is $15 or less per month, an annual return and payment are due by the following January 20. Wholesale businesses with a sales tax liability of $180 per year or less can file annually, as well. If total tax due in a year is more than $75,000, all state and local taxes must be remitted to the Department of Revenue by electronic funds transfer (EFT). Taxpayers owing less than $75,000 may choose to remit by EFT.
Insurance companies tax.	For companies maintaining a home office or regional home office in the state, 1%. For companies not maintaining a home office or regional home office in Colorado, 2% of gross premiums less reinsurance premiums and, for companies other than life, returned premiums. Captive insurers, the greater of $5,000 or the sum of (a) 0.5% of the first $25 million, plus 0.25% of the next $50 million, plus 0.1% of each dollar thereafter of the direct premiums collected and (b) 0.25% of the first $20 million, plus 0.1% of each dollar thereafter of assumed reinsurance premiums. Unauthorized insurers, 2.25%. Surplus line brokers, 3%. Foreign companies subject to retaliatory taxes.	Reports and payments—March 1. Insurers whose tax exceeded $5,000 for the preceding year pay an estimated tax on the last days of April, July and October and March 1.

Connecticut

Tax System.—Connecticut derives its revenue principally from a corporation business tax, a personal income tax, gasoline taxes, and sales and use taxes and from taxes imposed on specified businesses and privileges. An outline of the Connecticut tax system follows:

Tax	Basis—Rates	Due Dates
Corporation business tax.	Greater of 7.5% of net income, 3.1 mills per dollar of capital holdings (maximum $1 million), or the minimum tax of $250. Connecticut is phasing out the capital base tax beginning after the 2020 tax year. **Corporate tax surcharge.**—10% for tax years beginning before January 1, 2021 if gross income is $100 million or more and tax liability exceeds minimum tax (threshold exception does not apply to mandatory combined reporting groups). **Financial services companies.**—Greater of 7.5% of net income or $250.	Corporation business tax—by fifteenth day of the month next succeeding the due date of the corporation's corresponding federal income tax return for the income year (e.g., May 15 for calendar year taxpayers). Payments of estimated tax due on or before the 15th day of the 3rd, 6th, 9th and 12th months of the income year.

Tax	Basis—Rates	Due Dates
Personal income tax.	**Unmarried individuals and married individuals filing separately.**—3% on the first $10,000 of Connecticut taxable income; Connecticut taxable income over $10,000 but not over $50,000, $300 plus 5% of the excess over $10,000; over $50,000 but not over $100,000, $2,300 plus 5.5% of the excess over $50,000; over $100,000 but not over $200,000, $5,050 plus 6% of the excess over $100,000; over $200,000 but not over $250,000, $11,050 plus 6.5% of the excess over $200,000; over $250,000 but not over $500,000, $14,300 plus 6.9% of the excess over $250,000; over $500,000, $31,550 plus 6.99% of the excess over $500,000. **Heads of households.**—3% of the first $16,000 of Connecticut taxable income; Connecticut taxable income over $16,000 but not over $80,000, $480 plus 5% of the excess over $16,000; over $80,000 but not over $160,000, $3,680 plus 5.5% of the excess over $80,000; over $160,000 but not over $320,000, $8,080 plus 6% of the excess over $160,000; over $320,000 but not over $400,000, $17,680 plus 6.5% of the excess over $320,000; over $400,000 but not over $800,000, $22,880 plus 6.9% of the excess over $400,000; over $800,000, $50,480 plus 6.99% of the excess over $800,000. **Married individuals filing jointly and qualifying widow(er).**—3% of the first $20,000 of Connecticut taxable income; Connecticut taxable income over $20,000 but not over $100,000, $600 plus 5% of the excess over $20,000; over $100,000 but not over $200,000, $4,600 plus 5.5% of the excess over $100,000; over $200,000 but not over $400,000, $10,100 plus 6% of the excess over $200,000; over $400,000 but not over $500,000, $22,100 plus 6.5% of the excess over $400,000; over $500,000 but not over $1 million, $28,600, plus 6.9% of the excess over $500,000; over $1 million, $63,100 plus 6.99% of the excess over $1,000,000. **Trusts or estates.**—6.99% of Connecticut taxable income.	Reports and payments—April 15 or 15th day of the 4th month after close of tax year. Payments of estimated tax due on or before April 15th, June 15th, September 15th, and January 15th. Estimated tax from farming and fishing income due by January 15 of following taxable year.
	A net minimum tax equal to the lesser of (a) 19% of adjusted federal tentative minimum tax, or (b) 5.5% of adjusted federal alternative minimum taxable income is imposed on individuals, trusts and estates subject to the federal alternative minimum tax. Non- and part-year residents pay the same rate but multiplied by the ratio of the adjusted federal tentative minimum tax derived from sources within the state to the adjusted federal tentative minimum tax.	Reports and payments—on or before 15th day of 4th month after close of tax year. Payments of estimated tax due on or before April 15th, June 15th, September 15th, and January 15th.
Property tax.	All municipalities are required to assess property at uniform rate of 70% of true and actual value. Personal property of a telecommunications corporation taxed at state level at the rate of 47 mills, based on 70% of the fair market value of the property.	General property—Municipalities may require payment in a single payment or in equal semiannual or quarterly payments; single payment or first installment due July 1.

Tax	Basis—Rates	Due Dates
Admissions tax and dues or initiation fees tax.	10% admissions tax rate is imposed on admission charges to any place of amusement, entertainment, or recreation. However, the admissions tax rate on certain venues is reduced in two steps: (1) from 10% to 7.5% for sales that occur on or after July 1, 2019; and (2) from 7.5% to 5% for sales that occur on or after July 1, 2020. The lower tax rate applies to: the XL Center in Hartford; Dillon Stadium in Hartford; athletic events presented by a member team of the Atlantic League of Professional Baseball at the New Britain Stadium; Webster Bank Arena in Bridgeport; Harbor Yard Amphitheater in Bridgeport; Dodd Stadium in Norwich; Oakdale Theatre in Wallingford; and events, other than interscholastic athletic events, at Rentschler Field in East Hartford (interscholastic athletic events at Rentschler Field are exempt). The admissions tax rate on events at the Dunkin' Donuts Park in Hartford is first reduced and then eliminated as follows: (1) from 10% to 5% beginning July 1, 2019; and (2) from 5% to 0% (fully exempt) beginning July 1, 2020. The tax rate on admission charges to motion picture shows is 6%. 10% dues or initiation fees tax rate is imposed on any amount paid as dues or initiation fees to a social, athletic, or sporting club.	Reports and payments—due on or before last day of each month for preceding month.
Alcoholic beverages tax.	Excise—beer & cider, $7.20 per barrel; liquor coolers, $2.46 per wine gallon; still wine 21% or less absolute alcohol, 72¢ per gallon (18¢ per gal. if produced by a person who produces not more than 55,000 gallons of wine during the calendar year); sparkling wine and still wine over 21% absolute alcohol, $1.80 per gallon.	
Motor fuel excise tax; motor carrier road tax.	Motor fuels—25¢ per gallon of motor fuel (gasoline) sold, distributed or used. 25¢ per gallon of gasohol sold. Effective July 1, 2020 through June 30, 2021, the diesel fuel tax rate is 44.6¢ per gallon. Liquefied natural gas (LNG) and liquefied petroleum gas (LPG) is taxed at 26¢ per gallon.	Motor fuels—25th of each month.
	Motor carrier road tax—Amount of fuel used in operations within the state—same as motor fuels tax.	Motor carrier road tax—April 30, July 31, October 31, January 31 for preceding calendar quarter.
Cigarette tax; tobacco products tax.	$4.35 per pack of 20.	Report—25th day of each month; unstamped cigarettes, within 24 hours of possession.
	50% of wholesale sales price of tobacco products (tobacco products tax is reduced by 50% on modified risk tobacco products).	Report and payment—25th day of each month.
	$3 per ounce of snuff.	

Tax	Basis—Rates	Due Dates
Real estate conveyance tax; farm and forest land conveyance tax; tax on sale or transfer of controlling interest.	Real estate conveyance tax—state rate of 0.75% plus a municipal tax of 0.25%. The state rate on nonresidential interests (except unimproved land, including farm, forest, and open space land) is 1.25%, and the state rate on residential property transferred for a consideration of $800,000 or more is 0.75% on the first $800,000 of consideration paid, plus 1.25% on the remainder. Beginning July 1, 2020, the real estate conveyance tax rate for sales of residential property in excess of $2.5 million is 2.25% on the portion of the sales price that exceeds $2.5 million.	Payment—upon recording the deed or instrument.
Sales and use tax.	Sales—6.35% of gross receipts of retail sales of tangible personal property and enumerated services. The sales and use tax rate on canned or prewritten software that is electronically accessed or transferred, other than when purchased by a business for use by such business, and any additional content related to such software, is 6.35%. Hotel occupancy, 15%; bed and breakfast establishments, 11%; computer and data processing, 1%; certain luxury goods, 7.75%; rental or leasing of a passenger motor vehicle for 30 consecutive calendar days or less, 9.35%; machinery rental surcharge, 2.75%; tourism account surcharge, $1 per day; and vessels, vessel motors, and trailers used to transport vessels, 2.99%.	Sales and use tax reports and payments—the last day of the month following the end of the applicable period.
	Use—6.35% of sale price of tangible personal property stored, accepted, consumed or used within the state and enumerated services.	Use tax returns and payments are due April 15.
	Computer and data processing services—1%.	
Petroleum products gross earnings tax.	8.1%	Returns and payments—last day of January, April, July, and October.
Public utilities (gross earnings) taxes.	Community antenna television (CAT) systems, competitive video service providers, and companies providing video programming by satellite, 5%; railroads, 2% to 3.5%; municipal utilities, 5% (4% for residential service); electric transmission or distribution companies, 8.5% (6.8% for residential service).	Returns and payments—railroads, July 1; others, by the last days of January, April, July and October.

Tax	Basis—Rates	Due Dates
Insurance companies tax.	Domestic—1.5% of net direct insurance premiums received; 1.5% of net direct subscriber charges received by HMOs; 4% on risk retention groups or insurers, other than captive insurance companies or surplus lines insurers; 4% on surplus line brokers and domestic surplus line insurers; 0.38% on first $20 million of direct premiums for captive insurance companies, 0.285% on next $20 million, 0.19% on next $20 million, 0.072% on each additional dollar; 0.214% on first $20 million of assumed reinsurance premiums for captive insurance companies, 0.143% on next $20 million, 0.048% on next $20 million, 0.024% on each additional dollar; 2% assessment on net direct subscriber charges received by hospital and medical service corporations. Foreign—1.5% of all net direct premiums received. Unauthorized insurers—4% of gross premiums where Connecticut is the insured's home state. Foreign companies subject to retaliatory taxes.	Domestic insurers, foreign insurers, hospital and medical service corporations, nonprofit legal service corporations—returns and payments—March 1. Insureds procuring nonadmitted insurance independently file May 15, August 15, November 15, and February 15. Domestic and foreign insurers' declaration and payment of estimated tax due on or before the 15th day of the 3rd, 6th, 9th and 12th months of the calendar year.

Delaware

Tax System.—A general property tax is imposed locally in Delaware at uniform rates upon all real property within each taxing district. Personal property is not taxed. In addition, there are state taxes upon occupations, income, franchises and privileges and municipal license and inspection fees. An outline of the Delaware tax system follows:

Tax	Basis—Rates	Due Dates
Franchise tax.	**Authorized shares method.**—5,000 shares or less: $175; 5,001—10,000: $250; 10,000 or more shares: $250 plus $85 per each additional 10,000 shares or fractional shares. **Assumed capital value method.**—$500,000 or less of assumed no-par capital: $175; $500,001-$1 million of assumed no-par capital: $250; $1,000,000 or more of assumed no-par capital: $250 plus $85 of each additional $1 million or fraction of assumed no-par capital. Tax for assumed par value capital is $400 for each $1 million or fractional part, in excess of $1 million. **Regulated investment companies (RICs).**—$400 per $1 million of average gross assets for tax year. **Maximum tax.**—$200,000; $100,000 for RICs. **Minimum tax.**—$175 for authorized shares method; $400 for assumed capital value method.	**Annual return and payment.**—March 1. Installments of estimated tax of $5,000 or more due as follows: 40% due by June 1; 20% by September 1; 20% by December 1; and remainder by March 1 of following year.
Corporation income tax.	8.7% of taxable income derived from Delaware. Headquarters management corporations pay greater of 8.7% of taxable income or $5,000.	April 15 or the 15th day of 4th month after close of fiscal year.
Personal income tax.	2.2% for taxable income of $2,001–$5,000; 3.9% for taxable income of $5,001–$10,000; 4.8% for taxable income of $10,001–$20,000; 5.2% for taxable income of $20,001–25,000; 5.55% for taxable income of $25,001–$60,000; and 6.6% for taxable income above $60,000.	April 30 or 30th day of 4th month following close of fiscal tax year. Installments of estimated tax of $800 or more due as follows: 25% by April 30; 25% by June 15; 25% by September 15; and 25% by January 15 of following year.
Banks and trust companies tax.	8.7% for taxable income of $0–$20 million; 6.7% for taxable income of $20,000,001–$25 million; 4.7% for taxable income of $25,000,001–$30 million; 2.7% for taxable income of $30,000,001–$650 million; and 1.7% for taxable income of $650,000,001 or more. Banks and trust companies may elect to pay an alternative bank franchise tax equal to the sum of income tax liability plus a location benefit tax liability.	Final franchise tax report by January 30 of succeeding year and tax payment by March 1. Installments of estimated tax of $10,000 or more due as follows: 40% by June 1; 20% by September 1; 20% by December 1; and balance by March 1 of following year.
General property tax.	Fixed locally to meet budget. No state levy. Based on assessed value of real property for county, municipal, and school district purposes. In practice, property is valued at different ratios according to locality. Personal property exempt.	Returns and payment—various dates.
Lodging tax.	8% of rental for occupancies in a hotel, motel or tourist home.	Reports and payments—15th of the following month.

Tax	Basis—Rates	Due Dates
Alcoholic beverage tax.	Excise—beer, $4.85 per barrel.; cider, 16¢ per gallon; wine (except sacramental wines), 97¢ per gallon; spirits 25% alcohol or less, $2.50 per gallon; spirits more than 25% alcohol, $3.75 per gallon; 100-proof alcohol, $4.85 per gallon.	Excise—reports and payments: importers, 15th day of each month.
Gasoline tax.	Gasoline—23¢ per gallon of motor fuel sold or used. Special fuels—22¢ per gallon sold, delivered or used. Motor carriers fuel purchase tax—same rates as above on fuel consumed in Delaware operations.	Reports and payments—25th of each month. Motor carriers road tax—last day of April, July, October and January (annual reports and payments are authorized).
Cigarette tax; tobacco products tax.	Cigarettes—$2.10 per pack of 20; tobacco products—30% of wholesale sale price; moist snuff—$0.92 per ounce or fraction thereof; vapor products—$0.05 per fluid millimeter.	Reports—20th of each month. Payment—cigarettes, by purchase of stamps; tobacco products, 20th of following month.
Realty transfer tax.	3% on transfers of realty located in Delaware, provided value of property conveyed is more than $100, or 2.5% if the municipality or county has enacted a 1.5% local realty transfer tax. 2% on amounts exceeding $10,000 on contracts for improvements to realty.	Payment—by purchase of stamps.
Merchants and manufacturers tax; use tax on personal property leases.	Wholesalers generally, $75 per business location plus 0.3983% of gross receipts (less an $100,000 monthly deduction); food processors, $75 plus 0.1991% of gross receipts (less an $100,000 monthly deduction); commercial feed dealers, $75 plus 0.0996% of gross receipts (less an $100,000 monthly deduction); farm machinery, supplies, or materials retailers, $75 plus 0.0996% of gross receipts (less an $100,000 monthly deduction). For quarterly filers, if taxable gross receipts do not exceed a certain statutory limit during the lookback period, a deduction of $300,000 is allowed on the aggregate gross receipts for each quarter. Retailers generally, $75 license fee plus $25 per business location, plus 0.7468% of receipts from goods sold or services rendered (less an $100,000 monthly deduction); transient retailers, $25 license fee plus 0.7468% of gross receipts over $3,000; restaurant retailers, $75 license fee plus $25 per business location plus 0.6472% of receipts from goods sold in Delaware (less an $100,000 monthly deduction); grocery supermarket retailers, $75 license fee plus $25 per branch plus 0.3267% of gross receipts (less an $100,000 monthly deduction). For quarterly filers, if taxable gross receipts do not exceed a certain statutory limit during the lookback period, a deduction of $300,000 is allowed on the aggregate gross receipts for each quarter.	Merchants, manufacturers, and contractors: Returns and payments—20th of each month for preceding month. If the taxpayer's gross receipts during the lookback period do not exceed the statutory threshold, the report and payment are due on the last day of the month following the close of the quarter.

Tax	Basis—Rates	Due Dates
	Petroleum wholesalers pay $75 per business location, plus 0.3983%, plus additional adjustable hazardous substance tax, and a 0.2489% petroleum surtax on taxable gross receipts in excess of $100,000 from sales of petroleum or petroleum products. Petroleum retailers pay a $75 license fee, plus $25 per business location, plus 0.7468% and an additional hazardous substance tax on sales of petroleum or petroleum products in excess of $100,000. For gross receipts received after December 31, 2018, and before January 1, 2022, the rate of the additional hazardous substance tax is adjusted annually. For 2020, the rate is 1.5244%. For quarterly filers, if taxable gross receipts do not exceed a certain statutory limit during the lookback period, a deduction of $300,000 is allowed on the aggregate gross receipts for each quarter.	
	Contractors—$75 license fee plus 0.6472% of aggregate gross receipts (less an $100,000 monthly deduction). For quarterly filers, if taxable gross receipts do not exceed a certain statutory limit during the lookback period, a deduction of $300,000 is allowed on the aggregate gross receipts for each quarter.	
	Manufacturers—$75 per business location plus 0.126% of gross receipts (less a $1.25 million monthly deduction); automobile manufacturers, $75 per business location plus 0.0945% of gross receipts (less a $1.25 million monthly deduction); clean energy technology device manufacturers, $75 per business location plus 0.0945% of gross receipts (less a $1.25 million monthly deduction). For quarterly filers, if taxable gross receipts do not exceed a certain statutory limit during the lookback period, a deduction of $3.75 million is allowed on the aggregate gross receipts for each quarter.	
	Occupational licensees—$75 license fee plus $25 for each extra establishment, plus 0.3983% of aggregate gross receipts, less a $100,000 monthly deduction. For quarterly filers, if taxable gross receipts do not exceed a certain statutory limit during the lookback period, a deduction of $300,000 is allowed on the aggregate gross receipts for each quarter.	Additional tax—20th day of each month.
	Use tax on personalty leases—1.9914% of rent. Lessors—$75 license fee, plus $25 for each additional place of business in Delaware, plus 0.2987% of rental payments received, less a quarterly deduction of $300,000.	Lessor tax—returns quarterly.

Tax	Basis—Rates	Due Dates
Insurance companies tax.	**Insurers except wet marine and transportation insurers.**—1.75%, plus additional 0.25% tax on gross premiums written. **Wet marine and transportation insurers.**—5% on underwriting profits. **Captive insurance companies.**—0.002% on each $1 of direct premiums up to $200,000 per tax year, plus 0.001% on each $1 of assumed reinsurance premiums up to $110,000 per tax year. **Surplus lines and independently procured insurance.**—3% on gross premiums charged. **Corporate owned life insurance (COLI) premiums.**—2% on first $10 million of net premiums; 1.5% on $10,000,001 to $24,999,999 of net premiums; 1.25% on $25,000,000 to $99,999,999 of net premiums; and 1.0% on $100 million or more of net premiums. Domestic insurers also subject to annual privilege tax based on annual gross receipts equal to: $0 for less than $1 million; $10,000 for $1 million–$5 million; $25,000 for $5,000,001–$10 million; $45,000 for $10,000,001–$20 million; $65,000 for $20,000,001–$30 million; $85,000 for $30,000,001–$40 million; $95,000 for more than $40 million.	March 1, except wet marine and transportation insurers file June 1. Installments of estimated tax due as follows: 50% by April 15; 20% by June 15; 20% by September 15; and 10% by December 15.

District of Columbia

Tax System.—The tax system of the District of Columbia differs from the system of all of the states in that, instead of a number of local taxing bodies with one central authority, there is but one taxing body engaged in the assessment, levy, and collection of District taxes. In addition to the general property tax on all real and personal property in the District, there are also taxes on corporate and personal incomes, sales and use taxes, taxes on banks, utilities, and insurance companies, a realty transfer tax, and other excise taxes. An outline of the District's tax system follows:

Tax	Basis—Rates	Due Dates
General income tax; unincorporated business tax.	Individuals: After 2015—taxable income of: $0 - 10,000 x 4.0%; $10,001 - 40,000, $400 plus 6.0% of excess over $10,000; $40,001 - 60,000, $2,200 plus 6.5% of excess over $40,000; $60,001 - 350,000, $3,500 plus 8.5% of excess over $60,000; $350,001 - $1,000,000, $28,150 plus 8.75% of excess above $350,000; over $1,000,000, $85,025 plus 8.95% of excess over $1,000,000.	Returns—individuals, April 15th for calendar-year taxpayers or the 15th day of 4th month following the close of the fiscal year; corporations, 15th day of 4th month after end of income year.
	Withholding required, except for U.S. legislative employees.	Payments—in full when return is filed. Individual estimates of income not subject to withholding due April 15 and payments due April 15, June 15, September 15, and January 15. Estimated corporate income tax payments are due April 15, June 15, September 15, and December 15.
	Corporations, unincorporated businesses, and financial institutions (franchise tax): 8.25% for 2019.	
Ballpark Fee.	For gross receipts of $5 million to $8 million, $5,500; for $8,000,001 to $12 million, $10,800; for gross receipts of $12,000,001 to $16 million, $14,000; and for gross receipts of more than $16 million, $16,500	
General property tax.	The real property tax rates (including the special property tax rates) are (per $100 of assessed value): Class 1, $0.85; Class 2: $1.65 up to $5 million, $1.77 between $5 million and $10 million, and $1.89 for more than $10 million; Class 3, $5; and Class 4, $10.	Returns—personal property, in July.
	The tangible personal property tax rate is $3.40 per $100 of assessed value, and the first $225,000 of taxable value is excluded from tax.	Payments—real property, March 31 and September 15; personal property, in July.
Alcoholic beverages tax.	Excise—beer, $2.79 per barrel; champagne, sparkling wine, and any wine artificially carbonated, 45¢ per gallon; wine containing 14% or less alcohol by volume, 30¢ per gallon; wine containing more than 14% alcohol by volume, 40¢ per gallon; spirits and all other alcoholic beverages or alcohol, $1.50 per gallon.	

Tax	Basis—Rates	Due Dates
Motor fuels tax.	$.235 per gallon plus surcharge of $.053 per gallon; effective 10/1/2021 surcharge is increased to $.103 and adjusted annually thereafter.	Reports and payments—25th day of following month.
Motor vehicle excise tax.	Title issuance—Class I, 6% of fair market value for vehicles weighing 3,499 lbs. or less; Class II, 7% of fair market value if weight is 3,500 lbs. to 4,999 lbs; and Class III, 8% of fair market value if weight is 5,000 lbs. or more.	Payments—upon issuance of every certificate of title.
Cigarette tax; tobacco products tax.	$5.00 per pack of 20 ($4.50 tax plus $.50 surtax); the tax rate on other tobacco products is 91% of wholesale sales of other tobacco products. Other tobacco products—Reports and payments due by 21st day of following calendar quarter.	Cigarettes—Reports by 25th day of following month; payments by the purchase and affixation of stamps.
Real property transfer tax.	1.45% of consideration paid for transfers of title to all properties sold for $400,000 or greater; 1.1% of consideration paid for all other transfers. For qualifying first-time homebuyers purchasing homes for a price that does not exceed $625,000, 0.725%.	Tax due when deed submitted for recording. Deed must be accompanied by a return.
Sales and use taxes.	6% on all tangible property and selected services, tickets to legitimate theaters and entertainment venues; 8% on soft drinks; 10% on restaurant meals, liquor for consumption on premises, and rental vehicles; 10% for alcoholic beverages sold for off-the premises consumption; 10.25% the rental or leasing of vehicles and utility trailers, and tickets to baseball games or events at Nationals Park or Capital One Arena or items sold at the either park; 18% for parking motor vehicles in commercial lots; 14.95% for transient accommodations.	Sales and use—Returns—monthly, 20th of each month; annually, January 20 when tax liabilities are less than $50 per month. Payments—due at the time the return is filed.
Insurance companies tax.	1.7% on insurance companies other than accident and health insurance companies. Accident and health insurance companies 2%.	Reports—before March 1.

Florida

Tax System.—The Florida tax system consists of the general property tax, sales and use taxes, corporate franchise (income) tax, estate tax, public utility taxes and other special taxes listed below. A constitutional amendment provides that no levy of *ad valorem* taxes upon real or personal property, except intangible property, may be made for state purposes, thus effecting a partial separation of state and local taxes. An outline of the Florida tax system follows:

Tax	Basis—Rates	Due Dates
Corporate franchise (income) tax.	Corporations, banks and savings associations—4.458% of federal taxable income apportioned to Florida. Exemption equal to smaller of $50,000 or the sum of adjusted federal income apportioned to the state plus nonbusiness income allocated to the state. Effective for tax years before 2018, taxpayers had to pay the larger of the corporate income tax or a 3.3% alternative minimum tax.	Reports and payments—Taxpayers must file Form F-1120 by the 1st day of the 5th month following the close of the taxable year (May 1 for calendar year taxpayers) or the 15th day after the federal due date. Effective for tax years beginning after December 31, 2015 and before January 1, 2026, all June 30 year-end returns must be filed by the 1st day of the 4th month following the close of the taxable year or the 15th day after the federal due date. Declarations and payments of estimated tax required if estimated tax over $2,500. Payments are due before the 1st day of the 6th, 7th, 10th, and 1st month of the next taxable year (e.g., May 31, June 30, September 30 and December 31 for calendar year taxpayers).
General property tax; intangible personal property tax.	General property—rates fixed locally to meet budget. Assessed at full cash value of real and tangible personal property; no state levy on realty or tangible property.	Returns—tangible personal property, including railroad property, April 1. Payment—real property, due November 1; delinquent April 1. Installment payments allowed, due on last day of June, September, and December of current year and March of following year.
	Intangible personal property—A one-time nonrecurring tax of $2.00 per $1,000 of the principal amount of indebtedness is imposed on the just valuation of all notes, bonds, and other obligations for payment of money that are secured by mortgage, deed of trust, or other lien on real property located in Florida.	Returns and payments—payable upon recordation.

Tax	Basis—Rates	Due Dates
Alcoholic beverages excise tax.	Wines, wine coolers, and other beverages with 0.5% or more, but less than 17.259% alcohol by volume—$2.25 per gallon. Wines with 17.259% or more alcohol by volume—$3 per gallon. Natural sparkling wines—$3.50 per gallon. Ciders—$0.89 per gallon. Other beverages with less than 17.259% alcohol by volume—$2.25 per gallon. Other beverages with 17.259% or more, but less than 55.780% alcohol by volume—$6.50 per gallon. Other beverages with more than 55.780% alcohol by volume—$9.53 per gallon. Malt beverages—$0.48 per gallon.	
Motor and diesel fuel taxes; petroleum taxes.	Motor fuel—effective January 1, 2020, 18.3¢ per gallon. Oil inspection fee, 1/8¢ per gallon on gasoline, kerosene (except when used as aviation turbine fuel), and #1 fuel oils sold in Florida.	Gasoline—Reports and payments—20th of each month. Reports of inspection fees, due to the Commissioner of Agriculture on or before the 25th of each month.
	Diesel fuel—effective January 1, 2020, 18.3¢ per gallon. The county tax rate (ninth cent, SCETS, and local option tax rates) on diesel fuel: 14.9¢ per gallon statewide. The total state and county rates on diesel fuel: 33.2¢ per gallon statewide. Alternative fuels are taxed pursuant to a motor fuel equivalent gallon ratio.	Diesel fuel—Reports and payments—20th of each month. Quarterly and semiannual reports and payments may be permitted.
	Use tax on diesel fuel for business purposes—6% of cost of diesel fuel consumed, used or stored by a trade or business.	Reports and payments—purchaser or ultimate consumer must pay tax directly to state.
	Special and motor fuel use—The rate of tax includes the minimum motor fuel tax and diesel fuel tax, and any pollutant tax imposed by the state.	Special and motor fuel use—Reports and payments—annual returns, July 1; semiannual returns, January 1 and July 1; quarterly returns, January 1, April 1, July 1, and October 1.
	Inland protection tax, one of four taxes (including the perchloroethylene tax, coastal protection tax, and water quality tax) collectively known as the pollutants tax: the rates of tax, which depend on the balance in the Inland Protection Trust Fund, are: (1) 30¢ when the unobligated balance is between $100 million and $150 million; (2) 60¢ when the unobligated balance is above $50 million, but below $100 million; and (3) 80¢ when the unobligated balance is $50 million or less.	Petroleum taxes—Reports and payments—20th of each month.
	Aviation fuel tax—4.27¢ per gallon.	Aviation fuel tax—same as gasoline tax provisions.

Tax	Basis—Rates	Due Dates
Oil, gas and sulfur production taxes; solid minerals tax.	Production—Small well oil, 5% of gross value; oil, for tertiary and mature field recovery oil, a tiered rate structure based on the sale price or market price of a barrel of oil is in effect as follows: 1% of the gross value of oil on the value of oil $60 and below; 7% of the gross value of oil on the value of oil above $60 and below $80; 9% of the gross value of oil on the value of oil $80 and above); all other oil, 8% of gross value; escaped oil, 12.5% additional. Effective July 1, 2020 through June 30, 2021, the production of gas is taxed at the rate of $0.162 per MCF. Effective July 1, 2020 through June 30, 2021, sulphur production is taxed at the rate of $5.34 per ton.	Oil production tax—Reports and payments—25th day of the month following the month production occurred.
		Gas and sulfur production tax—Reports and payments—25th of 2nd month following end of each quarter. Declaration and payment of estimated tax due 25th day of each month.
	Solid minerals—Tax imposed on solid minerals, other than phosphate rock and heavy minerals, for 2020 is 8% of the taxable value of the minerals produced. For tax year 2020, the severance tax rate applicable to heavy minerals in Florida is $3.80 per ton. Lake belt area limerock and sand—the per-ton mitigation fee is $0.05. Phosphate rock—for tax years January 1, 2015 to December 31, 2022, the tax rate is $1.80 per ton.	Solid minerals tax—Reports and payments—April 1. Estimated tax payments due on 1st day of May, July, October, and January. Water treatment plant upgrade fee—on or before the 20th day of the month following the calendar month in which the sale occurs.
Cigarette and tobacco products taxes.	Cigarettes—Weighing not more than 3 lbs. per 1,000—16.95 mills each. Weighing more than 3 lbs. per 1,000 and not more than 6 in. long—33.9 mills each. Weighing more than 3 lbs. per 1,000 and more than 6 in. long—67.8 mills each. Cigarette surcharge—Weighing not more than 3 lbs. per 1,000—5¢ each. Weighing more than 3 lbs. per 1,000 and not more than 6 in. long—10¢ each. Weighing more than 3 lbs. per 1,000 and more than 6 in. long—20¢ each.	Reports—wholesalers, jobbers, and agents, 10th of each month; railroads and Pullman company, 10th of each month. Payment—by means of cash paid for stamps to be affixed to cigarette packages. Payment due by the 10th of the month following the month in which the stamps were sold.
	Tobacco products—25% of wholesale price to distributors; 25% of cost price to consumers. Surcharge on tobacco: 60% of wholesale sale price to distributors and consumers.	Reports and payments—10th of each month.
Document recording tax (i.e., the documentary stamp tax).	Bonds, debentures, certificates of indebtedness, promissory and nonnegotiable notes, assignments of salaries, wages or other compensation, 35¢ per $100 of face value. Instruments that convey an interest in realty, 70¢ per $100 of the consideration (60¢ per $100 in a county that imposes a surtax on documents). Promissory and nonnegotiable notes, assignments of salaries, wages or other compensation, 35¢ per $100 of value, not to exceed $2,450.	Payment—due at time of transfer or sale. For notes and wage assignments executed in connection with retail charge account services, tax paid quarterly.

Tax	Basis—Rates	Due Dates
Sales, use, rentals, and admissions taxes.	6% of retail sales, rentals, admission charges, use, consumption, distribution or storage for use or consumption in Florida of tangible personal property and selected services. Charges for the use of coin-operated machines—4%. Charges for electrical power or energy—4.35% (an additional 2.6% utility tax is imposed on electric power already subject to sales and use tax, for a combined rate of 6.95%). The per-ton indexed tax rate for the calculation of Florida use tax due on asphalt manufactured by a contractor for the contractor's own use is $0.82 per ton effective July 1, 2020 through June 30, 2021. Manufactured asphalt used in federal, state, and local government public works projects is exempt from the indexed tax.	Reports and payments—20th day of each month. Dealers who remitted $100 or less during the previous four calendar quarters may report and pay annually; dealers who remitted at least $100 but less than $500, report and pay semiannually; dealers who remitted at least $500 but less than $1,000, report and pay quarterly; dealers who remitted between $1,000 and $12,000 report quarterly and pay monthly.
Gross receipts tax on utility services.	Electric or gas light, heat, and power—2.5% of gross receipts. The natural or manufactured gas index prices per 1,000 cubic feet effective July 1, 2020 through June 30, 2021, are: (1) residential $21.54; (2) commercial $11.20; and (3) industrial $6.38.	Reports and payments—light, heat, or power, 20th day of the month for the preceding month. Returns may be filed (1) on a quarterly basis if the tax remitted for the preceding 4 calendar quarters did not exceed $1,000; (2) on a semiannual basis if the tax remitted for the preceding 4 calendar quarters did not exceed $500; or (3) on an annual basis if the tax remitted for the preceding 4 calendar quarters did not exceed $100.
	Communications services tax (CST)—The tax rates applicable to the sale of services originating or terminating within the states are as follows: (1) CST, 4.92%; (2) GRT on CST, 2.37%; and (3) second GRT, 0.15%. The combined rate is 7.44%. The tax rates applicable to the sale of satellite services are as follows: (1) CST, 9.07%; and (2) GRT on CST, 2.37%. The combined rate is 11.44%. Local rates vary among local taxing jurisdictions.	Reports and payments—same as for utility taxes.

Tax	Basis—Rates	Due Dates
Insurance companies tax.	Annuity policies—1%; wet marine and transportation insurance, 0.75%; surplus lines, 5%; mutual insurers, nonprofit self-insurance fund, medical malpractice self-insurance fund, and public housing authority self-insurance fund, 1.6%; all others, 1.75%.	Returns and payment—March 1 for premium tax, wet marine and transportation profits tax, and fire marshal assessment. April 15, June 15, October 15 and March 1 for estimated premium tax installments. Surplus lines tax payments due on May 15 for Q1 transactions, August 15 for Q2 transactions, November 15 for Q3 transactions, and February 15 for Q4 transactions. Surplus lines reports due on June 30 for Q1 transactions, September 30 for Q2 transactions, December 31 for Q3 transactions, and March 31 for Q4 transactions.
	Fire marshal assessment—1% of gross premiums from fire insurance on property in Florida. Foreign companies, other than those with a regional home office in Florida, are subject to retaliatory provisions.	

Georgia

Tax System.—Georgia's principal sources of revenue are personal and corporate income taxes and sales and use taxes. The gasoline tax is also an important revenue source. Lesser, but significant, amounts are raised by the tax on tobacco, the motor carriers tax, and taxes on alcoholic beverages and insurance companies. For counties and municipalities, the property tax remains the principal source of income. An outline of the Georgia tax system follows:

Tax	Basis—Rates	Due Dates
Corporation franchise (license) tax; annual report fee.	Corporation franchise—Graduated from $125 for $100,000, based on net worth, including capital stock and paid in and earned surplus of domestic corporations, and on the proportion of issued capital stock and surplus employed in the state of foreign corporations, to $5,000 for over $22 million. Beginning in tax year 2018 and beyond, corporations having net worth, including capital stock, paid-in surplus, and earned surplus of no more than $100,000 are exempt from corporate net worth tax.	Corporation franchise—returns and payments—April 15 or the 15th day of 4th month after beginning of tax period.
	Annual report (annual registration)—$50.	Annual report—April 1.
Corporate income tax.	Corporations—5.75% of federal taxable income, with adjustments. Upon the General Assembly and governor providing approval, the rate would decrease to 5.5% January 1, 2020. The rate returns to 6% January 1, 2026.	Returns and payments—April 15 or the 15th day of 4th month after close of fiscal year.
		Estimated tax payments—April 15, June 15, September 15, and December 15.
	Financial institutions—State occupation tax—0.25% of Georgia gross receipts.	Returns and payments—March 1.
Personal income tax.	Tax years beginning January 1, 2019 and expiring December 31, 2025: Heads of households, married persons filing jointly—1% of 1st $1,000 of taxable net income; 2% of next $2,000; 3% of next $2,000; 4% of next $2,000; 5% of next $3,000; over $10,000, 5.75%. Single persons—1% of 1st $750; 2% of next $1,500; 3% of next $1,500; 4% of next $1,500; 5% of next $1,750; over $7,000, 5.75%. Married persons filing separately—1% of 1st $500; 2% of next $1,000; 3% of next $1,000; 4% of next $1,000; 5% of next $1,500; over $5,000, 5.75%. Nonresidents—income from Georgia sources. Tax years beginning January 1, 2026: Heads of households, married persons filing jointly—1% of 1st $1,000 of taxable net income; 2% of next $2,000; 3% of next $2,000; 4% of next $2,000; 5% of next $3,000; over $10,000, 6%. Single persons—1% of 1st $750; 2% of next $1,500; 3% of next $1,500; 4% of next $1,500; 5% of next $1,750; over $7,000, 6%. Married persons filing separately—1% of 1st $500; 2% of next $1,000; 3% of next $1,000; 4% of next $1,000; 5% of next $1,500; over $5,000, 6%. Nonresidents—income from Georgia sources.	Returns and payments—April 15 or the 15th day of 4th month after close of fiscal year.
	Withholding required.	Estimated tax payments—15th day of April, June, September, and January of the following year.

Tax	Basis—Rates	Due Dates
General property tax.	General property—state and local rates fixed to meet budget. For tax years beginning after 2015, there is no state tax levy. Taxable tangible property is assessed at 40% of its fair market value.	General property—returns—April 1; railroads, airlines, and public utilities, March 1. Payments—by December 20, though counties may provide by resolution that all unpaid state or local property taxes are due on either November 15 or December 1 annually.
Alcoholic beverages tax.	Excise—Malt beverages: $1.08 per standard case of 24 12-oz. containers (4.5¢ per can), plus a uniform local beer tax of $1.20 per standard case (5¢ per can); Table wines up to 14% alcohol by volume manufactured inside state: 11¢ per liter; Table wines manufactured outside state: 40¢ cents per liter; Dessert wines over 14% and up to 21% alcohol by volume manufactured inside state: 27¢ per liter; Dessert wine manufactured outside state: 67¢ per liter; Fortified wines over 21% alcohol by volume: taxed as distilled spirits; Distilled spirits under 190 proof manufactured inside state: 50¢ per liter; Distilled spirits manufactured outside state: $1 per liter; Alcohol over 190 proof manufactured inside state: 70¢ per liter; Alcohol manufactured outside state: $1.40 per liter. * Note: Some localities also collect a local tax on distilled spirits (up to 22¢ per liter).	
Gasoline tax.	Effective January 1, 2020, through December 31, 2020, the state excise tax rate is 27.9¢ per gallon for most motor fuel types (gasoline, LPG, and special fuels including CNG) except that the rate is 31.3¢ per gallon for diesel and .01¢ per gallon on aviation gasoline.	Reports and payments—20th day of month for preceding calendar month.
Tobacco tax.	Cigarettes—37¢ per pack of 20.	Reports—by the 10th day of each month.
	Cigars—23% of the wholesale cost price.	Payments—by purchasing stamps or, for cigars, little cigars, and loose or smokeless tobacco, by alternative method of monthly reports.
	Loose or smokeless tobacco—10% of the wholesale cost price.	
Realty transfer tax.	$1 for the first $1,000 of value or fractional part of $1,000; 10¢ per additional $100 of value or fractional part of $100.	Payments—certification of payment issued by Superior Court clerks prior to recording.

Tax	Basis—Rates	Due Dates
Sales and use taxes.	Sales and use—4% of sales price.	Reports and payments—20th day of each month for the preceding calendar month. For dealers whose estimated tax liability for the month exceeds $60,000 (excluding local sales taxes), prepayments of not less than 50% of the estimated tax liability for the taxable period are due by the 20th day of the period. All taxpayers with a sales and use tax liability of more than $500 in connection with any return or report must file electronically.
Insurance companies tax.	State taxes—2.25% of gross direct premiums; reduced to 1.25% if 25% of total assets are invested in Georgia and to 0.5% if 75% of total assets are invested in Georgia. 1% additional on fire insurance companies. Surplus line brokers and independently procured coverages, 4%. Captive insurance company premiums—0.4% on the first $20 million, 0.3% on each dollar thereafter on direct premiums collected; 0.225% on the first $20 million of assumed reinsurance premium, 0.150% on next $20 million, 0.050% on next $20 million, and 0.025% of each dollar thereafter (annual maximum $100,000). Foreign companies subject to retaliatory taxes.	Reports and payments—March 1. If the tax for the preceding year was $500 or more, the current year's tax is due March 20, June 20, September 20, and December 20 based on estimated quarterly premiums. Additional tax for fire insurance companies—by April 1. Additional tax for surplus line brokers—15th day of April, July, October, and January.

Hawaii

Tax System.—The two main revenue producers for the state are the general net income tax and the general excise tax. Real property is subject to tax at rates fixed to meet county budgets. An outline of the Hawaii tax system follows:

Tax	Basis—Rates	Due Dates
General income tax.	*Married filing separately and single individuals:* not over $2,400, 1.40% of taxable income; over $2,400 but not over $4,800, $34 plus 3.20% of excess over $2,400; over $4,800 but not over $9,600, $110 plus 5.50% of excess over $4,800; over $9,600 but not over $14,400, $374 plus 6.40% of excess over $9,600; over $14,400 but not over $19,200, $682 plus 6.80% of excess over $14,400; over $19,200 but not over $24,000, $1,008 plus 7.20% of excess over $19,200; over $24,000 but not over $36,000, $1,354 plus 7.60% of excess over $24,000; over $36,000 but not over $48,000, $2,266 plus 7.90% of excess over $36,000; over $48,000 but not over $150,000, $3,214 plus 8.25% of excess over $48,000; over $150,000 but not over $175,000, $11,629 plus 9.00% of excess over $150,000; over $175,000 but not over $200,000, $13,879 plus 10.00% of excess over $175,000; over $200,000, $16,379 plus 11.00% of excess over $200,000. *Head of household:* rates range between 1.40% of the first $3,600 of taxable income and 11.00% of taxable income over $300,000. *Married filing jointly and surviving spouse:* rates range between 1.40% of the first $4,800 of taxable income and 11.00% of taxable income over $400,000. *Corporations*—first $25,000, 4.4%; next $75,000, 5.4% less $250; over $100,000, 6.4% less $1,250; plus 4% alternative rate on net capital gains. Corporations doing business in more than one state with no Hawaii activity except sales of $100,000 or less may elect instead to pay tax at 0.5% of annual gross sales.	Returns and payments—20th day of 4th month following close of income year. Estimated tax—declaration, 20th day of the 4th month of the current year; payments, 20th day of the 4th, 6th, 9th, and 13th months of the year.
Bank franchise (income) tax.	7.92% of net income of banks and other financial institutions or an alternative tax (if less than the franchise tax) on financial institutions having a net capital gain equal to the sum of (1) the franchise tax computed on the taxable income reduced by the amount of the net capital gain plus (2) 4% of the net capital gain for the tax year.	Returns and payments—20th day of 4th month following close of taxable year. Estimated tax declaration and payments—20th day of 4th, 6th, and 9th months of year, and of 1st month of following year.

Tax	Basis—Rates	Due Dates
General property tax.	State property tax laws were repealed, effective July 1, 2016. According to H.B. 2217, Laws 2016, "The legislature finds that article VIII, section 3, of the state constitution provides that the taxation of real property in the State has been transferred to the several counties. Pursuant to the Supreme Court of Hawaii's decision in State ex rel. Anzai v. City & County of Honolulu, 99 Hawaii 508, 57 P.3d 433 (2002), the need for numerous provisions in the Hawaii Revised Statutes governing the taxation of real property in the State lapsed decades ago, and those provisions are no longer of any force or effect." Rates are set by county councils except that rates for Kalawao County are set by the state. Realty is generally assessed at 100% of fair market value. Personal property is exempt.	Bills—mailed by July 20. Payments—installments due by August 20 and February 20.
Transient accommodations tax.	Tax rate is 10.25%. Tax is imposed on gross rental or gross rental proceeds from furnishing transient accommodations (i.e., a room, apartment, suite, single family dwelling, or the like that will be occupied by a person for less than 180 consecutive days). Tax imposed on the fair market rental value of resort time share vacation units at the rate of 10.25%.	Reports and payments—20th day of each calendar month; quarterly on or before April 20, July 20, October 20 and January 20 if liability is $4,000 or less annually; semiannual on or before July 20 and January 20 if liability does not exceed $2,000.
Alcoholic beverages taxes.	Distilled spirits, $5.98 per wine gallon; sparkling wine, $2.12 per wine gallon; still wine, $1.38 per wine gallon; cooler beverages, $0.85 per wine gallon; beer other than draft beer, $0.93 per wine gallon; draft beer, $0.54 per wine gallon.	
Fuel tax.	Rates in cents per gallon (effective July 1, 2020): Aviation fuel, 1¢; naphtha fuel (includes state (2¢) and county rates): Honolulu 2¢, Maui 2¢, Hawaii 2¢, Kauai 2¢; motor fuels and diesel oil (includes state (16¢) and county rates): Honolulu County 32.5¢, Maui County 40¢, Hawaii County 39¢, Kauai County 33¢; LP gas (includes state 5.2¢ and county rates): Honolulu County 10.6¢, Maui County 16.7¢, Hawaii County 12.8¢, Kauai County 10.8¢; alternative fuels (includes state and county rates): Honolulu County ethanol 4.8¢, methanol 3.7¢, biodiesel 12.3¢; Maui County ethanol 13.9¢, methanol 13.4¢, biodiesel 4.0¢; Hawaii County ethanol 5.7¢, methanol 4.4¢, biodiesel 4.0¢; Kauai County ethanol 4.9¢, methanol 3.8¢, biodiesel 4.0¢.	Reports and payments—20th day of each calendar month
Environmental response, energy, and food security tax.	$1.05 per barrel of petroleum product that is not aviation fuel, sold by a distributor to any retail dealer or end user.	Reports and payments—last day of each month.
Cigarette tax.	16¢ per cigarette or little cigar ($3.20 per pack of 20).	Reports—20th day of each calendar month. Payment—cigarette tax stamps purchased from Department of Taxation and affixed prior to distribution.

Tax	Basis—Rates	Due Dates
Tobacco products tax.	Tobacco products other than large cigars: 70% of the wholesale price. Large cigars: 50% of the wholesale price.	Reports and payments—20th day of each calendar month
Realty conveyance tax.	10¢ per $100 for properties with a value of less than $600,000; 20¢ per $100 for properties with a value of at least $600,000 but less than $1 million; 30¢ per $100 for properties with a value of $1 million but less than $2 million; 50¢ per $100 for properties with a value of at least $2 million but less than $4 million; 70¢ per $100 for properties with a value of at least $4 million but less than $6 million; 90¢ per $100 for properties with a value of at least $6 million but less than $10 million; and $1 per $100 for properties with a value of $10 million or greater. Sale of a condominium or single family residence for which the purchaser is ineligible for a homeowner's property tax exemption, rate is 15¢ per $100 for properties with a value of less than $600,000; 25¢ per $100 for properties with a value of at least $600,000 but less than $1 million; 40¢ per $100 for properties with a value of $1 million but less than $2 million; 60¢ per $100 for properties with a value of at least $2 million but less than $4 million; 85¢ per $100 for properties with a value of at least $4 million but less than $6 million; $1.10 per $100 for properties with a value of at least $6 million but less than $10 million; and $1.25 per $100 for properties with a value of $10 million or greater. Minimum tax, $1.	Payments—no later than 90 days after taxable transactions. Payments evidenced by seal.
General excise tax; use tax.	General excise—4%, 0.5%, or 0.15% of the value of products, gross proceeds or gross income according to type of business. 4% is generally the retail rate; 0.5% is generally the wholesale/manufacturer rate; and 0.15% is generally the insurance producer rate.	Returns and payments—20th day of each month; if annual liability will not exceed $4,000, quarterly on or before the 20th day of the month following the close of each quarter (April 20, July 20, October 20, and January 20); if annual liability does not exceed $2,000, semiannually on the 20th day of month following the close of semiannual period (July 20 and January 20). Annual reconciliation return due 20th day of 4th month after end of tax year.
	Use—4% of purchase price or value of property for use or consumption; certain purchases and imports (e.g. for resale), 0.5%. For taxable years beginning after December 31, 2018, intangible property is subject to use tax at the retail rate of 4%.	Returns and payments—20th day of the calendar month; if annual liability will not exceed $4,000, quarterly on or before April 20, July 20, October 20, and January 20 for calendar year filers; if annual liability does not exceed $2,000, semiannually on July 20 and January 20. Annual reconciliation return due 20th day of 4th month after end of tax year.

Tax	Basis—Rates	Due Dates
Public service company tax.	Tax based on gross income for preceding calendar year. Rates are 5.35% for scheduled route passenger carriers on land; 0.5% for sales to another utility for resale; 4% for all other revenues. The rate for utilities selling telecommunications services to an interstate or foreign telecommunications provider for resale is 0.5%. The rate for electric light or power businesses whose franchise does not provide for the payment of a tax, or that provides for a tax of less than 2.5%, is 2.5% of the gross receipts or the difference between the tax required under the franchise and 2.5% of the gross receipts from all electric light or power furnished to consumers during the preceding calendar year. Airlines, motor carriers, common carriers by water, and contract carriers other than motor carriers are subject to the general excise tax instead of the public service company tax.	Reports—20th day of the 4th month following the close of the tax year. Payments—20th day of the 4th month following the close of the tax year or in four equal installments, by the 20th day of the 4th, 6th, 9th and 12th months following the close of the tax year. If estimated liability exceeds $100,000, due in 12 equal installments by the 10th day of each month.
Insurance companies tax.	Authorized insurers, except life and ocean marine, 4.265%; life insurers, 2.75%; ocean marine insurers, 0.8775%; surplus lines brokers and surplus lines insurance independently procured through unauthorized insurers, for which Hawaii is a home state, 4.68%. Captive insurance companies, 0.25% on $0 to $25 million of gross premiums; 0.15% on more than $25 million to $50 million of gross premiums; 0.05% on more than $50 million to $250 million of gross premiums; and 0.00% on more than $250 million of gross premiums, provided that the annual maximum aggregate tax on gross premiums does not exceed $200,000.	Statements and payments—annually by March 1 and monthly by 20th day of month following month in which taxes accrue; surplus line brokers, quarterly by 45th day following end of calendar quarter.

Idaho

Tax System.—The Idaho tax system is based on the general income tax on individuals and corporations, the gasoline and special fuel taxes, and the sales and use taxes. A general property tax is imposed for local purposes, but the state's property tax is suspended so long as the sales and use taxes are in effect. Other significant revenue producers are alcoholic beverage taxes, cigarette and tobacco products taxes, and the insurance gross premiums tax. An outline of the Idaho tax system follows:

Tax	Basis—Rates	Due Dates
General income tax.	Individuals—2020 Rates: Single and married filing separately: at least 1 but less than $1,568—1.125%; $1,568 but less than $3,136—$17.64 plus 3.125% of the excess over $1,568; $3,136 but less than $4,704—$66.64 plus 3.625% of the amount over $3,136; $4,704 but less than $6,272—$123.48 plus 4.625% of the amount over $4,704; $6,272 but less than $7,840—$196.00 plus 5.625% of the amount over $6,272; $7,840 but less than $11,760—$284.20 plus 6.625% of the amount over $7,840; $11,760 and over—$543.90 plus 6.925% of the amount over $11,760. Married filing jointly, qualifying widow(er), and head of household: At least $1 but less than $3,136—1.125%; $3,136 but less than $6,272—$35.28 plus 3.125%; of the excess over $3,136; $6,272 but less than $9,408—$133.28 plus 3.625%; of the excess over $6,272; $9,408 but less than $12,544—$246.96 plus 4.625%; of the excess over $9,408; $12,544 but less than $15,680—$392.00 plus 5.625%; of the excess over $12,544; $15,680 but less than $23,520—$568.40 plus 6.625%; of the excess over $15,680; $23,520 and over—$1,087.80 plus 6.925%; of the excess over $23,520. Additional $10 tax for all persons filing returns.	Returns—April 15 or 15th day of 4th month after close of income year.

Tax	Basis—Rates	Due Dates
	Individuals—2019 Rates: Single and married filing separately: at least 1 but less than $1,541—1.125%; $1,541 but less than $3,081—$17.33 plus 3.125% of the excess over $1,541; $3,081 but less than $4,622—$65.47 plus 3.625% of the amount over $3,081; $4,622 but less than $6,162—$121.32 plus 4.625% of the amount over $4,622; $6,162 but less than $7,703—$192.57 plus 5.625% of the amount over $6,162; $7,703 but less than $11,554—$279.22 plus 6.625% of the amount over $7,703; $11,554 and over—$534.37 plus 6.925% of the amount over $11,554. Married filing jointly, qualifying widow(er), and head of household: At least $1 but less than $3,082—1.125%; $3,082 but less than $6,162—$34.66 plus 3.125%; of the excess over $3,082; $6,162 but less than $9,244—$130.94 plus 3.625%; of the excess over $6,162; $9,244 but less than $12,324—$242.64 plus 4.625%; of the excess over $9,244; $12,324 but less than $15,406—$385.14 plus 5.625%; of the excess over $12,324; $15,406 but less than $23,108—$558.44 plus 6.625%; of the excess over $15,406; $23,108 and over—$1,068.74 plus 6.925%; of the excess over $23,108. Additional $10 tax for all persons filing returns.	Returns—April 15 or 15th day of 4th month after close of income year.
	Individuals—2018 Rates: Single and married filing separately: at least 1 but less than $1,504—1.125%; $1,504 but less than $3,008—$16.92 plus 3.125% of the excess over $1,504; $3,008 but less than $4,511—$63.91 plus 3.625% of the amount over $3,008; $4,511 but less than $6,015—$118.42 plus 4.625% of the amount over $4,511; $6,015 but less than $7,519—$187.97 plus 5.625% of the amount over $6,015; $7,519 but less than $11,279—$272.56 plus 6.625% of the amount over $7,519; $11,279 and over—$521.63 plus 6.925% of the amount over $11,279. Married filing jointly, qualifying widow(er), and head of household: At least $1 but less than $3,008—1.125%; $3,008 but less than $6,016—$33.84 plus 3.125%; of the excess over $3,008; $6,016 but less than $9,022—$127.82 plus 3.625%; of the excess over $6,016; $9,022 but less than $12,030—$236.84 plus 4.625%; of the excess over $9,022; $12,030 but less than $15,038—$375.94 plus 5.625%; of the excess over $12,030; $15,038 but less than $22,558—$545.12 plus 6.625%; of the excess over $15,038; $22,558 and over—$1,043.26 plus 6.925%; of the excess over $22,558. Additional $10 tax for all persons filing returns.	
	Banks and corporations—6.925% of taxable income. Minimum tax, $20. Corporations must pay an excise tax of $10 when returns are filed.	Payments—with return. Estimated income and franchise tax payments are due from corporations required to make federal estimated payments. Federal due dates apply.
	General withholding required.	

Tax	Basis—Rates	Due Dates
General property tax.	County and municipal—fixed within statutory limits to meet budget. (The state property tax is not currently levied.)	Returns—March 15; mines, May 1; public utilities, and car and railroad companies, April 30. Payments—realty, December 20 and June 20; personalty, due on demand or, if no demand is made, December 20 and June 20.
Forest products tax.	Yield tax—3% of the stumpage value.	Reports—November 15 and May 15, by the county treasurer. Payments—by December 20 or June 20.
Alcoholic beverages taxes.	Excise—beer, $4.65 per 31-gallon barrel sold for use in the state. Wine, 45¢ per gallon. A 2% surcharge, based on the current price per unit, is levied on alcoholic liquor and all other merchandise sold in the state dispensary.	
Fuel taxes.	Gasoline and special fuel, 32¢ per gallon; propane, 23.2¢ per gallon; LNG, 34.9¢ per specially computed gallon; jet fuel, 6¢ per gallon; and aviation gasoline, 7¢ per gallon.	Reports and payments—last day of following month, generally.
Severance taxes.	Mine license tax—1% of net value of royalties received or ores mined.	Reports and payments—Mine license tax—15th day of 4th month following close of year.
	Oil and gas production tax—2.5% of gross income received by the producer of the oil or gas produced.	Oil and gas production tax—20th day of the next month following each quarter.
Cigarette tax; tobacco products tax.	57¢ per pack of 20 cigarettes.	Reports—by the 20th day of each month for the preceding month. Payments—by the purchase and affixation of stamps.
	Tobacco products other than cigarettes—40% of wholesale sales price.	Reports and payments—by the 20th day of each month for the preceding month.
Sales and use tax.	Sales—6% of retail sales price of taxable property and selected services. Additional local rate may apply.	Sales and use—Returns and payment—on or before the 20th of the following month. Persons who owe $750 or less per quarter may request permission to file quarterly or semiannual returns due the 20th day of the month following the reporting period. Annual or variable filing may be allowed for certain taxpayers.
	Use—6% of value of property used, stored, or consumed in Idaho.	

Tax	Basis—Rates	Due Dates
Utilities.	Electricity—1/2 mill per kilowatt hour of electricity and electrical energy generated, manufactured or produced in the state for sale, barter or exchange.	Electricity—last day of each month. Quarterly reports and payments may be allowed.
	Electrical Cooperatives—Cooperative electrical associations pay a tax of 3.5% of annual gross earnings after reduction.	Electrical Cooperatives—Reports filed at same time as property tax reports on other electric utilities. Payments due July 1.
	Natural Gas Cooperatives—Cooperative natural gas associations are subject to a tax of 3.5% of annual gross earnings, less the cost of the natural gas.	Natural Gas Cooperatives—Operating Property Statement must be filed. Payments due July 1.
	Wind Energy, Geothermal Energy, and Solar Energy Electrical Producers—The wind and geothermal energy tax is equal to 3% of the producer's gross wind and geothermal energy earnings. Solar energy tax is equal to 3.5% of the producer's gross solar energy earnings.	Wind Energy, Geothermal Energy, and Solar Energy Electrical Producers—Operating Property Statement must be filed. Payments due July 1.
Insurance tax.	1.5% (1.4% for insurers other than life insurers with 25% or more of its assets invested in specified Idaho companies, bonds, securities etc.). Title insurance, 1.5%. Surplus lines insurance, 1.5%. Health maintenance organization or hospital and medical service corporations, 4¢ per subscriber contract per month. Dental care services or dental insurance, 4¢ per month per contract. Self-funded plans 4¢ per month per beneficiary tax for all beneficiaries working or residing in Idaho. Foreign companies subject to retaliatory taxes.	Reports and payments—March 1. Prepayments required from insurers owing $400 or more for the preceding calendar year, due on or before June 15, September 15 and December 15, with any balance due on or before March 1.

Illinois

Tax System.—The Illinois revenue system was founded upon a general property tax at uniform rates upon all property within each taxing district. Since 1933, however, the tax has been entirely a local tax. The property tax has been supplemented by (1) state taxes, part of the revenue from which has been returned to the local governments, upon incomes, occupations, franchises and privileges and (2) municipal sales and license taxes and inspection fees that the legislature permits the local governments to exact. An outline of the Illinois tax system follows:

Tax	Basis—Rates	Due Dates
Corporation franchise tax.	Annual franchise tax—0.1% ($1.00 per $1,000) of paid-in capital for the 12-month period beginning on the first day of the anniversary month or the extended filing month of the corporation; minimum, $25; maximum, $2 million per year. Illinois phases out the franchise tax beginning after the 2019 tax year and repeals the tax after the 2023 tax year.	Reports—due before the first day of the anniversary month of the corporation or the extended filing month of the corporation.
	Initial franchise tax—0.15% ($1.50 per $1,000) of paid-in capital for the 12-month period beginning on the first day of the anniversary month in which the articles of incorporation are filed; minimum, $25.	Payments—initial and additional taxes due at the time of filing articles, certificates or reports of changes; annual franchise tax due before the first day of the anniversary month.
	Additional franchise tax—0.15% ($1.50 per $1,000) for each calendar month between the date of each increase in paid-in capital and its next anniversary month.	
Income tax.	Corporations—7% on federal taxable income after modifications.	Returns and payments—15th day of 4th month after close of tax year, except 15th day of 3rd month for corporate income taxpayers with a June 30 fiscal year end. Estimated payments—15th day of April, June, September and December (Individuals, April 15th, June 15th, September 15th, and January 15th after close of taxable year). Exempt organization return due 15th day of 5th month after close of tax year.
	Individuals, estates and trusts—4.95% on federal adjusted gross income after modifications.	
	Additional personal property replacement tax: Corporations, 2.5% of net income; subchapter S corporations, partnerships and trusts, 1.5% of net income.	

Tax	Basis—Rates	Due Dates
Real property tax.	General property—There is no set rate for property tax in Illinois. Tax bills are based on two factors, the equalized assessed value (EAV) of the property, and the amount of money the local taxing districts need to operate during the coming year. Most property is assessed at 33 1/3% of fair cash value, except for Cook County. Personal property is exempt.	General property—returns—realty, none required; railroads, on or before June 1. Payment—realty, equally on June 1 and September 1; Cook County (two installments), March 1 (55%) and August 1 (45%).
Hotel operators' occupation tax.	6% of 94% of gross rental receipts.	Reports and payments—monthly, due last day of following month; quarterly if average monthly liability does not exceed $200, due April 30, July 31, October 31, and January 31; annually if average monthly liability does not exceed $50, due January 31.
Hydraulic fracturing severance tax.	3% of oil or gas produced from a well in the first 24 months; 6% of gas severed from the well thereafter; based on average daily production (ADP) of oil from a well thereafter, if ADP is less than 25 barrels, 3%; if ADP is at least 25 barrels but less than 50 barrels, 4%; if ADP is at least 50 barrels, but less than 100 barrels, 5%; if ADP is at least 100 barrels, 6%. Oil is exempt if produced from a well that has ADP of less than 15 barrels for the 12-month period immediately preceding production.	Reports and payments—electronic returns must be accompanied by electronic fund transfer remittances from purchasers for oil and gas purchased during the month for which the return is filed on or before the last day of the following month.
Alcoholic beverages tax.	Alcoholic beverages—Per gallon—beer and cider with an alcohol content of 0.5% to 7%, 23.1¢; alcoholic liquor other than beer with alcohol content of 14% or less, $1.39; alcoholic liquor with an alcohol content of more than 14% and less than 20%, $1.39; alcoholic liquor with an alcohol content of 20% or more, $8.55.	
Motor fuel tax.	$0.387 per gallon gasoline/gasohol and compressed natural gas (CNG) from July 1, 2020, through June 30, 2021 (previously, $0.38 per gallon from July 1, 2019, through June 30, 2020); $0.462 on diesel fuel, liquefied petroleum gas (LPG), and liquefied natural gas (LNG) from July 1, 2020, through June 30, 2021 (previously, $0.455 per gallon from July 1, 2019, through June 30, 2020).	Reports and payments—Suppliers and distributors—20th day of each calendar month.

Tax	Basis—Rates	Due Dates
Motor fuel use tax.	Fuel used by commercial motor vehicles is subject to an additional use tax based on the average selling price of special fuel in the state. The rate is 6.25% of the average selling price of motor fuel purchased in IL. Fuel used by commercial motor vehicles is subject to an additional use tax based on the average selling price of special fuel in the state. The rate is 6.25% of the average selling price of motor fuel purchased in IL. From July 1, 2020, through December 31, 2020, the rates are $0.531 per gallon for gasoline/gasohol; $0.611 per gallon for diesel fuel or per DGE for liquefied natural gas (LNG); $0.607 per DGE for liquefied petroleum gas (LPG); and $0.49 per GGE for compressed natural gas (CNG).	Reports and payments—returns must be filed electronically and payments must be made electronically on or before the last day of the month following the quarter the return is filed.
	Environmental impact fee, $0.008 per gallon sold.	Returns and payments—20th of each month.
Cigarette tax.	149 mills per cigarette ($2.98 per package of 20).	Reports—15th of each month. Manufacturers, 5th of each month. Payment—Distributors, by purchase of tax stamps; Manufacturers, 5th day of each month.
	Tobacco products tax—36% of wholesale price of tobacco products sold or otherwise disposed of to a retailer or consumer; 15% of wholesale price of electronic cigarette products sold or otherwise disposed of to a retailer or consumer. Moist snuff—$0.30 per ounce.	Return and payment—15th day of each month.
Retailers' occupation (sales) tax; use tax.	Sales tax—6.25% of gross receipts from retail sales of tangible personal property and selected services; 1% tax on qualifying food, drugs, medical appliances, and modifications to make motor vehicle usable by disabled person.	Reports—Sales and use taxes: monthly, due 20th day of following month; quarterly if average monthly liability does not exceed $200, due 20th day of the month following each quarter; annually if average monthly liability does not exceed $50, due January 20. Monthly reports from large taxpayers making quarter-monthly payments due 20th day of following month.
	Use tax—6.25% of selling price or fair market value; 1% tax on qualifying food, drugs, medical appliances, and modifications to make motor vehicle usable by disabled person.	Payment—with report; four times monthly if average monthly liability is $20,000 or more. Retailers of motor fuel must prepay 6¢ per gallon of motor fuel and 5¢ per gallon of gasohol to their distributors, suppliers or other resellers.

Tax	Basis—Rates	Due Dates
Service occupation tax; service use tax.	Service occupation tax—6.25% of selling price of personalty, transferred by servicemen as an incident to "sales of service"; 1% on qualifying food, drugs, medical appliances, and modifications to make motor vehicle usable by disabled person.	Reports and payment—Service taxes: monthly, due 20th day of following month; quarterly if average monthly liability does not exceed $200, due 20th day of month following each quarter; annually if average monthly liability does not exceed $50, due January 20.
	Service use tax—6.25% of selling price of property transferred to the serviceman of property transferred as an incident to the sale of a service; 1% on qualifying food, drugs, medical appliances, and modifications to make motor vehicle usable by disabled person.	Payment—with report; 4 times monthly if average monthly liability is $20,000 or more.
Public utilities.	Gas revenue tax: 2.4¢ per therm or 5% of gross receipts, whichever results in a lower tax. Gas use tax: 2.4¢ per therm for delivering suppliers or 5% of purchase price for self-assessing purchasers.	Gas revenue tax—Reports and payments due on the 15th day of the third month following the close of the taxable period. Quarterly estimated payments are due on the 15th day of the 3rd, 6th, 9th, and 12th months of each taxable period. Gas use tax—Reports and payments due on the 15th of each month for the preceding calendar month. Annual or quarterly returns and payments may be authorized for purchasers or suppliers with low average monthly tax liabilities. Quarter-monthly estimated payments are required if average monthly tax liability is $10,000 or more, due on or before the 7th, 15th, 22nd, and last days of the month.
	Telecommunications infrastructure maintenance fee, 0.5% of gross charges.	Returns—on or before the 30th day of each month following the month for which the return is filed. Payments—due with the return.
	Electricity excise tax: based on number of kilowatt-hours used or consumed monthly graduating from 0.330¢ for the first 2,000 hours to 0.202¢ for anything in excess of 20 million hours. Electricity excise tax on purchases from municipal utilities and electrical cooperatives: 0.32¢ per kilowatt-hour or 5% of gross receipts, whichever results in a lower tax. For self-assessing purchasers, 5.1% of the purchase price. Electricity distribution tax: based on the number of kilowatt-hours distributed to a purchaser in Illinois. The rate escalates from 0.031¢ per kilowatt-hour for the first 500 million kilowatt-hours to 0.131¢ per kilowatt-hour in excess of 18 billion kilowatt-hours.	Report and payment—Electricity excise taxes—must be filed by the 15th of each month for the preceding calendar month; quarterly and annual filings may be authorized. Quarter-monthly payments may be required if monthly remittances average at least $10,000. Public utilities revenue tax—filed no later than the 15th day of the 3rd month following the close of the tax period. Estimated payments—15th day of 3rd, 6th, 9th, and 12th months of each tax period.

Tax	Basis—Rates	Due Dates
Insurance companies tax.	All companies doing any form of insurance business in Illinois must pay an annual privilege tax of 0.5% of the net premiums written in the state, except the rate is 0.4% for health insurance related premiums. Fire premiums tax, 1%. 3.5% on surplus line brokers that independently procure insurance directly from an unauthorized insurer. 0.5% on industrial insureds that independently procure insurance directly from an unauthorized insurer.	Report and payment—March 15. Surplus line agents—August 1 and February 1. Fire premiums tax—March 31. Estimated tax from companies with prior year tax liability of $5,000 or more—15th day of April, June, September and December.

Indiana

Tax System.—The revenue system for the State of Indiana was founded primarily on a property tax, which continues to be the main revenue producer for local purposes, but the sales and adjusted gross income taxes are the major sources of state revenue. In addition, there are the insurance company and motor carrier taxes, the revenue from which accrues to the state. Income from motor vehicle registration fees, gasoline tax and liquor taxes is divided between the state and local tax bodies. An outline of the Indiana tax system follows:

Tax	Basis—Rates	Due Dates
Income tax.	Individuals—3.23% after December 31, 2016 of adjusted gross income. Previously, 3.3% after December 31, 2014 and before January 1, 2017 and 3.4% before January 1, 2015.	Returns and payment—15th day of 4th month after close of taxable year
	Corporations—5.5% after June 30, 2019 and before July 1, 2020, 5.25% after June 30, 2020 and before July 1, 2021, and 4.9% after June 30, 2021; previously 8% of adjusted gross income after June 30, 2012 and before July 1, 2013, 7.5% after June 30, 2013 and before July 1, 2014, 7.0% of adjusted gross income after June 30, 2014 and before July 1, 2015, 6.5% after June 30, 2015 and before July 1, 2016, 6.25% after June 30, 2016 and before July 1, 2017, 6.0% after June 30, 2017 and before July 1, 2018, 5.75% after June 30, 2018 and before July 1, 2019; 5% of adjusted gross income derived from sources in a qualified area with an inactive or closed military base.	Returns and payment—later of 15th day of 4th month after close of tax year or one month after the federal return is due for corporations with federal returns due after the 15th day of the fourth month after close of the tax year. Estimated reports and payments—Individuals, at the time provided under federal law. For calendar year corporations, 20th day of April, June, September and December. For all other corporate taxpayers, by the 20th day of the 4th, 6th, 9th, and 12th months of the tax year.
Utilities receipts tax.	For taxable years beginning before January 1, 2021, the tax is imposed at a rate of 1.4%. For taxable years beginning after December 31, 2020, the rate of the tax will be adjusted annually. For taxable years beginning after December 31, 2020, and before January 1, 2022, the utility receipts tax rate will be 1.4%.	Estimated returns and payments—for taxpayers with estimated tax liability greater than $1,000—annual report due by April 15 of following year for calendar year filers.
Utility services use tax.	Prior to 2021, the tax is imposed at the rate of 1.4%. For calendar years beginning after December 31, 2020, the rate of the tax will be adjusted annually. For calendar year 2021, the utility services use tax rate will be 1.4%.	Reports and payments—by 30 days after end of month in which the services were purchased.
Financial institutions.	The financial institutions tax rate for all taxpayers is: (1) 6% for tax years after December 31, 2019, and before January 1, 2021; (2) 5.5% for tax years after December 31, 2020, and before January 1, 2022; (3) 5% for tax years after December 31, 2021, and before January 1, 2023; and (4) 4.9% for tax years after December 31, 2022.	Financial institutions tax—Reports and payments—15th day of the month after the taxpayer's federal tax return is due.

Tax	Basis—Rates	Due Dates
General property tax.	General property—The tax rate is the aggregate amount levied on each $100 of assessed valuation by all the taxing districts.	General property—Personal property returns May 15th. Payment—Unless an exception applies, equally on May 10 and November 10.
Alcoholic beverages tax.	Beer—$0.115 per gallon; liquor (21% or more alcohol)—$2.68 per gallon; wine (less than 21% alcohol)—$0.47 per gallon.	
Gasoline and special fuel taxes; motor carrier fuel tax.	Gasoline—30¢ per gallon. Special fuel—49¢ per gallon. Both effective July 1, 2019 through June 30, 2020. (As of press time, these rates have not yet been updated by the Indiana Department of Revenue)	Reports and payments—Gasoline—20th of each month; Special fuel—20th of each month.
	From July 1, 2019, to June 30, 2020, the motor carrier fuel tax rate is $0.49 per gallon of special fuel or alternative fuel, and $0.30 per gallon of gasoline, consumed by a carrier in its operations on highways in Indiana (same as gasoline and special fuel tax rates). (As of press time, these rates have not yet been updated by the Indiana Department of Revenue)	Motor carrier fuel tax—Reports and payments—by the last day of April, July, October and January.
Severance tax.	For petroleum—1% of value. For natural gas—$0.03 per 1,000 cubic feet. For oil—$0.24 per barrel.	Returns and payments—within 30 days after the last day of the month being reported.
Auto rental excise tax.	4% on vehicles weighing less than 11,000 lbs. for less than 30 days.	Payment and collection—the auto rental excise tax is imposed, paid, and collected in the same manner that the state gross retail tax (sales and use) is imposed, paid, and collected.
Cigarette tax; tobacco products tax.	20-pack cigarettes—$0.995. 25-pack cigarettes—$1.24375. Other tobacco products—24% wholesale price of tobacco products other than moist snuff. Moist snuff—$0.40 per ounce.	Reports by distributors—sales to other distributors, 15th of each month; interstate sales, 10th of each month. Payment—by purchase of stamps and affixing to individual packages.
	Tobacco products tax—24% of wholesale price.	Reports and payments—before 15th of each month.
Sales and use tax.	Sales and use—7%.	Returns and payment—monthly within 30 days after close of the month (within 20 days if average monthly liability for prior year exceeded $1,000).

Tax	Basis—Rates	Due Dates
Insurance tax.	Foreign companies and domestic companies electing to pay the tax—1.3% of gross premiums less allowable deductions, including consideration for reinsurance, dividends paid or credited, premiums returned, and unearned premiums.	Reports—March 1. Payments—estimated tax due on or before the 15th days of April, June, September and December; balance of tax due with annual report.
	Fire companies—An additional 0.5% of gross premiums less returned premiums and consideration received from reinsurance.	Fire companies—payments—before March 2.
	Surplus lines brokers—2.5%.	Surplus lines brokers—Financial statement—March 15; payments—February 1 and August 1.

Iowa

Tax System.—The Iowa tax system was originally based primarily on a general property tax. The property tax has now been replaced as a source of state revenue (although property continues to be taxed at all other levels of government) by corporate and special income taxes, a sales tax and various occupational and license taxes. The legislature has delegated broad licensing powers to municipalities, but such powers are limited to specific authorizations. An outline of the Iowa tax system follows:

Tax	Basis—Rates	Due Dates
General income tax.	Individuals—2020 Rates: Rates: First $1,666 of taxable income, 0.33%; over $1,667 to $3,332 x 0.67% minus $5.66; over $3,32 to $6,664 x 2.25% minus $58.31; over $6,664 to $14,994 x 4.14% minus $184.26; over $14,994 to $24,990 x 5.63% minus $407.68; over $24,990 to $33,320 x 5.96% minus $490.14; over $33,320 to $49,980 x 6.250 minus $586.77; over $49,980 to $74,970 x 7.44% minus $1,181.53; and over $74,970 and over x 8.530% minus $1,998.70; or an alternative minimum tax equal 6.7% of the taxpayer's minimum taxable income. 2021 Rates: First $1,676 of taxable income, 0.33%; over $1,676 to $3,352 x 0.67% minus $5.70; over $3,352 to $6,704 x 2.25% minus $58.66; over $6,704 to $15,084 x 4.14% minus $185.37; over $15,084 to $25,140 x 5.63% minus $410.12; over $25,140 to $33,520 x 5.96% minus $493.08; over $33,520 to $50,280 x 6.250 minus $590.29; over $50,280 to $75,420 x 7.44% minus $1,188.62; and over $75,420 and over x 8.530% minus $2,010.70; or an alternative minimum tax equal 6.7% of the taxpayer's minimum taxable income. Withholding required.	Returns and payment—last day of 4th month after end of tax year. Estimated payments—installments for calendar-year taxpayers on April 30, June 30, September 30, January 31; or installments for fiscal-year taxpayers on last day of 4th, 6th, and 9th months of current fiscal year and 1st month of the next fiscal year.
	Nonresidents—Same rates as above on income derived from Iowa.	
	Corporations—2020 Rates: first $25,000 of net taxable income, 6%; $25,001 to $100,000, 8%; $100,001 to $250,000, 10%; over $250,000, 12% or the greater of the income or franchise tax or the state alternative minimum tax, which equals 60% of the maximum Iowa corporate income tax rate (rounded to the nearest 0.1%) of the taxpayer's state alternative minimum taxable income. 2021 Rates: first $25,000 of net taxable income, 5.5%; $25,001 to $100,000, 5.5%; $100,001 to $250,000, 9%; over $250,000, 9.8% or the greater of the income or franchise tax or the state alternative minimum tax, which equals 60% of the maximum Iowa corporate income tax rate (rounded to the nearest 0.1%) of the taxpayer's state alternative minimum taxable income.	Returns and payment—last day of 4th month after end of tax year. Estimated payments—installments for calendar-year taxpayers on April 30, June 30, September 30, December 31; or installments for fiscal-year taxpayers on last day of 4th, 6th, 9th, and 12th months of the current fiscal year.
	Financial institutions (franchise)—5% of taxable net income.	Returns and payments—last day of 4th month after end of tax year.

Tax	Basis—Rates	Due Dates
General property tax.	Rates fixed locally on an annual basis to meet budget needs. Property is generally assessed at 100% of market value; agricultural property is assessed according to productivity. Personal property is exempt.	Payments—in full before September 1, or in installments by September 1 and March 1.
Grain handler's tax.	1/4 mill per bushel of grain handled.	Report—between January 1 and 60 days thereafter. Payment—same as general property tax.
Alcoholic beverage taxes.	Beer—$.19 per gallon or $5.89 per barrel of beer, prorated for lesser amounts. Wine—$1.75 per gallon or fraction.	Beer and wine—15th of each month.
Gasoline tax; special fuel tax.	Motor fuel—30¢ per gallon (30.5¢ per gallon, July 1, 2019 through June 30, 2020). Special fuel (diesel)—32.5¢ per gallon.	Reports and payments—last day of each month; importers must report and pay semimonthly, due on the last day of the month (for the first 15 days), and on the 15th of the following month (for the remainder).
Motor vehicle rental excise tax.	Automobile rental tax—5% of rental price.	Reports and payments—last days of April, July, October and January.
Cigarette and tobacco products tax.	Cigarettes and little cigars—6.8¢ per cigarette ($1.36 per pack of 20) or per little cigar.	Payment—by purchase of stamps. Reports—10th of each month.
	Tobacco products—50% of wholesale price of tobacco products (22% of wholesale price, plus an additional 28% of the wholesale price). Snuff is taxed at $1.19 per ounce.	Tobacco products—20th of each month.
Realty transfer tax.	$0.80 per $500. The first $500 is exempt.	Payment—when deed or other instrument conveying the property is presented for recording.

Tax	Basis—Rates	Due Dates
Sales tax; use (compensating) tax.	Sales tax—6% of gross receipts from sales of tangible personal property, utilities, admission to amusements, fairs and athletic events, operation of amusement devices and games of skill, printing services, vulcanizing, recapping and retreading services, service or warranty contracts, prepaid telephone calling cards, and solid waste collection services.	Sales—file quarterly by the last day of the month following the end of the quarter if annual liability is between $120 and $6,000. File annually by January 31 if annual liability is less than $120. File monthly by the 20th if annual liability is over $6,000 but not more than $60,000. If more than $60,000, electronic deposits are required on the 25th of the month of collection and the 10th of the following month.
	Use tax—6% of purchase price of tangible personal property for use within the state.	Use—last day of the month following the end of the quarter, except if monthly collections exceed $1,500, deposits are due on or before the 20th day of the month following the month of collection. Total quarterly amount due with quarterly report by the last day of the month following the end of the quarter. If annual use tax liability does not exceed $120, reports and payments due January 31.
Insurance companies tax.	Life insurance companies and health service associations: 1% of adjusted gross premiums. Insurers other than life insurance companies: 1%. Marine insurance underwriting profits: 6.5% of profits from insurance written in Iowa. Unauthorized insurers: 1% of gross premiums received.	Insurance premiums tax—Reports and payments—due March 1. Prepayment requirements for taxpayers with previous-year liability exceeding $1,000. Life insurance companies and health service associations, as well as insurers other than life insurance companies: 50% of the prior year's tax, due June 1, and an additional 50% of the prior year's tax, due August 15 of each year. Marine insurance underwriting profits: reports and payments due June 1.
	Foreign companies subject to retaliatory taxes.	

Kansas

Tax System.—The Kansas tax system was founded on a general property tax at uniform rates within each taxing district. The general property tax has been supplemented by taxes on incomes, sales, use, occupations and privileges. In the case of corporations, a franchise tax based on capital stock is also imposed. An outline of the Kansas tax system follows:

Tax	Basis—Rates	Due Dates
Income tax.	Individuals—for tax year 2019: married individuals filing jointly, Kansas taxable income over $5,000, but not over $30,000, 3.1%; over $30,000, but not over $60,000, $930 plus 5.25% of the excess over $30,000; and over $60,000, $2,505 plus 5.7% of the excess over $60,000. For single individuals and married individuals filing separately with Kansas taxable income over $2,500 but not over $15,000, 3.1%; over $15,000, but not over $30,000, the tax is $465 plus 5.25% of the excess over $15,000; and over $30,000, the tax is $1,252.50 plus 5.7% of the excess over $30,000. Married individuals filing joint returns with taxable income of $5,000 or less, and all other individuals with taxable income of $2,500 or less, will have a tax liability of zero.	Returns and payments—individuals and corporations—15th day of 4th month after end of income year. Domestic insurers, when federal income tax return is due.
	Nonresidents—same on income from sources in Kansas.	
	General withholding is required.	Payment of estimated tax is due on April 15, June 15, September 15, and January 15 (December 15 for corporations).
	Corporations: 4% on federal taxable income with modifications from business done in the state or derived from Kansas sources, plus a 3.0% surtax on taxable income in excess of $50,000.	Corporate income—annually, April 15 or the 15th day of the fourth month after end of income year.
Bank privilege (income) tax.	Banks—2.25% on net income, plus a 2.125% surtax on net income over $25,000. The tax on trust companies, savings and loan associations and development credit corporations is 2.25%, plus a 2.25% surtax on net income over $25,000. These taxes are in lieu of taxes on stock or assets.	Financial institutions—returns and payment due 15th day of 4th month after end of federal tax year. Quarterly payments of estimated tax required.
General property tax.	Real and tangible personal property—Valued at fair market value, unless specifically classified at a lower percentage. One mill for educational institutions, and 0.5 mill for institutions that care for the disabled.	Tangible personal property—returns—March 15. General property—returns—railroads and public utilities, March 20. Oil and gas property statements, April 1. Payment—December 20 and May 10 (in full on December 20 if $10 or less).

Tax	Basis—Rates	Due Dates
Alcoholic beverage tax.	Excise—beer and cereal malt beverage, 18¢ per gallon; wine, 14% alcohol or less, 30¢ per gallon; over 14%, 75¢ per gallon; alcohol and spirits, $2.50 per gallon.	
	Enforcement—8% of gross receipts.	
	Clubs, caterers, drinking establishments, temporary permit holders, and public venues—10% of gross receipts.	
Motor vehicle fuel and special fuel tax.	Motor vehicle fuel—24¢ per gallon. Special fuel—26¢ per gallon. LP gas—23¢ per gallon. E85 fuel—17¢ per gallon. CNG—24¢ per gallon. LNG—26¢ per gallon.	Reports and payments—25th of each month. Interstate motor fuel users—last day of January, April, July, and October.
	Additional 1¢ per gallon on petroleum products (other than aviation fuel) manufactured in or imported into Kansas, levied to fund storage tank release trust (tax may be suspended depending on fund balance).	Reports and payments—before the 25th of each month.
	Additional 1.5¢ per barrel (50 gals.) petroleum products inspection fee levied on the manufacturer, importer, exporter or distributor for first possession of petroleum products.	Reports and payments—25th of each month.
Severance tax.	Oil and gas, 8% of gross value; coal, $1 per ton.	Reports—due on or before the 20th day of the second month following the end of every calendar month in which oil, gas or coal is removed from a lease or production unit or mine.
		Payments—on or before the 20th day of the second month following the month of severance.
	Conservation fee fund tax—Oil and gas-rates set by State Corporation Commission: Oil, 144 mills per barrel; Gas, 20.50 mills per 1,000 cubic feet; Plugged well, 3.25¢ per foot of well depth ($35 minimum).	Same as for oil and gas tax (above).
Cigarette and tobacco products tax.	Cigarette tax—$1.29 per pack of 20 cigarettes; $1.61 per pack of 25 cigarettes. 5¢ per milliliter of consumable material for electronic cigarettes and a proportionate tax on all fractional parts thereof.	Cigarettes—report (wholesalers), 10th of each month. Payment, by purchase of stamps. Consumable materials—reports and payments, 20th of each month.
	Tobacco products—10% of wholesale sales price.	Tobacco products—reports and payments, 20th of each month.

Tax	Basis—Rates	Due Dates
Sales and use tax	STATE SALES TAX RATE—6.5% of gross receipts from retail sale, rental, or lease of tangible personal property and from the retail sale of specified services. STATE USE TAX RATE—6.5% of sales price of tangible personal property purchased for storage, use, or consumption. MOTOR VEHICLE RENTALS—Motor vehicle rentals are subject to an additional 3.5% excise tax imposed on gross receipts from the rental or lease of motor vehicles for a period of 28 or fewer days (short-term rentals).	SALES TAX—If a retailer's sales or use tax liability for any calendar year: (1) exceeds $4,000, monthly returns must be filed by the 25th of the following month, regardless of the accounting method used; (2) does not exceed $4,000, retailers must file quarterly returns by the 25th day of the month following each quarter; and (3) is not more than $400, retailers must file annual returns by January 25 of the following year. USE TAX—same as sales tax.
Private car companies tax.	Railroads leasing private cars—2.5% of gross earnings from use or operation of cars within state.	Report and payment—March 1.
Insurance companies tax.	Domestic companies, 2%; foreign companies, 2%; captive insurers, 2%.	Reports—60 days after January 1; payment, when assessed. Estimated taxes due June 15 and December 15.
	Agents, 6% of gross premiums; surplus lines, 6% of premiums allocated to Kansas.	Agents—report and payment due March 1. Surplus lines—report and payment due March 1.
	Fire insurance companies, 2% of all premiums on fire and lightning insurance covering Kansas risks the preceding year. Fire marshal tax, up to .80%.	Fire insurance companies tax—report and payment, April 1. Fire marshal—payment March 15.
	Professional and trade associations not subject to the Commissioner's jurisdiction, 1% of annual Kansas gross premiums.	Payment—May 1.

Kentucky

Tax System.—A general property tax is imposed on real and tangible personal property at uniform rates in the taxing districts where such property is located. The property tax is supplemented by (1) state taxes on franchises, incomes, privileges and occupations and (2) municipal taxes and inspection fees. An outline of the Kentucky tax system follows:

Tax	Basis—Rates	Due Dates
General income tax.	**Individuals.**—5% on federal adjusted gross income after state modifications.	**Annual returns and payments.**—April 15 (15th day of 4th month after end of income year).
	Estimated tax threshold.—More than $500 in expected tax liability.	**Estimated tax returns and payments.**—April 15th, June 15th, September 15th, and January 15th.
	Corporation income tax.—5% on federal taxable income after state modifications. **Limited liability entity tax (LLET).**—Lesser of 9 1/2¢ per $100 of gross receipts or 75¢ per $100 of gross profits. Exemption for gross receipts or profits of $3 million or less. Taxpayers with more than $3 million but less than $6 million of gross receipts or profits may reduce liability by an amount equal to $2,850 of gross receipts or $22,500 of gross profits multiplied by a fraction, numerator of which is $6 million minus gross receipts or profits for taxable year, and denominator of which is $3 million. Minimum tax is $175 for all taxpayers.	**Annual returns and payments.**—April 15 (15th day of 4th month after end of income year).
	Estimated tax threshold.—More than $5,000 in expected income tax and LLET liability.	**Estimated tax returns and payments.**—Due as follows: 25% by April 15; 25% by June 15; 25% by September 15; and 25% by December 15.
Bank franchise tax.	1.1% of net capital; minimum $300. Kentucky repeals the tax on January 1, 2021.	Reports and payments—March 15.
General property tax; public service companies tax.	General property—Aggregate of state and local fixed annually to meet local budget requirements. State rate on real property for 2020 is 12.2¢ per $100.	General property—personal property returns between January 1 and May 15; utilities, April 30. Payment of property taxes generally—December 31; public service companies, local taxes due 30 days after notice.
Alcoholic beverages tax.	Excise—sale and distribution, beer $2.50 per barrel; wine 50¢ per gallon; distilled spirits $1.92 per gallon; distilled spirits representing 6% or less of total volume of beverage, 25¢ per gallon.	Excise tax—Reports and payments, on or before the 20th of each month.
	Gross receipts—Wholesalers of wine and distilled spirits and distributors of beer: (1) for distilled spirits, 11% of wholesale sales; and (2) for wine and beer, 10% for wholesale sales.	Gross receipts tax—Reports and payments, on or before the 20th of each month.

Tax	Basis—Rates	Due Dates
Motor fuels tax; motor carrier fuel use tax; liquefied petroleum motor fuel tax.	Variable. Rate effective in 2020 was 26¢ per gallon on gas.	Reports and payments—25th day of each month, except last day of month following each quarter under the carrier gasoline use tax.
Oil production and severance taxes.	Oil production—4.5% of market value of crude petroleum produced.	Oil production reports and payment—20th of each month for the transporter.
	Coal severance—4.5% of gross value of coal severed and/or processed. Minimum tax, 50¢ per ton of severed coal. Tax limited to 50¢ per ton or 4% of the selling price per ton, whichever is less, on coal used for burning solid waste.	Coal severance—reports and payments, 20th of each month.
	Natural resources severance—4.5% of gross value of natural gas and other natural resources severed or processed. Tax limited to 12¢ per ton of clay and 14¢ per ton of limestone used to manufacture cement.	Natural resources severance—reports and payments, last day of each month.
Motor vehicle usage tax.	6% of retail sales price of motor vehicles or gross rental charge of U-Drive-Its, except 81% of such price for new trucks whose gross weight is over 10,000 lbs; minimum tax $6. $25 per month on dealers' loaner vehicles or usage tax.	Payment—when owner titles or registers a vehicle.
Cigarette tax and tobacco products excise tax.	CIGARETTES: $1.10 per pack of 20 cigarettes. TOBACCO PRODUCTS: tobacco products, other than snuff and chewing tobacco, 15% of actual price for which distributor sells product (retail distributors taxed at their total purchase price); snuff, 19¢ per each 1-1/2 ounces or portion thereof by net weight; chewing tobacco, 19¢ per single unit, 40¢ per each half-pound unit, or 65¢ per pound unit. VAPING PRODUCTS: $1.50 per cartridge; 15% on open vaping systems	Reports—20th of each month. Payment—for cigarettes, by purchase of stamps.
Realty transfer tax.	50¢ per $500 of value declared in the deed transferring title to realty.	Payment—collected by county clerk at time of recording.
Sales and use tax.	6% of gross receipts from retail sales, rentals, or leases of tangible personal property (including natural, artificial, and mixed gas; electricity; water; steam; and prewritten computer software) or digital property; 6% of gross receipts from the sale of specified services.	Reports and payments—due the 20th of each month. The Kentucky Department of Revenue may permit or require returns or tax payments for periods other than monthly. If the average monthly tax liability exceeds $10,000, the due date is the 25th day of the current month for the period from the 16th of preceding month through the 15th of current month.

Tax	Basis—Rates	Due Dates
Transient room (lodging) tax.	1% state-level tax applies to charges for the renting out of any suite, room, or cabin by motels, hotels, inns, and other accommodation businesses. The tax is imposed in addition to the 6% sales tax and any locally assessed transient room tax. The tax does not apply to the rental or lease of any room (or set of rooms) equipped with a kitchen, in an apartment building, and that is usually leased as a dwelling for 30 or more days by an individual or business that regularly holds itself out as exclusively providing apartments.	Payment—20th day of the following month.
Telecommunication/ utility taxes.	Utility gross receipts license tax—variable cannot exceed 3% of gross receipts derived from furnishing utility services, cable service, direct satellite broadcast and wireless cable service, and Internet protocol television service within a school district.	Payment—20th day of the following month.
	Telecommunications tax—1.3% of gross revenues from communications services, 2.4% of gross revenues from multi-channel video programming services, and 3% excise tax on multi-channel video and audio programming services.	Payment—20th day of the following month.
Insurance premiums tax.	**Life insurers.**—1.5% of taxable premiums, except domestic insurers may irrevocably elect to pay a combined premiums tax and tax of one-tenth of one cent ($0.001) on each $100 of taxable capital, then offset the capital tax against the premium tax. **Stock, mutual, and other insurers.**—2% of taxable premiums, plus 0.75% on premiums allocated to fire insurance. **Unauthorized insurers.**—2% of taxable insurance or reinsurance premiums. **Surplus lines brokers.**—3% of taxable premiums. **Captive insurers.**—0.4% on first $20 million of premium receipts; 0.3% on next $20 million of premium receipts; 0.2% on next $20 million of premium receipts; and 0.075% on each additional dollar of premium receipts. $5,000 minimum tax. **Surcharge (other than life and health insurers).**—$1.80 per $100 of premiums, assessments, or other charges, except for municipal premium taxes	**Annual returns and payments.**—March 1.
	Estimated tax threshold.—$5,000 or more in prior year's liability. No fixed-dollar threshold for surplus lines brokers.	**Quarterly tax returns and payments.**—1/3 of prior year's tax liability or estimated current year's tax liability by June 1, October 1, and March 1 of the following year. Tax on quarterly transactions by surplus lines brokers due April 30; July 31; October 30; and January 31.

Louisiana

Tax System.—The tax system was founded upon a general property tax assessed by the several parish assessors, subject to review and approval of the parish boards of equalization and the State Tax Commission. Assessments are made uniformly according to value within each taxing district. The property tax is supplemented by other state taxes, the revenue from which in many instances is shared by the local governments. These include taxes on sales, use, severance, incomes, franchises, occupations and privileges. Municipal license taxes and inspection fees are also exacted within local jurisdictions for purposes of revenue or regulation. An outline of the Louisiana tax system follows:

Tax	Basis—Rates	Due Dates
Corporation franchise tax.	The franchise tax is imposed at a rate of $1.50 for each $1,000, or major fraction thereof, on the first $300,000 of taxable capital, and at a rate of $3 for each $1,000, or major fraction thereof, which exceeds $300,000 of taxable capital. In-lieu fee of $10 provided for certain cooperatives. Initial tax of $110. Applicable to tax periods beginning between July 1, 2020, and June 30, 2021, the franchise tax of $1.50 for each $1,000 that is levied on the first $300,000 of taxable capital will not apply to small business corporations. During this time period, the initial franchise tax of $110 will also not apply to small business corporations.	Returns and payment—Initial return: Tax due immediately on taxpayer becoming subject to franchise tax; tax payable on or before 15th day of fourth month after the month in which tax is due. Annual return: Tax due on 1st day of each calendar or fiscal year; tax payable on or before 15th day of fourth month after the month in which tax is due.
Income tax.	Individuals—first $12,500 of taxable income—2%; next $37,500—4%; over $50,000—6%.	Returns and payment—May 15 for calendar year and 15th day of 5th month after close of income year for fiscal year. Estimated tax—declarations and payment due on 15th day of April, June, September, and January for calendar year and 15th day of the 4th, 6th, 9th months of income year and 1st month following close of the fiscal year.
	Corporations—4% of first $25,000 of Louisiana taxable income; 5% of next $25,000; 6% of next $50,000; 7% of next $100,000; 8% of Louisiana taxable income in excess of $200,000. Effective for taxable years beginning on and after January 1, 2019, for pass-through entities that elect to be taxed at the entity level—2% of first $25,000 of Louisiana taxable income; 4% of the next $75,000; 6% of Louisiana taxable income in excess of $100,000.	Returns and payments—Fiscal year—on or before the 15th day of the 5th month following the close of the accounting period. Calendar year—May 15.
	Withholding required.	Returns and payments—Quarterly returns and payments due on the last day of the month following the close of the quarterly period (April 30, July 31, October 31, and January 31).

Tax	Basis—Rates	Due Dates
General property tax.	Property is taxed at a rate equal to all lawful levies and is assessed at a percentage of fair market or use value.	Self-reporting forms are sent to assessors. Payment by December 31 except for Orleans Parish, which is February 1.
Alcoholic beverages tax.	Excise—Beverages of low alcoholic content (beer), $12.50 per barrel containing not more than 31 gallons. Malt beverages, $12.50 per barrel. Liquor, 80¢ per liter. Sparkling wines, 55¢ per liter. Still wines per liter: 14% or less alcohol, 20¢; 14% to 24%, 35¢; over 24%, 55¢.	Beverages of high alcoholic content (liquor and wine): Report filed and taxes paid on or before the 15th day of the month following the taxable month. Beverages of low alcoholic content (beer): Report filed and taxes paid within 20 days after the end of each calendar month.
Gasoline tax.	Gasoline and diesel fuel—16¢ per gallon, plus additional 4¢ per gallon, on gasoline and diesel fuel, for a total of 20¢ per gallon.	Reports and payments—Terminal operator monthly return—20th of next month; terminal operator annual return—last day of February following the end of the calendar year being filed; supplier/permissive supplier monthly return—22nd of next month; distributor/exporter/blender monthly return—20th of next month; importer monthly return—15th of next month.
Severance tax.	**Timber**—Trees and timber, 2.25% of current stumpage value as determined by the Louisiana Forestry Commission. Pulpwood, 5% of current stumpage value as determined by the Louisiana Forestry Commission.	Reports and payments—Tax returns filed by the last day of the month following the taxable month.
	Gas—The tax rate for natural gas and equivalent gas volumes of natural gasoline, casinghead gasoline, and other natural gas liquids per 1,000 cu. ft. at a base pressure of 15.025 lbs. per sq. in. absolute and at 60 degrees Fahrenheit is adjusted annually on July 1 and may never be less than 7¢. Full rate, 9.34¢ per thousand cu. ft., through June 30, 2021.	Reports and payments—Tax returns must be filed on or before the 25th day of the second month following the month to which the tax is applicable.
	Oil—(per barrel of 42 gals.)—Full rate oil/condensate, 12.5% of value.	Reports and payments—Tax returns filed on or before the 25th day of the second month following the month to which the tax is applicable.
Tobacco tax.	Cigarettes—$1.08 per pack.	Cigarettes and tobacco—reports—20th of each month. Payment—by purchase of stamps or use of metered stamping machines.
	Cigars—8% of invoice price if invoiced at $120 per 1,000 or less; 20% if invoiced at over $120 per 1,000.	
	Smokeless tobacco—20% of invoice price.	

Tax	Basis—Rates	Due Dates
Sales and use tax.	4.45% of retail sale, lease or rental, use, consumption, distribution or storage of tangible personal property and sales of specified services	Reports and payments—20th of each month for the preceding calendar month. If liability is less than $500 per month, returns and payments are due quarterly on the 20th of the first month of the next succeeding quarter.
Insurance companies gross premiums tax.	Life, health, accident, or service insurers—premiums of $7,000 or less, $140; over $7,000, $140 plus $225 per each additional $10,000 over $7,000.	Report—March 1. Payment—15th day of the month following the end of each quarter, except that 4th quarter's tax is due March 1; surplus line brokers remit tax on or before the 1st day of March, June, September and December.
	Health maintenance organizations (HMOs)—$550 for every $10,000 of gross annual premiums collected.	
	Fire, marine, transportation, casualty, surety, or other insurance—premiums of $6,000 or less, $185; over $6,000, $185 plus $300 per each additional $10,000 over $6,000.	
	Foreign and alien insurers (other than life) for support of municipal fire departments—2% of gross premiums on fire risks.	
	Fire marshal's tax—1.25% of gross premiums.	
	Insurers (other than life insurers)—additional 0.25% of annual premiums for insurance against loss or damage by fire on Louisiana property.	
	Surplus line brokers—4.85% per annum.	
	Foreign companies are subject to retaliatory taxes.	

Maine

Tax System.—Maine derives its revenue from taxes imposed on corporate and individual incomes and real and tangible personal property of residents, and from sales and use taxes, gasoline taxes, motor vehicle registration fees and the cigarette tax. An annual franchise tax on domestic corporations is imposed, and an annual license fee is required from foreign corporations. An outline of the Maine tax system follows:

Tax	Basis—Rates	Due Dates
Corporate annual report.	Domestic and foreign corporations annual report filing fees: domestic, $85; foreign, $150.	Annual report—determined by Secretary of State.
Corporate income tax.	Corporations—3.5% of the first $350,000 of Maine net income; Maine net income over $350,000 but not over $1.05 million, $12,250 plus 7.93% of net income over $350,000; over $1.05 million but not over $3.5 million, $67,760 plus 8.33% over $1.05 million; over $3.5 million, $271,845 plus 8.93% of net income over $3.5 million. Alternative minimum tax: repealed for tax years beginning after 2017.	Returns and payments—due when federal tax is due (April 15 for calendar-year taxpayers; 15th day of the 4th month following the close of the tax year for fiscal-year taxpayers); payments of estimated tax, 15th day of 4th, 6th, 9th and 12th months of fiscal year. If the corporation's tax year is a short year of fewer than 12 months, then the estimated tax must be paid in full by the 15th day of the last month of its tax year.
Franchise tax.	Financial institutions—1% of Maine net income for the tax year plus 8¢ per $1,000 of financial institution's Maine assets *or* 39¢ per $1,000 of financial institution's Maine assets.	Returns and payments—due on or before the 15th day of the 4th month following the end of the financial institution's fiscal year (April 15 for calendar-year taxpayers).

Tax	Basis—Rates	Due Dates
Personal income tax.	2021 tax year—*Single individuals and married persons filing separately:* Maine taxable income less than $22,450, 5.8%; $22,450 to $53,150, $1,302 plus 6.75% of excess over $22,450; $53,150 or more, $3,374 plus 7.15% of excess over $53,150. *Heads of households:* Less than $33,650, 5.8%; $33,650 to $79,750, $1,952 plus 6.75% of excess over $33,650; $79,750 or more, $5,064 plus 7.15% of excess over $79,750. *Married filing jointly and surviving spouses:* Less than $44,950, 5.8%; $44,950 to $106,350, $2,607 plus 6.75% of excess over $44,950; $106,350 or more, $6,752 plus 7.15% of excess over $106,350. 2020 tax year—*Single individuals and married persons filing separately:* Maine taxable income less than $22,200, 5.8%; $22,200 to $52,600, $1,288 plus 6.75% of excess over $22,200; $52,600 or more, $3,340 plus 7.15% of excess over $52,600. *Heads of households:* Less than $33,300, 5.8%; $33,300 to $78,900, $1,931 plus 6.75% of excess over $33,300; $78,900 or more, $5,009 plus 7.15% of excess over $78,900. *Married filing jointly and surviving spouses:* Less than $44,450, 5.8%; $44,450 to $105,200, $2,578 plus 6.75% of excess over $44,450; $105,200 or more, $6,679 plus 7.15% of excess over $105,200.	Returns and payments—due when federal tax return is due; payments of estimated tax, 15th day of 4th, 6th, 9th and 13th months of fiscal year. Farmer or fisherman, single payment by January 15 of following tax year.
General property tax.	General property—valuation of real and personal property based on 100% of current market value.	General property—assessed as of April 1; due date determined by local jurisdiction.
	Unorganized Territory Tax—set by the State Tax Assessor.	Payment—due upon receipt of bill. Interest accrues after October 1.
Alcoholic beverages tax.	Excise—malt liquor, plus premium: 35¢ per gallon; wine, plus premium: 60¢ per gallon.	Excise—at time of purchase or, for bonded manufacturers and wholesalers of malt liquor or wine, 15th of each month for preceding month.
Motor fuel taxes.	Gasoline—30.0¢ per gallon; diesel, 31.2¢; internal combustion fuel bought or used to propel a jet or turbojet engine aircraft, 3.4¢ per gallon.	Gasoline tax—reports and payments—distributors, exporters, importers, reports due 21st of each month; wholesalers, last day of each month.
Cigarette and tobacco products tax.	100 mills per cigarette ($2.00 per 20 cigarettes).	Payment—by affixing stamps.
	Tobacco products—smokeless tobacco, $2.02 per ounce. Packages containing smokeless tobacco that contain less than one ounce, also $2.02 per package.	Tobacco products—reports and payments—last day of each month.
Realty transfer tax.	$2.20 per $500 or fraction of value of the property; grantor and grantee each liable for half.	Payment—the tax is paid by affixing stamps to the document.

Tax	Basis—Rates	Due Dates
Sales and use tax.	Sales and use—5.5% general rate on tangible personal property and taxable services; 5.5% on automobile rentals of one year or more; 10% on rentals of automobiles for less than one year; 9% on rentals of rooms or shelter; 8% on the value of all food prepared by a retailer.	Reports and payments—15th of each month, less often for small taxpayers.
Insurance companies tax.	2% on domestic and foreign insurance companies; 1% on all gross direct premiums collected or contracted for on long-term care policies; 1% with respect to premiums written on qualified group disability policies, unless the premium is written by a large domestic insurer (any insurer domiciled in Maine with assets in excess of $5 billion), in which case the rate is 2.55%.	Reports and payments—Quarterly return and payment due April 30, June 25, and October 31. If tax is $1,000 or less, an annual return and payment due March 15 may be allowed. Annual reconciliation return due March 15 (final payment due with annual return). Additional tax on fire insurance companies paid on an estimated basis at the end of each calendar month.
	Fire insurance companies—additional 1.4% tax.	
	Surplus line brokers—3% of gross direct premiums, if Maine is the insured's home state.	
	Foreign companies subject to retaliatory taxes.	

Maryland

Tax System.—Maryland derives its revenue from taxes imposed on the income of individuals, estates and corporations, sales and use taxes and taxes imposed on specified businesses and privileges. Property taxes are levied by the local governments on real and tangible personal property and on certain intangible personal property for the benefit of the state and local governments. An outline of the Maryland tax system follows:

Tax	Basis—Rates	Due Dates
Income tax.	Individuals—2% of Maryland taxable income of $1 through $1,000; 3% of Maryland taxable income of $1,001 through $2,000; 4% of Maryland taxable income of $2,001 through $3,000; 4.75% of Maryland taxable income of $3,001 through $100,000; 5% of Maryland taxable income of $100,001 through $125,000; 5.25% of Maryland taxable income of $125,001 through $150,000; 5.5% of Maryland taxable of $150,001 through $250,000; 5.75% of Maryland taxable income in excess of $250,000. Joint filers, surviving spouse, head of household—2% of Maryland taxable income of $1 through $1,000; 3% of Maryland taxable income of $1,001 through $2,000; 4% of Maryland taxable income of $2,001 through $3,000; 4.75% of Maryland taxable income of $3,001 through $150,000; 5% of Maryland taxable income of $150,001 through $175,000; 5.25% of Maryland taxable income of $175,001 through $225,000; 5.5% of Maryland taxable of $225,001 through $300,000; 5.75% of Maryland taxable income in excess of $300,000. Tax preference items are taxable if over $10,000 for an individual return; $20,000 for a joint return. General withholding required according to tables prepared by Comptroller.	Returns and payments—Individuals, 15th day of 4th month after end of income year; corporations, 15th day of 4th month after end of tax year.
	Counties are authorized to impose local individual income taxes at a percentage of taxable income.	
	Corporations—8.25% of net income allocable to the state.	Estimates of personal income tax due April 15; payments due April 15, June 15, September 15. Final payment due January 15 following or January 31 with final income tax return. Corporate and partnership estimated tax declarations and payments due by 15th day of 4th, 6th, 9th and 12th months of tax year.

Tax	Basis—Rates	Due Dates
	Partnerships and S corporations—7.5% for nonresident individual members (including nonresident fiduciaries) and 8.25% for nonresident entity members. Effective for tax years beginning on or after January 1, 2020, the tax rate for pass-through entities that elect to be taxed at the entity level will be the sum of the lowest county tax rate imposed and the top marginal state tax rate for individuals applied to the sum of each individual member's distributive or pro rata share of the pass-through's taxable income. For corporation members, the tax rate is equal to the state corporate income tax rate (8.25%) applied to the sum of each member's distributive or pro rata share of the pass-through's taxable income.	
General property tax.	General property—aggregate of state and local rates fixed annually to meet budgets. Assessment of real property based on fair market value of property. All real property is valued once in every three-year cycle, based on exterior physical inspection of the property. Increases in value are phased in over three following years.	Homeowners must pay first installment of semiannual tax by September 30; second installment must be paid by December 31.
Admissions tax.	Local admissions taxes are authorized at up to 10% of gross receipts.	Reports and payments—For regular accounts, 10th of month following taxable event. Seasonal or alternative filing basis may also be assigned.
Alcoholic beverages tax.	Excise—distilled spirits and other alcoholic beverages except wines and beer, \$1.50 per gallon; wines, 40¢ per gallon (10.57¢ per liter); beer, 9¢ per gallon (2.3778¢ per liter).	
Gasoline tax.	Motor fuels—36.3¢ per gallon. 7¢ per gallon for aviation gasoline. 36.3¢ per gallon for gasohol.	Reports and payments—last day of month for preceding month or postmarked not later than two days prior to the last day of each month.
	Motor carrier road tax—same as motor fuels rate for type of fuel used that is in effect when return period begins.	Reports and payments—quarterly basis (last day of April, July, October, and January).
Tobacco tax.	\$2.00 per pack of 20 cigarettes; 10¢ for each cigarette in a package of more than 20 cigarettes and in a package of free samples.	Reports—wholesalers, 21st of month; manufacturers that distribute free samples of cigarettes, 15th of month (report the quantity of free sample cigarettes distributed during preceding month).
	Other tobacco products—30% of wholesale price.	Payment—by affixing stamps prior to sale.
State recordation tax.	Rate is set by counties and Baltimore City. Ground rents, redemption sum plus any other consideration.	Payment—when instrument recorded.

Tax	Basis—Rates	Due Dates
State transfer tax.	0.5% of consideration paid or to be paid for realty; 0.25% of consideration for sales of improved residential real property to first-time home buyers who occupy the property as a principal residence.	Payment—when instrument recorded.
Sales and use tax.	6% of taxable price. Alcoholic beverages—9% of taxable price. Short-term vehicle rentals—11.5%.	Reports and payments, retail sales—20th of each month. Comptroller may assign a less frequent filing schedule for taxpayers that remit less than $100 in tax per month.
Public service company franchise tax.	Gross receipts tax—telegraph, telephone, oil pipeline, electric or gas companies, 2% of gross receipts.	Reports and payments—March 15 (April 15, applicable to tax years beginning in tax year 2018 and thereafter). Estimated tax—initial declaration and quarterly reports due by April 15, June 15, September 15 and December 15.
Insurance companies tax.	2% of gross direct premiums; 2% on gross receipts received as a result of capitation payments made to a managed care organization, supplemental payments, and bonus payments, and subscription charges or other amounts paid to a health maintenance organization; 3% of gross premiums charged by unauthorized insurers; 3% of gross premiums less any returned premiums charged for surplus lines insurance. For 2019, health insurance provider fee assessment of 2.75% on all amounts used to calculate the entity's premium tax liability or the amount of the entity's premium tax exemption value for calendar 2018. For 2020 to 2023, the health provider fee assessment is 1% on all amounts used to calculate the entity's premium tax liability for the immediately preceding calendar year. Foreign companies subject to retaliatory taxes.	Reports and payments—March 15; estimated tax—initial declaration and quarterly reports due by April 15, June 15, September 15 and December 15. Unauthorized insurers' tax—report and payment due March 15 and September 15. Surplus lines brokers—report and payment due March 15 and September 15.

Massachusetts

Tax System.—Massachusetts derives its revenue from taxes imposed on the income of individuals and partnerships, from a corporation excise tax, measured by net income and tangible property or net worth, from sales and use taxes and from taxes imposed on specified businesses and privileges. General property taxes are levied by the local governments. An outline of the Massachusetts tax system follows:

Tax	Basis—Rates	Due Dates
Corporation excise (income) tax.	Corporations—Greater of: $2.60 per $1,000 on taxable tangible property or net worth, plus 8% on income attributable to state sources or fixed dollar minimum tax of $456.	Returns and payments—April 15 or 15th day of 4th month following close of fiscal tax year. Estimated tax payments due the 15th day of the 3rd, 6th, 9th and 12th months of the tax year, with fewer installments necessary if filing requirements are met later in the year.
	S corporations—Greater of: $2.60 per $1,000 on taxable tangible property or net worth, plus 1.97% on total receipts of $6 million or more, but less than 9 million; or 2.95% on total receipts of $9 million or more, or fixed dollar minimum tax of $456.	
Financial institutions excise (income) tax.	9% of net income. The minimum tax is $456.	Returns and payments—April 15 or 15th day of 4th month following close of fiscal tax year. Estimated tax payments due the 15th day of the 3rd, 6th, 9th and 12th months of the tax year.
Personal income tax.	Part A income (short-term capital gains): 12.00%; Part A income (interest and dividends): 5.05%; Part B income: 5.05%; and Part C income (long term capital gains): 5.05%.	Returns and payments—April 15 or 15th day of the 4th month following the close of fiscal tax year. Estimated tax payments and returns due April 15, June 15, September 15 and January 15, if expected tax liability that is not covered by withholding exceeds $400.
General property tax.	General property—fair cash value of real and personal property. Rates vary locally.	Reports—at time required in assessors' notices. Tax due July 1. In cities and towns with quarterly payments, preliminary payments may be required, generally on August 1 and November 1 (later dates may be approved by the Commissioner). In cities and towns with semiannual payments, the preliminary tax is due and payable October 1.

Tax	Basis—Rates	Due Dates
Room occupancy excise tax.	Massachusetts imposes a room occupancy excise tax of 5.7%. Each Massachusetts city and town has the option of levying up to an additional 6% (6.5% in Boston). A convention center financing fee of 2.75% is also imposed on room occupancies in Boston, Cambridge, Chicopee, Springfield, West Springfield and Worcester.	Returns and payments—20th of each month for previous month's rentals. Payment is due with return.
Alcoholic beverage tax.	Excise tax on manufacturers, wholesalers and importers—malt beverages, $3.30 per barrel. Other taxes per wine gallon as follows: still wine, including vermouth, 55¢; champagne and sparkling wines, 70¢; alcoholic beverages containing 15% or less alcohol by volume, $1.10 per gallon; alcoholic beverages containing 15% or more alcohol by volume, $4.05 per gallon; cider containing more than 3% but not more than 6% of alcohol by weight at 60 degrees Fahrenheit.	Reports and payments (excise)—due within 20 days after the expiration of the period covered.
Gasoline tax.	The total motor fuel rate for gasoline is 26.54¢ per gallon (state excise tax of 24¢ plus 2.54¢ of other state taxes/fees). Tax rates for special fuels (liquefied gases and propane), aviation fuel, and aircraft (jet) fuel are updated quarterly.	Reports and payments—Licensees dealing in imported fuel, 20th day of January, April, July, and October. Distributors and unclassified exporters and importers, 20th day of each month.
Motor vehicle excise tax.	An excise in the amount of $25 per $1,000 is assessed upon the value of the vehicle as determined in accordance with the depreciation schedule.	Reports—none required. Payment—30 days from date of bill.
Cigarette tax.	$3.51 per pack of 20; Little cigars taxed as cigarettes. Cigars and smoking tobacco—40% of wholesale price; smokeless tobacco—210% of wholesale price.	Reports—on or before the 20th of each month for previous month's sales. Payment—due with return.
Sales and use tax.	6.25% on the sales price or rental charge of tangible personal property or certain telecommunications services sold or rented in the Commonwealth. Cities and towns are authorized to impose an additional 0.75% local option sales tax on taxable sales of meals.	Returns and payment—for tax liability of $100 or less, payment and return due annually by the 20th of the month following the calendar year. For tax liability of $101 to $1,200, payment and return due quarterly by the 20th of the month following the calendar quarter. For tax liability of $1,201 or more, payment and return due monthly by the 20th of the following month.
Direct broadcast satellite television excise tax.	5% of gross revenues of direct broadcast satellite providers.	Returns and payment—by 20th of each month.
Tax on marijuana.	6.25% state sales tax; 10.75% state excise tax; and up to 3% local option for cities or towns.	Returns and payment—by 20th of each month.

Tax	Basis—Rates	Due Dates
Insurance taxes.	2.28% on taxable gross premiums of domestic and foreign casualty companies, plus up to 1% on total gross investment income of domestic companies.	Returns and payment—April 15; May 15 for ocean marine profits tax.
	2% on domestic and foreign life insurance company premiums.	
	5.7% on net underwriting profits from marine insurance.	Estimated tax payments due on the 15th day of the 3rd, 6th, 9th and 12th months of the tax year, with fewer installments necessary if filing requirements are met later in the year.
	Foreign companies are subject to retaliatory taxes.	

Michigan

Tax System.—The state and all of its political subdivisions derive revenue from general property taxation. All property, except that specifically exempted, is subject to taxation according to a uniform rule. This is qualified by the provisions for specific taxes in lieu of the property tax. The property tax has been supplemented by taxes on personal income, sales, use, business and privileges. An outline of the Michigan tax system follows:

Tax	Basis—Rates	Due Dates
Corporate income tax.	C corporations subject to tax at 6%. Financial institutions are subject to a franchise tax at a 0.29% rate.	Reports and payments—last day of 4th month after end of tax year. Calendar-year taxpayers must file quarterly returns and pay estimated tax by April 15, July 15, October 15, and January 15. Fiscal-year taxpayer returns due on the corresponding date for the taxpayer's fiscal year-end.
Michigan business tax.	4.95% business income tax; modified gross receipts tax, 0.8%, and until January 1, 2017, an annual surcharge of 21.99%. Financial institutions are subject to a franchise tax at a 0.29% rate, and until January 1, 2017 an annual surcharge of 23.4%. This is in lieu of the business income tax and the modified gross receipts tax. [CCH Note: After 2011, only certain taxpayers with certificated credits may elect to pay the MBT. Others will pay the corporate income tax.]	Reports and payments—last day of 4th month after end of tax year. Calendar-year taxpayers must file quarterly returns and pay estimated tax by April 15, July 15, October 15, and January 15. Fiscal-year taxpayer returns due on the corresponding date for the taxpayer's fiscal year-end.
Personal income tax.	Individuals, estates, and trusts—4.25% of taxable income.	Returns—calendar-year taxpayers, April 15; fiscal-year taxpayers, 15th day of 4th month after tax year. Estimated tax payments due 15th day of April, June, September and January. Fiscal-year taxpayers may substitute the appropriate dates that correspond to the calendar-year dates.
General property tax.	General property—Property assessed at 50% of true cash value. Intangibles are exempt.	Personal property—returns—February 20. Assessment roll (real property)—first Monday in March. Payment—generally, February 14.
Public service companies tax.	Property of companies subject to assessment by the State Tax Commission is assessed at 50% of its true cash value and taxable value as of the preceding December 31.	Returns—Companies with gross receipts of over $1 million by March 31; $1 million or less, by March 15. Payment—before August 1 and December 1, or all on July 1.

Tax	Basis—Rates	Due Dates
Low-grade iron ore properties tax.	The rated annual capacity of the plant in gross tons multiplied by .55% of the mine value per gross ton, based upon the projected natural iron analysis of the iron ore pellets or of the concentrated and/or agglomerated products, multiplied by the percent of construction completion of the low grade iron ore mining property; starting the calendar year after merchantable ore is commercially produced from a low grade iron ore mining property, 1.1% of mine value per ton based on average natural iron analysis of shipments for that year of pellets and concentrated and/or agglomerated products times average annual production of preceding five years.	Payment—same as general property tax.
Forest lands tax.	Commercial forests—annual specific tax of $1.30 per acre; increases by 5¢ on January 1, 2022, and every five years after that date.	Commercial reserves—same as general property tax.
Convention facility development tax.	3% of room charge in convention hotel located within a qualified local governmental unit if it has 81 to 160 rooms; 6% if more than 160 rooms. All other convention hotels, 1.5% if hotel has 81 to 160 rooms, 5% if more than 160 rooms.	Reports and payments—20th day of month following the month the tax accrued.
Alcoholic beverages tax.	Excise—beer, $6.30 per barrel; wine containing 16% or less alcohol, 13.5¢ per liter, or 20¢ per liter if containing more than 16% alcohol; mixed spirit drink, 48¢ per liter.	
Motor fuel tax.	All motor fuels and alternative fuels (including CNG, LPG, and LNG), 26.3¢ per gallon. Gasoline used in aircraft, 3¢ per gallon.	Reports and payments—20th of each month following reporting period. Motor fuel suppliers and alternative fuel dealers, monthly.
Motor carrier fuel (diesel fuel) tax.	26.3¢ per gallon.	Reports and payments—20th of each month following reporting period. Motor fuel suppliers and alternative fuel dealers, monthly.
Oil and gas severance tax.	Severance—5% of gross cash market value of gas or 6.6% of gross cash market value of oil (4% of gross cash market value of stripper well crude oil and crude oil from marginal properties), plus a fee (computed annually) not to exceed 1% of the gross cash market value of all oil and gas produced in the state.	Report and payment—25th of each month.
Tobacco products tax.	Cigarettes: $2 per pack of 20 cigarettes; Cigars: 32% of the wholesale price (tax may not exceed 50¢ per individual cigar through October 31, 2021). Other: 32% of the wholesale price of noncigarette smoking tobacco, and smokeless tobacco.	Reports and payments—20th of each month.

Tax	Basis—Rates	Due Dates
Realty transfer tax.	County tax—55¢ in counties of less than 2 million population and not more than 75¢ in a county with a population of 2 million or more for each $500 or fraction thereof of value of instrument. State tax—An additional state realty transfer tax is imposed at the rate of $3.75 for each $500, or fraction, of the total value of the property being transferred.	No reports. Payment by affixing stamps.
Sales and use tax.	Sales—6% of gross proceeds from retail sales of tangible personal property, electricity, gas and steam. However, sales for residential use of electricity, natural or artificial gas, or home heating fuels are taxed at 4%. Prepayment of gasoline—Effective November 1, 2020 through November 30, 2020, 10.4¢ per gallon (Effective December 1, 2020 through December 31, 2020, 10.4¢ per gallon). Prepayment of diesel fuel—Effective November 1, 2020 through November 30, 2020, 12.1¢ per gallon (Effective December 1, 2020 through December 31, 2020, 12.1¢ per gallon) (rate revised on monthly basis).	Sales—reports and payments—20th of each month (3/4 and reconciliation payment due on 20th if required to file EFT payments). Refiners and pipeline and marine terminal operators must report and make prepayments on or before the 10th and 25th of each month.
	Use—6% of sales price of tangible personal property purchased for storage, use or consumption, including electricity, natural or artificial gas, steam, rental of rooms and lodgings, and intrastate telephone and telegraph service. However, consumption of electricity, natural gas, and home heating fuels for residential use is taxed at 4%.	Use—reports and payments—20th of each month (3/4 and reconciliation payment due on 20th if required to file EFT payments).

Tax	Basis—Rates	Due Dates
Insurance companies tax.	Generally—1.25% of gross direct premiums. Comprehensive major medical, student, children's health insurance program, Medicaid, employer comprehensive, and employer associations and trusts policies written on risk located or residing in Michigan—0.8863% for 2020 (0.95%. for 2019). Surplus lines insurers and unauthorized insurers—2% of premiums written in Michigan and an additional 0.5% regulatory fee.	Returns and payment—Annual tax returns and payment due to Department of Treasury by March 1. Annual reports due to Commissioner of Insurance by March 1. Quarterly estimated tax returns and payments due April 15, July 15, October 15, and January 15 if estimated tax liability for the year is expected to exceed $800. Surplus lines returns and payment due February 15 and August 15.
	Foreign and alien insurers are subject to retaliatory tax.	Returns and payment—Annual statement due March 1. Quarterly estimated tax returns and payments due before April 30, July 31, October 31, and January 31.
	Surplus lines insurers, 2% on premiums written plus a 0.5% regulatory fee. Unauthorized insurers, 2% of premiums written plus a 0.5% regulatory fee.	Reports and payment—Surplus lines insurers, February 15 and August 15. Insureds and self-insurers dealing with unauthorized insurers, within 30 days after transaction. Payments—Surplus lines insurers and insureds dealing with unauthorized insurers, at the time of filing the report. Insurers and self-insurers dealing with unauthorized insurers, within 30 days after transaction.

Minnesota

Tax System.—The Minnesota tax system is founded on the general property tax. Money and credits are exempt. By far, the greater proportion of the property tax revenue is devoted to the support of municipal corporations and other local tax-levying bodies. Further revenue is derived from sales and use taxes, gasoline tax, motor vehicle taxes, cigarette and tobacco products taxes, liquor taxes, income taxes, insurance company taxes, estate tax, mining taxes, and several other miscellaneous taxes. Municipalities are given broad licensing power, but this power to license must be based on statutory enactment or charter provisions. An outline of the Minnesota tax system follows:

Tax	Basis—Rates	Due Dates
Income tax.	Corporations—9.8% of taxable income. An alternative minimum tax equal to the excess of 5.8% of Minnesota alternative minimum taxable income over the basic tax is imposed. Corporations are subject to an additional minimum tax ranging from $0 to $10,380 depending on the Minnesota property, payroll, and sales or receipts, and the type of corporation or partnership.	Reports and payments—15th day of 4th month after end of income year.
	Banks—Same as corporations.	
	Individuals—Inflation adjusted brackets for tax year **2020:** For married individuals filing joint returns and surviving spouses, 5.35% on the first $39,410, 6.80% if $39,411 to $156,570, 7.85% if $156,571 to $273,470, 9.85% if over $273,470. For single individuals, 5.35% on the first $26,960, 6.80% if $26,961 to $88,550, 7.85% if $88,551 to $164,400, 9.85% if over $164,400. For head of households, 5.35% on the first $33,190, 6.80% if $33,191 to $133,360, 7.85% if $133,361 to $218,540, 9.85% if over $218,540. For married filing separately and estates, 5.35% on the first $19,705, 6.80% if $19,706 to $78,285, 7.85% if $78,286 to $136,735, 9.85% if over $136,735. A 6.75% alternative minimum tax is imposed.	
	General withholding required.	Individual estimated tax payments—April 15, June 15, September 15, and January 15. Corporate estimated tax payments—due 15th day of the 3rd, 6th, 9th and 12th months of the taxable year.
General property tax.	General property—all real and personal property valued according to numerous classes from varying percentages of its market value.	General property—returns for utilities, March 31. Payments—May 15 and October 15 (or 21 days after postmark date on statement, whichever is later).

Tax	Basis—Rates	Due Dates
Alcoholic beverage taxes.	Beer, 3.2% alcohol or less, per barrel of 31 gallons, $2.40; over 3.2% alcohol, $4.60; wines per gallon, 14% alcohol or less, 30¢ per gallon; more than 14% alcohol but not exceeding 21%, 95¢ per gallon; more than 21% alcohol but not exceeding 24%, $1.82 per gallon; over 24% alcohol, $3.52 per gallon; sparkling wines, $1.82 per gallon; cider 15¢ per gallon; distilled spirits, liqueurs, cordials, and specialties regardless of alcohol content (excluding ethyl alcohol), $5.03 per gallon; low-alcohol dairy cocktails, 8¢ per gallon.	
Gasoline tax.	Rates (including a 0.5¢ surcharge) are: gasoline, diesel fuel, and special fuels, $0.285 per gallon. Motor carriers fuel tax—same rate as motor fuels.	Reports and payments—23rd day of each month. Motor carriers' reports due last day of April, July, October, and January; payments required with reports.
Severance taxes.	Mining occupation tax—applies to both ferrous and nonferous metals. The tax is paid in lieu of corporate franchise tax and is based on taxable income and imposed at the same rates as income tax.	Mining occupation tax—reports and payments, May 1.
	Net proceeds tax (applies to all mineral and energy resources except sand, silica sand, gravel, building stone, all clays, crushed rock, limestone, granite, dimension stone, horticultural peat, soil, iron ore and taconite) — additional 2% of net proceeds from mining.	Net proceeds tax—Payment due June 15 of the year succeeding the calendar year of the report.
Cigarette excise and tobacco products excise taxes.	Cigarette excise—The rate is 152 mills per cigarette ($0.152 per cigarette or $3.04 per pack of 20). "Little cigars" are taxed as cigarettes.	Reports and payments—18th day of each month; payment of taxes evidenced by stamp. If fiscal year liability is $250,000 or more, 81.4% June liability for following year is due two business days before June 30, along with report and payment of actual May liability. Reconciliation report and payment due August 18.
	Cigarette sales tax—6.5% of the weighted average retail price, adjusted annually.	
	Tobacco products excise—The excise tax on tobacco is equal to 95% of the wholesale sales price of the tobacco product; Moist snuff: 95% of wholesale sales price or $3.04 per container (whichever is greater).	
Mortgage registry tax.	Mortgage registry—0.0023% of amount of debt secured by real estate mortgage.	Payments—at time of registration or filing.
MinnesotaCare tax.	Hospitals, surgical centers, health care providers, and wholesale drug distributors—1.8% of gross revenues.	Hospitals and surgical centers—estimated tax payments due within 15 days of the end of the month. Others—quarterly estimated tax payments due April 15, July 15, October 15, and January 15.

Tax	Basis—Rates	Due Dates
Sales and use taxes.	6.875% sales and use tax on gross receipts from, or the sales price of, retail sales, and use, storage or consumption of tangible personal property; leases and rentals, digital products, and specified services also taxable. Alcoholic beverages, 9.375% (6.875% sales and use tax plus 2.5% liquor gross receipts tax). Sales of motor vehicles, 6.5% excise tax. Motor vehicle leases, 6.875%; additional 9.2% rental tax and 5% rental fee imposed on the lease or rental of 28 days or less of a passenger automobile, a van or a pickup truck. Cigarette sales tax—see Cigarette excise and tobacco products excise taxes above.	Reports and payments—20th day of each month for previous month. Quarterly and annual returns and payments allowed for small taxpayers. Annual use tax returns for businesses and annual sales tax returns generally due February 5.
Insurance companies tax.	2% of gross direct premiums, less return premiums, received on all direct business written within the state. Township mutual insurance companies—1%. Mutual property and casualty companies with assets of $5 million or less—1%. Mutual property and casualty companies with assets of $1.6 billion or less on December 31, 1989—1.26%, or 1% if they have less than $5 million in assets. 0.5% surcharge is imposed on Minnesota fire safety insurance premiums, less return premiums, on direct business received by insurance companies for homeowner's insurance policies, commercial fire policies, and commercial nonliability insurance policies. Surplus line insurers—3% of gross premiums paid, less return premiums, by an insured whose home state is Minnesota. Nonadmitted insurance—2% of gross premiums paid, less return premiums, by an insured whose home state is Minnesota. HMOs, nonprofit health service plan corporations, and community integrated service networks—1% tax. Foreign companies subject to retaliatory taxes.	Returns and payments—March 1. Estimated tax payments—March 15, June 15, September 15, and December 15. Surplus line insurers returns and payments—February 15 and August 15. Firefighters' relief surcharge returns and payments—April 30, June 30, and November 30. Fire safety insurance premium surcharge returns and payment—May 15, August 15, November 15, and February 15. If total insurance taxes and surcharges for last 12-month period ending June 30 totals $10,000 or more or taxpayer is required to pay any Minnesota business tax electronically, electronic payment of taxes is required.
Life insurance tax.	1.5% of gross premiums, less return premiums, received on all direct business by insurers or agents.	Reports—March 1. Payments—estimated payments due March 15, June 15, September 15, and December 15; reconciliation payments due March 1.

Mississippi

Tax System.—Mississippi imposes a general property tax for county, municipal, and district revenue, according to the rule of uniformity prescribed by the state Constitution. State taxes on privileges, excises, occupations, and income are imposed to supplement revenue from general property taxes. Municipalities and counties may not impose franchise taxes and may not tax any privilege that has been licensed for statewide purposes. An outline of the Mississippi tax system follows:

Tax	Basis—Rates	Due Dates
Corporation franchise tax.	First $100,000 of the value of the capital used, invested or employed is exempt. $2.00 for every $1,000 or fraction thereof of the value of the capital used, invested, or employed by the organization (minimum tax of $25) before 2021. $1.75 before 2022, $1.50 before 2023, $1.25 before 2024, $1.00 before 2025, $0.75 before 2026, $0.50 before 2027, and $0.25 before 2028.	Reports and payments—15th day of 3rd month following the close of the annual accounting period.
General income tax.	Individuals, corporations—3% of income between $2,000 and $5,000 in 2019; 3% of income between $3,000 and $5,000 in 2020; and 3% of income between $4,000 and $5,000 in 2021. No tax on income under $5,000 in 2022 and thereafter. 4% of next $5,000; 5% of amounts over $10,000.	Returns—April 15th or the 15th day of 4th month after close of taxable year.
		Payments—due with the return.
		Estimated income tax declarations and payments—due 15th day of 4th month; option to make payments on the 15th day of 4th, 6th, 9th, and 13th (12th in the case of corporations) months of income year.
General property tax.	General property—Taxable property is divided into 5 classes with assigned rates ranging from 10% to 30% of tax value. Rates are multiplied by local mill levy to determine tax.	General property lists—due April 1. Payments—due February 1. Payment may be authorized in 3 installments—50% on February 1; 25% on May 1; 25% on July 1.
	Banks—general property rates on adjusted net worth.	Bank statements—April 1; payments—December 1.
Alcoholic beverages excise tax.	Excise—42.68¢ per gallon on light wines and beer; $2.50[1] per gallon on distilled spirits; $1[1] per gallon on sparkling wine and champagne; 35¢[1] per gallon on wines. Annual privilege license tax of $10 for each 10,000 gallons, or any part thereof, of native wine produced by a native winery.	

Tax	Basis—Rates	Due Dates
Gasoline and fuel taxes.	Gasoline—18¢ per gallon (14.4¢ per gallon as of the first day of the month following the date upon which the Mississippi Transportation Commission and the State Treasurer certify that specified financial conditions are satisfied concerning the Four-Lane Highway Program and the Gaming Counties Infrastructure Program). Aviation gasoline—6.4¢ per gallon. Jet fuel—5.25¢ per gallon. Undyed diesel fuel—18¢ per gallon. The tax on compressed natural gas (CNG) and liquefied natural gas (LNG) for use in motor vehicles with a gross license tax weight of more than 10,000 lbs.—18¢ per 100 cubic feet; for vehicles with a weight of less 10,000 lbs. or less—the tax is $195 per year. The tax on railroad locomotive fuel (diesel)—0.75¢ per gallon. Tax on natural gas, locomotive fuel and compressed gas users—12¢ per 1,000 cubic feet upon any person using natural gas as a fuel in oil field or gas field production pumps in the state; 3¢ per 1,000 cubic feet upon any person using natural gas as a fuel in pipeline compressors or pumping stations or in engines or motors used for industrial purposes by a manufacturer or custom processor in this state; 0.75¢ per gallon upon any person using locomotive fuel in a railroad locomotive in this state; 2¢ per gallon upon any person using compressed gas as a fuel in oil field or gas field production pumps in this state; and 0.5¢ per gallon upon any person using compressed gas as a fuel in pipeline compressors or pumping stations or in engines or motors used for industrial purposes by a manufacturer or custom processor in this state.	Reports and payments—gasoline, ethanol, methanol, and special fuel distributors, 20th day of each month on fuels received the previous month.
	Lubricating oils—2¢ per quart (8¢ per gallon).	Reports and payments—lubricating oils, 20th day of each month.
Gas and oil severance taxes.	Gas—6% of value of natural gas produced and severed from soil or water, for sale, transport, storage, profit, or commercial use. Oil—6% of value at the point of production, 3% if oil is produced by an enhanced oil recovery method in which carbon dioxide or other approved method is used. Until July 1, 2023, reduced rate of 1.3% of value at the point of production for oil and natural gas produced from horizontally drilled wells or horizontally drilled recompletion wells from which production commences on and after July 1, 2013, for a period of 30 months from the date of the first sale of production.	Reports and payments—25th day of each month.
Salt severance tax.	3% of the value of the entire production of salt in the state.	Returns and payments—20th day of each month.

Tax	Basis—Rates	Due Dates
Timber or timber products tax.	Pine and soft woods used in manufacture of lumber and other products—$1 per 1,000 board feet (or 12¢ per ton).	Reports and payments—15th day of each month; quarterly by the 15th day of the month that follows the end of the quarter if tax does not exceed $3,600 per year.
	Hardwoods—75¢ per 1,000 board feet.	
	Lumber, including crossties—75¢ per 1,000 feet actual board measure.	
	Poles, piling, posts, staunchions, and other products not manufactured into lumber—$3.60 per 100 cubic feet.	
	For other timber products bought by the cubic foot—55¢ per 100 cubic feet for pine and other soft woods; 41¢ per 100 cubic feet for hardwoods.	
	Pulpwood, except pine—22.5¢ per standard cord of 128 cubic feet; pine pulpwood—30¢ per standard cord of 128 cubic feet.	
	Stumpwood, lightwood, or distillate—25¢ per ton of 2,000 lbs.	
	Turpentine crude gum—30¢ per barrel of 400 lbs.	
	All other timber products—75¢ per 1,000 board feet, or 37.5¢ per standard cord of 128 cubic feet.	
Tobacco tax.	Cigarettes—3.4¢ per cigarette (68¢ per pack of 20). Cigars, cheroots, stogies, snuff, chewing and smoking tobacco, and all other tobacco products other than cigarettes—15% of the manufacturer's list price. Additional tobacco equity tax—1.66¢ per cigarette, with exemptions for cigarettes manufactured by any manufacturer who is a party to the tobacco settlement agreement, and for cigarettes sold, purchased, or distributed in Mississippi for sale outside the state.	Reports and payments—cigarettes, by purchase of stamps; other tobacco products, 15th day of each month. Interstate commerce—15th day of each month.
Mineral documentary tax.	3¢ per mineral or royalty acre covered by conveyances or reservations of leasehold interests in nonproducing oil, gas, or other minerals for interests expiring 10 years or less from date of execution of instrument; 6¢ for terms between 10 and 20 years; 8¢ for terms exceeding 20 years. Minimum tax, $1.	Payments—by affixing stamps purchased at time of filing instruments.

Tax	Basis—Rates	Due Dates
Sales and use taxes.	Sales—7% of gross income, gross proceeds, purchase price, or value on most items of tangible personal property and on selected services. Reduced rates applicable to certain industries, including: manufacturing or processing machinery to be installed and/or used at a refinery; logging equipment; farm implements and tractors; dairy producer facilities; vehicles and aircraft; railroad track materials; mobile and manufactured homes; and various utility-related transactions.	Reports and payments—on or before the 20th day following the end of the reporting period, which can be monthly, quarterly, or annually. Monthly returns required if annual total payment is $3,600 or more, quarterly returns if between $600 and $3,599, and annual returns if less than $600. Taxpayers with a total average tax liability of at least $50,000 per month for the preceding calendar year must make an accelerated tax payment for June no later than June 25 each year.
	Use—imposed at same rate as under sales tax law on price or value of personal property used, stored, or consumed within Mississippi on which sales or use tax has not been paid to another state at a rate equal to or greater than the applicable Mississippi rate.	
Public utilities tax.	Electric—$22.50 per mile of pole line; pipe line—from $15 to $125 (depending on diameter); telephone—4¢ per telephone in service at end of calendar year or $25, whichever is greater; railroads—from $5 to $90 per mile.	Reports and payments—December 1.
Insurance companies tax.	Domestic and foreign—3% of gross premiums, less certain specified premiums. Surplus lines—4%. Fire insurance tax—additional 0.5%. Foreign companies subject to retaliatory taxes.	Reports and payments—March 1 (Annual Reconciliation and for October-December), April 20 (for January-March), June 20 (for April and May), July 20 (for June), and October 20 (for July-September). Audited financial reports due June 1.

[1] Pursuant to statute, the Mississippi Department of Revenue adds a 27.5% markup to the cost of alcoholic beverages.

Missouri

Tax System.—Missouri is divided into governmental units, for real property tax purposes, made up of counties, townships, and cities of the first through fourth classes. The county, however, is the principal unit for tax administration. The total real property tax is the aggregate of the levies from each of the governmental units in which the real property lies. Major sources of state revenue are the sales and use taxes, the income taxes, and the gasoline and fuel use taxes. An outline of the Missouri tax system follows:

Tax	Basis—Rates	Due Dates
Income tax.	Individuals (rates for 2020): Missouri taxable income not over $106, 0%; over $106 but not over $1,073, 1.5%; over $1,073 but not over $2,146, $16 plus 2% of excess over $1,073; over $2,146 but not over $3,219, $37 plus 2.5% of excess over $2,146; over $3,219 but not over $4,292, $64 plus 3% of excess over $3,219; over $4,292 but not over $5,365, $96 plus 3.5% of excess over $4,292; over $5,365 but not over $6,438, $134 plus 4% of excess over $5,365; over $6,438 but not over $7,511, $177 plus 4.5% of excess over $6,438; over $7,511 but not over $8,584, $225 plus 5% of excess over $7,511; over $8,584, $279 plus 5.4% of excess over $8,584. Top rate reduced by 0.1% for each year that the net general revenue collected in the previous fiscal year exceeds the highest amount of net general revenue in any one of the three fiscal years prior to such year by at least $150 million, with no more than five of these reductions to be made. Tax brackets adjusted annually for inflation. Withholding required.	Returns and payments—calendar year: April 15; fiscal year: 15th day of 4th month after close of tax year.
	Corporations and associations—4% (6.25% for tax years beginning before 2020)	Returns and payments—calendar year: April 15; fiscal year: 15th day of 4th month after close of tax year.
Financial institutions franchise tax.	Banks and other financial institutions—4.48% (7% for tax years beginning before 2020)	Returns and payments—April 15. Tax due for the calendar year in which a banking institution receives its certificate is payable on or before June 1 of the following year.
General property tax.	Real property—Tax is applied to a percentage of true value depending upon the property classification.	Returns—between January 1 and March 1, generally; for railroads and public utilities, April 15. Payments—December 31.
	Aggregate of rates for state, county, municipality, road, bridge, school, and other district purposes.	
Alcoholic beverages taxes.	Excise—beer and malt liquor, $1.86 per barrel; spirituous liquors, $2.00 per gallon; and wines, 30¢ per gallon.	

Tax	Basis—Rates	Due Dates
Motor fuel taxes.	Motor fuel—17¢ per gallon.	Reports and payments—Motor fuel—last day of the succeeding month, generally.
	Alternative fuels—from January 1, 2020, through December 31, 2024, a tax will be imposed on both compressed natural gas (CNG) and liquefied natural gas (LNG), if used as motor fuels, at a rate of 11¢ per gallon. After 2024, the tax rate on CNG will increase to 17¢.	
	Aviation fuel use—9¢ per gallon of aviation fuel used in propelling aircraft with reciprocating engines.	Aviation fuel use—last day of the succeeding month.
Cigarette tax.	8 1/2 mills per cigarette (17¢ per pack of 20).	Reports—20th day of each month. Payments—by means of purchases and affixations of stamps.
Tobacco products tax.	10% of manufacturer's invoice price.	Reports and payments—15th day of each month.
Sales and use tax.	4.225% of purchase price of tangible personal property and enumerated services. In lieu of regular use tax, a 4% special tax is imposed on motor vehicles, trailers, boats, and outboard motors.	Sales and use tax—If tax due is less than $100 per calendar quarter, tax returns and payments are due January 31 following the calendar year. If the tax due equals or exceeds $500 per calendar month, returns and payments are due by the 20th of the following month (last month of a quarter, due on the last day of the following month). If the tax due is less than $500 per calendar month but equals or exceeds $100 in a calendar quarter, returns and payments are due on the last day of the month following the end of the quarter (April, July, October, January). Quarter-monthly payments are due from large taxpayers.

Tax	Basis—Rates	Due Dates
Insurance companies tax.	Domestic and foreign insurers—2% of direct premiums received less cancelled or returned premiums. Mutual insurance companies—1% of annual premiums or assessments over $1 million; 2% on annual premiums or assessments over $5 million.	Returns—March 1. Payment—quarterly installments due on first day of March, June, September, and December, with a fifth reconciling installment due on June 1. Foreign mutual insurance companies other than life or fire, May 1.
	Foreign companies subject to additional retaliatory taxes. Surplus lines brokers and insureds who procure insurance from surplus lines insurers—5% of the entire gross premium for nonadmitted or surplus lines insurance policies for which the home state of the insured is Missouri.	Annual statement—March 2. Quarterly reports—not later than 45 days after the end of each calendar quarter ending March 31, June 30, September 30 and December 31. Payment—April 16.
	Captive insurance companies—38/100 of 1% on the first $20 million, 285/1000 of 1% on the next $20 million, 19/100 of 1% on the next $20 million, and 72/1000 of 1% on each dollar thereafter of direct premiums, and 214/1000 of 1% on the first $20 million, 143/1000 of 1% on the next $20 million, 48/1000 of 1% of the next $20 million, and 24/1000 of 1% on each dollar thereafter of assumed reinsurance premiums. Minimum tax of $7,500 and maximum tax of $200,000	Returns—February 1. Payment—May 1.

Montana

Tax System.—The tax system of Montana is founded on a classified property tax levied at uniform rates, plus taxes on incomes, occupations, and privileges. A net income franchise tax is imposed on corporations. An outline of the Montana tax system follows:

Tax	Basis—Rates	Due Dates
Corporate income; alternative corporate income tax; personal income tax.	Corporations—6.75% (7% for taxpayers electing water's-edge apportionment) of net income derived from Montana sources. Minimum tax, $50.	Corporation income—returns and payment—15th day of 5th month after close of income year. Payments of estimated tax (if tax liability is $5,000 or more) are due on the 15th days of the 4th, 6th, 9th and 12th months of tax year.
	Multistate corporations that do not rent or own real or personal property in Montana and whose in-state sales do not exceed $100,000 may elect to pay an alternative tax rate of 0.5% of gross receipts on Montana sales.	
	Personal income—**Rates for 2020:** $0 - 3,100 x 1.000% minus $0; $3,101 - 5,500 x 2.000% minus $31.00; $5,501 - 8,400 x 3.000% minus $86.00; $8,401 - 11,300 x 4.000% minus $170.00; $11,301 - 14,500 x 5.000% minus $283.00; $14,501 - 18,700 x 6.000% minus $428.00; $18,701 and over x 6.900% minus $596.00. **Rates for 2019:** $0 - 3,100 x 1.000% minus $0; $3,101 - 5,400 x 2.000% minus $31.00; $5,401 -8,200 x 3.000% minus $85.00; $8,201 - 11,100 x 4.000% minus $167.00; $11,101 - 14,300 x 5.000% minus $278.00; $14,301 - 18,400 x 6.000% minus $421.00; $18,401 and over x 6.900% minus $587.00.	Personal income—returns and payment—15th day of 4th month after close of income year. Payments of estimated tax are due 15th days of the 4th, 6th, and 9th months of tax year and 1st month of following year.
General property tax.	All taxable property in Montana is assessed at 100% of its market value, unless otherwise specified. Montana divides its real and personal property into 15 distinct classes (class one through five, class seven through ten, and class twelve through seventeen). Each class is taxed at a different percentage of market value, gross proceeds, or productive capacity. Aggregate of state, county, city and school rates fixed annually to meet state and local budgets. Property taxes on all classes of property in Montana have been frozen so that the total amount of taxes levied by each taxing unit is capped at the dollar amount levied for the 1996 tax year, subject to specified exceptions.	Payment—Generally required in two equal installments due November 30 of the tax year and May 31 of the following year. In all cases, due date applies, or 30 days after notice postmark, whichever is later. Special prepayment provisions apply for new industrial facilities, large-scale mineral development, and real property or improvements that were exempt and became taxable.
Sales and use tax (limited).	4% sales and use tax on accommodations and campgrounds, plus additional 4% lodging facility use tax on accommodation charge; 4% sales and use tax on base charge for rental vehicles.	Reports and payments—last day of month after end of each calendar quarter.

Tax	Basis—Rates	Due Dates
Alcoholic beverages tax.	Excise—beer, over 10,000 barrels produced per year, $4.30 per 31-gallon barrel; less than 10,000 barrels produced per year, $1.30 per barrel for the first 5,000 barrels, and $2.30 per barrel between 5,001 and 10,000 barrels.	
	Table wine—generally 27¢ per liter.	Payment—table wine, hard cider, 15th of each month; liquor, at time of sale and delivery in state; beer, end of each month.
	Cider—3.7¢ per liter.	
	Liquor—3% (less than 20,000 proof gallons); 8% (20,000 to 50,000 proof gallons); 13.8% (50,0001 to 200,000 proof gallons); 16% (over 200,000 proof gallons)	
Fuel taxes.	Gasoline license tax—32¢ per gallon of motor fuel distributed in Montana, except 5¢ per gallon for aviation gasoline.	Reports and payments—Gasoline, 25th of each month for the preceding calendar month.
	Special fuel use tax—29.45¢ per gallon of special fuel.	
	Petroleum storage tank cleanup fee—0.75¢ per gallon for gasoline, aviation gasoline, special fuel and heating oil distributed in the state.	Reports and payments—same as gasoline tax.
Compressed natural gas.	Compressed natural gas—7¢ per 120 cubic feet at 14.73 pounds per square inch absolute base pressure of compressed natural gas placed into the supply tank of a motor vehicle.	Reports and payments—quarterly returns with quarterly payments (last day of next calendar month following the quarter).
Liquefied petroleum gas.	5.18¢ per gallon of liquefied petroleum gas placed into the supply tank of a motor vehicle.	Reports and payments—quarterly returns with quarterly payments (last day of next calendar month following the quarter).
Oil and natural gas production tax.	Natural gas and oil are taxed on the gross taxable value of production on the basis of type of well and type of production according to the following schedule for working and nonworking interest owners.	Oil and natural gas production—Operators must report and pay the oil and natural gas production tax within 60 days after the end of each calendar quarter.
	Natural Gas—(a)(i) first 12 months of qualifying production, working interest 0.50%, nonworking interest 14.8%, (ii) after 12 months (A) pre-1999 wells, working and nonworking interest 14.8%, (B) post-1999 wells, working interest 9%, nonworking interest 14.8%; (b) stripper natural gas pre-1999 wells, working interest 11%, nonworking interest 14.8%; (c) horizontally completed well production (i) first 18 months of qualifying production, working interest 0.5%, nonworking interest 14.8%, (ii) after 18 months, working interest 9%, nonworking interest 14.8%.	

Tax	Basis—Rates	Due Dates
	Oil—(a) primary recovery production (i) first 12 months of qualifying production, working interest 0.5%, nonworking interest 14.8%, (ii) after 12 months (A) pre-1999 wells, working interest 12.5%, nonworking interest 14.8%, (B) post-1999 wells, working interest 9%, nonworking interest 14.8%; (b) stripper oil production (i) first 1 through 10 barrels a day production, working interest 5.5%, nonworking interest 14.8%, (ii) more than 10 barrels a day production, working interest 9%, nonworking interest 14.8%; (c)(i) stripper well exemption production, working interest 0.5%, nonworking interest 14.8%; (ii) stripper well bonus production, working interest 6%, nonworking interest 14.8%; (d) horizontally completed well production (i) first 18 months of qualifying production, working interest 0.5%, nonworking interest 14.8%, (ii) after 18 months (A) pre-1999 wells, working interest 12.5%, nonworking interest 14.8%, (B) post-1999 wells, working interest 9%, nonworking interest 14.8%; (e) incremental production (i) new or expanded secondary recovery production, working interest 8.5%, nonworking interest 14.8%, (ii) new or expanded tertiary production, working interest 5.8%, nonworking interest 14.8%; (f) horizontally recompleted wells (i) first 18 months, working interest 5.5%, nonworking interest 14.8%, (ii) after 18 months (A) pre-1999 wells, working interest 12.5%, nonworking interest 14.8%, (B) post-1999 wells, working interest 9%, nonworking interest 14.8%.	
Oil and gas conservation tax.	0.3% of market value of each barrel of crude petroleum or each 10,000 cubic feet of natural gas produced, saved and marketed or stored in Montana or exported.	Same as oil and gas production tax.
Coal severance tax.	Surface mining—10% of value for coal having a BTU rating per lb. of under 7,000 and 15% of value for coal having a BTU rating per lb. of 7,000 and over. Underground mining—3% of value on coal having a BTU rating per lb. of under 7,000 and 4% of value on coal having a BTU rating per lb. of 7,000 and over.	Reports and payments—within 30 days after end of each calendar quarter.
Cement tax.	22¢ per ton of cement and 5¢ per ton of gypsum products.	Reports and payments—within 30 days after each calendar quarter.
Metalliferous mines tax.	For concentrate shipped to a smelter, mill or reduction work, 1.81% if the gross value of the product is over $250,000. For gold, silver or platinum shipped to a refinery, 1.6% over $250,000.	Metalliferous mines—reports and payment—semiannually by August 15 for the reporting period ending June 30 and by March 31 for the reporting period ending December 31.
Micaceous minerals tax.	5¢ per ton of vermiculite, perlite, kerrite, maconite or other micaceous minerals produced.	Reports and payment—within 30 days after each calendar quarter.

Tax	Basis—Rates	Due Dates
Mineral production tax (resource indemnity and ground water assessment tax).	Mineral production tax—$25 (per year) plus 0.5% of gross value of products extracted from Montana if production exceeds $5,000, except as noted below. $25 plus 4% of gross value of product in excess of $625 for talc extracted from Montana and $25 plus 0.4% of gross value of product in excess of $6,250 for coal extracted from Montana. $25 plus 2% of gross value of product in excess of $1,250 for vermiculite extracted from Montana. $25 plus 10% of the gross value of product in excess of $250 for limestone extracted from Montana. $25 per year plus 1% of the gross value of product in excess of $2,500 for industrial garnets and associated by-products extracted from Montana.	Reports and payments—March 31.
Bentonite production tax.	Bentonite production tax rates are calculated every year. First 20,000 tons, exempt. 20,001 to 100,000 tons, $1.82 per ton. 100,001 to 250,000 tons, $1.75 per ton. 250,001 to 500,000 tons, $1.63 per ton. 500,001 to 1,000,000 tons, $1.46 per ton. 1,000,001 tons and more, $1.17 per ton. Royalties, 15% of the amount paid or apportioned in kind to the royalty owner.	Payments due semiannually, within 45 days after June 30 and December 31.
Cigarette tax; tobacco products tax.	$1.70 per pack of 20 cigarettes; when packages contain more than 20 cigarettes, the tax on each cigarette is equal to 1/20 the tax on a package containing 20 cigarettes.	Cigarette tax—payment by affixing insignia.
	Tobacco products, except cigarettes, 50% of wholesale price. Moist snuff is taxed at 85¢ per ounce. Licensed wholesalers are entitled to a collection and administrative expense discount.	Tobacco products—15th of each month.
Public utilities tax.	Electric companies—$.0002 per kilowatt hour of electricity generated, produced or manufactured. Electric distributors—$.00015 per kilowatt hour.	Electric—report and payment due on 30th day after each calendar quarter; telephone companies, 60th day after each calendar quarter.
	Telephone—excise tax imposed at rate of 3.75% on sales of retail telecommunications services.	
Insurance companies tax.	2.75% on all net premiums of authorized insurers. 0.75% for casualty insurers on net premiums from legal professional liability insurance. 2.5% on fire portion of specified risks. Foreign companies subject to retaliatory taxes. Captive insurers (direct), 0.4% on the first $20 million; 0.3% on each subsequent dollar collected, with $5,000 minimum and $100,000 maximum. Dormant captive insurers pay annual tax of $1,000.	Reports and payment—Annual return due March 1. Quarterly estimated tax payments due the 15th day of April, June, September, and December.

Nebraska

Tax System.—The major taxes comprising the tax system of Nebraska are corporate and individual income taxes, sales and use taxes, and gasoline and special fuel taxes. An initiative petition approved by the electorate at the 1966 general election amended the constitution to prohibit the state from levying a property tax. However, a locally imposed and collected general property tax on real and tangible personal property continues to be the most important source of local revenue. These taxes are supplemented by (1) state taxes on franchises, privileges or occupations, and (2) municipal taxes and inspection fees that the legislature authorizes the local governments to exact. An outline of the Nebraska tax system follows:

Tax	Basis—Rates	Due Dates
Corporation franchise tax.	Graduated from $26 for $10,000 or less based on domestic paid-up capital stock and foreign capital employed in Nebraska, to $23,990 for over $100 million. Foreign corporations pay double, but with a maximum tax of $30,000.	Reports and payments—April 15 of each even-numbered year.
Income tax.	Individuals—Tax year 2019: Rates for married couples filing jointly and qualified surviving spouses range between 2.46% of the first $6,440 of taxable income and $2,474.40 plus 6.84% of taxable income over $62,320. Rates for married couples filing separately range between 2.46% of the first $3,230 and $1,237.25 plus 6.84% of taxable income over $31,160. Rates for heads of household range between 2.46% of the first $6,020 and $1,787.31 plus 6.84% of taxable income over $46,200. Rates for single individuals range between 2.46% of the first $3,230 and $1,237.25 plus 6.84% of taxable income over $31,160. Corporations—5.58% of first $100,000 of taxable income and 7.81% of taxable income over $100,000.	Returns and payments (including payments of estimated tax)—due on the federal return and payment dates.
Financial institution franchise tax.	Lesser of $0.47 per $1,000 of average deposits or 3.81% of net income before taxes and extraordinary items.	Reports and payments—15th day of 4th month after end of taxable year (April 15 for calendar-year taxpayers).
General property tax.	General property—aggregate of local rates fixed annually to meet budget. Property is valued at its actual value.	General property—returns—tangible personal property, May 1; railroads, April 15. Payment—real, personal property, December 31 following date of levy; two installments (May 1 and September 1) to avoid delinquency; counties with a population of 100,000 or more, April 1 and August 1.
Lodging tax.	Lodging tax—state rate of 1% of total consideration. County rate may also apply.	Reports and payments—25th of the month.

Tax	Basis—Rates	Due Dates
Alcoholic beverages tax.	Excise—beer, 31¢ per gallon. Wine produced in farm wineries, 6¢ per gallon. Wine, except wine produced in farm wineries, 95¢ per gallon. Alcohol and spirits, $3.75 per gallon.	Reports and payments—25th of each month for preceding month.
Motor vehicle and special fuel tax.	Combined motor fuels total rate—33.2¢ effective July 1, 2020 through December 31, 2020. Rate is subject to change on January 1 and July 1 of each year.	Report and payment—20th day of the month following the reporting period.
	Aviation gasoline, 5¢ per gallon; aviation jet fuel, 3¢ per gallon.	Aviation fuel—20th day of each month for preceding month.
Oil and gas severance tax.	3% of value of resources severed at time of severance, except 2% of value on oil produced from wells averaging 10 barrels per day or less for all producing days during the tax year.	Reports and payments—last day of each month for preceding month.
Motor vehicle rental tax.	Up to 5.75% of rental contract amount for 31 days or less for motor vehicles with capacity of no more than 15 passengers.	Report and payment—February 15.
Cigarette tax; tobacco products tax.	64¢ per package containing not more than 20 cigarettes; over 20 cigarettes per package, 64¢ for the first 20 plus a proportional amount for each cigarette over 20.	Reports—10th day of each month for preceding month.
		Payment—by purchase of stamps prior to sale or delivery.
	Tobacco products tax—20% of wholesale price. The rate is 44¢ per ounce on snuff.	Reports and payments—10th day of each month for preceding month.
Documentary stamp tax.	$2.25 per $1,000 of value or fraction thereof.	Payment—affixation of stamps prior to recording.
Sales and use tax.	5.5% of gross receipts from retail sales of tangible personal property and certain services and upon the storage, use or other consumption in the state of tangible personal property. Local rate may also apply.	Reports and payments—20th day of each month for preceding month; quarterly and annual returns allowed for small taxpayers.
Insurance companies tax.	1% of gross premiums, except 0.5% for group sickness and accident insurance, and 1% for property and casualty insurance, excluding individual sickness and accident insurance.	Payment—March 1; prepayments from insurers whose annual tax for the preceding tax year was $4,000 or more due the 15th of April, June and September.
	Fire—gross premiums and assessments received for foreign fire insurance less return premiums on all direct business received in the state, 0.75%; domestic mutual companies and assessment associations pay 0.375%.	Payment—March 1.
	Nonadmitted insurers—3% of direct writing premiums plus fire insurance tax.	Report and payment—March 1, June 1, September 1, December 1

Nevada

Tax System.—The Nevada tax system is based on a general sales and use tax law, a commerce tax, and payroll excise taxes. In addition, the legislature has levied a live entertainment tax, a property tax, and certain excise and license taxes. An outline of the Nevada tax system follows:

Tax	Basis—Rates	Due Dates
Modified business tax on financial institutions.	2% of wages paid to employees. Beginning July 1, 2015, 2% rate also applies to businesses subject to the tax on the net proceeds of mining. (Note: The 2019 law allowing this rate to continue was invalidated by a district court in October 2020.)	On or before the last day of the month immediately following each calendar quarter for which the institution is required to pay an unemployment compensation contribution.
Modified business tax.	1.475% for quarterly wages paid in excess of $50,000 (Note: The 2019 law allowing this rate to continue was invalidated by a district court in October 2020). Prior to July 1, 2015, 1.17% for quarterly wages paid in excess of $85,000.	On or before the last day of the month immediately following each calendar quarter for which the business is required to pay an unemployment compensation contribution.
Commerce tax.	First imposed for tax year beginning on July 1, 2015. Based on gross revenue, with rates ranging from 0.051% to 0.331%, depending on industry.	On or before the 45th day following the end of the taxable year.
Bank branch excise tax.	Imposed on banks that maintain more than one branch office in any county in Nevada at a rate of $1,750 for each branch office in excess of one maintained by the bank in each county.	On or before the last day of the first month of each calendar quarter.
Live entertainment tax.	9% of the admission charge to a facility where live entertainment.	On or before the last day of each month.
General property tax.	General property—assessed at 35% of adjusted cash value of real and tangible personal property. Aggregate of state and local rates fixed to meet budget; not to exceed 5¢ per $1 of assessed valuation.	General property—Returns—July 31 (personal property). Payment—by 3rd Monday of August or in 4 equal installments on 3rd Monday of August and 1st Monday of October, January and March.
Net proceeds of minerals tax.	Dependent on the ratio of the net proceeds to the gross proceeds of the operation as a whole: the rate is 2% for a net-to-gross percentage of less than 10%; 2.5% for a percentage of at least 10% but less than 18%; 3% for a percentage of at least 18% but less than 26%; 3.5% for a percentage of at least 26% but less than 34%; 4% for a percentage of at least 34% but less than 42%; 4.5% for a percentage of at least 42% but less than 50%; and 5% for a percentage of 50% or more and where annual net proceeds exceed $4 million.	Reports—February 16. Payment—May 10.

Tax	Basis—Rates	Due Dates
Gaming tax.	State licenses, based on type and number of games operated.	Reports—as required. Payment—county licenses, quarterly in advance; state licenses, 24th day of the month following the month for which the fee is calculated; the additional state tax, due annually prior to December 31 for the ensuing calendar year.
Alcoholic beverage tax.	Excise—malt beverages, 16¢ per gal. Liquor, 0.5% through 14% alcohol, 70¢; more than 14% through 22% alcohol, $1.30; over 22% alcohol, $3.60 per gal.	
Motor vehicle fuel tax; special fuel tax; inspection fee.	Gasoline and gasohol—23¢ per gallon and diesel fuel—27¢ per gallon. (Does not include additional cleanup and inspection fees.)	Gasoline—Returns and payment—last day of each month. Suppliers reports—last day of month.
	Special fuel—Compressed natural gas, 21¢ per gallon. Liquefied petroleum gas, 6.4¢ per gallon. A55, 19¢ per gallon. Liquefied natural gas, 27¢ per gallon.	Special fuel—Suppliers' reports—last day of each month. Payment—with report.
Cigarette taxes.	Cigarettes—$1.80 per pack of 20 cigarettes.	Reports—dealers, not later than 25 days after the end of each month.
	Tobacco products—30% of wholesale price.	Payment—at time of purchase of tax stamps, unless authorized to defer payment.
Realty transfer tax.	$1.95 for each $500 of value or fraction thereof if the value is over $100. Additionally, for Washoe and Churchill Counties 10¢ is added; in Clark County 60¢ is added.	Payment—to be evidenced by county recorder.
Sales and use taxes.	Nevada sales and use taxes are imposed on a statewide basis at the rate of 6.85%. The components of the general rate are (1) a 2% state rate under the general Sales and Use Tax Act, (2) a 2.60% state rate under the Local School Support Tax Law, and (3) a 2.25% state-mandated local rate under the City-County Relief Tax Law. The general rate is increased by local taxes in certain counties.	Reports and payment—on or before last day of each month for the preceding month (quarterly for taxpayers having gross monthly sales of less than $10,000). Taxpayers with less than $1,500 in sales in the immediate proceeding year may request to file annually. Payment—July 1.
Insurance companies tax.	3.5% on amounts of net direct premiums written and net direct considerations written in Nevada. Rate of 2% for qualified risk retention groups. Special rates apply to captive insurers. Foreign companies subject to retaliatory taxes.	Reports and payment—March 15. Estimated payment—due quarterly on the last day of the last month of each calendar quarter.

New Hampshire

Tax System.—New Hampshire derives its revenue from the corporate profits tax, gasoline tax, vehicle registration fees and tobacco taxes, and from the taxation of banks, utilities and the income from intangibles, as well as from the general property tax. An outline of the New Hampshire tax system follows:

Tax	Basis—Rates	Due Dates
Business profits tax.	7.7% for tax periods ending on or after December 31, 2019; 7.5%, 7.7%, or 7.9% for tax periods ending on or after December 31, 2021 (depending on revenue collections) before net operating loss and special deductions, adjusted by state additions and deductions. All business organizations whose gross business income from all sources before expenses exceeds $50,000 must file.	Returns and estimated tax declarations—April 15 or the 15th day of 4th month after close of tax period. Payment—15th day of 4th, 6th, 9th, and 12th months.
Business enterprise tax.	0.6% for tax periods ending on or after December 31, 2019; 0.675%, 0.5%, or 0.6% for tax periods ending on or after December 31, 2021 (depending on revenue collections) of every business enterprise having gross business receipts in excess of $208,000 or an enterprise value tax base in excess of $104,000.	Reports and payments—March 15 or the 15th day of 3rd month for enterprises required to file a U.S. partnership return. 15th day of 4th month for all others.
Interest and dividends tax.	5% on interest from bonds, notes, money, debts, and savings deposits, and on dividends from shares in business or trusts paid to resident individuals.	Reports and payments—15th day of the 4th month. Estimated tax: 15th day of the 4th, 6th, 9th, and 12th months of the tax year (for calendar-year taxpayers, the final estimated payment is due January 15 of the following tax year).
Property tax.	Local property—fixed locally to meet budget.	General property—Reports—April 15; charitable organizations, except religious and educational organizations, June 1. Payments—December 1.
	State education property tax—The rate is set by the Commissioner of the Department of Revenue Administration at a level sufficient to generate revenue of $363 million when imposed on all persons and property subject to tax.	
Railroad tax.	Average state property rate. Railroad, express, and passenger car companies; also, companies other than rail companies owning cars operated for profit on railroad.	Reports—May 1. Payments—15 days after date of notice. Estimated tax—declaration, at time for filing annual return; payments, 15th day of April, June, September, and December.
Utility property tax.	$6.60 per $1,000 of the value of utility property.	Reports and payments—by January 15 of each year. Estimated taxes in four equal installments paid on the 15th day of April, June, September, and December.

Tax	Basis—Rates	Due Dates
Timber yield tax.	Timber, 10% of stumpage value.	Reports—Within 60 days after completion of operation or May 15, whichever comes first. Payments—within 30 days after mailing of tax bill.
Meals and rentals tax.	9% of rent for each room occupancy of fewer than 185 consecutive days; 9% of gross receipts from motor vehicle rentals for up to 180 days; and up to 9% of charges for meals of 36¢ or more.	Returns and payments—on or before the 15th day of each month following.
Medicaid enhancement tax.	The tax is 5.4% of net patient services revenue for the hospital's fiscal year ending during the calendar year in which the taxable period begins.	Reports—April 15 following expiration of the taxable period.
Alcoholic beverages tax.	Excise—beer wholesale distributors, beverage manufacturers, and brew pubs, 30¢ per gallon.	
Motor fuels tax.	Road toll tax on sale of fuels—22.2¢ per gallon. Road toll tax on special fuel—22.2¢ per gallon. Aviation fuel—An airways toll of 4¢ per gallon is imposed on motor fuel or fuel sold and used in the propulsion of aircraft. An airways toll of 2¢ per gallon is imposed on the sale of aviation jet fuel sold and used in the propulsion of private aircraft. However, all aircraft that are certified to operate under Part 121 of FAA rules and regulations are required to pay an airways toll of $0.005 per gallon on aviation jet fuel sold and used in the propulsion of aircraft.	Motor fuel—20th day of each month. Airways toll—20th day of each month.
Tobacco tax.	$1.78 per pack of 20 cigarettes sold at retail or at a proportional rate for packages containing more or less than 20 cigarettes. Tobacco products other than cigarettes, 65.03% of the wholesale sales price.	Reports—cigarette wholesalers, by 30th day following regular reporting period. Wholesalers of other tobacco products, 15th day following end of reporting period. Payments—by affixing stamps.
Realty transfer tax.	75¢ per $100, or fractional part thereof, of price or consideration for sale, grant, or transfer of real estate; imposed on both buyer and seller; minimum tax, $20.	Payments—by stamps affixed to document.
Communications services tax.	7% of gross charge.	Reports and payments—15th day of each month for preceding month. Estimated tax reports and payments from large taxpayers, 15th day of current month. Small taxpayers may be authorized to report and pay quarterly.

Tax	Basis—Rates	Due Dates
Insurance premiums tax.	Property and casualty and life insurers—1.25% of gross premiums (minimum, $200). Accident and health insurers—2%. Foreign insurance companies—3%. Unauthorized insurance—4% of gross premiums, except unauthorized marine insurance is 2% of gross premiums.	Reports—authorized insurers, March 1; unauthorized insurers, within 60 days of procurement.
		Payments—ocean marine companies, within one month of receiving notice of amount. Unauthorized insurers, March 1. Authorized insurers' tax payments required on annual basis on or before March 15.
	Surplus lines insurance—3% of gross premiums.	Returns and payments—during January.

New Jersey

Tax System.—The New Jersey tax system is based on a real property tax at uniform rates within each taxing district. Business personal property is assessed by the Director of the Division of Taxation. The property tax has been supplemented by taxes on income, occupations, privileges and taxable sales and use. An outline of the New Jersey tax system follows:

Tax	Basis—Rates	Due Dates
Corporation business tax; corporation income tax.	Corporation business (income) tax—9% of allocated net income. Corporations whose entire net income is $100,000 or less are taxed at 7.5%. Corporations with entire net income of $50,000 or less are taxed at 6.5%. Rates are applied to taxable net income, effective for privilege periods ending on or after July 31, 2019. There is a surtax on a taxpayer's allocated taxable net income. The surtax is 2.5% if the corporation has allocated taxable net income over $1 million for 2018 through December 31, 2023. Regulated investment companies pay minimum tax. *Minimum tax:* The minimum tax is based on gross receipts as follows: (1) gross receipts less than $100,000, $500; (2) gross receipts of $100,000 or more but less than $250,000, $750; (3) gross receipts $250,000 or more but less than $500,000, $1,000; (4) gross receipts of $500,000 or more but less than $1 million, $1,500; and (5) gross receipts of $1 million or more, $2,000. For privilege periods beginning in calendar year 2012 and thereafter, the minimum tax for corporations that are New Jersey S corporations is based on gross receipts as follows: (1) gross receipts less than $100,000, $375; (2) gross receipts of $100,000 or more but less than $250,000, $562.50; (3) gross receipts $250,000 or more but less than $500,000, $750; (4) gross receipts of $500,000 or more but less than $1 million, $1,125; and (5) gross receipts of $1 million or more, $1,500. For a taxpayer that is a member of an affiliated group or a controlled group pursuant to IRC Secs. 1504 or 1563 that has a total payroll of $5 million or more is the minimum tax is $2,000. For privilege periods ending on and after July 31, 2019, the minimum tax of each member of a combined group filing a mandatory or elective New Jersey combined return is $2,000 for the group privilege period.	Reports and payments—15th day of 4th month after close of taxable year. Installment payments of estimated tax due on or before the 15th day of the 4th, 6th, 9th, and 12th months of the current year.

Tax	Basis—Rates	Due Dates
Personal income taxes.	Personal income tax: *Single and married/civil union partner filing separately*: $0 - 20,000 x 1.4% minus $0; $20,001 - 35,000 x 1.75% minus $70; $35,001 - 40,000 x 3.5% minus $682.50; $40,001 - 75,000 x 5.52% minus $1,492.50; $75,001 - 500,000 x 6.37% minus $2,126.25; $500,001 - $1 million x 8.97% minus $14,513.75; over $1 million x 10.750% minus $32,313.75. *Married/civil union couple filing jointly, head of household, qualifying widow(er)/ surviving civil union partner*: $0 - 20,000 x 1.4% minus $0; $20,001 - 50,000 x 1.75% minus $70; $50,001 - 70,000 x 2.45% minus $420.00; $70,001 - 80,000 x 3.5% minus $1,154.50; $80,001 - 150,000 x 5.52% minus $2,775; $150,001 - $500,000 x 6.37% minus $4,042.50; $500,001 - $1 million x 8.97% minus $17,042.50; over $1 million x 10.75% minus $34,842.50.	Returns and payment—15th day of 4th month after end of fiscal year (calendar year, April 15). Estimated tax declarations due 15th day of April, June, September, and January in four equal installments. Fiscal-year taxpayers substitute corresponding months of the fiscal year.
General property tax.	General property—Aggregate of levies of all local levying bodies within whose jurisdiction the property lies. The taxable value of personal property of telephone, telegraph and messenger companies subject to local taxation is a percentage of true value corresponding to the average ratio of assessed to true value of real property in the taxing district.	Returns—Returns are not required for real property taxes. Taxpayers subject to the tax on telephone, etc., companies file returns on or before September 1. Payment—quarterly installments on February 1, May 1, August 1, and November 1.
Railroad property tax.	Railroad property—All property used for railroad purposes, other than main stem, tangible personal property, and facilities used in passenger service, which tax shall be assessed by the commissioner, $4.75 per $100 of true value.	Railroad property—Reports—property schedule, March 1. Payment—December 1.
Railroad franchise tax.	Railroad franchise—10% of net operating income allocated to New Jersey according to track mileage. $100 minimum if operating income is less than $1 million. $4,000 minimum if operating income exceeds $1 million.	Railroad franchise—Reports—schedule of revenue, April 1. Payment—June 15.
Casino control tax.	8% of gross revenues. Licenses—issuance fee, not less than $200,000. Slot machines, $500 per machine.	Report and payment—March 15.
Alcoholic beverage tax.	Excise—beer, 12¢ per gal. Liquors, $5.50 per gal. Still wines, vermouth, sparkling wines, 87.5¢ per gal. Cider, containing at least 3.2% but not more than 7% of alcohol by volume, 15¢ per gal.	

Tax	Basis—Rates	Due Dates
Gasoline (motor fuels) tax; fuel use tax.	Gasoline and gasohol, 10.5¢ per gallon; diesel, 13.5¢ per gallon; aviation fuel, 10.5¢ per gallon (additional tax is imposed on aviation fuel distributed to the general aviation airport at the rate of 2¢ per gallon). Liquefied petroleum gas and liquefied or compressed natural gas sold or used to propel motor vehicles on public highways, 5.25¢ per gallon.	Reports and payment—suppliers of motor fuels removed from the terminal system collect the tax and hold it in trust for the state and remit it on or before the 22nd day of the month following removal. Importers and jobbers, 20th day of the month following the sale.
Motor fuel use tax.	Same as the motor fuel tax rate for fuel used in operations in the state.	Reports and payments—last day of January, April, July and October.
Petroleum products gross receipts tax.	Petroleum products other than highway fuel and aviation fuel: 7% of gross receipts. Highway fuel and aviation fuel: 12.85% of gross receipts. Diesel fuel: 12.85%. Highway fuels are subject to an additional cents-per-gallon rate of 4¢.	Reports and payments—25th day of each month. Reconciliation return on or before the 25th day following the end of a quarterly period.
Cigarette tax; tobacco products tax.	$2.70 per pack of 20, whether sold, possessed for sale, use, consumption or storage for use within the state.	Reports—by 20th of each month. Payment—by stamps affixed to each package of cigarettes.
Tobacco products tax.	30% of wholesale sales or use of tobacco products other than cigarettes. Moist snuff, $0.75 per oz. on the net weight and a proportionate rate on all fractional parts of an ounce of the net weight of moist snuff. Liquid nicotine, $0.10 per fluid milliliter of liquid nicotine and a proportionate rate on fractional parts of a milliliter of liquid nicotine, as listed by the manufacturer. Container e-liquid, 10% of retail sales price.	Reports and payments—20th day of each month.
Realty transfer tax.	Basic fee: $1.75 per $500 of consideration ($1.25 state fee and $0.50 county fee). Additional fee: $0.75 per $500 of consideration in excess of $150,000. General purpose fee: $0.90 per $500 on the first $550,000 of the value recited in the deed of transfer; $1.40 on each $500 of the value between $550,000 and $850,000; $1.90 on each $500 of the value between $850,000 and $1,000,000; and $2.15 for each $500 of the value over $1,000,000. Supplemental fee: $0.25 for each $500 of consideration not in excess of $150,00; $0.85 for each $500 of consideration in excess of $150,000 but not in excess of $200,000; $1.40 for each $500 of consideration or fractional part thereof in excess of $200,000, plus, for a transfer of title to real property upon which there is new construction, an additional $1 for each $500 of consideration not in excess of $150,000.	Payment—prior to recordation.

Tax	Basis—Rates	Due Dates
Sales and use tax.	6.625% of taxable sales and uses, rentals, occupancies, admissions and selected services.	Returns and payment—20th day of the month following the quarter covered (April, July, October, January); if tax exceeds $500 for 1st or 2nd month of a quarter, due by the 20th of the following month.
Utilities—Excise tax on sewage and water corporations.	Excise on sewage and water corporations—5% of gross receipts; 2% if gross receipts are less than $50,000. Sewerage and water companies pay additional tax at the rate of 7.5% of gross receipts from New Jersey business for the preceding calendar year.	Reports—on gross receipts, February 1; on property, September 1. Payment—35%, 15 days after certification of apportionment, 35% on August 15, 30%, on November 15.
Surtax—Surtax for sewage and water companies.	0.625% of apportioned gross receipts taxes. If gross receipts are not more than $50,000, the tax is 0.25%; for businesses connected with lines or mains in the state, 0.9375%.	Payment—prepayment of 1/2 due by May 1.
Insurance companies tax.	All insurance companies other than marine—2% plus 0.1% of taxable premiums, less personal property taxes. Group accident, health, and legal insurance policies on New Jersey residents and legal insurance policies on New Jersey residents—1% plus 0.05%.	Reports and payments—Reports due on march 1. Stock, mutual and assessment insurance companies (domestic and foreign) prepay 1/2 of the prior year's tax on March 1. Domestic and foreign companies prepay an additional 1/2 of prior year's tax on or before each June 1.
	Foreign companies are subject to retaliatory taxes.	Reports—March 1.
Marine companies (state taxes).	5% plus 0.25% of the average annual underwriting profit.	Reports and payments—Reports due April 1. Payments due within 15 days after notice of amount of tax due.
Tax on insureds who procure or renew insurance with any unauthorized foreign or alien insurer.	5% of gross premium.	Reports and payments—30 days after the insurance was procured or renewed.
Surplus lines coverage.	5% of taxable premium receipts.	Reports and payments—quarterly.
Captive insurance companies (not combinable captive insurance companies).	0.38 of 1% on the first $20,000,000, 0.285 of 1% on the next $20,000,000, 0.19 of 1% on the next $20,000,000, and 0.072 of 1% on each dollar thereafter on direct premiums collected/contracted for on policies/contracts. Alternatively, 0.214 of 1% on the first $20,000,000 of assumed reinsurance premium, 0.143 of 1% on the next $20,000,000, 0.048 of 1% on the next $20,000,000, and 0.024 of 1% of each dollar thereafter.	Reports—March 1.

New Mexico

Tax System.—New Mexico imposes a general property tax, and also taxes on incomes, occupations, and privileges. Alcoholic beverages, motor fuels, natural resources, leased vehicles, cigarettes, and other tobacco products are subject to taxation. Various gross receipts taxes are also assessed. An insurance gross premiums tax is applicable as well. Finally, an annual franchise tax on both domestic and foreign corporations is imposed. An outline of the New Mexico tax system follows:

Tax	Basis—Rates	Due Dates
Franchise tax.	$50 per year, or prorated.	Returns and payments—by the 15th day of the 4th month after the end of the tax year (last day of month federal corporate income tax return is due if filing and paying electronically).
Income tax.	**Single individuals, estates, and trusts:** first $5,500, 1.7%; over $5,500 but not over $11,000, $93.50 plus 3.2% of excess over $5,500; over $11,000 but not over $16,000, $269.50 plus 4.7% of excess over $11,000; over $16,000, $504.50 plus 4.9% of excess over $16,000. **Heads of household, surviving spouses, and married individuals filing joint returns:** first $8,000, 1.7%; over $8,000 but not over $16,000, $136 plus 3.2% of excess over $8,000; over $16,000 but not over $24,000, $392 plus 4.7% of excess over $16,000; over $24,000, $768 plus 4.9% of excess over $24,000. **Married individuals filing separate returns:** first $4,000, 1.7%; over $4,000 but not over $8,000, $68 plus 3.2% of excess over $4,000; over $8,000 but not over $12,000, $196 plus 4.7% of excess over $8,000; over $12,000, $384 plus 4.9% of excess over $12,000. If general revenue growth from FY 2019 to FY 2020 is not more than 5%, then effective January 1, 2021, the following rates will take effect: **Single individuals, estates, and trusts:** first $5,500, 1.7%; over $5,500 but not over $11,000, $93.50 plus 3.2% of excess over $5,500; over $11,000 but not over $16,000, $269.50 plus 4.7% of excess over $11,000; over $16,000 but not over $210,000, $504.50 plus 4.9% of excess over $16,000; over $210,000, $10,010.50 plus 5.9% of excess over $210,000. **Heads of household, surviving spouses, and married individuals filing joint returns:** first $8,000, 1.7%; over $8,000 but not over $16,000, $136 plus 3.2% of excess over $8,000; over $16,000 but not over $24,000, $392 plus 4.7% of excess over $16,000; over $24,000 but not over $315,000, $768 plus 4.9% of excess over $24,000; over $315,000, $15,027 plus 5.9% of excess over $315,000. **Married individuals filing separate returns:** first $4,000, 1.7%; over $4,000 but not over $8,000, $68 plus 3.2% of excess over $4,000; over $8,000 but not over $12,000, $196 plus 4.7% of excess over $8,000; over $12,000 but not over $157,500, $384 plus 4.9% of excess over $12,000; over $157,500, $7,513.50 plus 5.9% of excess over $157,500.	Returns and payments—15th day of fourth month after tax year; estimated taxes—calendar-year taxpayers, April 15, June 15, and September 15 of calendar year, and January 15 of the following year; fiscal-year taxpayers 15th day of fourth, sixth, and ninth months of the fiscal year, and 15th day of the first month following that fiscal year.

Tax	Basis—Rates	Due Dates
	Corporations—Taxable income up to $500,000, 4.8% of taxable income; over $500,000 of taxable income, $24,000 plus 5.9% of excess over $500,000. Qualified corporate taxpayers may pay alternative tax of 0.75% of gross receipts from New Mexico sales.	Returns and payments—15th day of fourth month after tax year or April 15 for calendar-year taxpayers (last day of month federal corporate income tax return is due if filing and paying electronically); estimated taxes—15th day of the fourth, sixth, ninth, and 12th months of the current tax year.
	General withholding is required.	
General property tax.	General property—Aggregate of state and local rates fixed to meet budget, subject to limitations. Property is assessed at 33 1/3% of market value.	Payments—General property—by November 10 and April 10; prepayments, due July 10 and January 10, may be allowed if the tax due is $100 or more.
	Mining property—Assessment of mining property is based on production or market value, depending on the mineral produced.	Mining property—by November 10 and April 10.
Alcoholic beverages taxes.	Excise—beer, 41¢ per gallon and for microbrewed beer, 8¢ per gallon; spirituous liquors, $1.60 per liter; wine, 45¢ per liter; fortified wine, $1.50 per liter; alcoholic cider, 41¢ per gallon.	Reports and payments—by the 25th day of following month.
Gasoline tax; special fuel taxes.	17¢ per gallon of gasoline; and 21¢ per gallon of special fuel.	Reports and payments—Gasoline tax—by the 25th day of each following month. Special fuel suppliers tax—by the 25th day of the month following the month the fuel is received in the state. Special fuel users tax—by the 25th day of the month following the last day of the calendar quarter in which the special fuel is used. (The annual report and payment for small users are due January 25 following the tax year.)
Natural resources severance tax.	Gross value less rental and royalty payments and other deductions. Tax rates are: timber and nonmetallic minerals, 0.125%; surface coal, 57¢ per ton plus a per-ton indexed surtax; underground coal, 55¢ per ton plus a per-ton indexed surtax.	Reports and payments—by the 25th day of the month following the month in which the taxable event occurred.

Tax	Basis—Rates	Due Dates
Oil and gas severance tax.	Natural gas, natural gas from a new production well, oil or other liquid hydrocarbons, and carbon dioxide, 3.75% of the taxable value of the products. Oil and other liquid hydrocarbons from qualified enhanced recovery project, 1.875% of taxable value, under specified pricing circumstances.	Returns and payments—by the 25th day of the 2nd month following each calendar month.
Oil and gas ad valorem production tax.	District rate for nonresidential property imposed on the assessed value of products severed and sold from each production unit, generally.	Returns and payments—by the 25th day of the 2nd month following each calendar month.
Leased vehicle gross receipts tax.	5% of gross receipts from leasing small passenger vehicles plus a $2 per day per vehicle surcharge.	Leased vehicles—25th day of each month.
Cigarette tax; tobacco products tax.	$1.66 per pack of 20 cigarettes.	Payments—Cigarettes—for stamps, due by the 25th day of month following purchase.
	25% of the tobacco product's value.	Tobacco products—by the 25th day of the following month.
Gross receipts, governmental gross receipts and compensating tax.	Gross receipts—5.125% of gross receipts from sales of tangible personal property and services.	Gross receipts—Reports and payments due 25th of each month; semiannual or quarterly reports and payments allowed if liability is less than $200 per month.
	Compensating tax—5.125% of value of tangible personal property at time of acquisition, conversion or introduction into state; 5% of value of services at the time they were rendered.	Compensating tax—Reports and payments due 25th of each month; semiannual or quarterly reports and payments allowed if liability is less than $200 per month.
Insurance companies tax.	3.003% of gross premiums collected in the state, less all return premiums, including dividends paid or credited to policyholders or contract holders and premiums received for reinsurance on New Mexico risks.	Return—April 15 of following year; surplus lines brokers, within 60 days after each quarter. Payments—Estimated payments due on April 15, July 15, October 15, and January 15, with any adjustment due with the annual return (April 15).
	1% surtax on gross health insurance premiums and membership and policy fees received by the insurance company on hospital and medical expense incurred insurance or contracts; nonprofit health care service plan contracts, excluding dental or vision only contracts; and health maintenance organization subscriber contracts covering health risks within New Mexico during preceding calendar year, less all return health insurance premiums, including dividends paid or credited to policyholders or contract holders and health insurance premiums received for reinsurance on New Mexico risks.	
	Foreign companies subject to retaliatory taxes.	

Tax	Basis—Rates	Due Dates
Interstate telecommunications service.	Interstate telecommunications service—4.25% of interstate telecommunications gross receipts.	Interstate telecommunications service—Reports and payments due 25th of month following taxable event.
Railroad car company tax.	Railroad car companies—1 1/2% of gross earnings	Railroad car companies—Report and payment due March 1.
Rural electric cooperatives.	Rural electric cooperatives—$10 per 100 persons or fraction to whom electricity is supplied in the state.	Rural electric cooperatives—Payment due July 1.

New York

Tax System.—New York has not adopted the system of segregation of revenues for state and local purposes. The law permits the levy of income, property, franchise, sales and use, gross receipts, and miscellaneous taxes. An outline of the New York tax system follows:

Tax	Basis—Rates	Due Dates
Franchise taxes: business corporations; unrelated business tax.	Business corporations (**For tax year 2020**)—Greater of business income base of 6.5% (0% for qualified in-state manufacturers, 4.875% for qualified emerging technology companies (QETCs)); capital tax base of 0.025% (0.019% for qualified in-state manufacturers and QETCs) per dollar of allocated capital (up to $350,000 for qualified in-state manufacturers and QETCs or $5 million for other taxpayers); or fixed dollar minimum tax, ranging from $25 (if state receipts are not more than $100,000) to $200,000 (if state receipts are over $1 billion). Special fixed dollar minimum amounts apply to qualified New York manufacturers and QETCs, as well as non-captive REITs and RICs. Small business taxpayers: 6.5%. New York S corporations: subject only to the fixed dollar minimum tax, with special rates applicable. Metropolitan Commuter Transportation District surcharge: 29.4% of tax imposed. (**For tax year 2019**)—Greater of business income base of 6.5% (0% for qualified in-state manufacturers, 4.875% for qualified emerging technology companies (QETCs)); capital tax base of 0.05% (0.038% for qualified in-state manufacturers and QETCs) per dollar of allocated capital (up to $350,000 for qualified in-state manufacturers and QETCs or $5 million for other taxpayers); or fixed dollar minimum tax, ranging from $25 (if state receipts are not more than $100,000) to $200,000 (if state receipts are over $1 billion). Special fixed dollar minimum amounts apply to qualified New York manufacturers and QETCs, as well as non-captive REITs and RICs. Small business taxpayers: 6.5%. New York S corporations: subject only to the fixed dollar minimum tax, with special rates applicable. Metropolitan Commuter Transportation District surcharge: 28.9% of tax imposed.	Corporations: 15th day of 4th month after end of tax year. S corporations: 15th day of 3rd month after end of tax year. Estimated payments required for corporations that can reasonably expect tax in excess of $1,000, due in installments.
	Unrelated business income tax—9% or $250, whichever is greater, of unrelated business income of certain tax-exempt charitable organizations and trusts subject to the federal tax on unrelated business income.	Returns and payments—15th day of 5th month after close of taxable year.
	Banking corporations—**Note:** After tax year 2014, banks merged into corporate franchise tax.	

Tax	Basis—Rates	Due Dates
Personal income tax.	**For tax year 2020:** Single, Married Filing Separately: $0 - 8,500 x 4.000% minus $0; $8,501 - 11,700 x 4.500% minus $42.50; $11,701 - 13,900 x 5.250% minus $130.25; $13,901 - 21,400 x 5.900% minus $220.60; $21,401 - 80,650 x 6.090% minus $261.26; $80,651 -215,400 x 6.410% minus $519.33; $215,401 - 1,077,550 x 6.850% minus $1,467.09; $1,077,551 and over x 8.820% minus $22,694.82. Married Filing Jointly, Qualifying Widow(er): $0 - 17,150 x 4.000% minus $0; $17,151 - 23,600 x 4.500% minus $85.75; $23,601 - 27,900 x 5.250% minus $262.75; $27,901 - 43,000 x 5.900% minus $444.10; $43,001 -161,550 x 6.090% minus $525.80; $161,551 - 323,200 x 6.410% minus $1,042.75; $323,201 - 2,155,350 x 6.850% minus $2,464.83; $2,155,351 and over x 8.820% minus $44,925.22. Head of Household: $0 - 12,800 x 4.000% minus $0; $12,801 - 17,650 x 4.500% minus $64.00; $17,651 - 20,900 x 5.250% minus $196.37; $20,901 - 32,200 x 5.900% minus $332.22; $32,201 - 107,650 x 6.090% minus $393.40; $107,651 - 269,300 x 6.410% minus $737.87; $269,301 - 1,616,450 x 6.850% minus $1,922.79; $1,616,451 and over x 8.820% minus $33,766.85. **For tax year 2019:** Single, Married Filing Separately: $0 - 8,500 x 4.000% minus $0; $8,501 - 11,700 x 4.500% minus $42.50; $11,701 - 13,900 x 5.250% minus $130.25; $13,901 - 21,400 x 5.900% minus $220.60; $21,401 - 80,650 x 6.210% minus $286.94; $80,651 -215,400 x 6.490% minus $512.75; $215,401 - 1,077,550 x 6.850% minus $1,288.19; $1,077,551 and over x 8.820% minus $22,515.92. Married Filing Jointly, Qualifying Widow(er): $0 - 17,150 x 4.000% minus $0; $17,151 - 23,600 x 4.500% minus $85.75; $23,601 - 27,900 x 5.250% minus $262.75; $27,901 - 43,000 x 5.900% minus $444.10; $43,001 -161,550 x 6.210% minus $577.40; $161,551 - 323,200 x 6.490% minus $1,029.73; $323,201 - 2,155,350 x 6.850% minus $2,193.25; $2,155,351 and over x 8.820% minus $44,653.64. Head of Household: $0 - 12,800 x 4.000% minus $0; $12,801 - 17,650 x 4.500% minus $64.00; $17,651 - 20,900 x 5.250% minus $196.37; $20,901 - 32,200 x 5.900% minus $332.22; $32,201 - 107,650 x 6.210% minus $432.04; $107,651 - 269,300 x 6.490% minus $733.45; $269,301 - 1,616,450 x 6.850% minus $1,702.93; $1,616,451 and over x 8.820% minus $33,546.99. A supplemental tax (the tax table benefit recapture) is also computed for taxpayers with certain levels of income.	Personal income tax—on or before April 15 for calendar-year taxpayers, 15th day of 4th month after end of tax year for fiscal-year taxpayers. Payments of estimated income tax due April 15, June 15, September 15 and January 15. For farmers single due date is January 15 of succeeding year.

Tax	Basis—Rates	Due Dates
General property tax. (Assessed and collected locally.)	Aggregate of all levies for local purposes fixed annually by each locality to meet budget. Based on full value of real property including special franchises. Equalization rate in each locality determined by State Board of Real Property Tax Services. Personal property is exempt.	Returns—special franchises, 30 days after acquisition. Payment—generally by January 31 but payment date may vary according to locality.
Alcoholic beverage tax.	Excise—beer, 14¢ per gallon; cider and sparkling cider, 3.79¢ per gallon. Still wines, artificially carbonated sparkling wines, and natural sparkling wines, 30¢ per gallon. Liquor containing more than 2% but less than 24% alcohol, 67¢ per liter; liquor containing not more than 2% alcohol by volume, $0; all other liquor, $1.70 per liter.	
Motor fuel tax; fuel use tax; petroleum business tax.	Motor fuel tax, 8¢ per gallon.	Reports and payments—20th of each month. Larger taxpayers must make EFT payments or payments by certified check on or before the third business day following the 22nd day of each calendar month for that month.
	Pre-paid sales tax per gallon of motor fuel and diesel fuel is 16¢ in Region 1 and Region 2, and 15¢ in Region 3.	
	Petroleum business tax—2021 rates are announced in January 2021. *Tax rates for 2020:* 17.4¢ per gallon for motor fuel; 15.65¢ per gallon for highway diesel motor fuel; 9.5¢ per commercial gallon for non-highway diesel motor fuel; 17.4¢ per gallon for aviation gasoline; 7.0¢ per gallon for kero-jet fuel; and 8¢ for ethanol and gasohol. (Rates are indexed annually and include any applicable surcharge.) *Tax on carriers:* same as the total petroleum business tax rate on motor fuel and automotive-type diesel fuel imported into New York in the fuel tanks of vehicular units.	Petroleum business tax—20th day of each month. Larger taxpayers must make EFT payments or payments by certified check on or before the third business day following the 22nd day of each calendar month for that month.
Cigarette tax; tobacco products tax.	Cigarettes—$4.35 per pack of 20 cigarettes sold or used within state. If a pack of cigarettes contains more than 20 cigarettes, the tax on the cigarettes in excess of 20 is imposed at the rate of $1.0875 for each five cigarettes or fraction thereof. Little cigars also taxed at this rate.	Report—Sales tax, agents, 15th of each month. Use tax, within 24 hours. Payment—Sales tax, by means of stamps. Use tax, within 24 hours.
	Tobacco products—75% of wholesale price on cigars and tobacco products (other than little cigars and snuff). Snuff—$2 per ounce and a proportionate rate on any fractional amount for containers with more than one ounce.	Report and payment—20th of each month; use tax, within 24 hours.
Stock transfer tax.	Stock transfer tax—2.5¢ per share on transfers of stock or certificates of interest in property or accumulations other than by sale. Sale or agreement to sell at less than $5 per share, 1.25¢ per share; sale at $5 or more per share but less than $10, 2.5¢; sale at $10 or more but less than $20, 3.75¢; sale at $20 or more per share, 5¢. Maximum tax on a single transaction, $350.	Stock transfer tax—daily by clearing corporations; weekly by registered dealers in securities; or by purchase of stamps.

Tax	Basis—Rates	Due Dates
Mortgage recording tax.	Mortgage recording tax—50¢ for each $100 or major fraction of debt secured by real estate mortgage, including sales contracts under which vendees are entitled to possession. Additional tax is 25¢ for each $100 (30¢ per $100 in MCTD). Special additional tax is 25¢ for each $100. Local tax may be imposed by counties.	Mortgage recording tax—at time of recording instruments or making additional advances.
Realty transfer tax.	$2 per $500 of consideration or value of property conveyed; no tax if value is less than $500. Additional 1% tax on conveyance of residential realty for which the consideration is $1 million or more. The 2019 budget (Ch. 59 (S.B. 1509)) increased the rates, including the so-called mansion tax, on conveyances of real property in New York City. Specifically, the law increases the real estate transfer tax by 0.25% for conveyances of: (i) residential real property when the consideration is $3 million or more, and (ii) any other real property (i.e., commercial property) when the consideration is $2 million or more. The increased rate is in addition to the existing 0.4% real estate transfer tax on all conveyances. The law also imposes an additional mansion tax, ranging from 0.25% on transfers of $2 million or more to 2.9% on transfers of $25 million or more. This new/additional mansion tax is in addition to the existing 1% mansion tax on transfers of residential real property of $1 million or more. As a result of these increases and additional tax, the total combined top rate is 4.55% on the sale of residential properties valued at $25 million or above in New York City. The new rates go into effect on July 1, 2019, other than conveyances that are made pursuant to binding written contracts entered into on or before April 1, 2019, provided that the date of execution of such contract is confirmed by independent evidence or other facts and circumstances.	Report and payment—due 15th day after delivery of the instrument.
Sales and use tax.	4% of receipts from retail sales or the consideration given for the use of property or selected services. Additional state rate of 3/8% imposed in the Metropolitan Commuter Transportation District (MCTD). Additional 5% tax imposed on receipts from entertainment or information services provided by telephone, telegraph or interactive network services (if received exclusively in an aural manner). Additional 6% tax imposed on the short-term rental of passenger car rentals. In addition, there is a 6% special supplemental tax (total of 12%) on all passenger car rentals where delivery occurs within the MCTD, or where the passenger car is rented outside the MCTD for use within the MCTD. Also, there is an additional supplemental tax of 6% is imposed on passenger car rentals outside the MCTD (total of 12%).	Reports and payment—due 20 days after last days of Feb., May, Aug., and Nov. if taxable receipts are less than $300,000. If such receipts are $300,000 or more for any quarter of the preceding four quarters, reports and payments are due within 20 days after the end of each prior month. Annual returns must be filed on or before March 20th of each subsequent year. Information returns must be filed within 20 days following the 12-month period covered by the return. Larger taxpayers must make EFT payments or payments by certified check on or before the third business day following the 22nd day of each calendar month for that month.

Tax	Basis—Rates	Due Dates
Gross income tax on utility services; transportation and transmission corporations franchise tax.	Utility services gross income tax—2.5% on the gross income of telecommunications service providers. 2% for other utilities on gross income portion from transportation, transmission, or distribution.	Utility services gross income tax—on or before April 15 for year ending December 31 preceding.
	Transportation and transmission corporations franchise tax—1.5 mills per $1 of net value of capital stock allocated to New York; or 0.375 mills for each 1% of dividends provided that dividends paid in preceding calendar year amounted to 6% or more; or $75, whichever is greatest. Additional gross earnings tax: 0.375% of intrastate gross earnings.	Transportation and transmission corporations franchise and earnings taxes—Sec. 183: on or before March 15 (April 15 for tax years beginning after 2016). Sec. 184: on or before April 15.
	Telecommunication services tax—2.5% of gross receipts.	Telecommunication services—on or before April 15.
Insurance companies tax.	Franchise (income) and premiums taxes—Net income component is eliminated, except for life insurance companies, and tax is imposed on premiums only at rate of 1.75% for accident and health insurance contracts, 2% for other non-life premiums. Life insurance companies subject to 7.1% tax on allocated entire net income (alternative base/computation may apply; plus additional tax on subsidiary capital). A 17% Metropolitan Commuter Transportation District surcharge is imposed on insurance corporations and life insurance corporations with business activities in the District. Life insurance companies, additional franchise tax, 0.7% of gross direct premiums, less return premiums. Special rates apply to captive insurance companies. Foreign and alien fire insurance companies, $2 per $100 of premiums. Foreign mutual fire insurance companies, 2%.	Franchise and premiums taxes: Returns and payments—15th day of 4th month after end of tax year.
	Independently procured insurance—3.6% of the premiums paid, less returns thereon, for any person whose home state is New York and who purchases or renews a taxable insurance contract from an insurer not authorized to transact business in the state.	Independently procured insurance: Returns and payments—within 60 days of the end of the calendar quarter during which an independently procured insurance contract took effect or was renewed.
	Foreign companies subject to retaliatory taxes, unless organized or domiciled in a state or country that does not impose retaliatory taxes on New York insurers or provides for reciprocal exemptions.	
Metropolitan Commuter Transportation Mobility Tax (MCTMT).	For employers, 0.11% if quarterly payroll expense is over $312,500, but no greater than $375,000; 0.23% if quarterly payroll expense is no greater than $437,500; 0.34% if payroll expense exceeds $437,500 in any calendar quarter (for calendar quarters beginning before April 1, 2012, the rate was 0.34% for all employers). For individuals, 0.34% of net earnings from self-employment.	Due quarterly for employers. For individuals, due dates are the same as for personal income tax.

Tax	Basis—Rates	Due Dates
Employer Compensation Expense Tax (ECET).	Opt-in payroll tax. Affected employers subject to tax on annual payroll expenses exceeding $40,000 per employee. For employers opting in, the tax is phased in over three years, with a rate of 1.5% in 2019, 3% in 2020, and 5% beginning in 2021.	Tax due electronically on same dates applicable to employer withholding payments. Employers must file quarterly returns by the same due dates applicable to withholding returns.

North Carolina

Tax System.—North Carolina imposes a general property tax on all property for local purposes only. Intangible personal property is separately taxed. The state derives its revenue under the Revenue Act from personal and corporate income taxes, gasoline taxes, and sales and use taxes. The legislature has empowered counties, cities and towns to impose license taxes. An outline of the North Carolina tax system follows:

Tax	Basis—Rates	Due Dates
Corporation franchise tax.	$1.50 per $1,000 (.0015) of whichever yields highest tax: (1) net worth, (2) actual investment in North Carolina tangible property, or (3) 55% of the appraised value of real/tangible property. S corporations pay at the rate of $200 for the first $1 million of the tax base and $1.50 per $1,000 of the tax base that is more than $1 million. Minimum tax is $200 for all taxpayers.	Reports and payments—15th day of 4th month following the end of the income year.
Corporation income tax.	2.5% of taxable income.	Returns and payments—15th day of 4th month after close of income year. 15th day of 7th month following the close of income year for foreign corporations with no office or place of business in the U.S. Estimated tax payments due (if tax liability is $500 or more) by the 15th day of the 4th, 6th, 9th and 12th months of the tax year, depending on when filing requirements are first met.
Personal income tax.	5.25% on federal adjusted gross income after state modifications Estimated tax—If expected tax liability is $1,000 or more, payments due on the 15th day of April, June, September and January.	Returns and payments—April 15 for calendar-year returns; 15th day of 4th month after close of fiscal year for fiscal-year returns.
General property tax.	General property tax—fixed by cities and counties to meet budget. Based on true cash value of real property and tangible personal property.	General property tax—reports: property is listed during January; railroads and public service corporations, March 31. Payment, September 1, payable without penalty until January 6.
Alcoholic beverages tax.	Excise—malt beverages, 61.71¢ per gallon; unfortified wine, 26.34¢ per liter; fortified wine, 29.34¢ per liter; liquor, 30% of retail price.	Reports—on or before the 15th of each month.

Tax	Basis—Rates	Due Dates
Fuel taxes.	Motor fuels excise, diesel fuel excise, road tax: 36.1¢ per gallon for calendar year 2020.	Motor fuel—reports and payments: 22nd day of each month, with following exceptions: occasional importers, 3rd day of each month; terminal operators, 45 days after end of calendar year. Road tax—Reports and payments due on or before the last day of January, April, July, and October for preceding quarter.
	Inspection fee—0.25¢ per gallon of kerosene, motor fuel, aviation, and jet fuel.	Reports and payments—informational returns of licensed suppliers of kerosene, 22nd of each month; informational returns of kerosene terminal operators, 22nd of each month; inspection fee on motor fuel due when excise tax on motor fuel tax is payable (22nd of each month).
Severance taxes.	Condensates—3.5% of gross price paid. Effective January 1, 2021, the rate for condensates—5%. Gas—from 0.9% to 2.9% of market value. Effective January 1, 2021, the percentage rate for gas—from 0.9% to 5% of market value. Marginal gas—0.6% of market value. Effective January 1, 2021, the rate for marginal gas—0.8%. Oil—3.5% of gross price paid. Effective January 1, 2021, the rate for oil—5%.	Reports and payment—quarterly taxpayer returns due by the 25th day of the second month following the end of the quarter. Monthly taxpayer returns (for taxpayers consistently liable for $1,000 or more each month) due by the 25th day of the second month following the calendar month covered by the return. Payments are due upon filing of returns.
Primary forest product assessment.	50¢ per 1,000 board feet for softwood products measured in board feet; 40¢ per 1,000 board feet for hardwood and bald cypress products measured in board feet; 20¢ per cord for softwood products measured in cords; 12¢ per cord for hardwood and bald cypress products measured in cords.	Payment—last day of month following end of quarter.
Highway use tax.	A highway use tax is imposed at a 3% rate for the privilege of using the highways of North Carolina. The maximum tax is $2,000 for each certificate of title issued for a Class A or Class B motor vehicle that is a commercial motor vehicle, and for each certificate of title issued for a recreational vehicle.	Payment—to the Commissioner of Motor Vehicles when applying for a certificate of title for a motor vehicle.

Tax	Basis—Rates	Due Dates
Cigarette tax; tobacco products tax.	Cigarettes—2.25¢ per cigarette (45¢ per pack of 20). Tobacco products—12.8% of the cost price. The tobacco products tax is reduced by 25% or 50% on modified risk tobacco products depending on whether the product was issued a risk modification order or an exposure modification order by the FDA. Vapor products—5¢ per fluid milliliter of consumable product.	Reports and payments—20th of each month.
Realty transfer tax.	$1 per $500 or fractional part of the consideration or value of the interest or property conveyed.	Payment to the county where the realty is situated. Payment evidenced by tax stamps. Affixation of stamp not necessary; register of deeds may merely mark instrument to show tax was paid.
Sales and use tax.	Sales tax—4.75% on: (1) sales and purchases of tangible personal property, certain digital property, and certain services, including manufactured homes and modular homes sold at retail; (2) aircraft (maximum, $2,500 per article); (3) qualified jet engines; (4) repair, maintenance, and installation services (with certain exemptions); and (5) toll or private telecommunications services. Gross receipts derived from providing telecommunications and ancillary service, video programming, piped natural gas, electricity, and spirituous liquor are subject to the combined general rate of 7% for all transactions sourced to North Carolina. Aviation gasoline and jet fuel—7% combined general rate.	Returns and payments—payable when return is due. Taxpayers consistently liable for less than $100 in taxes per month may file on quarterly basis by last day of the month following the end of the quarter. Taxpayers consistently liable for at least $100 but less than $20,000 a month must file a return and pay taxes due on a monthly basis by the 20th day of the month following the calendar month covered by the return. Taxpayers consistently liable for at least $20,000 a month in state and local sales and use taxes must make a monthly prepayment of the next month's tax liability, which is due when the monthly return is due.
	Use tax—same rate on sales price of tangible personal property or taxable services stored, used, or consumed in the state.	

Tax	Basis—Rates	Due Dates
Public utilities tax; freight car line company tax.	Public utilities tax—repealed effective July 1, 2014. As of that date, the combined general sales and use tax rate applies to the gross receipts derived from sales of electricity and piped natural gas. Freight car line company tax—3% of intrastate gross earnings. Tax is in lieu of all ad valorem taxes.	Freight car line company tax—tax withheld by railroad company using or leasing cars of freight car line company. Railroad company must remit tax withheld together with a report, annually, on or before March 1 for preceding calendar year.
Public utility regulatory fee.	Applicable to jurisdictional revenues earned in each quarter, unless adjusted by the North Carolina Utilities Commission, the public utility fee is a percentage of a utility's jurisdictional revenues as follows: (1) 0.148% for noncompetitive jurisdiction revenues; (2) 0.04% for subsection (h) competitive jurisdictional revenues; and (3) 0.02% for subsection (m) competitive jurisdictional revenues.	Reports and payments—due to the North Carolina Utilities Commission on or before the 15th day of the second month following the end of each quarter.
Insurance companies tax.	1.9% on gross premiums from contracts issued by insurers, plus 0.74% on property coverage contracts. 1.9% on health maintenance organizations (HMOs). 2.5% on gross premiums from contracts for workers' compensation coverage. 5% for surplus lines insurance. 0.40% captive insurers tax on direct premiums of up to $20 million and 0.30% for premiums of $20 million or more, but not less than $5,000 or more than $100,000. Foreign companies subject to retaliatory taxes.	Reports and payments—March 15. Estimated payment (if $10,000 or more in business the prior year)—quarterly, three equal installments of *at least* 33 1/3% due April 15, June 15 and October 15 of tax year; if necessary, balance due by following March 15.

North Dakota

Tax System.—The North Dakota revenue system is founded on a general property tax at uniform rates within each taxing district. The general property tax has been supplemented by taxes on incomes, occupations, and privileges. An outline of the North Dakota tax system follows:

Tax	Basis—Rates	Due Dates
General income tax.	Individuals—: **2020 Rates**—Single: $0 - 40,125 x 1.10% minus $0; $40,126 - 97,150 x 2.04% minus $377.17; $97,151 - 202,650 x 2.27% minus $600.62; $202,651 - 440,600 x 2.64% minus $1,350.42; $440,601 and over x 2.90% minus $2,495.98. Married Filing Jointly, Qualifying Widow(er): $0 - 67,050 x 1.10% minus $0; $67,051 - 161,950 x 2.04% minus $630.27; $161,951 - 246,700 x 2.27% minus $1,002.75; $246,701- 440,600 x 2.64% minus $1,915.54; $440,601 and over x 2.90% minus $3,061.10. Married Filing Separately: $0 - 33,525 x 1.10% minus $0; $33,526 - 80,975 x 2.04% minus $315.13; $80,976 - 123,350 x 2.27% minus $501.38; $123,351 - 220,300 x 2.64% minus $957.77; $220,301 and over x 2.90% minus $1,530.55. Head of Household: $0 - 53,750 x 1.10% minus $0; $53,751 - 138,800 x 2.04% minus $505.25; $138,801- 224,700 x 2.27% minus $824.49; $224,701 - 440,600 x 2.64% minus $1,655.88; $440,601 and over x 2.90% minus $2,801.44. **2019 Rates**—Single: $0 - 39,450 x 1.10% minus $0; $39,451- 95,500 x 2.04% minus $370.83; $95,501 - 199,250 x 2.27% minus $590.48; $199,251 - 433,200 x 2.64% minus $1,327.70; $433,201 and over x 2.90% minus $2,454.02. Married Filing Jointly, Qualifying Widow(er): $0 - 65,900 x 1.10% minus $0; $65,901 - 159,200 x 2.04% minus $619.46; $159,201 - 242,550 x 2.27% minus $985.62; $242,551- 433,200 x 2.64% minus $1,883.05; $433,201 and over x 2.90% minus $3,009.37. Married Filing Separately: $0 - 32,950 x 1.10% minus $0; $32,951 - 79,600 x 2.04% minus $309.73; $79,601 - 121,275 x 2.27% minus $492.81; $121,276 - 216,600 x 2.64% minus $941.53; $216,601 and over x 2.90% minus $1,504.69. Head of Household: $0 - 52,850 x 1.10% minus $0; $52,851 - 136,450 x 2.04% minus $496.79; $136,451- 220,900 x 2.27% minus $810.62; $220,901 -433,200 x 2.64% minus $1,627.95; $433,201 and over x 2.90% minus $2,754.27.	Returns—calendar year, April 15; fiscal year, 15th day of 4th month after close of income year. Cooperatives, 15th day of 9th month after close of tax year.
	Corporate rates: Tax years beginning after 2014—first $25,000, 1.41%; $25,001 but not over $50,000, 3.55%; $50,001 or more, 4.31% If a corporation elects to use the water's edge method to apportion its income, the corporation will be subject to an additional 3.5% surtax on its North Dakota taxable income.	Payments—with returns. Individual and corporate estimated tax payments—4 equal installments.
Financial institutions privilege (income) tax.	For tax years beginning before 2013, 6.5% of federal taxable income with state adjustments. For subsequent years, taxpayers are transitioned to corporate income tax treatment.	Returns and payments—return and 2/7 of tax due April 15; remainder of tax due January 15 of following year.

Tax	Basis—Rates	Due Dates
General property tax.	General property tax—aggregate of state, county and municipal rates fixed annually to meet budget. Agricultural property assessed at productivity value. Residential and other property assessed at market value.	Returns—railroads, January 15 and April 1; utilities, May 1. Payments—January 1, but may be paid without penalty as follows: realty, 50% on March 1, 50% on October 15.
Alcoholic beverages taxes.	Excise (per wine gallon)—beer in bulk containers, 8¢; beer in bottles and cans, 16¢; wine containing less than 17% alcohol, 50¢; wine containing 17% to 24% alcohol, 60¢; distilled spirits, $2.50; alcohol, $4.05.	Payments—due on 15th day of each month.
Gasoline tax; special fuel tax.	Gasoline tax—23¢ per gallon of motor fuel used and sold. Special fuels tax—23¢ per gallon. Aviation fuel tax—8¢ per gallon. Additional 4% tax on fuel on which the aviation fuel tax is levied and refunded.	Reports and payments—25th day of each month.
Oil and gas gross production tax; coal severance tax; oil extraction tax.	Oil gross production tax—5% of gross value at well. Gas gross production tax—July 1, 2020, through June 30, 2021, $.0522 per mcf (rate determined annually by the State Tax Commissioner). Coal severance tax—37.5¢ per ton plus an additional 2¢ per ton. Oil extraction tax—5% of gross value at well of oil extracted; if the trigger price of $90 is exceeded for 3 consecutive months the oil extraction tax rate increases to 6% and will revert back to 5% after the trigger price is below $90 for 3 consecutive months.	Gas gross production tax reports and payments—on or before the 15th day of the 2nd month following production. Oil gross production tax, coal severance tax, and oil extraction tax reports and payments—on or before the 25th day of each month succeeding the month of production.
Motor vehicle excise tax.	Motor vehicle excise tax—5% of purchase price.	Payments—upon registration.
Aircraft excise tax.	Aircraft excise tax—5% of purchase price. Aircraft and helicopters used for application of agricultural chemicals or other agricultural material, 3% of purchase price.	Payments—upon registration.
Cigarette and tobacco products taxes.	Cigarette tax—44¢ per pack of 20. Cigars and pipe tobacco tax—28% of wholesale price. Snuff tax—60¢ per ounce. Chewing tobacco tax—16¢ per ounce.	Cigarette and tobacco products taxes, reports and payments—15th day of each month for the preceding month.

Tax	Basis—Rates	Due Dates
Sales and use taxes.	Sales tax—5% of gross receipts from retail sales of property, amusements, and specified services. Special taxes of 7% for alcoholic beverages, 3% for new farm machinery and irrigation equipment, and 3% for manufactured homes. Motor vehicles and aircraft subject to excise taxes, discussed above.	Reports and payments—last day of month following end of quarter (April 30, July 31, October 31, and January 31 for calendar year returns). If total taxable sales for the preceding year equal or exceed $333,000, monthly reports and payments are due on or before the last day of each month for the preceding month.
	Use tax—5% of purchase price.	Reports and payments—last day of month following end of quarter (April 30, July 31, October 31, and January 31 for calendar year returns). If total taxable sales for the preceding year equal or exceed $333,000, monthly reports and payments are due on or before the last day of each month for the preceding month.
Telecommunications carriers tax.	Telecommunications carriers—taxed on adjusted gross receipts in lieu of real and personal property taxes. Rate is 2.5% of adjusted gross receipts.	Telecommunications carriers—reports—May 1. Payments—January 1.
Coal conversion facilities.	Coal conversion facilities—2% of gross receipts; electrical generating plants—0.65 mill times 60% of the installed capacity of each unit times the number of hours in the taxable period plus 0.25 mill on each kilowatt hour of electricity produced for sale; coal gasification plants, the greater of 2% of gross receipts or 13.5¢ on each 1,000 cubic feet of synthetic natural gas produced for sale.	Coal conversion plants—reports and payments due on or before the 25th day of each month.
Insurance premiums tax.	Stock and mutual insurance company, nonprofit health service corporation, health maintenance organization, prepaid limited health service organization, and prepaid legal service organization doing business in the state—2% with respect to life insurance, 1.75% with respect to accident and sickness insurance and all other lines of insurance. Foreign companies subject to retaliatory taxes.	Reports and payments—March 1. Estimated reports and payments due quarterly.

Ohio

Tax System.—The revenue system of Ohio is founded upon a general property tax on real property and a classified property tax on tangible and intangible personal property. A corporate and personal income tax is also levied, as well as local income taxes. The taxes are supplemented by: state taxes, part of the revenue of which is returned to the local governments, upon occupations, franchises and privileges; and municipal licenses and inspection fees. An outline of the Ohio tax system follows:

Tax	Basis—Rates	Due Dates
Commercial activity tax.	For gross receipts greater than $150,000 and up to $1 million, a privilege tax of $150 is imposed. For tax periods beginning on or after January 1, 2014: $150,000-$1 million: $150; over $1 million-$2 million: $800; over $2 million-$4 million: $2,100; over $4 million: $2,600 plus 0.26%.	Returns and payment—Not later than the 10th day of the second month after the end of each calendar quarter, every taxpayer other than a calendar year taxpayer must file a tax return with the Tax Commissioner in the form prescribed by the Commissioner. Not later than the 10th day of May (for calendar years 2010 and beyond) following the end of each calendar year, every calendar year taxpayer must file a tax return with the Tax Commissioner in the form prescribed by the Commissioner.
Personal income tax.	Individuals and estates: $22,150 - $44,250 is $316.18, plus 2.850% of the amount over $22,150; $44,250 - $88,450 is $946.03, plus 3.326% of the amount over $44,250; $88,450 - $110,650 is $2,416.12, plus 3.802% of the amount over $88,450; $110,650 - $221,300 is $3,260.16, plus 4.413% of the amount over $110,650; and $221,300 and over is $8,143.14, plus 4.797% of the amount over $221,300. Rates are subject to inflation adjustments and general withholding is required.	Returns and payments—April 15. Declaration of estimated tax due on or before 15th day of 4th month of tax year if estimated tax in excess of withholding will exceed $500; estimated payment due with declaration and on or before 15th day of 4th, 6th, 9th and 13th months.

Tax	Basis—Rates	Due Dates
General property tax.	Real property—Aggregate of the local rates fixed to meet the budget, but the taxable value may not exceed 35% of the true or market value.	Payments—Real property and utility taxes, payable by December 31, if a full payment. If in two installments, then first half by December 31, and second half by June 20 of the following year.
	Tangible personal property—If used in a business, other than those provided below, currently 0%; natural gas company property or waterworks company for taxable property first subject to taxation in tax year 2017 and thereafter, assessed at 25%; pipeline, waterworks company for taxable property subject to taxation for tax years before 2017, or heating company property, assessed at 88%; water transportation company property, assessed at 25%; rural electric company's transmission and distribution property, assessed at 50% and its other taxable property, assessed at 25%; electric company's transmission and distribution property, assessed at 85%, and its other taxable property, assessed at 24%.	Tangible personal property: first half between February 15 and April 30; and second half by September 20.
Alcoholic beverage taxes.	Excise—Beer, $5.58 per barrel. Bottled beer, 0.0014 per oz. in containers of 12 ozs. or less and 0.0084 per 6 ozs. in containers of more than 12 ozs. Wines, per gal., 4% to 14% alcohol, 30¢; over 14% to 21% alcohol, 98¢; vermouth, $1.08; sparkling and carbonated wine and champagne, $1.48. Additional 2¢ per gal. tax levied on vermouth, sparkling and carbonated wine, champagne, and other wine. Bottled mixed drinks, $1.20 per gal.	
Motor fuel tax.	38.5¢ per gallon.	Reports and payments—By the last day of each month.
Resources severance taxes.	Coal, 10¢ per ton (plus an additional 1.2¢ per ton for surface-mined coal plus an additional 12¢, 14¢, or 16¢, depending on the amount remaining in a certain fund); The tax rate for clay, sandstone, shale, conglomerate, gypsum and quartzite is 1¢ per ton; The tax rate for dolomite, gravel, sand and limestone is 2¢ per ton; The tax rate for natural gas is 2.5¢ per 1,000 cubic feet; The tax rate for oil is 10¢ per barrel; The tax rate for salt is 4¢ per ton.	Returns and payments—payments are due May 15, August 15, November 15, and February 15 for the quarterly periods ending the last day of March, June, September and December, respectively. Electronic filing and payment are required.

Tax	Basis—Rates	Due Dates
Cigarette tax; tobacco products tax.	Cigarettes—8¢ per cigarette ($1.60 per pack of 20); county rates may also apply.	Reports—Wholesale dealers--By last day of each month following reporting period; users, by the 15th day of each month for the preceding month. Payment—Wholesalers and retailers, must remit the amount for tax stamps and/ or metered impressions using electronic funds transfer. Users, with the report.
	Tobacco products—17% of the wholesale price; little cigars, 37% of the wholesale price; premium cigars, the lesser of 17% of the wholesale price or 53¢.	Reports and payments—Distributors or importers, by the 23rd day of each month for the preceding month. Sellers of other tobacco products to consumers and persons storing, using, or otherwise consuming other tobacco products on which tax has not been paid must file returns on or before the last day of each month for the preceding month.
	Vapor products—1 cent per 0.1 milliliter of liquid vapor product or 1 cent per 0.1 grams of nonliquid vapor product.	Reports and payments—Vapor distributors are required to file returns and pay the tax by the 23rd day of each month. Reports and payment must be made electronically.
Sales tax; use tax.	Sales tax—Sales price of tangible personal property sold at retail, taxable services, rentals, lodgings, production and fabrication: 5.75%.	Report and payment—23rd day of each month for monthly returns (3/4 due on 23rd and reconciliation payment due on the 23rd of following month if required to file accelerated EFT payments). January 23 and July 23 for semi annual filers.
	Use tax—Storing, using or consuming (including rentals and production) of tangible personal property or receiving the benefit of a service—same rate as retail sales tax.	Report and payment—23rd day of each month for monthly returns (3/4 due on 23rd and reconciliation payment due on the 23rd of following month if required to file accelerated EFT payments). January 23 and July 23 for semi annual filers.

Tax	Basis—Rates	Due Dates
Public utilities tax.	Pipeline companies, 6.75%; all other public utilities, 4.75%. Minimum, $50. Electric and rural electric companies are not subject to the public utility tax, but are subject to the corporate franchise (income) tax. A kilowatt hour excise tax is imposed on electric distribution companies at the following rates per kilowatt hour of electricity distributed in a 30-day period by the company through a meter of an end-user: for the first 2,000 kilowatt hours, $0.00465; for the next 2,001 to 15,000 kilowatt hours, $0.00419; for 15,001 and higher kilowatt hours, $0.00363. Natural gas companies and combined electric and natural gas companies are subject to a natural gas company tax of 4$^{3}/_{4}$%.	Reports—Kilowatt hour excise tax returns—20th of each month for preceding month. Annual reports—railroads, September 1; express, telegraph companies, and all other public utilities subject to the public utility tax, August 1; natural gas companies and combined companies, within 45 days of the last day of March, June, September, and December; natural gas companies and combined companies with annual tax liability for preceding year of less than $325,000 may elect to file annual return within 45 days of December 31; estimated reports from taxpayers owing $1,000 or more due October 15; also on March 1 and June 1 if tax levied in prior year reached these levels. Payments—30 days after mailing notice of tax due; estimated payments from larger taxpayers (owing $1,000 or more) due October 15; also on March 1 and June 1 if tax levied in prior year reached these levels; kilowatt hour excise tax, by 20th day of month for preceding month; natural gas companies and combined companies, within 45 days of the last day of March, June, September, and December; natural gas companies electing to file annual return, within 45 days of December 31.

Tax	Basis—Rates	Due Dates
Insurance tax.	An annual franchise tax is imposed on both domestic and foreign insurance companies at the rate of 1.4% of the gross amount of premiums received from policies covering risks in Ohio. Balance of the premiums received by a health insurance corporation operated by an insurance company, 1%.	Reports—March 1; March 31 for tax summary and payments of tax by surplus lines brokers.
		Payments—domestic, 20 to 30 days after bill is mailed; foreign, partial payment equal to 1/2 of previous year's tax due October 15, balance due June 15 when the annual reports are filed.
	Additional fire marshal tax on fire insurance companies—0.75% of gross premiums.	
	Unauthorized and foreign risk retention groups—5% of gross premiums, fees, assessments, dues, etc., for subjects of insurance in Ohio.	

Oklahoma

Tax System.—The Oklahoma state and local revenue system consists of a locally administered general property tax and mortgage recording tax, and state-administered taxes on minerals, oil, and gas, plus state-administered taxes on franchises, incomes, gasoline, alcoholic beverages, sales, cigarettes, other tobacco products, motor vehicles, and insurance companies. An outline of the Oklahoma tax system follows:

Tax	Basis—Rates	Due Dates
Corporation franchise tax.	$1.25 per $1,000 or fraction thereof used, invested or employed in Oklahoma. Maximum, $20,000; minimum, $250. Moratorium on franchise tax for taxable periods beginning July 1, 2010, and ending before July 1, 2013.	Reports and payments—July 1 unless filed in conjunction with income tax return.
Business activity tax.	For the 2010-2012 tax years, the BAT is equal to the franchise tax paid or required to be paid for the taxable period ending before December 31, 2010. If no franchise tax was paid or required--an annual tax of $25. For tax years beginning after 2012, the BAT is repealed.	Reports and payments—July 1 unless filed in conjunction with income tax return.
General income tax.	Married persons filing jointly, surviving spouse, heads of household, not deducting federal income taxes[1]—0.5% of 1st $2,000 of taxable income (federal taxable income with adjustments); 1% of next $3,000; 2% of next $2,500; 3% of next $2,300; 4% of next $2,400; 5% on remainder. Single individuals, married persons filing separately, estates and trusts not deducting federal income taxes[1]—0.5% of 1st $1,000, 1%; next $1,500, 2%; next $1,250, 3%; next $1,150, 4%; next $2,300, 5% on remainder.	Personal income returns and payment—15th day of 4th month after end of income year or April 15. Declarations of estimated tax—15th day of 4th month of tax year or April 15. Payment of estimated tax—15th day of the 4th, 6th, 9th of tax year, and 1st month of following tax year.
	General withholding required.	
	Corporations—6% of Oklahoma taxable income, i.e., federal taxable income with adjustments.	Corporate income returns and payment—30 days after the federal due date. Declaration of estimated tax due on the 15th day of the 4th month of tax year with payments due on the 15th day of the 4th, 6th, 9th of tax year, and 1st month of following tax year.
	Pass-through entities are required to withhold 5% of any Oklahoma-source income distribution made to a nonresident member of an entity.	
Bank excise (income) tax.	6% of federal taxable income.	Reports and payments—15th day of 3rd month.
General property tax.	Aggregate of local rates fixed to meet budget, subject to limitations. No state levy.	Payments—November 1; installment payments—before January 1 and before April 1.
Alcoholic beverages taxes.	Excise tax—beer, $12.50 per 31-gallon barrel; distilled spirits, $1.47 per liter; all wine, except sparkling, 19¢ per liter; sparkling wine, 55¢ per liter.	

Tax	Basis—Rates	Due Dates
Motor fuel taxes.	Motor fuel tax—GASOLINE: 19¢ per gal.; DIESEL FUEL: 19¢ per gal; AIRCRAFT FUEL: 8/100¢ per gal.; COMPRESSED NATURAL GAS: 5¢ per specified volume.	Reports and payments—Suppliers, exporters, and importers, by the 27th day of following month, generally.
Severance taxes (gross production incentive tax).	Gross production incentive tax: Until July, 2021, the rate for oil and gas is 5%. After that, the rate is (1) 7% tax of the gross value of oil production based on a per-barrel measurement of 42 U.S. gallons of 231 cubic inches per gallon, computed at a temperature of 60 degrees Fahrenheit; and (2) 7% of the gross value of gas production.	Reports and payments—by the 1st day of the following calendar month.
Motor vehicle rental tax.	6% of gross receipts from motor vehicle rentals of 90 or fewer days.	Reports and payments—by the 20th day of the following month.
Cigarette tax; tobacco products tax.	Cigarettes—$2.03 per pack of 20.	Reports—Cigarettes—by the 10th day of the following calendar month.
	Tobacco products—CIGARS: $2.03 per pack of 20 Class A cigars (little cigars); 10¢ per Class B cigar; 12¢ per Class C cigar. CHEWING TOBACCO, SMOKELESS TOBACCO, AND SNUFF: 60% of factory list price. SMOKING TOBACCO: 80% of factory list price.	Tobacco products—by the 20th day of the following calendar month.
	For sales at a tribal store, if the tribe or nation has not entered into a compact with Oklahoma, the full state rate; for a compacting tribe or nation, the compact rate prevails.	Payments—by the purchase and affixation of stamps.
Documentary stamp tax.	75¢ per $500 of value (or fraction thereof) of deeds, etc., conveying realty when the consideration or value exceeds $100.	Payments—evidenced by stamps purchased from a county clerk and affixed to the deed, etc.
Sales & use tax.	Tax rate is 4.5%. Sales tax rate applies to gross receipts from the sale, lease, or rental of tangible personal property (including electricity, water, natural and artificial gas, steam, and prewritten computer software but excluding newspapers and periodicals) and specified services. Use tax rate applies to the sales price of tangible personal property purchased or brought into Oklahoma for storage, use, or consumption within the state, insofar as no sales tax was paid on such property. Motor vehicles subject to 1.25% sales and use tax and 3.25% excise tax on the value of the vehicle (excise tax rates vary for used and commercial motor vehicles).	Sales tax—Reports and payments—20th of each month; if tax for month does not exceed $50, 20th of January and July. Taxpayers owing an average of $2,500 or more per month in sales tax based on the previous fiscal year must participate in the Oklahoma Tax Commission's EFT and electronic data interchange program. Use tax—20th of each month.
Public utilities.	Rural electric cooperatives—2% of gross receipts.	Electric cooperatives—Reports and payments—20th of month.
	Freight car companies—4% of taxable gross revenue derived from use within state.	Freight line, equipment and mercantile companies—Reports, April 1. Payment—due after demand.

Tax	Basis—Rates	Due Dates
Insurance companies tax.	2.25% of gross premiums less returned premiums. Fire companies pay an additional, 5/16 of 1%. Foreign companies subject to retaliatory taxes.	Report and payment—March 1. Estimates and payments of premium taxes are due April 1, June 15, September 15 and December 15.
	Surplus lines tax—6% of gross premiums.	Surplus line brokers—Report—April 1. Payment—last day of the month following each quarter.
	Unauthorized insurance—6% of annual premiums.	Unauthorized insurance—Report and payment—30 days after premiums are determined.
	Captive insurance companies—0.2%, maximum tax $100,000, 0.1% of assumed reinsurance.	Captive insurance companies—Report and payment—March 1.

[1] Optional tables are enacted for taxpayers who deduct federal income taxes.

Oregon

Tax System.—The state imposes an income tax, gasoline tax, cigarette tax, inheritance tax, insurance companies tax, alcoholic beverage tax and motor vehicle fees. There are numerous other taxes and fees of minor importance, and municipalities are given the broad power to "license, regulate and control any lawful business, trade, occupation, profession or calling." Oregon does not impose a sales or use tax. An outline of the Oregon tax system follows:

Tax	Basis—Rates	Due Dates
Corporation excise (income) tax.	Corporation excise tax—6.6% on the first $1 million and 7.6% on taxable income in excess of $1 million. For tax years beginning after 2010 and before 2013, the rate in excess of $250,000 was 7.6%. Financial institutions are subject to the tax. Minimum tax: $150 if Oregon sales are less than $500,000; $500 if Oregon sales are $500,000 or more but less than $1 million; $1,000 if Oregon sales are $1 million or more but less than $2 million; $1,500 if Oregon sales are $2 million or more but less than $3 million; $2,000 if Oregon sales are $3 million or more but less than $5 million; $4,000 if Oregon sales are $5 million or more but less than $7 million; $7,500 if Oregon sales are $7 million or more but less than $10 million; $15,000 if Oregon sales are $10 million or more but less than $25 million; $30,000 if Oregon sales are $25 million or more but less than $50 million; $50,000 if Oregon sales are $50 million or more but less than $75 million; $75,000 if Oregon sales are $75 million or more but less than $100 million; and $100,000 if Oregon sales are $100 million or more. S and partnerships, $150.	Corporation excise tax—Reports and payments—15th day of month following due date of corresponding federal return. Estimated tax payments (for liability of $500 or more) due 15th day of 4th, 6th, 9th and 12th months of tax year.
	Corporation income tax—same as corporation excise tax. Qualified taxpayers with minimal Oregon sales may elect to pay alternative tax of 0.25% or 0.125% of gross sales in Oregon.	Corporation income tax—same as corporation excise tax above.
Personal income tax.	**Rates for 2020:** Single and married persons filing separately, 4.75% on first $3,600; over $3,601 to $9,050, 6.75% minus $72; over $9,051 to $125,000, 8.75% minus $252.99; over $125,001 9.9% minus $1,690.49. **Rates for 2019:** Single and married persons filing separately, 5% on first $3,550; over $3,551 to $8,900, 7% minus $68; over $8,901 to $125,000, 9% minus $238; over $125,001 9.9% minus $1,363. **Rates for 2018:** Single and married persons filing separately, 5% on first $3,450; over $3,451 to $8,700, 7% minus $69; over $8,701 to $125,000, 9% minus $243; over $125,001 9.9% minus $1,368. **Rates for 2017:** Single and married persons filing separately, 5% on first $3,400; over $3,401 to $8,500, 7% minus $68; over $8,501 to $125,000, 9% minus $238; over $125,001 9.9% minus $1,363. **Rates for 2016:** Single and married persons filing separately, 5% on first $3,350; over $3,151 to $8,450, 7% minus $67; over $8,451 to $125,000, 9% minus $236; over $125,001 9.9% minus $1,361.	Returns—same as due date of corresponding federal return. Estimated tax declarations—April 15.

Tax	Basis—Rates	Due Dates
	For married persons filing jointly, heads of households and qualifying widow(er)s, the tax is twice the tax that would be imposed on single persons if taxable income was cut in half.	Payment with return. Estimated tax payments due in four or fewer equal installments on or before April 15, June 15, September 15, and January 15.
General property tax.	General property tax—aggregate of state and local rates fixed to meet budget. Property subject to taxation includes all privately owned real property (e.g., land, buildings, and fixed machinery and equipment), manufactured homes, and personal property used in a business. Tax based on property assessment of the lesser of its real market value or its maximum assessed value.	Return—personal property, March 15; real property, when requested by county; public utilities, February 1, except Class 1 railroads, March 15. Payment—all taxes, November 15 or, if $40 or more, tax is payable in 3 equal installments due November 15, February 15 and May 15.
State lodging tax.	1.5% of consideration for sale, service, or furnishing of transient lodging.	Reports and payments—last day of month following end of each calendar quarter.
Alcoholic beverages tax; winery tax.	Excise—malt beverages, cider, $2.60 per 31-gal. barrel. Wines containing 14% alcohol or under, 67¢ per gallon (65¢ plus additional 2¢ per gallon). Wine containing over 14% alcohol, 77¢ per gallon (65¢ plus additional 10¢ per gallon plus additional 2¢ per gallon). Wine board tax—$25 per ton of vinifera grapes or imported vinifera or hybrid grape products for use in a licensed winery to make wine; for all other products used to make wine, $0.021 per gallon of wine made from those products.	
Motor fuel tax; fuel use tax.	Motor fuel tax—34¢ per gallon of motor fuel; aircraft fuel sold, distributed or used by a dealer, 11¢ per gallon; fuel for turbine engines, 3¢ per gallon. Fuel use tax—34¢ per gallon of motor fuel other than gasoline used in propelling motor vehicles on the highways.	Gasoline tax—Reports and payment—25th of each month. Fuel use tax—Reports, by 20th of each month; payment with report. Annual use fuel tax report and payment due January 20 if annual tax is less than $100; quarterly reports and payments due 20th day of April, July, October and January if monthly tax is less than $300.
Oil and gas gross production (privilege) tax.	6% of gross value at well on all oil and gas produced within the state.	Reports and payments—due on the 45th day following the preceding quarter.
Forest product taxes.	Forest Products Harvest Tax: $4.1322 per 1000 board ft.; Small Tract Forestland Tax: Eastern Oregon—$4.78 per 1000 board ft., Western Oregon—$6.15 per 1000 board ft.	Timber tax—Reports and payment—due by April 15.

Tax	Basis—Rates	Due Dates
Cigarette tax.	$1.33 per pack of 20.	Reports—due by distributors on or before the 20th day of January, April, July, and October. Payment—by stamps. Unpaid taxes due quarterly on or before the 20th day of January, April, July, and October by distributors. If not prepaid through the use of stamps, the tax is due and payable monthly on or before the 20th day of the month following the calendar month in which the distribution occurred.
	Tobacco products tax—65% of wholesale sales price, except tax imposed on cigars is limited to a maximum tax of 50¢ per cigar. Moist snuff, $1.78 per ounce, $2.14 minimum per retail customer.	Reports and payments—last day of January, April, July, and October for the preceding calendar quarter.
Public utilities tax.	Telecommunications and public utilities—subject to annual fee not exceeding 0.45% (0.35 for a telecommunications provider) of the utility's qualifying gross operating revenue in the preceding calendar year but may not be less than $10 ($100 for a telecommunications provider). Electric cooperatives—lesser of (1) 4% of all gross revenues from use or operation of transmission and distribution lines (exclusive of revenues from leasing lines to governmental agencies), less the cost of power to the association, or (2) sum of (a) an amount obtained by multiplying the real market value of the transmission and distribution lines for the current fiscal year by the maximum school tax rate allowable, plus (b) an amount obtained by multiplying the market value of the transmission and distribution lines for current fiscal year by $10 per $1,000 of market value, plus (c) an amount obtained by multiplying market value of transmission and distribution lines by tax rate for county for exempt bonded indebtedness. Railroads—Class I railroads subject to annual fee not exceeding 0.35% of combined gross operating revenues of Class I railroads derived in Oregon.	Reports—public utilities, annually, April 1, except for electric cooperatives, February 1. Payments—generally, 15 days after date of notice mailed (mailed on or after March 1); electric cooperatives, July 1.

Tax	Basis—Rates	Due Dates
Insurance companies tax.	Surplus lines licensees—2% of gross premiums, less return premiums and dividends paid plus a 0.3% fire marshal's tax.	Reports—annual financial statement, March 1, except for wet marine and transportation insurers, June 15. Payments—wet marine and transportation insurance, June 15; surplus lines licensees, quarterly on 45th day following quarterly period; all other insurers, April 1.
	Foreign and alien insurers writing wet marine and transportation insurance—5% of underwriting profit.	
	Insurers writing health plan policies—additional 1.5% of gross premiums.	
	Fire marshal tax—domestic and foreign—1.15% of gross premiums less return premiums and dividends.	Reports and payment—April 1.
	Foreign companies potentially subject to retaliatory taxes.	

Pennsylvania

Tax System.—The local governments in Pennsylvania are supported mainly by the ad valorem assessment and taxation of real estate; tangible personal property, for the most part, is not assessed. The counties secure further revenue from a tax on intangible personal property that has not been otherwise taxed by the state. There is no state tax levy on real property. Principal sources of state revenue are the sales and use taxes, corporate and personal income taxes, and gasoline taxes. The state previously levied a tax on the capital stock of domestic and foreign corporations, joint-stock associations, limited partnerships, and regulated investment companies, according to the value of such stock, and payment of this tax by the corporation exempted the shares of stock from taxation in the hands of the stockholders. The tax on corporate obligations issued by domestic corporations and foreign corporations, whose fiscal officer is within the jurisdiction of the state, is collected from the corporation, and this payment by the corporation exempts the security from taxation in the hands of the security holder. The corporation may, in turn, charge the security holder for this tax unless the obligation contains a covenant to the contrary. Public utilities are subject to gross receipts taxes, which are paid into the State Treasury. The state receives further revenue from taxes on bank shares, title and trust companies, and private bankers; taxes on the gross premiums of insurance companies; liquor taxes; and cigarette taxes. An outline of the Pennsylvania tax system follows:

Tax	Basis—Rates	Due Dates
Corporate net income tax.	9.99% of taxable income as reported on federal returns, with certain additions and deductions, allocated to Pennsylvania.	Reports—30 days after federal returns are due, or would be due if corporation required to file federally. Estimated payments are due on the 15th day of the 3rd, 6th, 9th, and 12th months of the tax year.
Personal income tax.	3.07% of taxable compensation; net profits; net gains or income from disposition of property; net gains or income from rents, royalties, patents or copyrights; dividends; interest from non-exempt obligations; gambling and lottery winnings other than Pennsylvania state lottery prizes; and net gains or income derived from estates or trusts. Withholding required. Nonresidents taxed at same 3.07% rate on income derived from Pennsylvania sources.	Returns and payments—April 15 for calendar-year taxpayers, or 15th day of 4th month after end of tax year for fiscal-year taxpayers. Estimated tax declarations if income other than compensation subject to withholding exceeds $8,000—April 15; payment—15th day of April, June, September, and January.

Tax	Basis—Rates	Due Dates
Financial institutions taxes.	Financial institutions taxes—national and state banks and trust companies having capital stock, located in Pennsylvania and title insurance companies, 0.89% of the taxable amount of the shares. Mutual thrift institutions, 11.5% of taxable net income. Private bankers, 1% of gross receipts.	Financial institutions taxes—all except private banks and mutual thrift institutions, March 15 for annual report and payment of tax balance for previous year. Private bankers, February 15. Mutual thrift institutions, annual report and payment of tax balance for previous year, April 15 or within 105 days after the close of their fiscal year; estimated tax payments due on 15th day of the 3rd, 6th, 9th, and 12th months of tax year.
General property tax.	General property tax—fixed locally to meet budget. No state tax. Based on fair market value of real property. Personal property is exempt.	General property tax—payment date varies by county. Some taxing districts may authorize installment payments.
Intangibles tax.	County intangibles tax (Personal property tax)—not to exceed 4 mills per $1 value of intangible personal property of resident individuals and corporations.	Intangibles tax—return and payment dates set by counties.
Capital stock/franchise tax.	Capital stock/franchise tax—Tax expired December 31, 2015. For tax years 2008 through 2011, 2.89 mills; 2012 tax year, 1.89 mills; 2013 tax year, 0.89 mills; 2014 tax year, 0.67 mills; 2015 tax year, 0.45 mills. Regulated investment companies—the sum of (1) the net asset value of the regulated investment company divided by $1 million, rounded to the nearest multiple of $75, and multiplied by $75, plus (2) the result of multiplying the personal income tax rate by the apportioned undistributed personal income tax income of the regulated investment company.	Returns—April 15 for calendar-year taxpayers; within 30 days after federal corporate income tax return due for fiscal-year taxpayers. Estimated payments due on the 15th day of 3rd, 6th, 9th, and 12th months of tax year.
Public utility realty tax.	Millage rates on which utility realty is assessed are calculated on yearly basis by dividing total realty tax equivalent by total state taxable value of all utility realty located in Pennsylvania. Also subject to an additional tax of 7.6 mills. There is no PURTA surcharge for 2012 through 2021.	Utility realty tax—Report and tentative payment due May 1. Notice of any changed assessment valuation or predetermined ratio given by August 1; any unpaid tax must be paid within 45 days of date of notification. Estimated tax due annually on or before April 15.
Hotel occupancy tax.	6% of the rent. Local taxes authorized.	Same as sales and use tax due dates.
Alcoholic beverages tax.	Excise—malt beverages, $2.48 per barrel sold or imported. Liquor sold by the Liquor Control Board, 18% of the net price of all liquors.	

Tax	Basis—Rates	Due Dates
Motor fuel taxes.	Oil company franchise tax—2020: $0.576 per gallon on liquid fuels (motor gasoline and gasohol); $0.741 per gallon on fuels (diesel). Aviation gasoline and other liquid fuels used in propeller-driven piston engine aircraft or aircraft engines, $0.059; jet fuels used in turbine-propeller jets, turbojets and jet-driven aircraft and aircraft engines, $0.019. Alternative fuel rates (2020)—hydrogen, $0.576/gasoline-gallon equivalent; compressed natural gas, $0.576/gasoline-gallon equivalent; propane/LPG, $0.425 per gallon; ethanol, $0.384 per gallon; methanol, $0.289 per gallon; E-85, $0.413 per gallon; M-85, $0.332 per gallon; and liquefied natural gas, $0.648. The rate for electricity is $0.0172/KWH.	Oil company franchise and alternative fuels reports and payment—20th day of each month.
Cigarette tax.	Cigarette tax—13¢ per cigarette sold or possessed within state ($2.60 per pack of 20).	Cigarette tax—returns, 20th day of each month; payment, purchase of stamps.
Other tobacco products tax.	Other tobacco products tax—40% of purchase price charged to retailer for electronic cigarettes. For other tobacco products, $0.55 per ounce; however, for tobacco products weighing less than 1.2 ounces per container, the minimum tax is $0.66 per package.	Other tobacco products tax—Wholesalers, retailers, unclassified importers, and manufacturers must file monthly reports and pay the tax by the 20th day of the month.
Realty transfer tax.	Realty transfer tax—1% of the value of real property within the state represented by the document conveying the property or an interest therein.	Payment—by affixation of documentary stamps.
Sales and use taxes.	6% of purchase price of tangible personal property and specified services.	Reports and payments—20th day of the month following the reporting period. Monthly, quarterly, and semi-annual returns authorized. A sales and use tax licensee whose total sales and use tax liability for the third calendar quarter of the preceding year equals or exceeds $25,000 is required to make a prepayment by the 20th of each month. Use tax returns from purchasers other than licensees—20th day of succeeding month.
Public utilities gross receipts tax.	59 mills per $1 (5.9%) on gross receipts from business of electric light, water power and hydroelectric corporations; 50 mills per $1 on gross receipts from business of transportation companies, telephone and telegraph companies (the gross receipts tax is not imposed on sales of natural gas).	Reports and payment—Annual report, estimated gross receipts tax, balance of tax due for the preceding year, March 15. Estimated taxes due March 15 of current year.

Tax	Basis—Rates	Due Dates
Insurance taxes.	Domestic, foreign, alien—2% of gross premiums; title insurance and trust companies—1.25% on each dollar of actual value of capital stock; surplus lines—3% on gross premiums, less premiums placed with unlicensed insurer other than risk retention groups; marine—5% of allocated underwriting profit; unauthorized insurers—2%.	Reports and payments—domestic, foreign, alien—Estimated taxes due March 15 of current year. Annual report and any remaining tax due by April 15 of following year. Title insurance companies—report and payments by March 15. Marine—annually, June 1. Surplus lines—annually January 31.

Rhode Island

Tax System.—The revenue system of Rhode Island is primarily based upon a general property tax assessed uniformly according to value within the taxing district by the cities and towns. Real and personal property not otherwise taxed is subject to this tax. The general property tax is supplemented by various other state taxes on occupations, franchises and privileges, a portion of the revenue from which is returned to the local governments. An outline of the Rhode Island tax system follows:

Tax	Basis—Rates	Due Dates
Business corporation tax.	Business corporation tax—business corporations, 7% of net income; minimum tax, $400. Regulated investment companies, real estate investment trusts and personal holding companies, greater of 10¢ per $100 gross income or $100. Up to a 4% rate reduction is allowed for development of new jobs. For tax years beginning on or after January 1, 2019, pass-through entities that elect to pay the state tax at the entity level pay the entity-level tax rate of 5.99%.	Business corporation tax reports and payments—April 15 (15th day of 4th month after close of tax year for fiscal-year filers); September 15 (15th day of 3rd month after close of tax year) for June 30 fiscal year end filers.
Bank excise (income) tax.	State banks—9% of net income or $2.50 per $10,000 of authorized capital stock (whichever is higher); minimum, $100. National banks—9% of net income; minimum, $100.	Banks—on or before date federal return due.
Personal income tax.	2020 tax year—Taxable income not over $65,250, 3.75%; over $65,250 but not over $148,350, 4.75%; over $148,350, 5.99%. General withholding required.	Returns and payments—15th day of fourth month after end of tax year. Declaration of estimated tax due 15th day of 4th month of tax year (or when federal declaration is due); payments due on 15th day of April, June, September, and January.
General property tax.	General property tax—fixed by cities and towns to meet budget. Based on full and fair cash value of real and personal property.	General property tax—dates vary with each locality.
Alcoholic beverages tax.	Excise—beer, $3.30 per 31 gallons; wines, $1.40¢ per gal.; sparkling wines, 75¢ per gal.; distilled liquor, $5.40 per gal.	
Motor fuel tax.	Motor fuels—34¢ per gallon on all taxable motor fuels.	Motor fuels—reports and payment, 20th of each month.
Rental vehicle surcharge.	Rental vehicle surcharge—8% of gross receipts from motor vehicle rentals for up to 30 consecutive days.	Remitted on quarterly basis according to schedule established by Tax Administrator. Annual report no later than February 15.

Tax	Basis—Rates	Due Dates
Cigarette and tobacco taxes.	Cigarettes and little cigars—$4.25 per pack of 20.	Reports—by 10th day of each month. Payment—by affixing stamps.
	Tobacco products tax—80% of wholesale cost of smokeless tobacco, cigars, and pipe tobacco other than snuff. Tax on cigars capped at $0.50 per cigar, and the tax on snuff is calculated by net weight. For snuff, the tax is $1.00 per ounce when the weight of snuff is greater than 1.2 ounces.	Tobacco products tax—same as cigarette tax.
Real estate conveyance tax.	$2.30 per $500 or fraction of consideration over $100.	No reports. Payment due when executing or presenting document for recording.
Sales and use tax.	7% of gross receipts from retail sales, rentals, and storage, use or consumption of all tangible personal property and selected services. Additional tax of 6% of total consideration charged for occupancy of any space furnished by any hotel. 1% local tax on meals and beverages and 1% local hotel tax are imposed statewide.	Reports and payments—20th of each month. Quarterly reports and payments authorized.
Insurance companies tax.	Domestic, foreign, and alien insurance companies, 2% of gross premiums (rate may be reduced after 2017 for certain companies creating new jobs). Captive insurers, 0.2% of first $20 million of direct premiums; 0.15% on next $20 million; 0.1% on next $20 million; thereafter 0.0375% on each dollar. Different rates apply for assumed reinsurance premiums of captive insurers. Surplus lines brokers, 4% of gross premiums.	Domestic and foreign insurers, payment due April 15. Captive insurers, payment due March 1. Surplus lines brokers, reports and payments due April 1.
	Foreign companies subject to retaliatory taxes.	

South Carolina

Tax System.—The revenue system of South Carolina is founded upon a general property tax assessed uniformly according to value within each taxing district. There is no state levy. There are state taxes on incomes, franchises, retail sales, occupations and privileges, a part of the revenue from which is returned to the local governments. An outline of the South Carolina tax system follows:

Tax	Basis—Rates	Due Dates
Income tax.	Individuals—**2020 rates:** $0 - 3,069 x 0.000% minus $0; $3,070 - 6,149 x 3.000% minus $92; $6,150 - 9,229 x 4.000% minus $154; $9,230 - 12,309 x 5.000% minus $246; $12,310 - 15,399 x 6.000% minus $369; $15,400 and over x 7.000% minus $523. **2019 rates:** $0 - 3,029 x 0.000% minus $0; $3,030 - 6,059 x 3.000% minus $91; $6,060 - 9,089 x 4.000% minus $152; $9,090 - 12,119 x 5.000% minus $242; $12,120 - 15,159 x 6.000% minus $364; $15,160 and over x 7.000% minus $515.	Returns—April 15th or 15th day of 4th month after close of fiscal year.
	General withholding is required.	
	Corporations—5% of entire net income.	Returns—Effective for tax years beginning after December 31, 2015, Form SC1120 must be filed by the 15th day of the fourth month following the close of the taxable year.
	Owner of pass-through business (active trade or business income)—3%.	Payment—corporations, with return and equally on or before the 15th day of 4th, 6th, 9th and 12th months following tax year if estimated tax exceeds $100. Individuals and fiduciaries: with return. Estimated personal income tax: payment, 15th day of the 4th, 6th, 9th and 13th months after beginning of taxable year.
Financial institutions tax.	Banks—4.5% of entire net income in the state. Savings and loan and similar associations, cooperative banks—6% of net income (not applicable in first three years of operation).	Returns—April 15th or 15th day of 4th month after close of fiscal year.
General property tax.	Aggregate of local rates fixed to meet budget. Property is classified and assessed at the following percentages of fair market value: primary residence, 4%; manufacturing and utility companies, 10.5%; commercial and residential non-owner occupied real property, 6%; privately owned agricultural real property, 4%; commercially owned agricultural real property, 6%; and all other personal property, 10.5%.	Returns reporting business personal property, manufacturers' property, and utility companies' property must be filed by the last day of the 4th month after the close of the taxpayer's accounting period year.
		Payment—January 15 to the state. Due dates for local taxes vary.

Tax	Basis—Rates	Due Dates
Admissions tax.	5% on paid admissions to places of amusement.	Reports and payments—20th day of each month.
Alcoholic beverages tax.	Beer and wine tax: Beer, license tax of 0.6¢ per oz. Wines, license tax of 90¢ per gal., plus an additional tax of 18¢ per gallon. Distilled spirits, 17¢ per 8 oz.	
Motor fuels taxes.	Motor fuels tax—24¢ per gallon on all gasoline or diesel fuel used or consumed in the state in producing or generating power for propelling motor vehicles. 0.25¢ per gallon inspection fee and a 0.5¢ environmental impact fee.	Suppliers—reports and payments due the 22nd day of each month.
Cigarette and tobacco tax.	Cigarette and tobacco tax—Cigarettes, 3.5 mills each, plus a surcharge of 2.5¢ per cigarette (57¢ per pack of 20). Other tobacco products—5% of manufacturer's price.	Cigarettes—reports and payment due by the 20th day of each month for preceding month. Tobacco products—reports and payment due by the 20th day of each month for preceding month.
Deed recording fee.	$1.85 for each $500 of value of realty when transfer of deed is recorded.	Payment—at time of recording the deed.
Sales and use taxes.	6% of retail sales price of tangible personal property or tangible personal property stored, used, consumed, or rented (5% for persons 85 and older; maximum tax of $500 for certain vehicles, aircraft, and boats, and self-propelled light construction equipment).	Sales tax—returns and payments—20th day of month. Use tax—returns and payments—20th day of each month.
Public utilities tax; hydroelectric companies tax.	Public utilities license tax—$1 per $1,000 of value of property owned and used in the state plus $3 per $1,000 of gross receipts. Minimum tax, $25.	Public utilities tax—reports and payments—15th day of 4th month following income year.
	Electric power companies tax—0.5 mill per kilowatt hour of electricity sold at wholesale or retail.	Electric companies tax—reports and payments—20th day of each month.
Insurance companies tax.	Life insurance companies, 0.75% of total premiums collected. All other insurance companies, 1.25% of total premiums collected. Fire insurance companies, aggregate 2.35% on premiums written on fire insurance. Captive insurance companies: 0.4% on first $20 million, 0.3% on each dollar over $20 million. Maximum tax, $100,000. Captive insurance companies (tax on assumed reinsurance premiums): 0.225% on first $20 million of assumed reinsurance premium; 0.150% on the next $20 million; 0.050% on the next $20 million; and 0.025% on each dollar of assumed reinsurance thereafter. Maximum tax, $100,000.	Reports—March 1.
	Foreign companies subject to retaliatory taxes.	Payments—on or before 1st day of March, June, September, and December.

South Dakota

Tax System.—South Dakota imposes a general property tax on both real and personal property, at uniform rates, in the taxing districts where such property is located. Personal property that is not centrally assessed is exempt. The property tax is supplemented by state taxes on the net incomes of banks and financial corporations, and on specified privileges and occupations, including retail sales, as well as by municipal taxes. Furthermore, alcoholic beverages, motor fuels, natural resources, cigarettes and other tobacco products, utilities, and insurance companies are also subject to taxation. An outline of the South Dakota tax system follows:

Tax	Basis—Rates	Due Dates
Bank and financial corporation excise tax.	6% on net income of $400 million or less; 5% on net income exceeding $400 million but not over $425 million; 4% on net income exceeding $425 million but not over $450 million; 3% on net income exceeding $450 million but not over $475 million; 2% on the net income exceeding $475 million but not over $500 million; 1% on the net income exceeding $500 million but not over $600 million; 0.5% on the net income exceeding $600 million but not over $1.2 billion; and 0.25% over $1.2 billion. Minimum, $200 per business location.	Reports and payments—final report and payment due within 15 days after the federal tax return is due.
General property tax.	Aggregate of state and local rates to meet budget requirements, subject to limitations. Based on the true and full value (taxable value) of the property. Personal property is exempt, except for specified centrally assessed operating property.	Returns—general property, during the first 6 months of year; public utilities, by April 15, except railroads; railroads, by May 1. Payments—by January 1; delinquent on May 1 and November 1. Realty tax totaling $50 or less is due in full by April 30. Entire amount of unpaid personal property tax becomes delinquent on May 1.
Alcoholic beverages taxes.	Occupational—malt beverages, $8.50 per 31-gal. barrel; light wines and diluted beverages (except sparkling wines) over 3.2% to 14% alcohol, 93¢ per gal., wines 15% to 20% alcohol, $1.45 per gal., wines 21% to 24% alcohol, and all natural and artificial sparkling wines containing alcohol, $2.07 per gal.; all cider containing alcohol by weight not more than 10%, 28¢ per gal.; and all other alcoholic beverages, $3.93 per gal. Plus 2% of the purchase price of alcoholic beverages, except for beer, purchased by a wholesaler.	

Tax	Basis—Rates	Due Dates
Motor fuels/special fuels excise taxes; petroleum fee.	Motor fuel, special fuel, and all other non-specified fuel, 28¢ per gal.; liquid petroleum gas and propane, 20¢ per gal.; biodiesel and biodiesel blends, 28¢ per gal.; liquid natural gas, 14¢ per gal.; compressed natural gas, 10¢ per gal.; ethyl and methyl alcohol, 14¢ per gal.; aviation gasoline, 6¢ per gal.; and jet fuel, 4¢ per gal.	Reports and payments—Generally, reports must be filed electronically by the 20th day of the calendar month following the monthly, quarterly, or semiannual reporting period, depending on the entity; payments, generally, must be remitted electronically by the 25th day of the calendar month following the requisite monthly, quarterly, or semiannual payment period, depending on the entity.
	Petroleum release compensation and tank inspection fee—2¢ per gal. of product	Payments—Generally, must be remitted electronically by the 25th day of the calendar month following the monthly, quarterly, or semiannual payment period, depending on the entity.
Severance taxes (energy minerals, conservation, and precious metals taxes).	Energy minerals—4.5% of the taxable value of any energy minerals severed and saved, plus $0.0024 per $1.00 of taxable value conservation tax.	Returns and payments—Energy minerals—within 30 days after the end of each calendar quarter.
	Precious metals—Gross yield tax—gold—$4 per ounce plus either $4 per ounce severed during a quarter if the average price of gold is $800 per ounce or greater; $3 if the average price is $700-$799 per ounce; $2 if the average price is $600-$699 per ounce; and $1 if the average price is $500-$599 per ounce.	Returns—Precious metals—by June 1.
	Net profits tax—gold and silver—10% of the net profits from the sale of gold and silver severed in the state.	Payments—25% of the estimated tax for the current year due by the last days of January, April, July, and October. Balance of the tax for the preceding year due by June 1.
	Owners' tax—8% of the value received for the right to sever gold and silver by an owner of a royalty interest, an overriding royalty, or a profits or working interest.	
Motor vehicle excise tax; motor vehicle rental tax.	Excise tax—4% of the purchase price of a vehicle used in the state (in lieu of the sales and use taxes).	Payments—Excise tax—upon the transfer of the title.
	Rental tax—4.5% for a vehicle rented 28 days or less (in addition to the sales and use taxes, but in lieu of the above excise tax).	Rental tax—at the time of the rental.
Farm machinery excise tax.	4.5% on gross receipts from the sale, resale, or lease of farm machinery, attachment units, and irrigation equipment used exclusively for agricultural purposes and on the use, storage, and consumption in South Dakota of such machinery and equipment.	Reports and payment—same as sales and use tax.
Large boat excise tax.	3% tax is imposed on the purchase price.	Payments—upon the original registration of the boat.

Tax	Basis—Rates	Due Dates
Cigarette tax; tobacco products tax.	Cigarettes—$1.53 for a package of 20.	Reports—Cigarettes—by the 15th day of following month. Payments—Cigarettes—evidenced by affixing stamps to package; amount due within 30 days after stamp purchase.
	Tobacco products—35% of the product's wholesale purchase price.	Reports and payments—Tobacco products—by the 15th day of following month.
Real estate transfer fee.	50¢ per $500 of value (or fraction thereof), payable by the grantor.	Payments—evidenced by an inked stamping after recordation.
Sales and use taxes.	Sales, service and use taxes—4.5% of gross receipts.	Reports and payments—All electronic returns are due on the 20th of the following month, and all electronic payments are due on the 25th of the following month. All paper returns and payments must be filed and paid by the 20th of the following month.
	Additional sales, service and use taxes—1.5% seasonal tourism tax (June—September) on gross receipts of hotels, rooming houses, campground sites, and other lodging places, passenger car rentals, amusement parks, and miscellaneous amusement and recreational services.	
	Contractors' excise tax—2% of the gross receipts of all prime contractors engaged in construction services or realty improvement projects in South Dakota.	
	Alternative contractors' excise tax—2% of gross receipts of all prime contractors and subcontractors engaged in realty improvement contracts for persons subject to the following taxes: railroad operating property, telephone companies, electric heating, water and gas companies, rural electric companies and rural water supply companies, or any municipal utility or telephone company but not to construction of a power generation facility that generates electricity with a nameplate capacity of at least 500 megawatts.	

Tax	Basis—Rates	Due Dates
Insurance companies tax.	Domestic companies—2.5% of premiums and 1.25% of the consideration for annuity contracts.	Reports and payments—Generally, on or before March 1 or quarterly; surplus line brokers, payment with annual report on or before April 1; quarterly, if tax exceeds $5,000.
	Domestic and foreign life insurance companies—2.5% on the first $100,000 of annual premiums, 0.08% of any premiums exceeding $100,000. Life insurance policies, other than credit life, of a face amount of $7,000 or less, 1.25% of premiums.	
	Annuities—1.25% of the first $500,000 of consideration for annuity contracts, 0.08% of any contract consideration exceeding $500,000.	
	Foreign companies—2.5% of premiums and 1.25% of the consideration for annuity contracts.	
	Foreign companies subject to retaliatory taxes—No retaliatory taxes on that portion of a life insurance policy's annual premiums exceeding $100,000 and that portion of the annual consideration on an annuity contract exceeding $500,000.	
	Unlicensed insurers—2.5% of premiums and 1.25% of consideration for annuity contracts.	
	Fire insurance companies pay additional tax of 0.5%.	
	Surplus line brokers, 2.5% of gross premiums.	
	Captive insurance companies—Must pay a supervision fee the greater of $5,000 per year or 0.08% on gross premiums, less return premiums. Prior to 2013, 0.25% of gross premiums, less return premiums, on risks and property. Minimum tax, $5,000.	Payments—on or before March 1.

Tennessee

Tax System.—Tennessee imposes a general property tax on all real estate and tangible personal property at uniform rates in the taxing district where such property is located. There is no state levy. The property tax is supplemented by (1) state taxes on sales, use, income, franchises, privileges and occupations and (2) municipal taxes and inspection fees. An outline of the Tennessee tax system follows:

Tax	Basis—Rates	Due Dates
Annual franchise tax.	Annual franchise tax—25¢ per $100 on greater of net worth or the value of real and tangible personal property; minimum, $100.	Annual franchise tax report and payment—15th day of 4th month following close of fiscal year.
Excise (income) tax.	Excise tax—6.5% of net earnings from business done by corporations, limited liability entities, and banks doing business in the state.	Excise tax—15th day of 4th month after close of tax year. Estimated tax payments due on the 15th day of the 4th, 6th, and 9th months of the current year and on the 15th day of the first month of the succeeding year.
Tax on income from stocks and bonds.	Hall income tax (applicable to individuals, partnerships, trusts, estates and associations):—1% for tax year 2020, and the tax is eliminated January 1, 2021. Previously, 4% for tax year 2017, 3% for tax year 2018, and 2% for tax year 2019. No withholding.	Returns and payment—April 15. For fiscal year taxpayers, by the 15th day of the 4th month following the end of the fiscal year.
General property tax.	Sum of county, municipal and school rates fixed to meet budget. No state levy except central assessment of public utilities and telecommunications tower properties. Realty is assessed at 55% of actual value for utilities, at 40% for commercial and industrial and at 25% for farm and residential property.	Payment—October 1. Cities—various dates.
Alcoholic beverage tax and wine gallonage tax.	Wine and high alcohol beer with alcohol content of more than 7%—$1.21 per gallon; distilled spirits with alcohol content of more than 7%—$4.40 per gallon; alcoholic beverages with alcohol content of 7% or less—$1.10 per gallon.	
Gasoline tax.	Gasoline tax—$0.26 per gallon of gasoline sold, distributed or stored in Tennessee. Clear diesel and dyed diesel used by a common carrier to transport—$0.27 per gallon.	Gasoline tax—suppliers and importers, 20th day of each month.
Alternative fuel taxes.	Compressed natural gas tax—21¢ per gallon. Liquefied natural gas (LNG) tax—22¢ per gallon for commercial users and out-of-state vehicles.	Compressed natural gas tax—25th of month following activity. Liquefied gas: Dealers—report and payment due on or before July 25 each year. Users—annual prepayment due based on weight; annual report and payment due on or before July 25.

Tax	Basis—Rates	Due Dates
Oil and natural gas severance tax.	3% of the sales price of oil and natural gas.	Reports and payments—oil, 20th of each month; gas, 20th of second month following period.
Coal severance tax.	$1 per ton severed.	Reports and payments—1st day of following month.
Cigarette and tobacco tax.	Cigarettes—3.1¢ per cigarette (62¢ per pack of 20 cigarettes), plus an enforcement and administration fee of 0.0005¢ per pack on dealers or distributors. Other tobacco products, including cigars, cheroots, stogies, manufactured tobacco, and snuff of all descriptions (whether made of tobacco or any substitute)—6.6% of the wholesale cost price.	Reports—15th of each month. Payment—by purchase of stamps.
Mortgage tax.	Mortgage tax—11.5¢ on each $100 of mortgage indebtedness in excess of $2,000.	Mortgage tax—at time of recording.
Realty transfer tax.	Realty transfer tax—37¢ per $100 of consideration or value of the property, whichever is greater, maximum of $100,000.	Real estate transfer tax—at time of recording.
Sales and use taxes.	7% of sales price of tangible personal property and taxable services sold at retail, or used, consumed, distributed, or stored in Tennessee. Aviation fuel is subject to a 4.5% special user privilege tax instead of sales tax. Video programming services, including cable television service, are not subject to sales and use tax but are subject to a 9% special user privilege tax. Tangible personal property sold to common carriers for use outside the state is subject to a 5.25% special user privilege tax instead of sales tax. Food and food ingredients for human consumption (not including alcoholic beverages, tobacco, candy, dietary supplements, or prepared foods) are taxed at 4%. The general state rate and applicable local rates apply to interstate telecommunications services. Motor vehicle rentals are subject to a 3% rental car tax surcharge, and an additional 2% county rental car tax is authorized. Water, gas, electricity, fuel oil, coal, and other energy used by manufacturers are not subject to sales or use tax but are instead subject to a 1.5% special user privilege tax. An additional state tax rate of 2.75% is imposed on the amount in excess of $1,600, but less than or equal to $3,200, on the sale or use of any single article of personal property. Single article tax applies only to motor vehicles, aircraft, watercraft, modular homes, manufactured homes, and mobile homes.	Reports and payments—20th of each month. Quarterly, semiannual, or annual filing periods allowed.
State business tax.	Industrial loan and thrift companies—0.3% of gross income; minimum $450, maximum $1,500. Other business classifications also subject to state or local tax at various retail and wholesale rates.	Reports and payments—15th day of 4th month following end of fiscal year.

Tax	Basis—Rates	Due Dates
Public utility (gross receipts) taxes.	Gas, water, electric utilities—3% of the gross receipts derived from intrastate business. For those who manufacture gas or distribute manufactured gas or natural gas—1.5% of the gross receipts.	All public utilities—Reports and payments due August 1. Tax may be paid in four equal installments due August 1, November 1, February 1 and May 1.
Insurance companies tax.	Domestic life insurance companies, 1.75% (minimum, $150) of gross premiums. Foreign life insurance companies, 1.75% of gross premiums received from citizens and residents of Tennessee (minimum, $150). Others, 2.5% of gross premiums on business done within the state (minimum, $150). Fire insurance companies pay an additional 0.75% tax on that portion of the premium applicable to the fire risk. Foreign companies are subject to retaliatory taxes. Title insurance companies, 2.5%; HMOs, including prepaid limited health service organizations, 6% of gross dollar amount collected. Surplus lines—5% for all types of premiums. Captive insurance company premiums—0.4% on the first $20 million, 0.3% on each dollar thereafter on direct premiums collected; 0.225% on first $20 million of assumed reinsurance premium, 0.15% on next $20 million, 0.05% on next $20 million, and 0.025% on each dollar thereafter (annual minimum aggregate premium tax $5,000, annual maximum $100,000).	Reports—Generally, March 1. Payments—Generally, June 1, August 20, December 1, and March 1.

Texas

Tax System.—The Texas revenue system is founded on a general property tax at uniform rates within each taxing district. The general property tax has been supplemented by taxes on franchises, sales and use, occupations and privileges. It should be noted that no state ad valorem tax can be levied for general revenue purposes. An annual franchise tax is levied on domestic and foreign corporations. An outline of the Texas tax system follows:

Tax	Basis—Rates	Due Dates
Corporate franchise tax/ business margin tax.	0.75% for most entities; 0.375% for qualifying wholesalers and retailers; and 0.331% for entities with $20 million or less in annualized total revenue using the E-Z computation.	Report and payment—May 15.
General property tax.	Aggregate of local rates fixed to meet budget. Texas has no state property tax. Taxable property is assessed at its market value as of January 1 of the tax year.	
	Imposed on all privately held real property and business tangible personal property, and on intangible property of certain savings and loan associations and insurance companies. Tangible personal property not held or used for production of income is exempt (there is a limited local option to tax such property).	Payment—January 31, delinquent if not paid by February 1.
Hotel occupancy tax.	6% of the cost of occupancy or right to use a room in a hotel or any other building in which the public may obtain sleeping accommodations if the charges are $15 or more each day. Local authorities may impose additional local hotel tax.	Reports and payments—on or before the 20th day of each month for the preceding month. Quarterly returns, due on the 20th day after the end of the quarter, are allowed if monthly liability is less than $500 for calendar month or $1,500 for calendar quarter.
Alcoholic beverages tax.	Mixed Beverage Gross Receipts Tax—6.7%, which is in addition to a separate 8.25% mixed beverage sales tax.	Mixed Beverage Gross Receipts Tax—Reports and payments—due on or before the 20th day of the month following each reporting period, even if there are no mixed beverage sales to report.
Gasoline taxes, special fuel taxes.	Gasoline and diesel fuel, 20¢ per gallon.	Reports and payments—Gasoline and diesel fuel taxes are paid monthly on the 25th day of each month for the preceding month.

Tax	Basis—Rates	Due Dates
Severance taxes.	Oil—4.6% of market value.	Oil—Reports and payment—25th day of each month for the preceding production month.
	Natural gas—7.5% of market value.	Natural gas—Reports and payment—monthly, 20th day of the second calendar month following production (August 15 for the production month of June of odd-numbered years); If qualified, yearly, February 20.
Motor vehicle sales or use tax.	6.25% of sales price, but standard presumptive value (SPV) may be used on private-party sales; $90 fee in lieu of use tax on new resident who brings previously registered vehicle into Texas.	Reports and payments—Tax generally paid to dealer upon purchase. Otherwise, purchaser must remit tax to county tax assessor-collector within 30 calendar days after vehicle is purchased in private-party sale or vehicle is brought into Texas; within 60 days after purchase or first use in Texas for active duty military personnel; or at time of title transfer for an even exchange or gift.
	Manufactured homes, 5% tax on 65% of sales price (3.25%) of initial sale of home by manufacturer, excluding shipping and delivery charges.	Reports and payment—Submitted by manufacturer by last day of each month.
	Boat and boat motor sales and use tax, 6.25% of total consideration. New residents, $15 per boat or boat motor brought into Texas.	Payment—20th working day after delivery to purchaser or entry into state.
Cigarette tax.	Cigarettes—$1.41 per pack of 20.	Cigarette reports—manufacturers and distributors, last day of each month. Payment—by means of stamps.
Tobacco products tax.	Cigars and tobacco products—chewing tobacco, snuff, and smoking tobacco, $1.22 per ounce; cigars weighing not more than 3 lbs. per 1,000, 1¢ per 10; cigars weighing more than 3 lbs. per 1,000 and retailing for not more than 3.3¢ each, $7.50 per 1,000; cigars with substantially no nontobacco ingredients weighing more than 3 lbs. per 1,000 and retailing for over 3.3¢ each, $11 per 1,000; cigars with a substantial amount of nontobacco ingredients weighing more than 3 lbs. per 1,000 and retailing for over 3.3¢ each, $15 per 1,000.	Tobacco reports and payments—last day of each month.

Tax	Basis—Rates	Due Dates
Sales and use taxes.	Sales—6.25% of sales price of taxable items and services. Additional local taxes, up to 2%, may be imposed, for a maximum combined state and local rate of 8.25%.	Reports and payment—Due on 20th day of the month following the end of the reporting period. Monthly returns required if taxpayer owes $1,500 or more per quarter. Quarterly returns may be filed if taxpayer has less than $1,500 to report per quarter. Annual returns may be filed if taxpayer has less than $1,000 to report for a calendar year and if authorized by Comptroller. To qualify for an additional timely filing/payment discount, monthly filers may prepay taxes on or before the 15th day of the month for which the prepayment is made, and quarterly filers may prepay taxes on or before the 15th day of the second month of the quarter for which the tax is due.
	Use—6.25% of sales price upon the storage, use or consumption of taxable items or services purchased, leased or rented for use in the state. Additional local taxes, up to 2%, may apply. Cities, counties, transit authorities, and special purpose districts may impose additional taxes, up to a maximum total local rate of 2%.	
Insurance companies tax.	1.6% on property and casualty insurance premiums; 1.75% on health and accident insurance premiums; 0.875% on first $450,000 for life insurance premiums, 1.75% on premiums over $450,000; 0.875% on first $450,000 of taxable gross revenues of HMOs, 1.75% on taxable gross revenues over $450,000; 1.35% on title insurance company premiums; 0.5% for captive insurance company premiums; 4.85% on surplus line insurers and unauthorized insurers premiums.	Returns and payment—licensed insurers, March 1; semiannual prepayments on March 1 and August 1 if net tax liability for previous calendar year in excess of $1,000. Independently procured—May 15. Surplus lines and title insurance—March 1; prepayments of surplus lines taxes due by 15th of month following month in which accrued taxes equal $70,000 or more. Unauthorized insurers—March 1.

Utah

Tax System.—Utah imposes a general property tax on real and personal property in the taxing units where such property is located. Intangible property, exempted from general property tax, is taxed on the income therefrom. Maximum rates of taxation of intangible property are provided. Property taxes are supplemented by taxes on incomes, sales, use, occupations, and privileges. An outline of the Utah tax system follows:

Tax	Basis—Rates	Due Dates
Corporate franchise and income taxes; corporate gross receipts tax.	Franchise and income taxes: 4.95%. Minimum tax, $100. Unrelated business income of exempt organizations is taxed at the corporate tax rate.	Returns and payments—15th day of 4th month after close of tax year. Estimated payments due 15th day of the 4th, 6th, 9th, and 12th months of the taxable year for corporations expecting to have current tax liability of $3,000 or more or that had a tax liability of $3,000 or more in the previous tax year. Unrelated business income tax returns due at same time as federal exempt organization business income tax returns.
	Corporate gross receipts tax on certain corporations not required to pay franchise or income tax—0.6250% if gross receipts exceed $10 million but not $500 million; 0.9375% if gross receipts exceed $500 million but not $1 billion; 1.2500% if gross receipts exceed $1 billion. Entities with ownership interests in a supplemental electricity-generating facility—0.6250% if gross receipts exceed $5 million but not $500 million; 0.9375% if gross receipts exceed $500 million but not $1 billion; 1.2500% if gross receipts exceed $1 billion.	Returns and payments—semiannually on or before the last day of July and January.
Personal income tax.	4.95%. Withholding required.	Returns—calendar: April 15; fiscal: 3 months and 15 days after close of tax year. Payments—with returns.
General property tax.	Aggregate of state and local rates fixed to meet budget.	Notices—general property, Nov. 1. Payments—personal property, within 30 days of notice; real property, November 30.
	Tangible personal property and real property, except residential property—Tax assessed at 100% of fair market value. Residential property owned by senior citizen claiming tax abatement for the poor—tax assessed at 35% of fair market value; other residential property—tax assessed at 55% of fair market value.	
Alcoholic beverages tax.	Excise—$13.10 per 31-gallon barrel on all beer; $13.10 per barrel.	

Tax	Basis—Rates	Due Dates
Gasoline tax; fuel use tax.	Motor fuels and gasohol tax—$0.314 per gallon of fuel sold or used, effective January 1, 2021 ($0.311 per gallon in 2020). Aviation fuel—$0.025 per gallon for fuel purchased for use by a federally certificated air carrier at Salt Lake International Airport ($0.040 per gallon at other airports); $0.090 per gallon for fuel purchased for use by a non-federally certificated air carrier. Compressed natural gas (CNG) and liquefied natural gas (LNG)—$0.171 per GGE/DGE, effective January 1, 2021 ($0.168 in 2020).	Motor fuels and special fuel taxes—reports and payments, last day of the month following reporting period.
	Special fuel (diesel)—same as motor fuel rate per gallon of special fuel sold or used.	
Environmental assurance fee.	Environmental assurance fee on petroleum products—$0.0065 per gallon on first sale or use of a petroleum product in Utah. Imposition depends on fund balance.	Assurance fee—returns and payments by last day of the month following month when sale occurs.
Recycling fee on lubricating oil.	Recycling fee on lubricating oil—4¢ per quart on the first sale of lubricating oil in the state.	Reports and payments—monthly or quarterly, depending on the vendor's frequency of sales and use tax reporting and paying.
Severance tax; oil and gas conservation tax.	3% of the value up to the first $13 per barrel for oil and up to and including $1.50 per MCF for natural gas, and 5% of the value from $13.01 and over per barrel for oil and $1.51 and over per MCF for natural gas. Liquid natural gas, 4% of value.	Reports and payments—June 1 for preceding year, except on or before June 1, September 1, December 1, and March 1 if preceding year's tax liability was $3,000 or more.
	Mining severance tax—After an initial $50,000 gross value exemption, a tax of 2.6% is imposed on the taxable value of metalliferous minerals sold or shipped out of the state. Taxable value of metalliferous minerals (all metals except beryllium) sold or otherwise disposed of, 30% of the gross proceeds. For metalliferous minerals sold or otherwise disposed of that are sold or shipped out of state in the form of ore, taxable value is 80% of the gross proceeds. Beryllium, taxable value 125% of direct mining costs incurred. Minerals remaining stockpiled for more than two years are subject to tax.	
	Conservation tax—$0.002 per $1 of market value at the well of oil and gas.	Payments—due quarterly on first day of June, September, December, and March.
	Brine shrimp royalty—3.25¢ per pound of brine shrimp eggs.	Reports—Feb. 15. Payments—April 30.
Cigarette tax.	Cigarettes—8.5¢ each on cigarettes weighing 3 lbs. or less per 1,000 ($1.70 per pack of 20; $2.125 per pack of 25); 9.963¢ each on cigarettes weighing more. (The tax rate will be increased by the same amount as any amount of reduction in the federal cigarette excise tax.)	Reports: Cigarette tax—Tobacco products excise tax—last day of month following each quarterly period.
	Excise tax on tobacco products, except cigarettes and moist snuff—86% of manufacturer's sales price; $1.83 per ounce for moist snuff.	Payments: Cigarette tax—by affixing stamps. Tobacco products excise tax—accompanies report.

Tax	Basis—Rates	Due Dates
Sales tax; use tax.	Sales and use taxes—4.85% general state sales tax rate; 2% on residential use of utility services; 1.75% on food and food ingredients. Sales tax based on total nonexempt cash and charge sales. Use tax based on total amount of cash and charge sales or purchases for storage, use, or other consumption in Utah. Nonnexus sellers of nonfood items in state taxed at combined state and local sales tax rate for the delivery location.	Sales tax—reports and payments—on or before the last day of the month following each calendar quarter. Taxpayers with a liability of $50,000 or more must report and pay the tax on or before the last day of each month. New businesses or businesses in good standing that expect or reported less than $1,000 in tax may file annually—due by January 31 following year end. Use tax—same as sales tax.
Public utilities regulation fee; emergency service charges; radio network charge.	Maximum rate—0.3% (0.15% for an electrical cooperative) of gross operating revenue from operations within the state; minimum tax, $50. 911 emergency service charge—71¢ per month on each access line in the state; unified statewide 911 emergency service charge—25¢ per month on access line in the state; radio network charge—52¢ per month.	Reports—April 15. Payments—July 1 for utilities fee; for the emergency and radio network charges, the last day of the month following the last day of the previous month or the previous quarter, depending on how or whether the person needs to file sales and use tax reports.
Insurance companies tax.	Generally, 2.25% of gross premiums less premiums returned or credited to policyholders on direct taxable business, premiums received for reinsurance of property or risks located in Utah, and dividends paid or credited to policyholders; plus, for motor vehicle insurers, an additional 0.01% of total premiums less premiums returned or credited to policyholders from policies covering Utah motor vehicle risks. On that portion of taxable premiums that is attributable to Utah variable life insurance premiums, 2.25% on the first $100,000 of Utah variable life insurance premiums paid and received by an admitted insurer in the preceding tax year and 0.08% of such premiums in excess of $100,000. Surplus line brokers, unauthorized insurers, 4.25% of gross premiums allocated to Utah, less returned premiums. Title insurers, 0.45%. Workers' compensation insurance writers, 2.75% effective January 1, 2020 (between 1% and 4.25% for 2011 through 2022, determined annually) on workers' compensation premiums received by all insurance carriers, including premiums received from state and local government agencies and public agency insurance mutuals. Foreign companies subject to retaliatory taxes.	Reports and statements, generally—March 1. Payments—March 31; surplus line brokers, 25th day of each month. Quarterly payments from insurers owing $10,000 or more in the preceding year, due on April 30, July 31, October 31, and March 31.

Vermont

Tax System.—Vermont derives its revenue from privilege, meals and rooms, sales and use, beverage, cigarettes and tobacco products, gasoline, income and estate and gift taxes, and from the taxation of other types of wealth. The state tax on real and personal property and intangibles has been superseded by the corporate and personal income taxes. The general property tax is for local purposes. An outline of the Vermont tax system follows:

Tax	Basis—Rates	Due Dates
General income tax.	Corporations (domestic and foreign)—not over $10,000 of net income, 6%; $10,001 to $25,000, $600 plus 7% of excess over $10,000; $25,001 and over, $1,650 plus 8.5% of excess over $25,000. Minimum tax, $750 for corporations with gross receipts over $5 million; $500 for corporations with gross receipts over $2 million and up to $5 million; $300 for corporations with gross receipts of $2 million or less; $75 for small farm corporations. Digital business entities may elect to be subject to special franchise tax.	Returns—15th day of 4th month after end of taxable year. Estimated tax required if estimated tax is over $500; estimated tax due with the declaration on the 15th day of the 4th, 6th, 9th and 12th months of the tax year.
	The income tax on individuals: **2020 rates:** Single: $0 -40,350 x 3.35% minus $0; $40,351 - 97,800 x 6.600% minus $1,311.37; $97,801 - 204,000 x 7.600% minus $2,289.37;$204,001 and over x 8.750% minus $4,635.37. Married Filing Jointly/Civil Union Filing Jointly: $0 - 67,450 x 3.350% minus 0; $67,451 - 163,000 x 6.600% minus $2,192.12; $163,001 - 248,350 x 7.600% minus $3,822.12; $248,351 and over x 8.750% minus $6,678.15. Married Filing Separately/Civil Union Filing Separately: $0 - 33,725 x 3.350% minus $0; $33,726 - 81,500 x 6.600% minus $1,096.06; $81,501 - 124,175 x 7.600% minus $1,911.06; $124,176 and over x 8.750% minus $3,339.07. Head of Household: $0 - 54,100 x 3.350% minus $0; $54,101 - 139,650 x 6.600% minus $1,758.25; $139,651 - 226,200 x 7.600% minus $3,154.75; $226,201 and over 8.750% minus $5,756.05. **2019 rates:** Single: $0 - 39,600 x 3.35% minus $0; $39,601 - 96,000 x 6.600% minus $1,287.00; $96,001 - 200,200 x 7.600% minus $2,247.00; $200,201 and over x 8.750% minus $4,549.30. Married Filing Jointly/Civil Union Filing Jointly: $0 - 66,150 x 3.350% minus 0; $66,151 - 159,950 x 6.600% minus $2,149.87; $159,951 - 243,750 x 7.600% minus $3,749.37; $243,751 and over x 8.750% minus $6,552.50. Married Filing Separately/Civil Union Filing Separately: $0 - 33,075 x 3.350% minus $0; $33,076 - 79,975 x 6.600% minus $1,074.94; $79,976 - 121,875 x 7.600% minus $1,874.69; $121,876 and over x 8.750% minus $3,276.25. Head of Household: $0 - 53,100 x 3.350% minus $0; $53,101 - 137,050 x 6.600% minus $1,725.75; $137,051 - 221,950 x 7.600% minus $3,096.25; $221,951 and over 8.750% minus $5,648.68. General withholding required.	For individuals, returns due on 15th day of 4th month after end of taxable year.

Tax	Basis—Rates	Due Dates
Bank franchise tax.	Banks and loan associations—0.000096 of the average monthly deposit held by the corporation.	Returns and payments—Beginning January 1, 2017, returns due quarterly by 25th day of month after quarter end. Payments due monthly on 25th day of following month.
Property tax.	Education property tax: homestead property—$1 per $100 of assessed valuation; nonresidential property $1.651 per $100 for fiscal year 2021.	Payment—varies locally; if no date fixed, within 30 days of mailing of notice.
	Land use change tax—10% of full fair market value of the changed land determined without regard to the use value appraisal.	Payment—within 30 days of mailing of notice.
Meals and rooms tax.	Meals and rooms—9%. Alcoholic beverages—10%.	Reports and payments—if annual tax is $500 or less, quarterly on the 25th day of April, July, October and January; otherwise, 25th of each month (for February, the 23rd).
Alcoholic beverages tax.	Excise—malt beverages, 26.5¢ per gallon if not more than 6% alcohol by volume and 55¢ per gallon if more than 6% alcohol by volume; vinous beverages, 55¢ per gallon; fortified wines and spirituous liquors, 5% to 25% of gross revenue.	
Gasoline and diesel fuel tax.	Gasoline—12.1¢ per gallon sold or used within the state. Additional motor fuel tax assessment (MFTA), subject to change on a quarterly basis, is imposed at a rate of the greater of: (1) 13.4¢ per gallon, or (2) 4% of the tax-adjusted retail price upon each gallon of motor fuel sold by the distributor, not to exceed 18¢. Additional motor fuel transportation infrastructure assessment (MFTIA), subject to change on a quarterly basis, is calculated based on the greater of: (1) 3.96¢ per gallon, or (2) 2% of the tax adjusted retail price upon each gallon of motor fuel sold by the distributor. Diesel—28¢ per gallon, plus a 3¢ per gallon motor fuel transportation infrastructure assessment and a 1¢ per gallon petroleum cleanup fee; 3¢ per gallon on railroad fuel used in the state.	Reports and payments—gasoline tax: 25th day of each month; diesel fuel tax: distributors and dealers report and pay on the last day of each month; railroad operators report and pay by the last day of October, January, April and July.
Motor vehicle purchase and use tax.	6% of the taxable cost of pleasure cars, motorcycles, motor homes, and other vehicles weighing up to 10,099 pounds, other than a farm truck. For other motor vehicles, the lesser of 6% of the taxable cost or $2,075.	Reports and payments due when registering or transferring registrations. Use tax report and payment at time of registration.
	9% use tax applies to short-term rental charges for pleasure vehicles.	Reports and payments—to be determined by the Commissioner.

Tax	Basis—Rates	Due Dates
Cigarette tax; tobacco products tax.	154 mills ($3.08 per pack of 20). Tax is calculated at 154 mills for each 0.0325 oz. of roll-your-own tobacco.	Cigarette tax report by wholesale dealers, 15th of each month; payment, by purchase and affixation of stamps.
	92% of wholesale price of tobacco products including electronic cigarettes and their paraphernalia; 2% deduction allowed for timely filing and payment.	Tobacco products tax report and payment—15th of each month.
	Cigars, $2 per cigar if the wholesale price is $2.18 to $9.99. If the wholesale price is $10 or more, $4 per cigar.	
	Snuff, $2.57 per oz. or fractional part thereof.	
	New smokeless tobacco, $2.57 per oz. or $3.08 per package if container is less than 1.2 oz.	
Capital gains tax on land.	From 5% to 80% of the gain, depending on (1) the number of years that the land was held and (2) the gain, calculated as a percentage of the basis.	Payment—buyers must withhold 10% of price if seller held land less than six years. Withheld tax due immediately. Returns and balance of tax due within 30 days after sale.
Property transfer tax.	1.25% (minimum $1) of value of property transferred. Property that used to be primary residences of the transferee are taxed at 0.5% of the first $100,000 in value, and at 1.25% of value over $100,000. A clean water surcharge of 0.2% is imposed on the value of property subject to the property transfer tax. The surcharge is scheduled to decrease to 0.04% effective July 1, 2027, and the surcharge is scheduled to be repealed effective July 1, 2039. There is no surcharge on the first $100,000 in value of property to be used for the principal residence of the transferee, or the first $200,000 in value of property transferred if the purchaser obtains a purchase money mortgage funded in part with a homeland grant through the Vermont Housing and Conservation Trust Fund, or that the Vermont Housing and Finance Agency or U.S. Department of Agriculture and Rural Development has committed to make or purchase.	Payment—payable to the commissioner at the time of transfer of title to property subject to tax.
Sales and use tax.	6% of sales price of taxable sales, purchases, services, charges, and rentals.	Returns and payment—tax due in one annual payment on or before January 25 if tax is $500 or less. Tax must be paid and returns filed quarterly on or before 25th of the month following the quarters ending on the last day of March, June, September, and December if tax is more than $500 but less than $2,500. In all other cases, tax and returns are due monthly on or before the 25th (23rd of February) of the following month.

Tax	Basis—Rates	Due Dates
Utilities taxes.	Telephone company tax—Net book value rate of tax is 2.37%. Alternative tax (in lieu of income tax) on companies that received less than $50 million in annual gross operating revenues within the state in prior year: from 2.25% to 5.25% of gross operating revenue, depending on gross operating revenues during the quarter.	Telephone net book value tax is to be paid in equal monthly installments on or before the 25th day of each month of each taxable year. Alternative tax—report, 25 days following the last day of the 3rd month of the tax year; payment—within 25 days following the last day of the 3rd, 6th, 9th, and 12th months of each tax year.
Insurance companies tax.	2% of annual premiums.	Returns—reconciliation return due the last day of February for the preceding year ending December 31. Payment—due with the reconciliation return if tax is expected to be less than $500 for the year; otherwise, quarterly returns and payments must be made the last day of May, August, November, and February.
	Foreign mutual fire insurance companies insuring only factories or mills—2% of gross premiums covering risks within the state less unabsorbed portion of premiums deposits.	Returns and payments—during month of February.
	Surplus lines brokers—3% premium receipts tax.	Surplus lines brokers—end of the month following each calendar quarter.
	Foreign companies subject to retaliatory taxes.	
	Captive insurance companies—Direct tax rate: if net taxable premiums equal $20 million or less, the amount is multiplied by 0.0038; if over $20 million but less than $40 million, multiply the excess over $20 million by 0.00285; if over $40 million but less than $60 million, multiply the excess over $40 million by 0.0019; and if over $60 million, multiply the excess over $60 million by 0.00072. Assumed tax rate: if net assumed reinsurance premiums are $20 million or less, multiply the amount by 0.00214; if over $20 million, but less than $40 million, multiply the excess over $20 million by 0.00143; if over $40 million but not more than $60 million, multiply the excess over $40 million by 0.00048; and if over $60 million, multiply the excess over $60 million by 0.00024. Minimum aggregate tax of $7,500; maximum aggregate tax of $200,000.	Returns and payments—March 15.

Virginia

Tax System.—Virginia has adopted a tax system of complete segregation of state and local sources of revenue. By this method real estate, tangible personal property, machinery and tools used in a manufacturing or mining business and merchants' capital are segregated for local taxation exclusively, while the state revenue is derived from taxes on income, corporate franchises, gasoline, cigarettes, sales and use, gross earnings of utilities, insurance companies and intangible personal property. An outline of the Virginia tax system follows:

Tax	Basis—Rates	Due Dates
Direct corporate income tax.	Corporate income—6% of net income from Virginia sources. Telecommunications companies are subject to a 0.5% minimum tax, if it is less than the corporate income tax, based on gross receipts for a calendar year. Certain electric suppliers are subject to a minimum tax if the corporate income tax net of any income tax credits is less than the minimum tax. The tax is 1.45% of gross receipts for the calendar year that ends during the taxable year minus the state's portion of the electric utility consumption tax billed to customers.	Returns and payments, corporations—15th day of 4th month after close of taxable year. Estimated corporate tax declaration and payments (if tax more than $1,000) due 15th day of 4th, 6th, 9th and 12th months of taxable year. Beginning January 1, 2013, all corporations are required to file annual income tax returns and make all payments electronically.
Personal income tax.	Personal income—Not over $3,000, 2%; over $3,000 but not over $5,000, $60 plus 3%; over $5,000 but not over $17,000, $120 plus 5%; over $17,000, $720 plus 5.75%. Withholding required.	Returns—calendar: May 1; fiscal: 15th day of 4th month after close of income year. Estimated tax declaration due May 1. Payment—May 1. Estimated payments due May 1, June 15, September 15, and January 15.
Bank franchise tax.	$1 on each $100 of net capital.	Returns—March 1. Payments—June 1.
General property tax.	Aggregate of local rates fixed to meet budget; rates based on fair market value of real property, tangible personal property, machinery, tools and merchant's capital. All general reassessments and annual assessments in localities having annual assessments of realty are at 100% of fair market value.	Returns—May 1. Payment—December 5.
Alcoholic beverages tax.	Excise—alcoholic beverages other than wine and vermouth, 20% of selling price; beer and wine coolers, 25.65¢ per gallon per barrel. Wine, 40¢ per liter.	Excise—reports, 10th of each month. Payment—sale of wine to retailers and wholesalers, at time of purchase; others, with monthly report.

Tax	Basis—Rates	Due Dates
Gasoline tax.	Gasoline—21.2¢ per gallon, effective July 1, 2020, through June 30, 2021; 26.2¢ per gallon effective July 1, 2021, through June 30, 2022, and the rate will be indexed annually effective July 1, 2022. Diesel—20.2¢ per gallon through June 30, 2021; 27¢ per gallon effective July 1, 2021, through June 30, 2022; and the rate will be indexed annually effective July 1, 2022. Aviation fuels—5¢ per gallon of aviation fuels. Alternative fuels—21.2¢ per gasoline gallon equivalent (GGE).	Motor fuel—Returns and payments—postmarked by 15th day of the 2nd month following the month for which the return and payment are due.
Forest products tax.	Pine products—lumber, $1.15 per 1,000 ft. board measure or log scale, International 1/4" Kerf Rule; hardwood, cypress and all other species, 22.5¢ per 1,000 feet board measure.	Reports and payments—quarterly, within 30 days after end of each calendar quarter. Annually—within 30 days after December 31 for any manufacturer of rough lumber that manufactures fewer than 500,000 board feet, any person who severs for sale 100 or fewer cords of fuel wood, or any person who severs 500 or fewer posts for fish net poles during any one calendar year.
Aircraft sales and use tax.	Aircraft sales and use tax—2% of the sales price of aircraft licensed for use in Virginia.	Payment—prior to applying for an aircraft license.
Motor vehicle sales tax.	Sales and use tax—4.15%. Special 3% tax on manufactured homes and 2% tax on mobile offices.	Sales and use tax—payable upon application for certificate of title.
Watercraft sales and use tax.	2%	Returns and payment—Dealers, 20th of each month. Purchasers, when applying for title.
Sales and use tax.	Sales tax—combined 5.3% of sales price, gross proceeds or cost price of tangible personal property, rentals, services or accommodations (consists of 4.3% state rate and 1% local rate imposed by all localities). Contractors' use tax, 4%. Vending machine sales, combined rate of 6.3% (consists of 5.3% state rate and 1% local rate). 2.5% on food for human consumption (consists of 1.5% reduced state rate and 1% local option tax).	Sales and use tax—returns and payment due on or before the 20th of each month for preceding month.
Cigarette excise tax; use tax on cigarettes.	Cigarettes—Excise tax—3¢ per cigarette (60¢ per pack of 20 cigarettes) (1.5% per cigarette, 30¢ per pack of 20 cigarettes prior to July 1, 2020). Roll-your-own tobacco, 10% of manufacturers sales price. Cigarette use tax, 1.5¢ per cigarette stored, used, or consumed in Virginia.	Reports—wholesalers by 20th of each month; retailers within one business day after receipt. Payment—by affixation of stamps, immediately upon receipt. Use tax—reports and payment—by 10th of each month.

Tax	Basis—Rates	Due Dates
Tobacco products tax.	20% of manufacturers sales price of the tobacco products (other than moist snuff, loose leaf tobacco, and liquid nicotine). Moist snuff—36¢ per ounce. Loose leaf tobacco products—42¢ for each unit less than 4 ounces; 80¢ for each unit that is at least 4 ounces but not more than 8 ounces; $1.40 for each unit more than 8 ounces but not more than 24 ounces; and units that exceed 24 ounces are taxed at 42¢ per unit plus 42¢ for each 4 ounce increment that exceeds 16 ounces. Liquid nicotine ("vape juice")— 6.6¢ per milliliter. Roll-your-own tobacco—10% of the manufacturer's sales price.	Returns and payment—20th of each month.
Recordation tax; Realty transfer tax.	Conveyances—25¢ per $100 consideration or fraction thereof. Realty transfers—50¢ per $500 of value or fraction thereof.	Payment—at time of recording.
Insurance companies tax.	Life—2.25% of direct gross premiums income or subscriber fee income, less return premiums, and premiums received for reinsurance on risks within the state.	Reports and payments—March 1. Workers' comp. insurers—within 30 days of December 31. Declarations and payments of estimated taxes from insurers expecting to owe more than $3,000 are due on the 15th day of the 4th, 6th, 9th, and 12th months.
	Mutual and industrial sick benefit—1% of direct gross premium income.	
	Dental or optometric and health services plans, 2.25% of direct gross subscriber fee income derived from all subscription contracts.	
	Workers' compensation insurers—2.5% of premiums received.	
	Foreign companies subject to retaliatory taxes.	

Washington

Tax System.—The revenue system of Washington is based primarily on the ad valorem assessment and taxation of property, but since 1933 the revenue needs of the state have been financed largely by occupation and other taxes. Although the state continues to receive a substantial income from property taxes, the greater part of such levies is used for the support of municipalities and other taxing districts. The yield from the revenue act taxes is devoted entirely to state purposes, and this is true of most of the other special taxes, the exceptions being the gasoline tax and the liquor taxes, a portion of each being redistributed locally. An outline of the Washington tax system follows:

Tax	Basis—Rates	Due Dates
Business and occupation tax.	Retailing (generally)—0.471% of gross proceeds of sales; Wholesaling—0.484% of gross proceeds of sales; Manufacturing—0.484% of value of products manufactured; Services and other activities—1.75% of gross income. Special rates applicable to certain industries.	Report and payment—25th of the following month for monthly filers.
General property taxes.	Aggregate of state and local rates fixed to meet budget. Assessed value is 100% of market value of real and tangible personal property, excluding open-space land, timber land, and agricultural land. Constitutional and statutory tax limitation, 1% of full, true and fair value.	Payment—in full by April 30 or in two equal installments on April 30 and October 31 if tax due is more than $50.
Leasehold excise tax.	Leasehold interests in exempt publicly owned real or personal property—12% plus 7% surtax of tax payable for a total state rate of 12.84%.	Return and payment—last day of following month. Department of Revenue may establish other return period.
Timber and forest lands taxes.	Timber harvesters pay a 5% tax on stumpage value of timber harvested.	Return and payment—last day of month following calendar quarter.
Alcoholic beverages tax.	Excise—Total tax—beer (per barrel), $8.08 per barrel (reduced rate of $4.782 applicable to first 60,000 barrels sold each year by small breweries); spirits liter tax paid by general public, $3.7708 (per liter); spirits liter tax paid by on-premises licensees (per liter), $2.4408; table wine (per liter), $0.2292; cider (per liter), $0.0814.	
Gasoline tax.	Gasoline and special fuel, 49.4¢ per gallon. Aircraft fuel rate is 11¢ per gallon.	Report and payment—gasoline, 25th of following month. Payment of motor fuel and special fuel taxes by electronic funds transfer due on 26th of following month.
Uranium and thorium milling tax.	5¢ per pound of uranium or thorium compound milled out of raw ore.	Quarterly basis.

Tax	Basis—Rates	Due Dates
Enhanced food fish tax.	Chinook, coho and chum salmon, and anadromous game fish (from Puget Sound), 5.62% of value at the point of landing; chinook, coho, and chum salmon, and anadromous game fish (harvested from ocean waters, the Columbia River, Willapa Bay, and Grays Harbor), 6.69%; pink and sockeye salmon, 3.37%; other food fish and shellfish except oysters, 2.25%; oysters, 0.09%; sea urchins and sea cucumbers, 2.25%. Rates include the additional 7% surtax.	Report and payment—25th day of following month.
Cigarette tax; tobacco products tax; vapor products tax.	Cigarettes—$3.025 per pack of 20 cigarettes.	Cigarettes—reports—wholesalers, 15th of each month; wholesalers selling cigarettes made by nonparticipating manufacturers, 25th of each month. Payment—stamps affixed upon receipt.
	Tobacco products—95% of taxable sales price on other tobacco products, including pipe and chewing tobacco; 95% of taxable sales price not to exceed 65¢ per cigar; little cigars, 15.125¢ per stick or $3.025 per pack of 20. Moist snuff rate based on net weight listed by manufacturer at rate of $2.526 per unit of 1.2 ounces or less and at a proportionate rate for larger units.	Tobacco products—reports—same as under business and occupation tax. Payment—with return.
	Vapor products—nine cents per milliliter of solution for accessible containers that are greater than five milliliters, and twenty-seven cents per milliliter of solution for other vapor products.	Payment-at time products brought into state.
Real estate excise tax.	The rate is 1.1% of the portion of the selling price less than or equal to $500,000 and 1.28% of the portion of the selling price that is greater than $500,000 and equal to or less than $1,500,000. The rate is 2.75% of the portion of the selling price that is greater than $1,500,000 and equal to or less than $3,000,000; and 3% of the portion of the selling price that is greater than $3,000,000.	Payment—with filing of affidavit form.
Retail sales tax.	State rate—6.5% of retail sales price on taxable property and services plus additional 0.3% on motor vehicle sales and additional 5.9% on retail car rentals. Local sales taxes also imposed. Use tax imposed at same rate as sales tax.	Report and payment—25th of each month for monthly filers.
Public utility tax.	Express, sewer, telegraph, and gas distribution, 3.852%; light and power, 3.873%; urban transportation, vessels under 65 ft., 0.642%; water distribution, 5.029%; log transportation, 1.3696%; motor transportation, railroad, railroad car, tugboat business, and all other public service businesses, 1.926%. Rates include the additional 7% surtax.	Report and payment—25th of following month for monthly filers.

Tax	Basis—Rates	Due Dates
Insurance premiums tax.	Life and other insurance—2%.	Reports—March 1 annually.
	Marine and foreign trade insurance—0.95% of gross underwriting profit allocable to state.	Payment—March 1 annually. Prepayment due from taxpayers owing $400 or more for preceding year—15th of June, September and December.
	Foreign insurance companies are subject to a retaliatory tax.	
	Health maintenance organizations and health care service contractors—2% of premiums and prepayments for health care services.	Report and payment—March 1. Prepayment—15th of June, September and December.

West Virginia

Tax System.—The West Virginia tax system is founded on the ad valorem assessment and taxation of property, but this source of revenue has now been supplemented with other taxes affording a substantial yield. The revenue from property taxes is mainly devoted to the support of municipal governments and other local tax levying bodies, with only a small portion going to the State Treasury. The state receives the entire revenue from the inheritance tax, insurance company taxes, the privilege tax on gross income, the taxes on utilities, the gasoline tax and liquor taxes. Both the state and local bodies share in license fees, but the proceeds of the consumers' sales and service tax are used entirely for support of the schools. The state collects both a personal income tax and a corporation net income tax. An outline of the West Virginia tax system follows:

Tax	Basis—Rates	Due Dates
Corporation net income tax.	6.5% of taxable income.	Returns and payment—April 15 for calendar year returns; fiscal returns, 15th day of fourth month after close of fiscal year. For unrelated business taxable income of exempt corporations, 15th day of the 5th month following the close of the tax year. Estimated tax declarations and payments due 15th day of 4th, 6th, 9th and 12th month of taxable year if taxable income exceeds $10,000.
Personal income tax.	*Individuals, individuals filing joint returns, heads of households, surviving spouses, and estates and trusts:* Less than $10,000, 3%; $10,000—$25,000, $300 plus 4% of excess over $10,000; $25,000—$40,000, $900 plus 4.5% of excess over $25,000; $40,000—$60,000, $1,575 plus 6% of excess over $40,000; over $60,000, $2,775 plus 6.5% of excess over $60,000. *Married individuals filing separate returns:* less than $5,000, 3%; $5,000—$12,500, $150 plus 4% of excess over $5,000; $12,500—$20,000, $450 plus 4.5% of excess over $12,500; $20,000—$30,000, $787.50 plus 6% of excess over $20,000; over $30,000, $1,387.50 plus 6.5% of excess over $30,000. General withholding required.	Returns and payment—15th day of the 4th month after end of income year. Estimated tax due 15th of April, June, September, and January, except for persons having total estimated tax of $40 or less or farmers, January 15.
General property tax.	Determined annually. Maximum levies: Class 1—50¢ per $100 actual value of real and personal property; Class 2—$1 per $100; Class 3—$1.50 per $100; Class 4—$2 per $100. Property is assessed at 60% of value.	Returns—general property between July 1 and October 1; business property, September 1; public utilities, May 1. Payment—September 1 and March 1.
Tax on corporations holding land.	5¢ for every acre over 10,000 acres.	Payment due before certificate of incorporation or of authority is issued.

Tax	Basis—Rates	Due Dates
Alcoholic beverages tax.	Excise—$5.50 per barrel of beer not in excess of 4.2% alcohol, and proportionately on smaller amounts. Retail purchases of liquor, 5% of purchase price. Wine, 26.406¢ per liter. Intoxicating liquors sold outside municipalities are taxed at 5% of the purchase price.	
Motor fuels tax.	Motor fuels excise tax—$0.357 per gallon effective for calendar year 2020. The 2020 rate is comprised of a flat rate ($0.205 per gallon) and an additional variable wholesale component ($0.152 per gallon).	Gasoline—reports and payments—last day of the calendar month for the preceding calendar month. Alternative fuels—reports and payments—on or before January 31 of every year, unless determined by the commissioner that payment must be made more frequently. If no tax is due, the return required by the commissioner must be completed and filed before January 31.
Motor carrier road tax.	Motor carrier road tax—same as motor fuels tax on gallons of motor and other fuel used by carriers in the state.	Motor carrier road tax—reports, last day of April, July, October, and January; payments, last day of January.
Severance taxes.	Coal—5% of the gross value of the coal produced. When thermal coal is sold for purposes of generating electricity, the severance tax rate is reduced as follows: 4.3% effective July 1, 2019; 3.7% effective July 1, 2020; 3% effective July 1, 2021. Coal is produced from the waste coal of prior mining—2.5%. These rates include the 0.35% additional severance tax on coal for the benefit of counties and municipalities. Minimum coal severance tax—75¢ per ton of coal produced for sale, profit, or commercial use during the taxable year. Special tax on coal production—2¢ per ton. The severance tax on limestone and sandstone was terminated effective July 1, 2019. Natural gas or oil—5%. The timber severance tax was terminated effective July 1, 2019. Other natural resources—5%. Coal refuse or gob piles—2.5%. Special reclamation tax on clean coal—27.9¢ per ton.	Annual return and payments—last day of the month following the tax year. Payments of natural gas or oil, timber, or other natural resource severance taxes—on or before the last day of the month following each quarter; if estimated tax exceeds $1,000 per month, due on or before the last day of each month for the preceding month. Payments of the minimum severance tax on coal, limestone or sandstone severance taxes—on or before the last day of the month for the preceding month. All payments for May due June 15. Except for the minimum severance tax on coal, if estimated tax due is $50 or less per month no installment payment is due.
Cigarette tax.	Cigarettes—$1.20 per each pack of 20 cigarettes or fraction thereof. Tobacco products—12% of the wholesale price of each tobacco product. E-cigarette liquid—7.5¢ per milliliter or fraction thereof.	Reports—15th day of each month by wholesalers, carriers, subjobbers, retail dealers and agents. Payment—cigarettes, by purchase of stamps or use of meters; other tobacco products, by invoice method.

Tax	Basis—Rates	Due Dates
Document recording tax.	Realty transfers—$1.10 for each $500 value or fraction thereof plus an additional minimum county excise tax of 55¢ per $500 of value. Counties may increase the excise tax to an amount not to exceed $1.65 for each $500 of value. Fee of $20 assessed upon the privilege of transferring real estate for consideration. In addition, county commissions may create a farmland protection program and impose an additional realty transfer tax with a maximum $1.10 for each $500 of value.	Payment—by affixing of documentary stamps at time of presentation for recording.
Consumers sales and service tax & use tax.	6% of the sales price of taxable services (excluding contracting, services rendered for resale or an employer, and personal & professional services) or of tangible personal property (except gasoline and special fuel) that is stored, consumed, or used within the state; 5% on gasoline and special and alternative fuels; 6% on mobile homes to be used as the owner's principal year-round residence based on 50% of the sales price or value of the home; 6% on other mobile homes; 6% on prepared food. Food and food ingredients are not subject to tax.	Returns and payment—Combined returns: due 20 days after end of month. Quarterly returns: if tax liability does not exceed $250 per month, 20th day of the 1st month in the next succeeding quarter (i.e., April 20, July 20, October 20, January 20). Annual return: if tax liability does not exceed $600 annually, 30 days after the close of the taxable year for federal and state income tax purposes.
Utilities tax.	In general—water companies (except municipally owned)—4.4%; natural gas and toll bridge companies—4.29%; all other public service or utility businesses, except electric utilities and gas storage businesses—2.86%.	Reports—if estimated liability exceed $1,000 per month, reports due on or before the last day of the succeeding month, except the report for May is due on or before June 15 of each year; if estimated liability is $1,000 or less per month, reports due on or before the last day of the month following each quarter. Taxpayers with a total tax liability of $200 or less in any year may request that they be allowed to file reports on or before the end of the month next following the close of the tax year. All taxpayers must report on or before the last day of the month following the end of the tax year. Payments—due with report.
	Electric light and power companies—For electricity generated in West Virginia, electric light and power companies, $22.78 multiplied by the taxable generating unit; if generating unit has flue and gas desulfurization system, $20.70. 5/100 of 1¢ times kilowatt hours sold where contract demands or usage at plant location exceeds 200,000 kilowatts per hour per year, whether electricity is produced in or out of state. For electricity sold in West Virginia but produced elsewhere, 19/100 of 1¢ times kilowatt hours sold.	

Tax	Basis—Rates	Due Dates
	Gas storage business—gas injected into or withdrawn from a gas storage business, 5¢ multiplied by the sum of the net number of dekatherms of gas injected into or withdrawn from the reservoir during a tax month.	
Insurance companies premiums tax.	2% of gross premiums less return premiums, plus additional 1% tax. Fire and casualty insurers, additional 1% of gross direct premiums. Surplus line brokers, 4.55% of gross premiums less return premiums. 1% of gross amount of annuity considerations less considerations returned; risk retention group, 2%; captive insurance companies, 5/10 of 1%. Surcharge on fire and casualty policies—.55% of gross direct premiums, except for surplus lines policies. Minimum tax for aggregate taxes, $200 per year. Foreign companies subject to retaliatory taxes.	Reports and payments—financial statement and annual tax return, March 1. Estimated quarterly payments, 25th day of month following quarter, except March 1 for fourth quarter; payments for captive insurance companies, due in February.
Soft drinks tax.	1¢ per 16.9 oz. (one-half liter) or fraction thereof of bottled soft drinks; 80¢/gallon or 84¢ per four liters of soft drink syrup or fraction thereof; 1¢/ounce or 1¢/28.35 grams of dry mixture or fraction thereof.	Reports—15th day of each month showing preceding month's operations. Payment—tax crowns (stamps) affixed to each unit.
Health care provider tax.	1.75% - 5.5% of gross receipts for enumerated health care services. Rates for certain services were phased out on 07/01/2010.	Returns and payments—on or before January 31; with fiscal returns due by the last day of the 1st month following close of fiscal year.

Wisconsin

Tax System.—The Wisconsin tax system is based on ad valorem levies on general property assessed by the state and its various taxing districts. Some specified businesses are taxed on other than an ad valorem basis and are not subject to the general property tax. The state also levies personal and corporate income, sales and use, and various excise taxes. An outline of the Wisconsin tax system follows:

Tax	Basis—Rates	Due Dates
Franchise and income taxes.	Corporations—7.9% of net income. **2020 Individual Rates:** For 2020, the rates for the first and second brackets are reduced to 3.54% and 4.65%. **2019 Individual Rates:** Single, Head of Household: $0 - 11,760 x 3.86% minus $0; $11,761 - 23,520 x 5.04% minus $138.77; $23,521 - 258,950 x 6.27% minus $428.07; $258,951 and over x 7.650% minus $4,001.58. Married Filing Jointly: $0 - 15,680 x 3.86% minus $0; $15,681 - 31,360 x 5.04% minus $185.02; $31,361 - 345,270 x 6.270% minus $570.75; $345,271 and over x 7.650% minus $5,335.48. Married Filing Separately: $0 - 7,840 x 3.86% minus $0; $7,841 - 15,680 x 5.04% minus $92.51; $15,681 - 172,630 x 6.270% minus $285.37; $172,631 and over x 7.650% minus $2,667.67. Urban mass transportation companies—50% of taxable income.	Returns and payments—C corporations, calendar year, April 15; fiscal year, by 15th day of 4th month following close of fiscal year; individuals, April 15.
General property tax.	General property tax—rates set by various taxation districts based on the total value of all property in the district, compared to the total budgetary needs of all the assessment jurisdictions covering the district. Department of Revenue sets rates for public utilities and commercial and industrial property.	Payment of taxes on real property due in full on or before January 31 or in two equal installments, January 31 and July 31. If total real property tax is less than $100, full payment due January 31. Personal property tax—on or before January 31.
Vessels tax.	Local tonnage tax on vessels—1¢ per net ton of the registered tonnage of steam vessels, barges, boats or other watercraft owned within the state and employed regularly in interstate traffic, in lieu of property taxes.	Vessels tax—returns and payments, January 1.
Forest crop/ managed forest tax.	Forest crop/managed forest tax—Forest crop law program generally closed to new entries in 1985. However, property enrolled in the program still is taxed at the rates set under the program, as adjusted. The managed forest land program tax rates are determined based on when parcel was entered into the program and the parcel's classification.	Returns and payments—January 31.
Alcoholic beverages tax.	Excise—intoxicating liquor, 85.86¢ per liter; wines: containing 14% alcohol or less, 6.605¢ per liter; containing more than 14% but not more than 21% alcohol, 11.89¢ per liter. Fermented malt beverages (beer), $2 per 31-gallon barrel. Cider containing not less than 0.5% or more than 7% alcohol by volume, 1.71¢ per liter.	

Tax	Basis—Rates	Due Dates
Fuel taxes.	Motor vehicle fuel and alternate fuel—motor vehicle and diesel fuels, 30.9¢ per gallon. Liquefied petroleum gas, 22.6¢ per gallon; compressed natural gas, 24.7¢ per gallon. General aviation fuel, 6¢ per gallon.	Reports—motor vehicle and alternate fuels, last day of each month; general aviation fuel, 20th day of each month; common carriers and other persons transporting motor vehicle fuel, general aviation fuel, or alternate fuels interstate, 30th day of month covered by report. Payments—motor vehicle fuel, 15th day of each month; alternate and general aviation fuels, payments accompany report.
	Petroleum inspection fee—2¢ per gallon.	
Metallic minerals occupation tax.	Percentage of net proceeds—rates change yearly and range from 0% to 15% based on net proceeds.	Reports and payments—June 15 following applicable tax year.
	Oil and gas severance tax—7% of market value of total production of oil or gas during previous year.	Reports and payments—same as metallic minerals tax.
Cigarette tax.	Cigarettes—126 mills each on cigarettes weighing 3 lbs. or less per 1,000 (12.6¢ per cigarette or $2.52 per pack of 20), plus 8 mills per cigarette minus the federal tax; 252 mills each on cigarettes weighing more than 3 lbs. per 1,000 (25.2¢ per cigarette or $5.04 per pack of 20), plus 16.8 mills per cigarette minus the federal tax.	Reports—permittees, 15th day of each month; users, within 15 days of importing more than 400 cigarettes. Payment—purchase of stamps or use of metering machine in lieu of stamps; users, accompanies report.
Tobacco products tax.	Tobacco products—71% of manufacturer's list price on domestic products; 71% of manufacturer's list price plus federal tax, duties and transportation costs to the U.S. on imported products; lesser of 71% of manufacturer's list price on cigars, not to exceed 50¢ per cigar; domestic moist snuff, 100% of manufacturer's list price.	Returns and payments—distributors, 15th day of each month.
Real estate transfer fee.	30¢ per $100 of value or fraction of realty transferred.	Reports and payments—at the time of recordation.
Sales and use taxes.	Sales tax, 5% of sales price; use tax, 5% of purchase price. 5% state vehicle rental fee for rental vehicles for 30 days or less and for limousines.	Returns and payments—on or before the last day of the month following each calendar quarter. If the tax for a quarter exceeds $1,200, monthly returns and payments may be required, due on the last day of the following month. If tho tax for a quarter exceeds $3,600, monthly returns and payments may be required, due on the 20th day of the following month.

Tax	Basis—Rates	Due Dates
Public utilities tax.	Telephone companies—tax imposed on real and tangible personal property; rate is prior year's net rate of the general property tax.	Reports—March 1. Payments—same for other public utilities, *i.e.,* May 10 and November 10.
	Car line companies—gross earnings in this state multiplied by the average net rate of taxation (tax withheld and paid by railroad companies).	Reports—April 15. Payments—September 10 of year prior to assessment and April 15 of the year of assessment.
	Electric cooperatives—apportionment factor multiplied by gross revenues multiplied by 3.19%.	Returns—March 15. Payments—May 10 and November 10 on estimated basis, one year in advance. Cooperatives with less than $2,000 liability pay full amount by May 10 of year of assessment.
	Light, heat, and power companies—0.97% of apportioned gas revenues and 3.19% of all other apportioned revenues.	Reports—March 1. Payments—May 10 and November 10 on estimated basis for current calendar year. Companies with less than $2,000 liability pay full amount by May 10 of year of assessment.
	Note: A license fee is imposed for selling electricity at wholesale; the fee amount is the apportionment factor multiplied by gross revenues from the sale of electricity at wholesale in the preceding year multiplied by 1.59%.	
Insurance companies tax.	Foreign fire insurers—2.375%. Foreign marine insurers—0.5%. Surplus lines insurers—3%.	Foreign fire, marine, casualty and life insurers reports—due March 1. Such insurers pay their estimated tax on or before the 15th day of April, June, September, and December.
	Fire companies also pay dues of 2% on premiums. Casualty, surety, and mortgage guaranty—2%. Life—foreign, 2% on gross premiums; domestic, generally same as foreign, but 3.5% tax on income may apply to some domestic life insurers. Foreign companies subject to retaliatory taxes.	

Wyoming

Tax System.—Wyoming derives its public revenue from taxes imposed on real and certain personal property of individuals and corporations and from taxes imposed upon classes of individuals and corporations carrying on specified kinds of business or engaging in particular transactions. An outline of the Wyoming tax system follows:

Tax	Basis—Rates	Due Dates
Corporation franchise (license) tax.	Domestic and foreign—$50 or $^{2}/_{10}$ of one mill on the dollar ($.0002), whichever is greater, based upon the sum of its capital, property, and assets located and employed in Wyoming.	Report and payment—first day of month of registration.
General property tax.	State and local rates fixed to meet budget. Property is assessed at 100% of fair market value for gross mineral and mine products, 11.5% for property used for industrial purposes and 9.5% for all other property.	Returns—listing of taxable property, March 1. Payment—in installments, 50% by November 10 and remaining 50% by May 10, or payment in full by December 31.
Alcoholic beverages tax.	Excise—wine, $.0075 per 100 ml.; spirituous liquor, $.025 per 100 ml.; malt beverages, $.005 per liter; manufactured wine shipped into state, 12% of retail price.	
Motor fuel tax.	Gasoline and diesel, 23¢ per gallon, plus 1¢ additional tax to fund environmental clean-up costs. Aviation fuel, 4¢ per gallon, plus 1¢ additional tax to fund environmental clean-up costs. A55, biodiesel, E-85, ethanol, methanol, gasohol, M-85, and propane are all taxed at the rate of 24 cents per gallon. Compressed natural gas (CNG) is sold at the rate of $0.24 per gasoline-gallon equivalent, liquefied petroleum gas (LPG) is sold at the rate of $0.24 per gasoline-gallon equivalent, and liquefied natural gas (LNG) is taxed at the rate of $0.24 per diesel-gallon equivalent.	Reports and payments—last day of each month for the preceding month.
Oil and gas conservation charge.	Assessed on fair market value of all oil and gas produced, transported, or sold in Wyoming—may not exceed $^{8}/_{10}$ of a mill ($0.0008); currently $^{5}/_{10}$ of a mill ($0.0005).	Payment—25th day of the 2nd month following the month in which the charge accrued.
Severance taxes.	Gross products tax—6% on crude oil, lease condensate, natural gas, and helium; 3.75% on value of underground coal; 4% of value of uranium and trona; 7% on surface coal; 2% on bentonite, sand and gravel, and oil shale or any other fossil fuel.	Reports and payments—monthly on 25th day of 2nd month following month of production; annually on February 25 if prior annual tax was under $30,000.
Cigarette tax.	30 mills per cigarette (60¢ per pack of 20 cigarettes) on sale by wholesaler or use or storage by consumer. 20% of wholesale purchase price of cigars, snuff, and other tobacco products, except moist snuff. $0.60 per ounce of moist snuff.	Returns—20th day of each month for preceding month. Payments—Cigarette tax paid by purchase and affixation of stamps or use of meters. Tobacco products are reported the 20th day of each calendar quarter for the preceding quarter, and payment must accompany the report.

Tax	Basis—Rates	Due Dates
Sales and use tax.	Sales and use taxes assessed at state rate of 4%. Additional local rate may apply.	Reports and payments—Due on or before last day of each month for preceding month's sales. If collected tax is less than $150 in any month, quarterly or annual reports and payments may be allowed, which are due on or before last day of month following each quarter or year. Vendor compensation credit for early payment allowed if taxes are paid by 15th day of the month that the taxes are due.
Insurance companies tax.	0.75% of net premiums, except 1% for annuity considerations. Effective April 1, 2020, an assessment of 0.75% is imposed on net premiums and net considerations of (1) private health benefit insurers, and (2) any plan which has entered into agreement with employee welfare benefit plans for air ambulance transport coverage. Applicable to life insurance policies issued on or after January 1, 2021, the tax rate is 0.75% on the first $100,000 of a life insurance policy's annual premium, and 0.075% on the portion of the annual premium exceeding $100,000. Wet marine and transportation insurers—0.75% of gross underwriting profit. Surplus lines insurance—3% of gross premiums charged, less any return premiums, for surplus lines insurance provided by a surplus lines broker. Foreign companies subject to retaliatory taxes.	Reports and payments—on or before March 1. Effective July 1, 2020, surplus lines broker reports and payments due quarterly on or before February 15, May 15, August 15 and November 15. Estimated payments—quarterly on or before the last day of the month immediately following the end of the calendar quarter for which payment is due. However, payment for the quarter ending December 31 is payable on or before March 1 of the succeeding year.

INCOME TAXES

The following pages contain charts on various topics relating to income-based taxes imposed by each state and the District of Columbia on corporations and individuals. Corporations are not subject to income-based taxes in Nevada, South Dakota (franchise tax on financial institutions only), Washington, and Wyoming. Individuals are not subject to income-based taxes in Alaska, Florida, Nevada, South Dakota, Texas, Washington, and Wyoming. Individuals in New Hampshire and Tennessee are taxed on interest and dividend income only.

Topics covered in this section include rates for corporations and individuals, allocation and apportionment (including UDITPA, MTC, and apportionment factors), combined reporting, and consolidated filing.

Estimated tax, withholding, and information returns are also covered, as well as conformity with federal income tax provisions, including bonus depreciation, net operating loss rules, IRC Sec. 179 asset expense deduction, and IRC Sec. 199 domestic production activities deduction.

In addition, there are charts dealing with the taxation of other types of entities, including limited liability companies, S corporations, utilities, insurance companies, and financial companies.

Table of 2020 Corporate Income Tax Rates

This chart shows the tax rates imposed on corporation income taxpayers by each state and the District of Columbia for the 2020 tax year. Minimum taxes are also included in the chart.

Jurisdiction	2020 Tax Year	Comment
Alabama	6.5% ***or*** taxpayers with $100,000 or less of gross sales within the state may pay 0.25% on such sales.	Gross sales option available only to taxpayers that do not own any property within the state.
Alaska	$0-$24,999: 0% $25,000-$48,999: 2% $49,000-$73,999: $480 plus 3% $74,000-$98,999: $1,230 plus 4% $99,000-$123,999: $2,230 plus 5% $124,000-$147,999: $3,480 plus 6% $148,000-$172,999: $4,920 plus 7% $173,000-$197,999: $6,670 plus 8% $198,000-$221,999: $8,670 plus 9% $222,000 or more: $10,830 plus 9.4%.	4.95% accumulated earnings tax imposed on first $100,000 of earnings and 6.93% of the excess. 12.6% personal holding company tax on apportioned income.
Arizona	4.9%	$50 minimum tax.
Arkansas	$0-$3,000: 1% $3,001-$6,000: 2% $6,001-$11,000: 3% $11,001-$25,000: 5% $25,001-$100,000: 6% $100,001 or more: 6.5%.	**Tax year 2021:** $0-$3,000: 1% $3,001-$6,000: 2% $6,001-$11,000: 3% $11,001-$25,000: 5% $25,001-$100,000: 6% $100,001 or more: 6.2%. **Tax years beginning on or after January 1, 2022:** $0-$3,000: 1% $3,001-$6,000: 2% $6,001-$11,000: 3% $11,001-$25,000: 5% $25,001 or more: 5.9%.
California	8.84%	$800 minimum tax. 10.84% rate on banks and financial corporations.
Colorado	4.63% ***or*** taxpayers with $100,000 or less of gross sales within the state may pay 0.5% on such sales.	Gross sales option available only to taxpayers that perform no activities in Colorado other than making sales and that do not own or rent any property within the state.

Jurisdiction	2020 Tax Year	Comment
Connecticut	*Greater of:* 7.5% of net income; 3.1 ($.0031) mills per dollar of capital holding; **or** $250 minimum tax. 10% surcharge is imposed for income tax years before January 1, 2021, if gross income is $100 million or more and tax liability exceeds minimum tax.	Financial service companies pay a tax equal to *greater of:* 7.5% of net income; **or** $250. Capital base tax decreases to: • 2.6 mills ($.0026) on each dollar of capital for the 2021 tax year; • 2.1 mills ($.0021) on each dollar of capital for the 2022 tax year; and • 1.1 mills ($.0011) on each dollar of capital for the 2023 tax year. Capital base tax no longer applies after the 2023 tax year.
Delaware	8.7%	**Headquarters management corporations**: 8.7% or $5,000 minimum tax, whichever is greater. **Banking organizations**: $0-$20,000,000: 8.7% $20,000,001-$25,000,000: 6.7% $25,000,001-$30,000,000: 4.7% $30,000,001-$650,000,000: 2.7% $650,000,001 or more: 1.7%. Banks and trust companies may elect to pay an alternative bank franchise tax.
District of Columbia	8.25%	**Minimum tax:** $250; or $1,000 for District gross receipts over $1 million. **Ball park fee imposed on gross receipts:** $5,000,000-$8,000,000: $5,500 $8,000,001-$12,000,000: $10,800 $12,000,001-$16,000,000: $14,000 $16,000,001 or more: $16,500.
Florida	4.458% minus exemption equal to smaller of: • $50,000; or • the sum of adjusted federal income apportioned to the state plus nonbusiness income allocated to the state.	Automatic rate reductions and refunds if net tax collections exceed forecasts in the 2020-2021 fiscal year.
Georgia	5.75%	
Hawaii	$0-$25,000: 4.4% $25,001-$100,000: 5.4% less $250 $100,001 or more: 6.4% less $1,250; ***or*** taxpayers with $100,000 or less of gross sales within the state may pay 0.5% on such sales. Alternative tax on capital gains is imposed at rate of 4%.	Gross sales option available only to taxpayers that have no business activity in the state other than sales and do not own or rent any property within the state. 7.92% rate on financial institutions.

Jurisdiction	2020 Tax Year	Comment
Idaho	6.925%, plus $10; ***or*** taxpayers with $100,000 or less of gross sales within the state may pay 1% on such sales.	$20 minimum tax. Gross sales option available only to taxpayers that do not own any property within the state.
Illinois	7% **plus** 2.5% personal property replacement tax.	7.99% rate for tax years after 2020, if voters approve constitutional amendment authorizing graduated personal income tax rates. Surcharge imposed on income from the sale or exchange of certain assets by: • any registrant organization under the Compassionate Use of Medical Cannabis Program; and • effective for tax years 2019-2027, gaming licensees.
Indiana	5.5% after June 30, 2019 and before July 1, 2020. 5.25% after June 30, 2020 and before July 1, 2021.	4.9% after June 30, 2021. 5% on adjusted gross income derived from sources within an area that contains an inactive or closed military base. **Financial Institutions Tax** 6.0% after December 31, 2019 and before January 1, 2021. 5.5% after December 31, 2020 and before January 1, 2022. 5.0% after December 31, 2021 and before January 1, 2023. 4.9% after December 31, 2022.
Iowa	$0-$25,000: 6% $25,000-$100,000: 8% minus $500 $100,000-$250,000: 10% minus $2,500 $250,000 or more: 12% minus $7,500.	5% franchise tax on financial institutions. **2021:** $0-$25,000: 5.5% $25,000-$100,000: 5.5% $100,000-$250,000: 9% $250,000 or more: 9.8%.
Kansas	4%, plus 3% surtax on taxable income over $50,000.	2.25% privilege tax on net income of financial institutions, plus a surtax (2.125% for banks and 2.25% for trust companies and savings and loan associations) for net income in excess of $25,000.
Kentucky	5%	Every corporation with over $3 million in gross receipts or gross profits must pay the greater of $175 or an annual limited liability entity tax (LLET) equal to lesser of: • 9.5 cents per $100 of Kentucky gross receipts; or • 75 cents per $100 of Kentucky gross profits. If gross receipts or gross profits are over $3 million but less than $6 million, gross receipts may be reduced by $2,850 or gross profits by $22,500 multiplied by a numerator of $6 million less the amount of gross receipts or gross profits for the taxable year, and a denominator of $3 million.

Jurisdiction	2020 Tax Year	Comment
Louisiana	$0-$25,000: 4% $25,001-$50,000: 5% $50,001-$100,000: 6% $100,001-$200,000: 7% $200,001 and over: 8%.	Pass-through entities that elect to be taxed as if filing as C corporations at the federal level are taxed at the following rates: $0-25,000: 2% $25,001-$100,000: 4% $100,001 and over: 6%.
Maine	$0-$350,000: 3.5% $350,001-$1,050,000: $12,250 plus 7.93% $1,050,001-$3,500,000: $67,760 plus 8.33% $3,500,001 or more: $271,845 plus 8.93%.	**Financial institutions franchise tax:** • 1% of net income, plus 8¢ per $1,000 of assets attributable to state sources; or • 39¢ per $1,000 of assets attributable to state sources.
Maryland	8.25%	For taxable years beginng on or after January 1, 2020, pass-through entities electing to pay the state tax at the entity level are subject to a rate at the sum of the lowest county tax rate imposed (2.25%) and the top marginal state tax rate for individuals (5.75%) applied to the sum of each individual member's distributive or pro rata share of the pass-through's taxable income. For corporation members, the tax rate is equal to the state corporate income tax rate (8.25%) applied to the sum of each member's distributive or pro rata share of the pass-through's taxable income.
Massachusetts	*Greater of:* $2.60 per $1,000 on taxable tangible property or net worth **plus** 8% on income attributable to state sources; ***or*** $456 fixed dollar minimum tax.	0.63% payroll tax on most employers for state medical and family leave program.
Michigan	Corporate income tax imposed at rate of 6%. Michigan Business Tax (MBT) imposed at rate of 4.95% and modified gross receipts tax imposed at rate of 0.8% on receipts of $350,000 or more.	MBT repealed Jan. 1, 2012, except for those taxpayers with certificated credits that elect to pay the MBT.
Minnesota	9.8%, plus minimum tax ranging from $0 to $10,380 based on property, payroll, and sales or receipts attributable to state sources.	
Mississippi	$3,000-$5,000: 3% $5,001-$10,000: 4% $10,001 or more: 5%.	The tax on the first $5,000 of income is being phased out by exempting $1,000 in 2018 and increasing that amount by $1,000 per year until 2022. The 3% rate will be: • $4,000-$5,000 in 2021 • no tax on income under $5,000 in 2022 and thereafter.

Jurisdiction	2020 Tax Year	Comment
Missouri	4%	**Financial Institutions Tax** 7%, but subject to reduction for tax years beginning after 2019 under provision requiring corresponding and proportionate reduction in the financial institutions tax rate when there is a reduction in the corporate tax rate.
Montana	6.75% ***or*** taxpayers with $100,000 or less of gross sales within the state may pay 0.5% on such sales. 7% for water's edge combined reporting groups.	$50 minimum tax. Gross sales option available only to taxpayers that do not own any property within the state.
Nebraska	$0 - $100,000: 5.58% $100,001 or more: $5,580 plus 7.81%.	
Nevada	N/A, because state does not tax general business corporation income.	
New Hampshire	**For tax periods ending on or after December 31, 2019, and before December 31, 2021:** 7.7% of taxable business profits for gross income over $50,000. 0.6% of business enterprise value base for gross income over $217,000 or enterprise value base over $108,000.	Thresholds for gross income and enterprise value base are indexed for inflation. **For tax periods ending on or after December 31, 2021:** 7.5%, 7.7% or 7.9%, depending on revenue collections, of taxable business profits. 0.5%, 0.6%, or 0.675%, depending on revenue collections, of business enterprise value base.

Jurisdiction	2020 Tax Year	Comment
New Jersey	*Greater of:* $0-$50,000: 6.5% $50,001-$100,000: 7.5% $100,001 or more: 9%; ***or*** alternative minimum assessment, if applicable; ***or*** fixed dollar minimum tax based on gross receipts. ***Fixed dollar minimum tax:*** $0-$99,999 gross receipts: $500 $100,000-$249,999 gross receipts: $750 $250,000-$499,999 gross receipts: $1,000 $500,000-$999,999 gross receipts: $1,500 $1,000,000 gross receipts or more: $2,000. ***Fixed dollar minimum tax (NJ S corporations):*** $0-$99,999 gross receipts: $375 $100,000-$249,999 gross receipts: $562.50 $250,000-$499,999 gross receipts: $750 $500,000-$999,999 gross receipts: $1,125 $1,000,000 gross receipts or more: $1,500. ***Surtax on corporations in 2020 and 2021:*** 2.5% if the corporation has allocated taxable net income over $1 million.	$2,000 minimum tax for members of affiliated or controlled group with total payroll of $5 million or more. $2,000 minimum tax for each member of a combined reporting group filing a combined return. **Pass-through Business Alternative Tax:** For electing entities the tax rate on the share of each distribution is: • under $250,000, 5.675% of the sum of distributive proceeds; • over $250,000 but not over $1,000,000, $14,187.50 plus 6.52% of the excess over $250,000; • over $1,000,000 but not over $5,000,000, $63,087.50 plus 9.12% of the excess over $1,000,000; or • over $5,000,000 $427,887.50 plus 10.9% of the excess over $5,000,000. If Connecticut, New York, and Massachusetts enact legislation having an identical effect, there will be an additional 17% surtax on income received from investment management services.
New Mexico	$0-$500,000: 4.8% over $500,00: 5.9%; ***or*** taxpayers with $100,000 or less of gross sales within the state may pay 0.75% on such sales.	Gross sales option available only to taxpayers whose only activity in the state consists of making sales, and who do not own or rent real estate in the state.
New York	*Greater of:* • business income base of 6.5% (0% for qualified in-state manufacturers, 4.875% for qualified emerging technology companies (QETCs)); • capital tax base of 0.025% (0.019% for qualified in-state manufacturers and QETCs) per dollar of allocated capital (up to $350,000 for qualified in-state manufacturers and QETCs or $5 million for other taxpayers); ***or*** • fixed dollar minimum tax based on receipts attributable to state sources. ***Fixed dollar minimum tax:*** ranges from $25 (if state receipts are not more than $100,000) to $200,000 (if state receipts are over $1 billion). ***Small business taxpayers:*** 6.5%.	After 2020, capital base tax is fully phased out at 0%. Special fixed dollar minimum tax amounts apply to qualified in-state manufacturers and QETCs, as well as non-captive REITs and RICs.
North Carolina	2.5%	

Jurisdiction	2020 Tax Year	Comment
North Dakota	$0-$25,000: 1.41% $25,001-$50,000: 3.55% $50,001 or more: 4.31%. 3.5% additional tax for water's edge combined reporting groups.	
Ohio	**Commercial activity tax (CAT):** 0.26% on gross receipts over $1 million. Annual minimum tax also applies as follows: $150,000-$1 million: $150 over $1 million-$2 million: $800 over $2 million-$4 million: $2,100 over $4 million: $2,600.	**Financial institutions tax (FIT):** Greater of: • 8 mills (.008) on the first $200 million in apportioned total equity capital, 4 mills (.004) on apportioned total equity capital greater than $200 million and less than $1.3 billion, and 2.5 mills (.0025) on apportioned total equity capital equal to or greater than $1.3 billion; or • $1,000.
Oklahoma	6%	
Oregon	*Greater of:* 6.6% on first $1 million or fraction thereof, 7.6% on taxable income over $1 million;**or** fixed dollar minimum tax based on Oregon sales. Taxpayers with $100,000 or less in gross sales within the state may pay 0.25% on such sales or 0.0125% on such sales if return on sales is less than 5%. ***Fixed dollar minimum tax:*** $0-$499,999: $150 $500,000-$999,999: $500 $1,000,000-$1,999,999: $1,000 $2,000,000-$2,999,999: $1,500 $3,000,000-$4,999,999: $2,000 $5,000,000-$6,999,999: $4,000 $7,000,000-$9,999,999: $7,500 $10,000,000-$24,999,999: $15,000 $25,000,000-$49,999,999: $30,000 $50,000,000-$74,999,999: $50,000 $75,000,000-$99,999,999: $75,000 $100,000,000 or over: $100,000.	Gross sales option available only to taxpayers that do not own any property within the state. **Corporate Activity Tax:** Beginning in 2020, corporations may be required to pay CAT. The tax for each calendar year will equal $250 plus the product of the taxpayer's taxable commercial activity in excess of $1 million multiplied by 0.57%.
Pennsylvania	9.99%	
Rhode Island	*Greater of:* net income tax of 7%; ***or*** minimum tax of $400.	**Registered personal holding companies, RICs, and REITs:** *Greater of:* 10 cents on each $100 of gross income; *or* $100. Pass-through entities electing to pay the state tax at the entity level are subject to a rate of 5.99%.
South Carolina	5%	4.5% rate on banks. 6% rate on most net income of savings and loan associations after first three years of operation.
South Dakota	N/A, because state does not tax general business corporation income.	
Tennessee	6.5%	

Jurisdiction	2020 Tax Year	Comment
Texas	0.75% for most entities. 0.375% for qualifying wholesalers and retailers. 0.331% for entities with $20 million or less in annualized total revenue using the E-Z computation.	Tax is imposed on lesser of 70% of total revenue, total revenue less $1,000,000, or 100% of total revenue after deductions for either compensation or cost of goods sold.
Utah	4.95%	$100 minimum tax.
Vermont	$0-$10,000: $0 plus 6% $10,001-$25,000: $600 plus 7% $25,001 and over: $1,650 plus 8.5%.	Minimum tax equal to the following: • $75 for small farm corporations; • $300 for corporations with $2 million or less in gross receipts; • $500 for corporations with gross receipts over $2 million; • $750 for corporations with gross receipts over $5 million.
Virginia	6%	**Telecommunication companies:** Greater of tax using corporate rate or 0.5% minimum tax on gross receipts. **Electric suppliers:** Greater of tax using corporate rate or 1.45% minimum tax on gross receipts.
Washington	N/A, because state does not tax general business corporation income.	
West Virginia	6.5%	
Wisconsin	7.9%	$25 up to $9,800 economic development surcharge if gross receipts are $4 million or more.
Wyoming	N/A, because state does not tax general business corporation income.	

Personal Income Table of 2020 Rates

This chart provides the 2020 tax rates that the states and the District of Columbia impose on personal income. The graduated rate information is presented in a format that includes a subtraction amount, which is used to properly reflect the cumulative tax calculated for the lower graduated rates. The use of this format for all of the states allows the rate information to be presented in a uniform way. The rates shown are state rates only. Local income taxes may apply.

Jurisdiction	2020 Tax Year	Comment
Alabama	Single, Head of Family, Married Filing Separately: $0 - 500 x 2.000% minus $0 $501 - 3,000 x 4.000% minus $10 $3,001 and over x 5.000% minus $40 Married Filing Jointly: $0 - 1,000 x 2.000% minus $0 $1,001 - 6,000 x 4.000% minus $20 $6,001 and over x 5.000% minus $80	
Arizona	Single, Married Filing Separately: $0 - 27,272 x 2.59% minus $0 $27,273 - 54,544 x 3.34% minus $205.00 $54,545 - 163,632 x 4.17% minus $657.00 $163,633 and over x 4.50% minus $1,197.00 Married Filing Jointly, Head of Household: $0 - 54,544 x 2.59% minus $0 $54,545 - 109,088 x 3.34% minus $409.00 $109,089 - 327,263 x 4.17% minus $1,315.00 $327,264 and over x 4.50% minus $2,394.00	Brackets indexed annually for inflation.
Arkansas	**Tax year 2020:** For net income under $22,200 rates range from 0% up to 3.4%. For net income from $22,200 to $79,300 rates range from 0.75% up to 5.9%. For net income over $79,300, rates range from 2% to 6.6%.	Bracketed numbers have not yet been indexed for inflation for 2020. Brackets indexed for inflation annually.

Jurisdiction	2020 Tax Year	Comment
California	Single, Married/RDP Filing Separately: $0 - $8,932 x 1.0% minus $0 $8,933 - $21,175 x 2.0% minus $89.32 $21,176 - $33,421 x 4.0% minus $512.82 $33,422 - $46,394 x 6.0% minus $1,181.24 $46,395 - $58,634 x 8.0% minus $2,109.12 $58,635 - $299,508 x 9.30% minus $2,871.36 $299,509 - $359,407 x 10.30% minus $5,866.44 $359,408 - $599,012 x 11.30% minus $9,460.51 $599,013 and over x 12.30% minus $15,450.63 Married/RDP Filing Jointly, Qualifying Widow(er): $0 - $17,864 x 1.0% minus $0 $17,865 - $42,350 x 2.0% minus $178.64 $42,351 - $66,842 x 4.0% minus $1,025.64 $66,843 - $92,788 x 6.0% minus $2,362.48 $92,789 - $117,268 x 8.0% minus $4,218.24 $117,269 - $599,016 x 9.30% minus $5,742.73 $599,017 - $718,814 x 10.30% minus $11,732.89 $718,815 - $1,198,024 x 11.30% minus $18,921.03 $1,198,025 and over x 12.30% minus $30,901.27 Head of Household: $0 - $17,876 x 1.0% minus $0 $17,877 - $42,353 x 2.0% minus $178.76 $42,354 - $54,597 x 4.0% minus $1,025.82 $54,598 - $67,569 x 6.0% minus $2,117.76 $67,570 - $79,812 x 8.0% minus $3,469.14 $79,813 - $407,329 x 9.30% minus $4,506.70 $407,330 - $488,796 x 10.30% minus $8,579.99 $488,797 - $814,658 x 11.30% minus $13,467.94 $814,659 and over x 12.30% minus $21,614.52 An additional 1% tax is imposed on taxable income in excess of $1 million.	Brackets indexed for inflation annually.

Jurisdiction	2020 Tax Year	Comment
Colorado	4.55% of federal taxable income, regardless of filing status.	Rate was 4.63% for tax years commencing prior to January 1, 2020. The rate decrease was approved via ballot initiative (Proposition 116) in the November 3, 2020, general election. Individual taxpayers are subject to an alternative minimum tax equal to the amount by which 3.47% of their CO alternative minimum taxable income exceeds their CO normal tax.
Connecticut	Single, Married Filing Separately: $0 - 10,000 x 3.000% minus $0 $10,001 - 50,000 x 5.000% minus $200 $50,001 - 100,000 x 5.500% minus $450 $100,001 -200,000 x 6.000% minus $950 $200,001 - 250,000 x 6.500% minus $1,950 $250,001 - 500,000 x 6.900% minus $2,950 $500,001 and over x 6.990% minus $3,400 Filing Jointly, Qualifying Widow(er): $0 - 20,000 x 3.000% minus $0 $20,001 - 100,000 x 5.000% minus $400 $100,001 - 200,000 x 5.500% minus $900 $200,001 - 400,000 x 6.000% minus $1,900 $400,001 - 500,000 x 6.500% minus $3,900 $500,001 - 1,000,000 x 6.900% minus $5,900 $1,000,001 and over x 6.990% minus $6,800 Head of Household: $0 - 16,000 x 3.000% minus $0 $16,001 - 80,000 x 5.000% minus $320 $80,001 - 160,000 x 5.500% minus $720 $160,001 - 320,000 x 6.000% minus $1,520 $320,001 - 400,000 x 6.500% minus $3,120 $400,001 - 800,000 x 6.900% minus $4,720 $800,001 and over x 6.990% minus $5,440	Resident estates and trusts are subject to 6.99% rate on all income.

Jurisdiction	2020 Tax Year	Comment
Delaware	$0 - 2,000 x 0.000% minus $0 $2,001 - 5,000 x 2.200% minus $44.00 $5,001 - 10,000 x 3.900% minus $129.00 $10,001 - 20,000 x 4.800% minus $219.00 $20,001 - 25,000 x 5.200% minus $299.00 $25,001 - 60,000 x 5.550% minus $386.50 $60,001 and over x 6.600% minus $1,106.50	
District of Columbia	$0 - 10,000 x 4.000% minus $0 $10,001 - 40,000 x 6.000% minus $200.00 $40,001 -60,000 x 6.500% minus $400.00 $60,001 - 350,000 x 8.500% minus $1,600.00 $350,001 - 1,000,000 x 8.7500% minus $2,475.00 $1,000,001 and over x 8.950% minus $4,475.00	
Georgia	Single: $0 - 750 x 1.000% minus $0 $751 - 2,250 x 2.000% minus $7.50 $2,251 - 3,750 x 3.000% minus $30.00 $3,751 - 5,250 x 4.000% minus $67.50 $5,251 - 7,000 x 5.000% minus $120.00 $7,001 and over x 5.75% minus $190.00 Married Filing Jointly, Head of Household: $0 - 1,000 x 1.000% minus $0 $1,001 - 3,000 x 2.000% minus $10.00 $3,001 - 5,000 x 3.000% minus $40.00 $5,001 - 7,000 x 4.000% minus $90.00 $7,001 - 10,000 x 5.000% minus $160.00 10,001 and over x 5.75% minus $260.00 Married Filing Separately: $0 - 500 x 1.000% minus $0 $501 - 1,500 x 2.000% minus $5.00 $1,501 - 2,500 x 3.000% minus $20.00 $2,501 - 3,500 x 4.000% minus $45.00 $3,501 - 5,000 x 5.000% minus $80.00 $5,001 and over x 5.75% minus $130.00	

Jurisdiction	2020 Tax Year	Comment
Hawaii	Single and Married Filing Separately: $0 - 2,400 x 1.400% minus $0 $2,401 - 4,800 x 3.200% minus $43.20 $4,801 - 9,600 x 5.500% minus $153.60 $9,601 - 14,400 x 6.400% minus $240.00 $14,401 - 19,200 x 6.800% minus $297.60 $19,201 - 24,000 x 7.200% minus $374.40 $24,001 - 36,000 x 7.600% minus $470.40 $36,001 - 48,000 x 7.900% minus $578.40 $48,001 -150,000 x 8.250% minus $746.40 $150,001 -175,000 x 9.000% minus $1,871.40 $175,001 - 200,000 x 10.000% minus $3,621.40 $200,001 and over x 11.00% minus $5,621.40 Married Filing Jointly, Surviving Spouse: $0 - 4,800 x 1.400% minus $0 $4,801 - 9,600 x 3.200% minus $86.40 $9,601 - 19,200 x 5.500% minus $307.20 $19,201 - 28,800 x 6.400% minus $480.00 $28,801 - 38,400 x 6.800% minus $595.20 $38,401 - 48,000 x 7.200% minus $748.80 $48,001 - 72,000 x 7.600% minus $940.80 $72,001 -96,000 x 7.900% minus $1,156.80 $96,001 -300,000 x 8.250% minus $1,492.80 $300,001 - 350,000 x 9.000% minus $3,742.80 $350,001 - 400,000 x 10.000% minus $7,242.80 $400,001 and over x 11.000% minus $11,242.80 Head of Household: $0 - 3,600 x 1.400% minus $0 $3,601 - 7,200 x 3.200% minus $64.80 $7,201 - 14,400 x 5.500% minus $230.40 $14,401 - 21,600 x 6.400% minus $360.00 $21,601 - 28,800 x 6.800% minus $446.40 $28,801 -36,000 x 7.200% minus $561.60 36,001 - 54,000 x 7.600% minus $705.60 $54,001 - 72,000 x 7.900% minus $867.60 $72,001 - 225,000 x 8.250% minus $1,119.60	

Jurisdiction	2020 Tax Year	Comment
	$225,001 - 262,500 x 9.000% minus $2,807.10 $262,501 - 300,000 x 10.00% minus $5,432.10 $300,001 and over x 11.000% minus $8,432.10	
Idaho	Single, Married Filing Separately: $0 - 1,567 x 1.125% minus $0 $1,568 - 3,135 x 3.125% minus $31.34 $3,136-4,703 x 3.625% minus $47.01 $4,704 - 6,271 x 4.625% minus $94.04 $6,272- 7,839 x 5.625% minus $156.75 $7,840 - 11,759 x 6.625% minus $235.14 $11,760 and over x 6.925% minus $270.42 Married Filing Jointly, Head of Household, Surviving Spouse: $0 - 3,135 x 1.125% minus $0 $3,136 - 6,271 x 3.125% minus $62.70 $6,272 - 9,407 x 3.625% minus $94.05 $9,408 - 12,543 x 4.625% minus $188.12 $12,544 - 15,679 x 5.625% minus $313.55 $15,680 – 23,519 x 6.625% minus $470.34 $23,520 and over x 6.925% minus $540.90	Brackets indexed for inflation annually.
Illinois	4.95% of federal AGI, regardless of filing status.	Surcharge imposed on income from the sale or exchange of certain assets by: • any registrant organization under the Compassionate Use of Medical Cannabis Program; and • effective for tax years 2019-2027, gaming licensees.
Indiana	3.23% of AGI, regardless of filing status.	Counties may impose an adjusted gross income tax on residents or on nonresidents, or a county option income tax.

Jurisdiction	2020 Tax Year	Comment
Iowa	$0 - 1,666 x 0.330% minus $0 $1,667 - 3,332 x 0.670% minus $5.66 $3,333 - 6,664 x 2.250% minus $58.31 $6,665 - 14,994 x 4.140% minus $184.26 $14,995 - 24,990 x 5.630% minus $407.68 $24,991 - 33,320 x 5.960% minus $490.14 $33,321 -49,980 x 6.250% minus $586.77 $49,981 - 74,970 x 7.440% minus $1,181.53 $74,971 and over x 8.530% minus $1,998.70	An alternative minimum tax of 6.7% of alternative minimum income is imposed if the minimum tax exceeds the taxpayer's regular income tax liability. The minimum tax is 75% of the maximum regular tax rate. Brackets indexed for inflation annually. **2021:** $0 - 1,676 x 0.330% minus $0 $1,676 - 3,352 x 0.670% minus $5.70 $3,352 - 6,704 x 2.250% minus $58.66 $6,704 - 15,084 x 4.140% minus $185.37 $15,084 - 25,140 x 5.630% minus $410.12 $25,140 -33,520 x 5.960% minus $493.08 $33,520 - 50,280 x 6.250% minus $590.29 $50,280 - 75,420 x 7.440% minus $1,188.62 $75,420 and over x 8.530% minus $2,010.70
Kansas	Single, Head of Household, Married Filing Separately: $0 - $2,500, tax liability is $0 $2,501 - $15,000 x 3.100% minus $0 $15,001 - 30,000 x 5.250% minus $322.50 $30,001 and over x 5.700% minus $457.50 Married Filing Jointly: $0 - $5,000, tax liability is $0 $5,001 - 30,000 x 3.100% minus $0 $30,001 - 60,000 x 5.250% minus $645.00 $60,001 and over x 5.700% minus $915.00	
Kentucky	5%	
Louisiana	Single, Head of household, Married Filing Separately: $0 - 12,500 x 2.000% minus $0 $12,501 - 50,000 x 4.000% minus $250.00 $50,001 and over x 6.000% minus $1,250.00 Married Filing Jointly, Qualifying Widow(er): $0 - 25,000 x 2.000% minus $0 $25,001 - 100,000 x 4.000% minus $500.00 $100,001 and over x 6.000% minus $2,500.00	

Jurisdiction	2020 Tax Year	Comment
Maine	Single and Married Filing Separately: $0 - 22,199 x 5.800% minus $0 $22,200 - 52,599 x 6.750% minus $210.89 $52,600 and over x 7.150% minus $421.29 Married Filing Jointly, Surviving Spouse: $0 - 44,449 x 5.800% minus $0 $44,450 - 105,199 x 6.750% minus $422.26 $105,200 and more x 7.150% minus $843.06 Head of household: $0 - 33,299 x 5.800% minus $0 $33,300 - 78,899 x 6.750% minus $316.34 $78,900 and more x 7.150% minus $631.94	**2021 Tax Year:** Single and Married Filing Separately: $0 - 22,450 x 5.800% minus $0 $22,450 - 53,150 x 6.750% minus $213.28 $53,150 and over x 7.150% minus $425.87 Married Filing Jointly, Surviving Spouse: $0 - 44,950 x 5.800% minus $0 $44,950 - 106,350 x 6.750% minus $427.03 $106,350 and more x 7.150% minus $852.42 Head of household: $0 - 33,650 x 5.800% minus $0 $33,650 - 79,750 x 6.750% minus $319.68 $79,750 and more x 7.150% minus $638.67. Brackets indexed for inflation annually.
Maryland	Single, Married Filing Separately, and Dependent Taxpayers: $0 - 1,000 x 2.000% minus $0 $1,001 -2,000 x 3.000% minus $10 $2,001 - 3,000 x 4.000% minus $30 $3,001-100,000 x 4.750% minus $52.50 $100,001-125,000 x 5.000% minus $302.50 $125,001 -150,000 x 5.250% minus $615 $150,001-$250,000 x 5.500% minus $990 over $250,000 x 5.750% minus $1,615 Married Filing Jointly, Head of Household, and Qualifying Widow/ Widower: $0 - 1,000 x 2.000% minus $0 $1,001 -2,000 x 3.000% minus $10 $2,001 - 3,000 x 4.000% minus $30 $3,001-150,000 x 4.75% minus $52.50 $150,001-175,000 x 5.000% minus $427.50 $175,001-225,000 x 5.250% minus $865 $225,001-$300,000 x 5.500% minus $1,427.50 over $300,000 x 5.750% minus $2,177.50	

Jurisdiction	2020 Tax Year	Comment
Massachusetts	12% on Part A income from short term capital gains, long term capital gains from collectibles, and long term capital gains from pre-1996 installment sales. 5% on Part A interest and dividend income. 5% on Part B income from wages, salaries, tips, pensions, business income, rents, etc. 5% on Part C income from long term capital gains, except long term capital gains from collectibles and pre-1996 installment sales. Effective beginning July 1, 2019, 0.75% payroll tax on most employers and employees for state medical and family leave program.	5.85% optional rate may be elected for Part A interest and dividend income, Part B income after exemptions, and Part C income.
Michigan	4.25%	For tax years beginning after 2022, tax rate may decrease if certain conditions are met.
Minnesota	Single: $0 - $26,960 x 5.350% minus $0 $26,961 - $88,550 x 6.800% minus $390.92 $88,551 - $164,400 x 7.850% minus $1,320.69 $164,401 and over x 9.850% minus $4,608.69 Married Filing Jointly: $0 - $39,410 x 5.350% minus $0 $39,411 - $156,570 x 6.800% minus $571.44 $156,571 - $273,470 x 7.850% minus $2,215.43 $273,471 and over x 9.850% minus $7,684.83 Married Filing Separately: $0 - $19,705 x 5.350% minus $0 $19,706 - $78,285 x 6.800% minus $285.72 $78,286 - $136,735 x 7.850% minus $1,107.71 $136,736 and over x 9.850% minus $3,842.41 Head of Household: $0 - $33,190 x 5.350% minus $0 $33,191 - $133,360 x 6.800% minus $481.25 $133,361 - $218,540 x 7.850% minus $1,881.53 $218,541 and over x 9.850% minus $6,252.33	A 6.75% alternative minimum tax is imposed. Brackets indexed for inflation annually.
Mississippi	$3,000 - 5,000 x 3.000% minus $0 $5,001 - 10,000 x 4.000% minus $50.00 $10,001 and over x 5.000% minus $150.00	The tax on the first $5,000 of income is being phased out by exempting $1,000 in 2018 and increasing that amount by $1,000 per year until 2022. The 3% rate will be: • $4,000-$5,000 in 2021 • no tax on income under $5,000 in 2022 and thereafter.

Jurisdiction	2020 Tax Year	Comment
Missouri	$0 - 106 x 0.000% minus $0 $107 - 1,073 x 1.500% minus $1.61 $1,074 - 2,146 x 2.000% minus $6.97 $2,147 - 3,219 x 2.500% minus $17.70 $3,220 - 4,292 x 3.000% minus $33.79 $4,293 - 5,365 x 3.500% minus $55.25 $5,366 - 6,438 x 4.000% minus $82.07 $6,439 - 7,511 x 4.500% minus $114.26 $7,512 - 8,584 x 5.000% minus $151.81 $8,585 and over x 5.400% minus $186.15	The top rate may be reduced by 0.1% for each year that the net general revenue collected in the previous fiscal year exceeds the highest amount of net general revenue in any one of the three fiscal years prior to such year by at least $150 million. However, no more than five of these reductions can be made.
Montana	$0 - 3,100 x 1.000% minus $0 $3,101 - 5,500 x 2.000% minus $31.00 $5,501 - 8,400 x 3.000% minus $86.00 $8,401 - 11,300 x 4.000% minus $170.00 $11,301 - 14,500 x 5.000% minus $283.00 $14,501 - 18,700 x 6.000% minus $428.00 $18,701 and over x 6.900% minus $596.00	Minimum tax, $1. Brackets indexed for inflation annually.
Nebraska	Single: $0 - 3,230 x 2.460% minus $0 $3,231 – 19,330 x 3.510% minus $33.91 $19,331 – 31,160 x 5.010% minus $323.87 $31,161 and over x 6.840% minus $894.09 Married Filing Jointly, Surviving Spouse: $0 - 6,440 x 2.460% minus $0 $6,441 - 38,680 x 3.510% minus $67.63 $38,681 – 62,320 x 5.010% minus $647.83 $62,321 and over x 6.840% minus $1,788.29 Married Filing Separately: $0 - 3,230 x 2.460% minus $0 $3,231 – 19,330 x 3.510% minus $33.91 $19,331 – 31,160 x 5.010% minus $323.87 $31,161 and over x 6.840% minus $894.09 Head of Household: $0 – 6,020 x 2.460% minus $0 $6,021 - 30,940 x 3.510% minus $63.21 $30,941 – 46,200 x 5.010% minus $527.31 $46,201 and over x 6.840% minus $1,372.77	Rates shown are for 2019 tax year. Brackets indexed for inflation annually.

Jurisdiction	2020 Tax Year	Comment
New Hampshire	5% on interest and dividends only, regardless of filing status.	
New Jersey	Single, Married/Civil Union Partner Filing Separately: $0 - 20,000 x 1.400% minus $0 $20,001 - 35,000 x 1.750% minus $70.00 $35,001 - 40,000 x 3.500% minus $682.50 $40,001 - 75,000 x 5.525% minus $1,492.50 $75,001 - 500,000 x 6.370% minus $2,126.25 $500,001 - $1,000,000 x 8.970% minus $15,126.25 $1,000,001 and over x 10.750% minus $32,926.25 Married/Civil Union Couple Filing Jointly, Head of Household, Qualifying Widow(er)/Surviving Civil Union Partner: $0 - 20,000 x 1.400% minus $0 $20,001 - 50,000 x 1.750% minus $70.00 $50,001 - 70,000 x 2.450% minus $420.00 $70,001 - 80,000 x 3.500% minus $1,154.50 $80,001 - 150,000 x 5.525% minus $2,775.00 $150,001 - 500,000 x 6.370% minus $4,042.50 $500,001 - $1,000,000 x 8.970% minus $17,042.50 $1,000,001 and over x 10.750% minus $34,842.50	If Connecticut, New York, and Massachusetts enact legislation having an identical effect, there will be an additional 17% surtax on income received from investment management services.

Jurisdiction	2020 Tax Year	Comment
New Mexico	Single: $0 - 5,500 x 1.700% minus $0 $5,501 - 11,000 x 3.200% minus $82.50 $11,001 -16,000 x 4.700% minus $247.50 $16,001 and over x 4.900% minus $279.50 Married Filing Jointly, Head of Household, Qualifying Widow(er): $0 - 8,000 x 1.700% minus $0 $8,001 - 16,000 x 3.200% minus $120.00 $16,001 - 24,000 x 4.700% minus $360.00 $24,001 and over x 4.900% minus $408.00 Married Filing Separately: $0 - 4,000 x 1.700% minus $0 $4,001 - 8,000 x 3.200% minus $60.00 $8,001 - 12,000 x 4.700% minus $180.00 $12,001 and over x 4.900% minus $204.00	Qualified nonresident taxpayers may pay alternative tax of 0.75% of gross receipts from sales in state. If revenue growth from FY 2019 to FY 2020 is not more than 5%, then effective January 1, 2021, the following rates will take effect: Single: $0 - 5,500 x 1.700% minus $0 $5,501 - 11,000 x 3.200% minus $82.50 $11,001 - 16,000 x 4.700% minus $247.50 $16,001 - 210,000 x 4.900% minus $279.50 $210,001 and over x 5.900% minus $2,379.50 Married Filing Jointly, Head of Household, Qualifying Widow(er): $0 - 8,000 x 1.700% minus $0 $8,001 - 16,000 x 3.200% minus $120.00 $16,001 - 24,000 x 4.700% minus $360.00 $24,001 -$315,000 x 4.900% minus $408.00 $315,001 and over x 5.900% minus $3,558.00 Married Filing Separately: $0 - 4,000 x 1.700% minus $0 $4,001 - 8,000 x 3.200% minus $60.00 $8,001 - 12,000 x 4.700% minus $180.00 $12,001 - 157,500 x 4.900% minus $204.00 $157,501 and over x 5.9% minus $1,779.00

Jurisdiction	2020 Tax Year	Comment
New York	Single, Married Filing Separately: $0 - 8,500 x 4.000% minus $0 $8,501 - 11,700 x 4.500% minus $42.50 $11,701 - 13,900 x 5.250% minus $130.25 $13,901 - 21,400 x 5.900% minus $220.60 $21,401 -80,650 x 6.090% minus $261.26 $80,651 - 215,400 x 6.410% minus $519.33 $215,401 - 1,077,550 x 6.850% minus $1,467.09 $1,077,551 and over x 8.820% minus $22,694.82 Married Filing Jointly, Qualifying Widow(er): $0 - 17,150 x 4.000% minus $0 $17,151 - 23,600 x 4.500% minus $85.75 $23,601 -27,900 x 5.250% minus $262.75 $27,901 - 43,000 x 5.900% minus $444.10 $43,001 - 161,550 x 6.090% minus $525.80 $161,551 - 323,200 x 6.410% minus $1,042.75 $323,201 - 2,155,350 x 6.850% minus $2,464.83 $2,155,351 and over x 8.820% minus $44,925.22 Head of Household: $0 - 12,800 x 4.000% minus $0 $12,801 - 17,650 x 4.500% minus $64.00 $17,651 - 20,900 x 5.250% minus $196.37 $20,901 - 32,200 x 5.900% minus $332.22 $32,201 - 107,650 x 6.090% minus $393.40 $107,651 - 269,300 x 6.410% minus $737.87 $269,301 - 1,616,450 x 6.850% minus $1,922.79 $1,616,451 and over x 8.820% minus $33,766.85	Supplemental tax imposed to recapture tax table benefit.
North Carolina	Flat tax of 5.25%.	

Jurisdiction	2020 Tax Year	Comment
North Dakota	Single: $0 - 40,125 x 1.10% minus $0 $40,126 - 97,150 x 2.04% minus $377.17 $97,151 -202,650 x 2.27% minus $600.62 $202,651 -440,600 x 2.64% minus $1,350.42 $440,601 and over x 2.90% minus $2,495.98 Married Filing Jointly, Qualifying Widow(er): $0 - 67,050 x 1.10% minus $0 $67,051 - 161,950 x 2.04% minus $630.27 $161,951 - 246,700 x 2.27% minus $1,002.75 $246,701-440,600 x 2.64% minus $1,915.54 $440,601 and over x 2.90% minus $3,061.10 Married Filing Separately: $0 - 33,525 x 1.10% minus $0 $33,526 - 80,975 x 2.04% minus $315.13 $80,976 -123,350 x 2.27% minus $501.38 $123,351 -220,300 x 2.64% minus $957.77 $220,301 and over x 2.90% minus $1,530.55 Head of Household: $0 - 53,750 x 1.10% minus $0 $53,751 - 138,800 x 2.04% minus $505.25 $138,801- 224,700 x 2.27% minus $824.49 $224,701 - 440,600 x 2.64% minus $1,655.88 $440,601 and over x 2.90% minus $2,801.44	Brackets indexed for inflation annually.
Ohio	$22,150 - 44,250 x 2.850% minus $631.28 $44,250 - 88,450 x 3.326% minus $841.91 $88,450 -110,650 x 3.802% minus $1,262.93 $110,650 - 221,300 x 4.413% minus $1,939.01 $221,300 and over x 4.797% minus $2,788.80	3% on taxable business income over the amount of the business income deduction. Rates shown reflect the annual adjustment for inflation.

Jurisdiction	2020 Tax Year	Comment
Oklahoma	Single, Married Filing Separately: $0 - 1,000 x 0.500% minus $0 $1,001 - 2,500 x 1.000% minus $5.00 $2,501 - 3,750 x 2.000% minus $30.00 $3,751 - 4,900 x 3.000% minus $67.50 $4,901 - 7,200 x 4.000% minus $116.50 $7,201 and over x 5.000% minus $188.50 Married Filing Jointly, Qualifying Widow(er), Head of Household: $0 - 2,000 x 0.500% minus $0 $2,001 - 5,000 x 1.000% minus $10.00 $5,001 - 7,500 x 2.000% minus $60.00 $7,501 - 9,800 x 3.000% minus $135.00 $9,801 - 12,200 x 4.000% minus $233.00 $12,201 and over x 5.000% minus $355.00	
Oregon	Single, Married Filing Separately: $0 - 3,600 x 4.750% minus $0 $3,601 - 9,050 x 6.750% minus $72.00 $9,051 - 125,000 x 8.750% minus $252.99 $125,001 and over x 9.9% minus $1,690.49 Married Filing Jointly, Qualifying Widow(er), Head of Household: $0 - 7,200 x 4.750% minus $0 $7,201 - 18,100 x 6.750% minus $144.00 $18,101 - 250,000 x 8.750% minus $506.00 $250,001 and over x 9.9% minus $3,381.00	Brackets indexed for inflation annually, except for taxable income of $125,000 or over.
Pennsylvania	3.07% of taxable compensation, net profits, net gains from the sale of property, rent, royalties, patents or copyrights, income from estates or trusts, dividends, interest, and winnings.	
Rhode Island	$0 - 65,250 x 3.750% minus $0 $65,251 - 148,350 x 4.750% minus $652.50 $148,351 and over x 5.990% minus $2,492.02	Brackets indexed for inflation annually.
South Carolina	$0 - 3,069 x 0.000% minus $0 $3,070 - 6,149 x 3.000% minus $92 $6,150 - 9,229 x 4.000% minus $154 $9,230 - 12,309 x 5.000% minus $246 $12,310 - 15,399 x 6.000% minus $369 $15,400 and over x 7.000% minus $523	Brackets indexed for inflation annually.

Jurisdiction	2020 Tax Year	Comment
Tennessee	1% upon interest and dividend income of individuals.	Tax year 2021 and beyond: 0%.
Utah	4.95%	
Vermont	Single: $0 - 40,350 x 3.35% minus $0 $40,351 - 97,800 x 6.600% minus $1,311.37 $97,801 - 204,000 x 7.600% minus $2,289.37 $204,001 and over x 8.750% minus $4,635.37 Married Filing Jointly/Civil Union Filing Jointly: $0 - 67,450 x 3.350% minus 0 $67,451 - 163,000 x 6.600% minus $2,192.12 $163,001 - 248,350 x 7.600% minus $3,822.12 $248,351 and over x 8.750% minus $6,678.15 Married Filing Separately/Civil Union Filing Separately: $0 - 33,725 x 3.350% minus $0 $33,726 - 81,500 x 6.600% minus $1,096.06 $81,501 - 124,175 x 7.600% minus $1,911.06 $124,176 and over x 8.750% minus $3,339.07 Head of Household: $0 - 54,100 x 3.350% minus $0 $54,101 - 139,650 x 6.600% minus $1,758.25 $139,651 - 226,200 x 7.600% minus $3,154.75 $226,201 and over 8.750% minus $5,756.05	Brackets indexed for inflation annually. Amount of tax increased by 24% for: • early withdrawals from qualified retirement plans, individual retirement accounts, and medical savings accounts; • recapture of the federal investment tax credit; and • qualified lump-sum distributions of pension income not included in federal taxable income.
Virginia	$0 - 3,000 x 2.000% minus $0 $3,001 - 5,000 x 3.000% minus $30.00 $5,001 - 17,000 x 5.000% minus $130.00 $17,001 and over x 5.750% minus $257.50	

Jurisdiction	2020 Tax Year	Comment
West Virginia	Single, Head of Household, Married Filing Jointly, Widower with Dependent Child: $0 - 10,000 x 3.000% minus $0 $10,001 - 25,000 x 4.000% minus $100.00 $25,001 -40,000 x 4.500% minus $225.00 $40,001 - 60,000 x 6.000% minus $825.00 $60,001 and over x 6.500% minus $1,125.00 Married Filing Separately: $0 - 5,000 x 3.000% minus $0 $5,001 - 12,500 x 4.000% minus $50.00 $12,501 - 20,000 x 4.500% minus $112.50 $20,001 - 30,000 x 6.000% minus $412.50 $30,001 and over x 6.500% minus $562.50	
Wisconsin	Single, Head of Household: $0 - 11,760 x 3.86% minus $0 $11,761 - 23,520 x 5.04% minus $138.77 $23,521 - 258,950 x 6.27% minus $428.07 $258,951 and over x 7.650% minus $4,001.58 Married Filing Jointly: $0 - 15,680 x 3.86% minus $0 $15,681 - 31,360 x 5.04% minus $185.02 $31,361 -345,270 x 6.270% minus $570.75 $345,271 and over x 7.650% minus $5,335.48 Married Filing Separately: $0 - 7,840 x 3.86% minus $0 $7,841 - 15,680 x 5.04% minus $92.51 $15,681 - 172,630 x 6.270% minus $285.37 $172,631 and over x 7.650% minus $2,667.67	Rates shown are for 2019 tax year. Rate reductions for 2020 for first and second brackets are scheduled to be determined by November 2020. Brackets indexed for inflation annually.

Alternative Minimum Tax

BEAT

The IRC Sec. 59A base erosion minimum tax applies to base erosion payments paid or accrued in tax years beginning after December 31, 2017.

Applicable taxpayers are required to pay, for any tax year, a tax equal to the base erosion minimum tax amount for the year. The base erosion and anti-abuse tax (BEAT) is paid in addition to any other income taxes imposed under Subtitle A (IRC Sec. 59A(a)).

The base erosion minimum tax amount for any tax year is the excess, if any, of:

- 10% (5% for tax years beginning in calendar year 2018) of the modified taxable income of the taxpayer for the tax year, over
- the regular tax liability for the tax year reduced (but not below zero) by the excess, if any, of:
  - the credits allowed against regular tax liability under Chapter 1 of the Code, over
  - the sum of (i) the credit allowed under IRC Sec. 38 (the general business credit) that is allocable to the research credit determined under IRC Sec. 41(a), plus (ii) the portion of the applicable IRC Sec. 38 credits that do not exceed 80% of the lesser of the amount of those credits or the base erosion minimum tax amount (IRC Sec. 59A(b)(1))

For tax years beginning after December 31, 2025, for purposes of determining the base erosion minimum tax amount, the 10% rate is increased to 12.5% of the taxpayer's modified taxable income and the regular tax liability is reduced (but not below zero) by the aggregate amount of allowable credits, rather than the excess described in item (2), above.

AMT

For tax years beginning after 2017, the federal alternative minimum tax (AMT) under IRC §§55-59 for corporations has been repealed. Any unused minimum tax credit of a corporation may be used to offset regular tax liability for any tax year. In addition, a portion of unused minimum tax credit is refundable in 2018 through 2021. The refundable portion is 50% (100% in 2021) of any excess minimum tax for the year over any credit allowable against regular tax for that year.

For tax years before 2018, under IRC §§55-59, corporations or LLCs taxed as corporations, except for certain qualifying small corporations, may be required to report and pay an alternative minimum tax (AMT) if:

- taxable income, before any net operating loss deduction, plus AMT adjustments and tax preference items is more than $40,000 or the allowable exemption amount, whichever is lower; or

• the corporation claims a general business credit, the qualified electric vehicle credit, or the credit for prior year minimum tax.

Alternative taxable income is determined by adjusting the corporation's taxable income calculated under the regular tax method by certain adjustments, preference items, and an exemption amount. The alternative taxable income is multiplied by 20% to determine the tentative minimum tax. The AMT equals the excess, if any, of the tentative minimum tax over the regular tax for the tax year. The AMT is reduced by AMT foreign tax credits.

This chart indicates whether each state imposes the BEAT or an AMT based on federal income tax law or based on some other computation method.

Jurisdiction	Alternative Minimum Tax	Comment
Alabama	No	
Alaska	Base erosion minimum tax imposed. **Tax years before 2018:** Alternative minimum tax imposed at rate of 18% of applicable federal AMT on tax preference items.	
Arizona	No	
Arkansas	No	
California	No base erosion minimum tax imposed. Alternative minimum tax (AMT) imposed at rate of 6.65% if sum of AMT adjustments, preference items, loss denials, and other items specified in IRC Sec. 59 (as modified by state adjustments), and state net income exceeds $40,000.	
Colorado	No	
Connecticut	No	
Delaware	No	Banks and trust companies may elect to pay an alternative bank franchise tax equal to the sum of income tax liability plus a location benefit tax liability. The income tax is imposed at the following graduated rates: $0-50,000,000: 7% 50,000,001-100,000,000: 5% $100,000,001-500,000,000: 3% $500,000,001-1,300,000,000: 1% over $1,300,000,001: 0.5%. The location benefit tax is $1,600,000 ($2,000,000 before 2012) plus a percentage of asset value based on the following formula: $0-5,000,000,000 in assets: 0.012% (0.015% before 2012) $5,000,000,001-20,000,000,000 in assets: 0.008% (0.010% before 2012) $20,000,000,001-$90,000,000,000 (100,000,000,000 before 2012) in assets: 0.004% (0.005% before 2012)

Jurisdiction	Alternative Minimum Tax	Comment
District of Columbia	No	
Florida	No **Tax years before 2018:** AMT imposed at rate of 3.3% on federal AMT base, after federal exemption amount or reduced exemption stated on federal return.	
Georgia	No	
Hawaii	No	
Idaho	No	
Illinois	No	
Indiana	No	
Iowa	AMT imposed at rate of 7.2% on apportioned federal AMT base adjusted as follows: • subtract depletion and tax exempt bond interest; • recompute federal adjusted current earnings to extent federal amount includes tax exempt interest; • reduce net operating loss by tax preferences and adjustments arising in year of NOL (deduction limited to 90% of AMTI); and • reduce federal exemption amount by 25% to extent state alternative minimum taxable income exceeds $150,000.	The AMT is repealed after 2020.
Kansas	No	
Kentucky	No	
Louisiana	No	
Maine	No	**Tax Years Before 2018**: AMT imposed at rate of 5.4% on apportioned federal AMT base adjusted as follows: • state taxable income addition modifications to extent not already included in federal base; • state taxable income subtraction modifications to extent not already eliminated from federal base; • recompute federal exemption amount; and • subtract any Pine Tree Development Zone credit.
Maryland	No	
Massachusetts	No	
Michigan	No	

Jurisdiction	Alternative Minimum Tax	Comment
Minnesota	5.8% tax imposed on excess of alternative minimum tax base over regular franchise tax liability.	
Mississippi	No	
Missouri	No	
Montana	No	
Nebraska	No	
Nevada	N/A, because state does not tax general business corporation income.	
New Hampshire	No	
New Jersey	Through July 31, 2019, alternative minimum assessment (AMA) imposed on taxpayers exempt from corporation business tax (CBT) under Pub.L. 86-272 that do not consent to pay CBT based on greater of gross profits or gross receipts computation method. **Gross profits of:** $0-1,000,000: AMA=0; $1,000,001-10,000,000: AMA=gross profits X .0025 X 1.11111 exclusion rate; $10,000,001-15,000,000: AMA=gross profits X .0035; $15,000,001-25,000,000: AMA=gross profits X .006; $25,000,001-37,500,000: AMA=gross profits X .007; and $37,500,001 or greater: AMA=gross profits X .008. **Gross receipts of:** $0-2,000,000: AMA=0; $2,000,001-20,000,000: AMA=gross receipts X .00125 X 1.11111 exclusion rate; $20,000,001-30,000,000: AMA=gross receipts X .00175; $30,000,001-50,000,000: AMA=gross receipts X .003; $50,000,001-75,000,000: AMA=gross receipts X .0035; and $75,000,001 or greater: AMA=gross receipts X .004.	Effective for tax years beginning on and after July 31, 2019, the alternative minimum assessment is repealed.
New Mexico	No	

Jurisdiction	Alternative Minimum Tax	Comment
New York	No	**Tax years before 2015:** Minimum taxable income tax (MTI) imposed at rate of 1.5% (1.36% for qualified in-state manufacturers and qualified emerging technology companies, 0.75% for eligible qualified in-state manufacturers) on entire net income allocated to state adjusted as follows: • addition of federal tax preference items; • addition or subtraction of certain federal adjustments used to compute federal AMT; • addition of state net operating loss deduction (NOLD); and • subtraction of alternative net operating loss deduction (ANOLD).
North Carolina	No	
North Dakota	No	
Ohio	No	
Oklahoma	No	
Oregon	No	
Pennsylvania	No	
Rhode Island	No	
South Carolina	No	
South Dakota	N/A, because state does not tax general business corporation income.	
Tennessee	No	
Texas	No	
Utah	No	
Vermont	No	
Virginia	No	0.5% minimum tax imposed on gross receipts of telecommunication companies in lieu of corporate income tax if income tax liability is less than minimum tax liability.
Washington	N/A, because state does not tax general business corporation income.	
West Virginia	No	
Wisconsin	No	
Wyoming	N/A, because state does not tax general business corporation income.	

Amended Return Deadline for Reporting Federal Changes—C Corporations

The following chart indicates the deadline for reporting a federal change or adjustment by a C Corporation, as well as, any attachments that must be filed.

Jurisdiction	C Corporations	Comment
Alabama	No deadline specified.	Attach RAR or any other itemized explanation of federal changes furnished by the IRS.
Alaska	File amended return within 60 days after final determination of federal adjustment.	Attach all documents related to the change, including RAR.
Arizona	Within 90 days after final determination of federal adjustment, either: • file amended return, or • file copy of final federal determination, concede accuracy or state errors, and request recomputation of tax by department.	Provide sufficient information for the department to recompute Arizona taxable income based on the RAR changes.
Arkansas	File amended return within 180 days after receipt of notice and demand for payment from IRS.	Prior to Oct. 1, 2015, amended return had to be filed within 90 days after receipt of notice and demand for payment from IRS.
California	File amended return or send a letter with copies of the federal changes within 6 months after final determination of federal change or filing amended federal return.	Attach copy of the final federal determination and all underlying data and schedules that explain or support the federal adjustments.
Colorado	File amended return within 30 days after final determination of federal change or filing amended federal return.	Include statement of reasons for difference. RAR showing federal return changes and state account number will be accepted for multistate corporations in lieu of an amended return.
Connecticut	File amended return within 90 days after final determination of federal change or filing federal amended return.	Attach IRS notification of changes or federal Form 1120X.
Delaware	File amended return within 90 days after final determination of federal adjustment or filing amended federal return.	Attach copy of federal amended return.
District of Columbia	File amended return within 90 days after final determination of federal change or filing amended federal return.	Provide detailed statement explaining the adjustments.
Florida	File amended return within 60 days after final determination of federal adjustment or assessment, payment, or collection of tax, whichever occurs first.	Attach copy of amended federal return, RAR, or other evidence of completed federal audit.
Georgia	File amended return within 180 days after final determination of federal adjustment.	Attach copy of federal Form 1120X or federal audit adjustments.

Jurisdiction	C Corporations	Comment
Hawaii	File amended return within 90 days after final determination of federal change or filing amended federal return.	Attach copy of the document issued by the federal government changing the federal taxable income of the corporation.
Idaho	File amended return within 120 days of a final determination.	Attach copies of all RARs and any other documents and schedules required to clarify the adjustments to taxable income.
Illinois	File amended return within 120 days after federal changes are agreed to or finally determined (two years and 120 days if claiming a refund resulting from the change).	Attach copy of federal finalization or proof of acceptance from IRS along with copy of amended federal form plus any other related forms, schedules, or attachments, if applicable. Examples of federal finalization include copy of: • federal refund check; • signed and dated audit report from the IRS, including copies of preliminary, revised, corrected, and superseding reports, if applicable; and/or • federal transcript verifying federal taxable income.
Indiana	File amended return within 180 days after the federal modification is made (120 days for modifications made before 2011).	Attach copy of amended federal return, RAR, audit report, and/or applicable federal waivers.
Iowa	File amended return within 60 days of final disposition of federal audit. File amended return within 6 months of federal audit finalization for refund claims arising after general three year limitation period.	Include amended federal return and copy of federal RAR, if applicable. Copy of federal RAR and notification of final federal adjustments provided by taxpayer will be acceptable in lieu of an amended return.
Kansas	File amended return within 180 days after the federal adjustment is paid, agreed to, or becomes final, whichever is earlier.	Attach copy of amended federal return, RAR, or adjustment letter with full explanation of changes made.
Kentucky	File federal adjustments report within 180 days after final determination date. **Tax years before April 15, 2020:** Taxpayers must: • notify Department of Revenue in writing within 30 days of federal audit initiation; and • submit copy of final federal determination within 180 days (30 days before April 27, 2018) of audit's conclusion.	
Louisiana	File amended return within 180 days of the final determination of the federal adjustments.	Attach statement disclosing nature and amounts of federal adjustments.
Maine	File amended return within 180 days after final determination of the federal change or correction or the filing of the federal amended return.	Attach copy of federal amended return or RAR. For returns reflecting federal net operating losses, attach copy of federal Form 1139.
Maryland	File amended return within 90 days after final determination of federal adjustment.	Attach copy of federal amended return or final IRS adjustment report.

Jurisdiction	C Corporations	Comment
Massachusetts	File amended return within 3 months after final determination of federal adjustment.	Attach copy of the federal RAR and supporting schedules.
Michigan	File amended return within 120 days after final determination of federal adjustment.	Attach copy of federal amended return or signed and dated IRS audit document.
Minnesota	File amended return, or mail letter to Department of Revenue detailing how the federal determination is incorrect or does not change the Minnesota tax, within 180 days after final determination of federal change or filing of federal amended return.	Attach copy of federal amended return or IRS audit report.
Mississippi	File amended return within 30 days after agreeing to the federal change.	Use Form 83-105 and check amended return box. Attach copy of federal amended return or RAR. If the taxpayer files consolidated for federal purposes, a pro forma amended federal return should be filed as well as the amended consolidated federal return.
Missouri	File amended return within 90 days after final determination of federal change or filing amended federal return.	Attach copy of federal amended return, RAR, closing agreement, and/or applicable court decision. If federal return was not amended, explain why the state return is being amended.
Montana	File amended return within 90 days after notice of federal change or filing amended federal return.	Attach the applicable forms and statements explaining all adjustments in detail.
Nebraska	File amended return within 60 days after a correction or change to the federal return. Taxpayers filing an amended federal return that results in a credit or refund must report the change or correction within 60 days after receiving proof that the IRS accepted the federal return.	Attach copy of federal amended return, IRS report, or other document that substantiates the adjustments claimed. Attach documentation showing that IRS accepted changes made on federal return.
Nevada	N/A, because state does not tax general business corporation income.	
New Hampshire	File amended return within 6 months after final determination of federal adjustment.	Attach copy of federal amended return or IRS adjustment report.
New Jersey	File amended return within 90 days after final determination of federal change or filing amended federal return.	
New Mexico	File amended return within 180 days after final determination of federal adjustment.	Attach copy of federal amended return or RAR.

Jurisdiction	C Corporations	Comment
New York	File amended return within 90 days after final determination of federal change (120 days for taxpayers making a combined report) or filing amended federal return.	Attach copy of federal Form 4549, Income Tax Examination Changes. If the corporation filed as part of a consolidated group for federal tax purposes but on a separate basis for state tax purposes, submit a statement indicating the changes that would have been made if the corporation had filed on a separate basis for federal tax purposes.
North Carolina	File amended return within 6 months after: • receiving notice of each federal change or correction; or • filing an amended federal return that results in an increase in state tax.	Include a complete explanation of reasons for filing an amended return, including specific schedule and line number references, on Schedule J of the return.
North Dakota	File amended return within 90 days after final determination of federal change or filing amended federal return.	Attach copy of federal amended return, Form 1139, or RAR. If corporation is included in a consolidated federal return, attach copy of amended pro forma separate company federal return, pages 1-4 of amended consolidated federal return, and schedule of gross income and deductions by company that supports the amended consolidated taxable income.
Ohio	No federal tax base. CAT is based on taxable gross receipts.	
Oklahoma	File amended return within 1 year after final determination of federal change.	Attach copy of federal Form 1120X or 1139 and proof of disposition by IRS or copy of RAR, when applicable.
Oregon	File amended return within 90 days after federal change or filing amended federal return.	Attach copy of federal amended return or RAR.
Pennsylvania	File amended return within six months after receipt of final federal change or correction or filing amended federal return.	Attach copy of federal amended return, statement of reasons for filing the amended return, and supporting forms or schedules.
Rhode Island	File amended return within 60 days after receipt of final determination of federal change.	Changes reported using Form RI-1120C and by checking the amended return box.
South Carolina	File amended return within 180 days after final determination of federal adjustment.	Attach copy of federal Forms 4549 and 870, along with other required information including an explanation of the adjustments, plus a copy of the original return.
South Dakota	N/A, because state does not tax general business corporation income.	

Jurisdiction	C Corporations	Comment
Tennessee	No deadline specified.	Submit a Franchise and Excise Tax Federal Income Revision Form, a letter of explanation, copies of pages from the RAR and federal Form 4549-B that reflect the examination changes, and (for taxpayers filing an amended federal return in relation to federal audit adjustments) a copy of the 1120X or the first page of the amended federal return. A taxpayer that files a consolidated federal return should enclose a schedule detailing the changes that apply to the entity for which the revisions are being reported or a reconciliation reflecting all adjustments by entity.
Texas	File amended return within 120 days after final determination of federal adjustment or filing amended federal return.	Attach cover letter of explanation, with enclosures necessary to support the amendment.
Utah	File amended return within 90 days after final determination of federal change or filing amended federal return.	Attach copy of federal amended return, IRS audit or adjustment report, or other explanation of changes.
Vermont	File amended return within 60 days after notice of federal change or filing federal amended return.	Attach copy of IRS report.
Virginia	File amended return within 1 year after final determination of federal change or filing federal amended return.	Attach copy of federal amended return, RAR, adjustment letter, or other form/ statement showing the nature of any federal change and date it became final.
Washington	N/A, because state does not tax general business corporation income.	
West Virginia	File amended return within 90 days after final determination of federal change or filing federal amended return.	Attach copy of RAR detailing adjustments.
Wisconsin	Mail report to department and/or file amended return within 90 days after final determination of federal change or filing amended federal return.	Send copy of final federal audit report.
Wyoming	N/A, because state does not tax general business corporation income.	

Amended Return Deadline for Reporting Federal Changes—Partnerships, LLPs, and LLCs

The following chart indicates the deadline for reporting a federal change or adjustment by a Partnership, LLP or LLC, as well as, any attachments that must be filed.

Jurisdiction	Partnerships, LLPs, and LLCs	Comment
Alabama	No deadline specified.	Attach RAR or any other itemized explanation of federal changes furnished by the IRS.
Alaska	File amended return within 60 days after final determination of federal adjustment.	Attach all documents related to the change, including RAR.
Arizona	Within 90 days after final determination of federal adjustment, either: • file amended return, or • file copy of final federal determination, concede accuracy or state errors, and request recomputation of tax by department.	Provide sufficient information for the department to recompute Arizona taxable income based on the RAR changes.
Arkansas	File amended return within 180 days after receipt of notice and demand for payment from IRS.	Prior to Oct. 1, 2015, amended return had to be filed within 90 days after receipt of notice and demand for payment from IRS.
California	File amended return within 6 months after final determination of federal change or filing amended federal return.	Attach copy of federal RAR or other notice of the adjustments.
Colorado	File amended return within 30 days after final determination of federal change or filing amended federal return.	Include statement of reasons for difference.
Connecticut	File amended return within 90 days after final determination of federal change or filing federal amended return.	
Delaware	File amended return within 90 days after final determination of federal change or filing amended federal return.	Attach copy of federal amended return and/or federal audit.
District of Columbia	File amended return within 90 days after final determination of federal change or filing amended federal return.	Provide detailed statement explaining the adjustments.
Florida	File amended return within 60 days after final determination of federal adjustment or assessment, payment, or collection of tax, whichever occurs first.	
Georgia	File amended return within 90 (previously 180) days after final determination of any federal change or correction.	Attach copy of amended federal partnership return. Detailed statement of federal audit adjustments must be mailed separately to Department of Revenue.

Jurisdiction	Partnerships, LLPs, and LLCs	Comment
Hawaii	File amended return within 90 days after federal change or filing amended federal return.	Attach copy of the document issued by the federal government changing the federal taxable income of the corporation.
Idaho	File amended return within 120 days of a final determination.	Attach copies of all RARs and any other documents and schedules required to clarify the adjustments to taxable income.
Illinois	File amended return within 120 days after federal changes are agreed to or finally determined (two years and 120 days if claiming a refund resulting from the change).	Attach copy of federal finalization or proof of acceptance from the IRS along with copy of amended federal form, if applicable. Examples of federal finalization include copy of: • audit report from the IRS; and/or • federal record of account verifying ordinary business income.
Indiana	File amended return within 180 days after the federal modification is made.	Attach copy of amended federal return, RAR, audit report, and/or applicable federal waivers.
Iowa	File amended return within 180 days (previously 60 days) of final disposition of federal audit.	Include amended federal return, if applicable. Copy of federal RAR and notification of final federal adjustments provided by taxpayer will be acceptable in lieu of an amended return.
Kansas	File amended return within 180 days after the federal adjustment is paid, agreed to, or becomes final, whichever is earlier.	Attach copy of amended federal return, RAR, or adjustment letter with full explanation of changes made.
Kentucky	90 days after the final determination date, taxpayers must • file a completed federal adjustments report; • notify direct partners or members of their distributive share of the federal adjustments; • file an amended composite or withholding return for direct partners or members; and • pay any tax that would have been due had the partnership correctly reported the federal adjustments. Direct partners or members have 180 days after the final determination date to: • file a federal adjustment report stating their distributive share of the adjustments reported to them; and • pay any tax due, including penalties and interest, as if the federal adjustments had been correctly reported. **Tax years before April 15, 2020:** Taxpayers must: • notify Department of Revenue in writing within 30 days of federal audit initiation; and • submit copy of final federal determination within 180 days (30 days before April 27, 2018) of audit's conclusion.	If taxpayer elects to pay tax for its partners or members, it has: • 90 days after the final determination date to provide notice of its election and to file a federal adjustments report; and • 180 days after the final determination date to pay the tax owed by its partners or members.

Jurisdiction	Partnerships, LLPs, and LLCs	Comment
Louisiana	File amended return within 60 days of the taxpayer's receipt of the federal adjustments.	Attach statement disclosing nature and amounts of federal adjustments.
Maine	N/A, because no return filing requirement for tax years after 2011.	Effective for taxable years beginning on or after January 1, 2018, partnerships are required to report and pay any amount due to the state resulting from a federal partnership-level audit no later than 180 days after the final determination date. The 180-day requirement also applies to partners required to file a federal adjustment report and who are included in a composite return or are subject to withholding.
Maryland	File amended return within 90 days after final determination of federal adjustment.	Attach copy of federal amended return or final IRS adjustment report.
Massachusetts	File amended return within 1 year after receipt of notice of final determination of federal change.	Attach copy of the federal RAR and supporting schedules.
Michigan	File amended return within 120 days after final determination of federal adjustment.	Attach copy of federal amended return or signed and dated IRS audit document.
Minnesota	File amended return, or mail letter to Department of Revenue detailing how the federal determination is incorrect or does not change the Minnesota tax, within 180 days after final determination of federal change or filing of federal amended return.	Attach copy of federal amended return or IRS audit report.
Mississippi	File amended return within 30 days after agreeing to the federal change.	Use Form 84-105 and check amended return box. Attach copy of federal amended return or RAR.
Missouri	File amended return within 90 days after final determination of federal change or filing amended federal return.	Attach copy of federal amended return, RAR, closing agreement, and/or applicable court decision.
Montana	File amended return within 90 days after notice of federal change or filing federal amended return.	Attach copy of federal amended return or IRS notice of corrections.
Nebraska	File amended return within 60 days after federal change or filing amended federal return.	Attach copy of federal amende return and all related schedules or other documentation explaining changes.
Nevada	N/A, because state does not tax pass-through income.	
New Hampshire	File amended return within 6 months after final determination of federal adjustment.	Attach copy of federal amended return or IRS adjustment report.
New Jersey	File amended return within 30 days after filing of federal amended return or 90 days after final determination of federal change.	

Jurisdiction	Partnerships, LLPs, and LLCs	Comment
New Mexico	File amended return within 180 days after final determination of federal adjustment.	Attach copy of federal amended return or RAR.
New York	File amended return within 90 days after final determination of federal change or filing amended federal return.	Attach copy of federal report of examination changes and signed statement indicating whether the taxpayer concedes the federal audit changes and, if not, then why.
North Carolina	File amended return within 6 months after: • receiving notice of each federal change or correction; or • filing an amended federal return that results in an increase in state tax.	
North Dakota	File amended return within 90 days after final determination of federal change or filing amended federal return.	Attach copy of federal amended return or IRS audit report.
Ohio	File amended return within 90 days after federal change or filing amended federal return.	Attach copy of federal amended return or RAR if refund requested.
Oklahoma	File amended return within 1 year after final determination of federal change.	Attach copy of federal amended return or RAR.
Oregon	File amended return within 90 days after federal change or filing amended federal return.	Attach copy of federal amended return or RAR.
Pennsylvania	File amended return within 30 days after determination of need to amend return.	Attach copy of federal amended return, statement of reasons for filing the amended return, and supporting forms or schedules.
Rhode Island	File amended return within 60 days after receipt of final determination of federal change.	Effective July 1, 2019, partnerships are required to make a supplemental return to report final federal adjustments arising from a partnership level audit or an administrative adjustment request within 180 days after receipt of notification of the final audit or adjustment. Changes reported using Form RI-1065 and by checking the amended return box.
South Carolina	File amended return within 180 days after final determination of federal adjustment.	Attach copy of federal amended return and all supporting schedules.
South Dakota	N/A, because state does not tax pass-through income.	
Tennessee	No deadline specified.	
Texas	File amended return within 120 days after final determination of federal adjustment or filing amended federal return.	Attach cover letter of explanation, with enclosures necessary to support the amendment.

Jurisdiction	Partnerships, LLPs, and LLCs	Comment
Utah	File amended return within 90 days after final determination of federal change or filing amended federal return.	Attach copy of federal amended return, IRS audit or adjustment report, or other explanation of changes.
Vermont	File amended return within 180 days after notice of federal change or filing federal amended return.	Attach copy of IRS report.
Virginia	File amended return within 1 year after final determination date of federal change or filing federal amended return.	No requirement to attach copy of amended federal return or IRS final determination letter.
Washington	N/A, because state does not tax pass-through income.	
West Virginia	File amended return within 90 days after final determination of federal change or filing amended federal return.	Attach copy of RAR detailing adjustments.
Wisconsin	File amended return within 90 days after final determination of federal change or filing amended federal return.	Send copy of federal amended return and/or final federal audit report.
Wyoming	N/A, because state does not tax pass-through income.	

Amended Return Deadline for Reporting Federal Changes—S Corporations

The following chart indicates the deadline for reporting a federal change or adjustment by an S Corporation, as well as, any attachments that must be filed.

Jurisdiction	S Corporations	Comment
Alabama	No deadline specified.	Attach RAR or any other itemized explanation of federal changes furnished by the IRS.
Alaska	File amended return within 60 days after final determination of federal adjustment.	Attach all documents related to the change, including RAR.
Arizona	Within 90 days after final determination of federal adjustment, either: • file amended return, or • file copy of final federal determination, concede accuracy or state errors, and request recomputation of tax by department.	Provide sufficient information for the department to recompute Arizona taxable income based on the RAR changes.
Arkansas	File amended return within 180 days after receipt of notice and demand for payment from IRS.	Prior to Oct. 1, 2015, amended return had to be filed within 90 days after receipt of notice and demand for payment from IRS.
California	File amended return or send a letter with copies of the federal changes within 6 months after final determination of federal change or filing amended federal return.	Attach copy of the final federal determination and all underlying data and schedules that explain or support the federal adjustments.
Colorado	File amended return within 30 days after final determination of federal change or filing amended federal return.	Include statement of reasons for difference.
Connecticut	File amended return within 90 days after final determination of federal change or filing federal amended return.	
Delaware	File amended return within 90 days after final determination of federal change or filing amended federal return.	Attach copy of federal amended return.
District of Columbia	File amended return within 90 days after final determination of federal change or filing amended federal return.	Provide detailed statement explaining the adjustments.
Florida	File amended return within 60 days after final determination of federal adjustment or assessment, payment, or collection of tax, whichever occurs first.	Attach copy of amended federal return, RAR, or other evidence of completed federal audit.
Georgia	File amended return within 180 days after final determination of any federal change or correction.	Attach copy of federal Form 1120S or federal audit adjustments.

Jurisdiction	S Corporations	Comment
Hawaii	File amended return within 90 days after federal change or filing amended federal return.	Attach copy of the document issued by the federal government changing the federal taxable income of the corporation.
Idaho	File amended return within 120 days of a final determination.	Attach copies of all RARs and any other documents and schedules required to clarify the adjustments to taxable income.
Illinois	File amended return within 120 days after federal changes are agreed to or finally determined (two years and 120 days if claiming a refund resulting from the change).	Attach copy of federal finalization or proof of acceptance from the IRS along with copy of amended federal form, if applicable. Examples of federal finalization include copy of: • audit report from the IRS; and/or • federal record of account verifying ordinary business income.
Indiana	File amended return within 180 days after the federal modification is made.	Attach copy of amended federal return, RAR, audit report, and/or applicable federal waivers.
Iowa	File amended return within 60 days of final disposition of federal audit.	Include amended federal return and copy of federal RAR, if applicable. Copy of federal RAR and notification of final federal adjustments provided by taxpayer will be acceptable in lieu of an amended return.
Kansas	File amended return within 180 days after the federal adjustment is paid, agreed to, or becomes final, whichever is earlier.	Attach copy of amended federal return, RAR, or adjustment letter with full explanation of changes made.
Kentucky	File federal adjustments report within 180 days after final determination date. **Tax years before April 15, 2020:** Taxpayers must: • notify Department of Revenue in writing within 30 days of federal audit initiation; and • submit copy of final federal determination within 180 days (30 days before April 27, 2018) of audit's conclusion.	
Louisiana	File amended return within 180 days of the final determination of the federal adjustments.	Attach statement disclosing nature and amounts of federal adjustments.
Maine	N/A, because no return filing requirement for tax years after 2011.	
Maryland	File amended return within 90 days after final determination of federal adjustment.	Attach copy of federal amended return or final IRS adjustment report.
Massachusetts	File amended return within 3 months after final determination of federal adjustment.	Attach copy of the federal RAR and supporting schedules.
Michigan	File amended return within 120 days after final determination of federal adjustment.	Attach copy of federal amended return or signed and dated IRS audit document.

Jurisdiction	S Corporations	Comment
Minnesota	File amended return, or mail letter to Department of Revenue detailing how the federal determination is incorrect or does not change the Minnesota tax, within 180 days after final determination of federal change or filing of federal amended return.	Attach copy of federal amended return or IRS audit report.
Mississippi	File amended return within 30 days after agreeing to the federal change.	Use Form 84-105 and check amended return box. Attach copy of federal amended return or RAR.
Missouri	File amended return within 90 days after final determination of federal change or filing amended federal return.	Attach copy of federal amended return, RAR, closing agreement, and/or applicable court decision.
Montana	File amended return within 90 days after notice of federal change or filing amended federal return.	Attach copy of federal amended return or IRS notice of corrections.
Nebraska	File amended return within 60 days after federal change or filing amended federal return.	Attach copy of federal amended return, IRS report, or other document that substantiates the adjustments claimed.
Nevada	N/A, because state does not tax pass-through income.	
New Hampshire	File amended return within 6 months after final determination of federal adjustment.	Attach copy of federal amended return or IRS adjustment report.
New Jersey	File amended return within 90 days after final determination of federal change or filing amended federal return.	
New Mexico	File amended return within 180 days after final determination of federal adjustment.	Attach copy of federal amended return or RAR.
New York	File amended return within 90 days after final determination of federal change or filing amended federal return.	Attach copy of federal Form 4549, Income Tax Examination Changes.
North Carolina	File amended return within 6 months after: • receiving notice of each federal change or correction; or • filing an amended federal return that results in an increase in state tax.	Include a complete explanation of reasons for filing an amended return, including specific schedule and line number references, on Schedule J of the return.
North Dakota	File amended return within 90 days after final determination of federal change or filing amended federal return.	Attach copy of federal amended return or IRS audit report.
Ohio	File amended return within 90 days after federal change or filing amended federal return.	Attach copy of federal amended return or RAR if refund requested.
Oklahoma	File amended return within 1 year after final determination of federal change.	Attach copy of federal amended return or RAR.

Jurisdiction	S Corporations	Comment
Oregon	File amended return within 90 days after federal change or filing amended federal return.	Attach copy of federal amended return or RAR.
Pennsylvania	File amended return within 30 days after determination of need to amend return.	Attach copy of federal amended return, statement of reasons for filing the amended return, and supporting forms or schedules.
Rhode Island	File amended return within 60 days after notice of final determination of federal change.	Changes reported using Form RI-1120S and by checking the amended return box.
South Carolina	File amended return within 180 days after final determination of federal adjustment.	Attach copy of federal Forms 4549 and 870, along with other required information including an explanation of the adjustments, plus a copy of the original return.
South Dakota	N/A, because state does not tax pass-through income.	
Tennessee	No deadline specified.	Submit a Franchise and Excise Tax Federal Income Revision Form, a letter of explanation, copies of pages from the RAR and federal Form 4549-B that reflect the examination changes, and (for taxpayers filing an amended federal return in relation to federal audit adjustments) a copy of the 1120X or the first page of the amended federal return. A taxpayer that files a consolidated federal return should enclose a schedule detailing the changes that apply to the entity for which the revisions are being reported or a reconciliation reflecting all adjustments by entity.
Texas	File amended return within 120 days after final determination of federal adjustment or filing amended federal return.	Attach cover letter of explanation, with enclosures necessary to support the amendment.
Utah	File amended return within 90 days after final determination of federal change or filing amended federal return.	Attach copy of federal amended return, IRS audit or adjustment report, or other explanation of changes.
Vermont	File amended return within 180 days after notice of federal change or filing federal amended return.	Attach copy of IRS report.
Virginia	File amended return within 1 year after final determination date of federal change or filing federal amended return.	No requirement to attach copy of amended federal return or IRS final determination letter.
Washington	N/A, because state does not tax pass-through income.	
West Virginia	File amended return within 90 days after final determination of federal change or filing amended federal return.	Attach copy of RAR detailing adjustments.

Jurisdiction	S Corporations	Comment
Wisconsin	Mail report to department and/or file amended return within 90 days after final determination of federal change or filing amended federal return.	Send copy of federal amended return and/ or final federal audit report.
Wyoming	N/A, because state does not tax pass-through income.	

Amended Return Forms—C Corporations

The following chart indicates the form that must be filed by a C Corporation when filing an amended return or reporting a federal return change or adjustment.

Jurisdiction	C Corporations	Comment
Alabama	Use Form 20C and check amended return box at top of return.	
Alaska	Use Form 6000 and check amended return box.	Electronic filing required.
Arizona	Use dedicated amended return Form 120X.	
Arkansas	Use Form AR1100CT and check amended return box. **Tax years before 2010:** Use dedicated amended return Form AR1100CTX. If a refund is sought, claim may be filed instead on taxpayer's letterhead containing specified information and grounds upon which refund is claimed.	
California	Use dedicated amended return Form 100X.	
Colorado	Use dedicated amended return Form 112X; attach pertinent schedules and documentation, with a statement of reasons for the difference.	
Connecticut	Use dedicated amended return Form CT-1120X, or if taxpayer is a combined return filer, use Form CT-1120CU and check the "Amended" box.	
Delaware	Use dedicated amended return Form 1100X.	
District of Columbia	Use Form D-20 for the year at issue, fill in amended return oval, and attach detailed statement of adjustment.	
Florida	Use dedicated amended return Form F-1120X.	
Georgia	Use Form 600 and check amended return block.	
Hawaii	Use Form N-30 for the year being amended and check the amended return box. If the return is being amended to take a farming NOL carryback deduction, also check the NOL box. Attach a completed Schedule AMD, Explanation of Changes on Amended Return.	
Idaho	Use Form 41 and check amended return box.	

Jurisdiction	C Corporations	Comment
Illinois	Use dedicated amended return Form IL-1120-X.	
Indiana	Use dedicated amended return Form IT-20X.	
Iowa	Use dedicated amended return Form 1120X.	
Kansas	Use Form K-120 and check amended return box.	
Kentucky	Use Form 720 and check amended return box or amended return—RAR box.	
Louisiana	Use Form CIFT-620 and mark amended return circle.	
Maine	Use Form 1120-ME and check amended return box. Schedule X must also be completed and included with the amended return.	Prior to 2016 tax year, use dedicated amended return Form 1120X-ME and check appropriate box identifying reason for filing amended return.
Maryland	Use dedicated amended return Form 500X.	
Massachusetts	Use Form 355 and check: • amended return box, if return does not report changes that result from filing a federal amended return or from a federal audit; • both the amended return and the federal amendment boxes, if return includes changes reported on an amended federal return; or • both the amended return and the federal audit boxes, if return incorporates changes that result from a federal audit.	Electronic filing required for certain taxpayers.
Michigan	For CIT, use dedicated amended return Form 4892. For MBT, use Form 4567 and check amended return box.	
Minnesota	Use dedicated amended return Form M4X.	
Mississippi	Use Form 83-105 and check amended return box.	
Missouri	Use Form MO-1120 and check the box indicating that it is an amended return.	
Montana	Use Form CIT; indicate at the top of the form that it represents an amended filing and check the box indicating the reason(s) for the amended return.	
Nebraska	Use dedicated amended return Form 1120XN.	

Jurisdiction	C Corporations	Comment
Nevada	N/A, because state does not tax general business corporation income.	
New Hampshire	For changes not based on IRS adjustment, use Form BT-SUMMARY and appropriate BET and/or BPT return(s), check "AMENDED" block, and attach all applicable schedules and federal pages. For changes based on IRS adjustment, use Form DP-87 CORP.	
New Jersey	Use Form CBT-100 for the appropriate tax year and write "AMENDED RETURN" on the front.	
New Mexico	Use Form CIT-1 for the appropriate tax year and check the box at the top of page 1 of the form to indicate the type of amended return.	
New York	Use Form CT-3 and mark the amended return box on the front page of the return.	
North Carolina	Use Form CD-405, fill in amended return circle, and include a complete explanation of changes on Schedule J. If additional tax is due, use Form CD-V Amended payment voucher.	
North Dakota	Use dedicated amended return Form 40-X and include a corrected Form 40, page 1, and supporting schedules.	
Ohio	Annual filers must use Form CAT 12 and check amended return box. Quarterly filers must file an amended return via the Ohio Business Gateway.	
Oklahoma	Use Form 512 and check amended return box. Explanation or statement of reasons should be provided on Schedule 512-X.	
Oregon	Use Form 20 or Form 20-I for the appropriate tax year and check "Amended" box.	

Jurisdiction	C Corporations	Comment
Pennsylvania	Generally, use Form RCT-101, check amended report box, and include Schedule AR. If the taxpayer files an amended federal return for a period for which the department issued an official notice of settlement, the change must be reported on an amended Form RCT-101. If the taxpayer files an amended federal return for a period for which the department did not issue an official notice of settlement, or if a change to federal taxable income is initiated by the IRS as part of an audit or examination (regardless of whether the corporate net income tax for that period was settled by the department), the change must be reported on Form RCT-128.	
Rhode Island	Use Form RI-1120C and check amended return box.	
South Carolina	Use Form SC 1120 and check amended return box.	
South Dakota	N/A, because state does not tax general business corporation income.	
Tennessee	Use Form FAE 170 and check amended return box.	
Texas	Use original report form and type or print "Amended Report" at the top.	
Utah	Use Form TC-20 for the year being amended and enter a code number on the "Amended Return" line that best corresponds to the reason for amending.	
Vermont	Use Form CO-411 and check amended return box.	
Virginia	Use Form 500, check amended return box and other applicable boxes to indicate reason for filing amended return, and provide explanation of changes.	
Washington	N/A, because state does not tax general business corporation income.	
West Virginia	Use Form WV/CNF-120 and check "Amended" or "RAR" box.	
Wisconsin	Use Form 4, check the amended return line on the front of the return, and include Schedule AR explaining any changes made.	
Wyoming	N/A, because state does not tax general business corporation income.	

Amended Return Forms—Partnerships, LLPs, and LLCs

The following chart indicates the form that must be filed by a Partnership, LLP, or LLC when filing an amended return or reporting a federal return change or adjustment.

Jurisdiction	Partnerships, LLPs, and LLCs	Comment
Alabama	Use Form 65 and check amended return box at top of return.	
Alaska	Use Form 6900 and check amended return box.	Electronic filing required.
Arizona	Use Form 165 and check amended return box.	
Arkansas	Use Form AR1050 and check amended return box.	
California	Use Form 565 and check amended return box.	
Colorado	Use Form 106 and check amended return box; attach pertinent schedules and documentation, with a statement of reasons for the difference.	
Connecticut	Use Form CT-1065/CT-1120SI and check amended return box.	
Delaware	Use Form 300 and check amended return box.	
District of Columbia	Use Form DC-65 for the year at issue and fill in amended return oval.	
Florida	Partnerships are not required to file amended returns.	
Georgia	Use Form 700 and check amended return block.	
Hawaii	Use Form N-20 and check amended return box. Attach a completed Schedule AMD, Explanation of Changes on Amended Return.	
Idaho	Use Form 65 and check amended return box.	
Illinois	Use dedicated amended return Form IL-1065-X.	
Indiana	Use Form IT-65 and check amended return box.	
Iowa	Use Form IA 1065 and check amended return box.	
Kansas	Use Form K-120S and check amended return box.	
Kentucky	Use Form 765 and check amended return box.	

Jurisdiction	Partnerships, LLPs, and LLCs	Comment
Louisiana	Use Form IT-565 and write "Amended" at top of form.	
Maine	N/A, because no return filing requirement. **Tax years before 2012**: Use Form 1065 ME/1120S-ME and check amended return box.	
Maryland	Use Form 510, check amended return box, and draw line through barcode on return.	
Massachusetts	Use Form 3 and fill in amended return or amended return due to federal change oval.	
Michigan	For MBT, use Form 4567 and check amended return box. For SBT, use dedicated amended return Form C-8000X or C-8044X.	
Minnesota	Use dedicated amended return Form M3X.	
Mississippi	Use Form 84-105 and check amended return box.	
Missouri	Use Form MO-1065 and check amended return box.	
Montana	Use Form PTE and check amended return box.	Beginning with tax year 2019, pass-through entities use Form PTE instead of PR-1.
Nebraska	Use Form 1065N and check amended return box.	
Nevada	N/A, because state does not tax pass-through income.	
New Hampshire	For changes not based on IRS adjustment, use Form BT-SUMMARY and appropriate BET and/or BPT return(s), check "AMENDED" block, and attach all applicable schedules and federal pages. For changes based on IRS adjustment, use Form DP-87 PART.	
New Jersey	Use Form NJ-1065 for the appropriate tax year and check the amended return box.	
New Mexico	Use Form PTE for the appropriate tax year and check the "amended" box.	
New York	Use Form IT-204 and mar the amended return box on the front page of the return.	
North Carolina	Use Form D-403 and fill in amended return circle.	

Jurisdiction	Partnerships, LLPs, and LLCs	Comment
North Dakota	Use Form 58, mark the amended return circle, and attach a statement explaining the reason(s) for filing the amended return.	
Ohio	CAT 12	
Oklahoma	Use Form 514 and place an "X" in amended return box.	
Oregon	Use Form 65 and check amended return box.	
Pennsylvania	Use Form PA-20S/PA-65 and mark "Amended Information Return" circle.	
Rhode Island	Use Form RI-1065 and check "Amended" box.	
South Carolina	Use Form SC 1065 and check amended return box.	
South Dakota	N/A, because state does not tax pass-through income.	
Tennessee	Use Form INC 250 and check amended return box.	
Texas	Use original report form and type or print "Amended Report" at the top.	
Utah	Use Form TC-65 for the year being amended and enter a number in the box entitled "Enter code 1-4 for amended return" that best corresponds to the reason for amending.	
Vermont	Use Form BI-471 and check amended return box.	
Virginia	Use Form 502, check amended return box, and provide explanation of changes.	
Washington	N/A, because state does not tax pass-through income.	
West Virginia	Use Form WV/SPF-100 and check amended return box.	
Wisconsin	Use Form 3, check item F on the front of the return, and include an explanation of any changes made.	
Wyoming	N/A, because state does not tax pass-through income.	

Amended Return Forms—S Corporations

The following chart indicates the form that must be filed by an S Corporation when filing an amended return or reporting a federal return change or adjustment.

Jurisdiction	S Corporations	Comment
Alabama	Use Form 20S and check amended return box at top of return.	
Alaska	Use Form 6000 and check amended return box.	Electronic filing required.
Arizona	Use Form 120S and check amended return box.	
Arkansas	Use Form AR1100S and check amended return box.	
California	Use dedicated amended return Form 100X.	
Colorado	Use Form 106 and check amended return box; attach pertinent schedules and documentation, with a statement of reasons for the difference.	
Connecticut	Use Form CT-1065/CT-1120SI and check amended return box.	
Delaware	Use Form 1100S.	
District of Columbia	Use Form D-20 for the year at issue, fill in amended return oval, and attach detailed statement of adjustment.	
Florida	If a federal return is filed, use dedicated amended return Form F-1120X.	
Georgia	Use Form 600S and check amended return block.	
Hawaii	Use Form N-35 for the year being amended and check amended return box. Attach a completed Schedule AMD, Explanation of Changes on Amended Return.	
Idaho	Use Form 41S and check amended return box.	
Illinois	Use dedicated amended return Form IL-1120-ST-X.	
Indiana	Use Form IT-20S and check amended return box.	
Iowa	Use Form IA 1120S and check amended return box.	
Kansas	Use Form K-120S and check amended return box.	
Kentucky	Use Form 720S and check amended return box.	

Jurisdiction	S Corporations	Comment
Louisiana	Use Form CIFT-620 and mark amended return circle.	
Maine	N/A, because no return filing requirement. **Tax years before 2012**: Use Form 1065 ME/1120S-ME and check amended return box.	
Maryland	Use Form 510, check amended return box, and draw line through barcode on return.	
Massachusetts	Use Form 355S and check: • amended return box, if return does not report changes that result from filing a federal amended return or from a federal audit; • both the amended return and the federal amendment boxes, if return includes changes reported on an amended federal return; or • both the amended return and the federal audit boxes, if return incorporates changes that result from a federal audit.	
Michigan	For MBT, use Form 4567 and check amended return box. For SBT, use dedicated amended return Form C-8000X or C-8044X.	
Minnesota	Use dedicated amended return Form M8X.	
Mississippi	Use Form 84-105 and check amended return box.	
Missouri	Use Form MO-1120S and check amended return box.	
Montana	Use Form PTE and check amended return box.	Beginning with tax year 2019, pass-through entities use Form PTE instead of CLT-4S.
Nebraska	Use Form 1120-SN and check amended return box.	
Nevada	N/A, because state does not tax pass-through income.	
New Hampshire	For changes not based on IRS adjustment, use Form BT-SUMMARY and appropriate BET and/or BPT return(s), check "AMENDED" block, and attach all applicable schedules and federal pages. For changes based on IRS adjustment, use Form DP-87 CORP.	
New Jersey	Use Form CBT-100S for the appropriate tax year and write "AMENDED RETURN" on the front.	

Jurisdiction	S Corporations	Comment
New Mexico	Use Form S-Corp for the appropriate tax year and check the "amended" box.	If Form PTE was filed in a tax year prior to 2011, use the Form PTE for that year.
New York	Use Form CT-3-S and mark the amended return box on the front page of the return.	
North Carolina	Use Form CD-401S, fill in amended return circle, and include a complete explanation of changes on Schedule J. If additional tax is due, use Form CD-V Amended payment voucher.	
North Dakota	Use Form 60, mark the amended return circle, and attach a statement explaining the reason(s) for filing the amended return.	
Ohio	CAT 12	
Oklahoma	Use Form 512-S and place an "X" in amended return box.	
Oregon	Use Form 20-S for the appropriate tax year and check "Amended" box.	
Pennsylvania	Use Form PA-20S/PA-65 and mark "Amended Information Return" circle.	
Rhode Island	Use Form RI-1120S and check amended return box.	
South Carolina	Use Form SC 1120S and check amended return box. Also, write "Amended" on face of return.	
South Dakota	N/A, because state does not tax pass-through income.	
Tennessee	Use Form FAE 170 and check amended return box.	
Texas	Use original report form and type or print "Amended Report" at the top.	
Utah	Use Form TC-20S for the year being amended and enter a code number on the "Amended Return" line that best corresponds to the reason for amending.	
Vermont	Use Form BI-471 and check amended return box.	
Virginia	Use Form 502, check amended return box, and provide explanation of changes.	
Washington	N/A, because state does not tax pass-through income.	
West Virginia	Use Form WV/SPF-100 and check amended return box.	

Jurisdiction	S Corporations	Comment
Wisconsin	Use Form 5S, check the amended return line in item D on the front of the return, and include an explanation of any changes made.	
Wyoming	N/A, because state does not tax pass-through income.	

Apportionment Formulas

A state is allowed by the U.S. Constitution to tax the income of a multistate corporation if the state applies a formula that fairly apportions a percentage of the corporation's income attributable to business activities inside and outside the state. An apportionment formula must have both internal and external consistency to satisfy the fairness requirement. An apportionment formula has internal consistency if the tax is structured so that every jurisdiction could impose an identical tax and no multiple taxation would occur. An apportionment formula has external consistency if the factors used in the formula reflect a reasonable sense of how income is generated.

At one time, most states utilized an evenly weighted three-factor apportionment formula, which consisted of property, payroll, and sales (or receipts) factors. However, the number of states that still weight each factor equally is decreasing. Many states have an apportionment formula with a double-weighted sales factor. In addition, the number of states that have adopted a one-factor sales formula is growing.

This chart shows the standard apportionment formulas used in each state for the 2020 tax year. Special apportionment rules that apply to specific industries, such as manufacturers, financial institutions, insurance companies, and transportation companies, are not included in the chart.

Jurisdiction	2020 Tax Year	Comment
Alabama	Three-factor formula with double-weighted sales factor.	
Alaska	Evenly weighted three-factor formula.	
Arizona	Three-factor formula with double-weighted sales factor or one-factor sales formula.	By electing to use one-factor sales formula, taxpayer agrees to release its name to Joint Legislative Budget Committee and to participate in an Economic Impact Analysis.
Arkansas	**Tax years before 2021:** Three-factor formula with double-weighted sales factor. **Tax years after 2020:** Single sales factor.	
California	One-factor sales formula.	
Colorado	One-factor sales formula.	
Connecticut	One-factor gross receipts formula.	
Delaware	One-factor sales formula.	
District of Columbia	One-factor sales formula.	
Florida	Three-factor formula with double-weighted sales factor. .	Corporations making capital expenditures of at least $250 million may elect one-factor sales formula.
Georgia	One-factor sales formula.	

Jurisdiction	2020 Tax Year	Comment
Hawaii	Evenly weighted three-factor formula.	
Idaho	Three-factor formula with double-weighted sales factor.	
Illinois	One-factor sales formula.	
Indiana	One-factor sales formula.	
Iowa	One-factor sales formula.	
Kansas	Evenly weighted three-factor formula.	If payroll factor exceeds 200% of average of property and sales factor, taxpayer may elect two-factor formula of property and sales.
Kentucky	One-factor receipts formula.	Schedule A must be completed and submitted with return.
Louisiana	One-factor sales formula.	
Maine	One-factor sales formula.	
Maryland	Three-factor formula with quintuple-weighted sales factor.	Single-sales factor formula phased in as follows: • 2021 Tax Year: Three-factor formula with sextuple-weighted sales factor; • 2022 Tax Year and Thereafter: One-factor sales formula.
Massachusetts	Three-factor formula with double-weighted sales factor.	
Michigan	One-factor sales formula for purposes of computing corporate income tax. One-factor sales formula for purposes of computing Michigan Business Tax (MBT).	MBT repealed Jan. 1, 2012, except for those taxpayers with certificated credits that elect to pay the MBT.
Minnesota	One-factor sales formula.	
Mississippi	No general apportionment formula. One-factor sales formula for taxpayers that are not required to use a designated apportionment formula based on specific type or line of in-state business activity.	
Missouri	One-factor sales formula.	
Montana	Evenly weighted three-factor formula.	
Nebraska	One-factor sales formula.	
Nevada	N/A, because state does not tax general business corporation income.	
New Hampshire	Three-factor formula with double-weighted sales factor.	
New Jersey	One-factor sales formula.	
New Mexico	Evenly weighted three-factor formula.	Optional one-factor sales formula for taxpayers whose principal business activity in state is a headquarters operation.

Jurisdiction	2020 Tax Year	Comment
New York	One-factor receipts formula.	
North Carolina	One-factor sales formula.	
North Dakota	Evenly weighted three-factor formula or elective single sales factor formula.	
Ohio	**Commercial Activity Tax (CAT):** N/A, because no general apportionment formula.	
Oklahoma	Evenly weighted three-factor formula; corporations meeting investment criteria may double-weight the sales factor.	
Oregon	One-factor sales formula.	
Pennsylvania	One-factor sales formula.	
Rhode Island	One-factor sales formula.	
South Carolina	One-factor sales formula.	
South Dakota	N/A, because state does not tax general business corporation income.	
Tennessee	Three-factor formula with triple-weighted sales factor.	
Texas	One-factor gross receipts formula.	

Jurisdiction	2020 Tax Year	Comment
Utah	Evenly weighted three-factor formula, unless election is made to use apportionment formula with the property factor, the payroll factor, plus 8 times the sales factor, divided by 10.	Sales factor weighted taxpayers must use a one factor sales formula. "Sales factor weighted taxpayer" means a taxpayer that does not meet the definition of an "optional apportionment taxpayer" and performs economic activities classified only in a 2002 or 2007 NAICS code other than a code within: • Sector 21, Mining; • Sector 31-33, Manufacturing, other than Subsector 3254, Pharmaceutical and Medicine Manufacturing, Subsector 3333, Commercial and Service Industry Machinery Manufacturing, Subsector 334, Computer and Electronic Product Manufacturing, or Code 336111, Automobile Manufacturing; • Sector 48-49, Transportation and Warehousing; • Sector 51, Information, other than Subsector 519, Other Information Services; • Sector 52, Finance and Insurance; or • Industry Group 2212, Natural Gas Distribution. A taxpayer is a "sales factor weighted taxpayer" if either it used the singles sales factor method in the previous taxable year or it generates greater than 50% of its total sales everywhere from economic activities classified in an NAICS code other than a code within one of the above-listed sectors or industry groups. A single sales factor apportionment requirement phases in for all corporations that are not sales factor weighted taxpayers or optional apportionment taxpayers. Phased-in sales factor weighted taxpayers must use an enhanced sales factor formula consisting of: • for 2020, the property factor, the payroll factor, plus 8 times the sales factor, divided by 10; and • after 2020, the sales factor, divided by 1. For taxable years beginning after 2018, optional apportionment taxpayers may use evenly weighted three-factor formula or the apportionment formula prescribed for phased-in sales factor weighted taxpayers. An optional apportionment taxpayer that chooses to use the phased in single sales factor method must continue using that method in subsequent years. "Optional apportionment taxpayer" generally means a taxpayer with a property factor fraction plus payroll factor fraction divided by two that is greater than 0.50.
Vermont	Three-factor formula with double-weighted sales factor.	
Virginia	Three-factor formula with double-weighted sales factor.	

Jurisdiction	2020 Tax Year	Comment
Washington	N/A, because state does not tax general business corporation income.	
West Virginia	Three-factor formula with double-weighted sales factor.	
Wisconsin	One-factor sales formula.	
Wyoming	N/A, because state does not tax general business corporation income.	

Apportionment—Airlines

The following chart indicates whether each state and the District of Columbia has a special corporation income tax apportionment formula for the airline industry. Where a state uses a special formula and/or special provisions for computing the factors of the formula, the special formula and/or provisions are noted.

Jurisdiction	Airlines	Comment
Alabama	Same formula as other corporations with special rules for computing each factor.	
Alaska	Three-factor formula with special rules for computing each factor, including the ratio of ground time in the state compared to total ground time everywhere.	"Ground time" means all time spent on the ground while loading and unloading passengers, freight, mail, or operating supplies, or during refueling operations, and does not include periods when the aircraft is: • not being loaded or unloaded; • not in service; or • idle due to strikes, repairs and maintenance, downshifts, or seasonal reduction of service.
Arizona	Single-factor formula based on revenue aircraft miles flown.	
Arkansas	One-factor formula based on receipts.	Effective for tax years beginning on or after January 1, 2021, a single sales factor apportionment formula is implemented in Arkansas.
California	Same formula as other corporations with special rules for computing sales factor (each factor for tax years before 2013).	
Colorado	Same formula as other corporations, with special rules for computing sales factor.	
Connecticut	Three-factor formula based on arrivals and departures; revenue tons handled; and originating revenue.	
Delaware	No	
District of Columbia	Same single factor formula as other corporations with special rules for computing sales factor.	
Florida	One-factor formula based on revenue miles.	
Georgia	Special three-factor formula.	
Hawaii	Special three-factor formula.	
Idaho	Same formula as other corporations with special rules for computing each factor.	

Jurisdiction	Airlines	Comment
Illinois	One-factor formula based on revenue miles traveled in the state over the revenue miles traveled everywhere.	Applies to airlines that receive an average of 80% or more of gross income over a 3-year period from: • transportation services; or • ancillary services. Transportation services include intermodal services that involve the single movement of freight by multiple carriers. Ancillary services include: • packing, warehousing, and freight packaging; • passenger food or beverage sales; • in-flight rental of pillows, blankets or headsets; and • airline baggage and reservation services.
Indiana	Three factor formula with special rules for computing each factor.	
Iowa	Formula based on total miles traveled to apportion gross receipt or gross revenues.	
Kansas	Same formula as other corporations with special rules for computing each factor.	
Kentucky	**Commercial passenger airlines:** Same formula as for other corporations, except special rules for computing factors. **Air freight forwarders:** Same formula as for other corporations, except special rules for computing factors.	
Louisiana	Effective January 1, 2016, one-factor formula based on gross apportionable income.	Prior to 2016, two-factor formula (property and income) with special rules for computing each factor.
Maine	No	
Maryland	Evenly weighted three-factor formula.	
Massachusetts	Same three-factor formula as other corporations with special rules for computing each factor.	
Michigan	One-factor formula based on revenue miles.	
Minnesota	Same formula as other corporations with special rules for computing each factor.	
Mississippi	Alternative two-factor (revenue passenger miles and revenue ton miles) and one-factor (flight miles) formulas.	
Missouri	Same evenly weighted three-factor formula with special rules for computing each factor, or optional one-factor mileage ratio formula.	

Jurisdiction	Airlines	Comment
Montana	Same formula as other corporations with special rules for computing each factor.	
Nebraska	Same formula as other corporations with special rules for computing each factor.	
Nevada	N/A, because state does not tax general business corporation income.	
New Hampshire	Same formula as other corporations with special rules for computing each factor.	
New Jersey	Same formula as for other corporations with special rules for computing the receipts factor.	
New Mexico	Same formula as other corporations with special rules for computing each factor.	
New York	Yes	For tax years before 2015, air freight forwarders and foreign airlines use a formula with a double-weighted receipts factor and special rules for computing the factors. Other taxpayers engaged in aviation activities use a three-factor formula with special rules for computing each factor. For tax years after 2014, aviation service providers use a single receipts factor, with special rules for computing the factor (generally based on arrivals and departures, revenue tons, and originating revenue; or, for air freight forwarding, based on pickup and delivery).
North Carolina	One-factor formula based on revenue ton miles.	
North Dakota	Same formula as other corporations with special rules for computing each factor.	
Ohio	No.	
Oklahoma	Same formula as other corporations with special rules for computing each factor.	
Oregon	Same formula as other corporations with special rules for computing each factor.	
Pennsylvania	One-factor formula based on revenue miles for transportation of property and two-factor formula based on revenue miles for transportation of passengers.	

Jurisdiction	Airlines	Comment
Rhode Island	**Taxable years beginning on or after January 1, 2015:** Same formula as other corporations with special rules for computing receipts. **Taxable years beginning before 2015:** Same formula as other corporations with special rules for computing each factor.	
South Carolina	One-factor formula based on revenue tons.	
South Dakota	N/A, because state does not tax general business corporation income.	
Tennessee	Two-factor formula (originating revenue and total air miles) with special rules for computing each factor.	
Texas	One-factor formula based on total miles.	
Utah	Same formula as other corporations with special rules for computing each factor.	
Vermont	No	
Virginia	No	
Washington	N/A, because state does not tax general business corporation income.	
West Virginia	No	
Wisconsin	Three-factor formula based on arrivals and departures, revenue tons, and originating revenue. Air freight forwarders use a three-factor formula based on arrivals and departures scheduled by affiliated carrier, revenue tons handled by affiliated carrier, and revenue.	
Wyoming	N/A, because state does not tax general business corporation income.	

Apportionment—Athletics

The following chart indicates whether each state and the District of Columbia has a special corporation income tax apportionment formula for the athletic teams. Where a state uses a special formula and/or special provisions for computing the factors of the formula, the special formula and/or provisions are noted.

Jurisdiction	Athletics	Comment
Alabama	No	
Alaska	No	
Arizona	No	
Arkansas	No	
California	Same formula as other corporations, except: • all property, payroll, and sales are deemed to be in the state for teams whose base of operations is in the state; • all property, payroll, and sales are deemed to be outside of the state for teams whose base of operations is in another state or country; and • special rules apply when a team whose base of operations is in the state is subject to an income-based tax in another state or country.	
Colorado	No	
Connecticut	No	
Delaware	No	
District of Columbia	No	
Florida	No	
Georgia	No	
Hawaii	No	
Idaho	No	
Illinois	No	
Indiana	No	
Iowa	No	
Kansas	No	
Kentucky	No	
Louisiana	No	
Maine	No	
Maryland	No	
Massachusetts	No	

Jurisdiction	Athletics	Comment
Michigan	No	
Minnesota	Same formula as other corporations, except that all income from the operation of an athletic team is assigned to the state in which the team's operation is based when the visiting team does not share in the gate receipts.	
Mississippi	No	
Missouri	No	
Montana	No	
Nebraska	No	
Nevada	N/A, because state does not tax general business corporation income.	
New Hampshire	No	
New Jersey	No	
New Mexico	No	
New York	No	
North Carolina	No	
North Dakota	No	
Ohio	Gross receipts may be sitused to Ohio using any reasonable, consistent, and uniform method of apportionment.	
Oklahoma	No	
Oregon	No	
Pennsylvania	No	
Rhode Island	No	
South Carolina	No	
South Dakota	N/A, because state does not tax general business corporation income.	
Tennessee	No	
Texas	No	
Utah	No	
Vermont	No	
Virginia	No	
Washington	N/A, because state does not tax general business corporation income.	

Jurisdiction	Athletics	Comment
West Virginia	No	
Wisconsin	Same formula as general business corporations, subject to following sales factor adjustments: Gate receipts, radio and television receipts, concessions and miscellaneous income are included. Income from player contract transactions, franchise fees, and similar sources are excluded.	
Wyoming	N/A, because state does not tax general business corporation income.	

Apportionment—Construction

The following chart indicates whether each state and the District of Columbia has a special corporation income tax apportionment formula for the construction industry. Where a state uses a special formula and/or special provisions for computing the factors of the formula, the special formula and/or provisions are noted.

Jurisdiction	Construction	Comment
Alabama	Same formula as other corporations with special rules for computing each factor and for accounting method used.	
Alaska	Three-factor formula with special rules for computing each factor and for accounting method used.	
Arizona	No	
Arkansas	Same formula as other corporations with special rules for computing each factor.	Effective for tax years beginning on or after January 1, 2021, a single sales factor apportionment formula is implemented in Arkansas.
California	Same formula as other corporations with special rules for computing sales factor (each factor prior to 2013 tax year) and for accounting method used.	
Colorado	Same formula as other corporations, with special rules for computing sales factor.	
Connecticut	No	
Delaware	No	
District of Columbia	No	
Florida	No	
Georgia	No	
Hawaii	Same formula as other corporations with special rules for computing each factor and for accounting method used.	
Idaho	Same formula as other corporations with special rules for computing each factor and for accounting method used.	
Illinois	No	
Indiana	No	
Iowa	One-factor formula based on gross receipts.	
Kansas	No	

Jurisdiction	Construction	Comment
Kentucky	Same formula as other corporations with special rules for computing each factor and for accounting method used.	
Louisiana	No	
Maine	No	
Maryland	No	
Massachusetts	No	
Michigan	No	
Minnesota	No	
Mississippi	One-factor formula based on contract receipts.	
Missouri	Same formula as other corporations with special rules for computing each factor and for accounting method used.	
Montana	Same formula as other corporations with special rules for computing each factor.	
Nebraska	No	
Nevada	N/A, because state does not tax general business corporation income.	
New Hampshire	No	
New Jersey	No	
New Mexico	Same formula as other corporations with special rules for computing each factor.	
New York	No	
North Carolina	No **Tax years before 2018:** One-factor formula based on sales.	
North Dakota	No	
Ohio	Gross receipts may be sitused to Ohio using any reasonable, consistent, and uniform method of apportionment. As a default, the number of properties anticipated to be built in Ohio compared to everywhere will be accepted. If the services are not for standardized buildings, square footage may be used as a method of apportionment unless it creates a distortion.	
Oklahoma	No	

Jurisdiction	Construction	Comment
Oregon	Same formula as other corporations with special rules for computing each factor.	
Pennsylvania	No	
Rhode Island	No	
South Carolina	No	
South Dakota	N/A, because state does not tax general business corporation income.	
Tennessee	No	
Texas	No	
Utah	Same formula as other corporations with special rules for computing each factor and for accounting method used.	
Vermont	No	
Virginia	One-factor formula for corporations that elect to report on the completed-contract basis.	
Washington	N/A, because state does not tax general business corporation income.	
West Virginia	No	
Wisconsin	No	
Wyoming	N/A, because state does not tax general business corporation income.	

Apportionment—Financial Corporations

The following chart indicates whether each state and the District of Columbia has a special corporation income tax apportionment formula for financial corporations. Where a state uses a special formula and/or special provisions for computing the factors of the formula, the special formula and/or provisions are noted.

Jurisdiction	Financial Corporations	Comment
Alabama	Three-factor formula for financial institution excise tax based on receipts, property, and payroll.	
Alaska	Three-factor formula with special rules for computing property and sales factors.	
Arizona	No	
Arkansas	Through 2020, three-factor formula with special rules for computing each factor.	For taxable years beginning on or after January 1, 2021, a single sales factor apportionment formula is implemented, including for financial institutions.
California	Equally weighted three-factor formula with special rules for computing receipts and property factors. If single-sales factor formula used, only special rule for sales factor applies.	
Colorado	Same formula as for other corporations, with special rules for computing each factor.	
Connecticut	One-factor formula based on receipts.	
Delaware	Yes, banks or trust companies electing to pay the alternative bank franchise tax must apply three-factor formula with double-weighted receipts factor and special rules for computing each factor.	
District of Columbia	Two-factor formula based on payroll and gross income.	
Florida	Same formula as other corporations with special rules for computing property and sales factors.	
Georgia	No	
Hawaii	Same formula as other corporations with special rules for computing receipts and property factors and special rules for international banks.	
Idaho	Same formula as other corporations with special rules for computing each factor.	
Illinois	One-factor formula based on gross receipts.	
Indiana	No	

Jurisdiction	Financial Corporations	Comment
Iowa	One-factor formula based on gross income.	
Kansas	Same formula as other corporations with special rules for computing each factor.	
Kentucky	Same formula as other corporations, except special rules for computing factors.	
Louisiana	No	
Maine	Three-factor formula with double-weighted receipts factor.	
Maryland	Three-factor formula with double-weighted receipt factor and special rules for computing each factor.	
Massachusetts	Three-factor formula (receipts, property, and payroll).	
Michigan	No.	
Minnesota	One-factor formula based on sales.	Same formula as other corporations for tax years before 2014 with special rules for computing each factor.
Mississippi	Same formula as other corporations with special rules for computing each factor.	
Missouri	One-factor sales apportionment formula.	
Montana	No	
Nebraska	No	
Nevada	N/A, because state does not tax general business corporation income.	
New Hampshire	Same formula as other corporations with special rules for computing property and sales factors.	
New Jersey	No	
New Mexico	Same formula as other corporations with special rules for computing each factor.	
New York	**Tax years before 2015:** Three-factor formula with special rules for computing each factor, except single receipts factor applies to certain taxpayers providing services to an investment company. **Tax years after 2014:** Same formula as other corporations under Article 9-A, and special rules for sourcing receipts from financial transactions.	

Jurisdiction	Financial Corporations	Comment
North Carolina	One-factor formula based on receipts for tax years after 2019. **Tax years before 2018:** One-factor formula for loan companies based on sales.	
North Dakota	Same formula as other corporations with special rules for computing each factor.	
Ohio	Gross receipts may be sitused to Ohio using any reasonable, consistent, and uniform method of apportionment. As a default, the number of locations in Ohio compared to everywhere will be accepted.	
Oklahoma	No	
Oregon	Same formula as other corporations with special rules for computing property and receipts factors.	
Pennsylvania	No	
Rhode Island	One-factor formula based on the domicile of customers.	
South Carolina	No	
South Dakota	N/A, because state does not tax general business corporation income.	
Tennessee	One-factor formula based on gross receipts.	For tax years after 2017, elective single receipts factor available for financial asset management companies.
Texas	Same formula as other corporations with special rules for excluding certain interest.	
Utah	Same formula as other corporations with special rules for computing property and receipts factors.	
Vermont	No	
Virginia	One-factor formula based on total business.	
Washington	N/A, because state does not tax general business corporation income.	
West Virginia	One-factor formula based on gross receipts.	
Wisconsin	One-factor receipts formula.	
Wyoming	N/A, because state does not tax general business corporation income.	

Apportionment—Motor Carriers

The following chart indicates whether each state and the District of Columbia has a special corporation income tax apportionment formula for motor carriers. Where a state uses a special formula and/or special provisions for computing the factors of the formula, the special formula and/or provisions are noted.

Jurisdiction	Motor Carriers	Comment
Alabama	Same formula as other corporations with special rules for computing each factor.	
Alaska	Three-factor formula with special rules for computing each factor, including a terminal days ratio based on the number of days spent in terminals in the state divided by the total number of days spent in terminals everywhere.	A terminal is any location where goods are loaded on or unloaded from interstate mobile transportation equipment. Time spent in terminals does not include periods when the interstate mobile transportation equipment is: • not being loaded or unloaded; • not in service; or • idle due to strikes, repairs and maintenance, downshifts, or seasonal reduction of service.
Arizona	No	
Arkansas	One-factor formula based on miles operated inside and outside the state.	Effective for tax years beginning on or after January 1, 2021, a single sales factor apportionment formula is implemented in Arkansas.
California	Same formula as other corporations with special rules for computing sales factor (each factor for tax years before 2013).	
Colorado	Same formula as other corporations, with special rules for computing sales factor.	
Connecticut	One-factor formula based on miles operated.	
Delaware	No	
District of Columbia	Same single factor formula as other corporations with special rules for computing sales factor.	
Florida	One-factor formula based on revenue miles.	
Georgia	Same formula as for other corporations with special rules for computing sales factor.	
Hawaii	No	
Idaho	Three-factor formula with special rules for computing each factor.	

Jurisdiction	Motor Carriers	Comment
Illinois	One-factor formula based on gross receipts from transportation services that both originates and terminates in the state, plus gross receipts from interstate transportation, multiplied by a fraction equal to the miles traveled in the state on all interstate trips divided by miles traveled everywhere on all interstate trips, over all gross receipts derived from transportation services.	Applies to carriers that receive an average of 80% or more of gross income over a 3-year period from: • transportation services; or • ancillary services. Transportation services include intermodal services that involve the single movement of freight by multiple carriers. Ancillary services include: • packing, warehousing, and freight packaging; and • truck and driver leasing or similar arrangements.
Indiana	Three factor formula with special rules for computing each factor.	
Iowa	One-factor formula based on total miles traveled.	
Kansas	One-factor formula based on miles operated.	
Kentucky	Same formula as other corporations with special rules for computing property and sales factors.	
Louisiana	Effective January 1, 2016, one-factor formula based on gross apportionable income.	Prior to 2016, two-factor formula based on property and income with special rules for computing each factor.
Maine	No	
Maryland	One-factor formula based on miles traveled.	
Massachusetts	Same three-factor formula as other corporations with special rules for computing each factor.	
Michigan	One-factor formula based on revenue miles.	
Minnesota	No	
Mississippi	One-factor formulas based on business income, vehicle miles, or gross receipts.	
Missouri	Same formula as other corporations with special rules for computing each factor. Optional one-factor mileage ratio formula.	
Montana	Same formula as other corporations with special rules for computing each factor.	
Nebraska	Same formula as other corporations, except special rules for transportation revenue based on mobile property miles.	
Nevada	N/A, because state does not tax general business corporation income.	

Jurisdiction	Motor Carriers	Comment
New Hampshire	Same formula as other corporations with special rules for computing each factor.	
New Jersey	Same formula as other corporations with special rules for computing receipts factor.	
New Mexico	Same formula as other corporations with special rules for computing each factor.	
New York	One-factor formula based on miles traveled.	
North Carolina	One-factor formula based on vehicle miles.	
North Dakota	Same formula as other corporations with special rules for computing each factor.	
Ohio	No.	
Oklahoma	Same formula as other corporations with special rules for computing each factor.	
Oregon	Same formula as other corporations with special rules for computing each factor.	
Pennsylvania	One-factor formula based on revenue miles. Two-factor formula based on revenue miles or transportation of property and passengers.	
Rhode Island	**Taxable years beginning on or after January 1, 2015:** Same formula as other corporations with special rules for computing receipts. **Taxable years beginning before 2015:** Same formula as other corporations with special rules for computing each factor.	
South Carolina	One-factor formula based on vehicle miles.	
South Dakota	N/A, because state does not tax general business corporation income.	
Tennessee	Two-factor formula based on gross receipts and mileage with special rules for computing each factor. One-factor formula based on rail and highway mileage transport of passengers and property by both rail and motor carrier.	

Jurisdiction	Motor Carriers	Comment
Texas	One-factor formula based on total miles.	
Utah	Same formula as other corporations with special rules for computing each factor.	
Vermont	No	
Virginia	One-factor formula based on vehicle miles.	
Washington	N/A, because state does not tax general business corporation income.	
West Virginia	One-factor formula based on vehicle miles.	
Wisconsin	Two-factor formula based on gross receipts and ton miles.	
Wyoming	N/A, because state does not tax general business corporation income.	

Apportionment—Others

The following chart indicates whether each state and the District of Columbia has a special corporation income tax apportionment formula for various industries, including investment and financial services, mineral production, oil and gas production, and film production. Where a state uses a special formula and/or special provisions for computing the factors of the formula, the special formula and/or provisions are noted.

Jurisdiction	Other Industries	Comment
Alabama	None	
Alaska	***Oil and gas production:*** Two-factor sales and extraction formula with special rules for computing each factor. ***Oil and gas production plus pipeline transportation:*** Three-factor formula (sales, property, and extraction) with special rules for computing each factor.	
Arizona	None	
Arkansas	Passive intangible holding companies: One-factor sales formula.	Effective for tax years beginning on or after January 1, 2021, a single sales factor apportionment formula is implemented in Arkansas.
California	***Unitary businesses with foreign operations:*** Same formula as other corporations, except applicable exchange rates used in computing factor(s). ***Franchisors:*** Same formula as other corporations, except payroll factor modified for employees traveling to franchise locations to provide administrative or advisory services and sales factor modified for various service fees and royalty payments. ***Commercial fishing:*** Same formula as other corporations, except port day ratio applied to each factor's numerator. ***Film and television producers, distributors, and television networks:*** Same formula as other corporations, except for pre-2013 years property factor modified for film costs and studio rental; for pre-2013 tax years, payroll factor modified for compensation such as talent salaries, residual and profit participation payments, payments made by producers to other corporations for actor and director services; and sales factor modified for gross receipts from theaters, television stations, video cassettes, and discs.	Film distributors were not covered by special apportionment regulation prior to 2011 tax year. If single sales factor apportionment formula used, only modifications to sales factor rules apply.
Colorado	None	

Jurisdiction	Other Industries	Comment
Connecticut	***Securities brokerages:*** One-factor formula based on brokerage commission and total margin interest paid. ***Credit card companies:*** One-factor formula based on receipts, interest, fees, and penalties.	
Delaware	***Asset Management Corporations:*** One-factor gross receipts formula. ***Worldwide Headquarters Corporations:*** Equally-weighted three-factor formula or optional one-factor sales formula for tax years after 2016.	
District of Columbia	None	
Florida	***Citrus growers:*** Same three-factor formula as other corporations or optional one-factor sales formula.	
Georgia	***Credit card processing services:*** One-factor formula based on gross receipts for qualifying rents. ***Public service corporations:*** One-factor formula based on gross operating revenues.	
Hawaii	None	
Idaho	None	
Illinois	***Federally regulated exchanges*:** Optional one-factor formula based on: • transactions executed on a physical trading floor located in the state; • all other matching, execution, or clearing transactions, including without limitation receipts from the provision of matching, execution, or clearing services to another entity, multiplied by 27.54%; and • all other sales in the state.	
Indiana	None	
Iowa	None	
Kansas	None	
Kentucky	***Enterprise zone brokerage service sales:*** Optional one-factor formula based on brokerage commissions and margin interest.	Election irrevocable for 5 years.

Jurisdiction	Other Industries	Comment
Louisiana	***Oil and gas companies:*** Three-factor formula with double weighted sales factor (effective January 1, 2016). ***Service businesses:*** One-factor sales formula (effective January 1, 2016). ***Merchandisers:*** One-factor sales formula.	Prior to 2016 for service businesses, two-factor sales and payroll formula.
Maine	No	
Maryland	***Brokerage services:*** One-factor receipts formula. ***Processing services:*** Same three-factor formula as other corporations, except numerator of sales factor determined using point of sale. ***Leasing and rental enterprises:*** Two-factor formula based on receipts and property with special rules for computing each factor. ***Film and television production:*** Same three-factor formula as other corporations, except property factor modified for film costs and studio rental; payroll factor modified for compensation such as talent salaries, residual and profit participation payments; sales factor modified for gross receipts from theatres, television stations, video cassettes, and discs.	
Massachusetts	***Courier and package delivery services:*** Same three-factor formula as other corporations with special rules for property and payroll factors.	Sales factor computed using sourcing rules for transportation and delivery services. **Tax years before 2014:** Same three-factor formula as other corporations with special rules for computing each factor.
Michigan	None	
Minnesota	***Certain mail-order and telephone solicitation businesses:*** One-factor sales formula. ***Investment companies:*** One-factor formula based on aggregate of gross payments collected.	

Jurisdiction	Other Industries	Comment
Mississippi	***Mineral and natural resource producers:*** One-factor sales factor formula that includes market value of minerals or natural resources produced. ***Medical or pharmaceutical supplier:*** Three-factor formula with double weighted payroll and property factors. ***Major medical laboratory service businesses:*** Effective January 1, 2019, one-factor sales factor formula for net business income.	
Missouri	***Bridge companies:*** Same evenly weighted three-factor formula or optional one-factor mileage ratio formula, except 50% of net income from interstate bridge operations is included.	
Montana	None	
Nebraska	None	
Nevada	N/A, because state does not tax general business corporation income.	
New Hampshire	None	
New Jersey	Asset management services provided to regulated investment companies; Same formula as for other corporations with special rules for computing the receipts factor.	
New Mexico	Taxpayers with headquarters operations in New Mexico may elect to use single-sales factor formula.	
New York	***Owners of cable TV rights:*** Same formula as other corporations, except special rule for receipts factor. ***Newspaper and periodical advertisers:*** Same formula as other corporations, except special situsing rules for receipts factor. ***Securities and commodities brokers:*** Same formula as other corporations, except receipts factor modified special situsing rules on commissions, margin interest, account maintenance fees, management or advisory service fees, interest on certain loans and advances, and gross income, including accrued interest or dividends, from certain principal transactions.	

Jurisdiction	Other Industries	Comment
North Carolina	None **Tax years before 2018:** One-factor sales formula.	
North Dakota	None	
Ohio	Yes	Ohio rules sets forth the situsing methods for various services.
Oklahoma	None	
Oregon	***Film and TV producers:*** Same one-factor sales formula as other corporations, except property factor modified for film costs and studio rental; payroll factor modified for compensation such as talent salaries, residual and profit participation payments; sales factor modified for gross receipts from theatres, television stations, video cassettes, and discs. ***Installment sales:*** Percentage-of-the-year formula. ***Lobbying expenses:*** One-factor dues received formula. ***Timber:*** Three-factor formula with double-weighted sales factor beginning July 1, 2005. ***Forest products:*** Three-factor formula with double-weighted sales factor before 2010.	
Pennsylvania	None	
Rhode Island	***Pension plan service companies:*** One-factor formula based on the domicile of customers.	
South Carolina	None	
South Dakota	N/A, because state does not tax general business corporation income.	
Tennessee	None	
Texas	***Newspaper and magazine advertisers:*** (Former franchise tax) Same one-factor receipts formula as other corporations, except advertising revenues apportioned on basis of distribution.	
Utah	***Securities and commodities brokers, dealers:*** Same formula as other corporations, except property factor modified by average value of securities or commodities used to produce income and sales factor modified by brokerage commissions, margin interest, and account maintenance fees.	

Jurisdiction	Other Industries	Comment
Vermont	None	
Virginia	***Retail companies:*** Triple-weighted sales factor for tax years beginning on or after July 1, 2012, but before July 1, 2014; quadruple-weighted sales factor for tax years beginning on or after July 1, 2014, but before July 1, 2015; and one-factor sales formula for tax years beginning on and after July 1, 2015. ***Certain enterprise data center operators***: Quadruple-weighted sales factor formula from July 1, 2016, until July 1, 2017, and one-factor sales formula beginning on July 1, 2017, and thereafter.	
Washington	N/A, because state does not tax general business corporation income.	
West Virginia	None	
Wisconsin	None	
Wyoming	N/A, because state does not tax general business corporation income.	

Apportionment—Pipelines

The following chart indicates whether each state and the District of Columbia has a special corporation income tax apportionment formula for pipeline corporations. Where a state uses a special formula and/or special provisions for computing the factors of the formula, the special formula and/or provisions are noted.

Jurisdiction	Pipelines	Comment
Alabama	No	
Alaska	Two-factor formula based on property and sales for taxpayers engaged only in pipeline transportation of oil or gas with special rules for computing each factor. Three-factor formula based on sales, property, and extraction for taxpayers engaged in pipeline transportation and oil and gas production with special rules for computing each factor.	
Arizona	No	
Arkansas	Same formula as other corporations with special rules for computing each factor.	Effective for tax years beginning on or after January 1, 2021, a single sales factor apportionment formula is implemented in Arkansas.
California	Same formula as other corporations with special rules for computing sales factor (and property factor for tax years before 2013).	
Colorado	No	
Connecticut	No	
Delaware	No	
District of Columbia	No	
Florida	One-factor formula based on revenue miles.	
Georgia	Same formula as for other corporations with special rules for computing sales factor.	
Hawaii	No	
Idaho	No	
Illinois	One-factor formula based on gross receipts from transportation services that both originates and terminates in the state, plus gross receipts from interstate transportation, multiplied by a fraction equal to the miles traveled in the state on all interstate trips divided by miles traveled everywhere on all interstate trips, over all gross receipts derived from transportation services.	Applies to pipline businesses that receive an average of 80% or more of gross income over a 3-year period from: • transportation services; or • ancillary services.

Jurisdiction	Pipelines	Comment
Indiana	Three factor formula with special rules for computing each factor.	
Iowa	One-factor formula transportation revenue based on traffic units.	
Kansas	No	
Kentucky	Same formula as other corporations with special rules for sales factor.	
Louisiana	Same formula as other corporations with special rules for computing sales factor.	
Maine	No	
Maryland	No	
Massachusetts	Same three-factor formula as other corporations, except sales factor is a fraction the numerator of which is the total number of traffic units in the state during the taxable year and the denominator of which is the total number of traffic units everywhere during the taxable year.	A traffic unit is the movement of one unit of product such as one barrel of oil, one barrel of gasoline or one thousand cubic feet of natural or casinghead gas, for a distance of one mile.
Michigan	One-factor formula based on miles transported.	
Minnesota	No	
Mississippi	Three-factor formula based on property, payroll, and traffic miles.	
Missouri	No	
Montana	No	
Nebraska	One-factor formula based on revenue miles.	
Nevada	N/A, because state does not tax general business corporation income.	
New Hampshire	No	
New Jersey	No	
New Mexico	No	
New York	Same formula as other corporations with special rules for computing receipts factor, based on transportation units.	
North Carolina	One-factor formula based on barrel miles. **Tax years after 2019:** One-factor formula based on traffic units.	
North Dakota	No	

Jurisdiction	Pipelines	Comment
Ohio	No.	
Oklahoma	Same formula as other corporations with special rules for computing each factor.	
Oregon	No	
Pennsylvania	One-factor formula based on revenue ton miles, revenue barrel miles, or revenue cubic miles.	
Rhode Island	No	
South Carolina	One-factor formula based on revenue ton miles, revenue barrel miles, or revenue cubic miles.	
South Dakota	N/A, because state does not tax general business corporation income.	
Tennessee	Two-factor formula based on gross receipts and pipeline miles with special rules for computing each factor.	
Texas	One-factor formula with special rules for natural gas production.	
Utah	No	
Vermont	No	
Virginia	No	
Washington	N/A, because state does not tax general business corporation income.	
West Virginia	No	
Wisconsin	Three-factor formula based on property, payroll and traffic units.	
Wyoming	N/A, because state does not tax general business corporation income.	

Apportionment—Railroads

The following chart indicates whether each state and the District of Columbia has a special corporation income tax apportionment formula for the railroad industry. Where a state uses a special formula and/or special provisions for computing the factors of the formula, the special formula and/or provisions are noted.

Jurisdiction	Railroads	Comment
Alabama	Same formula as other corporations with special rules for computing each factor.	
Alaska	Three-factor formula with special rules for computing each factor, including a terminal days ratio based on the number of days spent in terminals in the state divided by the total number of days spent in terminals everywhere.	A terminal is any location where goods are loaded on or unloaded from interstate mobile transportation equipment. Time spent in terminals does not include periods when the interstate mobile transportation equipment is: • not being loaded or unloaded; • not in service; or • idle due to strikes, repairs and maintenance, downshifts, or seasonal reduction of service.
Arizona	No	
Arkansas	Same formula as for other corporations with special rules for computing each factor. One-factor formula based on total mileage for private railcar operators.	Effective for tax years beginning on or after January 1, 2021, a single sales factor apportionment formula is implemented in Arkansas.
California	Same formula as other corporations with special rules for computing sales factor (each factor prior to 2013 tax year).	
Colorado	Same formula as other corporations, with special rules for computing sales factor.	
Connecticut	No	
Delaware	No	
District of Columbia	Same single factor formula as other corporations with special rules for computing sales factor.	
Florida	One-factor formula based on revenue miles.	
Georgia	One-factor formula for qualifying rents based on gross operating revenues.	
Hawaii	No	
Idaho	Three-factor formula with special rules for computing each factor.	

Jurisdiction	Railroads	Comment
Illinois	One-factor formula based on gross receipts from transportation services that both originates and terminates in the state, plus gross receipts from interstate transportation, multiplied by a fraction equal to the miles traveled in the state on all interstate trips divided by miles traveled everywhere on all interstate trips, over all gross receipts derived from transportation services.	Applies to railroads that receive an average of 80% or more of gross income over a 3-year period from: • transportation services; or • ancillary services. Transportation services include intermodal services that involve the single movement of freight by multiple carriers. Ancillary services include: • packing, warehousing, and freight packaging; • passenger food or beverage sales; and • railroad switching and transportation detention charges.
Indiana	Three factor formula with special rules for computing each factor.	
Iowa	One-factor formula based on car and locomotive miles traveled.	
Kansas	One-factor formula based on freight car miles.	
Kentucky	Same formula as other corporations with special rules for computing sales and property factor.	
Louisiana	Effective January 1, 2016, one-factor formula based on gross apportionable income.	Prior to 2016, two-factor formula based on property and income with special rules for computing each factor.
Maine	No	
Maryland	One-factor formula based on miles traveled.	
Massachusetts	Same three-factor formula as other corporations, except sales factor is determined by multiplying total receipts from transportation or delivery services by the percentage of the total passenger departures or property pickups and passenger arrivals or property deliveries that take place in the state relative to the departures/pickups and arrivals/deliveries that take place everywhere.	No special apportionment formula for tax years beginning before January 1, 2014.
Michigan	One-factor formula based on revenue miles.	
Minnesota	No	
Mississippi	One-factor formulas based on mileage.	
Missouri	Same evenly weighted three-factor formula with special rules for computing each factor, or optional one-factor mileage ratio formula.	
Montana	Same formula as other corporations with special rules for computing all three factors.	

Jurisdiction	Railroads	Comment
Nebraska	No	
Nevada	N/A, because state does not tax general business corporation income.	
New Hampshire	Same formula as other corporations with special rules for computing each factor.	
New Jersey	No	
New Mexico	Same formula as other corporations with special rules for computing each factor.	
New York	One-factor formula based on miles traveled.	
North Carolina	One-factor formula based on railway operating revenue.	
North Dakota	Same formula as other corporations with special rules for computing each factor.	
Ohio	No.	
Oklahoma	Same formula as other corporations with special rules for computing each factor.	
Oregon	Same formula as other corporations with special rules for computing each factor.	
Pennsylvania	One-factor formula based on revenue miles for transportation of property. Two-factor formula based on revenue miles for transportation of property and passengers.	
Rhode Island	No	
South Carolina	One-factor formula based on railway operating revenue.	
South Dakota	N/A, because state does not tax general business corporation income.	
Tennessee	Two-factor formula based on gross receipts and mileage with special rules for computing each factor. One-factor formula for taxpayers that transport passengers and property by both rail and motor carrier.	
Texas	One-factor formula based on total miles.	
Utah	Same formula as other corporations with special rules for computing each factor.	
Vermont	No	

Jurisdiction	Railroads	Comment
Virginia	One-factor formula based on revenue car miles.	
Washington	N/A, because state does not tax general business corporation income.	
West Virginia	No	
Wisconsin	Two-factor formula based on gross receipts and revenue ton miles for railroads and sleeping car companies.	
Wyoming	N/A, because state does not tax general business corporation income.	

Apportionment—Ship Transport

The following chart indicates whether each state and the District of Columbia has a special corporation income tax apportionment formula for the ship transport industry. Where a state uses a special formula and/or special provisions for computing the factors of the formula, the special formula and/or provisions are noted.

Jurisdiction	Ship Transport	Comment
Alabama	No	
Alaska	Three-factor formula with special rules for computing each factor, including a days-spent-in-port ratio based on number of 24-hour days spent in state ports during tax year divided by total number of days spent in all ports during tax year.	When determining whether 20% U.S. factor test is satisfied and must be included in a water's edge combined report, days-spent-in-port ratio must be used to attribute to U.S. that portion of property, payroll, and sales factors of the company and each of its affiliates.
Arizona	No	
Arkansas	No	
California	Same formula as other corporations with special rules for computing sales factor (each factor prior to 2013 tax year).	
Colorado	No	
Connecticut	No	
Delaware	No	
District of Columbia	Same single factor formula as other corporations with special rules for computing sales factor.	
Florida	One-factor formula based on revenue miles.	
Georgia	No	
Hawaii	Special three-factor formula.	
Idaho	No	
Illinois	One-factor formula based on gross receipts from transportation services that both originates and terminates in the state, plus gross receipts from interstate transportation, multiplied by a fraction equal to the miles traveled in the state on all interstate trips divided by miles traveled everywhere on all interstate trips, over all gross receipts derived from transportation services.	Applies to transportation businesses that receive an average of 80% or more of gross income over a 3-year period from: • transportation services; or • ancillary services. Transportation services include intermodal services that involve the single movement of freight by multiple carriers. Ancillary services include packing, warehousing, and freight packaging.
Indiana	Three factor formula with special rules for computing each factor.	

Jurisdiction	Ship Transport	Comment
Iowa	One factor gross receipts or gross revenues formula based on total miles.	
Kansas	No	
Kentucky	Same formula as for other corporations with special rules for computing property and sales factors.	
Louisiana	Effective January 1, 2016, one-factor formula based on gross apportionable income.	Prior to 2016, two-factor formula based on property and income with special rules for computing each factor.
Maine	No	
Maryland	One-factor formula based on miles traveled.	
Massachusetts	Same three-factor formula as other corporations, except sales factor is determined by multiplying total receipts from transportation or delivery services by the percentage of the total passenger departures or property pickups and passenger arrivals or property deliveries that take place in the state relative to the departures/pickups and arrivals/deliveries that take place everywhere.	No special apportionment formula for tax years beginning before January 1, 2014.
Michigan	One-factor formula based on receipts.	
Minnesota	No	
Mississippi	No	
Missouri	No	
Montana	No	
Nebraska	No	
Nevada	N/A, because state does not tax general business corporation income.	
New Hampshire	Same formula as other corporations with special rules for computing each factor.	
New Jersey	No	
New Mexico	No	
New York	N/A	Transportation companies are subject to tax under Art. 9, rather than the general corporate franchise tax. Generally, under Art. 9, vessel operators use a one-factor apportionment formula based on working days.
North Carolina	One-factor formula based on revenue ton miles.	
North Dakota	No	

Jurisdiction	Ship Transport	Comment
Ohio	No	
Oklahoma	No	
Oregon	Same formula as other corporations with special rules for computing each factor.	
Pennsylvania	One-factor formula based on days in port (high seas) or revenue miles (inland waters).	
Rhode Island	No	
South Carolina	One-factor formula based on revenue tons.	
South Dakota	N/A, because state does not tax general business corporation income.	
Tennessee	No	
Texas	One-factor formula based on total miles.	
Utah	No	
Vermont	No	
Virginia	No	
Washington	N/A, because state does not tax general business corporation income.	
West Virginia	No	
Wisconsin	No	
Wyoming	N/A, because state does not tax general business corporation income.	

Asset Expense Election–IRC § 179

Under IRC § 179, taxpayers may elect to expense in the year acquired, rather than depreciate, certain qualified property used in an active trade or business, up to a maximum dollar amount. The expense deduction is phased out on a dollar-for-dollar basis once the taxpayer's total investment in qualified depreciable property for the taxable year exceeds a threshold amount.

Current and historical dollar and investment limits (since 2003):

- $100,000 and $400,000 for the 2003 tax year (Jobs and Growth Tax Relief Reconciliation Act (JGTRRA) of 2003 (P.L.108-27));
- $102,000 and $410,000, as adjusted for inflation, for the 2004 tax year (American Jobs Creation Act of 2004 (AJCA) (P.L. 108-357));
- $105,000 and $420,000, as adjusted for inflation, for the 2005 tax year (American Jobs Creation Act of 2004 (AJCA) (P.L. 108-357));
- $108,000 and $430,000, as adjusted for inflation, for the 2006 tax year (American Jobs Creation Act of 2004 (AJCA) (P.L. 108-357));
- $125,000 and $400,000, for the 2007 tax year (Small Business and Work Opportunity Tax Act of 2007 (P.L. 110-28));
- $250,000 and $800,000, for the 2008 and 2009 tax years (Economic Stimulus Act (ESA) of 2008 (P.L. 110-185); American Recovery and Reinvestment Tax Act of 2009 (ARRA) (P.L. 111-5)); and
- $500,000 and $2,000,000, for tax years 2010-2015 (Small Business Jobs Act of 2010 (P.L. 111-240); American Taxpayer Relief Act of 2012 (ATRA) (P.L. 112-240); Tax Increase Prevention Act of 2014 (P.L. 113-295));
- $500,000 and $ 2,010,000, as adjusted for inflation, for the 2016 tax year (Protecting Americans from Tax Hikes Act of 2015 (PATH Act) (P.L. 114-113));
- $510,000 and $2,030,000, as adjusted for inflation, for the 2017 tax year (PATH Act); and
- $1 million and $2.5 million (as adjusted for inflation) for tax years after 2017 (Tax Cuts and Jobs Act (P.L. 115-97)).

This chart shows the tax treatment by each state and the District of Columbia of the IRC § 179 asset expense deduction.

Jurisdiction	Asset Expense Election—IRC § 179	Comment
Alabama	Subtraction from federal tax base allowed for qualified irrigation equipment equal to federal deduction limits that existed on January 1, 2011. No other adjustments to federal deduction limits required or allowed.	
Alaska	No adjustments to federal deduction limits required.	
Arizona	No adjustments to federal deduction limits required.	

Jurisdiction	Asset Expense Election—IRC § 179	Comment
Arkansas	Subtraction allowed equal to: • $25,000 for tax years after 2010; • $134,000 for 2010 tax year; • $133,000 for 2009 tax year.	
California	Addition to income required for: • amount that exceeds $25,000 expense deduction limit as reduced by $200,000 investment phase-out threshold; and • expenses claimed for "qualified real property," off-the-shelf computer software, and property used to furnish lodging. Taxpayers that do not make the IRC § 179 election are allowed an additional 20% first-year depreciation deduction for the cost of qualifying property, up to a $2,000 maximum additional deduction, in year the property is acquired.	Adjustments are computed on Form 3885.
Colorado	No adjustments to federal deduction limits required.	
Connecticut	**Tax years on or after January 1, 2018:** Addition required for 80% of federal deduction. Subtraction allowed for 25% of addback amount in each of the next 4 tax years. **Tax years before 2018:** No adjustments to federal deduction required.	
Delaware	No adjustments to federal deduction limits required.	
District of Columbia	Subtraction for expensing of assets is limited to $25,000 or $40,000 for qualified high technology companies.	Federal depreciation form and statement showing computation must be attached to state return.
Florida	No adjustments to federal deduction limits required.	Addition required for amount of federal deduction that exceeds: • $128,000 for tax years after 2007 and before 2015; and • $250,000 for 2010 taxable year. Subtraction allowed equal to 1/7 of addback amount in first and succeeding six tax years.
Georgia	No modification required.	Addition required for amount that exceeds $250,000 expense deduction limit as reduced by $800,000 investment phase-out threshold, for 2008-2013 taxable years.

Jurisdiction	Asset Expense Election—IRC § 179	Comment
Hawaii	Addition to federal tax base required for: • amount that exceeds $25,000 expense deduction limit as reduced by $200,000 investment phase-out threshold; and • off-the-shelf computer software.	
Idaho	No adjustments to federal deduction limits required.	
Illinois	No adjustments to federal deduction limits required.	
Indiana	Addition required for amount of federal deduction that exceeds $25,000.	**Tax years after 2017:** Adjustment required for certain exchanges that would have been eligible for nonrecognition of gain or loss under IRC Sec. 1031 as in effect on January 1, 2017.
Iowa	Addition to income required for amount of federal expense deduction limit that exceeds: • **2016-2017:** $25,000 as reduced by the $200,000 investment phase-out threshold; • **2018:** $70,000 as reduced by the $280,000 investment phase-out threshold; • **2019:** $100,000 as reduced by the $400,000 investment phase-out threshold. No adjustments to federal deduction limits required for: • tax years after 2009 and before 2016; and • tax years after 2019.	Adjustment is computed on Form 4562A.
Kansas	No adjustments to federal deduction limits required.	Expensing deduction from net income attributable to state sources allowed for the following property placed in service in the state during taxable years beginning after 2011: • depreciable machinery and equipment (excluding residential rental property, nonresidential real property, any railroad grading or tunnel bore or any other property with applicable recovery period over 25 years); and • certain canned computer software. Expense deduction is claimed by completing and enclosing Schedule 120EX with the annual return.

Jurisdiction	Asset Expense Election—IRC § 179	Comment
Kentucky	Addition to federal tax base required for full amount of federal deduction. Subtraction from federal tax base allowed for maximum expense deduction of $25,000 as reduced by maximum investment phase-out threshold of $200,000. **Tax years after 2019:** Subtraction from federal tax base allowed for maximum expense deduction of $100,000 as reduced by federal investment phase-out threshold.	Subtraction is computed by converting federal Form 4562 and ignoring lines and instructions on enhanced federal deduction limits.
Louisiana	No adjustments to federal deduction limits required.	
Maine	Addition to federal tax base required in tax years after 2017 for amount that exceeds inflation adjusted $500,000 expense deduction limit as reduced by inflation adjusted $2 million investment phase-out threshold. Subtraction from federal tax base allowed for: • 5% of former addition modification for property placed in service after 2002 beginning in tax year following year property was placed in service, with remaining 95% of modification recovered evenly over remainder of asset's life beginning in year 3; and • equal amounts of former addition modification for property placed in service in 2002 over remainder of asset's life beginning in 2004 tax year.	Addition to federal tax base required in tax years before 2011 for amount that exceeded $25,000 expense deduction limit as reduced by $200,000 investment phase-out threshold.
Maryland	Addition to federal tax base required for amount that exceeds $25,000 expense deduction limit as reduced by $200,000 investment phase-out threshold, except no addition required for certain manufacturing businesses effective for tax years after 2018. Subtraction allowed to extent amount claimed for federal purposes is less than amount permitted for state purposes.	Adjustment is computed on Form 500DM.
Massachusetts	No adjustments to federal deduction limits required.	
Michigan	No adjustments to federal deduction limits required.	

Jurisdiction	Asset Expense Election—IRC §179	Comment
Minnesota	Addition to federal tax base required in tax years after 2005 and before 2020 for 80% of amount that exceeds $25,000 expense deduction limit as reduced by $200,000 investment phase-out threshold, except no addition required for qualifying depreciable property acquired in like-kind exchange that did not qualify for gain or loss recognition deferral due to elimination of deferral under Tax Cuts and Jobs Act of 2017. Subtraction from federal tax base allowed equal to 1/5 of addback amount in first and succeeding four tax years.	
Mississippi	No adjustments to federal deduction limits required.	
Missouri	No adjustments to federal deduction limits required.	
Montana	No adjustments to federal deduction limits required.	
Nebraska	Subtraction from federal tax base allowed beginning on or after January 1, 2006, and in each of the four following taxable years, for 20% of enhanced federal deduction that was required as an addition adjustment for tax years 2003 through 2005.	
Nevada	N/A, because state does not tax general business corporation income.	
New Hampshire	Addition required for amount of federal deduction. Subtraction allowed for maximum expense deduction equal to: • $500,000 for property placed in service after 2017; • $100,000 for property placed in service after 2016; • $25,000 for property placed in service after 2011 and before 2017; and • $20,000 for property placed in service before 2012.	
New Jersey	Addition required for amount of federal deduction that exceeds $25,000.	
New Mexico	No adjustments to federal deduction limits required.	
New York	Addition to federal tax base required, except eligible farmers, for expense deduction amount relating to sport utility vehicles weighing over 6,000 pounds. No other adjustments to federal deduction limits required.	

Jurisdiction	Asset Expense Election—IRC § 179	Comment
North Carolina	Addition required equal to: • 85% of amount that exceeds $250,000 expense deduction limit as reduced by $800,000 investment phaseout threshold for 2010-2012 tax years; and • 85% of amount that exceeds $25,000 expense deduction limit as reduced by $200,000 investment phaseout threshold for tax years after 2012. Subtraction allowed for 20% of addback amount in over 5 years beginning with the tax year following the addback year.	
North Dakota	No adjustments to federal deduction limits required.	
Ohio	Taxable gross receipts computed without regard to federal expense deduction.	
Oklahoma	Addition to federal tax base required in 2009 tax year for amount of expense deduction that exceeds $175,000. No adjustments to federal deduction limits required for other tax years.	
Oregon	No adjustments to federal deduction limits required for tax years before 2009 or after 2010. Addition to federal tax base required in tax years 2009 and 2010 for amount of federal deduction that exceeds $134,000 expense deduction limit as reduced by $530,000 investment phase-out threshold.	Adjustment is computed on Depreciation Schedule for Individuals, Partnerships, Corporations, and Fiduciaries.
Pennsylvania	No adjustments to federal deduction limits required.	
Rhode Island	No adjustments to federal deduction limits required for assets placed in service after 2013. For assets placed in service before 2013, addition to federal tax base required for amount that exceeds $25,000 expense deduction limit as reduced by $200,000 investment phase-out threshold.	
South Carolina	No adjustments to federal tax base required.	
South Dakota	N/A, because state does not tax general business corporation income.	
Tennessee	No adjustments to federal deduction limits required.	

Jurisdiction	Asset Expense Election—IRC §179	Comment
Texas	Subtraction allowed for taxable entities that use cost of goods sold to compute margin limited to $25,000 expense deduction and $200,000 investment phaseout threshold.	
Utah	No adjustments to federal deduction limits required.	
Vermont	No adjustments to federal deduction limits required.	
Virginia	No adjustments to federal deduction limits required.	State generally decouples with provisions of the Tax Cuts and Jobs Act after 2017.
Washington	N/A, because state does not tax general business corporation income.	
West Virginia	No adjustments to federal deduction limits required.	
Wisconsin	Addition required for taxable years before 2014 equal to federal amount that exceeds $25,000 expense deduction limit as reduced by $200,000 investment phase-out threshold. No adjustments to federal deduction limits required for taxable years after 2013.	
Wyoming	N/A, because state does not tax general business corporation income.	

Bad Debt Deduction

Under IRC § 166, a taxpayer may take a deduction for debts that become wholly or partially worthless within the income year. The amount of the deduction is calculated by reference to the adjusted basis for determining loss from the sale of property. This chart shows the corporation income tax treatment by each state and the District of Columbia of the federal deduction for bad debts.

Jurisdiction	Bad Debt Deduction—IRC § 166	Comment
Alabama	Same as federal.	
Alaska	Same as federal.	
Arizona	Same as federal.	
Arkansas	Same as federal.	
California	Same as federal, except modifications required for banks, saving and loan associations, and other financial corporations.	
Colorado	Same as federal.	
Connecticut	Same as federal.	
Delaware	Same as federal.	
District of Columbia	Same as federal.	
Florida	Same as federal.	
Georgia	Same as federal.	
Hawaii	Same as federal.	
Idaho	Same as federal.	
Illinois	Same as federal.	
Indiana	Same as federal.	
Iowa	Same as federal.	
Kansas	Same as federal.	
Kentucky	Same as federal.	
Louisiana	Same as federal.	
Maine	Same as federal.	
Maryland	Same as federal.	
Massachusetts	Same as federal.	
Michigan	Same as federal.	
Minnesota	Same as federal.	
Mississippi	Same as federal.	
Missouri	Same as federal.	

Jurisdiction	Bad Debt Deduction—IRC §166	Comment
Montana	Same as federal, except reserve method.	
Nebraska	Same as federal.	
Nevada	N/A, because state does not tax general business corporation income.	
New Hampshire	Same as federal.	
New Jersey	Same as federal.	
New Mexico	Same as federal.	
New York	Same as federal.	
North Carolina	Same as federal.	
North Dakota	Same as federal.	
Ohio	Bad debts may be excluded from gross receipts.	
Oklahoma	Same as federal.	
Oregon	Same as federal, except modifications required for financial institutions that change accounting methods.	
Pennsylvania	Same as federal.	
Rhode Island	Same as federal.	
South Carolina	Same as federal.	
South Dakota	N/A, because state does not tax general business corporation income.	
Tennessee	Same as federal, except large banks may use the reserve method.	
Texas	Same as federal.	
Utah	Same as federal.	
Vermont	Same as federal.	
Virginia	Same as federal, except modifications required for saving and loan associations.	
Washington	N/A, because state does not tax general business corporation income.	
West Virginia	Same as federal, except reserve method allowed for all taxpayers.	
Wisconsin	Same as federal.	
Wyoming	N/A, because state does not tax general business corporation income.	

Banks and Financial Institutions

This chart shows the tax that is imposed by each state and the District of Columbia on banks and financial institutions.

Jurisdiction	Banks and Financial Institutions	Comment
Alabama	Excise tax on net income	
Alaska	Corporate net income tax	
Arizona	Corporate income tax	
Arkansas	Corporate income tax	
California	Corporation franchise tax imposed at higher rate.	
Colorado	Corporate income tax	
Connecticut	Corporation business tax	
Delaware	Bank franchise tax on net income; ***or*** Alternative bank franchise tax equal to sum of income tax liability plus location benefit tax liability.	
District of Columbia	Corporation franchise tax	
Florida	Bank franchise tax on net income	
Georgia	Corporate income and net worth taxes Gross receipts tax on depository institutions	
Hawaii	Franchise tax on entire net income	
Idaho	Corporate income tax	
Illinois	Corporate income and personal property replacement taxes	
Indiana	Franchise tax on apportioned income	
Iowa	Franchise tax on net income	
Kansas	Privilege tax on net income	
Kentucky	Bank franchise tax on net capital **Tax years after 2020:** Corporation income tax and limited liability entity tax (LLET)	
Louisiana	Bank shares tax	
Maine	Franchise tax on net income and assets	
Maryland	Corporate income tax	
Massachusetts	Financial institution excise tax on net income	
Michigan	Franchise tax on net capital.	
Minnesota	Corporate franchise tax	

Jurisdiction	Banks and Financial Institutions	Comment
Mississippi	Corporate income tax	Exemption for nonprofit mutual savings banks and nonprofit farm loan associations.
Missouri	Financial institutions franchise and corporate income taxes	Credit unions, savings and loans, and building and loans exempt from income tax.
Montana	Corporate income tax	
Nebraska	Franchise tax based on percentage of deposits	
Nevada	N/A, because state does not tax general business corporation income.	
New Hampshire	Business profits tax	
New Jersey	Corporation business tax	
New Mexico	Corporate income tax	
New York	**Tax years prior to 2015:** Bank franchise tax **Tax years after 2014:** Corporate franchise tax	
North Carolina	Corporate income tax	
North Dakota	Corporate income tax	Financial institution tax on taxable income for taxable years before 2013.
Ohio	Financial institutions tax on total equity capital attributable to state sources.	
Oklahoma	Bank and credit union privilege tax on net income Banks also subject to franchise tax	
Oregon	Corporation excise tax	
Pennsylvania	Bank and trust company shares tax Mutual thrift institution excise tax Private bankers gross receipts tax	
Rhode Island	Bank excise tax on net income or capital stock	
South Carolina	Bank tax on entire net income	
South Dakota	Bank franchise tax on net income	
Tennessee	Franchise and excise financial institution tax	
Texas	Revised franchise tax (margin tax) Franchise tax prior to 2008 tax year.	
Utah	Corporate franchise tax	
Vermont	Franchise tax measured by average monthly deposits held within state.	

Jurisdiction	Banks and Financial Institutions	Comment
Virginia	Bank franchise tax on net capital for banks, banking associations, and trust companies. Corporate income tax for savings and loan associations.	
Washington	N/A, because state does not tax general business corporation income.	
West Virginia	Corporate net income tax	
Wisconsin	Corporation franchise or income tax	
Wyoming	N/A, because state does not tax general business corporation income.	

Business Interest Expenses—IRC § 163(j)

Under IRC § 163(j), the deduction of business interest is limited for any tax year beginning after 2017 to the sum of the taxpayer's business interest income, floor plan financing, and 30 percent of adjusted taxable income (ATI). For taxpayers other than partnerships, the ATI limit is increased for the 2019 or 2020 tax year to 50 percent, unless the taxpayer elects to continue to use the 30 percent limit. For partnerships, the 50 percent limit applies only for the tax year beginning in 2020, with a special allocation of excess business interest expense to partners for the 2019 tax year unless the partner elects otherwise. A taxpayer may elect for any tax year beginning in 2020 to use its ATI from the 2019 tax year to calculate its limitation. The limitation generally applies to all taxpayers, but does not apply for small businesses with average gross receipts of $25 million or less (adjusted for inflation). Any disallowed interest generally may be carried forward indefinitely. In the case of a partnership or S corporation, the deduction limitation applies at the entity level, except that disallowed interest of the entity is allocated to each partner or shareholder as excess business interest. This chart shows the tax treatment by each state and the District of Columbia of the IRC § 163(j) deduction limitation.

Jurisdiction	Business Interest Expenses—IRC § 163(j)	Comment
Alabama	No adjustments to federal deduction limit allowed.	
Alaska	No adjustments to federal deduction limit allowed.	
Arizona	Addition required for amount of deduction that exceeds 30% for 2019 and 2020 tax years, if state does not update IRC conformity tie-in date.	
Arkansas	Subtraction allowed for amount that exceeds federal limit.	
California	Subtraction allowed for amount that exceeds federal limit.	
Colorado	Generally, no adjustments to federal deduction limit allowed. Addition required for amount of deduction that exceeds 30% for 2020 tax year.	
Connecticut	Subtraction allowed for amount that exceeds federal limit.	
Delaware	No adjustments to federal deduction limit allowed.	
District of Columbia	No adjustments to federal deduction limit allowed.	
Florida	Addition required for amount of deduction that exceeds 30% for 2019 and 2020 tax years, if state does not update IRC conformity tie-in date.	

Jurisdiction	Business Interest Expenses—IRC §163(j)	Comment
Georgia	Subtraction allowed for amount that exceeds federal limit.	
Hawaii	Addition required for amount of deduction that exceeds 30% for 2019 tax year.	
Idaho	Addition required for amount of deduction that exceeds 30% for 2019 and 2020 tax years.	
Illinois	No adjustments to federal deduction limit allowed.	
Indiana	Subtraction allowed for amount that exceeds federal limit.	
Iowa	After 2019, Iowa decouples from changes that limit the deduction of business interest expenses. Addition required for amount of deduction that exceeds 30% for 2019. **Tax years before 2019:** Subtraction allowed for amount that exceeds federal limit.	Iowa's decoupling does not apply in any tax year a taxpayer takes the additional first-year depreciation allowance under IRC Sec. 168(k). Iowa did not conform with CARES Act as it applies retroactively to 2019.
Kansas	No adjustments to federal deduction limit allowed.	
Kentucky	Addition required for amount of deduction that exceeds 30% for 2019 and 2020 tax years.	
Louisiana	No adjustments to federal deduction limit allowed.	
Maine	Addition required for amount of deduction that exceeds 30% for 2019 and 2020 tax years.	
Maryland	Addition required for amount of deduction that exceeds 30% for 2020 tax year.	
Massachusetts	No adjustments to federal deduction limit allowed.	
Michigan	No adjustments to federal deduction limit allowed.	
Minnesota	Addition required for amount of deduction that exceeds 30% for 2019 and 2020 tax years.	
Mississippi	Subtraction allowed for amount that exceeds federal limit.	
Missouri	Subtraction allowed for amount that exceeds federal limit.	
Montana	No adjustments to federal deduction limit allowed.	
Nebraska	No adjustments to federal deduction limit allowed.	

Jurisdiction	Business Interest Expenses—IRC § 163(j)	Comment
Nevada	N/A, because state does not tax general business corporation income.	
New Hampshire	Addition required for amount of deduction that exceeds 30% for 2020 tax year. **2019:** Subtraction allowed for amount that exceeds federal limit.	Adjustments are computed on Schedule IV.
New Jersey	No adjustments to federal deduction limit allowed.	Deduction limitation applied on pro-rata basis to interest paid to both related and unrelated parties, regardless of whether the related parties are subject to interest expense add-back requirements.
New Mexico	No adjustments to federal deduction limit allowed.	
New York	Addition required for amount of deduction that exceeds 30% for 2019 and 2020 tax years.	
North Carolina	Addition required for amount of deduction that exceeds 30% for 2019 and 2020 tax years.	
North Dakota	No adjustments to federal deduction limit allowed.	
Ohio	N/A, because the commercial activity tax is not considered an income tax and is not tied to federal income tax base.	
Oklahoma	No adjustments to federal deduction limit allowed.	
Oregon	No adjustments to federal deduction limit allowed.	
Pennsylvania	No adjustments to federal deduction limit allowed.	
Rhode Island	No adjustments to federal deduction limit allowed.	
South Carolina	Subtraction allowed for amount that exceeds federal limit. State does not adopt federal limitation on deduction of business interest expense.	
South Dakota	N/A, because state does not tax general business corporation income.	
Tennessee	No adjustments to federal deduction limit allowed. **Tax years after 2019:** Subtraction allowed for amount that exceeds federal limit.	
Texas	N/A, because franchise (margin) tax not tied to federal income base and interest may not be included in the amount of the cost of goods sold deduction.	

Jurisdiction	Business Interest Expenses—IRC § 163(j)	Comment
Utah	No adjustments to federal deduction limit allowed.	
Vermont	No adjustments to federal deduction limit allowed.	State has not conformed to the federal amendment increasing the adjusted taxable income limit from 30% to 50% for 2019 and 2020.
Virginia	Subtraction allowed for 20% of amount that exceeds federal limit.	State has not conformed to the federal amendment increasing the adjusted taxable income limit from 30% to 50% for 2019 and 2020.
Washington	N/A, because state does not tax general business corporation income.	
West Virginia	Addition required for amount of deduction that exceeds 30% for 2019 and 2020 tax years, if state does not update IRC conformity tie-in date.	
Wisconsin	Subtraction allowed for amount that exceeds federal limit.	
Wyoming	N/A, because state does not tax general business corporation income.	

Capital Loss Carryovers

Under IRC § 1212, a corporation may carry back a capital loss to each of the three tax years preceding the loss year and any excess may be carried forward for five years following the loss year. This chart covers the position of each state regarding capital loss carryovers under IRC § 1212.

Jurisdiction	Capital Loss Carryovers	Comment
Alabama	No adjustments to federal deduction required or allowed.	
Alaska	No adjustments to federal deduction required or allowed.	
Arizona	No adjustments to federal deduction required or allowed.	
Arkansas	Subtraction from gross income allowed for full amount of capital loss in year sustained.	
California	Addition required for capital loss carrybacks deducted in determining federal taxable income.	
Colorado	No adjustments to federal deduction required or allowed.	
Connecticut	Subtraction allowed for capital loss carryover not deducted in computing federal capital gain for each of the 5 income years following the loss year.	Subtraction applies only to taxpayers subject to tax that filed an annual return in the loss year.
Delaware	No adjustments to federal deduction required or allowed.	
District of Columbia	No adjustments to federal deduction required or allowed.	
Florida	Addition required for net capital loss carryover deducted from capital gains in computing federal taxable income for the tax year. Subtraction allowed for apportioned net capital loss carryover based on federal deduction and time periods.	Attach a schedule showing: • year(s) of loss; • apportionment fraction for the taxable year in which the loss occurred; and • amount of the carryover(s) previously deducted.
Georgia	No adjustments to federal deduction required or allowed.	A deduction is not allowed for losses that occurred in a year that the taxpayer was not subject to Georgia tax or for losses that were previously reported.
Hawaii	No adjustments to federal deduction required or allowed.	
Idaho	No adjustments to federal deduction required or allowed.	Addition required for capital loss carryovers incurred during a year in which a corporation transacts no business in the state, unless the corporation was included in combined report in which another group member does business in the state.
Illinois	No adjustments to federal deduction required or allowed.	

Jurisdiction	Capital Loss Carryovers	Comment
Indiana	No adjustments to federal deduction required or allowed.	
Iowa	No adjustments to federal deduction required or allowed.	The full amount of the federal capital loss carryover is carried back or forward and offset proportionally against allocable and apportionable income items of the carryback or carryforward year.
Kansas	No adjustments to federal deduction required or allowed.	
Kentucky	No adjustments to federal deduction required or allowed.	
Louisiana	No adjustments to federal deduction required or allowed.	
Maine	No adjustments to federal deduction required or allowed.	
Maryland	No adjustments to federal deduction required or allowed.	
Massachusetts	Addition required for amount of federal deduction.	
Michigan	**Corporate Income Tax** No adjustments to federal deduction required or allowed. **Michigan Business Tax (MBT)** No adjustments to federal deduction required or allowed.	
Minnesota	Addition required for capital losses deducted on federal return. Subtraction allowed for capital losses based on federal deduction, except with 15-year carryforward period and no carrybacks.	
Mississippi	Addition required for net capital loss carryover deducted from capital gains in computing federal taxable income for the tax year. Subtraction allowed for apportioned net capital loss carryover based on federal deduction and time periods.	Although Mississippi does not follow the federal provisions and capital losses must be computed separately for Mississippi purposes, the definition of relevant terms are the same as for federal purposes and losses may be carried over for five years.
Missouri	No adjustments to federal deduction required or allowed.	
Montana	Addition required for federal capital loss carryover utilized on federal return. Subtraction allowed for capital loss incurred in current year.	
Nebraska	Addition required for amount of federal carryover deduction. Subtraction from adjusted federal taxable income allowed for apportioned net capital loss carryover in each of the 5 years after the loss year.	Attach a detailed schedule that shows the computation of the capital loss carryover along with copies of the applicable federal Schedule D to substantiate the Federal capital (loss)/gain.

Jurisdiction	Capital Loss Carryovers	Comment
Nevada	N/A, because state does not tax general business corporation income.	
New Hampshire	No adjustments to federal deduction required or allowed.	
New Jersey	No adjustments to federal deduction required or allowed.	
New Mexico	No adjustments to federal deduction required or allowed.	
New York	No adjustments to federal deduction required or allowed.	Net capital losses earned in 2015 or later cannot be carried back to a tax year beginning before 2015.
North Carolina	Addition required for amount by which gains have been offset by capital loss carryovers. Subtraction allowed for capital losses that taxpayers cannot claim as a federal deduction under IRC § 1211(a).	
North Dakota	No adjustments to federal deduction required or allowed.	
Ohio	Taxable gross receipts computed without regard to federal deduction.	
Oklahoma	No adjustments to federal deduction required or allowed.	
Oregon	No adjustments to federal deduction required or allowed.	Adjustments may be required if taxpayer participated in tax amnesty program.
Pennsylvania	No adjustments to federal deduction required or allowed.	
Rhode Island	No adjustments to federal deduction required or allowed.	
South Carolina	Addition required for capital loss carrybacks deducted in determining federal taxable income.	
South Dakota	N/A, because state does not tax general business corporation income.	
Tennessee	Addition required for capital gains offset by capital loss carryover or carryback. Subtraction allowed for portion of current year capital loss not included in federal taxable income.	
Texas	No adjustments to federal deduction required or allowed.	
Utah	Addition required for capital gains offset by capital loss carryover. Subtraction allowed for capital loss incurred in current year or carried forward.	

Jurisdiction	Capital Loss Carryovers	Comment
Vermont	No adjustments to federal deduction required or allowed.	
Virginia	No adjustments to federal deduction required or allowed.	Special rules apply for certain utility/ transportation providers.
Washington	N/A, because state does not tax general business corporation income.	
West Virginia	No adjustments to federal deduction required or allowed.	
Wisconsin	No adjustments to federal deduction required or allowed.	
Wyoming	N/A, because state does not tax general business corporation income.	

Combined Reporting Requirements—Elective Combination

In a typical combined report, the business income of members of a unitary group is combined, intercompany transactions are eliminated, and the combined business income is apportioned among the states based on group-level apportionment percentages. Some states provide for a form of combined reporting known as worldwide combined reporting, which takes into account the business income of all members of a unitary group, including foreign affiliates. Some states employ a more limited form of combined reporting generally referred to as water's-edge reporting, under which unitary group members that are incorporated in a foreign country or that conduct most of their business abroad are excluded from the combined report. Under separate reporting, each legally distinct corporate entity's income is treated separately for tax purposes. This chart indicates whether each state and the District of Columbia allows corporations an option to elect to report their income on a worldwide or water's-edge combined basis. This chart does not cover states that mandate combined reporting and allow taxpayers to elect an alternative method of combined reporting than otherwise required by the mandate. Mandatory combined reporting is covered under the topic Combined Reporting Requirements—Mandatory Combinations.

Jurisdiction	Elective Combination	Comment
Alabama	No, separate reporting required.	
Alaska	No	
Arizona	No	
Arkansas	No, separate reporting required.	
California	Yes, unitary businesses that derive income wholly from state sources.	
Colorado	No	
Connecticut	Yes, combined pass through entity tax returns allowed effective for tax years after 2017.	**Tax years before 2016:** Water's edge combined reporting allowed for unitary businesses if: • taxpayers were included in a federal consolidated return; or • addback required for otherwise deductible interest expenses and costs paid, accrued, or incurred to one or more group members.
Delaware	No, separate reporting required.	
District of Columbia	No	Separate reporting required for tax years beginning before 2011.
Florida	No, separate reporting required.	
Georgia	No, separate reporting required.	
Hawaii	No	
Idaho	No	
Illinois	No	

Jurisdiction	Elective Combination	Comment
Indiana	No	
Iowa	No, separate reporting required.	
Kansas	No	
Kentucky	No	
Louisiana	No, separate reporting required.	
Maine	No	
Maryland	No, separate reporting required.	
Massachusetts	No	
Michigan	Yes, water's edge combined reporting allowed for tax years beginning after 2012 for affiliated groups.	
Minnesota	No	
Mississippi	Yes, water's-edge combined reporting allowed for income tax returns of affiliated corporations that are taxable in the state.	Foreign affiliates included only if required to file state tax return. Form 83-310 must be attached to designated reporting corporation's return.
Missouri	No, separate reporting required.	
Montana	No	
Nebraska	No	
Nevada	N/A, because state does not tax general business corporation income.	
New Hampshire	No	
New Jersey	No.	
New Mexico	**Taxable years beginning on or after January 1, 2020:** Worldwide combined reporting required for members of a unitary business group, unless the corporations properly elect to report and pay tax on taxable income as a water's-edge or consolidated group. **Taxable years before 2020:** Water's-edge combined reporting allowed for unitary businesses.	
New York	No	For tax years after 2014, a commonly owned group election is available to treat all corporations meeting the stock ownership test as a combined group, even if not engaged in a unitary business.
North Carolina	No, separate reporting required.	
North Dakota	No	
Ohio	No	

Jurisdiction	Elective Combination	Comment
Oklahoma	No, separate reporting required.	
Oregon	No, separate reporting required.	
Pennsylvania	No, separate reporting required.	
Rhode Island	Yes, applicable to tax years beginning after 2014, combined reporting allowed for affiliated groups.	
South Carolina	No, separate reporting required.	
South Dakota	N/A, because state does not tax general business corporation income.	
Tennessee	No	
Texas	No	
Utah	Yes, water's-edge combined reporting may be elected by nonunitary affiliated corporations that are doing business in the state and qualified to file a federal consolidated return.	
Vermont	No	
Virginia	Yes, water's edge combined reporting allowed for affiliated corporations.	Corporations may not elect and cannot be required to include any controlled foreign corporation if its income is derived from sources outside U.S..
Washington	N/A, because state does not tax general business corporation income.	
West Virginia	No	
Wisconsin	No	A controlled group election is available to include every member of a commonly controlled group in a combined report, regardless of whether each is actually engaged in the unitary business.
Wyoming	N/A, because state does not tax general business corporation income.	

Combined Reporting Requirements—Mandatory Combinations

In a typical combined report, the business income of members of a unitary group is combined, intercompany transactions are eliminated, and the combined business income is apportioned among the states based on group-level apportionment percentages. Some states provide for a form of combined reporting known as worldwide combined reporting, which takes into account the business income of all members of a unitary group, including foreign affiliates. Some states employ a more limited form of combined reporting generally referred to as water's-edge reporting, under which unitary group members that are incorporated in a foreign country or that conduct most of their business abroad are excluded from the combined report. Under separate reporting, each legally distinct corporate entity's income is treated separately for tax purposes. This chart indicates whether each state requires any corporations to report their income on either a worldwide or water's-edge combined basis, or allows corporations to elect between these two methods. This chart does not discuss whether states allow corporations an option to elect combined reporting when not mandated. Elective combined reporting is covered under the topic Combined Reporting Requirements— Elective Combinations.

Jurisdiction	Mandatory Combination	Comment
Alabama	No, separate reporting required.	
Alaska	Yes, water's-edge combined reporting required for affiliated corporations engaged in a unitary business. Worldwide combined reporting required for oil and gas corporations.	Foreign affiliates are excluded unless: • 20% or more of affiliate's average property, payroll, and sales factors are assigned to a location within U.S.; or • affiliate is a tax-haven corporation.
Arizona	Yes, water's-edge combined reporting required for unitary businesses that derive income from sources within and outside of the state, unless election is made to file a consolidated return.	
Arkansas	No, separate reporting required.	
California	Yes, worldwide combined reporting required for unitary businesses that derive income from sources within and outside of the state, unless a water's-edge election is made.	Foreign affiliates may be excluded by making a water's-edge election. Form 100-WE is used to make a water's-edge election. Form 100W is used to file a water's-edge return.
Colorado	Yes, water's-edge combined reporting required for affiliated corporations that meet three or more parts of six-part test for current and two preceding years.	Foreign affiliates are excluded if 80% or more of affiliate's average property and payroll factors are assigned to locations outside the U.S.

Jurisdiction	Mandatory Combination	Comment
Connecticut	Yes, water's-edge combined reporting required for unitary business groups that have common ownership and where at least one company is subject to the corporation business tax, unless a worldwide or affiliated group combined reporting election is made.	Foreign affiliates are excluded unless: • 20% or more of affiliate's average property, payroll, and sales factors are assigned to a location within U.S.; or • affiliate is a tax-haven corporation. $2.5 million cap on amount by which unitary group's tax liability computed on a combined bases is allowed to exceed group's tax liability computed on a separate basis.
Delaware	No, separate reporting required.	
District of Columbia	Yes, water's-edge combined reporting required for unitary businesses, unless a worldwide unitary combined reporting election is made.	
Florida	No, separate reporting required.	
Georgia	No, separate reporting required.	
Hawaii	Yes, water's-edge combined reporting required for unitary businesses, unless another method is permitted to fairly represent extent of taxpayer's business activity in the state.	
Idaho	Yes, worldwide combined reporting required for unitary businesses with more than 50% common ownership that transact business within and outside the state, unless a water's-edge election is made.	Foreign affiliates may be excluded under water's-edge election, unless included in federal return. Water's-edge election is made on Form 14.
Illinois	Yes, water's-edge combined reporting required for unitary businesses.	Foreign affiliates are excluded if 80% or more of affiliate's property and payroll are outside the U.S.
Indiana	No	
Iowa	No, separate reporting required.	
Kansas	Yes, water's-edge combined reporting required for corporations conducting a unitary business both within and outside the state.	Schedule K-121 must be filed with returns.

Jurisdiction	Mandatory Combination	Comment
Kentucky	Yes, water's-edge combined reporting required for unitary groups doing business in state, unless election is made to file consolidated return. **Tax years before 2019:** No, separate reporting required.	A combined group can only include corporations, the voting stock of which is more than 50% owned by a common owner or owners. Common ownership can be direct or indirect. A combined group must otherwise include members that: • are incorporated in the U.S. or formed under the laws of any state, the District of Columbia, or any U.S. territory or possession; • earn less than 80% of their income from sources outside the U.S., the District of Columbia, or any U.S. territory or possession; • earn more than 20% of income from intangible property or services that another member can deduct from its apportionable income; and • conduct business in a tax haven. A tax haven does not include a jurisdiction that has entered into a comprehensive income tax treaty with the U.S.
Louisiana	No, separate reporting required.	
Maine	Yes, water's-edge combined reporting required for affiliated corporations engaged in unitary business if more than 50% common ownership exists.	Corporations not required to file a federal return are excluded. Form CR must be attached to returns.
Maryland	No, separate reporting required.	**Tax years after 2005 and before 2011:** Pro-forma water's edge combined returns required for members of any affiliated corporate group, specifying: • difference between income tax computed using double-weighted sales factor and income tax computed using single sales factor where sales throwback rule was applicable; • amount and source of nonoperational income that was not apportionable to the state; and • if corporation was commercially domiciled in state, difference in tax where 100% of nonoperational income was allocated to the state.
Massachusetts	Yes, water's-edge combined reporting required for unitary businesses, unless worldwide election is made.	Foreign affiliates are excluded if the average of the affiliate's property, payroll, and sales factors outside the U.S. is 80% or more.
Michigan	Yes, water's-edge combined reporting required by unitary business groups for Michigan Business Tax (MBT) purposes in tax years after 2007 and for corporate income tax purposes in tax years after 2011.	
Minnesota	Yes, water's-edge combined reporting required for unitary businesses that have nexus with the state.	
Mississippi	No	

Jurisdiction	Mandatory Combination	Comment
Missouri	No, separate reporting required.	
Montana	Yes, worldwide combined reporting required for unitary businesses, unless a water's-edge election is made.	Foreign affiliates may be excluded by making a water's-edge election, unless more than 20% of affiliate's property and payroll are assigned to a location within U.S. or affiliate is incorporated in tax-haven jurisdiction. Form WE-Elect must be filed within the first 90 days of the tax year (or by the end of the tax period for tax periods of less than 90 days) for which the election is to become effective.
Nebraska	Yes, water's-edge combined reporting required for unitary businesses that derive income from business activity taxable within and outside the state.	Foreign affiliates are included if subject to the requirements of IRC § 243 in order for their distributions to qualify for the dividends-received deduction.
Nevada	N/A, because state does not tax general business corporation income.	
New Hampshire	Yes, water's-edge combined reporting required for unitary businesses.	Foreign affiliates are excluded if 80% or more of affiliate's property and payroll are assigned to locations outside U.S. and additional certification and reporting requirements are met. Form NH-1120-WE is used to file a water's-edge return.
New Jersey	Yes, water's-edge combined reporting required for corporations that: • have common ownership; • are a unitary business; and • include at least one company subject to the corporation business tax.	For privilege periods ending before July 31, 2019, New Jersey required separate reporting.
New Mexico	**Taxable years beginning on or after January 1, 2020:** Worldwide combined reporting required for members of a unitary business group, unless the corporations properly elect to report and pay tax on taxable income as a water's-edge or consolidated group. **Taxable years before 2020:** Water's-edge combined reporting required for unitary businesses providing retail sales of goods in a facility of more than 30,000 square feet under one roof in state, unless taxpayer has non-retail operations in state that employ at least 750 employees.	
New York	For tax years after 2014, full unitary water's-edge combined reporting is adopted with an ownership requirement of more than 50%.	Form CT-3-A is used to file on a combined basis. For tax years before 2015, water's-edge combined reporting required for related corporations with substantial intercorporate transactions, regardless of the transfer price for such intercorporate transactions.
North Carolina	No, separate reporting required.	

Jurisdiction	Mandatory Combination	Comment
North Dakota	Yes, worldwide combined reporting required for affiliated corporations engaged in unitary business if more than 50% common ownership exists, unless a water's-edge election is made.	Foreign affiliates are included unless a water's-edge election is made and 80% or more of affiliate's property and payroll are assigned to locations outside U.S.
Ohio	Combined taxpayers may not exclude receipts between members of the group for purposes of the CAT. Group members, other than the primary taxpayer, may request approval for separate filing together with the primary taxpayer using Form CAT RTFS.	
Oklahoma	No, separate reporting required.	
Oregon	No, separate reporting required.	Consolidated state returns are required for certain unitary members filing federal consolidated returns.
Pennsylvania	No, separate reporting required.	
Rhode Island	Applicable to tax years beginning after 2014, combined reporting required for unitary businesses.	For taxable years beginning on or after January 1, 2019, mandatory combined reporting is not applicable to pass-through entities that elect to be taxed at the entity level.
South Carolina	No, separate reporting required.	
South Dakota	N/A, because state does not tax general business corporation income.	
Tennessee	No, except combined reporting required for unitary groups of financial institutions and captive REIT affiliated groups.	
Texas	**Revised franchise (margin) tax:** Water's-edge combined reporting required for affiliated groups engaged in a unitary business. **Franchise tax:** No	Foreign affiliates excluded if 80% or more of affiliate's property and payroll are assigned to locations outside U.S..
Utah	Yes, water's-edge combined reporting required for affiliated corporations engaged in a unitary business, unless worldwide combined reporting election is made.	Foreign corporations are excluded from the water's-edge report unless 20% or more of their total business activity is in the U.S.
Vermont	Yes, water's-edge combined reporting required for affiliated corporations engaged in unitary business if more than 50% common ownership exists.	Foreign affiliates are excluded if 80% or more of affiliate's property and payroll are assigned to locations outside U.S.
Virginia	No	
Washington	N/A, because state does not tax general business corporation income.	

Jurisdiction	Mandatory Combination	Comment
West Virginia	Yes, water's-edge unitary combined reporting required for unitary business groups, unless worldwide combined reporting election is made or such method is required by the state.	Water's edge unitary combined reporting takes into account income and apportionment factors of members that meet certain requirements, including: • members incorporated in U.S. or its territories; • members with 20% or more U.S. apportionment factors; • DISCs, foreign sales corporations, and export trade corporations; • members with business income effectively connected with trade or business within U.S.; • controlled foreign corporations; • intangible holding companies; and • members doing business in tax-haven jurisdictions.
Wisconsin	Yes, water's-edge combined reporting required for commonly controlled corporations engaged in a unitary business.	Foreign corporations are excluded if 80% or more of the corporation's worldwide income is active foreign business income, unless the corporation elected to be included in a federal consolidated return, in which case it will be treated in the same way as a domestic corporation.
Wyoming	N/A, because state does not tax general business corporation income.	

Composite Returns—Partnerships, LLPs, and LLCs

In most states, partnerships, limited liability partnerships (LLPs), and limited liability companies (LLCs) classified as partnerships can file composite income tax returns for nonresident partners or members. Composite returns allow pass-through entities to report and pay tax for each participant's distributive share of the entity's income. Generally, participants cannot receive income from any other state sources. The filing of the composite return also relieves the participant of the requirement for filing a separate return. Most states limit participants in a composite return to nonresident individuals. Some states extend eligibility to nonresident pass through entities and corporations. Special rules may apply to the availability of net operating losses (NOLs), deductions, and credits.

This chart shows composite return options and requirements in each state and the District of Columbia. It provides information on participant eligibility, return forms, and special computation rules.

Jurisdiction	Partnerships, LLPs, and LLCs	Comment
Alabama	Composite returns using Form PTE-C are required to be filed by March 15 (15th day of third month following close of tax year for fiscal year taxpayers) on behalf of nonresident owners who are individuals, corporations, partnerships, LLPs, LLCs, trusts (including business trusts), and estates if there are one or more nonresident owners at any time during the taxable year, unless the partnership is a qualified investment partnership or publicly traded partnership that provides for certain inspections by the state tax agency. Composite tax is imposed at rate of 5% on nonresident owners' distributive shares of nonseparately stated income, separately stated income, and guaranteed payments allocated and apportioned to state, but excluding distributive shares of separately stated items of deduction or expense. Income or gain of one nonresident owner may not offset the loss of another owner, and a NOL carryforward may not offset income or gain.	**Coronavirus (COVID-19) Pandemic Filing/Payment Relief** July 15, 2020 filing and payment due date.
Alaska	Composite returns not authorized.	No personal income tax.

Jurisdiction	Partnerships, LLPs, and LLCs	Comment
Arizona	Composite returns using Form 140NR may be filed by April 15 (15th day of fourth month following close of tax year for fiscal year taxpayers) on behalf of at least 10 full-year nonresident individuals who have the same tax year and who have no other income, including income of any participant's spouse, from state sources other than allocable distributive income. Individuals who must make state estimated tax payments and deceased individuals may not be included in return. The Residency Status box for a Composite Return, on page 1 of the form, must be checked. Affidavits of qualification and powers of attorney must be executed by each participant. Each member's tax liability computed separately based on separate taxable income using appropriate tax table for tax year involved. Itemized deductions, net operating losses (NOLs), and tax credits not allowed.	**Coronavirus (COVID-19) Pandemic Filing/Payment Relief** July 15, 2020 filing and payment due date.
Arkansas	Composite returns using Form AR1000CR may be filed by April 15 on behalf of electing full-year nonresident individuals and business entities that do not have income or losses from other state sources. The composite return includes the distributive share of income or other gain that is passed through to the members. Tax is imposed at rate of 6.6%. No deductions or credits are allowed. Information must be submitted by CD if there are more than 10 participants. Withholding information returns, Form AR1099PT, must be filed for each participant.	Tax rate is 5.9% for tax years beginning after 2020. Tax rate was 6.9% for tax years prior to 2020. **Coronavirus (COVID-19) Pandemic Filing/Payment Relief:** July 15, 2020, return and payment due date.

Jurisdiction	Partnerships, LLPs, and LLCs	Comment
California	Group nonresident returns using Form 540NR may be filed on behalf of full-year nonresident individual partners if return is filed using calendar tax year and participants do not have income from state sources other than distributions reported on another group nonresident return. Tiered entities are not allowed to file a group return combining all of their business entities and individual nonresident partners on one group return. Tiered entities must file separate group nonresident returns for their electing individual nonresident partners and cannot include any business entities in the group nonresident return. Participants must be informed of terms and conditions of group return specified on form FTB 3864, which must be signed by authorized person or attorney-in-fact, and attached to return. Schedule 1067A must also be attached to return. Until 2030, tax is imposed at rate of 12.3% (13.3% if member has taxable income over $1 million). After 2030, tax is imposed at rate of 9.3% (10.3% if member has taxable income over $1 million). Individual deductions and credits may not be claimed on return, other than a deduction for deferred compensation contributions for participants with no other earned income and those credits directly attributable to the partnership's activity.	**Coronavirus (COVID-19) Pandemic Filing/Payment Relief** July 15, 2020 return due date. July 15, 2020 payment due date.
Colorado	Composite returns using Form 106 may be filed by April 15 on behalf of electing nonresident individuals, nonresident estates and trusts, and pass-through entities (to the extent their members/shareholders are nonresident individuals, estates, or trusts), if participants do not have income from other state sources. Tax is imposed at rate of 4.63%.	Temporary rate reduction from 4.63% to 4.50% for tax year 2019. **Coronavirus (COVID-19) Pandemic Filing/Payment Relief:** October 15, 2020, return due date. July 15, 2020, payment due date.

Jurisdiction	Partnerships, LLPs, and LLCs	Comment
Connecticut	Partnerships, LLPs, or LLCs can elect to pay composite income tax for nonresident individuals using Schedule CT-NR. Composite income tax tax equals each nonresident's distributive share of income from state sources multiplied by 6.99% and reduced by the nonresident's pass-through entity tax credit. Check composite return election box on pass-through entity tax return due March 15 (15th day of 3rd month after end of taxable year) and attach composite tax schedule.	Composite returns not authorized for 2018 tax year. **Tax Years Before 2018:** Filing of composite returns using Form CT-1065/CT-1120SI required by April 15 (15th day of fourth month after end of tax year) if partnership, LLP, or LLC: • was required to file a federal return; and • had income, gain, loss, or deduction from state sources. Composite tax applied at rate of 6.99% to all partners or members with $1,000 or more of distributive income from state sources. Composite payment based on distributive share of: • separately and nonseparately computed items from lines 1 to 12 of federal Schedule K-1; and • any modification to the S corporation's income, gain, loss or deduction.
Delaware	Composite returns using Form 200-C may be filed and tax paid at rate of 6.6% on behalf of electing full-year nonresident individuals who have the same tax year and do not have income from other state sources. Net operating losses (NOLs) and refundable credits are not allowed. Returns are due by April 30 (30th day of fourth month after close of taxable year of nonresidents).	
District of Columbia	Personal income tax is not applicable to nonresidents.	
Florida	Composite returns not authorized.	No personal income tax
Georgia	Composite returns using Form IT-CR may be filed on behalf of nonresidents that do not have income from other state sources. Permission is not required. Tax may be computed on behalf of individuals on basis of standard graduated rate schedule for applicable filing status without exemptions or deduction or on prorated basis with exemptions and deductions using entity's income. The return is due on April 15 for calendar year filers or within 3.5 months following close of the fiscal year. Tax is imposed on nonresident corporations and partnerships at rate of 5.75%.	

Jurisdiction	Partnerships, LLPs, and LLCs	Comment
Hawaii	Composite returns using Form N-15 may be filed 20th day of the fourth month following on behalf of electing nonresident individuals who do not have income from other state sources. Powers of attorney from each participant must be executed and attached to the initial composite return filed by the partnership. Composite payments based on participating partner's distributive share of Hawaii source income taxed at the partner's own individual tax rate, but with no standard deduction or personal exemption. Itemized deductions using ratio of state adjusted gross income to total adjusted gross income may not be claimed. Tax credits based on total adjusted gross income from all sources may not be claimed.	**Coronavirus (COVID-19) Pandemic Filing/Payment Relief** July 20, 2020 filing and payment due date.
Idaho	Composite returns may be filed using Form 65 on behalf of two or more nonresident individual owners (including grantor trusts, qualified subchapter S trusts, and single member LLCs treated as a disregarded entity) or beneficiaries of a trust or estate with income taxable in the state. The income that may be reported on the composite return includes an owner's share of any income, loss, deduction, or credit of the LLC that is required to be included on the individual's state return, except that deductions may not be claimed on behalf of the owner for: • net operating losses (NOLs); • capital losses; • capital gains; • informational items reported on federal Schedule K-1s; • items that are not deductible on federal return, unless specifically allowed under state law; • standard deduction; • personal exemptions; • itemized deductions related to the owner; and • items previously deducted by the entity on the owner's behalf. Tax is computed at the corporate tax rate (6.925%). The filing of a composite return is done in lieu of withholding. An entity is liable for tax on income not reported on a composite return or included in withholding.	
Illinois	Composite returns not authorized.	

Jurisdiction	Partnerships, LLPs, and LLCs	Comment
Indiana	Composite adjusted gross income tax returns using form IT-65 must be filed on behalf of nonresidents, even if nonresident has income from other state sources. The filing is due the 15th day of the 4th month following the close of the tax year. The tax is imposed at the rate of 3.23%.	Publicly traded partnerships are not required to file composite returns for their partners. For tax years before 2015, any shareholder that was a corporation or partnership was excluded from the composite return.
Iowa	Composite returns can be elected and filed using Form IA 1040C on behalf of nonresident individuals who do not have income from state sources, other than from the entity or another entity, if income exceeds the amount of one standard deduction for single taxpayers plus an amount of income necessary to create tax liability at the effective tax rate on the composite return sufficient to offset one personal exemption. The return is due by April 30. Tax is determined using personal income tax rate schedule (0.360% to 8.980% for 2018, 0.330% to 8.530% after 2018).	
Kansas	Composite returns using Form K-40C may be filed by April 15 (15th day of 4th month after close of tax year) for nonresident individuals that do not have income from other state sources. Not allowed for any tax year the entity is claiming a special tax credit or a net operating loss (NOL). Tax imposed at graduated rates of 3.1%, 5.25%, or 5.7% based on filing status and taxable income. Tax based on share of apportionable business income reduced by standard deduction and personal exemptions multiplied by nonresident allocation percentage.	
Kentucky	Composite income tax returns using Form 740NP-WH may be filed on behalf of electing nonresident individuals who are not subject to pass-through entity withholding requirements. Tax must be paid at the rate of 5% (6% for tax years before 2018) on distributive share of all items of pass-through income, including but not limited to interest, dividend, capital gains and losses, guaranteed payments, and rents. Return must be filed by April 15 (15th day of fourth month following close of tax year). A record of tax paid must be furnished to each participating nonresident by return due date.	Nonresident individual partners should not be included in composite returns if distributive share income was subject to withholding and reported. **Coronavirus (COVID-19) Pandemic Filing/Payment Relief** July 15, 2020 due date for returns and payments due on and after April 15, 2020 and before July 15, 2020. Penalty and interest calculation will begin July 16, 2020.

Jurisdiction	Partnerships, LLPs, and LLCs	Comment
Louisiana	Composite returns using Form R-6922 are required to be filed by May 15 (15th day of fifth month following close of tax year for fiscal year taxpayers) on behalf of nonresident owners who are individuals, estates, and trusts (other than tax-exempt trusts) that have not agreed to file individual returns, unless the partnership is an exempt publicly traded partnership. Composite tax is imposed at rate of 6% on nonresident owner's share of partnership's income attributable to the state, as reflected on the partnership's return for the taxable period. Nonresident owners must claim their respective share of any credit earned by partnership for applicable tax period in which credit was earned. Credits claimed on composite return may not be allowed or claimed on any other return submitted on behalf of or by owner for the same tax period.	**Coronavirus (COVID-19) Pandemic Filing/Payment Relief:** Return and payment due July 15, 2020. **Hurricane Laura Relief:** Filing and payment deadline extensions are available as a result of damage caused by Hurricane Laura for taxpayers located in parishes that have been declared federal disaster areas. Returns and payments originally due between August 24, 2020, and November 2, 2020, are extended to December 31, 2020, for corporate income, franchise, partnership, and partnership composite taxes. Returns and payments originally due between August 24, 2020, and November 2, 2020, are extended to November 30, 2020, for income withholding.
Maine	Composite returns using Form 1040ME may be filed on behalf of certain electing nonresident individuals, electing small business trusts (ESBTs), qualified subchapter S trusts (QSSTs), nonresident trusts, or nonresident estates. Nonresident individuals, trusts, and estates may not have income from other state sources (including spouse's income for married individuals filing jointly). Reportable income is that portion of the distributive share of income apportionable to Maine, based on sales of the partnership/S corporation. Form 1040ME is due April 15. Schedule 1040C-ME must also be completed. Tax is imposed at rate of 7.15%.	For 2017 tax year returns, due date for Form 1040ME has been extended to April 17, 2018, to conform with corresponding federal extension. **Coronavirus (COVID-19) Pandemic Filing/Payment Relief:** July 15, 2020, return and payment due date.
Maryland	Composite returns using Form 510C may be filed on behalf of electing nonresident individuals who do not have taxable income from other state sources. Statements of electing participants must be attached to return and signed by an authorized official. Credits may not be claimed, except estimated tax payments. Flow-through addition or subtraction modifications not allowed, except modifications required by state's decoupling from federal bonus depreciation, expensing, and extended net operating loss (NOL) provisions. Form 510C is due April 15. Tax is imposed at the rate of 7.5%.	Rate is determined by adding the highest individual rate plus the lowest county rate. **Coronavirus (COVID-19) Pandemic Filing/Payment Relief:** July 15, 2020, return and payment due date.

Jurisdiction	Partnerships, LLPs, and LLCs	Comment
Massachusetts	Composite returns using Form MA NRCR may be filed by April 15 on behalf of 2 or more electing full-year nonresident individuals, electing small business trusts (ESBTs), or the estate or trust of a deceased nonresident member. Composite returns may be filed by lower-tier entities on behalf of upper-tier entities. Tax is imposed at rate of 5.05% (5% for tax years after 2019) on taxable income and 12% on certain capital gains. Participants must waive right to claim deductions, exemptions and credits.	Electronic filing is mandated. **Coronavirus (COVID-19) Pandemic Filing/Payment Relief** July 15, 2020 due date for return filing and payment.
Michigan	Composite returns using Form 807 may be filed on behalf of 2 or more electing nonresident individuals, estates, or trusts, or pass-through entities with nonresident owners if participants do not have income from other state sources and do not claim certain credits and more than 1 personal exemption. Pages 1-5 of federal Form 1065, Form MI-1040H, a list of participants, a list of nonparticipants, and a list of Michigan resident members must be attached to return. Form 807 is due April 15. Tax on individuals imposed at rate of 4.25% based on electing nonresident members' shares of income available for distribution from the flow-through entity for doing business in, or deriving income from, sources within the state.	**Coronavirus (COVID-19) Pandemic Filing/Payment Relief** July 15, 2020 filing and payment due date.
Minnesota	Composite returns using Form M-3 may be filed by April 15 (15th day of fourth month following close of tax period for fiscal year taxpayers) on behalf of electing full-year nonresident individuals, or certain grantor trusts, who do not have income from state sources other than filing entity or other entities electing composite filing. Nonbusiness deductions, standard deductions, or personal exemptions are not allowed. Tax is imposed at rate of 9.85%. Composite income tax box on front of return must be checked.	

Jurisdiction	Partnerships, LLPs, and LLCs	Comment
Mississippi	Composite returns using Form 84-105 may be filed on behalf of electing nonresident individuals who do not carry on any other state activity. Election may not be revoked without written permission. Participants should be identified on Form 84-131 Schedule K by writing "composite" after each participant's name. Deduction of $5,000 or 10% of composite net income, whichever is less, is authorized in lieu of any individual exemption and deduction. Tax credits are allowed, as well as net operating loss and capital loss deductions, provided they are computed and tracked on an individual basis. Form 84-105 is due on March 15. Tax imposed on taxable income at following rates: • $0-$5,000: 3% • $5,001-$10,000: 4% • $10,001 or more: 5%	Tax on the first $5,000 of income phased out by exempting $1,000 in 2018 and increasing that amount by $1,000 per year until 2022. As a result, the 3% rate will be: • $1,000-$5,000 in 2018 • $2,000-$5,000 in 2019 • $3,000-$5,000 in 2020 • $4,000-$5,000 in 2021 • No tax on income under $5,000 in 2022 and thereafter.
Missouri	Composite returns using Form MO-1040 may be filed by April 15 on behalf of electing nonresident individuals, partnerships, S corporations, regular corporations, estates filing a federal Form 1041, and trusts that do not have income from other state sources. Tax is imposed at highest individual income tax rate applicable to individuals (6% prior to 2018, 5.9% for 2018, 5.4% for 2019) and applied to income from schedule in lieu of demonstrating exact amount of income, deductions and exemptions. "Composite Return" must be written at top of return. Composite box should be checked at top of entity's return. A schedule listing all participants, their identification number and income attributable to state sources must be attached to composite return. Schedule must be submitted electronically in spreadsheet format if more than 100 participants.	**Coronavirus (COVID-19) Pandemic** **Filing/Payment Relief** July 15, 2020 filing and payment due date.

Jurisdiction	Partnerships, LLPs, and LLCs	Comment
Montana	Composite returns using Form PTE may be filed by March 15 (15th day of third month following close of tax year for fiscal year filers) on behalf of electing nonresident individuals, foreign C corporations, tax-exempt entities, and second-tier pass-through entities that do not have income from state sources other than the filing entity and other composite returns. Participants must submit powers of attorney. Credits passed through to participants may not be used to reduce composite tax. Owners may subtract standard deduction and one personal exemption from distributive share of income, and applicable tax rate (1% to 6.9%) is applied to result. This figure is multiplied by the composite tax ratio, which is the entity's state source income over its total federal income.	Beginning with tax year 2019, pass-through entities use Form PTE instead of PR-1.
Nebraska	Composite returns not authorized.	
Nevada	N/A, because state does not tax pass-through income.	
New Hampshire	No, partnerships taxed in same manner as C corporations.	Personal income tax applies only to interest and dividend income and is not applicable to nonresidents.
New Jersey	Composite returns may be filed on behalf of electing full-year nonresident individuals who do not file on a fiscal year basis and do not have income from state sources other than the filing entity or other composite returns. Form NJ-1080C is due by April 15. Election to participate must be made each year by completing and filing Form NJ-1080E. List of participants and nonparticipants must be attached to return. Box labeled "Composite Return is filed for Nonresident Partners" should be checked at top of entity's return. Participants must waive right to claim exemptions, deductions, or credits. Tax is imposed at highest rate allowed.	Returns with 25 or more participants must be filed on diskette.
New Mexico	Composite returns not authorized.	

Jurisdiction	Partnerships, LLPs, and LLCs	Comment
New York	Group returns using Form IT-203-GR may be filed by April 15 (15th day of fourth month following close of tax year for fiscal year taxpayers) on behalf of at least 11 electing full-year nonresident individuals who have the same accounting period, if neither the participant nor the participant's spouse, has income from other state sources, or is subject to the separate tax on the ordinary income portion of lump-sum distribution. Participants must waive right to claim any standard or itemized deduction, dependent exemption, personal income tax credits, and net operating loss (NOL) carryback or carryover. Permission to file group returns must be requested by submitting Form TR-99, accompanied by powers of attorney from each participant, no later than 30 days following close of tax year. Group agent must be appointed. Tax imposed at rate of 8.82%.	
North Carolina	Composite returns not authorized.	For partnerships with nonresident partners, the managing partner must compute and pay the tax due for each nonresident partner. The manager may withhold the tax due from each nonresident partner's share of the partnership income. Withholding by pass-through entities is covered under the topic Withholding by Pass-Throughs.
North Dakota	Composite return using Form 58 may be filed by April 15 (15th day of fourth month following close of tax year for fiscal year taxpayers) on behalf of electing nonresident individuals and (for taxable years beginning after 2013) pass-through entities who do not have income from state sources except from the filing entity or other pass-through entities. Tax imposed at rate of 2.90%. No adjustments, deductions, or tax credits are allowed.	**COVID-19 Filing/Payment Relief:** July 15, 2020 return and payment due date.
Ohio	Not allowed for CAT.	CAT taxpayer filing groups may either file a combined return or a consolidated return.

Jurisdiction	Partnerships, LLPs, and LLCs	Comment
Oklahoma	Entities can elect to file composite returns using Form 514 on behalf of nonresidents. Form 514-PT must also be completed for participants. Tax imposed on nonresident individuals at highest marginal tax rate and on nonresident partners that are C corporations, S corporations, and partnerships at the rate of 6%. Partnership returns are due no later than 30 days after the due date established under the Internal Revenue Code.	
Oregon	Composite returns using Form OC may be filed on behalf of electing full-year nonresident individuals and C corporations with no commercial domicile in the state. Credits are not allowed, except corporate excise or income taxpayers are allowed the surplus credit (if applicable). Due date is the same as the tax year and due date for the majority of the electing owners' federal and Oregon tax returns. Tax imposed on nonresident individuals at standard graduated rate (5% to 9.9%) for applicable filing status and on nonresident corporate taxpayers at applicable corporate rate (6.6% or 7.6%) or at the minimum corporate rate (fixed dollar minimums).	
Pennsylvania	Nonresident consolidated income tax returns using Form PA-40 NRC may be filed on behalf of electing nonresident individual owners who do not have income from other state sources. PA Schedule NRC-I listing each of nonresident individual that received PA-20S/PA-65 Schedule NRK-1 must be completed. Return is due April 15. The tax rate is 3.07%. Election may not be changed.	
Rhode Island	Composite returns using Form RI-1040C may be filed on behalf of electing nonresident individuals who have the same taxable year and file Form RI-1040C-NE. The composite returns must include income from doing business in, or deriving income from sources in, Rhode Island. Form RI-1040C is due March 15. Tax imposed at rate of 5.99%.	

Jurisdiction	Partnerships, LLPs, and LLCs	Comment
South Carolina	Composite returns using Form SC1040 may be filed by April 15 (15th day of fourth month following close of tax year for fiscal year filers) on behalf of nonresident individuals, estates, and trusts. Composite return box and single filing status should be checked on return. Nonresidents may participate even if they have taxable income from other state sources. Tax imposed at rate of 7% on any income that does not qualify as active trade or business income, unless participant completes an I-338 composite return affidavit stating that the participant has no other taxable income from state sources.	**COVID-19 Filing/Payment Relief:** July 15, 2020 return and payment due date.
South Dakota	N/A, because state does not tax pass-through income.	
Tennessee	No, personal income tax applies only to stock and bond income and is not applicable to nonresidents.	
Texas	No personal income tax.	
Utah	Composite returns not authorized.	
Vermont	Composite returns using Form BI-471 may be filed by March 15 (15th day of third month following close of tax period for fiscal year taxpayers) on behalf of nonresidents. Election is binding for 5 years. Tax is imposed at rate of 7.6%.	Entities with more than 50 nonresident owners are required to file a composite return, including and paying tax for all nonresident owners.
Virginia	Unified returns using Form 765 may be filed by May 1 (15th day of fourth month following close of tax period for fiscal year taxpayers) on behalf of two or more nonresident individuals who are direct owners with state-source income for the taxable year from the pass-through entity (PTE) filing the return. Certain estates and trusts which qualify and have income passed through to their nonresident beneficiaries may also elect to file a unified return. Participants must sign consent form that continues in force until revoked in writing. Taxable income cannot be reduced by net operating loss (NOL) carryovers, charitable contributions, IRC § 179 expense deductions, or other deductions. Credits are not allowed, except flow-through credits. Amount of tax is computed by applying tax rates for individual income tax (2% to 5.75%). Schedule L providing participant information must be included with return.	Effective for tax years beginning after 2014, a PTE may file a composite return for only a portion of its qualified nonresident owners, provided that it pays the PTE withholding tax for any qualified nonresident owners who are not included in the composite return.

Jurisdiction	Partnerships, LLPs, and LLCs	Comment
Washington	N/A, because state does not tax pass-through income.	
West Virginia	Composite returns using Form IT-140NRC may be filed by March 15 (15th day of 3rd month after close of tax year) for electing nonresident individuals upon payment of $50 processing fee. Tax paid at rate of 6.5% on nonresident's share of distributive income. Participation by all nonresident distributees is not required. Nonresident return is required if participant has taxable income from other sources. If separate return is filed, nonresident must include income derived from the pass-through entity filing the composite return and may claim credit for income remitted with composite return.	
Wisconsin	Composite returns using Form 1CNP may be filed by April 15 on behalf of full-year nonresident individuals who do not derive any taxable income or deductible loss from other state sources. Participants may not claim any tax credit or amounts deductible as itemized deductions. Tax computed according to Form 1CNP worksheet or at rate of 7.65%.	**COVID-19 Filing/Payment Relief:** July 15, 2020 return and payment due date.
Wyoming	N/A, because state does not tax pass-through income.	

Composite Returns—S Corporations

Most states allow S corporations to file composite income tax returns on behalf of nonresident shareholders reporting and paying tax on each participant's pro rata share of income. Generally, participants may not derive income from any other state sources and the filing of the composite return relieves the participant of the requirement for filing a separate return. In most states, eligibility to participate in composite returns is limited to nonresident individuals. Some states have extended eligibility to nonresident pass through entities and corporations. Special rules may apply to the availability of net operating losses (NOLs), deductions, and credits. This chart indicates whether composite returns may be filed for nonresident shareholders, participant eligibility requirements, return forms, and special computation rules.

Jurisdiction	S Corporations	Comment
Alabama	Composite returns using Form PTE-C may be filed by March 15 (15th day of third month following close of tax period for fiscal year taxpayers) on behalf of some or all nonresident owners who are individuals, trusts, or estates if there are one or more nonresident owners at any time during the taxable year. Composite tax is imposed at rate of 5% on nonresident owners' distributive shares of nonseparately and separately stated income allocated and apportioned to state, but excluding distributive shares of separately stated items of deduction or expense. Income or gain of one nonresident owner may not offset the loss of another owner, and a NOL carryforward may not offset income or gain.	Composite returns must be filed on behalf of nonresident owners for whom a Schedule NRA consent agreement has not been filed (i.e., for owners that do not agree to file income tax returns, pay taxes, and consent to state income tax jurisdiction). **Coronavirus (COVID-19) Pandemic Filing/Payment Relief** July 15, 2020 filing and payment due date.
Alaska	Composite returns not authorized.	No personal income tax

Jurisdiction	S Corporations	Comment
Arizona	Composite returns using Form 140NR may be filed by April 15 (15th day of fourth month following close of tax year for fiscal year taxpayers) on behalf of at least 10 full-year nonresident individuals who have the same tax year and who have no other income, including income of any participant's spouse, from state sources other than allocable distributive income. Individuals who must make state estimated tax payments and deceased individuals may not be included in return. The Residency Status box for a Composite Return, on page 1 of the form, must be checked. Affidavits of qualification and powers of attorney must be executed by each participant. Each member's tax liability computed separately based on separate taxable income using appropriate tax table for tax year involved. Itemized deductions, net operating losses (NOLs), and tax credits not allowed.	**Coronavirus (COVID-19) Pandemic Filing/Payment Relief** July 15, 2020 filing and payment due date.
Arkansas	Composite returns using Form AR1000CR may be filed by April 15 on behalf of electing full-year nonresident individuals and business entities that do not have income or losses from other state sources. The composite return includes the distributive share of income or other gain that is passed through to the members. Tax is imposed at rate of 6.6%. No deductions or credits are allowed. Information must be submitted by CD if there are more than 10 participants. Withholding information returns using Form AR1099PT must be filed for each participant.	Tax rate is 5.9% for tax years beginning after 2020. Tax rate was 6.9% for tax years prior to 2020. **Coronavirus (COVID-19) Pandemic Filing/Payment Relief:** July 15, 2020, return and payment due date.

Jurisdiction	S Corporations	Comment
California	Group nonresident returns using Form 540NR may be filed on behalf of full-year nonresident individual shareholders if return is filed using calendar tax year and participants do not have income from state sources other than distributions reported on another group nonresident return. Tiered entities are not allowed to file a group return combining all of their business entities and individual nonresident members on one group return. Tiered entities must file separate group nonresident returns for their electing individual nonresident members and cannot include any business entities in the group nonresident return. Participants must be informed of terms and conditions of group return specified on form FTB 3864, which must be signed authorized person or attorney-in-fact, and attached to return. Schedule 1067A must also be attached to return. Until 2030, tax is imposed at rate of 12.3% (13.3% if member has taxable income over $1 million). After 2030, tax is imposed at rate of 9.3% (10.3% if member has taxable income over $1 million). Individual deductions not allowed. Credits not allowed except those directly attributable to the S corporation's activity.	**Coronavirus (COVID-19) Pandemic Filing/Payment Relief** July 15, 2020 return due date. July 15, 2020 payment due date.
Colorado	Composite returns using Form 106 may be filed by April 15 on behalf of electing nonresident individuals, nonresident estates and trusts, and pass-through entities (to the extent their members/shareholders are nonresident individuals, estates, or trusts), if participants do not have income from other state sources. Tax is imposed at rate of 4.63%.	Temporary rate reduction from 4.63% to 4.50% for tax year 2019. **Coronavirus (COVID-19) Pandemic Filing/Payment Relief:** October 15, 2020, return due date. July 15, 2020, payment due date.

Jurisdiction	S Corporations	Comment
Connecticut	S corporations can elect to pay composite income tax for nonresident individuals using Schedule CT-NR. Composite income tax tax equals each nonresident member's distributive share of the corporation's income from state sources multiplied by 6.99% and reduced by the member's pass-through entity tax credit. Check composite return election box on the pass-through tax entity return due March 15 (15th day of 3rd month after end of tax year) and attach composite tax schedule.	Composite returns not authorized for 2018 tax year. **Tax Years Before 2018:** Filing of composite returns using Form CT-1065/CT-1120SI required by April 15 (15th day of fourth month after end of tax year) if S corporation: • was required to file a federal return; and • had income, gain, loss, or deduction from state sources. Composite tax applied at rate of 6.99% to all shareholders with $1,000 or more of distributive income from state sources. Composite payment based on distributive share of: • separately and nonseparately computed items from lines 1 to 12 of federal Schedule K-1; and • any modification to the S corporation's income, gain, loss or deduction.
Delaware	Composite returns using Form 200-C may be filed and tax paid at rate of 6.6% on behalf of electing full-year nonresident individuals who have the same tax year and do not have income from other state sources. Net operating losses (NOLs) and refundable credits are not allowed. Returns are due by April 30 (30th day of fourth month after close of taxable year of nonresidents).	
District of Columbia	No, S corporations taxed in same manner as C corporations.	
Florida	Composite returns not authorized.	No personal income tax
Georgia	Composite returns using Form IT-CR may be filed on behalf of nonresidents that do not have income from other state sources. Permission is not required. Tax may be computed on behalf of individuals on basis of standard graduated rate schedule for applicable filing status without exemptions or deduction or on prorated basis with exemptions and deductions using entity's income. The return is due on April 15 for calendar year filers or within 3.5 months following close of the fiscal year. Tax is imposed on nonresident corporations and partnerships at rate of 5.75%.	

Jurisdiction	S Corporations	Comment
Hawaii	Composite returns using Form N-15 may be filed by April 20 (20th day of the fourth month following the close of the S corporation's tax year) on behalf of electing nonresident individuals who do not have income from other state sources. Powers of attorney from each participant must be executed and be retained by the corporation. Composite payments based on each shareholder's share of Hawaii taxable income taxed at the shareholder's own individual tax rate, but with no standard deduction or personal exemption. Itemized deductions using ratio of state adjusted gross income to total adjusted gross income may not be claimed. Tax credits based on total adjusted gross income from all sources may not be claimed.	**Coronavirus (COVID-19) Pandemic Filing/Payment Relief** July 20, 2020 filing and payment due date.
Idaho	Composite returns may be filed using Form 65 on behalf of two or more nonresident individual owners (including grantor trusts, qualified subchapter S trusts, and single member LLCs treated as a disregarded entity) or beneficiaries of a trust or estate with income taxable in the state. The income that may be reported on the composite return includes an owner's share of any income, loss, deduction, or credit of the LLC that is required to be included on the individual's state return, except that deductions may not be claimed on behalf of the owner for: • net operating losses (NOLs); • capital losses; • capital gains; • informational items reported on federal Schedule K-1s; • items that are not deductible on federal return, unless specifically allowed under state law; • standard deduction; • personal exemptions; • itemized deductions related to the owner; and • items previously deducted by the entity on the owner's behalf. Tax is computed at the corporate tax rate (6.925%). The filing of a composite return is done in lieu of withholding. An entity is liable for tax on income not reported on a composite return or included in withholding.	
Illinois	Composite returns not authorized.	

Jurisdiction	S Corporations	Comment
Indiana	Composite adjusted gross income tax returns using form IT-20 S must be filed on behalf of nonresidents, even if nonresident has income from other state sources. The filing is due the 15th day of the 4th month following the close of the tax year. The tax is imposed at the rate of 3.23%.	For tax years before 2015, any shareholder that was a corporation or partnership was excluded from the composite return.
Iowa	Composite returns can be elected and filed using Form IA 1040C on behalf of nonresident individuals who do not have income from state sources, other than from the entity or another entity, if income exceeds the amount of one standard deduction for single taxpayers plus an amount of income necessary to create tax liability at the effective tax rate on the composite return sufficient to offset one personal exemption. The return is due by April 30. Tax is determined using personal income tax rate schedule (0.360% to 8.980% for 2018, 0.330% to 8.530% after 2018).	
Kansas	Composite returns using Form K-40C may be filed by April 15 (15th day of 4th month after close of tax year) for nonresident individuals that do not have income from other state sources. Not allowed for any tax year the entity is claiming a special tax credit or a net operating loss (NOL). Tax imposed at graduated rates of 3.1%, 5.25%, or 5.7% based on filing status and taxable income. Tax based on share of apportionable business income reduced by standard deduction and personal exemptions multiplied by nonresident allocation percentage.	
Kentucky	Composite income tax returns using Form 740NP-WH may be filed on behalf of electing nonresident individuals who are not subject to pass-through entity withholding requirements. Tax must be paid at the rate of 5% (6% for tax years before 2018) on distributive share of all items of pass-through income, including but not limited to interest, dividend, capital gains and losses, guaranteed payments, and rents. Return must be filed by April 15 (15th day of fourth month following close of tax year). A record of tax paid must be furnished to each participating nonresident by return due date.	Nonresident individual shareholders should not be included in composite returns if distributive share income was subject to withholding and reported. **Coronavirus (COVID-19) Pandemic Filing/Payment Relief** July 15, 2020 due date for returns and payments due on and after April 15, 2020 and before July 15, 2020. Penalty and interest calculation will begin July 16, 2020.

Jurisdiction	S Corporations	Comment
Louisiana	No, S corporations taxed in same manner as C corporations.	**Coronavirus (COVID-19) Pandemic Filing/Payment Relief:** Return and payment due July 15, 2020. **Hurricane Laura Relief:** Filing and payment deadline extensions are available as a result of damage caused by Hurricane Laura for taxpayers located in parishes that have been declared federal disaster areas. Returns and payments originally due between August 24, 2020, and November 2, 2020, are extended to December 31, 2020, for corporate income, franchise, partnership, and partnership composite taxes. Returns and payments originally due between August 24, 2020, and November 2, 2020, are extended to November 30, 2020, for income withholding.
Maine	Composite returns using Form 1040ME may be filed on behalf of certain electing nonresident individuals, electing small business trusts (ESBTs), qualified subchapter S trusts (QSSTs), nonresident trusts, or nonresident estates. Nonresident individuals, trusts, and estates may not have income from other state sources (including spouse's income for married individuals filing jointly). Reportable income is that portion of the distributive share of income apportionable to Maine, based on sales of the partnership/S corporation. Form 1040ME is due April 15. Schedule 1040C-ME must also be completed. Tax is imposed at rate of 7.15%.	For 2017 tax year returns, due date for Form 1040ME has been extended to April 17, 2018, to conform with corresponding federal extension. **Coronavirus (COVID-19) Pandemic Filing/Payment Relief:** July 15, 2020, return and payment due date.
Maryland	Composite returns using Form 510C may be filed on behalf of electing nonresident individuals who do not have taxable income from other state sources. Statements of electing participants must be attached to return and signed by an authorized official. Credits may not be claimed, except estimated tax payments. Flow-through addition or subtraction modifications not allowed, except modifications required by state's decoupling from federal bonus depreciation, expensing, and extended net operating loss (NOL) provisions. Form 510C is due April 15. Tax is imposed at the rate of 7.5%.	Rate is determined by adding the highest individual rate plus the lowest county rate. **Coronavirus (COVID-19) Pandemic Filing/Payment Relief:** July 15, 2020, return and payment due date.

Jurisdiction	S Corporations	Comment
Massachusetts	Composite returns using Form MA NRCR may be filed by April 15 on behalf of 2 or more electing full-year nonresident individuals, electing small business trusts (ESBTs), or the estate or trust of a deceased nonresident member. Composite returns may be filed by lower-tier entities on behalf of upper-tier entities. Tax is imposed at rate of 5.05% (5% for tax years after 2019) on taxable income and 12% on certain capital gains. Participants must waive right to claim deductions, exemptions and credits.	Electronic filing is mandated.
Michigan	Composite returns using Form 807 may be filed on behalf of 2 or more electing nonresident individuals, estates, or trusts, or pass-through entities with nonresident owners if participants do not have income from other state sources and do not claim certain credits and more than 1 personal exemption. Pages 1-5 of federal Form 1120S, Form MI-1040H, a list of participants, a list of nonparticipants, and a list of Michigan resident members must be attached to return. Form 807 is due April 15. Tax on individuals imposed at rate of 4.25% based on electing nonresident members' shares of income available for distribution from the flow-through entity for doing business in, or deriving income from, sources within the state.	**Coronavirus (COVID-19) Pandemic Filing/Payment Relief** July 15, 2020 filing and payment due date.
Minnesota	Composite returns using Form M-8 may be filed by March 15 (15th day of third month following close of tax period for fiscal year taxpayers) on behalf of electing full-year nonresident individuals, or certain grantor trusts, who do not have income from state sources other than filing entity or other entities electing composite filing. Nonbusiness deductions, standard deductions, or personal exemptions are not allowed. Tax is imposed at rate of 9.85%. Composite income tax box on front of return must be checked.	

Jurisdiction	S Corporations	Comment
Mississippi	Composite returns using Form 84-105 may be filed on behalf of electing nonresident individuals who do not carry on any other state activity. Election may not be revoked without written permission. Participants should be identified on Form 84-131 Schedule K by writing "composite" after each participant's name. Deduction of $5,000 or 10% of composite net income, whichever is less, is authorized in lieu of any individual exemption and deduction. Tax credits are allowed, as well as net operating loss and capital loss deductions, provided they are computed and tracked on an individual basis. Form 84-105 is due on March 15. Tax imposed on taxable income at following rates: • $0-$5,000: 3% • $5,001-$10,000: 4% • $10,001 or more: 5%	Tax on the first $5,000 of income phased out by exempting $1,000 in 2018 and increasing that amount by $1,000 per year until 2022. As a result, the 3% rate will be: • $1,000-$5,000 in 2018 • $2,000-$5,000 in 2019 • $3,000-$5,000 in 2020 • $4,000-$5,000 in 2021 • No tax on income under $5,000 in 2022 and thereafter.
Missouri	Composite returns using Form MO-1040 may be filed by April 15 on behalf of electing nonresident individuals, partnerships, S corporations, regular corporations, estates filing a federal Form 1041, and trusts that do not have income from other state sources. Tax is imposed at highest individual income tax rate applicable to individuals (6% prior to 2018, 5.9% for 2018, 5.4% for 2019) and applied to income from schedule in lieu of demonstrating exact amount of income, deductions and exemptions. "Composite Return" must be written at top of return. A schedule listing all participants, their identification number and income attributable to state sources must be attached to composite return. Schedule must be submitted electronically in spreadsheet format if more than 100 participants.	**Coronavirus (COVID-19) Pandemic Filing/Payment Relief** July 15, 2020 filing and payment due date.

Jurisdiction	S Corporations	Comment
Montana	Composite returns using Form PTE may be filed by March 15 (15th day of third month following close of tax year for fiscal year filers) on behalf of nonresident individuals and tax-exempt entities that do not have income from state sources other than the electing entity and other pass-through entities that elected to file composite returns. Participants must submit powers of attorney. Credits passed through to participants may not be used to reduce composite tax. Individual owners may subtract standard deduction and one personal exemption from distributive share of income, and applicable personal income tax rate (1% to 6.9%) is applied to result. This figure is multiplied by the composite tax ratio, which is the entity's state source income over its total federal income.	Beginning with tax year 2019, S corporations use Form PTE instead of CLT-4S.
Nebraska	Composite returns not authorized.	
Nevada	N/A, because state does not tax pass-through income.	
New Hampshire	No, S corporations taxed in same manner as C corporations.	Personal income tax applies only to interest and dividend income and is not applicable to nonresidents.
New Jersey	Composite returns may be filed on behalf of electing full-year nonresident individuals who do not file on a fiscal year basis and do not have income from state sources other than the filing entity or other composite returns. Form NJ-1080C is due by April 15. Election to participate must be made each year by completing and filing Form NJ-1080E. List of participants and nonparticipants must be attached to return. Box labeled "Composite Return is filed for Nonresident Partners" should be checked at top of entity's return. Participants must waive right to claim exemptions, deductions, or credits. Tax is imposed at highest rate allowed.	Returns with 25 or more participants must be filed on diskette.
New Mexico	Composite returns not authorized.	

Jurisdiction	S Corporations	Comment
New York	Group returns using Form IT-203-S may be filed by April 15 (15th day of fourth month following close of tax year for fiscal year taxpayers) on behalf of at least 11 electing full-year nonresident individuals who have the same accounting period, if neither the participant nor the participant's spouse, has income from other state sources, or is subject to the separate tax on the ordinary income portion of lump-sum distribution. Participants must waive right to claim any standard or itemized deduction, dependent exemption, personal income tax credits, and net operating loss (NOL) carryback or carryover. Permission to file group returns must be requested by submitting Form TR-99, accompanied by powers of attorney from each participant, no later than 30 days following close of tax year. Group agent must be appointed. Tax imposed at rate of 8.82%.	
North Carolina	Composite returns using Form CD-401S may be filed by April 15 (15th day of 4th month after close of tax year) for nonresident individuals. Participants are not required to file separate returns, except nonresidents who have income from other state sources. Tax paid at rate of 5.25% based on nonresident's share of separately stated income, modifications, and credits. Losses from sales of Section 1231 property are not deductible.	
North Dakota	Composite return using Form 60 may be filed by April 15 (15th day of fourth month following close of tax year for fiscal year taxpayers) on behalf of electing nonresident individuals and trusts who do not have income from state sources except from the filing entity or other pass-through entities. Tax imposed at rate of 2.90%. No adjustments, deductions, or tax credits are allowed.	**COVID-19 Filing/Payment Relief:** July 15, 2020 return and payment due date.
Ohio	Not allowed for CAT.	CAT taxpayer filing groups may either file a combined return or a consolidated return.
Oklahoma	No	

Jurisdiction	S Corporations	Comment
Oregon	Composite returns using Form OC may be filed on behalf of electing full-year nonresident individuals and C corporations with no commercial domicile in the state. Credits are not allowed, except corporate excise or income taxpayers are allowed the surplus credit (if applicable). Due date is the same as the tax year and due date for the majority of the electing owners' federal and Oregon tax returns. Tax imposed on nonresident individuals at standard graduated rate (5% to 9.9%) for applicable filing status and on nonresident corporate taxpayers at applicable corporate rate (6.6% or 7.6%) or at the minimum corporate rate (fixed dollar minimums).	
Pennsylvania	Nonresident consolidated income tax returns using Form PA-40 NRC may be filed on behalf of electing nonresident individual owners who do not have income from other state sources. PA Schedule NRC-I listing each of nonresident individual that received PA-20S/PA-65 Schedule NRK-1 must be completed. Return is due April 15. The tax rate is 3.07%. Election may not be changed.	
Rhode Island	Composite returns using Form RI-1040C may be filed on behalf of electing nonresident individuals who have the same taxable year and file Form RI-1040C-NE. The composite returns must include income from doing business in, or deriving income from sources in, Rhode Island. Form RI-1040C is due March 15. Tax imposed at rate of 5.99%.	
South Carolina	Composite returns using Form SC1040 may be filed by April 15 (15th day of fourth month following close of tax year for fiscal filers) on behalf of nonresident individuals, estates, and trusts. Composite return box and single filing status should be checked on return. Nonresidents may participate even if they have taxable income from other state sources. Tax imposed at rate of 7% on any income that does not qualify as active trade or business income, unless participant completes an I-338 composite return affidavit stating that the participant has no other taxable income from state sources.	**COVID-19 Filing/Payment Relief:** July 15, 2020 return and payment due date.
South Dakota	N/A, because state does not tax pass-through income.	
Tennessee	No, S corporations taxed in same manner as C corporations.	

Jurisdiction	S Corporations	Comment
Texas	No personal income tax.	
Utah	Composite returns not authorized.	
Vermont	Composite returns using Form BI-471 may be filed by March 15 (15th day of third month following close of tax period for fiscal year taxpayers) on behalf of nonresidents. Election is binding for 5 years. Tax is imposed at rate of 7.6%.	Entities with more than 50 nonresident owners are required to file a composite return, including and paying tax for all nonresident owners.
Virginia	Unified returns using Form 765 may be filed by May 1 (15th day of fourth month following close of tax period for fiscal year taxpayers) on behalf of two or more nonresident individuals who are direct owners with state-source income for the taxable year from the pass-through entity (PTE) filing the return. Certain estates and trusts which qualify and have income passed through to their nonresident beneficiaries may also elect to file a unified return. Participants must sign consent form that continues in force until revoked in writing. Taxable income cannot be reduced by net operating loss (NOL) carryovers, charitable contributions, IRC § 179 expense deductions, or other deductions. Credits are not allowed, except flow-through credits. Amount of tax is computed by applying tax rates for individual income tax (2% to 5.75%). Schedule L providing participant information must be included with return.	Effective for tax years beginning after 2014, a PTE may file a composite return for only a portion of its qualified nonresident owners, provided that it pays the PTE withholding tax for any qualified nonresident owners who are not included in the composite return.
Washington	N/A, because state does not tax pass-through income.	
West Virginia	Composite returns using Form IT-140NRC may be filed by March 15 (15th day of 3rd month after close of tax year) for electing nonresident individuals upon payment of $50 processing fee. Tax paid at rate of 6.5% on nonresident's share of distributive income. Participation by all nonresident distributees is not required. Nonresident return is required if participant has taxable income from other sources. If separate return is filed, nonresident must include income derived from the pass-through entity filing the composite return and may claim credit for income remitted with composite return.	

Jurisdiction	S Corporations	Comment
Wisconsin	Composite returns using Form 1CNS may be filed by April 15 on behalf of full-year nonresident individuals who do not derive any taxable income or deductible loss from other state sources. Deductions and tax credits are not allowed. Tax computed according to Form 1CNS worksheet or at rate of 7.65%.	**COVID-19 Filing/Payment Relief:** July 15, 2020 return and payment due date.
Wyoming	N/A, because state does not tax pass-through income.	

Consolidated Returns

An affiliated group of corporations may elect to file a federal consolidated income tax return. Consolidated taxable income is computed by calculating the separate taxable incomes of the members, aggregating them, and increasing or decreasing the result by items that are computed on a consolidated basis. A federal "affiliated group" is defined as one or more chains of includible corporations connected through stock ownership with a common parent that is an includible corporation. The common parent must directly own 80% or more of at least one of the other includible corporations, and stock meeting the 80% test in each includible corporation other than the common parent must be owned directly by one or more of the other includible corporations. Includible corporations generally are domestic corporations except tax-exempt corporations, pass-through corporations such as S corporations, and life insurance companies.

The following chart shows whether each state and the District of Columbia permits the filing of consolidated returns by corporation income taxpayers.

Jurisdiction	Consolidated Returns	Comment
Alabama	Yes	Alabama affiliated group filing or required to file a federal consolidated return may elect to file AL consolidated return for same year.
Alaska	Yes	
Arizona	Yes	Permitted for affiliated groups filing federal consolidated return; may be required.
Arkansas	Yes	Members of federally defined affiliated group that have Arkansas income may elect.
California	No	Certain affiliated groups of railroad corporations may file consolidated returns. Also, affiliated corporations may be required to file a consolidated return to prevent tax evasion or to clearly reflect income earned from business in the state.
Colorado	Yes	Permitted for federally defined affiliated group if all consent.
Connecticut	No	
Delaware	No	Permitted for affiliated group of headquarters management corporations.
District of Columbia	No, for tax years beginning after 2010. Yes, for tax years beginning before 2011.	Permitted upon binding election by all corporations that are part of a federally defined and electing affiliated group subject to D.C. franchise tax on some part of their gross income, where all corporations have nexus with the District, and the return does not include any corporation that uses a different accounting method and period. Exception applies to any Qualified High Technology Company.

Jurisdiction	Consolidated Returns	Comment
Florida	Yes	Permitted if parent and all members of affiliated group that filed federal consolidated return consent.
Georgia	No	Effective April 12, 2005, corporations filing a federal consolidated return must file separate returns, unless prior approval is received.
Hawaii	Yes	Permitted for Hawaii-based affiliated groups with Hawaii source income where federal consolidated return requirements have been met.
Idaho	No	
Illinois	No	
Indiana	Yes	Permitted if all filing members of the affiliated group have adjusted gross income derived from activities in Indiana and all qualifying members of the affiliated group are included in the consolidated return.
Iowa	Yes	Permitted (and may be required) for affiliated group members with nexus to Iowa who also file a federal consolidated return; members of an affiliated group that are exempt from Iowa taxation cannot be included in the consolidated return.
Kansas	Yes	Required for affiliated groups that file a consolidated federal return and derive all of their income from Kansas sources; corporations that are members of an affiliated group that do not derive their entire income from Kansas sources and that have filed a federal return may file a Kansas consolidated return with permission.
Kentucky	**Tax years before 2019:** Mandatory nexus consolidated filing. **Tax years beginning on or after January 1, 2019:** Elective consolidated return filing for members of federal affiliated group.	Not applicable to REITs, RICs, S corporations, and corporations that realize an NOL whose Kentucky apportionment factors are de minimis.
Louisiana	No	
Maine	Yes	Permitted for members of affiliated group engaged in a unitary business. All members of unitary business with nexus must be included in the return. Income of unitary business is the net income of the entire group.
Maryland	No	
Massachusetts	No	

Jurisdiction	Consolidated Returns	Comment
Michigan	No, for the CIT and the MBT. Yes, for the SBT.	Affiliated groups that are Michigan taxpayers may be permitted or required to file a consolidated return if certain eligibility requirements are met for SBT purposes.
Minnesota	No	
Mississippi	No	
Missouri	Yes	Permitted for an affiliated group that files a federal consolidated return if at least 50% of the group's income is derived from Missouri sources. Effective August 28, 2018, requirement to have at least 50% of the group's income derived from Missouri sources is eliminated.
Montana	Yes	Permitted for federally defined affiliated groups that have common ownership of at least 80% of all classes of stock of each affiliated corporation, that have a unitary business operation, and that receive permission from the Department of Revenue.
Nebraska	No	
Nevada	N/A, because state does not tax general business corporation income.	
New Hampshire	No	
New Jersey	No	Affiliated or controlled groups may be required to file consolidated returns to prevent distortion of income. Required for businesses holding a license pursuant to the Casino Control Act. Permitted for air carriers.
New Mexico	Yes	Only permitted for corporations that have filed a federal consolidated return.
New York	No	Permitted only for corporate stockholders in a tax-exempt DISC.

Jurisdiction	Consolidated Returns	Comment
North Carolina	Yes	**Post-2011 tax years:** Allowed/required if the DOR determines that the corporation's reported income does not accurately reflect the corporation's income attributable to its business income in North Carolina. DOR required to follow specified procedures when requiring forced combination. **Pre-2012 tax years:** Allowed/required if taxpayer files a federal consolidated return and: • taxpayer is directed to file a consolidated return by the Department of Revenue pursuant to the taxpayer's written request or upon the Department's finding that the taxpayer's return does not disclose the true net earnings of the corporation because payments have been made in excess of fair compensation between such a corporation and its parent, subsidiary, or affiliate; or • taxpayer's circumstances fall within the Department's rules that require the filing of a consolidated return.
North Dakota	Yes	Taxpayers that compute their liability on a combined basis may elect to file a consolidated North Dakota return; two or more North Dakota domestic corporations affiliated as a parent and a subsidiary that file a federal consolidated return must file a combined report and consolidated return for North Dakota income tax purposes.
Ohio	Yes.	
Oklahoma	Yes	If federal return filed: permitted for two or more affiliated corporations that derive part of their income from Oklahoma sources; required if affiliates income is entirely from Oklahoma sources.
Oregon	Consolidated state return required for unitary members that file federal consolidated returns and that are not permitted or required to: • determine state taxable income on separate basis; or • use different apportionment factors than apply to other group members.	
Pennsylvania	No	
Rhode Island	Yes, for tax years before 2015.	Affiliated group may file a consolidated return if 1) all consent, 2) no members are FSCs, DISCs, S corporations, or corporations buying, selling, dealing in, or holding securities on own behalf, 3) all are subject to Rhode Island income tax, and 4) all have the same fiscal year.

Jurisdiction	Consolidated Returns	Comment
South Carolina	Yes	May be filed by 1) a parent and substantially controlled subsidiary, 2) two or more corporations substantially under the control of the same interests, 3) a corporation doing business entirely within South Carolina and a corporation engaged in a multistate business, or 4) two or more corporations doing multistate business.
South Dakota	N/A, because state does not tax general business corporation income.	
Tennessee	No	
Texas	No	
Utah	No	
Vermont	Yes, permitted for affiliated group if: • income is attributable to state sources and parent or other group member has taxable nexus; • federal return is filed on consolidated basis; and • fiscal year of group members is the same.	Effective beginning with 2014 tax year, election is irrevocable for five year period, including the year election is made.
Virginia	Yes	Permitted for federally defined affiliated corporation, but a consolidated return may not include corporations that are exempt from Virginia income tax, not affiliated, or that use different taxable years; called a "combined return."
Washington	N/A, because state does not tax general business corporation income.	
West Virginia	Allowed for tax years beginning prior to 2009 if affiliated group filed federal consolidated return and all members of group consent to election. Required for tax years beginning prior to 2009 at discretion of state if necessary to clearly reflect taxable income.	
Wisconsin	No	
Wyoming	N/A, because state does not tax general business corporation income.	

Credit for Taxes Paid to Another State—Resident

The following chart indicates whether a credit for taxes paid by a resident to another state is allowed.

Jurisdiction	Residents	Comment
Alabama	Yes	
Arizona	Yes	
Arkansas	Yes	
California	Yes	
Colorado	Yes	
Connecticut	Yes	A legal resident of another state or D.C. can claim the credit if: • the taxpayer lives at a residence in Connecticut for more than 183 days of the tax year; and • Connecticut residents who live in the other state or D.C. can claim a similar credit.
Delaware	Yes	
District of Columbia	Yes	No credit allowed for tax paid to another jurisdiction on income from intangible property, such as dividends or interest, the source of which is within the District. Credit is permitted to (1) District domiciliaries required to pay tax to another jurisdiction on income from intangible property derived from sources within that jurisdiction and (2) nondomiciliary statutory residents of the District required to pay tax on income from intangible property from sources other than the District to state of domicile.
Georgia	Yes	Credit allowed if resident engages in employment, has an established business, or has investment property with taxable situs in another state that levies a tax upon net income.
Hawaii	Yes	No credit allowed to individuals who took up residence in Hawaii after age 65 and prior to July 1, 1976, who are treated as nonresidents for purposes of computing income.
Idaho	Yes	Must be domiciled in Idaho to qualify.
Illinois	Yes	
Indiana	Yes	
Iowa	Yes	
Kansas	Yes	
Kentucky	Yes	

Jurisdiction	Residents	Comment
Louisiana	Yes	Effective July 1, 2015, to June 30, 2023, credit available only if other state provides similar credit for Louisiana income taxes paid on income derived from property located in, or from services rendered in, or from business transacted in Louisiana; credit limited to amount of Louisiana income tax that would have been imposed if the income earned in other state had been earned in Louisiana; and credit not allowed for income taxes paid to a state that allows nonresidents a credit against income taxes imposed by that state for taxes paid or payable to the state of residence. However, in *Smith v. Robinson*, No. 2018-CA-0728 (Dec. 5, 2018), the Louisiana Supreme Court held that the reciprocity limitation was an unconstitutional violation of the Dormant Commerce clause. In addition, credit not allowed for tax paid on income that is not subject to tax in state. For taxes paid after 2017, deduction available to owner of pass-through entity that pays other state's entity-level tax.
Maine	Yes	
Maryland	Yes	
Massachusetts	Yes	
Michigan	Yes	
Minnesota	Yes	
Mississippi	Yes	
Missouri	Yes	
Montana	Yes	
Nebraska	Yes	
New Hampshire	No	
New Jersey	Yes	
New Mexico	Yes	Credit limited to amount of taxpayer's New Mexico income tax liability on portion of income allocated or apportioned to New Mexico on which tax payable to other state is determined.
New York	Yes	Credit limited to items of income sourced to those other qualifying locations.
North Carolina	Yes	
North Dakota	Yes	
Ohio	Yes	

Jurisdiction	Residents	Comment
Oklahoma	Yes	Credit only on taxes paid in another state for wages and compensation for personal services, including retirement income and gambling proceeds.
Oregon	Yes	
Pennsylvania	Yes	
Rhode Island	Yes	Other state's tax must be imposed regardless of taxpayer's residence or domicile.
South Carolina	Yes	Department of Revenue may allow credit where taxpayer is considered resident of South Carolina and resident of other state.
Tennessee	Yes	Credit allowed to resident shareholder of S corporation incorporated and doing business in another state for tax paid to other state on income, distributions or dividends, if tax credit reciprocity agreement between Tennessee and other state.
Utah	Yes	
Vermont	Yes	If taxpayer domiciled in other jurisdiction is deemed resident of Vermont, income from intangibles not employed in a business, trade, or profession is considered derived from sources within jurisdiction of domicile and credit may be claimed if jurisdiction of domicile provides for a similar credit.
Virginia	Yes	
West Virginia	Yes, except taxpayers cannot claim credit for taxes paid on compensation earned in reciprocal agreement states.	
Wisconsin	Yes	Credit not allowed for income tax paid to Illinois, Indiana, Kentucky, or Michigan on personal service income earned in those states included under a reciprocity agreement. Credit may not be claimed if taxpayer is a shareholder, partner, or member of a pass-through entity that elected to be taxed at the entity level. Credit cannot exceed amount of net tax paid to Wisconsin on income taxable to both Wisconsin and other state (limit not applicable to income taxable both to Wisconsin and to Minnesota, Iowa, Illinois, or Michigan).

Credit for Taxes Paid to Another State—Nonresident

The following chart indicates whether a credit for taxes paid by a nonresident to another state is allowed.

Jurisdiction	Nonresidents	Comment
Alabama	No	
Arizona	Yes	Credit allowed for taxes paid to state or country of residence if state or country of residence either exempts Arizona residents from tax on income derived from that state or country or allows Arizona residents credit against taxes imposed by that state or country for taxes paid to Arizona. Other limitations apply.
Arkansas	Yes	Credit may not exceed what tax would be on the outside income, if added to the Arkansas income, and calculated at Arkansas income tax rates. Credit is limited to total income tax owed to other states on income reported as taxable income to both Arkansas and the other states, reported as income from all sources, and included as Arkansas income.
California	Yes	Allowed only if state of residence either does not tax California residents on income from sources within its borders or allows California residents credit for California taxes imposed on income derived from the state. State of residence may not permit its residents a credit for the taxed income also taxed by California.
Colorado	No	
Connecticut	No	A legal resident of another state or D.C. can claim the credit if: • the taxpayer lives at a residence in Connecticut for more than 183 days of the tax year; and • Connecticut residents who live in the other state or D.C. can claim a similar credit.
Delaware	No	
District of Columbia	No	Credit is permitted to (1) District domiciliaries required to pay tax to another jurisdiction on income from intangible property, such as dividends or interest, derived from sources within that jurisdiction, and (2) nondomiciliary statutory residents of the District required to pay tax on income from intangible property from sources other than the District to state of domicile.
Georgia	No	
Hawaii	No	
Idaho	No	

Jurisdiction	Nonresidents	Comment
Illinois	No	
Indiana	Yes	Allowed only if other state grants substantially similar credit to Indiana residents subject to other state's income tax or imposes an income tax on its residents derived from sources in Indiana and exempts from taxation the income of Indiana residents.
Iowa	No	
Kansas	No	
Kentucky	No	
Louisiana	No	
Maine	No	Separate nonresident credit is allowed to offset tax attributable to income not subject to Maine taxation.
Maryland	No	
Massachusetts	No	
Michigan	No	If nonresident's state of residence exempts a Michigan resident from taxation on income earned for personal services performed in that state, a reciprocal agreement may provide a similar tax exemption for that state's residents on income earned for personal services performed in Michigan.
Minnesota	Yes	Credit allowed if nonresident is required to file Minnesota return as a Minnesota resident and paid income tax to Minnesota and state of residence. Taxpayer must provide statement from other state's tax department stating they were not eligible to receive a credit for tax paid to Minnesota.
Mississippi	No	
Missouri	No	
Montana	No	
Nebraska	No	
New Hampshire	No	
New Jersey	No	
New Mexico	No	
New York	No	
North Carolina	No	
North Dakota	No	

Jurisdiction	Nonresidents	Comment
Ohio	Yes	Credit allowed against tax due for that portion of Ohio adjusted gross income that is not allocable to Ohio.
Oklahoma	No	
Oregon	Yes	Allowed only if state of residence either (1) does not tax income of Oregon residents derived from sources within that state or (2) allows Oregon residents a credit against that state's income tax for taxes paid or payable to Oregon.
Pennsylvania	No	
Rhode Island	No	
South Carolina	No	Department of Revenue may allow credit where taxpayer is considered resident of South Carolina and resident of other state.
Tennessee	No	Credit allowed to resident shareholder of S corporation incorporated and doing business in another state for tax paid to other state on income, distributions or dividends, if tax credit reciprocity agreement between Tennessee and other state.
Utah	No	
Vermont	No	If taxpayer domiciled in other jurisdiction is deemed resident of Vermont, income from intangibles not employed in a business, trade, or profession is considered derived from sources within jurisdiction of domicile and credit may be claimed if jurisdiction of domicile provides for a similar credit.
Virginia	Yes	Taxpayer must be a resident of Arizona, California, Oregon, or the District of Columbia and have Virginia source income as a nonresident. Income must be taxed by both Virginia and the other state.
West Virginia	Yes, if the state has a reciprocal agreement with nonresident's state of residence.	
Wisconsin	No	

Deadline for Reporting Federal Changes

This chart shows the deadline in each state and the District of Columbia for reporting federal return changes or adjustments.

Jurisdiction	Deadline for Reporting Federal Changes	Comment
Alabama	No deadline specified.	
Arizona	File within 90 days after final determination of federal adjustment.	
Arkansas	File within 180 days from the receipt of the notice and demand for payment from the IRS.	Prior to Oct. 1, 2015, file within 90 days from the receipt of the notice and demand for payment from IRS.
California	File within six months after final determination of federal adjustment or as otherwise required by the Franchise Tax Board.	
Colorado	File within 30 days after final determination of federal adjustment.	
Connecticut	File amended return within 90 days after final determination of federal adjustment.	
Delaware	File amended return within 90 days after final determination of federal adjustment.	
District of Columbia	File within 90 days after final determination of federal adjustment.	
Georgia	File within 180 days after final determination of federal adjustment.	
Hawaii	File within 90 days after final determination of federal adjustment.	
Idaho	File within 60 days after final determination of federal adjustment.	
Illinois	File amended return within: • 120 days after federal changes are agreed to or finally determined; or • 2 years and 120 days if claiming a refund resulting from the change.	
Indiana	File within 180 days after federal modification is made.	File within 120 days after federal modification if modification is made before 2011.
Iowa	Late payment penalty may be waived if taxpayer provides written notification of federal audit while it is in progress and voluntarily files an amended return within 60 days of final disposition of federal audit.	
Kansas	File within 180 days after the federal adjustment is paid, agreed to, or becomes final, whichever is earlier.	

Jurisdiction	Deadline for Reporting Federal Changes	Comment
Kentucky	Taxpayers must: • notify Department of Revenue in writing within 30 days of federal audit initiation; and • submit copy of final federal determination within 180 days (30 days before April 27, 2018) of audit's conclusion.	
Louisiana	File within 60 days of the taxpayer's receipt of the federal adjustments.	
Maine	File within 180 days after final determination of the federal change or correction or the filing of the federal amended return.	
Maryland	File within 90 days after final determination of federal adjustment.	
Massachusetts	File amended return within 1 year of notice of final federal determination.	
Michigan	File within 120 days after final determination of federal adjustment.	
Minnesota	File within 180 days after final determination of federal adjustment.	
Mississippi	File within 30 days after agreeing to the federal change.	Check amended return box on Form 80-105. Attach copy of federal amended return or RAR.
Missouri	File within 90 days after final determination of federal adjustment.	
Montana	File within 90 days after receiving official notice of the federal change or correction.	
Nebraska	File within 60 days after a correction or change to the federal return.	
New Hampshire	File within 6 months after final determination of federal adjustment.	
New Jersey	Must report within 90 days and must either concede the accuracy of the determination or state the grounds upon which the taxpayer contends the determination is erroneous.	
New Mexico	File within 180 days after final determination of federal adjustment (90 days prior to July 1, 2013).	
New York	File within 90 days after final determination of federal adjustment.	
North Carolina	File amended return within 6 months after: • receiving notice of each federal change or correction; or • filing an amended federal return that results in an increase in state tax.	

Jurisdiction	Deadline for Reporting Federal Changes	Comment
North Dakota	File within 90 days after final determination of federal adjustment.	
Ohio	File within 60 days after the federal adjustment has been agreed to or finally determined.	
Oklahoma	File within 1 year after final determination of the federal adjustment.	
Oregon	Must report within 90 days and must either concede the accuracy of the determination or state the grounds upon which the taxpayer contends the determination is erroneous.	
Pennsylvania	File within 30 days after receipt of federal final change or correction.	
Rhode Island	File within 90 days after receipt of federal final determination of change.	Effective July 1, 2019, partners are required to make a supplemental return to report final federal adjustments arising from a partnership level audit or an administrative adjustment request within 180 days after receipt of notification of the final audit or adjustment.
South Carolina	File within 180 days after final determination of federal adjustment.	
Tennessee	No deadline specified.	
Utah	File within 90 days after final determination of federal adjustment.	
Vermont	File within 180 days after notice of federal change or filing federal amended return.	
Virginia	File within 1 year after final determination of a change or correction by the IRS or another state.	
West Virginia	File within 90 days after the final determination of the federal adjustment.	
Wisconsin	File within 90 days after the final determination of the federal adjustment.	

Depletion Deduction

IRC Sec. 611 allows taxpayers who hold economic interests in oil and gas wells to deduct depletion. Taxpayers can compute the deduction using cost depletion or percentage depletion. Under IRC Sec. 612 cost depletion, a taxpayer amortizes the cost of oil and gas investments over the period of income production. Under IRC Sec. 613 percentage depletion, a taxpayer deducts a statutory percentage of the gross income from the oil and gas property, regardless of actual costs. Generally, the taxpayer must use whichever method results in the larger allowance.

This chart shows the tax treatment by each state and the District of Columbia of the federal depletion deduction for oil and gas interests.

Jurisdiction	Oil and Gas Depletion	Comment
Alabama	No adjustment to federal depletion deduction required.	A subtraction is allowed for the amount of the state percentage depletion allowance that exceeds the federal deduction, but this provision currently has no effect because the state percentage is lower than the federal percentage.
Alaska	Addition required for amount of federal percentage depletion deduction that exceeds cost depletion.	
Arizona	No adjustment to federal depletion deduction required.	
Arkansas	No adjustment to federal depletion deduction required.	
California	Addition required if federal deduction exceeds allowable state deduction due to state differences, including: • federal temporary suspension of 100% taxable income limitation for oil and gas production from marginal properties; and • increased federal refinery limitations for independent producers eligible to use percentage depletion method.	
Colorado	No adjustment to federal depletion deduction required.	For oil shale, subtraction allowed for amount of state percentage depletion allowance that exceeds federal deduction.
Connecticut	No adjustment to federal depletion deduction required.	
Delaware	Addition required for amount of federal percentage depletion deduction that exceeds cost depletion.	
District of Columbia	No adjustment to federal depletion deduction required.	
Florida	No adjustment to federal depletion deduction required.	

Jurisdiction	Oil and Gas Depletion	Comment
Georgia	No adjustment to federal depletion deduction required.	
Hawaii	No adjustment to federal depletion deduction required.	
Idaho	No adjustment to federal depletion deduction required.	
Illinois	No adjustment to federal depletion deduction required.	
Indiana	No adjustment to federal depletion deduction required.	
Iowa	Addition required for amount of federal percentage depletion deduction that exceeds cost depletion.	Repealed after 2022 if certain net general fund revenue amounts are met.
Kansas	No adjustment to federal depletion deduction required.	
Kentucky	No adjustment to federal depletion deduction required.	
Louisiana	Addition required for amount of federal depletion deduction. Subtraction allowed for amount of state percentage depletion allowance that exceeds federal cost depletion deduction, except state depletion allowance temporarily reduced by 28% from July 1, 2015, to June 30, 2018.	
Maine	No adjustment to federal depletion deduction required.	
Maryland	Addition required for amount of federal percentage depletion deduction that exceeds cost depletion.	
Massachusetts	No adjustment to federal depletion deduction required.	
Michigan	No adjustment to federal depletion deduction required.	
Minnesota	Addition required for amount of federal percentage depletion deduction. Subtraction allowed for amount of cost depletion for property on which percentage depletion was added back.	
Mississippi	Addition required for amount of federal depletion deduction that exceeds the cost basis of an asset.	
Missouri	No adjustment to federal depletion deduction required.	

Jurisdiction	Oil and Gas Depletion	Comment
Montana	No adjustment to federal depletion deduction required.	For purposes of computing state NOL deduction, addition required for amount of federal percentage depletion that exceeds cost depletion.
Nebraska	No adjustment to federal depletion deduction required.	
Nevada	N/A, because state does not tax general business corporation income.	
New Hampshire	No adjustment to federal depletion deduction required.	NH did not adopted the federal temporary suspension of the 100% taxable income limitation for oil and gas production from marginal properties. An addition is required for amount of federal deduction that exceeds the limitation.
New Jersey	No adjustment to federal depletion deduction required.	
New Mexico	No adjustment to federal depletion deduction required.	
New York	No adjustment to federal depletion deduction required.	
North Carolina	Addition required for amount by which federal percentage depletion allowance for oil and gas wells exceeds cost depletion allowance.	
North Dakota	No adjustment to federal depletion deduction required.	
Ohio	N/A, because deduction not allowed.	
Oklahoma	Subtraction allowed for amount of state percentage depletion allowance that exceeds federal deduction.	For major oil companies, deduction cannot exceed 50% of net income.
Oregon	Addition required for amount of federal depletion deduction that exceeds state cost depletion deduction. Subtraction allowed for amount of state cost depletion deduction that exceeds federal depletion deduction.	
Pennsylvania	No adjustment to federal depletion deduction required.	
Rhode Island	No adjustment to federal depletion deduction required.	
South Carolina	Taxpayers that allocate or apportion income have option of adding back depletion before apportionment and deducting depletion after apportionment on natural deposits located in state, with allowances limited to 50% of net income apportioned to state.	
South Dakota	N/A, because state does not tax general business corporation income.	

Jurisdiction	Oil and Gas Depletion	Comment
Tennessee	Addition required for amount of federal depletion deduction that exceeds cost depletion.	
Texas	Subtraction for cost of goods sold includes depletion expenses associated with and necessary for the production of goods.	
Utah	No adjustment to federal depletion deduction required.	
Vermont	No adjustment to federal depletion deduction required.	
Virginia	No adjustment to federal depletion deduction required.	
Washington	N/A, because state does not tax general business corporation income.	
West Virginia	No adjustment to federal depletion deduction required.	
Wisconsin	Addition required for taxable years before 2014 equal to amount of federal percentage depletion deduction that exceeds cost depletion. No adjustment to federal depletion deduction required for taxable years after 2013.	
Wyoming	N/A, because state does not tax general business corporation income.	

Depreciation Rules—IRC § 167, IRC § 168

IRC § 167 allows a deduction from federal taxable income for the exhaustion, wear and tear of property used in a trade or business, or of property held for the production of income. Under the Modified Accelerated Cost Recovery System (MACRS) and the Accelerated Cost Recovery System (ACRS) of IRC § 168, the cost or other basis of an asset is generally recovered over a specific recovery period. MACRS applies to tangible property generally placed in service after 1986 and the Accelerated Cost Recovery System (ACRS) applies to property placed in service after 1980 and before 1987. In addition, first-year bonus depreciation for qualified property has been allowed under IRC § 168(k) for most tax years beginning in 2001. Qualified property generally includes:

- new property with a recovery period of 20 years or less;
- certain computer software;
- qualified improvement property (qualified leasehold improvement property before 2016 tax year); and
- certain used property placed in service after September 27, 2017.

Current and historical bonus depreciation rates:

- 30% for qualified property placed in service after September 10, 2001 and before May 6, 2003 (Job Creation and Worker Assistance Act of 2002 (JCWAA) (P.L. 107-147));
- 50% for qualified property placed in service after May 5, 2003 and before January 1, 2005 (Jobs and Growth Tax Relief Reconciliation Act of 2003 (JGTRRA) (P.L. 108-27));
- 50% for qualified property placed in service after December 31, 2007 and before September 9, 2010 (Economic Stimulus Act of 2008 (P.L. 110-185); American Recovery and Reinvestment Tax Act of 2009 (P.L. 111-5); and Small Business Jobs Act of 2010 (P.L. 111-240));
- 100% for qualified property placed in service after September 8, 2010, and before January 1, 2012 (Tax Relief, Unemployment Insurance Reauthorization, Job Creation Act of 2010 (Tax Relief Act of 2010));
- 50% for qualified property placed in service after December 31, 2011 and before September 28, 2017 (Tax Relief Act of 2010) (P.L. 111-312); American Taxpayer Relief Act of 2012 (P.L. 112-240); Tax Increase Prevention Act of 2014 (P.L. 113-295); Protecting Americans from Tax Hikes Act of 2015 (PATH Act of 2015) (P.L. 114-113));
- 100% for property placed in service after September 27, 2017, and before January 1, 2024 (Tax Cuts and Jobs Act (P.L. 115-97));
- 80% for property placed in service after December 31, 2023, and before January 1, 2025;
- 60% for property placed in service after December 31, 2024, and before January 1, 2026;

• 40% for property placed in service after December 31, 2025, and before January 1, 2027;

• 20% for property placed in service after December 31, 2026, and before January 1, 2028; and

• 0% (bonus expires) for property placed in service after December 31, 2027 (Tax Cuts and Jobs Act (P.L. 115-97)).

This chart shows the tax treatment by each state and the District of Columbia of federal depreciation under IRC § 167, and IRC § 168, including bonus depreciation under IRC § 168(k). Many states follow federal depreciation rules for purposes of computing corporation income tax liability, but require adjustments to taxable income for bonus depreciation.

Jurisdiction	Regular and Bonus Depreciation—IRC § 167 and IRC § 168	Comment
Alabama	No adjustments to federal deduction required for tax years before and after 2008. Addition required for federal bonus depreciation claimed in tax year 2008.	
Alaska	Addition by oil and gas producers and pipelines required for federal deduction. Subtraction by oil and gas producers and pipelines allowed for depreciation based on federal provisions in effect on June 30, 1981, or financial statement depreciation. No other adjustments for federal deduction, including bonus depreciation, required.	
Arizona	Addition required for federal deduction, including bonus depreciation. Subtraction allowed for depreciation computed as if bonus depreciation had not been elected for federal purposes.	

Jurisdiction	Regular and Bonus Depreciation—IRC §167 and IRC §168	Comment
Arkansas	Subtraction allowed for depreciation computed using federal provisions in effect on January 1, 2019, without regard to bonus depreciation, for property purchased in tax years beginning after 2014.	Subtraction allowed for depreciation computed using federal provisions in effect on January 1, 2017, without regard to bonus depreciation, for property purchased in tax years beginning after 2014. Subtraction allowed for depreciation computed using federal provisions in effect on January 1, 2015, without regard to bonus depreciation, for property purchased in tax years beginning after 2013 and before 2015. Subtraction allowed for depreciation computed using federal provisions in effect on January 2, 2013, without regard to bonus depreciation, for property purchased in tax years beginning after 2011 and before 2014. Subtraction allowed for depreciation computed using federal provisions in effect on January 1, 2009, without regard to bonus depreciation, for property purchased in tax years beginning after 2008 and before 2012.
California	Addition required if federal deduction exceeds allowable state deduction due to state differences, including: • federal bonus depreciation; and • accelerated depreciation under ACRS and MACRS recovery systems. Subtraction allowed if state deduction exceeds federal deduction due to state differences, including: • depreciation computed using pre-1981 federal provisions; and • additional first-year depreciation under state provisions.	Adjustments computed on Form 3885.
Colorado	No adjustments to federal deduction, including bonus depreciation, required.	
Connecticut	Addition required for federal bonus depreciation. Subtraction allowed for depreciation computed without regard to federal bonus depreciation.	Subtraction adjustment computed on Form CT-1120 ATT.
Delaware	No adjustments to federal deduction, including bonus depreciation, required.	
District of Columbia	Subtraction allowed for depreciation computed without regard to federal bonus depreciation.	Federal depreciation form and statement showing computation must be attached to state return.

Jurisdiction	Regular and Bonus Depreciation—IRC §167 and IRC §168	Comment
Florida	Addition required for amount of federal bonus depreciation claimed on property placed in service in taxable years beginning after 2007 and before 2027. Subtraction allowed equal to 1/7 of addback amount in first and succeeding six tax years.	
Georgia	Addition required for amount of federal deduction, including bonus depreciation. Subtraction allowed for depreciation computed on a separate basis using Form 4562 without regard to federal bonus depreciation, as well as special depreciation and shortened recovery periods for certain property.	Federal and state depreciation forms must be attached to state return.
Hawaii	Addition required for federal deduction relating to: • federal bonus depreciation; • depreciation of property on Native American Indian reservations. Subtraction allowed using federal guidelines in effect before federal bonus depreciation provisions.	Adjustment computed by completing federal depreciation form. Federal form and any worksheet showing computation of adjustments must be attached to state return.
Idaho	Addition required for tax years before 2008 and after 2009 if federal deduction exceeds allowable state deduction due to federal bonus depreciation. Subtraction allowed for tax years before 2008 and after 2009 if federal deduction computed without regard to bonus depreciation is less than allowable state deduction. No adjustments to federal deduction, including bonus depreciation, required for tax years after 2007 and before 2010.	Adjustment computed by completing and attaching federal depreciation form or detailed computation.
Illinois	Addition required for federal bonus depreciation, except 100% bonus depreciation. Subtraction may be claimed for a portion of federal bonus depreciation: • the last tax year federal regular depreciation is claimed on the property; or • when the taxpayer sells, transfers, abandons, or otherwise disposes of the property. Subtraction adjustment is equal to: • 42.9% of depreciation on property for which 30% or 50% federal bonus depreciation was claimed in tax years beginning after 2001 and ending on or before December 31, 2005; and • 100% of depreciation on property for which 50% bonus depreciation was claimed in tax years beginning after December 31, 2005.	Adjustments computed on Form IL-4562, which must be attached to state return.

Jurisdiction	Regular and Bonus Depreciation—IRC §167 and IRC §168	Comment
Indiana	Addition required for federal bonus depreciation. Subtraction allowed for depreciation computed without regard to bonus depreciation.	
Iowa	Addition required for federal bonus depreciation. Subtraction allowed for depreciation computed without regard to bonus depreciation.	Adjustment computed on Schedule IA 4562A.
Kansas	Addition required for federal depreciation of (1) buildings or facilities for which state disabled access credit is claimed, and (2) the following types of property if state amortization deduction is claimed: • oil refineries; • oil or natural gas pipelines; • integrated coal or coke gasification nitrogen fertilizer plants; • biomass-to-energy plants; • renewable electric cogeneration facilities; • waste heat utilization systems at an electric generation facility; • biofuel storage and blending equipment; or • carbon dioxide capture, sequestration or utilization machinery and equipment. No other adjustments to federal deduction, including bonus depreciation, required.	
Kentucky	Addition required for federal bonus depreciation. Subtraction allowed for depreciation using federal provisions in effect on December 31, 2001.	Adjustment computed by converting federal form and attaching to state return.
Louisiana	No adjustments to federal deduction, including bonus depreciation, required.	

Jurisdiction	Regular and Bonus Depreciation—IRC §167 and IRC §168	Comment
Maine	Addition to federal tax base required equal to: • net increase in depreciation attributable to federal bonus depreciation on property placed in service in the state in 2013 tax year and thereafter for which a capital investment credit is claimed; • federal bonus depreciation on property placed in service in 2011 and 2012 tax years for which a capital investment credit is claimed; • net increase in depreciation attributable to federal bonus depreciation on property placed in service in 2011 tax year and thereafter for which a capital investment credit is not claimed; and • net increase in depreciation attributable to federal bonus depreciation on property placed in service in 2008 to 2010 tax years. Subtraction from federal tax base allowed equal to: • depreciation computed as though bonus depreciation had not been claimed on property placed in service in 2011 tax year and thereafter for which a capital investment credit is not claimed; • depreciation computed as though bonus depreciation had not been claimed on property placed in service in 2008 to 2010 tax years; • 5% of addition modification for property placed in service in 2003 to 2005 tax years beginning in tax year following year property was placed in service, with remaining 95% of modification recovered evenly over remainder of asset's life beginning in year 3; and • equal amounts of addition modification for property placed in service in 2002 tax year over remainder of asset's life beginning in 2004 tax year.	Capital investment credit allowed equal to: • 1.2% of net increase in deprecation deduction reported as addition to income for 2020 tax year and thereafter, excluding certain utility and telecommunications property; • 9% of net increase in depreciation deduction reported as addition to income for 2013 through 2019 tax years, excluding certain utility and telecommunications property; and • 10% of federal bonus depreciation claimed on property placed in service for tax years 2011 and 2012, excluding certain utility and telecommunications property.
Maryland	After 2018, addition required if federal deduction exceeds allowable state deduction due to decoupling from federal bonus depreciation, except for certain manufacturing businesses. Before 2019, addition required if federal deduction exceeds allowable state deduction due to decoupling from federal bonus depreciation and higher depreciation deduction for certain heavy duty SUV's. Subtraction allowed if state deduction exceeds federal deduction.	Adjustments computed on Form 500DM.
Massachusetts	Addition required for federal bonus depreciation.	

Jurisdiction	Regular and Bonus Depreciation—IRC §167 and IRC §168	Comment
Michigan	Addition required for federal bonus depreciation.	**Tax years after 2008 and before 2011:** MBT credit is available for portion of denied federal bonus depreciation deduction.
Minnesota	Addition required for 80% of federal bonus depreciation. Subtraction allowed for amount of addition adjustment over five following tax years.	State does not conform to federal bonus depreciation changes made by the Tax Cuts and Jobs Act.
Mississippi	Addition required for federal bonus depreciation. Subtraction allowed by computing depreciation without regard to bonus depreciation.	Adjustments computed by converting federal depreciation form.
Missouri	Addition required for 30% federal bonus depreciation on property purchased between July 1, 2002 and June 30, 2003. Subtraction allowed for depreciation on property purchased between July 1, 2002 and June 30, 2003 computed without regard to 30% bonus depreciation. No other adjustments required.	
Montana	No adjustments to federal deduction, including federal bonus depreciation, required.	
Nebraska	Subtraction from federal tax base allowed beginning on or after January 1, 2006, and in each of the four following taxable years, for 20% of the total amount of bonus depreciation that was required as an addition adjustment for tax years 2003 through 2005.	Adjustment computed on separate schedule that must be attached to state return.
Nevada	N/A, because state does not tax general business corporation income.	
New Hampshire	Addition required for federal bonus depreciation. Subtraction allowed for depreciation computed using federal provisions in effect on December 31, 2015, without regard to bonus depreciation, effective for taxable periods after 2016.	Subtraction was previously allowed for depreciation computed using federal provisions in effect on December 31, 2000, without regard to bonus depreciation, for taxable periods before 2017.
New Jersey	Subtraction allowed after recomputing depreciation without regard to federal deduction relating to: • federal bonus depreciation; • accelerated depreciation on property placed in service on or after 1981 and prior to July 7, 1993; • depreciation of safe harbor lease property; and • depreciation attributable to partnership interests.	Adjustment computed on Form CBT-100, Schedule S.

Jurisdiction	Regular and Bonus Depreciation—IRC §167 and IRC §168	Comment
New Mexico	No adjustments to federal deduction, including bonus depreciation, required.	
New York	Addition required for federal deduction relating to: • federal bonus depreciation on property, except qualified resurgence zone and New York Liberty Zone property, placed in service on or after June 1, 2003 in tax periods beginning after 2002; • depreciation of safe harbor lease property; • accelerated depreciation on property placed in service either in or outside the state after 1980 in tax periods beginning before 1985; and • accelerated depreciation on property placed in service outside the state in tax periods beginning after 1984 and before 1994, if an election was made to continue using depreciation under IRC §167. Subtraction allowed for depreciation computed without regard to disallowed federal provisions.	Adjustment computed on Form CT-399.
North Carolina	Addition required for 85% of federal bonus depreciation. Subtraction allowed for 20% of addback over next five tax years.	Addition also required for depreciation on a utility plant acquired by a natural gas local distribution company.
North Dakota	Addition required for federal deduction relating to: • accelerated depreciation on property placed in service in 1981 and 1982; and • depreciation of safe harbor lease property. No other adjustments to federal deduction, including bonus depreciation, required.	
Ohio	No adjustment required because CAT is not considered an income tax and is not tied to federal income tax base.	

Jurisdiction	Regular and Bonus Depreciation—IRC §167 and IRC §168	Comment
Oklahoma	Addition required for federal deduction relating to: • 80% of amount of bonus depreciation for assets placed in service after December 31, 2007, and before January 1, 2010; • 80% of amount of bonus depreciation for assets placed in service after September 10, 2001, and before September 11, 2004; and • depreciation of refinery property located in the state if an election was made to expense 100% of cost. Subtraction allowed for 25% of bonus depreciation addition adjustment over following four tax years. No adjustments to federal deduction, including bonus depreciation, required for tax years after 2010.	Certification report for refinery expense election must be enclosed with state return.
Oregon	Addition required for federal deduction relating to: • federal bonus depreciation after 2008 and before 2011; • accelerated depreciation in tax years prior to 2009 on property placed into service on or after January 1, 1981 and before January 1, 1985; and • depreciation of safe harbor lease property in tax years prior to 2009. Subtraction allowed if state deduction exceeds federal deduction due to state differences in depreciable basis of property, including differences relating to the disallowance of federal bonus depreciation and enhanced IRC § 179 expense deduction limits for 2009 and 2010 tax years.	Adjustment is computed on Depreciation Schedule for Individuals, Partnerships, Corporations, and Fiduciaries.
Pennsylvania	Addition required for: • 50% federal bonus depreciation; and • 100% bonus depreciation for property placed in service after September 27, 2017. Subtraction allowed for property placed in service after September 27, 2017 equal to federal depreciation determined under: • IRC Sec. 167; and • IRC Sec. 168, except IRC Sec. 168(k) does not apply. Subtraction allowed in current and subsequent tax years for property placed in service before September 28, 2017 equal to 3/7 of 50% bonus depreciation addition adjustment.	Adjustments computed on Schedule C-3 of corporate tax report. No addition required for 100% bonus depreciation for property acquired after September 8, 2010 and placed in service before 2012.
Rhode Island	Addition required for federal bonus depreciation.	

Jurisdiction	Regular and Bonus Depreciation—IRC §167 and IRC §168	Comment
South Carolina	Addition required if federal deduction exceeds allowable state deduction due to decoupling from federal bonus depreciation provisions. Subtraction allowed if state deduction exceeds federal deduction.	Schedule showing computation of differences must be attached to state return.
South Dakota	N/A, because state does not tax general business corporation income.	
Tennessee	Addition required for federal deduction relating to: • federal bonus depreciation; and • depreciation of safe harbor lease property.	
Texas	Federal bonus depreciation is not includable in franchise tax depreciation. If federal bonus depreciation is claimed, franchise tax depreciation must be recomputed using an appropriate federal depreciation method in effect for the federal tax year beginning January 1, 2007.	
Utah	Addition required for depreciation by purchaser-lessors of safe harbor lease property. Subtraction allowed for depreciation by seller-lessees of safe harbor lease property. No other adjustments to federal deduction, including federal bonus depreciation, required.	
Vermont	Addition required for federal bonus depreciation.	
Virginia	Addition to federal tax base required if federal deduction recomputed without regard to bonus depreciation exceeds allowable state deduction. Subtraction allowed if state deduction exceeds federal deduction.	State generally decouples with provisions of the Tax Cuts and Jobs Act after 2017.
Washington	N/A, because state does not tax general business corporation income.	
West Virginia	Addition required for federal depreciation of certain water and air pollution control facilities if election was made to expense costs. No other adjustments to federal deduction, including bonus depreciation, required.	

Jurisdiction	Regular and Bonus Depreciation—IRC §167 and IRC §168	Comment
Wisconsin	Addition required if federal deduction exceeds allowable state deduction due to state differences, including: • federal bonus depreciation; • depreciation of safe harbor lease property for taxable years beginning before 2014; and • depreciation for taxable years beginning before 2014 of certain assets placed in service before 1987. Adjustment allowed for tax years equal to 20% of the difference between the combined federal basis of all depreciated or amortized assets (as of last day of taxable year beginning in 2013) and the combined state adjusted basis of those assets, beginning in the first taxable year after 2013 and each of next four taxable years.	Subtraction allowed for tax years beginning before 2014 equal to excess of state deduction over federal deduction using federal depreciation provisions in effect on December 31, 2000.
Wyoming	N/A, because state does not tax general business corporation income.	

Determining Business and Nonbusiness Income

Under the Uniform Division of Income for Tax Purposes Act (UDITPA), "business income" is apportioned among the states in which the taxpayer has nexus, whereas the entire amount of an item of "nonbusiness income" is specifically allocated to a single state. UDITPA defines nonbusiness income as "all income other than business income." An item of income is classified by UDITPA as business income if it either arises from a transaction in the regular course of the taxpayer's business (transactional test), or from property that is an integral part of the taxpayer's business (functional test). This chart shows the rules for determining business and nonbusiness income in each state and the District of Columbia for purposes of computing corporation income tax liability. If an answer indicates a state "follows UDITPA approach" it means the state has adopted provisions that are substantially similar to UDITPA, but it does not mean the state has adopted UDITPA.

Jurisdiction	Transactional, Functional, and Other Tests	Comment
Alabama	Same as UDITPA, except that "business income" includes income from property "acquisition, management, or disposition" of property and gain/loss from the disposition of either property operationally related to taxpayer's trade or business or stock in another corporation that was operationally related to the taxpayer's trade or business.	
Alaska	Follows UDITPA approach.	
Arizona	Follows UDITPA approach.	
Arkansas	Follows UDITPA approach.	
California	Follows UDITPA approach.	
Colorado	Nonbusiness income can be either directly allocated to the appropriate state or apportioned to Colorado using single sales factor apportionment formula.	
Connecticut	Corporation's entire net income subject to apportionment.	State does not distinguish between business and nonbusiness income.
Delaware	Rents, royalties, interest, and gains and losses from the sale of capital assets and real property are allocated; other income apportionable.	
District of Columbia	Follows UDITPA approach, except that some interest and dividends from District sources are specifically excluded.	
Florida	Follows UDITPA approach.	

Jurisdiction	Transactional, Functional, and Other Tests	Comment
Georgia	Investment income (income from interest, intangibles, and real property rental) and sales of noninventory items are allocable income; all other income is apportionable business income.	
Hawaii	Follows UDITPA approach.	
Idaho	Follows UDITPA approach except that the definition of "business income" includes income from property "acquisition, management, or disposition" and adds the words "or necessary" after the word "integral" in the functional test for business income and establishes a rebuttable presumption in favor of apportionment for gains, losses, interest, and dividends from securities.	
Illinois	All income that may be constitutionally treated as apportionable business income is business income.	
Indiana	Follows UDITPA approach, but eliminates presumptions that income is business income.	
Iowa	Same as UDITPA, but adds "operationally related" and "unitary business" tests.	
Kansas	Same as UDITPA, except that taxpayers may elect that all income constitutes business income.	
Kentucky	"Apportionable income" includes income from: • transactions and activity in regular course of taxpayer's trade or business; and • tangible and intangible property if its acquisition, management, employment, development, or disposition is or was related to operation of taxpayer's trade or business. **Tax years before 2018:** "Business income" includes income from: • transactions and activity in regular course of taxpayer's trade or business; and • tangible and intangible property if its acquisition, management, or disposition constitutes integral parts of the taxpayers's regular trade or business operations.	

Jurisdiction	Transactional, Functional, and Other Tests	Comment
Louisiana	Rents and royalties from immovable or corporeal movable property; royalties or similar revenue from the use of patents, trademarks, copyrights, secret processes, and other similar intangible rights; income from estates, trusts, and partnerships; and income from construction, repair, or other similar services are allocated; all other income apportioned.	
Maine	Entire net income subject to apportionment.	
Maryland	A corporation's income "that is derived from or reasonably attributable to the part of its trade or business carried on in the state" is subject to the three-factor or the one-factor apportionment formula.	
Massachusetts	Income derived from unrelated activities is not subject to apportionment; income of Massachusetts-domiciled corporation that nondomiciliary states constitutionally barred from taxing is allocated to Massachusetts; all other income apportioned.	
Michigan	Entire tax base subject to apportionment.	
Minnesota	Income that cannot constitutionally be apportioned, including capital transactions serving solely as investments, must be allocated; all other income apportioned.	
Mississippi	Same as UDITPA, except that "business income" includes income from tangible and intangible property if the "acquisition, management, and/or disposition" of the property constitute integral parts of the taxpayer's regular trade or business.	
Missouri	Follows UDITPA approach.	
Montana	Follows UDITPA approach.	
Nebraska	Entire federal taxable income is presumed to be subject to apportionment; presumption may be rebutted.	
Nevada	N/A, because state does not tax general business corporation income.	
New Hampshire	Gross business profits (federal taxable income before deductions) are apportionable.	

Jurisdiction	Transactional, Functional, and Other Tests	Comment
New Jersey	All operational income is subject to "allocation" (NJ uses this term instead of "apportionment"); nonoperational income assigned to particular state.	
New Mexico	Generally follows UDITPA approach except that "business income" includes the "acquisition, management or disposition" of property and adds business or segment liquidation to definition of "business income".	
New York	Business income (net income minus investment income) is apportioned.	For tax years after 2014, business income (entire net income minus investment income and other exempt income) is apportioned.
North Carolina	All income apportionable under U.S. Constitution, including income that arises from: • transactions and activities in the regular course of the taxpayer's trade or business; and • tangible and intangible property if the acquisition, management, employment, development, or disposition of the property is or was related to the operation of the taxpayer's trade or business.	
North Dakota	Follows UDITPA approach.	
Ohio	Nonbusiness assets are not subject to the commercial activity tax.	
Oklahoma	Similar to UDITPA, by specifying allocable items.	
Oregon	Generally follows UDITPA approach except that "business income" includes "income from tangible and intangible property (a) if the acquisition, management, use, or rental and (b) the disposition of the property constitute integral parts of the taxpayer's regular trade or business".	
Pennsylvania	Follows UDITPA approach, but includes all income that is apportionable under the U.S. Constitution.	
Rhode Island	All net income subject to apportionment.	
South Carolina	N/A, because state has not adopted business and nonbusiness income classification.	Income that is not directly allocated is apportionable.
South Dakota	N/A, because state does not tax general business corporation income.	

Jurisdiction	Transactional, Functional, and Other Tests	Comment
Tennessee	Generally follows UDITPA approach except that "business income" includes the "acquisition, management or disposition" of property and adds business or segment liquidation to definition of "business earnings".	
Texas	For all reports due on or after January 1, 2008, apportioned by multiplying the margin by a fraction, the numerator of which is the gross receipts from business done in the state, and the denominator of which is the gross receipts from its entire business. All gross receipts from enumerated activities are subject to apportionment for purposes of the earned surplus component of the franchise tax applicable to all reports due before January 1, 2008.	
Utah	Follows UDITPA approach, with presumption that certain items are business income.	
Vermont	Follows UDITPA approach.	
Virginia	Dividends allocable; all other income apportionable.	
Washington	N/A, because state does not tax general business corporation income.	
West Virginia	Follows UDITPA approach.	
Wisconsin	Rents/royalties from nonbusiness property and income (gain/loss) from sale of nonbusiness property are allocated; all other income apportioned.	
Wyoming	N/A, because state does not tax general business corporation income.	

Dividends Received Deduction

Under IRC §243, corporations can deduct 70% of dividends received from domestic corporations. The deduction equals 80% for dividends received from 20%-or-more owned corporations.

IRC §245 allows a 70% deduction for the U.S.-source portion of dividends received from 10%-or-more-owned foreign corporations. The deduction equals 80% for the U.S.-source portion of dividends received from 20%-or-more-owned foreign corporations.

The dividends received deduction amounts for tax years beginning after 2017 decrease from:

- 70% to 50%; and
- 80% to 65% for 20%-or-more owned corporations.

Corporations include the federal deduction on line 29b of the federal return. Many states do not allow the federal deduction by requiring:

- a federal line 28 starting point for computing taxable income; or
- an addback for the deduction.

In general, these states allow a deduction for a percentage of dividends received. Other states allow a deduction based on:

- a percentage of the amount that exceeds the federal deduction limits; or
- a percentage equal to the federal amount.

This chart shows the dividends received deduction allowed by each state and the District of Columbia.

Jurisdiction	Dividends Received Deduction	Comment
Alabama	Addition required for dividends received from less-than-20%-owned corporations, to extent deducted in computing federal taxable income.	Subtraction allowed for dividends received from 20%-or-more-owned foreign corporations to extent deductible under federal law if received from a U.S. corporation.
Alaska	Federal deduction not allowed due to income tax starting point.	Subtraction for dividends received is based on allocated and apportioned dividends and is equal to same percentages as federal deduction, except water's edge filer's are limited to 80% of dividends received from 80/20 companies.
Arizona	Addition required for amount of federal deduction.	Subtraction allowed for 100% of dividends received from foreign corporations and 50% or more controlled domestic corporations.
Arkansas	Federal deduction not allowed due to income tax starting point.	Exemption from income allowed for 100% of dividends received from 80% controlled foreign subsidiaries.

Jurisdiction	Dividends Received Deduction	Comment
California	Federal deduction not allowed due to income tax starting point.	Subtraction allowed on Schedule H equal to: • 100% of dividends received from unitary subsidiaries if paid from unitary earnings and profits accumulated while both payee and payer were members of a combined report; • 75% of dividends received by water's edge group (100% for dividends derived from a construction project, the location of which is not under the taxpayer's control) from any more-than-50%-owned corporation with less than 20% U.S. factors; and • 85% of dividends received from 80%-or-more-owned insurance company subsidiaries. Subtraction computed on Schedule H.
Colorado	Same as federal due to income tax starting point.	No addition or subtraction adjustment required or allowed.
Connecticut	Federal deduction not allowed due to income tax starting point.	Subtraction allowed equal to: • 100% of dividends received from 20% or more owned corporations; and • 70% of dividends received from less than 20% owned domestic corporations. Taxpayer must reduce deduction by any related expenses claimed as a federal deduction or credit. Effective for tax years beginning after 2017, nondeductible expenses equal 5% of all dividends received during the tax year. Subtraction computed on Form CT-1120 ATT.
Delaware	Same as federal due to income tax starting point.	Subtraction allowed for 100% of foreign dividends included in federal taxable income if foreign tax was paid or accrued on those dividends.
District of Columbia	Federal deduction not allowed due to income tax starting point.	Exemption from gross income tax base allowed for 100% of dividends received from wholly-owned subsidiaries and dividends received from foreign sources not attributable to trade or business income.
Florida	Same as federal due to income tax starting point.	Subtraction allowed for 100% of foreign source dividends included in federal taxable income. Taxpayer must reduce amount subtracted by any related expenses claimed as a deduction.
Georgia	Same as federal due to income tax starting point.	Subtraction allowed equal to: • 100% of foreign source dividends included in federal taxable; and • 100% of dividends, less related expenses, received from affiliated domestic corporations by corporations engaged in business within the state and subject to state income tax, to the extent such dividends have been included in net income.

Jurisdiction	Dividends Received Deduction	Comment
Hawaii	Federal deduction not allowed due to income tax starting point.	Subtraction allowed equal to: • 100% of dividends received from a national banking association; • 100% of dividends received from a member of an affiliated group, including foreign affiliates; • 100% of dividends received by a small business investment company operating under the federal Small Business Investment Act; • 100% of dividends received from qualified high technology businesses on shares of stock obtained through options or warrants; and • 70% of dividends received from all other corporations, subject to statutory limitations.
Idaho	Addition required for amount of federal deduction.	Subtraction allowed equal to 85% of dividends received by water's-edge filers from foreign corporations, reduced to 80% if water's-edge spreadsheet not filed. Subtraction computed on Form 42.
Illinois	Same as federal due to income tax starting point.	Subtraction allowed for foreign dividends included in federal taxable income, equal to: • 100% of dividends received from wholly owned subsidiaries; • 65% (80% for tax years before 2018) of dividends received from 20%-or-more-owned corporations; and • 50% (70% for tax years before 2018) of dividends received from less-than-20%-owned corporations. Subtraction computed on Schedule J.
Indiana	Same as federal due to income tax starting point.	Subtraction allowed for foreign dividends included in federal taxable income, equal to: • 100% of dividends received from 80%-or-more-owned corporations; • 85% of dividends received from less-than-80% but more-than-50%-owned corporations; and • 50% of dividends received from less-than-50%-owned corporations.
Iowa	Same as federal due to income tax starting point.	Subtraction allowed for foreign dividends included in federal taxable income, equal to: • 100% of dividends received from 80%-or-more-owned corporations; • 80% of dividends received from less-than-80% but more-than-20%-owned corporations; and • 70% of dividends received from less-than-20%-owned corporations.
Kansas	Same as federal due to income tax starting point.	Subtraction allowed for 80% of foreign dividends included in federal taxable income. Subtraction allowed for dividend income on stock issued by Kansas Venture Capital, Inc.

Jurisdiction	Dividends Received Deduction	Comment
Kentucky	Federal deduction not allowed due to income tax starting point.	Subtraction allowed for 100% of dividends received from domestic and foreign corporations.
Louisiana	Addition required for amount of federal deduction.	Subtraction allowed for 100% of dividends that would otherwise be included in gross income (72% from July 1, 2015, to June 30, 2018). Temporary reduction applied to tax years beginning in 2015, 2016, and 2017, regardless of when original or amended return is filed.
Maine	Same as federal due to income tax starting point.	Subtraction allowed for 50% of dividends included in federal taxable income, net of related expenses and other related deductions, from affiliated corporations that are more than 50% owned and not included in combined report.
Maryland	Same as federal due to income tax starting point.	Subtraction for 100% of dividends received from 50%-or-more-owned foreign corporations.
Massachusetts	Federal deduction not allowed due to income tax starting point.	Subtraction allowed for 95% of dividends received from 15%-or-more-owned domestic and foreign corporations.
Michigan	Same as federal due to income tax starting point.	**Corporate Income Tax (CIT) and Michigan Business Tax (MBT)** To the extent included in federal taxable income, subtraction allowed for 100% of dividends received from persons other than U.S. persons and foreign operating entities.
Minnesota	Federal deduction not allowed due to income tax starting point.	Subtraction allowed equal to: • 80% of dividends received from 20%-or-more-owned corporations; and • 70% of dividends received from less-than-20%-owned corporations. Subtraction computed on Form DIV.
Mississippi	Federal deduction not allowed due to income tax starting point.	Subtraction allowed equal to: • 100% of dividend income already subject to state's income tax that can be specifically identified to recipient; and • 100% of dividends received by holding companies from subsidiaries, except to extent that subsidiary corporation is a real estate investment trust (REIT). See, *Mississippi Department of Revenue v. AT&T* (holding that provision limiting the dividends received deduction to dividends paid by an entity that does business and files a return in the state discriminated against interstate commerce and was unconstitutional)

Jurisdiction	Dividends Received Deduction	Comment
Missouri	Same as federal due to income tax starting point.	Subtraction allowed to the extent included in federal taxable income for dividends received from state sources determined using single or three-factor apportionment formula. Subtraction computed on Schedule MO-C if using single sales-factor apportionment formula.
Montana	Federal deduction not allowed due to income tax starting point.	Subtraction allowed for dividends received from domestic corporations equal to same percentages as federal deduction. For water's edge filers, dividends received from 80/20 companies are allowed at 100%.
Nebraska	Same as federal due to income tax starting point.	Subtraction allowed equal to 100% of foreign dividends included in federal taxable income.
Nevada	N/A, because state does not tax general business corporation income.	
New Hampshire	Federal deduction not allowed due to income tax starting point.	
New Jersey	Federal deduction not allowed due to income tax starting point.	Subtraction allowed equal to: • 95% of dividends received from 80%-or-more-owned subsidiaries included in federal taxable income (100% prior to 2017); and • 50% of dividends received from less-than-80% but more-than-50%-owned subsidiaries included in federal taxable income.
New Mexico	Same as federal due to income tax starting point.	Additional subtraction allowed to separate filers for foreign dividends included in federal taxable income, equal to: • 100% of dividends received from corporations that are more than 80% owned; • 80% of dividends received from 80% to 20%-owned corporations; and • 70% of dividends received from less-than-20%-owned corporations. Subtraction computed on Form CIT-D. Combined and consolidated filers may adjust their apportionment percentages by inclusion of the factors of foreign-source dividend payers.
New York	Federal deduction not allowed due to income tax starting point.	**Tax years before 2015:** Subtraction allowed equal to: • 100% of dividends received from more-than-50% owned subsidiaries; and • 50% of dividends that conform to IRC Sec. 246(c) holding requirements and that are received from 50%-or-less owned corporations. **Tax years after 2014:** Subtractions allowed for investment income and other exempt income, including exempt unitary corporation dividends.

Jurisdiction	Dividends Received Deduction	Comment
North Carolina	Same as federal due to income tax starting point.	Subtraction allowed equal to 100% of foreign dividends included in federal taxable income. Taxpayer must reduce deduction by any related expenses. Nondeductible expenses include up to 15% of the dividends.
North Dakota	Addition required for amount of federal deduction.	Water's edge filers exclude 70% of dividends from foreign affiliates.
Ohio	Exclusion allowed for dividends.	
Oklahoma	Same as federal due to income tax starting point.	No addition or subtraction adjustment required or allowed.
Oregon	Federal deduction not allowed due to income tax starting point.	Subtraction allowed equal to: • 100% of dividends received from members of same unitary group filing state consolidated tax return; • 80% of dividends received from 20%-or-more-owned corporations; and • 70% of dividends received from less-than-20%-owned corporations. Schedule and explanation for subtraction must be attached to state return.
Pennsylvania	Federal deduction not allowed due to income tax starting point.	Subtraction allowed on Schedule C-2 for amount of federal deduction and foreign dividends included in federal taxable income, equal to: • 100% of dividends received from 80%-or-more-owned corporations; • 80% of dividends received from less-than-80% but 20%-or-more-owned corporations; and • 70% of dividends received from less-than-20%-owned corporations.
Rhode Island	Federal deduction not allowed due to income tax starting point.	Subtraction allowed for amount of federal deduction and foreign dividends included in federal taxable income, equal to: • 100% of dividends received from 100%-owned corporations; • 80% of dividends received from more-than-20%-owned; and • 70% of dividends received from less-than-20%-owned foreign corporations.
South Carolina	Same as federal due to income tax starting point.	Subtraction allowed for a percentage of foreign dividends included in federal taxable income.
South Dakota	N/A, because state does not tax general business corporation income.	
Tennessee	Federal deduction not allowed due to income tax starting point.	Subtraction allowed equal to 100% of dividends received from 80%-or-more-owned foreign corporations.

Jurisdiction	Dividends Received Deduction	Comment
Texas	**Revised Franchise (Margin) Tax** Exclusion from total revenue allowed equal to: • dividends received from domestic corporation to same extent as federal deduction and to the extent relating dividend income is included in total revenue; and • 100% of dividends received from foreign corporations.	
Utah	Federal deduction not allowed due to income tax starting point.	Subtraction allowed equal to: • 100% of dividends from more-than-50%-owned domestic corporations and certain insurance companies; • 50% of dividends received from foreign subsidiaries that are unitary group members, unless included in combined report.
Vermont	Same as federal due to income tax starting point.	No addition or subtraction adjustment required or allowed.
Virginia	Same as federal due to income tax starting point.	Subtraction allowed for dividends included in federal taxable income equal to 100% of dividends from 50%-or-more-owned corporations.
Washington	N/A, because state does not tax general business corporation income.	
West Virginia	Same as federal due to income tax starting point.	No addition or subtraction adjustment required or allowed.
Wisconsin	Federal deduction not allowed due to income tax starting point.	Subtraction allowed equal to 100% of dividends received from 70%-or-more-owned corporations, less foreign taxes paid and claimed as a state tax deduction.
Wyoming	N/A, because state does not tax general business corporation income.	

Due Date for Annual Return

Generally, C corporations must file a federal income tax return, Form 1120 by April 15th following the close of the calendar year or the 15th day of the 4th month following the close of the corporation's fiscal year. However, for a C corporation with a fiscal year ending on June 30, the filing deadline will remain at September 15th until tax years beginning after December 31, 2025, when the due date will be moved to October 15th. For tax years beginning before 2016, C corporations had to file by March 15th following the close of the calendar year or the 15th day of the third month following the close of the fiscal year.

If the due date falls on a Saturday, Sunday, or legal holiday, the return may be filed on the next business day. This chart shows the state corporate income information return due dates in each state and the District of Columbia for the current tax year.

Electronic filing mandates and options are not covered in this chart. However, they are covered in a chart under the topic E-Filing: Mandates/Options for C and S Corporations.

Jurisdiction	C Corporations	Comment
Alabama	Form 20C must be filed by April 15 (or 15th day of 4th month after end of taxable year).	**Taxable years before 2016:** Form 20C had to be filed by the 15th day of the 3rd month after end of taxable year. **Coronavirus (COVID-19) Pandemic Filing/Payment Relief** July 15, 2020 filing and payment due date.
Alaska	Form 6000 must be filed by May 15 (15th day of fifth month after end of taxable year).	Form 6240 (payment voucher) is due, accompanied with full payment of outstanding tax liability, by April 15 (15th day of 4th month after end of taxable year). **Coronavirus (COVID-19) Pandemic Filing/Payment Relief** July 15, 2020 for returns and payments due on April 15, 2020 and before July 15, 2020. Waiver of penalties and interest if tax is paid by July 15. **Return due date for taxable years before 2016:** April 15 or 15th day of 4th month after end of taxable year (30 days after federal return due date). **Payment due date for taxable years before 2016:** March 15 or 15th day of 3rd month after end of taxable year.
Arizona	Form 120 must be filed by April 15 following close of calendar year or 15th day of 4th month after fiscal year.	**Coronavirus (COVID-19) Pandemic Filing/Payment Relief** July 15, 2020 filing and payment due date.

Jurisdiction	C Corporations	Comment
Arkansas	Form AR1100CT must be filed by April 15th following close of calendar year or 3.5 months after fiscal year.	**Taxable years before 2016:** Form AR1100CT must be filed by March 15th following close of calendar year or 2.5 months after fiscal year.
California	Form 100 must be filed by April 15 or the 15th day of 4th month after end of fiscal tax year.	**Taxable years before 2016:** Form 100 had to be filed by March 15 or the 15th day of 3rd month after end of fiscal tax year. **Coronavirus (COVID-19) Pandemic Filing/Payment Relief** July 15, 2020 return due date. July 15, 2020 payment due date.
Colorado	Form 112 must be filed by the 15th day of 4th month after tax year.	**Coronavirus (COVID-19) Pandemic Filing/Payment Relief:** October 15, 2020, return due date. July 15, 2020 payment due date.
Connecticut	Form CT-1120 must be filed by: • May 15 for calendar year taxpayers; • 15th day of 5th month after end of tax year for fiscal year taxpayers whose tax year ends on a date other than June 30; or • 15th day of 4th month after end of tax year for fiscal year taxpayers whose tax year ends on June 30. 15th day of the month following due date of federal return.	**Coronavirus (COVID-19) Pandemic Filing/Payment Relief** July 15, 2020 for returns and payments due between March 15 and July 15, 2020. **2016 Tax Year:** • May 1 for calendar year taxpayers; • 1st day of 5th month after end of tax year for fiscal year taxpayers whose tax year ends on a date other than June 30; or • 1st day of 4th month after end of tax year for fiscal year taxpayers whose tax year ends on June 30. 1st day of month following due date of federal return. **Taxable years before 2016:** April 1 or 1st day of 4th after end of fiscal tax year.
Delaware	Form 1100 must be filed by April 15 (15th day of 4th month after end of taxable year).	**Coronavirus (COVID-19) Pandemic Filing/Payment Relief** July 15, 2020 return and payment due date. **Tax years before 2016:** April 1 (1st day of 4th month after end of taxable year).
District of Columbia	Form D-20 must be filed by April 15, for calendar-year filers, or by the 15th day of the 4rd month following the close of the tax year for fiscal year filers.	**Coronavirus (COVID-19) Pandemic Filing/Payment Relief** July 15, 2020 due date.

Jurisdiction	C Corporations	Comment
Florida	Form F-1120 must be filed by the 1st day of the 5th month following the close of the taxable year or the 15th day after the federal due date. Effective for tax years beginning after December 31, 2015 and before January 1, 2026, all June 30 year-end returns must be filed by the 1st day of the 4th month following the close of the taxable year or the 15th day after the federal due date.	**Coronavirus (COVID-19) Pandemic Filing/Payment Relief** August 3, 2020 for returns originally due May 1, June 1, and July 1 2020 from corporations with fiscal years ending December 31, 2019, January 31, 2020, and February 29, 2020. June 1, 2020 for payments due May 1, 2020. No extension for payments originally due June 1 and July 1, 2020. **Tax years beginning on and after January 1, 2026:** Form F-1120 must be filed by the 1st day of the 5th month following the close of the taxable year or the 15th day after the federal due date. **Tax years before 2016:** Form F-1120 had to be filed by April 1 following close of calendar year or 1st day of 4th month after fiscal year.
Georgia	Form 600 must be filed by April 15th (15th day of the 4th month following the close of the fiscal year).	**Coronavirus (COVID-19) Pandemic Filing/Payment Relief** July 15, 2020. **Taxable years before 2016:** Form 600 had to be filed by March 15, or the 15th day of the 3rd month after the close of a fiscal year.
Hawaii	Form N-30 must be filed by the 20th day of 4th month after tax year.	**Coronavirus (COVID-19) Pandemic Filing/Payment Relief** July 20, 2020 filing and payment due date.
Idaho	Form 41 must be filed by April 15 or the 15th day of 4th month after end of fiscal tax year.	**Coronavirus (COVID-19) Pandemic Filing/Payment Relief** June 15, 2020.
Illinois	Form IL-1120 must be filed by: • April 15 for calendar year taxpayers; • 15th day of 4th month after end of taxable year for fiscal year taxpayers whose tax year ends on a date other than June 30; or • 15th day of 3rd month after end of taxable year for fiscal year taxpayers whose tax year ends on June 30.	**Coronavirus (COVID-19) Pandemic Filing/Payment Relief** July 15, 2020 return and payment due date. **Taxable years before 2016:** March 15 (15th day of 3rd month after end of taxable year).
Indiana	Form IT-20 must be filed by the 15th day of 4th month after tax year or if the federal due date is after the 15th day of the 4th month after the tax year the 15th day of the month following the federal due date.	**Coronavirus (COVID-19) Pandemic Filing/Payment Relief** Returns originally due April 15, 2020 or April 20, due on or before July 15. Returns originally due May 15, 2020, due on August 17, 2020.

Jurisdiction	C Corporations	Comment
Iowa	Form IA 1120 must be filed by the last day of 4th month after tax year.	**Coronavirus (COVID-19) Pandemic Filing/Payment Relief** Returns due on or after March 19, 2020, and before July 31, 2020, extended to July 31, 2020.
Kansas	Form K-120 must be filed by the 15th day of 4th month after tax year.	**Coronavirus (COVID-19) Pandemic Filing/Payment Relief** July 15, 2020 return and payment due date. Extension also applies to fiscal year returns due between April 15, 2020 and July 15, 2020.
Kentucky	Form 720 must be filed by April 15 (15th day of 4th month after end of taxable year).	**Coronavirus (COVID-19) Pandemic Filing/Payment Relief** July 15, 2020 due date for returns and payments due on and after April 15, 2020 and before July 15, 2020. Penalty and interest calculation will begin July 16, 2020.
Louisiana	Form CIFT-620 must be filed by May 15 following close of calendar year or 15th day of 5th month after fiscal year.	**Taxable years before 2016:** Form CIFT-620 had to be filed by April 15 following close of calendar year or 15th day of 4th month after fiscal year. **Coronavirus (COVID-19) Pandemic Filing/Payment Relief:** Return and payment due July 15, 2020. **Hurricane Laura Relief:** Filing and payment deadline extensions are available as a result of damage caused by Hurricane Laura for taxpayers located in parishes that have been declared federal disaster areas. Returns and payments originally due between August 24, 2020, and November 2, 2020, are extended to December 31, 2020, for corporate income, franchise, partnership, and partnership composite taxes. Returns and payments originally due between August 24, 2020, and November 2, 2020, are extended to November 30, 2020, for income withholding.
Maine	Form 1120-ME must be filed by April 15 or the 15th day of 4th month after end of fiscal tax year.	**Taxable years before 2016:** Form 1120-ME had to be filed by March 15, or the 15th day of the 3rd month after the close of a fiscal year. **Coronavirus (COVID-19) Pandemic Filing/Payment Relief:** July 15, 2020, return and payment due date.

Jurisdiction	C Corporations	Comment
Maryland	Form 500 must be filed by April 15th (15th day of the 4th month following the close of the fiscal year).	**Coronavirus (COVID-19) Pandemic Filing/Payment Relief:** July 15, 2020, return and payment due date. **Taxable years before 2016:** Form 600 had to be filed by March 15, or the 15th day of the 3rd month after the close of a fiscal year.
Massachusetts	Form 355 must be filed by April 15 (15th day of 4th month after end of taxable year).	**Coronavirus (COVID-19) Pandemic Filing/Payment Relief** Waiver of penalties if taxpayers file and pay by July 15, 2020. **Tax years before 2017:** Form 355 must be filed by March 15 (15th day of 3rd month after end of taxable year).
Michigan	Form 4891 for corporate income tax or Form 4567 for Michigan Business Tax must be filed by April 30 following close of calendar year or last day of 4th month after end of fiscal year.	Only taxpayers with certificated credits that have made an election may continue paying the Michigan Business Tax. **Coronavirus (COVID-19) Pandemic Filing/Payment Relief** July 15, 2020 income tax filing and payment due date.
Minnesota	Form M4 must be filed by April 15 (or 15th day of 4th month after end of taxable year).	**Taxable years before 2016:** Form M4 had to be filed by the 15th day of the 3rd month after end of taxable year.
Mississippi	Form 83-105 must be filed by April 15th following the close of the calendar year or the 15th day of the 4th month following the close of the fiscal year.	**Taxable years before 2016:** Form 83-105 had to be filed by the 15th day of 3rd month following the close of the fiscal year. **Coronavirus (COVID-19) Pandemic Filing/Payment Relief:** July 15, 2020, return and payment due date.
Missouri	Form MO-1120 must be filed by April 15 (or 15th day of 4th month after end of taxable year).	**Coronavirus (COVID-19) Pandemic Filing/Payment Relief** July 15, 2020 filing and payment due date.
Montana	Form CIT must be filed by May 15 or 15th day of fifth month after end of fiscal tax year.	
Nebraska	Form 1120N must be filed by April 15 (or 15th day of 4th month after end of taxable year).	**Coronavirus (COVID-19) Pandemic Filing/Payment Relief** July 15, 2020 return and payment due date. **Taxable years before 2016:** Form 1120N had to be filed by the 15th day of the 3rd month after end of taxable year.

Jurisdiction	C Corporations	Comment
Nevada	N/A, because state does not tax general business corporation or pass-through income.	
New Hampshire	Form NH-1120 must be filed by April 15th following the end of the tax period.	**Taxable years before 2016:** Form NH-1120 had to be filed by the 15th day of 3rd month following the close of the fiscal year.
New Jersey	Form CBT-100 must be filed by the 15th day of 4th month after tax year.	**Coronavirus (COVID-19) Pandemic Filing/Payment Relief** July 15, 2020 return and payment due date.
New Mexico	Form CIT-1 must be filed by 15th day of the 4th month. Taxpayers using electronic media to file and pay, returns due by the last day of the month federal return originally due.	**Taxable years before 2016:** Form CIT-1 had to be filed by the 15th day of the 3rd month following the end of the corporate tax year. **Coronavirus (COVID-19) Pandemic Filing/Payment Relief:** New Mexico corporate income tax returns due between April 15, 2020, and July 15, 2020, are due July 15, 2020. No interest or penalty will be imposed for failure to pay any corporate income tax that became due April 15, 2020, through July 15, 2020, provided that payment for the unpaid tax is made in full on or before April 15, 2021, and if the failure to pay was not an intentional attempt to evade the tax.
New York	Form CT-3 must be filed by April 15th following the close of the calendar year or the 15th day of the 4th month following the close of the fiscal year.	**COVID-19 Filing/Payment Relief:** July 15, 2020 return and payment due date. **Taxable years before 2016:** Form CT-3 had to be filed by the 15th day of the 3rd month following the close of the taxable year.
North Carolina	Form CD-405 must be filed by April 15 (15th day of 4th month after end of taxable year).	**Coronavirus (COVID-19) Pandemic Filing/Payment Relief** July 15, 2020 return due date and penalty waiver if tax is paid by that date.
North Dakota	Form 40 must be filed by April 15th (15th day of 4th month after end of taxable year).	**COVID-19 Filing/Payment Relief:** July 15, 2020 return and payment due date.
Ohio	Form CAT 12 must be filed by annual filers by May 10. **Quarterly returns:** Electronic filing required by: • May 10; • August 10; • November 10; and • February 10 (10th day of second month after end of each calendar quarter).	

Jurisdiction	C Corporations	Comment
Oklahoma	Form 512 must be filed by 30 days after due date of federal return.	**Coronavirus (COVID-19) Pandemic Filing/Payment Relief** April 15, 2020 return due date. July 15, 2020 payment due date on payments up to $10 million. **Taxable years before 2016:** Form 512 had to be filed by 15th day of 3rd month following close of the taxable year.
Oregon	Form 20/Form 20-I must be filed by May 15 (15th day of the month following due date of related federal return).	**Coronavirus (COVID-19) Pandemic Filing/Payment Relief** July 15, 2020 for return filing and payment deadline for 2019 tax year. Fiscal year return and payments due after May 15, 2020 are not extended. Estimated tax payments for tax year 2020 are not extended.
Pennsylvania	Form RCT-101 must be filed 30 days after due date of federal return.	**Coronavirus (COVID-19) Pandemic Filing/Payment Relief** August 14, 2020 return and payment due date. **Taxable years before 2016:** Form RCT-101 was due April 15th (15th day of 4th month after end of taxable year).
Rhode Island	Form 1120C must be filed by April 15. Effective for tax years beginning after December 31, 2015 and before January 1, 2026, all June 30 year-end returns must be filed by September 15.	Effective for tax years beginning after December 31, 2025, all June 30 year-end returns must be filed by October 15. **Taxable years before 2016:** Form 1120C had to be filed by the 15th day of the 3rd month following the close of the taxable year. **Coronavirus (COVID-19) Pandemic Filing/Payment Relief:** July 15, 2020, return and payment due date.
South Carolina	Form SC1120 must be filed by April 15 (the 15th day of the 4th month after the tax year).	**COVID-19 Filing/Payment Relief:** July 15, 2020 return and payment due date. **Taxable years before 2016:** Form SC1120 had to be filed by March 15 (the 15th day of the 3rd month after the tax year).
South Dakota	N/A, because state does not tax general business corporation or pass-through income.	
Tennessee	Form FAE 170 must be filed by April 15th (15th day of 4th month after end of taxable year).	**COVID-19 Filing/Payment Relief:** July 15, 2020 return and payment due date.

Jurisdiction	C Corporations	Comment
Texas	Forms 05-158a (Franchise Tax Report Page 1), 05-158b (Franchise Tax Report Page 2), 05-102 (Public Information Report) must be filed by May 15.	**Coronavirus (COVID-19) Pandemic Filing/Payment Relief** July 15, 2020 report and payment due date.
Utah	Form TC-20 must be filed by later of: • 15th day of 4th month after tax year; or • due date of the corresponding federal return.	**Coronavirus (COVID-19) Pandemic Filing/Payment Relief** July 15, 2020 filing and payment due date.
Vermont	Form CO-411 must be filed by April 15 (or 15th day of 4th month after end of taxable year).	**COVID-19 Filing/Payment Relief:** July 15, 2020 return and payment due date. **Taxable years before 2016:** Form CO-411 had to be filed by the 15th day of the 3rd month following the close of the calendar year or the 15th day of the 3rd month following the close of the fiscal year.
Virginia	Form 500 must be filed by the 15th day of 4th month after tax year.	**COVID-19 Filing/Payment Relief:** April 15, 2020 return due date. June 1, 2020 payment due date.
Washington	N/A, because state does not tax general business corporation or pass-through income.	
West Virginia	Form WV/CNF-120 must be filed by April 15th following the close of the calendar year or the 15th day of the 4th month following the close of the fiscal year.	**Coronavirus (COVID-19) Pandemic Filing/Payment Relief** July 15, 2020 return and payment due date. **Taxable years before 2016:** Form WV/CNF-120 must be filed by the 15th day of the 3rd month after the close of the taxable year for fiscal-year filers.
Wisconsin	Form 4 must be filed by April 15th (or 15th day of 4th month following close of fiscal year).	**COVID-19 Filing/Payment Relief:** July 15, 2020 return and payment due date. **Taxable years before 2016:** Form 4 had to be filed by the 15th day of the 3rd month following the close of the taxable year.
Wyoming	N/A, because state does not tax general business corporation or pass-through income.	

E-Filing: Application and Acknowledgement Process—Acknowledgement Process

The IRS electronically acknowledges the receipt of all transmissions of electronically filed returns within 48 hours. Each return in a transmission is either accepted or rejected for specific reasons. Returns which meet the processing criteria are considered filed as soon as the return is accepted. Accepted returns meet the processing criteria as soon as the return is signed electronically or through the receipt by the IRS of a paper signature. Rejected returns that fail to meet processing criteria are considered not filed. The acknowledgement identifies the source of the reject and provides text to explain why the transmission or return rejected. Electronic Return Originators (EROs) of federal individual income tax returns must, at the request of taxpayer, provide the Declaration Control Number (DCN) and the date the IRS accepted the electronic return data. The ERO must also, if requested, supply the electronic postmark if the transmitter provided one for the return. This chart shows whether each state and the District of Columbia acknowledge the receipt of electronically filed returns and the acknowledgement process.

Jurisdiction	Acknowledgement Process	Comment
Alabama	Within 5 business days of IRS acknowledgement for business returns. Within 3 business days of IRS acknowledgement for individual returns.	
Alaska	Same as federal.	
Arizona	Within 48 hours of IRS acknowledgement.	
Arkansas	Within 3 days of IRS acknowledgement.	
California	Within 2 days.	
Colorado	Within 1 to 2 business days.	
Connecticut	Within 1 day of IRS acknowledgement. Immediate by confirmation number after business return is filed online.	
Delaware	Within 48 hours.	
District of Columbia	Within 72 hours of IRS acknowledgement.	
Florida	Within 1-2 days of IRS acknowledgement.	
Georgia	Same as federal for corporations and partnerships. Within 2-5 business days for individual income taxpayers.	

Jurisdiction	Acknowledgement Process	Comment
Hawaii	Within 1-2 business days of IRS acknowledgement.	
Idaho	Within 1 business day.	
Illinois	Same as federal for corporation returns. Immediate acknowledgement by confirmation number for individual income tax returns.	
Indiana	Within 1 day.	
Iowa	Within 1 business day for IRS acknowledgement.	
Kansas	Within 1-2 business days.	
Kentucky	Within 3 days of IRS acknowledgement.	
Louisiana	Within 3 business days.	
Maine	Within 24 to 48 hours of transmission.	
Maryland	Within 48 hours.	
Massachusetts	Within 1 business day.	
Michigan	Within 3 business days of successful transmission to IRS.	
Minnesota	Within 1 calendar day.	
Mississippi	Within 24 hours of IRS acknowledgement.	
Missouri	Within 1 to 3 business days for individual income tax returns and within 1 business day for business income tax returns.	
Montana	Same as federal for business income tax returns. Within 4 working days of IRS acknowledgement for individual income tax returns.	
Nebraska	Within 1 to 3 business days.	
New Hampshire	Immediate acknowledgement by confirmation number after interest and dividends tax return is filed online.	
New Jersey	Immediate acknowledgement by confirmation number for partnership returns. Transmitters required to retrieve and forward acknowledgements to practitioners within 24 hours. Same as federal for individual income tax returns.	
New Mexico	Within 2 business days.	
New York	Within 3 business days.	

Jurisdiction	Acknowledgement Process	Comment
North Carolina	Within 24 hours of IRS acknowledgement.	
North Dakota	2 days.	
Ohio	Within 1 business day of IRS acknowledgement.	
Oklahoma	Within 1-2 business days of IRS acknowledgement.	
Oregon	Within 1 business day for corporate income tax returns. Within 24 hours for personal income tax returns.	
Pennsylvania	Within 3 days of IRS acknowledgement.	
Rhode Island	Within 2 business days of IRS acknowledgement.	
South Carolina	Within 2-3 days or less of IRS acknowledgement.	
Tennessee	Within 2 business days of IRS acknowledgement. Immediate acknowledgement by confirmation number after return is filed online.	
Texas	Immediate acknowledgement by confirmation number after franchise tax report is filed online.	
Utah	Within same day return is received.	
Vermont	Within 2 days of IRS acknowledgement.	
Virginia	Within 2 business days of IRS acknowledgement.	
West Virginia	Within 1-2 business days.	
Wisconsin	Within 48 to 72 hours.	

E-Filing: Application and Acknowledgement Process—Application Process

A business or organization, which may include a sole proprietorship, partnerships, corporation, or other entity, must be authorized by the IRS to participate in the IRS e-file program. Authorized IRS e-file Providers include Electronic Return Originator (EROs), Intermediate Service Providers, Online Providers, Transmitters, Software Developers, and Reporting Agents. Corporations and partnerships that are subject to electronic filing requirements and that do not use an Authorized IRS e-file Provider to prepare and transmit returns also must be authorized to file directly with the IRS. An application to participate in the IRS e-file program must be completed and submitted online at the IRS website. Alternatively, a paper application using Form 8633 must be completed and submitted by mail. Applicants must provide basic information about the business and its Principals and at least one Responsible Official. The applicant and all Principals and Responsible Officials listed on e-file applications must pass a suitability check, except applicants applying only as a Software Developer and Responsible Officials of self filing corporations or partnerships. Applicants that are accepted by the IRS for federal e-filing are assigned an Electronic Filing Identification Number (EFIN) or an Electronic Transmitter Identification Number (ETIN) for applicants that perform the activity of transmission and/or software development. This chart shows electronic filing application process for each state and the District of Columbia.

Jurisdiction	Application Process	Comment
Alabama	Automatic acceptance if accepted by IRS.	Federal EFIN/ETIN is used for state purposes.
Alaska	No automatic acceptance if accepted by IRS.	Federal EFIN/ETIN is used for state purposes.
Arizona	No automatic acceptance if accepted by IRS.	Federal EFIN/ETIN is used for state purposes.
Arkansas	Automatic acceptance if accepted by IRS.	Federal EFIN/ETIN is used for state purposes.
California	Automatic acceptance if accepted by IRS.	Federal EFIN/ETIN is used for state purposes.
Colorado	Automatic acceptance if accepted by IRS.	Federal EFIN/ETIN is used for state purposes.
Connecticut	Automatic acceptance if accepted by IRS. Taxpayer Service Center administrator must set up online filing account for business taxpayers and CT Tax Registration Number (CT REG), PIN, user ID, and password must be entered to login.	Federal EFIN/ETIN is used.
Delaware	Automatic acceptance if accepted by IRS.	Federal EFIN/ETIN is used for state purposes.
District of Columbia	No automatic acceptance if accepted by IRS.	Federal EFIN/ETIN is used for state purposes.

Jurisdiction	Application Process	Comment
Florida	Automatic acceptance if accepted by IRS.	Federal EFIN/ETIN is used for state purposes. Enroll online using Enrollment/ Authorization for e-Services no later than 30 days before first electronic filing date.
Georgia	Automatic acceptance if accepted by IRS.	Federal EFIN/ETIN is used for state purposes.
Hawaii	Automatic acceptance if accepted by IRS.	Federal EFIN/ETIN is used for state purposes.
Idaho	Automatic acceptance if accepted by IRS.	Federal EFIN/ETIN is used for state purposes.
Illinois	Automatic acceptance if accepted by IRS.	Federal EFIN/ETIN is used for state purposes.
Indiana	Automatic acceptance if accepted by IRS.	Federal EFIN/ETIN is used for state purposes.
Iowa	Automatic acceptance if accepted by IRS.	Federal EFIN/ETIN is used for state purposes.
Kansas	Automatic acceptance if accepted by IRS.	Federal EFIN/ETIN is used for state purposes.
Kentucky	Automatic acceptance if accepted by IRS.	Federal EFIN/ETIN is used for state purposes.
Louisiana	Automatic acceptance if accepted by IRS.	Federal EFIN/ETIN is used for state purposes.
Maine	Automatic acceptance if accepted by IRS.	Federal EFIN/ETIN is used for state purposes.
Maryland	Automatic acceptance if accepted by IRS.	Federal EFIN/ETIN is used for state purposes.
Massachusetts	Automatic acceptance if accepted by IRS.	Federal EFIN/ETIN is used for state purposes.
Michigan	Automatic acceptance if accepted by IRS.	Federal EFIN/ETIN is used for state purposes.
Minnesota	Automatic acceptance if accepted by IRS.	Federal EFIN/ETIN is used for state purposes.
Mississippi	Automatic acceptance if accepted by IRS.	Federal EFIN/ETIN is used for state purposes.
Missouri	Automatic acceptance if accepted by IRS.	Federal EFIN/ETIN is used for state purposes.
Montana	Automatic acceptance if accepted by IRS.	Federal EFIN/ETIN is used for state purposes.
Nebraska	Automatic acceptance if accepted by IRS.	Federal EFIN/ETIN is used for state purposes.
New Hampshire	9-digit SSN, FEIN, PTIN or state DIN must be entered online.	
New Jersey	Automatic acceptance if accepted by IRS.	Federal EFIN/ETIN is used for state purposes.

Jurisdiction	Application Process	Comment
New Mexico	Automatic acceptance if accepted by IRS.	Software Developers' products must be validated and certified by both the IRS and the State of New Mexico prior to filing production efile submittals. Federal EFIN/ETIN is used for state purposes.
New York	Automatic acceptance if accepted by IRS.	Federal EFIN/ETIN is used for state purposes.
North Carolina	Automatic acceptance if accepted by IRS.	Federal EFIN/ETIN is used for state purposes.
North Dakota	Letter of intent must be approved.	Federal EFIN/ETIN is used for state purposes.
Ohio	Business taxpayers must register online with FEIN or SSN to use Ohio Business Gateway (OBG) for CAT purposes. Automatic acceptance for individual income tax returns if accepted by IRS.	Federal EFIN/ETIN is used for state purposes.
Oklahoma	Automatic acceptance if accepted by IRS.	Federal EFIN/ETIN is used for state purposes.
Oregon	Automatic acceptance if accepted by IRS.	Federal EFIN/ETIN is used for state purposes.
Pennsylvania	Automatic acceptance if accepted by IRS.	Federal EFIN/ETIN is used for state purposes.
Rhode Island	Automatic acceptance if accepted by IRS.	Federal EFIN/ETIN is used for state purposes.
South Carolina	Automatic acceptance if accepted by IRS.	Federal EFIN/ETIN is used for state purposes.
Tennessee	Automatic acceptance if accepted by IRS. No registration requirements for online filing.	Federal EFIN/ETIN is used for state purposes.
Texas	Taxpayer ID number, WebFile number, SIC code, and NAICS code required for online filing of franchise tax returns.	
Utah	Automatic acceptance if accepted by IRS.	Federal EFIN/ETIN is used for state purposes.
Vermont	Automatic acceptance if accepted by IRS.	Federal ETIN is used for state purposes.
Virginia	Automatic acceptance if accepted by IRS.	Federal EFIN/ETIN is used for state purposes.
West Virginia	Automatic acceptance if accepted by IRS.	Federal EFIN/ETIN is used for state purposes.
Wisconsin	Automatic acceptance if accepted by IRS.	Federal EFIN/ETIN is used for state purposes.

E-Filing: Mandates/Options for C and S Corporations

Electronic filing of federal 1120 and 1120-S income tax returns is required for C and S corporations with assets of $10 million or more and that file 250 or more tax returns determined on a calendar year basis (including income tax returns, employment tax returns, excise tax returns, and information returns). All original returns filed by a corporation and other members of the organization's controlled group (as defined by IRC Sec. 1563(A)) are aggregated for the 250 count. Amended or corrected returns, foreign reporting forms, and tax shelter registration forms are not included in this count. Voluntary electronic filing is also allowed. IRS Notice 2005-88 provides waiver guidance for corporations that cannot meet the electronic filing requirements due to technology constraints or where compliance would result in an undue financial burden. This chart shows whether each state and the District of Columbia mandate or allow electronic filing for C and S corporation returns. Mandate thresholds, waivers and exceptions, and taxpayer opt out provisions are also covered in the chart.

Jurisdiction	Self Filers and Tax Preparers	Comment
Alabama	Mandated for corporations with assets of at least $5 million. Mandated for tax preparers who prepare 25 or more returns using tax preparation software.	No taxpayer opt-out. No penalties for failure to e-file. Mandate does not apply to tax preparers if file no more than 15 original returns.
Alaska	Mandated for corporations that are required to e-file federal return.	Penalty equal to greater of $25 or 1% of tax due before payments. Waiver for undue hardship. File electronic waiver application Form 773 within 30 days before return is due. Waiver valid for 5 years after first filing due date after waiver is granted.
Arizona	Allowed.	
Arkansas	Allowed.	
California	Mandated for taxpayers that file an original or amended return prepared using tax preparation software.	Waiver available for undue hardship or reasonable cause. Penalty for failure to e-file of $100 for initial failure and $500 for each subsequent failure, unless failure is due to reasonable cause and not willful neglect.
Colorado	Allowed. Mandated if claiming enterprise zone credit (include DR 1366, EZ Carryforward Schedule).	
Connecticut	Mandated for taxpayers registered for corporation business tax and composite income tax.	Form DRS-EWVR may be filed no later than 30 days before due date to request one-year waiver if taxpayer can show that filing and paying electronically creates an undue hardship. 10% penalty imposed for failure to file and remit electronically.
Delaware	Allowed.	

Jurisdiction	Self Filers and Tax Preparers	Comment
District of Columbia	DC participates in the Modernized e-File program for Corporation (D-20) and Unincorporated Business Franchise (D-30 with an EIN only) tax returns.	
Florida	Mandated for corporations required to e-file federal income tax returns or required to pay taxes by EFT if tax paid in prior fiscal year is $20,000 or more.	Form DR-654, Request for Waiver from Electronic Filing, may be used to request waiver in limited circumstances. Penalty of 5% of tax due, up to $250, if fail to e-file. Penalty of $10 per return if fail to e-file under EFT requirement.
Georgia	Mandated for corporations that: • are required to pay electronically; • voluntarily pay electronically; or • are required to e-file federal return. Mandated for any return preparer required to e-file federal return.	No opt-out, no waivers/exceptions to mandate.
Hawaii	Allowed.	Mandate authorized, but not yet implemented.
Idaho	Allowed.	
Illinois	Mandated for corporations that are required to e-file federal return.	
Indiana	Allowed for S corporations. Not allowed for C corporations.	
Iowa	Allowed.	
Kansas	Allowed.	
Kentucky	Mandated for corporations that report $1 million or more in federal gross receipts. Allowed for other corporations.	
Louisiana	Mandated if threshold amount is met.	For corporate income tax returns, e-filing is required if the "absolute value" of the taxpayer's assets is at least $500,000 for tax periods beginning in 2018, or $250,000 for tax periods beginning after 2018. Mandate authorized if taxpayer required to file substantially same return for federal tax purposes. Mandated for all returns filed by professional athletic teams or athletes for Sports Facility Assistance Fund. Penalty for failing to e-file athletic returns: $1,000 per failure.
Maine	Mandated for C corporations with total assets of $10 million or more. No tax return required for S corporations.	Waiver for undue hardship. S corporations must e-file withholding form (Form 941P-ME), unless taxpayer or preparer does not use MeF software.
Maryland	Allowed.	

Jurisdiction	Self Filers and Tax Preparers	Comment
Massachusetts	Mandated for: • corporations with any single or combined amount of gross receipts or sales or other income reported on federal returns that is over $100,000; • S corporations with gross income totaling more than $100,000, including income taxed to S corporation and S corporation's shareholders' pro rata share items; • S corporations filing composite returns on behalf individual nonresident members; • S corporations with a filing obligation, unless members consist entirely of resident individuals; or • S corporations entities that withhold tax on member's distributive share.	No exceptions or opt-out for mandated corporations. Any corporation that has reached any e-filing threshold and is required to file and pay electronically in one year must continue to file and pay electronically in subsequent years even if the corporation does not reach e-filing threshold in subsequent years.
Michigan	Mandated for all MBT and CIT returns prepared.	No taxpayer opt-out available. Exceptions to mandate in limited circumstances; file Form 4833, E-file Exceptions for Business Taxes. No penalties for failure to e-file.
Minnesota	Mandated for tax preparers that reasonably expect to file more than 10 C corporation and/or S corporation returns for current year.	Taxpayer opt-out available by checking box on return. Penalty of $5/return for each Form M4 and/or M8 return that is not filed electronically, including returns for taxpayers that opt-out of electronic filing.
Mississippi	Allowed.	Mandate authorized, but not yet implemented.
Missouri	Allowed.	
Montana	Allowed.	
Nebraska	Not allowed.	
New Hampshire	Allowed on state's website.	NH-1120 and Form BET may be filed online at https://www.efilenh.govconnect.com/web/introduction.asp.
New Jersey	For tax years beginning after 2014, mandated for all returns prepared by a paid tax preparer.	For tax years beginning after 2015, mandated for taxpayers who prepare and submit their own returns.
New Mexico	Allowed.	

Jurisdiction	Self Filers and Tax Preparers	Comment
New York	Mandated for tax preparers that prepared authorized tax documents for more than ten different taxpayers during any calendar year beginning after 2011, including tax documents for prior periods. Preparers are then mandated to begin e-file and e-pay beginning the next calendar year, providing they use tax software to prepare one or more tax documents that year. Any preparer mandated to e-file must continue to e-file in all subsequent years, regardless of the number of documents prepared and filed. Mandated for corporations that do not use a tax preparer to prepare Article 9-A general business corporation and S corporation tax returns, use tax preparation software approved by the state, and have broadband Internet access.	No taxpayer opt-out. The only exception to the mandate is the state does not support e-file for one or more of the forms associated with the filing. Corporations are subject to a $50 penalty for failure to e-file or e-pay and penalty for failure to file and paid preparers are subject to a $50 per document penalty for failure to e-file. Certain preparers filing returns (other than personal income tax returns) on or after December 31, 2010, are required to register electronically with New York Department of Taxation and Finance and pay annual fee of $100.
North Carolina	Allowed.	
North Dakota	Allowed.	
Ohio	Mandated for CAT filers.	Taxpayer opt-out for good cause. Penalty if fail to e-file of greater of $25 or 5% of amount due for 1st 2 quarters, $50 or 10% of amount due for 3 quarter and beyond. E-file using Ohio Business Gateway.
Oklahoma	Allowed.	
Oregon	Mandated for corporations that are required to e-file federal return.	Waiver for undue hardship.
Pennsylvania	Mandated for tax preparers who filed 11 or more reports (original or amended) for previous tax year.	Penalty for failure to e-file of 1% of tax due,up to $500, but not less than $10. Taxpayer opt-out by checking box on return. Waiver for undue hardship.
Rhode Island	Mandated for tax preparers that prepare more than 100 returns in previous year.	Taxpayer opt-out from mandate may be requested by written letter, which must be attached to paper return. Mandate waiver available for undue hardship. Preparers that fail to comply with mandate may, after a hearing to show cause, be precluded from preparing and filing state tax returns. Beginning January 1, 2020, every employer required to deduct and withhold tax, and who had an average tax amount of $200 or more per month for the previous calendar year, must file returns electronically.
South Carolina	Mandated for tax preparers that filed 100 or more returns for a tax period for same tax year.	Taxpayer opt-out on form letter, which is retained by preparer. Exemption from mandate available on grounds of financial hardship. Penalty of $50 per return for failure to e-file.
Tennessee	Mandated for all returns prepared using approved software provided certified by department.	

Jurisdiction	Self Filers and Tax Preparers	Comment
Texas	Allowed using WebFile system or approved tax preparation software. Mandated for No Tax Due Reports.	A list of approved providers is available at https://comptroller.texas.gov/taxes/franchise/approved-providers.php.
Utah	Allowed.	
Vermont	Mandated for tax preparers who prepare more than 25 returns per year.	Written requests for exemptions based on extraordinary circumstances will be considered.
Virginia	Mandated.	Waiver for undue hardship available for periods up to one year. New waiver requests must be submitted in writing annually.
West Virginia	Mandated for self filers who had total annual liability of $50,000 or more during prior tax year. Mandated for preparers that use software to prepare more than 25 tax returns.	Taxpayers receiving services from a preparer required to e-file can opt out on Form OPT-1. Waiver requests allowed for hardship. Requests made on: • Form WV-EFT-WR for taxpayer requests; or • Form HW-1 for preparer requests. Penalty of $25 for each return a preparer fails to e-file.
Wisconsin	Mandated.	Waiver for undue hardship can be requested using Form EFT-102.

E-Filing: Mandates/Options for Individuals

Applicable to returns filed after 2010, electronic filing of federal 1040 personal income tax returns is required for tax preparers who file more than 10 returns per calendar year. Voluntary electronic filing is also allowed. This chart shows whether each state and the District of Columbia mandate or allow electronic filing of resident, part-year resident, or nonresident individual income tax returns by self-filers and tax preparers. Mandate thresholds, waivers and exceptions, and taxpayer opt out provisions are also covered in the chart.

Jurisdiction	Self Filers and Tax Preparers	Comment
Alabama	Mandated for tax preparers that filed 11 or more resident or part-year resident returns using tax preparation software. Not allowed for nonresidents. 2D barcode returns do not count as e-filed returns.	Taxpayer opt-out on Form EOO, Taxpayer E-file Opt Out Election Form. Attach Form EOO to tax return with 2D barcode printed on return. Reasonable cause is exception to mandate. No penalty for failure to e-file.
Alaska	N/A, because state has no personal income tax.	
Arizona	Allowed for resident, nonresident, and part-year resident returns.	
Arkansas	Allowed for resident, nonresident, and part-year resident returns.	
California	Mandated for tax preparers that filed more than 100 resident, nonresident, and part-year resident returns and that file one or more returns for the current taxable year using tax preparation software.	Taxpayer opt-out on Form FTB 8454, e-file Opt-Out Record for Individuals. Form is retained. No exceptions or waivers to mandate. Penalty for failure to e-file of $50/return, if due to willful neglect and not reasonable cause.
Colorado	Allowed for resident, nonresident, and part-year resident returns. Mandated if claiming enterprise zone credit (include DR 1366, EZ Carryforward Schedule).	
Connecticut	Mandated for tax preparers that filed 50 or more resident, nonresident, and part-year resident income tax returns during previous tax year.	Form DRS-EWVR may be filed no later than 30 days before due date to request one-year waiver if taxpayer can show that filing and paying electronically creates an undue hardship. Taxpayer opt-out if letter signed by taxpayer is attached to taxpayer's paper return. No penalties for failure to e-file.
Delaware	Allowed for resident, nonresident, and part-year resident returns, except: • returns reporting a lump sum distribution; and • returns on which number of state exemptions claimed does not match number of federal exemptions, excluding additional exemptions for taxpayers 60 years of age or over.	
District of Columbia	Allowed for resident and part-year resident returns.	Nonresidents are not subject to the tax.

Jurisdiction	Self Filers and Tax Preparers	Comment
Florida	N/A because state has no personal income tax.	
Georgia	Mandated for resident, nonresident, and part-year residents that: • are required to pay electronically; • voluntarily pay electronically. Mandated for any return preparer required to e-file federal return.	
Hawaii	Allowed for resident, nonresident, and part-year resident returns.	
Idaho	Allowed for resident, nonresident, and part-year resident returns.	
Illinois	Mandated for tax preparers that filed 11 or more income tax returns during previous tax year and who are required to e-file federal return.	Taxpayer opt-out on Form IL-8948, Electronic Filing Opt-Out Declaration.
Indiana	Mandated for tax preparers who filed more than 10 resident/nonresident returns in 2012 calendar year.	Nonresidents and part-year residents may file online or through MeF. Taxpayers opt-out on Form IN-OPT, which should be retained by preparer for 5 years. No waivers/exceptions to mandate. Penalty of $50/return if fail to e-file, up to $25K/yr.
Iowa	Allowed for resident, nonresident, and part-year resident returns.	
Kansas	Mandated for paid tax preparer that prepares 50 or more resident, nonresident, and part-year resident income tax returns during any calendar year, in which case 90% of returns must be electronically filed.	No taxpayer opt-out. Tax practitioner may request hardship waiver in writing. No penalty for failure to e-file.
Kentucky	Mandated for tax preparers who submitted 11 or more resident, nonresident, part-year resident returns for previous tax year.	Taxpayer opt-out on Form 8948-K, Preparer Explanation for Not Filing Electronically. Attach form to paper return. Waiver for preparer if undue hardship. Penalty of $10/return if fail to e-file.
Louisiana	Mandated for tax preparers that prepare more than 100 state individual income tax returns in any calendar year.	Taxpayer opt-out not available. Waiver available for undue hardship. Mandate authorized if taxpayer required to file substantially same return for federal tax purposes. Mandated for all returns filed by professional athletic teams or athletes. Penalty for failing to e-file athletic returns: $1,000 per failure.
Maine	Mandated for tax preparers who submitted more than 10 resident, nonresident, part-year resident returns for previous tax year.	Taxpayer opt-out available. Written request required; tax preparer must note refusal in taxpayer's records. Waiver available for undue hardship (determined on case-by-case basis). Penalty of $50/return for failure to e-file in absence of reasonable cause.

Jurisdiction	Self Filers and Tax Preparers	Comment
Maryland	Mandated for tax preparer who prepares more than 100 personal income tax returns in prior tax year.	Taxpayer opt-out by checking box on Form 502/505. Waiver available for undue hardship or reasonable cause. Penalty of $50/return for failure to e-file, up to $500, unless failure is due to reasonable cause and not willful neglect.
Massachusetts	Mandated for all tax preparers unless preparers reasonably expect to file 10 or fewer resident, nonresident, part-year resident returns during the previous calendar year.	Taxpayer opt-out on Form EFO, Personal Income Tax Declaration of Paper Filing, which must be retained by tax practitioner. No exceptions/waivers to mandate. Penalty of $100/return for failure to e-file.
Michigan	Mandated for tax preparers that file 11 or more resident, nonresident, and part-year resident returns.	No taxpayer opt out available. No exceptions/waivers to mandate. No penalty for failure to e-file.
Minnesota	Mandated for tax preparers that reasonably expect to file more than 10 returns, including resident, nonresident, and part-year resident returns, for current year.	Taxpayer opt-out available by checking box on return. Waiver available in rare circumstances. Penalty of $5/return for each Form M1 return that is not filed electronically, including returns for taxpayers that opt-out of electronic filing.
Mississippi	Allowed for resident, nonresident, and part-year resident returns.	Mandate authorized, but not yet implemented.
Missouri	Allowed for resident, nonresident, and part-year resident returns.	
Montana	Allowed for resident, nonresident, and part-year resident returns.	
Nebraska	Mandated for tax preparers that file 25 or more resident, nonresident, and part-year resident returns in prior calendar year.	Taxpayer opt-out on E-file Opt-Out Record for individuals. Waiver for preparer if undue hardship. Penalty of $100 per return if fail to e-file.
New Hampshire	Allowed for residents and part-year resident returns.	Nonresidents are not subject to the interest and dividends tax.
New Jersey	Mandated for tax preparers that reasonably expect to prepare 11 or more resident returns, including those prepared for trusts and estates, during the taxable year.	Resident, nonresident, part-year resident returns can be e-filed. Taxpayer opt-out available on Form NJ-1040-O. Tax preparer must maintain completed and signed form in file. No waivers/exceptions to mandate. Penalty of $50/return if fail to e-file. Penalty may be abated if failure to e-file is due to reasonable cause.
New Mexico	Mandated for tax preparers filing more than 25 resident, nonresident, and part-year resident returns per year.	Taxpayer opt-out on Form RPD-41338, and checkbox in paid preparer's signature box on return must be marked. Tax preparer keeps copy of Form RPD-41338 for 3 years. No waivers or exceptions to mandate. Penalty of $5/return if fail to e-file.

Jurisdiction	Self Filers and Tax Preparers	Comment
New York	Mandated for tax preparers that prepared authorized tax documents for more than ten different taxpayers during any calendar year beginning after 2011, and that prepare one or more authorized tax documents using tax software in the subsequent calendar year. 2D barcode returns do not count as e-filed returns. Mandated for taxpayers that prepare their own returns or other tax documents using tax software, applicable to documents filed through 2019.	No taxpayer opt-out. No exception to mandate. Preparer penalty of $50/return or extension if fail to e-file, unless there is reasonable cause. Penalty of $500 if charge separate e-file fee; $1,000 for later occurrences. Preparers filing returns on or after December 31, 2009 are required to register electronically with New York Department of Taxation and Finance and pay annual fee of $100.
North Carolina	Allowed for resident, nonresident, and part-year resident returns.	
North Dakota	Allowed for resident, nonresident, and part-year resident returns.	
Ohio	Mandated for tax preparers who prepare more than 11 original (resident, nonresident, part-year resident) individual tax returns during any calendar year that begins after 2012.	Taxpayer opt-out available on Form IT EF OPT OUT. Waivers determined case-by-case; use Form IT WAIVER. Penalty of $50/return if fail to e-file.
Oklahoma	Mandated for tax preparers that filed more than 10 resident returns for prior tax year. Nonresident and part-year resident returns allowed only through MeF.	No taxpayer opt out. No exceptions to mandate. No penalties for failure to e-file.
Oregon	Mandated for tax preparers who expect to file 11 or more returns.	Taxpayer opt-out available on federal Form 8948, Preparer Explanation for Not Filing Electronically. Tax preparer must must check box 1 and write his or her Oregon license number at the top of the form. Waiver for undue hardship.
Pennsylvania	Mandated for tax preparers who filed 11 or more resident, nonresident, and part-year resident returns (original or amended) for previous tax year.	Penalty for failure to e-file of 1% of tax due, up to $500, but not less than $10. Taxpayer opt-out by checking box on return. Waiver for undue hardship.
Rhode Island	Mandated for tax preparers who prepare more than 100 resident, nonresident, and part-year resident returns in previous year.	Taxpayer opt-out available by writing letter; attach letter to paper return. Waiver available for undue hardship. Preparers that fail to comply with mandate may, after a hearing to show cause, be precluded from preparing and filing state tax returns.
South Carolina	Mandated for tax preparers that filed 100 or more resident, nonresident, and part-year resident returns for a tax period for same tax year.	Taxpayer opt-out with form letter. Exception to mandate if financial hardship. Penalty of $50 per return if fail to e-file.
Tennessee	Mandated for all returns filed by taxpayers using an approved software provider.	Waiver for hardship. Electronic filing of returns available through state's website at https://tntap.tn.gov/EServices/_/.
Texas	N/A, because state has no personal income tax.	

Jurisdiction	Self Filers and Tax Preparers	Comment
Utah	Mandated for tax preparers that filed 101 or more resident, nonresident, and part-year resident returns.	Taxpayer opt-out on Form TC-831, Request to Elect-out of Electronic Filing. Tax preparer retains form. Exception to mandate if undue hardship. No penalties for failure to e-file.
Vermont	Allowed for taxpayers filing resident, nonresident, and part-year resident returns. Mandated for tax practitioners preparing more than 25 tax returns per year, effective January 1, 2020.	
Virginia	Mandated for tax preparers that filed 50 or more resident, nonresident, and part-year resident income tax returns during a previous tax year.	Taxpayers opt out by providing code in election field on return. Request exception to mandate on Form VA-8454P, Paid Tax Preparer Hardship Waiver Request, and mail form in. No penalty for failure to e-file.
West Virginia	Mandated for self filers who had total annual liability of $50,000 or more during prior tax year. Mandated for preparers that use software to prepare more than 25 tax returns.	Taxpayers receiving services from a preparer required to e-file can opt out on Form OPT-1. Waiver requests allowed for hardship. Requests made on: • Form WV-EFT-WR for taxpayer requests; or • Form HW-1 for preparer requests. Penalty of $25 for each return a preparer fails to e-file.
Wisconsin	Mandated for tax preparers that filed 50 or more resident, nonresident, and part-year resident returns for prior tax year.	Taxpayers may opt out by writing "no e-file" before signature on return. Exception to mandate for undue hardship; preparers submit written request. No penalty for failure to e-file.

E-Filing: Mandates/Options for Partnerships, LLPs, and LLCs

Electronic filing of federal 1065 partnership returns by self filers and tax preparers is required for partnerships, limited liability partnerships (LLPs), and limited liability companies (LLCs), which are classified as partnerships for federal tax purposes, if the partnership or LLC has more than 100 partners or members. A waiver may be granted to partnerships or LLCs where compliance would result in an undue hardship. Voluntary electronic filing is also allowed. This chart shows whether each state and the District of Columbia mandate or allow electronic filing of partnership returns by self-filers and tax preparers. Mandate thresholds, waivers and exceptions, and taxpayer opt out provisions are also covered in the chart.

Jurisdiction	Self Filers and Tax Preparers	Comment
Alabama	Mandated for partnerships with 50 or more partners. Mandated for tax preparers who prepare 25 or more returns using tax preparation software.	No taxpayer opt-out. No penalties for failure to e-file. Mandate does not apply to tax preparers if file no more than 15 original returns.
Alaska	Mandated for partnerships that are required to e-file federal return.	Waiver for undue hardship. File electronic waiver application Form 773 within 30 days before return is due. Waiver valid for 5 years after first filing due date after waiver is granted.
Arizona	Allowed.	
Arkansas	Allowed.	
California	Mandated for taxpayers that file an original or amended return prepared using tax preparation software.	Waiver available for undue hardship or reasonable cause. Penalty for failure to e-file of $100 for initial failure and $500 for each subsequent failure, unless failure is due to reasonable cause and not willful neglect.
Colorado	Allowed. Mandated if claiming enterprise zone credit (include DR 1366, EZ Carryforward Schedule).	
Connecticut	Mandated for taxpayers registered for composite income tax.	Form DRS-EWVR may be filed no later than 30 days before due date to request one-year waiver if taxpayer can show that filing and paying electronically creates an undue hardship. 10% penalty imposed for failure to file and remit electronically.
Delaware	Allowed.	
District of Columbia	Allowed. DC participates in the Modernized e-File program for Partnership Return of Income (D-65).	
Florida	Not allowed.	
Georgia	Mandated for taxpayers who are required to e-file federal return. Mandated for any return preparer required to e-file federal return.	No opt-out, no waivers/exceptions to mandate.

Jurisdiction	Self Filers and Tax Preparers	Comment
Hawaii	Not allowed.	Mandate authorized, but not yet implemented.
Idaho	Allowed.	
Illinois	Mandated for partnerships that are required to e-file federal return.	
Indiana	Allowed.	
Iowa	Allowed.	
Kansas	Allowed.	
Kentucky	Mandated for partnerships, LLPs, and LLCs that report $1 million or more in federal gross receipts. Allowed for other pass-through entities.	
Louisiana	Not allowed.	Mandate authorized if taxpayer required to file substantially same return for federal tax purposes. Mandated for all returns filed by professional athletic teams or athletes for Sports Facility Assistance Fund. Penalty for failing to e-file athletic returns: $1,000 per failure.
Maine	N/A because no tax return required.	Withholding form (Form 941P-ME) must be e-filed, unless taxpayer or preparer does not use MeF software.
Maryland	Allowed.	
Massachusetts	Mandated for partnership with: • 25 or more members; • $50,000 or more in gross income, including gross receipts from a trade or business, gross income from the sale or rental of real or tangible personal property, or from royalties, interest, or dividends; • $100,000 or more in income or loss from the sale of stock and securities; • $50,000 or more in ordinary loss from trade or business activities; • pass-through entities filing composite returns on behalf individual nonresident members; • a pass-through entity with a filing obligation, unless members consist entirely of resident individuals; or • a pass-through entity that withholds tax on a member's distributive share.	No opt-out, no waivers/exceptions to mandate. Penalty of $100/return if fail to e-file. Any partnership that has reached any electronic filing threshold and is accordingly required to file and pay electronically in one year must continue to file and pay electronically in subsequent years even if the corporation or partnership does not reach the electronic filing threshold in subsequent years.
Michigan	Mandated for all MBT returns prepared.	No taxpayer opt-out available. Exceptions to mandate in limited circumstances; file Form 4833, E-file Exceptions for Business Taxes. No penalties for failure to e-file.
Minnesota	Mandated for tax preparers that reasonably expect to file more than 10 returns for current year.	Taxpayer opt-out available by checking box on return. Penalty of $5/return for each Form M3 return that is not filed electronically, including returns for taxpayers that opt-out of electronic filing.

Jurisdiction	Self Filers and Tax Preparers	Comment
Mississippi	Allowed.	Mandate authorized, but not yet implemented.
Missouri	Allowed.	
Montana	Mandated for partnerships that have more than 100 partners over course of year.	Failure to file penalty imposed unless partnership demonstrates that satisfactory software is not readily available or that a hardship will result.
Nebraska	Not allowed.	
New Hampshire	Allowed on state's website.	NH-1065 may be filed online at https://www.efilenh.govconnect.com/web/introduction.asp.
New Jersey	Mandated for all returns prepared by a paid tax preparer. Mandated for entities with 10 or more partners.	No opt-out, no waivers/exceptions to mandate. Penalty of $100 for each month for failure to e-file if mandated, plus 5% late filing penalty per month up to maximum of 25% of tax liability.
New Mexico	Allowed.	
New York	Mandated for tax preparers that prepared authorized tax documents for more than ten different taxpayers during any calendar year beginning after 2011, and that prepare one or more authorized tax documents using tax software in the subsequent calendar year. Mandated for partnerships that do not use a tax preparer, if they have broadband Internet access and use approved software to prepare the return.	No taxpayer opt-out. No exception to mandate. Preparer penalty of $50/return or extension if fails to e-file, unless there is reasonable cause. Partnerships subject to $50 penalty for failure to e-file or e-pay. Taxpayer penalty of failure to file if paper return filed when mandated to e-file. Certain preparers filing returns (other than personal income tax returns) on or after December 31, 2010, are required to register electronically with New York Department of Taxation and Finance and pay annual fee of $100.
North Carolina	Allowed.	
North Dakota	Allowed.	
Ohio	Mandated for CAT filers.	Taxpayer opt-out for good cause. Penalty if fail to e-file of greater of $25 or 5% of amount due for 1st 2 quarters, $50 or 10% of amount due for 3 quarter and beyond. E-file using Ohio Business Gateway.
Oklahoma	Allowed.	
Oregon	Accepted for e-filing.	Mandate authorized, but not yet implemented.
Pennsylvania	Mandated for tax preparers who filed 11 or more reports (original or amended) for previous tax year.	Taxpayer opt-out. Waiver available for undue hardship. Penalty of $10/return if fail to e-file.

Jurisdiction	Self Filers and Tax Preparers	Comment
Rhode Island	Mandated for tax preparers that prepare more than 100 returns in previous year.	Taxpayer opt-out from mandate may be requested by written letter, which must be attached to paper return. Mandate waiver available for undue hardship. Preparers that fail to comply with mandate may, after a hearing to show cause, be precluded from preparing and filing state tax returns. Beginning January 1, 2020, every employer required to deduct and withhold tax, and who had an average tax amount of $200 or more per month for the previous calendar year, must file returns electronically.
South Carolina	Not allowed.	
Tennessee	Mandated for all returns prepared using software program certified by department.	
Texas	Allowed using WebFile system or approved tax preparation software. Mandated for No Tax Due Reports.	A list of approved providers is available at https://comptroller.texas.gov/taxes/franchise/approved-providers.php.
Utah	Allowed.	
Vermont	Mandated for tax preparers who prepare more than 25 returns per year.	Written requests for exemptions based on extraordinary circumstances will be considered.
Virginia	Mandated.	Waiver for undue hardship available for periods up to one year. New waiver requests must be submitted in writing annually.
West Virginia	Mandated for self filers who had total annual liability of $50,000 or more during prior tax year. Mandated for preparers that use software to prepare more than 25 tax returns.	Taxpayers receiving services from a preparer required to e-file can opt out on Form OPT-1. Waiver requests allowed for hardship. Requests made on: • Form WV-EFT-WR for taxpayer requests; or • Form HW-1 for preparer requests. Penalty of $25 for each return a preparer fails to e-file.
Wisconsin	Mandated.	Waiver for undue hardship can be requested using Form EFT-102.

E-Filing: PIN Signatures

Individual income taxpayers must sign electronic federal income tax returns using either a self-selected PIN or authorizing an ERO to enter a PIN on their behalf by signing a completed signature authorization form after reviewing the return. EROs must also sign with a PIN. Taxpayers must complete and sign the appropriate Form 8879 authorizing an ERO to enter the taxpayers' PIN on the return before transmission. EROs may sign the forms by rubber stamp, mechanical device, such as signature pen, or computer software program. The signature must include either a facsimile of the individual ERO's signature or of the ERO's printed name. The ERO must retain the signature authorization form for three years from the return due date or the IRS received date, whichever is later. This chart shows whether PIN signatures are accepted by each state and the District of Columbia.

Jurisdiction	Individuals	Comment
Alabama	Not accepted in place of signature form.	Self-selected PIN signatures under consideration.
Alaska	N/A, because state has no personal income tax.	
Arizona	Federal PIN accepted, except for state-only returns.	Form AZ-8879, E-file Signature Authorization, must be completed and signed by taxpayer. Form must be retained for 4 years.
Arkansas	Federal PIN accepted.	
California	Self-select PIN, practitioner PIN, and ERO PIN accepted for individual income tax returns.	Form FTB 8879, e-file Signature Authorization for Individuals, must be completed and signed when an individual e-file return is being signed using the practitioner PIN method. Form must be retained by ERO for 4 years from due date of return or 4 years from date return is filed, whichever is later.
Colorado	Not accepted in place of signature form.	
Connecticut	Federal PIN accepted.	
Delaware	Not accepted in place of signature form.	
District of Columbia	Yes, Federal PIN accepted in place of signature form.	
Florida	N/A, because state has no personal income tax.	
Georgia	Not accepted in place of signature form.	
Hawaii	Not required.	Electronic submission considered as signed document.
Idaho	Federal PIN accepted.	

Jurisdiction	Individuals	Comment
Illinois	PIN assigned and required for online filing of individual income tax returns through tax preparation software.	
Indiana	Federal PIN accepted.	
Iowa	Federal PIN accepted, except returns using practitioner PIN or state-only returns.	
Kansas	Federal PIN accepted.	
Kentucky	Federal PIN accepted.	Signature form required if not used.
Louisiana	Federal PIN accepted.	Federal signature authorization form must be retained for 3 years from return due date or IRS received date, whichever is later. Form may be retained electronically in accordance with the federal recordkeeping guidelines. Signature form also required for information purposes.
Maine	Not required.	Paperless filing.
Maryland	Federal PIN accepted, except if using paid preparer.	
Massachusetts	Not accepted in place of signature form.	
Michigan	Federal PIN accepted, except for state-only returns.	State-only returns can be signed using shared secrets that consist of SSN(s), previous year's AGI or total household resources and previous year's tax due or refund amount.
Minnesota	Federal PIN accepted.	
Mississippi	Federal PIN accepted.	
Missouri	Federal PIN accepted.	
Montana	Not required.	
Nebraska	Federal PIN accepted.	
New Hampshire	Not required.	
New Jersey	Federal PIN accepted, but not required.	
New Mexico	Federal PIN accepted.	
New York	Not accepted in place of signature form.	
North Carolina	Federal PIN accepted.	
North Dakota	Federal or state PIN accepted.	
Ohio	Not accepted.	
Oklahoma	Federal PIN accepted.	
Oregon	Federal PIN accepted.	

Jurisdiction	Individuals	Comment
Pennsylvania	Federal PIN accepted, except for state-only returns.	Form PA-8879, e-file Signature Authorization, must be completed and signed by taxpayer(s) and ERO. Form must be retained by ERO for 3 years.
Rhode Island	Federal PIN accepted.	
South Carolina	Not accepted in place of signature form.	
Tennessee	N/A	Check certification box to sign online return.
Texas	N/A, because state has no personal income tax.	
Utah	Federal PIN accepted, except for state-only returns.	
Vermont	Federal PIN accepted.	
Virginia	Federal PIN accepted.	Form VA-8879, e-file Signature Authorization, must be completed and signed by taxpayer(s) and ERO. Form must be retained by ERO for 3 years from return due date or date return was filed, whichever is later.
West Virginia	Federal PIN accepted, except for state-only returns.	
Wisconsin	Not required.	

E-Filing: Signature Forms

For federal individual income tax returns, practitioners no longer submit a paper signature for e-filed returns by using Form 8453, U.S. Individual Income Tax Declaration for an IRS e-file Return. Rather, federal Form 8453 is used to transmit supporting paper documents that are required to be submitted to the IRS with e-filed returns. Form 8453 must be mailed to the IRS within 3 business days an acknowledgement for the e-filed return is received. This chart shows whether a signature form is required by each state and the District of Columbia for electronic filing of individual income tax returns.

Jurisdiction	Individuals	Comment
Alabama	Form AL8453, Individual Income Tax Declaration for Electronic Filing must be signed by individual taxpayer(s), electronic return originator (ERO), and paid preparer, if different from ERO.	Form must be retained by ERO for 3 years from due date of return or 3 years from date the return was filed, whichever is later.
Alaska	N/A, because state has no personal income tax.	
Arizona	Form AZ-8879, E-File Signature Authorization Form, must be completed and signed by the taxpayer(s).	Form must be retained for 4 years.
Arkansas	Form AR8453, Individual Income Tax Declaration for Electronic Filing, must be completed and signed by taxpayer(s), ERO, and paid preparer.	Form must be retained by ERO for 3 years. Form must be faxed if taxpayer claims: • developmentally disabled credit (AR1000RC5 or Renewal Letter); or • other state tax credit.
California	Form FTB 8453, California e-file Return Authorization for Individuals, must be completed and signed by the taxpayer, ERO, and paid preparer if taxpayer signs using paper method.	Form must be retained for 4 years from return due date or 4 years from filing date, whichever is later. Form may be scanned as PDF copy.
Colorado	Form DR 8453, Individual Income Tax Return Declaration for Electronic Filing, must be completed and signed by the taxpayer and ERO or preparer. Form may be signed using same methods as federal form.	Form for must be retained by ERO and taxpayer for 4 years from return due date.
Connecticut	Not required.	
Delaware	Form DE-8453, Individual Income Tax Declaration for Electronic Filing, must be completed and signed by taxpayers, EROs, and paid preparers.	Form must be retained for 3 years from due date of return or 3 years from date return was transmitted, whichever is later.
District of Columbia	Form D-40 E, Individual Income Tax Declaration for Electronic Filing must be completed and signed by taxpayer, ERO, and paid preparer.	Form must be retained for 3 years.
Florida	N/A, because state has no personal income tax.	

Jurisdiction	Individuals	Comment
Georgia	Form GA 8453 must be completed and signed by taxpayer(s), ERO, and paid preparer.	Forms must be retained 3 years.
Hawaii	Not required.	Electronic submission considered as signed document.
Idaho	Not required.	
Illinois	Form IL-8453, Individual Income Tax Electronic Filing Declaration, must be signed by taxpayer, ERO, and paid preparer.	Form must be retained for 3 years.
Indiana	Form IT-8879, Declaration of Electronic Filing, must be completed and signed by taxpayers, EROs, and paid preparers.	Form must be retained for 3 years.
Iowa	IA Form 8453, Individual Income Tax Declaration for an E-File Return, must be completed and signed by taxpayer, ERO, and paid preparer if practitioner PIN is used to sign return or return is state-only.	Form must be retained for 3 years from return due date or date return was filed. Facsimile of signature or printed name not required.
Kansas	Not required.	
Kentucky	Form 8879-K, Individual Income Tax Declaration For Electronic Filing must be completed and signed by the taxpayer, ERO, and paid preparer if federal PIN is not used.	Form must be retained for 3 years. Facsimile of ERO's signature or printed name not required.
Louisiana	Form LA 8453, Individual Income Tax Declaration for Electronic Filing must be completed and signed by the taxpayer, ERO, and paid preparer.	Form must be retained for 3 years.
Maine	Not required.	Paperless filing.
Maryland	Form EL101, Income Tax Declaration For Electronic Filing, must be completed and signed by taxpayer(s), ERO, and paid preparer.	Form must be retained by taxpayer or ERO for 3 years.
Massachusetts	Form M-8453, Individual Income Tax Declaration for Electronic Filing must be completed and signed by taxpayer, ERO and paid preparer, if not an ERO.	Form must be retained by ERO for 3 years.
Michigan	Form MI-8453, Individual Income Tax Declaration for Electronic Filing must be completed and signed by the taxpayer, ERO, and paid preparer if state-only return is filed.	Form must be retained by preparer for 6 years.
Minnesota	Not required.	
Mississippi	Form MS8453, Declaration of Electronic Filing, must be completed and signed by taxpayer, ERO, and paid preparer.	Form must be retained by ERO for 3 years.
Missouri	Not required.	

Jurisdiction	Individuals	Comment
Montana	Not required.	
Nebraska	Not required.	
New Hampshire	Check box at end of online interest and dividends tax return to verify accuracy and sign it.	
New Jersey	Not required.	
New Mexico	Form PIT-8453, Individual Income Tax Declaration for Electronic Filing and Transmittal, must be completed and signed by taxpayer, ERO, and paid preparer.	Form must be retained by ERO for 3 years. Form should be mailed if refund is $9,500 or more.
New York	Form TR-579-IT, E-File Signature Authorization for Individual Income Tax Returns, must be completed and signed by taxpayer(s), ERO, and paid preparer.	Form must be retained for three years.
North Carolina	Not required.	
North Dakota	Not required.	
Ohio	Not required because acceptance of perjury statement by taxpayer(s) treated as e-file signature.	
Oklahoma	Form 511-EF, Individual Income Tax Declaration for Electronic Filing, must be completed and signed by taxpayer(s), ERO, and paid preparer.	Form must be retained 3 years. Copy must be mailed with non-electronic forms or other documents required to be mailed.
Oregon	Form EF, Individual Income Tax Declaration for Electronic Filing, must be signed by taxpayer(s), ERO, or paid preparer for state-only returns.	Form must be retained for 3 years.
Pennsylvania	Form PA-8453, Individual Income Tax Declaration for Electronic Filing must be completed and signed by the taxpayer(s), ERO, and paid preparer.	Form must be retained by ERO for 3 years after return due date or date return was filed, whichever is later.
Rhode Island	Not required.	
South Carolina	Form SC8453, Individual Income Tax Declaration for Electronic Filing, must be completed and signed by taxpayer(s), ERO, and paid preparer with original signature, rubber stamp, or mechanical device.	Form must be retained by EROs and transmitters for 3 years after return due date or date return was filed, whichever is later.
Tennessee	Not required.	Check certification box to sign online return.
Texas	N/A, because state has no personal income tax.	
Utah	Not required.	
Vermont	Form 8879-VT, Vermont Individual Tax Declaration for Electronic Filing, must be completed and signed by taxpayer, ERO, and paid preparer.	Form must be retained for 3 years from return due date or from date return was transmitted, whichever is later.

Jurisdiction	Individuals	Comment
Virginia	Form VA-8453, Individual Income Tax Declaration for Electronic Filing, must be completed and signed by taxpayer(s), ERO, and paid preparer if PIN is not used.	Form must be retained by ERO for 3 years from return due date or date return was filed, whichever is later.
West Virginia	Form WV-8453, Individual Income Tax Declaration for Electronic Filing, must be completed and signed by taxpayer(s), ERO, and paid preparer if PIN is not used or state-only return is filed.	Form must be retained by taxpayer for no less than 3 years.
Wisconsin	Not required.	

E-Filing: Supported/Accepted Programs—Fed/State E-File Program

Federal/State e-file is a cooperative tax-filing effort between the IRS and most states, which allows providers to electronically file both federal and state returns in a single transmission. State Only returns are also accepted and forwarded to the Electronic Management System (EMS) if the state return was previously rejected by the state; is originated separately from the federal return; is a part-year residency return; is a non-resident state return; or is a married filing separately state return, but the federal return was filed jointly. The IRS provides state acknowledgement service on its EMS. Participating states can send their acknowledgements to EMS for transmitters to pick up when they pick up their federal acknowledgement. This chart shows whether each state and the District of Columbia participate in the Federal/State e-file program.

Jurisdiction	Fed/State Efile Program	Comment
Alabama	Participates in program.	
Alaska	N/A, because state has no personal income tax.	
Arizona	Participates in program.	
Arkansas	Participates in program.	
California	Does not participate in program.	
Colorado	Does not participate in program.	
Connecticut	Participates in program.	
Delaware	Participates in program.	
District of Columbia	Participates in program.	
Florida	Participates in program.	
Georgia	Participates in program.	
Hawaii	Participates in program.	
Idaho	Does not participate in program.	
Illinois	Does not participate in program.	
Indiana	Does not participate in program.	
Iowa	Participates in program.	
Kansas	Participates in program.	
Kentucky	Participates in program.	
Louisiana	Participates in program.	
Maine	Does not participate in program.	
Maryland	Participates in program.	
Massachusetts	Does not participate in program.	State had independent program, which is based on federal program.

Jurisdiction	Fed/State Efile Program	Comment
Michigan	Does not participate in program.	
Minnesota	Participates in program.	
Mississippi	Does not participate in program.	
Missouri	Participates in program.	
Montana	Participates in program.	
Nebraska	Does not participate in program.	
New Hampshire	Participates in program.	
New Jersey	Participates in program for personal income tax returns.	Electronic filing of partnership returns is not through fed/state program.
New Mexico	Participates in program.	
New York	Participates in program.	
North Carolina	Participates in program.	
North Dakota	Participates in program.	
Ohio	Does not participate in program.	
Oklahoma	Participates in program.	
Oregon	Participates in program.	
Pennsylvania	Participates in program.	
Rhode Island	Participates in program.	
South Carolina	Does not participate in program.	
Tennessee	Participates in program.	
Texas	Does not participate in program.	
Utah	Participates in program.	
Vermont	Participates in program.	
Virginia	Participates in program.	
West Virginia	Participates in program.	
Wisconsin	Participates in program.	

E-Filing: Supported/Accepted Programs—State Direct E-Filing Program

This chart shows whether each state and the District of Columbia has a direct electronic filing program that is separate and independent from the federal electronic filing program.

Jurisdiction	State Direct E-filing Program	Comment
Alabama	No direct state program that is independent of federal program.	
Alaska	No direct state program that is independent of federal program.	
Arizona	No direct state program that is independent of federal program.	
Arkansas	No direct state program that is independent of federal program.	
California	State has direct e-file program that is independent of federal program.	Current original personal income tax returns may be filed online by California residents with fewer than 11 dependents if taxpayer's last name has not changed since last filing, unless the taxpayer meets certain requirements. Additional information available at: https://www.ftb.ca.gov/file/ways-to-file/online/calfile/help-with-calfile.html.
Colorado	No direct state program that is independent of federal program.	
Connecticut	No direct state program that is independent of federal program.	
Delaware	No direct state program that is independent of federal program.	
District of Columbia	Yes, for extension and estimated payments, MYTaxDC.gov.	
Florida	No direct state program that is independent of federal program.	
Georgia	No direct state program that is independent of federal program.	
Hawaii	No direct state program that is independent of federal program.	
Idaho	No direct state program that is independent of federal program.	
Illinois	No direct state program that is independent of federal program.	
Indiana	No direct state program that is independent of federal program.	
Iowa	No direct state program that is independent of federal program.	

Jurisdiction	State Direct E-filing Program	Comment
Kansas	No direct state program that is independent of federal program.	
Kentucky	No direct state program that is independent of federal program.	
Louisiana	No direct state program that is independent of federal program.	
Maine	No direct state program that is independent of federal program.	
Maryland	No direct state program that is independent of federal program.	
Massachusetts	State has direct e-file program that is independent of federal program.	
Michigan	No direct state program that is independent of federal program.	
Minnesota	No direct state program that is independent of federal program.	
Mississippi	No direct state program that is independent of federal program.	
Missouri	No direct state program that is independent of federal program.	
Montana	No direct state program that is independent of federal program.	
Nebraska	No direct state program that is independent of federal program.	
New Hampshire	State website only allows online payment, but not filing, for business enterprise and business profits taxes. Estimate payments, extension payments, return payments, amended return payments, and tax notice payments may be made online.	https://www.efilenh.govconnect.com/web/introduction.asp
New Jersey	No direct state program that is independent of federal program.	
New Mexico	The Unified Login System, New Mexico's access portal for taxpayers (Taxpayer Access Portal), supports online filing for C and S corporations, LLC and LLPs.	
New York	No direct state program that is independent of federal program.	
North Carolina	No direct state program that is independent of federal program.	
North Dakota	No direct state program that is independent of federal program.	
Ohio	State has direct e-file program that is independent of federal program.	Ohio Business Gateway for annual and Quarterly CAT returns.

Jurisdiction	State Direct E-filing Program	Comment
Oklahoma	No direct state program that is independent of federal program.	
Oregon	No direct state program that is independent of federal program.	
Pennsylvania	No direct state program that is independent of federal program.	
Rhode Island	No direct state program that is independent of federal program.	
South Carolina	No direct state program that is independent of federal program.	
Tennessee	No direct state program that is independent of federal program.	
Texas	No direct state program that is independent of federal program.	
Utah	No direct state program that is independent of federal program.	
Vermont	No direct state program that is independent of federal program.	
Virginia	No direct state program that is independent of federal program.	
West Virginia	State has direct e-file program that is independent of federal program.	Application may be completed online at https://mytaxes.wvtax.gov/_//
Wisconsin	Forms 1CNS, 1CNP, and PW-1s can be filed via My Tax Account.	

E-Filing: Supported/Accepted Programs—State Online E-Filing

The Internal Revenue Service (IRS) allows individual taxpayers to self prepare and electronically file income tax returns online for free at the IRS website. Forms that are available for free online preparation and electronic filing include federal Form 1040 along with the most common forms and schedules filed by individual taxpayers. Taxpayers can fill in tax data, perform basic mathematical calculations, sign electronically, print for recordkeeping, and e-file the return. The IRS does not support preparation or filing of state income tax returns. This chart shows whether each state and the District of Columbia has an online electronic filing program.

Jurisdiction	State Online E-filing	Comment
Alabama	Current personal income tax returns may be filed online at: https://myalabamataxes.alabama.gov.	
Alaska	Corporate income tax returns may be filed and amended at: https://online-tax.alaska.gov/ATP/WebDoc/_/	
Arizona	No online filing through state web site.	
Arkansas	Arkansas Taxpayer Access Point can be found at: https://atap.arkansas.gov/_/.	
California	Personal income tax returns may be filed online at: https://www.ftb.ca.gov/file/ways-to-file/online/calfile/index.asp?WT.mc_id=akCFHome.	Current original personal income tax returns may be filed online by California residents with less than 11 dependents if taxpayer's last name has not changed since last filing, unless the taxpayer meets certain requirements.
Colorado	Current and prior personal income tax, corporation, partnership, and fiduciary returns may be filed online at: https://www.colorado.gov/revenueonline/_/.	Registration not required, but must have filed previous state tax return.
Connecticut	Current year personal and business income tax returns may be filed online at: https://portal.ct.gov/DRS/TSC/TSC-Online	
Delaware	Current or prior year personal income tax returns may be filed at: https://revenue.delaware.gov/online-filing/	
District of Columbia	The following forms may be filed online at MyTax.DC.gov: FR-127, Extension of Time to File Income Tax Return FR-120, Corporation Franchise Tax Extension FR-130, Unincorporated Franchise Tax Extension FR-165, Partnership Tax Extension D-77, Estate Tax Extension.	

Jurisdiction	State Online E-filing	Comment
Florida	Online filing available at: https://taxapps.floridarevenue.com/Corporate/Login.aspx	Forms F-1120A, F-1120ES, and F-7400 may be filed online.
Georgia	No online filing through a state website.	
Hawaii	Online filing available at: http://tax.hawaii.gov/eservices/.	Form N-13 filers who have less than $100,000 taxable income, do not itemize deductions, and do not claim adjustments to income, may file online.
Idaho	No online filing through a state website.	
Illinois	Resident, nonresident, part-year resident individuals may file online at: https://mytax.illinois.gov/_/.	For the individual "online" program, a state issued IL-PIN or a valid IL Drivers License is required. For other online products, taxpayer's business must be registered with state.
Indiana	Online filing at: http://www.in.gov/dor/4578.htm.	
Iowa	No online filing through a state website.	
Kansas	Personal income tax returns may be filed online at: https://www.ksrevenue.org/iiwebfile.html.	
Kentucky	Current personal income tax returns may be filed online at: KY File	
Louisiana	Current and prior personal income tax returns may be filed online at: https://esweb.revenue.louisiana.gov/IndividualIncomeTax/Login.aspx?ReturnUrl=%2fIndividualIncomeTax%2fdefault.aspx.	Registration not required, but must have filed previous state tax return.
Maine	Current year personal income tax returns may be filed online at: https://portal.maine.gov/ifile/.	No application or approval required. Filer supplies user name and password.
Maryland	Personal income tax returns may be filed online at: https://interactive.marylandtaxes.gov/Individuals/iFile_ChooseForm/default.asp.	

Jurisdiction	State Online E-filing	Comment
Massachusetts	Online filing at: https://www.mass.gov/dor/e-services/masstaxconnect.html. Corporate excise taxpayers may use MassTaxConnect to file returns and make payments. Partnerships may use MassTaxConnect to file returns and make payments beginning December 5, 2016. Personal income taxpayers may use MassTaxConnect to make payments beginning December 5, 2016. Online e-filing (WebFile for Individuals) allowed for eligible full-year resident individual income taxpayers until November 6, 2016.	
Michigan	No online filing through a state website.	
Minnesota	No online return filing through state website.	
Mississippi	No online filing through a state website.	
Missouri	No online filing through a state website.	
Montana	Personal income tax returns may be filed online at: https://tap.dor.mt.gov/_/.	
Nebraska	Personal income tax returns may be filed online at: http://www.revenue.nebraska.gov/electron/online_services.html.	
New Hampshire	Current or prior year personal income tax returns may be filed online at: http://www.nh.gov/revenue.	
New Jersey	Current year resident personal income tax returns and tenant homestead rebate applications may be filed online at http://www.njwebfile.com. Current year partnership returns for partnerships with 50 or fewer partners may be filed online at https://www1.state.nj.us/TYTR_BusinessFilings/jsp/common/Login.jsp?taxcode=43.	
New Mexico	Online Services at: http://tax.newmexico.gov/Online-Services/.	
New York	Personal income tax returns may be filed online at https://www.tax.ny.gov/pit/efile.	

Jurisdiction	State Online E-filing	Comment
North Carolina	Form D-410, Application for Extension for Filing Individual Income Tax Return, can be filed online at http://www.dornc.com/electronic/d410.html. Form CD-419, Application for Extension for Franchise and Corporate Income Tax, can be filed online at http://www.dornc.com/electronic/index.html#businesses.	
North Dakota	Resident personal income tax returns may be filed online with fillable forms at: https://www.nd.gov/tax/user/individuals/e-file/e-file-programs/nd-fillable-forms.	
Ohio	CAT and personal income tax returns may be filed online at: https://www.tax.ohio.gov/ohio_individual/individual/filefaster.aspx.	
Oklahoma	Online filing through a state website using OkTAP at: Tax Commission Free File|http://www.ok.gov/tax/Individuals/Income_Tax/E-File_Options/Free_File/.	Full-year residents meeting certain requirements may e-file on http://www.ok.gov/tax/Individuals/Income_Tax/E-File_Options/Free_File/.
Oregon	No online filing through a state website.	
Pennsylvania	Current personal income tax returns may be filed online at: http://www.revenue.pa.gov/OnlineServices/Pages/default.aspx.	
Rhode Island	No online filing through a state website.	
South Carolina	No online filing through a state website.	
Tennessee	Current or prior year personal income tax returns may be filed online at https://tntap.tn.gov/EServices/_//.	
Texas	Business franchise tax returns may be filed online at http://www.window.state.tx.us/taxes.	To file online, use WebFile number (XT followed by 6 digits) found in notification letter.
Utah	Online at: https://tap.tax.utah.gov/TaxExpress/_/	
Vermont	No online filing through a state website.	
Virginia	For individuals, resident returns may be filed online via Free Fillable Forms e-File. For corporations, certain form types may be filed online at https://www.business.tax.virginia.gov/VTOL/Login.seam.	

Jurisdiction	State Online E-filing	Comment
West Virginia	Online filing at: https://mytaxes.wvtax.gov/_//_/.	
Wisconsin	Personal income tax returns may be filed online at https:// www.revenue.wi.gov/Pages/WI-efile/ home.aspx.	

E-Filing: Supported/Accepted Programs—State Only Returns

State Only returns are accepted through the Federal/State Efile Program and forwarded to the Electronic Management System (EMS) if the state return was previously rejected by the state; is originated separately from the federal return; is a part-year residency return; is a non-resident state return; or is a married filing separately state return, but the federal return was filed jointly. This chart shows whether each state and the District of Columbia accept electronic filing of state returns for individual taxpayers separately without the filing of a federal return.

Jurisdiction	Individuals	Comment
Alabama	Accepted for e-filing.	
Alaska	N/A, because state has no personal income tax.	
Arizona	Accepted for e-filing.	
Arkansas	Not accepted for e-filing.	
California	Accepted for e-filing.	
Colorado	Accepted for e-filing.	
Connecticut	Accepted for e-filing.	
Delaware	Accepted for e-filing.	
District of Columbia	Accepted for e-filing.	
Florida	N/A because state has no personal income tax.	
Georgia	Accepted for e-filing.	
Hawaii	Accepted for e-filing.	
Idaho	Accepted for e-filing.	
Illinois	Accepted for e-filing.	
Indiana	Accepted for e-filing.	
Iowa	Accepted for e-filing.	
Kansas	Not accepted for e-filing.	
Kentucky	Accepted for e-filing.	
Louisiana	Accepted for e-filing.	
Maine	Accepted for e-filing.	
Maryland	Accepted for e-filing.	
Massachusetts	Accepted for e-filing.	State e-filing program for individual income taxpayers is independent of federal program.
Michigan	Accepted for e-filing.	
Minnesota	Accepted for e-filing.	

Jurisdiction	Individuals	Comment
Mississippi	Accepted for e-filing.	
Missouri	Accepted for e-filing.	
Montana	Accepted for e-filing.	
Nebraska	Accepted for e-filing.	
New Hampshire	A taxpayer must first file a paper return, extension request, or payment through the state website. After a first paper contact with the Department, taxpayers may file online.	State does not participate in federal e-file program.
New Jersey	Accepted for e-filing.	
New Mexico	Accepted for e-filing.	
New York	Accepted for e-filing.	
North Carolina	Accepted for e-filing.	
North Dakota	Accepted for e-filing.	
Ohio	Accepted for e-filing.	
Oklahoma	Not accepted for e-filing.	
Oregon	Accepted for e-filing.	
Pennsylvania	Accepted for e-filing.	
Rhode Island	Accepted for e-filing.	
South Carolina	Accepted for e-filing.	
Tennessee	Accepted for e-filing.	
Texas	N/A, because state has no personal income tax.	
Utah	Accepted for e-filing.	
Vermont	Accepted for e-filing.	
Virginia	Accepted for e-filing.	
West Virginia	Accepted for e-filing.	
Wisconsin	Accepted for e-filing.	

E-Filing: Tax Authority Contact Information

The following chart indicates the contact information for electronic filing. When it is available, information has been provided for both individual and corporate income tax returns. This information is intended only for electronic return originators or software developers; it should not be given to taxpayers.

Jurisdiction	Tax Authority Contact Information	Comment
Alabama	Tavares D. Mathews, Individual MeF Coordinator Demetria Gordon, Business MeF Coordinator, Corporate and Business Privilege Tax Nicci Adams, Business MeF Coordinator, Pass Through and Fiduciary Tax	E-mail: Individual.Efile@revenue.alabama.gov or corporate.efile@revenue.alabama.gov Phone: 334-353-9497 (Individual), 334-353-9129 (Corporate and Business Privilege Tax), or 334-353-0685 (Pass-Through and Fiduciary Tax) Web: https://revenue.alabama.gov/individual-corporate/software-vendor-information/alabama-business-modernized-electronic-filing-mef/
Alaska	Scott Mueller, for corporate income returns.	E-mail: scott.mueller@alaska.gov Web: http://tax.alaska.gov/ State does not impose a personal income tax.
Arizona	Arizona E-File team	E-mail: AZefile@azdor.gov Web: https://azdor.gov/e-file-services
Arkansas	Caroline Glover, for individual and corporate income returns	E-mail: Caroline.Glover@dfa.arkansas.gov or arefile@dfa.arkansas.gov Phone: 501-682-7925 Fax: 501-682-7393 Web: https://www.dfa.arkansas.gov/income-tax/arkansas-efile/
California	e-Programs Customer Service, for individual and corporate income returns	E-mail: e-file.coordinator@ftb.ca.gov or business.e-file.coordinator@ftb.ca.gov Phone: 916-845-0353 Fax: 916-855-5556 Web: https://www.ftb.ca.gov/tax-pros/efile/index.html or https://www.ftb.ca.gov/file/ways-to-file/online/calfile/index.asp
Colorado	Steve Asbell, for individual and corporate income returns	E-mail: Stephen.Asbell@state.co.us Phone: 303-866-3889 Fax: 303-866-3211 Web: https://www.colorado.gov/revenue
Connecticut	CT MeF coordinator, for individual and corporate income returns	E-mail: jim.annino@po.state.ct.us or CT.eFile@po.state.ct.us Phone: 860-297-4973 Fax: 860-297-4761 Web: https://portal.ct.gov/drs
Delaware	Christie Meaders for individual returns DE_DOR_Forms@delaware.gov for corporate income returns	E-mail: christie.meaders@delaware.gov or DE_DOR_Forms@delaware.gov Phone: (302) 577-8457 Fax: 302-577-8206 Web: https://revenue.delaware.gov/

Jurisdiction	Tax Authority Contact Information	Comment
District of Columbia	efile@dc.gov, for individual and corporate returns	E-mail: efile@dc.gov Phone: 202-442-6239 or (202) 442-6262 or (202) 442-6919 Fax: 202-442-6330 Web: https://otr.cfo.dc.gov/
Florida	e-vendor@floridarevenue.com, for corporate income tax returns	E-mail: e-vendor@floridarevenue.com or TAYLORLA@dor.state.fl.us Phone: 850-717-7381 Web: https://floridarevenue.com/pages/default.aspx State does not impose a personal income tax.
Georgia	GA.Vendors@dor.ga.gov, for individual and corporate income returns	E-mail: GA.Vendors@dor.ga.gov or electronic.filing@dor.ga.gov Phone: 404-417-2395 Fax: 404-417-4398 Web: https://dor.georgia.gov/software-vendor-information or https://dor.georgia.gov/
Hawaii	tax.efile@hawaii.gov, for individual and corporate income returns	E-mail: tax.efile@hawaii.gov Web: https://tax.hawaii.gov/eservices/ Phone: 808-587-4242 Fax: 808-587-1488
Idaho	Auston Holmes, for individual and business returns	E-mail: efilecoordinator@tax.idaho.gov Phone: 208-334-5360 Fax: 208-334-7650 Web: https://tax.idaho.gov/
Illinois	Rev.TaxLOI@illinois.gov for individual returns Stuart Wilcoxon for business returns	E-mail: rev.ildor.mefbit@illinois.gov or Rev.TaxLOI@illinois.gov Phone: (217)785-0574 or 217 524-4767 Fax: 217-782-7992 Web: https://www2.illinois.gov/rev/Pages/default.aspx
Indiana	Electronic Filing Coordinator, for individual and business returns	E-mail: AltFileMgr@dor.in.gov Phone: 317-615-2550 Fax: 317-233-1455 Web: https://www.in.gov/dor/
Iowa	IDRMeFDeveloper@iowa.gov, for individual and business returns	E-mail: IDRMeFDeveloper@iowa.gov or idr@iowa.gov Phone: 515-281-3114 Fax: 515-281-0431 Web: https://tax.iowa.gov/
Kansas	KDOR_IncomeEServ@ks.gov or KDOR_BusinessTaxEServices@ks.gov, for individual and corporate income returns	E-mail: KDOR_IncomeEServ@ks.gov or KDOR_BusinessTaxEServices@ks.gov Phone: 785-368-8222 Fax: 785-296-0153 Web: https://www.ksrevenue.org/
Kentucky	Sikitia Snow or Jeremy Sapp, for individual returns Chris Rains, for corporate returns	E-mail: Sikitia.Snow@ky.gov, Jeremy.Sapp@ky.gov, Christopher.Rains@ky.gov Phone: 502-564-5370 Fax: 502-564-0230 Web: https://revenue.ky.gov/Pages/index.aspx

Jurisdiction	Tax Authority Contact Information	Comment
Louisiana	Shanna Kelly, for individual and corporate income returns	E-mail: shanna.kelly@la.gov Phone: 225-219-2490 or 225-219-2492 or 225-219-2763 Fax: 225-219-2651 Web: https://revenue.louisiana.gov/
Maine	E-file Helpdesk, for individual and corporate income returns	E-mail: efile.helpdesk@maine.gov Phone: 207-624-9730 Fax: 207-287-6628 Web: https://www.maine.gov/revenue/developers/
Maryland	efil@marylandtaxes.gov for individual and business returns	E-mail: efil@marylandtaxes.gov Phone: 410-260-7753 or 410-260-7424 Fax: 410-974-2274 Web: https://www.marylandtaxes.gov/
Massachusetts	anfitformsapproval@dor.state.ma.us for individual and corporate income returns	E-mail: anfitformsapproval@dor.state.ma.us Phone: 617-887-5174 Fax: 617-887-5029 Web: https://www.mass.gov/orgs/massachusetts-department-of-revenue
Michigan	MIFormsEfile@michigan.gov for individual and corporate income returns	E-mail: MIFormsEfile@michigan.gov Phone: 517-636-4450 Fax: 517-636-6826 Web: https://www.michigan.gov/taxes/0,4676,7-238-44070---,00.html
Minnesota	Efile.DevSupport@state.mn.us for individual and corporate income tax returns	E-mail: Efile.DevSupport@state.mn.us Phone: 651-556-4818 Fax: 651-556-3130 Web: https://www.revenue.state.mn.us/minnesota-department-revenue
Mississippi	efile@dor.ms.gov for individual and corporate income returns	E-mail: efile@dor.ms.gov Phone: 601-923-7055 or (601) 923-7700 Fax: 601-923-7039 Web: https://www.dor.ms.gov/Pages/default.aspx
Missouri	elecfile@dor.mo.gov for individual and corporate income returns	E-mail: elecfile@dor.mo.gov or moforms@dor.mo.gov Phone: (573) 751-5714 Fax: (573) 522-4876 Web: https://dor.mo.gov/
Montana	David Berg, for individual and corporate income returns	E-mail: daberg@mt.gov Phone: 406-444-4070 Fax: 406-444-9372 Web: https://mtrevenue.gov/
Nebraska	Michael Behnke, for individual income tax returns	E-mail: michael.behnke@nebraska.gov Phone: 402-471-5649 or 402-471-5619 Fax: 402-471-5608 Web: http://www.revenue.nebraska.gov/
New Hampshire	Customer service, for individual returns	Phone: 603-230-5920 or 603-271-2191 Fax: 603-271-6121 Web: https://www.revenue.nh.gov/

Jurisdiction	Tax Authority Contact Information	Comment
New Jersey	MEFADMIN@treas.nj.gov for individual and corporate income returns	E-mail: MEFADMIN@treas.nj.gov Phone: 609-777-4216 or 609-292-9292 Fax: 609-777-2811 Web: https://www.state.nj.us/treasury/revenue/
New Mexico	TRD-MEFinfo@state.nm.us for individual and business returns	E-mail: TRD-MEFinfo@state.nm.us TRD-TaxReturnHelp@state.nm.us or cit.taxreturnhelp@state.nm.us Phone: (505) 827-0825 or 505-476-3174 Fax: 505-827-0469 Web: http://www.tax.newmexico.gov/
New York	NYSPITMEF@tax.ny.gov for individual returns BTBCTELF@tax.ny.gov for corporate income returns	E-mail: NYSPITMEF@tax.ny.gov or BTBCTELF@tax.ny.gov Phone: 518-457-6387 Fax: 518-485-0449 Web: https://www.tax.ny.gov/bus/efile/elf_business.htm
North Carolina	NCTaxEfile@ncdor.gov for individual and corporate returns	E-mail: NCTaxEfile@ncdor.gov Phone: 919-814-1500 or 1-877-252-3052 Fax: 919-715-6158 Web: https://www.ncdor.gov/
North Dakota	Lucas Asche, for individual and corporate income returns	E-mail: lasche@nd.gov or taxmef@nd.gov Phone: 701-328-3129 Fax: 701-328-0352 Web: www.nd.gov/tax/mef/
Ohio	Individual.MeF@tax.state.oh.us for individual returns PTE.MeF@tax.state.oh.us or MNPTax@tax.state.oh.us for business returns	E-mail: Individual.MeF@tax.state.oh.us or PTE.MeF@tax.state.oh.us or MNPTax@tax.state.oh.us Phone: 614-466-0197 or 1-844-238-0403 or 614-387-1965 Fax: 206-339-7828 Web: https://www.tax.ohio.gov/
Oklahoma	Crystal Cameron, for individual and corporate income returns	E-mail: efiledevelopers@tax.ok.gov or efile@tax.ok.gov Phone: 405-522-5723 Fax: 405-522-1711 Web: https://www.ok.gov/tax/
Oregon	E-file Coordinator, for individual returns Beth Buck, for corporate income returns	E-mail: electronic.filing@oregon.gov or BUS.ElectronicFiling@oregon.gov or TrustEstate.ElectronicFiling@oregon.gov Phone: 503-378-4988 or 503-945-8152 Fax: 503-945-8649 Web: https://www.oregon.gov/dor/Pages/index.aspx
Pennsylvania	Joe Henry, for individual returns Gabrielle Brandt, for corporate income returns	E-mail: jhenry@pa.gov Phone: 717-425-2859 Fax: 717-772-9310 Web: https://www.revenue.pa.gov/Pages/default.aspx E-mail: ra-corpefile@state.pa.us Phone: 717-787-7512
Rhode Island	Leo Lebeuf, for individual and corporate income returns	E-mail: Tax.VendorForms@tax.ri.gov or Leo.Lebeuf@tax.ri.gov Phone: 401-574-8983 Fax: 401-574-8913 Web: http://www.tax.ri.gov/

Jurisdiction	Tax Authority Contact Information	Comment
South Carolina	Keith Wicker, for individual and corporate returns	E-mail: Keith.Wicker@dor.sc.gov or indelf@sctax.org or mef@dor.sc.gov Phone: 803-896-1845 Fax: 803-896-1779 Web: https://dor.sc.gov/
Tennessee	Marian Scott, for individual and corporate income tax returns	E-mail: Marian.Scott@state.tn.us or efile.questions@tn.gov Phone: 615-741-8616 or 615-253-3251 Fax: 615-532-2299 Web: https://www.tn.gov/revenue.html
Texas	Help desk, for corporate income returns	E-mail: WebFileHelp@cpa.state.tx.us or XMLBusiness@cpa.state.tx.us Phone: 800-531-5441, ext. 33630, or 1-800-252-1381 Web: https://comptroller.texas.gov/taxes/ State does not impose a personal income tax.
Utah	Nicole Meagan, for individual and corporate income returns	E-mail: nlmeagan@utah.gov or mef@utah.gov Phone: 801-297-2732 Fax: 801-297-7698 Web: https://tax.utah.gov/
Vermont	Terri Eldred for individual and corporate income returns	E-mail: terri.eldred@vermont.gov Phone: 802-828-6828 Fax: 802-828-3754 Web: https://tax.vermont.gov/
Virginia	ind_efile@tax.virginia.gov for individual returns bus_efile@tax.virginia.gov for corporate income returns	E-mail: ind_efile@tax.virginia.gov or bus_efile@tax.virginia.gov or FID_eFile@tax.virginia.gov Phone: 804.367.9286 or 804-367-7011 Fax: 804-367-0224 Web: https://www.tax.virginia.gov/
West Virginia	TaxLOI@wv.gov for individual and corporate income returns	E-mail: TaxLOI@wv.gov Phone: 304-558-3333 Fax: 304-558-1150 Web: https://tax.wv.gov/Pages/default.aspx
Wisconsin	DORElectronicFiling@revenue.wi.gov for individual and corporate returns	E-mail: DORElectronicFiling@revenue.wi.gov or DORBusinessTax@wisconsin.gov Phone: 608-266-2776 or 608-266-2772 Fax: 608-264-6884 Web: https://www.revenue.wi.gov/Pages/home.aspx

EFT Requirements and Options (Corporate Income)

Federal Electronic Funds Transfer (EFT) tax payments may be made through the Electronic Federal Tax Payment System (EFTPS). Domestic corporations must deposit all income tax payments through EFTPS. Many states either have mandatory EFT programs or accept voluntary EFT payments for corporate income and personal income withholding taxes. This chart indicates states that mandate or allow EFT by corporations for the payment of income, estimated, or employee withholding taxes. This chart also sets forth EFT thresholds for each state. The threshold amount applies separately for each tax type unless otherwise noted. EFT requirements for payment of other taxes, such as sales and use, motor fuel, tobacco, and alcohol taxes, are not covered in this chart.

Jurisdiction	EFT Requirements and Options	Comment
Alabama	Mandated for payment of income, estimated, and employee withholding taxes if single tax payments total $750 or more. E-pay required if e-filing withholding, corporate income, or business privilege tax returns.	Voluntary EFT payments also allowed. Registration required on EFT:001, EFT Authorization Agreement Form, if making ACH credit payments. Noncompliance penalties may apply.
Alaska	Mandated for: • annual income tax payments of $150,000 or more; and • monthly or quarterly estimated tax payments of $100,000 or more.	Voluntary EFT payments also allowed.
Arizona	Mandated for payment of estimated taxes if corporate income tax liability during prior tax year is $20,000 or more. Mandated for payment of withholding taxes if average quarterly withholding tax liability during prior tax year is $5,000 or more.	The Department of Revenue may lower the EFT threshold to: • $10,000 or more for taxable year 2019; • $5,000 or more for taxable year 2020; and • $500 or more for taxable years after 2020. Voluntary EFT payments also allowed. Application required on Form ADOR 10366, Authorization Agreement for Electronic Funds Transfer and Disclosure Agreement for Credit Filers. On-line registration available for ACH Debit filers. Noncompliance penalties may apply.
Arkansas	Mandated for payment of estimated tax if quarterly liability is $20,000 or more based on prior year. Mandated for employee withholding tax if monthly withholding average is $20,000 or more.	Voluntary EFT payments also allowed. Form EFT-CT or Form EFT-WH, EFT Authorization Agreement required. Noncompliance penalties may apply.

Jurisdiction	EFT Requirements and Options	Comment
California	Mandated for payment of franchise or income tax if total tax liability exceeds $80,000 in any taxable year. Mandated for payment of estimated tax if any estimated installment payment exceeds $20,000. Mandated for extension payment exceeding $20,000. Mandated for payment of employee withholding taxes if cumulative average payment for deposit periods in the 12-month lookback period was $20,000 or more.	Voluntary EFT payments also allowed with FTB or EDD permission. Noncompliance penalty for corporate tax payments equal to 10% of amount paid. Waiver available if threshold mandates not met during prior tax year or if amounts not representative of actual tax liability. Waiver also available if permanent physical or mental impairment prevents use of a computer. Voluntary participation allowed with prior approval of FTB and completion of Form FTB 3815, Authorization for Electronic Funds Transfer (EFT). Effective January 1, 2017, mandated for payment of employee withholding taxes for employers with 10 or more employees. Mandated for all other employers beginning January 1, 2018. Noncompliance penalty of 15% of amount due. Waiver may be available by filing E-file and E-pay Mandate Waiver Request (DE 1245) if due to lack of automation, severe economic hardship, current exemption from federal government, or other good cause.
Colorado	Mandated for payment of employee withholding tax if annual estimated tax liability is more than $50,000.	If withholding tax threshold is met during the year, EFT not required until following fiscal year. Voluntary EFT payments also allowed. Registration required on Form DR-5785, Authorization for Electronic Funds Transfer (EFT) for Tax Payments.
Connecticut	Beginning in 2014, mandated for all taxpayers registered for corporation business tax (excluding combined return), composite income tax, business entity tax, or withholding tax. Taxpayers must be notified by state to pay tax by EFT. Prior to 2014, mandated for income and estimated tax if annual tax liability was $4,000 or more, and for employer withholding tax payments if annual tax liability was $2,000 or more, for 12-month lookback period. Taxpayers required to e-file returns, statements, and other documents also required pay taxes by EFT (does not apply to tax return preparers).	Voluntary EFT payments also allowed. Form EFT-1, Authorization Agreement for Electronic Funds Transfers, required for ACH Credit. Noncompliance penalties may apply. Waiver for undue hardship available effective Oct. 1, 2011. Prior to July 1, 2010, mandated for payment of income, estimated, and employee withholding taxes if prior year tax liability exceeded $10,000 for 12-month lookback period.
Delaware	Mandated for payment of employee withholding taxes for employers required to deposit federal employment taxes by EFT. Allowed for corporate tentative and S corporation estimated tax payments.	Electronic Funds Transfer Authorization Agreement required. Penalty imposed for noncompliance equal to lesser of 5% of amount or $500 per required payment.

Jurisdiction	EFT Requirements and Options	Comment
District of Columbia	Mandated for: • Estimated tax returns if quarterly estimated tax liability exceed $5,000; and • Ballpark fee if DC gross receipts are $5 million or more for the prior tax year.	Voluntary EFT payments also allowed. Electronic Taxpayer Service Center Registration Application required. Noncompliance penalties may apply. A new tax portal, MyTax.DC, will be phased in and begin replacing eTSC in late October 2016. MyTax.DC and eTSC will be cross linked for taxpayer convenience during the transition.
Florida	Mandated for payment of income and estimated taxes if tax paid in prior fiscal year is $20,000 or more or if filed a consolidated return for every applicable tax period in prior fiscal year. Also mandated for taxpayers required to e-file.	Voluntary EFT payments also allowed. DR-600, Enrollment and Authorization for e-Services Program required. Noncompliance penalties may apply.
Georgia	Mandated for: • corporate estimated income tax in excess of $10,000; • withholding tax in excess of $1,000. Threshold for withholding tax is lowered to $500 for tax periods beginning after 2010. Mandated for payment of employee withholding taxes that exceed $50,000 for the 12-month lookback period and for third party payroll providers who prepare or remit withholding tax for more than 250 employers.	Voluntary EFT payments are allowed. Form EFT-001, Georgia EFT ACH-Debit Taxpayer Registration/Authorization Form or Form EFT-002, Georgia EFT ACH-Credit Taxpayer Registration/ Authorization Form required. Noncompliance penalties may apply.
Hawaii	Mandated for payment of income and estimated taxes if tax liability is over $100,000 in any taxable year. Mandated for employee withholding taxes if tax liability exceeds $40,000 annually.	Notwithstanding tax liability thresholds, a person required to pay any federal taxes by EFT may also be required to pay state taxes by EFT. Voluntary EFT payments are also allowed. Form EFT-1, Authorization Agreement for Electronic Funds Transfer required. Noncompliance penalties may apply. Exemptions may be granted for good cause.
Idaho	Mandated for payment of corporate income and estimated tax, and employee withholding taxes if amount due is $100,000 or greater.	Voluntary EFT payments also allowed. Electronic Funds Transfer Authorization required. Noncompliance penalties may apply.
Illinois	Mandated if tax liability is equal to: • $20,000 or more of annual corporation income and/or replacement tax liability; • $200,000 or more of annual individual income tax liability; or • more than $12,000 of employer income tax withholding liability for the previous 1 year look-back period.	Voluntary EFT payments also allowed. Form EFT-1, Authorization Agreement for Electronic Funds Transfer required. Noncompliance penalties may apply.
Indiana	Mandated for payment of estimated tax if estimated quarterly tax liability for current year or average estimated quarterly tax liability for preceding year exceeds $5,000. Mandated for all withholding tax payments.	Voluntary EFT payments also allowed. Form EFT-1, Authorization Agreement for Electronic Funds Transfer required. Noncompliance penalties may apply. If using EFT for estimated tax, Form IT-6 is not required.

Jurisdiction	EFT Requirements and Options	Comment
Iowa	Mandated if more than $20,000 in estimated tax is remitted in a quarter or if estimated tax liability for preceding year exceeds $80,000. Mandated for employee withholding tax if remit over $10,000 monthly.	Allows electronic filing and payment as alternative to EFT. Voluntary EFT payments also allowed. Authorization Agreement for Electronic Funds Transfer by ACH Credit required for ACH Credit. Noncompliance penalties may apply.
Kansas	Mandated for payment of employee withholding taxes if total tax liability exceeds $45,000 in any calendar year.	Voluntary EFT payments also allowed. Authorization form required. Noncompliance penalties may apply.
Kentucky	Mandated for payment of employee withholding taxes if average payment per reporting period exceeds $25,000 in the 12-month lookback period.	Waivers may be granted in certain circumstances. Revenue Form 10A070, Authorization Agreement for Electronic Funds Transfer required. Noncompliance penalties may apply. Voluntary EFT payments also allowed, including estimated and extension payments for limited liability entities beginning January 2013.
Louisiana	Mandated for: • payment of tax due in connection with the filing of any return, report, or other document that exceeds $5,000; • taxpayers that file tax returns more frequently than monthly and, during the preceding 12-month period, the average total payments exceed $5,000 per month; and • taxpayers that file withholding tax returns and payments on behalf of other taxpayers and, during the preceding 12-month period, the average total payments for all tax returns filed exceed $5,000 per month.	Exemption for hardship allowed (effective June 12, 2017). Waivers may be granted in certain other circumstances. Voluntary EFT payments also allowed (Form R-20193-L, Authorization Agreement for ACH Debit and Credit Tax Payments, required). Noncompliance penalties may apply.
Maine	Mandated if combined tax liability to state for all tax types is equal to or greater than threshold amount during most recent 12-month lookback period. Threshold amounts for calendar years since 2008 ($400,000 prior to 2008) are as follows: • 2008 - $100,000; • 2009 - $50,000; • 2010 - $25,000; • 2011 - $18,000; • 2012 - $16,000; • 2013 - $14,000; • 2014 - $12,000; and • 2015 and beyond - $10,000.	Mandated taxpayer has 60 days or first applicable due date, whichever is later, after receipt of information and instructions to begin remittance of tax by EFT. Waivers may be granted in certain circumstances. Voluntary EFT payments also allowed. Form EFT required if ACH Teledebit telephone payment system or ACH Credit payment method used. Noncompliance penalties may apply.
Maryland	Mandated for payment of income, estimated, and employee withholding taxes if tax liability is for $10,000 or more.	Voluntary EFT payments also allowed. Form RAD072, Authorization Agreement for Electronic Funds Transfer required. Noncompliance penalties may apply.

Jurisdiction	EFT Requirements and Options	Comment
Massachusetts	Mandated for: • corporate excise tax payments, including estimated tax and extension payments, by corporations with any single or combined amount of gross receipts or sales greater than $100,000 or that previously met an electronic filing threshold; • corporate excise tax payments, including estimated tax and extension payments, by S corporations with gross income over $100,000; • corporate excise tax payments, including estimated tax payments, by financial institutions, insurance companies, and public utilities with income of $100,000 or more; • corporate excise tax payments by a principal reporting corporation on behalf of taxpayer members of a combined group; • composite income tax payments, including estimated tax and extension payments, by pass-through entities on behalf of nonresident S corporation shareholders, partners, and members; • income tax withholding and estimated tax payments by pass-through entities on behalf of nonexempt S corporation shareholders, partners, and members; • corporate excise and personal income tax extension payments of $5,000 or more; • income tax payments, including estimated tax payments, by fiduciaries with total net taxable income of $50,000 or more; • withholding, room occupancy, and sales and use tax payments by employers, operators, and vendors with combined tax liability of $5,000; • withholding tax payments by third party bulk filers; and • pension payers withholding income tax for payees.	Waivers may be granted in certain circumstances. Voluntary EFT payments also allowed. Registration required. Noncompliance penalties may apply.
Michigan	Mandated for payment of employee withholding taxes if tax liability averages $40,000 or more each month of previous calendar year.	Voluntary EFT payments also allowed. Form 2248, Electronic Funds Transfer (EFT) Debit Application or Form 2328, Electronic Funds Transfer (EFT) Credit Application required. Noncompliance penalties may apply.
Minnesota	Mandated for payment of estimated and employee withholding taxes if aggregate amount is $10,000 or more in prior fiscal year ending June 30. Mandated for third party bulk filers of withholding tax returns.	Voluntary EFT payments also allowed. Registration required. Noncompliance penalties may apply. Taxpayers required to pay business taxes electronically for one year must continue to do so for all future years. Taxpayers required to pay any business tax electronically must pay all Minnesota taxes electronically.

Jurisdiction	EFT Requirements and Options	Comment
Mississippi	Mandated for withholding tax payroll service providers.	EFT may be required for payment of tax amounts of $20,000 or more, but is not currently required for income, estimated, or employee withholding taxes. Voluntary EFT payments allowed for withholding tax. Registration Application for Electronic Funds Transfer required.
Missouri	Mandated for employers subject to quarter-monthly withholding payment requirement.	Voluntary EFT payments also allowed. DOR-4572, Electronic Filing Trading Partner Agreement (TPA) required.
Montana	Mandated for tax liabilities of $500,000 or more.	Voluntary EFT also allowed for payment of income, estimated, and employee withholding taxes. Registration required.
Nebraska	Mandated for all payments of income, estimated, and employee withholding taxes if taxpayer made tax payments above designated threshold for that same tax program in a prior tax year. The EFT threshold is phased-in as follows: • July 2013—$9,000; • July 2014—$8,000; • July 2015—$7,000; • July 2016—$6,000; and • July 2017—$5,000.	Voluntary EFT payments also allowed. Noncompliance penalties may apply. Form 27EFT, Authorization Agreement for Electronic Funds Transfer (EFT) of Tax Payments has been eliminated.
New Hampshire	Mandated for the payment of business profits tax and/or the business enterprise tax if tax liability is $100,000 or more for the most recently filed tax year.	Voluntary EFT payments also allowed. Registration required. Noncompliance penalties may apply.
New Jersey	Mandated for payment of income, estimated, and employee withholding taxes if prior year tax liability in any one tax is $10,000 or more. Effective for tax years beginning on or after Jan. 1, 2016, all taxpayers and tax preparers must file CBT returns and make payments electronically. The mandate includes all CBT returns, estimated payments, extensions, and vouchers.	EFT threshold not applicable to taxpayers that sell, store, deliver, transport, or generate natural gas or electricity. Voluntary EFT payments also allowed. Form EFT1-D, Authorization Agreement for Electronic Funds Transfer (EFT) for ACH debit or Form EFT1-C, Authorization Agreement for Electronic Funds Transfer (EFT) for ACH credit. Noncompliance penalties may apply.
New Mexico	Mandated (EFT or other special payment method) for combined reporting system (CRS) taxes (which includes employee withholding tax) if average CRS tax liability was $25,000 or more per month during the previous calendar year.	Voluntary EFT payments also allowed for CRS taxes and corporate income taxes. Noncompliance penalties may apply.
New York	Mandated for payment of employee withholding taxes if aggregate amount withheld in semiannual period is $35,000 or more. Mandated for estimated corporate franchise tax payments.	Exempt if the aggregate tax withheld, pursuant to most recent annual reconciliation of withholding, is less than $100,000. PrompTax Withholding Tax Enrollment Application required. May apply for permission to participate on a voluntary basis. Noncompliance penalties may apply.

Jurisdiction	EFT Requirements and Options	Comment
North Carolina	Mandated for taxpayers with average tax liability of at least $20,000 per month during a 12-month period. Also required for corporation estimated income tax if required to pay federal estimated income tax by EFT. Mandated for payment of employee withholding tax if liability averages $20,000 or more monthly.	Threshold applies separately for each tax group. Voluntary EFT payments also allowed. Form EFT-100, Electronic Funds Transfer Authorization Agreement required. Noncompliance penalties apply.
North Dakota	Voluntary EFT payment of income, estimated, and employee withholding taxes is allowed.	Form 301-EF Application for Withholding E-File Tax Participation required.
Ohio	Mandated for payment of CAT returns. Mandated for payment of former corporate franchise tax if total liability for taxes, less all nonrefundable credits, exceeds $50,000 for the second preceding tax year. Mandated for employee withholding tax if actual or required payments exceeded $84,000 during 12-month lookback period.	If combined franchise tax report, the tax liability is aggregated for purposes of determining the threshold. EFT Authorization Agreement required. Waivers may be granted in certain circumstances. Noncompliance penalties may apply.
Oklahoma	Voluntary EFT payment of income, estimated, and employee withholding taxes is allowed.	Authorization agreement required.
Oregon	Mandated for payment of estimated and employee withholding taxes if required to make federal tax payments by EFT.	Waivers may be granted in certain circumstances. Voluntary EFT payments also allowed. ACH Debit Authorization Agreement and Application for Combined Payroll Tax and Assessment, ACH Credit Agreement and Application for Combined Payroll Tax and Assessment, ACH Debit Authorization Agreement and Application for Estimated Corporate Excise and Income Tax, or ACH Credit Agreement and Application for Estimated Corporation Excise and Income Tax required. Noncompliance penalties may apply.
Pennsylvania	Mandated for payment of income, estimated, and employee withholding tax payments of $1,000 ($10,000 before 2014) or more.	Voluntary EFT payments also allowed. Form REV-331A, EFT Authorization Agreement required. Noncompliance penalties may apply.
Rhode Island	Mandated for payment of income, estimated, and employee withholding taxes if tax exceeds $10,000 or if required to make federal withholding tax payments by EFT. Mandated for payment of withholding tax for a person is required to withhold with 10 or more employees.	Voluntary EFT payments also allowed. Form RI-EFT-1, Authorization Agreement for Electronic Funds Transfer required. Penalty if fail to pay by EFT of lesser of 5% or $500, unless due to reasonable cause. Beginning January 1, 2020, every employer required to deduct and withhold tax, and who had an average tax amount of $200 or more per month for the previous calendar year, must file returns electronically.

Jurisdiction	EFT Requirements and Options	Comment
South Carolina	Allowed. Payments of income, estimated, and employee withholding taxes of $15,000 or more owed for a filing period during previous 12 months must be paid in cash or by EFT.	Seasonal filers exempt. Voluntary EFT payments also allowed. Application for Electronic Funds Transfer required. Noncompliance penalties may apply.
Tennessee	Mandated for payments related to franchise and excise tax returns (FAE 170), effective Jan. 1, 2014.	Electronic Funds Transfer Agreement required. Noncompliance penalties may apply.
Texas	Mandated for payment of franchise taxes if amount paid in preceding fiscal year in single tax payment category was $10,000 or more or if Comptroller reasonably anticipates that taxpayer will pay at least same amount in current fiscal year.	Waivers may be granted in certain circumstances. Voluntary EFT payments also allowed. TEXNET Enrollment Form, 00-107 required. Noncompliance penalties may apply.
Utah	Voluntary EFT payment of corporate income taxes and employee withholding taxes is allowed.	TC-86, Registration to Make Utah Tax Payments Through EFT ACH Credit required.
Vermont	Mandated for payment of employee withholding taxes if employer reasonably expects withholding to be $9,000 or more quarterly.	Voluntary payment of employee withholding taxes is also allowed. Electronic Funds Transfer Enrollment Form required.
Virginia	Mandated for payment of income, estimated, and employee withholding taxes if average monthly tax liability exceeds $20,000. Mandated for all payments and annual reconciliation submission of employee withholding tax, including pass-through entity withholding tax payments, effective January 1, 2015. Mandated for corporate estimated tax payments and annual income tax final payment, effective January 1, 2013.	Voluntary EFT payments also allowed. Registration required. Noncompliance penalties may apply.
West Virginia	Mandated for all business taxes if any single business tax during the previous tax is: • $25,000 or more for tax years before 2019; and • $50,000 or more for tax years beginning on or after January 1, 2019.	Noncompliance penalties may apply. Taxpayers can submit written request for waiver from mandatory EFT requirement by December 1 before each tax year using Form WV/EFT-WR.
Wisconsin	Mandated for payment of income and estimated taxes if net tax less refundable credits on prior year's return was $1,000 or more. Mandated for employee withholding tax if required deposits were $300 or more in prior calendar year. Mandated for pass-through entity nonresident withholding payments.	Waivers may be granted in certain circumstances. Voluntary EFT payments also allowed. Online registration request required. For withholding deposits, EFT Registration and Payment System no longer available after Dec. 31, 2009. System is replaced by *My Tax Account* service.

EFT Requirements and Options (Personal Income)

This chart indicates whether electronic payments are allowed or required.

Jurisdiction	EFT Requirements and Options	Comment
Alabama	Electronic payments are allowed but not required.	
Arizona	Electronic payments are allowed but not required.	
Arkansas	Electronic payments are allowed but not required.	
California	Electronic payments required if estimated tax installment or extension request payment exceeds $20,000, or if total annual tax liability exceeds $80,000.	
Colorado	Electronic payments are allowed but not required.	
Connecticut	May be required if prior year's tax liability exceeded $4,000 ($10,000 prior to July 1, 2010). Optional for other taxpayers.	Department notifies taxpayers who are required to pay by EFT.
Delaware	Online payments by direct debit or credit card up to $2,500 allowed, but not required, for individual income and estimated taxes.	
District of Columbia	Electronic payments are allowed but not required.	
Georgia	May be required if estimated tax payments exceed $500. Optional for other taxpayers.	
Hawaii	May be required if annual tax liability is greater than $100,000. Optional for other taxpayers.	Department notifies taxpayers who are required to pay by EFT.
Idaho	Electronic payments are allowed but not required.	
Illinois	Required if annual tax liability is $200,000 or more. Optional for other taxpayers.	Department notifies taxpayers who are required to pay by EFT.
Indiana	Electronic payments are allowed but not required.	
Iowa	Electronic payments are allowed but not required.	
Kansas	Electronic payments are allowed but not required.	
Kentucky	Electronic payments are allowed but not required.	
Louisiana	Electronic payments are allowed but not required.	

Jurisdiction	EFT Requirements and Options	Comment
Maine	Required if annual tax liability in most recent lookback period was more than threshold amount. Threshold amounts for calendar years since 2008 ($400,000 prior to 2008) are as follows: • 2008 - $100,000; • 2009 - $50,000; • 2010 - $25,000; • 2011 - $18,000; • 2012 - $16,000; • 2013 - $14,000; • 2014 - $12,000; and • 2015 and beyond - $10,000.	Department notifies taxpayers who are required to pay by EFT.
Maryland	Electronic payments are allowed but not required.	
Massachusetts	Electronic payments are allowed but not required.	
Michigan	Allowed.	
Minnesota	Electronic payments are allowed but not required.	
Mississippi	Electronic payments are allowed but not required.	
Missouri	Electronic payments are allowed but not required.	
Montana	Required for payments of $500,000 or more.	
Nebraska	Electronic payments are allowed but not required.	
New Hampshire	Electronic payments are allowed but not required.	
New Jersey	Electronic payments are allowed but not required.	
New Mexico	Electronic payments are allowed but not required.	
New York	Electronic payments are allowed but not required.	
North Carolina	Electronic payments are allowed but not required.	
North Dakota	Electronic payments are allowed but not required.	
Ohio	Electronic payments are allowed but not required.	
Oklahoma	Electronic payments are allowed but not required.	
Oregon	Electronic payments are allowed but not required.	

Jurisdiction	EFT Requirements and Options	Comment
Pennsylvania	Electronic payments are allowed but not required.	
Rhode Island	Not allowed.	
South Carolina	Electronic payments are allowed but not required.	Payments of $15,000 or more must be made in cash or by EFT.
Tennessee	Required if average payments are $10,000 or more. Optional for other taxpayers. Preparers using commercially available software must pay by EFT, effective Jan. 1, 2014.	Department notifies taxpayers who are required to pay by EFT.
Utah	Electronic payments are allowed but not required.	
Vermont	Electronic payments are allowed but not required.	
Virginia	Electronic payments are allowed but not required.	
West Virginia	Required for payments of $100,000 or more. Optional for other taxpayers.	Department notifies taxpayers who are required to pay by EFT.
Wisconsin	Estimated tax must be paid by EFT if estimated tax payments in prior taxable year were $2,000 or more. Optional for other taxpayers.	

Estimated Tax—S Corporations

The following chart indicates whether estimated tax payments are required on behalf of nonresident S corporation shareholders. Many states require the payment of estimated tax for nonresident shareholders only when an election is made to file a composite return and unwitheld income tax liability of shareholders included in the return is expected to exceed a threshold amount. Payment forms, due dates, and installment percentages are noted in the Comments column (due dates listed are for calendar year filers). The chart does not reflect whether S corporations are required to pay estimated taxes on entity-level income or to withhold taxes on behalf of nonresidents.

Composite return and payment requirements are covered in a chart under the topic Composite Returns—S Corporations. Rules requiring pass-through entities to withhold tax on behalf of owners (instead of paying estimated tax) are covered under the topic Withholding—S Corporations.

Jurisdiction	S Corporations	Comment
Alabama	Not required.	Voluntary payments on composite basis allowed with Form BIT-V (payment type PTE-C should be checked). Four equal installments are due on April 15, June 15, September 15, and December 15.
Alaska	N/A	No personal income tax.
Arizona	Not required.	Voluntary payments on composite basis allowed with Form 140ES. Four equal installments are due on April 15, June 15, September 15, and January 15.
Arkansas	Required if a composite return is filed and unwithheld liability of nonresident owner is $1,000 or more.	Payments made with Form AR1000CRES due in four equal installments on April 15, June 15, September 15, and January 15.
California	Required if a group (composite) return is filed and unwithheld liability of nonresident owner is $500 or more.	Payments made with Form 540-ES due on April 15, June 15, September 15, and January 15. Installment minimums equal to 30% for the first payment, 40% for the second payment, 0% for the third payment, and 30% for the fourth payment. For 2018 first payment, due date has been extended to April 17, 2018, to conform with corresponding federal extension.
Colorado	Required if a composite return is filed and unwithheld liability of nonresident owner is $1,000 or more.	Payments made with Form 106EP due in four equal installments on April 15, June 15, September 15, and January 15. **Coronavirus (COVID-19) Pandemic Filing/Payment Relief:** Penalties for estimated payments due on and after April 15, 2020, but on or before June 15, 2020, are waived until July 15, 2020.

Jurisdiction	S Corporations	Comment
Connecticut	S corporations must pay estimated pass-through entity tax. Effective for tax years after 2018, threshold is $1,000 or more of annual tax liability. No estimated composite tax payment requirements for nonresidents.	Shareholders can claim a credit for pass-through entity tax paid. **Coronavirus (COVID-19) Pandemic Filing/Payment Relief** July 15, 2020 for returns and payments due between March 15 and July 15, 2020.
Delaware	Required.	Payments made with Form 1100P due in four installments on April 15 (50%), June 15 (20%), September 15 (20%), and December 15 (10%).
District of Columbia	N/A	Taxed same as C corporations.
Florida	N/A	No personal income tax.
Georgia	Required if a composite return is filed and composite tax is $500 or more.	Payments made with Form CR-ES due in four equal installments on April 15, June 15, September 15, and January 15.
Hawaii	Not required.	Voluntary payments on composite basis allowed with Form N-1. Four equal installments are due on April 20, June 20, September 20, and January 20.
Idaho	Not required.	
Illinois	Not required.	Form IL-1120-ST-V for voluntary prepayment of pass-through withholding tax.
Indiana	Not required.	
Iowa	Not required.	Voluntary payments on composite basis allowed with Form IA 1040ES. Four equal installments are due on April 30, June 30, September 30, and January 31.
Kansas	Not required.	
Kentucky	Required for entities that must withhold for nonresident owners or that file composite returns on behalf of electing nonresident individual owners, if estimated tax liability is expected to exceed: • $500 for individual owners; or • $5,000 for corporate owners.	Payments made with Form 740NP-WH-ES due (1) in four equal installments on April 15, June 15, September 15, and January 15 for individual owners; or (2) in three installments on June 15 (50%), September 15 (25%), and December 15 (25%) for corporate owners. **Coronavirus (COVID-19) Pandemic Filing/Payment Relief** July 15, 2020 due date for returns and payments due on and after April 15, 2020 and before July 15, 2020. Penalty and interest calculation will begin July 16, 2020.
Louisiana	N/A	Taxed same as C corporations.

Jurisdiction	S Corporations	Comment
Maine	Not required.	Voluntary payments on composite basis allowed with Form 1040ES-ME. Four equal installments are due on April 15, June 15, September 15, and January 15. For 2018, due date for first installment has been extended to April 17, 2018, to conform with corresponding federal extension.
Maryland	Required if tax liability exceeds $1,000.	Payments made with Form 510D due in four equal installments on April 15, June 15, September 15, and December 15. **Coronavirus (COVID-19) Pandemic Filing/Payment Relief:** Due date for first and second quarter 2020 estimated payments extended to July 15, 2020.
Massachusetts	Required if a composite return is filed and unwithheld tax liability of nonresident owner is $400 or more.	Payments must be made electronically, through ACH debit, in four equal installments on April 15, June 15, September 15, and January 15.
Michigan	Not required.	
Minnesota	Required if a composite return is filed and the sum of its estimated minimum fee, nonresident withholding and composite income tax for all nonresident shareholders electing to participate in the composite return, less any credits, is $500 or more.	Payments made with Form M72 due in four equal installments on April 15, June 15, September 15, and January 15.
Mississippi	Required if a composite return is filed and unwithheld tax liability of nonresident owner is $200 or more.	Payments made with Form 84-300 due in four equal installments on April 15, June 15, September 15, and December 15.
Missouri	Required if a composite return is filed and unwithheld tax liability of nonresident owner is $100 or more.	Payments made with Form MO-1040ES due in four equal installments on April 15, June 15, September 15, and January 15.
Montana	Required if a composite return is filed and S corporation expects to owe a composite income tax liability of at least $500.	Payments made with Form SB due in four equal installments on April 15, June 15, September 15, and January 15.
Nebraska	Not required.	
Nevada	N/A, because state does not tax general business corporation or pass-through income.	
New Hampshire	N/A	Taxed same as C corporations.
New Jersey	Required if S corporation: • previously filed composite return; and • estimated total income tax liability for current year composite return exceeds $400.	Payments made with Form NJ-1040-ES due in four equal installments on April 15, June 15, September 15, and January 15.
New Mexico	Not required.	

Jurisdiction	S Corporations	Comment
New York	Required if tax liability of nonresident owner is more than $300. Not required if: • individual nonresident owner is included in a group (composite) return; or • individual nonresident owner certifies that he or she will comply with income tax filing requirements.	Payments made with Form IT-2658. Entire amount due with first payment or in four equal installments on April 15, June 15, September 15, and January 15.
North Carolina	Required if nonresident individual shareholder fails to file shareholder agreement to file return and pay tax.	Estimated tax due with S corporation's annual return.
North Dakota	Not required.	
Ohio	Required if a composite return is filed and unwithheld tax liability of nonresident owners is $500 or more.	Payments made with Form IT 4708ES due either in four equal installments on April 15, June 15, September 15, and January 15, or in four installments as follows: • April 15 - 22.5% of tax due for current year; • June 15 - 45% of current year tax due less previous payments; • September 15 - 67.5% of current year tax due less previous payments; and • January 15 - 90% of current year tax due less previous payments.
Oklahoma	Required if the amount that must be withheld from all nonresident shareholders for the taxable year expected to exceed $500.	Voluntary estimated withholding payments allowed by other S corporations. Payments made with Form OW-9-EW due in equal installments on April 30, July 31, October 31, and January 31.
Oregon	Required if a composite return is filed and unwithheld tax liability of nonresident owner is $1,000 or more for an individual or $500 or more for a corporation.	Payments made with Form OC-V due in four equal installments on April 15, June 15, September 15, and January 15 (or December 15 for corporate owners) where majority of electing owners are calendar year filers; or on the 15th day of the fourth, sixth, ninth, and 12th months following the beginning of the fiscal year where majority of electing owners are fiscal year filers.
Pennsylvania	Not required.	
Rhode Island	Required for S corporations withholding income tax on nonresident shareholders if the aggregate tax liability derived from or connected with state sources from the S corporation is expected to be $250 or more.	Payments made with Form RI 1096PT-ES due in four equal installments on April 15, June 15, September 15, and January 15. Pass-through entities that elect to pay tax at the entity level may opt to make estimated payments of entity-level tax using Form BUS-EST. **Coronavirus (COVID-19) Pandemic Filing/Payment Relief:** July 15, 2020, due date for April and June estimated payments.

Jurisdiction	S Corporations	Comment
South Carolina	Required on behalf of any nonresident shareholder participating in the composite return whose expected tax owed with the composite return will be $100 or more.	Payments made with Form SC1040ES due in four equal installments on April 15, June 15, September 15, and January 15. **COVID-19 Filing/Payment Relief:** July 15, 2020 due date for April 15 and June 15, 2020 installments.
South Dakota	N/A, because state does not tax general business corporation or pass-through income.	
Tennessee	Not required.	
Texas	N/A	No personal income tax.
Utah	Not required.	
Vermont	Required.	Payments made with Form WH-435 due in four equal installments on April 15, June 15, September 15, and January 15; however, an entity with a single owner and a tax liability of $250 or less in the prior year (or an entity with two or more owners and a tax liability of $500 or less in the prior year) may file entire estimated amount on January 15. A safe harbor catch-up payment is due by April 15. **COVID-19 Filing/Payment Relief:** July 15, 2020 due date for June 15, 2020 installment.
Virginia	Required if a unified (composite) return is filed and unwithheld liability of nonresident owner exceeds $150.	Payments made with Form 770ES due in four equal installments on May 1, June 15, September 15, and January 15.
Washington	N/A, because state does not tax general business corporation or pass-through income.	
West Virginia	Required for nonresident withholding tax.	Equal installments on: • April 15, June 15, September 15, and December 15; or • 15th day of the fourth, sixth, ninth and twelfth months of the tax year. **Coronavirus (COVID-19) Pandemic Filing/Payment Relief** July 15, 2020 due date for first and second quarter installments.
Wisconsin	Required for nonresident withholding tax.	Payments must be made electronically in four equal installments on March 15, June 15, September 15, and December 15. If electronic payment presents an undue hardship and a waiver is granted, payments made with Form PW-ES. **COVID-19 Filing/Payment Relief:** July 15, 2020 due date for June 15, 2020 installment.
Wyoming	N/A, because state does not tax general business corporation or pass-through income.	

Estimated Tax for Nonresident Owners—Partnerships, LLCs, and LLPs

The following chart indicates whether estimated tax payments are required on behalf of nonresident partners or LLC members. Many states require the payment of estimated tax for nonresident partners or members only when an election is made to file a composite return and unwitheld income tax liability of partners or members included in the return is expected to exceed a threshold amount. Payment forms, due dates, and installment percentages are noted in the Comments column (due dates listed are for calendar year filers). The chart does not reflect whether partnerships, LLPs, and LLCs are required to pay estimated taxes on entity-level income or to withhold taxes on behalf of nonresidents.

Rules requiring partnerships, LLPs, and LLCs to withhold tax on behalf of owners (instead of paying estimated tax) are covered under the topic Withholding—Partnerships, LLPs, and LLCs.

Jurisdiction	Partnerships, LLPs, and LLCs	Comment
Alabama	Not required.	Voluntary payments on composite basis allowed with Form BIT-V (payment type PTE-C should be checked). Four equal installments are due on April 15, June 15, September 15, and December 15.
Alaska	No	No personal income tax.
Arizona	Not required.	Voluntary payments on composite basis allowed with Form 140ES. Four equal installments are due on April 15, June 15, September 15, and January 15.
Arkansas	Required if a composite return is filed and unwithheld liability of nonresident owner is $1,000 or more.	Payments made with Form AR1000CRES due in four equal installments on April 15, June 15, September 15, and January 15.
California	Required if a group (composite) return is filed and unwithheld liability of nonresident owner is $500 or more.	Payments made with Form 540-ES due on April 15, June 15, September 15, and January 15. Installment minimums equal to 30% for the first payment, 40% for the second payment, 0% for the third payment, and 30% for the fourth payment. For 2018 first payment, due date has been extended to April 17, 2018, to conform with corresponding federal extension.
Colorado	Required if a composite return is filed and unwithheld liability of nonresident owner is $1,000 or more.	Payments made with Form 106EP due in four equal installments on April 15, June 15, September 15, and January 15. **Coronavirus (COVID-19) Pandemic Filing/Payment Relief:** Penalties for estimated payments due on and after April 15, 2020, but on or before June 15, 2020, are waived until July 15, 2020.

Jurisdiction	Partnerships, LLPs, and LLCs	Comment
Connecticut	Partnerships, LLPs, and LLCs must pay estimated pass-through entity tax. Effective for tax years after 2018, threshold is $1,000 or more of annual tax liability. No estimated composite tax payment requirements for nonresidents.	Partners and members can claim a credit for pass-through entity tax paid. **Coronavirus (COVID-19) Pandemic Filing/Payment Relief** July 15, 2020 for returns and payments due between March 15 and July 15, 2020.
Delaware	Required if a composite return is filed and unwithheld tax liability of nonresident owner is $400 or more.	Payments made with Form 200-ES due in four equal installments on April 30, June 15, September 15, and January 15.
District of Columbia	Not required.	
Florida	N/A	No personal income tax.
Georgia	Required if a composite return is filed and composite tax is $500 or more.	Payments made with Form CR-ES due in four equal installments on April 15, June 15, September 15, and January 15.
Hawaii	Not required.	
Idaho	Not required.	
Illinois	Not required.	Form IL-1065-V for voluntary prepayment of pass-through withholding tax.
Indiana	Not required.	
Iowa	Not required.	Voluntary payments on composite basis allowed with Form IA 1040ES. Four equal installments are due on April 30, June 30, September 30, and January 31.
Kansas	Not required.	
Kentucky	Required for entities that must withhold for nonresident owners or that file composite returns on behalf of electing nonresident individual owners, if estimated tax liability is expected to exceed: • $500 for individual owners; or • $5,000 for corporate owners.	Payments made with Form 740NP-WH-ES due (1) in four equal installments on April 15, June 15, September 15, and January 15 for individual owners; or (2) in three installments on June 15 (50%), September 15 (25%), and December 15 (25%) for corporate owners. **Coronavirus (COVID-19) Pandemic Filing/Payment Relief** July 15, 2020 due date for returns and payments due on and after April 15, 2020 and before July 15, 2020. Penalty and interest calculation will begin July 16, 2020.
Louisiana	Not required.	Voluntary payments on composite basis allowed with Form R-6922ES.
Maine	Not required.	Voluntary payments on composite basis allowed with Form 1040ES-ME. Four equal installments are due on April 15, June 15, September 15, and January 15. For 2018, due date for first installment has been extended to April 17, 2018, to conform with corresponding federal extension.

Jurisdiction	Partnerships, LLPs, and LLCs	Comment
Maryland	Required if tax liability exceeds $1,000.	Payments made with Form 510D due in four equal installments on April 15, June 15, September 15, and January 15. **Coronavirus (COVID-19) Pandemic Filing/Payment Relief:** Due date for first and second quarter 2020 estimated payments extended to July 15, 2020.
Massachusetts	Required if a composite return is filed and unwithheld tax liability of nonresident owner is $400 or more.	Payments must be made electronically, through ACH debit, in four equal installments on April 15, June 15, September 15, and January 15.
Michigan	Not required.	
Minnesota	Required if a composite return is filed and the sum of its estimated minimum fee, nonresident withholding and composite income tax for all nonresident partners electing to participate in the composite return, less any credits, is $500 or more.	Payments made with Form M71 due in four equal installments on April 15, June 15, September 15, and January 15.
Mississippi	Required if a composite return is filed and unwithheld tax liability of nonresident owner is $200 or more.	Payments made with Form 84-300 due in four equal installments on April 15, June 15, September 15, and January 15.
Missouri	Required if a composite return is filed and unwithheld tax liability of nonresident owner is $100 or more.	Payments made with Form MO-1040ES due in four equal installments on April 15, June 15, September 15, and January 15.
Montana	Required if a composite return is filed and partnership expects to owe a composite income tax liability of at least $500.	Payments made with Form PR due in equal installments on April 15, June 15, September 15, and January 15.
Nebraska	Not required.	
Nevada	N/A, because state does not tax general business corporation or pass-through income.	
New Hampshire	Not required.	
New Jersey	Required if: • entity previously filed composite return; and • estimated total income tax liability for current year composite return exceeds $400.	Payments made with Form NJ-1040-ES due in four equal installments on April 15, June 15, September 15, and January 15. Payments for partners made using Form NJ-1040-ES in 4 installments due on 15th day of the: • fourth; • sixth; • ninth; and • twelth month of tax year.
New Mexico	Not required.	

Jurisdiction	Partnerships, LLPs, and LLCs	Comment
New York	Required if tax liability of nonresident owner is more than $300. Not required if: • partnership is a publicly traded partnership; • individual nonresident owner is included in a group (composite) return; or • individual nonresident owner certifies that he or she will comply with income tax filing requirements.	Payments made with Form CT-2658 (corporate owners) or Form IT-2658 (individual owners). Entire amount due with first payment or in four equal installments on April 15, June 15, September 15, and January 15.
North Carolina	Not required.	
North Dakota	Not required.	
Ohio	Required if a composite return is filed and unwithheld tax liability of nonresident owners is $500 or more.	Payments made with Form IT 4708ES due either in four equal installments on April 15, June 15, September 15, and January 15, or in four installments as follows: • April 15 - 22.5% of tax due for current year; • June 15 - 45% of current year tax due less previous payments; • September 15 - 67.5% of current year tax due less previous payments; and • January 15 - 90% of current year tax due less previous payments.
Oklahoma	Required if the amount that must be withheld from all nonresident owners for the taxable year expected to exceed $500.	Voluntary estimated withholding payments allowed by other partnerships, LLPs and LLCs. Payments made with Form OW-9-EW due in equal installments on April 30, July 31, October 31, and January 31.
Oregon	Required if a composite return is filed and unwithheld tax liability of nonresident owner is $1,000 or more for an individual or $500 or more for a corporation.	Payments made with Form OC-V due in four equal installments on April 15, June 15, September 15, and January 15 (or December 15 for corporate owners) where majority of electing owners are calendar year filers; or on the 15th day of the fourth, sixth, ninth, and 12th months following the beginning of the fiscal year where majority of electing owners are fiscal year filers.
Pennsylvania	Not required.	
Rhode Island	Required for entities withholding income tax on nonresident owners if the aggregate tax liability derived from or connected with state sources from the entity is expected to be $250 or more.	Payments made with Form RI 1096PT-ES due in four equal installments on April 15, June 15, September 15, and January 15. Pass-through entities that elect to pay tax at the entity level may opt to make estimated payments of entity-level tax using Form BUS-EST. **Coronavirus (COVID-19) Pandemic Filing/Payment Relief:** July 15, 2020, due date for April and June estimated payments.

Jurisdiction	Partnerships, LLPs, and LLCs	Comment
South Carolina	Required on behalf of any nonresident parter participating in the composite return whose expected tax owed with the composite return will be $100 or more.	Payments made with Form SC1040ES due in four equal installments on April 15, June 15, September 15, and January 15. **COVID-19 Filing/Payment Relief:** July 15, 2020 due date for April 15 and June 15, 2020 installments.
South Dakota	N/A, because state does not tax general business corporation or pass-through income.	
Tennessee	Not required.	
Texas	N/A	No personal income tax.
Utah	Not required.	
Vermont	Required unless entity is engaged solely in business of operating federal new market tax credit projects in the state.	Payments made with Form WH-435 due in four equal installments on April 15, June 15, September 15, and January 15; however, an entity with a single owner and a tax liability of $250 or less in the prior year (or an entity with two or more owners and a tax liability of $500 or less in the prior year) may file entire estimated amount on January 15. A safe harbor catch-up payment is due by April 15. **COVID-19 Filing/Payment Relief:** July 15, 2020 due date for June 15, 2020 installment.
Virginia	Required if a unified (composite) return is filed and unwithheld liability of nonresident owner exceeds $150.	Payments made with Form 770ES due in four equal installments on May 1, June 15, September 15, and January 15.
Washington	N/A, because state does not tax general business corporation or pass-through income.	
West Virginia	Required for nonresident withholding tax.	Equal installments on: • April 15, June 15, September 15, and December 15; or • 15th day of the fourth, sixth, ninth and twelfth months of the tax year. **Coronavirus (COVID-19) Pandemic Filing/Payment Relief** July 15, 2020 due date for first and second quarter installments.
Wisconsin	Required for nonresident withholding tax.	Payments must be made electronically in four equal installments on March 15, June 15, September 15, and December 15. If electronic payment presents an undue hardship and a waiver is granted, payments made with Form PW-ES. **COVID-19 Filing/Payment Relief:** July 15, 2020 due date for June 15, 2020 installment.
Wyoming	N/A, because state does not tax general business corporation or pass-through income.	

Estimated Tax Requirements—AIM/ASIM

The following chart indicates whether a state will accept lower estimated tax payments for corporations that calculate their income using an annualized method (AIM) or adjusted seasonal income method (ASIM).

Jurisdiction	Annualized or Adjusted Seasonal Income Method (AIM/ASIM)	Comment
Alabama	Yes	
Alaska	Yes	
Arizona	Yes	
Arkansas	Yes	
California	Yes	
Colorado	Yes	
Connecticut	Yes	
Delaware	No	
District of Columbia	Yes	
Florida	No	
Georgia	Yes	
Hawaii	Yes	
Idaho	Yes	Only if income is annualized for federal purposes.
Illinois	Yes	
Indiana	Yes	
Iowa	Yes	
Kansas	Yes	
Kentucky	Yes **Tax years before 2019:** No	Convert federal Form 1120-W, Schedule A, to a Kentucky form by entering Kentucky at the top center of the worksheet.
Louisiana	Yes	
Maine	Yes	Taxpayer may establish through adequate records that the actual distribution of its tax liability supports a different allocation of the tax throughout the tax year.
Maryland	No	
Massachusetts	No	
Michigan	Yes	
Minnesota	Yes	
Mississippi	Yes	

Jurisdiction	Annualized or Adjusted Seasonal Income Method (AIM/ASIM)	Comment
Missouri	Yes	
Montana	Yes	
Nebraska	Yes	
Nevada	N/A, because state does not tax general business corporation or pass-through income.	
New Hampshire	Yes	
New Jersey	Yes	
New Mexico	Yes	
New York	Yes	
North Carolina	Yes	
North Dakota	Yes	
Ohio	No	
Oklahoma	Yes	
Oregon	Yes	
Pennsylvania	No	
Rhode Island	No	
South Carolina	Yes	
South Dakota	N/A, because state does not tax general business corporation or pass-through income.	
Tennessee	Yes	
Texas	There are no statutory or regulatory provisions regarding estimated taxes.	
Utah	Yes	A taxpayer that elects a different annualization period than the one used for federal purposes must make an election with the Utah Tax Commission at the same time required under IRC Sec. 6655.
Vermont	No	
Virginia	Yes	
Washington	N/A, because state does not tax general business corporation or pass-through income.	
West Virginia	Yes	
Wisconsin	Yes for AIM. No for ASIM.	
Wyoming	N/A, because state does not tax general business corporation or pass-through income.	

Estimated Tax Requirements—Installments/Forms

This chart shows the installment percentages, due dates, and form that must be filed for making state estimated tax payments for the current tax year, as well as, alternative payment methods authorized by states for corporations that meet the estimated tax threshold requirement after a specified date. In describing the alternative payment methods, this chart refers to calendar year taxpayers. Fiscal-year taxpayers should substitute the appropriate months.

Jurisdiction	Installments/Forms	Comment
Alabama	Four equal installments must be paid by the 15th of the fourth, sixth, ninth, and 12th months of taxable year.	**Coronavirus (COVID-19) Pandemic Filing/Payment Relief** July 15, 2020 due date for April 15, 2020, and June 15, 2020 installments.
Alaska	Four equal installments must be paid by the 15th of the fourth, sixth, ninth, and 12th months of the taxable year.	State does not provide for accelerated payment methods, even if threshold met after April. Form 6240, except electronic payments required for payments of $100,000 or more. **Coronavirus (COVID-19) Pandemic Filing/Payment Relief** July 15, 2020 for installments due on April 15, 2020 and before July 15, 2020. Waiver of penalties and interest if paid by July 15.
Arizona	Four equal installments must be paid by the 15th of the fourth, sixth, ninth, and 12th months of the taxable year.	State does not authorize alternative payment methods, even if threshold met after April. Form 120-ES
Arkansas	Four equal installments must be paid by the 15th of the fourth, sixth, ninth, and 12th months of the taxable year. In lieu of the fourth installment, taxpayer may file a return and pay tax by the last day of the first month following the close of the income year.	A taxpayer who first meets the threshold requirements between April 15 and September 15 payments may be made in equal installments with the first payment due at the time the declaration is filed and remaining payments due at the subsequent installment due dates. If threshold is met after September 15 and before the following January 15, estimated tax must be paid in full with the declaration. AR 1100-ESCT
California	Estimated tax in excess of $800 paid in three installments as follows: • 30% by the 15th day of the fourth month of the taxable year; • 40% by the 15th day of the sixth month of the taxable year; and • 30% by the 15th day of the 12th month of the taxable year.	Estimated tax payments of $800 or less paid in full on the 15th of the fourth month of the corporation's taxable year. A taxpayer who first meets the threshold filing requirements after April 1, must adjust the amount of the installment due, depending on the quarter in which the requirements are first met. Form 100-ES. **Coronavirus (COVID-19) Pandemic Filing/Payment Relief** July 15, 2020 due date for first and second quarters of 2020.

Jurisdiction	Installments/Forms	Comment
Colorado	Four equal installments due on the 15th of the fourth, sixth, ninth, and 12th months of the taxable year.	State does not authorize alternative payment methods, even if threshold met after April. Form 112-EP **Coronavirus (COVID-19) Pandemic Filing/Payment Relief:** Penalties for estimated payments due on and after April 15, 2020, but on or before June 15, 2020, are waived until July 15, 2020.
Connecticut	Payments due according to the following schedule: 30% by the 15th day of 3rd month of income year; 40% by 15th day of 6th month of income year; 10% by 15th day of 9th month of income year; and 20% by 15th day of 12th month of income year.	State does not authorize alternative payment methods, even if threshold met after April. Forms CT-1120 ESA; CT-1120 ESB; CT-1120 ESC; CT-1120 ESD. **Coronavirus (COVID-19) Pandemic Filing/Payment Relief** July 15, 2020 for returns and payments due between March 15 and July 15, 2020.
Delaware	Installments due as follows: • 50% on April 15 (April 1 for tax years before 2017) or 15th day of 4th month (1st day of 4th month for tax years before 2017) of corporation's fiscal year; • 20% on June 15 or 15th day of 6th month of corporation's fiscal year; • 20% on September 15 or 15th day of 9th month of corporation's fiscal year; and • 10% on December 15 or 15th day of 12th month of corporation's fiscal year. Installments for certain small businesses due in four equal installments of 25% by the same due dates as other corporations.	State does not authorize alternative payment methods, as there are no filing threshold requirements. Form 1100-T **Coronavirus (COVID-19) Pandemic Filing/Payment Relief** July 15, 2020 installment due date for April 15, 2020 installment.
District of Columbia	Four equal installments must be paid by the 15th of the fourth, sixth, ninth, and 12th months of the taxable year.	A taxpayer who first meets the threshold filing requirements after April 15, must spread the estimated tax payments equally over the remaining installments, depending on the date in which the requirements are first met. Form D-20ES
Florida	Equal installments of 25% due by: • May 31 or before 1st day of 6th month of taxpayer's fiscal-year; • June 30 or before 1st day of 7th month of taxpayer's fiscal- year; • September 30 or before 1st day of 10th month of taxpayer's fiscal-year; and • December 31 or before 1st day of following taxable year.	Form F-1120ES Effective for tax years before 2017, first installment of estimated tax was due April 30 or before 1st day of 5th month of taxpayer's fiscal-year. Effective for tax years beginning on or after January 1, 2017, and before January 1, 2026, first installment for taxpayers with a June 30 taxable year end is due before 1st day of 5th month of the taxable year. A taxpayer that first meets the threshold filing requirements after the first installment due date must spread the estimated tax payments equally over the remaining installments, depending on the date when the requirements are first met.

Jurisdiction	Installments/Forms	Comment
Georgia	Four equal installments due on the 15th of the fourth, sixth, ninth, and 12th months of the taxable year.	**Coronavirus (COVID-19) Pandemic Filing/Payment Relief** Payments due after April 15, 2020, and before July 15, 2020 due July 15, 2020. A taxpayer who first meets the threshold filing requirements after April 1, must spread the estimated tax payments equally over the remaining installments, depending on the quarter in which the requirements are first met. Form 602-ES
Hawaii	Four equal installments due on the 20th of the fourth, sixth, and ninth months of the current taxable year, and the 20th of the first month of the following taxable year.	A taxpayer who first meets the threshold filing requirements after April 20, must spread the estimated tax payments equally over the remaining installments, depending on the date in which the requirements are first met. Form N-3
Idaho	Four equal installments due on 15th of the fourth, sixth, ninth, and 12th months of the taxable year.	Form 41ES
Illinois	Four equal installments due on the 15th of the fourth, sixth, ninth, and 12th months of the taxable year	Form IL-1120-V Form IL-1120-ES for tax years before 2019.
Indiana	Four equal installments due on the 20th of the fourth, sixth, ninth, and 12th months of the taxable year.	State does not authorize alternative payment methods, even if threshold met after April. Form IT-6
Iowa	Four equal installments due on the last day of the fourth, sixth, ninth, and 12th months of the taxable year.	A taxpayer who first meets the threshold filing requirements after April 30, must spread the estimated tax payments equally over the remaining installments, depending on the date in which the requirements are first met. Form IA 1120ES
Kansas	Four equal installments must be paid by the 15th of the fourth, sixth, ninth, and 12th months of the taxable year.	A taxpayer who first meets the threshold filing requirements after April 1, must spread the estimated tax payments equally over the remaining installments, depending on the quarter in which the requirements are first met. Form K-120ES **Coronavirus (COVID-19) Pandemic Filing/Payment Relief** Waiver of penalty and interest for estimated tax payments due April 15, 2020 and made before July 15, 2020.

Jurisdiction	Installments/Forms	Comment
Kentucky	Equal installments of 25% due by: • April 15 or 15th day of the 4th month of the fiscal year; • June 15 or 15th day of the 6th month of the fiscal year; • September 15 or 15th day of the 9th month of the fiscal year; and • December 15 or 15th day of the 12th month of the fiscal year.	Form 720ES **Coronavirus (COVID-19) Pandemic Filing/Payment Relief** July 15, 2020 due date for returns and payments due on and after April 15, 2020 and before July 15, 2020. Penalty and interest calculation will begin July 16, 2020. **Tax years before 2019:** Installments due as follows: • 50% by June 15 or 15th day of the 6th month of the fiscal year; • 25% by September 15 or 15th day of the 9th month of the fiscal year; and • 25% by December 15 or 15th day of the 12th month of the fiscal year. A taxpayer that first met the threshold filing requirements after June 1, but prior to September 2, was required to pay 75% of the estimated tax liability on September 15 and 25% on December 15. A taxpayer that first met the filing threshold after September 1 was required to pay 100% of the liability by December 15.
Louisiana	Four equal installments must be paid by the 15th of the fourth, sixth, ninth, and 12th months of the taxable year.	A taxpayer who first meets the threshold filing requirements after April 1 must spread the estimated tax payments equally over the remaining installments, depending on the date in which the requirements are first met. Form CIFT-620ES
Maine	Four equal installments due on the 15th of the fourth, sixth, ninth, and 12th months of the taxable year.	For 2018, due date for first installment has been extended to April 17, 2018, to conform with corresponding federal extension. State does not authorize alternative payment methods, even if threshold met after April. Form 1120ES-ME **Coronavirus (COVID-19) Pandemic Filing/Payment Relief:** Estimated payments for first and second quarter of 2020 extended to July 15, 2020.
Maryland	Four equal installments due on the 15th of the fourth, sixth, ninth, and 12th months of the taxable year.	State does not authorize alternative payment methods, even if threshold met after April. Form 500D **Coronavirus (COVID-19) Pandemic Filing/Payment Relief:** Due date for first and second quarter 2020 estimated payments extended to July 15, 2020.

Jurisdiction	Installments/Forms	Comment
Massachusetts	Payments equal to 40%, 25%, 25%, and 10% due on the 15th of the third, sixth, ninth, and 12th months of the taxable year. 30-25-25-20% for new corporations employing less than 10 persons in their first full taxable year.	• 65-25-10% (55–25–20% for new corporations) on the 15th of the sixth, ninth, and 12th months of the taxable year for corporations that first meet threshold requirement after February and before June. • 90-10% (80–20% for new corporations) on the 15th of ninth and 12th months of the taxable year for corporations that first meet threshold requirement after May and before September. • 100% on the 15th of the 12th month for corporations that first meet the threshold after August and before December. Form 355-ES, except electronic payments required by certain corporations.
Michigan	Four equal installments due by 15th day of first month following each quarter.	No alternative payment methods authorized. Form 4913 for corporate income tax and MBT. **Coronavirus (COVID-19) Pandemic Filing/Payment Relief** July 15, 2020 due date for April 15, 2020 income tax installment.
Minnesota	Four equal installments due on the 15th of the third, sixth, ninth, and 12th months of the taxable year.	State does not authorize alternative payment methods, even if threshold met after March. Form M-18
Mississippi	Four equal installments due on the 15th of the fourth, sixth, ninth, and 12th months of the taxable year.	Taxpayers who first meet the threshold after April 15 and before September 16, may make payments in equal installments, with the first installment due when the threshold is first met and equal installments paid on each regular installment due date. A taxpayer that meets the threshold requirement after September 15, must pay the estimated tax in full at the time the threshold is met. Form 83-300 **Coronavirus (COVID-19) Pandemic Filing/Payment Relief:** First and second quarter 2020 estimated tax payments are extended to July 15, 2020.
Missouri	Four equal installments must be paid by the 15th of the fourth, sixth, ninth, and 12th months of the taxable year.	A taxpayer who first meets the threshold filing requirements after April 15, must spread the estimated tax payments equally over the remaining installments, depending on the date in which the requirements are first met. Form MO-1120ES. **Coronavirus (COVID-19) Pandemic Filing/Payment Relief** July 15, 2020 due date for April 15, 2020, and June 15 2020 installments.
Montana	Four equal installments due on the 15th of the fourth, sixth, ninth, and 12th months of the taxable year.	Form CT.

Jurisdiction	Installments/Forms	Comment
Nebraska	Four equal installments due on the 15th of the fourth, sixth, ninth, and 12th months of the taxable year.	A taxpayer who first meets the threshold filing requirements after April 1, must spread the estimated tax payments equally over the remaining installments, depending on the quarter in which the requirements are first met. Form 1120N-ES **Coronavirus (COVID-19) Pandemic Filing/Payment Relief** July 15, 2020 due date for April 15, 2020 installment.
Nevada	N/A, because state does not tax general business corporation or pass-through income.	
New Hampshire	Four equal installments due on the 15th of the fourth, sixth, ninth, and 12th months of the taxable year.	A taxpayer who first meets the threshold filing requirements after the first quarter or any subsequent quarter, must add the missed installment(s) to the first installment paid. Form NH-1120-ES.
New Jersey	Four equal installments due on the 15th of the fourth, sixth, ninth, and 12th months of the taxable year.	**Coronavirus (COVID-19) Pandemic Filing/Payment Relief** July 15, 2020 for payment originally due April 15, 2020. For 2018, due date for first installment has been extended to April 17, 2018, to conform with corresponding federal extension. Taxpayers with gross receipts of $50 million or more, pay 25% on the 15th of the fourth month, 50% on the 15th of the sixth month, and 25% on the 15th of the 12th month. Taxpayers with a preceding year's liability of $500 or less may make a single payment of 50% of the prior year's tax liability, due by the original due date of the prior year's tax return. Form CTB-150

Jurisdiction	Installments/Forms	Comment
New Mexico	Four equal installments due on the 15th of fourth, sixth, ninth, and 12th months of current taxable year.	State does not authorize alternative payment methods, even if threshold met after first installment date. Form CIT-ES **Coronavirus (COVID-19) Pandemic Filing/Payment Relief:** New Mexico corporate income tax returns due between April 15, 2020, and July 15, 2020, are due July 15, 2020. No interest or penalty will be imposed for failure to pay any corporate income tax that became due April 15, 2020, through July 15, 2020, provided that payment for the unpaid tax is made in full on or before April 15, 2021, and if the failure to pay was not an intentional attempt to evade the tax.
New York	25% of estimated tax liability must be paid by 15th of third month of taxable year and 1/3 of remaining balance of estimated tax liability must be paid by 15th of sixth, ninth, and twelfth months of taxable year.	For payments due before March 15, 2017, if prior year tax liability exceeds $100,000, first installment payment must be 40% of estimated tax liability. For payments due on or after March 15, 2017, if second preceding year's tax liability exceeds $100,000, first installment payment must be 40% of estimated tax liability. A taxpayer who first meets the threshold filing requirements after May 31 must spread the estimated tax payments equally over the remaining installments, depending on the date on which the requirements are first met. Form CT-300 for mandatory first installment. Form CT-400 for other installments.
North Carolina	Four equal installments due on the 15th of the fourth, sixth, ninth, and 12th months of the taxable year.	A taxpayer who first meets the threshold filing requirements after April 1, must spread the estimated tax payments equally over the remaining installments, depending on the quarter in which the requirements are first met. Form CD-429
North Dakota	Four equal installments must be paid by the 15th of the fourth, sixth, and ninth months of the current taxable year and on the 15th of the first month following the close of the taxable year.	**COVID-19 Filing/Payment Relief:** July 15, 2020 due date for April 15 and June 15, 2020 installments. State does not authorize alternative payment methods, even if threshold met after first installment date. Form 40-ES
Ohio	Calendar quarter taxpayers must file not later than the 10th day of the second month after the end of each calendar quarter. Calendar year taxpayer must file not later than May 10 for calendar years 2010 and beyond.	Forms CAT-12

Jurisdiction	Installments/Forms	Comment
Oklahoma	Four equal installments due on the 15th of the fourth, sixth, and ninth months of the taxable year and the 15th of the month following the close of the taxable year.	**Coronavirus (COVID-19) Pandemic Filing/Payment Relief** April 15, 2020 payment extended to July 1, 2020. Fourth installment may be waived if taxpayer files return and pays tax by the end of the month following the close of the taxable year. State does not authorize alternative payment methods, even if threshold met after first installment date. Form 0W-8-ESC
Oregon	Four equal installments due on the 15th of the fourth, sixth, ninth, and 12th months of the taxable year.	State does not authorize alternative payment methods, even if threshold met after first installment date. Form 20-V
Pennsylvania	Four equal installments due on the 15th of the third, sixth, ninth, and 12th months of the taxable year.	State does not authorize alternative payment methods. Form REV-857
Rhode Island	**After 2017** Four equal installments due on the 20th of the fourth, sixth, ninth, and 12th months of the taxable year. **Prior to 2018** 40% due on the 15th of the third month of the taxable year and 60% due on the 15th of the sixth month of the taxable year.	Prior to 2018, if filing threshold is met after March 1 and before June 1, 100% of the tax is due by June 15. After 2017, state does not authorize alternative payment methods. Form RI-1120ES **Coronavirus (COVID-19) Pandemic Filing/Payment Relief:** July 15, 2020, due date for April and June estimated payments.
South Carolina	Four equal installments due on the 15th of the fourth, sixth, ninth, and 12th months of the taxable year.	**COVID-19 Filing/Payment Relief:** July 15, 2020 due date for April 15 and June 15, 2020 installments. State does not authorize alternative payment methods. Form SC1120-CDP
South Dakota	N/A, because state does not tax general business corporation or pass-through income.	
Tennessee	Four equal installments due on the 15th of the fourth, sixth, and ninth months of the current taxable year and on the 15th of the first month following the close of the taxable year.	**COVID-19 Filing/Payment Relief:** July 15, 2020 due date for April 15, 2020 installment. State does not authorize alternative payment methods even if threshold is met after first quarter. Form FAE-172
Texas	There are no statutory or regulatory provisions regarding estimated taxes.	

Jurisdiction	Installments/Forms	Comment
Utah	Four equal installments due on the 15th of the fourth, sixth, ninth, and 12th months of the taxable year, or as otherwise modified by federal action.	For taxpayers basing payments on their current year's (rather than prior year's) liability, the percentages must equal the following: 22.5% for the first installment, 45% by the second installment; 67.5% by the third installment, and 90% by the fourth installment. For the first year a corporation is required to file a return, it is not subject to the estimated tax payment requirement provided it pays the $100 minimum tax by the due date, without extensions, of its return. **Coronavirus (COVID-19) Pandemic Filing/Payment Relief** July 15, 2020 due date for first and second quarters of 2020. Form TC-559
Vermont	Four equal installments due on the 15th of the fourth, sixth, ninth, and 12th months of the taxable year.	**COVID-19 Filing/Payment Relief:** July 15, 2020 due date for April 15 and June 15, 2020 installments. A taxpayer who first meets the threshold filing requirements after April, must spread the estimated tax payments equally over the remaining installments, depending on the month in which the requirements are first met. Form CO-414
Virginia	Four equal installments due on the 15th of the fourth, sixth, ninth, and 12th months of the taxable year.	**COVID-19 Payment Relief:** June 1, 2020 payment due date for April 15, 2020 installment. A taxpayer who first meets the threshold filing requirements after April 1, must spread the estimated tax payments equally over the remaining installments, depending on the quarter in which the requirements are first met. Form 500-ES
Washington	N/A, because state does not tax general business corporation or pass-through income.	
West Virginia	Four equal installments must be paid by the 15th of the fourth, sixth, ninth, and 12th months of taxable year.	A taxpayer who first meets the threshold filing requirements after April 1, must spread the estimated tax payments equally over the remaining installments, depending on the quarter in which the requirements are first met. Form WV/CNF-120ES **Coronavirus (COVID-19) Pandemic Filing/Payment Relief** July 15, 2020 due date for first and second quarter installments.

Jurisdiction	Installments/Forms	Comment
Wisconsin	Four equal installments due on the 15th of the fourth, sixth, ninth, and 12th months of the taxable year.	**COVID-19 Filing/Payment Relief:** July 15, 2020 due date for April 15 and June 15, 2020 installments. If corporation's fiscal year begins in April, first installment is due on 15th of third month of taxable year. Form Corp-ES
Wyoming	N/A, because state does not tax general business corporation or pass-through income.	

Estimated Tax Requirements—Safe Harbor Calculation

Under IRC § 6655, corporations must pay a penalty if sufficient estimated tax is not paid for the taxable year. The underpayment penalty can be avoided if estimated tax payments by the corporation are equal to the lesser of:

- 100% of the current year's tax liability; or
- 100% of the tax shown on the preceding year's return.

The required annual payment cannot be based on the tax shown on the preceding year's return if the preceding year was less than 12 months or if the corporation did not file a return for the preceding year showing a liability for tax. Corporations that had $1 million or more in taxable net income for any of the 3 tax years immediately preceding the current tax year can only use the tax shown on the prior year's return for the first installment and any reduction resulting from use of the previous year's figures must be recaptured in the next installment. Corporations that do not satisfy the current or prior year safe harbor calculation must pay a penalty. No penalty is imposed for an underpayment of estimated tax for any tax year if the tax shown on the return for that year or, if no return is filed, the amount of tax due is less than $500. In addition, a corporation that establishes that its annualized income installment or its adjusted seasonal installment is less than its required installment can use the annualized income or adjusted seasonal installment method as a basis for its required installment.

This chart provides the estimated tax safe harbor calculation for each state and the District of Columbia for determining whether corporation income taxpayers are subject to penalties for underpayment of estimated tax. States that allow the use of the annualized income or adjusted seasonal installment method for determining the amount of estimated tax installments are covered in a chart under the topic Estimated Tax Requirements—AIM/ASIM.

Jurisdiction	Safe Harbor Calculation	Comment
Alabama	Lesser of: • 100% of current year's tax liability; or • 100% of tax liability shown on preceding year's return.	If taxable net income for any of the 3 tax years immediately preceding current tax year was $1 million or more, prior year's tax liability can be only used for first installment and any reduction resulting from use of previous year's figures must be recaptured in next installment.
Alaska	Lesser of: • 100% of current year's tax liability; or • 100% of tax liability shown on preceding year's return.	If taxable net income for any of the 3 tax years immediately preceding current tax year was $1 million or more, prior year's tax liability can be only used for first installment.
Arizona	Lesser of: • 90% of current year's tax liability; or • 100% of tax liability shown on preceding year's return.	If taxable net income for any of the 3 tax years immediately preceding current tax year was $1 million or more, prior year's tax liability can be only used for first installment and any reduction resulting from use of previous year's figures must be recaptured in next installment.

Jurisdiction	Safe Harbor Calculation	Comment
Arkansas	Lesser of: • 90% of current year's tax liability; or • 100% of tax liability shown on preceding year's return.	
California	Lesser of: • 100% of tax shown on current year's return; • 100% of current year's tax liability computed on annualized income or annualized seasonal income basis; or • 100% of tax shown on preceding year's tax return. Safe harbor computed on cumulative basis. Q1 installment may not be less than minimum tax, except newly formed or qualified corporations.	If taxable net income for any of the 3 tax years immediately preceding current tax year was $1 million or more, prior year's tax liability can be only used for first installment and any reduction resulting from use of previous year's figures must be recaptured in next installment.
Colorado	Lesser of: • 70% of current year's tax liability; or • 100% of tax liability shown on preceding year's return.	If taxable net income for any of the 3 tax years immediately preceding current tax year was $1 million or more, prior year's tax liability can be only used for first installment and any reduction resulting from use of previous year's figures must be recaptured in next installment.
Connecticut	Lesser of: • 90% of current year's liability (including surtax); or • 100% of tax liability (including surtax) shown on preceding year's return.	Amount of estimated tax paid by installment due dates must equal the lesser of: • 30% of the prior year tax or 27% of the current year tax (including surtax); • 70% of the prior year tax or 63% of the current year tax (including surtax); • 80% of the prior year tax or 72% of the current year tax (including surtax); and • 100% of the prior year tax or 90% of the current year tax (including surtax).
Delaware	Equal to: • 80% of current year's tax liability; or • 100% of tax liability shown on preceding year's return.	Prior year safe harbor calculation applies only to corporations that had aggregate gross receipts from sales of tangible personal property and gross apportionable income that does not exceed $20 million (adjusted annually for inflation for any two of the three taxable years immediately preceding the taxable year for which estimated tax is being computed. **Tax years before 2017:** Prior year safe harbor calculation did not apply to large ccorporations that had Delaware taxable income of $200,000 or more for any of the 3 taxable years immediately preceding the current taxable year.
District of Columbia	Lesser of: • 90% of tax due on current year's return; • 100% of current year's tax liability, if no return is filed; or • 110% of tax liability shown on preceding year's return.	

Jurisdiction	Safe Harbor Calculation	Comment
Florida	Lesser of: • 90% of current year's tax liability; or • 100% of tax liability applying current year's tax rate to tax base shown on preceding year's return.	
Georgia	Lesser of: • 70% of current year's tax liability; • 70% of current year's tax liability computed on annualized basis; • 100% of tax liability shown on preceding year's return; or • 100% of tax liability applying current year's tax rate to tax base shown on preceding year's return.	
Hawaii	Lesser of: • 100% of current year's tax liability; or • 100% of tax liability shown on preceding year's return.	If taxable net income for any of the 3 tax years immediately preceding current tax year was $1 million or more, prior year's tax liability can be only used for first installment and any reduction resulting from use of previous year's figures must be recaptured in next installment.
Idaho	Lesser of: • 90% of current year's tax liability; • 100% of tax liability shown on preceding year's return.	
Illinois	Lesser of: • 90% of current year's tax liability; or • 100% of tax liability shown on preceding year's return.	**Coronavirus (COVID-19) Pandemic Filing/Payment Relief** Lesser of: • 90% of tax liability for 2020 tax year; or • 100% of tax liability shown on 2019 or 2018 return.
Indiana	Lesser of: • 20% of current year's tax liability for any quarterly payment; or • 25% of preceding year's final tax liability for any quarterly payment.	
Iowa	Equal to: • 100% of current year's tax liability computed on annualized income basis; • 100% of current year's tax liability; • 100% of tax liability shown on preceding year's return; or • 100% of tax liability applying current year's tax rate to tax base shown on preceding year's return.	
Kansas	Lesser of: • 90% of the current year's tax liability; • 90% of the current year's tax liability computed on annualized basis; or • 100% of tax liability shown on preceding year's return.	

Jurisdiction	Safe Harbor Calculation	Comment
Kentucky	Equal to lesser of: • 100% of the current year's tax liability; or • 100% of the preceding year's tax liability.	**Tax years before 2019:** Equal to: • 70% of current year's combined income tax and limited liability entity tax, as reduced by $5,000 statutory exemption; or • 100% of preceding year's combined income tax and limited liability entity tax if $25,000 or less.
Louisiana	Lesser of: • 80% of current year's tax liability; • 80% of current year's tax liability computed on annualized basis; • 100% of tax liability shown on preceding year's return; or • 100% of tax liability applying current year's tax rate to tax base shown on preceding year's return.	
Maine	Lesser of: • 90% of current year's tax liability; or • 100% of tax liability shown on preceding year's return.	If taxable net income for any of the 3 tax years immediately preceding current tax year was $1 million or more, prior year's tax liability can be only used for first installment and any reduction resulting from use of previous year's figures must be recaptured in next installment.
Maryland	Lesser of: • 90% of current year's tax liability; or • 110% of tax paid for preceding year.	
Massachusetts	Lesser of: • 90% of current year's tax liability; • 90% of current year's tax liability computed using preceding year's apportionment percentage; or • 100% of tax liability shown on preceding year's return.	If taxable net income for any of the 3 tax years immediately preceding current tax year was $1 million or more, prior year's tax liability can be only used for first installment and any reduction resulting from use of previous year's figures must be recaptured in next installment.
Michigan	Equal to: • 85% of current year's tax liability; or • 100% of preceding year's tax liability if paid in four equal installments and liability, including surcharge, was $20,000 or less.	
Minnesota	Lesser of: • 100% of current year's tax liability; or • 100% of tax liability shown on preceding year's return.	If taxable net income for any of the 3 tax years immediately preceding current tax year was $1 million or more, prior year's tax liability can be only used for first installment and any reduction resulting from use of previous year's figures must be recaptured in next installment.
Mississippi	Lesser of: • 90% of current year's tax liability; or • 100% of tax liability shown on preceding year's return.	If taxable net income for any of the 3 tax years immediately preceding current tax year was $1 million or more, prior year's tax liability can be only used for first installment and any reduction resulting from use of previous year's figures must be recaptured in next installment.

Jurisdiction	Safe Harbor Calculation	Comment
Missouri	Lesser of: • 90% of current year's tax liability; • 90% of current year's tax liability computed on annualized basis; • 90% of current year's tax liability over 3, 5, 8, and 11 month periods; • tax liability computed by applying current year's tax rate to tax base shown on preceding year's return; or • 100% of tax liability shown on preceding year's return.	If taxable net income for any of the 3 taxable years immediately preceding current tax year is $1 million or more: • 90% of current year's tax liability; • 90% of current year's tax liability computed on annualized basis; • 90% of current year's tax liability over 3, 5, 8, and 11 month periods; or • 90% of current year's tax liability computed on annualized basis for the months preceding an installment date.
Montana	Lesser of: • 80% of current year's tax liability; • 80% of current year's tax liability computed on annualized income or adjusted seasonal income basis. • 100% of tax liability shown on preceding year's return.	
Nebraska	Lesser of: • 100% of tax liability shown on current year's return; • 100% of tax liability shown on preceding year's return; • 100% of tax liability applying current year's tax rate to tax base shown on preceding year's return; or • 100% of current year's tax liability computed on annualized income or adjusted seasonal income basis.	If taxable net income for any of the 3 tax years immediately preceding current tax year was $1 million or more, prior year's tax liability can be only used for first installment and any reduction resulting from use of previous year's figures must be recaptured in next installment.
Nevada	N/A, because state does not tax general business corporation or pass-through income.	
New Hampshire	Lesser of: • 90% of tax liability shown on current year's return; • 90% of current year's tax liability computed on annualized income basis; • 100% of tax liability shown on preceding year's return; or • 100% of tax liability applying current year's tax rate to tax base shown on preceding year's return.	
New Jersey	Lesser of: • 90% of tax liability shown on current year's return; • 90% of current year's tax liability computed on annualized income basis; • 100% of tax liability shown on preceding year's return; or • 100% of tax liability applying current year's tax rate to tax base shown on preceding year's return.	

Jurisdiction	Safe Harbor Calculation	Comment
New Mexico	Lesser of: • 80% of current year's tax liability; • 80% of current year's tax liability for each quarter computed on period-by-period basis; • 100% of preceding year's tax liability; • 110% of preceding year's tax liability if return has not been filed and extended due date has not expired before current year's first installment.	
New York	Lesser of: • 91% of current year's tax liability; • 91% of current year's tax liability computed on annualized income or adjusted seasonal income basis; • 100% of tax liability shown on preceding year's return; or • 100% of tax liability applying current year's tax rate to tax base shown on preceding year's return.	If taxable net income for any of the 3 tax years immediately preceding current tax year was $1 million or more, required percentage of current year's tax liability is 100% instead of 91%, and exceptions based on preceding year's returns do not apply.
North Carolina	Lesser of: • 90% of current year's tax liability; or • 100% of tax liability shown on preceding year's return.	Large corporations as defined under IRC §6655 can only use prior year's tax liability for safe harbor calculation.
North Dakota	Lesser of: • 90% of current year's tax liability; or • 100% of net tax liability shown on preceding year's return.	
Ohio	Equal to: • 95% of prior quarter's taxable gross receipts and 70% of actual tax liability if rule-based estimation is elected; or • 95%-105% of each quarter's taxable gross receipts if statutory-based estimation.	
Oklahoma	Lesser of: • 70% of current year's tax liability; • 70% of current year's tax liability computed on annualized income basis; or • 100% of tax liability shown on preceding year's return.	
Oregon	Lesser of: • 100% of current year's tax liability; • 100% of current year's tax liability computed on annualized income or adjusted seasonal income basis; or • 100% of tax liability shown on preceding year's return.	If taxable net income for any of the 3 tax years immediately preceding current tax year was $1 million or more, prior year's tax liability can be only used for first installment and any reduction resulting from use of previous year's figures must be recaptured in next installment.
Pennsylvania	Equal to: • 90% of current year's tax liability; or • 100% of tax liability applying current year's tax rate and certain adjustments to tax base shown on return for second preceding tax year.	

Jurisdiction	Safe Harbor Calculation	Comment
Rhode Island	Equal to: • 80% of current year's tax liability; • 100% of tax liability applying current year's tax rate to tax base shown on preceding year's return.	
South Carolina	Lesser of: • 100% of current year's tax liability; or • 100% of tax liability shown on preceding year's return.	If taxable net income for any of the 3 tax years immediately preceding current tax year was $1 million or more, prior year's tax liability can be only used for first installment and any reduction resulting from use of previous year's figures must be recaptured in next installment.
South Dakota	N/A, because state does not tax general business corporation or pass-through income.	
Tennessee	Lesser of: • 25% of 80% of current year's combined franchise and excise tax liability for any quarterly payment; or • 25% of preceding year's combined franchise and excise tax liability for any quarterly payment; or • 25% of preceding year's combined franchise and excise tax liability computed for any quarterly payment on annualized basis if preceding year was less than 12 months.	
Texas	No requirement for filing of estimated tax reports or payments.	
Utah	Lesser of: • 90% of current year's tax liability; • 90% of current year's tax liability computed on annualized income or adjusted seasonal income basis; or • 100% of tax liability shown on preceding year's return.	$100 minimum tax may be paid on 15th day of twelfth month instead of four equal installments if: • prepayment requirement is satisfied in current year and prior year's tax liability was $100; or • prepayment requirement was satisfied in prior year and current year's tax liability is $100.
Vermont	Lesser of: • 90% of current year's tax liability; or • 100% of tax liability applying current year's tax rate to tax base shown on preceding year's return.	**Tax years before June 5, 2013:** Lesser of • 80% of current year's tax liability; or • 100% of tax liability applying current year's tax rate to tax base shown on preceding year's return.
Virginia	Lesser of: • 90% of current year's tax liability; • 90% of current year's tax liability computed on annualized income basis; • 100% of tax liability shown on preceding year's return; or • 100% of tax liability applying current year's tax rate to tax base shown on preceding year's return.	
Washington	N/A, because state does not tax general business corporation or pass-through income.	

Jurisdiction	Safe Harbor Calculation	Comment
West Virginia	Lesser of: • 90% of current year's tax liability; • 100% of tax liability shown on preceding year's return; or • 100% of tax liability applying current year's tax rate to tax base shown on preceding year's return.	
Wisconsin	Lesser of: • 90% of current year's tax liability; • 90% of tax and surcharge computed on annualized basis; or • 100% of tax liability shown on preceding year's return if net income for current year is less than $250,000.	
Wyoming	N/A, because state does not tax general business corporation or pass-through income.	

Estimated Tax Requirements—Threshold

The following chart indicates the threshold at which C corporation taxpayers are required to make estimated tax payments.

Jurisdiction	Threshold	Comment
Alabama	Estimated liability of $500 or more.	
Alaska	Estimated liability of $500 or more.	
Arizona	Estimated liability of $1,000 or more.	$1,000 threshold applies to combined and consolidated filers.
Arkansas	Estimated liability of $1,000 or more.	
California	All general corporations required to make estimated payments regardless of estimated liability.	
Colorado	Estimated liability exceeds $5,000.	
Connecticut	Estimated liability exceeds $1,000.	
Delaware	Declaration of tentative tax required even if estimated tax liability is zero and no remittance is required.	
District of Columbia	Estimated liability exceeds $1,000.	
Florida	Estimated liability exceeds $2,500.	
Georgia	Estimated net income exceeds $25,000.	
Hawaii	Estimated liability of $500 or more.	
Idaho	Estimated liability of $500 or more.	
Illinois	Estimated income and replacement tax liability exceeds $400.	
Indiana	Estimated adjusted gross income tax liability exceeds $2,500.	
Iowa	Estimated liability exceeds $1,000.	
Kansas	Estimated liability exceeds $500.	
Kentucky	Estimated liability exceeds $5,000.	
Louisiana	Estimated liability of $1,000 or more.	
Maine	Estimated liability for current or prior year of $1,000 or more.	
Maryland	Estimated liability exceeds $1,000.	
Massachusetts	Estimated liability exceeds $1,000.	
Michigan	Estimated liability that exceeds $800. **Tax years prior to 2008:** Estimated liability exceeds $600.	Return not required for tax years less than 4 months long.
Minnesota	Estimated liability exceeds $500.	

Jurisdiction	Threshold	Comment
Mississippi	Estimated liability exceeds $200.	
Missouri	Estimated liability of $250 or more.	
Montana	Estimated liability of $5,000 or more.	
Nebraska	Estimated liability of $400 or more.	
Nevada	N/A, because state does not tax general business corporation or pass-through income.	
New Hampshire	Estimated liability of $200 or more.	
New Jersey	Prior year's tax liability exceeds $500.	Taxpayer's whose prior year's liability equals $500 or less, may in lieu of making the quarterly estimated tax payments, make a single installment payment of 50% of estimated tax liability, due on or before the original due date for filing the annual return.
New Mexico	Estimated liability exceeds $5,000.	
New York	Estimated liability exceeds $1,000.	
North Carolina	Estimated liability of $500 or more.	
North Dakota	Current and prior year's liability exceeds $5,000.	
Ohio	No threshold.	Estimated taxes allowed for calendar quarter commercial activity (CAT) taxpayers.
Oklahoma	Estimated liability of $500 or more.	
Oregon	Estimated liability of $500 or more.	
Pennsylvania	All general corporations required to make estimated payments regardless of estimated liability.	
Rhode Island	Estimated liability exceeds $500.	
South Carolina	Estimated liability of $100 or more.	
South Dakota	N/A, because state does not tax general business corporation or pass-through income.	
Tennessee	Combined franchise and excise tax liability for current year $5,000 or more.	
Texas	There are no statutory or regulatory provisions regarding estimated taxes.	
Utah	Current or preceding year's corporation franchise or income tax liability of $3,000 or more.	$3,000 threshold applies to combined filers.
Vermont	Estimated liability exceeds $500.	
Virginia	Estimated liability exceeds $1,000.	

Jurisdiction	Threshold	Comment
Washington	N/A, because state does not tax general business corporation or pass-through income.	
West Virginia	Estimated taxable income exceeds $10,000.	
Wisconsin	Estimated sum of net tax and economic development surcharge is $500 or more.	Payments not required if no liability for prior tax year and the current year's net income is $250,000 or less.
Wyoming	N/A, because state does not tax general business corporation or pass-through income.	

Estimated Tax Requirements—Underpayment Penalties

Under IRC § 6655, corporations must pay a penalty if sufficient estimated tax is not paid for the taxable year. The underpayment amount is the excess of the required installment over any installment paid on or before the due date. The penalty is equal to interest at the current underpayment rate from the installment due date to the earlier of:

- the date underpayment is actually paid; or
- 15th day of fourth month after the close of the tax year.

This chart provides the penalties imposed by each state and the District of Columbia on corporations for the underpayment of estimated taxes. The chart also shows the form used to compute the underpayment penalty. Safe harbor calculations for determining whether corporation income taxpayers are subject to penalties for underpayment of estimated tax are covered in a chart under the topic Estimated Tax Requirements—Safe Harbor Calculation.

Jurisdiction	Underpayment Penalties	Comment
Alabama	10% penalty on quarterly underpayment amount. Interest at current underpayment rate imposed from installment due date to earlier of: • date underpayment is actually paid; or • 15th day of third month after close of tax year.	Form 2220AL
Alaska	Interest at current underpayment rate imposed from installment due date to earlier of date underpayment is actually paid or: • 15th day of 3rd month after close of tax year for S corporations; • 15th day of 4th month after close of tax year for C corporations; or • September 15 for C corporations with June 30 fiscal year end.	Form 6220
Arizona	Interest imposed at current underpayment rate, up to 10% of amount not paid, from installment due date to earlier of: • date underpayment is actually paid; or • 15th day of fourth month after close of tax year.	Form 220
Arkansas	10% per year penalty.	Form AR2220
California	Interest at current underpayment rate imposed from installment due date to earlier of: • date underpayment is actually paid; or • 15th day of third month after close of tax year.	Form 5806

Jurisdiction	Underpayment Penalties	Comment
Colorado	Interest at current underpayment rate imposed from installment due date to earlier of: • date underpayment is actually paid; or • 15th day of fourth month after close of tax year.	Form DR 0205
Connecticut	Interest at current underpayment rate imposed from installment due date to earlier of: • date underpayment is actually paid; or • 15th day of 5th month (1st day of 4th month for tax years before 2017) after close of tax year.	Form 1120I
Delaware	1.5% per month penalty from due date of payment to date tax was paid.	
District of Columbia	Interest at current underpayment rate imposed from installment due date to earlier of: • date underpayment is actually paid; or • 15th day of third month after close of tax year.	
Florida	12% per year penalty and interest at current underpayment rate imposed from installment due date to earlier of: • date underpayment is actually paid; or • 1st day of fifth month after close of tax year.	
Georgia	9% per year penalty imposed from installment due date to earlier of: • date underpayment is actually paid; or • 15th day of third month after close of tax year.	Form 600 UET
Hawaii	8% per year penalty imposed at rate of 2/3 of 1% per month from installment due date to earlier of: • date underpayment is actually paid; or • 20th day of fourth month after close of tax year.	Form N-220
Idaho	Interest at current underpayment rate imposed from installment due date to earlier of: • date underpayment is actually paid; or • 15th day of fourth month after close of tax year.	Form 41ESR
Illinois	Penalty equal to: • 2% on amounts paid within 30 days of original due date; and • 10% on amounts paid later than 30 days after original due date until all unpaid amounts are satisfied.	Form IL-2220

Jurisdiction	Underpayment Penalties	Comment
Indiana	10% per quarter penalty.	Schedule IT-2220
Iowa	Interest at current underpayment rate imposed from installment due date to earlier of: • date underpayment is actually paid; or • 15th day of fourth month after close of tax year.	Form IA-2220
Kansas	Interest at current underpayment rate imposed from installment due date to earlier of: • date underpayment is actually paid; or • 15th day of fourth month after close of tax year.	Schedule K-220
Kentucky	Interest imposed at current underpayment rate from installment due date to earlier of: • date underpayment is actually paid; or • 15th day of fourth month after close of tax year.	Form 2220-K **Tax years before 2019:** 10% penalty on underpayment amount, but not less than $25.
Louisiana	12% per year penalty.	**COVID-19 penalty relief:** Penalties and interest for late filing and late payment will be waived for returns with an original due date between March 11, 2020, and July 15, 2020, if the delay was due to COVID-19. The waiver applies to taxpayers whose health was impacted by COVID-19, or taxpayers who relied on a tax preparer whose health was impacted by COVID-19, if the taxpayer or tax preparer was diagnosed with COVID-19 between March 11, 2020, and July 15, 2020. The waiver will not apply to any tax return filed or any tax payment submitted after November 15, 2020.
Maine	For 2018, 0.5% per month penalty (0.5833% for 2017) from installment due date to earlier of: • date underpayment is actually paid; or • 15th day of fourth month after close of tax year.	Form 2220ME
Maryland	10% per year penalty and interest imposed at 1/12th of current underpayment rate per month from installment due date.	Form 500UP
Massachusetts	Interest imposed at current underpayment rate from installment due date to earlier of: • date underpayment is actually paid; or • 15th day of third month after close of tax year.	Form M-2220

Jurisdiction	Underpayment Penalties	Comment
Michigan	Penalty from earlier of date underpayment is actually paid or 30th day of four month after close of tax year imposed at following rates: • 5% on amounts unpaid for 0-60 days; • 10% on amounts unpaid for 61-90 days; • 15% on amounts unpaid for 91-120 days; • 20% on amounts unpaid for 121-150 days; • 25% on amounts unpaid for 151 or more days. Interest imposed at current underpayment rate from installment due date to earlier of: • date underpayment is actually paid; • due date for next quarterly payment; or • due date of annual return.	CIT Form 4899 MBT Form 4582
Minnesota	Interest imposed at current underpayment rate from installment due date to earlier of: • date underpayment is actually paid; or • 15th day of third month after close of tax year.	Schedule M15C
Mississippi	10% per quarter penalty. 7/10 of 1% per month interest imposed from installment due date to earlier of: • date underpayment is actually paid; or • due date for next quarterly payment.	Form 83-305
Missouri	Interest imposed at current underpayment rate from installment due date to earlier of: • date underpayment is actually paid; or • 15th day of fourth month after close of tax year.	Form MO-2220
Montana	12% interest imposed from installment due date to earlier of: • date underpayment is actually paid; or • 15th day of fifth month after close of tax year.	Form CIT-UT
Nebraska	Interest imposed at current underpayment rate from installment due date to earlier of: • date underpayment is actually paid; or • 15th day of third month after close of tax year.	Form 2220N
Nevada	N/A, because state does not tax general business corporation or pass-through income.	

Jurisdiction	Underpayment Penalties	Comment
New Hampshire	Interest imposed at current underpayment rate from installment due date to earlier of: • date underpayment is actually paid; or • due date of annual return.	Form DP2210/2220
New Jersey	Interest imposed at current underpayment rate from installment due date to earlier of: • date underpayment is actually paid; or • 15th day of fourth month after close of tax year.	Form CTB-160-A for taxpayers with gross receipts of less than $50 million. Form CTB-160-B for taxpayers with gross receipts of $50 million or more.
New Mexico	2% per month penalty up to maximum of 20% of underpayment amount. Interest imposed at current underpayment rate from installment due date to earlier of: • date underpayment is actually paid; or • due date of annual return.	Form RPD-41287 for corporations with seasonal or annualized income computing safe harbor based on tax liability for each quarter. **Coronavirus (COVID-19) Pandemic Filing/Payment Relief:** No interest or penalty will be imposed for failure to pay any corporate income tax that became due April 15, 2020, through July 15, 2020, provided that payment for the unpaid tax is made in full on or before April 15, 2021, and if the failure to pay was not an intentional attempt to evade the tax.
New York	Interest imposed at current underpayment rate from installment due date to earlier of: • date underpayment is actually paid; or • 15th day of third month after close of tax year. 7.5% per year penalty if no underpayment rate set.	Form CT-222
North Carolina	Interest imposed at current underpayment rate from installment due date to earlier of: • date underpayment is actually paid; or • 15th day of third month after close of tax year.	Form CD-429B
North Dakota	12% interest imposed from installment due date to earlier of: • date underpayment is actually paid; or • 15th day of fourth month after close of tax year.	Form 40-UT No interest accrues if estimated tax is based on annualized or seasonal adjusted income method.
Ohio	10% penalty. Interest imposed at current underpayment rate from installment due date to earlier of: • date underpayment is actually paid; or • date assessment was issued.	

Jurisdiction	Underpayment Penalties	Comment
Oklahoma	20% interest imposed from installment due date to earlier of: • date underpayment is actually paid; or • 15th day of third month after close of tax year.	Form OW-8-P
Oregon	Interest imposed at current underpayment rate on full or partial monthly basis from installment due date to earlier of: • date underpayment is actually paid; or • due date of next installment.	Beginning 2018, interest is computed on an annualized basis instead of monthly or partial month basis. Form 37
Pennsylvania	Interest imposed at current underpayment rate from installment due date to earlier of: • date underpayment is actually paid; or • 15th day of fourth month after close of tax year.	120% of current interest rate for understatements in excess of 25%.
Rhode Island	5% per year penalty. Interest imposed at current underpayment rate from installment due date to earlier of: • date underpayment is actually paid; or • 15th day of fourth month after close of tax year.	Form RI-2220
South Carolina	Interest imposed at current underpayment rate from installment due date to earlier of: • date underpayment is actually paid; or • 15th day of fourth month after close of tax year.	Form SC2220
South Dakota	N/A, because state does not tax general business corporation or pass-through income.	
Tennessee	2% per month penalty up to maximum of 24%. Interest imposed at current underpayment rate from installment due date to earlier of: • date underpayment is actually paid; or • 15th day of fourth month after close of tax year.	Before tax year 2016, 5% per month penalty up to maximum of 25%. Form FAE 170
Texas	N/A, because estimated tax reports or payments not required.	
Utah	Interest imposed at current underpayment rate plus 4% from installment due date to earlier of: • date underpayment is actually paid; or • 15th day of fourth month after close of tax year.	

Jurisdiction	Underpayment Penalties	Comment
Vermont	1% per month penalty up to maximum of 25%. Interest imposed at current underpayment rate from installment due date to earlier of: • date underpayment is actually paid; or • 15th day of third month after close of tax year.	
Virginia	Interest imposed at current underpayment rate from installment due date to earlier of: • date underpayment is actually paid; or • 15th day of fourth month after close of tax year.	Form 500C
Washington	N/A, because state does not tax general business corporation or pass-through income.	
West Virginia	Interest imposed at current underpayment rate from installment due date to earlier of: • date underpayment is actually paid; or • 15th day of third month after close of tax year.	Form CNF-120U
Wisconsin	12% interest imposed from installment due date to earlier of: • date underpayment is actually paid; or • date on which corporation is required to file its return.	Form U.
Wyoming	N/A, because state does not tax general business corporation or pass-through income.	

FDII and GILTI Deduction–IRC §250

Under IRC Sec. 250, a deduction is allowed for domestic corporations in an amount equal to the sum of:

- 37.5%of its FDII, plus
- 50% of its GILTI, if any, and the amount treated as a dividend received by the corporation and attributable to its GILTI.

The deduction is available for tax years beginning after December 31, 2017, and before January 1, 2026. For tax years beginning after December 31, 2025, the deduction for FDII is 21.875% and 37.5% for GILTI.

The amount of the deduction is limited based on taxable income. If the sum of a domestic corporation's FDII and GILTI amounts exceeds its taxable income, then the amount of the FDII and GILTI deduction is similarly reduced by an amount determined by the excess.

A domestic corporation's foreign-derived intangible income (FDII) is the portion of its intangible income, determined according to a codified formula, that is derived from serving foreign markets.

Global intangible low-taxed income is the excess of a U.S. shareholders net controlled foreign corporations (CFCs) tested income over net deemed tangible income return for the year.

Corporations should use federal Form 8993 to figure out the eligible deduction for FDII and GILTI. The federal deduction is included on Form 1120, Schedule C.

This chart shows the treatment of the deduction for FDII and GILTI income for corporations by each state and the District of Columbia.

Jurisdiction	FDII and GILTI Deduction–IRC §250	Comment
Alabama	Same as federal due to income tax starting point.	
Alaska	Federal deduction not allowed due to income tax starting point.	
Arizona	For tax years after 2018, addition required for amount of federal deduction under IRC Sec. 250(a)(1)(B) (GILTI).	
Arkansas	No modifications because state does not conform to IRC Sec. 250.	
California	No modifications because state does not conform to IRC Sec. 250.	
Colorado	Same as federal due to income tax starting point.	
Connecticut	Federal deduction not allowed due to income tax starting point.	
Delaware	Same as federal due to income tax starting point.	

Jurisdiction	FDII and GILTI Deduction–IRC § 250	Comment
District of Columbia	Federal deduction not allowed due to income tax starting point.	
Florida	Same as federal due to income tax starting point.	
Georgia	Same as federal due to income tax starting point.	Deduction applies if income is included in state taxable net income.
Hawaii	No modifications because state does not conform to IRC Sec. 250.	
Idaho	Same as federal due to income tax starting point.	
Illinois	Addition required for amount of federal deduction.	
Indiana	Addition required for deduction allowed in computing GILTI.	
Iowa	Same as federal due to income tax starting point. **Tax years before 2018:** No modifications because state does not conform to IRC Sec. 250.	
Kansas	Same as federal due to income tax starting point.	
Kentucky	Addition required for deduction allowed in computing GILTI and any expenses related to that income.	
Louisiana	Same as federal due to income tax starting point.	
Maine	Addition required for deduction allowed in computing GILTI.	
Maryland	Same as federal due to income tax starting point.	
Massachusetts	Addition required for amount of federal deduction.	
Michigan	Same as federal in computing FDII due to income tax starting point. Addition required for federal deduction allowed in computing GILTI.	
Minnesota	Addition required for amount of any special deduction under IRC Sec. 250.	
Mississippi	Federal deduction not allowed due to income tax starting point.	
Missouri	Same as federal due to income tax starting point.	GILTI income is treated as dividend income and qualifies for state dividends received deduction.

Jurisdiction	FDII and GILTI Deduction–IRC § 250	Comment
Montana	FDII: Deduction allowed based on federal FDII deduction that represents amounts related to entities included in Montana group or return. GILTI: For water's edge and worldwide filers, state's deduction for certain dividends is allowed rather than federal GILTI deduction amount. For separate company, domestic or limited combination filers, deduction generally allowed based on federal GILTI deduction amounts associated with the entity or group included in the Montana return. But if any of the GILTI is from subsidiaries included in the state limited combination filing, an intercompany dividend elimination is allowed instead of the federal GILTI deduction.	
Nebraska	Same as federal due to income tax starting point.	
Nevada	N/A, because state does not tax general business corporation income.	
New Hampshire	No modifications because state does not conform to IRC Sec. 250.	
New Jersey	For privilege periods beginning on and after January 1, 2018, federal deduction allowed if: • Deduction is taken for federal tax purposes; and • income is included on taxpayer's federal and state tax returns.	
New Mexico	Same as federal due to income tax starting point.	Prior to 2020, federal deduction not allowed due to income tax starting point.
New York	Addition required for federal deduction allowed in computing FDII and, for tax years after 2018, GILTI.	
North Carolina	Addition required for deduction allowed in computing FDII and GILTI.	
North Dakota	Same as federal in computing FDII due to income tax starting point. Addition required for federal deduction allowed in computing GILTI.	
Ohio	**Commercial Activity Tax:** Excludes dividends and distributions from corporations and distributive or proportionate share of receipts and income from a pass-through entity for purposes of calculating the CAT.	
Oklahoma	Same as federal due to income tax starting point.	

Jurisdiction	FDII and GILTI Deduction–IRC § 250	Comment
Oregon	For tax years after 2018, addition required for amount of federal deduction under IRC Sec. 250 (GILTI).	
Pennsylvania	Federal deduction not allowed due to income tax starting point.	GILTI income is treated as dividend income and qualifies for state dividends received deduction.
Rhode Island	Rhode Island allows a subtraction from federal taxable income for the deduction from foreign-derived intangible income (FDII) and global intangible low-taxed income (GILTI).	
South Carolina	Addition required for deduction allowed in computing FDII and GILTI.	
South Dakota	N/A, because state does not tax general business corporation income.	
Tennessee	Federal deduction not allowed due to income tax starting point.	
Texas	No modifications because state does not conform to IRC Sec. 250.	
Utah	Federal deduction not allowed due to income tax starting point.	
Vermont	Same as federal due to income tax starting point.	
Virginia	Same as federal due to income tax starting point.	Subtraction allowed equal to the net inclusion of GILTI after considering the offset of any deduction allowed, including IRC Sec. 250.
Washington	N/A, because state does not tax general business corporation income.	
West Virginia	Same as federal due to income tax starting point.	
Wisconsin	No modifications because state does not conform to IRC Sec. 250.	
Wyoming	N/A, because state does not tax general business corporation income.	

Federal Form Attachment Requirements (Corporate Income)

The following chart indicates whether the state requires federal form 1120 to be attached to the state return. Additional or alternative attachment requirements are noted in the "Comments" column, including those states that require Schedule M-3 (Form 1120), Net Income (Loss) Reconciliation for Corporations With Total Assets of $10 Million or more, to be attached.

Jurisdiction	C Corporations	Comment
Alabama	Yes	Complete copy of the appropriate federal return with necessary supporting schedules must be attached to Form 20C. Members of affiliated group filing federal consolidated return must attach copy of federal Form 851, copy of supporting schedules, and copy of consolidated Federal Form 1120.
Alaska	Yes, copy of entire federal return and supporting schedules. Copy of federal return must be attached for each affiliated taxpayer electing to file consolidated state return. Copy of Form 990-T must be attached for exempt organizations.	If federal return exceeds 50 pages, copy of pages 1 through 5, Schedule D and supporting schedules, and if applicable: • Form 8453 or Form 8879, if electronically filed • Schedule M-3 (taxpayers with $10 million or more in total assets) • Form 2220 (underpayment of estimated tax) and supporting schedules • Form 3800 (general business credit) • Form 4797 (sales of business property) • Form 851 (affiliations schedule) and schedules prepared for the computation of consolidated taxable income • Form 8866 (interest computation under look-back method for property depreciated under income forecast method) or 8697 (interest computation under look-back method for completed long-term contracts) • Form 8611 (recapture of low-income housing credit)
Arizona	No	
Arkansas	Yes	Copy of the completed federal Form 1120, 1120S, or other form, including all schedules and documents.

Jurisdiction	C Corporations	Comment
California	Yes, if federal reconciliation method is used.	Corporations filing federal Schedule M-3 must attach either: • a copy of the Schedule M-3 (spreadsheet format allowed) and related attachments; or • a complete copy of federal return. Attach, if applicable: • Form 926 (return by a U.S. transferor of property to a foreign corporation) • Form 1066 (U.S. real estate mortgage investment conduit (REMIC) income tax return) • Form 3115 (application for change in accounting method) • Form 5471 (information return of U.S. persons with respect to certain foreign corporations) • Form 5472 (information return of a 25% foreign-owned U.S. corporation or a foreign corporation engaged in a U.S. trade or business) • Form 8886 (reportable transaction disclosure statement) • Form 8938 (statement of specified foreign financial assets) • Form 8975 (country-by-country report) and accompanying Schedule A (tax jurisdiction and constituent entity information) • Schedule UTP (uncertain tax position statement) If first time reportable transaction disclosed on return, duplicate Form 8886 must be mailed separately to FTB.
Colorado	No	
Connecticut	Complete copy of federal return as filed with the IRS including all schedules.	Attach, if applicable: • Form 1120H (tax exempt homeowners' association) • Form 1120-POL (tax exempt political organizations and associations)
Delaware	Yes, copy of federal return, including all federal schedules and exhibits.	Attach, if applicable: • Spreadsheets of all income and deduction items for members of federal affiliated groups reconciling each member's separate items with consolidated totals • Form 1118 (foreign tax credit) • Form 1139 (application for tentative refund relating to NOL carryback) • Form 5884 (work opportunity credit)
District of Columbia	No	If applicable, federal Forms 4562, 4797, and Schedule UTP must be attached to Form D-20. If a federal Schedule M-3 (Form 1120) was filed with the federal return it must be attached to Form D-20.

Jurisdiction	C Corporations	Comment
Florida	Yes	Copy of actual federal income tax return filed with the IRS must be attached to Form F-1120. Where applicable, federal Forms 4562, 851 (or Florida Form F-851), 1122, 4626, Schedule D, Schedule M-3, and any supporting details for Schedules M-1 and M-2.
Georgia	Yes	Federal return and all federal schedules supporting the federal return must be attached to Form 600.
Hawaii	No	Corporations claiming a depreciation deduction must attach a completed federal Form 4562.
Idaho	Yes	If applicable, also attach federal approval of change in accounting method or period and/or Form 4562.
Illinois	Copy of pages 1 through 5 of federal return	Attach, if applicable: • Schedule L (transactions by exempt organizations with interested persons) • Schedules M1 and M2 (foregin corporation reconciliation of income/loss and analysis of unappropriated retained earnings per books) • Schedule M-3 (taxpayers with $10 million or more in total assets) • Form 982 (reduction of tax attributes due to discharge of indebtedness) • Form 8886 (reportable transaction disclosure statement) Attach, if standard federal return is not filed: • 1120-H (income tax return for homeowners associations); • Page 1 (and Schedule A if filed) of Form 1120-L (life insurance company income tax return); • Page 1 (and Schedule A if filed) of Form 1120-PC (property and casualty insurance company income tax return); • Form 1120-POL (income tax return for certain political organizations); or • Form 1120-SF (income tax return for settlement funds). Corporations included in consolidated federal tax return must provide pro forma copy of federal Forms 1120, 1120-L, 1120-PC, and all applicable schedules, as if separate federal return had been filed.
Indiana	Yes	Copies of pages 1 through 5 and Schedule M-3 of the federal return must be attached to Indiana IT-20.
Iowa	Yes	Complete copy of federal return as filed with the IRS and federal Form 4626 must be attached to Form IA 1120. Federal affiliated group members filing consolidated federal returns must attach pages 1 through 5 of consolidated federal return.

Jurisdiction	C Corporations	Comment
Kansas	Copy of pages 1 through 5 of federal return or consolidated return.	If the return is a consolidated return, enclose a company-by-company spreadsheet of income and expense to total the consolidated federal taxable income and a company-by-company spreadsheet of the consolidated balance sheet, including Schedules M-1 and M-2. Federal schedules to support any Kansas modifications claimed on Form K-120, and federal Forms 851, 1118, and 5471, if applicable, must be attached to Form K-120.
Kentucky	Yes, copy of all pages of federal return.	Attach, if applicable: • Form 1125-A (cost of goods sold) • Form 1125-E (compensation of officers) • Form 851 (affiliations schedule) • Form 4562 (depreciation and amortization) • Form 4797 (sales of business property) • Schedule D (capital gains and losses) • Form 3800 (general business credit) • Form 5884 (work opportunity credit) • Form 1120, Schedule L attachments • Form 3115 (application for change in accounting method) • Form 1128 (application to adopt, change, or retain a tax year) • Form 6765 (credit for increasing research activities)
Louisiana	Corporations granted permission to use separate accounting method must attach federal return.	
Maine	Copy of pages 1 through 5 of federal return must be attached. Corporations included in federal consolidated filing must attach pages 1 through 5 of federal return. Exempt organizations must attach a copy of corporation's federal return. If applicable, federal Schedule(s) K-1, and federal Forms 851, 4626, 5884, and 8844.	
Maryland	Yes	Copy of actual federal return through schedule M2 as filed with the IRS must be attached to Form 500. Corporations included in federal consolidated filing must file separate Maryland returns with copy of consolidated federal return through schedule M2 attached. Each filing must also include columnar schedules of income and expense and balance sheet items required for federal filing, reconciling separate items of each member to consolidated totals.
Massachusetts	No	Exact copy of federal return, including all applicable schedules and any other documentation required to substantiate entries made on state return, must be made available to Department of Revenue upon request.

Jurisdiction	C Corporations	Comment
Michigan	Pages 1 through 5 of federal Form 1120 must be attached.	Forms 851, 4562, 4797, Schedule D must be attached. If filing as part of a consolidated federal return, attach a pro forma or consolidated schedule.
Minnesota	Yes, copies of all federal returns and all supporting schedules, as filed with the IRS, except: • Form 1118 (foreign tax credit); • Form 1122 (consolidated return authorization and consent of subsidiary corporation); • Form 3115 (application for change in accounting method); • Form 5471 (information return of U.S. persons with respect to certain foreign corporations); • Form 5472 (information return of a 25% foreign-owned U.S. corporation or a foreign corporation engaged in a U.S. trade or business); and • Form 5713 (international boycott report).	The federal return will be accepted in PDF format on a CD.
Mississippi	Yes	Copy of federal return filing must be attached. Combined filers must attach the consolidated Federal Form 1120 pages 1 through 5, Schedule M-3, and a complete Pro-Forma Federal Return. Corporations excluding extraterritorial income on federal return must attach federal Form 8873 to Form 83-105. If federal bonus depreciation claimed on federal return, federal Form 4562 must be completed twice and attached to Form 83-122. Taxpayers who elect installment method for federal income tax purposes should include both a federal Form 6252 and a schedule of any differences between the federal and Mississippi amounts.
Missouri	Yes	Federal affiliated group members not filing Missouri consolidated returns must attach pro forma federal Form 1120 with all pertinent schedules, as well as pages 1 through 5 of actual consolidated federal income tax return. Taxpayers filing reportable transaction disclosure statements must include a copy of federal Form 8886. Taxpayers reporting uncertain tax positions to the IRS must attach a copy of their federal Schedule UTP. Taxpayers excluding gain from sale of low income housing project must attach federal Form 4797. Taxpayers required to recapture federal low income housing credit must attach federal Form 8611.

Jurisdiction	C Corporations	Comment
Montana	Yes	Completed copy of federal Form 1120 must be attached. If federal return is voluminous, pages 1-5 of return must be attached along with specified schedules, including copy of Schedules M-3 and N. Members of federal consolidated group or combined reporting group must attach copy of pages 1-5 of ultimate parent company's consolidated federal return (full signed copy of ultimate parent's Form 1120 must be attached if consolidated group member is filing separate Montana return).
Nebraska	Copy of federal return and supporting schedules, as filed with the IRS, must be attached.	At a minimum, copy of the first five pages, Schedule D, Form 4797, and other supporting schedules must be attached. If a consolidated federal return is filed, copy of consolidating schedules or workpapers for income and expenses, cost of goods sold, and balance sheets, as well as Form 851, must also be attached.
Nevada	N/A, because state does not tax general business corporation income.	
New Hampshire	Yes	Federal consolidating schedules, supporting schedules and statements must also be attached to Business Profits Tax (BPT) returns.
New Jersey	No	Corporations included in consolidated federal filing must complete all schedules on own separate basis and attach copy of federal Form 851 to Form CBT 100. Corporations filing unconsolidated federal Form 1120 with IRS may attach Schedules M-1 and M-2, federal Form 1120, in lieu of completing Schedules C and C-1, Form CBT 100. Corporations deducting IRC Sec. 78 gross-up must attach federal Form 1118. Federal Form 4562 and a rider/schedules with information shown on Federal Form 1120, Schedule D and/or Form 4797 must be attached if releveant.
New Mexico	Pages 1 through 5 of federal Form 1120 must be attached to Form CIT-1.	Corporations filing under separate corporate entity or combined filing methods must attach pages 1 through 5 of simulated federal Form 1120. Other attachments may be required.

Jurisdiction	C Corporations	Comment
New York	Complete copy of federal return must be attached. Federal affiliated group members included in consolidated filings must complete and attach pro forma federal return reflecting federal taxable income that would have been reported on separate federal return and attach copy of federal consolidated workpaper indicating separate taxable income before elimination of intercorporate transaction included in federal consolidated return. If applicable, return must include disclosure Form DTF-686 with copy of federal Form 8886 attached.	
North Carolina	No, unless taxpayer does not complete Sch. G showing federal taxable income and state adjustments.	Attach, if applicable: • Pro forma federal tax return for taxpayer included in federal consolidated group • Schedules M1 and M2 (foregin corporation reconciliation of income/loss and analysis of unappropriated retained earnings per books) • Schedule M-3 (taxpayers with $10 million or more in total assets) Complete federal return must be available upon request.
North Dakota	Yes	Complete copy of federal return as filed with the IRS must be attached.
Ohio	No for CAT.	
Oklahoma	Yes	Complete copy of federal return must be attached to Form 512.
Oregon	Yes	Complete copy of federal return.
Pennsylvania	Yes	Complete copy of federal Income Tax return, on separate company basis, with all supporting schedules, must be attached. Federal Schedules L, M-1 and M-2 regardless of federal requirements.
Rhode Island	Yes	Copy of all pages and all schedules of federal return must be attached to Form RI-1120C.
South Carolina	Yes	Completed copy of federal return must be attached to SC 1120.
South Dakota	N/A, because state does not tax general business corporation income.	
Tennessee	No	
Texas	No	
Utah	Yes	First five pages of federal return must be attached to Form TC-20. Include federal Schedule M-3 (Form 1120) and federal Form 1125-A, if applicable.

Jurisdiction	C Corporations	Comment
Vermont	Pages 1 through 5, as appropriate, of federal return must be attached.	If affiliates are not part of the same federal consolidated group attach one federal return for each separate member. Attach Form 4562 (depreciation and amortization) as filed and pro forma, if applicable. Copies of federal statements regarding other income and deductions, net operating loss, and taxes and licenses.
Virginia	Copy of federal return as filed with IRS must be attached to state return.	
Washington	N/A, because state does not tax general business corporation income.	
West Virginia	Yes. Pages 1 through 5 of the signed federal income tax return as filed with the IRS.	If filing separate West Virginia and consolidated federal, attach pro forma federal, consolidated federal Form 851 (Affiliation Schedule), plus spreadsheets of the income and expenses, and balance sheet entries for every corporation included in the consolidated return. Attach schedules of other states with property, paid salaries or sales of tangible personal property protected by P.L. 86-272.
Wisconsin	Copy of federal return must be attached even if corporation had no state activity.	
Wyoming	N/A, because state does not tax general business corporation income.	

Federal Form Attachment Requirements (Personal Income)

Most states do not require that resident taxpayers attach a complete copy of federal Form 1040, including all schedules, to their state return. Some states require nonresident and part-year residents to attach a copy of their federal return. Many states require that all or selected supporting federal forms or schedules must be attached to a taxpayer's state return. This chart indicates states that impose a requirement for the current tax year that a complete copy of their federal personal income tax return, including all schedules, must be attached to the state personal income tax return. The chart also shows states that require attachment of only selected federal forms or schedules.

Jurisdiction	Federal Form Attachment	Comment
Alabama	Taxpayers must attach the appropriate federal form/schedule when making Alabama modifications. The state does not provide the following forms and schedules: • Schedules C (business income) and F (farm income); • Form 2106 (unreimbursed employee business expenses); • Form 3903 (moving expenses); • Form 4684 (casualty or theft losses); • Form 4797 (other gains/losses); • Form 6252 (installment sale income), and • Form 8283 (noncash charitable contributions of $500 or more).	
Arizona	Copy of federal return not required. Taxpayers who itemize must attach copy of federal Schedule A.	
Arkansas	Copy of federal return required for part-year residents and nonresidents. For residents, taxpayers must attach the following federal schedules and forms, if applicable: • Schedule listing disaster loss; • Schedule C (business income); • Schedule D (capital gains/losses); • Schedule E (rents, royalties, etc.); • Schedule F (farm income); • Form 2106 (unreimbursed employee business expenses); • Form 2441 or 1040A, Schedule 2 (child care credit); • Form 4684 (casualty or theft losses); • Form 4797 (other gains/losses); • Form 4952 (investment interest deduction); • Form 5329 (IRA withdrawal); • Form 8283 (noncash charitable contributions of $500 or more); and • Form 8606 (nondeductible contributions to IRA).	

Jurisdiction	Federal Form Attachment	Comment
California	Copy of federal return required for part-year residents and nonresidents. Also attach all federal Form(s) W-2 and W-2G received and any Form(s) 1099 showing state tax withheld. Resident taxpayers who attach federal forms or schedules other than Schedule A or B to federal Form 1040 must attach federal Form 1040 and all supporting schedules and forms. Taxpayers who itemize for state purposes, but not for federal purposes, must attach a pro forma copy of federal Schedule A to their state return. If applicable, attach federal Form 8886 (Reportable Transaction Disclosure Statement).	If first time reportable transaction disclosure on return, send a duplicate copy of federal Form 8886 to Franchise Tax Board. The FTB may impose penalties if taxpayer fails to file federal Form 8886, Form 8918 (Material Advisor Disclosure Statement), or any other required information.
Colorado	Copy of federal return not required.	
Connecticut	Copy of federal return not required. Attach, if applicable, federal Form 1310 (claiming refund due a deceased taxpayer).	
Delaware	Copy of pages 1 and 2 of federal return, plus all schedules required to be filed with federal return, must be attached and, if applicable: • Form 2106 or 2106EZ (unreimbursed employee expense credit); • Form 2441 (child and dependent care expense credit); • Schedule A; • Form 5884 (work opportunity credit); and • Schedule EIC.	Civil union individuals must include a pro forma federal return completed "as if" the filing status elected by the taxpayers for the Delaware return is married/civil union filing a joint, separate, or combined separate return.
District of Columbia	Copy of federal return not required.	
Georgia	Copy of federal return not required. Taxpayers must attach the following federal schedules and forms, if applicable: • Pages 1 and 2 of federal Form 1040, if federal adjusted gross income is $40,000 or more, or less than the total income on W-2(s); • Form 2441 or 1040A Schedule 2 (child and dependent care expense credit); • Schedule A (itemized deductions); and • Copy of federal return when claiming combat zone pay exclusion.	

Jurisdiction	Federal Form Attachment	Comment
Hawaii	Copy of federal return required for part-year residents and nonresidents. Attach, if applicable: • Form 1116 (foreign tax credit); • Form 1128 (application to adopt, change, or retain tax year); • Form 2106 or Form 2106-EZ (unreimbursed employee expense deduction); • Form 2120 (multiple support declaration); • Form 4562 (depreciation deduction); • Form 4684 (casualty or theft losses); • Form 4835 (farm rental income and expenses); • Form 5213 (hobby losses); • Form 6198 (at risk limitations); • Form 6252 (installment sale income); • Form 6781 (gains and losses); • Form 8283 (charitable contributions over $500); • Form 8332 (noncustodial parent dependent deduction); • Form 8582 (passive activity loss limitations); • Form 8814 (parent's election to report child's interest and dividends); • Form 8824 (like-kind exchanges); and • Form 8829 (business use of home expenses). Copies of all federal forms used as substitutes for state forms also must be attached.	
Idaho	Complete copy of the federal return must be attached.	
Illinois	Copy of federal return not required. Taxpayers must attach the following federal schedules and forms, if applicable: • Form 1040NR (federal nonresident alien income tax return); • Page 1 of Form 1040 or 1040A to support subtraction for Social Security, disability, and retirement income; • Form 1099-R or Form SSA-1099, if Form 1040, page 1, does not clearly identify reported retirement income and Social Security benefits; • Schedule D, (capital gains and losses) for gain on sale or exchange of employer securities; • Schedule B or Schedule 1, for interest and dividend income from U.S. retirement bonds; or • Form 8886 (Reportable Transaction Disclosure Statement).	

Jurisdiction	Federal Form Attachment	Comment
Indiana	Copy of federal return not required. Taxpayers must attach federal Schedule A from federal Form 1045; and federal Schedule R, if applicable.	
Iowa	Copy of federal return not required, unless: • nonresident or part-year resident credit is claimed; or • Illinois resident is requesting refund for Iowa income tax withheld in error. Attach, if applicable: • Schedules C or C-EZ (net business income or loss), D (capital gains), E (rental, pass activity, and royalty losses), and F (farming income or losses); • Form 3903 (moving expenses); • Form 4797 (sales of business property); • Form 1116 (foreign tax credit); and • Form 2441 (child care expense credit).	
Kansas	Copy of federal return not required, unless taxpayer is nonresident. Attach, if applicable: • Schedules A-F; and • Form 1116 (foreign tax credit).	
Kentucky	Copy of federal return and all supporting schedules required for nonresidents and part-year residents. Not required for residents, unless farm, business, or rental income or loss is received. Attach, if applicable: • Form 1128 (application to adopt, change, or retain a tax year); • Form 2106 or Form 2106-EZ (employee business expenses); • Form 2120 (multiple support declaration); • Form 2441 (child and dependent care expenses); • Form 3115 (application for change in accounting method); • Form 4562 (depreciation and amortization); • Form 4684 (casualties or thefts); • Form 4952 (investment interest expense deduction); • Form 8283 (noncash charitable contributions); • Form 8332 (custodial parent dependent exemption release); and • Form 8889 (health savings account deduction).	

Jurisdiction	Federal Form Attachment	Comment
Louisiana	Copy of federal return not required, unless: • disaster relief credits claimed on federal return as a result of Hurricane Katrina or Hurricane Rita; or • claiming deduction for capital gain from sale of state business. Attach, if applicable, Form 3800 and other appropriate federal forms for disaster relief credit.	
Maine	Copy of federal return not required, unless nonresident credit is claimed. Attach, if applicable: • Form 4562 (depreciation and amortization); and • Schedule K-1 (beneficiary's share of income, deductions, credits, etc.).	
Maryland	Copy of federal return not required.	
Massachusetts	Copy of federal return not required. Enclose federal Schedule F (farm income or loss), if applicable.	
Michigan	Copy of federal return not required. Taxpayers must attach the following schedules and forms, if applicable: • Schedule B or 1040A Schedule 1 (interest and dividend income if over $5,000); • Schedule C or C-EZ (business income and losses); • Schedule D (gains and losses); • Schedule E (rent, royalty, partnership income); • Schedule F (farm income or losses); • Schedule R or 1040A Schedule 3 (credit for elderly or disabled); • Form 1040NR (Nonresident Alien Income Tax Return); • Form 2555 (foreign earned income); • Form 3903 or 3903-F (moving expenses); • Form 4797 (gains and losses); • Form 6198 (deductible loss from activity); • Form 8829 (expenses for business use of home). Taxpayers claiming credit for repayment of amounts previously reported as income must attach pages 1 and 2 of federal Form 1040 and Schedule A, if applicable.	
Minnesota	Complete copy of federal return and schedules must be attached. Attach, if applicable: • Form 6251 (alternative minimum tax return); and • Form 8886 (reportable transaction disclosure statement).	Copy of Form 8886 also must be mailed to Department of Revenue when taxpayer first discloses reportable transaction. Penalties apply for noncompliance.

Jurisdiction	Federal Form Attachment	Comment
Mississippi	Copy of federal return not required. Taxpayers must attach the following federal schedules and forms, if applicable: • Schedule C or C-EZ (business income and losses); • Schedule D (gains and losses); • Schedule E (rent, royalty, partnership income); • Schedule F (farm income or losses); • Form 2106 (unreimbursed employee expense deduction); • Form 3903 or 3903-F (moving expenses); and • Form 4684 (casualty and theft losses). If amount of state taxable income entered on Form 80-105 differs from amount of federal taxable income entered on a federal return, separate reconciling schedules must be attached.	
Missouri	Copy of federal return must be attached. Attach, if applicable: • Schedule A (itemized deductions); • Form 1045 (net operating loss); • 1099-R, Form W-2P, and/or Form SSA-1099 (pension, social security, and/or social security disability exemption); • Form 4255 (recapture taxes); • Form 4797 (capital gain exclusion on sale of low income housing); • Form 4972 (lump sum distribution); • Form 8839 (special needs adoption credit); • Form 8611 (recapture taxes); • Form 8826 (disabled access credit); • Form 8828 (recapture taxes); • Form 8959 (additional medicare tax); and • Schedule K-1.	Attachment of Form 8886 (reportable transaction disclosure statement), if applicable, is also recommended by Department of Revenue.

Jurisdiction	Federal Form Attachment	Comment
Montana	Copy of federal return must be attached by nonresident and part-year resident taxpayers. Pages 1 and 2 of federal return must be attached if head-of-household filing status is used. Attach, if applicable: • Schedule B (interest and dividend income); • Schedule C or C-EZ (business income and losses); • Schedule D (gains and losses); • Schedule E (rent, royalty, partnership income); • Schedule F (farm income or losses); • Schedule SE (self-employment tax); • Form 1310 (statement of person claiming refund of deceased taxpayer); • Form 2106 or 2106-EZ (unreimbursed employee business expenses); • Form 3468 (historic property preservation credit); • Form 3903 or 3903-F (moving expenses); • Form 4797 (gains and losses); • Form 4972 (lump sum distribution); • Form 8839 (adoption expenses); • Form 8889 (health savings account deduction); and • Form 8903 (domestic production activities).	
Nebraska	Copy of federal return not required, unless entering a federal tax liability. Copy of pages 1 and 2 of federal return must be attached if claiming earned income credit. Taxpayers must attach the following federal schedules and forms, if applicable: • Schedule D (special capital gain deduction); • Schedule R (credit for elderly or disabled); and • Form 2441 (child/dependent care credit).	
New Hampshire	Copy of federal return not required.	

Jurisdiction	Federal Form Attachment	Comment
New Jersey	Copy of federal return not required. Part-year residents with income below annual filing threshold ($10,000 single or married filing separately, $20,000 married filing jointly) must attach copy of federal return. Taxpayers must attach the following federal schedules and forms, if applicable: • Schedule B (interest and dividend income); • Schedule C or C-EZ (business income and losses); • Form 2106 or 2106-EZ (unreimbursed employee business expenses); • Form 3903 or 3903-F (moving expenses); • Form 8283 (qualified conservation contributions); • Form 8853 (Archer MSA contributions); and • Schedule K-1.	
New Mexico	Copy of federal return not required. However, state may request copy of federal return and attachments.	
New York	Copy of federal return not required. Taxpayers must attach the following federal schedules and forms, if applicable: • Schedule C or C-EZ (business income and losses); • Schedule D (gains and losses); • Schedule E (rent, royalty, partnership income); • Schedule F (farm income or losses); and • Form 4797 (gains and losses). Copy of federal Form 8886 (Reportable Transaction Disclosure Statement) and any related information submitted to IRS must be attached, if applicable.	
North Carolina	Copy of federal return not required. Copy of federal return must be attached if federal return bears out-of-state address and taxpayer did not file electronically. Taxpayers with gross income meeting filing threshold who were not required to file federal return must complete and attach federal return. Taxpayers filing separate state return who filed joint federal return must complete and attach federal return as married filing separately or schedule showing computation of separate federal taxable income and include copy of joint federal return if that return bears out-of-state address.	
North Dakota	Complete copy of federal return, including supplemental forms and schedules, must be attached.	

Jurisdiction	Federal Form Attachment	Comment
Ohio	Copy of federal return not required. Taxpayers with zero or negative federal adjusted gross income must attach copy of federal return to state return. Investors in pass-through entities claiming credit for tax paid on Ohio Form IT-4708 or IT-1140 must attach federal Form K-1s that reflect amount of Ohio tax paid.	
Oklahoma	Copy of federal return must be attached if: • state AGI differs from federal; • claiming earned income credit; • claiming child care credit; • medical or health savings account deduction; • Police Corps Program deduction; • social security benefits subtracted; • lump sum distributions added; • out-of-state income; or • claiming exception to estimated payment requirements due to at least 66-2/3% of gross income this year or last year from farming. Nonresidents and part-year residents must attach copy of federal return. Taxpayers must attach the following federal schedules and forms, if applicable: • Schedule A (itemized deductions); • Schedule D (gains from exempt federal obligations, capital gains); • Schedule E (rent, royalty, partnership income); • Schedule F (farm income); • Form 2441 or 1040A Schedule 2 (child care expense credit); • Form 4562 (depreciation); • Form 8606 (nondeductible IRAs); • Form 8885 and Form 3800 (Indian employment exclusion); and • copy of federal NOL computation.	
Oregon	Copy of federal return must be attached. Federal schedules should not be attached, unless requested. Form 8886 checkbox must be marked on returns by taxpayers who are required to file federal disclosure form for listed or reportable transactions.	

Jurisdiction	Federal Form Attachment	Comment
Pennsylvania	Copy of federal return not required. Taxpayer must attach all applicable federal schedules, where allowed, if state schedules are not used. Federal Schedule K-1 must be attached if taxpayer did not receive the corresponding PA K-1, if applicable. Page 1 of federal Form 1040 must be attached if claiming deduction for medical savings account or health savings account contributions. Nonresident and part-year resident taxpayers who file paper copies of the PA-40 must also include a copy of page one of federal return.	
Rhode Island	Copy of federal return not required.	
South Carolina	Complete copy of federal return and schedules must be attached if taxpayer was required to use federal Schedules C, D, E, or F or if filing Schedule NR (part year/nonresident), Form SC1040TC (non-refundable credits), Form I-319 (tuition tax credit), or Form I-335 (active trade or business income). Taxpayers must attach federal Form 8332 (release of claim to exemption), if applicable.	
Tennessee	Copy of federal return not required.	
Utah	Copy of federal return not required. Attach, if applicable Form 8379 (injured spouse allocation).	
Vermont	For married or civil union filing separately and using Income Adjustment Schedule IN-113, pages 1 and 2 of federal return must be attached. Taxpayers must attach the following federal forms, if applicable: • Form 1310 (person claiming refund due a deceased taxpayer); or • Form 2441 (child and dependent care expenses).	
Virginia	Copy of federal return not required. Nonresident and part-year resident taxpayers must attach complete copy of federal return. Taxpayers must attach federal Schedules C, C-EZ, E and F, and Form 1310 (person claiming refund due a deceased taxpayer), if applicable.	
West Virginia	Copy of federal return not required. Copy of federal Schedule R (Part II) may be substituted for WV Schedule H (disabled taxpayer). If applicable, attach federal Form 8886 (Reportable Transaction Disclosure Statement).	

Jurisdiction	Federal Form Attachment	Comment
Wisconsin	Complete copy of federal return with supporting schedules and forms must be attached.	

Federal Income Taxes Paid

This chart indicates whether each state and the District of Columbia allow taxpayers computing personal income tax liability to claim a subtraction adjustment for federal income taxes paid.

Jurisdiction	Federal Income Taxes Paid	Comment
Alabama	Subtraction from adjusted gross income allowed.	
Arizona	No adjustments to federal tax base allowed.	
Arkansas	No adjustments to adjusted gross income allowed.	
California	No adjustments to federal tax base allowed.	
Colorado	No adjustments to federal tax base allowed.	
Connecticut	No adjustments to federal tax base allowed.	
Delaware	No adjustments to federal tax base allowed.	
District of Columbia	No adjustments to federal tax base allowed.	
Georgia	No adjustments to federal tax base allowed.	
Hawaii	No adjustments to federal tax base allowed.	
Idaho	No adjustments to federal tax base allowed.	
Illinois	No adjustments to federal tax base allowed.	
Indiana	No adjustments to federal tax base allowed.	
Iowa	Subtraction from federal tax base allowed.	
Kansas	No adjustments to federal tax base allowed.	
Kentucky	No adjustments to federal tax base allowed.	

Jurisdiction	Federal Income Taxes Paid	Comment
Louisiana	Subtraction from federal tax base allowed for federal income tax liability. Increased by: • federal disaster relief credits; • federal net investment income taxes; and • federal tax decrease from deduction for certain net disaster losses (2015 to 2017 tax years only). Reduced by: • Social Security taxes; • federal self-employment taxes; • federal taxes on exempt income; and • federal additional Medicare taxes.	
Maine	No adjustments to federal tax base allowed.	
Maryland	No adjustments to federal tax base allowed.	
Massachusetts	No adjustments to federal tax base allowed.	
Michigan	No adjustments to federal tax base allowed.	
Minnesota	No adjustments to federal tax base allowed.	
Mississippi	No adjustments to federal tax base allowed.	
Missouri	Subtraction from federal tax base allowed for up to $5,000, or $10,000 if filing status is married filing joint return.	
Montana	No adjustments to federal tax base allowed.	
Nebraska	No adjustments to federal tax base allowed.	
New Hampshire	N/A	Tax on individuals is imposed only on interest and dividend income.
New Jersey	No adjustments to gross income allowed.	
New Mexico	No adjustments to federal tax base allowed.	
New York	No adjustments to federal tax base allowed.	
North Carolina	No adjustments to federal tax base allowed.	
North Dakota	No adjustments to federal tax base allowed.	
Ohio	No adjustments to federal tax base allowed.	

Jurisdiction	Federal Income Taxes Paid	Comment
Oklahoma	No adjustments to federal tax base allowed. Subtraction from federal tax base allowed for tax years prior to 2006.	
Oregon	Subtraction from federal tax base allowed for up to $6,250 depending on federal adjusted gross income.	
Pennsylvania	No adjustments to gross income allowed.	
Rhode Island	No adjustments to federal tax base allowed.	
South Carolina	No adjustments to federal tax base allowed.	
Tennessee	N/A	Tax imposed only on interest and dividend income.
Utah	No adjustments to federal tax base allowed. Subtraction from adjusted income allowed for 50% of federal income tax liability for tax years prior to 2008.	
Vermont	No adjustments to federal tax base allowed.	
Virginia	No adjustments to federal tax base allowed.	
West Virginia	No adjustments to federal tax base allowed.	
Wisconsin	No adjustments to federal tax base allowed.	

Federal Return Attachment—Partnerships, LLPs, and LLCs

This chart shows whether the states and the District of Columbia require partnerships, limited liability partnerships (LLPs), and limited liability companies (LLCs) to attach federal form 1065 to the entity's state return. The "Comments" column notes additional attachment requirements.

Jurisdiction	Partnerships, LLPs, and LLCs	Comment
Alabama	Yes	
Alaska	Yes, copy of signed federal return.	
Arizona	No	
Arkansas	No	Partnerships are not required to attached copies of the federal return to their state return.
California	Partnerships filing federal Schedule M-3 must attach either: • a copy of the Schedule M-3 (spreadsheet format okay) and related attachments; or • a complete copy of federal return.	Attach, If applicable: • Form 8825 (rental real estate income and expenses of a partnership or an S corporation) • Form 8832 (entity classification election) • Form 8886 (reportable transaction disclosure statement) If first time reportable transaction, disclose on return, duplicate 8886 must be mailed separately to FTB.
Colorado	No	
Connecticut	Yes, attach completed copy of federal return, if filing paper form. Retain copy of federal return for 3 years if filing electronically.	Federal Schedule K-1s should not be sent with state return.
Delaware	Copy of federal return, including all schedules other than Schedule K-1.	
District of Columbia	Yes	Copy of federal K-1 and schedule showing the distribution of income for all members of the partnership.
Florida	No	
Georgia	Yes	
Hawaii	No	Partnerships, LLPs, and LLCs claiming a depreciation deduction must attach a completed federal Form 4562. LLCs electing to be classified as a partnership by filing federal Form 8832 must attach federal Form 8832 to the Form N-20 covering the first taxable year in which it carries on business in the state, derives income from sources in the state, or makes distributions that are received by a partner who is a resident or carries on business in the state and is subject to tax in the state.

Jurisdiction	Partnerships, LLPs, and LLCs	Comment
Idaho	Copy of federal return, including all Schedules K-1.	If applicable, also attach federal approval of change in accounting method or period and/or Form 4562.
Illinois	Yes, attach copy of federal return.	Attach, if applicable: • Schedule M-3 (taxpayers with $10 million or more in total assets) • Form 8886 (reportable transaction disclosure statement) • Schedule D (capital gains and losses) • Form 4797 (sales of business property) • Form 6252 (installment sale income)
Indiana	Copy of pages 1 through 5 of federal return and Schedule M-3.	
Iowa	Yes	
Kansas	Copy of pages 1-5 of federal return, Schedule M-1, Schedule M-2, and any additional federal schedules to support any state modifications.	
Kentucky	Yes, copy of all pages of federal return.	Attach, if applicable: • Form 1125-A (cost of goods sold) • Form 4797 (sales of business property) • Schedule D (capital gains and losses) • Form 5884 (work opportunity credit) • Schedules for items on Form 1120S, Schedule L (book balance sheet items), that state "attach schedule." • Form 4562 (depreciation and amortization) • Form 8825 (rental real estate income) • Form 6765 (credit for increasing research activities)
Louisiana	Partnerships granted permission to use separate accounting method must attach federal return.	
Maine	No return filing requirement for tax years beginning after 2011.	**Tax years before 2012 :** Yes
Maryland	Attach schedule K and K-1.	
Massachusetts	No	
Michigan	Pages 1-5 of federal Form 1065 (no K-1s), as well as Schedule D, Forms 4797, 8825, must be attached.	
Minnesota	Copy of federal return, Schedules K and K-1, and other federal schedules.	
Mississippi	Yes	
Missouri	Yes	
Montana	Yes	
Nebraska	Copy of federal return and supporting schedules.	If applicable, attach federal approval of change in accounting period for first return showing the change.

Jurisdiction	Partnerships, LLPs, and LLCs	Comment
Nevada	N/A, because state does not tax pass-through income.	
New Hampshire	Copy of pages 1-5 of federal return, plus applicable schedules.	
New Jersey	Copy of pages 1-5 of federal return, plus federal Schedule D and any federal extension request forms.	
New Mexico	Pages 1 through 5 of federal Form 1065 must be attached. Additional attachments may be required.	LLCs electing to be taxed as S corporations for federal income tax purposes must attach pages 1 through 5 of federal Form 1120S. Additional attachments may be required.
New York	No	If applicable, New York return must include disclosure Form DTF-686 with copy of federal Form 8886 attached. If federal Schedule M-3 was filed, copy must be attached.
North Carolina	Yes, attach copy of federal return and all supporting schedules, unless ordinary income (loss) items from return are transferred to state return.	
North Dakota	Yes	
Ohio	No for CAT.	
Oklahoma	Copy of federal return and Schedules K-1s.	
Oregon	Yes	
Pennsylvania	Yes	
Rhode Island	Yes	
South Carolina	Yes	
South Dakota	N/A, because state does not tax pass-through income.	
Tennessee	No	At the Commissioner of Revenue's discretion, taxpayers may be required to file a copy of the federal tax forms filed with the IRS.
Texas	No	
Utah	No	Partnerships are not required to attached copies of the federal return to their state return.
Vermont	Copies of first 5 pages of federal return must be attached.	
Virginia	Copy of federal return with Schedule K must be attached to state return.	If federal return is so voluminous that it is impractical to include a complete copy, attach federal form along with Schedule K and a statement that complete return will be made available upon request.

Jurisdiction	Partnerships, LLPs, and LLCs	Comment
Washington	N/A, because state does not tax pass-through income.	
West Virginia	Yes, attach copy of signed federal return.	Attach Schedule M-3 (taxpayers with $10 million or more in total assets), if applicable.
Wisconsin	Yes	
Wyoming	N/A, because state does not tax pass-through income.	

Federal Return Attachment—S Corporations

Jurisdiction	S Corporations	Comment
Alabama	Yes	
Alaska	Yes, copy of entire federal return and supporting schedules.	Attach Form 8453-S or Form 8879-S, if electronically filed. If corporate level taxes are imposed, attach copies of schedules and forms calculating federal tax and state tax.
Arizona	No	
Arkansas	Yes	
California	Yes, if federal reconciliation method is used.	Corporations filing federal Schedule M-3 must attach either: • a copy of the Schedule M-3 (spreadsheet format allowed) and related attachments, or • a complete copy of federal return. Attach, if applicable: • Form 926 (return by a U.S. transferor of property to a foreign corporation) • Form 970 (application to use LIFO inventory method) • Form 3115 (application for change in accounting method) • Form 5471 (information return of U.S. persons with respect to certain foreign corporations) • Form 5472 (information return of a 25% foreign owned U.S. corporation or a foreign corporation engaged in a U.S. trade or business • Form 8825 (rental real estate income and expenses of a partnership or an S corporation) • Form 8869 (qualified subchapter S subsidiary election) • Form 8886 (reportable transaction disclosure statement) • Form 8938 (statement of specified foreign financial assets) • Form 8975 (country-by-country report) and accompanying Schedule A (tax jurisdiction and constituent entity information) If first time reportable transaction disclosed on return, duplicate Form 8886 must be mailed separately to FTB.
Colorado	No	
Connecticut	Yes, attach completed copy of federal return, if filing paper form. Retain copy of federal return for 3 years if filing electronically.	Federal Schedule K-1s should not be sent with state return.
Delaware	Copy of federal return, including Schedule K and K-1, and if applicable Form 5884 (new jobs credit).	

Jurisdiction	S Corporations	Comment
District of Columbia	No	If applicable, attach: • federal Forms 851, 4562, 4797, 5471, 5472, 8833, 8868, 8886, and 8975 (including Schedule A); • federal Schedules D, J, M, M-3; and • Federal UTP.
Florida	Yes	
Georgia	Yes	
Hawaii	No	Page 4 of federal return and Schedule M-3, if applicable, must be attached to Form N-35. Corporations must attach a federal Form 4562 if claiming a depreciation deduction and a federal Form T if claiming a timber depletion deduction. If it is the first year the LIFO inventory method was either adopted or extended to inventory goods not previously valued under the LIFO method, a copy of federal Form 970 or a statement must be attached to Form N-35. If a QSub election is made for an existing corporation, the parent corporation must attach a copy of federal Form 8869 to the first Form N-35 filed after the election.
Idaho	Copy of federal return, including all Schedules K-1.	If applicable, also attach federal approval of change in accounting method or period and/or Form 4562. Copy of federal election or notice approving federal election must be attached to first state return.
Illinois	Yes, attach copy of federal return.	Attach, if applicable: • Schedule M-3 (taxpayers with $10 million or more in total assets) • Form 982 (reduction of tax attributes due to discharge of indebtedness) • Form 8886 (reportable transaction disclosure statement)
Indiana	Copy of pages 1 through 5 of federal return and Schedule M-3.	
Iowa	Yes	
Kansas	Copy of pages 1-4 of federal return, Schedule M-1, Schedule M-2, and any additional federal schedules to support any state modifications.	

Jurisdiction	S Corporations	Comment
Kentucky	Yes, copy of all pages of federal return.	Attach, if applicable: • Form 1125-A (cost of goods sold) • Form 4797 (sales of business property) • Schedule D (capital gains and losses) • Form 5884 (work opportunity credit) • Schedules for items on Form 1120S, Schedule L (book balance sheet items), that state "attach schedule." • Form 4562 (depreciation and amortization) • Form 8825 (rental real estate income) • Form 6765 (credit for increasing research activities)
Louisiana	Corporations granted permission to use separate accounting method must attach federal return.	
Maine	No return filing requirement for tax years beginning after 2011.	**Tax years before 2012:** Yes
Maryland	Attach a copy of Schedule K from federal Form 1120S, as well as a Schedule K-1 for each nonresident shareholder, and a copy of federal return through schedule M2.	
Massachusetts	No	Exact copy of federal return, including all applicable schedules and any other documentation required to substantiate entries made on state return, must be made available to Department of Revenue upon request.
Michigan	Pages 1 through 4 of federal Form 1120-S (no K-1s), as well as Forms 851, 4562, 4797, 8825, Schedule D, must be attached.	
Minnesota	Copy of federal return, Schedules K and K-1, and other federal schedules.	
Mississippi	Yes	
Missouri	Yes	Taxpayers filing reportable transaction disclosure statements must include a copy of federal Form 8886.
Montana	Yes	
Nebraska	Copy of federal return and supporting schedules.	If applicable, attach federal approval of change in accounting period for first return showing the change.
Nevada	N/A, because state does not tax pass-through income.	
New Hampshire	Copy of pages 1-5 of federal return, plus applicable schedules.	
New Jersey	Yes	
New Mexico	Pages 1 through 5 of federal Form 1120S must be attached. Additional attachments may be required.	

Jurisdiction	S Corporations	Comment
New York	Yes	If applicable, New York return must include disclosure Form DTF-686 with copy of federal Form 8886 attached.
North Carolina	Yes, attach copy of federal return and all supporting schedules, unless ordinary income (loss) items from return are transferred to state return.	Attach, if applicable: • Schedule L (book balance sheet items) • Schedule M-1 (reconciliation of income (loss) per books with income (loss) per return) • Schedule M-3 (taxpayers with $10 million or more in total assets)
North Dakota	Yes	
Ohio	No for CAT.	
Oklahoma	Copy of federal return and Schedules K-1s.	
Oregon	Yes	
Pennsylvania	Yes	
Rhode Island	Yes	
South Carolina	Yes	
South Dakota	N/A, because state does not tax pass-through income.	
Tennessee	No	At the Commissioner of Revenue's discretion, taxpayers may be required to file a copy of the federal tax forms filed with the IRS.
Texas	No	
Utah	Yes	First five pages of federal return must be attached to Form TC-20S. Include federal Schedule M-3 (Form 1120S) and federal Form 1125-A, if applicable.
Vermont	Copies of first 5 pages of federal return must be attached.	
Virginia	Copy of federal return with Schedule K must be attached to state return.	If federal return is so voluminous that it is impractical to include a complete copy, attach federal form along with Schedule K and a statement that complete return will be made available upon request.
Washington	N/A, because state does not tax pass-through income.	
West Virginia	Yes, attach copy of signed federal return.	Attach Schedule M-3 (taxpayers with $10 million or more in total assets), if applicable.
Wisconsin	Yes	
Wyoming	N/A, because state does not tax pass-through income.	

Global Intangible Low-Taxed Income (GILTI)—IRC § 951A

Global Intangible Low-Taxed Income (GILTI) is the excess of a U.S. shareholders net controlled foreign corporations (CFCs) tested income over net deemed tangible income return for the year. A person who is a U.S. shareholder of any CFC is required to include its GILTI (IRC § 951A) in gross income for the tax year. The provision applies to tax years of foreign corporations beginning after December 31, 2017, and to tax years of U.S. shareholders with which or within which such tax years of foreign corporations end.

A corporation computes GILTI on a separate federal form. It reports the resulting amount as taxable dividend income on federal Form 1120. So, a corporation computing income tax liability in a state with a federal taxable income starting point must include GILTI, unless the state allows a deduction.

This chart shows the tax treatment of GILTI income for corporations by each state and the District of Columbia. The chart does not cover states that provide apportionment factor relief or other apportionment adjustments for GILTI. Adjustments for foreign dividends received and foreign source income other than dividends are addressed in other charts.

Jurisdiction	Global Intangible Low-Taxed Income (GILTI)—IRC § 951A	Comment
Alabama	No subtraction allowed.	
Alaska	Subtraction allowed equal to foreign dividends received deduction.	
Arizona	Subtraction allowed under foreign dividends received deduction for tax years after 2018.	
Arkansas	No subtraction allowed.	
California	N/A, because state does not conform to IRC Sec. 951A.	
Colorado	Subtraction allowed for a portion of GILTI income under foreign dividends received deduction.	
Connecticut	Subtraction allowed equal to dividends received deduction.	
Delaware	No subtraction allowed.	
District of Columbia	No subtraction allowed.	
Florida	Subtraction allowed for all amounts included in federal taxable income, effective retroactively to tax years beginning on or after January 1, 2018.	
Georgia	Subtraction allowed for income specified in IRC Sec. 951A.	
Hawaii	N/A, because state does not conform to IRC Sec. 951A.	
Idaho	No subtraction allowed.	

Jurisdiction	Global Intangible Low-Taxed Income (GILTI)—IRC §951A	Comment
Illinois	Subraction allowed equal to: • 100% of GILTI from wholly owned foreign subsidiaries; • 65% of GILTI from 20%-or-more-owned foreign corporations; and • 50% of GILTI from less-than-20%-owned foreign corporations. Taxpayers must exclude IRC Sec. 250 deduction.	Subtraction computed on Schedule J.
Indiana	Subtraction allowed equal to foreign source dividend deduction.	
Iowa	Subtraction allowed to the extent GILTI included on the Iowa return.	
Kansas	No subtraction allowed.	
Kentucky	Subtraction allowed equal to dividends received deduction for 100% of GILTI.	
Louisiana	GILTI treated as dividend income. Subtraction allowed under the dividends received deduction.	Because no portion of GILTI income is taxable for Louisiana corporation income tax purposes, any deduction taken on the federal return related to GILTI income must be added back on Schedule F of the CIFT-620.
Maine	Subtraction allowed for a portion of GILTI included in federal gross income.	
Maryland	No subtraction allowed.	
Massachusetts	GILTI treated as dividend income. Subtraction allowed under the dividends received deduction.	
Michigan	Subtraction allowed for GILTI less IRC Sec. 250 deduction amount. Treated as a dividend from a foreign entity, similar to subpart F income.	
Minnesota	N/A, because state does not conform to IRC Sec. 951A.	
Mississippi	GILTI treated as foreign income that is not taxed.	
Missouri	No subtraction allowed.	
Montana	No subtraction allowed.	
Nebraska	No subtraction allowed.	
Nevada	N/A, because state does not tax general business corporation income.	
New Hampshire	Subtraction allowed for GILTI.	
New Jersey	No subtraction allowed.	
New Mexico	Subtraction allowed for GILTI. Taxpayers must exclude IRC Sec. 250 deduction.	Prior to 2020, no subtraction allowed.

Jurisdiction	Global Intangible Low-Taxed Income (GILTI)—IRC §951A	Comment
New York	For tax years after 2018, subtraction allowed for 95% of GILTI required to be included in federal gross income, without regard to the IRC Sec. 250 deduction, received from a corporation that is not part of the taxpayer's combined report. For tax years before 2019, no subtraction allowed.	
North Carolina	Subtraction allowed.	
North Dakota	Subtraction allowed for a portion of GILTI income as a foreign dividend for water's edge filers.	
Ohio	**Commercial Activity Tax:** Excludes dividends and distributions from corporations and distributive or proportionate share of receipts and income from a pass-through entity for purposes of calculating the CAT.	
Oklahoma	Taxpayers should report GILTI income as dividend income.	
Oregon	Subtraction allowed equal to dividends received deduction.	
Pennsylvania	GILTI treated as a dividend and included in corporate income tax base in the year recognized. The actual distribution is treated as previously taxed income.	
Rhode Island	No subtraction allowed.	
South Carolina	N/A, because state does not conform to IRC Sec. 951A.	
South Dakota	N/A, because state does not tax general business corporation income.	
Tennessee	Subtraction allowed for GILTI amounts included in federal taxable income, with an addition then required for 5% of the amount included in FTI before the deduction allowed under IRC Sec. 250.	
Texas	N/A, because state does not conform to IRC Sec. 951A.	
Utah	No subtraction allowed.	
Vermont	No subtraction allowed.	
Virginia	For tax years after 2017, subtraction allowed to the extent GILTI included in taxpayer's federal taxable income.	
Washington	N/A, because state does not tax general business corporation income.	
West Virginia	No subtraction allowed.	

Jurisdiction	Global Intangible Low-Taxed Income (GILTI)—IRC § 951A	Comment
Wisconsin	N/A, because state does not conform to IRC Sec. 951A.	
Wyoming	N/A, because state does not tax general business corporation income.	

Information Returns—Annuities

All persons engaged in a trade or business and making certain payments must file a federal information return (IRC § 6041). For example, distributions from annuities of $10 or more must be reported on federal Form 1099-R. This chart shows the state information return filing threshold amounts for annuity payments, if such returns are required to be filed with the state.

Jurisdiction	Annuities—Form 1099-R	Comment
Alabama	$1,500	
Arizona	Required if state withholding included.	
Arkansas	$2,500	If state taxes are withheld, filing is required regardless of the threshold amount.
California	Same as federal.	
Colorado	No threshold.	Only if tax withheld.
Connecticut	$10	
Delaware	Same as federal.	
District of Columbia	$600	
Georgia	Report all amounts.	Only file forms when Georgia withholding occurred.
Hawaii	$600	
Idaho	Same as federal.	If Idaho income tax withheld.
Illinois	Not required	Maintain and make available on request for a period 3 years from later of: • due date; or • date tax paid.
Indiana	$10	Only required if state or local income tax withheld.
Iowa	$10	Only file forms containing Iowa tax withholding.
Kansas	Same as federal.	
Kentucky	$600	
Louisiana	Not required	
Maine	$600	
Maryland	Amounts not reported on federal information return.	
Massachusetts	Same as federal.	
Michigan	Not required	
Minnesota	$600	
Mississippi	$600	

Jurisdiction	Annuities—Form 1099-R	Comment
Missouri	$1,200	
Montana	$600	
Nebraska	Not required	
New Hampshire	Not required	
New Jersey	$1,000	
New Mexico	$10	Every payer must file an annual statement of withholding (1099-R) for each individual from whom some portion of an annuity has been deducted and withheld.
New York	No threshold	Only if tax withheld.
North Carolina	Report all amounts.	
North Dakota	No threshold.	Only if tax withheld.
Ohio	Report all amounts.	Only applies to forms 1099R that show whithholding.
Oklahoma	$750	
Oregon	Same as federal.	If issuing more than 10 returns, where the recipient, winner, or the payer has an Oregon address.
Pennsylvania	$10	Only applies to forms 1099R that show whithholding.
Rhode Island	$100	
South Carolina	$800	
Tennessee	Not required	
Utah	Not required	
Vermont	Same as federal.	
Virginia	No threshold.	Required if Virginia income tax withheld or recipient worked or lived in the state for any part of year.
West Virginia	$600	
Wisconsin	$600	Report any amount if Wisconsin tax withheld.

Information Returns—Dividends

All persons engaged in a trade or business and making certain payments must file a federal information return (IRC §6041). For example, dividend payments of $10 or more ($600 or more for liquidations) must be reported on federal Form 1099-DIV (Treas. Reg. §§1.6042–2, 1.6043–2). This chart shows the state information return filing threshold amounts for dividend payments, if such returns are required to be filed with the state.

Jurisdiction	Dividends—Form 1099-DIV	Comment
Alabama	$1,500	
Arizona	Required if state withholding included.	
Arkansas	Report all amounts.	If state taxes are withheld, filing is required regardless of the threshold amount.
California	Same as federal.	
Colorado	No threshold.	Only if tax withheld.
Connecticut	Not required	
Delaware	N/A because filing not required.	
District of Columbia	$10	
Georgia	Amount of dividend paid to the shareholder.	
Hawaii	$10	
Idaho	Not required	
Illinois	Not required	Maintain and make available on request for a period 3 years from later of: • due date; or • date tax paid.
Indiana	Not required	
Iowa	$10	Only file forms containing Iowa tax withholding.
Kansas	Same as federal.	
Kentucky	$600	
Louisiana	Not required	
Maine	$10	
Maryland	Amounts not reported on federal information return.	
Massachusetts	Same as federal.	
Michigan	Not required	
Minnesota	$10	
Mississippi	$600	

Jurisdiction	Dividends—Form 1099-DIV	Comment
Missouri	$100	
Montana	$10	
Nebraska	Not required	
New Hampshire	Not required	
New Jersey	$1,000	
New Mexico	Not required	
New York	Not required	
North Carolina	Same as federal, if amounts not reported for federal purposes.	
North Dakota	No threshold.	Only if tax withheld.
Ohio	Not required	
Oklahoma	$750	
Oregon	Not required	
Pennsylvania	$10	
Rhode Island	$100	
South Carolina	$200	
Tennessee	Not required.	Applied to corporations with stockholders in the state, prior to July 1, 2010.
Utah	Not required	
Vermont	Same as federal	
Virginia	No threshold.	Required if Virginia income tax withheld or recipient worked or lived in the state for any part of year.
West Virginia	$600	
Wisconsin	Not required	

Information Returns—Due Date

All persons engaged in a trade or business and making certain payments must file a federal information return (IRC § 6041). Generally, information returns filed on federal 1099 forms for any calendar year must be filed with the IRS by February 28 for paper returns, or March 31 if filed electronically, of the following year (Treas. Reg. § 1.6041-6), except for information on nonemployee compensation. If the due date falls on a Saturday, Sunday, or legal holiday, the return may be filed on the next business day. Many states also require the filing of information returns that are similar to the federal 1099 forms. This chart shows the state information return due dates for those forms, if such returns are required to be filed with the state.

Jurisdiction	Due Date—Form 1099 Series (Except Nonemployee Compensation)	Comment
Alabama	March 15.	
Arizona	February 28, if state withholding included.	
Arkansas	February 28.	
California	March 31 for electronic returns. Paper filing not required if hard copies filed with IRS (unless different figures are required to be reported for state and federal purposes).	
Colorado	Not required	
Connecticut	January 31. 1099-K due 30 days after federal.	March 31 prior to 2018. Electronic filing is required for taxpayers who file 25 or more 1099s.
Delaware	February 28 for paper forms. March 31 for online electronic submission.	Follows federal specifications for electronic filing of 1099 forms.
District of Columbia	February 28.	
Georgia	January 31 for 1099-MISC. February 28 for all other 1099s.	
Hawaii	February 28.	
Idaho	Last day of February.	
Illinois	Not required	Maintain and make available on request for a period 3 years from later of: • due date; or • date tax paid.
Indiana	31 days after the end of the calendar year.	
Iowa	February 15	
Kansas	February 28.	

Jurisdiction	Due Date—Form 1099 Series (Except Nonemployee Compensation)	Comment
Kentucky	January 31 using: • electronic filing for employers who issue 26 or more withholding statements; or • Form K-5 for employers who issue less than 26 withholding statements.	State follows federal specifications for electronic filing.
Louisiana	January 31	
Maine	January 31.	February 28 for returns filed for calendar years beginning before 2017.
Maryland	January 31	
Massachusetts	Last day of February for taxpayers filing fewer than 50 forms on paper. March 31 for taxpayers filing 50 or more form who must file electronically.	
Michigan	Later of (1) January 31 or (2) date federal form is due.	
Minnesota	Same as federal, if state withholding included.	
Mississippi	February 28 for paper 1099s (less than 25) March 31 for electronic 1099s.	
Missouri	February 28.	
Montana	February 28.	
Nebraska	January 31, if state withholding included.	
New Hampshire	Not required	
New Jersey	February 15.	
New Mexico	Last day of February. January 31 for Form 1099-R (tax years after 2018). March 31 for Form 1099-MISC required to be electronically filed.	
New York	January 31. 1099-K due 30 days after federal.	
North Carolina	January 31.	Payers of nonwage compensation must file Form NC-1099PS and/or Form NC-1099-ITIN, unless required to file federal Form 1099-MISC.
North Dakota	January 31.	
Ohio	Same as federal, but only if state withholding included.	
Oklahoma	February 28.	
Oregon	January 31 for required 1099s.	Information returns 1099-MISC, 1099-G, or 1099-R must be electronically filed if issuing more than 10.

Jurisdiction	Due Date—Form 1099 Series (Except Nonemployee Compensation)	Comment
Pennsylvania	February 28 for paper forms. March 31 for online electronic submissions.	
Rhode Island	February 28.	
South Carolina	March 15.	
Tennessee	Not required	
Utah	Not required	
Vermont	February 28 for paper forms. March 31 for online electronic submission. 1099-K due 30 days after federal.	
Virginia	Same as federal, if Virginia income tax withheld or recipient worked or lived in the state for any part of year. 1099-K due 30 days after federal.	
West Virginia	February 28	
Wisconsin	January 31	

Information Returns—Interest

All persons engaged in a trade or business and making certain payments must file a federal information return (IRC §6041). For example, interest income of $10 or more ($600 or more under certain circumstances) must be reported on federal Form 1099-INT (Treas. Reg. §§1.6041–1, 1.6049–6). This chart shows the state information return filing threshold amounts for interest payments, if such returns are required to be filed with the state.

Jurisdiction	Interest—Form 1099-INT	Comment
Alabama	$1,500	
Arizona	Required if state withholding included.	
Arkansas	Report all amounts.	If state taxes are withheld, filing is required regardless of the threshold amount.
California	Same as federal.	
Colorado	No threshold.	Only if tax withheld.
Connecticut	Not required	
Delaware	N/A because filing not required.	
District of Columbia	$10	
Georgia	Report all amounts.	Only file forms when Georgia withholding occurred.
Hawaii	$10	
Idaho	Not required	
Illinois	Not required	Maintain and make available on request for a period 3 years from later of: • due date; or • date tax paid.
Indiana	Not required	
Iowa	$10	Only file forms containing Iowa tax withholding.
Kansas	Same as federal.	
Kentucky	$600	
Louisiana	Not required	
Maine	$10	
Maryland	Report any amount not reported on federal information return.	
Massachusetts	Same as federal.	
Michigan	Not required	
Minnesota	$10	
Mississippi	$600	

Jurisdiction	Interest—Form 1099-INT	Comment
Missouri	$100	
Montana	$10	
Nebraska	Not required	
New Hampshire	Not required	
New Jersey	$1,000	
New Mexico	Not required	
New York	Not required	
North Carolina	Same as federal, if amounts not reported for federal purposes.	
North Dakota	No threshold.	Only if tax withheld.
Ohio	Not required	
Oklahoma	$750	
Oregon	Not required	
Pennsylvania	Not required	
Rhode Island	$100	
South Carolina	$200	
Tennessee	Not required	
Utah	Not required	
Vermont	Same as federal.	
Virginia	No threshold.	Required if Virginia income tax withheld or recipient worked or lived in the state for any part of year.
West Virginia	$600	
Wisconsin	Not required	

Information Returns—Nonemployee Compensation

All persons engaged in a trade or business and making certain payments must file a federal information return (IRC § 6041). For example, nonemployee compensation of $600 or more must be reported on federal Form 1099-NEC (Treas. Reg. § 1.6041–1). Nonemployee compensation includes fees, commissions, prizes, and awards for services performed as a nonemployee, such as professional service fees (e.g., to attorneys, accountants, architects, contractors, engineers, etc.), witnesses or expert fees in a legal adjudication, travel reimbursements, directors' fees, and golden parachute payments. This chart shows the state information return filing threshold amounts for nonemployee compensation payments, if such returns are required to be filed with the state.

Jurisdiction	Nonemployee Compensation—Form 1099-NEC	Comment
Alabama	$1,500	
Arizona	Required if state withholding included.	
Arkansas	$2,500	If state taxes are withheld, filing is required regardless of the threshold amount.
California	Same as federal.	
Colorado	No threshold.	Only if tax withheld.
Connecticut	Same as federal.	
Delaware	Same as federal.	
District of Columbia	Same as federal.	
Georgia	Report all amounts.	Only file forms when Georgia withholding occurred.
Hawaii	Same as federal.	
Idaho	Same as federal.	If issued for transactions related to property located or utilized in state or for services performed in state.
Illinois	Not required.	Maintain and make available on request for a period 3 years from later of: • due date; or • date tax paid.
Indiana	Required if state withholding included.	
Iowa	Required if state withholding included.	Only file forms containing Iowa tax withholding.
Kansas	Same as federal.	
Kentucky	$600	
Louisiana	Required if state withholding included.	
Maine	$600	
Maryland	Required if state withholding included.	

Jurisdiction	Nonemployee Compensation—Form 1099-NEC	Comment
Massachusetts	Same as federal.	
Michigan	Same as federal.	
Minnesota	Required if state withholding included.	
Mississippi	$3,000	
Missouri	$1,200	
Montana	Same as federal.	
Nebraska	Required if state withholding included.	
New Hampshire	Not required.	
New Jersey	$1,000	
New Mexico	Not required.	
New York	Not required, but must keep records of information returns available for review by the Tax Department.	
North Carolina	$1,500	
North Dakota	Same as federal.	
Ohio	Required if state withholding included.	
Oklahoma	$750	
Oregon	Same as federal.	If issuing more than 10 returns, where the recipient, winner, or the payer has an Oregon address.
Pennsylvania	Same as federal.	
Rhode Island	$100	
South Carolina	$800	
Tennessee	Not required.	
Utah	Not required.	
Vermont	Same as federal.	
Virginia	No threshold.	Required if Virginia income tax withheld or recipient worked or lived in the state for any part of year.
West Virginia	$600	
Wisconsin	Same as federal.	

Information Returns—Premiums

All persons engaged in a trade or business and making certain payments must file a federal information return (IRC § 6041). This chart shows the state information return filing threshold amounts for premium payments, if such returns are required to be filed with the state.

Jurisdiction	Premiums	Comment
Alabama	$1,500	
Arizona	Required if state withholding included.	
Arkansas	$2,500	If state taxes are withheld, filing is required regardless of the threshold amount.
California	Report all amounts.	
Colorado	Not required	
Connecticut	Not required	
Delaware	Not required	
District of Columbia	$600	
Georgia	Report all amounts.	Only file forms when Georgia withholding occurred.
Hawaii	$600	
Idaho	Not required	
Illinois	Not required	Maintain and make available on request for a period 3 years from later of: • due date; or • date tax paid.
Indiana	Not required	
Iowa	Same as federal.	Only file forms containing Iowa tax withholding.
Kansas	Same as federal.	
Kentucky	$600	
Louisiana	Not required	
Maine	$600	
Maryland	Amounts not reported on federal information return.	
Massachusetts	Same as federal.	
Michigan	Not required	
Minnesota	$600	
Mississippi	$600	
Missouri	$1,200	
Montana	$600	

Jurisdiction	Premiums	Comment
Nebraska	Not required	
New Hampshire	Not required	
New Jersey	$1,000	
New Mexico	Not required	
New York	Not required	
North Carolina	Same as federal, if amounts not reported for federal purposes.	
North Dakota	Same as federal.	
Ohio	Not required	
Oklahoma	$750	
Oregon	Not required	
Pennsylvania	Not required	
Rhode Island	$100	
South Carolina	$800	
Tennessee	Not required	
Utah	Not required	
Vermont	Same as federal.	
Virginia	No threshold.	Required if Virginia income tax withheld or recipient worked or lived in the state for any part of year.
West Virginia	$600	
Wisconsin	Not required	

Information Returns—Rents/Royalties

All persons engaged in a trade or business and making certain payments must file a federal information return (IRC §6041). For example, rent payments of $600 or more or royalty payments of $10 or more must be reported on federal Form 1099-MISC (IRC §6050N; Treas. Reg. §§1.6041–1, 1.6050N-1). This chart shows the state information return filing threshold amounts for rent and royalty payments, if such returns are required to be filed with the state.

Jurisdiction	Rents/Royalties—Form 1099-MISC	Comment
Alabama	$1,500	
Arizona	Required if state withholding included.	
Arkansas	$2,500	If state taxes are withheld, filing is required regardless of the threshold amount.
California	Same as federal.	
Colorado	No threshold.	Only if tax withheld.
Connecticut	Same as federal.	
Delaware	Same as federal.	
District of Columbia	$600	
Georgia	Report all amounts.	Only file forms when Georgia withholding occurred.
Hawaii	$600	
Idaho	Same as federal.	If issued for transactions related to property located or utilized in Idaho or for services performed in Idaho.
Illinois	Not required	Maintain and make available on request for a period 3 years from later of: • due date; or • date tax paid.
Indiana	Not required	
Iowa	Report all amounts.	Only file forms containing Iowa tax withholding.
Kansas	Same as federal.	
Kentucky	$600	
Louisiana	$1,000	
Maine	$600	
Maryland	Report any amount not reported on federal information return.	
Massachusetts	Same as federal.	
Michigan	Same as federal.	
Minnesota	$600	

Jurisdiction	Rents/Royalties—Form 1099-MISC	Comment
Mississippi	$600	
Missouri	$1,200	
Montana	Rent: $600 Royalties: $10	
Nebraska	Not required	
New Hampshire	Not required	
New Jersey	$1,000	
New Mexico	N/A	Information returns are only required of persons paying rents and royalties from oil and gas properties located in New Mexico who are required to file federal information return Form 1099-MISC or New Mexico Form RPD-41285 on such payments.
New York	Not required	
North Carolina	Same as federal, if amounts not reported for federal purposes.	
North Dakota	Rent: $600 Royalties: $10	Applicable to taxable years beginning after 2013, for an oil and gas royalty payment remitter that is exempt from the withholding requirement under the production threshold exemption, an annual return is required to report royalty payments meeting a $600 quarterly threshold or a $1,000 annual threshold.
Ohio	Not required	
Oklahoma	$750	
Oregon	Same as federal.	If issuing more than 10 returns, where the recipient, winner, or the payer has an Oregon address.
Pennsylvania	Same as federal.	
Rhode Island	$100	
South Carolina	$800	
Tennessee	Not required	
Utah	Not required	
Vermont	Same as federal.	
Virginia	No threshold.	Required if Virginia income tax withheld or recipient worked or lived in the state for any part of year.
West Virginia	$600	
Wisconsin	$600	

Insurance Companies—Corporation Income Tax

Most states do not impose a corporate income tax on insurance companies doing business in their state, if the insurance company is subject to a tax on gross premiums. This chart shows whether corporation income tax is imposed on insurance companies either in lieu of, or in addition to, a gross premiums tax by each state and the District of Columbia.

Jurisdiction	Corporation Income Tax	Comment
Alabama	No	
Alaska	No	
Arizona	No	
Arkansas	No	
California	No	
Colorado	No	
Connecticut	No	
Delaware	No	
District of Columbia	No	
Florida	Yes	
Georgia	No	
Hawaii	No	
Idaho	No	
Illinois	Yes	
Indiana	Yes, if election to pay gross premiums tax not made. No, foreign insurers.	Check box on front of corporate adjusted gross income tax return.
Iowa	No	
Kansas	No	
Kentucky	No	
Louisiana	Yes	While insurance companies are not subject to the 1986 Corporation Income Tax Act, they continue to be taxed under the income tax provisions predating the 1986 Act. However, an offset is available against the income tax for gross premiums taxes that an insurance company pays.
Maine	No	
Maryland	No	
Massachusetts	No	
Michigan	No	
Minnesota	No	

Jurisdiction	Corporation Income Tax	Comment
Mississippi	Yes	
Missouri	No	
Montana	No	
Nebraska	Yes	
Nevada	N/A, because no corporation income tax.	
New Hampshire	Yes, business profits tax imposed.	
New Jersey	No	
New Mexico	No	
New York	Insurance franchise tax.	Additional franchise tax based on gross premiums for life insurers.
North Carolina	No	Mutual insurance companies are subject to tax on their unrelated business income.
North Dakota	No	
Ohio	No	
Oklahoma	No	
Oregon	Yes	
Pennsylvania	No	
Rhode Island	No	
South Carolina	No	
South Dakota	N/A, because no corporation income tax.	
Tennessee	No	
Texas	No	Subject to tax if in violation of an order of the Texas Department of Insurance final after appeal or no longer subject to appeal.
Utah	No	
Vermont	No	
Virginia	No	
Washington	N/A, because no corporation income tax.	
West Virginia	No	
Wisconsin	Yes, except domestic life insurers, foreign insurers, and certain other exempt insurers.	
Wyoming	N/A, because no corporation income tax.	

Insurance Companies—Premiums Tax

Most states do not impose a corporate income tax on insurance companies doing business in their state, but rather impose a tax on gross premiums. This chart shows the types of insurers and insurance that is subject to premiums tax in each state and the District of Columbia.

Jurisdiction	Premiums Tax	Comment
Alabama	Yes, applicable to: • Life, accident, and health insurers; • Non-profit hospitalization insurers; • Surplus lines brokers; • Unauthorized or nonadmitted insurers, including independently procured insurance; • Captive insurers; • Mutual aid associations; and • All other insurers doing business in the state.	
Alaska	Yes, applicable to: • Life, accident, and health insurers; • Property and casualty insurers; • Surplus lines brokers; • Unauthorized or nonadmitted insurers; • Risk retention groups; • Wet marine and transportation insurers; • Title insurers; and • All other insurers doing business in the state.	
Arizona	Yes, applicable to: • Life, accident, and health insurers; • Property and casualty insurers; • Surplus line brokers; • Nonadmitted insurers; • Captive insurers; • Title insurers; • Legal services insurers; and • All other insurers doing business in the state.	
Arkansas	Yes, applicable to: • Life, accident, and health insurers; • Property and casualty insurers; • Surplus lines brokers; • Unauthorized or nonadmitted insurers; • Captive insurers; • Title insurers; • Legal services insurers; • Travel insurers, effective for policies sold beginning on or after October 1, 2019; • All other insurers doing business in the state.	

Jurisdiction	Premiums Tax	Comment
California	Yes, applicable to: • Life, accident, and health insurers; • Surplus lines brokers; • Home protection insurers; • Nonadmitted insurers; • Risk retention groups; • Title insurers; and • All other insurers doing business in the state.	
Colorado	Yes, applicable to: • Life, accident, and health insurers; • Property and casualty insurers; • Surplus lines brokers; • Unauthorized or nonadmitted insurers; • Captive insurers; • Title insurers; • All other insurers doing business in the state.	
Connecticut	Yes, applicable to: • Life, accident, and health insurers; • Property and casualty insurers; • Surplus lines brokers; • Unauthorized or nonadmitted insurers; • Risk retention groups; • Captive insurers; and • All other insurers doing business in the state.	
Delaware	Yes, applicable to: • Life, accident, and health insurers; • Property and casualty insurers; • Workers' compensation and employers' liability insurers; • Self-procured insurance from unauthorized or nonadmitted insurers; • Surplus lines brokers; • Captive insurers; • Risk retention and purchasing groups; and • All other insurers doing business in the state.	
District of Columbia	Yes, applicable to: • Life, accident, and health insurers; • Property and casualty insurers; • Surplus lines brokers; • Captive insurers; • Title insurers; and • All other insurers doing business in the state.	

Jurisdiction	Premiums Tax	Comment
Florida	Yes, applicable to: • Life, accident, and health insurers; • Property and casualty insurers; • Wet marine and transportation insurers; • Self-insurance funds; • Captive insurers; • Legal expense insurance corporations; and • Surplus lines brokers; • Risk retention groups; • Title insurers; • Mutual insurers; • Travel insurers, effective July 1, 2020; and • All other insurers doing business in the state.	
Georgia	Yes, applicable to: • Life, accident, and health insurers; • Health maintenance organizations; • Property and casualty insurers; • Surplus lines brokers; • Unauthorized or nonadmitted insurers; • Captive insurers; • Risk retention groups; and • All other insurers doing business in the state.	
Hawaii	Yes, applicable to: • Life, accident, and health insurers; • Property and casualty insurers; • Surplus lines brokers; • Captive insurers; • Title insurers; • And all other insurance doing business in the state.	
Idaho	Yes, applicable to: • Life, accident, and health insurers; • Property and casualty insurers; • Surplus lines brokers; • Risk retention groups; • Title insurers; and • All other insurers doing business in the state.	
Illinois	Yes, applicable to: • Life, accident, and health insurers; • Property and casualty insurers; • Surplus lines brokers; • Captive insurers; • Risk retention groups; • Industrial insureds that independently procure insurance directly from an unauthorized insurer; and • All other insurers doing business in the state.	

Jurisdiction	Premiums Tax	Comment
Indiana	Yes, applicable to: • Life, accident, and health insurers; • Property and casualty insurers; • Surplus lines brokers; • Captive insurers; • Nonadmitted insurers; • Title insurers; and • All other insurers doing business in the state.	
Iowa	Yes, applicable to: • Life, accident, and health insurers; • Property and casualty insurers; • Surplus lines brokers; • Unauthorized or nonadmitted insurers; • Captive insurers; • Risk retention and purchasing groups; and • All other insurers doing business in the state.	
Kansas	Yes, applicable to: • Life, accident, and health insurers; • Property and casualty insurers; • Surplus lines brokers; • Unauthorized or nonadmitted insurers; • Captive insurers; and • All other insurers doing business in the state.	
Kentucky	Yes, applicable to: • Life, accident, and health insurers; • Property and casualty insurers; • Domestic mutual, domestic mutual fire or cooperative and assessment fire insurance companies; • Surplus lines brokers for insurance placed with state residents; • Unauthorized or nonadmitted insurers; • Risk retention groups; • Captive insurers; and • All other insurers doing business in the state.	
Louisiana	Yes, applicable to: • Life, accident, and health insurers; • Property and casualty insurers; • Surplus lines brokers; • Nonadmitted insurers; • Captive insurers; and • All other insurers doing business in the state.	
Maine	Yes, applicable to: • Life, accident, and health insurers; • Property and casualty insurers; • Surplus lines brokers; • Nonadmitted insurers; • Risk retention groups; and • All other insurers doing business in the state.	

Jurisdiction	Premiums Tax	Comment
Maryland	Yes, applicable to: • Life, accident, and health insurers; • Property and casualty insurers; • Surplus lines brokers; • Nonadmitted insurers; and • All other insurers doing business in the state.	
Massachusetts	Yes, applicable to: • Life, accident, and health insurers; • Property and casualty insurers; • Surplus lines brokers; • Nonadmitted insurers; • Health care service providers; and • Risk retention groups.	
Michigan	Yes, applicable to: • Life, accident, and health insurers; • Property and casualty insurers; • Surplus lines brokers; • Unauthorized insurers; and • All other insurers doing business in the state.	
Minnesota	Yes, applicable to: • Life, accident, and health insurers; • Property and casualty insurers; • Surplus lines brokers; • Nonadmitted insurers; • Risk retention groups; • Title insurers; and • All other insurers doing business in the state.	
Mississippi	Yes, applicable to: • Life, accident, and health insurers; • Property and casualty insurers; • Surplus lines brokers; • Nonadmitted insurers; • Captive insurers; • Risk retention groups; • Title insurers; and • All other insurers doing business in the state.	
Missouri	Yes, applicable to: • Life, accident, and health insurers; • Property and casualty insurers; • Surplus lines brokers; • Nonadmitted insurers; • Captive insurers; • Risk retention groups; and • All other insurers doing business in the state.	
Montana	Yes, applicable to: • Life, accident, and health insurers; • Property and casualty insurers; • Surplus lines brokers; • Nonadmitted insurers; • Captive insurers; • Risk retention groups; • Title insurers; and • All other insurers doing business in the state.	

Jurisdiction	Premiums Tax	Comment
Nebraska	Yes, applicable to: • Life, accident, and health insurers; • Property and casualty insurers; • Surplus lines brokers; • Nonadmitted insurers; • Captive insurers; • Title insurers; and • All other insurers doing business in the state.	
Nevada	Yes, applicable to: • Life, accident, and health insurers; • Property and casualty insurers; • Surplus lines brokers; • Nonadmitted insurers; • Captive insurers; • Risk retention groups; • Title insurers; and • All other insurers doing business in the state.	
New Hampshire	Yes, applicable to: • Life, accident, and health insurers; • Property and casualty insurers; • Surplus lines brokers; • Nonadmitted insurers; • Risk retention groups; • Title insurers; and • All other insurers doing business in the state.	
New Jersey	Yes, applicable to: • Life, accident, and health insurers; • Property and casualty insurers; • Surplus lines brokers; • Unauthorized or nonadmitted insurers; • Captive insurers; • Ocean marine insurers; • Workers' compensation insurers; and • All other insurers doing business in the state.	
New Mexico	Yes, applicable to: • Life; • Property and casualty insurers; • Surplus lines brokers; • Unauthorized or nonadmitted insurers; • Vehicle insurers; • Risk retention groups (through 2019); and • All other insurers doing business in the state.	
New York	Yes, applicable to: • Life, accident, and health insurers; • Property and casualty insurers; • Surplus lines brokers; • Unauthorized or nonadmitted insurers; • Captive insurers; and • All other insurers doing business in the state.	

Jurisdiction	Premiums Tax	Comment
North Carolina	Yes, applicable to: • Life, accident, health, and title insurers; • Property and casualty insurers; • Self insurers; • Health maintenance organizations (HMOs); • Hospital and dental service corporations; • Risk purchasing groups; • Nonadmitted surplus lines insurers; • Captive insurance companies, except foeign captive companies beginning July 1, 2018; and • All other insurers doing business in the state.	
North Dakota	Yes, applicable to: • Life, accident, and health insurers; • Property and casualty insurers; • Surplus lines brokers; • Unauthorized or nonadmitted insurers; • Risk retention and purchasing groups; and • All other insurers doing business in the state.	
Ohio	Yes, applicable to: • Life, accident, and health insurers; • Property and casualty insurers; • Surplus lines brokers; • Unauthorized or nonadmitted insurers; • Risk retention groups; and • All other insurers doing business in the state.	
Oklahoma	Yes, applicable to: • Life, accident, and health insurers; • Property and casualty insurers; • Surplus lines brokers; • Unauthorized or nonadmitted insurers; • Captive insurers; • Risk retention groups; and • All other insurers doing business in the state.	
Oregon	Yes, applicable to: • Health insurers; • Fire insurers; • Surplus lines insurers	
Pennsylvania	Yes, applicable to: • Life, accident, and health insurers; • Property and casualty insurers; • Surplus lines brokers; • Unauthorized or nonadmitted insurers; • Captive insurers; • Risk retention groups; • Title insurers; and • All other insurers doing business in the state.	

Jurisdiction	Premiums Tax	Comment
Rhode Island	Yes, applicable to: • Life, accident, and health insurers; • Property and casualty insurers; • Surplus lines brokers; • Unauthorized or nonadmitted insurers; • Captive insurers; • Title insurers; and • All other insurers doing business in the state.	
South Carolina	Yes, applicable to: • Life, accident, and health insurers; • Property and casualty insurers; • Surplus lines brokers; • Unauthorized or nonadmitted insurers; • Captive insurers; • Risk retention and purchasing groups; • Workers' compensation insurers; and • All other insurers doing business in the state.	
South Dakota	Yes, applicable to: • Life, accident, and health insurers; • Property and casualty insurers; • Surplus lines brokers; • Unauthorized or nonadmitted insurers; • Risk retention groups; • Bail bond insurers; and • All other insurers doing business in the state.	
Tennessee	Yes, applicable to: • Life, accident, and health insurers; • Property and casualty insurers; • Surplus lines brokers; • Unauthorized or nonadmitted insurers; • Captive insurers; • Risk retention groups; • Title insurers; • Workers' compensation insurers; and • All other insurers doing business in the state.	
Texas	Yes, applicable to: • Life, accident, and health insurers; • Property and casualty insurers; • Surplus lines brokers; • Unauthorized or nonadmitted insurers; • Title insurers; • Captive insurance companies; • Legal services insurers; and • All other insurers doing business in the state.	

Jurisdiction	Premiums Tax	Comment
Utah	Yes, applicable to: • Life, accident, and health insurers; • Property and casualty insurers; • Surplus lines brokers; • Unauthorized or nonadmitted insurers; • Purchasing groups; and • All other insurers doing business in the state.	
Vermont	Yes, applicable to: • Life, accident, and health insurers; • Property and casualty insurers; • Surplus lines brokers; • Unauthorized or nonadmitted insurers; • Captive insurers; and • All other insurers doing business in the state.	
Virginia	Yes, applicable to: • Life, accident, and health insurers; • Property and casualty insurers; • Surplus lines brokers; • Unauthorized or nonadmitted insurers; • Captive insurers; and • All other insurers doing business in the state.	
Washington	Yes, applicable to: • Life, accident, and health insurers; • Property and casualty insurers; • Surplus lines brokers; • Unauthorized or nonadmitted insurers; • Risk retention groups; and • All other insurers doing business in the state.	
West Virginia	Yes, applicable to: • Life, accident, and health insurers; • Property and casualty insurers; • Surplus lines brokers; • Nonadmitted insurers; • Captive insurers; • Risk retention and purchasing groups; and • All other insurers doing business in the state.	
Wisconsin	Yes, applicable to: • Life, accident, and health insurers; • Property and casualty insurers; • Surplus lines brokers; • Unauthorized or nonadmitted insurers; • Mortgage guaranty insurers; and • All other insurers doing business in the state.	

Jurisdiction	Premiums Tax	Comment
Wyoming	Yes, applicable to: • Life, accident, and health insurers; • Property and casualty insurers; • Surplus lines brokers; • Unauthorized or nonadmitted insurers; • Risk retention groups; • Title insurers; and • All other insurers doing business in the state.	

IRC Conformity and Taxable Income Starting Point—IRC Conformity

The following chart indicates which states have incorporated the Internal Revenue Code (IRC) by reference and thus use federal taxable income as the starting point for calculating state corporate taxable income. Some states do not incorporate the code by reference, but instead adopt specific provisions of the code and/or use federal taxable income as the starting point for determining state corporate taxable income. States that conform to the IRC generally may specifically exclude certain IRC sections, such as those relating to depreciation and net operating loss deductions. Such exceptions to general conformity provisions are not discussed in the chart below.

Jurisdiction	IRC Conformity	Comment
Alabama	IRC incorporated as amended to extent of provisions directly referenced by state code.	
Alaska	IRC incorporated by reference as currently amended.	
Arizona	IRC incorporated by reference as of January 1, 2020, for tax years after 2019. IRC incorporated by reference as of January 1, 2019, for tax years after 2018.	IRC incorporated by reference as of January 1, 2018, for tax years after 2017. IRC incorporated by reference as of January 1, 2017, for tax years after 2016. IRC incorporated by reference as of January 1, 2016, for tax years after 2015. IRC incorporated by reference as of January 1, 2015, for tax years after 2014.
Arkansas	Only certain IRC provisions are incorporated as amended through specified dates.	
California	IRC incorporated as of January 1, 2015, with modifications, for tax years beginning after 2014. IRC incorporated as of January 1, 2009, with modifications, for tax years beginning after 2009 and before 2015.	
Colorado	IRC incorporated by reference as currently amended.	
Connecticut	IRC incorporated by reference as currently amended.	
Delaware	IRC not incorporated by reference, but starting point for computing taxable income is federal taxable income as currently defined by the IRC.	
District of Columbia	IRC incorporated by reference as currently amended.	
Florida	IRC incorporated by reference as of January 1, 2020.	

Jurisdiction	IRC Conformity	Comment
Georgia	IRC incorporated by reference as of March 27, 2020, with modifications, for taxable years beginning on or after January 1, 2019.	IRC incorporated by reference, with modifications, as of: • January 1, 2019 for taxable years beginning on or after January 1, 2018; • February 9, 2018 for taxable years beginning on or after January 1, 2017; • January 1, 2017 for taxable years beginning on or after January 1, 2016; • January 1, 2016 for taxable years beginning on or after January 1, 2015; and • January 1, 2015 for taxable years beginning on or after January 1, 2014.
Hawaii	IRC incorporated by reference as of March 27, 2020, for taxable years beginning after 2019.	IRC incorporated by reference as of December 31, 2018, for taxable years beginning after 2018. IRC incorporated by reference as of February 9, 2018, for taxable years beginning after 2017. IRC incorporated by reference as of December 31, 2016, for taxable years beginning after 2016. IRC incorporated by reference as of December 31, 2015, for taxable years beginning after 2015. Various IRC provisions inoperative.
Idaho	IRC incorporated by reference as of January 1, 2020, effective retroactively to January 1, 2020.	IRC incorporated by reference as of January 1, 2019, effective retroactively to January 1, 2019. IRC incorporated by reference as of January 1, 2018, for years beginning after 2017. IRC incorporated by reference as of January 1, 2017, effective retroactively to January 1, 2017. However, IRC incorporated by reference as of December 21, 2017, for tax year 2017. IRC incorporated by reference as of January 1, 2016, effective retroactively to January 1, 2016. IRC provisions added, amended, or deleted prior to conformity provision update, are applicable on effective date of federal changes, including retroactive provisions.
Illinois	IRC incorporated by reference as currently amended.	
Indiana	IRC incorporated by reference as of January 1, 2020, for taxable years beginning after 2019.	IRC incorporated by reference as of January 1, 2019, for taxable years beginning after 2018. IRC incorporated by reference as of February 11, 2018, for taxable years beginning after 2017. IRC incorporated by reference as of January 1, 2016, for taxable years beginning after 2015. IRC incorporated by reference as of January 1, 2015, for taxable years beginning after 2014.

Jurisdiction	IRC Conformity	Comment
Iowa	IRC incorporated by reference as of January 1, 2015.	**2019:** IRC incorporated by reference as of March 24, 2018. **2020:** IRC incorporated by reference as currently amended. **Previously:** IRC temporarily incorporated by reference as January 1, 2016, for the 2015 tax year only. IRC incorporated by reference as of January 1, 2014, for tax years after 2013. IRC incorporated by reference as of January 1, 2013, for tax years after 2012.
Kansas	IRC incorporated by reference as currently amended.	
Kentucky	IRC incorporated by reference as amended on December 31, 2018, effective for tax years after 2018. IRC incorporated by reference as amended on December 31, 2017, effective for tax years after 2017 and before 2019.	It does not apply to any IRC amendments made after conformity date, except those extending provisions that would otherwise expire on that date. IRC incorporated by reference as amended on December 31, 2015, applicable to: • fiscal year-end taxpayers with tax years beginning on or after April 27, 2016; and • calendar year-end taxpayers beginning January 1, 2017. IRC incorporated by reference as amended on December 31, 2013, effective for taxable years beginning after 2013 and before: • April 27, 2017 for fiscal year-end taxpayers; or • January 1, 2017 for calendar year-end taxpayers.
Louisiana	IRC incorporated by reference as currently amended.	
Maine	IRC incorporated by reference as amended on December 31, 2019, for taxable years beginning on or after 2019.	IRC incorporated by reference as amended on December 31, 2018, for taxable years beginning on or after 2018. IRC incorporated by reference as amended on March 23, 2018, for taxable years beginning after 2016. IRC incorporated by reference as of December 31, 2016, for taxable years beginning in 2016. IRC incorporated by reference as of December 31, 2015, for taxable years beginning in 2015. IRC incorporated by reference as of December 31, 2014, for taxable years beginning in 2014. IRC incorporated by reference as of December 31, 2013, for taxable years beginning in 2013.
Maryland	IRC incorporated by reference as currently amended, unless Comptroller determines that impact of federal amendment on state income tax revenue for fiscal year that begins during calendar year in which amendment is enacted will be $5 million or more.	

Jurisdiction	IRC Conformity	Comment
Massachusetts	IRC incorporated by reference as currently amended.	
Michigan	IRC incorporated by reference for purposes of corporate income tax (CIT) as of January 1, 2018, or at taxpayer's option, as in effect for the taxable year.	Michigan business tax (MBT) repealed and replaced by CIT effective January 1, 2012, except for those taxpayers with certificated credits that elect to pay the MBT. IRC incorporated by reference for purposes of MBT as of January 1, 2008, or at taxpayer's option, as in effect for the taxable year.
Minnesota	IRC adopted as amended through December 31, 2018.	
Mississippi	IRC as amended to date, to the extent provisions are adopted.	
Missouri	IRC incorporated by reference as currently amended.	
Montana	IRC not incorporated by reference but federal taxable income is starting point for calculating state tax.	
Nebraska	IRC incorporated by reference as currently amended.	
Nevada	N/A, because state does not tax general business corporation income.	
New Hampshire	IRC incorporated by reference as of December 31, 2018, effective for taxable periods beginning on or after January 1, 2020.	IRC incorporated by reference as of: • December 31, 2016, effective for taxable periods beginning on or after January 1, 2018; • December 31, 2015, effective for taxable periods beginning on or after January 1, 2017; and • December 31, 2000, before 2017.
New Jersey	IRC not incorporated by reference, but federal taxable income, after certain additions and subtractions, is prima facie deemed to be entire net income.	
New Mexico	IRC incorporated by reference as currently amended.	
New York	IRC not incorporated by reference but federal taxable income is starting point for calculating state tax.	
North Carolina	IRC incorporated by reference as of May 1, 2020.	
North Dakota	IRC incorporated by reference as currently amended.	
Ohio	IRC incorporated by reference as currently amended.	
Oklahoma	IRC incorporated by reference as currently amended.	

Jurisdiction	IRC Conformity	Comment
Oregon	December 31, 2018 for tax years after 2018, or if related to definition of taxable income, as applicable to tax year of taxpayer.	December 31, 2017 for tax years after 2017, or if related to definition of taxable income, as applicable to tax year of taxpayer. December 31, 2016 for tax years after 2016, or if related to definition of taxable income, as applicable to tax year of taxpayer. December 31, 2015 for tax years after 2015, or if related to definition of taxable income, as applicable to tax year of taxpayer. December 31, 2014 for tax years after 2014, or if related to definition of taxable income, as applicable to tax year of taxpayer. December 31, 2013 for tax years after 2013, or if related to definition of taxable income, as applicable to tax year of taxpayer.
Pennsylvania	IRC not incorporated by reference but various provisions are adopted on a current basis and federal taxable income is starting point for calculating state tax.	
Rhode Island	IRC not incorporated by reference, but starting point for computing taxable income is federal taxable income as currently defined by the IRC.	
South Carolina	IRC incorporated by reference through December 31, 2019.	
South Dakota	N/A, because state does not tax general business corporation income.	
Tennessee	IRC not incorporated by reference, but starting point for computing taxable income is federal taxable income as currently defined by the IRC.	
Texas	IRC incorporated by reference as of January 1, 2007 for franchise (margin) tax reports due after 2007 tax year, not including any changes made by federal law after that date, and any regulations adopted under that code applicable to that period. IRC incorporated by reference for federal tax year beginning after 1995 and before 1997 for franchise tax reports due prior to 2008.	
Utah	IRC incorporated by reference as currently amended for tax year in which taxable income is determined.	

Jurisdiction	IRC Conformity	Comment
Vermont	IRC incorporated by reference as of December 31, 2019, for tax years beginning after 2018.	IRC incorporated by reference as of December 31, 2018, for tax years beginning after 2017. IRC incorporated by reference as of December 31, 2017, for tax years beginning after 2016. IRC incorporated by reference as in effect for 2016 taxable year, for tax years beginning after 2015. IRC incorporated by reference as in effect for 2015 taxable year, for tax years beginning after 2014. IRC incorporated by reference as in effect for 2014 taxable year, for tax years beginning after 2013. Federal amendments made subsequent to IRC conformity date impacting tax year at issue administratively recognized.
Virginia	IRC incorporated by reference as of December 31, 2019, effective February 17, 2020, and retroactively applicable to tax years after 2017.	IRC incorporated by reference as of December 31, 2018, effective February 15, 2019. IRC incorporated by reference as of February 9, 2018, effective February 22, 2018. IRC incorporated by reference as of December 31, 2016, effective February 3, 2017. IRC incorporated by reference as of December 31, 2015, effective February 5, 2016.
Washington	N/A, because state does not tax general business corporation income.	
West Virginia	IRC and federal laws relating to determination of federal taxable income in effect after December 31, 2019, and before January 1, 2020, adopted for purposes of computing taxable income.	For tax years that began before the conformity date, the law in effect for each of those years applies to that year. IRC not incorporated except as specifically adopted.
Wisconsin	IRC incorporated by reference as of December 31, 2017, with modifications, for taxable years beginning after 2017.	IRC incorporated by reference as of December 31, 2016, with modifications, for taxable years beginning after 2016. IRC incorporated by reference as of December 31, 2013, with modifications, for taxable years beginning after 2013. IRC incorporated by reference as of December 31, 2010, with modifications, for taxable years beginning after 2010.
Wyoming	N/A, because state does not tax general business corporation income.	

IRC Conformity and Taxable Income Starting Point—Starting Point

The following chart indicates the line on federal Form 1120 that constitutes the starting point for calculation of state taxable income.

Jurisdiction	C Corporation Starting Point	Comment
Alabama	Line 30	
Alaska	Line 28	
Arizona	Line 30	
Arkansas	Line 28 for multistate corporations. For corporations operating only in Arkansas, reconciliation required for each state line item amount, lines 7 through 14 and Lines 16 through 26, that is different from amounts listed on federal return. If amounts are the same for both federal and state returns, enter dollar amounts on lines 15, 27, and 29 through 46.	
California	Line 28 if using federal reconciliation method.	
Colorado	Line 30	
Connecticut	Line 28	
Delaware	Line 30	
District of Columbia	Line 28 reconciliation	Reconciliation required to explain any differences between net income reported for federal purposes and that reported for DC purposes. Reconciliation starts with federal taxable income before net operating loss deduction and special deductions.
Florida	Line 30	
Georgia	Line 30	
Hawaii	Line 28	
Idaho	Line 30	
Illinois	Line 30	
Indiana	Line 28	
Iowa	Line 28	
Kansas	Line 30	
Kentucky	Line 28	
Louisiana	Line 30	
Maine	Line 30	
Maryland	Line 28, minus line 29b	
Massachusetts	Line 28	

Jurisdiction	C Corporation Starting Point	Comment
Michigan	Line 30	
Minnesota	Line 28	
Mississippi	Line 28	
Missouri	Line 30	
Montana	Line 28	
Nebraska	Line 30	
Nevada	N/A, because state does not tax general business corporation income.	
New Hampshire	Line 28	
New Jersey	Line 28	
New Mexico	Line 28	
New York	Line 28	
North Carolina	Line 28, minus line 29b	
North Dakota	Line 30	
Ohio	No federal tax base. CAT is based on taxable gross receipts.	
Oklahoma	Line 30 for unitary taxpayers. Lines 1-30 as reported on federal return for nonunitary taxpayers.	
Oregon	Line 28	
Pennsylvania	Line 28	
Rhode Island	Line 28	
South Carolina	Line 30	
South Dakota	N/A, because state does not tax general business corporation income.	
Tennessee	Line 28	
Texas	Lines 1c and 4-10 for franchise (margin) tax reports due after 2007 tax year Line 28 for franchise tax reports due prior to 2008.	
Utah	Line 28	
Vermont	Line 30, plus line 29a **Tax years before 2018**: Line 28, minus line 29b	
Virginia	Line 30	
Washington	N/A, because state does not tax general business corporation income.	
West Virginia	Line 30	

Jurisdiction	C Corporation Starting Point	Comment
Wisconsin	Line 28	
Wyoming	N/A, because state does not tax general business corporation income.	

Limitation Periods for Assessment and Refund—Refunds

The federal limitation period for filing a claim for a refund is the later of 3 years from the time the return was filed or 2 years from the time the tax was paid, or if no return was filed by the taxpayer, the claim must be filed within 2 years from the time the tax was paid. This chart reflects the general statute of limitation (SOL) periods that apply in each state and the District of Columbia to refund claims by corporate income taxpayers. Special limitation periods relating to assessments, appeal orders, deficiency determinations, NOL carrybacks, capital losses, bad debts, computation changes resulting from federal audits, or other types of claims are not reflected in the chart.

Jurisdiction	Refunds	Comment
Alabama	Later of 3 yrs. from date filed or 2 yrs. from date paid. 2 yrs. from date paid if return not timely filed.	
Alaska	Later of 3 yrs. from date filed or 2 yrs. from date paid. 2 yrs. from date paid if return not timely filed.	Refund claim Form 611N will no longer be accepted for any tax year beginning August 21, 2013.
Arizona	4 yrs. from later of due date or date filed.	
Arkansas	Later of 3 yrs. from date filed or 2 yrs. from date paid.	
California	Later of 4 yrs. from date filed (if timely), 4 yrs. from due date, or 1 yr from date paid.	
Colorado	Federal statute of limitations period, plus one year.	
Connecticut	3 yrs. from date due.	
Delaware	Later of 3 yrs. from last date prescribed for filing or 2 yrs. from date paid. 2 yrs. from date paid in cases of failure to file.	
District of Columbia	3 yrs. from later of date due or date paid.	
Florida	3 yrs. from date paid.	
Georgia	3 yrs. from later of date due or date paid.	
Hawaii	Later of 3 yrs. from either date filed or due date, or 2 yrs. from date paid.	
Idaho	Later of 3 yrs. from original due date or date filed.	
Illinois	Later of 3 yrs. from date filed or 1 yr from date paid.	

Jurisdiction	Refunds	Comment
Indiana	3 yrs. from later of due date or date paid.	
Iowa	Later of 3 yrs. from due date or 1 yr. from date paid.	
Kansas	Later of 3 yrs. from date due or 2 yrs. from date paid.	
Kentucky	**Corporation income tax:** 4 yrs. from date paid. **Limited liability entity tax:** Later of 180 days after final assessment or 4 years from date paid.	
Louisiana	Later of 3 yrs. from end of calendar year in which due or 1 yr. from date paid.	
Maine	3 yrs. from later of date filed or date paid.	
Maryland	Later of 3 yrs. from date filed or 2 yrs. from date paid.	
Massachusetts	Later of 3 yrs. from date filed, 2 yrs. from date assessed, or 1 yr. from date paid. In cases of untimely filing, later of 3 yrs. from date due or 2 yrs. from date paid.	
Michigan	4 yrs. from date due.	
Minnesota	3.5 yrs. from due date.	
Mississippi	3 yrs. from later of due date or date paid.	
Missouri	Later of 3 yrs. from date filed or 2 yrs. from date paid.	
Montana	Later of 3 yrs. from due date or 1 yr. from date paid or filed.	
Nebraska	Later of 3 yrs. from date filed or 2 yrs. from date paid.	
Nevada	N/A, because state does not tax general business corporation income.	
New Hampshire	Later of 3 yrs. from due date or 2 yrs. from date paid.	
New Jersey	4 yrs. from date paid.	
New Mexico	Later of 3 yrs. from end of calendar year in which tax was due or tax was paid.	
New York	Later of 3 yrs. from date filed or 2 yrs. from date paid.	

Jurisdiction	Refunds	Comment
North Carolina	Later of 3 yrs. from due date or 2 yrs. from date paid.	
North Dakota	3 yrs. from later of due date or date filed.	
Ohio	4 yrs. from date paid.	
Oklahoma	3 yrs. from due date.	
Oregon	Later of 3 yrs. from date filed or 2 yrs. from date paid.	
Pennsylvania	3 yrs. from date paid.	
Rhode Island	3 yrs. from date paid.	
South Carolina	Later of 3 yrs. from date filed or 2 yrs. from date paid.	
South Dakota	N/A, because state does not tax general business corporation income.	
Tennessee	3 yrs. from end of calendar year in which paid.	
Texas	4 yrs. from date due.	
Utah	Later of 3 yrs. from due date or 2 yrs. from date paid.	
Vermont	Later of 3 yrs. from date due or 6 mos. after federal refund received.	
Virginia	Later of 3 yrs. from due date or 2 yrs. from date paid.	
Washington	N/A, because state does not tax general business corporation income.	
West Virginia	Later of 3 yrs. from due date or 2 yrs. from date paid. 2 yrs. from date paid in cases of failure to file.	
Wisconsin	4 yrs. from date due.	
Wyoming	N/A, because state does not tax general business corporation income.	

Limitation Periods for Assessment and Refund—Standard Limitation Periods

The Internal Revenue Service generally has 3 years from the filing of a federal income tax return to assess a tax. The statute of limitations (SOL) period for state income tax audits and deficiency assessments generally range from 3 to 4 years from the later of the return due date or the date the return was filed. This chart shows the standard limitations period for assessments in each state and the District of Columbia.

Jurisdiction	Standard Limitation Periods	Comment
Alabama	3 yrs. from later of due date or date filed.	
Alaska	3 yrs. from date filed.	
Arizona	4 yrs. from later of due date or date filed.	
Arkansas	3 yrs. from later of due date or date filed.	
California	4 yrs. from later of due date, without regard to any extension, or date filed.	
Colorado	Federal statute of limitations period, plus one year.	
Connecticut	3 yrs. from later of due date or date return received.	
Delaware	3 yrs. from later of due date or date filed.	
District of Columbia	3 yrs. from later of due date or date filed.	
Florida	3 yrs. from later of due date or date filed.	
Georgia	3 yrs. from later of due date or date filed.	
Hawaii	3 yrs. from later of due date or date filed.	
Idaho	3 yrs. from later of due date, without regard to extensions, or date return filed.	
Illinois	3 yrs. from later of due date or date filed.	
Indiana	3 yrs. from later of due date or date filed.	
Iowa	3 yrs. from later of due date or date filed.	
Kansas	3 yrs. from later of due date, date return filed, or date tax paid or within 1 year after an amended return is filed.	

Jurisdiction	Standard Limitation Periods	Comment
Kentucky	4 yrs. from later of due date or date filed.	
Louisiana	3 yrs. from end of calendar year in which due.	
Maine	3 yrs. from later of due date or date filed.	
Maryland	3 yrs. from later of due date or date filed.	
Massachusetts	3 yrs. from later of due date or date filed.	
Michigan	4 yrs. from later of due date or date filed.	
Minnesota	3.5 yrs. from later of due date or date filed.	
Mississippi	3 yrs. from later of due date or date filed.	
Missouri	3 yrs. from later of due date or date filed.	
Montana	3 yrs. from later of due date or date return filed.	
Nebraska	3 yrs. from later of due date, without regard to extensions, or date filed.	
Nevada	N/A, because state does not tax general business corporation or pass-through income.	
New Hampshire	3 yrs. from later of due date or date return filed, or if no return required, 3 yrs. from later of date tax due or paid.	
New Jersey	4 yrs. from later of due date or date filed.	
New Mexico	3 yrs. from end of calendar year in which tax due.	
New York	3 yrs. from later of due date or date filed.	For assessments based on amended return changes or corrections, the later of 1 year from the date the amended return was filed or 3 years from the date the original return was filed.
North Carolina	3 yrs. from later of due date or date filed.	
North Dakota	3 yrs. from later of due date or date filed.	
Ohio	4 yrs. from later of due date or date filed.	
Oklahoma	3 yrs. from later of due date or date filed.	
Oregon	3 yrs. from date filed.	

Jurisdiction	Standard Limitation Periods	Comment
Pennsylvania	3 yrs. from later of due date or date filed.	
Rhode Island	3 yrs. from later of due date or date filed.	
South Carolina	3 yrs. from later of due date or date filed.	
South Dakota	N/A, because state does not tax general business corporation or pass-through income.	
Tennessee	3 yrs. from end of calendar year in which filed.	
Texas	4 yrs. from due date.	
Utah	3 yrs. from date filed.	
Vermont	3 yrs. from later of due date or date filed.	
Virginia	3 yrs. from due date.	
Washington	N/A, because state does not tax general business corporation or pass-through income.	
West Virginia	3 yrs. from later of date due or date filed.	
Wisconsin	4 yrs. from later of due date or date filed.	
Wyoming	N/A, because state does not tax general business corporation or pass-through income.	

Limitation Periods for Assessment and Refund—Understatements, Fraud, or Failure to File

The assessment period for federal income tax purposes is extended from 3 to 6 years when more than 25% of gross income is omitted from a taxpayer's income tax return. There is no statute of limitations on assessment of federal income tax if the taxpayer fails to file a return or files a false or fraudulent return with intent to evade tax. This chart shows special limitations periods applicable in each state and the District of Columbia for assessments of income tax audits and deficiency assessments if a taxpayer files a state income tax return with a substantial understatement of liability, fails to file a return, or files a fraudulent return.

Jurisdiction	Understatements, Fraud, or Failure to File	Comment
Alabama	6 yrs. from due date or date filed if understatement exceeds 25%. No limit in cases of fraud or failure to file.	
Alaska	6 yrs. from date filed if understatement exceeds 25%. No limit in cases of fraud or failure to file.	
Arizona	6 yrs. from date filed if understatement exceeds 25%. 7 yrs. in case of failure to file. No limit in case of fraud.	
Arkansas	6 yrs. from later of due date or date filed if understatement exceeds 25%. No limit in cases of fraud or failure to file.	
California	6 yrs. from date filed if understatement exceeds 25%. No limit in cases of fraud or failure to file.	
Colorado	No limit in cases of fraud or failure to file.	
Connecticut	6 yrs. from date filed if understatement exceeds 25%. No limit in cases of fraud or failure to file.	
Delaware	6 yrs. from later of due date or date filed if understatement exceeds 25%. No limit in cases of fraud or failure to file.	
District of Columbia	6 yrs. from later of due date or date filed if understatement exceeds 25%. No limit in cases of fraud or failure to file.	
Florida	No limit in cases of underpayment, fraud or failure to file or pay.	Standard limitations period applies if taxpayer provides voluntary disclosure of tax liability before contact by state.

Jurisdiction	Understatements, Fraud, or Failure to File	Comment
Georgia	6 yrs. from date filed if understatement exceeds 25%. No limit in cases of fraud or failure to file.	
Hawaii	6 yrs. from date filed if understatement exceeds 25%. No limit in cases of fraud or failure to file.	
Idaho	No limit in cases of fraud or failure to file.	
Illinois	6 yrs. from later of due date or date filed, if understatement exceeds 25%. No limit in cases of fraud or failure to file.	
Indiana	6 yrs. from later of due date or date filed, if understatement exceeds 25%. No limit in cases of fraud or failure to file.	
Iowa	6 yrs. from later of due date or date filed, if understatement exceeds 25%. No limit in cases of fraud or failure to file.	
Kansas	No limit in cases of fraud.	
Kentucky	6 yrs. from later of due date or date filed, if understatement exceeds 25%. No limit in cases of fraud or failure to file.	
Louisiana	No limit in cases of fraud or failure to file.	
Maine	6 yrs. from date filed, if understatement exceeds 50%. No limit in cases of fraud or failure to file.	
Maryland	No limit in cases of fraud or failure to file.	
Massachusetts	6 yrs. from date filed if understatement exceeds 25%. No limit in cases of fraud or failure to file.	**Failure to file look-back policies:** • 7 years in general; or • 3 years for foreign corporations or other foreign entities that voluntarily disclose nonfiling. Special look-back policy applies to certain corporations engaged in business relating to: • in-state ownership and use of intangible property; or • in-state lending and ancillary loan activity.
Michigan	2 yrs. from date fraud or failure to file discovered.	

Jurisdiction	Understatements, Fraud, or Failure to File	Comment
Minnesota	6.5 yrs. from later of due date or date filed if understatement exceeds 25%. No limit in cases of fraud or failure to file.	
Mississippi	No limit in cases of fraud.	
Missouri	6 yrs. from later of due date or date filed, if understatement exceeds 25%. No limit in cases of fraud or failure to file.	
Montana	No limit in cases of fraud or failure to file.	
Nebraska	6 yrs. from later of due date or date filed, if understatement exceeds 25%. No limit in cases of fraud or failure to file.	
Nevada	N/A, because state does not tax general business corporation or pass-through income.	
New Hampshire	6 yrs. from date filed, if understatement exceeds 25%. No limit in cases of fraud or failure to file.	
New Jersey	No limit in cases of fraud or failure to file.	
New Mexico	6 yrs. from end of calendar year in which tax due, if understatement exceeds 25%. 7 yrs. in case of failure to file. 10 yrs. in case of fraud.	
New York	6 yrs. from later of due date or date filed, if understatement exceeds 25%. No limit in cases of fraud or failure to file.	
North Carolina	No limit in cases of fraud or failure to file.	
North Dakota	6 yrs. from later of due date or date filed, if understatement exceeds 25%. 10 yrs. in case of failure to file. No limit in cases of fraud.	
Ohio	No limit in cases of fraud or failure to file.	
Oklahoma	No limit in cases of fraud or failure to file return.	
Oregon	5 yrs. from date filed, if understatement exceeds 25%. No limit in cases of fraud or failure to file.	
Pennsylvania	No limit in cases of fraud or failure to file.	

Jurisdiction	Understatements, Fraud, or Failure to File	Comment
Rhode Island	6 yrs. from later of due date or date filed, if understatement exceeds 25%. No limit in cases of fraud or failure to file.	
South Carolina	6 yrs. from later of due date or date filed, if understatement is 20% or more. No limit in cases of fraud or failure to file.	
South Dakota	N/A, because state does not tax general business corporation or pass-through income.	
Tennessee	No limit in cases of fraud or failure to file.	
Texas	No limit, if understatement exceeds 25%, or in cases of fraud or failure to file.	
Utah	No special limitations period (general 3-yr. limitations period applies) for assessment attributable to substantial understatements. No limit in cases of fraud or failure to file.	
Vermont	No limit in cases of fraud or failure to file.	
Virginia	No limit in cases of fraud or failure to file.	
Washington	N/A, because state does not tax general business corporation or pass-through income.	
West Virginia	No limit in cases of fraud or failure to file.	
Wisconsin	6 yrs. from later of due date or date filed if understatement exceeds 25% and additional income for such year exceeds $100. No limit in cases of fraud or failure to file.	
Wyoming	N/A, because state does not tax general business corporation or pass-through income.	

Limited Liability Companies: Recognition of Federal Election

The following chart indicates whether states recognize the federal pass-through treatment of limited liability companies (LLCs) for state tax purposes. Most states follow the federal classification of LLCs provided under the federal check-the-box regulations, so that an LLC treated as a partnership for federal tax purposes is also treated as partnership for state tax purposes. The chart does not address state recognition of entity classification for single-member limited liability companies (SMLLCs). The chart also does not address whether the states impose any entity-level tax on LLCs. Entity-level taxes are addressed in the charts under the topic Limited Liability Companies: Taxation.

Jurisdiction	LLCs	Comment
Alabama	Same as federal.	
Alaska	Same as federal.	
Arizona	Same as federal.	
Arkansas	Same as federal.	
California	Same as federal.	
Colorado	Same as federal.	
Connecticut	Same as federal.	
Delaware	Same as federal.	
District of Columbia	Same as federal.	
Florida	Same as federal.	
Georgia	Same as federal.	
Hawaii	Same as federal.	
Idaho	Same as federal.	
Illinois	Same as federal.	
Indiana	Same as federal.	
Iowa	Same as federal.	
Kansas	Same as federal.	
Kentucky	Same as federal.	
Louisiana	Same as federal.	Effective for tax periods beginning on and after January 1, 2019, pass-through entities may elect to be taxed as if filing as a C corporation at the federal level.
Maine	Same as federal.	
Maryland	Same as federal.	
Massachusetts	Same as federal.	
Michigan	Same as federal.	

Jurisdiction	LLCs	Comment
Minnesota	Same as federal.	
Mississippi	Same as federal.	
Missouri	Same as federal.	
Montana	Same as federal.	
Nebraska	Same as federal.	
Nevada	N/A, because state does not tax pass-through income.	
New Hampshire	Federal election recognized.	
New Jersey	Same as federal.	
New Mexico	Same as federal.	
New York	Same as federal.	
North Carolina	Same as federal.	
North Dakota	Same as federal.	
Ohio	Subject to CAT.	
Oklahoma	Same as federal.	
Oregon	Same as federal.	
Pennsylvania	Same as federal.	
Rhode Island	Same as federal.	
South Carolina	Same as federal.	
South Dakota	N/A, because state does not tax pass-through income.	
Tennessee	Same as federal.	State follows federal classification but generally requires certain additions and subtractions for losses and income received from pass-through entities subject to the excise tax.
Texas	Federal provisions and classification not recognized.	Franchise tax imposed.
Utah	Same as federal.	
Vermont	Same as federal.	
Virginia	Same as federal.	
Washington	N/A, because state does not tax pass-through income.	
West Virginia	Same as federal.	
Wisconsin	Same as federal.	
Wyoming	N/A, because state does not tax pass-through income.	

Limited Liability Companies: Taxation

Jurisdiction	LLCs	Comment
Alabama	Business privilege tax imposed on taxable net worth.	
Alaska	No entity-level tax measured by income or net worth/capital value.	
Arizona	No entity-level tax measured by income or net worth/capital value.	
Arkansas	Minimum franchise tax imposed.	
California	Fee imposed on income attributable to state sources as follows: $250,000-$499,999: $900 $500,000-$999,999: $2,500 $1,000,000-4,999,999: $6,000 $5,000,000 or more: $11,790 $800 minimum tax.	
Colorado	No entity-level tax measured by income or net worth/capital value.	
Connecticut	Pass-through entity tax imposed a rate of 6.99% for tax years after 2017. $250 biennial assessment, known as business entity tax (BET) for tax years before 2020.	
Delaware	$300 annual tax imposed on LLCs. $75 annual tax imposed on each series LLC, effective beginning August 1, 2019. No other entity-level tax measured by income or net worth/capital value.	
District of Columbia	Franchise tax imposed on taxable income.	
Florida	No entity-level tax measured by income or net worth/capital value.	
Georgia	No entity-level tax measured by income or net worth/capital value.	
Hawaii	No entity-level tax measured by income or net worth/capital value.	
Idaho	Nondistributed income is taxed at the corporate rate. $10 tax unless all income or loss is distributed or otherwise reportable and entity does not have taxable income attributable to state sources.	
Illinois	1.5% personal property replacement income tax.	
Indiana	No entity-level tax measured by income or net worth/capital value.	
Iowa	No entity-level tax measured by income or net worth/capital value.	

Jurisdiction	LLCs	Comment
Kansas	No entity-level tax measured by income or net worth/capital value.	
Kentucky	Every limited liability pass-through entity with over $3 million in gross receipts or gross profits must pay the greater of $175 or an annual limited liability entity tax (LLET) equal to lesser of: • 9.5 cents per $100 of Kentucky gross receipts; or • 75 cents per $100 of Kentucky gross profits. If gross receipts or gross profits are over $3 million but less than $6 million, gross receipts may be reduced by $2,850 or gross profits by $22,500 multiplied by a numerator of $6 million less the amount of gross receipts or gross profits for the taxable year, and a denominator of $3 million.	
Louisiana	No entity-level tax measured by income or net worth/capital value.	Effective for tax periods beginning on and after January 1, 2019, pass-through entities may elect to be taxed as if filing as a C corporation at the federal level.
Maine	No entity-level tax measured by income or net worth/capital value.	
Maryland	No entity-level tax measured by income or net worth/capital value.	Beginning with tax year 2020, state allows pass-through entities to elect to be taxed at the entity level.
Massachusetts	No entity-level tax measured by income or net worth/capital value.	
Michigan	No entity-level tax measured by income or net worth/capital value, unless LLC has certificated credits and has elected to pay the Michigan Business Tax (MBT).	
Minnesota	Graduated minimum fee imposed based on in-state property, payroll, and sales or receipts. Otherwise, no entity-level tax measured by income or net worth/capital value.	
Mississippi	No entity-level tax measured by income or net worth/capital value.	
Missouri	No entity-level tax measured by income or net worth/capital value.	
Montana	No entity-level tax measured by income or net worth/capital value.	
Nebraska	No entity-level tax measured by income or net worth/capital value.	
Nevada	N/A, because state does not tax pass-through income.	

Jurisdiction	LLCs	Comment
New Hampshire	Business profits tax based on gross income. Business enterprise tax based on compensation, interest, and dividends.	
New Jersey	No entity-level tax measured by income or net worth/capital value.	**Pass-through business alternative tax.** After 2019, an LLC with at least one member subject to New Jersey income tax on the proceeds of the pass-through entity can elect to pay the pass-through business alternative income tax.
New Mexico	No entity-level tax measured by income or net worth/capital value.	
New York	Fee based on prior year gross income attributable to state sources imposed as follows: • $0 - $100,000: $25 • $100,001 - $250,000: $50 • $250,001 - $500,000: $175 • $500,001 - $1,000,000: $500 • $1,000,001 - $5,000,000: $1,500 • $5,000,001 - $25,000,000: $3,000 • $25,000,001 or more: $4,500	No entity-level tax measured by income or net worth/capital value for taxable years beginning before 2008.
North Carolina	No entity-level tax measured by income or net worth/capital value.	
North Dakota	No entity-level tax measured by income or net worth/capital value.	
Ohio	CAT imposed on gross receipts.	
Oklahoma	For tax years after 2018, LLCS may elect to pay income tax at the entity level.	
Oregon	No entity-level tax measured by income or net worth/capital value.	**Corporate Activity Tax:** Beginning in 2020, LLCs may be required to pay CAT.
Pennsylvania	No entity-level tax measured by income or net worth/capital value.	
Rhode Island	**Tax years after 2016:** Fee equal to $400 minimum tax, otherwise no entity-level tax measured by income or net worth/ capital value. **Tax year 2016:** Fee equal to $450 minimum tax, otherwise no entity-level tax measured by income or net worth/ capital value. **Tax years prior to 2016:** Fee equal to $500 minimum tax, otherwise no entity-level tax measured by income or net worth/ capital value.	For tax years beginning on or after January 1, 2019, a pass-through entity may elect to pay the state tax at the entity level. Such entities that make the election are subject to a tax rate of 5.99%.
South Carolina	No entity-level tax measured by income or net worth/capital value.	

Jurisdiction	LLCs	Comment
South Dakota	N/A, because state does not tax pass-through income.	
Tennessee	Excise tax imposed on net earnings and franchise tax imposed on net worth or actual value of tangible property. Hall income tax imposed on interest and dividend income that exceeds $1,250, less corresponding tax credit against excise tax liability.	Hall income tax rate reduced to 1% for 2020. Repealed beginning January 1, 2021.
Texas	Revised franchise (margin) tax imposed if total revenues exceed $1,000,000 as adjusted for inflation ($1,180,000 for 2020-2021, $1,130,000 for 2018-2019, $1,110,000 for 2016-2017).	
Utah	No entity-level tax measured by income or net worth/capital value.	
Vermont	$250 minimum tax, otherwise no entity-level tax measured by income or net worth/capital value.	
Virginia	No entity-level tax measured by income or net worth/capital value.	
Washington	N/A, because state does not tax pass-through income.	
West Virginia	No entity-level tax measured by income or net worth/capital value.	
Wisconsin	No entity-level tax measured by income or net worth/capital value.	Beginning with tax year 2019, state allows pass-through entities treated as partnerships to elect to be taxed at the entity level. Economic development surcharge imposed for tax years before 2013 on gross receipts of $4 million or more equal to greater of $25 or 0.2% (0.002) of net income attributable to the state, but not more than $9,800.
Wyoming	N/A, because state does not tax pass-through income.	

Lump Sum Distributions

Federal law offers taxpayers born before January 2, 1936 or their beneficiaries, who receive lump-sum distributions from qualified retirement plans the choice of (1) including the entire taxable portion of the distribution in their federal adjusted gross income (AGI) for the year or (2) calculating a separate tax on the entire taxable portion of the distribution by applying a 10-year averaging method. Taxpayers who elect to apply the 10 year averaging method must use federal Form 4972 to calculate the amount of federal tax due on their distribution and then add that amount to the amount of tax otherwise due on federal form 1040 after federal AGI and federal taxable income are determined. Thus, since most states begin the calculation of personal income tax liability with federal AGI or federal taxable income, lump-sum distributions for which federal 10-year averaging has been elected would not be included in the state tax base in those states, and would be effectively exempted at the state level, unless the state required that the distributions be added to federal AGI or taxable income as part of the state personal income tax calculation.

This chart shows the tax treatment by each state and the District of Columbia of lump-sum distributions.

Jurisdiction	Lump Sum Distributions	Comment
Alabama	Gross income must include lump sum distributions.	
Arizona	Addition to federal tax base required for amount reported on federal Form 4972.	
Arkansas	10-year averaging option allowed in computing adjusted gross income.	Form AR1000TD required.
California	10-year averaging option allowed for computing state tax liability.	Schedule G-1 required.
Colorado	Addition to federal tax base required for amount reported on federal Form 4972. Subtraction allowed equal to state pension exclusion.	
Connecticut	Addition to federal tax base required for amount reported on federal Form 4972.	
Delaware	10-year averaging option allowed for computing state tax liability.	Form 329 required.
District of Columbia	Addition to federal tax base required for amount reported on federal Form 4972.	
Georgia	Addition to federal tax base required for amount reported on federal Form 4972.	
Hawaii	10-year averaging option allowed for computing state tax liability.	Form N-152 required.

Jurisdiction	Lump Sum Distributions	Comment
Idaho	Addition to federal tax base required for amount reported on federal Form 4972.	
Illinois	Addition to federal tax base required for amount reported on federal Form 4972.	
Indiana	Addition to federal tax base required for amount reported on federal Form 4972.	
Iowa	Tax imposed equal to 25% of tax reported on federal Form 4972.	
Kansas	Tax imposed equal to 13% of tax reported on federal Form 4972.	
Kentucky	10-year averaging option allowed for computing state tax liability. Addition required for portion of distribution on which capital gains rate elected for federal tax purposes. Subtraction allowed for up to $31,110 ($41,110 for tax years before 2018) of amount reported on Form 4972-K.	Form 4972-K and Schedule P required.
Louisiana	No adjustments to federal tax base required for amount reported on federal Form 4972.	
Maine	Prior to 2013, tax imposed equal to 15% of tax reported on federal Form 4972 (7.5% for 2012 tax year). Tax eliminated for tax years after 2012.	
Maryland	Addition to federal tax base required for ordinary income portion and 40% of capital gains portion of amount reported on federal Form 4972.	
Massachusetts	Gross income must include amount received from private employer plans in excess of employee contributions.	
Michigan	Addition to federal tax base required for lump-sum distributions reported on federal Form 4972.	
Minnesota	5-year averaging option allowed for computing state tax liability. Addition required for portion of distribution on which capital gains rate elected for federal tax purposes.	Form M-1LS required.
Mississippi	No adjustments to federal tax base required for amount reported on federal Form 4972.	
Missouri	Tax imposed equal to 10% of tax reported on federal Form 4972.	Copy of federal Form 4972 must be attached to return.
Montana	Tax imposed equal to 10% of tax reported on federal Form 4972.	Copy of federal Form 4972 must be attached to return.

Jurisdiction	Lump Sum Distributions	Comment
Nebraska	Tax imposed equal to 29.6% of tax reported on federal Form 4972.	
New Hampshire	N/A, because tax imposed only on interest and dividend income.	
New Jersey	Gross income must include amount received in excess of employee contributions.	
New Mexico	5-year averaging option allowed for computing state tax liability if federal 10-year averaging method used on federal Form 4972.	
New York	10-year averaging option allowed for computing state tax liability.	Form IT-230 required.
North Carolina	No adjustments to federal tax base required for amount reported on federal Form 4972 for tax years after 2013. For tax years prior to 2014, addition to federal tax base required for amount reported on federal Form 4972.	
North Dakota	Addition to federal tax base required for amount reported on federal Form 4972.	
Ohio	Addition to federal tax base required for amount reported on federal Form 4972.	Lump sum distribution credit may be claimed equal to $50 senior citizen tax credit multiplied by taxpayer's expected remaining life years.
Oklahoma	Addition to federal tax base required for amount reported on federal Form 4972. Subtraction may be claimed equal to state pension exclusion.	
Oregon	Addition to federal tax base required for amount reported on federal Form 4972.	
Pennsylvania	Taxable income may exclude lump sum distributions.	
Rhode Island	Tax imposed equal to 25% of tax reported on federal Form 4972.	
South Carolina	10-year averaging option allowed for computing state tax liability.	Form SC4972 required.
Tennessee	N/A, because tax imposed only on interest and dividend income.	
Utah	Addition to federal tax base required for amount reported on federal Form 4972.	
Vermont	Tax imposed equal to 24% of tax reported on federal Form 4972.	

Jurisdiction	Lump Sum Distributions	Comment
Virginia	Addition to federal tax base required for amount reported on federal Form 4972, less minimum distribution allowance and amount excludable for federal tax purposes.	
West Virginia	Addition to federal tax base required for amount reported on federal Form 4972.	
Wisconsln	Addition to federal tax base required for amount reported on federal Form 4972 less any federal estate tax attributable to such distribution.	

Mortgage Interest—IRC § 163(h)

Under IRC § 163(h), individuals can claim a home mortgage interest itemized deduction. The interest must be paid or accrued on acquisition indebtedness used to buy, build, or substantially improve a qualified residence of the taxpayer.

Before 2018 and after 2025, the total amount of debt used for the home mortgage deduction cannot exceed $1 million ($500,000 if married filing separately).

For tax years 2018 through 2025, the dollar limit is reduced to $750,000 ($375,000 if married filing separately) for debt incurred after December 15, 2017. Interest on a home equity loan is no longer deductible. There are exceptions if the taxpayer:

- entered into a binding written contract before December 15, 2017, to close on the purchase of a principal residence before January 1, 2018, if the residence is purchased before April 1, 2018; or
- refinances an existing acquisition debt for the original loan amount, but the exception expires after the expiration of the original loan, or the earlier of the expiration of the loan or the first refinance or 30 years.

This chart indicates whether each state and the District of Columbia allows this federal itemized deduction.

Jurisdiction	Mortgage Interest—IRC § 163(h)	Comment
Alabama	Allowed	
Arizona	Allowed, including interest equal to the amount of the federal credit under IRC § 25 for interest on home mortgages.	
Arkansas	Allowed, except limited to interest from debt on the cost of the principal and/or second residence, plus improvements.	State does not conform to limitations enacted in Tax Cuts and Jobs Act.
California	Allowed, including interest equal to the amount of the federal credit under IRC § 25 for interest on home mortgages.	State does not conform to limitations enacted in Tax Cuts and Jobs Act. Certain payments made to the California Housing Finance Agency by first-time home buyers are considered mortgage interest and are deductible.
Colorado	N/A, because state itemized deductions not allowed.	
Connecticut	N/A, because state itemized deductions not allowed.	
Delaware	Allowed	
District of Columbia	Allowed	
Georgia	Allowed, including interest equal to the amount of the federal credit under IRC § 25 for interest on home mortgages.	

Jurisdiction	Mortgage Interest—IRC § 163(h)	Comment
Hawaii	Allowed	State does not conform to limitations enacted in Tax Cuts and Jobs Act.
Idaho	Allowed	
Illinois	N/A, because state itemized deductions not allowed.	
Indiana	N/A, because state itemized deductions not allowed.	
Iowa	Allowed, including interest equal to the amount of the federal credit under IRC § 25 for interest on home mortgages.	
Kansas	Allowed, equal to: • 100% of the interest for tax years beginning after 2019; • 75% of the interest for the 2019 tax year; and • 50% of the interest for tax years after 2014 and before 2019.	Form K-40, Schedule S.
Kentucky	Allowed.	Complete Form 740 or Form 740NP, Schedule A, and enclose with return.
Louisiana	Allowed.	
Maine	Allowed.	
Maryland	Allowed.	
Massachusetts	Not allowed.	State allowable deductions differ from federal itemized deductions.
Michigan	Not allowed.	
Minnesota	Allowed, except: • qualified residence interest excludes home equity interest; • acquisition indebtedness must not exceed $750,000 for indebtedness incurred on or after December 16, 2017; and • mortgage insurance premiums treated as interest under IRC 163(h)(3)(E) are excluded. Deductions reduced if taxpayer's income exceeds specified threshold amounts.	For tax years prior to 2019, this itemized deduction was allowed without modification. For tax year 2018, taxpayers could either claim the standard deduction or elect to itemize deductions, regardless of the election made on their 2018 federal income tax return. Itemized deductions were required to be calculated as they were allowed under the IRC as amended through December 16, 2016.
Mississippi	Allowed.	
Missouri	Allowed.	
Montana	Allowed.	
Nebraska	Allowed.	
New Hampshire	N/A.	Tax on individuals is imposed only on interest and dividend income.
New Jersey	Not allowed.	
New Mexico	Allowed.	

Jurisdiction	Mortgage Interest—IRC § 163(h)	Comment
New York	Allowed.	State does not conform to limitations enacted in Tax Cuts and Jobs Act.
North Carolina	Allowed, except limited to $20,000.	Complete and attach Supplemental Schedule S.
North Dakota	Allowed.	
Ohio	Not allowed.	
Oklahoma	Allowed, except limited by a $17,000 total of itemized deductions.	
Oregon	Allowed.	
Pennsylvania	Not allowed.	
Rhode Island	N/A, because state itemized deductions not allowed.	
South Carolina	Allowed.	
Tennessee	N/A	Tax imposed only on interest and dividend income.
Utah	N/A, because state itemized deductions not allowed.	
Vermont	N/A, because state itemized deductions not allowed.	
Virginia	Allowed.	
West Virginia	N/A, because state itemized deductions not allowed.	
Wisconsin	N/A, because state itemized deductions not allowed.	

Net Operating Loss (Corporate Income)

Under IRC § 172, NOLs sustained in tax years before 2018 may be carried back two years and then carried forward 20 years to offset taxable income in the carryback and carryforward years. Taxpayers may elect to waive the carryback period. Effective in 2018 and future tax years, NOLs may no longer be carried back, but may be carried forward indefinitely.

This chart shows the corporation income tax treatment by each state and the District of Columbia regarding carryback/carryforward periods, including extended carryback periods.

Jurisdiction	Carryback and Carryforward Periods	Comment
Alabama	0 back 15 forward	Carryforward extended 1 year for NOLs incurred in 2001.
Alaska	Same as federal.	
Arizona	0 back 5 forward for tax years before 2012. 20 forward for tax years after 2011.	
Arkansas	**Tax years before 2020:** 0 back 5 forward **2020 tax year:** 0 back 8 forward **Tax years on or after 2021:** 0 back 10 forward	
California	0 back 20 forward	**2013-2018 tax years:** 2 back 20 forward **2008-2012 tax years:** 0 back 20 forward **2000-2007 tax years:** 0 back 10 forward Carryover period extended for losses not claimed as a result of 2020-2022 suspension: • 1 year for losses incurred during 2021 tax year; • 2 years for losses incurred during 2020 tax year; • 3 years for losses incurred before 2020 tax year. Carryover period extended for losses not claimed as a result of 2008-2011 suspension: • 1 year for 2010 tax year losses; • 2 years for 2009 tax year losses; • 3 years for 2008 tax year losses; • 4 years for losses before 2008.

Jurisdiction	Carryback and Carryforward Periods	Comment
Colorado	**Tax years after 2020:** 0 back 20 forward **Tax years after 2017 and before 2021:** 0 back Carryforward period same as federal **Tax years before 2018:** 0 back 20 forward	Carryforward period extended 1 year for 2011-2013 tax year losses when portion of NOL is limited.
Connecticut	0 back 20 forward	
Delaware	Same as federal.	
District of Columbia	0 back Same as federal forward	
Florida	0 back Same as federal forward	
Georgia	0 back Same as federal forward	
Hawaii	0 back Same as federal forward	Hawaii does not conform to the extended carryback periods for the 2001, 2002, 2008, and 2009 tax years.
Idaho	2 back 20 forward	15 forward for tax years before 2000.
Illinois	0 back 12 forward	Carryover suspended for tax years ending after December 31, 2010 and before December 31, 2012.
Indiana	0 back 20 forward	**Tax years before 2012:** 2 back 20 forward.
Iowa	0 back 20 forward	**Tax years before 2009:** 2 back 20 forward
Kansas	3 back for any unused NOL after end of carryforward period or after final return is filed. 10 forward	
Kentucky	0 back Same as federal forward	
Louisiana	**Returns Filed After June 30, 2015** 0 back 20 forward **Returns Filed Before July 1, 2015** 3 back 15 forward	

Jurisdiction	Carryback and Carryforward Periods	Comment
Maine	0 back Same as federal forward	Carryforward period is extended for the number of years NOL is suspended with respect to tax years beginning in 2009, 2010 and 2011.
Maryland	**Tax year 2020:** 0 back Same as federal forward **Tax years 2018 and 2019:** Same as federal. **Tax years before 2018:** Same as federal, except extended carryback periods.	
Massachusetts	0 back 20 forward. **Tax years before 2010:** 0 back 5 forward	
Michigan	0 back 10 forward	
Minnesota	0 back 15 forward	
Mississippi	2 back 20 forward	
Missouri	Same as federal, except limited to: • 2 back • 20 forward	
Montana	3 back 7 forward for tax years before 2018 10 forward for tax years after 2017	
Nebraska	0 back 20 forward	**Tax years before 2014:** 0 back 5 forward
Nevada	N/A, because state does not tax general business corporation income.	
New Hampshire	0 back 10 forward	
New Jersey	0 back 20 forward	Carryforward is extended 2 years for suspended NOLs in 2003 and 2004 privilege periods. **Privilege periods before July 1, 2009:** 0 back 7 forward
New Mexico	0 back 20 forward	**Tax years before 2013:** 0 back 5 forward

Jurisdiction	Carryback and Carryforward Periods	Comment
New York	2 back for tax years before 2015 3 back for tax years after 2014. 20 forward	For NOLs incurred after 2014, a 3-year carryback is allowed, but no NOL can be carried back to a tax year beginning before 2015. For NOLs incurred before 2015, a prior NOL conversion subtraction is computed on Form CT-3.3
North Carolina	0 back 15 forward	
North Dakota	0 back Same as federal forward	
Ohio	N/A, because deduction not allowed.	
Oklahoma	**Tax years after 2017:** Same as federal. **Tax years before 2018:** 0 back 20 forward	Oklahoma does not conform to the extended carryback period for the 2008 tax year.
Oregon	0 back 15 forward	
Pennsylvania	0 back 20 forward	
Rhode Island	0 back 5 forward	
South Carolina	**Tax years after 2020:** Same as federal. **Tax years 2018-2020:** 0 back, indefinite forward **Tax years before 2018:** 0 back, 20 forward.	
South Dakota	N/A, because state does not tax general business corporation income.	
Tennessee	0 back 15 forward	
Texas	N/A, because deduction not allowed.	
Utah	0 back Same as federal forward **Tax years before 2018:** 3 back 15 forward	
Vermont	0 back 10 forward	
Virginia	Same as federal, except extended carryback periods.	Virginia does not conform to federal NOL changes for tax years after 2017.
Washington	N/A, because state does not tax general business corporation income.	

Jurisdiction	Carryback and Carryforward Periods	Comment
West Virginia	Same as federal, except it does not conform to carryback periods for NOLs from 2018, 2019, and 2020 tax years.	
Wisconsin	0 back 20 forward	**Tax years before 2014:** 0 back 15 forward
Wyoming	N/A, because state does not tax general business corporation income.	

Net Operating Loss (Personal Income)

A federal net operating loss (NOL) deduction is available to taxpayers under IRC § 172. A taxpayer sustains an NOL for a tax year if deductions exceed the taxpayer's gross income for that year. A loss from operating a business is the most common reason for an NOL. Partnerships and S corporations generally cannot use an NOL. However, partners or shareholders can use their separate shares of the partnership's or S corporation's business income and business deductions to figure their individual NOLs.

The NOL for a tax year must be computed without including any NOL carrybacks or carryforwards from other tax years. The determination of a taxpayer's NOL must also exclude:

- personal or dependency exemptions;
- nonbusiness deductions in excess of nonbusiness income;
- capital losses in excess of capital gains;
- the domestic production activities deduction under IRC § 199 (tax years before 2018);
- the 20% deduction for qualified business income from a pass-through entity under IRC § 199A (tax years after 2017); and
- the deduction for foreign-derived intangible income (FDII) under IRC § 250 (tax years after 2017).

Effective for tax years beginning after 2020, IRC § 172 limits the federal NOL deduction for NOLs that arise in tax years after 2017 to 80% of taxable income. IRC § 172 provides net operating loss (NOL) carryback and carryforward periods of:

- 2 back and 20 forward for tax years before 2018;
- 5 back and indefinitely forward for 2018, 2019, and 2020 tax years; and
- 0 back and indefinitely forward for tax years beginning after 2020.

Taxpayers may elect to waive the carryback period.

This chart shows how each state and the District of Columbia treats the federal NOL deduction. The chart also shows NOL carryback and carryforward periods. In some states, the NOL subtraction adjustment is not based on the federal deduction or a federal tax base starting point. Generally, modifications for nonresident taxpayers apply only to income from state sources.

Jurisdiction	Net Operating Losses (NOLs)—IRC § 172	Comment
Alabama	Subtraction from income is allowed for NOLs attributable to trade or business, sale of assets used in a trade or business, or personal casualties or thefts. **Carryback/Carryforward periods:** • 2 back • 15 forward	Irrevocable election may be made to waive carryback. NOL is computed using Form NOL-85 and applied in carryback or carryforward year using Form NOL-85A. Form NOL-85A must be attached to annual or amended return.

Jurisdiction	Net Operating Losses (NOLs)—IRC §172	Comment
Arizona	No adjustments to federal tax base required for federal deduction or carryback/carryforward periods, except addition for: • the amount of any NOL carryover claimed federally when restoring an amount under a claim of right that exceeds the NOL carryover allowable for state purposes; and • any extended carryback that was claimed federally for 2008 or 2009 NOLs. Subtraction from income allowed for: • the amount of any NOL carryover allowable for state purposes when restoring an amount under a claim of right that exceeds the NOL carryover claimed federally; and • any general NOL carryforward that would have been allowed if federal extended NOL carryback election had not been made.	State has not conformed to: • suspension of the 80% taxable income limit for tax years before 2021; or • the carryback periods for NOLs from 2018, 2019, and 2020 tax years.
Arkansas	Subtraction from income allowed for NOLs computed on separate basis from federal deduction and carryback/ carryforward periods. **Carryback/Carryforward periods for tax years before 2020:** • 0 back • 5 forward **Carryback/Carryforward periods for tax year 2020:** • 0 back • 8 forward **Carryback/Carryforward periods for tax years after 2020:** • 0 back • 10 forward 10 year carryforward for certain steel manufacturers. 15 year carryforward for certain medical companies.	Statement showing how NOL was calculated and year loss occurred must be attached to return.

Jurisdiction	Net Operating Losses (NOLs)—IRC §172	Comment
California	Addition to income required for amount of federal NOL deduction. Subtraction from income allowed for NOL computed using federal provisions, except taxable income limit and carryforward/carryback periods. **Carryforward/carryback periods for tax years after 2018:** • 0 back • 20 forward **Carryforward/carryback periods for 2013-2018 tax years:** • 2 back (75% limit for 2014, 50% for 2013) • 20 forward **Carryforward/carryback periods for 2008-2012 tax years:** • 0 back • 20 forward **Carryforward/carryback periods for 2000-2007 tax years:** • 0 back • 10 forward	NOL suspended in 2020, 2021, and 2022 tax years for taxpayers with net business income or modified adjusted gross income of $1,000,000 or more (based on federal AGI). NOL also suspended in 2010 and 2011 tax years for taxpayers with modified adjusted gross income of $300,000 or more (based on federal AGI). NOL also suspended in 2008 and 2009 tax years for taxpayers with taxable income of $500,000 or more. Carryover period extended for losses not claimed as a result of 2020-2022 suspension: • 1 year for losses incurred during 2021 tax year; • 2 years for losses incurred during 2020 tax year; • 3 years for losses incurred before 2020 tax year. Carryover period extended for losses not claimed as a result of 2008-2011 suspension: • 1 year for losses incurred during 2010 tax year; • 2 years for losses incurred during 2009 tax year; • 3 years for losses incurred during 2008 tax year; • 4 years for losses incurred before 2008 tax year. NOL is computed on Form 3805V and amount is entered as a positive number on Schedule CA (540 or 540NR).
Colorado	Addition required for amount of federal deduction that exceeds 80% of taxable income for NOLs from tax years after 2017 and before 2021. **Carryback/Carryforward periods:** No adjustments to federal provisions required.	
Connecticut	No adjustments to federal tax base required for federal deduction or carryback/carryforward periods.	
Delaware	No adjustments to federal tax base required for federal deduction or carryback/carryforward periods, except addition required for NOL carrybacks exceeding $30,000. Subtraction from federal tax base allowed in later tax years for amount of carryback addback.	
District of Columbia	No adjustments to federal tax base required for federal deduction or carryback/carryforward periods.	

Jurisdiction	Net Operating Losses (NOLs)—IRC §172	Comment
Georgia	No adjustments to federal tax base for federal deduction or carryback/ carryforward periods, except addition for: • 5 year carryback that was claimed for NOLs attributable to Gulf Opportunity Zone losses, Kansas disaster area losses, or other disaster area losses; • extended carryback that was claimed for NOLs attributable to small business losses incurred in 2008 and 2009; and • NOL carryover that was claimed from years when taxpayer was not subject to state's income tax.	
Hawaii	Addition to federal tax base required for: • amount of federal deduction that exceeds 80% of taxable income for NOLs from 2018, 2019, and 2020; and • amount of federal deduction from federally exempt interest income. Subtraction from federal tax base allowed for amount attributable to nondeductible interest expenses on indebtedness incurred to purchase tax-exempt bonds, or if taxpayer is a nonresident incurred to purchase out-of-state property or to conduct out-of-state business. **Carryback/Carryforward periods:** • 0 back • Same as federal forward	Hawaii does not conform to the extended carryback periods for the 2001, 2002, 2008, and 2009 tax years.
Idaho	Addition required for amount of federal deduction. Subtraction from income allowed for NOLs computed on separate basis from federal deduction and carryback/ carryforward rules. **Carryback/Carryforward periods:** • 2 back for up to $100,000 ($50,000 for married individuals filing separately) • 20 forward	**Tax years after 2012:** Carryback may be claimed by filing amended return within one year after end of loss year. **Tax years before 2013:** Irrevocable election could be made to waive carryback.
Illinois	No adjustments to federal tax base required for federal deduction or carryback/carryforward periods.	
Indiana	Addition to federal tax base required for amount of federal deduction. Subtraction from income allowed for NOLs equal to federal net operating loss adjusted for certain modifications. **Carryback/Carryforward periods:** • 0 back • 20 forward.	Adjustment is computed on Schedule IT-40NOL.

Jurisdiction	Net Operating Losses (NOLs)—IRC § 172	Comment
Iowa	Subtraction from income allowed for NOLs computed similar to federal deduction. **Carryback/Carryforward periods:** • 2 back • 20 forward 5 year carryback and 20 year carryforward for farming losses. 3 year carryback and 20 year carryforward for casualty and disaster area losses.	Election to waive carryback period allowed after 2019. Adjustment is computed on Form IA 123.
Kansas	No adjustments to federal tax base required for federal deduction or carryback/carryforward periods. **Tax years before 2017:** Addition to federal tax base required for federal NOL carryforward deduction. **Tax years before 2013:** Subtraction from federal tax base allowed for NOLs computed using federal provisions. **Carryback/Carryforward periods:** • 0 back • 10 forward	
Kentucky	Addition to federal tax base required for amount of federal deduction. Subtraction from federal adjusted gross income allowed for NOLs based on IRC § 172, except limited to 80% of taxable income. **Carryback/Carryforward periods:** • 0 back • Same as federal forward	Adjustment is computed on Schedule KNOL, which must be attached to annual return.
Louisiana	No adjustments to federal tax base required for federal deduction or carryback/carryforward periods.	

Jurisdiction	Net Operating Losses (NOLs)—IRC §172	Comment
Maine	Addition to federal tax base required for: • federal carryback deduction to prior tax years; • federal carryover deduction used to offset state addition modifications in loss year; • federal carryover deduction for any taxable year beginning in 2009, 2010, or 2011; and • federal carryover deduction disallowed by 80% taxable income limit and previously allowed as state tax subtraction for tax years after 2017. Subtraction from federal tax base allowed for: • recapture of NOL addition modifications for federal carryback or carryforward, excluding tax years 2009, 2010, and 2011; • recapture of NOL subtraction modifications denied for tax years 2009, 2010, and 2011 beginning with the 2012 tax year; and • federal NOL carryforward deductions disallowed by 80% taxable income limit for tax years after 2017.	
Maryland	No adjustments to federal tax base required for federal deduction or carryback/carryforward periods, except net addition modification (NAM) required for: • federal deduction if total addition modifications exceed total subtraction modifications in loss year when applying corresponding NOL to carryback/carryforward income year; • extended carryback that was claimed for NOLs incurred during 2001, 2002, 2008, 2009, or 2020 tax years; and • carryforward incurred in 2020 that exceeds 80% of taxable income for tax year.	Copies of federal return, including Schedules A and B or equivalent schedules, must be submitted with state return. Copy of loss year federal return must also be attached to carryback or carryforward year. If extended federal carryback was claimed: • Form 500DM must be completed and attached to annual return; and • amended return must be filed for carryback year.
Massachusetts	No NOL subtraction from income.	
Michigan	Addition to federal tax base required for amount of federal deduction. Subtraction from federal tax base allowed for NOLs, which are subject to allocation and apportionment and computed on a separate basis from federal deduction to account for other state differences. **Carryback/Carryforward periods:** No adjustments to federal provisions required.	

Jurisdiction	Net Operating Losses (NOLs)—IRC § 172	Comment
Minnesota	Addition to federal tax base required for amount of federal NOL carryback that exceeds 2 years. **Carryback/Carryforward periods:** • 2 back • 20 forward	Losses from sale of certain preferred stock treated as ordinary losses for federal purposes must be treated as capital losses when computing NOLs for state purposes. State has not conformed to: • suspension of the 80% taxable income limit for tax years before 2021; or • the carryback periods for NOLs from 2018, 2019, and 2020 tax years.
Mississippi	Subtraction from income is allowed for NOLs attributable to trade or business, which is computed on separate basis from federal deduction and carryback/carryforward rules. **Carryback/Carryforward periods:** • 2 back • 20 forward	Irrevocable election may be made to waive carryback. Adjustment is computed on Schedule N.
Missouri	Addition to federal tax base required for amount of federal deduction attributable to carryback in excess of two years or carryover in excess of 20 years. Subtraction from federal tax base allowed for addback amount in tax years subsequent to loss year.	
Montana	Addition to federal tax base required for amount of federal deduction. Subtraction from federal tax base allowed for NOL recomputed in accordance with federal provisions and state adjustments. **Carryback/Carryforward periods:** Same as federal.	Taxpayers can make irrevocable state election to waive carryback. Subtraction is computed on Form NOL.
Nebraska	Addition to federal tax base required for amount of federal deduction. Subtraction from federal tax base allowed for NOL that taxpayers compute by applying: • federal NOL; • state addition and subtraction adjustments; and • federal carryback/carryforward periods.	Complete and attach Form NOL worksheet. Also attach forms and worksheets supporing federal NOL. Attach worksheets to taxpayer's return.
New Hampshire	N/A	Tax imposed on interest and dividends and only deduction is personal exemption.
New Jersey	No NOL subtraction from income. After 2011, certain business losses may be carried forward for up to 20 years.	Losses in one income category apply only against income within same category. Net loss in one income category cannot be applied against income or gains in another category. After 2011, taxpayers allowed to net gains and losses derived from one or more specified business-related categories of gross income.

Jurisdiction	Net Operating Losses (NOLs)—IRC §172	Comment
New Mexico	Addition to federal tax base required for amount of federal deduction. Subtraction from federal tax base allowed for NOL recomputed to account for state differences. **Carryback/Carryforward periods:** • 0 back • 20 forward (5 forward before 2013)	Subtraction adjustment is computed on Schedule PIT-ADJ.
New York	Addition required for tax years after 2012 equal to amount of federal NOL deduction that exceeds federal taxable income computed without the NOL deduction. No adjustments to carryback periods for tax years before 2018 or to carryforward periods. For 2018, 2019, and 2020, addition required for federal 5-year carryback and 80% of taxable income limitation.	Beginning with tax year 2013, if amount of allowed state NOL is limited, the difference between state and federal NOLs is accounted for with an addition modification.
North Carolina	Addition to federal tax base required for: • NOL carryforards that exceed 80% taxable income limit for tax years 2018-2020; • NOL carrybacks from tax years 2018-2020; and • NOL carryforwards/carrybacks that a taxpayer does not absorb and will carryfoward to later tax years. Subtraction from federal adjusted gross income allowed for tax years 2021-2025 equal to 20% of addback for: • carryforwards that exceed 80% taxable income limit for tax years 2018-2020; and • NOL carrybacks from tax years from 2018-2020.	
North Dakota	No adjustments to federal tax base required for federal deduction or carryback/carryforward periods.	
Ohio	No adjustments to federal tax base required for federal deduction or carryback/carryforward periods, except carryback and carryforward cannot include five-sixths of NOL deduction attributable to IRC Sec. 168(k) bonus depreciation or IRC Sec. 179 expense deduction.	
Oklahoma	Addition to federal tax base required for amount of federal deduction. Subtraction from federal tax base allowed for NOL computed separately by reference to federal provisions. **Carryback/Carryforward periods:** No adjustments to federal provisions required, except carryback period is limited to 2 years for tax years beginning after December 31, 2007, and ending before January 1, 2009.	

Jurisdiction	Net Operating Losses (NOLs)—IRC § 172	Comment
Oregon	No adjustments to federal tax base required for federal deduction or carryback/carryforward periods, except addition required for: • extended carryback that was claimed for NOLs attributable to small business losses incurred in 2008 and 2009; and • NOLs that are not attributable to state sources.	
Pennsylvania	No NOL subtraction from income.	Business losses may be offset against business income. Losses may not be offset from one class of income against gains from another class.
Rhode Island	No adjustments to federal tax base required for federal deduction, except: • NOL must be adjusted to reflect state modifications to federal adjusted gross income; • NOL cannot include any loss sustained during any taxable year in which the taxpayer was not subject to state income tax; • extended carryback for NOLs incurred during taxable years ending during 2001 and 2002 was not allowed for state purposes; and • state deduction cannot exceed federal deduction. **Carryback/Carryforward periods:** • 0 back • 20 forward	
South Carolina	Addition to federal tax base required if amount of federal deduction is larger than allowable state NOL. Subtraction from federal tax base allowed if state NOL is larger than federal deduction. **Carryback/Carryforward periods:** Tax years before 2018: 0 back, 20 forward Tax years 2018-2020, 0 back, indefinite forward Tax years after 2020: Same as federal	Worksheet must be attached to annual return or maintained with taxpayer's records. State has not conformed to suspension of 80% taxable income limit for tax years before 2021.
Tennessee	N/A	Tax imposed on certain interest and dividends.
Utah	No adjustments to federal tax base required for federal deduction or carryback/carryforward periods.	
Vermont	No adjustments to federal tax base required for federal deduction or carryforward/pre-2018 carryback periods.	State has not conformed to: • suspension of the 80% taxable income limit for tax years before 2021; or • the carryback periods for NOLs from 2018, 2019, and 2020 tax years.

Jurisdiction	Net Operating Losses (NOLs)—IRC §172	Comment
Virginia	No adjustments to federal tax base required for federal deduction or carryback/carryforward periods, except addition required for extended carryback that was claimed for NOLs incurred during taxable years: • 2001 and 2002 • 2008 and 2009	State has not conformed to: • suspension of the 80% taxable income limit for tax years before 2021; or • the carryback periods for NOLs from 2018, 2019, and 2020 tax years.
West Virginia	No adjustments to federal tax base required for federal deduction or carryback/carryforward periods.	State does not conform to: • suspension of the 80% taxable income limit for tax years before 2021; or • the carryback periods for NOLs from 2018, 2019, and 2020 tax years.
Wisconsin	Addition to federal tax base required for amount of federal deduction. Subtraction from federal tax base allowed for NOL computed separately to account for state adjustments. **Carryback/Carryforward periods:** Tax years before 2014: 0 back, 15 forward Tax years after 2013: 2 back, 20 forward	

Payment by Credit Card

The following chart indicates whether a state allows taxpayers to make personal income tax payments by major credit card. This chart does not cover the types of credit cards accepted, information on the state's credit card service provider(s), or service charges imposed to offset the cost of accepting credit card payments.

Jurisdiction	Credit Card Payment	Comment
Alabama	Allowed	Credit card payments may be made over the Internet or by telephone (1-800-272-9829).
Arizona	Allowed	Credit card payments may be made over the Internet.
Arkansas	Allowed	Credit card payments may be made over the Internet or by telephone (1-800-272-9829).
California	Allowed	Credit card payments may be made over the Internet or by telephone (1-800-272-9829).
Colorado	Allowed	Credit card payments may be made over the Internet.
Connecticut	Allowed	Credit card payments may be made over the Internet or by telephone (1-800-272-9829).
Delaware	Allowed	Payments of up to $2,500 can be made by credit card over the Internet.
District of Columbia	Allowed	Credit card payments may be made over the Internet or by telephone (1-800-272-9829).
Georgia	Allowed	Credit card payments may be made over the Internet or by telephone (1-800-272-9829).
Hawaii	Allowed	Credit card payments may be made over the Internet. The maximum amount that can be charged to a credit card is $99,999.99 per transaction.
Idaho	Allowed	Credit card payments may be made (1) over the Internet; (2) by telephone (1-800-972-7660); or (3) in person at any Tax Commission office.
Illinois	Allowed	
Indiana	Allowed	Credit card payments may be made over the Internet or by telephone (1-800-272-9829).
Iowa	Allowed	Credit card payments may be made over the Internet or by telephone (current tax payments: 1-800-272-9829; billed delinquent payments: 1-866-243-1383).

Jurisdiction	Credit Card Payment	Comment
Kansas	Allowed	Credit card payments may be made over the Internet or by telephone (1-800-272-9829).
Kentucky	Allowed	
Louisiana	Allowed	Credit card payments may be made over the Internet or by telephone (1-888-272-9829).
Mainc	Not allowed	
Maryland	Allowed	Credit card payments may be made over the Internet or by telephone (1-800-272-9829). If taxpayer did not file a Maryland tax return for the previous tax year, taxpayer must use the Internet payment method to pay by credit card.
Massachusetts	Allowed	
Michigan	Allowed	
Minnesota	Allowed	Credit card payments may be made over the Internet or by telephone (1-855-947-2966).
Mississippi	Allowed	Credit card payments may be made over the Internet or by telephone (1-800-272-9829).
Missouri	Allowed	Credit card payments may be made over the Internet or by telephone (1-888-929-0513).
Montana	Allowed	Credit card payments may be made over the Internet.
Nebraska	Allowed	Credit card payments may be made over the Internet or by telephone (1-800-272-9829).
New Hampshire	Allowed	
New Jersey	Allowed	Credit card payments may be made over the Internet or by telephone (1-800-272-9829).
New Mexico	Allowed	Credit card payments may be made over the Internet.
New York	Allowed	Beginning June 16, 2015, individuals will not be able to use a credit card to pay a balance due when filing a 2014 personal income tax return or to make an estimated tax payment. The department anticipates that individuals will be able to resume using credit cards starting in January 2016. Credit card payments may be made over the Internet or by telephone (1-888-972-9697). Credit cards cannot be used to pay any tax due on an amended return.

Jurisdiction	Credit Card Payment	Comment
North Carolina	Allowed	Credit card payments may be made over the Internet.
North Dakota	Allowed	Credit card payments may be made over the Internet or by telephone (1-888-638-2937).
Ohio	Allowed	Credit card payments may be made over the Internet or by telephone (1-800-272-9829).
Oklahoma	Allowed	Credit card payments may be made over the Internet or by telephone (1-866-289-0455).
Oregon	Allowed	Credit card payments may be made over the Internet or by telephone (1-888-972-9673).
Pennsylvania	Allowed	Credit card payments may be made over the Internet or by telephone (1-800-272-9829).
Rhode Island	Allowed	Credit card payments may be made over the Internet or by telephone (1-800-272-9829).
South Carolina	Allowed	Credit card payments may be made over the Internet.
Tennessee	Allowed	Credit card payments may be made over the Internet.
Utah	Allowed	Credit card payments may be made over the Internet.
Vermont	Allowed	Credit card payments may be made over the Internet.
Virginia	Allowed	Credit card payments may be made over the Internet or by telephone (1-800-272-9829).
West Virginia	Allowed	Credit card payments may be made over the Internet or by telephone (1-800-272-9829).
Wisconsin	Allowed	Credit card payments may be made over the Internet or by telephone (1-800-272-9829).

Payroll Factor Rules

Under the Uniform Division of Income for Tax Purposes Act (UDITPA), the payroll factor for apportioning the income of multistate corporations is a fraction, the numerator of which is the total amount paid in a state for compensation and the denominator of which is the total compensation paid everywhere. Compensation is defined as wages, salaries, commissions and any other form of remuneration paid to employees for personal services. Neither UDITPA nor the Multistate Tax Commission (MTC) Model Apportionment Regulations specifically address whether officer compensation is included in the payroll factor.

This chart shows whether states that have a corporation income tax apportionment formula with a payroll factor include employee and officer compensation in the factor.

Jurisdiction	Employee and Officer Compensation	Comment
Alabama	Wages, salaries, commissions, and any other form of remuneration paid to employees for personal services rendered. Officer income not specifically included or excluded.	Prior to June 25, 2016: Compensation included wages, salaries, commissions, board, rent, housing, lodging, benefits, services, or any form of compensation paid to employees, including officers, in return for personal services connected with production of business income.
Alaska	Wages, salaries, commissions, board, rent, housing, lodging, benefits, services, or any form of compensation paid to employees, including officers, in return for personal services connected with production of business income.	
Arizona	Wages, salaries, commissions, board, rent, housing, lodging, benefits, services, or any form of compensation paid to employees, including officers, in return for personal services connected with production of business income.	
Arkansas	Wages, salaries, commissions, board, rent, housing, lodging, benefits, services, or any form of compensation paid to employees, including officers, in return for personal services connected with production of business income.	For taxable years beginning on or after January 1, 2021, single sales factor formula is implemented. The payroll factor will no longer be applicable.
California	N/A, because standard apportionment formula does not include a payroll factor.	**Tax years before 2013:** Wages, salaries, commissions, board, rent, housing, lodging, benefits, services, or any form of compensation paid to employees, including officers, in return for personal services connected with production of business income.
Colorado	N/A, because standard apportionment formula does not include a payroll factor.	

Jurisdiction	Employee and Officer Compensation	Comment
Connecticut	N/A, because standard apportionment formula does not include a payroll factor.	**Tax years before 2016:** Wages, salaries, and other compensation paid to employees, including officers.
Delaware	Wages, salaries and other compensation paid to employees, except general executive officers, including compensation resulting from taxpayer's proportionate ownership as general or limited partner in an active partnership.	
District of Columbia	N/A for tax years after 2014, because standard apportionment formula does not include a payroll factor.	For tax years through 2014, wages, salaries, commissions, and other compensation paid to employees, including officers, in return for personal services connected with the production of business income.
Florida	Wages, salaries, commissions, deferred compensation, board, rent, housing, lodging, benefits, services, or any form of compensation paid to employees, including officers, in return for personal services.	
Georgia	N/A, because standard apportionment formula does not include a payroll factor.	
Hawaii	Wages, salaries, commissions, board, rent, housing, lodging, benefits, services, or any form of compensation paid to employees, including officers, in return for personal services connected with production of business income.	
Idaho	Wages, salaries, commissions, board, rent, housing, lodging, benefits, services, or any form of compensation paid to employees, including officers, in return for personal services connected with production of business income.	
Illinois	N/A, because standard apportionment formula does not include a payroll factor.	
Indiana	N/A, because standard apportionment formula does not include a payroll factor.	**Tax years before 2011** Wages, salaries, commissions, board, rent, housing, lodging, benefits, services, or any form of compensation paid to employees, including officers, in return for personal services connected with production of business income.
Iowa	N/A, because standard apportionment formula does not include a payroll factor.	

Jurisdiction	Employee and Officer Compensation	Comment
Kansas	Wages, salaries, commissions, board, rent, housing, lodging, benefits, services, or any form of compensation paid to employees, including officers, in return for personal services connected with production of business income.	
Kentucky	N/A, because standard apportionment formula does not include a payroll factor. **Tax years before 2018:** Wages, salaries, commissions, board, rent, housing, lodging, benefits, services, or any form of compensation paid to employees, including officers, in return for personal services connected with production of business income.	
Louisiana	Wages, salaries, or any form of compensation paid to employees, including officers, in return for personal services connected with production of business income.	
Maine	N/A, because standard apportionment formula does not include a payroll factor.	
Maryland	Wages, salaries, and compensation paid to employees, including officers, for personal services.	
Massachusetts	Wages, salaries, commissions, bonuses, employee travel or allowances in excess of expenses, board, housing, personal use of automobile, employer contributions to qualified cash or deferred arrangement, employer contributions to nonqualified deferred compensation plans, benefits, services, or any form of compensation paid to employees, including officers, in return for personal services connected with production of business income.	
Michigan	N/A, because standard apportionment formula does not include a payroll factor.	
Minnesota	N/A for tax years after 2014, because standard apportionment formula does not include a payroll factor.	**Tax years before 2015:** Wages and salaries paid to employees, including officers.
Mississippi	Wages, salaries, commissions, board, rent, housing, lodging, benefits, services, or any form of compensation paid to employees, including officers, in return for personal services connected with production of business income.	

Jurisdiction	Employee and Officer Compensation	Comment
Missouri	Wages, salaries, commissions, board, rent, housing, lodging, benefits, services, or any form of compensation paid to employees, including officers, in return for personal services connected with production of business income.	N/A for taxpayers electing single-factor sales apportionment formula.
Montana	Wages, salaries, commissions, board, rent, housing, lodging, benefits, services, or any form of compensation paid to employees, including officers, in return for personal services connected with production of business income.	
Nebraska	N/A, because standard apportionment formula does not include a payroll factor.	
Nevada	N/A, because state does not tax general business corporation income.	
New Hampshire	Wages, salaries, commissions, or any form of compensation paid to employees, including officers, in return for personal services connected with production of business income.	
New Jersey	N/A for tax years after 2013, because standard apportionment formula does not include a payroll factor.	For tax years through 2013, wages, salaries, and other personal service compensation paid to employees, including officers.
New Mexico	Wages, salaries, commissions, board, rent, housing, lodging, benefits, services, or any form of compensation paid to employees, including officers, in return for personal services connected with production of business income.	
New York	N/A, because standard apportionment formula does not include a payroll factor.	
North Carolina	N/A, because standard apportionment formula does not include a payroll factor. **Tax years before 2018:** Wages, salaries, commissions, board, rent, housing, lodging, benefits, services, or any form of compensation paid to employees, except general executive officers, in return for personal services connected with production of business income.	

Jurisdiction	Employee and Officer Compensation	Comment
North Dakota	Gross wages, salaries, commissions, board, rent, housing, lodging, benefits, services, or any form of compensation paid to employees, including officers, before deductions for deferred compensation plans or flexible spending plans, in return for personal services connected with production of business income.	
Ohio	N/A	
Oklahoma	Compensation paid to employees for services, excluding officers' compensation.	
Oregon	N/A, because standard apportionment formula does not include a payroll factor.	
Pennsylvania	N/A, because standard apportionment formula does not include a payroll factor.	**Tax years before 2013:** Wages, salaries, commissions, or any form of compensation, whether or Excluded as part of the deduction of wages and salaries of the taxpayer, paid to employees, including officers.
Rhode Island	N/A, because standard apportionment formula does not include a payroll factor.	Included wages, salaries, and other compensation paid to employees, including officers for tax years before 2015.
South Carolina	N/A, because standard apportionment formula does not include a payroll factor.	**Tax years before 2011:** Wages, salaries, commissions, and other personal service compensation paid to employees, except general executive officers.
South Dakota	N/A, because state does not tax general business corporation income.	
Tennessee	Wages, salaries, commissions, share of compensation in pass-through entity, board, rent, housing, lodging, benefits, services, or any form of compensation paid to employees, including officers, in return for personal services connected with production of business income.	
Texas	N/A, because standard apportionment formula does not include a payroll factor.	
Utah	Wages, salaries, commissions, board, rent, housing, lodging, benefits, services, or any form of compensation paid to employees, including officers, in return for personal services connected with production of business income.	

Jurisdiction	Employee and Officer Compensation	Comment
Vermont	Wages, salaries, commissions, board, rent, housing, lodging, benefits, services, or any form of compensation paid to employees, including officers, in return for personal services connected with production of business income.	
Virginia	Wages, salaries, commissions paid or accrued, or any form of compensation paid to employees in return for personal services connected with production of business income. Officer income not specifically included or excluded.	
Washington	N/A, because state does not tax general business corporation income.	
West Virginia	Wages, salaries, commissions, board, rent, housing, lodging, benefits, services, or any form of compensation paid to employees, including officers, in return for personal services connected with production of business income.	
Wisconsin	N/A, because standard apportionment formula does not include a payroll factor.	
Wyoming	N/A, because state does not tax general business corporation income.	

Property Factor Rules—Owned Property

Under the Multistate Tax Commission (MTC) Model Apportionment Regulations, owned property must be included in the property factor of the apportionment formula and must be valued at its original cost. Original cost is the basis of the property for federal income tax purposes, prior to any federal adjustments, at the time of acquisition by the taxpayer, adjusted by subsequent capital additions or improvements and partial disposition by reason of sale, exchange, abandonment, or other method. If the original cost of property is unascertainable, the property is included in the factor at its fair market value as of the date of acquisition by the taxpayer. This chart shows whether owned property is included by each state and the District of Columbia in the property factor of the standard apportionment formula for determining corporate income tax liability.

Jurisdiction	Owned Property	Comment
Alabama	Included at: • original cost of property at time of acquisition, as adjusted by subsequent capital additions or improvements and partial disposition by sale, exchange, or abandonment; or • market value at date of acquisition if original cost is unascertainable.	
Alaska	Included at: • original cost representing federal basis of property at time of acquisition, as adjusted by subsequent capital additions or improvements and partial disposition by sale, exchange, or abandonment; or • market value at date of acquisition if original cost is unascertainable.	
Arizona	Included at: • original cost representing federal basis of property at time of acquisition, as adjusted by subsequent capital additions or improvements and partial disposition by sale, exchange, abandonment, or other similar event; or • fair market value at date of acquisition if original cost is unascertainable.	
Arkansas	Included at: • original cost representing federal basis of property at time of acquisition, as adjusted by subsequent capital additions or improvements and partial disposition by sale, exchange, or abandonment; or • market value at date of acquisition if original cost is unascertainable.	For taxable years beginning on or after January 1, 2021, single sales factor formula is implemented. The property factor will no longer be applicable.

Jurisdiction	Owned Property	Comment
California	N/A, because standard apportionment formula does not include a property factor.	Prior to 2013 tax year, included at: • original cost representing federal basis of property at time of acquisition, as adjusted by subsequent capital additions or improvements and partial disposition by sale, exchange, or abandonment; or • market value if original cost is unascertainable.
Colorado	N/A, because standard apportionment formula does not include a property factor.	
Connecticut	Included at net book value.	
Delaware	Included at original cost, less value of income from property that is separately allocated or excluded as non-business income.	
District of Columbia	Included at: • original cost, plus the cost of additions and improvements; or • market value at date of acquisition if original cost is unascertainable or zero.	N/A for tax years after 2014, because standard apportionment formula does not include a property factor.
Florida	Included at: • original cost representing federal basis of property at time of acquisition, as adjusted by subsequent capital additions or improvements and partial disposition by sale, exchange, or abandonment; or • market value at date of acquisition if original cost is unascertainable. Excluded if in-state property is dedicated exclusively to research and development activities performed under sponsored research contracts with a state university or certain nonpublic universities.	
Georgia	N/A, because standard apportionment formula does not include a property factor.	
Hawaii	Included at: • original cost representing federal basis of property at time of acquisition, as adjusted by subsequent capital additions or improvements and partial disposition; or • market value at date of acquisition if original cost is unascertainable.	

Jurisdiction	Owned Property	Comment
Idaho	Included at: • original cost representing federal basis of property at time of acquisition, as adjusted by subsequent capital additions or improvements and partial disposition by sale, exchange, or abandonment; or • market value at date of acquisition if original cost is unascertainable.	
Illinois	N/A, because standard apportionment formula does not include a property factor.	
Indiana	N/A, because standard apportionment formula does not include a property factor.	Prior to 2011 tax year, included at: • original cost; or • market value if original cost is unascertainable.
Iowa	N/A, because standard apportionment formula does not include a property factor.	
Kansas	Included at: • original cost representing federal basis of property at time of acquisition, as adjusted by subsequent capital additions or improvements and partial disposition by sale, exchange, or abandonment; or • market value at date of acquisition if original cost is unascertainable.	
Kentucky	N/A, because standard apportionment formula does not include a property factor. **Tax years before 2018:** Included at: • original cost; or • market value at date of acquisition if original cost is unascertainable, nominal, or zero.	
Louisiana	Included at cost, less reasonable reserve for depreciation, depletion, and obsolescence.	
Maine	N/A, because standard apportionment formula does not include a property factor.	
Maryland	Included at original cost.	

Jurisdiction	Owned Property	Comment
Massachusetts	Included at: • original cost representing federal basis of property at time of acquisition, as adjusted by subsequent capital additions or improvements and partial disposition by sale, exchange, or abandonment (but not adjusted for subsequent depreciation); or • market value at date of acquisition if original cost is unascertainable.	
Michigan	N/A, because standard apportionment formula does not include a property factor.	
Minnesota	N/A, because standard apportionment formula does not include a property factor.	Included at original cost for tax years before 2014, as adjusted by subsequent capital additions or improvements and partial disposition by sale, exchange, or abandonment.
Mississippi	Included at net book value.	
Missouri	Included at: • original cost representing federal basis of property at time of acquisition, as adjusted by subsequent capital additions or improvements and partial disposition by sale, exchange, or abandonment; or • market value at date of acquisition if original cost is unascertainable.	N/A for taxpayers electing single-factor sales apportionment formula.
Montana	Included at: • original cost representing federal basis of property at time of acquisition, as adjusted by subsequent capital additions or improvements and partial disposition by sale, exchange, or abandonment; or • market value at date of acquisition if original cost is unascertainable.	
Nebraska	N/A, because standard apportionment formula does not include a property factor.	
Nevada	N/A, because state does not tax general business corporation income.	
New Hampshire	Included at original cost representing federal basis of property at time of acquisition, as adjusted by subsequent sale, exchange, abandonment, or other such disposition.	
New Jersey	N/A, because standard apportionment formula does not include a property factor.	Prior to 2013 tax year, included at book value.

Jurisdiction	Owned Property	Comment
New Mexico	Included at: • original cost representing federal basis of property at time of acquisition, as adjusted by subsequent capital additions or improvements and partial disposition by sale, exchange, or abandonment; or • market value at date of acquisition if original cost is unascertainable.	
New York	N/A, because standard apportionment formula does not include a property factor.	
North Carolina	N/A, because standard apportionment formula does not include a property factor. **Tax years before 2018:** Included at: • original cost representing federal basis of property at time of acquisition, as adjusted by subsequent capital additions or improvements and partial disposition by sale, exchange, abandonment, or any other type of disposition; or • market value at date of acquisition if original cost is unascertainable.	
North Dakota	Included at original cost representing federal basis of property at time of acquisition, as adjusted by subsequent capital additions or improvements and partial disposition by sale, exchange, or abandonment.	
Ohio	N/A, because computation of Commercial Activity Tax (CAT) does not use an apportionment formula, but there are rules for situsing gross receipts.	
Oklahoma	Included at original cost.	
Oregon	N/A, because standard apportionment formula does not include a property factor.	
Pennsylvania	N/A, because standard apportionment formula does not include a property factor.	Prior to 2013 tax year, included at original cost.
Rhode Island	N/A, because standard apportionment formula does not include a payroll factor.	Included at average net book for tax years before 2015.
South Carolina	N/A, because standard apportionment formula does not include a property factor.	Prior to 2011 tax year, value was the original cost plus any additions or improvements without regard to deductions for depreciation, amortization, write-downs, or similar charges.
South Dakota	N/A, because state does not tax general business corporation income.	

Jurisdiction	Owned Property	Comment
Tennessee	Included at: • original cost representing federal basis of property at time of acquisition, as adjusted by subsequent capital additions or improvements and partial disposition by sale, exchange, or abandonment; or • market value at date of acquisition if original cost is unascertainable.	
Texas	N/A, because standard apportionment formula does not include a property factor.	
Utah	Included at original cost representing state basis of property at time of acquisition, as adjusted by subsequent capital additions or improvements and partial disposition by sale, exchange, or abandonment.	
Vermont	Included at original cost.	
Virginia	Included at original cost representing federal basis of property at time of acquisition, as adjusted by subsequent capital additions or improvements and partial disposition by sale, exchange, or abandonment.	
Washington	N/A, because state does not tax general business corporation income.	
West Virginia	Included at: • original cost, as adjusted by subsequent capital additions or improvements and partial or total disposition by sale, exchange, abandonment, loss or destruction or other alienation of, or loss of, the property; or • current market value where original cost is unavailable or cannot be obtained.	
Wisconsin	N/A, because standard apportionment formula does not include a property factor.	
Wyoming	N/A, because state does not tax general business corporation income.	

Property Factor Rules—Rented Property

Under the Multistate Tax Commission (MTC) Model Apportionment Regulations, rented property must be included in the property factor of the apportionment formula and is valued at eight times its net annual rental rate, less the aggregate annual subrental rates paid by subtenants of the taxpayer. However, subrents are not deducted when they constitute business income. If property owned by others is used by the taxpayer at no charge or rented by the taxpayer for a nominal rate, the net annual rental rate for the property is determined on the basis of a reasonable market rental rate for the property. This chart shows whether rented property is included by each state and the District of Columbia in the property factor of the standard apportionment formula for determining corporate income tax liability.

Jurisdiction	Rented Property	Comment
Alabama	Included at: • eight times net annual rental rate, less aggregate subrents representing nonbusiness income; or • reasonable market rental rate if rented at no charge or nominal rate.	
Alaska	Included at: • eight times net annual rental rate, less aggregate subrents representing nonbusiness income; or • reasonable market rental rate if rented at no charge or nominal rate.	
Arizona	Included at: • eight times net annual rental rate, less aggregate subrents representing nonbusiness income; or • reasonable market rental rate if rented at no charge or nominal rate.	
Arkansas	Included at: • eight times net annual rental rate, less aggregate subrents representing nonbusiness income; or • reasonable market rental rate if rented at no charge or nominal rate.	For taxable years beginning on or after January 1, 2021, single sales factor formula is implemented. The property factor will no longer be applicable.
California	N/A, because standard apportionment formula does not include a property factor.	Prior to 2013 tax year, included at: • eight times net annual rental rate, less aggregate subrents representing nonbusiness income; or • reasonable market rental rate if rented at no charge or nominal rate.
Colorado	N/A, because standard apportionment formula does not include a property factor.	
Connecticut	Included at eight times gross rents payable during income year or period.	
Delaware	Included at eight times annual rental.	

Jurisdiction	Rented Property	Comment
District of Columbia	Included at: • eight times net annual rental rate, less aggregate subrents (payments for leased property capitalized as rent for federal tax purposes are included only to the extent of their capitalized value for federal tax purposes); or • reasonable rental rate if rented at no charge or nominal rate.	N/A for tax years after 2014, because standard apportionment formula does not include a property factor.
Florida	Included at: • eight times net annual rental rate, less aggregate subrents representing nonbusiness income; or • reasonable market rental rate if rented at no charge or nominal rate. Excluded if in-state property is dedicated exclusively to research and development activities performed under sponsored research contracts with a state university or certain nonpublic universities.	
Georgia	N/A, because standard apportionment formula does not include a property factor.	
Hawaii	Included at: • eight times net annual rental rate, less aggregate subrents representing nonbusiness income; or • reasonable market rental rate if rented at no charge or nominal rate.	
Idaho	Included at: • eight times net annual rental rate, less aggregate subrents representing nonbusiness income; or • reasonable market rental rate if rented at no charge or nominal rate by the taxpayer.	
Illinois	N/A, because standard apportionment formula does not include a property factor.	
Indiana	N/A, because standard apportionment formula does not include a property factor.	Prior to 2011 tax year, included at eight times net annual rental rate, less aggregate subrents representing nonbusiness income.
Iowa	N/A, because standard apportionment formula does not include a property factor.	
Kansas	Included at eight times net annual rental rate, less aggregate subrents representing nonbusiness income.	

Jurisdiction	Rented Property	Comment
Kentucky	N/A, because standard apportionment formula does not include a property factor. **Tax years before 2018:** Included at: • eight times net annual rental rate, less aggregate subrents; or • reasonable market rental rate if rented at no charge or nominal rate.	
Louisiana	Excluded.	
Maine	N/A, because standard apportionment formula does not include a property factor.	
Maryland	Included at: • eight times expenses associated with privilege of occupying or using the property; or • capitalized reasonable market rental rate if rented at no charge or below market rate.	
Massachusetts	Included at: • eight times net annual rental rate, less aggregate subrents; or • fair market rental value if rented at no charge or nominal rate.	
Michigan	N/A, because standard apportionment formula does not include a property factor.	
Minnesota	N/A, because standard apportionment formula does not include a property factor.	Included for tax years before 2014 at eight times net annual rental rate, less aggregate subrents. If subrents produce a negative or clearly inaccurate value, alternative method may be required or requested.
Mississippi	Included at eight times net annual rental rate, less aggregate subrents.	
Missouri	Included at: • eight times net annual rental rate, less aggregate subrents representing nonbusiness income; or • reasonable market rental rate if rented at no charge or nominal rate.	N/A for taxpayers electing single-factor sales apportionment formula.
Montana	Included at: • eight times net annual rental rate, less aggregate subrents representing nonbusiness income; or • reasonable market rental rate if rented at no charge or nominal rate.	
Nebraska	N/A, because standard apportionment formula does not include a property factor.	
Nevada	N/A, because state does not tax general business corporation income.	

Jurisdiction	Rented Property	Comment
New Hampshire	Included at eight times net annual rental rate, less aggregate subrents (business organizations renting property in the regular course of a trade or business may not deduct rental income as subrents).	
New Jersey	N/A, because standard apportionment formula does not include a property factor.	Prior to 2013 tax year, included at eight times net annual rental rate, which includes amounts paid or accrued in addition to or in lieu of rent (such as taxes).
New Mexico	Included at: • eight times net annual rental rate, less aggregate subrents representing nonbusiness income; or • reasonable market rental rate if rented at no charge or nominal rate.	
New York	N/A, because standard apportionment formula does not include a property factor.	
North Carolina	N/A, because standard apportionment formula does not include a property factor. **Tax years before 2018:** Included at eight times net annual rental rate, less aggregate subrents representing nonapportionable income.	
North Dakota	Included at: • eight times net annual rental rate, less aggregate subrents representing nonbusiness income; or • reasonable market rental rate if rented at no charge or nominal rate.	
Ohio	N/A, because computation of Commercial Activity Tax (CAT) does not use an apportionment formula, but there are rules for situsing gross receipts.	
Oklahoma	Included at eight times net annual rental rate, less aggregate subrents.	
Oregon	N/A, because standard apportionment formula does not include a property factor.	
Pennsylvania	N/A, because standard apportionment formula does not include a property factor.	Prior to 2013 tax year, included at eight times net annual rental rate, less aggregate subrents.
Rhode Island	N/A, because standard apportionment formula does not include a payroll factor.	Included at eight times net annual rental rate, less aggregate subrents for tax years before 2015.
South Carolina	N/A, because standard apportionment formula does not include a property factor.	Prior to 2011 tax year, included in property factor of standard apportionment formula at eight times net annual rental rate.

Jurisdiction	Rented Property	Comment
South Dakota	N/A, because state does not tax general business corporation income.	
Tennessee	Included at: • eight times net annual rental rate, less aggregate subrents; or • reasonable market rental rate if rented at no charge or nominal rate.	
Texas	N/A, because standard apportionment formula does not include a property factor.	
Utah	Included at: • eight times net annual rental rate, less aggregate subrents representing nonbusiness income; or • reasonable market rental rate if rented at no charge or nominal rate.	
Vermont	Included at eight times net annual rental rate.	
Virginia	Included at eight times net annual rental rate, less amounts paid as service charges or incidental day-to-day expenses.	
Washington	N/A, because state does not tax general business corporation income.	
West Virginia	Included at eight times net annual rental rate.	
Wisconsin	N/A, because standard apportionment formula does not include a property factor.	
Wyoming	N/A, because state does not tax general business corporation income.	

Public Utilities

This chart shows whether each state and the District of Columbia tax public utilities based on income, net worth, or capital stock. The chart does not cover other forms of state tax or regulatory fees imposed on public utilities, such as gross receipts or gross revenue taxes.

Jurisdiction	Public Utilities	Comment
Alabama	Corporate income tax	
Alaska	Corporate net income tax	
Arizona	Corporate income tax	
Arkansas	Corporate income tax	
California	Corporation franchise (income) tax	
Colorado	Corporate income tax	
Connecticut	Corporation business tax	
Delaware	Corporate income tax	
District of Columbia	Corporation franchise tax	
Florida	Corporate income tax	
Georgia	Corporate income tax and net worth tax	
Hawaii	Corporate income tax and public service company tax on ratio of net income to gross income.	
Idaho	Corporate income tax	
Illinois	Corporate income tax and personal property replacement tax	
Indiana	Adjusted gross income tax	
Iowa	Corporate income tax	
Kansas	Corporate income tax	
Kentucky	Corporate income tax	
Louisiana	Corporation income tax and franchise tax	
Maine	Corporate income tax	
Maryland	Corporate income tax	
Massachusetts	Corporate excise tax	Public service corporation franchise tax for taxable years before January 1, 2014.
Michigan	Corporate income tax	**Tax years prior to 2012:** Michigan Business Tax (MBT)
Minnesota	Corporate franchise tax	

Jurisdiction	Public Utilities	Comment
Mississippi	Corporate income tax and privilege tax	
Missouri	Corporate income tax	
Montana	Corporate income tax	
Nebraska	Corporate income tax	
Nevada	N/A, because state does not tax general business corporation income.	
New Hampshire	Business profits tax	
New Jersey	Corporation business tax, except exemption for utilities subject to sales and use tax or gross receipts excise and franchise taxes.	
New Mexico	Corporate income tax	
New York	Corporation franchise tax	
North Carolina	Corporate income tax	
North Dakota	Corporation income tax	
Ohio	Commerical Activity Tax (CAT) for electric and telephone companies. Corporation franchise tax for electric and telephone companies in tax years prior to 2010.	
Oklahoma	Corporate income tax	
Oregon	Corporation excise tax	
Pennsylvania	Corporate net income tax	
Rhode Island	Exempt from business corporation tax	
South Carolina	Corporate income tax, except exemption for regional transportation authorities, certain rural electric cooperatives, and certain nonprofit water supply and/or sewerage disposal corporations.	
South Dakota	N/A, because state does not tax general business corporation income.	
Tennessee	Franchise and excise tax	
Texas	Revised franchise tax (margin tax)	
Utah	Corporate franchise tax	
Vermont	Corporate income tax	
Virginia	Corporate income tax for most utilities. 1.45% minimum tax imposed on certain electric suppliers in lieu of corporate income tax if income tax liability is less than minimum tax liability.	

Jurisdiction	Public Utilities	Comment
Washington	N/A, because state does not tax general business corporation income.	
West Virginia	Corporate net income tax	
Wisconsin	Corporation franchise or income tax, except exemption for certain electric cooperatives.	
Wyoming	N/A, because state does not tax general business corporation income.	

Qualified Business Income—IRC § 199A

Under IRC Sec. 199A, as enacted by the Tax Cuts and Jobs Act of 2017, individuals, trusts and estates with income from partnerships, S corporations and sole proprietorships can claim a special deduction for tax years beginning after December 31, 2017, and before January 1, 2026. The deduction is generally the lesser of:

- combined qualified business income; or
- 20% of the excess (if any) of taxable income over net capital gain.

For individual taxpayers, the Code Sec. 199A deduction is not allowed in determining adjusted gross income. The deduction is taken after determining federal adjusted gross income. The deduction is available to all taxpayers whether they claim itemized deductions or claim the standard deduction.

This chart indicates whether each state and the District of Columbia allow the IRC Sec. 199A deduction for individuals. Generally, states use federal taxable income, federal adjusted gross income, or federal gross income as the starting point to calculate state personal income tax. Because the federal deduction is taken after that point, most states do not require any adjustment.

Jurisdiction	Qualified Business Income—IRC § 199A	Comment
Alabama	No addition or subtraction adjustment required or allowed.	
Arizona	No addition or subtraction adjustment required or allowed.	
Arkansas	No statutory, regulatory, or administrative guidance.	
California	No addition or subtraction adjustment required or allowed.	IRC conformity provision specifically excludes federal deduction.
Colorado	Generally, no addition adjustment required. **Tax Years 2021-2022** Addition required for the amount of the federal qualified business income deduction taken if AGI exceeds $500,000 (for single filers) or $1 million (for married taxpayers filing jointly). Taxpayers who report farm income on their federal tax return are exempt from addback requirement.	
Connecticut	No addition or subtraction adjustment required or allowed.	
Delaware	No addition or subtraction adjustment required or allowed.	
District of Columbia	No addition or subtraction adjustment required or allowed.	
Georgia	No addition or subtraction adjustment required or allowed.	IRC conformity provision specifically excludes federal deduction.

Jurisdiction	Qualified Business Income—IRC §199A	Comment
Hawaii	No addition or subtraction adjustment required or allowed.	IRC conformity provision specifically excludes federal deduction.
Idaho	Subtraction adjustment allowed.	
Illinois	No addition or subtraction adjustment required or allowed.	
Indiana	No addition or subtraction adjustment required or allowed.	
Iowa	No addition or subtraction adjustment required or allowed in 2018.	Beginning in 2019, taxpayers are allowed a percentage of the deduction. The percentage is: • 25% for tax years after 2018 but before 2021; • 50% for the 2021 tax year; and • 75% after 2021.
Kansas	No addition or subtraction adjustment required or allowed.	
Kentucky	Addition required for federal deduction.	
Louisiana	No addition or subtraction adjustment required or allowed.	
Maine	No addition or subtraction adjustment required or allowed.	
Maryland	No addition or subtraction adjustment required or allowed.	
Massachusetts	Subtraction from income not allowed.	
Michigan	No addition or subtraction adjustment required or allowed.	
Minnesota	No addition adjustment required.	
Mississippi	No statutory, regulatory, or administrative guidance.	
Missouri	No addition or subtraction adjustment required or allowed.	
Montana	No addition or subtraction adjustment required or allowed.	
Nebraska	No addition or subtraction adjustment required or allowed.	
New Hampshire	No addition or subtraction adjustment required or allowed.	Tax on interest and dividends only.
New Jersey	Addition required for federal deduction.	
New Mexico	No addition or subtraction adjustment required or allowed.	
New York	No addition or subtraction adjustment required or allowed.	
North Carolina	No addition or subtraction adjustment required or allowed.	

Jurisdiction	Qualified Business Income—IRC §199A	Comment
North Dakota	No addition adjustment required.	
Ohio	No addition or subtraction adjustment required or allowed.	
Oklahoma	No addition or subtraction adjustment required or allowed.	
Oregon	No addition or subtraction adjustment required or allowed.	
Pennsylvania	No statutory, regulatory, or administrative guidance.	
Rhode Island	No addition or subtraction adjustment required or allowed.	
South Carolina	Addition adjustment required.	IRC conformity provision specifically excludes federal deduction.
Tennessee	No addition or subtraction adjustment required or allowed.	Tax on certain dividends and interest income.
Utah	No addition or subtraction adjustment required or allowed.	
Vermont	No addition or subtraction adjustment required or allowed.	
Virginia	No addition or subtraction adjustment required or allowed.	
West Virginia	No addition or subtraction adjustment required or allowed.	
Wisconsin	No addition or subtraction adjustment required or allowed.	IRC conformity provision specifically excludes federal deduction.

Reciprocal Personal Income Tax Agreements

Various states have adopted reciprocal personal income tax agreements with one or more states, including the District of Columbia, that allow income to be taxed in the state of residence even though it is earned in another state, as long as the income-source state is a party to the reciprocity agreement. States enter into such agreements because, in addition to greatly reducing the administrative reporting burden, no revenue loss is anticipated. Even taking into account such variables as the number of nonresidents working in a state, the tax rate, and taxpayer income levels, the taxable revenue shared may be roughly equivalent in both states. Reciprocity agreements put into operation an exception to the source-tax rule that the state in which income is earned has the primary right to tax that income. Generally, reciprocal agreements apply only to compensation, which may be limited to wages, salaries, tips commissions, and/or bonuses received for personal and/or professional services. Thus, even though New Jersey has a reciprocity agreement with Pennsylvania, income such as that arising from self-employment or a gain from a sale of property would be subject to tax under the source-tax rule in the income-source state. However, states may specify that certain income is not covered under reciprocity agreements, such as lottery winnings.

This chart shows whether each state and the District of Columbia have entered into reciprocity agreements with other jurisdictions.

Jurisdiction	Reciprocal Agreements	Comment
Alabama	No reciprocal tax agreements.	
Arizona	CA, IN, OR, VA	
Arkansas	No reciprocal tax agreements.	
California	No reciprocal tax agreements.	
Colorado	No reciprocal tax agreements.	
Connecticut	No reciprocal tax agreements.	
Delaware	No reciprocal tax agreements.	
District of Columbia	MD, VA	
Georgia	No reciprocal tax agreements.	
Hawaii	No reciprocal tax agreements.	
Idaho	No reciprocal tax agreements.	
Illinois	IA, KY, MI, WI	
Indiana	KY, MI, OH, PA, WI	
Iowa	IL	
Kansas	No reciprocal tax agreements.	
Kentucky	IL, IN, MI, OH, VA, WV, WI	

Jurisdiction	Reciprocal Agreements	Comment
Louisiana	No reciprocal tax agreements.	
Maine	No reciprocal tax agreements.	
Maryland	DC, PA, VA, WV	
Massachusetts	No reciprocal tax agreements.	
Michigan	IL, IN, KY, MN, OH, WI	
Minnesota	MI, ND	Agreement with WI terminated on January 1, 2010.
Mississippi	No reciprocal tax agreements.	
Missouri	No reciprocal tax agreements.	
Montana	ND	
Nebraska	No reciprocal tax agreements.	
New Hampshire	No reciprocal tax agreements.	
New Jersey	PA	
New Mexico	No reciprocal tax agreements.	
New York	No reciprocal tax agreements.	
North Carolina	No reciprocal tax agreements.	
North Dakota	MN, MT	
Ohio	IN, KY, MI, PA, WV	
Oklahoma	No reciprocal tax agreements.	
Oregon	No reciprocal tax agreements.	
Pennsylvania	IN, MD, NJ, OH, VA, WV	
Rhode Island	No reciprocal tax agreements.	
South Carolina	No reciprocal tax agreements.	
Tennessee	No reciprocal tax agreements.	
Utah	No reciprocal tax agreements.	
Vermont	No reciprocal tax agreements.	
Virginia	DC, KY, MD, PA, WV	
West Virginia	KY, MD, OH, PA, VA	
Wisconsin	IL, IN, KY, MI	Agreement with MN terminated on January 1, 2010.

Related Party Expense Addback Requirements

Jurisdiction	Related Party Expenses	Comment
Alabama	Addback required for interest and intangible expenses and costs directly or indirectly paid, accrued or incurred to, or in connection directly or indirectly with one or more direct or indirect transactions, with one or more related members.	***Addition not required if:*** • amount was taxed by a state or foreign nation with U.S. income tax treaty; • principal purpose of transaction not tax avoidance and related member not primarily engaged in activities involving intangibles or financing of related entities; • adjustments are unreasonable; **or** • taxpayer agrees to alternative adjustments and computations. Complete and attach Schedule AB, Add-Back Form.
Alaska	No adjustment for federal deduction required.	
Arizona	No adjustment to federal deduction required.	
Arkansas	Addback required for interest and intangible expenses and costs paid to related party.	***Not required if:*** • amount is taxed by a state or foreign country with U.S. income tax treaty; • transaction not intended to avoid tax and made at arm's-length; • taxpayer agrees to alternative apportionment method; or • related member is in non-tax location where it has 50 full-time employees, owns property valued over $1 million, and generates revenue over $1 million.
California	No adjustment to federal deduction required.	
Colorado	No adjustment to federal deduction required.	

Jurisdiction	Related Party Expenses	Comment
Connecticut	Addition to federal taxable income required for all related member interest and intangible expenses. Subtraction from federal taxable income allowed for amounts subject to an addback exception.	***Addition not required if:*** • addition is unreasonable; • taxpayer agrees to alternative method of apportionment or calculation; • related member paid intangible expenses to an unrelated party during same tax year and principal purpose of related party transaction not tax avoidance; • interest paid to a related member located in foreign country with U.S. income tax treaty; • interest paid at arm's length rates and not for tax avoidance purpose to a related member that was subject to tax on that income by a state or foreign country at rate equal to the state's rate; • interest paid at arm's length rates and not for tax avoidance purpose to a related member that was subject to the state's insurance premiums tax; or • the taxpayer and related member are both members of a combined group required to file a combined unitary tax return. Calculate addition and exceptions on Form CT-1120AB.
Delaware	Addition to federal taxable income required for amount of interest, including discounts, paid on intercorporate obligations representing advances, loans or similar contractual transactions between affiliated corporations if creditor corporation eliminated the interest income from its state taxable income. Subtraction from federal taxable income allowed for interest income received on intercorporate obligations if: • debtor and creditor corporations are subject to Delaware taxation on that income; and • debtor corporation does not claim a deduction for the interest payments in determining its entire net income.	

Jurisdiction	Related Party Expenses	Comment
District of Columbia	Deduction allowed for interest or intangible expense directly or indirectly paid to, accrued or incurred by, or in connection directly or indirectly with, one or more direct or indirect transactions with one or more related members if: • principal purpose of transaction not tax avoidance; • amount was paid at arm's-length rates and terms; and • related member directly or indirectly paid the expense, or the expense was accrued or incurred by a person who is not a related member; or amount was taxed by a state or foreign nation with U.S. income tax treaty at rate of 4.5% or more. Deduction allowed equal to the amount received from related members as royalties, interest, or similar income from intangibles if: • interest or expense payment to such member is denied under DC law; or • there is a similar deduction denial or addition modification of a state or foreign nation with U.S. income tax treaty.	
Florida	No adjustment to federal deduction required.	
Georgia	Addback required in tax years after 2005 for interest and intangible expenses and costs directly or indirectly paid, accrued, or incurred to, or in connection directly or indirectly with one or more direct or indirect transactions with, one or more related members.	Exceptions to addback may be claimed as subtraction if: • amount was received in arm's length transaction and taxed by a state on separate reporting basis; • transaction had valid business purpose and amount was paid at arm's length rates to related member domiciled in foreign nation with U.S. tax treaty; or • transaction had valid business purpose and related member paid costs and expense to unrelated party during same taxable year. Adjustments computed on Form IT-Addback.
Hawaii	No adjustment to federal deduction required.	
Idaho	No adjustment to federal deduction required.	

Jurisdiction	Related Party Expenses	Comment
Illinois	Addition to federal taxable income required for interest, intangible, and insurance premium expenses paid to 80/20 companies or noncombination rule companies (tax years before 2017) if the amounts exceed taxable dividends received. Subtraction from federal taxable income allowed for: • interest income received from each affiliated company; • intangible income received from each affiliated company; and • effective for tax years before 2017, insurance reimbursements received from each affiliated insurance company.	***Addition not required if:*** • amount is taxed by another state or foreign country that does not mandate unitary reporting; • principal purpose of transaction not tax avoidance, amount was paid at arm's-length rates and terms, and affiliate paid interest or expenses to an unrelated party during same tax year; • interest paid at arm's lenghth rates and terms and not for tax avoidance purpose; • addition is unreasonable; or • taxpayer agrees to alternative apportionment. Compute modifications on Schedule 80/20 and attach schedule to return.
Indiana	Addback required for intangible expenses and any directly related intangible interest expenses involving member(s) of same affiliated group or foreign corporation, that reduced taxable income for federal income tax purposes.	***Not required if:*** taxpayer and all recipients included in same consolidated or combined return; taxpayer agrees to alternative apportionment; addback is unreasonable; or disclosure is made and evidence shows that: • amount is taxed by another state or foreign country that is recipient's commercial domicile; • transaction has valid business purpose and made at commercially reasonable rate or comparable arm's length terms; • transaction has valid business purpose and recipient regularly engages in intangible transactions with unrelated parties on substantially similar terms; • payment received from unrelated party, and on behalf of unrelated party, paid to recipient in arm's length transaction; • recipient paid equal or greater amount to unrelated party during taxable year; or • recipient engaged in substantial business activities involving intangibles or other substantial business activities separate from those business activities.
Iowa	No adjustment to federal deduction required.	
Kansas	No adjustment to federal deduction required.	

Jurisdiction	Related Party Expenses	Comment
Kentucky	Addition to federal taxable income required for related member intangible expenses, intangible interest expenses, and management fees. Subtraction from federal taxable income allowed for arm's length amount of related party expenses if the taxpayer is not required to file a consolidated return and the transaction: • is undertaken directly or indirectly with one or more of its shareholders, members, partners, or affiliated corporations; and • does not fall within the scope of the addback requirement or one of its exceptions.	***Addition not required if:*** • taxpayer and recipient included in consolidated return; • payment was subject to income tax in another state or a foreign country with U.S. tax treaty, related member engaged in substantial business activities unrelated to intangibles or financing of related members, and transaction made at commercially reasonable rate and arm's-length terms; • related member regularly engages in transactions with unrelated parties on terms identical to transaction; or • taxpayer agrees to alternative apportionment formula; Complete and attach Schedule RPC, Related Party Costs Disclosure Statement.
Louisiana	**Tax Years After 2015:** Addback required for interest expenses and costs, intangible expenses and costs, and management fees directly or indirectly paid, accrued, or incurred to, or in connection directly or indirectly with one or more direct or indirect transactions, with one or more related members. **Tax Years Before 2016:** No adjustment to federal deduction required.	***Not required if:*** • amount is taxed by a state or foreign country with U.S. income tax treaty; • principal purpose of transaction not tax avoidance; • related member paid amount to unrelated member during same taxable year; or • addback is unreasonable.
Maine	No adjustment to federal deduction required.	
Maryland	Addback required for interest expense or intangible expense directly or indirectly paid, accrued, or incurred to, or in connection directly or indirectly with one or more direct or indirect transactions with, one or more related members.	***Not required if:*** • tax avoidance not principle purpose of transaction; • expense paid at arm's length interest rate or price; • during same taxable year, related member paid the expense to an unrelated person; • the related member and expense was subject to income tax in a state, U.S. possession, or foreign nation with U.S. tax treaty and aggregate effective tax rate paid on amount was at least 4%; or • in the case of interest expense, taxpayer and related party are banks.

Jurisdiction	Related Party Expenses	Comment
Massachusetts	Addition to federal taxable income for related member interest and intangible expenses, including losses from factoring or discounting transactions.	***Addition not required if:*** • adjustment is unreasonable; • taxpayer agrees to alternative apportionment; • related member is not a controlled foreign corporation and is a resident of a foreign county with a U.S. tax treaty; • related member is taxed on corresponding income by a state or foreign country at similar tax rate; or • related member paid expenses to unrelated party during same tax year and principal purpose of transaction not tax avoidance. Complete and file: • Schedule ABI to claim interest addback exceptions; and/or • Schedule ABIE to claim intangible expense addback exceptions.
Michigan	Addback required for royalty, interest, or other expenses paid to related persons for use of intangible assets if such person is not included in taxpayer's unitary business group.	Addback not required if transaction has business purpose other than tax avoidance, is conducted at arm's-length rates and terms, and: • is a pass through of another transaction between a third party and related person with comparable rates and terms; • results in double taxation; • is unreasonable; or • related person is organized under laws of foreign nation which has comprehensive income tax treaty with U.S.
Minnesota	No adjustment to federal deduction required.	
Mississippi	Addback required for interest and intangible expenses and costs directly or indirectly paid, accrued to or incurred, in connection directly or indirectly with one or more direct or indirect transactions with one or more related members.	***Not required if:*** • related member paid amount to unrelated member during same taxable year; or • related member not primarily engaged in activities involving intangibles and transaction has valid business purpose other than tax avoidance.
Missouri	No adjustment to federal deduction required.	
Montana	No adjustment to federal deduction required.	
Nebraska	No adjustment to federal deduction required.	
Nevada	N/A, because state does not tax general business corporation income.	
New Hampshire	No adjustment to federal deduction required.	

Jurisdiction	Related Party Expenses	Comment
New Jersey	Addback required for interest, interest expenses and costs, and intangible expenses and costs directly or indirectly paid, accrued or incurred to, or in connection directly or indirectly with one or more direct or indirect transactions with one or more related members.	***Not required if:*** • taxpayer agrees to alternative apportionment; • amount paid to related member located in foreign nation with U.S. tax treaty; • interest paid to an independent lender and taxpayer guarantees debt; • addback is unreasonable; • related member paid amount to unrelated person during income year and principal purpose of transaction not tax avoidance; or • principal purpose of transaction not tax avoidance; interest paid at arm's interest rate; related member and payment is subject to income tax in a state, U.S. possession, or foreign nation at rate of 6% or more.
New Mexico	No adjustment to federal deduction required.	
New York	Addback required for royalty payments made to related member.	***Not required if:*** • amount included in related member's tax base, related member paid all or part of amount to unrelated party, and transaction between taxpayer and related member had valid business purpose; • related member was subject to income tax, the tax base included the royalty payment, and the aggregate effective tax rate was at least 80% of the state's rate; • related member organized in foreign country, income from transaction subject to comprehensive income tax treaty, related member taxed by foreign country at rate equal to state's rate, and amount paid in transaction with valid business purpose and arm's-length terms; or • taxpayer and department agree to alternative adjustments.

Jurisdiction	Related Party Expenses	Comment
North Carolina	Addback required for: • royalty payments, including interest expense payments, made to related member for use of copyrights, patents, and trademarks in the state if claimed as a federal deduction and election is made for recipient to exclude royalty income from its income; and • effective for tax years after 2015, net interest expense paid to related member. Subtraction allowed for: • royalty payments received for use of copyrights, patents, and trademarks in the state if payer is a related member and election is made for payer to exclude the royalty payments from its expense deduction; • effective for tax years after 2015 and before 2017, interest expense paid to related member equal to greater of (1) 15% of taxpayer's adjusted taxable income or (2) taxpayer's proportionate share of interest paid to a person who is not a related member during same taxable year; and • effective for tax years beginning on or after January 1, 2017, interest expense paid to related member equal to taxpayer's proportionate share of interest paid to a person who is not a related member during same taxable year.	***Royalty addback not required if:*** • related member includes amount as taxable income on the state's corporation income tax return for same taxable year and amount is not deducted by related party; • related member paid, accrued, or incurred payment to unrelated member; or • related member organized in foreign country with U.S. income tax treaty that taxes payments at rate equal or greater than the state's rate. ***Limit on subtraction for interest expense does not apply if:*** • state imposes tax on related member's interest income; • another state imposes income or gross receipts tax on related member's interest income, except interest eliminated by combined or consolidated return requirements does not qualify as interest that is subject to tax; • related member organized in foreign country with U.S. income tax treaty that taxes payments at rate equal or greater than the state's rate; or • related member is a bank.
North Dakota	No adjustment to federal deduction required.	
Ohio	No adjustment required because CAT is not considered an income tax and is not tied to federal income tax base.	
Oklahoma	No adjustment to federal deduction required.	
Oregon	Addback required if: • intangible asset owned by one entity and used by another for royalty or other fee; • both owner and user owned by same interests; • owner and user not included in same tax return; and • transaction results in either tax evasion or taxable income not clearly reflective of in-state business activity.	

Jurisdiction	Related Party Expenses	Comment
Pennsylvania	Effective for tax years after December 31, 2014, addback required for an intangible expense or cost, or an interest expense or cost, paid, accrued or incurred directly or indirectly in connection with one or more transactions with an affiliated entity.	*Not required if:* • the transaction did not have the principal purpose of tax avoidance and was done at arm's length rate and terms; • the affiliated entity was domiciled in a foreign nation which has in force a comprehensive tax treaty with the United States providing for the allocation of all categories of income subject to taxation, or the withholding of tax, on royalties, licenses, fees and interest for the prevention of double taxation; or • the affiliated entity directly or indirectly paid, accrued or incurred a payment to a person who is not an affiliated entity, if the payment is paid, accrued or incurred on the intangible expense or cost, or interest expense or cost, and is equal to or less than the taxpayer's proportional share of the transaction.
Rhode Island	No adjustment to federal deduction required.	
South Carolina	Addback required for accrual of expense or interest if payee is related person and payment not made in taxable year of accrual or before payer's income tax return due for taxable year of accrual.	Disallowed deductions allowed when payment made. Holder must include payment in income in year debtor is entitled to take deduction. Interest deduction not allowed for accrual or payment of interest on obligations issued as dividends or paid instead of paying dividends, unless purpose of transaction not tax avoidance.
South Dakota	N/A, because state does not tax general business corporation income.	

Jurisdiction	Related Party Expenses	Comment
Tennessee	Addition required for intangible expenses paid, accrued, or incurred in connection with transactions with one or more affiliates. Subtraction allowed for intangible expenses if transaction is disclosed and if: • affiliate is registered for and paying the state's Excise Tax; • affiliate is in a foreign nation that is a signatory to income tax treaty with U.S. or affiliate is not otherwise required to be registered for or to pay the state's Excise Tax. Subtraction allowed for intangible income if intangible expense is included in affiliate's taxable net earnings and is not deducted by affiliate. **Tax years on or after July 1, 2012 and before July 1, 2016:** Addition required for intangible expense or interest expense paid, accrued, or incurred to, or in connection directly or indirectly with transactions with one or more affiliates. Subtraction allowed for intangible expense upon application if it is determined that principal purpose of transaction is not tax avoidance or upon notice if: • affiliate is located in foreign nation with comprehensive U.S. income tax treaty; • affiliate paid expense to unrelated entity during same taxable year; or • affiliate's intangible income is taxed by another state that does not allow combined or consolidated filing in which affiliate's income may be offset by taxpayer's deduction. Subtraction allowed for intangible income if intangible expense is included in affiliate's taxable net earnings and is not deducted by affiliate.	Negligence penalty imposed if taxpayer: • fails to disclose transaction; or • fails to make addition. Form IE, Intangible Expense Disclosure, must be filed.
Texas	No adjustment to federal deduction required.	
Utah	For tax years beginning after 2019, addition to unadjusted income required for royalty or other expense paid to a related party for use of an intangible asset owned by the related entity.	**Addition not required if:** • for the same tax year, the related entity is subject to state or foreign income taxes on the royalty or other expense; or • the corporation paying the royalty or other expense never owned the intangible asset.
Vermont	No adjustment to federal deduction required.	

Jurisdiction	Related Party Expenses	Comment
Virginia	Addback required for interest and intangible expenses and costs associated with intangible property transactions with related entity. Subtraction allowed to related entity for interest and intangible expenses and costs received from a related corporation that added the amounts back to federal taxable income.	***Addition for interest expenses not required if:*** • related member has substantial business operations relating to interest-generating activities and pays at least 5 full-time employees to manage and administer such activities; • interest expense not associated with activities involving intangibles; • transaction has valid business purpose other than tax avoidance or reduction and payments made at arm's length rates and terms;**and** • (1) amount is subject to income or capital-based tax imposed by a state or foreign government; (2) payments made under pre-existing contract at arm's length rates and terms; (3) related member engages in transactions with unrelated members generating annual revenue over $2 million; or (4) transaction undertaken at arm's length rates and terms and related member uses funds that are either borrowed from or paid by unrelated member or debt incurred involves specified business purposes. ***Addition for intangible expenses not required if:*** • amount is subject to income or capital-based tax imposed by a state or foreign government; • related member derives at least 1/3 of gross revenues from licensing of intangible property to non-related member and transaction was made at rates and terms comparable to rates and terms of agreements that related member has entered into with non-related members for licensing of intangible property; or • related member directly or indirectly paid, accrued or incurred a portion of the payment to non-related members and transaction had principal business purpose other than tax avoidance. Schedule 500AB, Related Entity Add Backs and Exceptions, must be filed.
Washington	N/A, because state does not tax general business corporation income.	

Jurisdiction	Related Party Expenses	Comment
West Virginia	Addition to federal taxable income required for related member interest and intangible expenses.	***Addition not required if:*** • related member paid intangible expenses to an unrelated party during same tax year and related party transaction was undertaken for valid business purpose; • related party interest expense transaction was undertaken for a valid business purpose and reflects arm's length terms; • related member was subject to state tax on the income at a similar rate; • related member organized in a foreign country with a U.S. income tax treaty, its income is taxed by that country at rate equal to the state's rate, and related party transaction undertaken for valid business purpose and reflects arm's length terms; or • taxpayer agrees to alternative adjustments and computations.
Wisconsin	Addback required for interest expenses, rental expenses, intangible expenses, and management fees directly or indirectly paid, accrued, or incurred to, or in connection directly or indirectly with one or more direct or indirect transactions with, one or more related entities. Subtraction allowed to related entity for income corresponding to expense disallowed under addback requirement.	***Addback not required if amount disclosed and:*** • related entity paid amount to unrelated party during same taxable year; • related entity is a holding company or subsidiary of a holding company, with certain exceptions; • related entity, other than a captive REIT, and expense were subject to income or receipts tax applied at aggregate effective tax rate of at least 80%; or • transaction was primarily motivated by business purpose other than tax avoidance, economic position of taxpayer was changed in meaningful way apart from tax effects, and expenses or fees were paid, accrued, or incurred using terms reflecting arm's-length relationship. Schedule RT, Related Entity Expenses Disclosure, may be required. Schedule RT-1, Statement of Disallowed Related Entity Expenses, is used to substantiate subtraction.
Wyoming	N/A, because state does not tax general business corporation income.	

Repatriation or Transition Income—IRC § 965

Under IRC Sec. 965, a tax is imposed on the accumulated foreign earnings of certain foreign corporations to implement transition to a new participation exemption (territorial) system of taxation. The transition tax applies to deferred earnings of CFCs or foreign corporations that are at least 10-percent owned by a domestic corporation (i.e., specified foreign corporations). Under the transition rule, the corporation's Subpart F income for the last tax year beginning before January 1, 2018, is increased by the greater of its accumulated post-1986 foreign earnings determined as of:

- November 2, 2017; or
- December 31, 2017.

U.S. shareholders of the corporation must include in their income a proportionate share of the corporation's Subpart F income (mandatory inclusion). A portion of the mandatory income inclusion is deductible. The deduction effectively results in a reduced tax rate of:

- 15.5% for deferred earnings held in cash; and
- 8% percent for other deferred earnings.

The transition tax can be paid in installments over an 8-year period. The first installment must be paid on the due date (determined without regard to extensions) of the tax return for the last tax year that begins before January 1, 2018 (the tax year of the mandatory inclusion).

This chart shows the tax treatment of IRC Sec. 965 income by each state and the District of Columbia. The chart does not cover states that provide apportionment factor relief or other apportionment adjustments for that income.

Jurisdiction	Repatriation or Transition Income—IRC § 965	Comment
Alabama	Addition required for IRC Sec. 965 income net of related deduction and other federal adjustments. Subtraction allowed for: • IRC Sec. 965 expenses; • IRC Sec. 965 income net of related deduction if received from 20%-or-more-owned controlled foreign corporations; and • IRC Sec. 965 income tax included in taxable income after dividends received deduction and exclusion of nonbusiness income.	Statement for dividends received deduction should be attached to return providing the name, taxpayer ID and ownership interest of the controlled foreign corporation. Complete Federal Income Tax Deduction Worksheet IRC Section 965 for tax deduction and attach to return. Also, attach copy of federal IRC Sec. 965 Transition Tax Statement to return.
Alaska	Addition required for IRC Sec. 965 gross income. Subtraction allowed equal to foreign dividends received deduction.	Attach copy of federal IRC 965 Transition Tax Statement to return.

Jurisdiction	Repatriation or Transition Income—IRC § 965	Comment
Arizona	Subtraction allowed for IRC Sec. 965 income included in federal taxable income. Addition required for IRC Sec. 965(c) deduction. **2017 Tax Return:** No addition required for IRC Sec. 965 income or deduction because it is not included in federal taxable income starting point.	
Arkansas	No modifications because state does not conform to IRC Sec. 965.	Unless conformity legislation is passed, state will continue to tax income as dividends are actually paid.
California	No modifications because state does not conform to IRC Sec. 965.	Net income excluded from return.
Colorado	Addition required for IRC Sec. 965 income net of related deduction. Subtraction allowed for amount of federal deduction or credit claimed for foreign taxes paid on IRC Sec. 965 income.	Submit copy of federal IRC 965 Transition Tax Statement with return.
Connecticut	Addition required for IRC Sec. 965 gross income. Subtraction allowed equal to dividends received deduction, less 5% of related expenses.	Subtraction computed on Form CT-1120 ATT, Schedule I.
Delaware	No legislation or guidance on treatment of IRC Sec. 965 repatriation (transition) tax.	
District of Columbia	No legislation or guidance on treatment of IRC Sec. 965 repatriation (transition) tax	
Florida	No modifications. Subtraction allowed if income flows through to federal taxable income (e.g. REIT flow-through income).	
Georgia	Addition required for expenses related to IRC Sec. 965 income net of related deduction.	IRC Sec. 965 income net of related deduction excluded from taxable income.
Hawaii	No modifications because state does not conform to IRC Sec. 965.	
Idaho	No modification required for IRC Sec. 965 income or deduction.	

Jurisdiction	Repatriation or Transition Income—IRC §965	Comment
Illinois	Subraction allowed equal to: • 100% of IRC Sec. 965 income from wholly owned foreign subsidiaries; • 65% of IRC Sec. 965 income from 20%-or-more-owned foreign corporations; and • 50% of IRC Sec. 965 income from less-than-20%-owned foreign corporations. Taxpayers must exclude IRC Sec. 965(c) deduction. **2017 Tax Year:** Addition required for IRC Sec. 965 income net of related deduction. Subtraction allowed equal to: • 100% of IRC Sec. 965 income from wholly owned foreign subsidiaries; • 80% of IRC Sec. 965 income from 20%-or-more-owned foreign corporations; and • 70% of IRC Sec. 965 income from less-than-20%-owned foreign corporations.	Subtraction computed on Schedule J. Addition for 2017 tax year entered on Schedule M.
Indiana	Addition required for IRC Sec. 965 gross income. Subtraction allowed equal to foreign source dividends deduction.	
Iowa	No modifications because state does not conform to IRC Sec. 965.	Net income excluded from return.
Kansas	No legislation or guidance on treatment of IRC Sec. 965 repatriation (transition) tax.	
Kentucky	No modifications because state does not conform to IRC Sec. 965.	
Louisiana	Addition required for balance of IRC Sec. 965 income net of related deduction after applying: • dividends received deduction; and • apportionment percentage. Subtraction allowed for federal income tax paid on IRC Sec. 965 income apportioned and taxed by the state.	Complete corporate income tax section of Form R-620-965, Internal Revenue Code Section 965 Income & FIT Deduction Worksheet, and attach to return. Also, attach copy of federal IRC Sec. 965 Transition Tax Statement to return.
Maine	Addition required for IRC Sec. 965 gross income. Subtraction allowed for 80% of deferred foreign income included in addback amount.	
Maryland	Addition required for IRC Sec. 965 net income. Subtraction allowed equal to deduction for dividends received from related foreign corporations.	Attach copy of federal IRC 965 Transition Tax Statement to return.
Massachusetts	Addition required on 2017 return for IRC Sec. 965 gross income. Subtraction allowed equal to dividends received deduction.	Complete and file Schedule FCI. Include copy of federal Form 965.
Michigan	Addition required for IRC Sec. 965 income reported for federal purposes. Subtraction allowed equal to foreign dividends received deduction.	

Jurisdiction	Repatriation or Transition Income—IRC § 965	Comment
Minnesota	Addition required for amount of any special deduction under IRC Sec. 965. Subtraction allowed for amount of deferred foreign income recognized because of IRC Sec. 965.	Include copy of federal IRC 965 Transition Tax Statement with return.
Mississippi	Repatriation dividends are considered nonbusiness income as foreign sourced dividends for Mississippi purposes. The dividends will be allocated to Mississippi under nonbusiness allocation rules, if applicable.	
Missouri	Addition required for: • IRC Sec. 965 net income; and • IRC Sec. 78 gross-up amounts associated with the IRC Sec. 965 transition tax. Subtraction allowed for: • IRC Sec. 965 income equal to dividends received deduction; and • IRC Sec. 965 transition tax.	Attach or electronically include copy of federal IRC 965 Transition Tax Statement when filing return.
Montana	Subtraction allowed for: • 80% of IRC Sec. 965 inclusion income received by water's edge filers; • 100% of IRC Sec. 965 inclusion income received by worldwide filers from members of worldwide group; or • 965(c) deduction for separate company, domestic or limited combination filers for amounts received from entity or group of entities included in return. **2017 Tax Year:** Addition required for gross income from IRC Sec. 965 dividends. Subtraction allowed for: • 80% of IRC Sec. 965 dividends received by water's edge filers; • 100% of IRC Sec. 965 dividends received by worldwide filers from unitary subsidiaries included in return; or • 100% of IRC Sec. 965 dividends received by separate company, domestic or limited combination filers from unitary subsidiaries included in return.	Attach copy of federal IRC 965 Transition Tax Statement to return. For water's edge filers, if any of the 965 inclusion income is from subsidiaries included in the water's edge filing, such as those incorporated in tax haven countries, then taxpayer deducts 100% of the inclusion income related to these entities. A similar provision applies for limited combination filers.
Nebraska	Addition required for IRC Sec. 965 gross income. Subtraction allowed for IRC Sec. 965(c) deduction.	Submit copy of federal IRC 965 Transition Tax Statement with return.
Nevada	N/A, because state does not tax general business corporation income.	
New Hampshire	No modifications because state does not conform to IRC Sec. 965.	
New Jersey	Addition required for: • IRC Sec. 965 net income; • IRC Sec. 965(c) deduction; and • IRC Sec. 965 exemptions or credits. Subtraction allowed equal to dividends received exclusion.	Include copy of federal IRC 965 Transition Tax Statement with Form CBT-DIV 2017 Supplemental.

Jurisdiction	Repatriation or Transition Income—IRC § 965	Comment
New Mexico	Addition required for IRC Sec. 965 net income. Subtraction allowed equal to foreign source dividends deduction.	Include copy of IRC Sec. 965 Transition Tax Statement and 2017 CIT-DFI schedule along with the original or amended CIT-1 return.
New York	The IRC Sec. 965(a) inclusion amount received from corporations not included in taxpayer's combined return is considered gross exempt CFC income. Addition required for: • IRC Sec. 965(c) deduction; and • interest deductions related to IRC Sec. 965 income, unless safe harbor election is made.	Attach copy of the federal and pro-forma, if applicable, IRC Sec. 965 Transition Tax Statement, along with accompanying worksheets used to compute the IRC § 965 amounts, to return.
North Carolina	Subtraction allowed for IRC Sec. 965 income included in federal taxable income. Addition required for IRC Sec. 965(c) deduction. **2017 Tax Return:** No addition required for IRC Sec. 965 income or deduction because it is not included in federal taxable income starting point.	
North Dakota	Addition required for: • IRC Sec. 965 income; and • IRC Sec. 965(c) deduction.	File copy of federal IRC 965 Transition Tax Statement with return. For worldwide combined filers, the IRC Sec. 965 inclusion attributable to a CFC included in the combined report is deducted as an intercompany dividend elimination. For water's edge filers, 70% of the IRC Sec. 965 inclusion is deductible as a foreign dividend.
Ohio	N/A, because Commercial Activity Tax (CAT) is not considered an income tax and is not tied to federal income tax base.	
Oklahoma	Addition required for IRC Sec. 965 income included in federal transition tax statement.	IRC Sec. 965 income is considered dividend income. Include copy of federal IRC 965 Transition Tax Statement. Installment payments allowed if taxpayer elects to pay federal tax in installments. Include a schedule reflecting income tax related to the § 965 income and amount of installment payments that will be remitted each year.
Oregon	Addition required for IRC Sec. 965 gross income. Subtraction allowed equal to dividends received deduction.	Report addition and subtraction adjustments on Schedule OR-ASC-CORP. Include copy of federal IRC 965 Transition Tax Statement with return.
Pennsylvania	Addition required for IRC Sec. 965 income net of related deduction. Subtraction allowed equal dividends received deduction.	Compute adjustments on REV-798A, Schedule RTT.

Jurisdiction	Repatriation or Transition Income—IRC § 965	Comment
Rhode Island	Addition required for IRC Sec. 965 income net of related deduction. Subtraction allowed equal to dividends received deduction for income received from nonunitary foreign subsidiaries.	Complete Schedule 965 and include with return. Also include copy of federal IRC 965 Transition Tax Statement.
South Carolina	Modifications may be required because state does not conform to IRC Sec. 965.	
South Dakota	N/A, because state does not tax general business corporation income.	
Tennessee	Subtraction allowed for IRC Sec. 965 income included in federal taxable income. Addition required for 5% of the amount included in federal taxable income before the IRC Sec. 965(c) deduction.	For 2017 tax year, no modification required for IRC Sec. 965 income or deduction because it is not included in federal taxable income starting point.
Texas	No modifications because state does not conform to IRC Sec. 965.	
Utah	Addition required for IRC Sec. 965 gross income. Subtraction allowed equal to dividends received exclusion.	Complete and file Form TC-20R. Also attach copy of federal IRC 965 Transition Tax Statement. Installment payments allowed if taxpayer: • elects to pay federal tax in installments; and • apportions deferred IRC Sec. 965 income to state. Installments due by: • due date of return for first taxable year in which corporation reports deferred IRC Sec. 965 income; and • due date of returns for next 7 years.
Vermont	Addition required for IRC Sec. 965 income net of related deduction.	
Virginia	Conforms to IRC Sec. 965, but no guidance on treatment of repatriation or transition income.	
Washington	N/A, because state does not tax general business corporation income.	
West Virginia	No legislation or guidance on treatment of IRC Sec. 965 repatriation (transition) tax.	
Wisconsin	Modifications may be required because state does not conform to IRC Sec. 965.	Modifications reported on Schedule 4V, Additions to Federal Income, and Schedule 4W, Subtractions from Federal Income.
Wyoming	N/A, because state does not tax general business corporation income.	

Return Due Dates

The federal individual income tax return is due on or before the 15th day of the 4th month following the close of the tax year or April 15 in the case of a calendar-year taxpayer. If the due date falls on a Saturday, Sunday, or legal holiday, the return may be filed on the next succeeding day that is not a Saturday, Sunday, or legal holiday.

Most states follow the federal deadline. This chart shows the state personal income tax return due dates and forms for the current tax year.

Electronic filing mandates and options are not covered in this chart. However, they are covered in a chart under the topic E-Filing: Mandates/Options for Individuals.

Jurisdiction	Due Date and Form	Comment
Alabama	Form 40 or Form 40NR (nonresidents) must be filed by the due date of the corresponding federal return.	**Coronavirus (COVID-19) Pandemic Filing/Payment Relief** July 15, 2020 filing and payment due date.
Arizona	Form 140, Form 140PY (part-year residents), or Form 140NR must be filed by April 15th or 15th day of 4th month after close of fiscal year.	**Coronavirus (COVID-19) Pandemic Filing/Payment Relief** July 15, 2020 filing and payment due date.
Arkansas	Form AR1000 or AR1000NR (part-year and nonresidents) must be filed by April 15th or 3.5 months after close of fiscal year.	**Coronavirus (COVID-19) Pandemic Filing/Payment Relief:** July 15, 2020, return and payment due date.
California	Form 540 or Form 540NR (part-year and nonresidents) must be filed by April 15 or 15th day of 4th month after close of fiscal year.	**Coronavirus (COVID-19) Pandemic Filing/Payment Relief** July 15, 2020 filing and payment due date.
Colorado	Form 104 or Form 104PN (part-year and nonresidents) must be filed by April 15th or 15th day of 4th month after close of tax year.	**Coronavirus (COVID-19) Pandemic Filing/Payment Relief:** October 15, 2020, return due date. July 15, 2020, payment due date.
Connecticut	Form CT-1040 or Form CT-1040NR/PY (part-year and nonresidents) must be filed by April 15th or 15th day of 4th month after close of fiscal year.	**Coronavirus (COVID-19) Pandemic Filing/Payment Relief** July 15, 2020 return and payment due date.
Delaware	Form 200-01 or Form 200-02 (part-year and nonresidents) must be filed by April 30 or 30th day of 4th month after close of fiscal year.	**Coronavirus (COVID-19) Pandemic Filing/Payment Relief** July 15, 2020 return and payment due date.
District of Columbia	Form D-40 must be filed by April 15th or 15th day of 4th month after close of fiscal year.	**Coronavirus (COVID-19) Pandemic Filing/Payment Relief** July 15, 2020 due date.

Jurisdiction	Due Date and Form	Comment
Georgia	Form 500 must be filed by April 15th or 15th day of 4th month after close of fiscal year.	**Coronavirus (COVID-19) Pandemic Filing/Payment Relief** July 15, 2020.
Hawaii	Form N-11 (residents) or Form N-15 (part-year and nonresidents) must be filed by April 20th, or 20th day of 4th month after close of fiscal year.	**Coronavirus (COVID-19) Pandemic Filing/Payment Relief** July 20, 2020 filing and payment due date.
Idaho	Form 40 or Form 43 (part-year and nonresidents) must be filed by April 15th or 15th day of 4th month after close of fiscal year.	**Coronavirus (COVID-19) Pandemic Filing/Payment Relief** June 15, 2020.
Illinois	Form IL-1040 must be filed by April 15th or 15th day of 4th month after close of fiscal year.	**Coronavirus (COVID-19) Pandemic Filing/Payment Relief** July 15, 2020 return and payment due date.
Indiana	Form IT-40 or Form IT-40PNR (part-year and nonresidents) must be filed by April 15th or 15th day of 4th month after close of fiscal year.	**Coronavirus (COVID-19) Pandemic Filing/Payment Relief** Returns originally due April 15, 2020, due on or before July 15.
Iowa	Form IA 1040 must be filed by April 30th or last day of 4th month after close of fiscal year.	**Coronavirus (COVID-19) Pandemic Filing/Payment Relief** Returns due on or after March 19, 2020, and before July 31, 2020, extended to July 31, 2020.
Kansas	Form K-40 must be filed by April 15th or 15th day of 4th month after close of fiscal year.	**Coronavirus (COVID-19) Pandemic Filing/Payment Relief** July 15, 2020 return and payment due date. Extension also applies to fiscal year returns due between April 15, 2020 and July 15, 2020.
Kentucky	Form 740 or Form 740-NP (part-year and nonresidents) must be filed by April 15th or 15th day of 4th month after close of fiscal year.	**Coronavirus (COVID-19) Pandemic Filing/Payment Relief** July 15, 2020 due date for returns and payments due on and after April 15, 2020 and before July 15, 2020. Penalty and interest calculation will begin July 16, 2020.

Jurisdiction	Due Date and Form	Comment
Louisiana	Form IT-540 or Form IT-540B (nonresidents and part-year residents) must be filed by May 15th or 15th day of 5th month after close of fiscal year.	**Coronavirus (COVID-19) Pandemic Filing/Payment Relief:** Return and payment due July 15, 2020. **Hurricane Laura Relief:** Filing and payment deadline extensions are available as a result of damage caused by Hurricane Laura for taxpayers located in parishes that have been declared federal disaster areas. Returns and payments originally due between August 24, 2020, and November 2, 2020, are extended to December 31, 2020, for corporate income, franchise, partnership, and partnership composite taxes. Returns and payments originally due between August 24, 2020, and November 2, 2020, are extended to November 30, 2020, for income withholding.
Maine	Form 1040ME must be filed by April 15th or 15th day of 4th month after close of fiscal year.	**Coronavirus (COVID-19) Pandemic Filing/Payment Relief:** July 15, 2020, return and payment due date.
Maryland	Form 502 or Form 505 (nonresidents) must be filed by April 15th or 15th day of 4th month after close of fiscal year.	**Coronavirus (COVID-19) Pandemic Filing/Payment Relief:** July 15, 2020, return and payment due date.
Massachusetts	Form 1 or Form 1-NR/PY (part-year and nonresidents) must be filed by April 15th or 15th day of 4th month after close of fiscal year.	**Coronavirus (COVID-19) Pandemic Filing/Payment Relief** July 15, 2020 due date for return filing and payment.
Michigan	Form MI-1040 must be filed by April 15th or 15th day of 4th month after close of fiscal year.	**Coronavirus (COVID-19) Pandemic Filing/Payment Relief** July 15, 2020 filing and payment due date.
Minnesota	Form M1 must be filed by April 15th or 15th day of 4th month after close of fiscal year.	**Coronavirus (COVID-19) Pandemic Filing/Payment Relief** July 15, 2020 filing and payment due date.
Mississippi	Form 80-105 or Form 80-205 (part-year and nonresidents) must be filed by April 15th or 15th day of 4th month after close of fiscal year.	**Coronavirus (COVID-19) Pandemic Filing/Payment Relief:** July 15, 2020, return and payment due date.
Missouri	Form MO-1040 must be filed by April 15th or 15th day of 4th month after close of fiscal year.	**Coronavirus (COVID-19) Pandemic Filing/Payment Relief** July 15, 2020 filing and payment due date.
Montana	Form 2 must be filed by April 15th or 15th day of 4th month after close of fiscal year.	**COVID-19 Filing/Payment Relief:** July 15, 2020 return and payment due date.

Jurisdiction	Due Date and Form	Comment
Nebraska	Form 1040N must be filed by April 15th or 15th day of 4th month after close of fiscal year.	**Coronavirus (COVID-19) Pandemic Filing/Payment Relief** July 15, 2020 return and payment due date.
New Hampshire	Form DP-10 must be filed by April 15th or 15th day of 4th month after close of fiscal year.	
New Jersey	Form NJ-1040 or Form NJ-1040NR (nonresidents) must be filed by April 15th or 15th day of 4th month after close of fiscal year.	**Coronavirus (COVID-19) Pandemic Filing/Payment Relief** July 15, 2020 return and payment due date.
New Mexico	Form PIT-1 must be filed by April 15th or 15th day of 4th month after close of fiscal year. Due date is April 30th (or 30th day of 4th month after close of fiscal year) if both filing and payment are submitted electronically.	**Coronavirus (COVID-19) Pandemic Filing/Payment Relief:** New Mexico personal income tax returns due between April 15, 2020, and July 15, 2020, due by July 15, 2020. No interest or penalty will be imposed for failure to pay any personal income tax that became due April 15, 2020, through July 15, 2020, provided that payment for the unpaid tax is made in full on or before April 15, 2021, and the failure to pay was not an intentional attempt to evade the tax.
New York	Form IT-201 or Form IT-203 (part-year and nonresidents) must be filed by April 15th or 15th day of 4th month after close of fiscal year.	**COVID-19 Filing/Payment Relief:** July 15, 2020 return and payment due date.
North Carolina	Form D-400 must be filed by April 15th or 15th day of 4th month after close of fiscal year.	**Coronavirus (COVID-19) Pandemic Filing/Payment Relief** July 15, 2020 return due date and penalty waiver if tax is paid by that date.
North Dakota	Form ND-1 must be filed by April 15th or 15th day of 4th month after close of fiscal year.	**COVID-19 Filing/Payment Relief:** July 15, 2020 return and payment due date.
Ohio	Form IT-1040 must be filed by April 15th or 15th day of 4th month after close of fiscal year.	**Coronavirus (COVID-19) Pandemic Filing/Payment Relief** July 15, 2020 return and payment due date.
Oklahoma	Form 511 or Form 511NR (part-year and nonresidents) must be filed by April 15th or 15th day of 4th month after close of fiscal year. April 20th for calendar-year electronic filers.	**Coronavirus (COVID-19) Pandemic Filing/Payment Relief** April 15, 2020 return due date. July 15, 2020 payment due date on payments up to $1 million for non-corporate tax filers.
Oregon	Form 40, Form 40P (part-year residents), or Form 40N (nonresidents) must be filed by April 15th or 15th day of 4th month after close of fiscal year.	**Coronavirus (COVID-19) Pandemic Filing/Payment Relief** July 15, 2020 return and payment due date.

Jurisdiction	Due Date and Form	Comment
Pennsylvania	Form PA-40 must be filed by April 15th or 15th day of 4th month after close of fiscal year.	**Coronavirus (COVID-19) Pandemic Filing/Payment Relief** July 15, 2020 filing and payment due date.
Rhode Island	Form RI-1040 or Form RI-1040NR (part-year and nonresidents) must be filed by April 15th or 15th day of 4th month after close of fiscal year.	**Coronavirus (COVID-19) Pandemic Filing/Payment Relief:** July 15, 2020, return and payment due date.
South Carolina	Form SC1040 must be filed by April 15th or 15th day of 4th month after close of fiscal year.	**COVID-19 Filing/Payment Relief:** July 15, 2020 return and payment due date.
Tennessee	Form INC-250 must be filed by April 15th or 15th day of 4th month after close of fiscal year.	**COVID-19 Filing/Payment Relief:** July 15, 2020 return and payment due date.
Utah	Form TC-40 must be filed by due date of the corresponding federal return.	**Coronavirus (COVID-19) Pandemic Filing/Payment Relief** July 15, 2020 filing and payment due date.
Vermont	Form IN-111 must be filed by April 15th or 15th day of 4th month after close of fiscal year.	**COVID-19 Filing/Payment Relief:** July 15, 2020 return and payment due date.
Virginia	Form 760, Form 760PY (part-year residents), or Form 763 (nonresidents) must be filed by May 1st or 15th day of 4th month after close of fiscal year.	**COVID-19 Filing/Payment Relief:** May 1, 2020 return due date for calendar year filers. June 1, 2020 payment due date.
West Virginia	Form WV/IT-140 must be filed by April 15th or 15th day of 4th month after close of fiscal year.	**Coronavirus (COVID-19) Pandemic Filing/Payment Relief** July 15, 2020 return and payment due date.
Wisconsin	Form 1 or Form 1NPR (part-year and nonresidents) must be filed by April 15th or 15th day of 4th month after close of fiscal year.	**COVID-19 Filing/Payment Relief:** July 15, 2020 return and payment due date.

Return Filing Extensions (Corporate Income)

An automatic six-month federal extension is available to corporation income taxpayers, if Form 7004 is filed by the original due date of the return. Effective for tax years after 2015, C corporations with a June 30 fiscal year end are allowed a 7-month federal extension through 2025. Effective for tax years beginning after December 31, 2025, an automatic six-month federal extension is available to all corporation income taxpayers.

Most states automatically provide an equivalent filing extension if the taxpayer has received a federal filing extension or filed for a state extension by the original due date of the return. The duration of some state extension periods differ from the federal extension and some states recognize federal extensions beyond the 6-month automatic extension.

For states that recognize the federal extension, a copy of the federal extension generally must be attached to the state return when filed. Some states provide for an automatic extension, but do not require the taxpayer to file any paper or electronic extension request. An extension of time to file a return is not an extension of time to pay any tax due. Payment of tax is generally required to avoid penalties and interest. Some states allow or recognize extensions on behalf of a consolidated group, while others require each group member to file a separate extension request.

The following chart shows the return filing extension rules in effect for each state and the District of Columbia for the current tax year.

Jurisdiction	C Corporations	Comment
Alabama	6-month automatic extension. No paper or electronic extension request required.	100% of outstanding tax liability must be paid by original due date to avoid penalties. Electronic pay mandated if single tax payment totals $750 or more.
Alaska	Automatic extension equal to federal extension period plus 30 days.	100% of outstanding tax liability must be paid by original due date to avoid penalties. Federal extension must be attached to return. If federal extension is attached, check the box on the front page of the return.
Arizona	Automatic extension equal to federal extension period. 6-month automatic extension if Form 120EXT is filed by the original due date.	90% of outstanding tax liability must be paid with Form 120EXT by original due date to avoid penalties. Payment may be made over Internet without 120EXT unless Arizona extension requested. If filing under extension, do not attach copy of extension to return, but check box on front page of return.
Arkansas	6-month automatic extension if federal extension is filed by original due date of return. Additional 60-day state extension may be requested on Form AR1155. 180-day extension may be requested if Form AR1155 is postmarked by original due date.	100% of outstanding tax liability must be paid with Voucher 5 by original due date to avoid penalties. If federal extension granted, check box on front page of return. Original copy of state extension confirmation must be attached to face of return when filed.

Jurisdiction	C Corporations	Comment
California	7-month automatic extension for corporations in good standing (6-months for 2016-2018 tax years). No paper or electronic extension request required.	100% of outstanding tax liability must be paid with Form FTB 3539, unless payment is made by EFT or Web Pay, by original due date to avoid interest and penalties. EFT required if extension payment exceeds $20,000.
Colorado	6-month automatic extension. No paper or electronic extension request required.	90% of outstanding tax liability must be paid with Form DR-158-C by original due date to avoid penalties.
Connecticut	6-month automatic extension if federal extension and Form CT-1120 EXT is filed by original due date of return. 6-month extension for reasonable cause if Form CT-1120 EXT is filed by original due date of return.	90% of tax liability must be paid with Form CT-1120 EXT by original due date of return to avoid penalties. Electronic filing available. Affiliated corporations filing either combined return or unitary return must attach Form CT-1120CC to state extension form for the initial income year an affiliate is included.
Delaware	6-month automatic extension if federal extension or Form 1100-EXT is filed by original due date of return. Additional extension may be granted for good cause by submitting letter to Division of Revenue.	100% of outstanding tax liability must be paid with Form 1100-T-EXT by original due date to avoid penalties. Federal extension or approval letter for additional state extension must be attached to return when filed. "Extension" box must be checked on the front page of the return. Affiliated corporations filing a consolidated federal return must file separate extension requests for each affiliated group member.
District of Columbia	6-month automatic extension if Form FR-120 is filed by original due date of return and tax due is paid. For combined filers, 7-month automatic extension if Form FR-120 is filed by original due date of return and tax due is paid.	100% of outstanding tax liability must be paid by original due date to avoid penalties. Blanket requests for extensions will not be accepted. Extension must be attached to return. Qualified high technology companies must submit a completed DC Form QHTC-CERT with the extension request. If liability exceeds $5,000, it must be paid electronically.
Florida	Automatic extension if federal extension and Form F-7004 is filed by original due date of return. Extension may be granted if Form F-7004 is filed by original due date of return and good cause is shown for extension. Extension period equal to: • 6 months for a taxable year that ends other than June 30; or • 7 months for a taxable year that ends June 30.	100% of outstanding tax liability must be paid with F-7004 by original due date to avoid penalties. Extension must be attached to return and box checked on the front page of the return. Extension is void if tax liability is not paid or if amount paid is underpaid by the greater of $2,000 or 30% of tax shown when filed. **Effective for taxable years before 2016:** Automatic extension equal to earlier of 6 months or 15 days after expiration of federal extension if federal extension and Form F-7004 filed by original due date of return. Extension of 6 months for good cause if Form F-7004 filed by original due date of return.

Jurisdiction	C Corporations	Comment
Georgia	6-month automatic extension if federal extension is filed by original due date of return. 6-month extension may be granted if Form IT-303 is filed by original due date of return and reasonable cause, including why application for federal extension not made, is shown.	100% of outstanding tax liability must be paid with Form IT-560C by original due date to avoid penalties. Copy of federal extension must be attached to return when filed. State extension form must be completed in triplicate and one copy attached to return when filed. Extension box must be checked on the front page of the return. Corporations filing consolidated returns must file a separate extension application for filing net worth tax for each subsidiary.
Hawaii	6-month automatic extension.	100% of outstanding tax liability must be paid with Form N-301 by original due date to avoid penalties. Form N-301 may be filed electronically.
Idaho	6-month automatic extension. No paper or electronic extension request required.	80% of current year's outstanding tax liability or 100% of prior year's tax liability must be paid with Form 41ES by original due date of return to avoid penalties. Payments of $50 or less not required.
Illinois	Automatic extension equal to: • 6-months for calendar year taxpayers and fiscal year taxpayers whose tax year ends on a date other than June 30 (7-months for taxable years before 2016); • 7-months for fiscal year taxpayers whose tax year ends on June 30; or • one month beyond federal extension period, if longer. No paper or electronic extension request required.	100% of outstanding tax liability must be paid with Form IL-1120-V by original due date, unless paid by electronic funds transfer, to avoid penalties. Federal extension must be attached to return when filed if longer than state automatic extension period.
Indiana	Automatic extension equal to federal extension plus 30 days. Automatic state extension, equal to federal extension period, if written request is filed and outstanding tax liability equal to penalty safe harbor threshold is paid by original due date of return. Additional extension may be granted if written request is made by federal or state extended due date and reasonable cause is shown.	90% of outstanding tax liability must be paid with Form IT-6 by original due date to avoid penalties. Federal extension form must be attached and extension box must be checked on front page of return.
Iowa	6-month automatic extension. No paper or electronic extension request required.	90% of outstanding tax liability must be paid with Form 42-019 by original due date to avoid penalties.
Kansas	6-month automatic extension if federal extension is filed by original due date of return.	90% of outstanding tax liability must be paid with Form K-120V by original due date to avoid penalties. Federal extension must be attached to return when filed. No extension necessary if taxpayer entitled to refund.

Jurisdiction	C Corporations	Comment
Kentucky	Automatic extension equal to federal extension period; **or** 7-month (6-month for tax years before 2019) automatic state extension if Form 720EXT is filed by the original due date of the return.	100% of outstanding tax liability must be paid with Form 720EXT by original due date to avoid interest and penalties. Copy of extension must be attached to return when filed. An extension of time for filing a consolidated return operates as an extension for all affiliated group members.
Louisiana	7-month extension may be requested with electronic application filed by original due date of return.	State authorized to grant extension if taxpayer has automatic federal extension. Method for notification to state that automatic federal extension was obtained to be established by rule (although rule has not yet been established). 100% of outstanding tax liability must be paid by original due date to avoid interest and penalties. Effective June 4, 2020, if a disaster or emergency is declared by the Louisiana Governor or the U.S. President, the Department of Revenue may extend tax return filing and payment deadlines by no more than six months. Interest may accrue during the extension in the case of a governor-declared disaster, but not during a presidentially-declared disaster.
Maine	Automatic extension equal to federal extension (additional 30 days allowed prior to 2017). No paper or electronic extension request required.	90% of outstanding tax liability must be paid with Form 1120EXT-ME by original due date and remaining balance must be paid when the return is filed to avoid penalties. **Coronavirus (COVID-19) Pandemic Filing/Payment Relief:** Form 1120ME (Corporate Income Tax Return) or 2019 Maine Form 1120B-ME (Franchise Tax Return) otherwise due on extension by October 15, 2020, may be filed by November 16, 2020.
Maryland	7-month automatic extension provided Form 500E is filed by original due date of return.	100% of outstanding tax liability must be paid with Form 500E or by EFT by original due date to avoid penalties. Extension requests may be submitted electronically if no tax is due, unless it is the corporation's first filing. Affiliated corporations that file consolidated federal returns must file separate state extension for each member corporation.

Jurisdiction	C Corporations	Comment
Massachusetts	6-month automatic extension (7-month for combined report filers) if greater of: • 50% of total amount of tax liability ultimately due; or • minimum corporate excise has been paid by original due date of return No paper or electronic extension request required.	6-month automatic extension for any taxpayer corporation included in a combined report that is required to pay the non-income measure of corporate excise tax, but has a different taxable year than that of the combined group. 50% of tax liability must be paid with Form 355-7004 or electronically by original due date of return or extension will be void. Penalties and interest will also apply. Additional extension for good cause may be requested if Form 355-7004 is filed by the extended due date. **Effective for returns due before November 30, 2015:** 6-month automatic extension if: • no tax is due and 100% of tax liability has been paid by original due date of return; or • Form 355-7004 is filed and the greater of 50% of the tax due or the minimum tax has been paid by original due date of return.
Michigan	8-month state extension if Form 4 postmarked by original due date of return.	100% of outstanding tax liability must be paid with Form 4 by original due date to avoid penalties.
Minnesota	7-month automatic extension or automatic extension equal to federal extension period, if it is longer. No paper or electronic extension request required.	90% of outstanding tax liability must be paid electronically, by phone, or through the Payment Voucher System by the original due date and the remaining 10% must be paid by the extended due date to avoid penalties.
Mississippi	6-month automatic extension if federal extension is filed and no tax is due. 6-month automatic extension if Form 83-180 is filed by original due date of return.	100% of outstanding tax liability must be paid with Form 83-180 by original due date to avoid penalties. Proof of federal extension must be made available upon request. Effective for tax years beginning after December 31, 2015, Form 83-180 must be filed by April 15th following the close of the calendar year or the 15th day of the 4th month following the close of the fiscal year.
Missouri	6-month automatic extension if federal extension is filed by original due date of return. Additional extensions may be granted for cause if Form MO-7004 is filed by extended due date. 6-month automatic extension if Form MO-7004 is filed by original due date of return. Additional extensions may be granted for reasonable cause if Form MO-7004 is filed by extended due date.	100% of outstanding tax liability must be paid with Form MO-7004 by the original due date to avoid penalties. Federal extension must be attached to the MO-7004 or to the return if no MO-7004 was filed. An approved MO-7004 must be attached to the return when filed. Must check box to indicate type of return/ extension filed. Blanket and consolidated requests for extension not accepted. Separate extensions must be submitted for each affiliated group member if filing a federal consolidated income tax return and not qualifying to file a consolidated state return.

Jurisdiction	C Corporations	Comment
Montana	6-month automatic extension. Additional time may be granted for good cause. No paper or electronic extension request required.	100% of outstanding tax liability must be paid by the original due date to avoid penalties.
Nebraska	6-month automatic extension if federal extension is filed by original due date of return. Additional one-month extension may be granted if Form 7004N is filed by extended due date. 7-month automatic extension available if Form 7004N is filed by original due date of return.	100% of outstanding tax liability must be paid electronically or with Form 7004N by original due date to avoid penalties. Any federal extension must be attached to return when filed. If additional extension beyond federal extension is sought, attach federal extension to Form 7004N. Members of a unitary group filing a single return using the combined income approach should only request one extension for the entire group. The name, address, Federal ID number, and Nebraska ID number of each corporation included in the combined return must be listed on Form 7004N.
Nevada	N/A, because state does not tax general business corporation or pass-through income.	
New Hampshire	7-month automatic extension if 100% of tax due is paid or Form BT-EXT is filed by original due date of return.	100% of outstanding tax liability must be paid electronically or with Form BT-EXT by original due date to avoid penalties.
New Jersey	6-month automatic extension if Form CBT-200-T is filed by original due date of return.	90% of outstanding current year tax liability, or 100% of previous year's tax base, whichever is less, must be paid electronically or with Form CBT-200-T by original due date to avoid penalties.
New Mexico	6-month automatic extension if federal extension is filed by original due date of return. Additional extension may be granted for cause if written request or Form RPD-41096 is filed by extended due date. 60-day extension may be granted for cause if written request or Form RPD-41096 is filed by original due date of return. Additional extensions may be granted for good cause.	100% of tax liability must be paid with Form RPD-41096, unless previously paid, to avoid interest. Extension must be attached to any request for additional filing extensions and also must be attached to return when filed.
New York	6-month automatic extension if estimated tax is paid and Form CT-5, or Form CT-5.3 for corporations filing combined returns, is filed by original due date of return. Additional extensions of up to two additional 3-month periods may be granted if Form CT-5.1 is filed by previous extended due date.	90% of current year's tax liability, including MTA surcharge, or 100% of prior year's tax liability, must be paid with Form CT-5 or CT-5.3 by original due date of return, and any remaining tax liability must be paid by extended due date, to avoid penalties. Electronic filing mandated. A corporation being added to a combined group or a group of corporations forming a new combined group must each file their own separate CT-5.

Jurisdiction	C Corporations	Comment
North Carolina	Automatic extension equal to federal extension period. 6-month automatic extension if Form CD-419 is filed by original due date of return. **Tax years before 2019:** 6-month automatic extension if Form CD-419 is filed by original due date of return.	100% of outstanding tax liability must be paid with Form CD-419 by original due date to avoid penalties. Electronic filing and payment available.
North Dakota	For tax years after 2015, automatic extension to federal extended due date plus one month. For tax years before 2016, automatic extension equal to federal extension period. Extension may be obtained for good cause if Form 101 is filed by original due date of return.	100% of outstanding tax liability must be paid with Form 40-EXT, or a letter containing specified information along with a state extension approval, to avoid interest. Extension must be attached to return when filed and appropriate box must be checked on front page of return.
Ohio	Extensions for CAT filers not addressed.	
Oklahoma	6-month automatic extension if federal extension is filed by original due date of return and no tax is due. Additional 1-month extension may be granted if Form 504 is filed by extended due date. 7-month automatic extension if Form 504 is filed by original due date of return.	90% of outstanding tax liability must be paid electronically or with Form 504-C by original due date of return to avoid penalties. Copy of extension request must be included with return when filed. If federal extension is filed, appropriate box must be checked on front page of return and copy of federal extension must be included with return when filed.
Oregon	Automatic extension equal to federal extension period. 6-month automatic extension if Form 7004 with "For Oregon only" marked on top of form is attached to return.	90% of tax liability must be paid with Form 20V by original due date of return to avoid penalties. Extension box should be checked on Form 20V at time of remittance. Copy of extension must be attached to return as the last item prior to the federal corporation return. "Extension filed" box must be checked on front page of return.
Pennsylvania	Automatic extension equal to federal extension period. 60 day state extension may be granted if: Form REV-853 is filed or online request is submitted by original due date of return.	100% of outstanding tax liability must be paid with Form REV-853, or submitted by EFT for taxes of $1,000 or more, by original due date of return to avoid penalties. Both copy of federal extension request and state extension approval letter must be attached to return in front of any supporting schedules. For automatic extension, federal extension form must be attached and extension box must be checked on front page of return.
Rhode Island	6-month automatic extension if Form RI-7004 is filed by original due date of return. 7-month automatic extension for June 30 fiscal-year filers (2016 to 2025 tax years).	100% of outstanding tax liability must be paid by original due date to avoid penalties.

Jurisdiction	C Corporations	Comment
South Carolina	6-month automatic extension if federal extension filed. 6-month automatic state extension if Form SC-1120-T is filed by original due date of return.	90% of outstanding tax liability must be paid with Form SC1120-T by original due date of return to avoid penalties. Electronic filing and payment available. Corporations filing a consolidated return should file a single state extension. A federal extension will be accepted if all corporations filing in the state are included in one or more federal extensions.
South Dakota	N/A, because state does not tax general business corporation or pass-through income.	
Tennessee	6-month automatic extension if federal extension or Form FAE 173 is filed by original due date of return.	Taxpayers included in a federal consolidated return that have tax due must file Form FAE 173 or an electronic extension request by the original due date. 90% of current year's tax liability or 100% of prior year's tax liability, whichever is less, must be paid with either Form FAE-173 or copy of federal extension by original due date of return to avoid penalties. Extension request need not be filed by original due date if payment requirement has already been met.
Texas	6-month automatic extension for annual reports if Form 05-164 is filed by original due date of report. 3-month automatic extension of annual reports for EFT filers if Form 05-164 is filed by original due date of report. 3-month additional extension if form is filed by initial 3-month extended due date. 45-day automatic extension for initial reports if Form 05-164 is filed by original due date of report.	90% of current year's outstanding tax liability, or 100% of prior year's tax liability, must be paid by original due date of annual report and remaining balance must be paid by extended due date, to avoid penalties. Penalty for EFT filers will be waived if amount paid equals at least 90% of tax due, or 100% of prior year's tax liability, and balance is paid by first extended due date. 90% of tax liability must be paid by the original due date of initial reports to avoid penalties. Combined groups can only use the 100% of prior revised franchise tax liability option if all members filed a franchise tax report in the previous year. Groups that include newly taxable entities or no-nexus members must use the 90% option. An affiliate list on Form 05-165 also must be submitted with the extension. Electronic filing available.
Utah	6-month automatic extension. For 2019 tax year, automatic extension until last day of federal extension. No paper or electronic extension request required.	90% of outstanding tax liability (minimum tax if greater), or 100% of prior year's tax must be paid by original due date of return (or, for 2019 tax year, automatically extended return due date) to avoid penalties unless payment extension granted. The tax used to compute the 90% amount includes the interest on installment sales and the recapture of low-income housing credit on the return.

Jurisdiction	C Corporations	Comment
Vermont	Automatic federal extension period plus 30 days if federal extension, or Form BA-403 is filed by original due date of return.	100% of outstanding tax liability must be paid with Form BA-403 by original due date to avoid penalties. Copy of federal extension request must be filed with return. "Extended return" box must be checked on front page of return. Electronic filing available.
Virginia	6-month automatic extension or 30 days after federal extended due date, whichever is later. No paper or electronic extension request required.	90% of outstanding tax liability must be paid electronically with 500CP eForm, the taxpayer's Business Online Services Account, or by a ACH credit transaction by original due date of return to avoid penalties.
Washington	N/A, because state does not tax general business corporation or pass-through income.	
West Virginia	Automatic extension equal to federal extension period. 6-month state extension for cause if written request is made by extended due date.	100% of outstanding tax liability must be paid with Form WV-CNF-120T by original due date of return to avoid penalties. Copy of federal extension must be attached to return and extended due date entered at top of return.
Wisconsin	Automatic extension to federal extended due date plus 30 days. State-only 7-month automatic extension or until original due date of corresponding federal return, whichever is later.	No penalty applies, but tax not paid by original due date of return is subject to interest. If relying on federal extension, copy must be attached to return. Box must be checked on front page of return and extended due date entered.
Wyoming	N/A, because state does not tax general business corporation or pass-through income.	

Return Filing Extensions (Personal Income)

An automatic six-month federal extension is available to individual taxpayers, if Form 4868 is filed by the original due date of the return. Most states automatically provide an equivalent filing extension if the taxpayer has received a federal filing extension or filed for a state extension by the original due date of the return. The duration of some state extension periods differ from the federal extension. A copy of the federal extension generally must be attached to the state return when filed. An extension of time to file a return is not an extension of time to pay any tax due. Payment of tax is generally required to avoid penalties and interest. The following chart shows the return filing extension rules in effect for each state. Special rules that govern extensions for individuals or military personnel outside the U.S. are not covered in the chart.

Jurisdiction	General Taxpayers	Comment
Alabama	6-month automatic extension for tax years beginning on or after January 1, 2008. No paper or electronic extension request required. **For tax years prior to 2008**: 6-month automatic extension if Form 4868A is filed by original due date of return.	100% of outstanding tax liability must be paid by original due date of return to avoid penalties. Electronic payment mandated if single tax payment totals $750 or more.
Arizona	6-month automatic extension if federal extension or Form 204 is filed by original due date of return.	100% of tax liability must be paid by original due date of return to avoid late payment penalty. 90% of tax liability must be paid by original due date of return to avoid extension underpayment penalty. Mark envelope for state extension, "Extension Request." Applicable extension box must be marked on front of return.
Arkansas	6-month automatic extension if federal extension is filed by original due date of return. 180-day automatic extension if Form AR1055 is filed by original due date of return.	100% of outstanding tax liability must be paid by original due date of return to avoid penalties. Copy of federal extension not required when return is filed. Check extension box on front of return.
California	6-month automatic extension. No paper or electronic extension request required.	100% of outstanding tax liability must be paid with FTB 3519, unless payment is made by EFT or Web Pay, by original due date of return to avoid penalties. EFT required if extension payment exceeds $20,000.
Colorado	6-month automatic extension. No paper or electronic extension request required.	90% of outstanding tax liability must be paid with DR 158-I by original due date of return to avoid penalties.
Connecticut	6-month automatic extension if federal extension is filed by original due date of return. Form CT-1040EXT must be filed if tax is owed and payment is other than by credit card. 6-month state extension upon showing of good cause if Form CT-1040EXT is filed by original due date of return.	90% of outstanding tax liability must be paid with Form CT-1040EXT by original due date of return to avoid penalties. Electronic filing available. Payment extension available upon showing of undue hardship and filing Form CT-1127.

Jurisdiction	General Taxpayers	Comment
Delaware	Automatic extension equal to federal extension period if no balance due and federal application form is filed by original due date of return;**or** 5 1/2-month automatic state extension if Form 1027 is filed by original due date of return. Additional state extension available by submitting copy of federal extension.	100% of outstanding tax liability must be paid with Form 1027 by original due date of return to avoid penalties. Blanket requests for extensions will not be granted. Copy of federal or state extension must be attached to return when filed. Electronic filing available.
District of Columbia	6-month automatic extension if Form FR-127 is filed by original due date of return.	100% of tax liability must be paid by original due date of return to avoid penalties. Copy of extension request form must be attached to return when filed.
Georgia	6-month automatic extension if federal extension is filed by original due date of return. 6-month state extension if Form IT-303 is filed by original due date of return and reasonable cause is shown.	100% of tax liability must be paid by original due date of return to avoid penalties. Copy of federal extension must be attached to return when filed. State extension form must be completed in triplicate and one copy attached to return when filed.
Hawaii	6-month automatic extension.	100% of outstanding tax liability must be paid with Form N-101A by original due date of return to avoid penalties. Electronic filing available.
Idaho	6-month automatic extension. No paper or electronic extension request required.	80% of current year's tax liability or 100% of total tax reported for preceding tax year must be paid with Form 51 by original due date of return to avoid penalties.
Illinois	Automatic extension equal to federal extension period; **or** 6-month automatic state extension. No paper or electronic extension request required.	100% of tax liability must be paid with Form IL-505-I by original due date of return to avoid penalties. Copy of federal extension must be attached to return when filed.
Indiana	7-month automatic extension if federal extension is filed by original due date of return. 7-month automatic extension if Form IT-9 is filed by original due date of return. Prior to 2014 tax year, 60-day automatic extension if Form IT-9 was filed by original due date of return.	90% of tax liability must be paid by original due date of return to avoid penalties. Copy of federal extension must be attached when return is filed. Electronic filing available.
Iowa	6-month automatic extension. No paper or electronic extension request required.	90% of tax liability must be paid by original due date of return to avoid penalties.
Kansas	6-month automatic extension. No paper or electronic extension request required.	90% of outstanding tax liability must be paid with K-40V by original due date of return to avoid penalties. Extension payment box on K-40V must be checked. If federal extension is filed, copy must be enclosed when return is filed.

Jurisdiction	General Taxpayers	Comment
Kentucky	Automatic extension equal to federal extension period if federal application form is filed by original due date of return; **or** 6-month state extension may be granted for reasonable cause if Form 740EXT is filed by original due date of return. Inability to pay is not a valid reason.	75% of outstanding tax liability must be paid by original return due date to avoid penalties. Payment must accompany lower portion of federal extension application or payment voucher section of Form 740EXT. Copy of extension must be attached to return when filed. Electronic filing available.
Louisiana	6-month extension may be requested by original due date of return with: • a Department paper form; • electronic application for extension; or • copy of federal extension form.	100% of outstanding tax liability must be paid by original due date of return to avoid interest and penalties. Copy of federal extension form must be submitted with Form R-2867. Effective June 4, 2020, if a disaster or emergency is declared by the Louisiana Governor or the U.S. President, the Department of Revenue may extend tax return filing and payment deadlines by no more than six months. Interest may accrue during the extension in the case of a governor-declared disaster, but not during a presidentially-declared disaster.
Maine	6-month automatic extension. Additional time to file may be requested in writing prior to expiration of automatic extension period. Total extension period generally cannot exceed 8 months.	90% of outstanding tax liability must be paid with Form 1040EXT-ME or electronically by original due date of return to avoid penalties.
Maryland	6-month automatic extension if federal extension or Form 502E is filed by original due date of return.	100% of tax liability must be paid with Form 502E by original due date of return to avoid penalties. Electronic filing and payment available.
Massachusetts	6-month automatic extension if 80% of any outstanding tax liability has been paid by original due date of return. No paper or electronic extension request required.	80% of outstanding tax liability must be paid with Form 4868 or electronically by original due date of return or extension will be void. Penalties and interest will also apply. **Tax returns before December 5, 2016:** 6-month automatic extension if: • no tax was due and 100% of outstanding tax liability was paid by original due date of the return; or • Form M-8736 was filed and 80% of outstanding tax liability was paid by original due date of return.
Michigan	6-month automatic extension if copy of federal extension or Form 4 is filed by original due date of return.	No extension request required if no tax is due or taxpayer is due a refund. Copy of federal or state extension must be attached to return when filed.
Minnesota	6-month automatic extension. No paper or electronic extension request required.	90% of outstanding tax liability must be paid with Form M13 by original due date of return to avoid penalties.
Mississippi	6-month automatic extension if federal extension or Form 80-106 is filed by due date of original return and no tax is due.	100% of outstanding tax liability must be paid with Form 80-106 by original due date of return to avoid penalties.

Jurisdiction	General Taxpayers	Comment
Missouri	6-month automatic extension if federal extension is filed or Form MO-60 is filed and tax paid by original due date of return.	100% of outstanding tax liability must be paid with Form MO-60 by original due date of return to avoid penalties. Copy of federal extension must be attached to return when filed.
Montana	6-month automatic extension. Prior to 2010 tax year, 6-month automatic extension only if federal extension was filed and tax paid by original due date of return.	Penalties avoided if: • 90% of outstanding current year tax liability paid with Form EXT-13 (EXT-12 for 2012 tax year); • 100% of previous year's tax liability paid with Form EXT-13 (EXT-12 for 2012 tax year); or • beginning with 2012 tax year, total tax liability for current year is $200 or less. Prior to 2010 tax year, extension indicator box had to be checked and, unless return was filed electronically, a copy of federal extension had to be attached when return was filed. For post-2011 reporting periods, no penalty or interest imposed on taxpayers who owe $200 or less if paid by extended due date.
Nebraska	6-month automatic extension if federal extension is filed by original due date of return.	Copy of federal extension or schedule with electronic confirmation number and explanation must be attached to return when filed. Form 4868N is not necessary if a federal extension has been filed or if the return is being e-filed by a paid tax preparer.
New Hampshire	7-month automatic extension if no tax due, otherwise Form DP-59-A must be filed and postmarked by original due date of return.	100% of tax liability must be submitted with extension form or by electronic means before midnight on return due date to avoid penalties.
New Jersey	6-month automatic extension if federal extension or Form NJ-630 is filed by original due date of return. Additional extension may be granted if exceptional circumstances exist.	80% of tax liability must be paid with Form NJ-630 by original due date of return to avoid penalties. If federal extension is filed, extension box or electronic filing confirmation number must be filled in at top of return and copy of extension must be enclosed with return when filed.
New Mexico	6-month automatic extension if federal extension is filed by original due date of return. Additional extension for good cause may be requested on Form RPD-41096. 60-day automatic extension if Form RPD-41096 is postmarked by original due date of return. Additional extension up to 12 months may be granted upon showing of good cause.	100% of tax liability must be paid by original due date of return to avoid interest. Penalties waived during extension period.

Jurisdiction	General Taxpayers	Comment
New York	6-month automatic extension if Form IT-370 is filed by original due date of return.	90% of outstanding tax liability must be paid with Form IT-370 by original due date of return to avoid penalties. Electronic filing generally required for tax preparers. Electronic payment optional if department website used, required if tax preparation software used. For tax years before 2011, copy of federal extension could be filed in place of Form IT-370 if taxpayer expected refund or anticipated owing no tax.
North Carolina	Automatic extension equal to federal extension period. 6-month automatic extension if Form D-410P is filed by original due date of return. **Tax years before 2019:** 6-month automatic state extension if Form D-410P is filed by original due date of return.	90% of tax liability must be paid by original due date of return to avoid penalties. Electronic filing available.
North Dakota	6-month automatic extension if federal extension is filed by original due date of return. Reasonable extension of time may be granted for good cause if Form 101 is filed and postmarked by due date of original return.	100% of tax liability must be paid by extended due date of return to avoid penalties. Circle next to "Extension" must be filled in at top of return.
Ohio	6-month automatic extension if federal extension is filed by original due date of return.	90% of tax liability must be paid with Form IT 40P by original due date of return to avoid penalties. Copy of federal extension form, extension confirmation number, or extension acknowledgement must be attached to return when filed.
Oklahoma	6-month automatic extension if federal extension or Form 504 is filed by due date of original return.	90% of tax liability must be paid with Form 504 by original due date of return to avoid penalties. Copy of federal extension must be enclosed when return is filed.
Oregon	6-month automatic extension if federal extension or Form 40-EXT is filed by original due date of return.	90% of tax liability must be paid with Form 40-EXT by original due date of return to avoid penalties. Extension should not be attached to return. Copy should be retained with taxpayer's records. Extension box must be checked at top of return.
Pennsylvania	6-month automatic extension if federal extension is filed by original due date of return and no tax is due. 6-month extension if Form Rev-276 is filed before original due date of return and adequate explanation of reason for delay is provided.	100% of tax due must be paid using Form Rev-276, electronic funds transfer, or credit card, by original due date of return to avoid penalties. Extension request oval must be filled in at top of return. Copy of federal extension must be submitted by return due date.
Rhode Island	6-month automatic extension if federal extension or Form RI-4868 is filed by original due date of return.	100% of tax due must be paid with Form RI-4868 by original due date of return to avoid penalties. Copy of extension must be attached to front of return when filed. If federal extension was filed electronically, acknowledgement must be attached to front of return when filed.

Jurisdiction	General Taxpayers	Comment
South Carolina	6-month automatic extension if federal extension or Form SC-4868 is filed by original due date of return.	90% of tax liability must be paid with Form SC-4868 by original due date of return to avoid penalties. Copy of extension must be attached to back of return when filed. Extension box should be checked on front of return. Electronic filing available.
Tennessee	6-month automatic extension if federal extension is filed by original due date of return or Form INC-251 is attached to return when filed.	100% of tax liability must be paid by extended due date of return to avoid penalties. Copy of extension must be attached to return when filed. Electronic filing available.
Utah	6-month automatic extension. For 2019 tax year, automatic extension until last day of federal extension. No paper or electronic extension request required.	90% of current year tax or 100% of previous year's tax must be paid by original due date of return (or, for 2019 tax year, automatically extended return due date) to avoid penalties. Payments of outstanding tax liability may be made with Form TC-546 or online.
Vermont	6-month automatic extension if Form IN-151 is filed by original due date of return. Return may be filed up to 60 days after due date without being charged a late file penalty even if Form IN-151 is not filed.	100% of tax liability must be paid by original due date of return to avoid penalties.
Virginia	6-month automatic extension. No paper or electronic extension request required.	90% of outstanding tax liability must be paid with Form 760IP by original due date of return to avoid penalties.
West Virginia	6-month automatic extension if federal extension or Schedule-L is filed by original due date of return.	100% of tax due must be paid with Schedule L by original due date of return to avoid penalties. Date of federal extension period, or "Federal Extension Granted" and confirmation number if granted electronically, must be written at top of return. Extended due date must be written in appropriate box. Copy of federal extension must be enclosed with return when filed.
Wisconsin	6-month automatic extension if federal extension is filed by original due date of return.	No paper or electronic extension application required prior to filing return. Copy of federal extension, or statement indicating which federal extension provision taxpayer wants to apply for state purposes, must be enclosed with return when filed.

S Corporations: Recognition of Federal Election

The following chart indicates whether states conform to the federal pass-through treatment of S corporations if the corporation has filed a valid S corporation election for federal tax purposes. Most states generally recognize the federal S corporation election, but some states require compliance with additional filing requirements and conditions. The chart does not address state recognition of qualified Subchapter S subsidiary (QSSS) elections. The chart also does not reflect whether the states impose any entity-level tax on S corporations. Entity-level taxes are addressed in the charts under the topic S Corporations: Taxation.

Jurisdiction	S Corporations	Comment
Alabama	State recognizes federal S corporation election.	
Alaska	State recognizes federal S corporation election.	
Arizona	State recognizes federal S corporation election.	
Arkansas	**Tax years before 2018:** State does not recognize federal S corporation election. **Tax years beginning on and after January 1, 2018:** Same as federal.	For tax years prior to 2018, election form AR1103, must be filed in duplicate within first 75 days of first tax year. Copy of federal S corporation acceptance form and consent to election by all shareholders must be attached to state election form.
California	State recognizes federal S corporation election.	
Colorado	State recognizes federal S corporation election.	
Connecticut	State recognizes federal S corporation election.	
Delaware	State recognizes federal S corporation election.	
District of Columbia	State does not recognize federal S corporation election.	S corporations taxed in same manner as other corporations.
Florida	State recognizes federal S corporation election.	No pass-through of income to shareholders because no state individual income tax.
Georgia	State recognizes federal S corporation election.	Recognized as long as all shareholders are subject to tax in state.
Hawaii	State recognizes federal S corporation election.	
Idaho	State recognizes federal S corporation election.	Copy of federal election or notice approving federal election must be attached to first state return.
Illinois	State recognizes federal S corporation election.	

Jurisdiction	S Corporations	Comment
Indiana	State recognizes federal S corporation election.	
Iowa	State recognizes federal S corporation election.	
Kansas	State recognizes federal S corporation election.	
Kentucky	State recognizes federal S corporation election.	
Louisiana	State does not recognize federal S corporation election.	S corporations taxed in same manner as other corporations. Effective for tax periods beginning on and after January 1, 2019, pass-through entities may elect to be taxed as if filing as a C corporation at the federal level.
Maine	State recognizes federal S corporation election.	
Maryland	State recognizes federal S corporation election.	
Massachusetts	State recognizes federal S corporation election.	
Michigan	State recognizes federal S corporation election.	
Minnesota	State recognizes federal S corporation election.	
Mississippi	State recognizes federal S corporation election.	
Missouri	State recognizes federal S corporation election.	
Montana	State recognizes federal S corporation election.	
Nebraska	State recognizes federal S corporation election.	
Nevada	N/A, because state does not tax pass-through income.	
New Hampshire	State does not recognize federal S corporation election.	S corporations required to pay business profits tax.
New Jersey	State does not recognize federal S corporation election.	Federal S corporations must make separate state election on Form CBT-2553.
New Mexico	State recognizes federal S corporation election.	
New York	State does not recognize federal S corporation election.	S corporations must make separate election with state, unless mandatory state S election applies.
North Carolina	State recognizes federal S corporation election.	

Jurisdiction	S Corporations	Comment
North Dakota	State recognizes federal S corporation election.	
Ohio	Subject to CAT.	
Oklahoma	State recognizes federal S corporation election.	Except as provided for in the Pass-Through Entity Tax Equity Act of 2019, under which an S corporation elects to pay a pass-through entity tax.
Oregon	State recognizes federal S corporation election.	
Pennsylvania	State recognizes federal S corporation election.	Federal election automatically applies unless S corporation elects out with approval of all shareholders.
Rhode Island	State recognizes federal S corporation election.	
South Carolina	State recognizes federal S corporation election.	
South Dakota	N/A, because state does not tax pass-through income.	
Tennessee	State does not recognize federal S corporation election.	S corporations taxed in same manner as other corporations.
Texas	State recognizes S corporation election, but entity taxed in same manner as other corporations.	Franchise tax imposed.
Utah	State recognizes federal S corporation election.	
Vermont	State recognizes federal S corporation election.	
Virginia	State recognizes federal S corporation election.	
Washington	N/A, because state does not tax pass-through income.	
West Virginia	State recognizes federal S corporation election.	
Wisconsin	State recognizes federal S corporation election.	
Wyoming	N/A, because state does not tax pass-through income.	

S Corporations: Taxation

Jurisdiction	S Corporations	Comment
Alabama	Business privilege tax imposed on taxable net worth.	
Alaska	No entity-level tax measured by income or net worth/capital value.	
Arizona	No entity-level tax measured by income or net worth/capital value.	
Arkansas	No entity-level tax measured by income or net worth/capital value.	
California	Income tax imposed at 1.5% (3.5% for financial S corporations). $800 minimum tax.	Alternative minimum tax not imposed on S corporations.
Colorado	No entity-level tax measured by income or net worth/capital value.	
Connecticut	Pass-through entity tax imposed a rate of 6.99% for tax years after 2017. $250 biennial assessment, known as business entity tax (BET) for tax years before 2020.	
Delaware	Franchise tax imposed on authorized number of shares or assumed capital value.	
District of Columbia	Franchise tax imposed on taxable income.	
Florida	No entity-level tax measured by income or net worth/capital value.	
Georgia	Graduated tax imposed on net worth tax including issued capital stock, paid-in surplus, and earned surplus.	
Hawaii	No entity-level tax measured by income or net worth/capital value.	
Idaho	$20 minimum tax and $10 additional tax unless all income or loss is distributed or otherwise reportable and S corporation does not have any taxable income attributable to state sources, otherwise no entity-level tax measured by income or net worth/capital value.	An S corporation filing an Idaho corporate return must pay tax upon its net recognized built-in gain and its excess net passive investment income apportionable or allocable to the state.
Illinois	1.5% personal property replacement income tax.	
Indiana	No entity-level tax measured by income or net worth/capital value.	
Iowa	No entity-level tax measured by income or net worth/capital value.	
Kansas	No entity-level tax measured by income or net worth/capital value.	

Jurisdiction	S Corporations	Comment
Kentucky	Every S corporation with over $3 million in gross receipts or gross profits must pay the greater of $175 or an annual limited liability entity tax (LLET) equal to lesser of: • 9.5 cents per $100 of Kentucky gross receipts; or • 75 cents per $100 of Kentucky gross profits. If gross receipts or gross profits are over $3 million but less than $6 million, gross receipts may be reduced by $2,850 or gross profits by $22,500 multiplied by a numerator of $6 million less the amount of gross receipts or gross profits for the taxable year, and a denominator of $3 million.	
Louisiana	Franchise tax imposed on issued and outstanding capital stock, surplus, and undivided profits.	Effective for tax periods beginning on and after January 1, 2019, pass-through entities may elect to be taxed as if filing as a C corporation at the federal level.
Maine	No entity-level tax measured by income or net worth/capital value.	
Maryland	No entity-level tax measured by income or net worth/capital value.	Beginning with tax year 2020, state allows pass-through entities to elect to be taxed at the entity level.
Massachusetts	*Greater of:* $2.60 per $1,000 on taxable tangible property or net worth **plus** • 2% on total receipts of $6 million or more, but less than 9 million; or • 3% on total receipts of $9 million or more *or* $456 fixed dollar minimum tax.	**2019 Net Income Tax Rates:** • 1.97% on total receipts of $6 million or more, but less than 9 million; or • 2.95% on total receipts of $9 million or more **2016-2018 Net Income Tax Rates:** • 1.93% on total receipts of $6 million or more, but less than 9 million; or • 2.9% on total receipts of $9 million or more. **2015 Net Income Tax Rates:** • 1.9% on total receipts of $6 million or more, but less than 9 million; or • 2.85% on total receipts of $9 million or more.
Michigan	No entity-level tax measured by income or net worth/capital value, unless S corporation has certificated credits and has elected to pay the Michigan Business Tax (MBT).	
Minnesota	Graduated minimum fee imposed based on property, payroll, and sales or receipts attributable to state sources. Otherwise, no entity-level tax measured by income or net worth/capital value.	
Mississippi	Franchise tax imposed on capital, surplus, undivided profits and true reserves employed in the state.	

Jurisdiction	S Corporations	Comment
Missouri	No entity-level tax measured by income or net worth/capital value.	
Montana	No entity-level tax measured by income or net worth/capital value.	
Nebraska	Biennial occupation (franchise) fee based on paid-up capital stock.	
Nevada	N/A, because state does not tax pass-through income.	
New Hampshire	Business profits tax based on gross income. Business enterprise tax based on compensation, interest, and dividends.	
New Jersey	**Fixed dollar minimum tax after 2011:** $0-$99,999 gross receipts: $375 $100,000-$249,999 gross receipts: $562.50 $250,000-$499,999 gross receipts: $750 $500,000-$999,999 gross receipts: $1,125 $1,000,000 gross receipts or more: $1,500.	Corporation business tax (CBT) imposed at corporate tax rate on entire net income of corporations that have not made S corporation election for state purposes or that have income subject to federal taxation. **Pass-through business alternative tax.** After 2019, an S corporation with at least one member subject to New Jersey income tax on the proceeds of the pass-through entity can elect to pay the pass-through business alternative income tax.
New Mexico	Franchise tax.	
New York	Fixed dollar minimum tax based on receipts attributable to state sources imposed as follows: $0 - $100,000 receipts: $25 $100,001 - $250,000 receipts: $50 $250,001 - $500,000 receipts: $175 $500,001 - $1,000,000 receipts: $300 $1,000,001 - $5,000,000 receipts: $1,000 $5,000,001 - $25,000,000 receipts: $3,000 over $25,000,000 receipts: $4,500. Otherwise no entity-level tax measured by income or net worth/ capital value.	Reduced fixed dollar minimum tax amounts apply to qualified in-state manufacturers and qualified emerging technology companies.
North Carolina	Effective beginning on or after January 1, 2019, franchise tax imposed at rate of $200 for first $1 million of the tax base and $1.50 per $1,000 of the tax base that is more than $1 million. $200 minimum tax.	Franchise tax imposed on largest of: • net worth (capital stock, surplus and undivided profits for tax years before 2017); • actual investment in tangible property in the state; or • 55% of appraised value of real/tangible property in the state.
North Dakota	No entity-level tax measured by income or net worth/capital value.	
Ohio	CAT imposed on gross receipts.	

Jurisdiction	S Corporations	Comment
Oklahoma	Franchise tax imposed for prior tax years on capital used, invested, or employed in the state.	**Pass-through Entity Tax:** An S corporation can elect to pay the pass-through entity tax, the amount of tax due is the sum of total tax attributable to each shareholder.
Oregon	$150 minimum tax, otherwise no entity-level tax measured by income or net worth/capital value.	**Corporate Activity Tax:** Beginning in 2020, S corporations may be required to pay CAT.
Pennsylvania	No entity-level tax measured by income or net worth/capital value.	
Rhode Island	**Tax years after 2016:** Fee equal to $400 minimum tax, otherwise no entity-level tax measured by income or net worth/ capital value. **Tax year 2016:** Fee equal to $450 minimum tax, otherwise no entity-level tax measured by income or net worth/ capital value. **Tax years prior to 2016:** Fee equal to $500 minimum tax, otherwise no entity-level tax measured by income or net worth/ capital value.	For tax years beginning on or after January 1, 2019, a pass-through entity may elect to pay the state tax at the entity level. Such entities that make the election are subject to a tax rate of 5.99%.
South Carolina	Corporation license fee (franchise tax) imposed on total capital and paid-in surplus.	
South Dakota	N/A, because state does not tax pass-through income.	
Tennessee	Excise tax imposed on net earnings and franchise tax imposed on net worth or actual value of tangible property.	
Texas	Revised franchise (margin) tax imposed if total revenues exceed $1,000,000 as adjusted for inflation ($1,180,000 for 2020-2021, $1,130,000 for 2018-2019, $1,110,000 for 2016-2017).	
Utah	No entity-level tax measured by income or net worth/capital value.	
Vermont	$250 minimum tax, otherwise no entity-level tax measured by income or net worth/capital value.	
Virginia	No entity-level tax measured by income or net worth/capital value.	Bank franchise tax may apply.
Washington	N/A, because state does not tax pass-through income.	
West Virginia	No entity-level tax measured by income or net worth/capital value.	

Jurisdiction	S Corporations	Comment
Wisconsin	Franchise tax imposed at rate of 7.9% on interest income attributable to the state. Economic development surcharge imposed on gross receipts of $4 million or more equal to greater of $25 or 0.2% (0.002) of net income attributable to the state, but not more than $9,800.	Beginning with tax year 2018, state allows S corporations to elect to be taxed at the entity level.
Wyoming	N/A, because state does not tax pass-through income.	

Sales Factor Rules—Destination Test

Under the Uniform Division of Income for Tax Purposes Act (UDITPA) and Multistate Tax Commission (MTC) Model Apportionment Regulations, sales of tangible personal property, except sales to the United States Government, are in the state if the property is delivered or shipped to a purchaser within the state, regardless of the f.o.b. point or other conditions of the sale. The MTC regulations further provide that property is deemed to be delivered or shipped to a purchaser within the state if the recipient is located in the state, even though the property is ordered from outside the state. Property is delivered or shipped to a purchaser within the state if the shipment terminates in the state, even though the property is subsequently transferred by the purchaser to another state. This chart shows whether each state and the District of Columbia follow the destination test for determining the sales factor of the general apportionment formula and computing corporation income tax liability.

Jurisdiction	Destination Test	Comment
Alabama	Yes	
Alaska	Yes	
Arizona	Yes	
Arkansas	Yes	
California	Yes	
Colorado	Yes	
Connecticut	Yes	
Delaware	Yes	
District of Columbia	Yes	
Florida	Yes	
Georgia	Yes, except when property is picked up by an out-of-state customer at taxpayer's place of business in the state for transport out of the state.	
Hawaii	Yes	
Idaho	Yes	
Illinois	Yes	Sales of tangible personal property are not from state if seller and purchaser would be members of same unitary business group but for the fact that either seller or purchaser is a person with 80% or more of total business activity outside of the United States and property is purchased for resale.
Indiana	Yes	

Jurisdiction	Destination Test	Comment
Iowa	Yes, except when property is picked up by an out-of-state customer at taxpayer's place of business in the state for transport out of the state.	
Kansas	Yes	
Kentucky	Yes	
Louisiana	Yes	
Maine	Yes	
Maryland	Yes	
Massachusetts	Yes	
Michigan	Yes	
Minnesota	Yes	
Mississippi	Yes	
Missouri	Yes	
Montana	Yes	
Nebraska	Yes	
Nevada	N/A, because state does not tax general business corporation income.	
New Hampshire	Yes.	
New Jersey	Yes	
New Mexico	Yes	
New York	Yes	
North Carolina	Yes	
North Dakota	Yes	
Ohio	Yes for gross receipts.	
Oklahoma	Yes	
Oregon	Yes	
Pennsylvania	Yes	
Rhode Island	Yes	
South Carolina	Yes	
South Dakota	N/A, because state does not tax general business corporation income.	
Tennessee	Yes	
Texas	Yes	
Utah	Yes	
Vermont	Yes	

Jurisdiction	Destination Test	Comment
Virginia	Yes	
Washington	N/A, because state does not tax general business corporation income.	
West Virginia	Yes	
Wisconsin	Yes	
Wyoming	N/A, because state does not tax general business corporation income.	

Sales Factor Rules—Income-Producing Activity and Cost of Performance Sourcing

Under the income-producing activity and costs of performance sourcing rules, sales other than sales of tangible personal property are sourced to the taxing state, if the income-producing activity is performed entirely in the state. Sales are also sourced to the state, if the income-producing activity is performed both inside and outside the taxing state, but a greater proportion of the income-producing activity is performed in the state based on costs of performance. This income-producing activity and cost of performance method applies to income from service, rental income from real or tangible personal property, income from intangibles, and income from the sale of real property. This chart shows whether each state and the District of Columbia use the income-producing activity and cost of performance method for determining the sales factor of the general apportionment formula and computing corporation income tax liability.

Jurisdiction	Application of Rule	Comment
Alabama	No, for taxable years beginning on or after December 31, 2010.	Yes, for taxable years beginning before December 31, 2010.
Alaska	Yes	
Arizona	Yes, except multistate service providers that elect a combination of income-producing activity and market-based sourcing for taxable years after 2013.	For a multistate service provider that is a regionally accredited institution of higher education with at least one university campus in Arizona on which at least 2,000 students reside, the election will apply only to the treatment of sales for educational services.
Arkansas	Yes, except income attributed to sources based percentage method for apportioning business income, rather than based on cost of performance.	
California	No, for tax years after 2012.	Yes, for tax years prior to 2013, except for taxpayers after 2010 tax year that elect to use single sales factor apportionment formula.
Colorado	Yes for services, using direct cost of performance or using time spent in the performance of the service for purely personal services.	
Connecticut	No	
Delaware	No	Receipts from state sources include income activity that is performed within the state.
District of Columbia	Yes, for tax years before 2015.	
Florida	Yes	
Georgia	No	
Hawaii	Yes, except for intangibles and services for tax years beginning after 2019.	No, for intangibles and services for tax years beginning after 2019.

Jurisdiction	Application of Rule	Comment
Idaho	Yes	
Illinois	No, except for: • tax years before 2009; and • interest, net gains, and other items of income from intangible personal property received by a taxpayer who is not a dealer in that property.	
Indiana	No, except for: • broadcasting services; and • telecommunication services. Yes, before 2019.	
Iowa	No	
Kansas	Yes	
Kentucky	Yes, for tax years before 2018.	
Louisiana	No	
Maine	No, except when the customer for services or the purchaser of intangible property is the federal government.	
Maryland	No	
Massachusetts	No	Yes, for tax years before 2014.
Michigan	Yes, tax years prior to 2008.	
Minnesota	No	
Mississippi	Yes, except receipts attributed to state to extent such receipts represent activities actually performed within the state, rather than based on cost of performance.	
Missouri	Yes, for taxable years beginning before 2020.	No, for taxable years beginning after 2019.
Montana	Yes, for tax years beginning before 2018.	
Nebraska	Yes, prior to tax year 2014 No, after tax year 2013.	
Nevada	N/A, because state does not tax general business corporation income.	
New Hampshire	Yes, for tax years before 2021.	Market-based sourcing adopted effective January 1, 2021 and applicable to tax periods ending before December 31, 2021.
New Jersey	Yes for services performed both inside and outside the state, using cost of performance, amount of time spent in the performance of such services, or some other reasonable method.	
New Mexico	No, for tax years after 2019. Yes, for tax years before 2020.	

Jurisdiction	Application of Rule	Comment
New York	No	
North Carolina	Yes for services, except receipts attributed to state based on proportion of time spent in performing such services in the state, rather than based on cost of performance. **Tax years after 2019:** Yes for services, if taxpayer makes net loss apportionment election.	
North Dakota	Yes	
Ohio	Letter from Ways and Means Ranking Member Neal to Chairman Brady No	
Oklahoma	No	
Oregon	Yes	
Pennsylvania	Yes, for intangibles and receipts from other than: • sale, lease, rental or other use of real property; • rental, lease or licensing of tangible property; and • services.	
Rhode Island	No	
South Carolina	Yes for services, except receipts attributed to state to extent activity is performed within the state, rather than based on cost of performance.	
South Dakota	N/A, because state does not tax general business corporation income.	
Tennessee	Yes, effective for tax years before July 1, 2016. No, effective for tax years beginning on or after July 1, 2016.	Taxpayers may elect to apply sourcing method in effect (earnings producing activity sourcing) before January 1, 2016 if: • application of market based sourcing results in lower apportionment factor; • the election results in a higher apportionment factor; and • the taxpayer has net earnings for that tax year.
Texas	No	
Utah	Yes, prior to 2009 tax year.	
Vermont	Yes, until January 1, 2020.	
Virginia	Yes	
Washington	N/A, because state does not tax general business corporation income.	
West Virginia	Yes	
Wisconsin	No	Yes, for taxable years before 2009.

Jurisdiction	Application of Rule	Comment
Wyoming	N/A, because state does not tax general business corporation income.	

Sales Factor Rules—Throwback or Throwout Rules

Under the Uniform Division of Income for Tax Purposes Act (UDITPA) throwback rule, sales of tangible personal property are thrown back to the state from which the property was shipped if the seller is not taxable in the destination state or if the purchaser is the U.S. government. Under an alternative throwout rule, which is not addressed by UDITPA, sales made to states in which the taxpayer is not taxable are thrown out of both the numerator and the denominator of the sales factor.

In combined reporting states, the question is whether "taxpayer" means the specific member of the unitary group making the sale or all members of the group. In states that follow the Joyce rule, the taxpayer means only the group member that made the sale and throwback is avoided only if the selling member has nexus in the destination state. In states that follow the Finnigan rule, taxpayer means all members of the unitary group and throwback is avoided if any group member has nexus in the destination state.

This chart shows whether each state and the District of Columbia follow a sales factor throwback or throwout rule and, in combined reporting states, the Joyce or Finnigan rule.

Jurisdiction	Sales of Tangible Personal Property	Comment
Alabama	Throwback rule applies to sales of tangible personal property if: • property shipped from state to purchaser in another state and taxpayer is not taxable in destination state; • property shipped from state to U.S. government.	
Alaska	Throwback rule applies to sales of tangible personal property if: • property shipped from state to purchaser in another state and taxpayer is not taxable in destination state; • property shipped from state to U.S. government.	Throwback rule for combined reporting groups is avoided only if selling member has nexus with destination state (Joyce).
Arizona	No throwback or throwout rule.	
Arkansas	Throwback rule applies to sales of tangible personal property if: • property shipped from state to purchaser in another state and taxpayer is not taxable in destination state; • property shipped from state to U.S. government.	

Jurisdiction	Sales of Tangible Personal Property	Comment
California	Throwback rule applies to sales of tangible personal property if: • property shipped from state to purchaser in another state and taxpayer is not taxable in destination state; • property shipped from state to U.S. government.	Throwback rule for combined reporting groups is avoided if any group member has nexus with destination state (Finnigan).
Colorado	Throwback rule applies if: • sales of tangible personal property are shipped from state to purchaser in another state and taxpayer is not taxable in destination state; and • taxpayer's commercial domicile is in the state and patents and copyrights are used in a state in which taxpayer is not taxable.	Throwback rule for combined reporting groups is avoided only if selling member has nexus with destination state (Joyce).
Connecticut	Yes, if property is not held primarily for sale to customers in the ordinary course of trade or business.	**Tax years before 2016:** No throwback or throwout rule.
Delaware	No throwback or throwout rule.	
District of Columbia	Throwback rule applies to sales of tangible personal property if: • property shipped from District to purchaser in another state and taxpayer is not taxable in destination state; and • property shipped from District to U.S. government.	Throwback rule for combined reporting groups is avoided only if selling member has nexus with destination state (Joyce).
Florida	No throwback or throwout rule.	
Georgia	No throwback or throwout rule.	
Hawaii	Throwback rule applies to sales of tangible personal property if: • property shipped from state to purchaser in another state and taxpayer is not taxable in destination state; • property shipped from state to U.S. government.	Throwback rule for combined reporting groups is avoided only if selling member has nexus with destination state (Joyce).
Idaho	Throwback rule applies to sales of tangible personal property if: • property shipped from state to purchaser in another state and taxpayer is not taxable in destination state; • property shipped from state to U.S. government.	Throwback rule for combined reporting groups is avoided only if selling member has nexus with destination state (Joyce).
Illinois	Throwback rule applies to sales of tangible personal property if: • property shipped from state to purchaser in another state and taxpayer is not taxable in destination state; • property shipped from state to U.S. government.	Exception to throwback for premises owned or leased by person who has independently contracted with seller for printing of newspapers, periodicals or books. Throwback rule for combined reporting groups is avoided only if selling member has nexus with destination state (Joyce).

Jurisdiction	Sales of Tangible Personal Property	Comment
Indiana	No throwback or throwout rule.	Prior to 2016, throwback rule applied to sales of tangible personal property if: • property shipped from state to purchaser in another state and taxpayer was not taxable in destination state; • property shipped from state to U.S. government. Throwback rule for combined reporting groups was avoided if any group member had nexus with destination state (Finnigan).
Iowa	No throwback or throwout rule.	
Kansas	Throwback rule applies to sales of tangible personal property if: • property shipped from state to purchaser in another state and taxpayer is not taxable in destination state; • property shipped from state to U.S. government.	Throwback rule for combined reporting groups is avoided if any group member has nexus with destination state (Finnigan).
Kentucky	Throwback rule applies to sales of tangible personal property if property shipped from state to U.S. government.	
Louisiana	Throwback rule applies to sales of tangible personal property if: • taxpayer is not taxable in the state to which the sale is assigned; or • state of assignment cannot be determined or reasonably approximated.	**Tax years before 2016:** No throwback or throwout rule.
Maine	Throwout rule applies to sales of tangible personal property shipped from state to purchaser in another state and taxpayer is not taxable in destination state. Throwback rule applies to sales of tangible personal property shipped from state to U.S. government.	Throwout rule for combined reporting groups is avoided if any group member has nexus with destination state (Finnigan).
Maryland	No throwback or throwout rule.	
Massachusetts	Throwback rule applies to sales of tangible personal property if: • property shipped from state to purchaser in another state and taxpayer is not taxable in destination state; and • property is not sold by agent of taxpayer who is chiefly situated at, connected with, or sent out from taxpayer's owned or rented business premises outside of state.	Throwback rule for combined reporting groups is avoided if any group member has nexus with destination state (Finnigan).
Michigan	No throwback or throwout rule.	
Minnesota	No throwback or throwout rule.	

Jurisdiction	Sales of Tangible Personal Property	Comment
Mississippi	Throwback rule applies to sales of tangible personal property if: • property shipped from state to purchaser in another state and taxpayer is not taxable in destination state; • property shipped from state to U.S. government.	Throwback rule for combined reporting groups is avoided only if selling member has nexus with destination state (Joyce).
Missouri	Throwback rule applies to sales of tangible personal property if: • property shipped from state to purchaser in another state and taxpayer is not taxable in destination state; • property shipped from state to U.S. government.	
Montana	Throwback rule applies to sales of tangible personal property if: • property shipped from state to purchaser in another state and taxpayer is not taxable in destination state; • property shipped from state to U.S. government.	Throwback rule for combined reporting groups is avoided if any group member has nexus with destination state (Finnigan). **Tax years before 2018:** Throwback rule for combined reporting groups is avoided only if selling member has nexus with destination state (Joyce).
Nebraska	No throwback or throwout rule.	
Nevada	N/A, because state does not tax general business corporation income.	
New Hampshire	Throwback rule applies to sales of tangible personal property if: • property shipped from state to purchaser in another state and taxpayer is not taxable in destination state; • property shipped from state to U.S. government.	Throwback rule for combined reporting groups is avoided only if selling member has nexus with destination state (Joyce).
New Jersey	No throwback or throwout rule.	
New Mexico	Throwback rule applies to sales of tangible personal property if: • property shipped from state to purchaser in another state and taxpayer is not taxable in destination state; • property shipped from state to U.S. government. Throwback rule for property shipped to state where taxpayer is not taxable does not apply if: • taxpayer is manufacturer electing alternative apportionment formula for tax years after 2013; or • taxpayer's principal business activity in state is "headquarters operation" and elects to use single-sales factor apportionment formula for tax years after 2014.	Throwback rule for combined reporting groups is avoided only if selling member has nexus with destination state (Joyce).
New York	No throwback or throwout rule.	

Jurisdiction	Sales of Tangible Personal Property	Comment
North Carolina	No statutory throwback or throwout rule.	For corporations permitted to apportion income, only those sales made within North Carolina are required to be included in the numerator of the sales factor. However, sales of a corporation which is not required to file an income tax return in another state are considered to be in North Carolina.
North Dakota	Throwback rule applies to sales of tangible personal property if: • property shipped from state to purchaser in another state and taxpayer is not taxable in destination state; • property shipped from state to U.S. government.	Throwback rule for combined reporting groups is avoided only if selling member has nexus with destination state (Joyce).
Ohio	No throwback or throwout rule.	
Oklahoma	Throwback rule applies to sales of tangible personal property if: • property shipped from state to purchaser in another state and taxpayer is not doing business in destination state; • property shipped from state to U.S. government.	
Oregon	Throwback rule applies to sales of tangible personal property if: • property shipped from state to purchaser in another state and taxpayer is not taxable in destination state; • property shipped from an office, store, warehouse, factory, or other place of storage in the state to U.S. government.	Sale of goods shipped from a public warehouse is not considered to take place in the state if the person storing the goods is an affiliate or related party and: • taxpayer's only activity in state is storage of goods in the public warehouse; or • taxpayer's only activities in state are storage of goods in public warehouse and presence of employees within state are solely for soliciting sales.
Pennsylvania	No throwback or throwout rule.	
Rhode Island	Throwback rule applies to sales of tangible personal property if property shipped from state to purchaser in another state and taxpayer is not taxable in destination state.	
South Carolina	No throwback or throwout rule.	
South Dakota	N/A, because state does not tax general business corporation income.	
Tennessee	Throwback rule applies to sales of tangible personal property if property shipped from state to U.S. government.	
Texas	No throwback or throwout rule.	

Jurisdiction	Sales of Tangible Personal Property	Comment
Utah	Throwback rule applies to sales of tangible personal property if: • property shipped from state to purchaser in another state and taxpayer is not taxable in destination state; • property shipped from state to U.S. government.	Throwback rule for combined reporting groups is avoided if any group member has nexus with destination state (Finnigan).
Vermont	Throwback rule applies to sales of tangible personal property if: • property shipped from state to purchaser in another state and taxpayer is not taxable in destination state; • property shipped from state to U.S. government.	Throwback rule for combined reporting groups is avoided only if selling member has nexus with destination state (Joyce).
Virginia	No throwback or throwout rule.	
Washington	N/A, because state does not tax general business corporation income.	
West Virginia	Throwout rule applies to sales assigned to state in which taxpayer is not subject to tax.	Throwout rule for taxpayers subject to combined reporting after 2008 is avoided only if selling member has nexus with destination state (Joyce).
Wisconsin	Throwback rule applies if: • Tangible personal property is shipped or sold from within the state by any taxpayer that is not taxable in the shipping/delivering state or destination state; or • Tangible personal property is shipped from within the state to U.S. government.	For taxable years beginning before 2009, throwback was 50% rather than 100%. Throwback rule for combined reporting groups in tax years after 2008 is avoided if any group member has nexus with destination state (Finnigan).
Wyoming	N/A, because state does not tax general business corporation income.	

Social Security Benefits

Under federal law, taxpayers may be required to include a portion of their Social Security benefits in their taxable adjusted gross income (AGI). Most states begin the calculation of state personal income tax liability with federal AGI, or federal taxable income, and in those states, the portion of Social Security benefits subject to federal personal income tax is subject to state personal income tax, unless state law allows taxpayers to subtract the federally taxed portion of their benefits from their federal AGI in the computation of their state AGI. This chart shows the tax treatment by each state and the District of Columbia of Social Security benefits.

Jurisdiction	Social Security Benefits	Comment
Alabama	Exclusion from gross income allowed for all benefits.	
Arizona	Subtraction allowed for federal taxable benefits.	
Arkansas	Subtraction allowed for federal taxable benefits.	
California	Subtraction allowed for federal taxable U.S. benefits.	
Colorado	Subtraction allowed for federal taxable benefits up to maximum of: • $24,000 for taxpayers who are 65 and older; and • $20,000 for taxpayers who are 55 and older or those who are second party beneficiaries to such taxpayers.	
Connecticut	Subtraction allowed equal to: • 100% of federal taxable benefits if federal AGI is less than $60,000 and filing status is filing jointly, qualifying widow(er), or head of household; • 100% of federal taxable benefits if federal AGI is less than $50,000 and filing status is single or filing separately; or • 75% of federal taxable benefits as computed on state Social Security benefit adjustment worksheet.	**Tax years after 2018:** Subtraction allowed equal to: • 100% of federal taxable benefits if federal AGI is less than $100,000 and filing status is filing jointly, qualifying widow(er), or head of household; • 100% of federal taxable benefits if federal AGI is less than $75,000 and filing status is single or filing separately; or • 75% of federal taxable benefits as computed on state Social Security benefit adjustment worksheet.
Delaware	Subtraction allowed for federal taxable benefits.	
District of Columbia	Subtraction allowed for federal taxable benefits.	
Georgia	Subtraction allowed for federal taxable benefits.	
Hawaii	Subtraction allowed for federal taxable benefits.	
Idaho	Subtraction allowed for federal taxable benefits.	

Jurisdiction	Social Security Benefits	Comment
Illinois	Subtraction allowed for federal taxable benefits.	
Indiana	Subtraction allowed for federal taxable benefits.	
Iowa	Subtraction allowed for federal taxable benefits.	For tax years before 2013, subtraction allowed equal to: • 89% of federal taxable benefits for 2013 tax year; • 77% of federal taxable benefits for 2012 tax year; • 67% of federal taxable benefits for 2011 tax year; • 55% of federal taxable benefits for 2010 tax year; • 43% of federal taxable benefits for 2009 tax year; and • 32% of federal taxable benefits for 2007 and 2008 tax years.
Kansas	Subtraction allowed for federal taxable benefits if federal AGI is $75,000 or less.	
Kentucky	Subtraction allowed for federal taxable benefits.	
Louisiana	Subtraction allowed for federal taxable benefits.	
Maine	Subtraction allowed for federal taxable benefits.	
Maryland	Subtraction allowed for federal taxable benefits.	
Massachusetts	Exclusion from gross income allowed for all benefits.	
Michigan	Subtraction allowed for federal taxable benefits.	
Minnesota	No adjustment allowed for federal taxable benefits.	
Mississippi	Exclusion from gross income allowed for all benefits.	
Missouri	Subtraction allowed for amount included in federal tax base if state AGI is $100,000 or less for married taxpayers filing jointly or $85,000 or less for any other filing status. Subtraction reduced dollar for dollar on income in excess of threshold amount for taxpayer's filing status.	
Montana	Addition to federal tax base required if state taxable benefits exceed federal taxable benefits. Subtraction allowed for all or part of federal taxable benefits that exceed state taxable benefits.	

Jurisdiction	Social Security Benefits	Comment
Nebraska	Subtraction allowed for federal taxable benefits if taxpayer's federal adjusted gross income is less than or equal to $58,000 for joint filers or $43,000 for all other filers.	For tax years prior to 2014, no adjustment allowed for federal taxable benefits.
New Hampshire	N/A, because tax imposed only on interest and dividend income.	
New Jersey	Exclusion from gross income allowed for all benefits.	
New Mexico	No adjustment allowed for federal taxable benefits.	
New York	Subtraction allowed for federal taxable benefits.	
North Carolina	Subtraction allowed for federal taxable benefits.	
North Dakota	Subtraction allowed for federal taxable benefits if taxpayer's federal adjusted gross income is less than or equal to $100,000 for joint filers or $50,000 for all other filers.	For tax years prior to 2019, no adjustment allowed for federal taxable benefits.
Ohio	Subtraction allowed for federal taxable benefits.	
Oklahoma	Subtraction allowed for federal taxable benefits.	
Oregon	Subtraction allowed for federal taxable benefits.	
Pennsylvania	Exclusion from taxable income allowed for all benefits.	
Rhode Island	**Prior to 2016 Tax Year** No adjustment allowed for federal taxable benefits. **After 2015 Tax Year** Subtraction allowed for federal taxable benefits, if federal AGI is below threshold. AGI limits are adjusted annually for inflation.	**2019 income limit:** $85,150 if filing status is single, married filing separately, or head of household; and $106,400 if filing status is married filing jointly or qualifying widow(er).
South Carolina	Subtraction allowed for federal taxable benefits.	
Tennessee	N/A, because tax imposed only on interest and dividend income.	
Utah	No adjustment allowed for federal taxable benefits.	

Jurisdiction	Social Security Benefits	Comment
Vermont	**Tax years before 2018:** No adjustment allowed for federal taxable benefits. **Tax years after 2017:** Subtraction allowed for amount included in federal tax base if federal AGI is $60,000 or less for joint filers or $45,000 or less for other filers. Subtraction reduced for income in excess of threshold.	
Virginia	Subtraction allowed for federal taxable benefits.	
West Virginia	No adjustment allowed for federal taxable benefits. **Tax years after 2019:** Subtraction allowed if federal AGI does not exceed: • $50,000 for a single individual or married individual filing separately; or • $100,000 for married couple filing jointly. Equal to: • 35% of federal taxable benefits for tax years beginning on and after January 1, 2020; • 65% of federal taxable benefits for tax years beginning on and after January 1, 2021; and • 100% of federal taxable benefits for tax years beginning on and after January 1, 2022.	
Wisconsin	Subtraction allowed for federal taxable benefits.	

Standard Deduction

Under IRC Sec. 63, most individual taxpayers who do not itemize their deductions can subtract a standard deduction amount from adjusted gross income to arrive at taxable income. The basic standard deduction amount depends on filing status. The dollar amount of the standard deduction changes every year based on cost-of-living adjustments. An additional standard deduction is provided for elderly/blind taxpayers. The federal standard deduction for 2017 is: $12,700 for joint filers and surviving spouses, $6,350 for single and married filing separately, and $9,350 for heads of household. The federal standard deduction for 2018 are: $24,000 joint filers and surviving spouses, $12,000 for single and married filing separately, and $18,000 for heads of household. This chart identifies whether the state allows a standard deduction and an additional deduction for elderly/blind taxpayers that is the same or similar to the federal deductions.

Jurisdiction	Standard Deduction	Comment
Alabama	$2,000 up to $2,500 if filing status is single; $2,000 up to $3,750 if filing status is married filing separately; $4,000 up to $7,500 if filing status is married filing jointly; and $2,000 up to $4,700 if filing status is head of family.	Standard deduction amount ranges based on AGI. No additional deduction for elderly/blind taxpayers. Effective for tax years beginning 2018 and beyond, increased optional standard deduction available.
Arizona	**2020 Tax Year:** $24,800 if filing status is married filing jointly; $18,650 if filing status is head of household; and $12,400 if filing status is single or married filing separately. **2019 Tax Year:** $24,400 if filing status is married filing jointly; $18,350 if filing status is head of household; and $12,200 if filing status is single or married filing separately.	No additional deduction for elderly/blind taxpayers. **2018 Tax Year:** $10,613 if filing status is married filing jointly or head of household; and $5,312 if filing status is single or married filing separately. **2017 Tax Year:** $10,336 if filing status is married filing jointly or head of household; and $5,183 if filing status is single or married filing separately. **2016 Tax Year:** $10,189 if filing status is married filing jointly or head of household; and $5,099 if filing status is single or married filing separately. **2015 Tax Year:** $10,173 if filing status is married filing jointly or head of household; and $5,091 if filing status is single or married filing separately. Amount adjusted annually for inflation. For tax years beginning after 2018, standard deduction increased by 25% of the amount of charitable contribution deduction taxpayer could have claimed if taxpayer elected to itemize deductions.
Arkansas	$2,200 if filing status is other than married filing jointly; and $4,400 if filing status is married filing jointly.	No additional deduction for elderly/blind taxpayers. **Tax years before 2015:** $2,000 if filing status is other than married filing jointly; and $4,000 if filing status is married filing jointly.

Jurisdiction	Standard Deduction	Comment
California	**2020 tax year:** $4,601 if filing status is single or married/RDP filing separately; and $9,202 if filing status is married/RDP filing jointly, surviving spouse, or head of household. **2019 tax year:** $4,537 if filing status is single or married/RDP filing separately; and $9,074 if filing status is married/RDP filing jointly, surviving spouse, or head of household.	No additional deduction for elderly/blind taxpayers, sales and use taxes, property taxes, or motor vehicle taxes. **2018 tax year:** $4,401 if filing status is single or married/RDP filing separately; and $8,802 if filing status is married/RDP filing jointly, surviving spouse, or head of household. **2017 tax year:** $4,236 if filing status is single or married/RDP filing separately; and $8,472 if filing status is married/RDP filing jointly, surviving spouse, or head of household. **2016 tax year:** $4,129 if filing status is single or married/RDP filing separately; and $8,258 if filing status is married/RDP filing jointly, surviving spouse, or head of household. **2015 tax year:** $4,044 if filing status is single or married/RDP filing separately; and $8,088 if filing status is married/RDP filing jointly, surviving spouse, or head of household.
Colorado	Same as federal due to income tax starting point.	
Connecticut	No standard deduction.	
Delaware	$3,250 if filing status is other than married filing jointly; $6,500 if filing status is married filing jointly; and $2,500 up to a maximum of $5,000 for taxpayers who are 65 and older or blind.	

Jurisdiction	Standard Deduction	Comment
District of Columbia	Same as federal.	No additional deduction for elderly/blind taxpayers. January 1, 2013 to December 31, 2017, adjusted annually for cost of living. **2018 tax year and after:** Same as federal. **2017 tax year:** $5,650 if single or married filing separately; $7,800 for head of household; $10,275 for married/registered domestic partners filing jointly, qualifying widow(ers) with dependent child and married/registered domestic partners filing separately on same return. **2016 tax year:** $5,250 if single or married filing separately; $6,550 for head of household; $8450 for married/registered domestic partners filing jointly, qualifying widow(ers) with dependent child and married/registered domestic partners filing separately on same return. **2015 tax year:** $5,200 if single or married filing separately; $6,500 for head of household; $8,350 for married/registered domestic partners filing jointly, qualifying widow(ers) with dependent child and married/registered domestic partners filing separately on same return.
Georgia	$4,600 if filing status is single or a head of household; $3,000 if filing status is married taxpayer filing separately; $6,000 if filing status is married filing jointly; $1,300 for each taxpayer who is 65 or older; and $1,300 for each taxpayer who is blind.	**Before 2018:** $2,300 if filing status is single or a head of household; $1,500 if filing status is married taxpayer filing separately; $3,000 if filing status is married filing jointly; $1,300 for each taxpayer who is 65 or older; and $1,300 for each taxpayer who is blind.
Hawaii	$2,200 if filing status is single or married filing separately; $3,212 if filing status is head of household; $4,400 if filing status is married filing jointly or qualifying widow(er).	No additional deduction for elderly/blind taxpayers, real property taxes, disaster losses, or motor vehicle sales taxes.
Idaho	Same as federal.	
Illinois	No standard deduction.	
Indiana	No standard deduction.	

Jurisdiction	Standard Deduction	Comment
Iowa	**2020 tax year:** $2,110 if filing status is single or married filing separately; and $5,210 if filing status is married filing jointly, head of household, or qualified widow(er). **2021 tax year:** $2,130 if filing status is single or married filing separately; and $5,240 if filing status is married filing jointly, head of household, or qualified widow(er).	No additional deduction for elderly/blind taxpayers. **2019 tax year:** $2,080 if filing status is single or married filing separately; and $5,120 if filing status is married filing jointly, head of household, or qualified widow(er). **2018 tax year:** $2,030 if filing status is single or married filing separately; and $5,000 if filing status is married filing jointly, head of household, or qualified widow(er). **2017 tax year:** $2,000 if filing status is single or married filing separately; and $4,920 if filing status is married filing jointly, head of household, or qualified widow(er). **2016 tax year:** $1,970 if filing status is single or married filing separately; and $4,860 if filing status is married filing jointly, head of household, or qualified widow(er). **2015 tax year:** $1,950 if filing status is single or married filing separately; and $4,810 if filing status is married filing jointly, head of household, or qualified widow(er).
Kansas	$3,000 if filing status is single; $3,750 if filing status is married filing separately; $5,500 if filing status is head of household; $7,500 if filing status is married filing jointly. **Additional deduction for elderly/ blind taxpayers:** $850 if single or head of household taxpayer is 65 years or older; and $850 if taxpayer is blind. $700 for each married taxpayer who is 65 years or older; and $700 for each taxpayer who is blind.	
Kentucky	**2020 tax year:** $2,650. **2019 tax year:** $2,590. **2018 tax year:** $2,530. **2017 tax year:** $2,480. **2016 tax year:** $2,460. **2015 tax year:** $2,440.	No additional deduction for elderly/blind taxpayers. Amount adjusted annually for inflation.
Louisiana	$4,500 if filing status is single or married filing separately; $9,000 for all other taxpayers; $1,000 for each taxpayer who is 65 or older; and $1,000 for each taxpayer who is blind.	Amounts represent combined standard deduction and personal exemption.

Jurisdiction	Standard Deduction	Comment
Maine	Same as federal, except amount is subject to phaseout for taxpayers with state AGI exceeding: • $80,000 for single taxpayers and married taxpayers filing separate returns; • $120,000 for taxpayers filing as heads of households; and • $160,000 for taxpayers filing married joint returns or as a surviving spouse. **2020 tax year:** $12,400 for single taxpayers and married taxpayers filing separate returns; $18,650 for taxpayers filing as heads of household; and $24,800 for taxpayers filing married joint returns or surviving spouses. **2021 tax year:** $12,550 for single taxpayers and married taxpayers filing separate returns; $18,800 for taxpayers filing as heads of household; and $25,100 for taxpayers filing married joint returns or surviving spouses.	State AGI phase-out thresholds adjusted annually for inflation. **2019 tax year:** $12,200 for single taxpayers and married taxpayers filing separate returns; $18,350 for taxpayers filing as heads of household; and $24,400 for taxpayers filing married joint returns or surviving spouses. **2018 tax year:** $12,000 for single taxpayers and married taxpayers filing separate returns; $18,000 for taxpayers filing as heads of household; and $24,000 for taxpayers filing married joint returns or surviving spouses. **2016 and 2017 tax years:** $11,600 for single taxpayers and married taxpayers filing separate returns; $17,400 for taxpayers filing as heads of household; and $23,200 for taxpayers filing married joint returns or surviving spouses. **Prior to 2016 tax year** Before 2016, standard deduction was the same as federal, except that for 2013 tax year standard deduction was $10,150 for joint filers and $5,075 for married taxpayers filing separate returns.
Maryland	$1,500 to $2,250 if filing status single or married filing separately; or $3,000 up to $4,500 if filing status is married filing jointly, head of household, or qualifying widow(er).	15% of state AGI. After 2018 tax year, standard deduction amounts adjusted annually for inflation. **Tax years before 2018:** $1,500 to $2,000 if filing status single or married filing separately; or $3,000 to $4,000 if filing status is married filing jointly, head of household, or qualifying widow(er).
Massachusetts	No standard deduction.	
Michigan	No standard deduction.	

Jurisdiction	Standard Deduction	Comment
Minnesota	**Tax year 2020:** • $24,800 for married couples filing join returns; • $12,400 for singles; and • $18,650 heads of households. Additional deduction for senior and/or blind taxpayers: • $1,300 for married taxpayers and surviving spouses; and • $1,650, for other taxpayers. Deduction for dependents is limited to the greater of: • $1,100; or • $350, plus the individual's earned income (not to exceed the regular standard deduction amount). **Tax year 2019:** • $24,400 for married couples filing join returns; • $12,200 for singles; and • $18,350 heads of households. Additional deduction for senior and/or blind taxpayers: • $1,300 for married taxpayers and surviving spouses; and • $1,650, for other taxpayers. Deduction for dependents is limited to the greater of: • $1,100; or • $350, plus the individual's earned income (not to exceed the regular standard deduction amount).	Standard deduction reduced if income exceeds specified threshold amounts. For tax year 2020, the applicable threshold amounts are: • $197,850; or • $98,925 for married taxpayers filing a separate return. For tax year 2019, the applicable threshold amounts are: • $194,650; or • $97,325 for married taxpayers filing a separate return. **Tax year 2018:** For tax year 2018, $6,500 if filing status is single or married taxpayer filing separately; $9,550 if filing status is head of household; and $13,000 if filing status is married filing jointly. Taxpayers who are elderly or blind are allowed an additional standard deduction of $1,300. The amount is increased to $1,600 if taxpayer is also unmarried and not a widow(er). Taxpayers may either claim the standard deduction or elect to itemize deductions, regardless of the election made on their 2018 federal income tax return.
Mississippi	$2,300 if filing status is single or married filing separately; $4,600 if filing status is married filing jointly or qualifying widow(er); and $3,400 if filing status is head of household.	No additional deduction for elderly/blind taxpayers.
Missouri	Same as federal.	

Jurisdiction	Standard Deduction	Comment
Montana	20% of state AGI, subject to minimum and maximum amounts per tax year. **2020 tax year:** $2,130 up to $4,790 if filing status is single or married filing separately; or $4,260 up to $9,580 if filing status is married filing jointly or head of household.	**2019 tax year:** $2,090 up to $4,710 if filing status is single or married filing separately; or $4,180 up to $9,420 if filing status is married filing jointly or head of household. **2018 tax year:** $2,030 up to $4,580 if filing status is single or married filing separately; or $4,060 up to $9,160 if filing status is married filing jointly or head of household. **2017 tax year:** $2,000 up to $4,510 if filing status is single or married filing separately; or $4,000 up to $9,020 if filing status is married filing jointly or head of household. **2016 tax year:** $1,980 up to $4,460 if filing status is single or married filing separately; or $3,960 up to $8,920 if filing status is married filing jointly or head of household. **2015 tax year:** $1,940 up to $4,370 if filing status is single or married filing separately; or $3,880 up to $8,740 if filing status is married filing jointly or head of household.
Nebraska	$6,900, if filing status is single or married filing separately; $10,100, if filing status is head of household; $13,800, if filing status is married filing jointly or qualifying widow(er); and $8,500 to $19,000 based on filing status for each taxpayer who is 65 or older and each taxpayer who is blind.	**Tax year 2018:** $6,750, if filing status is single or married filing separately; $9,900, if filing status is head of household; $13,500, if filing status is married filing jointly or qualifying widow(er); and $8,350 to $18,700 based on filing status for each taxpayer who is 65 or older and each taxpayer who is blind. **Tax year 2017:** $6,350, if filing status is single or married filing separately; $9,350, if filing status is head of household; $12,700, if filing status is married filing jointly or qualifying widow(er); and $7,600 to $17,700 based on filing status for each taxpayer who is 65 or older and each taxpayer who is blind. **Tax year 2016:** $6,300, if filing status is single or married filing separately; $9,300, if filing status is head of household; $12,600, if filing status is married filing jointly or qualifying widow(er); and $7,550 to $17,600 based on filing status for each taxpayer who is 65 or older and each taxpayer who is blind.
New Hampshire	No standard deduction.	
New Jersey	No standard deduction.	
New Mexico	Same as federal.	

Jurisdiction	Standard Deduction	Comment
New York	**Tax years after 2016:** $3,100 if filing status is single and claimed as a dependent on another taxpayer's return; $8,000 if filing status is single or married filing separately; $16,050 if filing status is married filing jointly or qualifying widow(er) with dependent child; and $11,200 if filing status is head of household. **Tax year 2016:** $3,100 if filing status is single and claimed as a dependent on another taxpayer's return; $7,950 if filing status is single or married filing separately; $15,950 if filing status is married filing jointly or qualifying widow(er) with dependent child; and $11,150 if filing status is head of household. **Tax year 2015:** $3,100 if filing status is single and claimed as a dependent on another taxpayer's return; $7,900 if filing status is single or married filing separately; $15,850 if filing status is married filing jointly or qualifying widow(er) with dependent child; and $11,100 if filing status is head of household. **Tax year 2014:** $3,100 if filing status is single and claimed as a dependent on another taxpayer's return; $7,800 if filing status is single or married filing separately; $15,650 if filing status is married filing jointly or qualifying widow(er) with dependent child; and $10,950 if filing status is head of household.	No additional deduction for elderly/blind taxpayers. Deduction indexed for tax years 2013 through 2017.

Jurisdiction	Standard Deduction	Comment
North Carolina	$10,000 if filing status is single or married filing separately; $20,000 if filing status is married filing jointly or qualifying widow(er); $15,000 if filing status is head of household.	**Tax Years after 2019:** $10,750 if filing status is single or married filing separately; $21,500 if filing status is married filing jointly or qualifying widow(er); $16,125 if filing status is head of household. **Tax Years after 2016 and before 2019:** $8,750 if filing status is single or married filing separately; $17,500 if filing status is married filing jointly or qualifying widow(er); $14,000 if filing status is head of household. **2016 Tax Year:** $8,250 if filing status is single or married filing separately; $16,500 if filing status is married filing jointly or qualifying widow(er); $13,200 if filing status is head of household. **2014 and 2015 tax years:** $7,500 if filing status was single or married filing separately; $15,000 if filing status was married filing jointly or qualifying widow(er); $12,000 if filing status was head of household. **2012 and 2013 tax years:** $3,000 if filing status was single or married filing separately; $6,000 if filing status was married filing jointly or qualifying widow(er); $4,400 if filing status was head of household. Additional deduction allowed in tax years before 2014 for each taxpayer who was 65 or older and each taxpayer who was blind.
North Dakota	Same as federal due to income tax starting point.	
Ohio	No standard deduction.	

Jurisdiction	Standard Deduction	Comment
Oklahoma	**Tax years after 2016**: $6,350 if filing status is single or married filing separately; $12,700 if filing status is married filing jointly or qualifying widow(er); $9,350 if filing status is head of household.	No additional deduction for elderly/blind taxpayers. **2016 tax year** $6,300 if filing status is single or married filing separately; $12,600 if filing status is married filing jointly or qualifying widow(er); $9,300 if filing status is head of household. **2015 tax year** $6,300 if filing status is single or married filing separately; $12,600 if filing status is married filing jointly or qualifying widow(er); $9,250 if filing status is head of household. **2014 tax year** $6,200 if filing status is single or married filing separately; $12,400 if filing status is married filing jointly or qualifying widow(er); $9,100 if filing status is head of household.
Oregon	**2020 Tax Year** • $2,315 if filing status is single or married filing separately; • $4,630 if filing status is married filing jointly or qualifying widow(er); or • $3,725 if filing status is head of household.	Addition to federal tax base required for amount of federal standard deduction. **2019 Tax Year** • $2,270 if filing status is single or married filing separately; • $4,545 if filing status is married filing jointly or qualifying widow(er); or • $3,655 if filing status is head of household. **2018 Tax Year** • $2,215 if filing status is single or married filing separately; • $4,435 if filing status is married filing jointly or qualifying widow(er); or • $3,570 if filing status is head of household. **2017 Tax Year** • $2,175 if filing status is single or married filing separately; • $4,350 if filing status is married filing jointly or qualifying widow(er); or • $3,500 if filing status is head of household. **2016 Tax Year** • $2,155 if filing status is single or married filing separately; • $4,315 if filing status is married filing jointly or qualifying widow(er); or • $3,475 if filing status is head of household. **2015 Tax Year** • $2,145 if filing status is single or married filing separately; • $4,295 if filing status is married filing jointly or qualifying widow(er); or • $3,455 if filing status is head of household.

Jurisdiction	Standard Deduction	Comment
Pennsylvania	No standard deduction.	
Rhode Island	**2020 tax year:** $8,900 if filing status is single or married filing separately; $17,800 if filing status is married filing jointly or qualifying widow(er); and $13,350 if filing status is head of household.	**2019 tax year:** $8,750 if filing status is single or married filing separately; $17,500 if filing status is married filing jointly or qualifying widow(er); and $13,100 if filing status is head of household. **2018 tax year:** $8,525 if filing status is single or married filing separately; $17,050 if filing status is married filing jointly or qualifying widow(er); and $12,800 if filing status is head of household. **2017 tax year:** $8,375 if filing status is single or married filing separately; $16,750 if filing status is married filing jointly or qualifying widow(er); and $12,550 if filing status is head of household. **2016 tax year:** $8,300 if filing status is single or married filing separately; $16,600 if filing status is married filing jointly or qualifying widow(er); and $12,450 if filing status is head of household. **2015 tax year:** $8,275 if filing status is single or married filing separately; $16,550 if filing status is married filing jointly or qualifying widow(er); and $12,400 if filing status is head of household. **2014 tax year:** $8,100 if filing status is single or married filing separately; $16,250 if filing status is married filing jointly or qualifying widow(er); and $12,200 if filing status is head of household. **2013 tax year:** $8,000 if filing status is single or married filing separately; $16,000 if filing status is married filing jointly or qualifying widow(er); and $12,000 if filing status is head of household. Amounts indexed for inflation.
South Carolina	Same as federal due to income tax starting point.	
Tennessee	No standard deduction.	
Utah	No standard deduction.	Credit allowed equal to 6% of the federal standard deduction with phaseout based on income.

Jurisdiction	Standard Deduction	Comment
Vermont	**Tax year 2019:** $6,150 if single or married filing separately; $9,200 for head of household; $12,300 for married filing jointly or surviving spouse; $1,000 additional deduction if taxpayer or taxpayer's spouse is 65 or older; and $1,000 additional deduction if taxpayer or taxpayer's spouse is blind.	Adjusted annually for inflation. **Tax year 2018:** $6,000 if single or married filing separately; $9,000 for head of household; $12,000 for married filing jointly or surviving spouse; $1,000 additional deduction if taxpayer or taxpayer's spouse is 65 or older; and $1,000 additional deduction if taxpayer or taxpayer's spouse is blind. **Tax years before 2018:** Same as federal due to income tax starting point.
Virginia	$3,000, if filing status is single or married filing separately and $6,000, if filing status is married filing jointly.	**Tax Years 2019-2025:** • $4,500, if filing status is single or married filing separately; and • $9,000, if filing status is married filing jointly. No additional deduction for elderly/blind taxpayers.
West Virginia	No standard deduction.	
Wisconsin	**2020 Tax year:** $0 up to $20,470 based on state income and filing status. **2019 Tax year:** $0 up to $20,110 based on state income and filing status.	**2018 Tax year:** $0 up to $19,580 based on state income and filing status. **2017 Tax year:** $0 up to $19,210 based on state income and filing status. **2016 Tax year:** $0 up to $19,010 based on state income and filing status. **2015 Tax year:** $0 up to $18,460 based on state income and filing status.

Starting Point

This chart indicates the starting point for calculating taxable personal income used by each state. Generally, states use federal taxable income, federal adjusted gross income, or federal gross income as the starting point to calculate the base upon which state personal income tax is imposed.

Jurisdiction	Starting Point	Comment
Alabama	Gross income.	
Arizona	Federal adjusted gross income.	
Arkansas	Gross income.	
California	Federal adjusted gross income.	
Colorado	Federal taxable income.	
Connecticut	Federal adjusted gross income.	
Delaware	Federal adjusted gross income.	
District of Columbia	Federal gross income.	
Georgia	Federal adjusted gross income.	
Hawaii	Federal adjusted gross income.	
Idaho	Federal adjusted gross income.	
Illinois	Federal adjusted gross income.	
Indiana	Federal adjusted gross income.	
Iowa	"Net income" defined by statute as federal adjusted gross income, but each item of income from federal return must reported on line-by-line basis incorporating state adjustments where required to determine gross income.	
Kansas	Federal adjusted gross income.	
Kentucky	Federal adjusted gross income.	
Louisiana	Federal adjusted gross income.	
Maine	Federal adjusted gross income.	
Maryland	Federal adjusted gross income.	
Massachusetts	Federal gross income.	
Michigan	Federal adjusted gross income.	
Minnesota	Federal adjusted taxable income. **Tax years before 2019:** Federal taxable income.	
Mississippi	Gross income.	
Missouri	Federal adjusted gross income.	

Jurisdiction	Starting Point	Comment
Montana	Federal adjusted gross income.	
Nebraska	Federal adjusted gross income.	
New Hampshire	Gross income.	Tax on interest and dividends only.
New Jersey	Gross income.	
New Mexico	Federal adjusted gross income.	
New York	Federal adjusted gross income.	
North Carolina	Federal adjusted gross income.	
North Dakota	Federal taxable income.	
Ohio	Federal adjusted gross income.	
Oklahoma	Federal adjusted gross income.	
Oregon	Federal adjusted gross income.	
Pennsylvania	Gross income.	
Rhode Island	Federal adjusted gross income.	
South Carolina	Federal taxable income.	
Tennessee	Certain dividends and interest income.	
Utah	Federal adjusted gross income.	
Vermont	Federal taxable income (through 2017 tax year).	Beginning with 2018 tax year, federal adjusted gross income.
Virginia	Federal adjusted gross income.	
West Virginia	Federal adjusted gross income.	
Wisconsin	Federal adjusted gross income.	

Start-Up and Organizational Expenditures—IRC § 195, IRC § 248, and IRC § 709

The federal American Jobs Creation Act of 2004 (AJCA) (P.L. 108-357) allows taxpayers to elect a deduction of up to $5,000 for start-up or organizational expenses incurred in the tax year in which a trade, business, corporation, or partnership begins (IRC § 195, § 248, and § 709). The $5,000 must be reduced, but not below zero, by any amount in excess of $50,000. Start-up or organizational expenses that cannot be deducted may be amortized over a 15-year period. The Small Business Jobs Act of 2010 (P.L. 111-240) increases the expense deduction from $5,000 to $10,000, effective for tax years beginning in 2010. In addition, the threshold limit for reducing the deduction is increased from $50,000 to $60,000.

This chart shows the income tax treatment by each state and the District of Columbia of the federal start-up and organizational expense deduction.

Jurisdiction	Start-Up and Organizational Expenditures—IRC § 195, IRC § 248, and IRC § 709	Comment
Alabama	No adjustments to federal deduction required.	
Alaska	No adjustments to federal deduction required.	
Arizona	No adjustments to federal deduction required.	
Arkansas	Subtraction from taxable income allowed equal to: • federal deduction allowed under IRC § 195 in effect on January 1, 2001; • federal deduction allowed under IRC § 248 in effect on January 1, 2005; and • federal deduction allowed under IRC § 709 in effect on January 1, 2007.	
California	No adjustments to federal deduction required.	
Colorado	No adjustments to federal deduction required.	
Connecticut	No adjustments to federal deduction required.	
Delaware	No adjustments to federal deduction required.	
District of Columbia	Subtraction from gross income allowed equal to federal deduction.	
Florida	No adjustments to federal deduction required.	
Georgia	No adjustments to federal deduction required.	
Hawaii	No adjustments to federal deduction required.	

Jurisdiction	Start-Up and Organizational Expenditures—IRC § 195, IRC § 248, and IRC § 709	Comment
Idaho	No adjustments to federal deduction required.	
Illinois	No adjustments to federal deduction required.	
Indiana	No adjustments to federal deduction required.	Addition required for amount of federal deduction that exceeds $5,000 limit for tax years after 2009 and before 2013.
Iowa	No adjustments to federal deduction required.	
Kansas	No adjustments to federal deduction required.	
Kentucky	No adjustments to federal deduction required.	
Louisiana	No adjustments to federal deduction required.	
Maine	No adjustments to federal deduction required.	
Maryland	No adjustments to federal deduction required.	
Massachusetts	No adjustments to federal deduction required.	
Michigan	No adjustments to federal deduction required.	
Minnesota	No adjustments to federal deduction required.	
Mississippi	No adjustments to federal deduction required.	
Missouri	No adjustments to federal deduction required.	
Montana	No adjustments to federal deduction required.	
Nebraska	No adjustments to federal deduction required.	
Nevada	N/A, because state does not tax general business corporation income.	
New Hampshire	Addition to gross business profits required for amount that exceeds allowable federal deduction in effect on December 31, 2000.	
New Jersey	No adjustments to federal deduction required.	
New Mexico	No adjustments to federal deduction required.	

Jurisdiction	Start-Up and Organizational Expenditures—IRC § 195, IRC § 248, and IRC § 709	Comment
New York	No adjustments to federal deduction required.	
North Carolina	No adjustments to federal deduction required.	
North Dakota	No adjustments to federal deduction required.	
Ohio	Taxable gross receipts computed without regard to federal deduction.	
Oklahoma	No adjustments to federal deduction required.	
Oregon	No adjustments to federal deduction required.	
Pennsylvania	No adjustments to federal deduction required.	
Rhode Island	No adjustments to federal deduction required.	
South Carolina	No adjustments to federal deduction.	
South Dakota	N/A, because state does not tax general business corporation income.	
Tennessee	No adjustments to federal deduction required.	
Texas	Addition required for amount of federal deduction.	
Utah	No adjustments to federal deduction required.	
Vermont	No adjustments to federal deduction required.	
Virginia	No adjustments to federal deduction required.	
Washington	N/A, because state does not tax general business corporation income.	
West Virginia	No adjustments to federal deduction required.	
Wisconsin	No adjustments to federal deduction required, except for tax years beginning in 2010.	Wisconsin did not conform to the provision increasing the deduction for tax years beginning in 2010.
Wyoming	N/A, because state does not tax general business corporation income.	

State, Local, and Foreign Taxes—IRC Sec. 164

Under IRC Sec. 164, state, local, and foreign taxes may be deducted as itemized deductions on Schedule A of Form 1040 for federal income tax purposes. Taxes eligible for deduction are:

- state, local, and foreign income taxes;
- state and local sales taxes in lieu of deducting state and local income taxes;
- state, local, and foreign real property taxes; and
- state and local personal property taxes.

However, for tax years 2018 through 2025, taxpayers cannot deduct foreign real property taxes. During the same time period, taxpayers may only deduct a total amount of up to $10,000 ($5,000 if married filing separate) of the following state and local taxes:

- income taxes, or general sales taxes if elected instead of income taxes;
- real estate taxes;
- and personal property taxes.

This chart indicates whether each state allows the federal itemized deduction for state, local, and foreign taxes.

Jurisdiction	State, Local, and Foreign Taxes—IRC Sec. 164	Comment
Alabama	Allowed, except limited to: • state, local, and foreign real property taxes; • state and local personal property taxes; and • no $10,000 limit ($5,000 for married taxpayer filing a separate return) on state and local tax deductions for the 2018 to 2025 tax years.	Form 40, Schedule A
Arizona	Allowed.	Form 140 Schedule A
Arkansas	Allowed, except for: • sales and use taxes; and • state income taxes. The following limitations on deductibility for the 2018 to 2025 tax years do not apply: • the $10,000 limit ($5,000 for married taxpayer filing a separate return) on state and local tax deductions; and • the foreign real property tax deduction.	Form AR1000F and Form AR3

Jurisdiction	State, Local, and Foreign Taxes—IRC Sec. 164	Comment
California	Allowed, except for: • state, local, and foreign income taxes; • foreign real property taxes (no federal deduction is available for 2018 to 2025 tax years); and • sales and use taxes. These disallowed federal tax deductions must be subtracted from federal itemized deductions in computing California itemized deductions. In addition, California does not conform to the federal $10,000 limit ($5,000 for married taxpayer filing a separate return) on state and local tax deductions for the 2018 to 2025 tax years.	Form 540, Schedule CA If adjusted gross income (AGI) exceeds threshold amount, itemized deduction is reduced by lesser of: • 6% of excess AGI over threshold amount; or • 80% of itemized deductions otherwise allowed for tax year. Threshold amounts adjusted annually for inflation.
Colorado	Allowed, except for state income taxes.	Form 104 and Schedule 104AD
Connecticut	N/A, because state itemized deductions not allowed.	
Delaware	Allowed, except taxpayer must reduce deduction by: • income taxes paid to Delaware; and • any credit claimed for tax paid to another state.	Downward adjustment for Delaware income taxes paid does not apply to real property and local income taxes up to: • $10,000; or • $5,000 for married taxpayers filing separate or combined returns.
District of Columbia	Allowed, except for: • state and local income taxes; and • no $10,000 limit ($5,000 for married taxpayer filing a separate return) on real estate tax deductions for the 2018 to 2025 tax years.	Form D-40 Itemized deductions reduced by 5% if adjusted gross income exceeds $200,000 ($100,000 if married filing separate).
Georgia	Not allowed.	Form 500, Schedule 3
Hawaii	Allowed, except Hawaii imposes income limitations in deducting: • state, local, and foreign income taxes; and • state and local sales taxes if elected instead of state and local income taxes. In addition, the federal $10,000 limit ($5,000 for married taxpayer filing a separate return) on state and local tax deductions for the 2018 to 2025 tax years does not apply.	Form N-11, Worksheet A-2 Hawaii does not follow IRC Sec. 68(f), which temporarily repeals the overall limitation on itemized deductions for tax years 2018 through 2025. The applicable thresholds are those that were operative for federal tax year 2009.
Idaho	Allowed, except for: • state and local income taxes; and • state and local sales taxes in lieu of deducting state and local income taxes.	Form 40
Illinois	N/A, because state itemized deductions not allowed.	
Indiana	N/A, because state itemized deductions not allowed.	Form IT-40, Schedule 1

Jurisdiction	State, Local, and Foreign Taxes—IRC Sec. 164	Comment
Iowa	Allowed, except for Iowa income taxes. In addition, the federal $10,000 limit ($5,000 for married taxpayer filing a separate return) on state and local tax deductions for the 2018 to 2025 tax years does not apply.	Form IA 1040, Schedule A
Kansas	Allowed only for real estate and personal property taxes. Equal to: • 100% of the taxes for tax years beginning after 2019; • 75% of the taxes for the 2019 tax year; and • 50% of the taxes for tax years after 2014 and before 2019.	Form K-40, Schedule S.
Kentucky	Not allowed. **Tax years before 2018** Allowed, except limited to: • local income taxes; • real property taxes; and • personal property taxes.	Complete Form 740 or Form 740NP, Schedule A, and enclose with return. Itemized deductions for tax years before 2018 were subject to the phaseout limitation for high-income individuals that existed under the IRC as of December 31, 2006.
Louisiana	Allowed.	Form IT-540
Maine	Allowed, as modified by: • adding property taxes not claimed as a federal itemized deduction as a result of the $10,000 limitation on federal itemized deductions for state and local taxes (for tax years beginning after 2017); and • subtracting any income or sales and use taxes imposed by Maine or any other taxing jurisdiction. Beginning with 2018 tax year, itemized deduction phased out for taxpayers with state AGI exceeding $80,000 for single taxpayers and married taxpayers filing separate returns, $120,000 for taxpayers filing as heads of households, and $160,000 for taxpayers filing married joint returns or as a surviving spouse.	Form 1040ME, Schedule 2 Itemized deductions limited as follows (adjusted annually for inflation): • $29,050 for 2018 tax year; • $28,600 for 2017 tax year; • $28,450 for 2016 tax year; • $28,350 for 2015 tax year; • $27,950 for 2014 tax year; • $27,500 for 2013 tax year. State AGI phase-out thresholds adjusted annually for inflation. For 2016 and 2017 tax years, itemized deduction phased out for taxpayers with state AGI exceeding $70,000 for single taxpayers and married taxpayers filing separate returns, $105,000 for taxpayers filing as heads of households, and $140,000 for taxpayers filing married joint returns or as a surviving spouse.
Maryland	Allowed, except for state and local income taxes.	Form 502
Massachusetts	Not allowed.	State allowable deductions differ from federal itemized deductions.
Michigan	N/A, because state itemized deductions not allowed.	

Jurisdiction	State, Local, and Foreign Taxes—IRC Sec. 164	Comment
Minnesota	Allowed, in an amount equal to sum of taxpayer's taxes paid for: • up to $10,000 ($5,000 if married filing separate) of state, local, and foreign property taxes; • foreign income, war profits, and excess profits taxes not reduced by the federal foreign tax credit; and • foreign subnational taxes that did not qualify for the state credit for taxes paid to another state. Deductions reduced if taxpayer's income exceeds specified threshold amounts.	For taxpayers before 2019, this deduction was allowed, with modifications to state and local income taxes, or general sales taxes, and personal property taxes. For tax year 2018, taxpayers could either claim the standard deduction or elect to itemize deductions, regardless of the election made on their 2018 federal income tax return. Itemized deductions were required to be calculated as they were allowed under the IRC as amended through December 16, 2016.
Mississippi	Allowed, except for: • state and local income taxes; and • state and local sales taxes in lieu of deducting state and local income taxes.	Form 80-108, Schedule A
Missouri	Allowed, except for state and local income taxes.	Form MO-1040, Form MO-A
Montana	Allowed, except for state income taxes.	Form 2, Itemized Deduction Schedule
Nebraska	Allowed, except for state and local income taxes.	Form 1040N
New Hampshire	N/A, because state itemized deductions not allowed.	
New Jersey	Allowed, except limited to property taxes paid on a personal residence up to $15,000 ($10,000 before 2018).	Form NJ-1040, Worksheet H
New Mexico	Allowed, except for: • state and local income taxes; and • state and local sales taxes in lieu of deducting state and local income taxes.	Form PIT-1, Line 10 Worksheet
New York	Allowed, as federal itemized deductions existed before the TCJA, except for: • state, local, and foreign income taxes; and • state and local sales taxes. Itemized deductions limited for high-income taxpayers.	Form IT-201, Form IT-196
North Carolina	Allowed only for real property taxes up to $20,000.	Complete and attach Supplemental Schedule S.
North Dakota	Allowed.	Form ND-1
Ohio	Not allowed.	Form IT-1040
Oklahoma	Allowed, except for: • state and local income taxes; and • state and local sales taxes in lieu of deducting state and local income taxes. If the amount of state and local taxes deducted on the federal return is limited, taxable income on the state return shall be increased only by the amount actually deducted after any such limitations are applied.	Form 511, Schedule 511-D Itemized deductions, other than charitable contributions and medical expenses, limited to $17,000 annually for tax years after 2017.

Jurisdiction	State, Local, and Foreign Taxes—IRC Sec. 164	Comment
Oregon	Allowed, except for: • Oregon income taxes; and • state and local sales taxes	Form 40, Schedule OR-A
Pennsylvania	N/A, because state itemized deductions not allowed.	
Rhode Island	N/A, because state itemized deductions not allowed.	
South Carolina	Allowed, except for: • state, local, and foreign income taxes; and • state and local sales taxes in lieu of deducting state and local income taxes.	Form SC1040
Tennessee	N/A, because state itemized deductions not allowed.	
Utah	N/A, because state itemized deductions not allowed.	Taxpayers that itemize deductions for federal purposes are allowed a nonrefundable state tax credit equal to 6% of the difference between: • the taxpayer's federal itemized deductions; and • any state or local income tax claimed on the taxpayer's federal return for the taxable year. For tax years beginning after 2017, "state or local income tax" means the lesser of: • the amount of state or local income tax the taxpayer pays and reports on the federal return for the taxable year, regardless of whether the taxpayer is allowed an itemized deduction for the full amount paid; or • $10,000. Credits are phased out at 1.3 cents per dollar of income over $12,000 for single/married filing separately, $18,000 for heads of household, and $24,000 for joint filers/qualifying widow(er), adjusted annually for inflation.
Vermont	N/A, because state itemized deductions not allowed beginning with tax year 2018.	**Tax years before 2018:** Starting point adopted federal itemized deductions with modifications.
Virginia	Allowed, except for: • state and local income taxes; and • state and local sales taxes in lieu of deducting state and local income taxes. For tax years after 2018, real and personal property taxes not otherwise deducted because of the federal limitation on the state and local tax deduction may be subtracted.	Form 760, Schedule A
West Virginia	N/A, because state itemized deductions not allowed.	

Jurisdiction	State, Local, and Foreign Taxes—IRC Sec. 164	Comment
Wisconsin	N/A, because state itemized deductions not allowed.	

Taxability of Bond Interest (Corporate Income)—Other States' Bonds

Many states exempt interest income from bonds issued by the state or its localities, while taxing interest income received from bonds issued by other states and localities. In other states, interest income from bonds is taxable whether or not it is received from in-state or out-of-state bonds. In *Kentucky Department of Revenue v. Davis*, U.S. Supreme Court, Dkt. 06-666, May 19, 2008, the U.S. Supreme Court upheld the traditional state tax treatment of municipal bond interest, under which a state exempts from income taxes the interest on bonds issued by the state and its own localities, but not the interest on bonds issued by other states and their localities. The Court ruled that Kentucky, the state in which the case before it arose, and other states with similar taxing regimes do not violate the Commerce Clause by limiting the exemption to the interest on in-state bonds. The exemption permissibly favors a traditional government function and is critical to the functioning of the municipal financial market. Furthermore, it does not represent the sort of protectionism the Commerce Clause was designed to prevent. This chart shows the corporation income tax treatment by each state and the District of Columbia of interest from bonds issued by other states and localities. The chart does not address state tax treatment of gain or loss on the sale of bonds or the amortization of premium discounts.

Jurisdiction	Other States' Bonds	Comment
Alabama	Taxable	
Alaska	Exempt	
Arizona	Taxable	
Arkansas	Taxable	
California	Taxable	
Colorado	Taxable	
Connecticut	Taxable	
Delaware	Taxable	
District of Columbia	Taxable	
Florida	Taxable	
Georgia	Taxable	
Hawaii	Taxable	
Idaho	Taxable	
Illinois	Taxable	
Indiana	**Prior to 2012** Exempt **After 2011** Taxable	

Jurisdiction	Other States' Bonds	Comment
Iowa	Taxable	
Kansas	Taxable	
Kentucky	Taxable	
Louisiana	Exempt	
Maine	Taxable	
Maryland	Taxable	
Massachusetts	Taxable	
Michigan	Taxable	
Minnesota	Taxable	
Mississippi	Taxable	
Missouri	Taxable	
Montana	Taxable	
Nebraska	Taxable	
Nevada	N/A, because state does not tax general business corporation income.	
New Hampshire	Exempt	
New Jersey	Taxable	
New Mexico	Taxable	
New York	Taxable	
North Carolina	Taxable	
North Dakota	Taxable	
Ohio	Exempt	
Oklahoma	Taxable	
Oregon	Taxable	
Pennsylvania	Exempt	
Rhode Island	Taxable	
South Carolina	Taxable	
South Dakota	N/A, because state does not tax general business corporation income.	
Tennessee	Taxable	
Texas	Exempt	
Utah	Taxable	
Vermont	Taxable	
Virginia	Taxable	

Jurisdiction	Other States' Bonds	Comment
Washington	N/A, because state does not tax general business corporation income.	
West Virginia	Taxable	
Wisconsin	Taxable	
Wyoming	N/A, because state does not tax general business corporation income.	

Taxability of Bond Interest (Corporate Income)—State's Own Bonds

Many states exempt interest income from bonds issued by the state or its localities, while taxing interest income received from bonds issued by other states and localities. In other states, interest income from bonds is taxable whether or not it is received from in-state or out-of-state bonds. In *Kentucky Department of Revenue v. Davis*, U.S. Supreme Court, Dkt. 06-666, May 19, 2008, the U.S. Supreme Court upheld the traditional state tax treatment of municipal bond interest, under which a state exempts from income taxes the interest on bonds issued by the state and its own localities, but not the interest on bonds issued by other states and their localities. The Court ruled that Kentucky, the state in which the case before it arose, and other states with similar taxing regimes do not violate the Commerce Clause by limiting the exemption to the interest on in-state bonds. The exemption permissibly favors a traditional government function and is critical to the functioning of the municipal financial market. Furthermore, it does not represent the sort of protectionism the Commerce Clause was designed to prevent. This chart shows the corporation income tax treatment by each state and the District of Columbia of interest from bonds issued by that state and its localities. The chart does not address state tax treatment of gain or loss on the sale of bonds or the amortization of premium discounts.

Jurisdiction	State's Own Bonds	Comment
Alabama	Exempt	
Alaska	Exempt	
Arizona	Exempt	
Arkansas	Exempt	
California	Exempt for corporation income tax purposes. Taxable for corporation franchise tax purposes.	
Colorado	Exempt	
Connecticut	Taxable	
Delaware	Exempt	
District of Columbia	Exempt	
Florida	Taxable	
Georgia	Exempt	
Hawaii	Exempt	
Idaho	Exempt	
Illinois	Taxable	Income from certain specified obligations is exempt. Interest from all other obligations is taxable.
Indiana	Exempt	

Jurisdiction	State's Own Bonds	Comment
Iowa	Taxable	Income from certain specified obligations is exempt. Interest from all other obligations is taxable.
Kansas	Exempt	
Kentucky	Exempt	
Louisiana	Exempt	
Maine	Exempt	
Maryland	Exempt	
Massachusetts	Taxable	
Michigan	Exempt	
Minnesota	Taxable	
Mississippi	Exempt	
Missouri	Exempt	
Montana	Taxable	Income from certain specified obligations is exempt. Interest from all other obligations is taxable.
Nebraska	Exempt	
Nevada	N/A, because state does not tax general business corporation income.	
New Hampshire	Exempt	
New Jersey	Taxable	
New Mexico	Exempt	
New York	Taxable	
North Carolina	Exempt	
North Dakota	Exempt	
Ohio	Exempt	
Oklahoma	Taxable	Income from certain specified obligations is exempt. Interest from all other obligations is taxable.
Oregon	Taxable	
Pennsylvania	Exempt	
Rhode Island	Exempt	
South Carolina	Exempt	
South Dakota	N/A, because state does not tax general business corporation income.	
Tennessee	Taxable	
Texas	Exempt	

Jurisdiction	State's Own Bonds	Comment
Utah	Taxable	Credit allowed for percentage of gross interest income from bonds issued by the state and its agencies and instrumentalities.
Vermont	Exempt	
Virginia	Exempt	
Washington	N/A, because state does not tax general business corporation income.	
West Virginia	Taxable	Income from certain specified obligations is exempt. Interest from all other obligations is taxable.
Wisconsin	Taxable	Income from certain specified obligations is exempt from the income tax. Interest from all other obligations is taxable.
Wyoming	N/A, because state does not tax general business corporation income.	

Taxability of Bond Interest (Corporate Income)—U.S. Bonds

This chart shows the corporation income tax treatment by each state and the District of Columbia of federal bond interest.

Jurisdiction	U.S. Bonds	Comment
Alabama	Exempt	
Alaska	Exempt	
Arizona	Exempt	
Arkansas	Exempt	
California	Exempt for corporation income tax purposes. Taxable for corporation franchise tax purposes.	
Colorado	Exempt	
Connecticut	Taxable	Exempt from state taxation under 31 U.S.C. § 3124, except for nondiscriminatory franchise or nonproperty tax imposed on corporations. However, unlike individual taxpayers, state does not provide any subtraction adjustment to income tax starting point for corporation business taxpayers.
Delaware	Exempt	
District of Columbia	Exempt	
Florida	Taxable	Exempt from state taxation under 31 U.S.C. § 3124, except for nondiscriminatory franchise or nonproperty tax imposed on corporations. However, state does not provide any subtraction adjustment to income tax starting point.
Georgia	Exempt	
Hawaii	Exempt	
Idaho	Exempt	
Illinois	Exempt	
Indiana	Exempt	
Iowa	Exempt	
Kansas	Exempt	
Kentucky	Exempt	
Louisiana	Exempt	
Maine	Exempt	
Maryland	Exempt	
Massachusetts	Taxable	

Jurisdiction	U.S. Bonds	Comment
Michigan	Exempt	
Minnesota	Taxable	
Mississippi	Exempt	
Missouri	Exempt	
Montana	Taxable	
Nebraska	Exempt	
Nevada	N/A, because state does not tax general business corporation income.	
New Hampshire	Exempt	
New Jersey	Taxable	
New Mexico	Exempt	
New York	Taxable	
North Carolina	Exempt	
North Dakota	Exempt	
Ohio	Exempt	
Oklahoma	Exempt	
Oregon	Exempt	
Pennsylvania	Exempt	
Rhode Island	Exempt	
South Carolina	Exempt	
South Dakota	N/A, because state does not tax general business corporation income.	
Tennessee	Taxable	
Texas	Exempt	
Utah	Taxable	Credit allowed for percentage of gross interest income from federal government obligations.
Vermont	Exempt	
Virginia	Exempt	Interest on obligations of federal authorities, commissions, or instrumentalities that is exempt for federal tax but not from state tax is taxable.
Washington	N/A, because state does not tax general business corporation income.	
West Virginia	Exempt	Interest on obligations of federal authorities, commissions, or instrumentalities that is exempt for federal tax but not from state tax is taxable.

Jurisdiction	U.S. Bonds	Comment
Wisconsin	Exempt under income tax. Taxable under franchise tax.	
Wyoming	N/A, because state does not tax general business corporation income.	

Taxability of Bond Interest (Personal Income)—Other States' Bonds

Jurisdiction	Other States' Bonds	Comment
Alabama	Taxable	
Arizona	Taxable	
Arkansas	Taxable	
California	Taxable	
Colorado	Taxable	
Connecticut	Taxable	
Delaware	Taxable	
District of Columbia	Exempt	
Georgia	Taxable	
Hawaii	Taxable	
Idaho	Taxable	
Illinois	Taxable	
Indiana	**After 2011** Taxable **Prior to 2012** Exempt	
Iowa	Taxable	
Kansas	Taxable	
Kentucky	Taxable	
Louisiana	Taxable	Interest from obligations of another state or political subdivision of another state that was not reported on federal return is taxable if obligations were purchased after 1979.
Maine	Taxable	
Maryland	Taxable	
Massachusetts	Taxable	
Michigan	Taxable	
Minnesota	Taxable	
Mississippi	Taxable	
Missouri	Taxable	
Montana	Taxable	
Nebraska	Taxable	
New Hampshire	Taxable	
New Jersey	Taxable	

Jurisdiction	Other States' Bonds	Comment
New Mexico	Taxable	Interest from obligations of Puerto Rico, Guam, and other U.S. territories and possessions is exempt.
New York	Taxable	
North Carolina	Taxable	
North Dakota	Exempt	
Ohio	Taxable	
Oklahoma	Taxable	
Oregon	Taxable	
Pennsylvania	Taxable	
Rhode Island	Taxable	
South Carolina	Taxable	
Tennessee	Taxable	
Utah	Taxable	Interest from non-Utah state and local bonds acquired after 2002 is taxable only if the other state or locality imposes an income-based tax on Utah government bonds.
Vermont	Taxable	
Virginia	Taxable	
West Virginia	Taxable	
Wisconsin	Taxable	

Taxability of Bond Interest (Personal Income)—State's Own Bonds

Jurisdiction	State's Own Bonds	Comment
Alabama	Exempt	
Arizona	Exempt	
Arkansas	Exempt	
California	Exempt	
Colorado	Exempt	Interest from bonds issued by CO or any of its political subdivisions on or after May 1, 1980 is exempt. Additionally, interest from specified obligations issued prior to May 1, 1980 is exempt under CO law.
Connecticut	Exempt	
Delaware	Exempt	
District of Columbia	Exempt	
Georgia	Exempt	
Hawaii	Exempt	
Idaho	Exempt	
Illinois	Taxable	Interest income from specified obligations is exempt and may be subtracted from adjusted gross income.
Indiana	Exempt	
Iowa	Taxable	Interest income from specified obligations is exempt.
Kansas	Exempt	
Kentucky	Exempt	
Louisiana	Exempt	
Maine	Exempt	
Maryland	Exempt	
Massachusetts	Exempt	
Michigan	Exempt	
Minnesota	Exempt	
Mississippi	Exempt	
Missouri	Exempt	
Montana	Exempt	
Nebraska	Exempt	
New Hampshire	Exempt	
New Jersey	Exempt	

Jurisdiction	State's Own Bonds	Comment
New Mexico	Exempt	
New York	Exempt	
North Carolina	Exempt	
North Dakota	Exempt	
Ohio	Exempt	
Oklahoma	Taxable	Income from obligations issued by OK or any of its political subdivisions is exempt if so provided by the statute authorizing issuance of the obligation or if it is a local governmental obligation issued after July 1, 2001, for a purpose other than to provide financing for nonprofit corporate projects.
Oregon	Exempt	
Pennsylvania	Exempt	
Rhode Island	Exempt	
South Carolina	Exempt	
Tennessee	Exempt	
Utah	Exempt	Income from certain general obligation bonds for capital facilities and to facilitate highway construction is also exempt.
Vermont	Exempt	
Virginia	Exempt	
West Virginia	Exempt	
Wisconsin	Taxable	Income from specified obligations is exempt.

Taxability of Bond Interest (Personal Income)—U.S. Bonds

Jurisdiction	U.S. Bonds	Comment
Alabama	Exempt	
Arizona	Exempt	
Arkansas	Exempt	
California	Exempt	
Colorado	Exempt	
Connecticut	Exempt	Interest on obligations of federal authorities, commissions, or instrumentalities that is exempt for federal tax, but not from state tax, is taxable.
Delaware	Exempt	
District of Columbia	Exempt	
Georgia	Exempt	
Hawaii	Exempt	
Idaho	Exempt	
Illinois	Exempt	
Indiana	Exempt	
Iowa	Exempt	
Kansas	Exempt	
Kentucky	Exempt	
Louisiana	Exempt	
Maine	Exempt	Interest on obligations of federal authorities, commissions, or instrumentalities that is exempt for federal tax, but not from state tax, is taxable.
Maryland	Exempt	
Massachusetts	Exempt	
Michigan	Exempt	
Minnesota	Exempt	
Mississippi	Exempt	
Missouri	Exempt	
Montana	Exempt	
Nebraska	Exempt	
New Hampshire	Exempt	
New Jersey	Exempt	
New Mexico	Exempt	

Jurisdiction	U.S. Bonds	Comment
New York	Exempt	
North Carolina	Exempt	
North Dakota	Exempt	
Ohio	Exempt	
Oklahoma	Exempt	
Oregon	Exempt	
Pennsylvania	Exempt	
Rhode Island	Exempt	
South Carolina	Exempt	
Tennessee	Exempt	
Utah	Exempt	
Vermont	Exempt	
Virginia	Exempt	Interest on obligations of federal authorities, commissions, or instrumentalities that is exempt for federal tax, but not from state tax, is taxable.
West Virginia	Exempt	
Wisconsin	Exempt	

Taxes Paid Deduction—Federal Income Taxes

Most states do not allow taxpayers to deduct federal income tax paid in computing corporation income tax liability. This chart shows whether each state and the District of Columbia allow a deduction for income taxes paid to the U.S..

Jurisdiction	Federal Income Taxes	Comment
Alabama	Subtraction adjustment allowed for taxes paid on income attributable to state sources.	
Alaska	No deduction allowed.	
Arizona	No deduction allowed.	
Arkansas	No deduction allowed.	
California	No deduction allowed.	
Colorado	No deduction allowed.	
Connecticut	No deduction allowed.	
Delaware	No deduction allowed.	
District of Columbia	No deduction allowed in computing tax base.	
Florida	No deduction allowed.	
Georgia	No deduction allowed.	
Hawaii	No deduction allowed.	
Idaho	No deduction allowed.	
Illinois	No deduction allowed.	
Indiana	No deduction allowed.	
Iowa	Subtraction adjustment allowed for 50% of tax paid.	
Kansas	No deduction allowed.	
Kentucky	No deduction allowed.	
Louisiana	Subtraction adjustment allowed for taxes paid on income attributable to state sources.	
Maine	No deduction allowed.	
Maryland	No deduction allowed.	
Massachusetts	No deduction allowed.	
Michigan	No deduction allowed.	
Minnesota	No deduction allowed.	
Mississippi	No deduction allowed.	

Jurisdiction	Federal Income Taxes	Comment
Missouri	Subtraction adjustment allowed for 50% of taxes paid on income attributable to state sources.	
Montana	No deduction allowed.	
Nebraska	No deduction allowed.	
Nevada	N/A, because state does not tax general business corporation income.	
New Hampshire	No deduction allowed.	
New Jersey	No deduction allowed.	
New Mexico	No deduction allowed.	
New York	No deduction allowed.	
North Carolina	No deduction allowed.	
North Dakota	No adjustment allowed for tax years after 2003.	
Ohio	No deduction allowed.	
Oklahoma	No deduction allowed.	
Oregon	No deduction allowed.	
Pennsylvania	No deduction allowed.	
Rhode Island	No deduction allowed.	
South Carolina	No deduction allowed.	
South Dakota	N/A, because state does not tax general business corporation income.	
Tennessee	No deduction allowed.	
Texas	No deduction allowed.	
Utah	No deduction allowed.	
Vermont	No deduction allowed.	
Virginia	No deduction allowed.	
Washington	N/A, because state does not tax general business corporation income.	
West Virginia	No deduction allowed.	
Wisconsin	No deduction allowed.	
Wyoming	N/A, because state does not tax general business corporation income.	

Taxes Paid Deduction—Foreign Taxes Paid

A corporation computing taxable income for federal income tax purposes may annually choose to take either a credit or a deduction for foreign taxes paid or accrued. Generally, if a corporation elects the benefits of the foreign tax credit (FTC) for any tax year, no portion of the foreign taxes are allowed as a deduction in that year or any subsequent tax year. None of the states have a credit equivalent to the federal FTC. In many states, no adjustment to the tax base is required or allowed for the amount of the federal deduction or the amount disallowed as a federal deduction if the FTC is claimed by the taxpayer. Other states require an addition to the tax base for the amount of the federal deduction. Some states allow a subtraction for the amount disallowed as a federal deduction if the FTC is claimed by the taxpayer. This chart indicates states that require or allow an adjustment to taxable income when either a federal deduction or credit is claimed for foreign taxes paid.

Jurisdiction	Foreign Taxes Paid	Comment
Alabama	Subtraction allowed for amount of federal deduction disallowed if foreign tax credit is claimed.	
Alaska	Addition required for amount of federal deduction.	
Arizona	Addition required for amount of federal deduction.	
Arkansas	Subtraction allowed for amount of foreign taxes paid.	
California	Addition required for amount of federal deduction.	
Colorado	Addition required for amount of federal deduction.	Subtraction allowed for amount equal to federal deduction or, if federal foreign tax credit is claimed, a portion of foreign source income included federal taxable income.
Connecticut	No adjustment required or allowed.	
Delaware	Addition required for amount of federal deduction.	
District of Columbia	Addition required for amount of federal deduction for reconciliation purposes.	Subtraction of income taxes not allowed in computing tax base.
Florida	No addition required for federal deduction.	Subtraction allowed for foreign taxes taken as credits under IRC Sec. 901 to any corporation that derived less than 20% of its gross income or loss for its tax year ending in 1984 from sources within the U.S.
Georgia	Addition required for amount of federal deduction.	
Hawaii	No adjustment required or allowed.	

Jurisdiction	Foreign Taxes Paid	Comment
Idaho	No adjustment required or allowed.	
Illinois	No adjustment required or allowed.	
Indiana	Addition required for amount of federal deduction.	
Iowa	No adjustment required or allowed.	
Kansas	Addition required for amount of federal deduction.	
Kentucky	Addition required for amount of federal deduction.	
Louisiana	No adjustment required or allowed.	
Maine	No adjustment required or allowed.	
Maryland	No adjustment required or allowed.	
Massachusetts	Addition required for amount of federal deduction.	
Michigan	Addition required.	
Minnesota	Addition required for amount of federal deduction.	
Mississippi	Addition required for amount of federal deduction.	
Missouri	No adjustment required or allowed.	
Montana	Addition required for amount of federal deduction.	
Nebraska	Subtraction allowed for portion of federal deduction disallowed if foreign tax credit is claimed.	
Nevada	N/A, because state does not tax general business corporation income.	
New Hampshire	Addition required for amount of federal deduction.	
New Jersey	Addition required for amount of federal deduction.	
New Mexico	No adjustment required or allowed.	
New York	No addition required for amount of federal deduction.	For tax years before 2015, addition required for amount of federal deduction.
North Carolina	Addition required for amount of federal deduction.	
North Dakota	Addition required for amount of federal deduction.	
Ohio	No adjustment required or allowed.	
Oklahoma	Addition required for amount of federal deduction.	

Jurisdiction	Foreign Taxes Paid	Comment
Oregon	Addition required for amount of federal deduction.	
Pennsylvania	Addition required for amount of federal deduction.	
Rhode Island	No adjustment required or allowed.	
South Carolina	Addition required for amount of federal deduction.	
South Dakota	N/A, because state does not tax general business corporation income.	
Tennessee	No adjustment required or allowed.	
Texas	No adjustment required or allowed.	
Utah	Addition required for amount of federal deduction.	
Vermont	No adjustment required or allowed.	
Virginia	Addition required for amount of federal deduction.	
Washington	N/A, because state does not tax general business corporation income.	
West Virginia	Addition required for amount of federal deduction.	
Wisconsin	Subtraction allowed for amount of federal deduction disallowed if foreign tax credit is claimed and income is subject to state's franchise or income tax.	Subtraction computed on Sch. W.
Wyoming	N/A, because state does not tax general business corporation income.	

Taxes Paid Deduction—State and Local Income Taxes

State and local taxes relating to a taxpayer's trade or business or activities for the production of income are generally deductible for federal income tax purposes in the year in which the taxes are paid or accrued. Most states do not allow a deduction for state or local taxes measured by income. Such states require an addition adjustment in computing state income tax liability for state and local taxes deducted on the federal return. States that allow a deduction generally limit it to income taxes paid to other states and do not extend the deduction to amounts paid to the taxing state or its localities. This chart shows whether each state and the District of Columbia allow a corporation income tax deduction for income taxes paid to states or localities.

Jurisdiction	State and Local Income Taxes	Comment
Alabama	Addition required for amount of federal deduction.	
Alaska	Addition required for amount of federal deduction.	
Arizona	Addition required for amount of federal deduction.	
Arkansas	Subtraction adjustment allowed, except for Arkansas taxes.	
California	Addition required for amount of federal deduction, including for taxes such as the: • Illinois personal property replacement income tax; and • New Hampshire business profits tax. No addition required for Texas franchise (margin) tax.	
Colorado	Addition required for Colorado income taxes.	
Connecticut	Addition required for amount of federal deduction.	
Delaware	Addition required for amount of federal deduction.	
District of Columbia	No deduction allowed in computing tax base.	
Florida	Addition required for amount of federal deduction, except local taxes.	
Georgia	Addition required for amount of federal deduction, except Georgia income taxes.	
Hawaii	No adjustment required for amount of federal deduction.	
Idaho	Addition required for amount of federal deduction.	

Jurisdiction	State and Local Income Taxes	Comment
Illinois	Addition required for Illinois income and replacement taxes.	
Indiana	Addition required for amount of federal deduction, including but not limited to taxes such as the: • Indiana riverboat wagering tax; • Texas Franchise (Margin) Tax; • Washington Business and Occupation Tax; and • West Virginia Business and Occupation Tax.	
Iowa	Addition required for Iowa income taxes.	
Kansas	Addition required for amount of federal deduction, including: • Texas Revised Franchise (Margin) Tax, if determined by deducting cost of goods sold or compensation from gross receipts; and • Michigan Business Tax (MBT) based on income. No addition required for Ohio Commercial Activity Tax (CAT).	
Kentucky	Addition required for amount of federal deduction.	
Louisiana	Addition required for Louisiana income taxes.	
Maine	Addition required for amount of federal deduction, except addition does not apply to: • Ohio Commercial Activities Tax (CAT); • Texas Revised Franchise (Margin) Tax; and • Michigan Business Tax (MBT) based on gross receipts.	
Maryland	Addition required for amount of federal deduction.	

Jurisdiction	State and Local Income Taxes	Comment
Massachusetts	Addition required for amount of federal deduction, including but not limited to taxes such as the: • Delaware Gross Receipts Tax (Merchants' and Manufacturers' License Taxes); • Indiana Gross Income Tax; • Los Angeles City Tax; • Louisiana Franchise Tax; • Michigan Business Tax based on gross receipts; • New Hampshire Business Profits Tax; • New Hampshire Insurance Premiums Tax; • Ohio Commercial Activities Tax (CAT); • Ohio Franchise Tax; • Pennsylvania Franchise Tax; • San Francisco Business Tax (including the San Francisco Payroll Expense Tax); • Texas Franchise (Margin) Tax; • Washington Business and Occupation Tax; and • West Virginia Business and Occupation Tax.	
Michigan	Addition required for amount of federal deduction.	
Minnesota	Addition required for amount of federal deduction, excluding: • Ohio Commercial Activities Tax (CAT); • Texas Revised Franchise (Margin) Tax; and • Michigan Business Tax (MBT) based on gross receipts.	
Mississippi	Addition required for amount of federal deduction.	
Missouri	Addition required for amount of federal deduction.	
Montana	Addition required for amount of federal deduction.	
Nebraska	No adjustment required for amount of federal deduction.	
Nevada	N/A, because state does not tax general business corporation income.	
New Hampshire	Addition required for amount of federal deduction.	
New Jersey	Addition required for amount of federal deduction, including: • Ohio Commercial Activities Tax (CAT), • Texas Revised Franchise (Margin) Tax, and • Washington Business and Occupation Tax (B&O tax)	

Jurisdiction	State and Local Income Taxes	Comment
New Mexico	No adjustment required for amount of federal deduction.	
New York	Addition required for amount of federal deduction.	New York City taxes not added back.
North Carolina	Addition required for amount of federal deduction.	
North Dakota	Addition required for amount of federal deduction.	
Ohio	No adjustment required for amount of federal deduction.	
Oklahoma	Addition required for amount of federal deduction.	
Oregon	Addition required for amount of federal deduction, except local taxes.	
Pennsylvania	Addition required for amount of federal deduction. The following states do not impose an income tax subject to addback: • Nevada; • South Dakota; • Texas (unless paid based on net earned surplus); • Washington; and • Wyoming.	
Rhode Island	Addition required for Rhode Island business corporation and franchise taxes.	
South Carolina	Addition required for amount of federal deduction, including the: • District of Columbia Unincorporated Business Tax; • Michigan Business Tax; • New Hampshire Business Profits Tax; and • Texas Franchise (Margin) Tax. No addition required for: • Ohio Commercial Activities Tax (CAT); • Washington Business and Occupation Tax; and • West Virginia Business and Occupation Tax.	
South Dakota	N/A, because state does not tax general business corporation income.	
Tennessee	Addition required for Tennessee excise tax.	
Texas	No adjustment required for amount of federal deduction.	
Utah	Addition required for amount of federal deduction.	
Vermont	Addition required for amount of federal deduction.	

Jurisdiction	State and Local Income Taxes	Comment
Virginia	Addition required for amount of federal deduction, excluding: • Texas Revised Franchise (Margin) Tax; and • Kentucky Limited Liability Entity Tax.	
Washington	N/A, because state does not tax general business corporation income.	
West Virginia	Addition required for amount of federal deduction.	
Wisconsin	Addition required for amount of federal deduction, including the: • Michigan Business Tax; • New Hampshire Business Profits Tax; and • Texas Franchise (Margin) Tax. No addition required for: • Ohio Commercial Activities Tax (CAT); • Washington Business and Occupation Tax; and • West Virginia Business and Occupation Tax.	Local income taxes not added back.
Wyoming	N/A, because state does not tax general business corporation income.	

UDITPA Conformity

The Uniform Division of Income for Tax Purposes Act (UDITPA) is a model law for apportioning the income of a corporation that is taxable in two or more states. UDITPA breaks income into two classes: business income, which is apportionable, and nonbusiness income, which is allocable. UDITPA also provides for the use of an equally-weighted three-factor formula consisting of a sales factor, property factor, and payroll factor.

This chart indicates whether each state and the District of Columbia has adopted UDITPA for the purposes of computing corporation income tax liability or has enacted substantially similar statutory or regulatory provisions. Variations from UDITPA apportionment formula are covered in a chart under the topic Apportionment Formulas.

Jurisdiction	UDITPA Conformity	Comment
Alabama	Yes	
Alaska	Yes	
Arizona	Yes, with modifications.	
Arkansas	Yes, with modifications.	Modifies treatment of capital gains and losses from property sales. Requires apportionment of income attributed to activity within and outside state. Effective for taxable years beginning on or after January 1, 2021, single sales factor apportionment formula implemented.
California	Yes, with modifications.	
Colorado	No	
Connecticut	No	
Delaware	No, but similar statute.	
District of Columbia	No, but substantially similar provisions.	
Florida	No, but many similar provisions.	
Georgia	No, but some similar provisions.	
Hawaii	Yes, with modifications.	
Idaho	Yes, with modifications.	
Illinois	No, but many similar provisions.	
Indiana	No, but many similar provisions.	
Iowa	No, but some similar provisions.	

Jurisdiction	UDITPA Conformity	Comment
Kansas	Yes, with modifications.	Differences include special apportionment factors for certain industries, inclusion of public utilities as businesses subject to apportionment, an election of equally-weighted property and sales factor formula for certain taxpayers, and special rules for 2 or more corporations contriving to evade taxes through intercompany transactions.
Kentucky	Yes, with many modifications.	
Louisiana	No, but some similar provisions.	
Maine	Yes, with modifications.	
Maryland	No	
Massachusetts	No	
Michigan	No	
Minnesota	No	
Mississippi	No, but some similar provisions.	
Missouri	Yes, with modifications.	
Montana	Yes, with modifications.	
Nebraska	No, but some similar provisions.	
Nevada	N/A, because state does not tax general business corporation income.	
New Hampshire	No, but many similar provisions.	
New Jersey	No	
New Mexico	Yes, with modifications.	
New York	No	
North Carolina	No, but many similar provisions.	
North Dakota	Yes, with modifications.	Provisions differ regarding public utilities and allocation of gain or loss on sale of partnership interest.
Ohio	No, but many similar provisions.	
Oklahoma	No, but many similar provisions.	
Oregon	Yes, with modifications.	
Pennsylvania	Yes, with modifications.	
Rhode Island	No, but some similar provisions.	
South Carolina	No	
South Dakota	N/A, because state does not tax general business corporation income.	
Tennessee	No, but many similar provisions.	

Jurisdiction	UDITPA Conformity	Comment
Texas	No	
Utah	Yes, with modifications.	
Vermont	No, but some similar provisions.	
Virginia	No	
Washington	N/A, because state does not tax general business corporation income.	
West Virginia	No	
Wisconsin	No, but many similar provisions.	
Wyoming	N/A, because state does not tax general business corporation income.	

Withholding—Partnerships, LLPs, and LLCs

Under the Multistate Tax Commission's (MTC) proposed statutory language on pass-through entity nonresident withholding requirements, general and limited partnerships, limited liability partnerships (LLPs), and limited liability companies (LLCs) that are not taxed as a corporation must withhold and pay income tax on the share of income of the entity distributed to each nonresident partner or member. The withholding requirements apply both to nonresident individuals and nonresident business entities. Many states have adopted similar nonresident withholding requirements. Some states have extended the withholding requirements to resident partners and members. This chart shows whether each state and the District of Columbia require partnerships, LLPs, and LLCs to withhold on partner or member income.

States that require pass-through entities to file estimated returns and pay estimated tax, instead of withholding, on behalf of owners are covered under the topic Estimated Tax—Partnerships, LLCs, and LLPs. States that require pass through entities to file composite returns and make composite payments, instead of withholding on behalf of owners are covered under the topics Composite Returns—Partnerships, Composite Returns—LLCs, and Composite Returns—LLPs.

Jurisdiction	Partnerships, LLPs, and LLCs	Comment
Alabama	N/A, because withholding not required.	
Alaska	N/A, because withholding not required.	No personal income tax.
Arizona	N/A, because withholding not required.	
Arkansas	Withholding required for the following nonresident owners: • individuals; • trusts; and • C corporations (2018 tax year and thereafter).	
California	Withholding required for the following domestic nonresident owners: • individuals; • corporations; • partnerships, LLPs, and LLCs; • trusts; and • estates. Withholding required for the following foreign (non-U.S.) partners: • nonresident alien individuals; • corporations; • partnerships, LLPs, and LLCs; • trusts; and • estates.	

Jurisdiction	Partnerships, LLPs, and LLCs	Comment
Colorado	Withholding required for the following nonresident owners: • individuals; • trusts; and • estates.	
Connecticut	N/A, because withholding not required.	Pass-through entity tax applies for tax years after 2017. Composite return and payment requirements apply for tax years before 2018.
Delaware	N/A, because withholding not required.	
District of Columbia	N/A, because withholding not required.	Personal income tax not applicable to nonresidents.
Florida	N/A, because withholding not required.	No personal income tax.
Georgia	Withholding required for the following nonresident owners: • individuals; • corporations, except C corporations that meet certain conditions; • partnerships, LLPs, and LLCs; and • fiduciaries.	
Hawaii	N/A, because withholding not required.	
Idaho	Withholding required for nonresident individuals (including grantor trusts, qualified subchapter S trusts, and single member LLCs treated as a disregarded entity).	
Illinois	Withholding required for the following nonresident owners: • individuals; • corporations; • partnerships, LLPs, and LLCs; • trusts; and • estates.	
Indiana	Withholding required for the following nonresident owners: • individuals, except residents of reverse credit states who pay income tax at equivalent or higher rate; • C corporations not registered with the state; • partnerships, LLPs, and LLCs; • S corporations; • trusts; and • estates.	
Iowa	Withholding required for nonresident individuals.	

Jurisdiction	Partnerships, LLPs, and LLCs	Comment
Kansas	N/A, because withholding not required after July 1, 2014.	Prior to July 1, 2014, withholding required for the following nonresident owners: • individuals; • corporations; • partnerships, LLPs, and LLCs; • trusts; and • estates.
Kentucky	Withholding required for the following nonresident owners: • individuals; • C corporations doing business in the state only through ownership interests in the entity; • trusts; and • estates.	
Louisiana	N/A, because withholding not required.	
Maine	Withholding required for the following nonresident owners: • individuals; • corporations; • partnerships, LLPs, and LLCs; • trusts; and • estates.	
Maryland	Withholding required for the following nonresident owners: • individuals; • corporations; • partnerships, LLPs, and LLCs; and • trusts.	
Massachusetts	Withholding required for the following owners: • individuals; • corporations; • partnerships, LLPs, and LLCs; • trusts; and • estates.	Tax is calculated by multiplying withholding rate by lesser of 80% of shareholder's distributive share for the taxable year, or 100% of shareholder's prior year distributive share.
Michigan	N/A, because withholding not required for tax years beginning after July 1, 2016.	For tax years beginning before July 1, 2016, withholding required for the following nonresident owners: • individuals; • C corporations; • S corporations; • partnerships, LLPs, and LLCs; • trusts; and • estates. In addition, for tax years beginning before July 1, 2016, withholding required for each member that is a corporation or flow through entity, if business income of withholding entity that is attributable to state sources exceeds $200,000.
Minnesota	Withholding required for nonresident individuals.	

Jurisdiction	Partnerships, LLPs, and LLCs	Comment
Mississippi	Withholding optional for resident or nonresident individuals, except for individuals who fail to pay or report taxes, in which case entity is jointly and severally liable for the individual's tax liability.	
Missouri	Withholding required for nonresident individuals.	
Montana	Withholding required for the following nonresident owners: • individuals; • corporations; • partnerships, LLPs, and LLCs; • trusts; and • estates.	
Nebraska	Withholding required for nonresident individuals.	
Nevada	N/A, because state does not tax pass-through income.	
New Hampshire	N/A, because partnerships, LLPs, and LLCs taxed at entity level.	
New Jersey	N/A, because withholding not required.	State effectively requires withholding for the nonresident partner tax through estimated tax payment requirements.
New Mexico	Withholding required for the following nonresident owners: • individuals; • corporations; • partnerships, LLPs, and LLCs; • trusts; and • estates.	
New York	N/A, because withholding not required.	
North Carolina	Withholding required for the following nonresident owners: • individuals; • corporations; • partnerships, LLPs, and LLCs; • trusts other than grantor trusts; and • estates.	
North Dakota	Withholding required for the following nonresident owners: • individuals; • S corporations (taxable years beginning after 2013); • partnerships, LLPs, and LLCs (taxable years beginning after 2013); and • trusts.	

Jurisdiction	Partnerships, LLPs, and LLCs	Comment
Ohio	Withholding required for the following nonresident owners: • individuals; • nonexempt S corporations, partnerships, LLPs, and LLCs (investing entities); • trusts; and • estates.	Withholding required for C corporation investors prior to 2009 tax year.
Oklahoma	Withholding required for the following nonresident owners: • individuals • C corporations; • S corporations; • partnerships, LPs, LLPs, and LLCs and; • trusts.	
Oregon	Withholding required for the following nonresident owners: • individuals; and • C corporations.	
Pennsylvania	Withholding required for the following nonresident owners: • individuals; • inter vivos or testamentary trusts; and • decedents' estates.	
Rhode Island	Withholding required for the following nonresident owners: • individuals; • corporations; • partnerships, LLPs, and LLCs; and • trusts.	For tax years beginning on or after January 1, 2019, a pass-through entity may elect to pay the state tax at the entity level. Such entities that make the election do not have to comply with the provisions regarding withholding on nonresident owners.
South Carolina	Withholding required for nonresident individuals and C corporations.	
South Dakota	N/A, because state does not tax pass-through income.	
Tennessee	N/A, because partnerships LLPs, and LLCs taxed at entity level.	
Texas	**Revised Franchise (Margin) Tax:** N/A, because partnerships (except certain general partnerships), LLPs, and LLCs taxed at entity level. **Franchise Tax prior to 2008 tax year:** N/A for partnerships and LLPs, because withholding not required. N/A for LLCs, because taxed at entity level.	No personal income tax.

Jurisdiction	Partnerships, LLPs, and LLCs	Comment
Utah	Withholding required for the following: • nonresident individuals; • resident or nonresident corporations; • resident or nonresident partnerships, LLPs and LLCs; • resident or nonresident trusts; and • resident or nonresident estates.	
Vermont	N/A, because withholding not required.	
Virginia	Withholding required for the following nonresident owners: • individuals; and • corporations.	
Washington	N/A, because state does not tax pass-through income.	
West Virginia	Withholding required for the following nonresident owners: • individuals; • corporations; • partnerships, LLPs, and LLCs; • trusts; and • estates.	
Wisconsin	Withholding required for the following nonresident owners: • individuals; • corporations; • partnerships, LLPs, and LLCs; • trusts; and • estates.	
Wyoming	N/A, because state does not tax pass-through income.	

Withholding—S Corporations

Under the Multistate Tax Commission's (MTC) proposed statutory language on pass-through entity nonresident withholding requirements, S corporations must withhold and pay income tax on the share of income of the entity distributed to each nonresident shareholder. The withholding requirements apply both to nonresident individuals and nonresident business entities. Many states have adopted similar nonresident withholding requirements. Some states have extended the withholding requirements to resident shareholders. This chart shows whether each state and the District of Columbia require S corporations to withhold on shareholder income.

States that require S corporations to file estimated returns and pay estimated tax, instead of withholding, on behalf of shareholders are covered under the topic Estimated Tax—S Corporations. States that require S corporations to file composite returns and make composite payments, instead of withholding, on behalf of shareholders are covered under the topic Composite Returns—S Corporations.

Jurisdiction	S Corporations	Comment
Alabama	N/A, because withholding not required.	
Alaska	N/A, because withholding not required.	No personal income tax.
Arizona	N/A, because withholding not required.	
Arkansas	Withholding required for the following nonresident owners: • individuals; • trusts; and • C corporations (2018 tax year and thereafter).	
California	Withholding required for the following domestic nonresident owners: • individuals; • trusts; and • estates.	
Colorado	Withholding required for the following nonresident owners: • individuals; • trusts; and • estates.	
Connecticut	N/A, because withholding not required.	Pass-through entity tax applies for tax years after 2017. Composite return and payment requirements apply for tax years before 2018.
Delaware	N/A, because withholding not required.	
District of Columbia	N/A, because withholding not required.	S corporations taxed at entity level in same manner as other corporations.
Florida	N/A, because withholding not required.	No personal income tax.

Jurisdiction	S Corporations	Comment
Georgia	Withholding required for the following nonresident owners: • individuals; and • fiduciaries.	
Hawaii	Withholding required for the following nonresident owners: • individuals; • trusts; and • estates.	
Idaho	Withholding required for nonresident individuals (including grantor trusts, qualified subchapter S trusts, and single member LLCs treated as a disregarded entity).	
Illinois	Withholding required for the following nonresident owners: • individuals; • trusts; and • estates.	
Indiana	Withholding required for the following nonresident owners: • individuals, except residents of reverse credit states who pay income tax at equivalent or higher rate; • trusts; and • estates.	
Iowa	Withholding required for nonresident individuals.	
Kansas	N/A, because withholding not required after July 1, 2014.	Prior to July 1, 2014, withholding required for the following nonresident owners: • individuals; • trusts; and • estates.
Kentucky	Withholding required for the following nonresident owners: • individuals; • trusts; and • estates.	
Louisiana	N/A, because S corporations taxed at entity level.	
Maine	Withholding required for the following nonresident owners: • individuals; • trusts; and • estates.	
Maryland	Withholding required for the following nonresident owners: • individuals; and • trusts.	
Massachusetts	Withholding required for the following owners: • individuals; • trusts; and • estates.	Tax is calculated by multiplying withholding rate by lesser of 80% of shareholder's distributive share for the taxable year, or 100% of shareholder's prior year distributive share.

Jurisdiction	S Corporations	Comment
Michigan	N/A, because withholding not required for tax years beginning after July 1, 2016.	For tax years beginning before July 1, 2016, withholding required for the following nonresident owners: • individuals; • C corporations; • S corporations; • partnerships, LLPs, and LLCs; • trusts; and • estates. In addition, for tax years beginning before July 1, 2016, withholding required for each member that is a corporation or flow through entity, if business income of withholding entity that is attributable to state sources exceeds $200,000.
Minnesota	Withholding required for nonresident individuals.	
Mississippi	Withholding required for nonresident individuals who: • fail to file nonresident agreement to pay tax; or • fail to file a return and to pay tax.	
Missouri	Withholding required for nonresident individuals.	
Montana	Withholding required for the following nonresident owners: • individuals; • trusts; and • estates.	
Nebraska	Withholding required for nonresident individuals.	
Nevada	N/A, because state does not tax pass-through income.	
New Hampshire	N/A, because S corporations taxed at entity level.	
New Jersey	Withholding required for nonresident individuals who are not initial shareholders and who fail to consent to state S corporation election.	
New Mexico	Withholding required for the following nonresident owners: • individuals; • trusts; and • estates.	
New York	N/A, because withholding not required.	
North Carolina	N/A, because withholding not required.	
North Dakota	Withholding required for the following nonresident owners: • individuals; and • trusts.	

Jurisdiction	S Corporations	Comment
Ohio	Withholding required for the following nonresident owners: • individuals; • trusts; and • estates.	
Oklahoma	Withholding required for the following nonresident owners: • individuals; and • trusts.	
Oregon	Withholding required for nonresident individuals.	
Pennsylvania	Withholding required for the following nonresident owners: • individuals; • inter vivos or testamentary trusts; and • decedents' estates.	
Rhode Island	Withholding required for the following nonresident owners: • individuals; and • trusts.	
South Carolina	Withholding required for nonresident individuals.	
South Dakota	N/A, because state does not tax pass-through income.	
Tennessee	N/A, S corporations taxed at entity level.	
Texas	N/A, because S corporations taxed at entity level.	No personal income tax.
Utah	Withholding required for the following owners: • nonresident individuals; • resident or nonresident businesses; • resident or nonresident trusts; and • resident or nonresident estates.	
Vermont	N/A, because withholding not required.	
Virginia	Withholding required for nonresident individuals.	
Washington	N/A, because state does not tax pass-through income.	
West Virginia	Withholding required for the following nonresident owners: • individuals; • trusts; and • estates.	

Jurisdiction	S Corporations	Comment
Wisconsin	Withholding required for the following nonresident owners: • individuals; • trusts; and • estates.	
Wyoming	N/A, because state does not tax pass-through income.	

Withholding Returns and Deposits—Annual Reconciliation

For federal income tax purposes, employers must annually file Form W-3, Transmittal of Wage and Tax Statements, and Copy A of all Forms W-2, Wage and Tax Statement, that were issued for the previous calendar year. These forms are filed with the Social Security Administration and then forwarded to the IRS and are due by January 31. All states that impose a personal income tax require withholding of tax by employers. The frequency of remittance of tax to the state varies, as does the frequency of returns. This chart shows the annual reconciliation due dates and forms in effect for each state and the District of Columbia. If the due date falls on a Saturday, Sunday, or legal holiday, states generally allow the return to be filed on the next business day.

Jurisdiction	Annual Reconciliation	Comment
Alabama	Form A-3 must be filed by February 28.	Employers and agents submitting 25 or more state W-2 and/or 1099 statements with state tax withheld must submit form electronically through the state's website.
Arizona	Form A-1R must be filed by February 28.	
Arkansas	Form AR3MAR must be filed by January 31. Prior to 2018, Form ARSMAR must be filed by February 28 or 30 days after termination of business.	
California	None	
Colorado	Form DR 1093 must be filed by January 31 following the close of the calendar year.	
Connecticut	Form CT-W3 must be filed by January 31.	Electronic filing and payment required effective for tax periods beginning after 2013. Due date for tax periods before 2015 was March 31 and for tax periods before 2014, February 28 for paper filing or March 31 for electronic filing.
Delaware	Form W-3 must be filed by January 31 (February 28 for tax years before 2016).	
District of Columbia	Form FR-900B must be filed by January 31.	
Georgia	Form G-1003 must be filed by February 28.	
Hawaii	Form HW-3 must be filed by February 28.	
Idaho	Form 967 must be filed by last day of January.	
Illinois	None	
Indiana	Form WH-3 must be filed by January 31.	

Jurisdiction	Annual Reconciliation	Comment
Iowa	Form 44-007/VSP must be filed by February 28.	
Kansas	Form KW-3/KW-3E must be filed by January 31.	Entities reporting for 51 or more employees or payees must file electronically.
Kentucky	Form K-3 must be filed by January 31.	
Louisiana	Form L-3 must be filed by January 31.	
Maine	Form W-3ME must be filed by February 28.	Employers that are registered for state income tax withholding must electronically file all original annual reconciliation forms.
Maryland	Form MW-508 must be filed by January 31 (February 28 prior to July 1, 2016).	Prior to July 1, 2016, the due date was February 28. Employers with 25 or more W-2 wage statements to report are required to file electronically.
Massachusetts	Form M-941A must be filed by January 31.	
Michigan	Form MI-W3 must be filed by February 28 for tax years before 2018 (January 31 beginning with tax year 2018).	
Minnesota	Form MW5 must be filed by January 31.	
Mississippi	Form 89-140 must be filed by January 31 for paper filers or February 28 for magnetic filers.	
Missouri	Form W-3 must be filed by February 28.	
Montana	Form MW-3 must be filed by February 28.	
Nebraska	Form W-3N must be filed by January 31.	
New Hampshire	Withholding not required.	Personal income tax applies only to interest and dividend income.
New Jersey	Form NJ-W-3M must be filed by February 28.	
New Mexico	Form RPD-41072 must be filed by February 28.	
New York	Form NYS-45 must be filed by January 31.	
North Carolina	Form NC-3 must be filed electronically by January 31.	
North Dakota	Form 307 must be filed January 31.	
Ohio	Form IT-941 must be filed January 31.	

Jurisdiction	Annual Reconciliation	Comment
Oklahoma	The annual report must be filed by February 28 of the following year, using the Tax Commissioner's electronic data interchange program.	
Oregon	Form WR must be filed January 31.	
Pennsylvania	Form Rev-1667R must be filed January 31.	
Rhode Island	Form RI-W3 must be filed January 31.	
South Carolina	Form WH-1606 must be filed by the last day of February.	
Tennessee	Withholding not required.	Personal income tax applies only to stock and bond income.
Utah	Form TC-941R must be filed by February 28 for paper filing or March 31 for eletronic filing.	
Vermont	Beginning July 1, 2016, Form WH-434 must be filed by January 31. Prior to July 1, 2016, Form WH-434 was due February 28.	
Virginia	Form VA-6 must be filed by January 31.	Employers who furnish 50 or more employee withholding statements must file the W-2 statements electronically.
West Virginia	Form WV/IT-103 must be filed January 31. **Tax years before 2018:** Form WV/IT-103 must be filed February 28.	Employers who withhold less than $600 annually or employ certain domestic employees file form WV/IT-101A due January 31 of the succeeding year.
Wisconsin	Form WT-7 must be filed January 31.	

Withholding Returns and Deposits—Monthly Deposits

For federal income tax purposes, the timing and frequency of an employer's deposits for an employer that files federal Form 941 are determined on an annual basis based on its deposit history during a look-back period ending on June 30 of the preceding year. An employer is either a monthly depositor or a semiweekly depositor for each calendar year, depending on the amount of employment taxes it accumulated during the look-back period. All states that impose a personal income tax require withholding of tax by employers. The frequency of remittance of tax to the state varies, as does the frequency of returns. This chart shows the monthly deposit due dates and forms in effect for each state and the District of Columbia. 15th day entries indicate the day of the month following the end of the period. If the due date falls on a Saturday, Sunday, or legal holiday, states generally allow the return to be filed on the next business day.

Jurisdiction	Monthly Deposits	Comment
Alabama	Form A-6 must be filed by 15th day.	Payments of $750 or more must be paid and filed electronically via the state's website.
Arizona	Form A1-WP must be filed by 15th day.	Federal deposit schedule if average withholding during preceding four calendar quarters exceeds $1,500.
Arkansas	Form AR941M must be filed by 15th day.	
California	Form DE 88ALL must be filed by 15th day if $350 or more in accumulated withholding.	Quarterly if less than $350 in accumulated withholding. Federal deposit schedule if $500 or more of accumulated withholding.
Colorado	Form DR 1094 must be filed by 15th day.	
Connecticut	Form CT-WH must be filed by 15th day.	Weekly if withholding is $10,000 or more during 12-month lookback period. Electronic filing and payment required effective for tax periods beginning after 2013.
Delaware	Form W1 must be filed by 15th day.	
District of Columbia	Form FR-900M must be filed by 20th day.	
Georgia	Form GA-V must be filed by 15th day.	Semi-weekly deposits required if withholding more than $50,000 in the aggregate during the lookback period (12 months period ending June 30 of preceding calendar year).
Hawaii	Form HW-14 must be filed by 15th day.	Federal semiweekly payment schedule if annual withholding exceeds $40,000 or if required to make federal semiweekly deposits.
Idaho	Form 910 must be filed by 20th day.	Semimonthly if annual withholdings is $240,000 or more or monthly withholding average is $20,000.

Jurisdiction	Monthly Deposits	Comment
Illinois	Form IL-941 must be filed by 15th day.	
Indiana	Form WH-1 must be filed by 20th day if average monthly withholding is greater than $1,000, otherwise 30th day.	
Iowa	Form 44-101 must be filed by 15th day.	No monthly deposit for 3rd month of quarter. Balance due paid with quarterly return.
Kansas	Form KW-5 must be filed by 15th day.	
Kentucky	Form K-1 must be filed by 15th day for first 11 months of year. Form K-3 must be filed by 31st day for last month of calendar year.	
Louisiana	Form L-1 or L-1V voucher must be filed by last day.	Semi-monthly if total state income tax withheld from employees is $5,000 or more (must pay via electronic funds transfer). For wages paid during the first 15 days of a calendar month, the due date is the last calendar day of that month. For wages paid between the 16th day and the last day of a calendar month, the due date is the 15th day of the following month.
Maine	Monthly deposit not required.	Semiweekly if withholding is $18,000 or more during 12-month lookback period (Form 900ME).
Maryland	Form MW-506 must be filed by 15th day.	If withholding is $15,000 or more during 12-month lookback period and $700 of withholding has accumulated in any pay period, deposit due on 3rd business day following payroll, unless waiver is obtained permitting monthly filing. **Coronavirus (COVID-19) Pandemic Filing/Payment Relief:** Withholding payments due for periods including February, March, April and May, 2020, may be submitted by July 15, 2020.
Massachusetts	Form M-942 must be filed by 15th day.	
Michigan	Form 5080 must be filed by 20th day.	
Minnesota	Form MW5 must be filed by 15th day.	Semi-weekly deposits if withholding is more than $1,500 in the previous quarter and the IRS requires semi-weekly deposits of federal withholding taxes.
Mississippi	Form 89-105 must be filed by 15th day.	
Missouri	Form MO-941 must be filed by 15th day, except for the third month of a quarter in which case the due date is the last day of the succeeding month.	Quarter-monthly deposits if withholding is $9,000 or more in each of at least two months during the prior 12 months.

Jurisdiction	Monthly Deposits	Comment
Montana	Form MW-1 must be filed by 15th day.	Federal deposit schedule if withholding during 12-month lookback period is $12,000 or more.
Nebraska	Form 501N must be filed by 15th day.	
New Hampshire	Withholding not required.	Personal income tax applies only to interest and dividend income.
New Jersey	Form NJ-500 must be filed by 15th day of the month following the close of the month.	Weekly payment required if prior year withholding tax liability $10,000 greater, deposit due Wed. following the week containing payday.
New Mexico	Form CRS-1 must be filed by 25th day.	**Coronavirus (COVID-19) Pandemic Filing/Payment Relief:** Withholding returns and payments due between March 25, 2020, and July 25, 2020, may be submitted by July 25, 2020. No interest or penalty will be imposed for failure to pay any withholding tax that became due March 25, 2020, through July 25, 2020, provided that payment for the unpaid taxes is made in full on or before April 25, 2021, and the failure to pay was not an intentional attempt to evade the tax.
New York	Monthly deposit not required.	Form NYS-1 must be filed by 3rd or 5th business day after each payroll that results in accumulated withholding of $700 or more during a calendar quarter.
North Carolina	Form NC-5 must be filed by 15th day, except January 31st for December payments.	Same as federal if average monthly withholding is $2,000 or more. Next business day deposit requirement for withholding of $100,000 or more does not apply. Semi-weekly filers must file quarterly reconciliation, Form NC-5Q, on the last day (10 day automatic extension if no additional tax is due.)
North Dakota	Monthly deposit not required.	
Ohio	Form IT-501 must be filed by 15th day.	
Oklahoma	Form WTH-10001 must be filed by 20th day.	Follows federal semi-weekly deposit schedule.
Oregon	Form OTC must be filed by 15th day.	
Pennsylvania	Form PA-501 must be filed by 15th day.	December deposit is due by January 31.
Rhode Island	Form RI-941M must be filed by 20th day.	Last day of following month for March, June, September, and December returns.
South Carolina	Form WH-1601 must be filed by 15th day.	
Tennessee	Withholding not required.	Personal income tax applies only to stock and bond income.

Jurisdiction	Monthly Deposits	Comment
Utah	Form TC-941PC must be filed by last day.	
Vermont	Form WH-431 must be filed by 25th day.	January deposit is due by February 23. Semi-weekly payment requirement applies to those required to make semi-weekly payments of federal withholding.
Virginia	Form VA-5 must be filed by 25th day.	
West Virginia	Form WV/IT-101V must be filed by 15th day.	
Wisconsin	Form WT-6 must be filed by last day.	Semi-monthly if more than $5,000 withheld in any quarter. For taxes withheld during the first 15 days of a calendar month, the due date is the last calendar day of that month. For taxes withheld between the 16th day and the last day of a calendar month, the due date is the 15th day of the following month.

Withholding Returns and Deposits—Quarterly Returns

For federal income tax purposes, the quarterly tax returns are made on Form 941, Employer's Quarterly Federal Tax Return, which states the amount of federal income and FICA taxes withheld for that quarter. The form is due at the end of the month following the end of the quarter. All states that impose a personal income tax require withholding of tax by employers. The frequency of remittance of tax to the state varies, as does the frequency of returns. This chart shows the quarterly return due dates and forms in effect for each state. If the due date falls on a Saturday, Sunday, or legal holiday, states generally allow the return to be filed on the next business day.

Jurisdiction	Quarterly Returns	Comment
Alabama	Form A-1 must be filed by April 30, July 31, October 31, and January 31 (last day of month after end of quarter).	Payments of $750 or more must be paid and filed electronically via the state's website.
Arizona	Form A1-QRT must be filed by April 30, July 31, October 31, and January 31 (last day of month after end of quarter).	
Arkansas	Quarterly withholding not required.	
California	Form DE 9 and Form DE 9C must be filed by April 30, July 31, October 31, and January 31 (last day of month after end of quarter).	
Colorado	Form 1094 must be filed by April 30, July 31, October 31, and January 31 (last day of month after end of quarter).	
Connecticut	Form CT-941 must be filed by April 30, July 31, October 31, and January 31 (last day of month after end of quarter).	Electronic filing and payment required effective for tax periods beginning after 2013.
Delaware	Form W1Q must be filed by April 30, July 31, October 31, and January 31 (last day of month after end of quarter).	
District of Columbia	Quarterly withholding not required.	
Georgia	Form G-7 must be filed by April 30, July 31, October 31, and January 31 (last day of month after end of quarter).	
Hawaii	Form HW-14 must be filed by April 15, July 15, October 15, and January 15 (15th of month after end of quarter).	
Idaho	Form 910 must be filed by April 30, July 31, October 31, and January 31 (last day of month after end of quarter).	

Jurisdiction	Quarterly Returns	Comment
Illinois	Form IL 941 must be filed by April 30, July 31, October 31, and January 31 (last day of month after end of quarter).	
Indiana	Form WH-1 must be filed by April 30, July 31, October 31, and January 31 (last day of month after end of quarter).	
Iowa	Form 44-095 must be filed by April 30, July 31, October 31, and January 31 (last day of month after end of quarter).	
Kansas	Form KW-5 must be filed by April 25, July 25, October 25, and January 25 (25th of month after end of quarter).	
Kentucky	Form K-1 must be filed for first three quarters of calendar year by April 30, July 31, and October 31 (last day of month after end of quarter). Form K-3 for must be filed for fourth quarter and annual reconciliation by January 31.	
Louisiana	Form L-1 must be filed by April 30, July 31, October 31, and January 31 (last day of month after end of quarter).	
Maine	Form 941ME must be filed by April 30, July 31, October 31, and January 31 (last day of month after end of quarter).	Employers that are registered for state income tax withholding must electronically file all original quarterly forms.
Maryland	Form MW-506 must be filed by April 15, July 15, October 15, and January 15 (15th of month after end of quarter)	
Massachusetts	Form 941 must be filed by April 30, July 31, October 31, and January 31 (last day of month after end of quarter).	
Michigan	Form 5080 must be filed by April 20, July 20, October 20, and January 20 (20th of month after end of quarter).	
Minnesota	Form MW5 must be filed by April 30, July 31, October 31, and January 31 (last day of month after end of quarter).	
Mississippi	Form 89-105 must be filed by April 15, July 15, October 15, and January 15 (15th of month after end of quarter)	
Missouri	Form MO-941 must be filed by April 30, July 31, October 31, and January 31 (last day of month after end of quarter).	
Montana	Quarterly withholding not required.	

Jurisdiction	Quarterly Returns	Comment
Nebraska	Form 941N must be filed by April 30, July 31, October 31, and January 31 (last day of month after end of quarter).	
New Hampshire	Withholding not required.	Personal income tax applies only to interest and dividend income.
New Jersey	Form NJ-927/NJ-927-W must be filed by April 30, July 30, October 30, and January 30 (30th of month after end of quarter).	
New Mexico	Form CRS-1 must be filed by April 25, July 25, October 25, and January 25 (25th of month after end of quarter).	Semi-annually if combined taxes due are less than $1,200 for the semi-annual period or an average less than $200 per month for the 6-month period. **Coronavirus (COVID-19) Pandemic Filing/Payment Relief:** Withholding returns and payments due between March 25, 2020, and July 25, 2020, may be submitted by July 25, 2020. No interest or penalty will be imposed for failure to pay any withholding tax that became due March 25, 2020, through July 25, 2020, provided that payment for the unpaid taxes is made in full on or before April 25, 2021, and the failure to pay was not an intentional attempt to evade the tax.
New York	Form NYS-45 must be filed by April 30, July 31, October 31, and January 31 (last day of month after end of quarter).	
North Carolina	Form NC-5 must be filed by April 30, July 31, October 31, and January 31 (last day of month after end of quarter).	
North Dakota	Form 306 must be filed by April 30, July 31, October 31, and January 31 (last day of month after end of quarter).	
Ohio	Form IT-501 must be filed by April 30, July 30, October 30, and January 30 (30th of month after end of quarter).	
Oklahoma	Form WTH-10001 must be filed by April 20, July 20, October 20, and January 20 (20th of month after end of quarter).	
Oregon	Form OQ must be filed by April 30, July 31, October 31, and January 31 (last day of month after end of quarter).	
Pennsylvania	Form PA-W-3 must be filed by April 30, July 31, October 31, and January 31 (last day of month after end of quarter).	

Jurisdiction	Quarterly Returns	Comment
Rhode Island	Form RI-941Q must be filed by April 30, July 31, October 31, and January 31 (last day of month after end of quarter).	
South Carolina	Form WH-1605 must be filed by April 30, July 30, October 30, and January 30 (30th of month after end of quarter).	
Tennessee	Withholding not required.	Personal income tax applies only to stock and bond income.
Utah	Form TC-941 must be filed by April 30, July 31, October 31, and January 31 (last day of month after end of quarter).	
Vermont	Form WH-431 must be filed by April 25, July 25, October 25, and January 25 (25th of month after end of quarter).	
Virginia	Form VA-5 must be filed by April 30, July 31, October 31, and January 31 (last day of month after end of quarter).	
West Virginia	Form WV/IT-101Q must be filed by April 30, July 30, October 30, and January 30 (30th of month after end of quarter).	
Wisconsin	Form WT-6 must be filed by April 30, July 31, October 31, and January 31 (last day of month after end of quarter).	

SALES AND USE TAXES

The following pages contain charts summarizing various sales and use tax topics. Alaska, Delaware, Montana, New Hampshire, and Oregon do not impose a general, statewide sales and use tax.

Topics covered include state rates, the tax basis (including the components), nexus, taxability of specific transactions (arranged by topic), statutes of limitations, validity periods for exemption and resale certificates, taxpayer remedies, and collection discounts.

Sales and Use Tax Rates

Rate listed below is the general state rate. Most states authorize additional local sales and use taxes, which are not included.

Jurisdiction	2020 Rates	Comment
Alabama	4%	
Arizona	5.6%	
Arkansas	6.5%	Food rate is 1.5%.
California	7.25%	The 7.25% current total statewide base includes 1% that goes to city and county (local) funds and operations.
Colorado	2.9%	An additional state sales tax rate applies to sales of marijuana and marijuana products.
Connecticut	6.35%	7.75% on motor vehicles that cost more than $50,000 (with certain exceptions), jewelry that costs more than $5,000, and certain clothing, footwear, and other items that cost more than $1,000.
District of Columbia	6%	
Florida	6%	
Georgia	4%	Effective July 1, 2015, sales of motor fuel for highway use exempt from 4% state sales and use tax rate. Prior to July 1, 2015, sales of motor fuel for highway use exempt from first 3% of state sales and use tax, but subject to remaining 1% of state sales and use tax.
Hawaii	4%	0.5% rate for wholesalers/ manufacturers.
Idaho	6%	
Illinois	6.25%	Grocery food, drugs, medical appliances, and modifications to make a motor vehicle usable by a disabled person are taxed at 1%.
Indiana	7%	
Iowa	6%	
Kansas	6.5%	6.15% July 1, 2013 - June 30, 2015.
Kentucky	6%	
Louisiana	4.45%	
Maine	5.5%	
Maryland	6%	
Massachusetts	6.25%	
Michigan	6%	

Jurisdiction	2020 Rates	Comment
Minnesota	6.875%	
Mississippi	7%	
Missouri	4.225%	Total rate of 4.225% consists of general sales/use tax of 4%, additional sales tax of 0.10% for soil/water conservation and state parks, and additional sales tax of 0.125% for wildlife conservation. Grocery food taxed at reduced rate of 1.225%.
Nebraska	5.5%	Adjusted biennially.
Nevada	6.85%	
New Jersey	6.625%	
New Mexico	5.125%	Compensating tax rate on services is 5%. Rate on services increases to 5.125% on July 1, 2021.
New York	4%	
North Carolina	4.75%	
North Dakota	5%	
Ohio	5.75%	
Oklahoma	4.5%	
Pennsylvania	6%	
Rhode Island	7%	
South Carolina	6%	
South Dakota	4%	
Tennessee	7%	The rate on food is 5%. Additional tax of 2.75% imposed on any single item sold in excess of $1,600 but not more than $3,200.
Texas	6.25%	
Utah	4.85%	Food and food ingredients are taxed at reduced rate of 1.75%.
Vermont	6%	
Virginia	4.3%	Additional 1% local rate imposed in all localities. Additional 0.7% state tax imposed in the localities that make up Northern Virginia and Hampton Roads regions. Grocery food taxed at reduced rate of 2.5% (1.5% state tax and 1% local option tax).
Washington	6.5%	
West Virginia	6%	Reduced rates apply to long-term vehicle lease payments, and to sales and uses of motor vehicles, gasoline, and certain fuels.

Jurisdiction	2020 Rates	Comment
Wisconsin	5%	
Wyoming	4%	

Administrative Appeals

The following chart describes the time period in which a taxpayer must file an appeal of a department decision with the appropriate administrative entity outside of the taxing authority. Appeals to the taxing authority or judicial entity are addressed in Department Appeals and Judicial Appeals.

Jurisdiction	Administrative Appeals	Comment
Alabama	State does not have administrative appeal body.	
Arizona	Petition must be filed with State Board of Tax Appeals within 30 days after receipt of the decision or order.	
Arkansas	State does not have administrative appeal body.	
California	State does not have administrative appeal body.	
Colorado	State does not have administrative appeal body.	
Connecticut	State does not have administrative appeal body.	
District of Columbia	District does not have administrative appeal body.	
Florida	State does not have administrative appeal body.	
Georgia	State does not have administrative appeal body.	
Hawaii	Petition must be filed with District Board of Review within 30 days after mailing date of notice of assessment.	
Idaho	Petition must be filed with Board of Tax Appeals within 91 days after notice of redetermination is received.	
Illinois	State does not have administrative appeal body.	Board of Appeals actions may be commenced within 180 days after liability has become final for relief from penalties and interest or for an offer in compromise; liability may not be contested.
Indiana	State does not have administrative appeal body.	
Iowa	Petition must be filed within 30 days from the date of notice of recalculation or denial.	
Kansas	Notice of appeal must be filed with State Board of Tax Appeals within 30 days after final decision.	

Jurisdiction	Administrative Appeals	Comment
Kentucky	Petition must be filed with the Kentucky Claims Commission (formerly the Kentucky Board of Tax Appeals) within 30 days after date of decision.	
Louisiana	Petition must be filed with Board of Tax Appeals within 60 days after notice of deficiency or decision.	
Maine	State does not have administrative appeal body.	
Maryland	Petition must be filed with Tax Court within 30 days after mailing notice of decision.	Tax Court is an administrative, not judicial, entity.
Massachusetts	Petition must be filed with Appellate Tax Board within 60 days after date of notice of decision or within six months after application for abatement is deemed to be denied.	
Michigan	Petition must be filed with Tax Tribunal within 60 days after decision.	If the taxpayer has filed a request appointing an official representative to receive copies of letters and notices from the Department of Treasury, the 60 day period does not begin to accrue until both the taxpayer and its representative has been served with the final assessment.
Minnesota	Notice of appeal must be filed with Tax Court within 60 days after Commissioner of Revenue's order.	Tax Court is an administrative, not judicial, entity.
Mississippi	Petition must be filed with Board of Tax Appeals within 60 days from the date of the Board of Review's order.	
Missouri	Petition must be filed with Administrative Hearing Commission within 60 days after mailing or delivery of decision, whichever is earlier.	
Nebraska	State does not have administrative appeal body.	
Nevada	Petition must be filed with Department and Tax Commission within 30 days after service of decision.	
New Jersey	State does not have administrative appeal body.	
New Mexico	State does not have administrative appeal body.	
New York	Petition must be filed with Tax Appeals Tribunal within 30 days after notice of decision.	
North Carolina	Notice of intent to file a petition must be filed with Tax Review Board within 30 days after final decision.	Petition must be filed with Tax Review Board within 60 days after notice of intent.

Jurisdiction	Administrative Appeals	Comment
North Dakota	State does not have administrative appeal body.	
Ohio	Petition must be filed with Board of Tax Appeals within 60 days after service of notice of decision.	
Oklahoma	State does not have administrative appeal body.	
Pennsylvania	Petition must be filed with Board of Finance and Revenue within 60 days after notice of decision.	
Rhode Island	State does not have administrative appeal body.	
South Carolina	Petition must be filed with Administrative Law Judge within 30 days after decision mailed or delivered.	
South Dakota	State does not have administrative appeal body.	
Tennessee	State does not have administrative appeal body.	
Texas	State does not have administrative appeal body.	
Utah	State does not have administrative appeal body.	
Vermont	State does not have administrative appeal body.	
Virginia	State does not have administrative appeal body.	
Washington	Petition must be filed with Board of Tax Appeals within 30 days after mailing notice of decision.	
West Virginia	Petition must be filed with Office of Tax Appeals within 60 days of receipt of assessment notice.	
Wisconsin	Petition must be filed with Tax Appeals Commission within 60 days of Department of Revenue determination or redetermination.	
Wyoming	An appeal directly to the Board of Equalization must be filed within 30 days of decision.	

Affiliate Nexus

This chart indicates whether the presence of an affiliated or related entity in a state can create nexus for a seller. Note that state nexus statutes are subject to federal constitutional restrictions. However, in *South Dakota v. Wayfair*, Inc. (Dkt. No. 17-494, June 21, 2018), the U.S. Supreme Court overruled *Quill Corp. v. North Dakota* (504 U.S. 298 (1992)) and held that physical presence is no longer required to establish sales and use tax nexus.

Jurisdiction	Affiliate Nexus	Comment
Alabama	Yes	Nexus is established if an out-of-state vendor and an in-state business maintaining one or more locations within Alabama are related parties and they: (1) use an identical or substantially similar name, tradename, trademark, or goodwill, to develop, promote, or maintain sales; (2) pay for each other's services contingent upon the volume or value of sales; (3) share a common business plan or substantially coordinate their business plans; or (4) the in-state business provides services to, or that inure to the benefit of, the out-of-state business related to developing, promoting, or maintaining the in-state market.
Arizona	Yes	If the related entity's activities help establish or maintain a market for the seller.
Arkansas	No	
California	Yes	Applicable April 1, 2019, the term "retailer" includes any retailer that, in the preceding or current calendar year, has total combined sales of tangible personal property for delivery in California by the retailer and all persons related to the retailer that exceed $500,000. For purposes of this section, a person is related to another person if the persons are two corporations that are members of the same controlled group.
Colorado	No	Affiliate nexus provisions were repealed effective June 1, 2019.
Connecticut	Yes	If the related entity is a retailer engaged in a similar line of business in the state.
District of Columbia	Yes	If the related entity acts on behalf of the seller.
Florida	Yes	Every dealer who makes a mail order sale must collect sales or use tax when the dealer, while not having nexus, is a corporation that is a member of an affiliated group of corporations, as provided, and any parent or subsidiary corporation in the affiliated group has nexus with Florida.

Jurisdiction	Affiliate Nexus	Comment
Georgia	Yes	With certain exceptions, the definition of "dealer" includes an affiliate that sells at retail, offers for sale at retail in Georgia, or engages in the regular or systematic solicitation of a consumer market in Georgia through a related dealer located in Georgia. There is rebuttable presumption that a "dealer" is one who makes sales of tangible personal property or services that are subject to sales and use tax if a "related member" (other than a common carrier acting in its capacity as such) that has substantial nexus in Georgia (1) sells a similar line of products as the person and does so under the same or a similar business name; or (2) uses trademarks, service marks, or trade names in Georgia that are the same or substantially similar to those used by the person.
Hawaii	Yes	If the related entity acts on behalf of the seller.
Idaho	Yes	If the seller that had at least $100,000 in sales in Idaho in the previous year and other statutory requirements are met.
Illinois	Yes	Having or maintaining in Illinois, directly or by a subsidiary, an office, distribution house, sales house, warehouse or other place of business constitutes maintaining a business.
Indiana	No	
Iowa	Yes	"Affiliate nexus" provisions apply.
Kansas	Yes	"Affiliate nexus" provisions apply.
Kentucky	Yes	The definition of "retailer engaged in business in this state" includes a retailer who maintains, operates, or uses in Kentucky an office, place of distribution, sales or sample room, warehouse, storage place, or other place of business through a subsidiary or any other related entity.
Louisiana	Yes	Click-through and affiliate nexus provisions are applicable to remote sellers effective April 1, 2016.
Maine	Yes	If the related entity acts on behalf of the seller.
Maryland	Yes	If the related entity acts on behalf of the seller.
Massachusetts	Yes	If the related entity's activities help create or maintain a market for the seller.
Michigan	Yes	If the related entity acts on behalf of the seller.
Minnesota	Yes	If the related entity or affiliate acts on behalf of the seller. An affiliate includes a related party that uses the retailer's facilities or employees in Minnesota to advertise, promote, or facilitate sales of items by the retailer to purchasers in Minnesota or for the provision of services to the retailer's purchasers in Minnesota, such as accepting returns of purchases for the retailer, providing assistance in resolving customer complaints of the retailer, or providing other services.
Mississippi	Yes	If the related entity acts on behalf of the seller.

Jurisdiction	Affiliate Nexus	Comment
Missouri	Yes	Presumption of nexus if the affiliated entity: sells a similar line of products under a similar business name; maintains a place of business that facilitates the delivery of property or services sold by the vendor or allows the vendor's customers to pick up property sold by the vendor; delivers, installs, assembles, or performs maintenance services for the vendor's customers in the state; or conducts any other activities in the state that are significantly associated with the vendor's ability to maintain a market in the state.
Nebraska	Yes	If the seller is owned or controlled by the same interests that own or control a retailer engaged in a similar line of business in the state. However, in Quill Corp. v. North Dakota, the U.S. Supreme Court held that under the Commerce clause, a vendor must have a physical presence in a state in order for that state to require the vendor to collect tax.
Nevada	Yes	
New Jersey	Yes	Activities occurring in New Jersey that create nexus include, but are not limited to: having employees, independent contractors, agents, or other representatives (including salespersons, consultants, customer representatives, service or repair technicians, instructors, delivery persons, and independent representatives or solicitors acting as agents of the business) working in New Jersey.
New Mexico	Yes	If the related entity acts on behalf of the seller.

Jurisdiction	Affiliate Nexus	Comment
New York	Yes	If the related entity acts on behalf of the seller and certain conditions are met. Under certain conditions, a vendor includes out-of-state sellers (remote affiliates) of taxable tangible personal property or services that are affiliated with businesses in New York (New York affiliates). In such a situation, a New York business and an out-of-state seller are affiliated with each other if one owns, directly or indirectly, more than 5% of the other or if more than 5% of each is owned, directly or indirectly, by the same person or by an affiliated group of persons. Remote affiliates are vendors and must register for sales tax purposes and begin to collect and remit sales tax when they are affiliated with a business in New York and either of the following conditions is met: –Condition I: A New York affiliate who is a sales tax vendor uses a trademark, service mark, or trade name in New York that is the same as that used in New York by the remote affiliate, or –Condition II: A New York affiliate engages in activities in New York that benefit the remote affiliate in its development or maintenance of a market for its goods or services in New York, to the extent that those activities are sufficient for the remote affiliate to satisfy the nexus requirements of the U.S. Constitution. For purposes of determining whether this condition is met, the Department will consider whether the direct or indirect ownership exceeds 50%, (i.e., if one owns, directly or indirectly, more than 50% of the other or if more than 50% of each person is owned, directly or indirectly, by the same person or by an affiliated group of persons). Condition II will be considered to be met if the percentage of direct or indirect ownership exceeds 50% and the New York affiliate engages in any activities that are more than de minimis and that promote the development or maintenance of a market for the remote affiliate's products or services in New York.
North Carolina	No	
North Dakota	Yes	If the related entity acts on behalf of the seller.
Ohio	Yes	If the seller is a member of an affiliated group with least one member that has nexus, and the activities of that member establish or maintain a market in Ohio for the seller.
Oklahoma	Yes	"Maintaining a place of business in this state" includes having or maintaining in Oklahoma permanently or temporarily (including through a subsidiary) a physical place of business. "Affiliate nexus" provisions also apply.
Pennsylvania	Yes	If the related entity acts on behalf of the seller, or provides services that benefit, support or complement the remote seller's business activity.
Rhode Island	Yes	If the related entity acts on behalf of the seller. Also, the existence and/or presence of certain non-collecting retailer's, referrer's, or retail sale facilitator's in-state software on the devices of in-state customers constitutes physical presence of the non-collecting retailer, referrer, or retail sale facilitator in Rhode Island.

Jurisdiction	Affiliate Nexus	Comment
South Carolina	Yes	If the related entity/affiliate sells similar merchandise and uses common trade names, trademarks or logos or if the South Carolina affiliate is used to accept returns, take orders, perform customer service, or distribute advertising materials on the corporation's behalf. Also, the corporation has nexus if it authorizes an affiliated company to install, deliver, service, or repair merchandise in South Carolina. A corporation also has nexus if it uses an affiliated company to investigate, handle or resolve customer issues, or provide training or technical assistance.
South Dakota	Yes	If the related entity acts on behalf of the seller.
Tennessee	No	
Texas	Yes	(1) If retailer holds a substantial ownership interest in, or is substantially owned by, a person with a business location in Texas and either (a) sells a substantially similar line of products under a substantially similar business name as the person located in Texas or (b) uses facilities or employees of the Texas business to advertise, promote sales, or perform other activity to establish a marketplace in Texas; (2) if retailer holds a substantial ownership interest in, or is substantially owned by, a person that (a) maintains a distribution center, warehouse, or similar location in Texas and (b) delivers property sold by the retailer to consumers.
Utah	Yes	If the related entity engages in advertising, marketing, or sales activities on behalf of the seller.
Vermont	Yes	If the seller owns or controls a person engaged in the same manner or similar line of business in the state.
Virginia	Yes	If the seller and the related entity are owned or controlled by the same interests. Virginia has legislation that requires certain remote sellers that utilize in-state facilities to collect Virginia sales tax. The law establishes a presumption that a dealer has nexus with the state if any commonly controlled person maintains a distribution center, warehouse, fulfillment center, office, or similar location in Virginia that facilitates the delivery of tangible personal property sold by the dealer to its customers. The presumption may be rebutted by demonstrating that the activities conducted by the commonly controlled person in Virginia are not significantly associated with the dealer's ability to establish or maintain a market in the state. A "commonly controlled person" means any person that is a member of the same "controlled group of corporations," as defined in IRC § 1563(a), as the dealer or any other entity that bears the same ownership relationship to the dealer as a corporation that is a member of the same controlled group of corporations. The law took effect on September 1, 2013 (the law provided that it is effective on the earlier of September 1, 2013, or upon passage of federal legislation granting states the authority to require remote sellers to collect taxes on goods shipped to in-state purchasers. Because no such federal legislation has been enacted, the effective date is September 1, 2013.)

Jurisdiction	Affiliate Nexus	Comment
Washington	Yes	An affiliated company that performs activities significantly associated with the out-of-state taxpayer's ability to establish or maintain a market in Washington creates nexus.
West Virginia	Yes	A retailer is considered to do business in West Virginia if it (1) solicits orders by mail, has physical presence in the state, and economically benefits from an authorized installation, servicing, or repair facility in the state owned or operated by a related person; (2) has a franchisee or licensee operating in the state under its trade name; or (3) has, maintains, occupies, or uses through a subsidiary an office, distribution house, sales house, warehouse, or other place of business in the state. "Affiliate nexus" provisions also apply.
Wisconsin	Yes	If the seller's affiliate in Wisconsin uses facilities or employees in Wisconsin to advertise, promote, or facilitate sales of items by the seller to purchasers in Wisconsin or for providing services to the seller's purchasers in Wisconsin, including accepting returns of purchases or resolving customer complaints.
Wyoming	Yes	If the related entity acts on behalf of seller.

Clothing

Temporary sales tax holiday exemptions not included.

Jurisdiction	Clothing	Comment
Alabama	Taxable	
Arizona	Taxable	
Arkansas	Taxable	
California	Taxable	Exemptions allowed for (1) new children's clothing sold to nonprofit organizations for free distribution to elementary school children and (2) used clothing sold by certain thrift stores benefiting the chronically ill.
Colorado	Taxable	
Connecticut	Taxable	Clothing and footwear that costs more than $1,000 is subject to the luxury goods tax. Certain exemptions apply.
District of Columbia	Taxable	
Florida	Taxable	
Georgia	Taxable	
Hawaii	Taxable	
Idaho	Taxable	Exemption applies to purchases of clothes and footwear by nonsale clothiers that provide free clothes to the needy.
Illinois	Taxable	
Indiana	Taxable	
Iowa	Taxable	
Kansas	Taxable	
Kentucky	Taxable	
Louisiana	Taxable	
Maine	Taxable	
Maryland	Taxable	
Massachusetts	Exempt	Exemption limited to clothing and footwear costing $175 or less. Certain clothing and footwear designed for athletic activity or protective use are taxable.
Michigan	Taxable	
Minnesota	Exempt	Accessories, most protective equipment, sports and recreational articles, and fur clothing are taxable.

Jurisdiction	Clothing	Comment
Mississippi	Taxable	Clothing, footwear, and accessories used as wardrobes in production of motion pictures are exempt.
Missouri	Taxable	
Nebraska	Taxable	
Nevada	Taxable	
New Jersey	Exempt	Fur clothing, clothing accessories or equipment, sport or recreational equipment, or protective equipment are taxable. Protective equipment is only exempt when purchased for the daily work of the user and worn as part of a work uniform or work clothing.
New Mexico	Taxable	
New York	Exempt	Exemption limited to clothing and footwear costing less than $110 per item or pair. Clothing and footwear costing $110 or more per item or pair are taxable.
North Carolina	Taxable	Separately stated alteration charges in connection with the sale of clothing are exempt.
North Dakota	Taxable	
Ohio	Taxable	Narrow exemption for protective clothing used exclusively in a regulated manufacturing area.
Oklahoma	Taxable	
Pennsylvania	Exempt	Accessories, fur articles, ornamental and formal wear, and sports clothing are taxable.
Rhode Island	Exempt	Accessories and special clothing designed primarily for athletic or protective use are taxable. Clothing exemption only applies to $250 of sales price per item.
South Carolina	Taxable	Certain protective clothing required for working in a clean room environment is exempt.
South Dakota	Taxable	
Tennessee	Taxable	Exemption applies to used clothing sold by certain nonprofit organizations.
Texas	Taxable.	
Utah	Taxable	
Vermont	Exempt	Clothing accessories or equipment, protective equipment, and sport or recreational equipment are taxable.

Jurisdiction	Clothing	Comment
Virginia	Taxable	Exemptions apply to: certain protective clothing furnished to employees engaged in research activities, mining, and manufacturing; and foul-weather clothing worn by commercial watermen.
Washington	Taxable	
West Virginia	Taxable	
WIsconsIn	Taxable	
Wyoming	Taxable	

Collection Discounts Allowed Seller

The following chart indicates whether a state allows a collection discount that reimburses a seller for expenses incurred in acting as the collecting agent and remitting sales tax before it becomes delinquent. Where state law specifies the applicability of the discount to multiple locations, it is noted in the chart.

Jurisdiction	Collection Discounts Allowed	Comment
Alabama	5% of the first $100 of tax due and 2% of excess amount; maximum of $400 per month.	Single discount.
Arizona	Credit allowed equal to 1% of tax due, not to exceed $10,000 per calendar year.	Single discount.
Arkansas	2% of tax due; maximum of $1,000 per month.	Single discount.
California	None	
Colorado	Effective July 1, 2011 through June 30, 2014, the vendor's fee is 2.22%.	Effective July 1, 2009 through June 30, 2011, the vendor's fee was temporarily eliminated.
Connecticut	None	
District of Columbia	None	
Florida	2.5% of the first $1,200 of tax due (mail order dealers may negotiate an allowance of up to 10%).	Per business location.
Georgia	3% of the first $3,000 of tax due and 0.5% of excess amount.	Per registration number.
Hawaii	None	
Idaho	None	
Illinois	Greater of 1.75% of tax due or $5 per calendar year.	
Indiana	0.83% if total annual sales tax collected was less than $60,000; 0.6% if total annual sales tax collected was between $60,000 and $600,000; and 0.3% if total annual sales tax collected was more than $600,000.	Certain utilities not entitled to allowance. Effective for reporting periods beginning after June 30, 2008, collection allowances are: 0.73% if total sales tax collected was less than $60,000; 0.53% if total sales tax collected was between $60,000 and $600,000; and 0.26% if total sales tax collected was more than $600,000.
Iowa	None	
Kansas	None	

Jurisdiction	Collection Discounts Allowed	Comment
Kentucky	1.75% of the first $1,000 of tax due; through June 30, 2013, 1% of amount exceeding $1,000; effective July 1, 2013, 1.5% of amount exceeding $1,000. Through June 30, 2013, allowance is capped at $1,500 per reporting period; effective July 1, 2013, allowance is capped at $50 per reporting period.	
Louisiana	1.5% of tax due after August 1, 2020; 0.935% of tax due prior to then.	Total vendor compensation is capped at $1,500 per month for dealers with one or more business locations.
Maine	None	However, retailers are allowed to retain "breakage" as compensation for collection of tax. Under the bracket system, when the tax due in a sales tax return is less than the actual tax collected from customers, the excess collected is "breakage".
Maryland	Credit equal to 1.2% of first $6,000 of tax due and 0.9% of excess. Limited to $500 per return, or $500 for all returns for vendors eligible to file consolidated returns.	Credit does not apply to any sales and use tax that a vendor is required to pay for any taxable purchase or use made by the vendor.
Massachusetts	None	
Michigan	Vendor may deduct greater of: (1) for payments made before the 12th day of the month, 0.75% of tax due at a rate of 4% for the preceding month (maximum $20,000 of tax due); for payments made between the 12th and the 20th, 0.5% of the tax due at a rate of 4% for the preceding month (maximum $15,000 of tax due); or (2) the tax collected at a rate of 4% on $150 of taxable purchase price for prior month.	
Minnesota	None	
Mississippi	2% of tax due; maximum of $50 per month and $600 per year.	Per business location.
Missouri	2% of tax due.	
Nebraska	2.5% of the first $3,000 remitted each month.	Per business location.
Nevada	Effective Jan. 1, 2009, the rate is 0.25% of tax due.	The 0.25% rate was set to be temporary and expire July 1, 2009, but the expiration date was later repealed. Prior to Jan. 1, 2009, the rate was 0.5%.
New Jersey	None	
New Mexico	None	
New York	Credit equal to 5% of tax due; maximum of $200 per quarterly (or longer) period.	
North Carolina	None	

Jurisdiction	Collection Discounts Allowed	Comment
North Dakota	1.5% of tax due; maximum of $110 per month	Per business location.
Ohio	0.75% of tax due.	A vendor that has selected a certified service provider as its agent is not entitled to the discount if the certified service provider receives a monetary allowance.
Oklahoma	1%; maximum of $2,500 per month, per permit. (Repealed effective July 1, 2017.)	
Pennsylvania	Discount is the lesser of: (1) 1% of the amount of tax collected or (2) $25 per return for a monthly filer, $75 per return for a quarterly filer, or $150 per return for a semiannual filer.	
Rhode Island	None	
South Carolina	2% of tax due (3% if tax due is less than $100); maximum discount is $3,000 per year ($3,100 if filing electronically; $10,000 for out-of-state taxpayers filing voluntarily).	
South Dakota	None	Effective July 1 after $10 million is accumulated in tax relief fund created from additional revenue received by state from sellers that voluntary register to collect under Streamlined Sales and Use Tax (SST) Agreement, monthly filers are allowed credit of 1.5% of gross amount of tax due (may not exceed $70 per month).
Tennessee	2% of the first $2,500 and 1.15% of the excess amount per report (only allowed to out-of-state taxpayers filing voluntarily).	
Texas	0.5% of tax due plus 1.25% of the amount of any prepaid tax.	Discounts for timely filing do not apply to holders of direct pay permits.
Utah	1.31% of state tax and 1% of local, public transit, and municipal energy sales and use tax (monthly taxpayers).	Effective 7/1/07, monthly filers who remit the 2.75% tax collected on sales of food and food ingredients may retain an amount equal to the sum of (1) 1.31% of the amount the seller is required to remit under the provision imposing a 2.75% tax on food and food ingredients and (2) 1.31% of the difference between the amounts the seller would have remitted under the provision imposing a general 4.75% tax and the amounts the seller must remit under the provision imposing a 2.75% tax on food and food ingredients.
Vermont	Seller who collects tax is allowed to retain any amount lawfully collected in excess of the tax imposed.	

Jurisdiction	Collection Discounts Allowed	Comment
Virginia	3% (4% food tax) if monthly taxable sales are less than $62,501; 2.25% (3% food tax) if $62,501 to $208,000; 1.5% (2% food tax) if over $208,000.	For returns filed for sales on and after 7/1/05, dealer is allowed a single discount at the percentages listed, applicable to the first 3% of state tax due for a given period.
Washington	None	
West Virginia	None	
Wisconsin	0.5% of the tax payable on retail sales or $10, whichever is greater, up to $1,000 for each reporting period, and not to exceed tax liability. Certified service providers ineligible.	
Wyoming	Early payment credit, 1.95% of first $6,250 of taxes due, then 1% of amount over $6,250. Maximum credit of $500 per month.	Credit allowed only if taxes are remitted on or before 15th day of month that they are due.

Components of Basis—Bad Debts

The following chart indicates whether bad debts may be claimed as a deduction, refund, or credit.

Jurisdiction	Bad Debts	Comment
Alabama	Refund or credit.	
Arizona	Deduction	
Arkansas	Deduction	
California	Deduction	
Colorado	Deduction	
Connecticut	Credit	
District of Columbia	Deduction	
Florida	Refund or credit.	
Georgia	Deduction	
Hawaii	Deduction	
Idaho	Refund or credit.	
Illinois	Credit	
Indiana	Deduction	
Iowa	Deduction	
Kansas	Deduction	
Kentucky	Deduction	
Louisiana	Refund	
Maine	Credit	
Maryland	Refund or credit.	
Massachusetts	Refund	
Michigan	Deduction	
Minnesota	Deduction	
Mississippi	Credit	
Missouri	Refund or credit.	
Nebraska	Deduction	When the bad debt amount exceeds the taxable sales for the period in which the bad debt is written off, a refund claim may be filed.
Nevada	Deduction	Prior to January 1, 2006, a bad debt credit was authorized.
New Jersey	Deduction	
New Mexico	Deduction	

Jurisdiction	Bad Debts	Comment
New York	Refund or credit.	
North Carolina	Deduction	
North Dakota	Deduction	
Ohio	Deduction	When the bad debt amount exceeds the taxable sales in a reporting period, a refund claim may be filed.
Oklahoma	Deduction	
Pennsylvania	Refund	
Rhode Island	Deduction	
South Carolina	Deduction	
South Dakota	Deduction	
Tennessee	Credit	
Texas	Deduction or refund.	
Utah	Deduction	
Vermont	Refund or credit.	
Virginia	Credit	
Washington	Refund or credit.	The refund or credit is limited to the seller.
West Virginia	Deduction	
Wisconsin	Deduction	
Wyoming	Credit	

Components of Basis—Coupons and Cash Discounts

The following chart indicates whether or not coupons and cash discounts are included in the tax base.

Jurisdiction	Coupons and Cash Discounts	Comment
Alabama	Cash discounts, retailers coupons not included; manufacturers coupons included.	
Arizona	Cash discounts, retailers coupons not included; manufacturers coupons included.	
Arkansas	Cash discounts, retailers coupons, membership discounts not included; manufacturers coupons, motor vehicle rebates included.	
California	Retailer cash discounts and retailer coupons are not included. Where a manufacturer or third party reimburses the retailer (e.g. a manufacturer's coupon), the amount of the discount or coupon is included.	
Colorado	Discounts, retailers coupons, discounts, rebates, credits not included; manufacturers coupons, early payment discounts included.	
Connecticut	Cash discounts and manufacturers and retailers coupons not included; rebate amounts included.	
District of Columbia	Cash discounts at time of sale, trade discounts, and quantity discounts at time of sale not included.	
Florida	Cash discounts at time of sale, retailers coupons not included; manufacturers coupons included.	
Georgia	The "sales price" does not include discounts, including cash, term, or coupons not reimbursed by a third party.	
Hawaii	Cash discounts not included. Manufacturer-reimbursed coupons included.	
Idaho	Retailer discounts (to the extent they represent price adjustments), trade discounts, discounts offered as inducement to continue telecommunications services, retailers coupons, retailers rebates, and manufacturers rebates on motor vehicle sales not included; manufacturers coupons, manufacturers rebates (other than motor vehicle rebates), cash discounts offered as inducements for prompt payment included.	

Jurisdiction	Coupons and Cash Discounts	Comment
Illinois	ROT, SOT: Discounts, retailers coupons not included; reimbursed coupons included.	
Indiana	Cash and term discounts, retailers coupons not included; manufacturers coupons included.	
Iowa	Discounts, retailers coupons, motor vehicle rebates to purchasers not included; manufacturers coupons included.	
Kansas	The "sales or selling price" does not include discounts, including cash, term, or coupons not reimbursed by a third party.	
Kentucky	"Gross receipts" or "sales price" does not include cash discounts or include coupons not reimbursed by a third party.	
Louisiana	Cash discounts, retailers coupons, motor vehicle rebates offered as price reductions not included; manufacturers coupons included.	
Maine	Discounts, retailers coupons not included; manufacturers coupons, manufacturers rebates included.	
Maryland	Discounts at time of sale and retailers coupons are not included. Early payment discounts, rebates to the buyer from a third party, and coupons for which vendor can be reimbursed or compensated in any form by a third party are included.	
Massachusetts	Cash discounts at time of sale, trade discounts, manufacturers and retailers coupons not included; discounts for early payment included.	
Michigan	Cash, trade, and quantity discounts given directly by the seller, retailers coupons not included; manufacturers coupons, manufacturers rebates included.	
Minnesota	Discounts not reimbursed by third party, such as retailer coupons, not included; discounts reimbursed by third party, such as manufacturer coupons, included.	
Mississippi	Cash discounts, retailers coupons not included; manufacturers coupons included.	
Missouri	Cash discounts, retailers coupons not included; manufacturers coupons excluded.	

Jurisdiction	Coupons and Cash Discounts	Comment
Nebraska	Cash discounts, retailers coupons, motor vehicle rebates used to reduce the selling price not included; manufacturers coupons, cash rebates, deal-of-the day certificates included.	
Nevada	Cash discounts, retailers coupons not included; reimbursed coupons included.	
New Jersey	Discounts that represent a price reduction, such as a trade discount, volume discount, or cash and carry discount, early payment discounts, and retailers coupons not included; reimbursed coupons, rebates included.	
New Mexico	Cash discounts, retailers coupons not included; manufacturers coupons included.	
New York	Discounts that represent a price reduction, such as a trade discount, volume discount or cash and carry discount, and retailers coupons are not included; manufacturer's coupons, reimbursed coupons, and early payment discounts included.	
North Carolina	Cash discounts, trade discounts, retailers coupons not included; manufacturers coupons included.	
North Dakota	Discounts, retailers coupons not included; manufacturers coupons, manufacturers rebates included if the seller receives consideration from the manufacturer and other criteria are met.	
Ohio	Cash and term discounts, retailers coupons not included; reimbursed coupons included.	The value of a gift card or certificate redeemed by a consumer in purchasing tangible personal property is excluded from tax if (1) the vendor is not reimbursed and (2) the gift card or certificate is distributed through a customer award, loyalty, or promotional program.
Oklahoma	"Gross receipts," "gross proceeds," or "sales price" does not include cash discounts or include coupons not reimbursed by a third party.	
Pennsylvania	Discounts at time of sale and retailers and manufacturers coupons not included if separately stated; discounts after sale included.	
Rhode Island	Discounts allowed by a seller, including cash, term, or coupons that are not reimbursed by a third party not included; consideration received by a seller from third parties, including manufacturer's coupons, included if certain criteria are met.	

Jurisdiction	Coupons and Cash Discounts	Comment
South Carolina	Cash discounts at time of sale, retailers coupons, discounts on the sale of items from the exchange of points from a customer loyalty awards program, not included; timely payment discounts deductible by retailer on subsequent report; manufacturers coupons and manufacturers rebates included.	When property is transferred to a customer, through a customer loyalty awards program, for no consideration, nominal consideration, or an amount significantly below cost, there is a rebuttable presumption that the property is a promotional item withdrawn from inventory, and the retailer is liable for sales tax based on the fair market value of the property.
South Dakota	Discounts, retailers coupons not included; reimbursed coupons included.	
Tennessee	Discounts, including cash, term, or coupons not reimbursed by a third party that are allowed by seller not included.	
Texas	Cash discounts and retailers and manufacturers coupons not included.	
Utah	Cash discounts, retailers coupons, and term discounts not included; manufacturers coupons included.	
Vermont	Discounts allowed by a seller, including cash, term, or coupons that are not reimbursed by a third party not included; consideration received by a seller from third parties included if certain criteria are met.	
Virginia	Cash, trade, and early payment discounts, and retailers coupons not included; manufacturers coupons included.	
Washington	Discounts, retailers coupons not included; manufacturers coupons included.	The redemption of a deal-of-the-day voucher is taxed based on the amount paid for the voucher plus any other consideration received by the seller from the customer (e.g., cash, check, or credit card amount), provided the seller is not reimbursed by a third party.
West Virginia	The "sales price" does not include discounts, including cash, term, or coupons not reimbursed by a third party.	
Wisconsin	Discounts allowed by a seller, including cash, term, or coupons that are not reimbursed by a third party not included; consideration received by a seller from third parties included if certain criteria are met.	
Wyoming	Cash and term discounts and retailers coupons not included; manufacturers coupons included.	

Components of Basis—Excise Taxes

Jurisdiction	Excise Taxes	Comment
Alabama	Included, except for federal taxes retailers must collect from consumers, certain separately stated state taxes on alcoholic beverages, and municipal privilege tax.	
Arizona	Included, except for federal retail excise tax on autos, heavy trucks, and fuel.	
Arkansas	Gross receipts, gross proceeds, or sales price includes any tax imposed on the seller but does not include any tax imposed directly on the consumer that is separately stated on the invoice or other document given to the purchaser.	
California	Federal excise taxes on retail sales, local rapid transit district sales and use taxes, state motor vehicle fees and taxes that are added to or measured by a vehicle's price, and diesel fuel excise tax not included; federal manufacturers and importers excise taxes on gasoline, diesel, or jet fuel for which the purchaser is entitled to a direct income tax credit or refund also not included; import duties not included if the importer of record is a consignee and the consignee is the buyer; state motor vehicle fuel license taxes included; other manufacturers and importers excise taxes included.	
Colorado	Direct federal taxes excluded and state sales and use taxes not included; indirect federal manufacturers taxes included.	
Connecticut	Federal taxes imposed on retail sales, state cabaret tax not included; federal manufacturers or importers excise taxes and all taxes imposed on a basis other than the proceeds from retail sales included.	
District of Columbia	Separately stated federal retailers excise taxes not included.	
Florida	Separately stated federal retailers excise taxes, separately stated municipal public service taxes, separately stated motor vehicle warranty fee not included; federal manufacturers excise tax, municipal utility fees, state tire and battery fees, rental car surcharge included, state utility gross receipts tax included if the cost is separately itemized and passed on to customers; other taxes included.	Taxable admissions do not include any federal taxes.

Jurisdiction	Excise Taxes	Comment
Georgia	Excluded: (1) separately stated federal retailers' excise tax, (2) state motor fuel excise tax on gasoline and other motor fuel, (3) state excise tax on cigarettes. Included: federal excise taxes on (1) gasoline and diesel fuel; (2) tires, tubes, and accessories; and (3) cigarettes.	
Hawaii	Certain state and federal liquid fuel taxes; state liquor tax; state cigarette and tobacco products taxes; federal excise taxes on articles sold at retail; federal taxes imposed on sugar manufactured in Hawaii; state rental motor vehicle surcharge taxes; state nursing home facility taxes not included.	
Idaho	Federal importers and manufacturers excise taxes included; federal taxes on retail sales not included.	
Illinois	ROT: federal taxes collected from customer, federal excise taxes on retail sales, state motor fuel tax, state tire fee not included; federal excise taxes on manufacture, import taxes, tax on non-retail sale, state liquor tax, cigarette tax included.	
Indiana	Federal or state taxes collected as agent, federal retailers tax if imposed solely on sale of personal property and collected by a merchant as a separate item in addition to the price, manufacturers excise tax, and federal and state fuel tax not included.	
Iowa	Taxes imposed on sales subject to Iowa sales and use tax, federal excise tax on first retail sale of a vehicle not included, federal excise tax on communication services of local and toll telephone and teletypewriter exchange services not included; federal excise taxes on alcohol, tobacco, fuel, and tires, and state cigarette tax included.	
Kansas	Federal manufacturers' excise tax paid by manufacturer included; "sales or selling price" includes all taxes imposed on the seller but excludes separately stated taxes legally imposed directly on the consumer.	
Kentucky	"Gross receipts" or "sales price" includes all taxes imposed on the retailer but excludes separately stated taxes legally imposed directly on the purchaser; federal tax on retail sales excluded from tax base; federal manufacturers' excise tax or federal import duty included in tax base.	
Louisiana	Excise taxes included.	

Jurisdiction	Excise Taxes	Comment
Maine	Federal tax on retail sales not included; federal manufacturers, importers, alcohol, and tobacco excise taxes included.	
Maryland	Consumer excise taxes imposed directly on buyer, certain county utility taxes, admissions taxes, electricity surcharges, and certain taxes imposed on leased property not included.	
Massachusetts	Federal retail excise tax on trucks not included; taxes with incidence on vendor included.	
Michigan	Taxes legally imposed directly on the consumer that are separately stated on the invoice, bill of sale, or similar document, not included; taxes imposed on the seller and federal manufacturers' excise taxes, included.	
Minnesota	Separately stated taxes imposed directly on consumers, separately stated federal excise taxes imposed at retail level not included. Federal excise taxes imposed at the wholesale/lessor or other level included.	
Mississippi	Federal retailers excise tax, tax levied on income from transportation, telegraphic dispatches, telephone conversations, and electric energy, and certain state gasoline tax not included.	
Missouri	Federal manufacturers excise tax, excise tax on retail sales of fuel, vehicles, sporting goods, firearms, communications, and certain transportation, and state tobacco tax not included; local tobacco tax imposed on seller included.	
Nebraska	Occupation taxes, import duties, manufacturer's excise taxes, property taxes included. Federal luxury excise tax excluded.	
Nevada	Federal taxes imposed on retail sales not included; manufacturers and importers excise taxes included.	
New Jersey	Excise taxes imposed on consumers not included; other federal, state, and local excise taxes included.	
New Mexico	Gross receipts taxes, federal communication excise tax, air transportation excise tax, not included; federal manufacturers excise tax, cigarette tax included.	

Jurisdiction	Excise Taxes	Comment
New York	Excise taxes imposed on manufacturers, importers, producers, distributors, or distillers are included. Excise taxes imposed directly on consumers (other than cigarette taxes) not included (i.e., federal excise taxes on special motor fuels, communication services, taxable transportation, and state taxes on gasoline).	
North Carolina	Separately stated taxes imposed directly on consumers not included; federal excise taxes imposed on manufacturer included.	
North Dakota	Included	
Ohio	Excise taxes imposed on consumers not included; excise taxes imposed on manufacturers, distributors, wholesalers, and retailers, included.	
Oklahoma	Under definitions of "gross receipts," "gross proceeds," and "sales price," separately stated taxes imposed directly on consumers not included. Federal excise taxes levied on retailers and manufacturers included.	
Pennsylvania	State taxes and taxes that represent cost to vendor, including manufacturers excise, gross receipts, and mercantile taxes, included.	
Rhode Island	Any taxes legally imposed directly on the consumer that are separately stated excluded; manufacturers, importers, and retailers excise taxes included.	
South Carolina	Federal taxes imposed on retail sales, local sales and use taxes, and local hospitality taxes and accommodations fees imposed directly on customers not included; federal manufacturers and importers excise taxes, local hospitality taxes and accommodations fees imposed on retailers included.	
South Dakota	Separately stated taxes imposed directly on consumers not included.	
Tennessee	Separately stated taxes imposed directly on consumers not included.	
Texas	Certain federal excise taxes included.	
Utah	Excise taxes included.	
Vermont	Separately stated taxes legally imposed directly on the consumer not included.	

Jurisdiction	Excise Taxes	Comment
Virginia	Separately stated federal retailers excise tax, state and local sales and use taxes, and local excise taxes on meals and lodging not included; federal manufacturers excise tax and taxes on alcoholic beverages and tobacco included.	
Washington	Any separately stated tax imposed on consumers not included; taxes imposed on sellers included.	
West Virginia	"Sales price" does not include any taxes legally imposed directly on the consumer that are separately stated on the invoice. Any excise tax imposed before imposition of West Virginia sales tax included. Federal, state, and local taxes simultaneously imposed on the property or service purchased not included.	
Wisconsin	Excluded from the basis are separately stated taxes legally imposed directly on the purchaser and separately stated taxes imposed on the seller, provided the seller may, but is not required to, pass on to and collect the tax from the user or consumer. These include the federal communications tax imposed upon telegraph service and telephone service; various local Wisconsin taxes; Wisconsin state vehicle rental fee; federal luxury tax; federal and Wisconsin motor vehicle excise taxes refunded; police and fire protection fee; low-income assistance fees; landline and wireless 911 charges; and state universal service fund fee. Included in the basis are the Wisconsin fermented malt beverage and intoxicating liquors taxes; federal stamp taxes and manufacturer's or importer's excise tax not imposed directly on the purchaser; federal, county, or municipal fuel taxes included in the price of alternate fuels and general aviation fuel subject to the sales tax; Wisconsin cigarette and tobacco products taxes; foreign export gallonage taxes on fuels; federal gas guzzler tax; federal medical device excise tax; federal universal service fund fee; dry cleaning and dry cleaning products fees; Wisconsin Public Service Commission fees; certain telephone and telecommunications surcharges; state-issued video service franchise fee; petroleum inspection fee; and Wisconsin motor fuel taxes.	Retroactively to September 1, 2014, any federal excise tax imposed on a seller of a heavy truck or trailer sold at retail is exempt from sales and use tax.
Wyoming	Separately stated taxes imposed directly on consumers not included; other taxes included.	

Components of Basis—Finance Charges

If charges are excluded when separately stated, it is noted in the Comment column.

Jurisdiction	Finance Charges	Comment
Alabama	Excluded	Must be separately stated.
Arizona	Excluded	Must be separately stated.
Arkansas	No specific provisions.	
California	Excluded	Must be separately stated.
Colorado	Excluded	Must be separately stated.
Connecticut	Included	
District of Columbia	Excluded	Must be separately stated.
Florida	Excluded	Must be separately stated.
Georgia	Excluded	Must be separately stated to be excluded from the "sales price."
Hawaii	Included	
Idaho	Excluded	
Illinois	Excluded	
Indiana	Excluded	Must be separately stated.
Iowa	Excluded	Must be separately stated.
Kansas	Excluded	Must be separately stated to be excluded from the "sales or selling price."
Kentucky	Excluded	Must be separately stated to be excluded from the "gross receipts" or "sales price."
Louisiana	Excluded	
Maine	Excluded	Must be separately stated.
Maryland	Excluded	Must be separately stated.
Massachusetts	Excluded	Must be separately stated.
Michigan	Excluded	Must be separately stated.
Minnesota	Excluded	Must be separately stated.
Mississippi	Excluded	Included prior to July 1, 2014. Excluded if credit extended by third-party creditor.
Missouri	Excluded	
Nebraska	Excluded	Must be separately stated.
Nevada	Excluded	Must be separately stated.
New Jersey	Excluded	

Jurisdiction	Finance Charges	Comment
New Mexico	Excluded	
New York	Excluded	
North Carolina	Excluded	Must be separately stated.
North Dakota	Excluded	Must be separately stated.
Ohio	Excluded	Must be separately stated.
Oklahoma	Excluded	Must be separately stated to be excluded from the "gross receipts," "gross proceeds," or "sales price."
Pennsylvania	Excluded	Must be separately stated.
Rhode Island	Excluded	Must be separately stated.
South Carolina	Excluded	Must be separately stated.
South Dakota	Excluded	Must be separately stated.
Tennessee	Excluded	Must be separately stated.
Texas	Excluded	Must be separately stated.
Utah	Excluded	Must be separately stated.
Vermont	Excluded	Must be separately stated.
Virginia	Excluded	Must be separately stated.
Washington	Excluded	Must be separately stated.
West Virginia	Excluded	Must be separately stated to be excluded from the "sales price."
Wisconsin	Excluded	Must be separately stated.
Wyoming	Excluded	Must be separately stated.

Components of Basis—Installation Charges

If charges are excluded when separately stated, it is noted in the Comment column.

Jurisdiction	Installation Charges	Comment
Alabama	Excluded	Must be separately stated.
Arizona	Excluded	Must be separately stated.
Arkansas	Excluded	Must be separately stated.
California	Excluded	
Colorado	Excluded	Must be separately stated.
Connecticut	Excluded	Must be separately stated.
District of Columbia	Excluded	Must be separately stated.
Florida	Included	
Georgia	Excluded	Must be separately stated.
Hawaii	Included	
Idaho	Excluded	Must be separately stated.
Illinois	Included	Excluded if separately contracted.
Indiana	Excluded	Must be separately stated.
Iowa	Included	Excluded if separately contracted.
Kansas	Included	Certain installation services related to construction are excluded.
Kentucky	Excluded	Must be separately stated to be excluded from "gross receipts" or "sales price."
Louisiana	Excluded	Must be separately stated.
Maine	Excluded	Must be separately stated.
Maryland	Excluded	Must be separately stated.
Massachusetts	Excluded	
Michigan	Included, as long as they are incurred before the completion of the transfer of ownership of tangible personal property from the seller to the purchaser.	
Minnesota	Included	
Mississippi	Included	
Missouri	Excluded	Must be separately stated or the price of the tangible personal property constitutes less than 10% of the total sale price.
Nebraska	Included, as long as the property being installed is taxable.	Installation charges of sewer and water service providers are not gross receipts and are not taxable.

Jurisdiction	Installation Charges	Comment
Nevada	Excluded	Must be separately stated.
New Jersey	Included	Excluded if installation constitutes real property addition or capital improvement.
New Mexico	Included	
New York	Included	Excluded if installation constitutes real property addition, capital improvement, or in certain other situations.
North Carolina	Included	The general sales and use tax rate applies to the sales price of, or the gross receipts derived from, repair, maintenance, and installation services. Certain exceptions apply.
North Dakota	Excluded	Must be separately stated.
Ohio	Included	Installation charges for exempt property or property that will become a part of a production, transmission, transportation, or distribution system for the delivery of a public utility service, are not taxable.
Oklahoma	Excluded	Must be separately stated to be excluded from "gross receipts," "gross proceeds," or "sales price."
Pennsylvania	Included	
Rhode Island	Excluded	Must be separately stated.
South Carolina	Excluded	Must be separately stated.
South Dakota	Included	
Tennessee	Included	
Texas	Included	
Utah	Excluded	Must be separately stated.
Vermont	Excluded	Must be separately stated.
Virginia	Excluded	Must be separately stated.
Washington	Included	
West Virginia	Included	
Wisconsin	Included	
Wyoming	Included	

Components of Basis—Installment Sales

Jurisdiction	Installment Sales	Comment
Alabama	Payments reported as received.	Lay-away sales taxable at transfer of title.
Arizona	Payments reported as received.	Lay-away sales taxable at transfer of title or when transaction nonrefundable.
Arkansas	No specific provisions.	
California	Total sales price reported at time of sale.	Lay-away sales taxable at transfer of title.
Colorado	Payments reported as received.	
Connecticut	Total sales price reported at time of sale.	
District of Columbia	Total sales price reported at time of sale.	
Florida	Total sales price reported at time of sale.	
Georgia	No specific provisions.	
Hawaii	Reporting of payments depends on whether seller/lessor is cash or accrual basis taxpayer.	If seller/lessor is an accrual basis taxpayer, the transaction is reported by classifying purchase price as retailing income at inception of lease, and the finance charge is accrued as interest income ratably in accordance with the lease agreement, whether received by seller/lessor or not. If seller/lessor is a cash basis taxpayer, monthly payments received are reported by allocating the amount received between the purchase price of the property and the finance charge.
Idaho	Total sales price reported at time of sale.	Lay-away sales taxable at transfer of title.
Illinois	Payments reported as received.	
Indiana	No specific provisions.	
Iowa	Total payment reported at time of delivery.	
Kansas	Payments reported as received.	If accrual basis, total sales price reported at time of sale.
Kentucky	Payments reported as received.	If accrual basis, total sales price reported at time of sale.
Louisiana	Total sales price reported at time of sale.	
Maine	Total sales price reported at time of sale.	
Maryland	Total sales price reported at time of sale.	

Jurisdiction	Installment Sales	Comment
Massachusetts	Total sales price reported at time of sale.	
Michigan	Total sales price reported at time of sale.	
Minnesota	Payments reported as received.	If accrual basis, total sales price reported at time of sale.
Mississippi	Total sales price reported at time of sale.	
Missouri	Payments reported as received.	If accrual basis, total sales price reported at time of sale. Lay-away sales taxed when sale complete.
Nebraska	Payments reported as received.	Retailers maintaining their books and records on the accrual basis, may choose to report such sales on a cash basis by deferring remittance of sales tax not yet collected on credit, conditional, and installment sales.
Nevada	No specific provisions.	
New Jersey	Total sales price reported at time of sale.	
New Mexico	Payments reported as received.	Seller must elect to treat payments reported as received.
New York	Total sales price reported at time of sale.	
North Carolina	Payments reported as received.	If accrual basis, total sales price reported at time of sale.
North Dakota	Payments reported as received when payment of principal sum is extended over a period longer than 60 days from date of sale.	Exception applies if purchaser is billed in full in intervals of less than 60 consecutive days, even though credit terms may allow purchaser to extend principal payments beyond 60 consecutive days.
Ohio	Total sales price reported at time of sale.	
Oklahoma	Total sales price reported at time of sale.	
Pennsylvania	Seller must require purchaser to pay full amount of tax due on entire purchase price at time of purchase or within 30 days after purchase.	
Rhode Island	No specific provisions.	
South Carolina	Payments reported as received or total sales price reported at time of sale, at taxpayer's election.	Lay-away payments taxed as received as long as title has been transferred to the property being held by the seller for the purchaser (e.g., as security). If both title and possession remain with the seller, sales tax on lay-away payments is remitted with the return for the month in which the item was transferred to the customer.

Jurisdiction	Installment Sales	Comment
South Dakota	Payments reported as received.	
Tennessee	Total sales price reported at time of sale.	Lay-away sales taxable upon delivery to customer.
Texas	Payments reported as received.	If accrual basis, total sales price reported at time of sale.
Utah	Total sales price reported at time of sale.	
Vermont	Total sales price reported at time of sale.	Certain vendors may request permission to report payments as received.
Virginia	Total sales price reported at time of sale.	Lay-away sales taxable upon delivery to customer.
Washington	Total sales price reported at time of sale.	
West Virginia	Total sales price reported at time of sale.	Lay-away sales taxable upon delivery to customer.
Wisconsin	Payments reported when purchaser takes possession of the property.	
Wyoming	Total sales price reported at time of sale.	If title passes at a future date, payments taxed as received.

Components of Basis—Returns and Repossessions

Where treatment differs for repossessed goods, it is noted in the Comments column.

Jurisdiction	Returns and Repossessions	Comment
Alabama	Deductible, if full sales price refunded.	A deduction or credit is allowed for the unpaid purchase price of repossessed property.
Arizona	Not included in gross receipts.	No specific provisions on repossessions.
Arkansas	Deductible, if full purchase price and tax were returned to customer.	A deduction is not allowed for property that has been repossessed or voluntarily returned without a full refund.
California	Deductible, if the purchaser receives a full refund of the sales price including tax, and the purchaser is not required to purchase other property at a price greater than the returned merchandise in order to obtain a refund or credit.	Repossessions are deductible if the entire amount paid by the purchaser is refunded, or if a credit for a worthless account is allowable.
Colorado	Deductible, if full sale price and tax refunded.	A deduction is allowed for the uncollected selling price of repossessed property.
Connecticut	Not included in gross receipts, if property is returned within 90 days from the purchase date.	No specific provisions on repossessions.
District of Columbia	A refund is allowed, if property is returned within 90 days of sale and full purchase price including tax is refunded to purchaser.	No deduction or refund is allowed for repossessed property.
Florida	Deductible if tax has not been remitted. If tax has been remitted, a credit is allowed.	A deduction is allowed for the unpaid balance of repossessed property.
Georgia	Deductible, if the property is returned within 90 days from the sale date, and the entire sales price is refunded to the purchaser. For property returned after 90 days, dealer may request a credit memorandum.	No specific provisions on repossessions.
Hawaii	Amount refunded not included in gross proceeds.	No specific provisions on taxability of repossessions. Repossession services are taxable.
Idaho	Deductible, if the sale price is refunded, and the purchaser is not required to purchase other merchandise at a greater price.	A bad debt adjustment is allowed for property that is repossessed and seasonably resold.
Illinois	Deductible, if the amount charged including tax is refunded to the purchaser.	A credit is allowed for the uncollected portion of the sale price of repossessed property.
Indiana	No specific provisions.	
Iowa	Amount refunded not included in gross receipts.	A seller may claim a bad debt credit for repossessed merchandise.

Jurisdiction	Returns and Repossessions	Comment
Kansas	Deductible, if the amount charged including tax is refunded to the purchaser.	Resales of repossessed goods by a retailer are reportable as part of the retailer's gross receipts; retailers and financial institutions accrue tax on the use of repossessed goods other than for retention, demonstration, or display in the regular course of business.
Kentucky	Property repossessed by the seller may not be classed as returned goods or deductible bad debt.	
Louisiana	Deductible before tax has been remitted; refund allowed after tax has been remitted.	No deduction or refund is allowed for repossessed property.
Maine	Deductible, if the full sale price is refunded.	A deduction is not allowed for repossessed property unless the retailer incurs a loss, based on either the fair market value of the property or the resale price.
Maryland	Deductible	A credit is allowed for repossessed property. The amount is the difference between the tax on the unpaid balance and the tax on the value of the item at the time of repossession.
Massachusetts	Deductible, if the property is returned within 90 days from the sale date (180 days for motor vehicles), and the entire amount charged, less vendor's handling fees, has been refunded.	No specific provisions on repossessions.
Michigan	Deductible	No specific provisions on repossessions.
Minnesota	Deductible, if the sales tax is refunded to the purchaser.	A repossession is not considered a deductible return.
Mississippi	Deductible, if the total sales price is refunded to the purchaser.	A deduction is allowed for the uncollected portion of the selling price of repossessed property.
Missouri	Deductible, if the full sales price including tax is refunded to the purchaser.	No specific provisions on repossessions.
Nebraska	Deductible	A credit is allowed for the unpaid balance of repossessed property. A credit is not allowed if the retailer remitted the tax on a cash accounting basis or collected the full tax from the purchaser at the time of purchase.
Nevada	Deductible, if the full sales price is refunded, and the purchaser is not required to purchase other property at a greater price than the returned property in order to obtain a refund.	No specific provisions on repossessions.
New Jersey	Not deductible; a regulation allowing a deduction has been authorized but not implemented.	A retailer may file a refund claim for overpaid sales tax on repossessed property; a deduction is not allowed.

Jurisdiction	Returns and Repossessions	Comment
New Mexico	Deductible	A retailer that reports on an accrual basis may deduct amounts written off as uncollectible debt for the amount credited to a buyer from whom property was repossessed.
New York	Tax that has not been remitted may be deducted during current reporting period. A credit or a refund is allowed for tax that has already been remitted.	No specific provisions on repossessions.
North Carolina	A refund or a credit is allowed if the entire amount charged including tax is refunded to the purchaser.	A deduction is not allowed for repossessed property.
North Dakota	A credit is allowed, if the purchase price including tax is refunded to the purchaser.	A credit is allowed for tax paid on the unpaid balance of the original sale of the repossessed property.
Ohio	Amounts refunded not included in receipts.	No specific provisions on repossessions.
Oklahoma	Deductible, if the full purchase price including tax is refunded to the purchaser.	A credit is allowed for the unpaid portion of repossessed property.
Pennsylvania	Deductible, if the sale amount and tax have been refunded to the purchaser.	A deduction is not allowed for repossessed property.
Rhode Island	Deductible, if the full sale price including tax but excluding handling charges is refunded to the purchaser, and the merchandise is returned within 120 from the purchase date.	A deduction is not allowed for repossessed property.
South Carolina	Amounts refunded not included in gross proceeds.	No specific provisions on repossessions.
South Dakota	Amounts refunded not included in gross receipts.	No specific provisions on repossessions.
Tennessee	Deductible, if the purchase price including tax is refunded to the purchaser.	If the unpaid purchase price of repossessed property exceeds $500, a dealer may claim a credit equal to the difference between the sales tax paid at the time of the original purchase and the amount of sales tax that would be owed for the portion of the purchase price that was paid by the purchaser, plus the sales tax on the first $500 of the unpaid balance.
Texas	Credit allowed for tax on fully refunded amount.	A credit is allowed for the unpaid portion of the purchase price of repossessed property.
Utah	Adjustment and credit allowed if tax reported and paid in full. Credit amount may not exceed sales tax on portion of purchase price remaining unpaid at time the goods are returned.	Credit allowed to seller of a motor vehicle for tax that the seller collected on vehicle that has been repossessed and that the seller resells. Credit is equal to the product of the portion of the vehicle's purchase price that was subject to tax and remains unpaid after resale of the vehicle, and the tax rate.

Jurisdiction	Returns and Repossessions	Comment
Vermont	Deductible, if the full price including tax is refunded to the purchaser.	A vendor may apply for a refund for tax paid on the unpaid balance of repossessed property.
Virginia	Deductible, if the sales price is refunded or credited to the account of the purchaser.	The unpaid balance on repossessed property is deductible.
Washington	Deductible, if the full selling price including tax is refunded to the purchaser. If property is not returned within the guaranty period or if the full selling price is not refunded, a presumption is raised that the property returned is not returned goods but rather an exchange or repurchase by the vendor.	No specific provision on repossessions.
West Virginia	Deductible	No specific provisions on repossessions.
Wisconsin	Deduction allowed for the amount of the purchase price refunded to the buyer if tax refunded to buyer.	Repossession of property not included in tax base if the only consideration is cancellation of the purchaser's obligation to pay the remaining balance of the purchase price. A deduction for repossessed property is not allowed unless the entire consideration paid by the purchaser is refunded, or a deduction for worthless accounts is allowable.
Wyoming	Deductible, if the full sales price including tax is refunded to the purchaser.	A deduction is not allowed for repossessed property.

Computers: Canned Software—Delivered on Tangible Personal Property

Jurisdiction	Delivered on Tangible Personal Property	Comment
Alabama	Taxable	
Arizona	Taxable	
Arkansas	Taxable	
California	Taxable	
Colorado	Taxable	
Connecticut	Taxable	
District of Columbia	Taxable	
Florida	Taxable	Software used predominantly for research and development may qualify for exemption.
Georgia	Taxable	
Hawaii	Taxable	
Idaho	Taxable	
Illinois	Taxable	
Indiana	Taxable	
Iowa	Taxable	
Kansas	Taxable	
Kentucky	Taxable	
Louisiana	Taxable	
Maine	Taxable	
Maryland	Taxable	
Massachusetts	Taxable	
Michigan	Taxable	
Minnesota	Taxable	
Mississippi	Taxable	
Missouri	Taxable	
Nebraska	Taxable	
Nevada	Taxable	
New Jersey	Taxable	
New Mexico	Taxable	
New York	Taxable	
North Carolina	Taxable	

Jurisdiction	Delivered on Tangible Personal Property	Comment
North Dakota	Taxable	
Ohio	Taxable	
Oklahoma	Taxable	
Pennsylvania	Taxable	
Rhode Island	Taxable	
South Carolina	Taxable	Broadcasting software sold to a radio station, television station, or cable television system is exempt.
South Dakota	Taxable	
Tennessee	Taxable	Exemptions may apply for the use of software developed and fabricated by an affiliated company or for fabrication of software by a person for that person's own use or consumption.
Texas	Taxable	
Utah	Taxable	
Vermont	Taxable	
Virginia	Taxable	Software used directly and exclusively in exempt research and development activities may qualify for exemption.
Washington	Taxable	
West Virginia	Taxable	
Wisconsin	Taxable	
Wyoming	Taxable	

Computers: Canned Software—Downloaded

This chart indicates whether sales or licenses of prewritten computer software delivered electronically are subject to tax.

Jurisdiction	Downloaded	Comment
Alabama	Taxable	
Arizona	Taxable	
Arkansas	Exempt	Software delivered electronically or by "load and leave" not taxable.
California	Exempt	Prewritten program transferred by remote telecommunications exempt, provided that purchaser does not obtain possession of any tangible personal property (such as storage media) in the transaction.
Colorado	Exempt	
Connecticut	Taxable	Effective October 1, 2019, the sales and use tax rate on canned downloaded software that is electronically accessed or transferred, other than when purchased by a business for use by such business, and any additional content related to such software, is increased from 1% to 6.35%. Until October 1, 2019, if no tangible personal property is delivered to purchaser along with the downloaded software, canned downloaded software is taxed at the reduced 1% rate applicable to computer and data processing services.
District of Columbia	Taxable	
Florida	Exempt	
Georgia	Exempt	Documentation must indicate method of delivery. If software is delivered both electronically and through a tangible medium, the transaction is treated as a taxable sale of tangible personal property unless the software qualifies as custom software.
Hawaii	Taxable	
Idaho	Exempt	Electronically delivered, remotely accessed (cloud), and "load and leave" software exempt.
Illinois	Taxable	
Indiana	Taxable	
Iowa	Taxable	Pursuant to tax reform (S.F. 2417), Iowa Code § 423.3(67) repealed as of January 1, 2019
Kansas	Taxable	

Jurisdiction	Downloaded	Comment
Kentucky	Taxable	
Louisiana	Taxable	
Maine	Taxable	
Maryland	Exempt	Exempt as long as the transaction does not include the transfer of any tangible personal property.
Massachusetts	Taxable	
Michigan	Taxable	
Minnesota	Taxable	
Mississippi	Taxable	
Missouri	Exempt	
Nebraska	Taxable	
Nevada	Exempt	
New Jersey	Taxable	Downloaded software is exempt only if used directly and exclusively in the conduct of the purchaser's business, trade, or occupation.
New Mexico	Taxable	
New York	Taxable	
North Carolina	Taxable	Only computer software that meets certain descriptions is exempt.
North Dakota	Taxable	
Ohio	Taxable	
Oklahoma	Exempt	
Pennsylvania	Taxable	
Rhode Island	Taxable	
South Carolina	Exempt	Exempt as long as no part of the software is transferred by tangible means.
South Dakota	Taxable	
Tennessee	Taxable	
Texas	Taxable	
Utah	Taxable	
Vermont	Taxable	
Virginia	Exempt	Exempt as long as the transaction does not include the transfer of any tangible personal property.
Washington	Taxable	

Jurisdiction	Downloaded	Comment
West Virginia	Taxable	Exemptions may apply for high technology businesses, certain education software, software directly used in communications or incorporated into a manufactured product, or software used to provide data processing services.
Wisconsin	Taxable	
Wyoming	Taxable	

Computers: Custom Software—Delivered on Tangible Personal Property

Jurisdiction	Delivered on Tangible Personal Property	Comment
Alabama	Exempt	Cost of tangible medium used to transfer custom software programming to customer taxable.
Arizona	Exempt	
Arkansas	Taxable	
California	Exempt	
Colorado	Exempt	
Connecticut	Taxable	Software taxable at 1% rate for computer and data processing services; tangible personal property taxable at general state sales/use tax rate. Custom software may be exempt if purchased in connection with exempt machinery under the biotechnology, manufacturing, or commercial printers/ publishers exemption.
District of Columbia	Taxable	
Florida	Exempt	The charge that a computer technician makes for a customized software package that includes such items as instructional material, pre-punched cards, or programmed tapes is construed to be a service charge and exempt.
Georgia	Exempt	
Hawaii	Taxable	
Idaho	Exempt	
Illinois	Exempt	
Indiana	Exempt	
Iowa	Taxable	Pursuant to tax reform (S.F. 2417)
Kansas	Exempt	
Kentucky	Exempt	
Louisiana	Exempt	
Maine	Exempt	
Maryland	Exempt	
Massachusetts	Exempt	
Michigan	Exempt	
Minnesota	Exempt	When purchased with a computer, exempt only if charges for custom software are separately stated.

Jurisdiction	Delivered on Tangible Personal Property	Comment
Mississippi	Taxable	
Missouri	Exempt	Tax does not apply to the amount charged to the customer for customized software. The seller of the customized software is subject to tax on the purchase of any tangible personal property or taxable services used to provide the nontaxable service.
Nebraska	Taxable	
Nevada	Exempt	Exempt only if charges for custom software or programming are separately stated.
New Jersey	Exempt	If a purchaser receives custom software in some tangible medium, the transfer of the disc or CD to the purchaser is deemed to be an incidental part of the sale of exempt software development and design services.
New Mexico	Taxable	
New York	Exempt	
North Carolina	Exempt	
North Dakota	Exempt	When purchased with equipment, exempt only if charges for custom software are separately stated.
Ohio	Exempt	Custom system software for business use is a taxable computer service. Programming of custom application software is not a taxable sale.
Oklahoma	Exempt	Exempt if tangible personal property transferred with custom software is incidental to sale of the software. If a computer is purchased with custom software and the charges are not separately stated, the entire purchase is taxable.
Pennsylvania	Exempt	
Rhode Island	Exempt	
South Carolina	Taxable	Broadcasting software sold to a radio station, television station, or cable television system is exempt.
South Dakota	Taxable	
Tennessee	Taxable	Exemptions may apply for the use of software developed and fabricated by an affiliated company or for fabrication of software by a person for that person's own use or consumption.
Texas	Taxable	
Utah	Exempt	

Jurisdiction	Delivered on Tangible Personal Property	Comment
Vermont	Exempt	
Virginia	Exempt	Exempt if true object of sale is to provide exempt custom programming service and tangible personal property transferred is not critical to the transaction; separately stated charges for tangible personal property are taxable. Taxable if true object of sale is to provide tangible personal property. Information conveyed via tangible means (e.g., diskette, computer tape, report, etc.) generally is taxable except for information customized to a particular customer's needs and sold to that particular customer.
Washington	Exempt	
West Virginia	Taxable	
Wisconsin	Exempt	
Wyoming	Exempt	

Computers: Custom Software—Downloaded

This chart indicates whether sales or licenses of custom computer software delivered electronically are subject to tax.

Jurisdiction	Downloaded	Comment
Alabama	Exempt	
Arizona	Exempt	
Arkansas	Exempt	Software delivered electronically or by "load and leave" not taxable.
California	Exempt	
Colorado	Exempt	
Connecticut	Taxable	Effective October 1, 2019, the sales and use tax rate on custom downloaded software that is electronically accessed or transferred, other than when purchased by a business for use by such business, and any additional content related to such software, is increased from 1% to 6.35%. Until October 1, 2019, if no tangible personal property is delivered to the purchaser along with the downloaded software, custom downloaded software is taxed at the reduced 1% rate applicable to computer and data processing services.
District of Columbia	Taxable	
Florida	Exempt	
Georgia	Exempt	
Hawaii	Taxable	
Idaho	Exempt	
Illinois	Exempt	
Indiana	Exempt	
Iowa	Taxable	Pursuant to tax reform (S.F. 2417), Iowa Code § 423.3(67) repealed as of January 1, 2019.
Kansas	Exempt	
Kentucky	Exempt	
Louisiana	Exempt	
Maine	Exempt	
Maryland	Exempt	
Massachusetts	Exempt	
Michigan	Exempt	
Minnesota	Exempt	

Jurisdiction	Downloaded	Comment
Mississippi	Taxable	
Missouri	Exempt	Tax does not apply to the amount charged to the customer for customized software. The seller of the customized software is subject to tax on the purchase of any tangible personal property or taxable services used to provide the nontaxable service.
Nebraska	Taxable	
Nevada	Exempt	
New Jersey	Exempt	
New Mexico	Taxable	
New York	Exempt	
North Carolina	Exempt	
North Dakota	Exempt	When purchased with equipment, exempt only if charges for custom software are separately stated.
Ohio	Exempt	Custom system software for business use is a taxable computer service. Programming of custom application software is not a taxable sale.
Oklahoma	Exempt	
Pennsylvania	Exempt	
Rhode Island	Exempt	
South Carolina	Exempt	Exempt as long as the transaction does not include the transfer of any tangible personal property.
South Dakota	Taxable	
Tennessee	Taxable	Exemptions may apply for the use of software developed and fabricated by an affiliated company or for fabrication of software by a person for that person's own use or consumption.
Texas	Taxable	
Utah	Exempt	
Vermont	Exempt	
Virginia	Exempt	Exempt as long as the transaction does not include the transfer of any tangible personal property.
Washington	Exempt	
West Virginia	Taxable	
Wisconsin	Exempt	
Wyoming	Exempt	

Computers: Customization of Canned Software

Jurisdiction	Customization of Canned Software	Comment
Alabama	Taxable	Separately stated charges for modifications to canned software prepared exclusively for a particular customer are exempt only to extent of modification.
Arizona	Taxable	Charges for modification of prewritten software for the specific use of an individual customer are exempt if separately stated on the sales invoice and records.
Arkansas	Exempt	Modification or enhancement of canned software may be exempt programming service if reasonable, separate charge given to purchaser.
California	Taxable	Separately stated charges for modifications to canned software prepared exclusively for a particular customer exempt only to extent of modification.
Colorado	Exempt	
Connecticut	Taxable	Taxable at reduced rate for computer and data processing services.
District of Columbia	Taxable	
Florida	Exempt	
Georgia	Taxable	Prewritten computer software, even though modified to the specifications of a purchaser, remains prewritten computer software. However, if there is a separately stated charge on the dealer's invoice for the modification or enhancement, the charge is not subject to tax.
Hawaii	Taxable	
Idaho	Exempt	If charge separately stated and customization prepared exclusively for a customer.
Illinois	Exempt	Modified software held for general or repeated sale/lease is taxable.
Indiana	Taxable	If modification or enhancement is designed and developed to the specifications of a specific purchaser, software remains prewritten computer software. Where there is a reasonable, separately stated charge for such a modification or enhancement, the modification or enhancement is not prewritten computer software and is exempt.
Iowa	Taxable	Pursuant to tax reform (S.F. 2417)

Jurisdiction	Customization of Canned Software	Comment
Kansas	Taxable	Separately stated charges for modifications to canned software prepared exclusively for a particular customer exempt.
Kentucky	Exempt	If prewritten software is modified or enhanced for a specific user and the charge for the modification or enhancement is reasonable and is separately stated on the invoice to the customer, the modification or enhancement does not fall under the definition of "prewritten computer software."
Louisiana	Exempt	"Custom computer software" is computer software that is prepared, created, adapted, or modified: (1) to the special order of a particular purchaser, licensee, or user; or (2) to meet the specific needs or requirements of a particular purchaser, licensee, or user, regardless of the means by which such software is furnished, delivered, or transmitted, and regardless of whether such software incorporates or consists of preexisting routines, utilities, or other computer software components.
Maine	Taxable	Separately stated charges for modifications to canned software prepared exclusively for a particular customer exempt only to extent of modification.
Maryland	Exempt	Exempt if the service aspect of the transaction predominates over sale of canned software.
Massachusetts	Exempt	Charges for customization must be separately stated.
Michigan	Taxable	Exempt if separately stated and identified.
Minnesota	Exempt	Must be separately stated.
Mississippi	Taxable	
Missouri	Taxable	Programming changes to canned software to adapt it to a customer's equipment or business processes are in the nature of fabrication or production labor that are a part of the sale and are taxable.
Nebraska	Taxable	Software that alters existing software is considered separate from the existing software and is taxable.
Nevada	Taxable	Exempt if charges for modifications are separately stated.

Jurisdiction	Customization of Canned Software	Comment
New Jersey	Taxable	A separately stated, commercially reasonable charge for the professional service of modifying canned software for a customer is exempt.
New Mexico	Taxable	
New York	Taxable	Reasonable, separately stated charges for modifications to canned software prepared exclusively for a particular customer exempt only to extent of modification. Modified software may be exempt if used directly and predominantly in production of property for sale or for research and development.
North Carolina	Taxable	Exempt if charges for modifications are separately stated.
North Dakota	Taxable	Exempt if charges for modifications are separately stated.
Ohio	Taxable	Reasonable, separately stated charges for modifications to canned software prepared exclusively for a particular customer exempt only to extent of modification.
Oklahoma	Taxable	Reasonable, separately stated charges for modifications to canned software prepared exclusively for a particular customer exempt only to extent of modification.
Pennsylvania	Taxable	Maintenance, updates, and support services, except for separately invoiced help desk or call center support services, for canned software are taxable. Reasonable, separately stated charges for modifications to canned software prepared exclusively for a particular customer may be exempt.
Rhode Island	Taxable	Modifications to prewritten computer software that are designed to make the software conform to a purchaser's specifications are exempt, if the charges are separately stated.
South Carolina	Taxable	Modifications to canned software prepared exclusively for a particular customer are considered to be taxable custom programs.
South Dakota	Taxable	
Tennessee	Taxable	Prewritten software that is modified to the specifications of a purchaser remains prewritten software. However, where there is a separately stated charge for a modification, the modification is not considered prewritten software.

Jurisdiction	Customization of Canned Software	Comment
Texas	Taxable	Taxable if performed by person who sold the canned software. Charges to customize canned software not sold by the person doing the customization are exempt.
Utah	Taxable	Charges for modifications to canned software that are reasonable and separately stated and identified on the invoice are exempt.
Vermont	Exempt	If canned software is received in a tangible form, custom software services must be separately invoiced to retain exemption as professional services.
Virginia	Taxable	Canned software that is modified to any degree does not become exempt custom software.
Washington	Exempt	
West Virginia	Taxable	
Wisconsin	Taxable	Reasonable, separately stated charges for canned software modifications or enhancements designed and developed to the specifications of a specific purchaser exempt.
Wyoming	Taxable	

Department Appeals

The following chart describes the time period in which a taxpayer must file a protest or appeal of an assessment with the taxing authority. Appeals to other administrative or judicial entities are addressed in Administrative Appeals and Judicial Appeals.

Jurisdiction	Department Appeals	Comment
Alabama	Petition must be filed with the Department of Revenue, Administrative Law Division within 30 days after the date of entry of the assessment.	
Arizona	Petition must be filed with the Department of Revenue within 45 days after receipt of notice of deficiency assessment or within such additional time as the Department allows.	
Arkansas	Petition must be filed with the Director of the Department of Finance and Administration within 30 days after receipt of the notice of assessment.	
California	Petition for redetermination must be filed with the State Board of Equalization within 30 days after service of notice of deficiency assessment.	
Colorado	Petition must be filed with the Executive Director of the Department of Revenue within 30 days after mailing of notice of deficiency.	
Connecticut	Petition must be filed with the Commissioner of Revenue Services within 60 days after service of notice.	
District of Columbia	Petition must be filed with the Mayor within 30 days after notice of deficiency.	
Florida	Petition must be filed with the Department of Revenue within 60 days after issuance of proposed assessment.	
Georgia	Petition must be filed with the Revenue Commissioner within 30 days after date of notice of assessment, or within another time limit specified with the notice.	
Hawaii	Petition under expedited appeals and dispute resolution program must be filed after issuance of notice of proposed assessment.	
Idaho	Petition must be filed with the Tax Commission within 63 days after mailing notice of deficiency.	
Illinois	Petition must be filed with the Department of Revenue within 60 days after issuance of notice of deficiency.	
Indiana	Petition must be filed with the Department of Revenue within 60 days after date of notice of assessment.	
Iowa	Petition must be filed with the Director of Revenue within 60 days after date of notice of assessment.	
Kansas	Informal conference may be requested with the Secretary of Revenue within 60 days after mailing of notice.	

Jurisdiction	Department Appeals	Comment
Kentucky	Effective July 1, 2018, petition must be filed with the Department of Revenue within 60 days after date of notice of assessment (previously, 45 days).	
Louisiana	Petition must be filed with the Secretary of Revenue and Taxation within 30 days after notice of deficiency or assessment.	15 days if notice based on failure to file return.
Maine	Petition must be filed with the State Tax Assessor within 60 days after receipt of notice of assessment.	
Maryland	Petition must be filed with the Comptroller within 30 days after mailing notice of Comptroller's action.	
Massachusetts	Informal conference may be requested with the Commissioner of Revenue within 30 days of notice.	
Michigan	Informal conference may be requested with the Department of Treasury within 60 days after receipt of notice of intent to assess.	
Minnesota	Petition must be filed with the Commissioner of Revenue within 60 days of notice of action.	
Mississippi	Petition must be filed with the Board of Review within 60 days from the date of the Department's action.	
Missouri	Petition for informal review must be filed with the Director of Revenue within 60 days after the assessment is delivered or sent by certified mail, whichever is earlier.	
Nebraska	Petition must be filed with the Tax Commissioner within 60 days after service of notice of deficiency.	
Nevada	Petition must be filed with the Department of Taxation within 45 days after service of notice of assessment.	
New Jersey	Petition must be filed with the Director of the Division of Taxation within 90 days after service of notice of assessment.	
New Mexico	Petition must be filed with the Secretary of Taxation and Revenue within 90 days.	
New York	Petition must be filed with the Division of Tax Appeals within 90 days after mailing notice of determination.	
North Carolina	Petition must be filed with the Secretary of Revenue within 30 days after mailing or delivery of notice of proposed assessment.	
North Dakota	Petition must be filed with the Tax Commission within 30 days after notice of determination.	
Ohio	Petition must be filed with the Tax Commissioner within 60 days after service of notice of assessment.	
Oklahoma	Petition must be filed with the Tax Commission within 60 days after mailing of notice of assessment.	
Pennsylvania	Notice of intention to file petition must be filed with the Department of Revenue within 60 days after mailing notice of assessment.	

Jurisdiction	Department Appeals	Comment
Rhode Island	Petition must be filed with the Tax Administrator within 30 days after mailing notice of assessment.	
South Carolina	Petition must be filed with the Department of Revenue within 90 days after date of proposed assessment.	
South Dakota	Petition must be filed with the Secretary of Revenue within 30 days after date of certification of assessment.	
Tennessee	Informal conference may be requested with the Commissioner of Revenue within 30 days after date of notice of assessment.	
Texas	Petition must be filed with the Comptroller of Public Accounts within 60 days after issuance of notice of determination.	Prior to September 1, 2017, within 30 days after notice was served.
Utah	Petition must be filed with the Tax Commission within 30 days after mailing notice of deficiency.	
Vermont	Petition must be filed with the Commissioner of Taxes within 60 days after notice of determination.	
Virginia	Petition must be filed with the Tax Commissioner within 90 days after notice of assessment.	
Washington	Petition must be filed with the Department of Revenue within 30 days after issuance of notice of assessment.	The appeals division may grant an extension of time to file a petition if the taxpayer's request is made within the thirty-day filing period.
West Virginia	State does not have department appeal procedures. Taxpayer must file an administrative appeal.	
Wisconsin	Petition must be filed with the Department of Revenue within 60 days after receipt of notice of determination.	
Wyoming	State does not have department appeal procedures. Taxpayer must file an administrative appeal.	

Digital Products

This chart indicates whether sales of digital products transferred electronically, including downloaded music, videos, and books, are subject to tax.

Jurisdiction	Digital Products	Comment
Alabama	Taxable	
Arizona	Taxable	
Arkansas	Taxable	
California	Exempt	
Colorado	Taxable	
Connecticut	Taxable	Effective October 1, 2019, the sales and use tax rate on digital goods is increased from 1% to 6.35%. Until October 1, 2019, digital goods are taxed at a reduced rate of 1% applicable to computer and data processing services. "Digital goods" are defined as electronically accessed or transferred audio, visual, or audiovisual works, reading materials, or ring tones.
District of Columbia	Taxable	
Florida	Exempt	
Georgia	Exempt	
Hawaii	Taxable	
Idaho	Taxable	Digital music, digital books, digital videos, and digital games are taxable when the purchaser has a permanent right to use such software and regardless of the method of delivery or access. If the right to use is conditioned upon continued payment from the purchaser (e.g., a paid subscription), it is not a permanent right of use.
Illinois	Exempt	
Indiana	Taxable	Taxable if seller grants end user a right of permanent use that is not conditioned upon continued payment by the purchaser.
Iowa	Taxable	Pursuant to tax reform (S.F. 2417), Iowa Code § 423.3(67) repealed as of January 1, 2019.
Kansas	Exempt	
Kentucky	Taxable	
Louisiana	Taxable	Transactions in which the customer pays an access fee or subscription fee to obtain the use but not ownership of a website or software are not taxable.

Jurisdiction	Digital Products	Comment
Maine	Taxable	
Maryland	Exempt	Not expressly enumerated as taxable in the taxing statute.
Massachusetts	Exempt	
Michigan	Exempt	
Minnesota	Taxable	Students' digital textbooks and instructional materials exempt. Presentations accessed as digital audio and audiovisual works exempt. Effective for sales and purchases made after June 30, 2017, jukebox music purchased by an operator is exempt (whether in digital or tangible form).
Mississippi	Taxable	
Missouri	Exempt	
Nebraska	Taxable	
Nevada	Exempt	
New Jersey	Taxable	New Jersey imposes tax on specified digital products. "Specified digital product" means an electronically transferred digital audio-visual work, digital audio work, or digital book; provided however, that a digital code which provides a purchaser with a right to obtain the product shall be treated in the same manner as a specified digital product. Specified digital products are subject to tax regardless of whether the sale of the product is for permanent or less than permanent use and regardless of whether continued payment is required. Exemptions are provided for: specified digital products that are accessed but not delivered electronically; video programming services, including video on demand television services; and for broadcasting services, including content to provide such services.
New Mexico	Taxable	

Jurisdiction	Digital Products	Comment
New York	Exempt	E-books do not constitute taxable information services if they satisfy the following criteria: (1) the purchase of the product does not entitle the customer to additional goods and services and any revisions done to the e-book are for the limited purpose of correcting errors; (2) the product is provided as a single download; (3) the product is advertised or marketed as an e-book or a similar term; (4) if the intended or customary use of the product requires that it be updated or that a new or revised edition be issued from time to time (i.e., an almanac), the updates or the new or revised editions are not issued more frequently than annually; and (5) the product is not designed to work with software other than the software necessary to make the e-book legible on a reading device (e.g., Kindle, Nook, iPad, iPhone or personal computer). Effective March 1, 2012, electronic news services and electronic periodicals will be exempt.
North Carolina	Taxable	
North Dakota	Exempt	
Ohio	Taxable	Digital music purchased from and electronically delivered by a jukebox or other single-play commercial music machine is exempt.
Oklahoma	Exempt	
Pennsylvania	Taxable	Exempt before 8/1/16
Rhode Island	Taxable	
South Carolina	Exempt	Not expressly enumerated as taxable in the taxing statute. However, charges to stream television, movies, music, and similar content are taxable as communications services.
South Dakota	Taxable	
Tennessee	Taxable	Exempt if tangible equivalent is exempt.
Texas	Taxable	
Utah	Taxable	
Vermont	Taxable	
Virginia	Exempt	
Washington	Taxable	Digital goods that are streamed or remotely accessed are also taxable. Digital goods include photographs transferred electronically to the end user.
West Virginia	Exempt	

Jurisdiction	Digital Products	Comment
Wisconsin	Taxable	Tax applies to "specified digital goods" (digital audio works, digital audiovisual works, and digital books) and "additional digital goods" (greeting cards, finished artwork, periodicals, video or electronic games, and newspapers or other news or information products). Digital goods that would be exempt if sold in tangible form are exempt.
Wyoming	Taxable	Taxable when sold to end user with rights for permanent use.

Direct Pay Permits

The following chart indicates whether direct pay permits are allowed. Where limitations are placed on the issuance of permits, it is noted in the Comments column.

Jurisdiction	Direct Pay Permits	Comment
Alabama	Allowed	Limited to electric cooperatives, telephone companies, manufacturers, transportation companies, processors of tangible personal property and mining, quarrying, or compounding businesses.
Arizona	Allowed	Limited to taxpayers that made purchases of at least $500,000 during the calendar year preceding application.
Arkansas	Allowed	
California	Allowed	Specified requirements must be met.
Colorado	Allowed	Limited to taxpayers that purchased at least $7 million of commodities, services, or tangible personal property subject to tax during the calendar year preceding application.
Connecticut	Allowed	Specified requirements must be met.
District of Columbia	Not Allowed	
Florida	Allowed	Limited to certain specified taxpayers.
Georgia	Allowed	Exceptions apply.
Hawaii	Not Allowed	
Idaho	Allowed	Limited to sales of tangible personal property. Not applicable when engaging contractors improving real property.
Illinois	Allowed	Specified requirements must be met. Not applicable to food, beverages, property required to be titled or registered with government agency, or transactions subject to Service Occupation or Service Use Tax.
Indiana	Allowed	
Iowa	Allowed	Limited to taxpayers accruing tax liability of more than $4,000 in semi-monthly period. Permit not applicable in situations such as for sales of gas, electricity, heat, pay television service, communication service, tax on motor vehicles and on vehicles rented for 60 or fewer days.

Jurisdiction	Direct Pay Permits	Comment
Kansas	Allowed	Limited to taxpayers making annual purchases of at least $1 million of tangible personal property for business use and not for resale or purchasing substantial amounts of property for business use under circumstances making it difficult to determine whether property is taxable or exempt.
Kentucky	Allowed	Limited to certain specified taxpayers that meet specified requirements.
Louisiana	Allowed	Limited to certain specified taxpayers that meet specified requirements.
Maine	Allowed	Limited to manufacturers and utilities. Not applicable to purchases of food, beverages, hotel accommodations, and telephone service, or to certain rentals and construction contracts.
Maryland	Allowed	Limited to taxpayers that have effective rate agreements with the Comptroller of the Treasury.
Massachusetts	Allowed	Specified requirements must be met.
Michigan	Allowed	
Minnesota	Allowed	Not applicable to purchases of food, beverages, taxable lodgings, admissions to places of amusement athletic events or the privilege of use of amusement devices, motor vehicles, and certain taxable services.
Mississippi	Allowed	Limited to certain specified taxpayers. May be issued to public utilities, effective July 1, 2005.
Missouri	Allowed	Limited to taxpayers making annual purchases over $750,000.
Nebraska	Allowed	Limited to taxpayers making annual purchases of at least $3 million, excluding purchases for which a resale certificate could be used. Direct pay permit holders must pay the tax on or before the 20th day of the month following the date of the taxable purchase, lease, or rental.
Nevada	Allowed	Effective January 1, 2006, Nevada allows taxpayers to obtain direct pay permits.
New Jersey	Allowed	
New Mexico	Not Allowed	
New York	Allowed	
North Carolina	Allowed	Limited to purchases of tangible personal property and telecommunications services.

Jurisdiction	Direct Pay Permits	Comment
North Dakota	Allowed	Not applicable to purchases of food, beverages, taxable lodging, and admissions to places of amusement or athletic events or the privilege of use of amusement devices.
Ohio	Allowed	Limited to (1) taxpayers purchasing goods and services where its impossible to determine at the time of purchase whether purchases are taxable or exempt or (2) taxpayers whose number of purchase transactions of goods or services exceeds 5,000 annually or whose state sales and use tax paid on these purchases exceeds $250,000 annually.
Oklahoma	Allowed	Limited to taxpayers making purchases of at least $800,000 annually in taxable items.
Pennsylvania	Allowed	Not applicable to purchases of certain motor vehicles, trailers, semi-trailers, or tractors; prepared food or beverages at any eating place; or occupancy or accommodations subject to hotel occupancy tax.
Rhode Island	Allowed	
South Carolina	Allowed	
South Dakota	Allowed	Limited to taxpayers making purchases of at least $3 million annually in taxable goods and services. Not applicable to purchases of food, beverages, taxable lodgings, admissions to places of amusement and athletic events, motor vehicles, telecommunication services and utilities.
Tennessee	Allowed	Limited to exceptional circumstances or taxpayer hardship.
Texas	Allowed	Limited to taxpayers making purchases of at least $800,000 annually in taxable items for the taxpayer's own use and not for resale.
Utah	Allowed	Effective July 1, 2006, a direct pay permit may be issued to a seller that obtains a license, is subject to mandatory EFT, has a record of timely payment of taxes, and has the ability to determine the appropriate location of a transaction for each transaction for which the seller makes a purchase using the permit. Not applicable to purchases of food, accommodations, admissions, motor vehicles, common carrier or telecommunications services, or utilities.
Vermont	Allowed	

Jurisdiction	Direct Pay Permits	Comment
Virginia	Allowed	Limited to manufacturers, mine operators, and public service corporations.
Washington	Allowed	Limited to taxpayers who make purchases of over $10 million per calendar year or have an expected cumulative tax liability of at least $240,000 in the current calendar year.
West Virginia	Allowed	Limited to certain specified taxpayers.
Wisconsin	Allowed	Specified requirements must be met.
Wyoming	Allowed	Limited to taxpayers making purchases of at least $5 million in a calendar year.

Drop Shipments

This chart indicates whether a state allows a seller with nexus to accept a resale exemption from a purchaser/re-seller without nexus on a transaction in which the seller drop ships property to a consumer in the state on behalf of the purchaser/re-seller.

Jurisdiction	Drop Shipments	Comment
Alabama	Yes	
Arizona	Yes	
Arkansas	Yes	
California	No	California generally does not allow a seller with nexus to accept a resale exemption from a purchaser without nexus when the seller drop ships property to an in-state consumer. If an out-of-state retailer (true retailer) holds a permit, and it issues the drop shipper a resale certificate for the sale, the drop shipper is relieved of the responsibility to report and pay the tax.
Colorado	Yes	
Connecticut	No	Drop shipper required to collect tax if customer is not engaged in business in CT. However, the CT Supreme Court has held that a drop shipper did not deliver property in CT where property was shipped F.O.B. factory.
District of Columbia	No	If the reseller registers in the District, it may obtain and use a resale certificate.
Florida	Depends on circumstances	Registered dealers located in Florida are required to collect tax. A registered nonresident dealer's sales of tangible personal property to an unregistered nonresident purchaser that are drop shipped into Florida are not subject to Florida sales and use tax unless: (1) the taxpayer ships the property to the Florida customer from the taxpayer's facility in Florida; (2) the taxpayer ships the property to the Florida customer from the taxpayer's facility located outside Florida, but uses transportation owned or leased by the taxpayer; or (3) the taxpayer ships the property to the Florida customer from the taxpayer's facility located outside Florida, but the terms of the delivery require the taxpayer to collect the sales price, in whole or in part, from the Florida customer at the time of delivery of the property to the customer.
Georgia	Yes	Exceptions apply.

Jurisdiction	Drop Shipments	Comment
Hawaii	No	If purchaser/re-seller has nexus, drop shipper is subject to tax at wholesale rate. If purchaser/re-seller does not have nexus, drop shipper is subject to tax at retail rate.
Idaho	Yes	
Illinois	Yes	
Indiana	Yes	
Iowa	Yes	
Kansas	Yes	
Kentucky	Yes	
Louisiana	Yes	
Maine	Yes	
Maryland	No	
Massachusetts	No	
Michigan	Yes	
Minnesota	Yes	
Mississippi	No	MS drop shipper must collect tax from out-of-state retailer except if MS consumer is: direct pay permit holder; licensed dealer making a purchase for resale; or exempt entity that provides an exemption certificate to drop shipper.
Missouri	Yes	
Nebraska	Yes	
Nevada	Yes	
New Jersey	Yes	
New Mexico	Yes	
New York	Yes	
North Carolina	Yes	
North Dakota	Yes	
Ohio	Yes	
Oklahoma	Yes	
Pennsylvania	Yes	
Rhode Island	Yes	
South Carolina	Yes	
South Dakota	Yes	

Jurisdiction	Drop Shipments	Comment
Tennessee	No	If TN customer is exempt, purchaser/ reseller may provide TN customer's exemption certificate or resale certificate along with the purchaser's home state resale certificate. Effective July 1, 2015, drop shipper may claim a resale exemption (included in definition of "resale").
Texas	Yes	
Utah	Yes	
Vermont	Yes	
Virginia	Yes	
Washington	Yes	Purchaser must provide SST exemption certificate, or MTC exemption certificate.
West Virginia	Yes	
Wisconsin	Yes	
Wyoming	Yes	

Economic Nexus

This chart indicates whether a state has economic nexus provisions. In general, economic nexus means that if a remote seller passes a state's economic threshold for total revenue or number of transactions in that state, they are legally obligated to collect and remit sales and use tax in that state. No physical presence is required.

Note that state nexus statutes are subject to federal constitutional restrictions. However, in *South Dakota v. Wayfair, Inc.* (Dkt. No. 17-494, June 21, 2018), the U.S. Supreme Court overruled *Quill Corp. v. North Dakota* (504 U.S. 298 (1992)) and held that physical presence is no longer required to establish sales and use tax nexus.

Jurisdiction	Economic Nexus	Comment
Alabama	Yes	Out-of-state sellers who lack an Alabama physical presence but are making retail sales of tangible personal property into the state have a substantial economic presence in Alabama for sales and use tax purposes and are required to register for a license and to collect and remit tax, when: (a) the seller's retail sales of tangible personal property sold into the state exceed $250,000 per year based on the previous calendar year's sales; and (b) the seller conducts one or more of the activities described in Section 40-23-68, Code of Alabama.
Arizona	Yes	Effective October 1, 2019, an economic nexus test is established for both remote sellers and marketplace facilitators. A remote seller, not facilitated by a marketplace facilitator, will be required to pay TPT on retail sales of property if their gross proceeds or gross income with Arizona customers is more than: • $200,000 for 2019; • $150,000 for 2020; and • $100,000 for 2021 and thereafter. A marketplace facilitator will be required to pay TPT on retail sales of property if their gross proceeds or gross income with Arizona customers is more than $100,000.
Arkansas	Yes	Remote sellers and marketplace facilitators are required to collect sales tax if, in the previous or current calendar year, it had aggregate sales within the state, or deliveries to locations within the state, exceeding: $100,000; or 200 transactions.
California	Yes	Applicable April 1, 2019, retailers located outside California (remote sellers) are required to register with the CDTFA and collect California use tax if, in the preceding or current calendar year, the total combined sales of tangible personal property for delivery in California by the retailer and all persons related to the retailer exceed $500,000.
Colorado	Yes	Remote retailers are required to collect Colorado sales tax if they have $100,000 or more in annual sales into Colorado. Retailers must also collect state-collected local sales tax and special district tax. Retailers should contact home rule cities for guidance.

Jurisdiction	Economic Nexus	Comment
Connecticut	Yes	Effective July 1, 2019, out-of-state retailers that make retail sales of tangible personal property or services from outside Connecticut to a destination within Connecticut must collect and remit sales or use tax if: —they made at least 200 Connecticut sales during the preceding 12-month period ending September 30; and —their gross receipts are $100,000 or more during that period.
District of Columbia	Yes	Statute includes economic sales thresholds.
Florida	No	
Georgia	Yes	Effective for calendar year 2019, a remote seller is a "dealer" with nexus if they have in the previous or current calendar year from retail sales of tangible personal property for electronic or physical delivery within Georgia, or for use, consumption, distribution, or storage in Georgia: (1) more than $250,000 in gross revenue; or (2) at least 200 separate retail sales of tangible personal property. Effective January 1, 2020, the thresholds are: (1) more than $100,000 in gross revenue; or (2) at least 200 separate retail sales of tangible personal property.
Hawaii	Yes	Effective July 1, 2018, and applicable to taxable years beginning after 2017, a business is subject to general excise tax if, in the current or immediately preceding calendar year, it makes: —$100,000 or more in Hawaii sales of tangible personal property, services, or intangible property; or —200 or more separate Hawaii sales of tangible personal property, services, or intangible property.
Idaho	Yes	Remote sellers must collect and remit state-level Idaho sales and use tax if they (1) lack physical presence in Idaho; and (2) have over $100,000 in Idaho sales in the previous or current calendar year.
Illinois	Yes	Remote retailers are required to collect tax use and service use tax if either threshold is met for a 12-month period: (1) their sales of property to customers in Illinois are $100,000 or more; or (2) they enter into 200 or more sales transactions in Illinois. Effective July 1, 2020, the economic nexus thresholds trigger a retailers' occupation tax collection requirement for remote retailers in place of the use tax collection requirement.
Indiana	Yes	Sellers are liable for collecting Indiana sales tax if one of two sales thresholds are met for 12 months. Sellers meet the threshold for a given period if: —their gross revenue from sales into Indiana is more than $100,000; or —they enter into 200 or more separate transactions in Indiana. Effective July 1, 2019, marketplace facilitators are retail merchants when they engage in certain activities for sellers on their marketplace. The marketplace may be physical or on the internet. A marketplace facilitator must collect sales tax if: —it has economic nexus with Indiana; and —the retailer itself does not have nexus with Indiana.

Jurisdiction	Economic Nexus	Comment
Iowa	Yes	Effective January 1, 2019, retailers are required to collect Iowa sales tax if they have gross revenue from Iowa sales of $100,000 or more, or make 200 or more separate Iowa sales transactions, in the previous or current calendar year. Note that effective July 1, 2019, the 200 separate sale threshold for remote sellers is eliminated. Therefore, remote sellers will only be subject to the $100,000 annual taxable sales threshold. In South Dakota v. Wayfair, Inc. (Dkt. No. 17-494, June 21, 2018), the U.S. Supreme Court overruled Quill Corp. v. North Dakota (504 U.S. 298 (1992)) and held that physical presence is no longer required to establish sales and use tax nexus.
Kansas	No	
Kentucky	Yes	Effective July 1, 2018, remote sellers must collect Kentucky sales and use tax if, in the previous or current calendar year: (1) their gross receipts from Kentucky sales exceeds $100,000; or (2) they have at least 200 separate in-state sales transactions of property. Effective July 1, 2019, the economic nexus thresholds also apply to (1) remote retailers who sell through marketplaces, and (2) marketplace providers (through their own sales or from sales made in their marketplaces).
Louisiana	Yes	Applies to remote dealers with sales into the state in excess of $100,000 or 200 or more separate transactions.
Maine	Yes	Remote sellers with either 200 or more taxable transactions in Maine or sales exceeding $100,000 in the state, must collect tax.
Maryland	Yes	A remote seller has economic nexus if during the current or prior year: gross revenue from sales of property or services into Maryland is more than $100,000; or property or services are sold into Maryland 200 or more times.
Massachusetts	Yes	Sellers with over $500,000 in sales and more than 100 transactions into the state in the preceding calendar year, must register, collect and remit. Effective October 1, 2019, remote retailers must register and collect Massachusetts sales or use tax if, in the previous or current year, their annual gross sales into Massachusetts exceed $100,000.
Michigan	Yes	After September 30, 2018, remote sellers with over $100,000 in sales to Michigan or 200 or more transactions in the prior calendar year, have nexus.
Minnesota	Yes	Remote retailers must collect and remit tax if, over the prior 12-month period, they make either: (1) 200 or more retail sales shipped to Minnesota; or (2) $100,000 or more in retail sales shipped to Minnesota.
Mississippi	Yes	A "person doing business in this state," who is consequently required to collect and remit sales or use tax, includes any marketplace facilitator, marketplace seller, or remote seller with sales that exceed $250,000 in any consecutive 12-month period.

Jurisdiction	Economic Nexus	Comment
Missouri	No	
Nebraska	Yes	Remote sellers with over $100,000 in sales or 200 or more transactions in the state annually, must collect tax.
Nevada	Yes	A remote seller has economic nexus if during the current or prior calendar year: —gross revenue from sales of property or services into Nevada is more than $100,000; or —property or services are sold into Nevada 200 or more times.
New Jersey	Yes	Sales tax collection is required in New Jersey if, during the current or prior calendar year, a remote seller exceeds: (i) $100,000 in gross revenue from delivery of tangible personal property, specific digital products, or services into New Jersey; or (ii) 200 or more separate transactions in New Jersey.
New Mexico	Yes	
New York	Yes	A business that has no physical presence in New York, but meets the following requirements in the immediately preceding four sales tax quarters, is required to register and collect/remit sales tax: (i) makes more than $500,000 in sales of tangible personal property delivered in New York,**and** (ii) makes more than 100 sales of tangible personal property delivered in New York.
North Carolina	Yes	A remote seller is required to register, and collect and remit North Carolina sales and use tax if, in the previous or current calendar year, the retailer had one or more of the following: (1) the remote seller has gross sales in excess of $100,000 sourced to North Carolina; or (2) the remote seller has 200 or more separate transactions sourced to North Carolina ("threshold").
North Dakota	Yes	Out-of-state sellers with no physical presence in North Dakota are subject to sales and use tax if, in the previous calendar year or the current calendar year the seller's gross sales from the sale of tangible personal property and other taxable items delivered in North Dakota exceed $100,000. Such a seller is required to remit sales or use tax and must follow all applicable procedures and requirements as if the seller has a physical presence in North Dakota. Remote sellers must register and begin collecting North Dakota sales and use tax on the earlier of: -60 days after meeting the threshold, or - the following calendar year. NOTE: Previously, North Dakota had a 200 or more separate transactions threshold, too. It was eliminated retroactively to tax years beginning on or after January 1, 2019. Effective October 1, 2019, a marketplace facilitator meeting the $100,000 in sales threshold is required to collect tax on sales of property and services delivered into North Dakota, which are made by a marketplace seller through the marketplace facilitator.

Jurisdiction	Economic Nexus	Comment
Ohio	Yes	A seller or marketplace facilitator has substantial nexus if, in the current or preceding calendar year, it (i) has gross receipts exceeding $100,000 from sales into Ohio, or (ii) engages in 200 or more separate sales transactions in Ohio.
Oklahoma	Yes	**Remote sellers:** By July 1, 2018, and by June 1 of each calendar year starting in 2019, a "remote seller" who had at least $10,000 ($100,000 effective November 1, 2019) in aggregate Oklahoma sales in the preceding 12-calendar-month period must file an election with the Oklahoma Tax Commission to: (1) collect and remit sales and use tax due on tangible personal property and obtain a sales tax permit, or (2) through October 31, 2019, comply with notice and reporting requirements. The notice and reporting option is no longer available to remote sellers effective November 1, 2019. **Marketplace facilitators and referrers:** By July 1, 2018, and by June 1 of each calendar year starting in 2019, a "remote seller," "marketplace facilitator," or "referrer" who had at least $10,000 in aggregate Oklahoma sales in the preceding 12-calendar-month period must file an election with the Oklahoma Tax Commission to: (1) collect and remit sales and use tax due on tangible personal property and obtain a sales tax permit, or (2) comply with notice and reporting requirements.
Pennsylvania	Yes	Beginning July 1, 2019, persons making more than $100,000 in Pennsylvania sales in the previous 12 months must: — register for a license; and —collect, report, and remit sales tax. Effective through June 30, 2019: By March 1, 2018, and by June 1 of each subsequent calendar year, remote sellers, marketplace facilitators, and referrers with aggregate sales of tangible personal property subject to Pennsylvania sales and use tax of $10,000 or more in the previous 12-calendar-month period must file an election with the Department of Revenue to either: —collect and remit the sales tax, or —comply with certain notice and reporting requirements.
Rhode Island	Yes	Applies to remote dealers with sales into the state in excess of $100,000 or 200 or more separate transactions.
South Carolina	Yes	Economic nexus occurs when gross sales into South Carolina are more than $100,000 in this or the last calendar year.
South Dakota	Yes	Effective November 1, 2018, remote retailers are required to collect South Dakota sales tax if they have $100,000 or more in annual sales into South Dakota, or make 200 or more separate annual sales transactions into South Dakota.

Jurisdiction	Economic Nexus	Comment
Tennessee	Yes	A dealer with no physical presence in Tennessee must register with the Tennessee Department of Revenue and collect and remit sales or use tax if the dealer: (1) engages in the regular or systematic solicitation of consumers in Tennessee through any means; and (2) made sales that exceeded $100,000 (prior to October 1, 2020, $500,000) to consumers in Tennessee during the previous 12-month period.
Texas	Yes	Sales tax collection will be required in Texas if, during the preceeding 12 calendar months, a remote seller exceeds: (i) $500,000 in total Texas revenue. The initial 12 calendar months for calculating a remote seller's Texas revenues is July 1, 2018, through June 30, 2019.
Utah	Yes	A sales tax collection obligation is imposed on remote sellers that: (1) have more than $100,000 in gross revenue in the state or (2) make at least 200 separate transactions in the state.
Vermont	Yes	A "vendor" having nexus with Vermont includes a person making sales of tangible personal property from outside Vermont to a destination within Vermont and not maintaining a place of business or other physical presence in Vermont who: —engages in regular, systematic, or seasonal solicitation of sales of tangible personal property in Vermont; and —has made sales from outside Vermont to destinations within Vermont of at least $100,000 or totaling at least 200 individual sales transactions during any 12-month period preceding the monthly period at issue. Effective June 1, 2019, the definition of "vendor" is expanded to include certain marketplace facilitators and marketplace sellers.
Virginia	Yes	Remote sellers are required to register, collect and remit retail sales and use if they have: (i) more than $100,000 in annual gross revenue from sales in Virginia; or (ii) at least 200 sales transactions in Virginia.
Washington	Yes	Remote sellers with more than $100,000 in gross retail sales in Washington in the current or prior calendar year, must register and collect sales tax.

Jurisdiction	Economic Nexus	Comment
West Virginia	Yes	Effective January 1, 2019, any out-of-state vendor who, as of July 1, 2018, is not required to collect and remit state and municipal sales and use taxes, either because they do not have in-state physical presence or they have not voluntarily agreed to collect and remit the tax, who delivers more than $100,000 of goods or services into West Virginia, or engages in 200 or more separate transactions for the delivery of goods and services into West Virginia, during calendar year 2018, will be required to collect and remit taxes on all sales made on and after January 1, 2019 that are delivered into West Virginia. This collection requirement applies to out-of-state vendors that currently do not collect state and municipal sales and use taxes but meet either the $100,000 threshold, or the 200 transactions threshold, during calendar year 2018. Vendor responsibility for collection and remittance of these taxes will be determined annually each year thereafter. In addition, collection requirements apply to sales by marketplace facilitators or referrers made on and after July 1, 2019.
Wisconsin	Yes	Beginning October 1, 2018, remote retailers must register and collect Wisconsin sales or use tax if, in the previous or current year, their: annual gross sales into Wisconsin exceed $100,000; or annual number of separate sales transactions into Wisconsin is 200 or more.
Wyoming	Yes	Remote sellers with over $100,000 in sales to Wyoming or 200 or more transactions in the current or prior calendar year, have nexus.

Electronic Filing of Sales Tax Returns

The following chart indicates whether a state allows taxpayers to file sales and use tax returns electronically.

Jurisdiction	Electronic Filing	Comment
Alabama	Yes	Required for all taxpayers.
Arizona	Yes	Amended returns cannot be filed electronically.
Arkansas	Yes	
California	Yes	Single-outlet retailer accounts and businesses with only one location that pre-pay on a quarterly basis may file electronically. Only Form BOE-401-A (with Schedules A and T only) and Form BOE-401-EZ may be filed electronically.
Colorado	Yes	
Connecticut	Yes	
District of Columbia	Yes	
Florida	Yes	Required for any taxpayer: (1) who has paid the tax or fee in the prior state fiscal year (July 1 through June 30) in an amount of $20,000 or more; (2) who files a consolidated return; or (3) who has two or more places of business for which the combined tax and/or fee payments equal or exceed $20,000 for the prior state fiscal year.
Georgia	Yes	Required for taxpayers who are required pay by EFT. Optional for other taxpayers.
Hawaii	Yes	
Idaho	Yes	
Illinois	Yes	
Indiana	Yes	Retail merchants that register with the department after December 31, 2009 are required to report and remit sales and use taxes using the department's online filing program.
Iowa	Yes	Fuel tax returns are required by statute to be filed electronically.
Kansas	Yes	
Kentucky	Yes	Consumer use tax returns cannot be filed electronically.
Louisiana	Yes	Required for motor vehicle leasing and rental businesses. Optional for other taxpayers.
Maine	Yes	

Jurisdiction	Electronic Filing	Comment
Maryland	Yes	
Massachusetts	Yes	Required for taxpayers who had a combined tax liability in the preceding calendar year of at least $5,000 (previously, $10,000) in wage withholding, state and local room occupancy excise, and sales and use taxes (including sales taxes imposed on meals and telecommunications services). Businesses that registered after August 31, 2003 and taxpayers with zero tax returns must also file electronically. Optional for all other taxpayers.
Michigan	Yes	
Minnesota	Yes	Required, unless taxpayer's religious beliefs prohibits use of electronics.
Mississippi	Yes	The Mississippi Department of Revenue uses an online filing and payment system called Taxpayer Access Point (TAP).
Missouri	Yes	The following types of businesses are allowed to file their sales and use tax returns electronically: those that owed no sales taxes and those with less than 150 locations.
Nebraska	Yes	Amended returns cannot be filed electronically. As of July 1, 2011, the Tax Commissioner requires taxpayers subject to the EFT mandate for sales tax payments to also e-file their sales tax returns, Forms 10. Taxpayers are subject to EFT if they have made payments of $5,000 or more in the prior tax year.
Nevada	Yes	
New Jersey	Yes	Required for all taxpayers.
New Mexico	Yes	
New York	Yes	Required for monthly and quarterly sales tax filers who meet these three conditions: (1) do not use a tax preparer to prepare the required filings; (2) use a computer to prepare, document or calculate the required filings or related schedules, or is subject to the corporation tax e-file mandate; and (3) have broadband Internet access. Tax preparers are also required to electronically file returns for annual sales tax filers.
North Carolina	Yes	
North Dakota	Yes	
Ohio	Yes	
Oklahoma	Yes	Required for taxpayers who owed an average of $2,500 or more per month in total sales taxes in the previous fiscal year. Optional for other taxpayers.
Pennsylvania	Yes	A third party preparer must e-file all sales, use, and hotel occupancy tax returns for all calendar years following a calendar year in which the preparer files 10 or more sales, use, and hotel occupancy tax returns.
Rhode Island	Yes	Required for taxpayers who are required to pay by EFT. Optional for other taxpayers.

Jurisdiction	Electronic Filing	Comment
South Carolina	Yes	Taxpayers owing $15,000 or more per month may be mandated to file electronically.
South Dakota	Yes	
Tennessee	Yes	Required if tax required to be paid in connection with a return is $1,000 or more. Effective January 1, 2013, required if average sales tax liability is $500 or more. Optional for other taxpayers.
Texas	Yes	Required for taxpayers who are required to pay by EFT. Optional for other taxpayers.
Utah	Yes	
Vermont	Yes	
Virginia	Yes	Beginning with the July 2012 return (due August 20, 2012), monthly filers of the ST-9 and ST-9CO must submit their returns and payments electronically. Quarterly filers will be required to file and pay electronically beginning with the September 2013 return, due October 21, 2013. To meet this electronic filing requirement, the returns must be filed using eForms, Business iFile or Web Upload. Taxpayers that are unable to make the necessary changes to file and pay electronically may request a temporary waiver from the department. Such request must be in writing and provide the following information: business name, Virginia tax account number, contact person, phone number, e-mail address (optional), mailing address, the reason for the request, and the date when the retail sales taxes can be filed and paid electronically.
Washington	Yes	All monthly and quarterly filers are required to file and pay electronically.
West Virginia	Yes	For tax years beginning on or after January 1, 2009, required for taxpayers who had a total annual remittance for any single tax type of $100,000 or more in the immediately preceding tax year. Effective for tax years beginning on or after January 1, 2013, this threshold is lowered to $50,000. The threshold amount is reduced to $25,000 for tax years beginning on or after January 1, 2014, and then to $10,000 for tax years beginning on or after January 1, 2015. For tax years beginning on or after January 1, 2016, the threshold is increased to $25,000.
Wisconsin	Yes	
Wyoming	Yes	

Electronic Payment of Sales Tax

The following chart indicates whether a state allows taxpayers to make sales and use tax payments electronically.

Jurisdiction	Electronic Payments	Comment
Alabama	Yes	Required for taxpayers making individual payments of $750 or more.
Arizona	Yes	Required for taxpayers whose tax liability in the prior year was $1 million or more.
Arkansas	Yes	Required if average monthly tax liability for the preceding year exceeded $20,000.
California	Yes	Required if estimated monthly tax liability is $10,000 or more.
Colorado	Yes	Required for taxpayers whose sales tax liability for the previous calendar year exceeded $75,000.
Connecticut	Yes	Required if prior year liability exceeded $10,000 for the 12-month period ending the preceding June 30.
District of Columbia	Yes	Required when the payment due for the tax period exceeds $25,000 and for payments made by third party bulk filers.
Florida	Yes	Required if tax paid in the prior state fiscal year was $30,000 or more. All consolidated sales tax and solid waste and surcharge filers must remit payments electronically.
Georgia	Yes	For tax periods from Jan. 1, 2010 - Dec. 31, 2010, EFT required for payments exceeding $1,000; for tax periods from Jan. 1, 2011, forward, EFT required for payments exceeding $500.
Hawaii	Yes	Required for taxpayers whose annual tax liability exceeds $100,000 in any taxable year.
Idaho	Yes	Required when the amount due is $100,000 or more.
Illinois	Yes	Required for taxpayers whose state and local sales and use tax liability in the preceding calendar year was at least $200,000. Taxpayers who file electronic returns are also required to make electronic payments.

Jurisdiction	Electronic Payments	Comment
Indiana	Yes	Required if taxpayer's estimated monthly tax liability for current tax year or the average monthly tax liability for the preceding year exceeds $10,000. Beginning January 1, 2010, the department may require a person who is paying outstanding tax using periodic payments to make the payments by electronic funds transfer through an automatic withdrawal from the person's account at a financial institution.
Iowa	Yes	Required for all taxpayers.
Kansas	Yes	Required if total sales tax liability exceeds $45,000 in any calendar year.
Kentucky	Yes	Required if: (1) average payment per reporting period is at least $10,000; (2) payment is made on behalf of 100 or more taxpayers; (3) aggregate of funds to be remitted on behalf of others is at least $10,000 for each tax being remitted; or (4) average payment of sales tax per reporting period during 12-month period ending on September 30 of the year immediately preceding the current calendar year exceeds $25,000.
Louisiana	Yes	Required if tax due in connection a return exceeds $5,000.
Maine	Yes	Required for any taxpayer with a combined tax liability of $100,000 or more for all tax types during the previous calendar year. Effective January 1, 2009, threshold decreases to $50,000; effective January 1, 2010, threshold decreases to $25,000.
Maryland	Yes	Required if tax of $10,000 or more is due in connection with a return.
Massachusetts	Yes	Required for taxpayers who are required to file electronic returns. Optional for other taxpayers.
Michigan	Yes	Required if total sales and use tax liability for preceding calendar year was at least $720,000.
Minnesota	Yes	Taxpayers with sales and use tax liability of $10,000 or more during the preceding fiscal year ending June 30 must make all payments for periods in subsequent calendar years by EFT, unless prohibited by religious beliefs.

Jurisdiction	Electronic Payments	Comment
Mississippi	Yes	The Mississippi Department of Revenue uses an online filing and payment system called Taxpayer Access Point (TAP). Required for taxpayers owing $20,000 or more in connection with a return and for taxpayers who have received notification from the Tax Commissioner.
Missouri	Yes	May be required for taxpayers required to remit on a quarter-monthly basis.
Nebraska	Yes	Taxpayers are subject to EFT if they have made payments of $5,000 or more in the prior tax year.
Nevada	Yes	
New Jersey	Yes	Required for taxpayers whose tax liability for the prior year was $10,000 or more.
New Mexico	Yes	Taxpayers whose average tax payment during the previous calendar year was $25,000 or more are required to pay by EFT or another method specified by statute.
New York	Yes	Required if, on or after June 1, the taxpayer's liability for the June 1 through May 31 period immediately preceding was more than $500,000 for state and local sales and use taxes or more than $5 million for prepaid state and local sales and use taxes on motor fuel and diesel motor fuel.
North Carolina	Yes	Required for taxpayers whose tax liability was at least $240,000 during a 12-month period.
North Dakota	Yes	
Ohio	Yes	Taxpayers must use commissioner approved electronic method. Certain direct pay permit holders are required to use EFT.
Oklahoma	Yes	Required for taxpayers who owed an average of $2,500 per month during previous fiscal year.
Pennsylvania	Yes	Required for payments of $1,000 or more.
Rhode Island	Yes	Required if the seller's average monthly sales and use tax liability in the previous calendar year was at least $200.
South Carolina	Yes	Taxpayers who paid $15,000 or more for any one filing period during the past year in sales, use, accommodations, local option, or special local taxes can be required to pay by EFT.
South Dakota	Yes	

Jurisdiction	Electronic Payments	Comment
Tennessee	Yes	Required if tax required to be paid in connection with a return is $1,000 or more. Effective January 1, 2013, required if average sales tax liability is $500 or more.
Texas	Yes	Required for taxpayers who paid a total of $10,000 or more in a single category of payments or taxes during the preceding state fiscal year if the Comptroller reasonably anticipates the taxpayer will pay at least that amount during the current fiscal year.
Utah	Yes	Required for taxpayers whose liability for state, local, public transit, municipal energy, and short-term leases and rentals of motor vehicles sales and use taxes was $96,000 or more in the previous tax year.
Vermont	Yes	May be required for any taxpayer required to pay a federal tax by EFT or for any taxpayer who has submitted to the Tax Department two or more protested or otherwise uncollectible checks with regard to any state tax payment in the prior two years.
Virginia	Yes	Beginning with the July 2012 return (due August 20, 2012), monthly filers of the ST-9 and ST-9CO must submit their returns and payments electronically. Quarterly filers will be required to file and pay electronically beginning with the September 2013 return, due October 21, 2013. To meet this electronic filing requirement, the returns must be filed using eForms, Business iFile or Web Upload. Taxpayers that are unable to make the necessary changes to file and pay electronically may request a temporary waiver from the department. Such request must be in writing and provide the following information: business name, Virginia tax account number, contact person, phone number, e-mail address (optional), mailing address, the reason for the request, and the date when the retail sales taxes can be filed and paid electronically.
Washington	Yes	Required for taxpayers filing returns on a monthly or quarterly basis.

Jurisdiction	Electronic Payments	Comment
West Virginia	Yes	Effective for tax years prior to January 1, 2012, required for taxpayers with sales and use tax liability of $100,000 or more during the previous taxable year or reporting period; effective for tax years beginning on or after January 1, 2012, the threshold is reduced to $10,000; for tax years beginning on or after January 1, 2013, the threshold is increased to $50,000; for tax years beginning on or after January 1, 2014, the threshold is reduced to $25,000; for tax years beginning on or after January 1, 2015, the threshold is reduced to $10,000; for tax years beginning on or after January 1, 2016, the threshold is increased to $25,000. Required for both county and municipal special district excise taxes and for sales taxes collected within an economic opportunity development district, regardless of amount.
Wisconsin	Yes	Required if aggregate amount of general, county, and stadium sales and use taxes due in the prior calendar year was $300 or more.
Wyoming	Yes	

Exemption Certificate Validity Periods

Jurisdiction	Exemption Certificate Validity Periods	Comment
Alabama	Valid as long as no change in character of purchaser's operation and the tangible personal property purchased is the kind usually purchased for the purpose indicated.	
Arizona	Valid for the period set out on certificate.	
Arkansas	No stated expiration period.	Seller may require purchaser to complete Form ST391 to prove entitlement to exemption.
California	Valid until revoked in writing by issuer, unless issued for specific transaction, in which case certificate is generally valid for one year.	
Colorado	Charitable exemption certificates do not expire. Contractor's exemption certificates expire at the end of the job.	
Connecticut	Valid for three years from the issue date provided the exemption remains in effect.	An exemption certificate may be issued for a single exempt purchase or may be used for a continuing line of purchases of the same type provided the certificate is marked "Blanket Certificate." Most blanket certificates are valid for three years from the issue date if the exemption remains in effect.
District of Columbia	Validity periods vary depending on the type of certificate.	
Florida	Each sales tax exemption certificate expires five years after the date of issuance.	Upon expiration, the certificate is subject to review and reissuance procedures.
Georgia	Until revoked in writing.	
Hawaii	Does not expire.	New application must be filed if there is material change in facts.
Idaho	No stated expiration period.	
Illinois	Exemption certificate validity periods vary depending on the purchaser.	Exemption certificates, including blanket certificates, for manufacturing, production agriculture, and coal and aggregate mining should be updated at least every three years.
Indiana	Does not expire.	
Iowa	Fuel exemption certificates valid up to 3 years.	
Kansas	Exemption certificates are generally valid provided there is a recurring business relationship between the buyer and seller of no more than 12 months elapsing between sales. Tax-exempt entity exemption certificates contain an expiration date.	

Jurisdiction	Exemption Certificate Validity Periods	Comment
Kentucky	The Kentucky Department of Revenue recommends that certificates be updated every four years. The new and expanded industry certificate is project-specific.	
Louisiana	Generally valid indefinitely.	Direct pay, resale, and manufacturing exemption certificates automatically renewed for up to three years unless taxpayer no longer qualified for the exemption.
Maine	No stated expiration period.	
Maryland	Expires five years after issuance.	Governmental entity certificates do not expire. All other exemption certificates will expire on September 30, 2017 and, upon reissuance, at 5-year intervals.
Massachusetts	No stated expiration period.	
Michigan	Expires after four years unless shorter period is agreed upon.	Renewal of a blanket exemption certificate is not required if there is a recurring business relationship between buyer and seller. A "recurring business relationship" exists when a period of not more than 12 months elapses between sales transactions.
Minnesota	Does not expire unless information changes; should be updated every three to five years.	
Mississippi	No stated expiration period.	Seller must obtain and maintain adequate records to substantiate exemption.
Missouri	Valid for 5 years.	Must be updated every 5 years or when the certificate expires by its terms, whichever is earlier.
Nebraska	Valid indefinitely.	A blanket certificate remains valid if sales occur between the seller and purchaser at least once every 12 months.
Nevada	Valid for five years.	
New Jersey	No stated expiration period.	Division of Taxation recommends that a seller request a new certificate from a buyer every few years.
New Mexico	There is no stated validity period for a New Mexico nontaxable transaction certificate, other than that for utilities consumed in manufacturing (type 12).	Type 12 NTTCs expire after three years.
New York	No stated expiration period.	A blanket certificate is valid until it is revoked in writing, the vendor knows it is fraudulent, or the department provides notice that the purchaser may not make exempt purchases.

Jurisdiction	Exemption Certificate Validity Periods	Comment
North Carolina	Blanket certificate remains valid provided purchaser is making recurring purchases.	If single purchase box is not checked on Form E-595E indicating certificate is being used for a single purchase, certificate will be treated as a blanket certificate. A blanket certificate continues in force as long as the purchaser is making recurring purchases (i.e., at least one purchase within a period of 12 consecutive months) or until it is otherwise cancelled by the purchaser.
North Dakota	Valid until exemption no longer applies.	
Ohio	No stated expiration period.	
Oklahoma	Blanket exemption certificates are valid provided there is a recurring business relationship between the buyer and seller of no more than 12 months elapsing between sales.	
Pennsylvania	No expiration date.	A taxpayer claiming an exemption as a charitable, religious, or educational institution may be required to renew its exemption every three years.
Rhode Island	Blanket exemption certificates remain valid so long as the purchaser is making recurring purchases (at least one transaction within a period of 12 consecutive months) or until cancelled by the purchaser.	
South Carolina	There is no stated expiration period for an exemption certificate.	The Department advises that a certificate is valid as long as the business is in operation.
South Dakota	Blanket certificates are valid indefinitely so long as the purchaser is making recurring purchases (at least one purchase within a period of 12 consecutive months) or until cancelled by the purchaser.	
Tennessee	Blanket exemption certificates remain valid so long as the purchaser is making recurring purchases (at least one transaction within a period of 12 consecutive months) or until cancelled by the purchaser.	
Texas	No stated expiration period.	
Utah	There is no expiration period for a Utah exemption certificate if no more than a 12-month period elapses between sales transactions.	
Vermont	Valid indefinitely.	Exemption certificate for fuel and electricity (Form S-3F) valid for three years. Exemption certificate for registrable motor vehicles other than cars and trucks (Form S-3V) valid for single purchase.

Jurisdiction	Exemption Certificate Validity Periods	Comment
Virginia	Valid until notice from Department of Taxation that certificate is no longer acceptable or is revoked.	Expiration date is stated on certificates for nonprofit organizations.
Washington	A blanket exemption certificate is valid as long as the purchaser has a "recurring business relationship" with the seller. Such a relationship is found where there is at least one sale transaction within a period of twelve consecutive months.	
West Virginia	Blanket certificates are effective so long as the purchaser makes at least one purchase within a period of 12 consecutive months, or until the certificate is otherwise cancelled by the purchaser.	
Wisconsin	Continuous certificates valid indefinitely but should be reviewed periodically.	
Wyoming	No stated expiration period.	

Food and Meals—Caterers

This chart indicates whether sales made by caterers are taxable. Unless otherwise indicated, the taxable charge includes charges for any services related to the preparation or service of food or beverages. Exemptions may apply to sales made to certain purchasers.

Jurisdiction	Caterers	Comment
Alabama	Taxable	Caterer's service charge is not taxable if caterer prepares food not furnished by caterer. Voluntary gratuities that are distributed to employees are not taxable.
Arizona	Taxable	Gratuities that are distributed to employees are not taxable.
Arkansas	Taxable	Gratuities that are distributed to employees are not taxable.
California	Taxable	Voluntary gratuities that are distributed to employees are not taxable.
Colorado	Taxable	Gratuities that are distributed to employees are not taxable.
Connecticut	Taxable	Effective October 1, 2019, the Connecticut sales and use tax rate on meals sold by eating establishments and caterers, is increased from 6.35% to 7.35%. The 7.35% rate is comprised of the 1% sales and use tax rate on such sales that applies in addition to the 6.35% state sales and use tax. Gratuities that are distributed to employees are not taxable.
District of Columbia	Taxable	Voluntary gratuities that are distributed to employees are not taxable.
Florida	Taxable	Voluntary gratuities that are distributed to employees are not taxable.
Georgia	Taxable	Eligible food and beverages sold for off-premises consumption are not taxable if the caterer does not assist in serving, cooking, heating, or providing any other on-site service related to consumption following delivery to customer. Voluntary gratuities are not taxable.
Hawaii	Taxable	
Idaho	Taxable	Prepared food or beverage supplied by retailer free of charge to its employees is exempt if retailer sells prepared food or beverages in its normal course of business. Voluntary gratuities distributed to employees are not taxable. When a gratuity is negotiated before a sale the amount is subject to tax.

Jurisdiction	Caterers	Comment
Illinois	Taxable	Gratuities that are distributed to employees are not taxable.
Indiana	Taxable	Gratuities that are distributed to employees are not taxable.
Iowa	Taxable	Voluntary gratuities that are distributed to employees are not subject to tax.
Kansas	Taxable	Tax applies to entire charge.
Kentucky	Taxable	Voluntary gratuities that are distributed to employees are not taxable.
Louisiana	Taxable	Gratuities that are distributed to employees are not taxable.
Maine	Taxable	Incidental charges for tables, chairs, rentals of equipment are not subject to tax. Gratuities that are distributed to employees are not taxable.
Maryland	Taxable	Voluntary gratuities that are distributed to employees are not taxable.
Massachusetts	Taxable	Caterer's service charge is not taxable if caterer prepares food owned by client at a fixed location on an ongoing basis. Delivery charges and gratuities that are distributed to employees are not taxable.
Michigan	Taxable	Gratuities that are distributed to employees are not taxable.
Minnesota	Taxable	Tax applies to entire charge. Special rules may apply.
Mississippi	Taxable	Gratuities that are distributed to employees are not taxable.
Missouri	Taxable	Optional set-up, serving, and takedown services and delivery charges are not taxable. Voluntary gratuities are not taxable.
Nebraska	Taxable	Voluntary gratuities that are distributed to employees are not taxable.
Nevada	Taxable	Gratuities that are distributed to employees are not taxable.
New Jersey	Taxable	Gratuities that are distributed to employees are not taxable.
New Mexico	Taxable	Gratuities that are distributed to employees are not taxable.
New York	Taxable	Gratuities that are distributed to employees are not taxable.
North Carolina	Taxable	Gratuities that are distributed to employees are not taxable.
North Dakota	Taxable	Tips and gratuities exempt if certain requirements satisfied.
Ohio	Taxable	Not taxable if food is sold for off-premises consumption.

Jurisdiction	Caterers	Comment
Oklahoma	Taxable	Voluntary gratuities that are distributed to employees are not taxable.
Pennsylvania	Taxable	Separately stated gratuity exempt.
Rhode Island	Taxable	
South Carolina	Taxable	Voluntary gratuities that are distributed to employees are not taxable.
South Dakota	Taxable	Voluntary gratuities that are distributed to employees are not taxable.
Tennessee	Taxable	Charges for optional services are not taxable. Voluntary gratuities that are distributed to employees are not taxable.
Texas	Taxable	Mandatory gratuities up to 20% and voluntary gratuities that are distributed to employees are not taxable.
Utah	Taxable	Voluntary gratuities that are distributed to employees are not taxable.
Vermont	Taxable	Exempt from sales tax but subject to meals and rooms tax. Tips exempt if certain requirements satisfied.
Virginia	Taxable	Mandatory gratuities up to 20% and voluntary gratuities that are distributed to employees are not taxable.
Washington	Taxable	Voluntary gratuities that are distributed to employees are not taxable.
West Virginia	Taxable	Gratuities that are distributed to employees are not taxable.
Wisconsin	Taxable	Tips exempt if certain requirements satisfied.
Wyoming	Taxable	Gratuities or tips, whether offered by customer or invoiced by seller, are not taxable at any place where meals are regularly served to the public.

Food and Meals—Grocery Food

The chart below sets forth the taxability of non-prepared grocery food. Many states that exempt grocery food exclude certain items such as soft drinks, candy, and confections. Food prepared by a grocery is taxable in all states as meals.

Jurisdiction	Grocery Food	Comment
Alabama	Taxable	
Arizona	Exempt	
Arkansas	Taxable	Food and food ingredients taxed at reduced state rate of 1.5%, plus any applicable local rate. Food items ineligible for reduced rate taxed at regular state rate. State rate will fall from 1.5% to 0.125% if certain budget conditions met.
California	Exempt	Certain meals are taxed. Exceptions apply.
Colorado	Exempt	Certain items are taxable including carbonated water, chewing gum, seeds and plants to grow food, prepared salads and salad bars, cold sandwiches, deli trays, candy, soft drinks and hot/cold beverages served in unsealed cups through a vending machine.
Connecticut	Exempt	Effective October 1, 2019, the Connecticut sales and use tax rate on meals sold by grocery stores is increased from 6.35% to 7.35%. The 7.35% rate is comprised of the 1% sales and use tax rate on such sales that applies in addition to the 6.35% state sales and use tax.
District of Columbia	Exempt	
Florida	Exempt	
Georgia	Exempt	This exemption for the sale of "food and food ingredients" to an individual consumer for off-premises human consumption does not apply to any local sales and use tax. "Food and food ingredients" does not include prepared food, alcoholic beverages, dietary supplements, drugs, over-the-counter drugs, or tobacco.
Hawaii	Taxable	Food purchased with federal food coupons or vouchers exempt.
Idaho	Taxable	
Illinois	Taxable	Taxed at reduced rate of 1%. Candy, soft drinks, alcoholic beverages, and food prepared for immediate consumption do not qualify for the 1% rate.
Indiana	Exempt	
Iowa	Exempt	
Kansas	Taxable	Certain exemptions may apply.
Kentucky	Exempt	Exemption applies with regard to "food and food ingredients" for human consumption. "Food and food ingredients" does not include "candy," "tobacco," "alcoholic beverages," "soft drinks," "dietary supplements," "prepared food," or food sold through vending machines.

Jurisdiction	Grocery Food	Comment
Louisiana	Exempt	Exemption applies to food sold for preparation and consumption in the home.
Maine	Exempt	The exemption for food products for home consumption is limited to "grocery staples."
Maryland	Exempt	
Massachusetts	Exempt	
Michigan	Exempt	
Minnesota	Exempt	
Mississippi	Taxable	
Missouri	Taxable	Taxed at reduced rate.
Nebraska	Exempt	
Nevada	Exempt	
New Jersey	Exempt	
New Mexico	Exempt	
New York	Exempt	The exemption does not apply to candy, confectionery, and certain drinks.
North Carolina	Exempt	Sales of food are subject to local taxes.
North Dakota	Exempt	
Ohio	Exempt	All food, including prepared food, is exempt if sold for off-premises consumption.
Oklahoma	Taxable	Exemptions apply to sales to and/or by churches, nonprofit schools, and certain nonprofit organizations serving the needy or elderly. Purchases of food using food stamps are also exempt.
Pennsylvania	Exempt	Depends upon the type of food and the location from which food is sold.
Rhode Island	Exempt	
South Carolina	Exempt	Unprepared food that can be purchased with federal food stamps is exempt from state sales and use tax, but may be subject to other local sales and use taxes.
South Dakota	Taxable	
Tennessee	Taxable	Food and food ingredients are subject to a reduced sales and use tax rate of 4% plus the applicable local rate.
Texas	Exempt	
Utah	Taxable	Subject to local taxes. Food and food ingredients are taxed at reduced rate of 1.75%.
Vermont	Exempt	

Jurisdiction	Grocery Food	Comment
Virginia	Taxable	Taxed at reduced rate of 1.5% (1% local option tax also applies).
Washington	Exempt	
West Virginia	Exempt	Sales and use tax ceased applying to sales of grocery food on July 1, 2013. Previously, the state-level rate applicable to sales of grocery food was 6% prior to January 1, 2006; 5% from January 1, 2006, through June 30, 2007; 4% from July 1, 2007, through June 30, 2008; 3% from July 1, 2008, through December 31, 2011; 2% from January 1, 2012, through June 30, 2012; and 1% from July 1, 2012, through June 30, 2013.
Wisconsin	Exempt	
Wyoming	Exempt	Food for domestic home consumption is exempt.

General Nexus Rules and Internet Sales—General Rules

This chart indicates when an out-of-state seller is required to collect tax. Note that state nexus statutes are subject to federal constitutional restrictions. However, in *South Dakota v. Wayfair, Inc.* (Dkt. No. 17-494, June 21, 2018), the U.S. Supreme Court overruled *Quill Corp. v. North Dakota* (504 U.S. 298 (1992)) and held that physical presence is no longer required to establish sales and use tax nexus.

Jurisdiction	General Rules	Comment
Alabama	Sellers maintaining a place of business in Alabama, engaging in specific activities or business relationships, or who have retail sales exceeding a certain economic threshold (substantial economic presence) are required to collect the state's tax.	In *South Dakota v. Wayfair, Inc.* (Dkt. No. 17-494, June 21, 2018), the U.S. Supreme Court overruled *Quill Corp. v. North Dakota* (504 U.S. 298 (1992)) and held that physical presence is no longer required to establish sales and use tax nexus. *Notice and reporting requirements:* The Department of Revenue is authorized to require non-collecting remote sellers to report Alabama sales to the Department and notify Alabama customers of their use tax obligations. The requirements would apply to out-of-state sellers who do not collect sales, use, or simplified sellers use tax on Alabama sales. Effective January 1, 2019, marketplace facilitators will be required to: (i) collect and remit simplified sellers use tax on all marketplace sales including those of marketplace sellers, or (ii) report such sales to the Department of Revenue and provide customer notifications.
Arizona	Retailers maintaining a place of business in the state are required to collect tax.	In *South Dakota v. Wayfair, Inc.* (Dkt. No. 17-494, June 21, 2018), the U.S. Supreme Court overruled *Quill Corp. v. North Dakota* (504 U.S. 298 (1992)) and held that physical presence is no longer required to establish sales and use tax nexus.
Arkansas	Retailers doing business or engaging in business in the state are required to collect tax.	In *South Dakota v. Wayfair, Inc.* (Dkt. No. 17-494, June 21, 2018), the U.S. Supreme Court overruled *Quill Corp. v. North Dakota* (504 U.S. 298 (1992)) and held that physical presence is no longer required to establish sales and use tax nexus.

Jurisdiction	General Rules	Comment
California	Retailers engaged in business in this state are required to collect tax.	In *South Dakota v. Wayfair, Inc.* (Dkt. No. 17-494, June 21, 2018), the U.S. Supreme Court overruled *Quill Corp. v. North Dakota* (504 U.S. 298 (1992)) and held that physical presence is no longer required to establish sales and use tax nexus. Applicable April 1, 2019, retailers located outside California (remote sellers) are required to register with the CDTFA and collect California use tax if, in the preceding or current calendar year, the total combined sales of tangible personal property for delivery in California by the retailer and all persons related to the retailer exceed $500,000 (economic nexus). Moreover, applicable October 1, 2019, a "marketplace facilitator" is defined as a person who contracts with marketplace sellers to facilitate for consideration, regardless of whether deducted as fees from the transaction, the sale of the marketplace seller's products through a marketplace operated by the person or a related person and who fulfills certain conditions. A "marketplace" is a physical or electronic place, including the Internet, where a marketplace seller sells or offers for sale tangible personal property for delivery in California regardless of whether the property, marketplace seller, or marketplace has a physical presence in California.
Colorado	Retailers doing business in the state are required to collect tax. Effective December 1, 2018, economic nexus applies to out-of-state retailers.	In *South Dakota v. Wayfair, Inc.* (Dkt. No. 17-494, June 21, 2018), the U.S. Supreme Court overruled *Quill Corp. v. North Dakota* (504 U.S. 298 (1992)) and held that physical presence is no longer required to establish sales and use tax nexus.
Connecticut	Retailers engaged in business in the state are required to collect tax.	In *South Dakota v. Wayfair, Inc.* (Dkt. No. 17-494, June 21, 2018), the U.S. Supreme Court overruled *Quill Corp. v. North Dakota* (504 U.S. 298 (1992)) and held that physical presence is no longer required to establish sales and use tax nexus. Connecticut imposes economic (effective December 1, 2018), click-through, and affiliate nexus.
District of Columbia	Retailers engaging in business in the District are required to collect tax.	In *South Dakota v. Wayfair, Inc.* (Dkt. No. 17-494, June 21, 2018), the U.S. Supreme Court overruled *Quill Corp. v. North Dakota* (504 U.S. 298 (1992)) and held that physical presence is no longer required to establish sales and use tax nexus.

Jurisdiction	General Rules	Comment
Florida	Dealers making sales in the state are required to collect tax.	In *South Dakota v. Wayfair, Inc.* (Dkt. No. 17-494, June 21, 2018), the U.S. Supreme Court overruled *Quill Corp. v. North Dakota* (504 U.S. 298 (1992)) and held that physical presence is no longer required to establish sales and use tax nexus. Florida imposes affiliate nexus.
Georgia	"Retailers," "dealers," and those engaging in certain activities in the state, must collect tax on taxable sales in Georgia. Also effective January 1, 2019, "dealer" is expanded to include those who in the previous or current calendar year from retail sales of tangible personal property for electronic or physical delivery within Georgia, and for use, consumption, distribution, or storage in Georgia: (1) had more than $250,000 in gross revenue, or (2) conducted at least 200 separate retail sales of tangible personal property.	In *South Dakota v. Wayfair, Inc.* (Dkt. No. 17-494, June 21, 2018), the U.S. Supreme Court overruled *Quill Corp. v. North Dakota* (504 U.S. 298 (1992)) and held that physical presence is no longer required to establish sales and use tax nexus.
Hawaii	Persons engaging in business in the state are required to collect tax.	In *South Dakota v. Wayfair, Inc.* (Dkt. No. 17-494, June 21, 2018), the U.S. Supreme Court overruled*Quill Corp. v. North Dakota* (504 U.S. 298 (1992)) and held that physical presence is no longer required to establish sales and use tax nexus. Effective July 1, 2018, and applicable to taxable years beginning after 2017, a business is subject to general excise tax if, in the current or immediately preceding calendar year, it makes: —$100,000 or more in Hawaii sales of tangible personal property, services, or intangible property; or —200 or more separate Hawaii sales of tangible personal property, services, or intangible property.
Idaho	Retailers engaged in business in the state are required to collect tax.	In *South Dakota v. Wayfair, Inc.* (Dkt. No. 17-494, June 21, 2018), the U.S. Supreme Court overruled *Quill Corp. v. North Dakota* (504 U.S. 298 (1992)) and held that physical presence is no longer required to establish sales and use tax nexus.
Illinois	1) Physical presence; or 2) Sales of property to Illinois customers are $100,000 or more, or enter into 200 or more sales transactions in Illinois.	In *South Dakota v. Wayfair, Inc.* (Dkt. No. 17-494, June 21, 2018), the U.S. Supreme Court overruled*Quill Corp. v. North Dakota* (504 U.S. 298 (1992)) and held that physical presence is no longer required to establish sales and use tax nexus. Illinois has enacted physical presence and economic/sales presence standards. Nexus can be created by attending trade shows, although a safe harbor exists.

Jurisdiction	General Rules	Comment
Indiana	Retail merchants engaged in business in the state are required to collect tax.	In *South Dakota v. Wayfair, Inc.* (Dkt. No. 17-494, June 21, 2018), the U.S. Supreme Court overruled *Quill Corp. v. North Dakota* (504 U.S. 298 (1992)) and held that physical presence is no longer required to establish sales and use tax nexus.
Iowa	Retailers making taxable sales of tangible personal property (or, effective January 1, 2019, specified digital products) in the state are required to collect tax.	In *South Dakota v. Wayfair, Inc.* (Dkt. No. 17-494, June 21, 2018), the U.S. Supreme Court overruled *Quill Corp. v. North Dakota* (504 U.S. 298 (1992)) and held that physical presence is no longer required to establish sales and use tax nexus.
Kansas	Retailers doing business in the state are required to collect tax.	In *South Dakota v. Wayfair, Inc.* (Dkt. No. 17-494, June 21, 2018), the U.S. Supreme Court overruled *Quill Corp. v. North Dakota* (504 U.S. 298 (1992)) and held that physical presence is no longer required to establish sales and use tax nexus.
Kentucky	Retailers engaged in business in this state are required to collect tax. Also, effective July 1, 2018, a retailer has nexus when they sell tangible personal property or digital property delivered or transferred electronically to a Kentucky purchaser if: (1) they sold such property to a Kentucky purchaser in at least 200 separate transactions in the previous or current calendar year; or (2) their gross receipts from the sale of such property to Kentucky purchasers in that period exceeds $100,000.	In *South Dakota v. Wayfair, Inc.* (Dkt. No. 17-494, June 21, 2018), the U.S. Supreme Court overruled *Quill Corp. v. North Dakota* (504 U.S. 298 (1992)) and held that physical presence is no longer required to establish sales and use tax nexus.
Louisiana	"Dealers" are required to collect tax.	In *South Dakota v. Wayfair, Inc.* (Dkt. No. 17-494, June 21, 2018), the U.S. Supreme Court overruled *Quill Corp. v. North Dakota* (504 U.S. 298 (1992)) and held that physical presence is no longer required to establish sales and use tax nexus. Click-through and affiliate nexus provisions are applicable to remote sellers effective April 1, 2016.
Maine	Sellers with a substantial physical presence in the state are required to collect tax.	In *South Dakota v. Wayfair, Inc.* (Dkt. No. 17-494, June 21, 2018), the U.S. Supreme Court overruled *Quill Corp. v. North Dakota* (504 U.S. 298 (1992)) and held that physical presence is no longer required to establish sales and use tax nexus.
Maryland	"Vendors" are required to collect tax.	In *South Dakota v. Wayfair, Inc.* (Dkt. No. 17-494, June 21, 2018), the U.S. Supreme Court overruled *Quill Corp. v. North Dakota* (504 U.S. 298 (1992)) and held that physical presence is no longer required to establish sales and use tax nexus.

Jurisdiction	General Rules	Comment
Massachusetts	Vendors engaged in business in the commonwealth are required to collect tax.	In *South Dakota v. Wayfair, Inc.* (Dkt. No. 17-494, June 21, 2018), the U.S. Supreme Court overruled *Quill Corp. v. North Dakota* (504 U.S. 298 (1992)) and held that physical presence is no longer required to establish sales and use tax nexus.
Michigan	Seller that engage in specified activities are required to collect tax.	In *South Dakota v. Wayfair, Inc.* (Dkt. No. 17-494, June 21, 2018), the U.S. Supreme Court overruled *Quill Corp. v. North Dakota* (504 U.S. 298 (1992)) and held that physical presence is no longer required to establish sales and use tax nexus. After September 30, 2018, Michigan imposes economic nexus.
Minnesota	Retailers maintaining a place of business in this state are required to collect tax.	In *South Dakota v. Wayfair, Inc.* (Dkt. No. 17-494, June 21, 2018), the U.S. Supreme Court overruled *Quill Corp. v. North Dakota* (504 U.S. 298 (1992)) and held that physical presence is no longer required to establish sales and use tax nexus.
Mississippi	Sellers who maintain a place of business or do business in the state, or who purposefully or systematically exploit the Mississippi market are required to collect tax.	In *South Dakota v. Wayfair, Inc.* (Dkt. No. 17-494, June 21, 2018), the U.S. Supreme Court overruled *Quill Corp. v. North Dakota* (504 U.S. 298 (1992)) and held that physical presence is no longer required to establish sales and use tax nexus. Nexus may exist for sellers lacking a physical presence in Mississippi if they "purposefully or systematically exploit the Mississippi market" and if their sales into the state exceed $250,000 for the prior 12 months. Exploiting the Mississippi market includes direct mail marketing, telemarketing, many types of advertising, and online emails and messaging to Mississippi customers.
Missouri	Vendors engaged in business in Missouri, having physical presence in or sufficient contact with the state, or engaging in specific business activities or business relationships, must collect tax.	In *South Dakota v. Wayfair, Inc.* (Dkt. No. 17-494, June 21, 2018), the U.S. Supreme Court overruled *Quill Corp. v. North Dakota* (504 U.S. 298 (1992)) and held that physical presence is no longer required to establish sales and use tax nexus.
Nebraska	Sellers engaged in business in this state are required to collect tax.	In *South Dakota v. Wayfair, Inc.* (Dkt. No. 17-494, June 21, 2018), the U.S. Supreme Court overruled *Quill Corp. v. North Dakota* (504 U.S. 298 (1992)) and held that physical presence is no longer required to establish sales and use tax nexus. Nebraska imposes economic nexus on remote sellers.

Jurisdiction	General Rules	Comment
Nevada	Retailers maintaining a place of business in this state are required to collect tax. However, Nevada does not define the term "retailer maintaining a place of business."	In *South Dakota v. Wayfair, Inc.* (Dkt. No. 17-494, June 21, 2018), the U.S. Supreme Court overruled *Quill Corp. v. North Dakota* (504 U.S. 298 (1992)) and held that physical presence is no longer required to establish sales and use tax nexus.
New Jersey	"Sellers" are required to collect tax.	In *South Dakota v. Wayfair, Inc.* (Dkt. No. 17-494, June 21, 2018), the U.S. Supreme Court overruled *Quill Corp. v. North Dakota* (504 U.S. 298 (1992)) and held that physical presence is no longer required to establish sales and use tax nexus. New Jersey imposes the following types of nexus: economic, click-through, marketplace, and affiliate.
New Mexico	Sellers that attempts to exploit New Mexico's markets by carrying on an activity in the state are required to collect tax.	In *South Dakota v. Wayfair, Inc.* (Dkt. No. 17-494, June 21, 2018), the U.S. Supreme Court overruled *Quill Corp. v. North Dakota* (504 U.S. 298 (1992)) and held that physical presence is no longer required to establish sales and use tax nexus.
New York	Vendors making sales or maintaining a place of business in the state, vendors engaged in specified activities or business relationships, including certain Internet retailers, are required to collect tax in New York.	In *South Dakota v. Wayfair, Inc.* (Dkt. No. 17-494, June 21, 2018), the U.S. Supreme Court overruled *Quill Corp. v. North Dakota* (504 U.S. 298 (1992)) and held that physical presence is no longer required to establish sales and use tax nexus. New York imposes the following types of nexus: economic, click-through, affiliate, and marketplace providers.
North Carolina	Retailers engaged in business in the state are required to collect tax.	In *South Dakota v. Wayfair, Inc.* (Dkt. No. 17-494, June 21, 2018), the U.S. Supreme Court overruled *Quill Corp. v. North Dakota* (504 U.S. 298 (1992)) and held that physical presence is no longer required to establish sales and use tax nexus. North Carolina imposes click-through and economic nexus.

Jurisdiction	General Rules	Comment
North Dakota	Retailers maintaining a place of business in this state are required to collect tax.	In *South Dakota v. Wayfair, Inc.* (Dkt. No. 17-494, June 21, 2018), the U.S. Supreme Court overruled *Quill Corp. v. North Dakota* (504 U.S. 298 (1992)) and held that physical presence is no longer required to establish sales and use tax nexus. Out-of-state sellers with no physical presence in North Dakota are subject to sales and use tax if, in the previous calendar year or the current calendar year: - the seller's gross sales from the sale of tangible personal property and other taxable items delivered in North Dakota exceed $100,000, or - the seller sold tangible personal property and other taxable items for delivery in North Dakota in 200 or more separate transactions. Such a seller is required to remit sales or use tax and must follow all applicable procedures and requirements as if the seller has a physical presence in North Dakota.
Ohio	Sellers who have substantial nexus with the state are required to collect tax.	In *South Dakota v. Wayfair, Inc.* (Dkt. No. 17-494, June 21, 2018), the U.S. Supreme Court overruled *Quill Corp. v. North Dakota* (504 U.S. 298 (1992)) and held that physical presence is no longer required to establish sales and use tax nexus. A seller or marketplace facilitator has substantial nexus if, in the current or preceding calendar year, it (i) has gross receipts exceeding $100,000 from sales into Ohio, or (ii) engages in 200 or more separate sales transactions in Ohio.
Oklahoma	Oklahoma tax must be collected by any vendor maintaining a place of business in Oklahoma who sells taxable tangible personal property or services to persons within Oklahoma. By July 1, 2018, and by June 1 of each calendar year starting in 2019, a marketplace facilitator, remote seller, or referrer who had at least $10,000 in aggregate Oklahoma sales in the preceding 12-calendar-month period must (1) elect to obtain a sales tax permit and collect sales tax, or (2) comply with notice and reporting requirements.	In *South Dakota v. Wayfair, Inc.* (Dkt. No. 17-494, June 21, 2018), the U.S. Supreme Court overruled *Quill Corp. v. North Dakota* (504 U.S. 298 (1992)) and held that physical presence is no longer required to establish sales and use tax nexus.
Pennsylvania	Sellers maintaining a place of business in the state are required to collect tax.	In *South Dakota v. Wayfair, Inc.* (Dkt. No. 17-494, June 21, 2018), the U.S. Supreme Court overruled *Quill Corp. v. North Dakota* (504 U.S. 298 (1992)) and held that physical presence is no longer required to establish sales and use tax nexus.

Jurisdiction	General Rules	Comment
Rhode Island	Retailers engaging in business in the state are required to collect tax.	In *South Dakota v. Wayfair, Inc.* (Dkt. No. 17-494, June 21, 2018), the U.S. Supreme Court overruled *Quill Corp. v. North Dakota* (504 U.S. 298 (1992)) and held that physical presence is no longer required to establish sales and use tax nexus. The existence and/or presence of certain non-collecting retailer's, referrer's, or retail sale facilitator's in-state software on the devices of in-state customers constitutes physical presence of the non-collecting retailer, referrer, or retail sale facilitator in Rhode Island.
South Carolina	Sellers that engage in specified activities, such as maintaining a place of business in South Carolina or soliciting sales by an agent or salesman, are required to collect tax.	In *South Dakota v. Wayfair, Inc.* (Dkt. No. 17-494, June 21, 2018), the U.S. Supreme Court overruled *Quill Corp. v. North Dakota* (504 U.S. 298 (1992)) and held that physical presence is no longer required to establish sales and use tax nexus.
South Dakota	Retailers maintaining a place of business in the state are required to collect tax. Effective November 1, 2018, economic nexus applies to out-of-state retailers. Effective March 1, 2019, economic nexus applies to marketplace providers.	In *South Dakota v. Wayfair, Inc.* (Dkt. No. 17-494, June 21, 2018), the U.S. Supreme Court overruled *Quill Corp. v. North Dakota* (504 U.S. 298 (1992)) and held that physical presence is no longer required to establish sales and use tax nexus.
Tennessee	"Dealers" are required to collect tax.	In *South Dakota v. Wayfair, Inc.* (Dkt. No. 17-494, June 21, 2018), the U.S. Supreme Court overruled *Quill Corp. v. North Dakota* (504 U.S. 298 (1992)) and held that physical presence is no longer required to establish sales and use tax nexus. Tennessee imposes economic and click-through nexus. However, enforcement of the economic nexus provision is delayed and litigation is pending.
Texas	Retailers engaged in business in this state are required to collect tax.	In *South Dakota v. Wayfair, Inc.* (Dkt. No. 17-494, June 21, 2018), the U.S. Supreme Court overruled *Quill Corp. v. North Dakota* (504 U.S. 298 (1992)) and held that physical presence is no longer required to establish sales and use tax nexus.

Jurisdiction	General Rules	Comment
Utah	Sellers that engage in specified activities are required to collect tax.	In *South Dakota v. Wayfair, Inc.* (Dkt. No. 17-494, June 21, 2018), the U.S. Supreme Court overruled *Quill Corp. v. North Dakota* (504 U.S. 298 (1992)) and held that physical presence is no longer required to establish sales and use tax nexus. Effective January 1, 2019, a seller not otherwise obligated to pay or collect and remit sales and use tax is so obligated provided certain conditions are met. That obligation applies to sellers of tangible personal property, products transferred electronically, or services in Utah who, in the previous or current calendar year: (1) receive more than $100,000 from the sale of such property, products transferred electronically, or services in Utah; or (2) sell such property, products transferred electronically, or services in Utah in 200 or more separate transactions.
Vermont	"Vendors" are required to collect tax.	In *South Dakota v. Wayfair, Inc.* (Dkt. No. 17-494, June 21, 2018), the U.S. Supreme Court overruled *Quill Corp. v. North Dakota* (504 U.S. 298 (1992)) and held that physical presence is no longer required to establish sales and use tax nexus.
Virginia	Dealers maintaining a place of business in Virginia, or engaging in specified activities or business relationships, are required to collect tax.	In *South Dakota v. Wayfair, Inc.* (Dkt. No. 17-494, June 21, 2018), the U.S. Supreme Court overruled *Quill Corp. v. North Dakota* (504 U.S. 298 (1992)) and held that physical presence is no longer required to establish sales and use tax nexus.
Washington	Persons who maintain in the state a place of business or stock of goods or engage in business activities in the state are required to collect tax.	In *South Dakota v. Wayfair, Inc.* (Dkt. No. 17-494, June 21, 2018), the U.S. Supreme Court overruled *Quill Corp. v. North Dakota* (504 U.S. 298 (1992)) and held that physical presence is no longer required to establish sales and use tax nexus. Remote businesses with more than $100,000 in sales in Washington in the current or prior calendar year, must collect sales tax.
West Virginia	Retailers engaging in business in the state are required to collect tax.	In *South Dakota v. Wayfair, Inc.* (Dkt. No. 17-494, June 21, 2018), the U.S. Supreme Court overruled *Quill Corp. v. North Dakota* (504 U.S. 298 (1992)) and held that physical presence is no longer required to establish sales and use tax nexus.
Wisconsin	Retailers engaged in business in the state are required to collect tax.	In *South Dakota v. Wayfair, Inc.* (Dkt. No. 17-494, June 21, 2018), the U.S. Supreme Court overruled *Quill Corp. v. North Dakota* (504 U.S. 298 (1992)) and held that physical presence is no longer required to establish sales and use tax nexus.

Jurisdiction	General Rules	Comment
Wyoming	"Vendors" are required to collect tax.	In *South Dakota v. Wayfair, Inc.* (Dkt. No. 17-494, June 21, 2018), the U.S. Supreme Court overruled *Quill Corp. v. North Dakota* (504 U.S. 298 (1992)) and held that physical presence is no longer required to establish sales and use tax nexus.

General Nexus Rules and Internet Sales—Internet Sales

This chart indicates whether using a website to make sales to a state's residents can create nexus for a seller. Note that state nexus statutes are subject to federal constitutional restrictions. However, in *South Dakota v. Wayfair, Inc.* (Dkt. No. 17-494, June 21, 2018), the U.S. Supreme Court overruled *Quill Corp. v. North Dakota* (504 U.S. 298 (1992)) and held that physical presence is no longer required to establish sales and use tax nexus.

Jurisdiction	Internet Sales	Comment
Alabama	May create nexus	In *South Dakota v. Wayfair, Inc.* (Dkt. No. 17-494, June 21, 2018), the U.S. Supreme Court overruled *Quill Corp. v. North Dakota* (504 U.S. 298 (1992)) and held that physical presence is no longer required to establish sales and use tax nexus. *Notice and reporting requirements:* The Department of Revenue is authorized to require non-collecting remote sellers to report Alabama sales to the Department and notify Alabama customers of their use tax obligations. The requirements would apply to out-of-state sellers who do not collect sales, use, or simplified sellers use tax on Alabama sales. Effective January 1, 2019, marketplace facilitators will be required to: (i) collect and remit simplified sellers use tax on all marketplace sales including those of marketplace sellers, or (ii) report such sales to the Department of Revenue and provide customer notifications. *Economic nexus (substantial economic presence):* Out-of-state sellers who lack an Alabama physical presence but who are making retail sales of tangible personal property into the state have a substantial economic presence in Alabama for sales and use tax purposes and are required to register for a license with the department and to collect and remit tax, when: (a) the seller's retail sales of tangible personal property sold into the state exceed $250,000 per year based on the previous calendar year's sales; and (b) the seller conducts one or more of the activities described in Section 40-23-68, Code of Alabama. The Department announced that its existing economic nexus rule (810-6-2-.90.03), which took effect January 1, 2016, will be applied prospectively for sales made on or after October 1, 2018. While the rule was technically effective January 1, 2016, its validity was in question pending the outcome of the *Wayfair* decision. Because *Wayfair* removed the constitutional impediments to the rule, it will be enforced going forward. Remote sellers with annual Alabama sales in excess of the rule's $250,000 small seller exception should register for the Alabama Simplified Sellers Use Tax Program (SSUT) and begin collecting no later than October 1, 2018.
Arizona	No	In *South Dakota v. Wayfair, Inc.* (Dkt. No. 17-494, June 21, 2018), the U.S. Supreme Court overruled *Quill Corp. v. North Dakota* (504 U.S. 298 (1992)) and held that physical presence is no longer required to establish sales and use tax nexus.
Arkansas	Yes	In *South Dakota v. Wayfair, Inc.* (Dkt. No. 17-494, June 21, 2018), the U.S. Supreme Court overruled *Quill Corp. v. North Dakota* (504 U.S. 298 (1992)) and held that physical presence is no longer required to establish sales and use tax nexus.

Jurisdiction	Internet Sales	Comment
California	Yes	Applicable April 1, 2019, the definition of "retailer engaged in business in this state" is amended to include any retailer that, in the preceding or current calendar year, has total combined sales of tangible personal property for delivery in California by the retailer and all persons related to the retailer that exceed $500,000 (economic nexus). Moreover, applicable October 1, 2019, a "marketplace facilitator" is defined as a person who contracts with marketplace sellers to facilitate for consideration, regardless of whether deducted as fees from the transaction, the sale of the marketplace seller's products through a marketplace operated by the person or a related person and who fulfills certain conditions. A "marketplace" is a physical or electronic place, including the Internet, where a marketplace seller sells or offers for sale tangible personal property for delivery in California regardless of whether the property, marketplace seller, or marketplace has a physical presence in California.
Colorado	Yes	In *South Dakota v. Wayfair, Inc.* (Dkt. No. 17-494, June 21, 2018), the U.S. Supreme Court overruled *Quill Corp. v. North Dakota* (504 U.S. 298 (1992)) and held that physical presence is no longer required to establish sales and use tax nexus.
Connecticut	Yes	In *South Dakota v. Wayfair, Inc.* (Dkt. No. 17-494, June 21, 2018), the U.S. Supreme Court overruled *Quill Corp. v. North Dakota* (504 U.S. 298 (1992)) and held that physical presence is no longer required to establish sales and use tax nexus. Connecticut imposes click-through nexus. Being "engaged in business" in Connecticut specifically includes selling tangible personal property or services through an agreement with a person located in Connecticut, under which that person, for a commission or other consideration that is based on the sale of tangible personal property or services by the retailer, directly or indirectly refers potential customers, whether by a link on an Internet web site or otherwise, to the retailer, provided the cumulative gross receipts from sales by the retailer to customers in the state who are referred to the retailer by all such persons with this type of agreement with the retailer is in excess of $2,000 ($250,000 effective December 1, 2018) during the four preceding four quarterly periods ending on the last day of March, June, September and December.
District of Columbia	No	In *South Dakota v. Wayfair, Inc.* (Dkt. No. 17-494, June 21, 2018), the U.S. Supreme Court overruled *Quill Corp. v. North Dakota* (504 U.S. 298 (1992)) and held that physical presence is no longer required to establish sales and use tax nexus. The District of Columbia has no specific rules enacted.

Jurisdiction	Internet Sales	Comment
Florida	Yes	In *South Dakota v. Wayfair, Inc.* (Dkt. No. 17-494, June 21, 2018), the U.S. Supreme Court overruled *Quill Corp. v. North Dakota* (504 U.S. 298 (1992)) and held that physical presence is no longer required to establish sales and use tax nexus. Every dealer who makes a mail order sale is subject to the power of the state to levy and collect sales and use tax when the dealer, by purposefully or systematically exploiting the market provided by Florida by any media-assisted, media-facilitated, or media-solicited means, including computer-assisted shopping, creates nexus with Florida.
Georgia	May create nexus	In *South Dakota v. Wayfair, Inc.* (Dkt. No. 17-494, June 21, 2018), the U.S. Supreme Court overruled *Quill Corp. v. North Dakota* (504 U.S. 298 (1992)) and held that physical presence is no longer required to establish sales and use tax nexus. "Click-through" nexus provisions apply. Effective July 18, 2012, the definition of "dealer"; was expanded to include any person who enters into an agreement with one or more persons who are Georgia residents under which the resident(s), for a commission or other consideration, based on completed sales, directly or indirectly refers potential customers (whether by a link on an Internet website, an in-person oral presentation, telemarketing, or otherwise) to the person, if the cumulative gross receipts from sales by the person to customers in Georgia who are referred to the person by all residents with this type of an agreement with the person is more than $50,000 during the preceding 12 months. The presumption that such a person qualifies as a "dealer" in Georgia is rebuttable.
Hawaii	May create nexus	In *South Dakota v. Wayfair, Inc.* (Dkt. No. 17-494, June 21, 2018), the U.S. Supreme Court overruled *Quill Corp. v. North Dakota* (504 U.S. 298 (1992)) and held that physical presence is no longer required to establish sales and use tax nexus. Effective July 1, 2018, and applicable to taxable years beginning after 2017, a business is subject to general excise tax if, in the current or immediately preceding calendar year, it makes: —$100,000 or more in Hawaii sales of tangible personal property, services, or intangible property; or —200 or more separate Hawaii sales of tangible personal property, services, or intangible property.
Idaho	Yes	In *South Dakota v. Wayfair, Inc.* (Dkt. No. 17-494, June 21, 2018), the U.S. Supreme Court overruled *Quill Corp. v. North Dakota* (504 U.S. 298 (1992)) and held that physical presence is no longer required to establish sales and use tax nexus. Effective July 1, 2018, the definition of "retailer engaged in business in this state" includes any retailer that has an agreement, directly or indirectly, with one or more persons engaged in business in Idaho which, for a commission or other consideration, the persons refer potential purchasers to the retailer directly, whether by a link on an internet website, written or oral presentation, or otherwise, and the cumulative gross receipts from sales by the retailer to purchasers who are referred by all retailers engaged in business in the state with such an agreement are greater than $10,000 during the immediately preceding 12 months.

Jurisdiction	Internet Sales	Comment
Illinois	Yes	In *South Dakota v. Wayfair, Inc.* (Dkt. No. 17-494, June 21, 2018), the U.S. Supreme Court overruled *Quill Corp. v. North Dakota* (504 U.S. 298 (1992)) and held that physical presence is no longer required to establish sales and use tax nexus. When a retailer has a commission contract with an Illinois person and that person refers customers to the seller via a website link that allows the retailer to track the referrals, nexus may exist. In addition, Illinois has an economic/sales presence standard.
Indiana	Yes	In *South Dakota v. Wayfair, Inc.* (Dkt. No. 17-494, June 21, 2018), the U.S. Supreme Court overruled *Quill Corp. v. North Dakota* (504 U.S. 298 (1992)) and held that physical presence is no longer required to establish sales and use tax nexus. Nexus exists with Indiana to the extent allowed under federal law.
Iowa	Yes	In *South Dakota v. Wayfair, Inc.* (Dkt. No. 17-494, June 21, 2018), the U.S. Supreme Court overruled *Quill Corp. v. North Dakota* (504 U.S. 298 (1992)) and held that physical presence is no longer required to establish sales and use tax nexus.
Kansas	May create nexus	In *South Dakota v. Wayfair, Inc.* (Dkt. No. 17-494, June 21, 2018), the U.S. Supreme Court overruled *Quill Corp. v. North Dakota* (504 U.S. 298 (1992)) and held that physical presence is no longer required to establish sales and use tax nexus. "Click-through" nexus provisions apply. There is a rebuttable presumption that a retailer is a "retailer doing business in this state" if the retailer enters into an agreement with one or more Kansas residents under which the resident, for a commission or other consideration, directly or indirectly refers potential customers, whether by a link or an Internet website, by telemarketing, by an in-person oral presentation, or otherwise, to the retailer, if the cumulative gross receipts from sales by the retailer to customers in Kansas who are referred to the retailer by all residents with this type of an agreement with the retailer is more than $10,000 during the preceding 12 months.
Kentucky	No	In *South Dakota v. Wayfair, Inc.* (Dkt. No. 17-494, June 21, 2018), the U.S. Supreme Court overruled *Quill Corp. v. North Dakota* (504 U.S. 298 (1992)) and held that physical presence is no longer required to establish sales and use tax nexus.
Louisiana	Yes	In *South Dakota v. Wayfair, Inc.* (Dkt. No. 17-494, June 21, 2018), the U.S. Supreme Court overruled *Quill Corp. v. North Dakota* (504 U.S. 298 (1992)) and held that physical presence is no longer required to establish sales and use tax nexus. Click-through and affiliate nexus provisions are applicable to remote sellers effective April 1, 2016.

Jurisdiction	Internet Sales	Comment
Maine	Yes	In *South Dakota v. Wayfair, Inc.* (Dkt. No. 17-494, June 21, 2018), the U.S. Supreme Court overruled *Quill Corp. v. North Dakota* (504 U.S. 298 (1992)) and held that physical presence is no longer required to establish sales and use tax nexus. When a retailer enters into an agreement with a person, under which the person refers potential customers in Maine to the seller for a commission by a link on an Internet website.
Maryland	No	In *South Dakota v. Wayfair, Inc.* (Dkt. No. 17-494, June 21, 2018), the U.S. Supreme Court overruled *Quill Corp. v. North Dakota* (504 U.S. 298 (1992)) and held that physical presence is no longer required to establish sales and use tax nexus.
Massachusetts	May create nexus	In *South Dakota v. Wayfair, Inc.* (Dkt. No. 17-494, June 21, 2018), the U.S. Supreme Court overruled *Quill Corp. v. North Dakota* (504 U.S. 298 (1992)) and held that physical presence is no longer required to establish sales and use tax nexus. Statute indicates nexus may exist.
Michigan	Yes	In *South Dakota v. Wayfair, Inc.* (Dkt. No. 17-494, June 21, 2018), the U.S. Supreme Court overruled *Quill Corp. v. North Dakota* (504 U.S. 298 (1992)) and held that physical presence is no longer required to establish sales and use tax nexus. There is a rebuttable presumption that a retailer is engaged in business in Michigan if the retailer enters into an agreement with one or more Michigan residents under which the resident, for a commission or other consideration, directly or indirectly refers potential customers, whether by a link or an Internet website, by an in-person oral presentation, or otherwise, to the retailer, if the cumulative gross receipts from sales by the retailer to customers in Michigan who are referred to the retailer by all residents with this type of an agreement with the retailer is more than $10,000 during the preceding 12 months. Also, the seller's total cumulative gross receipts from sales to customers in Michigan must be greater than $50,000 during the immediately preceding 12 months. After September 30, 2018, a seller that has sales exceeding $100,000 or 200 or more sales transactions in Michigan in the prior calendar year, has nexus.
Minnesota	Yes	In *South Dakota v. Wayfair, Inc.* (Dkt. No. 17-494, June 21, 2018), the U.S. Supreme Court overruled *Quill Corp. v. North Dakota* (504 U.S. 298 (1992)) and held that physical presence is no longer required to establish sales and use tax nexus. Statute indicates nexus may exist.

Jurisdiction	Internet Sales	Comment
Mississippi	May create nexus	In *South Dakota v. Wayfair, Inc.* (Dkt. No. 17-494, June 21, 2018), the U.S. Supreme Court overruled *Quill Corp. v. North Dakota* (504 U.S. 298 (1992)) and held that physical presence is no longer required to establish sales and use tax nexus. Nexus may exist for sellers lacking a physical presence in Mississippi if they "purposefully or systematically exploit the Mississippi market" and if their sales into the state exceed $250,000 for the prior 12 months. Exploiting the Mississippi market includes direct mail marketing, telemarketing, many types of advertising, and online emails and messaging to Mississippi customers.
Missouri	Yes	In *South Dakota v. Wayfair, Inc.* (Dkt. No. 17-494, June 21, 2018), the U.S. Supreme Court overruled *Quill Corp. v. North Dakota* (504 U.S. 298 (1992)) and held that physical presence is no longer required to establish sales and use tax nexus. Click-through nexus: There is a presumption of nexus if a vendor enters into an agreement with a state resident, under which the resident, for a commission or other consideration, refers potential customers, through a link on an Internet website or otherwise, to the vendor, and the vendor's cumulative gross receipts from sales to Missouri customers referred by residents with such an agreement exceeded $10,000 in the preceding 12 months. This presumption may be rebutted by showing that the Missouri resident did not engage in activity within Missouri that was significantly associated with the vendor's market in Missouri in the preceding 12 months.
Nebraska	May create nexus	In *South Dakota v. Wayfair, Inc.* (Dkt. No. 17-494, June 21, 2018), the U.S. Supreme Court overruled *Quill Corp. v. North Dakota* a (504 U.S. 298 (1992)) and held that physical presence is no longer required to establish sales and use tax nexus. Remote sellers with more than $100,000 of sales or 200 or more transactions in Nebraska have nexus.
Nevada	May create nexus	In *South Dakota v. Wayfair, Inc.* (Dkt. No. 17-494, June 21, 2018), the U.S. Supreme Court overruled *Quill Corp. v. North Dakota* (504 U.S. 298 (1992)) and held that physical presence is no longer required to establish sales and use tax nexus. Nevada does not provide statutory or regulatory guidance on nexus for sales and use tax purposes.

Jurisdiction	Internet Sales	Comment
New Jersey	Yes	In *South Dakota v. Wayfair, Inc.* (Dkt. No. 17-494, June 21, 2018), the U.S. Supreme Court overruled *Quill Corp. v. North Dakota* (504 U.S. 298 (1992)) and held that physical presence is no longer required to establish sales and use tax nexus. *Click-through nexus*: A person making sales of taxable tangible personal property, specified digital products, or services is presumed to be soliciting business through an independent contractor or other representative if the person making sales enters into an agreement with an independent contractor having physical presence in New Jersey or other representative having physical presence in New Jersey, for a commission or other consideration, under which the independent contractor or representative directly or indirectly refers potential customers, whether by a link on an Internet website or otherwise, and the cumulative gross receipts from sales to customers in New Jersey who were referred by all independent contractors or representatives that have this type of an agreement with the person making sales are in excess of $10,000 during the preceding four quarterly periods ending on the last day of March, June, September, and December. This presumption may be rebutted by proof that the independent contractor or representative with whom the person making sales has an agreement did not engage in any solicitation in New Jersey on behalf of the person that would satisfy the nexus requirements of the U.S. Constitution during the four quarterly periods in question.
New Mexico	No	In *South Dakota v. Wayfair, Inc.* (Dkt. No. 17-494, June 21, 2018), the U.S. Supreme Court overruled *Quill Corp. v. North Dakota* (504 U.S. 298 (1992)) and held that physical presence is no longer required to establish sales and use tax nexus. No specific rules enacted have been enacted.

Jurisdiction	Internet Sales	Comment
New York	Yes	In *South Dakota v. Wayfair, Inc.* (Dkt. No. 17-494, June 21, 2018), the U.S. Supreme Court overruled *Quill Corp. v. North Dakota* (504 U.S. 298 (1992)) and held that physical presence is no longer required to establish sales and use tax nexus. *Click-through nexus:* New York has a rebuttable presumption that certain Internet retailers of taxable tangible personal property or services are sales tax vendors required to register and collect state and local sales taxes. Specifically, New York's statutes define a vendor required to collect tax to include a seller that enters into a commission agreement with a New York resident under which the resident directly or indirectly refers potential customers, whether by a link on an internet website or otherwise, to the seller and such referrals result in gross receipts in excess of $10,000 during the preceding four quarterly periods. The presumption is deemed rebutted where the seller is able to establish that the only activity of its resident representative in New York on behalf of the seller is a link provided on the representatives' Web site to the seller's Web site and none of the resident representatives engage in any solicitation activity in the state targeted at potential New York customers on behalf of the seller. *Marketplace providers:* Effective June 1, 2019, Marketplace providers are required to collect and remit sales tax on taxable sales of tangible personal property that they facilitate.
North Carolina	Yes	In *South Dakota v. Wayfair, Inc.* (Dkt. No. 17-494, June 21, 2018), the U.S. Supreme Court overruled *Quill Corp. v. North Dakota* (504 U.S. 298 (1992)) and held that physical presence is no longer required to establish sales and use tax nexus. Click-through nexus is imposed. A retailer is presumed to be soliciting or transacting business by an independent contractor, agent, or other representative if the retailer enters into an agreement with a North Carolina resident who, pursuant to the agreement and for a commission or other consideration, directly or indirectly refers potential customers, whether by link on an Internet Web site or otherwise, to the retailer. The presumption applies only if the cumulative gross receipts from sales by the retailer to North Carolina purchasers who are referred to the retailer by all residents with this type of agreement with the retailer is in excess of $10,000 during the preceding four quarterly periods. The presumption may be rebutted by proof that the resident with whom the retailer has an agreement did not engage in any solicitation in North Carolina on behalf of the seller that would satisfy the nexus requirement of the U.S. Constitution during the four quarterly periods in question.

Jurisdiction	Internet Sales	Comment
North Dakota	Yes	In *South Dakota v. Wayfair, Inc.* (Dkt. No. 17-494, June 21, 2018), the U.S. Supreme Court overruled *Quill Corp. v. North Dakota* (504 U.S. 298 (1992)) and held that physical presence is no longer required to establish sales and use tax nexus. Out-of-state sellers with no physical presence in North Dakota are subject to sales and use tax if, in the previous calendar year or the current calendar year: - the seller's gross sales from the sale of tangible personal property and other taxable items delivered in North Dakota exceed $100,000, or - the seller sold tangible personal property and other taxable items for delivery in North Dakota in 200 or more separate transactions. Such a seller is required to remit sales or use tax and must follow all applicable procedures and requirements as if the seller has a physical presence in North Dakota.
Ohio	Yes	In *South Dakota v. Wayfair, Inc.* (Dkt. No. 17-494, June 21, 2018), the U.S. Supreme Court overruled *Quill Corp. v. North Dakota* (504 U.S. 298 (1992)) and held that physical presence is no longer required to establish sales and use tax nexus. A seller or marketplace facilitator has substantial nexus if, in the current or preceding calendar year, it (i) has gross receipts exceeding $100,000 from sales into Ohio, or (ii) engages in 200 or more separate sales transactions in Ohio.
Oklahoma	May create nexus	In *South Dakota v. Wayfair, Inc.* (Dkt. No. 17-494, June 21, 2018), the U.S. Supreme Court overruled *Quill Corp. v. North Dakota* (504 U.S. 298 (1992)) and held that physical presence is no longer required to establish sales and use tax nexus. Any retailer making sales of tangible personal property to purchasers in Oklahoma by the Internet that has contracted with an entity to provide and perform installation or maintenance services for the retailer's purchasers in Oklahoma comes within the definition of a "retailer."
Pennsylvania	Yes	In *South Dakota v. Wayfair, Inc.* (Dkt. No. 17-494, June 21, 2018), the U.S. Supreme Court overruled *Quill Corp. v. North Dakota* (504 U.S. 298 (1992)) and held that physical presence is no longer required to establish sales and use tax nexus. Click-through nexus: The DOR has stated that a remote seller has nexus if the seller: has a contractual relationship with an entity or individual physically located in PA whose website has a link that encourages purchasers to place orders with the remote sellers, and the in-state entity or individual receives consideration for the contractual relationship with the remote seller; or regularly solicits orders from PA customers via the website of an entity or individual physically located in PA, such as via click-through technology.

Jurisdiction	Internet Sales	Comment
Rhode Island	Yes	In *South Dakota v. Wayfair, Inc.* (Dkt. No. 17-494, June 21, 2018), the U.S. Supreme Court overruled *Quill Corp. v. North Dakota* (504 U.S. 298 (1992)) and held that physical presence is no longer required to establish sales and use tax nexus. Click-through nexus: There is a presumption of nexus if a retailer enters into an agreement with a state resident, under which the resident, for a commission or other consideration, refers potential customers, through a link on an Internet website or otherwise, to the retailer, if the retailer's cumulative gross receipts from sales to Rhode Island customers referred by residents with such an agreement exceeded $5,000 during the preceding 4 quarterly periods. The presumption can be rebutted by proof that the state resident did not engage in any solicitation on behalf of the seller that would satisfy the nexus requirements of the U.S. Constitution during the four quarterly periods in question. In addition, the existence and/or presence of certain non-collecting retailer's, referrer's, or retail sale facilitator's in-state software on the devices of in-state customers constitutes physical presence of the non-collecting retailer, referrer, or retail sale facilitator in Rhode Island.
South Carolina	No	In *South Dakota v. Wayfair, Inc.* (Dkt. No. 17-494, June 21, 2018), the U.S. Supreme Court overruled *Quill Corp. v. North Dakota* (504 U.S. 298 (1992)) and held that physical presence is no longer required to establish sales and use tax nexus. A business that sells tangible personal property over the Internet and operates a website maintained on a server owned by the business and located in South Carolina, has nexus. Other exceptions may also apply.
South Dakota	Yes	In *South Dakota v. Wayfair, Inc.* (Dkt. No. 17-494, June 21, 2018), the U.S. Supreme Court overruled *Quill Corp. v. North Dakota* (504 U.S. 298 (1992)) and held that physical presence is no longer required to establish sales and use tax nexus. Out-of-state sellers with no physical presence in South Dakota are subject to sales and use tax if, in the previous calendar year or the current calendar year: —the seller's gross sales from the sale of tangible personal property and other taxable items delivered in South Dakota exceed $100,000, or —the seller sold tangible personal property and other taxable items for delivery in South Dakota in 200 or more separate transactions. Such a seller is required to remit sales or use tax and must follow all applicable procedures and requirements as if the seller has a physical presence in South Dakota.

Jurisdiction	Internet Sales	Comment
Tennessee	Yes	In *South Dakota v. Wayfair, Inc.* (Dkt. No. 17-494, June 21, 2018), the U.S. Supreme Court overruled *Quill Corp. v. North Dakota* (504 U.S. 298 (1992)) and held that physical presence is no longer required to establish sales and use tax nexus. A dealer is presumed to have a representative, agent, salesperson, canvasser, or solicitor operating in Tennessee for the purpose of making sales and is presumed to have a substantial nexus with Tennessee provided: (a) the dealer enters into an agreement or contract with one or more persons located in Tennessee under which the person, for a commission or other consideration, directly or indirectly refers potential customers to the dealer, whether by a link on an Internet website or any other means; and (b) the dealer's cumulative gross receipts from retail sales made by the dealer to customers in Tennessee who are referred to the dealer by all residents with this type of an agreement with the dealer exceed $10,000 during the preceding 12 months.
Texas	Yes	In *South Dakota v. Wayfair, Inc.* (Dkt. No. 17-494, June 21, 2018), the U.S. Supreme Court overruled *Quill Corp. v. North Dakota* (504 U.S. 298 (1992)) and held that physical presence is no longer required to establish sales and use tax nexus. Statute indicates nexus may exist. A person whose only activity in Texas is conducted as a user of Internet hosting is not engaged in business in Texas.
Utah	No	In *South Dakota v. Wayfair, Inc.* (Dkt. No. 17-494, June 21, 2018), the U.S. Supreme Court overruled *Quill Corp. v. North Dakota* (504 U.S. 298 (1992)) and held that physical presence is no longer required to establish sales and use tax nexus. Thus, the commissioner can require remote sellers to collect sales tax.
Vermont	Yes	In *South Dakota v. Wayfair, Inc.* (Dkt. No. 17-494, June 21, 2018), the U.S. Supreme Court overruled *Quill Corp. v. North Dakota* (504 U.S. 298 (1992)) and held that physical presence is no longer required to establish sales and use tax nexus. Nexus exists if seller qualifies as a "vendor." Also, Vermont has enacted a click-through nexus provision.

Jurisdiction	Internet Sales	Comment
Virginia	No	In *South Dakota v. Wayfair, Inc.* (Dkt. No. 17-494, June 21, 2018), the U.S. Supreme Court overruled *Quill Corp. v. North Dakota* (504 U.S. 298 (1992)) and held that physical presence is no longer required to establish sales and use tax nexus. Virginia has legislation that requires certain remote sellers that utilize in-state facilities to collect Virginia sales tax. The law establishes a presumption that a dealer has nexus with the state if any commonly controlled person maintains a distribution center, warehouse, fulfillment center, office, or similar location in Virginia that facilitates the delivery of tangible personal property sold by the dealer to its customers. The presumption may be rebutted by demonstrating that the activities conducted by the commonly controlled person in Virginia are not significantly associated with the dealer's ability to establish or maintain a market in the state. The law takes effect on the earlier of September 1, 2013, or the effective date of federal legislation authorizing the states to require a seller to collect taxes on sales of goods to in-state purchasers without regard to the location of the seller. If, however, such federal legislation is enacted prior to August 15, 2013, and the effective date of that federal legislation is after September 1, 2013, but on or before January 1, 2014, then the provisions become effective on January 1, 2014.
Washington	May create nexus	In *South Dakota v. Wayfair, Inc.* (Dkt. No. 17-494, June 21, 2018), the U.S. Supreme Court overruled *Quill Corp. v. North Dakota* (504 U.S. 298 (1992)) and held that physical presence is no longer required to establish sales and use tax nexus. Until July 1, 2019, remote sellers and marketplace facilitators with gross receipts of at least $10,000 sourced to Washington in the current or preceding calendar year must elect to collect sales tax or comply with notice and reporting requirements. Remote sellers with more than $100,000 in Washington sales in the current or prior calendar year, must collect sales tax.
West Virginia	Yes	In *South Dakota v. Wayfair, Inc.* (Dkt. No. 17-494, June 21, 2018), the U.S. Supreme Court overruled *Quill Corp. v. North Dakota* (504 U.S. 298 (1992)) and held that physical presence is no longer required to establish sales and use tax nexus. Sellers who purposefully or systematically exploit the market in the state by any media-assisted, media-facilitated, or media-solicited means, including computer-assisted shopping, create nexus with the state for purposes of sales and use tax.
Wisconsin	Yes	Beginning October 1, 2018, remote retailers must register and collect Wisconsin sales or use tax if, in the previous or current year, their: annual gross sales into Wisconsin exceed $100,000; or annual number of separate sales transactions into Wisconsin is 200 or more.

Jurisdiction	Internet Sales	Comment
Wyoming	Yes	In *South Dakota v. Wayfair, Inc.* (Dkt. No. 17-494, June 21, 2018), the U.S. Supreme Court overruled *Quill Corp. v. North Dakota* (504 U.S. 298 (1992)) and held that physical presence is no longer required to establish sales and use tax nexus. "Vendor" defined as including every person who engages in regular or systematic solicitation by three or more separate transmittances of advertisements in any 12 month period in a consumer market in Wyoming by the distribution of catalogs. "Vendor" includes remote sellers to the extent provided by Wyo. Stat. Ann. Sec. 39-15-501 (during the pendency of the Department's declaratory judgment action, it is prohibited from enforcing the remote seller tax remittance obligations).

Judicial Appeals

The following chart describes the time period in which a taxpayer must seek judicial review of a department decision or decision by an administrative entity. Appeals to the taxing authority or administrative entity are addressed in Department Appeals and Administrative Appeals.

Jurisdiction	Judicial Appeals	Comment
Alabama	Suit must be filed with the Circuit Court within 30 days after the date of final assessment.	
Arizona	Suit must be filed with the Tax Court within 30 days after the date of final decision.	
Arkansas	Suit must be filed with the Circuit Court within one year after date of final determination.	Suit must be filed within 30 days if bond posted rather than tax paid.
California	Suit must be filed in a court of competent jurisdiction in a city or county in which the Attorney General has an office within 90 days after mailing of notice of Board's action.	
Colorado	Suit must be filed with the District Court within 30 days after the mailing of the determination.	
Connecticut	Suit must be filed with the Superior Court for the District of New Britain within one month after service of notice.	
District of Columbia	Suit must be filed with the Superior Court within six months after date of final determination or denial of refund claim.	
Florida	Suit must be filed with the Circuit Court within 60 days after date of final assessment, in lieu of proceeding under the Administrative Procedure Act.	Appeal must be filed with the Appellate Court within 30 days of rendition of the order appealed from if proceeding under the APA.
Georgia	Suit must be filed with the Superior Court within 30 days after date of decision.	
Hawaii	Notice of appeal must be filed with the Tax Appeal Court within 30 days after mailing date of notice of assessment if direct review.	Notice of appeal must be filed within 30 days after date decision was filed by State Board of Review if administrative review had been taken.
Idaho	Suit must be filed with the District Court within 91 days after notice of redetermination is received.	Within 28 days after Board of Tax Appeals decision is mailed.
Illinois	Suit must be filed with the Circuit Court within 35 days after date the administrative decision is served.	
Indiana	Suit must be filed with the Tax Court within 180 days of issuance of letter of findings.	

Jurisdiction	Judicial Appeals	Comment
Iowa	Suit must be filed with the District Court within 30 days after date of State Board's decision.	
Kansas	Suit must be filed with the District Court within 30 days after rehearing order entered or denied by the State Board of Tax Appeals.	
Kentucky	Notice of appeal must be filed with the Kentucky Claims Commission (formerly the Kentucky Board of Tax Appeals) within 30 days of the final order. Statement of appeal must be filed with the Circuit Court within 30 days after notice of appeal is filed.	
Louisiana	Suit must be filed with the District Court within 30 days after decision of Board of Tax Appeals.	
Maine	Suit must be filed with the Superior Court within 60 days after receipt of notice.	
Maryland	Suit must be filed with the Circuit Court within 30 days after the latest of: date of action, date of agency's notice of action, or date taxpayer received notice.	
Massachusetts	Suit must be filed with the Appeals Court within 60 days of entry of judgment of the Board.	
Michigan	Suit must be filed with the Court of Claims within 90 days after assessment, decision, or order.	Decisions of the Court of Claims or Tax Tribunal may be appealed to the Court of Appeals.
Minnesota	Writ of certiorari must be obtained from the state Supreme Court within 60 days after Tax Court order entered.	
Mississippi	Suit must be filed with the Chancery Court within 60 days from the date of the Board of Tax Appeal's order.	
Missouri	Suit must be filed with the Court of Appeals within 30 days after notice of final decision mailed or delivered.	
Nebraska	Suit must be filed with the District Court within 30 days after service of final decision.	
Nevada	Suit must be filed with the District Court within 30 days of the Commission's decision.	
New Jersey	Suit must be filed with the Tax Court within 90 days of the date of Director's decision.	Tax Court decisions may be appealed to the Appellate Division of the Superior Court.

Jurisdiction	Judicial Appeals	Comment
New Mexico	Suit must be filed with Court of Appeals within 30 days of mailing or delivery of administrative hearing decision.	If administrative hearing not held, suit must be filed with the District Court for Santa Fe County within 90 days after denial of claim or 90 days after expiration of Secretary's time for action.
New York	Suit must be filed with the Appellate Division of the Supreme Court, Third Division, within four months after notice of determination.	
North Carolina	Suit must be filed with the District Court within 30 days after receipt of decision.	
North Dakota	Appeal must be filed with the District Court within 30 days after notice of Commissioner determination.	
Ohio	Suit must be filed with the Court of Appeals or State Supreme Court within 30 days after entry of decision in Board's journal.	
Oklahoma	Suit must be filed with the State Supreme Court within 30 days after mailing of decision.	
Pennsylvania	Appeal must be filed with the Commonwealth Court within 30 days after entry of the order by the Board of Finance and Revenue.	
Rhode Island	Suit must be filed with the Sixth Division of the District Court within 30 days after mailing of notice of final decision.	
South Carolina	Suit must be filed with the Circuit Court within 30 days of receipt of Administrative Law Judge's decision.	
South Dakota	Suit must be filed with the Circuit Court within 30 days after notice of final decision served.	
Tennessee	Suit must be filed with the Chancery Court within 90 days after mailing notice of assessment.	
Texas	Suit must be filed with the District Court within 30 days after denial of rehearing motion or within 90 days after filing protest.	
Utah	Suit must be filed with the District Court within 30 days after mailing notice of agency action.	
Vermont	Appeal must be filed with the Superior Court within 30 days after decision or action of Commissioner.	
Virginia	Suit must be filed with the Circuit Court within the later of three years after assessment or one year after Commissioner's determination.	

Jurisdiction	Judicial Appeals	Comment
Washington	An appeal of a Board of Tax Appeals decision must be filed with the Superior Court within 30 days after the decision. For a tax refund, the appeal must be filed to the superior court of Thurston county, within the time limitation for a refund provided in chapter 82.32 RCW or, if an application for refund has been made to the department within that time limitation, then within 30 days after rejection of the application, whichever is later.	
West Virginia	Suit must be filed with the Circuit Court within 60 days after receipt of notice of decision.	
Wisconsin	Petition must be filed within 30 days after service of decision or disposition of rehearing request.	
Wyoming	Suit must be filed with the District Court within 30 days after service of decision.	

Leases and Rentals—Motor Vehicles

Jurisdiction	Motor Vehicles	Comment
Alabama	Taxable	Taxed at reduced rate.
Arizona	Taxable	Rentals for 180 days or less subject to additional surcharge.
Arkansas	Taxable	Sales tax due on lease payments made to lessor during lease term. Additional short-term rental vehicle excise tax (10%) due on rentals for less than 30 days. Long-term (30 days or more) rental vehicle excise tax (1.5%) expired on June 30, 2015.
California	Taxable	
Colorado	Taxable	A $2 motor vehicle daily rental fee is also imposed.
Connecticut	Taxable	Rentals for less than 31 days subject to additional surcharges. Leases/rentals of certain passenger cars utilizing hybrid technology exempt.
District of Columbia	Taxable	Taxed at special rate.
Florida	Taxable	Additional surcharge applies to first 30 days of term of any lease/rental.
Georgia	Taxable	Lease payments for vehicles leased for more than 31 consecutive days for which a state and local title ad valorem tax (TAVT) is paid are exempt from sales and use tax.
Hawaii	Taxable	Certain rentals subject to additional surcharge.
Idaho	Taxable	
Illinois	Exempt	Rentals for one year or less subject to automobile renting occupation and use tax.
Indiana	Taxable	Rentals for less than 30 days subject to additional auto rental excise tax.
Iowa	Taxable	Rentals for 60 days or less subject to additional automobile rental excise tax. Leases for 12 months or more exempt from general use tax, but subject to long-term lease tax.
Kansas	Taxable	Rentals for 28 days or less subject to additional motor vehicle rental excise tax.
Kentucky	Exempt	Exempt from general sales/use tax if motor vehicle usage tax paid. Vehicles not subject to motor vehicle usage tax are subject to general sales/use tax.
Louisiana	Taxable	
Maine	Taxable	Long-term auto rentals subject to tax at 5%. Short-term rentals of autos, or pickup trucks and vans with a gross vehicle weight of less than 26,000 pounds, for periods of less than one year subject to tax at 10%.
Maryland	Taxable	Leases for 180 days or less taxed at special rate. Leases for one year or more exempt.
Massachusetts	Taxable	Rentals in Boston subject to additional surcharge.

Jurisdiction	Motor Vehicles	Comment
Michigan	Taxable	Subject to use tax.
Minnesota	Taxable	Rentals for 28 days or less subject to additional motor vehicle rental fee and tax.
Mississippi	Taxable	Subject to general sales tax at special rates. Additional rental vehicle tax imposed on rentals for a period of 30 days or less.
Missouri	Taxable	Lessor/renter who paid tax on previous purchase, lease, or rental of vehicle, should not collect tax on subsequent lease/rental or sublease/subrental.
Nebraska	Taxable	For leases of one year or more, lessors may elect to pay tax on cost of vehicle in lieu of collecting tax on lease proceeds. Rentals for 31 days or less subject to additional fee. The sales and use tax on lease and rental payments of motor vehicles is sourced to the primary property location associated with each lease payment.
Nevada	Taxable	Short-term leases subject to additional fees.
New Jersey	Taxable	Rentals for 28 days or less subject to additional fee. Leases/rentals of new or used zero-emission vehicles exempt.
New Mexico	Taxable	Subject to additional leased vehicle gross receipts tax and additional surcharge.
New York	Taxable	Subject to additional special tax on passenger car rentals. Accelerated sales tax payment provisions apply to long-term leases.
North Carolina	Exempt	Exempt from general sales/use tax, but subject to highway use tax or alternate gross receipts tax.
North Dakota	Exempt	Leases for one year or more exempt from general sales/use tax, but subject to motor vehicle excise tax. Rentals for less than 30 days subject to general sales/use tax and surcharge.
Ohio	Taxable	
Oklahoma	Taxable	Rentals of 90 days or less subject to motor vehicle rental tax. Otherwise, subject to motor vehicle excise tax. Leases for 12 months or more exempt from sales and use tax if owner paid motor vehicle excise tax.
Pennsylvania	Taxable	Leases for 30 days or more subject to additional motor vehicle lease tax. Rentals for less than 30 days subject to additional rental tax and fee. Carsharing subject to fee.
Rhode Island	Taxable	For rentals of 30 days or less, car rental companies must collect additional surcharge.
South Carolina	Taxable	Maximum tax is $300 for each lease. Rentals for 90 days or less subject to vehicle license fee.
South Dakota	Taxable	Rentals for 28 days or less subject to additional vehicle rentals tax. Leases/rentals for more than 28 days exempt.

Jurisdiction	Motor Vehicles	Comment
Tennessee	Taxable	Rentals for 31 days or less subject to additional surcharge.
Texas	Exempt	Leases for more than 180 days exempt from general sales/use tax, but subject to motor vehicle sales/use tax. Rentals for 30 days or less subject to gross rental receipts tax at rate of 10% (6.25% for rentals longer than 30 days).
Utah	Taxable	Leases/rentals for 30 days or less subject to additional motor vehicle rental tax.
Vermont	Exempt	Charges at end of lease for excess wear and tear or excess mileage taxable. Rentals for less than one year subject to rental car use tax.
Virginia	Taxable	Subject to motor vehicle rental tax. Rental of any daily rental vehicle subject to additional tax and additional fee. Certain exceptions apply.
Washington	Taxable	In addition to retail sales tax, a rental car tax is paid by the consumer on rental of passenger car for period of 30 days or less at rate of 5.9%. A motor vehicle sales tax applies to every rental not subject to the rental car tax at rate of 0.3% of net price paid, used to finance transportation improvements. A sales and use tax exemption applies to leases of certain new clean alternative fuel vehicles.
West Virginia	Exempt	Tax is imposed on monthly motor vehicle lease payments for vehicles leased by West Virginia residents for a contractually specified period of more than 30 days.
Wisconsin	Taxable	Additional fee on rentals for 30 days or less.
Wyoming	Taxable	Exempt where rental is computed from gross receipts of the operation, provided operator has a valid interstate authority or permit. Additional surcharge is imposed on rentals of rental vehicles for 31 days or less.

Leases and Rentals—Tangible Personal Property

Jurisdiction	Tangible Personal Property	Comment
Alabama	Taxable	Subject to a privilege or license tax (rental tax).
Arizona	Taxable	
Arkansas	Taxable	For rentals of less than 30 days, tax paid on basis of rental payments to lessor, regardless of whether lessor paid sales or use tax at time of purchase of property.
California	Taxable	
Colorado	Taxable	Exempt if lease/rental for 3 years or less and lessor paid sales/use tax upon acquisition.
Connecticut	Taxable	
District of Columbia	Taxable	
Florida	Taxable	
Georgia	Taxable	
Hawaii	Taxable	
Idaho	Taxable	
Illinois	Exempt	Exempt from sales tax. Rental purchase agreement occupation or use tax may apply.
Indiana	Taxable	
Iowa	Taxable	
Kansas	Taxable	
Kentucky	Taxable	
Louisiana	Taxable	
Maine	Taxable	Only leases deemed by state tax assessor to be in lieu of purchase are treated as sales. In a "straight" lease, lessor pays tax on purchase price, no tax charged to lessee.
Maryland	Taxable	
Massachusetts	Taxable	
Michigan	Taxable	Lessor may elect to pay use tax on rental/lease receipts in lieu of payment of sales/use tax on cost of property upon acquisition.
Minnesota	Taxable	
Mississippi	Taxable	
Missouri	Taxable	
Nebraska	Taxable	
Nevada	Taxable	Only leases deemed by Tax Commission to be in lieu of a transfer of title, exchange, or barter are treated as sales.

Jurisdiction	Tangible Personal Property	Comment
New Jersey	Taxable	
New Mexico	Taxable	
New York	Taxable	
North Carolina	Taxable	
North Dakota	Taxable	Rental is not taxable if the lessor paid tax on the purchase of the property.
Ohio	Taxable	
Oklahoma	Taxable	
Pennsylvania	Taxable	
Rhode Island	Taxable	Lessor may elect to pay tax on cost of property upon acquisition or collect tax on total rental/lease charges.
South Carolina	Taxable	70% of gross proceeds from the rental of portable toilets are exempt.
South Dakota	Taxable	
Tennessee	Taxable	
Texas	Taxable	
Utah	Taxable	
Vermont	Taxable	Rentals of furniture in furnished apartments or houses for residential use are exempt.
Virginia	Taxable	
Washington	Taxable	
West Virginia	Taxable	
Wisconsin	Taxable	
Wyoming	Taxable	

Manufacturing and Machinery—Machinery

The following chart does not include office equipment.

Jurisdiction	Machinery	Comment
Alabama	Taxable	Taxed at a reduced rate.
Arizona	Exempt	Exempt if used directly in manufacturing, processing, fabricating, job printing, refining or metallurgical operations.
Arkansas	Taxable	Exemptions available for certain replacement and repair of machinery and equipment and purchases used in new or expanding facility.
California	Exempt	Operative July 1, 2014, and before July 1, 2030, a partial exemption is applicable to the gross receipts from the sale, storage, use, or other consumption in California of certain qualified tangible personal property, including machinery and equipment, purchased for use by certain qualified persons to be used primarily in any stage of manufacturing, processing, refining, fabricating, or recycling of tangible personal property.
Colorado	Exempt	Purchase must be over $500. Exemption limited to $150,000 for qualifying purchases of used machinery.
Connecticut	Exempt	
District of Columbia	Taxable	
Florida	Exempt	Florida provides an exemption for industrial machinery and equipment purchased by eligible manufacturing businesses. There are also exemptions for industrial M&E used exclusively for spaceport activities or to manufacture, process, compound, or produce tangible personal property for sale (limited to new or expanding businesses), industrial M&E used under federal procurement contracts, and industrial M&E used in semiconductor, defense, or space technology production.
Georgia	Exempt	
Hawaii	Taxable	
Idaho	Exempt	
Illinois	Exempt	
Indiana	Exempt	
Iowa	Exempt	
Kansas	Exempt	
Kentucky	Taxable	Exemption available for purchases used in new and expanded industry. Refund available for purchases of energy-efficiency machinery or equipment used at a Kentucky manufacturing plant for an energy efficiency project.
Louisiana	Exempt	

Jurisdiction	Machinery	Comment
Maine	Exempt	Exemption available for specific activities.
Maryland	Exempt	
Massachusetts	Exempt	
Michigan	Exempt	
Minnesota	Exempt	Capital equipment exemption.
Mississippi	Taxable	Taxed at a reduced rate. Special rate for manufacturing machinery used at refinery.
Missouri	Exempt	
Nebraska	Exempt	Exemption includes repair and replacement parts and purchases of installation, repair, or maintenance services performed on exempt machinery.
Nevada	Taxable	
New Jersey	Exempt	
New Mexico	Taxable	Credit available for certain machinery.
New York	Exempt	
North Carolina	Exempt	Effective July 1, 2018, the privilege tax is repealed and such items are exempt from sales and use tax. Until July 1, 2018, mill machinery and mill machinery parts and accessories are exempt from sales and use tax but are subject to a 1% privilege tax with an $80 cap per article.
North Dakota	Taxable	Exemption available for certain purchases used in new or expanding plant.
Ohio	Exempt	
Oklahoma	Exempt	
Pennsylvania	Exempt	
Rhode Island	Exempt	
South Carolina	Exempt	
South Dakota	Taxable	
Tennessee	Exempt	
Texas	Exempt	
Utah	Exempt	Machinery and equipment that is used to manufacture an item sold as tangible personal property and that has an economic life of three or more years is exempt. Certain machinery and equipment used in the amusement industry.
Vermont	Exempt	
Virginia	Exempt	

Jurisdiction	Machinery	Comment
Washington	Exempt	The exemption does not apply to machinery and equipment primarily used for activities taxable under the state public utility tax.
West Virginia	Exempt	
Wisconsin	Exempt	
Wyoming	Exempt	

Manufacturing and Machinery—Raw Materials

Jurisdiction	Raw Materials	Comment
Alabama	Exempt	Materials that do not become an ingredient or component of manufactured tangible personal property for sale are taxable.
Arizona	Exempt	Tax applies to materials that are consumed but not incorporated into manufactured property. Materials incorporated into manufactured property qualify for resale exemption.
Arkansas	Exempt	Resale exemption applies to materials that do become a recognizable integral part of the product. Other materials are taxable.
California	Exempt	Tax applies to materials that are consumed but not incorporated into manufactured property manufactured.
Colorado	Exempt	Sales of materials that will become ingredients or components of manufactured property are wholesale sales. Materials used as an aid in manufacturing are taxable.
Connecticut	Exempt	Exemption applies to materials that become an ingredient or component of manufactured property or are used directly in an industrial plant in the actual fabrication of finished products to be sold.
District of Columbia	Exempt	Resale exemption applies to materials that will be incorporated into manufactured property. Other materials are taxable.
Florida	Exempt	Materials must become an ingredient component of the finished product.
Georgia	Exempt	
Hawaii	Taxable	Sales to a licensed manufacturer of materials that will be incorporated into a saleable product are taxed at the wholesale rate.
Idaho	Exempt	
Illinois	Exempt	Materials that are consumed but not physically incorporated into manufactured property are taxable.
Indiana	Exempt	
Iowa	Exempt	
Kansas	Exempt	
Kentucky	Exempt	
Louisiana	Exempt	
Maine	Exempt	
Maryland	Exempt	
Massachusetts	Exempt	
Michigan	Exempt	

Jurisdiction	Raw Materials	Comment
Minnesota	Exempt	
Mississippi	Exempt	
Missouri	Exempt	
Nebraska	Exempt	
Nevada	Exempt	
New Jersey	Exempt	Exemption applies to materials that become a component of a product and to essential materials used to cause a chemical or refining process.
New Mexico	Exempt	
New York	Exempt	
North Carolina	Exempt	Materials must become an ingredient or component of manufactured property.
North Dakota	Exempt	
Ohio	Exempt	Exemption applies to materials that are incorporated as components of manufactured property or are consumed directly in producing tangible personal property.
Oklahoma	Exempt	
Pennsylvania	Exempt	Exemption applies to property predominantly used directly in manufacturing. Materials that will be incorporated as ingredients or components of manufactured products qualify for resale exemption.
Rhode Island	Exempt	
South Carolina	Exempt	
South Dakota	Exempt	
Tennessee	Exempt	
Texas	Exempt	Exemption applies to materials that become an ingredient or component of manufactured property. Materials directly consumed in manufacturing are exempt if they are necessary for the operation or cause a chemical or physical change to the product.
Utah	Exempt	
Vermont	Exempt	
Virginia	Exempt	
Washington	Exempt	
West Virginia	Exempt	
Wisconsin	Exempt	
Wyoming	Exempt	

Manufacturing and Machinery—Utilities/Fuel

Jurisdiction	Utilities/Fuel	Comment
Alabama	Taxable	Wood residue, coke, or coal sold to manufacturers, or stored by manufacturers, exempt.
Arizona	Taxable	
Arkansas	Taxable	Natural gas and electricity used by manufacturers directly in manufacturing process or used by certain electric power generators taxed at reduced rate. Natural gas and electricity purchased for use in steel manufacturing or in tile manufacturing tile are exempt.
California	Exempt	Gas, electricity, and water, including steam, geothermal steam, brines, and heat are exempt when delivered to consumers through mains, lines, or pipes. Fuel oil is taxable.
Colorado	Exempt	Temporarily taxable effective March 1, 2010 through June 30, 2012, with exceptions for (1) fuel or energy used for agricultural purposes, railroad transportation services, or the generation of electricity; (2) gas for electricity for residential use, and (3) gasoline and special fuel that is subject to excise tax.
Connecticut	Exempt	Gas, electricity and heating fuel must be used in metered premises and 75% of gas electricity or fuel, or 75% of premises, must be used for manufacturing.
District of Columbia	Exempt	
Florida	Exempt	
Georgia	Taxable	Electricity used directly in manufacture of product is exempt if cost of electricity exceeds 50% of cost of all materials used in product, including electricity. From July 1, 2008, to December 31, 2010, partial exemption applies to certain fuels used in manufacturing or processing tangible personal property for resale.
Hawaii	Taxable	Certain utilities exempt from general excise tax, subject to public service company tax.
Idaho	Exempt	Matter used to produce heat by burning, including wood, coal, petroleum and gas is exempt.
Illinois	Exempt	
Indiana	Exempt	
Iowa	Exempt	
Kansas	Exempt	
Kentucky	Exempt	Energy and energy producing fuels used in manufacturing, processing, refining, or fabricating exempt to the extent that cost of the energy or fuel exceeds 3% of the cost of production.
Louisiana	Taxable	Purchases of business utilities are generally taxable at 2%.
Maine	Exempt	95% of sale price of fuel and electricity used at manufacturing facility exempt.

Jurisdiction	Utilities/Fuel	Comment
Maryland	Exempt	
Massachusetts	Exempt	
Michigan	Exempt	
Minnesota	Exempt	Transportation, transmission, or distribution of certain fuels through pipes, lines, tanks, or mains taxable.
Mississippi	Taxable	Reduced rate applies to electricity, current, power, steam, coal, natural gas, liquefied petroleum gas, or other fuel sold to or used by a qualified technology intensive enterprise. Fuel, electricity, and natural gas used directly in manufacture of motor vehicles exempt. Electricity used directly in electrolysis process in sodium chlorate production exempt. Effective July 1, 2014, exemption allowed for electricity, current, power, steam, coal, natural gas, liquefied petroleum gas, or other fuel sold to certain manufacturers; poultry, livestock, fish, milk, other food producers or processors; and commercial fishermen.
Missouri	Exempt	
Nebraska	Exempt	Electricity, gas, coal, corn and wood used as fuel, fuel oil, diesel fuel, propane, gasoline, coke, nuclear fuel, and butane exempt if more than 50% of amount purchased is used directly in processing, manufacturing, or refining.
Nevada	Taxable	Gas, electricity, and water, when delivered to consumers through mains, lines, or pipes, are exempt. "Domestic fuels," including wood, coal, petroleum, and gas, are exempt. Purchases of tangible personal property that will be incorporated into a manufactured article to be sold are exempt.
New Jersey	Exempt	The purchase of natural gas distributed through a pipeline, electricity, and utility service is taxable.
New Mexico	Exempt	100% of receipts received on or after January 1, 2017, and 80% of receipts received in calendar year 2016.
New York	Exempt	
North Carolina	Exempt	The exemption for electricity sold to a manufacturer is inapplicable to electricity used at a facility at which the primary activity is not manufacturing.
North Dakota	Taxable	Exemptions include natural gas and fuels used for heating purposes, steam used for agricultural processing, electricity, and water.
Ohio	Exempt	
Oklahoma	Exempt	
Pennsylvania	Exempt	Exempt if predominantly used directly in manufacturing or processing operations.
Rhode Island	Exempt	
South Carolina	Exempt	
South Dakota	Taxable	

Jurisdiction	Utilities/Fuel	Comment
Tennessee	Taxable	Effective July 1, 2015, a special user privilege tax is imposed in lieu of sales and use tax. Until July 1, 2015, generally subject to tax at a reduced rate. Certain specified exemptions apply.
Texas	Exempt	Gas and electricity directly used in manufacturing exempt.
Utah	Exempt	
Vermont	Exempt	
Virginia	Exempt	
Washington	Taxable	
West Virginia	Exempt	Gasoline and special fuels taxable.
Wisconsin	Exempt	
Wyoming	Exempt	

Medical Devices

The types of medical devices that are exempt vary greatly from state to state. Some states limit the exemption to prosthetic devices (which replace organic material), while others include durable medical equipment and mobility enhancing equipment in the exemption.

Jurisdiction	Medical Devices	Comment
Alabama	Taxable	Certain devices exempt if payment made by Medicare/Medicaid.
Arizona	Exempt	Prescription required.
Arkansas	Exempt	Prescription required.
California	Exempt	Prescription required.
Colorado	Exempt	If price greater than $100, prescription required.
Connecticut	Exempt	
District of Columbia	Exempt	Prescription required for some devices.
Florida	Exempt	Prescription required.
Georgia	Exempt	Exemptions apply to the sale or use of any durable medical equipment or prosthetic device sold or used pursuant to a prescription, and to the sale or use of all mobility enhancing equipment prescribed by a physician.
Hawaii	Exempt	Prescription required.
Idaho	Exempt	Prescription required.
Illinois	Taxable	Taxed at 1% reduced rate.
Indiana	Exempt	Prescription required.
Iowa	Exempt	Prescription required for some devices.
Kansas	Exempt	Prescription required.
Kentucky	Exempt	Prescription generally required.
Louisiana	Exempt	Prescription required.
Maine	Exempt	
Maryland	Exempt	A prescription is required for certain surgical or orthopedic devices.
Massachusetts	Exempt	Prescription required for some devices.
Michigan	Exempt	Prescription required.
Minnesota	Exempt	Durable medical equipment taxable unless sold for home use or if paid for or reimbursed by Medicare or Medicaid, regardless of whether sold for home use.

Jurisdiction	Medical Devices	Comment
Mississippi	Exempt	Exemptions allowed for durable medical equipment, home medical supplies, prosthetics, orthotics, hearing aids, hearing devices, prescription eyeglasses, oxygen, and oxygen equipment if prescribed and if other requirements are met. Payment not required to be made by any particular person.
Missouri	Exempt	Effective August 28, 2016, all sales, rentals, repairs, and parts of durable medical equipment are also exempt, as well as for parts for certain types of health care related equipment.
Nebraska	Exempt	For mobility enhancing equipment, a prescription is required. For durable medical equipment, home medical supplies, oxygen equipment, and prosthetic devices, a prescription is required and they must be of the type eligible for coverage under the medical assistance program established pursuant to the Medical Assistance Act.
Nevada	Exempt	
New Jersey	Exempt	
New Mexico	Taxable	Exempt only if delivered by a licensed practitioner incidental to the provision of a service and the value of the device is included in the cost of the service.
New York	Exempt	
North Carolina	Exempt	Prescription required for some devices.
North Dakota	Exempt	
Ohio	Exempt	Prescription required. Medical oxygen and medical oxygen-dispensing equipment, not sold for home use, is also exempt when purchased by hospitals, nursing homes, or other medical facilities, regardless of whether the sale is made pursuant to a prescription.
Oklahoma	Taxable	Some devices exempt; others exempt if prescribed and payment made under Medicare/Medicaid.
Pennsylvania	Exempt	
Rhode Island	Exempt	
South Carolina	Exempt	Some devices are exempt only if sold under a prescription.
South Dakota	Exempt	Prescription required.
Tennessee	Exempt	
Texas	Exempt	Prescription required for some devices.

Jurisdiction	Medical Devices	Comment
Utah	Exempt	Prescription required.
Vermont	Exempt	
Virginia	Exempt	
Washington	Taxable	Some devices exempt if sold under prescription.
West Virginia	Exempt	Prescription required.
Wisconsin	Exempt	Durable medical equipment must be for use in a person's home to qualify for exemption.
Wyoming	Exempt	

Medical Services

Jurisdiction	Medical Services	Comment
Alabama	Exempt	
Arizona	Exempt	
Arkansas	Exempt	
California	Exempt	
Colorado	Exempt	
Connecticut	Exempt	
District of Columbia	Exempt	
Florida	Exempt	
Georgia	Exempt	
Hawaii	Taxable	
Idaho	Exempt	
Illinois	Exempt	
Indiana	Exempt	
Iowa	Exempt	
Kansas	Exempt	
Kentucky	Exempt	
Louisiana	Exempt	
Maine	Exempt	
Maryland	Exempt	
Massachusetts	Exempt	
Michigan	Exempt	
Minnesota	Exempt	
Mississippi	Exempt	
Missouri	Exempt	
Nebraska	Exempt	
Nevada	Exempt	
New Jersey	Exempt	

Jurisdiction	Medical Services	Comment
New Mexico	Taxable	Receipts from payments by federal government exempt. Health care practitioners may deduct from gross receipts payments they receive from managed health care providers or health care insurers for commercial contract services or Medicare Part C services provided by a health care practitioner. Receipts from fee-for-service payments by a health care insurer do not qualify.
New York	Exempt	
North Carolina	Exempt	
North Dakota	Exempt	
Ohio	Exempt	
Oklahoma	Exempt	
Pennsylvania	Exempt	
Rhode Island	Exempt	
South Carolina	Exempt	
South Dakota	Exempt	
Tennessee	Exempt	
Texas	Exempt	
Utah	Exempt	
Vermont	Exempt	
Virginia	Exempt	
Washington	Exempt	
West Virginia	Exempt	
Wisconsin	Exempt	
Wyoming	Exempt	

Medicines

In all states except Illinois, prescription medicines are exempt from sales and use taxes. The chart below reflects the taxability of nonprescription medicines.

Jurisdiction	Medicines	Comment
Alabama	Taxable	Prescription medicine is exempt.
Arizona	Taxable	Prescription medicine is exempt.
Arkansas	Taxable	Prescription medicine is exempt.
California	Taxable	Prescription medicine is exempt.
Colorado	Taxable	Prescription medicine is exempt.
Connecticut	Exempt	Prescription medicine is exempt. Applicable April 1, 2015, certain nonprescription drugs or medicines are exempt.
District of Columbia	Exempt	Prescription and nonprescription medicine is exempt.
Florida	Taxable	Prescription medicine is exempt.
Georgia	Taxable	Prescription medicine is exempt. Over-the-counter drugs are taxable even if dispensed under a prescription or purchased on a physician's advice.
Hawaii	Taxable	Prescription medicine is exempt.
Idaho	Taxable	Prescription medicine is exempt.
Illinois	Taxable	Prescription and nonprescription medicine is taxed at a lower rate.
Indiana	Taxable	Prescription medicine is exempt.
Iowa	Taxable	Prescription medicine is exempt.
Kansas	Taxable	Prescription medicine is exempt (excluding that used in the performance or induction of an abortion).
Kentucky	Taxable	Prescription medicine is exempt. Over-the-counter drugs for which a prescription has been issued are exempt.
Louisiana	Taxable	Prescription medicine is exempt.
Maine	Taxable	Prescription medicine is exempt.
Maryland	Exempt	Prescription and nonprescription medicine is exempt.
Massachusetts	Taxable	Prescription medicine is exempt.
Michigan	Taxable	Medicine that can only be legally dispensed by prescription is exempt. The sale of over-the-counter drugs legally dispensed pursuant to a prescription is also exempt.
Minnesota	Exempt	Prescription and nonprescription medicine is exempt.
Mississippi	Taxable	Prescription medicine is exempt.
Missouri	Taxable	Prescription medicine is exempt. Nonprescription drugs purchased/used by disabled persons are also exempt.

Jurisdiction	Medicines	Comment
Nebraska	Taxable	Prescription medicine is exempt.
Nevada	Taxable	Prescription medicine is exempt. Nonprescription medicine is exempt if furnished by medical personnel.
New Jersey	Exempt	Prescription and nonprescription medicine is exempt.
New Mexico	Taxable	Prescription medicine is exempt.
New York	Exempt	Prescription and nonprescription medicine is exempt.
North Carolina	Taxable	Prescription medicine is exempt.
North Dakota	Taxable	Prescription medicine is exempt.
Ohio	Taxable	Prescription medicine is exempt.
Oklahoma	Taxable	Prescription medicine is exempt.
Pennsylvania	Exempt	Prescription and nonprescription medicine is exempt.
Rhode Island	Taxable	Prescription medicine is exempt.
South Carolina	Taxable	Prescription medicine is exempt. Over-the-counter drugs are exempt if sold to health care clinic that provides free medical and dental care to all of its patients. An exemption is available for injectable medicines and biologics.
South Dakota	Taxable	Prescription medicine is exempt. Nonprescription medicine is exempt if furnished by medical personnel.
Tennessee	Taxable	Prescription medicine is exempt.
Texas	Exempt	Prescription medicine is exempt. Nonprescription medicine is exempt if required to be labeled with a "Drug Facts" panel in accordance with FDA regulations.
Utah	Taxable	Prescription medicine is exempt.
Vermont	Exempt	Prescription and nonprescription medicine is exempt.
Virginia	Exempt	Prescription and nonprescription medicine is exempt.
Washington	Taxable	Prescription medicine is exempt. Naturopathic medicines prescribed, dispensed or used by a licensed naturopath in the treatment of a patient are also exempt.
West Virginia	Taxable	Prescription medicine is exempt.
Wisconsin	Taxable	Prescription medicine is exempt. Nonprescription medicine is exempt if furnished by medical personnel.
Wyoming	Taxable	Prescription medicine is exempt.

Newspapers

Jurisdiction	Newspapers	Comment
Alabama	Taxable	
Arizona	Taxable	
Arkansas	Exempt	
California	Taxable	Newspapers published least four times but not more than 60 times per year are exempt if sold by subscription and delivered by mail or common carrier. Certain newspapers published or distributed by exempt organizations are also exempt.
Colorado	Exempt	
Connecticut	Exempt	
District of Columbia	Taxable	
Florida	Taxable	Exempt if sold by subscription and delivered by mail.
Georgia	Taxable	
Hawaii	Taxable	Subscriptions to newspapers issued at least four times per year are exempt from use tax.
Idaho	Taxable	Taxable if the single copy price exceeds 11 cents.
Illinois	Exempt	
Indiana	Exempt	
Iowa	Exempt	
Kansas	Taxable	
Kentucky	Taxable	
Louisiana	Exempt	If distributed at no cost.
Maine	Exempt	Exemption applies to publications issued at least every three months.
Maryland	Taxable	Newspapers distributed by the publisher at no charge are exempt.
Massachusetts	Exempt	
Michigan	Exempt	Exempt if (1) accepted as second class mail or as a controlled circulation publication, (2) qualified to accept legal notices for publication in Michigan, or (3) of general circulation established at least two years and published at least weekly.
Minnesota	Exempt	Exemption applies to publications issued at least every three months.
Mississippi	Exempt	Exemption applies to daily or weekly newspapers.
Missouri	Taxable	
Nebraska	Exempt	Exemption applies to newspapers regularly issued at intervals not exceeding one week.

Jurisdiction	Newspapers	Comment
Nevada	Exempt	Exemption applies to newspapers regularly issued at intervals not exceeding one week.
New Jersey	Exempt	
New Mexico	Exempt	
New York	Exempt	Effective March 1, 2012, electronic news services and electronic periodicals will be exempt.
North Carolina	Taxable	Newspapers sold through a coin-operated vending machine are subject to the general state and applicable local and transit sales and use taxes on 50% of the sales price.
North Dakota	Exempt	
Ohio	Exempt	
Oklahoma	Exempt	
Pennsylvania	Exempt	Exemption applies to newspapers of general circulation qualified to carry legal advertisements.
Rhode Island	Exempt	
South Carolina	Exempt	
South Dakota	Taxable	
Tennessee	Exempt	Exemption applies to newspapers regularly distributed at least twice per month.
Texas	Exempt	
Utah	Exempt	
Vermont	Exempt	
Virginia	Taxable	Exempt if sold by subscription.
Washington	Exempt	The purchase of machinery and equipment used directly in printing newspapers or other materials qualifies for the manufacturing machinery exemption.
West Virginia	Taxable	Exempt if delivered to consumers by route carrier.
Wisconsin	Exempt	
Wyoming	Exempt	

Occasional Sales

Jurisdiction	Occasional Sales	Comment
Alabama	Exempt	Includes exemption provisions for a retailer selling property, if the transaction is not in the regular course of business.
Arizona	Exempt	Includes exemption provisions for a retailer selling property, if the transaction is not in the regular course of business.
Arkansas	Exempt	
California	Exempt	
Colorado	Taxable	
Connecticut	Exempt	Includes exemption provisions for a retailer selling property, if the transaction is not in the regular course of business.
District of Columbia	Exempt	
Florida	Exempt	Includes exemption provisions for a retailer selling property, if the transaction is not in the regular course of business.
Georgia	Exempt	Includes exemption provisions for a retailer selling property, if the transaction is not in the regular course of business.
Hawaii	Exempt	Includes exemption provisions for a retailer selling property, if the transaction is not in the regular course of business.
Idaho	Exempt	
Illinois	Exempt	Includes exemption provisions for a retailer selling property, if the transaction is not in the regular course of business.
Indiana	Exempt	Includes exemption provisions for a retailer selling property, if the transaction is not in the regular course of business.
Iowa	Exempt	Includes exemption provisions for a retailer selling property, if the transaction is not in the regular course of business.
Kansas	Exempt	Includes exemption provisions for a retailer selling property, if the transaction is not in the regular course of business.
Kentucky	Exempt	
Louisiana	Exempt	Includes exemption provisions for a retailer selling property, if the transaction is not in the regular course of business.
Maine	Exempt	Includes exemption provisions for a retailer selling property, if the transaction is not in the regular course of business.
Maryland	Exempt	Exemption applies only if the sale price is less than $1,000 and the sale is not made through an auctioneer or dealer.

Jurisdiction	Occasional Sales	Comment
Massachusetts	Exempt	Includes exemption provisions for a retailer selling property, if the transaction is not in the regular course of business.
Michigan	Exempt	No use tax exemption. Includes exemption provisions for a retailer selling property, if the transaction is not in the regular course of business.
Minnesota	Exempt	Includes exemption provisions for a retailer selling property, if the transaction is not in the regular course of business.
Mississippi	Exempt	
Missouri	Exempt	Exemption does not apply if gross receipts from all such sales in calendar year exceed $3,000. Includes exemption provisions for a retailer selling property, if the transaction is not in the regular course of business.
Nebraska	Exempt	
Nevada	Exempt	
New Jersey	Exempt	
New Mexico	Exempt	Includes exemption provisions for a retailer selling property, if the transaction is not in the regular course of business.
New York	Exempt	Exemption applies only to first $600 of receipts from such sales in calendar year.
North Carolina	Exempt	
North Dakota	Exempt	Includes exemption provisions for a retailer selling property, if the transaction is not in the regular course of business.
Ohio	Exempt	Exemption does not include motor vehicles; watercraft or outboard motors that are required to be titled under Sec. 1548.06, Ohio R.C.; watercraft documented with the U.S. Coast Guard; or snowmobiles or all-purpose vehicles.
Oklahoma	Taxable	
Pennsylvania	Exempt	Includes exemption provisions for a retailer selling property, if the transaction is not in the regular course of business.
Rhode Island	Exempt	Includes exemption provisions for a retailer selling property, if the transaction is not in the regular course of business.
South Carolina	Exempt	
South Dakota	Exempt	
Tennessee	Exempt	Excluded from the definition of "business." Occasional sales of aircraft, motor vehicles, and vessels are taxable.
Texas	Exempt	

Jurisdiction	Occasional Sales	Comment
Utah	Exempt	Includes exemption provisions for a retailer selling property, if the transaction is not in the regular course of business.
Vermont	Exempt	
Virginia	Exempt	Includes exemption provisions for a retailer selling property, if the transaction is not in the regular course of business.
Washington	Exempt	No use tax exemption. Includes exemption provisions for a retailer selling property, if the transaction is not in the regular course of business.
West Virginia	Exempt	Includes exemption provisions for a retailer selling property, if the transaction is not in the regular course of business.
Wisconsin	Exempt	Beginning January 1, 2018, the exemption applies if the seller's total taxable sales price from sales of tangible personal property, other taxable items, or taxable services is less than $2,000 during a calendar year. Before January 1, 2018, the exemption applies to persons not required to hold a seller's permit only if gross receipts for calendar year are less than $1,000 ($1,000 threshold does not apply to nonprofit organizations). A sale of any tangible personal property or taxable services is not considered an occasional sale if at the time of such sale the seller holds or is required to hold a seller's permit. However, a sale of business assets after cessation of business may qualify for exemption.
Wyoming	Taxable	Exemption applies only to occasional sales by religious or charitable organizations.

Occasional Sales of Motor Vehicles

Jurisdiction	Occasional Sales of Motor Vehicles	Comment
Alabama	Exempt	Exempt from general sales/use tax, but subject to separate tax.
Arizona	Exempt	
Arkansas	Taxable	
California	Taxable	Motor vehicle sales specifically excluded from occasional sales exemption. Separate sales tax exemption exists for sales by non-dealers, but purchaser subject to use tax. Use tax exemptions may apply for certain family and/or corporate transfers/ sales.
Colorado	Taxable	
Connecticut	Taxable	Motor vehicle sales specifically excluded from occasional sales exemption. Separate sales tax exemption exists for sales by non-dealers, but purchaser subject to use tax. Use tax exemptions may apply for certain family and/or corporate transfers/ sales.
District of Columbia	Exempt	Exempt from general sales/use tax, but subject to separate tax.
Florida	Taxable	Exemptions may apply for certain family and/or corporate transfers/sales.
Georgia	Exempt	
Hawaii	Exempt	
Idaho	Taxable	Exemptions may apply for certain family and/or corporate transfers/sales.
Illinois	Exempt	Sales by individuals and non-dealers are exempt from retailers' occupation tax and general use tax, but are subject to vehicle use tax.
Indiana	Taxable	Exemptions may apply for certain family and/or corporate transfers/sales.
Iowa	Taxable	Exempt from sales tax, but purchaser subject to use tax. Use tax exemptions may apply for certain family and/or corporate transfers/sales. Motor vehicles sales specifically excluded from occasional sales exemption.
Kansas	Taxable	Exemptions may apply for certain family, corporate, or LLC transfers/sales.
Kentucky	Exempt	Exempt from general sales/use tax, but subject to separate tax.
Louisiana	Taxable	
Maine	Taxable	Exemptions may apply for certain family and/or corporate transfers/sales.
Maryland	Exempt	Exempt from general sales/use tax, but subject to motor vehicle excise tax. Short-term rentals are taxable.

Jurisdiction	Occasional Sales of Motor Vehicles	Comment
Massachusetts	Taxable	Exemptions may apply for certain family and/or corporate transfers/sales.
Michigan	Taxable	Exemptions may apply for certain family and/or corporate transfers/sales.
Minnesota	Exempt	Exempt from general sales/use tax, but subject to separate tax.
Mississippi	Taxable	Effective July 1, 2005, taxed at 5% rate (3% prior to that date). Exemptions may apply for certain family and/or corporate transfers/sales.
Missouri	Taxable	
Nebraska	Taxable	Exemptions may apply for certain corporate transfers/ sales.
Nevada	Taxable	Exemptions may apply for certain family and/or corporate transfers/sales.
New Jersey	Taxable	Exemptions may apply for certain family and/or corporate transfers/sales.
New Mexico	Exempt	Exempt from general sales/use tax, but subject to separate tax.
New York	Taxable	Exemptions may apply for certain family and/or corporate transfers/sales.
North Carolina	Exempt	Exempt from general sales/use tax, but subject to separate tax.
North Dakota	Exempt	Exempt from general sales/use tax, but subject to separate tax.
Ohio	Taxable	
Oklahoma	Taxable	Exempt from general sales/use tax, but subject to vehicle excise tax.
Pennsylvania	Taxable	Exemptions may apply for certain family and/or corporate transfers/sales.
Rhode Island	Taxable	Exemptions may apply for certain family and/or corporate transfers/sales.
South Carolina	Exempt	Exempt from general sales/use tax, but subject to casual excise tax. Exemptions may apply for certain family and/or corporate transfers/sales.
South Dakota	Exempt	Exempt from general sales/use tax, but subject to separate tax.
Tennessee	Taxable	Exemptions may apply for certain family and/or corporate transfers/sales.
Texas	Exempt	Exempt from general sales/use tax, but subject to separate tax.
Utah	Taxable	
Vermont	Exempt	Exempt from general sales/use tax, but subject to separate tax.

Jurisdiction	Occasional Sales of Motor Vehicles	Comment
Virginia	Exempt	Exempt from general sales/use tax, but subject to separate tax.
Washington	Taxable	
West Virginia	Exempt	
Wisconsin	Taxable	Exemptions may apply for certain family and/or corporate transfers/sales.
Wyoming	Taxable	

Optional Maintenance Contracts

Jurisdiction	Optional Maintenance Contracts	Comment
Alabama	Exempt	
Arizona	Exempt	Agreement must be sold as a separate and distinct item and separately stated on sales invoice.
Arkansas	Taxable	
California	Exempt	
Colorado	Exempt	Must be purchased separately.
Connecticut	Taxable	
District of Columbia	Taxable	
Florida	Taxable	
Georgia	Exempt	Charge must be separately stated.
Hawaii	Taxable	Wholesale rate applies to a dealer's furnishing of goods or services to a purchaser of tangible personal property to fulfill a warranty obligation of the manufacturer of the property.
Idaho	Exempt	Charge must be separately stated.
Illinois	Exempt	Charge must be separately stated.
Indiana	Taxable	Maintenance contracts are taxable if there is a reasonable expectation that tangible personal property will be provided.
Iowa	Taxable	
Kansas	Taxable	
Kentucky	Exempt	Exempt if the retailer separately states the charge for the contract in its books and records and on the customer's invoice.
Louisiana	Taxable	
Maine	Exempt	Charge must be separately stated.
Maryland	Exempt	
Massachusetts	Exempt	Charge must be separately stated.
Michigan	Exempt	Charge must be separately stated.
Minnesota	Taxable	Total sales price of optional bundled maintenance contract taxable if the price of the taxable products is more than minimal, but such contracts are not taxable if the price of the taxable products is minimal. For optional unbundled maintenance contracts, only the sales prices of separately stated taxable items are taxable.
Mississippi	Taxable	Motor vehicle service contracts are exempt.
Missouri	Exempt	Charge must be separately stated.

Jurisdiction	Optional Maintenance Contracts	Comment
Nebraska	Taxable	A maintenance agreement is taxable if the property covered or the services provided are taxable. Agreements covering only real estate, fixtures, or structures are exempt.
Nevada	Exempt	Agreement must be billed separately. The value of property transferred in connection with the agreement must not exceed 51% of the cost of the agreement.
New Jersey	Taxable	
New Mexico	Taxable	
New York	Taxable	
North Carolina	Taxable	Optional service contracts are subject to the general rate of tax provided the contracts meet the definition of "service contract." Service contracts on motor vehicles are exempt.
North Dakota	Exempt	Charge must be separately stated.
Ohio	Taxable	
Oklahoma	Exempt	Charge must be separately stated.
Pennsylvania	Taxable	
Rhode Island	Exempt	Charge must be separately stated.
South Carolina	Taxable	Exempt if the property covered by the contract is exempt. Motor vehicle extended service and warranty contracts are exempt. The sale of a warranty, service, or maintenance contract is not taxable if purchased after the purchase of the tangible personal property.
South Dakota	Taxable	
Tennessee	Taxable	
Texas	Taxable	
Utah	Taxable	
Vermont	Exempt	When a contract includes the replacement of parts, the service provider may charge the customer tax at the time the contract is sold or may sell the contract without charging or collecting tax. If tax is charged when the contract is sold, no additional tax should be collected from the customer when repairs are made or property is replaced under the contract. If no tax is charged for a service contract, the service provider must maintain sufficient records to report the parts and supplies used in performing the contract and must remit use tax on all such items.
Virginia	Exempt	Maintenance contracts that provide only repair labor are exempt. Contracts that provide both parts and labor are subject to tax on one-half the total charge for the contract. Contracts that provide parts only are taxable.
Washington	Taxable	

Jurisdiction	Optional Maintenance Contracts	Comment
West Virginia	Taxable	
Wisconsin	Taxable	Exempt if contract relates to exempt items.
Wyoming	Exempt	Charge must be separately stated.

Parts Purchased for Use in Performing Service Under Optional Maintenance Contracts

Jurisdiction	Parts Purchased for Use in Performing Service Under Optional Maintenance Contracts	Comment
Alabama	Taxable	Tax is not due on the purchase of or withdrawal from inventory of parts used in performing services free of charge for a customer under the terms of a manufacturer's extended service contract sold to the customer by the dealer.
Arizona	Taxable	
Arkansas	Exempt	
California	Taxable	
Colorado	Taxable	
Connecticut	Exempt	Repairers are liable for tax on purchases of non-integral parts.
District of Columbia	Taxable	
Florida	Exempt	
Georgia	Taxable	
Hawaii	Taxable	
Idaho	Taxable	
Illinois	Taxable	
Indiana	Exempt	
Iowa	Exempt	
Kansas	Exempt	
Kentucky	Taxable	Taxable to the repairer.
Louisiana	Exempt	
Maine	Taxable	
Maryland	Taxable	Taxable to the repairer. Exempt if a separate charge to the customer is made for the materials.
Massachusetts	Taxable	
Michigan	Taxable	Taxable to the repairer.
Minnesota	Taxable	Parts may be exempt if contract is taxable. For optional unbundled maintenance contracts, only the sales prices of separately stated taxable items are taxable.
Mississippi	Exempt	

Jurisdiction	Parts Purchased for Use in Performing Service Under Optional Maintenance Contracts	Comment
Missouri	Taxable	
Nebraska	Exempt	If the agreement does not provide full coverage, the amount charged for parts is taxable.
Nevada	Taxable	
New Jersey	Exempt	
New Mexico	Exempt	
New York	Exempt	
North Carolina	Taxable	The sale or renewal of a service contract sold at retail is subject to the general state and applicable local and transit sales and use tax rates, regardless of whether the tangible personal property covered in the service contract becomes a part of or is affixed to real property.
North Dakota	Taxable	
Ohio	Exempt	
Oklahoma	Taxable	
Pennsylvania	Exempt	
Rhode Island	Taxable	
South Carolina	Taxable	Parts are exempt if the maintenance contract was given without charge, at the time of original purchase of the defective property, the tax was paid on the sale of the defective part or on the sale of the property of which the defective part was a component, and the warrantee is not charged for any labor or materials. The sale of a warranty, service, or maintenance contract is not taxable if purchased after the purchase of the tangible personal property.
South Dakota	Exempt	
Tennessee	Exempt	
Texas	Exempt	
Utah	Exempt	

Jurisdiction	Parts Purchased for Use in Performing Service Under Optional Maintenance Contracts	Comment
Vermont	Taxable	When a contract includes the replacement of parts, the service provider may charge the customer tax at the time the contract is sold or may sell the contract without charging or collecting tax. If tax is charged when the contract is sold, no additional tax should be collected from the customer when repairs are made or property is replaced under the contract. If no tax is charged for a service contract, the service provider must maintain sufficient records to report the parts and supplies used in performing the contract and must remit use tax on all such items.
Virginia	Exempt	
Washington	Exempt	The obligor must provide a reseller permit to the supplier. If a customer is required to pay an amount for parts not fully covered under an agreement, the additional amount is taxable.
West Virginia	Exempt	
Wisconsin	Exempt	
Wyoming	Taxable	

Periodicals

Jurisdiction	Periodicals	Comment
Alabama	Taxable	
Arizona	Taxable	
Arkansas	Taxable	Exempt if sold by subscription.
California	Taxable	Periodicals issued at least every three months but not more than 60 times per year are exempt if sold by subscription and delivered by mail or common carrier. Certain periodicals published or distributed by exempt organizations are also exempt.
Colorado	Taxable	
Connecticut	Taxable	Exempt if sold by subscription.
District of Columbia	Taxable	
Florida	Taxable	Exempt if sold by subscription and delivered by mail.
Georgia	Taxable	
Hawaii	Taxable	Subscriptions to periodicals issued at least four times per year are exempt from use tax.
Idaho	Taxable	Taxable if the single copy price exceeds 11 cents.
Illinois	Exempt	
Indiana	Taxable	
Iowa	Taxable	
Kansas	Taxable	
Kentucky	Taxable	
Louisiana	Taxable	
Maine	Exempt	Exemption applies to periodicals issued at average intervals not exceeding three months.
Maryland	Taxable	Periodical subscriptions sold by an elementary or secondary school for fundraising purposes are exempt.
Massachusetts	Exempt	
Michigan	Exempt	Publication is exempt if (1) accepted as second class mail or as a controlled circulation publication, (2) qualified to accept legal notices for publication in Michigan, or (3) of general circulation established at least two years and published at least weekly.
Minnesota	Taxable	Exempt if sold by subscription and issued at average intervals not exceeding three months.
Mississippi	Taxable	Certain periodicals of exempt scientific, literary, or educational organizations and subscription sales of all magazines are exempt.
Missouri	Taxable	

Jurisdiction	Periodicals	Comment
Nebraska	Taxable	
Nevada	Taxable	
New Jersey	Exempt	
New Mexico	Taxable	
New York	Exempt	Effective March 1, 2012, electronic news services and electronic periodicals will be exempt.
North Carolina	Taxable	Magazines sold by subscription and delivered by mail are exempt.
North Dakota	Taxable	Periodicals sold by subscription are exempt. Periodicals furnished by a nonprofit organization to its members free or because of membership fees are exempt.
Ohio	Taxable	Exempt if distributed as a controlled circulation publication.
Oklahoma	Exempt	
Pennsylvania	Taxable	Exempt if sold by subscription.
Rhode Island	Taxable	
South Carolina	Taxable	Exempt if used in a course of study in primary and secondary schools and institutions of higher learning or for students' use in the school library or sold to publicly supported state, county, or regional libraries.
South Dakota	Taxable	
Tennessee	Exempt	Exemption applies to periodicals printed entirely on newsprint or bond paper and regularly distributed at least twice monthly. Magazines that are distributed and sold to consumers through U.S. mail or common carrier are exempt if the only activities carried on by the seller or distributor in Tennessee are the printing, storage, labeling, and delivery to the mail or carrier.
Texas	Taxable	Periodical subscriptions sold for a semiannual or longer period and entered as second-class mail are exempt.
Utah	Taxable	
Vermont	Taxable	
Virginia	Taxable	Periodicals sold by subscription are exempt if issued at regular intervals not exceeding three months.
Washington	Taxable	Periodical subscriptions sold for fundraising purposes by educational institutions and certain nonprofit organizations are not taxable. The purchase of machinery and equipment used directly in printing newspapers or other materials qualifies for the manufacturing machinery exemption.
West Virginia	Taxable	

Jurisdiction	Periodicals	Comment
Wisconsin	Exempt	Exemption applies to periodicals sold by subscription and regularly issued at average intervals not exceeding 3 months (6 months by educational associations and certain nonprofit corporations), controlled circulation publications sold to commercial publishers for distribution without charge or mainly without charge or regularly distributed by or on behalf of publishers without charge or mainly without charge to the recipient and of shoppers guides which distribute no less than 48 issues in a 12-month period.
Wyoming	Taxable	

Pollution Control Equipment

The following chart indicates whether a state provides any exemptions for pollution control equipment.

Jurisdiction	Pollution Control Equipment	Comment
Alabama	Yes	Exemption applies to devices and facilities acquired for the reduction of air or water pollution and materials used in structures built primarily to reduce pollution.
Arizona	Yes	Machinery and equipment used to prevent land, water, or air pollution is exempt when purchased by businesses in the following industries: manufacturing, processing, fabricating, job printing, refining, mining, metallurgical operations, telecommunications, electricity production or transmission, and research and development.
Arkansas	Yes	Exemption applies to tangible personal property, including catalysts, chemicals, reagents, and solutions, that are installed and used by manufacturing and processing facilities to prevent or reduce air or water pollution that might result from the operation of the facility.
California	Yes	Exemption applies to transfers between the California Pollution Control Financing Authority and any participating party of title to tangible personal property that constitutes a project or pollution control facility.
Colorado	Yes	A refund is allowed for tax paid on pollution control equipment during the state fiscal year if state revenues for the fiscal year exceed a certain threshold.
Connecticut	Yes	Exemptions apply to tangible personal property incorporated into or used in the operation of industrial waste treatment or air pollution control facilities, any project of the Connecticut Resources Recovery Authority, and facilities that convert solid waste into energy.
District of Columbia	No	
Florida	Yes	Exemption applies to any facility, device, fixture, equipment, machinery, specialty chemical, or bioaugmentation product used primarily for the control or abatement of pollution or contaminants in manufacturing, processing, compounding, or producing for sale items of tangible personal property at a fixed location.
Georgia	Yes	Exemptions apply to machinery and equipment (and related machinery and equipment repair, replacement, and component parts) used primarily for reducing or eliminating air or water pollution; machinery incorporated into a water conservation facility; and machinery and equipment for use in combating air and water pollution and any industrial material bought for further processing in the manufacture of tangible personal property for sale or any part of the industrial material or by-product which becomes a wasteful product contributing to pollution problems and which is used up in a recycling or burning process.

Jurisdiction	Pollution Control Equipment	Comment
Hawaii	Yes	Exemptions apply to tangible personal property furnished for the construction, reconstruction, erection, operation, use, maintenance, or furnishing of an air pollution control facility and to all of the gross proceeds arising from an air pollution control facility.
Idaho	Yes	Exemption applies to pollution control equipment required to meet state or federal air and water quality standards. Effective July 1, 2007, exemption applies to tangible personal property acquired and primarily used for the purpose of meeting air or water quality standards, rules, or regulations of a state or federal agency.
Illinois	Yes	Exemption applies to low sulfur dioxide emission coal fueled devices.
Indiana	Yes	Exemption applies to tangible personal property acquired by a person engaged in the business of manufacturing, processing, refining, mining, or agriculture if the property constitutes, is incorporated into, or is consumed in the operation of a device, facility, or structure predominantly used and acquired for the purpose of complying with any state, local, or federal environmental quality statutes, regulations, or standards.
Iowa	Yes	Exemption applies to air and water pollution control equipment used by a manufacturer.
Kansas	Yes	Machinery and equipment qualify for the manufacturing for resale exemption when used to control pollution at a plant or facility where pollution is produced by the manufacturing or processing operation.
Kentucky	Yes	Through December 31, 2030, an exemption applies to the sale, rental, storage, use, or other consumption of tangible personal property used to construct, repair, renovate, or upgrade a coal-based near zero emission power plant. Prior to July 1, 2018, an exemption applied to property certified as a pollution control facility.
Louisiana	Yes	Certain equipment is taxable. The Louisiana Department of Revenue issued tables of rates and exemptions effective July 1, 2018 through June 30, 2025 listing exemptions and applicable rates.
Maine	Yes	Exemption applies to sale of an air or water pollution control facility, including parts, accessories, and materials for the construction, repair or maintenance of the facility.
Maryland	Yes	Exemption applies to an item required to conform to air or water pollution laws and normally considered part of real property.
Massachusetts	No	
Michigan	Yes	Exemption applies to property installed as a component part of an air or water pollution control facility.

Jurisdiction	Pollution Control Equipment	Comment
Minnesota	Yes	Exemptions apply to pollution control equipment purchased by a steel reprocessing firm if necessary to meet state or federal emission standards; equipment for processing solid or hazardous waste at a resource recovery facility; and materials, supplies, and equipment for the construction, improvement, or expansion of a waste-to energy resource recovery facility if the facility uses biomass or mixed municipal solid waste as a primary fuel to generate steam or electricity.
Mississippi	Exempt	Exemption applies to qualifying pollution control equipment sold to manufacturers or custom processors for industrial use.
Missouri	Exempt	Exemption applies to machinery, equipment, appliances, and devices used solely for preventing, abating, or monitoring air or water pollution and to materials and supplies required for the installation, construction, or reconstruction of such equipment.
Nebraska	Yes	A refund is allowed for tax paid on purchases of tangible personal property incorporated into an air or water pollution control facility.
Nevada	No	
New Jersey	Yes	New Jersey provides exemptions for equipment used to treat effluent from primary wastewater treatment facilities; recycling equipment; and zero-emission vehicles.
New Mexico	No	
New York	Yes	Exemption applies to machinery and equipment used for disposing of industrial waste as a part of a process for preventing water or air pollution if purchased by a manufacturer and used predominantly to actually treat, bury, or store waste materials from a production process, and if over 50% of the waste treated, buried or stored results from the production process.
North Carolina	Yes	Sales of pollution abatement equipment and chemicals to manufacturers are exempt from sales and use tax but are, until July 1, 2018, subject to a 1% privilege tax. As of that date, the privilege tax is repealed and the items remain exempt from sales and use tax.
North Dakota	Yes	Exemptions apply to environmental upgrade equipment used in qualifying power plants, oil refineries, and gas processing plants; and machinery and equipment purchased for use in a new or expanded recycling facility.
Ohio	Yes	Exemption applies to materials or parts incorporated into a certified air, noise, or industrial water pollution control facility.
Oklahoma	Yes	Exemption applies to machinery, equipment, fuels, and chemicals incorporated into and directly used or consumed in the process of treatment to substantially reduce the volume or harmful properties of hazardous waste at treatment facilities specifically permitted by the Hazardous Waste Management Act.

Jurisdiction	Pollution Control Equipment	Comment
Pennsylvania	Yes	Exemption applies to machinery, equipment, and supplies used to control, abate, or prevent air, water, or noise pollution generated in a manufacturing, processing, mining, or public utility operation.
Rhode Island	Yes	Exemptions apply to tangible personal property incorporated into or used and consumed in the operation of an air or water pollution control facility; and to tangible personal property used or consumed in the operation of equipment, the exclusive function of which is the recycling, reuse, or recovery of materials from the treatment of hazardous waste generated by the taxpayer.
South Carolina	Yes	Exemption applies to machines necessary to comply with a federal or South Carolina agency's order for the prevention or abatement of air, water, or noise pollution caused or threatened by any machine used in manufacturing, processing, recycling, compounding, mining, or quarrying tangible personal property for sale.
South Dakota	No	
Tennessee	Exempt	Exemptions apply to any system used primarily to eliminate, prevent, or reduce air or water pollution or to treat or recycle hazardous waste; and chemicals and supplies used in a pollution control facility.
Texas	Yes	Exemptions apply to offshore spill response containment property and to repair, remodeling, and restoration services performed on personal property if required by law to protect the environment.
Utah	Yes	Exemption applies to property, materials, or services used in the construction of or installed in certified pollution control facilities.
Vermont	No	
Virginia	Yes	Exemption applies to pollution control equipment and facilities that have been certified by the Department of Taxation as having been constructed, reconstructed, erected, or acquired in conformity with the state program or requirements for the abatement or control of water or air pollution.
Washington	Yes	Exemptions apply to pollution control equipment installed and used in a manufacturing, testing, or research and development operation to prevent air or water pollution or contamination that might otherwise result from the operation; and tangible personal property, labor and services used in the construction or installation of air pollution control facilities at a thermal electric generation facility.
West Virginia	Yes	Exemption applies to sales of tangible personal property or services to persons engaged in the business of manufacturing, transportation, transmission, communication, or the production of natural resources and used in pollution control or environmental quality or protection activity directly relating to the activity of manufacturing, transportation, communication, transmission, or the production of natural resources.

Jurisdiction	Pollution Control Equipment	Comment
Wisconsin	Yes	Exemptions available for vehicles used for waste reduction, certain waste treatment facility property, waste reduction and recycling equipment, biomass used for fuel sold for residential use, and wind-, solar-, and certain gas-powered products.
Wyoming	No	

Resale Certificate Validity Periods

Jurisdiction	Resale Certificate Validity Periods	Comment
Alabama	Resale certificates not required.	
Arizona	Valid for the period set out on certificate.	
Arkansas	No stated expiration period.	
California	Valid until revoked in writing by the issuer.	
Colorado	Colorado does not have an official resale certificate form.	
Connecticut	Must be renewed every three years from the date it was issued.	A resale certificate may be issued for one purchase or may be issued as a blanket certificate for a continuing line of purchases. To use a resale certificate for a continuing line of purchases, the purchaser must mark the certificate a "Blanket Certificate." The certificate must be renewed at least every three years from the date it is issued.
District of Columbia	One year	
Florida	Annual resale certificates are issued each year.	Annual resale certificates expire each year on December 31. Active and registered dealers automatically receive a new Florida Annual Resale Certificate for Sales Tax (Form DR-13) every year.
Georgia	Until revoked in writing.	
Hawaii	Until revoked in writing.	
Idaho	No stated expiration period.	
Illinois	Valid indefinitely, but should be updated at least every three years.	
Indiana	Does not expire.	
Iowa	Certificate valid for up to 3 years.	
Kansas	The resale certificate is valid provided there is a recurring business relationship between the buyer and seller of no more than 12 months elapsing between sales.	
Kentucky	Valid provided there is no change in the character of the purchaser's operation and the purchases are of tangible personal property of the kind usually purchased by the purchaser for resale.	
Louisiana	Valid for the period indicated on the certificate.	Sale for resale exemption certificates automatically renewed for up to three years unless taxpayer no longer qualified for the exemption.

Jurisdiction	Resale Certificate Validity Periods	Comment
Maine	Valid for five years.	Provisional resale certificates issued between January 1st and September 30th effective for the duration of the calendar year in which it is issued and for the two subsequent calendar years. Provisional resale certificates issued between October 1st and December 31st effective until the end of the third succeeding calendar year. Beginning September 14, 2013, the assessor will issue a resale certificate to the retailer effective for five calendar years if certain conditions are met. Before September 14, 2013, the Assessor will issue a resale certificate, on or before the expiration date, effective for the next three calendar years. Any subsequent annual resale certificate issued effective for the next five calendar years.
Maryland	Valid until revoked by either taxpayer or Comptroller.	
Massachusetts	No stated expiration period.	
Michigan	Expires after four years unless shorter period agreed to.	Renewal of a blanket exemption certificate is not required if there is a recurring business relationship between buyer and seller. A "recurring business relationship" exists when a period of not more than 12 months elapses between sales transactions.
Minnesota	Does not expire unless information changes; should be updated every three to five years.	
Mississippi	No stated expiration period. Contractor's Material Purchase Certificate is valid for the job identified on the certificate.	Seller must obtain and maintain adequate records to substantiate resale exemption.
Missouri	Valid as long as no change in character of purchaser's operation, and the purchases are of tangible personal property or taxable services of a sort that the purchaser usually purchases for resale.	
Nebraska	Valid indefinitely.	A blanket resale certificate remains valid if sales occur between the seller and purchaser at least once every 12 months.
Nevada	Valid until revoked in writing.	Department recommends updating every two to three years.
New Jersey	No stated expiration period.	Division of Taxation recommends that a seller request a new certificate from a buyer every few years.
New Mexico	New Mexico resale certificates have no stated expiration period.	

Jurisdiction	Resale Certificate Validity Periods	Comment
New York	No stated expiration period.	Must be delivered to vendor within 90 days of transaction and be properly completed (all required entries were made).
North Carolina	Blanket certificate remains valid provided purchaser is making recurring purchases.	If single purchase box is not checked on Form E-595E indicating certificate is being used for a single purchase, certificate will be treated as a blanket certificate. A blanket certificate continues in force as long as the purchaser is making recurring purchases (i.e., at least one purchase within a period of 12 consecutive months) or until it is otherwise canceled by the purchaser.
North Dakota	New certificate should be taken every two years.	
Ohio	No stated expiration period.	
Oklahoma	Blanket certificates are valid provided there is a recurring business relationship between the buyer and seller of no more than 12 months elapsing between sales.	
Pennsylvania	No expiration date.	Sales tax license must be renewed every five years.
Rhode Island	Resale certificates have no stated expiration period.	
South Carolina	Valid until cancelled or revoked in writing.	
South Dakota	New certificate should be requested each year.	
Tennessee	Valid until revoked writing by the purchaser.	
Texas	No stated expiration period.	
Utah	Valid indefinitely.	Department recommends updating every year.
Vermont	Valid indefinitely.	
Virginia	Valid until notice from Department of Taxation that certificate is no longer acceptable or is revoked.	

Jurisdiction	Resale Certificate Validity Periods	Comment
Washington	Permits issued to other qualifying businesses are valid for a period of 48 months. A reseller permit issued to a business with limited contacts with the Department of Revenue is valid for 24 months. Reseller permits issued to qualifying contractors after July 1, 2013 will be valid for 24 months. As of July 1, 2011, the department may issue, renew, or reinstate permits to contractors for a period of 24 months if it is satisfied that the contractor is entitled to make wholesale purchases.	Resale certificates have been replaced by Department-issued reseller permits.
West Virginia	Blanket certificates are effective so long as the purchaser makes at least one purchase within a period of 12 consecutive months, or until the certificate is otherwise cancelled by the purchaser.	
Wisconsin	Valid indefinitely, but should be reviewed periodically.	
Wyoming	No stated expiration period.	

Return Due Dates

This chart lists sales and use tax return due dates.

Jurisdiction	Return Due Dates	Comment
Alabama	20th of month following reporting period.	
Arizona	20th of month following reporting period.	
Arkansas	20th of month following reporting period.	
California	Last day of month following reporting period.	
Colorado	20th of month following reporting period.	If taxpayer's accounting period does not end on the last day of the month, return is due on 20th day following the last day of the accounting period.
Connecticut	Last day of the month following the end of the applicable monthly, quarterly, or annual period.	Effective October 1, 2015, and applicable to periods ending on or after December 31, 2015, the deadline for remittance of sales and use taxes and the filing of returns is the last day of the month following the applicable monthly, quarterly, or annual period.
District of Columbia	20th of month following reporting period.	
Florida	20th of month following reporting period.	
Georgia	20th of month following reporting period.	
Hawaii	General excise tax and use tax return due 20th day of month following reporting period.	
Idaho	20th of month following reporting period.	
Illinois	20th of month following reporting period.	
Indiana	Monthly filers: (1) 20th of month following reporting period if average monthly sales and use tax liability in preceding year exceeded $1,000, or if filing combined sales/withholding tax return and withholding tax return is due by 20th; (2) 30th of month following reporting period if average monthly sales and use liability in preceding year did not exceed $1,000. Annual filers: last day of month following reporting period.	
Iowa	Last day of month following reporting period.	
Kansas	25th of month following reporting period.	
Kentucky	20th of month following reporting period.	If the average monthly tax liability exceeds $10,000, the due date is the 25th day of the current month for the period from the 16th of preceding month through the 15th of current month.
Louisiana	20th of month following reporting period.	

Jurisdiction	Return Due Dates	Comment
Maine	15th of month following reporting period.	
Maryland	20th of month following reporting period.	
Massachusetts	20th of month following reporting period.	
Michigan	20th of month following reporting period.	Due to COVID-19, returns and payments due March 20, 2020, April 20, 2020, and May 20, 2020 may be submitted to the department by June 20, 2020, without penalty or interest.
Minnesota	20th of month following reporting period.	
Mississippi	Monthly, quarterly filers: 20th of month following reporting period. 4-week accounting period filers: 20th day following end of reporting period.	
Missouri	Monthly filers: 20th of month following reporting period. Quarterly, annual filers: last day of month following reporting period.	
Nebraska	20th of month following reporting period.	
Nevada	Last day of month following reporting period.	
New Jersey	20th of month following reporting period.	
New Mexico	25th of month following reporting period.	
New York	Monthly filers: 20th of month following reporting period. Quarterly filers: last day of month following reporting period.	
North Carolina	Monthly filers: 20th of month following reporting period. Quarterly filers: last day of month following quarter.	
North Dakota	Last day of month following quarter.	
Ohio	23rd of month following reporting period.	
Oklahoma	20th of month following reporting period.	
Pennsylvania	20th of month following reporting period.	
Rhode Island	Monthly filers: 20th of month following reporting period. Quarterly filers: last day of month following reporting period.	
South Carolina	20th of month following reporting period.	Taxpayers affected by COVID-19 may file returns due between April 1, 2020 and June 1, 2020 by June 1, 2020.
South Dakota	20th of month following reporting period. EFT remitters: 23rd of month following reporting period.	
Tennessee	20th of month following reporting period.	

Jurisdiction	Return Due Dates	Comment
Texas	20th of month following reporting period.	
Utah	Last day of month following reporting period.	
Vermont	25th (23rd of February) of month following reporting period.	
Virginia	20th of month following reporting period.	As a result of COVID-19, the Department of Revenue will consider requests from sales tax dealers for an extension of the due date for filing and payment of the February 2020 sales tax return due March 20, 2020. If the request is granted, the Department will allow filing and payment of such return on April 20, 2020 with a waiver of any penalties that would have applied.
Washington	Monthly filers: 25th of month following reporting period. Other filing periods: last day of month following reporting period.	Due date for annual filers is April 15. From February 29, 2020 through the end of the state of emergency, the department will provide the following payment extension (upon request): 60 days for monthly filers. The due date for the first quarterly return is extended to June 30, 2020. The due date for annual filers is extended to June 15, 2020.
West Virginia	20th of month following reporting period.	
Wisconsin	Last day of month following reporting period.	20th of month following reporting period if sales and use tax liability exceeds $3,600 per quarter and Department of Revenue provides written notice of earlier due date.
Wyoming	Last day of month following reporting period.	

Sales for Resale

The following chart indicates whether a state accepts the Multistate Tax Commission Uniform Multijurisdiction Exemption Certificate (MTC) and/or the Border States Uniform Sales for Resale Certificate (BSC) and any limitations on acceptance.

Jurisdiction	Multistate Certificates	Comment
Alabama	MTC	Retailer remains responsible to determine validity of exemption claim.
Arizona	BSC, MTC	May only be used for sales for resale.
Arkansas	MTC	
California	BSC, MTC	May only be used for sales for resale.
Colorado	MTC	May not be used for sales for resale of taxable services.
Connecticut	MTC	May only be used for sales for resale.
District of Columbia	No	
Florida	MTC	May only be used for sales for resale; must include purchaser's Florida tax registration number and registration date.
Georgia	MTC	The purchaser's state of registration number will be accepted in lieu of Georgia's registration number when the purchaser is located outside Georgia, does not have nexus with Georgia, and the tangible personal property is delivered by drop shipment to the purchaser's customer located in Georgia.
Hawaii	MTC	May not be used for sales for resale of taxable services. May be used by seller to claim either lower tax rate or no tax.
Idaho	MTC	
Illinois	MTC	May not be used for sales for resale of taxable services or for subsequent lease. Illinois registration or resale number must be included.
Indiana	No	
Iowa	MTC	
Kansas	MTC	
Kentucky	MTC	(1) Kentucky does not permit the use of the certificate to claim a resale exclusion for the purchase of a taxable service. (2) The certificate is not valid as an exemption certificate. Its use is limited to use as a resale certificate subject to the provisions of Ky. Rev. Stat. Ann. § 139.270 (Good Faith). (3) The use of the certificate by the purchaser constitutes the issuance of a blanket certificate in accordance with Ky. Admin. Reg. 103 § 31:111.
Louisiana	No	
Maine	MTC	May not be used for sales for subsequent lease.

Jurisdiction	Multistate Certificates	Comment
Maryland	MTC	Vendors may accept resale certificates that bear the exemption number issued to a religious organization.
Massachusetts	No	
Michigan	MTC	Effective for four years unless shorter period agreed to and stated on certificate.
Minnesota	MTC	May not be used for sales for resale of taxable services in most situations. May be used for items to be used only once in production and never again.
Mississippi	No	
Missouri	MTC	Improper use of certificate may subject purchaser to tax, penalty, and interest. Delivery outside of state may still subject transaction to Missouri tax.
Nebraska	MTC	Blanket certificate valid for three years.
Nevada	MTC	
New Jersey	MTC	
New Mexico	BSC, MTC	May not be used for sales for resale of taxable services. May be used for sales for resale and purchases for ingredients or components if certificate not issued in state and buyer not required to be registered in state.
New York	No	
North Carolina	MTC	May only be used for sales for resale, except may not be used by contractors who intend to use the property.
North Dakota	MTC	
Ohio	MTC	Buyer must specify reason for exemption and deliver certificate before or during return period for filing returns.
Oklahoma	MTC	Oklahoma allows this certificate in lieu of a copy of the purchaser's sales tax permit as one of the elements of "properly completed documents," which is one of the three requirements that must be met prior to a vendor being relieved of liability. The other two requirements are that the vendor must have the certificate in his possession at the time the sale is made, and must accept the documentation required under Okla. Admin. Code § 710:65-7-6 in good faith. Absent strict compliance with these requirements, Oklahoma holds a seller liable for sales tax due on sales where the claimed exemption is found to be invalid, for whatever reason, unless the Oklahoma Tax Commission determines that the purchaser should be pursued for collection of the tax resulting from improper presentation of a certificate.
Pennsylvania	MTC	May only be used for sales for resale; must include purchaser's Pennsylvania license number.
Rhode Island	MTC	May only be used for sales for resale, where property will be resold in same form.
South Carolina	MTC	

Jurisdiction	Multistate Certificates	Comment
South Dakota	MTC	May be used for sales of services for resale if not used by purchaser and delivered or resold to current customer without alteration.
Tennessee	MTC	
Texas	BSC, MTC	Resale of items must be within the geographical limits of the U.S. (and its territories or possession).
Utah	MTC	
Vermont	MTC	
Virginia	No	
Washington	MTC	May be used for sales of chemicals to be used in processing. Must be renewed at least every four years.
West Virginia	No	
Wisconsin	MTC	May only be used for sales for resale.
Wyoming	No	

Sales Tax Holiday

The following chart indicates whether a state authorizes a sales tax holiday during the year

Jurisdiction	Sales Tax Holidays - 2020	Comment
Alabama	Yes	July 17-19: clothing (not accessories or protective or recreational equipment) with sales price of $100 or less per item; single purchases, with a sales price of $750 or less, of computers, computer software, school computer equipment; noncommercial purchases of school supplies, school art supplies, and school instructional materials with sales price of $50 or less per item; noncommercial book purchases with sales price of $30 of less per book. February 21-23: severe weather preparedness items that cost $60 or less, except for portable generators and power cords used to provide light or communications or preserve food in the event of a power outage, which are covered as long as they cost $1,000 or less.
Arizona	No	
Arkansas	Yes	Aug. 1-2: clothing items under $100, clothing accessory or equipment under $50, school art supply, school instructional material, and school supply.
California	No	
Colorado	No	
Connecticut	Yes	August 16-22: clothing and footwear (not athletic or protective clothing or footwear, jewelry, handbags, luggage, umbrellas, wallets, watches, and similar items) that cost less than $100 per item.
District of Columbia	No	
Florida	Yes	May 29-June 4: specified disaster preparedness items. August 7-9: clothing, footwear, wallets, and bags that cost $60 or less, school supplies that cost $15 or less, and on the first $1,000 of the sales price of personal computers and related accessories purchased for noncommercial home or personal use. Neither holiday applies to sales made in a theme park, entertainment complex, public lodging establishment, or airport.
Georgia	No	
Hawaii	No	
Idaho	No	
Illinois	No	
Indiana	No	
Iowa	Yes	August 7-8: clothing and footwear (not accessories, rentals, athletic or protective) with sales price of less than $100 per item.
Kansas	No	
Kentucky	No	

Jurisdiction	Sales Tax Holidays - 2020	Comment
Louisiana	November 20 and 21.	First $2,500 of consumer purchases for recover from Hurricanes Laura and Delta and COVID-19.
Maine	No	
Maryland	Yes	February 15-17: Energy Star products and solar water heaters. August 9-15: Items of clothing (not accessories) and footwear with a taxable price of $100 or less.
Massachusetts	Yes	
Michigan	No	
Minnesota	No	
Mississippi	Yes	July 24-25: Clothing or footwear (not accessories, rentals, or skis, swim fins, or skates) with sales price under $100 per item. Aug 28-30: Firearms, ammunition, and hunting supplies, including archery equipment
Missouri	Yes	August 7-9: noncommercial purchases of clothing (not accessories) with taxable value of $100 or less per item; school supplies up to $50 per purchase; computer software with taxable value of $350 or less; personal computers and computer peripherals up to $1,500; and graphing calculators with a taxable value of $150 or less. Localities may opt out. If less than 2% of retailer's merchandise qualifies, retailer must offer a tax refund in lieu of tax holiday. April 19-25: Retail sales of Energy Star certified new appliances of up to $1,500 per appliance.
Nebraska	No	
Nevada	No	
New Jersey	No	
New Mexico	Yes	August 7-9: footwear and clothing (not accessories or athletic or protective clothing) with sales price of less than $100 per item; school supplies with sales price of less than $30 per item; computers with sales price of $1,000 or less per item; computer peripherals with sales price of $500 or less per item; book bags, backpacks, maps and globes with sales price less than $100 per item; and handheld calculators with sales price of less than $200 per item. Retailers are not required to participate.
New York	No	Items of clothing and footwear sold for less than $110 are exempt from the state's sales and use tax.
North Carolina	No	
North Dakota	No	
Ohio	Yes	August 7-9. The following items will be exempt: school supplies with a price of $20 or less, clothing with a price of $75 or less, and school instructional materials with a price of $20 or less.

Jurisdiction	Sales Tax Holidays - 2020	Comment
Oklahoma	Yes	August 7-9. Applies to the sale of any article of clothing or footwear (excluding accessories, rentals, and athletic or protective clothing) that is designed to be worn on or about the human body and that has a sales price of less than $100.
Pennsylvania	No	
Rhode Island	No	
South Carolina	Yes	August 7-9: clothing (not rentals), clothing accessories, footwear, school supplies, computers, printers, printer supplies, computer software, bath wash clothes, bed linens, pillows, bath towels, shower curtains, bath rugs.
South Dakota	No	
Tennessee	Yes	July 31-August 2: the following items are exempt from sales or use tax: (1) clothing (not accessories), school supplies, and school art supplies with sales price of $200 or less per item; and (2) electronic devices with sales price of $3,000 or less per item. This is a one-time holiday held during 2020 only. August 7-9: food and drink sold by restaurants and limited service restaurants is exempt from sales tax. This is a one-time holiday held during 2020 only.

Jurisdiction	Sales Tax Holidays - 2020	Comment
Texas	Yes	April 25-27: Emergency preparation items: (i) a portable generator used to provide light or communications or to preserve perishable food in the event of a power outage, provided the sales price of the generator is less than $3,000; (ii) a storm protection device manufactured, rated, and marketed specifically to prevent damage to a glazed or non-glazed opening during a storm or an emergency or rescue ladder, provided that the sales price of the device or ladder is less than $300; or (iii) a reusable or artificial ice product; a portable, self-powered light source; a gasoline or diesel fuel container; a AAA cell, AA cell, C cell, D cell, 6 volt, or 9 volt battery, or a package containing more than one battery, other than an automobile or boat battery; a nonelectric cooler or ice chest for food storage; a tarpaulin or other flexible waterproof sheeting; a ground anchor system or tie-down kit; a mobile telephone battery or battery charger; a portable self-powered radio, including a two-way radio or weatherband radio; a fire extinguisher, smoke detector, or carbon monoxide detector; a hatchet or axe; a self-contained first aid kit; or a nonelectric can opener, provided that the sales price of the item listed in (3) is less than $75. May 23-25: the following Energy Star products: air conditioners (sales price up to $6,000), clothes washers, ceiling fans, dehumidifiers, dishwashers, incandescent or fluorescent lightbulbs, programmable thermostats, and refrigerators (sales price up to $2,000). Aug 7-9: clothing and footwear (not accessories, athletic, protective, or rentals), school supplies, and school backpacks with sales price of less than $100 per item. April 28-30: emergency preparation items: (i) a portable generator used to provide light or communications or to preserve perishable food in the event of a power outage, provided the sales price of the generator is less than $3,000; (ii) a storm protection device manufactured, rated, and marketed specifically to prevent damage to a glazed or non-glazed opening during a storm or an emergency or rescue ladder, provided that the sales price of the device or ladder is less than $300; or (iii) a reusable or artificial ice product; a portable, self-powered light source; a gasoline or diesel fuel container; a AAA cell, AA cell, C cell, D cell, 6 volt, or 9 volt battery, or a package containing more than one battery, other than an automobile or boat battery; a nonelectric cooler or ice chest for food storage; a tarpaulin or other flexible waterproof sheeting; a ground anchor system or tie-down kit; a mobile telephone battery or battery charger; a portable self-powered radio, including a two-way radio or weatherband radio; a fire extinguisher, smoke detector, or carbon monoxide detector; a hatchet or axe; a self-contained first aid kit; or a nonelectric can opener, provided that the sales price of the item listed in (3) is less than $75.
Utah	No	
Vermont	No	

Jurisdiction	Sales Tax Holidays - 2020	Comment
Virginia	Yes	August 7-9: Combined annual tax holiday for school supplies and clothing, Energy Star and WaterSense products, and hurricane preparedness items. School supplies and clothing: clothing and footwear with selling price of $100 or less per item, and school supplies with selling price of $20 or less per item. Energy Star and WaterSense: noncommercial purchases of Energy Star and WaterSense qualified products with a sales price of $2,500 or less per item. Hurricane preparedness: portable generators with selling price of $1,000 or less, gas-powered chain saws with a sales price of $350 or less, chainsaw accessories with a sales price of $60 or less per item, and other hurricane preparedness items with selling price of $60 or less.
Washington	No	
West Virginia	No	Effective July 1, 2021, certain back-to-school items are exempt from West Virginia consumers sales, service, and use tax if the sale or purchase occurs on: the first Sunday of August; or the previous Friday and Saturday; or the following Monday.
Wisconsin	No	
Wyoming	No	

Services—Generally

This chart indicates whether services are subject to sales and use tax.

Jurisdiction	Services Generally	Comment
Alabama	Services are generally not taxable.	
Arizona	Specified services are taxable.	
Arkansas	Specified services are taxable.	
California	Services are generally not taxable.	
Colorado	Specified services are taxable.	
Connecticut	Specified services are taxable.	
District of Columbia	Specified services are taxable.	
Florida	Specified services are taxable.	
Georgia	Specified services are taxable.	
Hawaii	Services are taxable unless specifically exempted.	
Idaho	Specified services are taxable.	
Illinois	Services are generally not taxable.	Service Occupation Tax (SOT) is imposed on tangible personal property that is transferred incidental to a service transaction.
Indiana	Services are generally not taxable.	
Iowa	Specified services are taxable.	
Kansas	Specified services are taxable.	
Kentucky	Specified services are taxable.	
Louisiana	Specified services are taxable.	
Maine	Specified services are taxable.	
Maryland	Specified services are taxable.	
Massachusetts	Specified services are taxable.	
Michigan	Specified services are taxable.	
Minnesota	Specified services are taxable.	
Mississippi	Specified services are taxable.	
Missouri	Specified services are taxable.	
Nebraska	Specified services are taxable.	
Nevada	Specified services are taxable.	
New Jersey	Specified services are taxable.	
New Mexico	Services are taxable unless specifically exempted.	

Jurisdiction	Services Generally	Comment
New York	Specified services are taxable.	
North Carolina	Specified services are taxable.	
North Dakota	Specified services are taxable.	
Ohio	Specified services are taxable.	
Oklahoma	Specified services are taxable.	
Pennsylvania	Specified services are taxable.	
Rhode Island	Specified services are taxable.	
South Carolina	Specified services are taxable.	
South Dakota	Services are taxable unless specifically exempted.	
Tennessee	Specified services are taxable.	
Texas	Specified services are taxable.	
Utah	Specified services are taxable.	
Vermont	Specified services are taxable.	
Virginia	Specified services are taxable.	
Washington	Specified services are taxable.	
West Virginia	Taxable	Services are taxable unless specifically exempted.
Wisconsin	Specified services are taxable.	
Wyoming	Specified services are taxable.	

Services—Janitorial

The following chart indicates the taxability of janitorial services. Where a state's treatment of services that might be considered janitorial differs from the general treatment, it is noted in the Comments column.

Jurisdiction	Janitorial	Comment
Alabama	Exempt	
Arizona	Exempt	
Arkansas	Taxable	
California	Exempt	
Colorado	Exempt	
Connecticut	Taxable	Janitorial or maintenance services performed on a casual-sale basis are not taxable. Janitorial services for the disabled may be exempt.
District of Columbia	Taxable	
Florida	Taxable	Nonresidential cleaning services, including janitorial services on a contract or fee basis, are taxable. Residential cleaning services are exempt.
Georgia	Exempt	Not included in the definition of a taxable "retail sale."
Hawaii	Taxable	
Idaho	Exempt	
Illinois	Exempt	
Indiana	Exempt	
Iowa	Taxable	
Kansas	Exempt	The waxing of floors is taxable.
Kentucky	Exempt	Not expressly enumerated as taxable in the taxing statute.
Louisiana	Taxable	The furnishing of cleaning services, including the cleaning and renovation of furniture, carpets and rugs, is taxable. However, the cleaning and restoration of miscellaneous items other than furniture and structural cleaning are exempt provided certain conditions are met and the charge for each is separately stated.
Maine	Exempt	
Maryland	Taxable	Cleaning of a commercial or industrial building is taxable. Cleaning for individuals is exempt.
Massachusetts	Exempt	
Michigan	Exempt	
Minnesota	Taxable	
Mississippi	Exempt	
Missouri	Exempt	

Jurisdiction	Janitorial	Comment
Nebraska	Taxable	
Nevada	Exempt	
New Jersey	Taxable	
New Mexico	Taxable	
New York	Taxable	Interior cleaning and maintenance service agreements of 30 days or more are taxable.
North Carolina	Exempt	
North Dakota	Exempt	
Ohio	Taxable	
Oklahoma	Exempt	Not expressly enumerated as taxable in the taxing statute.
Pennsylvania	Taxable	
Rhode Island	Exempt	
South Carolina	Exempt	
South Dakota	Taxable	
Tennessee	Exempt	Cleaning real property, such as windows, walls, and carpeting is exempt. Cleaning personal property, including furniture, rugs, and draperies, is taxable.
Texas	Taxable	
Utah	Exempt	Assisted cleaning or washing of tangible personal property is taxable.
Vermont	Exempt	
Virginia	Exempt	
Washington	Exempt	Janitorial services does not include cleaning the exterior walls of buildings, the cleaning of septic tanks, special clean up jobs required by construction, fires, floods, etc., painting, papering, repairing, furnace or chimney cleaning, snow removal, sandblasting, or the cleaning of plant or industrial machinery or fixtures.
West Virginia	Taxable	Janitorial services performed on or in connection with new construction, reconstruction, alteration, expansion, or remodeling of a building are exempt.
Wisconsin	Exempt	Routine and repetitive janitorial services, including those provided by temporary employees, are exempt. Specialized cleaning of tangible personal property taxable; specialized cleaning of real property exempt. Janitor fees included in rental of certain school or government facilities may be taxable, depending on use of facility.
Wyoming	Exempt	However, generally, services for repair, alteration, or improvement of tangible personal property are taxable.

Services—Repair (Labor)

Jurisdiction	Labor Only	Comment
Alabama	Exempt	Labor charges are not taxable when billed for labor expended in repairing or altering existing tangible personal property belonging to another in order to restore the property to its original condition or usefulness without producing new parts. When repair work includes the sale of repair parts in conjunction with repairs to existing tangible personal property belonging to another, only the sales price of the repair parts is taxable provided the charges for the repair parts and the charges for the repair labor are billed separately on the invoice to the customer. If a repairman fabricates repair parts which are used in conjunction with repairs to existing tangible personal property belonging to another, the total charge for the parts, including any labor charges incurred in making, producing, or fabricating the parts, is taxable even if the fabrication labor charges are billed to the customer as a separate item.
Arizona	Exempt	Repairs to tangible personal property permanently attached to real property are taxable under the contracting classification.
Arkansas	Taxable	Special exemptions apply.
California	Exempt	
Colorado	Exempt	
Connecticut	Taxable	Special exemptions apply.
District of Columbia	Taxable	
Florida	Taxable	Charges for repairs of tangible personal property that require labor or service only are taxable unless the repairer can establish that repairer furnished no tangible personal property that was incorporated into or attached to the repaired item.
Georgia	Exempt	
Hawaii	Taxable	
Idaho	Exempt	
Illinois	Exempt	
Indiana	Exempt	
Iowa	Taxable	The tax applies to labor for "enumerated services." Most repairs of tangible personal property fall under an enumerated service. Where the repair is not an enumerated service, the charge for labor is exempt if separately stated.
Kansas	Taxable	Exceptions apply.
Kentucky	Exempt	
Louisiana	Taxable	Special exemptions apply.
Maine	Exempt	

Jurisdiction	Labor Only	Comment
Maryland	Exempt	
Massachusetts	Exempt	
Michigan	Exempt	
Minnesota	Exempt	
Mississippi	Taxable	An exclusion is allowed for repair services when the repaired property is delivered to the customer in another state by common carrier or in the seller's equipment.
Missouri	Exempt	
Nebraska	Taxable	Charges for repair labor are taxable when the item of property being repaired is taxable and is not annexed to real property. Most charges for labor to repair motor vehicles are not taxable.
Nevada	Exempt	
New Jersey	Taxable	
New Mexico	Taxable	
New York	Taxable	Certain exceptions apply.
North Carolina	Taxable	The general sales and use tax rate applies to the sales price of, or the gross receipts derived from, repair, maintenance, and installation services. Certain exceptions apply.
North Dakota	Exempt	
Ohio	Taxable	Repair services for exempt tangible personal property is not taxable.
Oklahoma	Exempt	
Pennsylvania	Taxable	Certain exemptions exist for the repair of wearing apparel, shoes, and exempt tangible personal property, and repairs involving real estate.
Rhode Island	Exempt	
South Carolina	Exempt	
South Dakota	Taxable	
Tennessee	Taxable	
Texas	Taxable	Certain exemptions exist for the repair of aircraft, certain ships and boats, motor vehicles, and computer programs.
Utah	Taxable	May be exempt if the tangible personal property being repaired is exempt.
Vermont	Exempt	
Virginia	Exempt	
Washington	Taxable	

Jurisdiction	Labor Only	Comment
West Virginia	Taxable	Exceptions apply. Repairs that result in a capital improvement to a building or other structure or to real property are tax-exempt contracting services.
Wisconsin	Taxable	Repairs of aircraft and aircraft parts are exempt.
Wyoming	Taxable	

Services—Transportation

The following chart indicates the taxability of services related to intrastate transportation of persons or property. The chart does not include transportation/delivery services in connection with the sale of tangible personal property.

Jurisdiction	Transportation	Comment
Alabama	Exempt	Exemption limited to transportation services of the kind and nature that would be regulated by the state Public Service Commission or similar regulatory body if sold by a public utility.
Arizona	Taxable	Taxpayers subject to motor carrier fee or light motor vehicle fee exempt. Certain transportation services provided by railroads, ambulances, dial-a-ride programs, or special needs programs exempt.
Arkansas	Exempt	
California	Exempt	
Colorado	Exempt	
Connecticut	Exempt	Effective July 1, 2011, certain intrastate transportation services provided by livery services are taxable.
District of Columbia	Exempt	
Florida	Taxable	Certain intrastate transportation services provided by livery services are taxable. Certain exceptions apply.
Georgia	Exempt	Charter and sightseeing services provided by urban transit systems taxable. Common carrier charges for the intrastate transport of persons taxable. Fares for taxicabs and cars for hire taxable.
Hawaii	Taxable	Certain inter-island transport of agricultural commodities, stevedoring and towing services, county transportation system services, and helicopter rides not taxable.
Idaho	Taxable	Intrastate unscheduled air transportation for hire of freight and passengers generally taxable. Interstate transportation services exempt.
Illinois	Exempt	
Indiana	Exempt	
Iowa	Taxable	Pursuant to tax reform (S.F. 2417).
Kansas	Exempt	Not expressly enumerated as taxable in the taxing statute.
Kentucky	Exempt	Not expressly enumerated as taxable in the taxing statute.
Louisiana	Exempt	
Maine	Exempt	
Maryland	Exempt	
Massachusetts	Exempt	

Jurisdiction	Transportation	Comment
Michigan	Exempt	
Minnesota	Exempt	
Mississippi	Exempt	
Missouri	Taxable	Exempt if provided on contract basis, when no ticket is issued. Transportation by limousines, taxis, and buses that are not required to be licensed by the Division of Motor Carrier and Railroad Safety are exempt. Federal law prohibits taxation of receipts from the intrastate transportation of persons for hire in air commerce.
Nebraska	Exempt	
Nevada	Exempt	
New Jersey	Exempt	However, the following transportation charges are taxable: transportation services originating in New Jersey and provided by a limousine operator, except such services provided in connection with funeral services; transportation or transmission of natural gas and electricity (utility service); and delivery charges. Effective May 1, 2017, transportation services originating in New Jersey and provided by a limousine operator will no longer be subject to tax.
New Mexico	Taxable	
New York	Taxable	Sales tax is imposed on specified transportation services, whether or not any tangible personal property is transferred in conjunction therewith, and regardless of whether the charge is paid in New York or out-of-state, as long as the service is provided in New York. Certain exceptions apply.
North Carolina	Exempt	
North Dakota	Exempt	Passenger transportation and freight transportation by common carrier specifically exempt.
Ohio	Taxable	Transportation of persons by aircraft or motor vehicle, except ambulance or transit bus, is taxable. Charges by delivery companies that are not making sales of tangible personal property generally exempt.
Oklahoma	Taxable	Exceptions apply.
Pennsylvania	Exempt	
Rhode Island	Taxable	Tax applies to taxicab services, limousine services, and other road transportation services, including charter bus service and all other transit and ground passenger transportation. Certain exceptions apply.
South Carolina	Exempt	
South Dakota	Taxable	Certain railroad, river/canal, and air transportation; trucking and courier services; and local and suburban passenger transportation, except limousine service, exempt.
Tennessee	Exempt	

Jurisdiction	Transportation	Comment
Texas	Exempt	Transportation services provided on a stand-alone basis exempt. Transportation services that are incident to the performance of a taxable service are taxable.
Utah	Taxable	
Vermont	Exempt	
Virginia	Exempt	Separately stated transportation charges are exempt.
Washington	Exempt	Towing services, and similar automotive transportation services, are taxable. Charges for moving existing structures/buildings are taxable.
West Virginia	Taxable	Businesses regulated by the Public Service Commission exempt.
Wisconsin	Exempt	
Wyoming	Taxable	Transportation by ambulance or hearse and certain transportation of freight/property, raw farm products, and drilling rigs exempt. Transportation of employees to/from work exempt when paid or contracted for by employee or employer.

Shipping

The following chart indicates whether shipping and postage charges in conjunction with the sale of tangible personal property are included in the tax base.

Jurisdiction	Shipping Charges	Comment
Alabama	Excluded if (1) charges are separately stated and paid directly or indirectly by the purchaser, and (2) delivery is by common carrier or the U.S. Postal Service.	Transportation charges are not separate and identifiable if included with other charges and billed as "shipping and handling" or "postage and handling."
Arizona	Excluded if charges are separately stated.	
Arkansas	Included	If shipment includes both exempt and taxable property, the seller should allocate the delivery charge and must tax the percentage allocated to the taxable property. Charges billed to buyer by a carrier other than the seller are excluded.
California	Excluded if charges are separately stated and delivery is made directly to the purchaser by independent contractor, common carrier or the U.S. Postal Service.	Charges imposed by the seller to transport property, and property sold for a "delivered price," are not subject to tax, provided that (1) delivery charges are stated as a separate entry on the invoice or other bill of sale; and (2) goods are shipped to the purchaser via U.S. mail, independent contractor, or common carrier, rather than the seller's vehicles; and (3) transportation occurs after the property is sold. Tax does not apply to separately stated charges for transportation of land fill material if (1) the charges are reasonable; (2) consideration received is solely for the transport of the material to a specific site; and (3) the material is transferred without charge.
Colorado	Excluded if charges are (1) separable from the sales transaction, and (2) separately stated.	
Connecticut	Included	Charges to deliver exempt items are excluded.
District of Columbia	Excluded if charges are separately stated and delivery occurs after the sale.	
Florida	Excluded if charges are (1) separately stated, and (2) optional.	Separately stated charges for transportation after title passes to the buyer are also excluded.
Georgia	Included	Exceptions apply.
Hawaii	Included	Charges for items shipped outside the state are excluded.

Jurisdiction	Shipping Charges	Comment
Idaho	Excluded if charges are separately stated.	Charges by a manufactured homes dealer to transport the home to a buyer are included.
Illinois	Excluded if charges are separately contracted for.	
Indiana	Included	
Iowa	Excluded if charges are separately contracted for and separately stated.	If shipment includes both exempt and taxable property, the seller should allocate the delivery charge and must tax the percentage allocated to the taxable property.
Kansas	Included	If shipment includes both exempt and taxable property, the seller should allocate the delivery charge and must tax the percentage allocated to the taxable property.
Kentucky	Included	
Louisiana	Excluded if charges are separately stated and delivery occurs after the sale.	
Maine	Excluded if (1) shipment is made direct to the purchaser, (2) charges are separately stated, and (3) the transportation occurs by means of common carrier, contract carrier or the United States mail.	
Maryland	Excluded if charges are separately stated.	
Massachusetts	Excluded if charges (1) reflect the costs of preparing and delivering goods to a location designated by the buyer, (2) are separately stated on the invoice to the buyer, and (3) are set in good faith and reasonably reflect the actual costs incurred by the vendor.	
Michigan	Included	Charges are excluded: (1) if the retailer is engaged in a separate delivery business; or (2) if incurred after the transfer of ownership. If shipment includes both exempt and taxable property, the seller should allocate the delivery charge and must tax the percentage allocated to the taxable property.
Minnesota	Included	Shipping charges are excluded if the product being shipped is exempt. If shipment includes both exempt and taxable property, the seller should allocate the delivery charge on the basis of the sales price or weight of the property being delivered and must tax the percentage allocated to the taxable property.
Mississippi	Included	

Jurisdiction	Shipping Charges	Comment
Missouri	Included	Included if the charge is part of the sale of tangible personal property, whether or not it is separately stated. Also included if charge is not part of the sale of tangible personal property but is separately stated. Excluded if the charge is not part of the sale of tangible personal property if separately stated. If parties intend delivery charges to be part of the sale of tangible personal property, it is included even when the delivery charge is separately stated. Effective August 28, 2017, usual and customary delivery charges that are stated separately from the sale price are not subject to sales and use tax.
Nebraska	Included	If shipment includes both exempt and taxable property, the seller should allocate the delivery charge and must tax the percentage allocated to the taxable property. Delivery charges are exempt when the charges relate to the sale of exempt property or the purchaser paid the delivery charge to a delivery/freight company separately.
Nevada	Excluded if (1) charges are separately stated, and (2) title passes to the purchaser before shipment pursuant to a written agreement.	If shipment includes both exempt and taxable property, the seller should allocate the delivery charge and must tax the percentage allocated to the taxable property.
New Jersey	Included	Regardless if separately stated. Delivery charges are not taxable if the sale itself is not taxable. If a shipment includes both exempt and taxable property, the seller should allocate the delivery charge by using: (1) a percentage based on the total sales price of the taxable property compared to the total sales price of all property in the shipment; or (2) a percentage based on the total weight of the taxable property compared to the total weight of all property in the shipment. The seller must tax the percentage of the delivery charge allocated to the taxable property but is not required to tax the percentage allocated to the exempt property.
New Mexico	Included	If the transportation costs are paid by the seller to the carrier.
New York	Included	Separately stated charges to ship promotional materials are excluded.
North Carolina	Included	If shipment includes both exempt and taxable property, the seller should allocate the delivery charge and must tax the percentage allocated to the taxable property.

Jurisdiction	Shipping Charges	Comment
North Dakota	Included	Shipping charges are excluded if the product being shipped is exempt. If shipment includes both exempt and taxable property, the seller should allocate the delivery charge on the basis of the sales price or weight of the property being delivered and must tax the percentage allocated to the taxable property.
Ohio	Included	If shipment includes both exempt and taxable property, the seller should allocate the delivery charge and must tax the percentage allocated to the taxable property. Charges paid by customer to delivery company (not imposed/collected by retailer) are not taxable.
Oklahoma	Included	If shipment includes both exempt and taxable property, the seller should allocate the delivery charge and must tax the percentage allocated to the taxable property. Excluded where separately stated.
Pennsylvania	Included	Charges made in conjunction with nontaxable transactions are excluded. Charges for delivery made and billed by someone other than seller of item being delivered not taxable.
Rhode Island	Included, if the property sold is taxable.	If the property sold is exempt, delivery charges are not taxable. If a shipment includes both exempt and taxable property, the seller should allocate the delivery charges by using: (1) a percentage based on the total sales prices of the taxable property compared to the total sales prices of all property in the shipment; or (2) a percentage based on the total weight of the taxable property compared to the total weight of all property in the shipment. The seller must tax the percentage of the delivery charge allocated to the taxable property but does not have to tax the percentage allocated to the exempt property.
South Carolina	Included	Charges for transportation after title has passed to the purchaser are excluded.
South Dakota	Included	If shipment includes both exempt and taxable property, the seller should allocate the delivery charge and must tax the percentage allocated to the taxable property. Freight charges paid directly to freight company (not to seller) by purchaser are exempt.
Tennessee	Included	Delivery charges paid by buyer to an independent third-party hired by buyer are excluded.

Jurisdiction	Shipping Charges	Comment
Texas	Included	Shipping charges incident to the sale or lease/rental of taxable tangible personal property or the performance of taxable services that are billed by the seller/ lessor to the purchaser/lessee are taxable. A third-party carrier that only provides transportation and does not sell the item being delivered is not responsible for collecting tax.
Utah	Excluded if charges are separately stated.	
Vermont	Included	Separately stated delivery charges for direct mail excluded.
Virginia	Excluded if charges are separately stated.	
Washington	Included	Charges incurred after purchaser has taken receipt of the goods and charges to deliver exempt items are excluded.
West Virginia	Included	Excluded if (1) separately stated, (2) delivery is by common carrier, and (3) customer pays the delivery charge directly to the carrier.
Wisconsin	Included	Separately stated delivery charges for direct mail excluded. If shipment includes both exempt and taxable property, the seller should allocate the delivery charge on the basis of the sales price or weight of the property being delivered and must tax the percentage allocated to the taxable property.
Wyoming	Excluded if charges are separately stated.	

Statutes of Limitations

This chart states the period in which sales and use taxes may be assessed. Generally, there is no limitation period for assessments where no return was filed or a fraudulent return was filed.

Jurisdiction	Assessments	Comment
Alabama	3 years from later of return due date or return filing date.	If base understated by more than 25%, 6 years from later of return due date or return filing date.
Arizona	4 years from later of return due date or return filing date.	If receipts understated by more than 25%, 6 years from return filing date.
Arkansas	3 years from later of return due date or return filing date.	If receipts understated by more than 25%, six years from the date the return was filed.
California	3 years from later of the end of the calendar month following the quarterly period for which the assessment relates, or the return filing date.	8 years from the end of the calendar month following the quarterly period if no return was filed.
Colorado	3 years from later of tax due date or return filing date.	
Connecticut	3 years from the later the end of the calendar month following the tax period, or the date the return was filed.	
District of Columbia	3 years from return filing date.	6 years from return filing date if tax understated by more than 25%.
Florida	3 years from later of return due date, tax due date, or return filing date, or any time a right to a refund or credit is available to the taxpayer.	
Georgia	3 years from later of return due date or return filing date.	
Hawaii	3 years from later of annual return due date or filing date.	
Idaho	3 years from later of return due date or return filing date.	7 years from return due date if no return was filed.
Illinois	3 years from the month or period in which the taxable gross receipts were received (assessments issued on January 1 or July 1).	
Indiana	3 years from later of the return filing date or the end of the calendar year containing the period for which the return was filed.	
Iowa	3 years from return filing date.	
Kansas	3 years from return filing date.	In the case of a false or fraudulent return, 2 years from the date fraud was discovered.
Kentucky	4 years from later of return due date or return filing date.	

Jurisdiction	Assessments	Comment
Louisiana	3 years from the end of the calendar year in which the tax payment was due.	
Maine	3 years from later of return due date or return filing date. If tax understated by 50% or more, 6 years from return filing date.	
Maryland	4 years from tax due date.	No limitations period if proof of fraud or gross negligence.
Massachusetts	3 years from later of return due date or return filing date.	
Michigan	4 years from later of return due date or return filing date.	For cases involving fraud, 2 years from the date fraud was discovered.
Minnesota	3.5 years from later of return due date or return filing date.	If taxes underreported by more than 25%, 6.5 years from later of return due date or return filing date.
Mississippi	3 years from return filing date.	
Missouri	3 years from later of return due date or return filing date.	
Nebraska	3 years from later of date the return was filed or the last day of the calendar month following the tax period.	For cases where a return has not been filed, a false or fraudulent return has been filed with the intent to evade the tax, or an amount has been omitted from a return that is in excess of 25% of the amount of tax stated, 6 years after the last day of the calendar month following the period in which the amount is proposed to be determined.
Nevada	3 years from later of return filing date or the last day of the calendar month following the tax period.	8 years from the last day of the month following the tax period if no return is filed.
New Jersey	4 years from return filing date.	
New Mexico	3 years from the end of the calendar year in which the tax payment was due.	If taxes underreported by more than 25%, 6 years from the end of the calendar year in which the tax payment was due. 7 years from the end of the calendar year in which the tax payment was due if no return was filed. 10 years from the end of the calendar year in which the tax payment was due if fraudulent return was filed.
New York	3 years from later of return due date or return filing date.	
North Carolina	3 years from later or return due date or return filing date.	
North Dakota	3 years from later of return due date or return filing date.	If tax understated by 25% or more, 6 years from later of return due date or return filing date. 6 years from return due date if no return was filed.

Jurisdiction	Assessments	Comment
Ohio	4 years from later of return due date or return filing date.	Statute of limitations period does not apply if the taxpayer has not filed a return, if the commissioner has information that the taxpayer has collected taxes but failed to remit to the state, or the taxpayer and commissioner have waived the limitations period in writing.
Oklahoma	3 years from later of return due date or return filing date.	
Pennsylvania	3 years from later of return filing date or the end of the year in which the liability arose.	
Rhode Island	3 years from later of return filing date or the 15th day of the month following the month in which the return was due.	
South Carolina	3 years from later of date the return was filed or due to be filed.	3 year statute of limitations period does not apply (i) if there is a fraudulent intent to evade taxes; (ii) a taxpayer has failed to file a return, (iii) there has been an understatement of tax by 20% or more; (iv) taxpayer has given consent in writing to waive limitation; and (v) tax imposed is a use tax and assessment is based on information obtained from state, local, regional or national tax administration organization.
South Dakota	3 years from return filing date.	
Tennessee	3 years from the end of the calendar year in which the return was filed.	
Texas	4 years from tax due date.	No limitation period if tax understated by 25% or more.
Utah	3 years from return filing date.	
Vermont	3 years from later of return due date or return filing date.	If tax understated by 20% or more, 6 years from return filing date.
Virginia	3 years from tax due date.	6 years from tax due date if no return was filed or fraudulent return was filed.
Washington	4 years from the close of the tax year in which the liability arose.	Statute of limitations period does not apply to a taxpayer that has not registered, that has committed fraud or misrepresentation, or has executed a written waiver of the limitation.
West Virginia	3 years from later of return due date or return filing date.	
Wisconsin	Generally 4 years from return filing date.	Period may be extended if taxpayer consents in writing.
Wyoming	3 years from the date of delinquency.	

Trade-Ins

The following chart indicates whether or not the value of a trade-in is included in the sales price for sales tax purposes.

Jurisdiction	Trade-Ins	Comment
Alabama	Included	Certain exclusions.
Arizona	Excluded	
Arkansas	Included	Exclusion allowed for certain items, e.g. vehicles, trailers, and aircraft.
California	Included	
Colorado	Excluded	
Connecticut	Excluded	
District of Columbia	Included	
Florida	Excluded	
Georgia	Excluded	
Hawaii	Excluded	
Idaho	Excluded	Exclusion not allowed on sale of a new manufactured home or a modular building.
Illinois	Excluded	
Indiana	Excluded	
Iowa	Excluded	
Kansas	Excluded	
Kentucky	Excluded	
Louisiana	Excluded	
Maine	Included	Exclusion allowed for certain items, e.g. vehicles, boats, aircraft, chain saws, and trailers. Separately stated charges are excluded.
Maryland	Included	
Massachusetts	Included	Exclusion allowed for certain items, e.g. vehicles, boats, and aircraft.
Michigan	Included	Credit for the agreed-upon value of a titled watercraft used as part payment of the purchase price of a new or used watercraft is excluded. The agreed-upon value of a motor vehicle (up to a specified maximum limit) or a recreational vehicle used as part payment of the purchase price of a new or used motor vehicle or a new or used recreational vehicle, is excluded. Credit for the core charge attributed to a recycling fee, deposit, or disposal fee for a motor vehicle or recreational vehicle part or battery is excluded.
Minnesota	Excluded	
Mississippi	Excluded	

Jurisdiction	Trade-Ins	Comment
Missouri	Excluded	Exclusion not applicable to certain manufactured home sales.
Nebraska	Excluded	
Nevada	Excluded	
New Jersey	Excluded	Credit for trade-in on property of the same kind accepted in part payment and intended for resale if the amount is separately stated on the invoice, bill of sale, or similar document given to the purchaser is specifically excluded from the sales price. Exclusion not allowed on certain sales of manufactured or mobile homes.
New Mexico	Excluded	Exclusion not allowed on trade-in of manufactured home.
New York	Excluded	
North Carolina	Included	
North Dakota	Excluded	Exclusion not allowed on trade-in of used mobile home.
Ohio	Included	Exclusion allowed on sales of certain items, e.g. watercraft and new vehicles.
Oklahoma	Included	
Pennsylvania	Excluded	
Rhode Island	Included	Certain exclusions apply.
South Carolina	Excluded	
South Dakota	Excluded	
Tennessee	Excluded	
Texas	Excluded	
Utah	Excluded	
Vermont	Excluded	
Virginia	Excluded	
Washington	Excluded	
West Virginia	Excluded	
Wisconsin	Excluded	Exclusion not allowed on sale of certain manufactured or modular homes.
Wyoming	Excluded	

Vending Machine Sales—Food

The following chart indicates the taxability of sales of food made through vending machines but does not specify upon whom the liability for the tax falls.

Jurisdiction	Food	Comment
Alabama	Taxable	Food, food products, coffee, milk, milk products, and substitutes for these products taxed at reduced rate.
Arizona	Exempt	Food for consumption on premises is taxable.
Arkansas	Exempt	Registered vending device operators exempt from general gross receipts tax, but subject to either special vending device sales/use tax or vending device decal fee.
California	Taxable	33% of cold food receipts taxable.
Colorado	Exempt	Certain items are taxable including carbonated water, chewing gum, seeds and plants to grow food, prepared salads and salad bars, cold sandwiches, deli trays, candy, soft drinks and hot/cold beverages served in unsealed cups through a vending machine.
Connecticut	Exempt	Candy, carbonated and alcoholic beverages, cigarettes, tobacco products, and items not intended for human consumption are not considered food products and are taxable. All sales for 50 cents or less exempt.
District of Columbia	Taxable	
Florida	Taxable	Sales for less than 10 cents exempt. Food/drink sales in school cafeterias, food/drink sales for 25 cents or less through coin-operated machines sponsored by certain charitable organizations, and receipts from machines operated by churches exempt.
Georgia	Taxable	
Hawaii	Taxable	
Idaho	Taxable	Sales for 11 cents or less exempt. Sales for 12 cents through $1 taxed at 117% of vendor's acquisition cost. Sales for more than $1 taxed on retail sales price.
Illinois	Taxable	Reduced tax rate of 1% applies to food sold through vending machines, except soft drinks, candy, and hot foods are subject to the full tax rate. Bulk vending machine sales of unsorted food items (e.g, nuts) are exempt.
Indiana	Taxable	Sales for 8 cents or less exempt. Sales may be exempt because of tax-exempt status of person or organization that makes the sale.
Iowa	Taxable	Applies to items sold for consumption on premises, items prepared for immediate consumption off premises, candy, candy-coated items, candy products, and certain beverages.
Kansas	Taxable	
Kentucky	Taxable	Sales of 50 cents or less through coin-operated bulk vending machines exempt.

Jurisdiction	Food	Comment
Louisiana	Exempt	Sales to dealer for resale through coin-operated vending machines taxable; subsequent resale exempt. Food products sold through a distributor's own vending machines are subject to use tax on the distributor's cost of the items sold.
Maine	Taxable	Exemption for sales of products for internal human consumption when sold through vending machines operated by a person more than 50% of whose retail gross receipts are from sales through vending machines.
Maryland	Taxable	Taxed at special rate. Snack food, milk, fresh fruit/ vegetables, and yogurt are exempt.
Massachusetts	Taxable	Exempt if machine sells only snacks and/or candy with a sales price of less than $3.50.
Michigan	Taxable	Food or drink heated or cooled to an average temperature above 75 degrees Fahrenheit or below 65 degrees Fahrenheit before sale is taxable. Milk, juices, fresh fruit, candy, nuts, chewing gum, cookies, crackers, chips, and nonalcoholic beverages in sealed container exempt.
Minnesota	Exempt	Prepared food, candy, soft drinks, and dietary supplements sold through vending machines, snack boxes, or honor boxes are taxable. Vending machine sales are also taxable if the vending machine is located on the property of – or operated by – a school or a tax-exempt or nonprofit organization.
Mississippi	Exempt	Food/drinks sold through vending machines serviced by full-line vendors exempt.
Missouri	Taxable	Sales made on religious, charitable, and public elementary or secondary school premises exempt.
Nebraska	Taxable	
Nevada	Taxable	Prepared food intended for immediate consumption taxable.
New Jersey	Taxable	Taxed at 70% of retail vending machine price. Sales for 25 cents or less by retailer primarily engaged in coin-operated machine sales exempt. Food/drink sold in school cafeterias and milk exempt.
New Mexico	Taxable	
New York	Taxable	Sales for 10 cents or less by vendor primarily engaged in vending machine sales exempt. Candy and certain beverages sold for 75 cents or less (effective June 1, 2014, $1.50 or less) are exempt. Certain sales intended for off-premises consumption and certain bulk vending machine sales exempt.
North Carolina	Taxable	Taxed at 50% of sales price. Sales for one cent exempt.
North Dakota	Taxable	Sales for 15 cents or less exempt.

Jurisdiction	Food	Comment
Ohio	Taxable	Sales of food for off-premises consumption exempt. Sales of automatic food vending machines that preserve food with a shelf life of forty-five days or less by refrigeration and dispense it to the consumer, are exempt.
Oklahoma	Taxable	Sales from coin-operated devices for which certain license fees have been paid are exempt.
Pennsylvania	Exempt	Specific items taxable, including soft drinks, meals, sandwiches, hot beverages, and items dispensed in heated form or served cold but normally heated in operator-provided oven/microwave. Sales on school or church premises exempt.
Rhode Island	Taxable	Sales in school areas designated primarily for students/ teachers exempt.
South Carolina	Taxable	Vendors making sales solely through vending machines are deemed to be users or consumers of certain property they purchase for sale through vending machines (not cigarettes or soft drinks in closed containers, which are subject to business license tax at wholesale level).
South Dakota	Taxable	
Tennessee	Taxable	Certain nonprofit entities may pay gross receipts tax in lieu of sales tax.
Texas	Taxable	Taxed on 50% of receipts. Candy and soft drinks fully taxable. Sales of food, candy, gum, or items designed for a child's use/play for 50 cents or less through coin-operated bulk vending machines exempt.
Utah	Taxable	Sales of food and food ingredients or prepared food from a vending machine are exempt if the proceeds of each sale do not exceed $1, and the seller or operator of the vending machine reports an amount equal to 150% of the cost of the items as goods consumed. f the food and food ingredients or prepared food as goods consumed.
Vermont	Exempt	Food sold through vending machines is exempt from sales and use tax but subject to meals and rooms tax.
Virginia	Taxable	Rate and base vary depending on placement/use of machine.
Washington	Taxable	Taxed on 57% of receipts. Hot prepared foods and soft drinks are fully taxable.
West Virginia	Taxable	
Wisconsin	Exempt	Candy, soft drinks, dietary supplements, and prepared food are taxable.
Wyoming	Taxable	Food that qualifies as food for domestic home consumption is exempt.

Vending Machine Sales—Merchandise

The following chart indicates the taxability of sales made through vending machines but does not specify upon whom the liability for the tax falls.

Jurisdiction	Merchandise	Comment
Alabama	Taxable	
Arizona	Taxable	Tax is due on gross proceeds or gross income from the business of operating or conducting video games and pinball machines.
Arkansas	Exempt	Registered vending device operators exempt from general gross receipts tax, but subject to either special vending device sales/use tax or vending device decal fee. Devices that sell only cigarettes, newspapers, magazines, or postage stamps not taxable as vending devices. Owners and operators of coin-operated pinball machines, coin-operated music machines, coin-operated mechanical games, and similar devices are subject to a 3% gross receipts tax.
California	Taxable	
Colorado	Taxable	Sales of tangible personal property for 15 cents or less is exempt. No tax on coin-operated video games or amusement devices.
Connecticut	Taxable	Sales of $0.50 or less and sales of food products are exempt.
District of Columbia	Taxable	No guidance on customer use of video games and amusement devices.
Florida	Taxable	Sales for less than $0.10 are exempt. Food or drink for human consumption sold for $0.25 or less through a coin-operated vending machine sponsored by a nonprofit corporation is exempt.
Georgia	Taxable	
Hawaii	Taxable	
Idaho	Taxable	Sales for 11 cents or less exempt. Sales for 12 cents through $1 taxed at 117% of vendor's acquisition cost. Sales for more than $1 taxed on retail sales price.
Illinois	Taxable	Bulk vending machine sales exempt. An annual privilege tax applies to the use of all coin-in-the-slot-operated amusement devices.
Indiana	Taxable	Sales for 8 cents or less exempt. Sales may be exempt because of tax-exempt status of person or organization that makes the sale.
Iowa	Taxable	Iowa sales and use taxes are imposed on a broad range of amusement and recreational activities. The sales price derived from the operation of all forms of amusement devices and from games of skill, games of chance, raffles, and bingo games operated and conducted within the state are taxable.
Kansas	Taxable	
Kentucky	Taxable	Sales of 50¢ or less through coin-operated bulk vending machines are exempt.

Jurisdiction	Merchandise	Comment
Louisiana	Exempt	Sales of tangible personal property to dealer for resale through coin-operated vending machines taxable. Subsequent resale exempt. Coin video games are also exempt.
Maine	Taxable	Items sold through vending machines (other than items for internal human consumption) are taxable retail sales. Chewing gum is not considered an item for internal human consumption. Coin video games are exempt.
Maryland	Taxable	Taxed at special rate. Sales for 75 cents or less through bulk vending machines exempt. Coin video games are exempt and taxed under the Admissions and Amusement Tax.
Massachusetts	Taxable	Sales for 10 cents or less exempt. No guidance has been provided on the taxability of coin-operated video games or amusement devices.
Michigan	Taxable	Amounts paid to use coin-operated video games and other amusement devices are not taxable.
Minnesota	Taxable	Coin video games are taxable.
Mississippi	Taxable	Sales of food and drink for human consumption through vending machines serviced by full line vendors are exempt.
Missouri	Taxable	Photocopies, tobacco products, and sales made on religious, charitable, and public elementary or secondary school premises exempt.
Nebraska	Taxable	Gross receipts from the operation of mechanical amusement devices, including coin-operated video games, are subject to the mechanical amusement device tax, not the sales tax.
Nevada	Taxable	Sales and use tax is not imposed on the use of coin-operated video games or amusement devices.
New Jersey	Taxable	Sales for 25 cents or less by retailer primarily engaged in coin-operated machine sales exempt.
New Mexico	Taxable	Charges for use of a vending machine device that performs a service, such as entertainment, are taxable.
New York	Taxable	Sales for 10 cents or less and bulk vending machine sales for 50 cents or less exempt if vendor primarily engaged in vending machine sales.
North Carolina	Taxable	Taxed at 50% of sales price. Tobacco and newspapers sold through a coin-operated vending machine are fully taxable.
North Dakota	Taxable	Sales for 15 cents or less exempt.
Ohio	Taxable	The gross receipts from the operation of coin-operated video games are not taxable.
Oklahoma	Taxable	Sales from vending machines are taxable. Sales from coin-operated devices for which an annual license fee is paid are exempt.
Pennsylvania	Taxable	

Jurisdiction	Merchandise	Comment
Rhode Island	Taxable	Sales made from machines located in certain facilities by licensed operators who are blind are exempt. Coin video games are exempt.
South Carolina	Taxable	Vendors making sales solely through vending machines are deemed to be users or consumers of certain property they purchase for sale through vending machines (not cigarettes or soft drinks in closed containers, which are subject to business license tax at wholesale level). Coin video games are exempt.
South Dakota	Taxable	Also, jukeboxes, video games; pinball machines; arcades and other mechanical games and coin-operated devices used for commercial purposes are taxable.
Tennessee	Taxable	Certain nonprofit entities may pay gross receipts tax in lieu of sales tax when the value of merchandise sold through the vending machines they operate is less than $0.25.
Texas	Taxable	Candy and soft drinks fully taxable. Sales of food, candy, gum, or items designed for a child's use/play for 50 cents or less. Coin-operated bulk vending machines exempt. Coin-operated (or token) amusement devices, such as video games and pinball machines are exempt.
Utah	Taxable	Payments for use of content on computer devices is not taxable.
Vermont	Taxable	
Virginia	Taxable	Rate and base vary depending on placement/use of machine.
Washington	Taxable	Coin-operated video games are not taxable.
West Virginia	Taxable	
Wisconsin	Taxable	
Wyoming	Taxable	Postage stamps exempt. Fees charged to play coin-operated arcade or video games are not taxable.

PROPERTY TAX

The following pages contain charts summarizing various property tax topics. Topics covered include administrative appeals, assessment dates, the legal basis of assessments, real property delinquency dates, real property lien dates, and real property payment dates.

Taxes on tangible personal property and inventories, as well as personal property return dates, are also covered.

Administrative Appeals

Jurisdiction	Administrative Appeals	Comment
Alabama	A taxpayer may appeal any final assessment entered by the department by filing a notice of appeal with the Tax Tribunal within 30 days from the date of entry of the final assessment.	
Alaska	A state oil or gas tax assessment must be appealed within 20 days after an assessment notice is mailed. A municipal property tax assessment must be appealed no later than 30 days after a property tax statement is mailed.	
Arizona	Petitions must be filed within 60 days after the valuation notice mailing date.	
Arkansas	Assessments must be appealed to the county board of equalization by the third Monday in August.	
California	Between July 2 and September 15 (November 30 if assessee does not receive tax bill by August 1).	Appeals of supplemental taxes and of taxes for which a timely notice was not sent must be filed within 60 days of either the notice or the mailing of the tax bill.
Colorado	Written petitions must be filed by June 1.	
Connecticut	Appeals must be filed by February 20, for the March hearing or by March 20 if the Assessor or the Board of Assessors has received an extension.	
Delaware	The Board of Assessment for Kent County hears appeals from April 1 through April 15; in Sussex County, the Board of Assessment Review hears appeals from February 15 through March 1; and the Board of Assessment Review in New Castle County hears appeals from March 15 through April 30. Appeals of quarterly supplemental assessments may be made within 30 days from the date the notice is sent.	
District of Columbia	Certified petition must be filed within 45 days of the original assessment notice, generally.	
Florida	A petition for review of valuation issues must be filed no later than the 25th day following mailing of the notice of assessment. A petition for review of denial of an exemption, an application for agricultural or high-water recharge classification, or deferral must be filed no later than the 30th day following notice.	
Georgia	Appeals must be filed within 45 days from the date of notice mailing.	

Jurisdiction	Administrative Appeals	Comment
Hawaii	Hawaii County, Maui County: April 9 preceding the tax year; Honolulu County: January 15 preceding the tax year; Kauai County: December 31 preceding the tax year.	
Idaho	An appeal of an assessment listed on the real or personal property roll must be filed by the fourth Monday of June. An appeal of an assessment listed on the subsequent property roll must be filed by the fourth Monday of November.	
Illinois	Appeals must be filed on or before 30 days after the date of publication of the assessment list. In Cook County, they must be filed within at least 20 days after receipt of Board of Appeals meeting notice.	
Indiana	If a taxpayer disagrees with the determination reached by a county property tax assessment board of appeals, and has gone through a preliminary conference with the county property tax assessment board of appeals, the taxpayer may file a petition for review by the Indiana Board within 45 days on a form prescribed by the Indiana Board.	
Iowa	Appeals to the board of review must be made on or after April 2 to and including April 30.	
Kansas	As a prerequisite for a formal protest, an appeal to a county appraiser must first be filed within 30 days after receipt of the notice of valuation for real property or by May 15 for personal property. An appeal of a county appraiser decision may be filed with a hearing officer or board within 18 days of the date that the final determination of the appraiser was mailed. A written appeal of an officer's or board's decision, or of the classification and appraisal of certain complex property by an independent appraiser, must be filed with the State Board of Tax Appeals within 30 days after the date of the order from which the appeal is taken.	
Kentucky	Before a formal appeal may be filed, a conference with the property valuation administrator (PVA) must be filed within the 13-day tax roll inspection period, which begins on the first Monday in May. An appeal of the PVA assessment must be filed with the board of assessment appeals within one workday following the conclusion of the tax roll inspection period.	

Jurisdiction	Administrative Appeals	Comment
Louisiana	Appeals of the board of review must be filed with the tax commission within 10 business days of the board's decision.	
Maine	Written appeals of property tax must be filed with the board of assessment review (or to the county commissioners if no board is adopted) within 60 days after the notice of the decision from which the appeal is taken or after the application is denied.	
Maryland	Appeals to an assessment supervisor must be made no later than 45 days from the receipt of the assessment notice.	
Massachusetts	Appeals of a local board of assessors must be filed with the county commissioners within three months after either the assessor's decision or the date the application is denied. Appeals of the commissioners' decision must be filed with the appellate tax board within three months of the decision.	
Michigan	Petitions to the Tax Tribunal must be filed by May 31 of the tax year involved for commercial real property, industrial real property, developmental real property, commercial personal property, industrial personal property, or utility personal property. Petitions to the Tax Tribunal must be filed by July 31 of the tax year involved for agricultural real property, residential real property, timber-cutover real property, or agricultural personal property.	For an assessment dispute as to the valuation or exemption of property, the assessment must be protested before the board of review before the tribunal acquires jurisdiction. The date for filing property tax appeals in the Tax Tribunal has been extended to August 31, 2020 if the deadline originally fell after May 27, 2020 and before September 1, 2020.
Minnesota	Petitions must be filed with the local board of appeal and equalization during the board's annual April and May meetings.	
Mississippi	Written objections to a municipal or county tax assessment must be filed with the governing body of the municipality or the county board of supervisors during the August annual meeting.	
Missouri	Appeals are heard by the county board of equalization and must be filed with the county clerk before the third Monday in June.	

Jurisdiction	Administrative Appeals	Comment
Montana	Generally protests must be filed with the county tax appeal board no later than 30 days after receipt of notice of classification and approval. For class three and class four property, within 30 days from date of assessment notice for reduction of appraised value to be considered for both years of the two-year appraisal cycle. For class 10 property, any time but only once each valuation cycle.	
Nebraska	On or before June 30th.	
Nevada	Appeals must be made to the county board of equalization by January 15. Appeals from the county board to the state board of equalization must be made by March 10.	
New Hampshire	Appeals to the board of tax and land appeals must be filed by September 1. Motions for a rehearing of the board's decision must be filed within 30 days of the clerk's date on the board's order or decision.	
New Jersey	Petitions must be filed with county board of taxation by the later of April 1 or 45 days from the date the taxing district completes the bulk mailing of the notification of assessment.	
New Mexico	File petition with local county assessor by the later of April 1 of the property tax year to which the valuation notice applies or 30 days after the assessor's mailing of this notice, generally.	
New York	A complaint may be filed any time before the time fixed for review by the local board of assessment review, which is generally the fourth Tuesday in May.	
North Carolina	The taxpayer must request a hearing with the county board of review in writing or by personal appearance prior to the board's adjournment. If the taxpayer requests review of a decision made by the board, notice of which was mailed fewer than 15 days prior to the board's adjournment, the request for a hearing thereon may be made within 15 days after notice of the board's decision was mailed.	

Jurisdiction	Administrative Appeals	Comment
North Dakota	Appeals of an assessment must be filed with the township board, normally by the first Monday in April, or with the city board, normally by the second Tuesday in April. Appeals of the local board must be filed with the county board of equalization during the county board's meeting in the first 10 days in June. Appeals of the county board must be filed with the state board of equalization during the state board's meeting on the second Tuesday in August.	
Ohio	Within 60 days after notice is mailed, taxpayer may file petition for reassessment with Tax Commissioner. If no appeal is taken from Commissioner's decision, the determination becomes final subject to appeal to the Board of Tax Appeals.	
Oklahoma	Written complaints must be filed with the county assessor by 30 days from the date that a notice of valuation was mailed; if the valuation has not increased from the prior year, complaints must be filed by the first Monday in May. Appeals of an assessor's decision must be filed within 10 working days of the date of the final action notice.	
Oregon	A value reduction petition must be filed after tax statements are mailed and before December 31.	
Pennsylvania	For Philadelphia County, the first Monday of October. For Allegheny County, the appeal date is set by ordinance. For counties of Class 2A and the third through eighth classes, for new or changed assessments, 40 days after notice of assessment; for all other matters, September 1 or date designated by county commissioners.	
Rhode Island	Appeals to local assessors must be made within 90 days of the first tax payment due date.	
South Carolina	Written objections must be filed with the county assessor within 90 days after the assessment notice is mailed provided the objection is for a tax year when a notice is sent. Appeals of an assessor's decision to the county board of appeals must be filed within 30 days after the date of the assessor's response.	
South Dakota	An appeal must be filed with the clerk of the local board of equalization by the Thursday preceding the third Monday in March. An appeal to the Office of Hearing Examiners must be filed with the county auditor by the third Friday in May.	

Jurisdiction	Administrative Appeals	Comment
Tennessee	To protest an assessment, taxpayers must appear before the county board of equalization during its meeting. Appeals to the state board of equalization must be filed the later of August 1 or 45 days after notice of the local board's decision was sent.	
Texas	Written notice to the appraisal review board must be filed the later of June 1 or 30 days after the appraisal notice is delivered. For property taxes imposed for a tax year beginning on or after January 1, 2018, the later of May 15 or 30 days after the appraisal notice is delivered.	
Utah	Appeals for real property valuation or equalization must be filed with the county board of equalization the later of 45 days after the valuation notice is mailed or September 15; for personal property, appeals must be filed no later than (1) the expiration of time for filing a signed statement if one is requested or (2) within 60 days after the notice is mailed. Appeals to the state tax commission must be filed with the county auditor within 30 days of the county board's final action.	
Vermont	Appeals to the local board of civil authority must be filed with the town clerk within 14 days of the lister's decision. Appeals to the director of the division of property valuation and review must be filed within 30 days of the local board's decision notice.	
Virginia	Appeal dates vary by locality; appeal date must be a minimum of 30 days from the final date for the assessing officer to hear objections.	
Washington	Appeals to the county board of equalization must be filed by the later of (1) July 1, (2) within 30 days after a notice is mailed, or (3) within 30 days after a notice is electronically transmitted (4) within a time limit of 60 days adopted by the county legislative authority. Appeals to the board of tax appeals must be filed within 30 days after the county board's notice is mailed.	
West Virginia	Applications must be made before the county commission during its annual February 1 meeting.	Taxpayers may elect to file a petition for review with the assessor within eight business days of receiving a notice of increased assessment.

Jurisdiction	Administrative Appeals	Comment
Wisconsin	After an informal review by the local assessor, review may be sought with the board of review, which meets during the 45-day period beginning on the 4th Monday of April (by the 3rd Monday of May in Milwaukee and Madison). Written or oral notice to the clerk is required at least 48 hours prior to the scheduled meeting. Written complaints to the Department of Revenue must be filed either within 20 days after receipt of the board's determination notice or within 30 days of the date specified on the affidavit if no notice is received. Appeals to the state tax commission must be filed within 60 days of the determination.	
Wyoming	Appeals to the county board of equalization must be made within 30 days of the notification of assessment. Appeals to the state board of equalization must be made within 30 days of the local board's decision.	

Assessment/Valuation Date

Jurisdiction	Assessment/Valuation Date	Comment
Alabama	October 1.	
Alaska	January 1.	
Arizona	January 1.	
Arkansas	January 1.	
California	July 1.	
Colorado	January 1.	
Connecticut	October 1.	
Delaware	Varies by county.	
District of Columbia	January 1.	
Florida	July 1.	
Georgia	January 1.	
Hawaii	Honolulu County, January 31; Kauai County, March 15; Hawaii County: April 19; Maui County: April 19.	
Idaho	January 1.	
Illinois	June 1.	In Cook County, as soon as the assessor reasonably can.
Indiana	January 1 (also applicable to mobile homes including manufactured homes subject to assessment under IC 6-1.1-7).	Mobile homes are assessed in the year following the year containing the related assessment date for other property. The annual assessment date for mobile homes is January 15 in a year ending before January 1, 2017, and January 1 in a year beginning after December 31, 2016.
Iowa	January 1.	
Kansas	January 1.	
Kentucky	January 1.	
Louisiana	January 1.	In Orleans Parish, status of property on August 1 of each year determines tax treatment for following calendar year.
Maine	April 1.	
Maryland	January 1.	
Massachusetts	January 1.	
Michigan	December 31.	
Minnesota	January 2.	
Mississippi	January 1.	Personal property is assessed as of March 1.

Jurisdiction	Assessment/Valuation Date	Comment
Missouri	January 1.	
Montana	First Monday in August.	
Nebraska	January 1.	
Nevada	July 1.	
New Hampshire	April 1.	
New Jersey	October 1.	
New Mexico	January 1.	
New York	March 1.	Generally, taxable status date is March 1 and valuation date is July 1 of previous year.
North Carolina	January 1.	
North Dakota	February 1.	
Ohio	First Monday in August.	
Oklahoma	January 1.	
Oregon	January 1.	
Pennsylvania	First Monday of September (Allegheny County), third Monday of September (Philadelphia County), or July 1 (all other counties).	
Rhode Island	December 31.	
South Carolina	December 31.	
South Dakota	Valuation date, November 1; assessment date, the following June 1.	Centrally assessed property is assessed in early July.
Tennessee	January 1.	
Texas	January 1.	
Utah	May 22.	
Vermont	April 1.	
Virginia	January 1.	
Washington	January 1.	
West Virginia	July 1.	
Wisconsin	January 1.	
Wyoming	January 1	

Construction Work in Progress

The following chart outlines the timing of valuation and assessment of construction work in progress and/or new construction. In general, states will either assess and tax property under construction on a pro rata basis as the construction is progressing, or will make an assessment and collect tax on the property as new construction upon its completion. Certain county-specific information is also included.

Jurisdiction	Construction Work in Progress	Comment
Alabama	An improvement to real property that is partially complete as of October 1 of a tax year must be reported to the local property tax assessor and be assessed as incomplete for the tax year.	
Alaska	Property committed primarily to the production or pipeline transportation of oil or gas or to the operation or maintenance of oil or gas production or transportation facilities must be assessed at its full and true value as of the date that construction commences. Tax is then prorated according to the time remaining in the assessment year. Additionally, a four-year exemption from municipal property taxes is authorized for certain real property improvements.	
Arizona	Construction work in progress becomes taxable when the work has progressed to a degree that it is useful for its eventual purpose.	
Arkansas	No specific statutory provisions.	
California	Property under construction is taxable throughout the construction process, with the value of the construction being determined as of each lien date during the process.	As of the date of completion of the construction, the newly constructed property will be appraised at its full value, which also will be the newly constructed property base-year value.
Colorado	Property under construction after January 1 is assessed on July 1 of that year. If construction is completed by July 1, the valuation is prorated at the same ratio as the number of months it is completed bears to the full year. If completed after July 1, the valuation added is one-half the difference between the valuation on January 1 and on July 1.	
Connecticut	Assessment is made on a prorated basis for construction completed after the assessment date.	Partially completed new construction is assessed based on the value of the partially completed new construction as of October 1st.
Delaware	No specific statutory provisions.	
District of Columbia	Construction work in progress is taxable at estimated market value when 65% of the estimated construction is completed.	

Jurisdiction	Construction Work in Progress	Comment
Florida	Any improvement to real property that is not substantially completed on January 1 has no value placed on it.	
Georgia	Taxpayers are responsible for filing timely returns when improvements have been made to real property since it was last returned for taxation.	
Hawaii	For all four counties, in assessing a building for property tax purposes, consideration must be given to any new construction, improvement, modification, or repair that results in a higher assessed value.	
Idaho	Improvements, other than additions to existing improvements, constructed upon real property are not subject to property taxation during the year of construction, other than that portion that is actually in place as of January 1 of each calendar year. A prorated occupancy tax is imposed in lieu of a property tax during the construction year.	A provisional property tax exemption may be granted for property that is under construction for a tax-exempt purpose.
Illinois	Owner is liable for increased taxes on a proportional basis due to the construction of new or added buildings, structures, or other improvement from the date when either the occupancy permit is issued or the improvement is habitable and fit for occupancy or intended customary use.	
Indiana	Construction work in progress is valued at 10% of the true tax value of the cost of the property.	
Iowa	Although Iowa has no specific statutory provisions on construction in progress, individual lots within a subdivision plat must not be assessed in excess of the total assessment of the land as acreage or unimproved property for five years after the recording of the plat or until the lot is actually improved with permanent construction, whichever occurs first.	
Kansas	Construction incomplete as of the January 1 assessment date is valued at the fair market value as of that date.	If there is added value attributable to the construction in progress on January 1st, the property will be classified based upon its intended use, and not as a vacant lot.
Kentucky	No specific statutory provisions.	
Louisiana	Assessment is to be made on the basis of the condition of the buildings on the first day of January.	

Jurisdiction	Construction Work in Progress	Comment
Maine	The valuation of construction in progress varies by district. Personal property used or intended to be used in construction in progress may be eligible for a Business Equipment Tax Exemption or a Business Equipment Tax Reimbursement.	
Maryland	Substantially completed improvements from construction that add at least $100,000 in value will result in revaluation in any year of a three-year cycle.	Improvements adding at least $100,000 in value will be valued on the date of finality, the semiannual date of finality, or quarter date of finality, following substantial completion.
Massachusetts	Construction work in progress becomes taxable once an occupancy permit is issued and is assessed on a prorated basis.	
Michigan	Value of new construction is 50% of the true cash value.	
Minnesota	Construction work in progress is assessed annually to the extent completed on January 2.	
Mississippi	A newly constructed home remains exempt from property tax until it is first leased, rented, sold, or occupied.	
Missouri	New construction or an improvement to existing property that occurs between January 1 of an odd-numbered year and January 1 of an even-numbered year will have its true value determined as of January 1 of the odd-numbered year.	
Montana	Construction of improvements does not become taxable until completed, with partial exemptions further applying during the first five years following completion.	
Nebraska	Improvements become taxable to the extent completed on December 31 prior to January 1 assessment date.	
Nevada	A closed assessment roll may be reopened to reflect changes in improvements resulting from new construction occurring before July 1.	
New Hampshire	No specific statutory provisions.	However, in certain cities and towns that adopt provisions for the semi-annual collection of taxes and for properties that have physically changed in valuation, the partial payment of taxes assessed on April 1 is computed using the current year's appraisal multiplied by one-half of the previous year's tax rate.

Jurisdiction	Construction Work in Progress	Comment
New Jersey	Construction work in progress on the October 1 assessment date of any year and completed before January 1 is assessed on the basis of the property's value on the first day of the month following completion.	
New Mexico	Construction work in progress, in connection with business property, is valued at 50% of the actual amounts expended as of December 31 of the preceding calendar year, according to the taxpayer's accounting records.	
New York	No specific statutory provisions.	
North Carolina	Partially completed buildings are appraised in accordance with the degree of completion as of January 1.	
North Dakota	Construction work in progress is exempt for up to five years if approved by a city or county governing body.	
Ohio	Construction work in progress is valued based on its value or percentage of completion as it existed on January 1.	
Oklahoma	When a building is constructed upon land after January 1, the value of the building is added to the assessed value of the land upon which the building is constructed, at its fair cash value, for the next ensuing year. However, after the building is completed, it is deemed to have an assessment value of the fair cash value of only the materials used in the building until the building and the underlying land are conveyed to a bona fide purchaser or are occupied or used for any purpose other than as a sales office or is leased, whichever occurs first.	
Oregon	A new commercial building or structure, or an addition to an existing commercial building or structure is generally not taxable until construction is complete; however, noncommercial property may be assessed before construction is complete.	
Pennsylvania	Improvements on buildings not exempt as dwellings are taxable on a prorated basis; residential buildings will not be valued or assessed until occupied, conveyed, or 30 months after building permit is issued.	
Rhode Island	Completed construction work in progress becomes taxable either from the date that the certificate of occupancy is issued or the date that the property is first used, whichever occurs first, prorated for the assessment year in which the construction is completed.	Separate laws exists for each town taxing construction work in progress.

Jurisdiction	Construction Work in Progress	Comment
South Carolina	New structures cannot be assessed for property tax until completed for the intended use.	
South Dakota	Newly constructed improvements are taxable when the improvements reach a value of $10,000 or $30,000, depending on the structure.	
Tennessee	An improvement that is incomplete on January 1 is assessed based on the fair market value of the materials used. If the improvement is subsequently completed and ready for use before the following September 1, the assessment is corrected to reflect the value of the structure at the time of completion. The corrected assessment is then prorated for the portion of the year following the date of completion.	
Texas	No specific statutory provisions.	
Utah	Construction work in progress is valued at full cash value projected upon completion reduced by qualifying allocable preconstruction costs on non-residential property.	
Vermont	Towns may exempt for up to three years construction work in progress up to the first $75,000 of appraised value of homes, dwelling houses, or farms.	
Virginia	New buildings are assessed at their actual value at the time of assessment, whether entirely completed or not.	
Washington	New construction is assessed as of July 31 each year.	
West Virginia	Buildings become taxable when they are fit for use, but construction materials are taxed as personal property.	
Wisconsin	The value of a structure as if it were completed, multiplied by the percentage of completion; or a blanket percentage reduction in value throughout a development in progress.	
Wyoming	No specific statutory provisions. In using an historical cost method of valuing property, construction work in progress is included to the extent it is taxable and not otherwise valued.	

Freeport Exemptions

Jurisdiction	In-Transit/Freeport (Temporary Storage)	Comment
Alabama	Exempt	Personal property consigned to or stored in a facility for shipment outside Alabama is exempt. The exemption may not exceed 36 months.
Alaska	Taxable	No exemption specified by law.
Arizona	Exempt	The following property is exempt: (1) property moving through Arizona to a destination outside the state; (2) property consigned to an Arizona warehouse from a point outside Arizona for storage or assembly in transit to a destination outside Arizona; and (3) commodities held in an Arizona warehouse for resale on a contract subject to the rules of a regulated commodity market.
Arkansas	Exempt	Property in transit to destination in Arkansas taxable only in taxing district of its destination. Property in transit through the state and property manufactured, processed, or refined in the state and stored for out-of-state shipment are exempt.
California	Exempt	Property moving in intrastate commerce on the lien date is taxable. Property moving in interstate or foreign commerce, whether entering or leaving the state, is exempt.
Colorado	Taxable	While no property law provision specifically addresses in-transit property, apparently property in-transit traveling out of state would not be taxable whereas property in-transit traveling into the state would be taxable at its destination.
Connecticut	Exempt	Exemptions apply to (1) merchandise shipped into Connecticut and held in storage in its original package in the name of, or for the account of, the producer or manufacturer in a public commercial storage warehouse and (2) merchandise produced or manufactured in Connecticut that is in a public commercial warehouse or wharf and that is intended to be shipped outside the state in the package or container in which it is stored.
Delaware	Exempt	Personal property is generally exempt in Delaware.
District of Columbia	Exempt	Exemptions apply for personal property held in a public warehouse for shipment outside the District.

Jurisdiction	In-Transit/Freeport (Temporary Storage)	Comment
Florida	Exempt	Exempt provided the in-state storage does not exceed 180 days; tangible personal property physically present in the state on or after January 1 that is in the state for 30 days or less also is exempt.
Georgia	Exempt	Foreign merchandise in transit is exempt while located at the port of original entry or port of export even if it is held in a warehouse where it is assembled, bound, joined, processed, disassembled, divided, cut, broken in bulk, relabeled, or repackaged.
Hawaii	Hawaii County, Honolulu County, Kauai County, and Maui County generally do not tax personal property.	No specific ordinances on topic. However, "property" definition generally excludes personal property.
Idaho	Exempt	Exemptions apply to personal property that is shipped into Idaho, stored in warehouses, and designated for reshipment out of the state, and to property that is shipped into the state, stored in its original package in a warehouse, and owned by a person who has no domicile or business situs in the state.
Illinois	Exempt	Personal property is generally exempt in Illinois.
Indiana	Exempt	Inventory is not subject to assessment. All personal property is subject to tax unless specifically exempted.
Iowa	Exempt	Although no specific exemption is authorized, most personal property is exempt in Iowa.
Kansas	Exempt	Exemptions apply for in-transit property moving through the state in interstate commerce, except taxable public utility inventories, even if it is warehoused in Kansas prior to reaching its final destination outside the state.
Kentucky	Exempt	Exemptions apply for personal property shipped into Kentucky and placed in a warehouse or distribution center for the purpose of further shipment to an out-of-state destination.
Louisiana	Exempt	Exemptions apply to raw materials, goods, commodities, articles and personal property held in storage while in transit through Louisiana, which are moving in interstate commerce through or over the territory of the state, or that are held in storage within Louisiana, having been shipped from outside Louisiana for storage in transit to a final destination outside Louisiana.

Jurisdiction	In-Transit/Freeport (Temporary Storage)	Comment
Maine	Exempt	Exemptions apply for in-transit property that is moving through the state in interstate commerce.
Maryland	Taxable	No specific exemption is authorized, although local governing bodies may authorize payments in lieu of property taxes for business stock consisting of foreign imports if the foreign imports are in their original packages and are in the possession of a business engaged in importing.
Massachusetts	Exempt	Personal property that is stored in its original package in a public warehouse is exempt if owned by a person who does not have a domicile or place of business in the state.
Michigan	Exempt	Exemptions apply for products, materials, and goods (except alcoholic beverages) in a public warehouse, U.S. customs port of entry bonded warehouse, dock, or port facility if designated as in-transit to out-of-state destinations.
Minnesota	Exempt	No statutory provision but state has indicated that exemptions apply for goods in transit that are shipped into the state.
Mississippi	Exempt	Exemptions from state, county, and municipal taxes apply for commodities that are: (1) in transit; (2) assembled or stored on wharves, in railway cars, or in warehouses at ports of entry designated by the federal government; and (3) intended for import or export into, through, or from Mississippi. At the discretion of a county or municipality, exemptions from local taxes apply for personal property that is: (1) moving in interstate commerce through the state, (2) consigned or transferred to a licensed free port warehouse in the state for storage in transit to a final destination outside the state, (3) manufactured in Mississippi and stored in separate facilities, structures, places or areas maintained by a manufacturer, licensed as a free port warehouse, for temporary storage and handling pending transit to a final destination outside the state, or (4) consigned or transferred to a licensed free port warehouse within the state, for storage pending transit to not more than one other location in the state for production or processing into a component or part that is then transported to a final destination outside of the state.

Jurisdiction	In-Transit/Freeport (Temporary Storage)	Comment
Missouri	Exempt	Exemptions apply for personal property moving through the state in interstate commerce, even if it is warehoused in the state prior to reaching its final destination outside the state.
Montana	Exempt	Exemptions apply for merchandise produced outside Montana that is in transit through the state and that is consigned to a storage facility in the state prior to shipment to a final destination outside the state.
Nebraska	Taxable	No exemption specified by law.
Nevada	Exempt	Exemptions apply for property moving in interstate commerce through or over Nevada or consigned to a Nevada warehouse from outside the state for storage in transit to a final destination outside the state.
New Hampshire	Exempt	Personal property is generally exempt in New Hampshire.
New Jersey	Exempt	Personal property is generally exempt in New Jersey. The metal content of ores and unrefined metals owned by nonresidents of New Jersey and stopped in transit through the state for the purpose of refining is exempt.
New Mexico	Exempt	Exemptions apply for personal property being transported in interstate commerce to a destination outside the state, even if it is consigned to an in-state warehouse or factory.
New York	Exempt	Personal property is generally exempt in New York.
North Carolina	Exempt	Exemptions apply to: (1) property that has been imported from a foreign country through a North Carolina seaport terminal and which is stored at the terminal while awaiting further shipment for the first 12 months of storage; (2) property shipped into North Carolina for the purpose of repair, alteration, maintenance, or servicing and reshipment to the owner outside the state; (3) motor vehicle chassis belonging to nonresidents and temporarily in-state to have a body mounted upon them.
North Dakota	Exempt	Although no specific exemption is authorized, most personal property is exempt in North Dakota.

Jurisdiction	In-Transit/Freeport (Temporary Storage)	Comment
Ohio	Exempt	Exemptions apply for merchandise and agricultural products shipped into Ohio for storage purposes only (without further manufacturing or processing), held in a facility not owned or controlled by the owner of the merchandise, and subsequently shipped out of Ohio to anyone. Due to a phase-out of the underlying tax base initiated in 2005, the tax effectively on personal property has become moot, except as it relates to certain utilities. The tax has not been repealed, but its tax basis, in most instances, has been reduced to 0%.
Oklahoma	Exempt	A general "in-transit" exemption applies to personal property moving through the state if the property is forwarded at through rates from the point of origin to the point of destination and not detained in Oklahoma for more than 90 days. The specific "freeport exemption," however, applies to goods, wares, and merchandise moving through the state, but temporarily held for assembly, storage, manufacturing, processing, or fabricating purposes, if the holding period is not for more than nine months.
Oregon	Exempt	Exemptions apply for property moving in interstate or foreign commerce, whether entering or leaving the state, while it remains in transit.
Pennsylvania	Exempt	Exempt as personal property. No specific provisions on in-transit property.
Rhode Island	Taxable	Manufactured property brought into the state for finishing and returned to a nonresident owner is exempt.
South Carolina	Exempt	Exemptions apply for property moving in interstate commerce through the state or consigned to an in-state warehouse from outside the state for storage while in transit to an out-of-state destination.
South Dakota	Exempt	Exempt as personal property. No specific provisions on in-transit property.
Tennessee	Exempt	Exemptions apply to (1) property moving in interstate commerce, (2) property consigned to an in-state warehouse for storage while in transit to a final destination outside the state, and (3) property transported from outside the state to an in-state plant, warehouse, or establishment for storage or repackaging and held for eventual sale or other disposition outside the state.

Jurisdiction	In-Transit/Freeport (Temporary Storage)	Comment
Texas	Exempt	An exemption applies to property that is (1) acquired in or imported into the state to be forwarded outside the state, (2) detained in state for assembling, storing, manufacturing, processing, or fabricating purposes, and (3) transported outside the state within 175 days.
Utah	Exempt	An exemption applies to property that is held for shipment to a final destination outside the state within 12 months.
Vermont	Taxable	No specific statutes on topic.
Virginia	Exempt	Exemptions apply to domestic merchandise scheduled for export while in inventory located in a foreign trade zone within Virginia and cargo merchandise, and equipment in transit that is stored, located or housed temporarily in a marine or airport terminal in Virginia prior to being transported by vessels or aircraft to a point outside Virginia.
Washington	Exempt	A proportional exemption is allowed to account for property in transit.
West Virginia	Exempt	
Wisconsin	Taxable	Goods and merchandise located in storage in a commercial storage warehouse or on a public wharf are assessed to the property owner, not the warehouse owner.
Wyoming	Exempt	

Intangible Property

For purposes of this chart, the term "taxable" applies only in those jurisdictions in which the authority to tax intangible property has been exercised, while the term "exempt" applies both to jurisdictions that have enacted specific exemptions for intangible property, and to those that have the authority to tax intangible property but have not done so.

Jurisdiction	Intangible Property	Comment
Alabama	Taxable	Specified intangibles, such as certain bonds and hoarded money, are taxable.
Alaska	Exempt	
Arizona	Exempt	
Arkansas	Exempt	Intangible property of taxpayers subject to assessment by the Arkansas Public Service Commission is not included in the general exemption on intangible property.
California	Exempt	Taxable property may be assessed and valued by assuming the presence of intangible assets or rights necessary to put taxable property to beneficial or productive use.
Colorado	Exempt	
Connecticut	Exempt	
Delaware	Exempt	
District of Columbia	Exempt	
Florida	Exempt	A non-reoccurring tax is imposed on notes, bonds, or other obligations of money that are secured by a mortgage deed or other lien of real property. A recurring tax on the lease of real property owned by a government and leased to a nongovernmental entity is also due with rental payments.
Georgia	Exempt	A separate intangible recording tax applies only to long-term notes secured by real estate.
Hawaii	Hawaii County, Honolulu County, Kauai County, and Maui County generally do not tax personal property.	No specific ordinances on topic. However, "property" definition generally excludes personal property.
Idaho	Exempt	
Illinois	Exempt	Personal property tax is not levied on any personal property with a situs in Illinois.
Indiana	Exempt	
Iowa	Exempt	
Kansas	Exempt	

Jurisdiction	Intangible Property	Comment
Kentucky	Exempt	All intangible property except that assessed under the financial institution deposit tax or corporation and public utility taxes is exempt from state and local ad valorem tax.
Louisiana	Exempt	Public service properties, bank stocks, and credit assessments on premiums written in the state by insurance companies and loan and finance companies are taxable.
Maine	Exempt	There is an excise tax, as opposed to an ad valorem tax, on the assets of financial institutions to meet the administrative costs of supervision.
Maryland	Exempt	
Massachusetts	Exempt	
Michigan	Exempt	
Minnesota	Exempt	
Mississippi	Taxable	Money on hand and evidence of indebtedness bearing interest in excess of the maximum rate allowed by law are taxable. Statutory exemptions exist for most other categories.
Missouri	Exempt	
Montana	Exempt	
Nebraska	Exempt	
Nevada	Exempt	
New Hampshire	Exempt	
New Jersey	Exempt	
New Mexico	Exempt	
New York	Exempt	
North Carolina	Exempt	Leasehold interests in exempted real property taxable.
North Dakota	Exempt	
Ohio	Taxable	Due to a phase-out of the underlying tax base initiated in 2005, the tax effectively on personal property has become moot, except as it relates to certain utilities. The tax has not been repealed, but its tax basis, in most instances, has been reduced to 0%. Intangible property of certain charities is exempt.
Oklahoma	Exempt	
Oregon	Exempt	

Jurisdiction	Intangible Property	Comment
Pennsylvania	Taxable	County option tax can be imposed on specified intangibles owned by resident individuals and corporations.
Rhode Island	Exempt	
South Carolina	Exempt	
South Dakota	Exempt	
Tennessee	Exempt	Only certain intangibles of insurance companies and loan and investment companies are taxable.
Texas	Exempt	Only certain intangibles of insurance companies and savings and loan associations are taxable.
Utah	Exempt	
Vermont	Exempt	
Virginia	Exempt	
Washington	Exempt	
West Virginia	Exempt	
Wisconsin	Exempt	
Wyoming	Exempt	Water rights and reservoir rights are subject to tax.

Legal Basis for Assessment

Jurisdiction	Assessment/Valuation Basis	Comment
Alabama	Specified percentages of fair and reasonable market value.	
Alaska	Full and true value.	
Arizona	Specified percentages of either full cash value or limited property value.	
Arkansas	No more than 20% of true and full market or actual value.	
California	Full value.	Full value means full cash value, fair market value, or such other value as constitutionally or statutorily prescribed.
Colorado	29% of actual value of all nonresidential property. Residential property assessed based on a ratio of valuation.	The residential rate is 7.2% of actual value for the property tax years commencing on or after January 1, 2017.
Connecticut	70% of the true and actual value.	
Delaware	True value in money.	
District of Columbia	Estimated market value.	
Florida	Just value.	
Georgia	Specified percentages (generally 40%) of fair market value.	
Hawaii	Hawaii County, Honolulu County, Maui County, Kauai County: Percentage of fair market value.	
Idaho	Full market value.	
Illinois	33 1/3% of fair cash value.	Special percentages apply within Cook County.
Indiana	True tax value.	
Iowa	100% of actual value except for certain classes of property.	
Kansas	Fair market value in money.	
Kentucky	Fair cash value.	
Louisiana	Specified percentages of fair market value, or for certain property types, use value.	
Maine	Just value, which is 100% of current market value.	
Maryland	Specified percentages of full cash value.	
Massachusetts	Specified percentages of fair cash value.	
Michigan	50% of true cash value.	

Jurisdiction	Assessment/Valuation Basis	Comment
Minnesota	Specified percentages of market value.	
Mississippi	True value.	Specified percentages are applied to the true value to determine assessed value.
Missouri	Specified percentages of true value in money.	
Montana	100% of market value.	
Nebraska	Actual value for real property, net book value for personal property.	
Nevada	35% of taxable value, generally.	
New Hampshire	Market value.	
New Jersey	True market value.	
New Mexico	One-third of market value.	
New York	Current full value (market value).	Under the use standard for valuation, improved property is assessed for its current use, while property that is put to no current use is assessed for its highest and best use.
North Carolina	True value in money.	
North Dakota	Specified percentages of assessed value.	
Ohio	Specified percentages of true value in money (not to exceed 35% of true value)	
Oklahoma	Between 11% and 13.5% of fair cash value.	
Oregon	The assessed value of property equals the lesser of its maximum assessed value (the greater of 103% of assessed value from the prior year or 100% of the maximum assessed value from the prior year) or the property's real market value.	
Pennsylvania	Predetermined ratio applied to actual value.	
Rhode Island	Full and fair cash value.	
South Carolina	Specified percentages of true value in money.	
South Dakota	True and full value in money.	
Tennessee	Specified percentages of appraised or market value.	
Texas	Market value.	
Utah	Specified percentages of fair market value.	

Jurisdiction	Assessment/Valuation Basis	Comment
Vermont	1% of listed value (fair market value).	
Virginia	Fair market value.	
Washington	100% of true and fair value in money.	
West Virginia	60% of true and actual value.	
Wisconsin	Full cash value.	
Wyoming	Generally 9.5% (11.5% for industrial property) of fair market value. 100% of gross products for mines, minerals.	

Personal Property Renditions

Jurisdiction	Personal Property Return/Rendition Date	Comment
Alabama	January 1.	
Alaska	Varies locally.	
Arizona	April 1.	
Arkansas	May 31.	
California	April 1.	Penalties apply for statements filed after May 7. Statements may be amended without penalty prior to May 31.
Colorado	April 15.	
Connecticut	November 1.	
Delaware	Exempt	
District of Columbia	July 31.	
Florida	April 1.	
Georgia	From January 1 to April 1.	
Hawaii	Exempt	
Idaho	March 15.	
Illinois	Exempt	
Indiana	May 15.	
Iowa	Exempt	
Kansas	March 15.	
Kentucky	May 15.	
Louisiana	Later of April 1 or within 45 days of receipt of forms from assessor. In Jefferson Parish, 45 days after receipt of forms from assessor.	
Maine	Varies locally.	
Maryland	April 15.	
Massachusetts	March 1.	
Michigan	February 20.	
Minnesota	Exempt	
Mississippi	April 1.	
Missouri	March 1.	
Montana	March 1.	

Jurisdiction	Personal Property Return/Rendition Date	Comment
Nebraska	On or before May 1.	For tax year 2020, return must be filed by May 1, 2020 or before July 15, 2020.
Nevada	July 31.	
New Hampshire	Exempt	
New Jersey	Exempt	Business tangible personal property, exclusive of inventories, is subject to local property taxes if used in the business of local exchange telephone, telegraph and messenger systems, companies, corporations or associations that were subject to the public utilities gross receipts tax as of April 1, 1997.
New Mexico	For centrally assessed property, by the last day of February. For most other property, generally no annual report is due.	
New York	Exempt	
North Carolina	First business day in January through January 31.	
North Dakota	Exempt	
Ohio	Forms generally are not required for tax years after 2008 or, for certain telecommunication property, 2010. For certain utilities, between February 15 and April 30.	Due to a phase-out of the underlying tax base initiated in 2005, the tax on personal property effectively has become moot, except as it relates to certain utilities. The tax has not been repealed, but its tax basis, in most instances, has been reduced to 0%.
Oklahoma	March 15.	
Oregon	March 15.	
Pennsylvania	Intangible personal property only. Deadline either set within January 1 and 15 or January 1st if not set.	
Rhode Island	January 31.	
South Carolina	April 30.	
South Dakota	Exempt	
Tennessee	March 1.	
Texas	April 15 For rendition statements and property reports for property located in an appraisal district in which one or more taxing units exempt freeport property, the date is April 1, effective January 1, 2018	
Utah	May 15 or, for counties of the first class, the later of 60 days following request or May 15.	
Vermont	April 1.	

Jurisdiction	Personal Property Return/Rendition Date	Comment
Virginia	May 1.	
Washington	April 30.	
West Virginia	July 1 through October 1.	Corporate property reports due between the first day of the assessment year and September 1.
Wisconsin	March 1.	
Wyoming	March 1.	

Real Property Delinquency Date

Jurisdiction	Real Property Delinquency Date	Comment
Alabama	January 1.	
Alaska	Varies locally.	
Arizona	1/2 November 1, 1/2 May 1.	Taxes that are unpaid are delinquent after 5:00 p.m. on the due dates.
Arkansas	October 16.	
California	1/2 December 10, 1/2 April 10.	
Colorado	May 1 for taxpayers making payments in full; or for taxpayers paying 1/2 in Feb and 1/2 in June, delinquent on June 16.	
Connecticut	Unpaid tax or tax installments become delinquent on the first day of the month following the month in which the tax became due.	
Delaware	October 1.	September 2 for New Castle County.
District of Columbia	1/2 April 1, 1/2 September 16.	
Florida	Later of April 1 following year in which assessed or immediately after 60 days have expired from mailing of original tax notice.	
Georgia	December 20.	Subject to variations in some counties.
Hawaii	1/2 August 21, 1/2 February 21.	
Idaho	December 21; or 1/2 December 21, 1/2 June 21.	
Illinois	1/2 on June 2, 1/2 on September 2, or the day after the date specified on the real estate tax bill as the due date for the first or second installment.	
Indiana	1/2 May 11, 1/2 November 11.	
Iowa	1/2 October 1, 1/2 April 1.	
Kansas	December 21; or 1/2 December 21, 1/2 May 11.	
Kentucky	January 1.	
Louisiana	December 31. February 1 for Orleans Parish.	
Maine	Varies locally.	
Maryland	October 1.	
Massachusetts	November 1, or 30 days after tax bill mailed if mailed after October 1.	
Michigan	March 1.	March 1 for summer levy.

Jurisdiction	Real Property Delinquency Date	Comment
Minnesota	1/2 May 16 (or 21 days after tax notice is postmarked, if later), 1/2 October 16.	
Mississippi	February 2.	Property taxes also may be payable in installments and become delinquent if the following schedule is not met: 50% due by February 1; 25% due by May 1; and 25% due by July 1.
Missouri	January 1.	
Montana	1/2 December 1 (or 30 days after tax notice is postmarked, if later), 1/2 June 1.	
Nebraska	1/2 May 1, 1/2 September 1.	For counties with a population of more than 100,000, 1/2 April 1 and 1/2 August 1.
Nevada	Day after third Monday in August.	For quarterly installments, day after third Monday in August and first Mondays in October, January, and March. There is a 10-day grace period following payment due date before penalty imposed.
New Hampshire	December 2.	Subject to variations in some cities/ towns.
New Jersey	1/4 February 2, 1/4 May 2, 1/4 August 2, 1/4 November 2.	
New Mexico	30 days after due date.	
New York	Varies locally.	
North Carolina	January 6.	
North Dakota	January 1. Installment payments: 1/2 March 2, 1/2 October 16.	
Ohio	1/2 January 1, 1/2 June 21.	
Oklahoma	November 2 for property owners, January 1 for mortgage servicers.	Special rules apply to installment payments.
Oregon	May 16.	
Pennsylvania	Delinquent for all taxing districts as of December 31 of each calendar year.	
Rhode Island	Varies locally.	
South Carolina	Later of January 16 or 30 days after mailing of tax notice.	
South Dakota	1/2 May 1, 1/2 November 1.	
Tennessee	March 1.	
Texas	February 1; or 1/2 December 1, 1/2 July 1 (if locality has elected split payment option).	
Utah	December 1.	

Jurisdiction	Real Property Delinquency Date	Comment
Vermont	Varies locally.	
Virginia	December 6.	Subject to variations in some localities.
Washington	May 1; or 1/2 May 1, 1/2 November 1.	
West Virginia	October 1 for first installment; April 1 for second installment.	On or after April 1 of each year, the sheriff may prepare and publish a notice stating that the taxes assessed for the previous year have become delinquent.
Wisconsin	February 1; or 1/2 February 1, 1/2 August 1.	
Wyoming	November 11 and May 11, unless all taxes are paid by December 31	

Real Property Lien Date

Jurisdiction	Real Property Lien Date	Comment
Alabama	October 1.	
Alaska	January 1.	
Arizona	January 1.	
Arkansas	First Monday in January.	
California	January 1.	
Colorado	January 1.	
Connecticut	October 1.	
Delaware	Varies locally.	
District of Columbia	January 1.	
Florida	January 1.	
Georgia	Varies locally.	
Hawaii	July 1.	
Idaho	January 1.	
Illinois	January 1.	
Indiana	May 10.	
Iowa	September 1.	Lien attaches at time tax due and payable.
Kansas	November 1.	
Kentucky	January 1.	
Louisiana	December 31.	
Maine	9 to 12 months from commitment date.	
Maryland	July 1.	
Massachusetts	January 1.	
Michigan	December 1, a day set by a city or village charter, or a tax day designated as such by a county, township, city, or village treasurer.	July 1 for summer levy.
Minnesota	January 2.	
Mississippi	January 1.	
Missouri	January 1.	
Montana	January 1.	
Nebraska	December 31.	
Nevada	July 1.	
New Hampshire	October 1.	

Jurisdiction	Real Property Lien Date	Comment
New Jersey	January 1.	
New Mexico	January 1.	
New York	Varies locally.	
North Carolina	January 1.	
North Dakota	January 1.	
Ohio	January 1.	
Oklahoma	November 1, generally. For specified grantor/grantee conveyances, October 1.	
Oregon	July 1.	
Pennsylvania	Varies locally.	
Rhode Island	December 31.	
South Carolina	December 31.	
South Dakota	January 1.	
Tennessee	January 1.	
Texas	January 1.	
Utah	January 1.	
Vermont	Varies locally.	
Virginia	December 6.	
Washington	January 1.	
West Virginia	July 1.	
Wisconsin	January 1.	
Wyoming	Perpetual	

Real Property Payment Date

Jurisdiction	Real Property Payment Date	Comment
Alabama	October 1.	For municipal taxes, varies locally.
Alaska	Varies locally.	
Arizona	1/2 October 1, 1/2 March 1.	
Arkansas	One-fourth is payable from first business day in March through the third Monday in April; one-fourth, or a first installment of one-half if no payment was made, is payable from the third Monday in April through the third Monday in July; and one-half is payable from the third Monday in July through October 15.	
California	1/2 November 1, 1/2 February 1.	Payments for property on unsecured roll are due January 1.
Colorado	For taxpayers paying 2 equal payments: 1/2 due last day of February, 1/2 due June 15. For taxpayers making payment in full: due April 30.	
Connecticut	July 1.	Municipalities may provide for single, semi-annual, or quarterly payments.
Delaware	July 1 (New Castle County); June 1 (Kent County); July 1 (Sussex County).	
District of Columbia	1/2 March 31, 1/2 September 15.	
Florida	November 1.	Election to pay in quarterly installments available.
Georgia	December 20.	Subject to variations in some counties, and installment payments permitted in certain counties.
Hawaii	Two equal installments due August 20 and February 20.	
Idaho	December 20; or 1/2 December 20, 1/2 June 20.	
Illinois	1/2 June 1, 1/2 September 1, unless county has created different deadlines. For Cook County, March 1 (55% of estimate), August 1 (balance based on actual tax bill).	
Indiana	1/2 May 10, 1/2 November 10.	
Iowa	1/2 September 1, 1/2 March 1.	
Kansas	1/2 December 20, 1/2 May 10.	For tax amounts of $10 or less, full payment due December 20.
Kentucky	December 31. 2% discount for payment by November 1.	
Louisiana	November 15.	

Jurisdiction	Real Property Payment Date	Comment
Maine	Varies locally.	
Maryland	July 1.	County or municipal corporation governing bodies must provide a semiannual payment schedule for small business property with a tax bill of $100,000 or less for tax years beginning after June 30, 2012.
Massachusetts	July 1.	Localities may allow semi-annual or quarterly tax payments.
Michigan	February 14; July 1 for summer levy.	Different provisions apply to villages and fourth class cities.
Minnesota	1/2 May 15, 1/2 October 15.	
Mississippi	February 1.	For counties authorizing partial payment, 1/2 of payment is due February 1, 1/4 is due May 1, and 1/4 is due July 1.
Missouri	December 31.	Locality may allow installment payments.
Montana	1/2 November 30, 1/2 May 31.	
Nebraska	Due December 31, with installment payments due on May 1 and September 1 (April 1 and August 1 in larger counties).	
Nevada	Third Monday in August; or 1/4 third Monday in August and 1/4 on each of the first Mondays in October, January, March.	
New Hampshire	December 1.	Locality may allow semiannual installment payments.
New Jersey	Quarterly installments due February 1, May 1, August 1, November 1.	Municipalities may allow a grace period for payments of up to an additional ten calendar days. Retroactively effective to July 1, 2017, taxpayers are permitted to make dedicated prepayments toward anticipated property taxes, regardless of whether any tax bills have been issued prior to prepayment.
New Mexico	1/2 November 10, 1/2 April 10.	Prepayment option may be available that results in four installments.
New York	Later of January 31, or 30 days after receipt of tax roll and warrant.	Installment payments may be made.
North Carolina	September 1.	
North Dakota	January 1.	Installment payments may be made.
Ohio	December 31; or 1/2 December 31, 1/2 June 20.	
Oklahoma	November 1; or 1/2 December 31, 1/2 March 31.	

Jurisdiction	Real Property Payment Date	Comment
Oregon	November 15; or 1/3 November 15, 1/3 February 15, 1/3 May 15.	
Pennsylvania	Varies locally.	
Rhode Island	Varies locally.	
South Carolina	September 30 through January 15.	May vary by locality.
South Dakota	April 30 and October 31.	Electronic installment payments may be permitted.
Tennessee	County taxes due on first Monday of October. Payment dates for municipal taxes vary by municipality.	Municipalities that collect their own property taxes may opt to accept partial tax payments.
Texas	January 31.	1/2 December 1, 1/2 July 1, if governing body of taxing unit has adopted split-payment option.
Utah	November 30.	
Vermont	Varies locally.	
Virginia	December 5.	Unless another date is set by the locality.
Washington	April 30; or 1/2 April 30, 1/2 October 31.	
West Virginia	1/2 September 1, 1/2 March 1.	
Wisconsin	January 31; or 1/2 January 31, 1/2 July 31.	
Wyoming	December 31; or 1/2 September 1, 1/2 March 1.	

Real Property Tax Year

Jurisdiction	Real Property Tax Year	Comment
Alabama	October-September.	
Alaska	Calendar year.	
Arizona	Calendar year.	
Arkansas	Calendar year.	
California	July 1 - June 30.	
Colorado	Calendar year.	
Connecticut	October-September.	
Delaware	Varies locally.	
District of Columbia	October-September.	
Florida	Calendar year.	
Georgia	Calendar year.	
Hawaii	July 1-June 30.	
Idaho	Calendar year.	
Illinois	Calendar year.	
Indiana	January 1.	
Iowa	Calendar year.	
Kansas	Calendar year.	
Kentucky	Calendar year.	
Louisiana	Calendar year.	
Maine	April-March.	
Maryland	July-June.	
Massachusetts	July 1 - June 30 Assessed on the preceding January 1.	
Michigan	Calendar year.	
Minnesota	Calendar year.	
Mississippi	Calendar year.	
Missouri	Calendar year.	
Montana	Calendar year.	
Nebraska	Calendar year.	
Nevada	July-June.	
New Hampshire	April-March.	
New Jersey	Municipalities operate on a calendar year or fiscal year basis.	Real property is assessed on October 1.

Jurisdiction	Real Property Tax Year	Comment
New Mexico	Calendar year.	
New York	July-June.	
North Carolina	Calendar year.	
North Dakota	Calendar year.	
Ohio	Calendar year.	
Oklahoma	Calendar year.	
Oregon	July 1 - June 30.	
Pennsylvania	Varies locally.	
Rhode Island	December 31.	
South Carolina	Calendar year.	
South Dakota	Calendar year.	
Tennessee	Calendar year.	
Texas	Calendar year.	
Utah	Calendar year.	
Vermont	April-March.	
Virginia	Calendar year.	
Washington	Calendar year.	
West Virginia	July-June.	
Wisconsin	Calendar year.	
Wyoming	Calendar year.	

Tangible Personal Property

Jurisdiction	Tangible Personal Property	Comment
Alabama	Taxable	Taxable unless a specific exemption applies. Most personal-use property is exempt.
Alaska	Taxable	Alaska authorizes municipal taxes on personal property and state tax on personal property used for oil and gas exploration, production, and pipeline transportation. Municipalities are authorized to levy a flat tax on personal property, except that household furniture and personal effects are exempt.
Arizona	Taxable	Taxable unless a specific exemption applies. The first $50,000 (indexed for inflation) of business personal property and household goods is exempt. The exemption amount is adjusted annually.
Arkansas	Taxable	Taxable unless a specific exemption applies. Personal property used within the home is exempt.
California	Taxable	Taxable unless a specific exemption applies. Household goods and personal effects are exempt.
Colorado	Taxable	Taxable unless a specific exemption applies. Exemption for business inventories, household goods and motor vehicles is adjusted biennially to account for inflation.
Connecticut	Taxable	Taxable unless a specific exemption applies. Specific household and personal effects are exempt.
Delaware	Exempt	
District of Columbia	Taxable	Only personal property used in a trade or business is taxable. Specific exemptions may apply.
Florida	Taxable	Taxable unless a specific exemption applies. Household goods and personal effects are exempt.
Georgia	Taxable	Taxable unless a specific exemption applies. Household goods, personal effects, and the first $7,500 of otherwise taxable personal property are exempt.
Hawaii	Hawaii County, Honolulu County, Kauai County, and Maui County generally do not tax personal property.	No specific ordinances on topic. However, "property" definition generally excludes personal property.

Jurisdiction	Tangible Personal Property	Comment
Idaho	Taxable	Taxable unless a specific exemption applies. The first $100,000 of business personal property is annually exempt, generally. A purchased taxable personal property item is generally exempt if it has an acquisition cost of $3,000 or less.
Illinois	Exempt	
Indiana	Taxable	Taxable unless a specific exemption applies. Household goods are exempt.
Iowa	Exempt	Most personal property is exempt, although some items of personal property are deemed to be real property.
Kansas	Taxable	Taxable unless a specific exemption applies. Household items, business inventories, and other specified properties are exempt.
Kentucky	Taxable	Taxable unless a specific exemption applies. Household goods are exempt.
Louisiana	Taxable	Taxable unless a specific exemption applies. Personal property used in the home is exempt.
Maine	Taxable	Taxable unless a specific exemption applies. Exemptions are provided for household goods, apparel, farming utensils, mechanics' tools, and de minimis property (less than $1,000).
Maryland	Taxable	Exempt from state property tax; may be subject to a local property tax. Multiple exemptions apply. Only certain personal property used in connection with a business or profession is taxable.
Massachusetts	Taxable	Taxable unless a specific exemption applies. Household effects of residents kept at their domiciles are exempt.
Michigan	Taxable	Taxable unless a specific exemption applies. Household goods are exempt.
Minnesota	Taxable	Only specified items of personal property are taxable. Household goods are exempt.
Mississippi	Taxable	Taxable unless a specific exemption applies. Specified household goods are exempt.
Missouri	Taxable	Taxable unless a specific exemption applies. Household goods are exempt.
Montana	Taxable	Taxable unless a specific exemption applies. Household goods and furniture are exempt.

Jurisdiction	Tangible Personal Property	Comment
Nebraska	Taxable	A personal property tax exemption is available on the first $10,000 of valuation of tangible personal property in each tax district in which a personal property tax return is required to be filed. Only depreciable property that is used in a trade or business or for the production of income and that has a determinable life longer than one year is taxable.
Nevada	Taxable	Taxable unless a specific exemption applies. Household goods and furniture used by a single household and owned by a member of that household are exempt.
New Hampshire	Exempt	
New Jersey	Exempt	Only business personal property used by specified utilities and petroleum refineries is taxable.
New Mexico	Taxable	Only specified items of personal property are taxable. Household items are not included in the list of taxable property.
New York	Exempt	
North Carolina	Taxable	Taxable unless a specific exemption applies. Nonbusiness property generally is not taxable.
North Dakota	Taxable	Only centrally assessed property of certain entities is taxable.
Ohio	N/A	Due to a phase-out of the underlying tax base initiated in 2005, the tax on personal property effectively has become moot, except as it relates to certain utilities. The tax has not been repealed, but its tax basis, in most instances, has been reduced to 0%.
Oklahoma	Taxable	Taxable unless a specific exemption applies. Household goods are exempt, subject to a $100 cap, although counties may enact a full exemption.
Oregon	Taxable	Only personal property used in a trade or business is taxable.
Pennsylvania	Exempt	
Rhode Island	Taxable	Taxable unless a specific exemption applies. Household goods and furniture are exempt.
South Carolina	Taxable	Taxable unless a specific exemption applies. Household goods, wearing apparel, and furniture used in the owner's home are exempt.

Jurisdiction	Tangible Personal Property	Comment
South Dakota	Exempt	Only the personal property of centrally assessed utilities and railroads is taxable.
Tennessee	Taxable	Only personal property used in a business or profession is taxable.
Texas	Taxable	Unless a locality elects otherwise, only income-producing personal property is taxablc.
Utah	Taxable	Taxable unless a specific exemption applies. Household goods used exclusively by their owner in maintaining a home are exempt.
Vermont	Taxable	Taxable unless a specific exemption applies. Personal wearing apparel, household furniture, and equipment are exempt.
Virginia	Taxable	Taxable unless a specific exemption applies. Household goods and personal effects are exempt only if a local authority enacts the exemption.
Washington	Taxable	Taxable unless a specific exemption applies. Household goods and personal effects are exempt.
West Virginia	Taxable	Taxable unless a specific exemption applies. Household goods and personal effects are exempt; $200 exemption for property used for profit.
Wisconsin	Taxable	Taxable unless a specific exemption applies. Household goods and personal effects are exempt.
Wyoming	Taxable	Taxable unless a specific exemption applies. Personal property used for personal or family use (excluding mobile homes) is exempt.

Taxation of Inventories

Jurisdiction	Inventories	Comment
Alabama	Exempt	Stocks of goods, wares, and merchandise are exempt.
Alaska	Taxable	Inventory exemption may be enacted by each municipality.
Arizona	Exempt	
Arkansas	Taxable	Inventory of merchants and manufacturers is taxable.
California	Exempt	
Colorado	Exempt	Inventory is constitutionally exempt.
Connecticut	Exempt	
Delaware	Exempt	
District of Columbia	Exempt	
Florida	Exempt	
Georgia	Exempt	
Hawaii	Hawaii County, Honolulu County, Kauai County, and Maui County generally do not tax personal property.	No specific ordinances on topic. However, "property" definition generally excludes personal property.
Idaho	Exempt	
Illinois	Exempt	
Indiana	Exempt	
Iowa	Exempt	
Kansas	Exempt	
Kentucky	Taxable	Merchants' inventories and manufacturers' finished goods ready for sale, raw materials, and goods in process are subject to state property tax.
Louisiana	Taxable	Inventory is taxable, unless it is being held in the state for storage purposes only.
Maine	Exempt	
Maryland	Exempt	Business stock of person engaged in a manufacturing or commercial business is exempt.
Massachusetts	Taxable	Inventories held by corporations are exempt; inventories held by unincorporated businesses are taxable.
Michigan	Exempt	Inventory is exempt, unless it is held for lease or federal depreciation or depletion deductions have been claimed.

Jurisdiction	Inventories	Comment
Minnesota	Exempt	
Mississippi	Taxable	Counties and municipalities may elect an exemption for manufactured products that are held by the manufacturer and located within the county or municipality.
Missouri	Exempt	
Montana	Exempt	
Nebraska	Exempt	
Nevada	Exempt	
New Hampshire	Exempt	
New Jersey	Exempt	
New Mexico	Exempt	Inventory generally exempt, unless federal depreciation or depletion deductions have been claimed.
New York	Exempt	
North Carolina	Exempt	
North Dakota	Exempt	
Ohio	N/A	Due to a phase-out of the underlying tax base initiated in 2005, the tax effectively on personal property has become moot, except as it relates to certain utilities. The tax has not been repealed, but its tax basis, in most instances, has been reduced to 0%.
Oklahoma	Taxable	
Oregon	Exempt	
Pennsylvania	Exempt	
Rhode Island	Exempt	
South Carolina	Exempt	
South Dakota	Exempt	Inventory is exempt unless it is owned by a centrally assessed utility.
Tennessee	Exempt	Inventory of merchandise held for sale or exchange by persons subject to the state business and occupation tax is exempt.
Texas	Taxable	
Utah	Exempt	
Vermont	Taxable	Inventory is taxable, although municipalities may elect an exemption.
Virginia	Taxable	Inventory generally is taxable as merchants' capital, although local taxing authorities may enact an exemption.

Jurisdiction	Inventories	Comment
Washington	Exempt	
West Virginia	Taxable	
Wisconsin	Exempt	A merchant's stock-in-trade, manufacturers' materials and finished products, and livestock are exempt, but property held for rental is taxable.
Wyoming	Exempt	

PRACTICE AND PROCEDURE

The following pages contain charts summarizing facets of state tax practice and procedure. Topics covered include interest rates, installment payments, mailing rules, taxpayer representation, whole dollar reporting, record retention, and abatement of penalties and interest. Also included are managed audit programs and state contact information.

Abatement of Penalties and Interest

The state taxing authority of most states, including the District of Columbia, or its director secretary, or authority representative, has the authority to abate or waive penalties or interest due on delinquent taxes if certain criteria are met. The criteria for abatement vary from state to state but generally fall within one of four categories:

(1) Good Cause - some states allow abatement of penalties or interest if the taxpayer can show good cause for the failure to pay the tax or file the return or report. Some states use one of the following phrases to convey the same concept: reasonable cause, reasonable diligence, good faith, or excusable failure. While many states with these types of provisions provide statutory or regulatory guidance, many leave interpretation of the terms up to the taxing authority;

(2) Department Fault - many states allow abatement of penalties or interest if the penalty or interest was incurred as a result of the taxpayer's reliance on the erroneous advice of taxing authority personnel. In such cases, the taxpayer must have supplied the personnel with all of the necessary facts to render the advice given. In addition, abatement is also allowed where the taxing authority unreasonably delayed the taxpayer and caused penalties or interest to be incurred;

(3) Uncollectible - penalties and interest may sometimes be abated when the taxing authority determines that the amounts due are uncollectible or that the cost of collecting the outstanding amount outweighs the amount that would be collected;

(4) Compromise/Closing Agreement - the final method of abatement of penalties or interest is in conjunction with a compromise of tax or a closing agreement related to disputed outstanding amounts. While this is more in the nature of a settlement of a dispute rather than an abatement, some states limit their abatement provisions to these agreements.

Although most states treat abatements of penalties and interest similarly for all taxes, property taxes are generally the exception. The chart below does not necessarily reflect the States' positions on abatements relating to property taxes.

Jurisdiction	Abatement of Penalties and Interest	Comment
Alabama	Penalties: Good Cause *or* Department Fault Interest: No	
Alaska	Penalties: Compromise/Closing Agreement Interest: No	
Arizona	Penalties: Good Cause *or* Department Fault Interest: Department Fault	
Arkansas	Penalties: Department Fault Interest: Department Fault	

Jurisdiction	Abatement of Penalties and Interest	Comment
California	Penalties: Good Cause *or* Department Fault Interest: Department Fault *or* Uncollectible	
Colorado	Penalties: Good Cause Interest: Good Cause	
Connecticut	Penalties: Uncollectible Interest: Uncollectible	
Delaware	Penalties: Good Cause *or* Department Fault *or* Uncollectible Interest: Good Cause *or* Department Fault *or* Uncollectible	
District of Columbia	Penalties: Good Cause *or* Department Fault Interest: Department Fault	
Florida	Penalties: Good Cause *or* Department Fault *or* Compromise/Closing Agreement Interest: Compromise/Closing Agreement *or* Uncollectible	
Georgia	Penalties: Good Cause Interest: Good Cause	
Hawaii	Penalties: Good Cause *or* Uncollectible Interest: Good Cause *or* Uncollectible	
Idaho	Penalties: Good Cause Interest: No	
Illinois	Penalties: Reasonable Cause *or* Department Fault Interest: No	
Indiana	Penalties: Good Cause Interest: No	
Iowa	Penalties: Department Fault Interest: Department Fault	
Kansas	Penalties: Good Cause *or* Department Fault *or* Uncollectible Interest: Good Cause *or* Department Fault	
Kentucky	Penalties: Good Cause *or* Department Fault Interest: Department Fault	
Louisiana	Penalties: Good Cause *or* Department Fault Interest: Good Cause *or* Department Fault	
Maine	Penalties: Reasonable Cause Interest: Good Cause	
Maryland	Penalties: Good Cause Interest: Good Cause	

Jurisdiction	Abatement of Penalties and Interest	Comment
Massachusetts	Penalties: Good Cause *or* Department Fault Interest: Good Cause	
Michigan	Penalties: Good Cause Interest: No	
Minnesota	Penalties: Good Cause *or* Department Fault Interest: Good Cause *or* Department Fault	
Mississippi	Penalties: Good Cause Interest: Good Cause	
Missouri	Penalties: Good Cause *or* Department Fault Interest: Department Fault	
Montana	Penalties: Good Cause *or* Uncollectible Interest: Good Cause *or* Uncollectible (only if penalty abated, and then at a maximum of $500)	
Nebraska	Penalties: Good Cause Interest: Department Fault or Extreme Hardship	
Nevada	Penalties: Good Cause *or* Department Fault Interest: Good Cause *or* Department Fault	
New Hampshire	Penalties: Good Cause *or* Department Fault *or* Uncollectible Interest: Good Cause *or* Department Fault *or* Uncollectible	
New Jersey	Penalties: Good Cause *or* Department Fault Interest: Good Cause *or* Department Fault	
New Mexico	Penalties: Department Fault *or* Compromise/Closing Agreement Interest: Department Fault *or* Compromise/Closing Agreement	
New York	Penalties: Good Cause *or* Department Fault Interest: Department Fault	
North Carolina	Penalties: Good Cause Interest: Can be reduced or waived if taxpayer files for bankruptcy	
North Dakota	Penalties: Good Cause Interest: Good Cause	
Ohio	Penalties: Good Cause Interest: No	
Oklahoma	Penalties: Good Cause *or* Uncollectible Interest: Good Cause *or* Uncollectible	

Jurisdiction	Abatement of Penalties and Interest	Comment
Oregon	Penalties: Good Cause *or* Uncollectible Interest: Good Cause, Department Fault *or* Uncollectible	
Pennsylvania	Penalties: Good Cause *or* Department Fault Interest: Department Fault	Income tax penalties eligible for abatement limited to $300 or less.
Rhode Island	Penalties: Department Fault, Uncollectible, *or* Compromise/Closing Agreement Interest: Department Fault, Uncollectible, *or* Compromise/Closing Agreement	
South Carolina	Penalties: Good Cause *or* Department Fault Interest: Yes, up to 30 days for administrative convenience.	
South Dakota	Penalties: Good Cause *or* Department Fault Interest: Good Cause *or* Department Fault	
Tennessee	Penalties: Good Cause *or* Department Fault Interest: No	
Texas	Penalties: Good Cause Interest: Good Cause	
Utah	Penalties: Good Cause Interest: Good Cause	
Vermont	Penalties: Any reason Interest: Any reason	
Virginia	Penalties: Good Cause *or* Department Fault Interest: Department Fault	
Washington	Penalties: Good Cause Interest: Department Fault	
West Virginia	Penalties: Good Cause, Department Fault, *or* Uncollectible Interest: Department Fault	
Wisconsin	Penalties: Department Fault Interest: Department Fault (rates also may be reduced for equitable reasons (Applies to income tax only))	
Wyoming	Penalties: Good Cause Interest: No	

Installment Payments

Many states allow taxpayers to pay past due taxes in installments, rather than in a lump sum payment. Some states require a showing of financial hardship or have other requirements that must be met before entering into an installment agreement. Other states merely give the taxing body the authority to enter agreements at its own discretion.

For states that allow installment payments, a written installment agreement is usually required. The agreement generally may be terminated by the state if the taxpayer fails to comply with the terms of the agreement, or fails to comply with other tax laws of the state. Some states may also terminate based on other factors, such as an improvement in the taxpayer's financial condition.

Although some states allow installment payments under the state's taxpayers' bill of rights, this chart identifies those states that have formal, statutory or regulatory, provisions regarding installment payments. This chart does not address estimated tax payments or property tax payments.

Jurisdiction	Installment Payment Provisions	Comment
Alabama	Installments allowed only after final assessment and termination of appeals.	Maximum length is 12 months. May be terminated for change in financial condition.
Alaska	No formal provisions. However, for state oil and gas tax the Department is authorized to provide for installment payments.	
Arizona	Installments allowed.	Financial report must be filed and taxpayer must be current in all filings.
Arkansas	Installments allowed only if liability is less than $2,000.	
California	FTB - Installments allowed. SBE - Installments allowed.	The FTB must enter into an agreement to accept full payment of personal income tax liability in installments if all of the following apply: (1) liability, excluding interest, penalties, and additions, is $10,000 or less; (2) within last five years taxpayer has not failed to file a return, not failed to make a payment, or entered into an installment agreement; (3) taxpayer cannot currently pay liability; (4) the installment agreement is for a maximum of three years; and (5) taxpayer complies with tax law provisions while agreement is in effect. For a variety of taxes and fees it administers, the California Department of Tax and Fee Administration may enter into installment agreements for taxes, penalties and interest.
Colorado	No formal provisions. However, the Department will accept installment payments before proceeding to other collection methods.	

Jurisdiction	Installment Payment Provisions	Comment
Connecticut	No formal provisions.	
Delaware	No formal provisions. However, the Division of Revenue may allow payments on an installment basis.	Taxpayers should contact the local office of the Delaware Division of Revenue for details about completing an Installment Agreement Request.
District of Columbia	No formal provisions. However, installment payments may be part of an agreement in compromise.	
Florida	Installments allowed.	
Georgia	No formal provisions.	Taxpayers should contact the Georgia Department of Revenue to request a payment agreement.
Hawaii	Installments allowed.	
Idaho	Installments allowed.	
Illinois	Installments allowed.	
Indiana	No formal provisions. Although there is no official policy, according to the Indiana Department of Revenue, the Department's Collection Division will work with all taxpayers to help them comply with the law.	
Iowa	Installments allowed.	Extreme financial hardship required. Penalties and interest must be included.
Kansas	Installments allowed.	Length and condition determined by taxpayer's financial condition.
Kentucky	Installments allowed.	20% collection fee may be imposed. May be terminated for change in financial condition.
Louisiana	Louisiana law provides for payment of past due taxes by installment with regard to real and personal property.	
Maine	No formal provisions.	
Maryland	Installments allowed only if taxpayer is current with all filings.	
Massachusetts	Installments allowed.	May be terminated if significant change in financial condition.
Michigan	No formal provision, however, taxpayers who meet certain requirement are allowed to make installment payments.	Qualifying taxpayers may be required to complete a Collection Information Statement, which lists their income, expenses, assets, and liabilities. Such taxpayers also are required to sign an Installment Agreement, which includes a payment amount determined by the Department of Treasury. Taxpayers who are granted installment agreements must file and pay all taxes and estimated payments when they are due. Penalties and interest continue to accrue.

Jurisdiction	Installment Payment Provisions	Comment
Minnesota	Installments allowed.	Taxpayers must submit a financial statement.
Mississippi	Installments allowed for personal income tax, otherwise no formal provisions.	
Missouri	An agreement in compromise may allow for installment payments.	
Montana	No formal provisions.	
Nebraska	Installments allowed.	
Nevada	Installments allowed.	Maximum length is 12 months.
New Hampshire	Installments allowed to facilitate the collection of delinquent taxes.	
New Jersey	Installments allowed.	
New Mexico	Installments allowed.	Security may be required. Maximum length is 5 years.
New York	Installments allowed.	May be terminated for change in financial condition.
North Carolina	Installments allowed.	Penalties may be waived in agreement. May be terminated for change in financial condition.
North Dakota	No formal provisions. However, the Accounts Receivable Section of the Office of the State Tax Commissioner may allow payment plans to collect delinquent taxes.	
Ohio	Installments allowed for delinquent real and personal property taxes, otherwise no formal provisions.	
Oklahoma	Installments allowed only when continued business operations are enjoined.	
Oregon	Installments allowed.	May be terminated if significant change in financial condition.
Pennsylvania	Installments allowed with approval of state treasurer.	May be terminated if significant change in financial condition. Maximum length is 7 years.
Rhode Island	A taxpayer who is unable to pay the tax liability in full may request an installment agreement specifying the amount of payments possible.	Taxpayer must review Instructions to Form RI 9465, Installment Agreement Request. Within 30 days, the Division of Taxation will notify the taxpayer whether the request is approved or denied, or if more information is needed.
South Carolina	Installments allowed.	Maximum length is 1 year.
South Dakota	No formal provisions.	
Tennessee	Installments allowed.	

Jurisdiction	Installment Payment Provisions	Comment
Texas	Installments allowed.	Maximum length is 3 years.
Utah	Installments allowed.	May be terminated if substantial change in financial condition.
Vermont	No formal provisions.	
Virginia	Installments allowed.	May be terminated if collection is in jeopardy or significant change in financial condition.
Washington	No formal provisions. However, taxpayers for whom immediate payment of taxes will create an extreme financial hardship may ask the Department of Revenue about a payment plan.	Taxpayers will be asked to provide financial records to demonstrate their inability to pay the taxes in full. In most cases, payment plans for delinquent taxes require a tax warrant to be issued and filed.
West Virginia	Installments allowed.	
Wisconsin	Installments allowed.	Application must include reasons for installments and proposed payment plan.
Wyoming	Installments allowed if payment would result in severe inconvenience.	

Interest Rates on Overpayments—2020

Interest rates on overpayments are set either by statute or by regulation pursuant to a statutory formula. Interest rates based on the prevailing federal short-term rate (STR), as determined by Internal Revenue Code Sec. 6621(b), or the prevailing prime or discount rate at leading commercial banks generally are rounded to the nearest whole number. This chart shows the interest rate that is imposed by each state and the District of Columbia on an annual or quarterly basis for the overpayment of income tax.

Jurisdiction	Interest Rates on Overpayments—2020	Comment
Alabama	Jan-Mar: 5% Apr-June: 5% Jul-Sep: 3%	Adjusted quarterly.
Arizona	Jan-Mar: 5% Apr-Jun: 5% Jul-Sep: 3%	Adjusted quarterly.
Arkansas	10%	Rate specified in statute.
California	5%	Jan-Jun 2021: 3% Adjusted semiannually.
Colorado	7%	Adjusted annually.
Connecticut	8% (2/3 of 1% each month)	Rate specified in statute.
Delaware	6% (1/2 of 1% per month).	Rate specified in statute.
District of Columbia	1% above the primary credit discount rate for the Richmond Federal Reserve Bank as of the previous September 30, rounded to the nearest whole number, but not to exceed 6% in the aggregate.	Rate specified in statute.
Georgia	7.75%	
Hawaii	4% (1/3 of 1% per month).	Rate specified in statute.
Idaho	5%	Adjusted annually. **2021:** 2%
Illinois	Jan-Jul: 5% Jul-Dec: 3%	Adjusted semiannually.
Indiana	4%	Adjusted annually.
Iowa	7%	Adjusted annually. **2021 Rate:** 6%
Kansas	6%	4% for 2021 tax year. Adjusted annually.
Kentucky	3%	1% for 2021 tax year. Adjusted annually.
Louisiana	5.75%	Adjusted annually. Beginning January 1, 2022, interest rate on refunds is set at 3% above the judicial rate.

Jurisdiction	Interest Rates on Overpayments—2020	Comment
Maine	7%	5% for 2021. Adjusted annually.
Maryland	10.5% or 3% above prime, whichever is greater.	2021: 10% or 3% above prime, whichever is greater. 2022: 9.5% or 3% above prime, whichever is greater. 2023 and after: 9% or 3% above prime, whichever is greater.
Massachusetts	Jan-Mar: 4% Apr-Jun: 4% Jul-Sep: 2% Oct-Dec: 2%	Adjusted quarterly.
Michigan	Jan-Jun: 6.4% Jul-Dec: 5.63%	Jan-Jun 2021: 4.25% Adjusted semiannually.
Minnesota	5%	Adjusted annually.
Mississippi	9.6%	
Missouri	Jan-Mar: 2.1.% Apr-Jun: 2.0% Jul-Sep: 1.9% Oct-Dec: 1.8%	Jan-Mar 2021: 1.2.% Adjusted quarterly.
Montana	5%	Adjusted annually.
Nebraska	5%	3% for tax years after 2020. Adjusted biennially.
New Hampshire	4%	For 2021, the rate will be 2%. Adjusted annually.
New Jersey	4.75%	If tax is not refunded within 6 months, interest on overpayments is paid at the prime rate compounded annually. Rate adjusted annually.
New Mexico	Jan-Mar: 5% Apr-Jun: 5% Jul-Sep: 3% Oct-Dec: 3%	Adjusted quarterly.
New York	Jan-Mar: 4%	Adjusted quarterly.
North Carolina	Jan-Jun: 5% Jul-Dec: 5%	Adjusted semiannually.
North Dakota	12%	Rate specified in statute.
Ohio	5%	Adjusted annually. **2021:** 3%
Oklahoma	15%	Rate specified in statute.
Oregon	6% 10% for tier 2 interest.	
Pennsylvania	5%	Adjusted annually.
Rhode Island	5%	3.25% for 2021. Adjusted annually.

Jurisdiction	Interest Rates on Overpayments—2020	Comment
South Carolina	Jan-Mar: 5%	Adjusted quarterly. Rates reduced by 3% through June 30, 2020.
Tennessee	July 2019-June 2020: 9.5%	Adjusted annually.
Utah	4%	**2021:** 2% Adjusted annually.
Vermont	5.5%	Adjusted annually.
Virginia	Jan-Mar: 7%	Adjusted quarterly.
West Virginia	Jan-Dec: 7.75%	Adjusted annually.
Wisconsin	3%	Rate specified in statute.

Interest Rates on Underpayments—2020

Interest rates on underpayments are set either by statute or by regulation pursuant to a statutory formula. Interest rates based on the prevailing federal short-term rate (STR), as determined by Internal Revenue Code Sec. 6621(b), or the prevailing prime or discount rate at leading commercial banks generally are rounded to the nearest whole number. This chart shows the interest rate that is imposed by each state and the District of Columbia on an annual or quarterly basis for the underpayment of income tax.

Jurisdiction	Interest Rates on Underpayments—2020	Comment
Alabama	Jan-Mar: 5% Apr-June: 5% Jul-Sep: 3%	Adjusted quarterly.
Arizona	Jan-Mar: 5% Apr-Jun: 5% Jul-Sep: 3%	Adjusted quarterly.
Arkansas	10%	Rate specified in statute.
California	5%	Jan-Jun 2021: 3% Adjusted semiannually.
Colorado	7%	4% if paid within 30 days of notice of underpayment, or if cured voluntarily without notification. Adjusted annually.
Connecticut	12% (1% each month)	Rate specified in statute.
Delaware	6% (1/2 of 1% per month).	Rate specified in statute.
District of Columbia	10%	Rate specified in statute.
Georgia	7.75%	
Hawaii	8% (2/3 of 1% per month).	Rate specified in statute.
Idaho	5%	Adjusted annually. **2021:** 2%
Illinois	Jan-Jul: 5% Jul-Dec: 3%	Adjusted semiannually.
Indiana	4%	Adjusted annually.
Iowa	7%	Adjusted annually. **2021 Rate:** 6%
Kansas	6%	4% for 2021 tax year. Adjusted annually.
Kentucky	7%	5% for 2021 tax year. Adjusted annually.

Jurisdiction	Interest Rates on Underpayments—2020	Comment
Louisiana	8.75%	Adjusted annually. **COVID-19 relief:** Penalties and interest for late filing and late payment will be waived for returns with an original due date between March 11, 2020, and July 15, 2020, if the delay was due to COVID-19. The waiver applies to taxpayers whose health was impacted by COVID-19, or taxpayers who relied on a tax preparer whose health was impacted by COVID-19, if the taxpayer or tax preparer was diagnosed with COVID-19 between March 11, 2020, and July 15, 2020. The waiver will not apply to any tax return filed or any tax payment submitted after November 15, 2020.
Maine	7%	5% for 2021. Adjusted annually.
Maryland	10.5% or 3% above prime, whichever is greater.	2021: 10% or 3% above prime, whichever is greater. 2022: 9.5% or 3% above prime, whichever is greater. 2023 and after: 9% or 3% above prime, whichever is greater.
Massachusetts	Jan-Mar: 6% Apr-Jun: 6% Jul-Sep: 4% Oct-Dec: 4%	Compounded daily and adjusted quarterly.
Michigan	Jan-Jun: 6.4% Jul-Dec: 5.63%	Jan-Jun 2021: 4.25% Adjusted semiannually.
Minnesota	5%	Adjusted annually.
Mississippi	9.6%	
Missouri	5%	2021: 3% Adjusted quarterly.
Montana	5%	Adjusted annually.
Nebraska	5%	3% for tax years after 2020. Adjusted biennially.
New Hampshire	7%	For 2021, the rate will be 5%. Adjusted annually.
New Jersey	6.25%	Quarterly adjustments allowed if prime rate varies by more than 1% from previously determined rate.
New Mexico	Jan-Mar: 5% Apr-Jun: 5% Jul-Sep: 3% Oct-Dec: 3%	Adjusted quarterly.
New York	Jan-Mar: 7.5%	Adjusted quarterly.
North Carolina	Jan-Jun: 5% Jul-Dec: 5%	Adjusted semiannually.

Jurisdiction	Interest Rates on Underpayments—2020	Comment
North Dakota	12%	Rate specified in statute.
Ohio	5%	Adjusted annually. **2021:** 3%
Oklahoma	15%	Rate specified in statute.
Oregon	6% 10% for tier 2 interest.	
Pennsylvania	5%	Adjusted annually.
Rhode Island	18%	18% for 2021. Adjusted annually.
South Carolina	Jan-Mar: 5%	Adjusted quarterly.
Tennessee	July 2019-June 2020: 9.5%	Adjusted annually.
Utah	4%	**2021:** 2% Adjusted annually.
Vermont	7.5%	Adjusted annually.
Virginia	Jan-Mar: 7%	Adjusted quarterly.
West Virginia	Jan-Dec: 9.25%	Adjusted annually.
Wisconsin	18% (delinquent) 12% (nondelinquent)	Rate specified in statute.

Interest Rates on Overpayments—2019

Interest rates on overpayments are set either by statute or by regulation pursuant to a statutory formula. Interest rates based on the prevailing federal short-term rate (STR), as determined by Internal Revenue Code Sec. 6621(b), or the prevailing prime or discount rate at leading commercial banks generally are rounded to the nearest whole number. This chart shows the interest rate that is imposed by each state and the District of Columbia on an annual or quarterly basis for the overpayment of income tax.

Jurisdiction	Interest Rates on Overpayments—2019	Comment
Alabama	Jan-Mar: 6% Apr-June: 6% Jul-Sep: 5% Oct-Dec: 5%	Adjusted quarterly.
Arizona	Jan-Mar: 6% Apr-Jun: 6% Jul-Sep: 5% Oct-Dec: 5%	Adjusted quarterly.
Arkansas	10%	Rate specified in statute.
California	Jan-Jun: 5% Jul-Dec: 6%	Adjusted semiannually.
Colorado	7%	Adjusted annually.
Connecticut	8% (2/3 of 1% each month)	Rate specified in statute.
Delaware	6% (1/2 of 1% per month).	Rate specified in statute.
District of Columbia	1% above the primary credit discount rate for the Richmond Federal Reserve Bank as of the previous September 30, rounded to the nearest whole number, but not to exceed 6% in the aggregate.	Rate specified in statute.
Georgia	7.5%	
Hawaii	4% (1/3 of 1% per month).	Rate specified in statute.
Idaho	5%	Adjusted annually.
Illinois	Jan-Jul: 6 Jul-Dec: 5%	Adjusted semiannually.
Indiana	3%	Adjusted annually.
Iowa	6%	Adjusted annually.
Kansas	6%	Adjusted annually.
Kentucky	3%	Adjusted annually.
Louisiana	6%	Adjusted annually.
Maine	6%	Adjusted annually.
Maryland	11% or 3% above prime, whichever is greater.	

Jurisdiction	Interest Rates on Overpayments—2019	Comment
Massachusetts	Jan-Mar: 5% Apr-Jun: 5% Jul-Sep: 4% Oct-Dec: 4%	Adjusted quarterly.
Michigan	Jan-Jun: 5.9% Jul-Dec: 6.39%	Adjusted semiannually.
Minnesota	5%	Adjusted annually.
Mississippi	9.6%	Rate reductions scheduled annually through 2019.
Missouri	Jan-Mar: 1.5% Apr-Jun: 1.7% Jul-Sep: 5.0% Oct-Dec: 5.0%	Adjusted quarterly.
Montana	5%	Adjusted annually.
Nebraska	5%	Adjusted biennially.
New Hampshire	3%	Adjusted annually.
New Jersey	5.25%	If tax is not refunded within 6 months, interest on overpayments is paid at the prime rate compounded annually. Rate adjusted annually.
New Mexico	Jan-Mar: 6% Apr-Jun: 6% Jul-Sep: 5% Oct-Dec: 5%	Adjusted quarterly.
New York	Jan-Mar: 5% Apr-Jun: 5% Jul-Sep: 4% Oct-Dec: 4%	Adjusted quarterly.
North Carolina	Jan-Jun: 6% Jul-Dec: 5%	Adjusted semiannually.
North Dakota	12%	Rate specified in statute.
Ohio	5%	Adjusted annually.
Oklahoma	15%	Rate specified in statute.
Oregon	6% 10% for tier 2 interest.	
Pennsylvania	6%	Adjusted annually.
Rhode Island	5.25%	Adjusted annually.
South Carolina	Jan-Mar: 6% Apr-Jun: 6% Jul-Sep: 5% Oct-Dec: 5%	Adjusted quarterly. Rates reduced by 3% through June 30, 2020.
Tennessee	July 2018-June 2019: 8.75% July 2019-June 2020: 9.5%	Adjusted annually.
Utah	3%	Adjusted annually.
Vermont	4.75%	Adjusted annually.

Jurisdiction	Interest Rates on Overpayments—2019	Comment
Virginia	Jan-Mar: 8% Apr-Jun: 8% Jul-Sep: 7% Oct-Dec: 7%	Adjusted quarterly.
West Virginia	Jan-Dec: 8.25%	Adjusted annually.
Wisconsin	3%	Rate specified in statute.

Interest Rates on Underpayments—2019

Interest rates on underpayments are set either by statute or by regulation pursuant to a statutory formula. Interest rates based on the prevailing federal short-term rate (STR), as determined by Internal Revenue Code Sec. 6621(b), or the prevailing prime or discount rate at leading commercial banks generally are rounded to the nearest whole number. This chart shows the interest rate that is imposed by each state and the District of Columbia on an annual or quarterly basis for the underpayment of income tax.

Jurisdiction	Interest Rates on Underpayments—2019	Comment
Alabama	Jan-Mar: 6% Apr-June: 6% Jul-Sep: 5% Oct-Dec: 5%	Adjusted quarterly.
Arizona	Jan-Mar: 6% Apr-Jun: 6% Jul-Sep: 5% Oct-Dec: 5%	Adjusted quarterly.
Arkansas	10%	Rate specified in statute.
California	Jan-Jun: 5% Jul-Dec: 6%	Adjusted semiannually.
Colorado	7%	4% if paid within 30 days of notice of underpayment, or if cured voluntarily without notification. Adjusted annually.
Connecticut	12% (1% each month)	Rate specified in statute.
Delaware	6% (1/2 of 1% per month).	Rate specified in statute.
District of Columbia	10%	Rate specified in statute.
Georgia	7.5%	
Hawaii	8% (2/3 of 1% per month).	Rate specified in statute.
Idaho	5%	Adjusted annually.
Illinois	Jan-Jul: 6% Jul-Dec: 5%	Adjusted semiannually.
Indiana	3%	Adjusted annually.
Iowa	7%	Adjusted annually.
Kansas	6%	Adjusted annually.
Kentucky	7%	Adjusted annually.
Louisiana	9%	Adjusted annually.
Maine	6%	Adjusted annually.
Maryland	11% or 3% above prime, whichever is greater.	

Jurisdiction	Interest Rates on Underpayments—2019	Comment
Massachusetts	Jan-Mar: 7% Apr-Jun: 7% Jul-Sep: 6% Oct-Dec: 6%	Compounded daily and adjusted quarterly.
Michigan	Jan-Jun: 5.9% Jul-Dec: 6.39%	Adjusted semiannually.
Minnesota	5%	Adjusted annually.
Mississippi	9.6%	Rate reductions scheduled annually through 2019.
Missouri	5%	Adjusted annually.
Montana	5%	Adjusted annually.
Nebraska	5%	Adjusted biennially.
New Hampshire	6%	Adjusted annually.
New Jersey	8.25%	Quarterly adjustments allowed if prime rate varies by more than 1% from previously determined rate.
New Mexico	Jan-Mar: 6% Apr-Jun: 6% Jul-Sep: 5% Oct-Dec: 5%	Adjusted quarterly.
New York	Jan-Mar: 8.5% Apr-Jun: 8.5% Jul-Sep: 7.5% Oct-Dec: 7.5%	Adjusted quarterly.
North Carolina	Jan-Jun: 6% Jul-Dec: 5%	Adjusted semiannually.
North Dakota	12%	Rate specified in statute.
Ohio	5%	Adjusted annually.
Oklahoma	15%	Rate specified in statute.
Oregon	6% 10% for tier 2 interest.	
Pennsylvania	6%	Adjusted annually.
Rhode Island	18%	Adjusted annually.
South Carolina	Jan-Mar: 6% Apr-Jun: 6% Jul-Sep: 5% Oct-Dec: 5%	Adjusted quarterly.
Tennessee	July 2018-June 2019: 8.75% July 2019-June 2020: 9.5%	Adjusted annually.
Utah	3%	Adjusted annually.
Vermont	6.75%	Adjusted annually.

Jurisdiction	Interest Rates on Underpayments—2019	Comment
Virginia	Jan-Mar: 8% Apr-Jun: 8% Jul-Sep: 7% Oct-Dec: 7%	Adjusted quarterly.
West Virginia	Jan-Dec: 9.75%	Adjusted annually.
Wisconsin	18% (delinquent) 12% (nondelinquent)	Rate specified in statute.

Interest Rates on Overpayments—2018

Interest rates on overpayments are set either by statute or by regulation pursuant to a statutory formula. Interest rates based on the prevailing federal short-term rate (STR), as determined by Internal Revenue Code Sec. 6621(b), or the prevailing prime or discount rate at leading commercial banks generally are rounded to the nearest whole number. This chart shows the interest rate that is imposed by each state and the District of Columbia on an annual or quarterly basis for the overpayment of income tax.

Jurisdiction	Interest Rates on Overpayments—2018	Comment
Alabama	Jan-Mar: 4% Apr-June: 5% Jul-Sep: 5% Oct-Dec: 5%	6% for Jan-Mar 2019. Adjusted quarterly.
Arizona	Jan-Mar: 4% Apr-Jun: 5% Jul-Sep: 5% Oct-Dec: 5%	Adjusted quarterly.
Arkansas	10%	Rate specified in statute.
California	Jan-Dec: 4%	5% for Jan-Jun 2019. Adjusted semiannually.
Colorado	7%	Adjusted annually.
Connecticut	8% (2/3 of 1% each month)	Rate specified in statute.
Delaware	6% (1/2 of 1% per month).	Rate specified in statute.
District of Columbia	1% above the primary credit discount rate for the Richmond Federal Reserve Bank as of the previous September 30, rounded to the nearest whole number, but not to exceed 6% in the aggregate.	Rate specified in statute.
Georgia	7.5%	
Hawaii	4% (1/3 of 1% per month).	Rate specified in statute.
Idaho	4%	5% for 2019. Adjusted annually.
Illinois	Jan-Jul: 4% Jul-Dec: 5%	Jan-Jul 2019: 6% Adjusted semiannually.
Indiana	3%	Adjusted annually.
Iowa	6%	Adjusted annually.
Kansas	5%	Adjusted annually.
Kentucky	2%	Adjusted annually.
Louisiana	5%	Adjusted annually.
Maine	6%	Adjusted annually.

Jurisdiction	Interest Rates on Overpayments—2018	Comment
Maryland	12% or 3% above prime, whichever is greater.	2019: 11% or 3% above prime, whichever is greater. 2020: 10.5% or 3% above prime, whichever is greater. 2021: 10% or 3% above prime, whichever is greater. 2022: 9.5% or 3% above prime, whichever is greater. 2023 and after: 9% or 3% above prime, whichever is greater.
Massachusetts	Jan-Mar: 3% Apr-Jun: 4% Jul-Sep: 4% Oct-Dec: 4%	Adjusted quarterly.
Michigan	Jan-Jun: 5.15% Jul-Dec: 5.41%	5.9% for Jan-June 2019. Adjusted semiannually.
Minnesota	4%	Adjusted annually.
Mississippi	9.6%	Rate reductions scheduled annually through 2019.
Missouri	Jan-Mar: 0.6% Apr-Jun: 1.0% Jul-Sep: 1.2% Oct-Dec: 1.3%	Adjusted quarterly.
Montana	4%	Adjusted annually.
Nebraska	3%	5% for 2019-2020. Adjusted biennially.
New Hampshire	3%	Adjusted annually.
New Jersey	4.25%	5.25% for 2019. If tax is not refunded within 6 months, interest on overpayments is paid at the prime rate compounded annually. Rate adjusted annually.
New Mexico	Jan-Mar: 4% Apr-Jun: 5% Jul-Sep: 5% Oct-Dec: 5%	Adjusted quarterly.
New York	Jan-Mar: 3% Apr-Jun: 4% Jul-Sep: 4% Oct-Dec: 4%	5% for Jan-Mar 2019. Adjusted quarterly.
North Carolina	Jan-Jun: 5% Jul-Dec: 5%	Jan-Jun 2019: 6% Adjusted semiannually.
North Dakota	12%	Rate specified in statute.
Ohio	4%	**2019 Rate:** 5% Adjusted annually.
Oklahoma	15%	Rate specified in statute.
Oregon	5% 9% for tier 2 interest.	
Pennsylvania	4%	Adjusted annually.

Jurisdiction	Interest Rates on Overpayments—2018	Comment
Rhode Island	4.25%	5.25% for 2019. Adjusted annually.
South Carolina	Jan-Mar: 4% Apr-Jun: 5% Jul-Sep: 5% Oct-Dec: 5%	Adjusted quarterly. Rates reduced by 3% from July 1, 2016, to June 30, 2019.
Tennessee	July 2017-June 2018: 8% July 2018-June 2019: 8.75%	Adjusted annually.
Utah	3%	Adjusted annually.
Vermont	4%	4.75% for 2019. Adjusted annually.
Virginia	Jan-Mar: 6% Apr-Jun: 7% Jul-Sep: 7% Oct-Dec: 7%	Adjusted quarterly.
West Virginia	Jan-Dec: 7.25%	2019: 8.25% Adjusted annually.
Wisconsin	3%	Rate specified in statute.

Interest Rates on Underpayments—2018

Interest rates on underpayments are set either by statute or by regulation pursuant to a statutory formula. Interest rates based on the prevailing federal short-term rate (STR), as determined by Internal Revenue Code Sec. 6621(b), or the prevailing prime or discount rate at leading commercial banks generally are rounded to the nearest whole number. This chart shows the interest rate that is imposed by each state and the District of Columbia on an annual or quarterly basis for the underpayment of income tax.

Jurisdiction	Interest Rates on Underpayments—2018	Comment
Alabama	Jan-Mar: 4% Apr-June: 5% Jul-Sep: 5% Oct-Dec: 5%	6% for Jan-Mar 2019. Adjusted quarterly.
Arizona	Jan-Mar: 4% Apr-Jun: 5% Jul-Sep: 5% Oct-Dec: 5%	Adjusted quarterly.
Arkansas	10%	Rate specified in statute.
California	Jan-Dec: 4%	5% for Jan-Jun 2019. Adjusted semiannually.
Colorado	7%	4% if paid within 30 days of notice of underpayment, or if cured voluntarily without notification. Adjusted annually.
Connecticut	12% (1% each month)	Rate specified in statute.
Delaware	6% (1/2 of 1% per month).	Rate specified in statute.
District of Columbia	10%	Rate specified in statute.
Georgia	7.5%	
Hawaii	8% (2/3 of 1% per month).	Rate specified in statute.
Idaho	4%	5% for 2019. Adjusted annually.
Illinois	Jan-Jul: 4% Jul-Dec: 5%	Jan-Jul 2019: 6% Adjusted semiannually.
Indiana	3%	Adjusted annually.
Iowa	6%	Adjusted annually.
Kansas	5%	Adjusted annually.
Kentucky	6%	7% for 2019. Adjusted annually.
Louisiana	8%	Adjusted annually.
Maine	6%	Adjusted annually.

Jurisdiction	Interest Rates on Underpayments—2018	Comment
Maryland	12% or 3% above prime, whichever is greater.	2019: 11% or 3% above prime, whichever is greater. 2020: 10.5% or 3% above prime, whichever is greater. 2021: 10% or 3% above prime, whichever is greater. 2022: 9.5% or 3% above prime, whichever is greater. 2023 and after: 9% or 3% above prime, whichever is greater.
Massachusetts	Jan-Mar: 5% Apr-Jun: 6% Jul-Sep: 6% Oct-Dec: 6%	Compounded daily and adjusted quarterly.
Michigan	Jan-Jun: 5.15% Jul-Dec: 5.41%	5.9% for Jan-June 2019. Adjusted semiannually.
Minnesota	4%	Adjusted annually.
Mississippi	9.6%	Rate reductions scheduled annually through 2019.
Missouri	4%	Adjusted annually.
Montana	4%	Adjusted annually.
Nebraska	3%	5% for 2019-2020. Adjusted biennially.
New Hampshire	6%	Adjusted annually.
New Jersey	7.25%	8.25% for 2019. Quarterly adjustments allowed if prime rate varies by more than 1% from previously determined rate.
New Mexico	Jan-Mar: 4% Apr-Jun: 5% Jul-Sep: 5% Oct-Dec: 5%	Adjusted quarterly.
New York	Jan-Mar: 7.5% Apr-Jun: 7.5% Jul-Sep: 7.5% Oct-Dec: 7.5%	8.5% for Jan-Mar 2019. Adjusted quarterly.
North Carolina	Jan-Jun: 5% Jul-Dec: 5%	Jan-Jun 2019: 6% Adjusted semiannually.
North Dakota	12%	Rate specified in statute.
Ohio	4%	**2019 Rate:** 5% Adjusted annually.
Oklahoma	15%	Rate specified in statute.
Oregon	5% 9% for tier 2 interest.	
Pennsylvania	4%	Adjusted annually.
Rhode Island	18%	Adjusted annually. Rate will remain unchanged for 2019.

Jurisdiction	Interest Rates on Underpayments—2018	Comment
South Carolina	Jan-Mar: 4% Apr-Jun: 5% Jul-Sep: 5% Oct-Dec: 5%	Adjusted quarterly.
Tennessee	July 2017-June 2018: 8% July 2018-June 2019: 8.75%	Adjusted annually.
Utah	3%	Adjusted annually.
Vermont	6%	6.75% for 2019. Adjusted annually.
Virginia	Jan-Mar: 6% Apr-Jun: 7% Jul-Sep: 7% Oct-Dec: 7%	Adjusted quarterly.
West Virginia	Jan-Dec: 8.75%	2019: 9.75% Adjusted annually.
Wisconsin	18% (delinquent) 12% (nondelinquent)	Rate specified in statute.

Mailing Rules—Delivery Rules

The chart below indicates those states that extend the postmark rule to private delivery services.

Jurisdiction	Delivery Rules	Comment
Alabama	Yes	
Alaska	No	
Arizona	No	
Arkansas	No	
California	Yes	
Colorado	Yes	
Connecticut	Yes	
Delaware	No	
District of Columbia	Yes	
Florida	No	
Georgia	Yes	
Hawaii	Yes	
Idaho	Yes	
Illinois	No	
Indiana	No	
Iowa	No	
Kansas	Yes	
Kentucky	No	
Louisiana	Yes	
Maine	Yes	
Maryland	No	
Massachusetts	Yes	
Michigan	No	
Minnesota	Yes	
Mississippi	No	
Missouri	Yes	
Montana	No	
Nebraska	No	
Nevada	No	
New Hampshire	Yes	

Jurisdiction	Delivery Rules	Comment
New Jersey	Yes	
New Mexico	Yes	
New York	Yes	
North Carolina	No	
North Dakota	Yes	
Ohio	Yes	
Oklahoma	Yes	
Oregon	Yes	
Pennsylvania	No	
Rhode Island	Yes	
South Carolina	Yes	
South Dakota	No	
Tennessee	Yes	
Texas	Yes	
Utah	No	
Vermont	No	
Virginia	No	
Washington	No	
West Virginia	Yes	
Wisconsin	Yes	
Wyoming	No	

Mailing Rules—Postmark

Most states provide that a return or payment is considered timely filed if the return or payment is placed in a properly addressed envelope and postmarked not later than the due date of the return or payment, regardless of when the return or payment is actually received by the tax authority. The chart below indicates those states that follow the postmark rule.

Weekends and holidays: All states provide that when a return or payment is due on a Saturday, Sunday, or legal holiday, the due date is extended to the first business day following the Saturday, Sunday, or legal holiday.

Jurisdiction	Postmark	Comment
Alabama	Yes	
Alaska	Yes	
Arizona	Yes	
Arkansas	Yes	
California	Yes	
Colorado	Yes	
Connecticut	Yes	
Delaware	Yes	
District of Columbia	Yes	
Florida	Yes	
Georgia	Yes	
Hawaii	Yes	
Idaho	Yes	
Illinois	Yes	
Indiana	Yes	
Iowa	Yes	
Kansas	Yes	
Kentucky	Yes	
Louisiana	Yes	
Maine	Yes	
Maryland	Yes	
Massachusetts	Yes	
Michigan	Yes	
Minnesota	Yes	
Mississippi	Yes	

Jurisdiction	Postmark	Comment
Missouri	Yes	
Montana	Yes	
Nebraska	Yes	
Nevada	Yes	
New Hampshire	Yes	
New Jersey	Yes	
New Mexico	Yes	
New York	Yes	
North Carolina	Yes	
North Dakota	Yes	
Ohio	Yes	
Oklahoma	Yes	
Oregon	Yes	
Pennsylvania	Yes	
Rhode Island	Yes	
South Carolina	Yes	
South Dakota	Yes	
Tennessee	Yes	
Texas	Yes	
Utah	Yes	
Vermont	Yes	
Virginia	Yes	
Washington	Yes	
West Virginia	Yes	
Wisconsin	Yes	
Wyoming	Yes	

Managed Auditsw

The following chart indicates whether a state has a managed audit program. Managed audits allow a taxpayer (or qualified third party) to perform an audit under guidelines set by the state.

Jurisdiction	Managed Audit Programs	Comment
Alabama	No	
Arizona	Yes	Managed audit applications may be submitted beginning in 2006.
Arkansas	No	
California	Yes	Pilot program terminated 1/1/03. New program in effect beginning 1/1/04.
Colorado	Yes	
Connecticut	Yes	
District of Columbia	No	
Florida	Yes	State offers Certified Audit Program. Certified audits must be performed by qualified third parties.
Georgia	Yes	Managed audit agreement is unique for each taxpayer.
Hawaii	No	
Idaho	Yes	Taxpayers seeking information on managed audits should contact Idaho State Tax Commission.
Illinois	No	
Indiana	No	
Iowa	No	
Kansas	Yes	
Kentucky	No	
Louisiana	No	
Maine	No	State has no formal provisions but Maine Revenue Services may make informal arrangements to permit the taxpayer to perform some audit procedures.
Maryland	Yes	
Massachusetts	No	
Michigan	Yes	Taxpayers seeking information on managed audits should contact Department of Treasury Audit Discovery Division.

Jurisdiction	Managed Audit Programs	Comment
Minnesota	No	Field auditors may allow taxpayers to examine their own records during the course of a field audit if the auditor believes the taxpayer understands the issue to be examined.
Mississippi	No	
Missouri	No	
Nebraska	No	
Nevada	No	
New Jersey	No	New Jersey utilizes an "effective use tax rate program."
New Mexico	Yes	
New York	No	
North Carolina	Yes	Generally limited to businesses that do not make a large number of retail sales.
North Dakota	No	
Ohio	Yes	
Oklahoma	No	
Pennsylvania	Yes	
Rhode Island	Yes	
South Carolina	No	
South Dakota	No	
Tennessee	No	
Texas	Yes	
Utah	Yes	Specific industries are selected for the self-review program.
Vermont	No	
Virginia	No	
Washington	Yes	
West Virginia	No	
Wisconsin	Yes	Available for sales and use tax.
Wyoming	No	

Record Retention

All states require taxpayers to maintain records to indicate the amount due for each tax administered by the state. Most states specify the period for which these records must be retained, while some states merely require that the records be kept without identifying a retention period.

The chart below indicates the specified record retention period (in years) for each state and tax. The retention period may be extended due to audit, appeal, or agreement.

Jurisdiction	Record Retention	Comment
Alabama	Corporate Income: 3 years Personal Income: 3 years Sales and Use: 3 years Motor Fuels: 3 years Cigarettes/ Tobacco: 3 years Personal Income Withholding: 3 years	
Alaska	Corporate Income: 3 years Motor Fuels: 3 years Cigarettes/Tobacco: 3 years	State does not impose personal income tax, sales and use tax, or personal income withholding tax.
Arizona	Corporate Income: 4 years Personal Income: 4 years Sales and Use: 6 years Motor Fuels: 3 years Cigarettes/ Tobacco: 4 years Personal Income Withholding: Not specified	
Arkansas	Corporate Income: 6 years Personal Income: 6 years Sales and Use: 6 years Motor Fuels: 2 years (certain taxpayers 6 years or until fuel consumed) Cigarettes/ Tobacco: 3 years Personal Income Withholding: 6 years	
California	Corporate Income: not more than 8 years (for adjustment period) Personal Income: not specified Sales and Use: 4 years Motor Fuels: 4 years Cigarettes/ Tobacco: 4 years Personal Income Withholding: not specified	Records must be kept for: the period of time in which the taxpayer's franchise or income tax liability is subject to adjustment, but not to exceed 8 years from the due date; the period of time during which a protest is pending before the FTB; the period of time during which an appeal is pending before the State Board of Equalization; or the period of time during which a refund lawsuit is pending in a state or federal court.
Colorado	Corporate Income: 4 years Personal Income: 4 years Sales and Use: 3 years Motor Fuels: 3 years Cigarettes/ Tobacco: 3 years Personal Income Withholding: 4 years	

Jurisdiction	Record Retention	Comment
Connecticut	Corporate Income: not specified Personal Income: not specified Sales and Use: 3 years Motor Fuels: 3 years Cigarettes/ Tobacco: not specified Personal Income Withholding: 4 years	
Delaware	Corporate Income: 3 years Personal Income: not specified Sales and Use: 3 years (leases of tangible personal property) Motor Fuels: 3 years Cigarettes/ Tobacco: not specified Personal Income Withholding: not specified	State generally does not impose a sales and use tax. Records must be kept for use tax on leases of tangible personal property.
District of Columbia	The District does not specify the retention period.	
Florida	Corporate Income: 3 years Sales and Use: 5 years Motor Fuels: 3 years Cigarettes/ Tobacco: 3 years	State does not impose personal income tax or personal income withholding tax.
Georgia	Corporate Income: 3 years Personal Income: 4 years Sales and Use: 3 years Motor Fuels: 3 years Cigarettes/ Tobacco: 3 years Personal Income Withholding: 4 years	
Hawaii	Corporate Income: 3 years Personal Income: 3 years Sales and Use: 3 years Motor Fuels: 5 years Cigarettes/ Tobacco: 5 years Personal Income Withholding: 3 years	
Idaho	Corporate Income: not specified Personal Income: not specified Sales and Use: 4 years Motor Fuels: 3 years Cigarettes/ Tobacco: cigarette wholesalers, 4 years; tobacco distributors, 5 years Personal Income Withholding: 4 years	
Illinois	Corporate Income: No specific time limit Personal Income: No specific time limit Sales and Use: 3 years Motor Fuels: 4 years Cigarettes/ Tobacco: 3 years Personal Income Withholding: January 31 of the fourth year after the calendar year in which the tax was deducted	
Indiana	Corporate Income: 3 years Personal Income: 3 years Sales and Use: 3 years Motor Fuels: 3 years Cigarettes/ Tobacco: 3 years Personal Income Withholding: 5 years	

Jurisdiction	Record Retention	Comment
Iowa	Corporate Income: 3 years Personal Income: 3 years Sales and Use: 5 years Motor Fuels: 3 years Cigarettes/ Tobacco: 2 years Personal Income Withholding: 3 years	
Kansas	Corporate Income: 3 years Personal Income: 3 years Sales and Use: 3 years Motor Fuels: 3 years Cigarettes/ Tobacco: 3 years Personal Income Withholding: 3 years	
Kentucky	Corporate Income: 4 years Personal Income: 4 years Sales and Use: 4 years Motor Fuels: 5 years Cigarettes/ Tobacco: 4 years Personal Income Withholding: 4 years	
Louisiana	Corporate Income: 3 years Personal Income: 3 years Sales and Use: 3 years Motor Fuels: 2 years Cigarettes/ Tobacco: 3 years Personal Income Withholding: 3 years	
Maine	Corporate Income: 3 years Personal Income: 3 years Sales and Use: 6 years Motor Fuels: 4 years Cigarettes/ Tobacco: 6 years Personal Income Withholding: 6 years	
Maryland	Corporate Income: 10 years (retention period recommended by the Department) Personal Income: 10 years (retention period recommended by the Department) Sales and Use: 4 years Motor Fuels: 4 years Cigarettes/ Tobacco: 6 years Personal Income Withholding: 10 years	
Massachusetts	Corporate Income: 3 years Personal Income: 3 years Sales and Use: 3 years Motor Fuels: 3 years Cigarettes/ Tobacco: 3 years Personal Income Withholding: 3 years	
Michigan	Corporate Income: not specified Personal Income: 6 years Sales and Use: 4 years Motor Fuels: 4 years Cigarettes/Tobacco: 4 years Personal Income Withholding: not specified	
Minnesota	Corporate Income: 4 years Personal Income: 4 years Sales and Use: not specified Motor Fuels: 3.5 years Cigarettes/ Tobacco: 3.5 years (retailers and subjobbers: 1 year; public warehouses: 1 year) Personal Income Withholding: not specified	

Jurisdiction	Record Retention	Comment
Mississippi	Corporate Income: not specified Personal Income: not specified Sales and Use: 3 years Motor Fuels: 3 years Cigarettes/Tobacco: 3 years Personal Income Withholding: 3 years	
Missouri	Corporate Income: 4 years Personal Income: 4 years Sales and Use: 3 years Motor Fuels: 3 years Cigarettes/ Tobacco: 3 years Personal Income Withholding: not specified	
Montana	Corporate Income: 3 years if reproduced or are of no further value Personal Income: 3 years if reproduced or are of no further value Motor Fuels: 3 years Cigarettes/Tobacco: 3 years Lodging Facility Use Tax: 5 years Personal Income Withholding: 5 years	State does not have a sales and use tax.
Nebraska	Corporate Income: not specified Personal Income: not specified Sales and Use: 3 years Motor Fuels: 3 years Cigarettes/ Tobacco: 3 years Personal Income Withholding: not specified	
Nevada	Business Tax: 4 years Sales and Use: 4 years Motor Fuels: 4 years Cigarettes/ Tobacco: 3 years	Business tax imposed. State does not have a corporate tax, personal income tax, or personal income withholding.
New Hampshire	Business Profits Tax: 3 years Business Enterprise Tax: 3 years Meals and Room Tax: 3 years Motor Fuels: 4 years (3 years for retailers) Cigarettes/ Tobacco: 3 years Personal Income Withholding: not specified	State does not impose a sales tax, only a meals and room tax.
New Jersey	Corporate Income: 5 years Personal Income: not specified Sales and Use: 4 years Motor Fuels: 4 years Cigarettes/ Tobacco: 4 years Personal Income Withholding: not specified	
New Mexico	Corporate Income: 3 years Personal Income: 3 years Sales and Use: 3 years Motor Fuels: 3 years Cigarettes/ Tobacco: 3 years Personal Income Withholding: 3 years	
New York	Corporate Income: not specified Personal Income: 3 years Sales and Use: 3 years Motor Fuels: 3 years Cigarettes/ Tobacco: 3 years Personal Income Withholding: 4 years	

Jurisdiction	Record Retention	Comment
North Carolina	Corporate Income: not specified Personal Income: not specified Sales and Use: not specified Motor Fuels: 3 years Cigarettes/Tobacco: 3 years Personal Income Withholding: not specified	
North Dakota	Corporate Income: 3 years Personal Income: 3 years Sales and Use: 3.25 years Motor Fuels: 3 years Cigarettes/ Tobacco: not specified Personal Income Withholding: 3 years	
Ohio	Corporate Income: 4 years Personal Income: 4 years Sales and Use: 4 years Motor Fuels: 4 years Cigarettes/ Tobacco: 3 years Personal Income Withholding: 3 years	
Oklahoma	Corporate Income: not specified Personal Income: not specified Sales and Use: 3 years Motor Fuels: not specified Cigarettes/ Tobacco: 3 years Personal Income Withholding: not specified	
Oregon	Record retention based on variable limitations periods Motor Fuels: 3 years Cigarettes/Tobacco: 5 years	State does not have a sales and use tax.
Pennsylvania	Corporate Income: 3 years Personal Income: 4 years Sales and Use: 3 years Motor Fuels: 2 years Cigarettes/ Tobacco: 4 years Personal Income Withholding: not specified	
Rhode Island	Corporate Income: not specified Personal Income: not specified Sales and Use: 3 years Motor Fuels: not specified Cigarettes/ Tobacco: 3 years Personal Income Withholding: not specified	
South Carolina	Corporate Income: 4 years Personal Income: 4 years Sales and Use: 4 years Motor Fuels: 4 years Cigarettes/ Tobacco: 4 years Personal Income Withholding: 4 years	
South Dakota	Corporate Income: 6 years (banks and financial institutions only) Sales and Use: 3 years Motor Fuels: 3 years Cigarettes/ Tobacco: 3 months	State does not have a personal income tax.
Tennessee	Business and Occupation Tax: 3 years Personal Income: not specified Sales and Use: 3 years Motor Fuels: 3 years Cigarettes/ Tobacco: 3 years Personal Income Withholding: not specified	

Jurisdiction	Record Retention	Comment
Texas	Corporate Income: not specified Sales and Use: 4 years Motor Fuels: 4 years Cigarettes/Tobacco: 4 years	State does not have a personal income tax.
Utah	Corporate Income: not specified Personal Income: not specified Sales and Use: 3 years Motor Fuels: 3 years Cigarettes/ Tobacco: 3 years Personal Income Withholding: not specified	
Vermont	Corporate Income: not specified Personal Income: not specified Sales and Use: 3 years Motor Fuels: 3 years Cigarettes: 6 years Tobacco: 3 years Personal Income Withholding: not specified	
Virginia	Corporate Income: 3 years Personal Income: 3 years Sales and Use: 3 years Motor Fuels: 3 years Cigarettes/ Tobacco: 3 years Personal Income Withholding: 3 years	
Washington	Business and Occupation Tax: 5 years Sales and Use: 5 years Motor Fuels: 5 years Cigarettes/ Tobacco: 5 years	State has a business and occupation tax, not a corporate or personal income tax.
West Virginia	Corporate Income: 3 years (record retention period recommended by the Department) Personal Income: permanently Sales and Use: 3 years Motor Fuels: 3 years Cigarettes/ Tobacco: 3 years Personal Income Withholding: 5 years	
Wisconsin	Corporate Income: 4 years Personal Income: 4 years Sales and Use: 4 years Motor Fuels: not specified Cigarettes/ Tobacco: not specified Personal Income Withholding: not specified	
Wyoming	Corporate Income: not specified Personal Income: not specified Sales and Use: 3 years Motor Fuels: 3 years Cigarettes/ Tobacco: 3 years Personal Income Withholding: not specified	

State Contacts

Jurisdiction	State Contacts	Comment
Alabama	Alabama Department of Revenue Office of the Commissioner P.O. Box 327001 Montgomery, AL 36132-7001 (334) 242-1175 ADOR Website	
Arizona	Arizona Department of Revenue Taxpayer Information and Assistance P.O. Box 29086 Phoenix, AZ 85038-9086 (602) 255-3381 or (800) 352-4090 AZ DOR Website	
Arkansas	Arkansas Department of Finance and Administration Sales and Use Tax Unit P.O. Box 1272 Little Rock, AR 72203-1272 (501) 682-1895 E-mail: sales.tax@rev.state.ar.us AR DFA Website	
California	California State Board of Equalization 450 N Street P.O. Box 942879 Sacramento, CA 94279-001 (800) 400-7115 CA SBE Website	
Colorado	Colorado Department of Revenue 1375 Sherman St. Denver, CO 80261 (303) 238-7378 DOR Website	
Connecticut	Connecticut Department of Revenue Services 25 Sigourney St. Hartford, CT 06106-5032 (860) 297-5962 or (800) 382-9462 (in CT) CT DRS Website	
District of Columbia	Office of Tax and Revenue Office of the Chief Financial Officer 941 N. Capitol St. NE 8th Fl. Washington, DC 20002 (202) 727-4829 E-mail: otr.ocfo@dc.gov DC OTR Website	
Florida	Florida Department of Revenue Taxpayer Services 1379 Blountstown Hwy. Tallahassee, FL 32304-2716 (800) 352-3671 FL DOR Website	

Jurisdiction	State Contacts	Comment
Georgia	Georgia Department of Revenue 1800 Century Blvd, NE Atlanta, GA 30345 (877) 423-6711, option 1 GA DOR Website	
Hawaii	Hawaii Department of Taxation Oahu District Office Princess Ruth Keelikolani Building 830 Punchbowl Street Honolulu, HI 96813-5094 (808) 587-4242 or (800) 222-3229 HI DOT Website	
Idaho	Idaho State Tax Commission P.O. Box 36 800 Park Blvd., Plaza IV Boise, ID 83722-0410 (208) 334-7660 or (800) 972-7660 ID Tax Commission Website	
Illinois	Illinois Department of Revenue P.O. Box 19044 62794-9044 (217) 524-4772 or (800) 732-8866 IL DOR Website	
Indiana	Indiana Department of Revenue 100 N. Senate Ave. Indianapolis, IN 46204 Phone: (317) 233-4015 IN DOR Website	
Iowa	Iowa Department of Revenue Taxpayer Services P.O. Box 10457 Des Moines, IA 50306-0457 (515) 281-3114 or (800) 367-3388 (Iowa, Rock Island, Moline, Omaha) E-mail: idr@iowa.gov IA DOR Website	
Kansas	Kansas Department of Revenue Tax Assistance Docking State Office Building Room 150 915 SW Harrison Street Topeka, KS 66612 (785) 368-8222 KS DOR Website	
Kentucky	Kentucky Department of Revenue 200 Fair Oaks Ln. Frankfort, KY 40602 (502) 564-8139 KY DOR Website	
Louisiana	Louisiana Department of Revenue Sales Tax Division P.O. Box 3138 Baton Rouge, LA 70821-3138 (225) 219-7356 LA DOR Website	

Jurisdiction	State Contacts	Comment
Maine	Maine Department of Revenue Services Sales, Fuel & Special Tax Division P.O. Box 1065 Augusta, ME 04332-1605 (207) 626-9693 Email: sales.tax@maine.gov ME DRS Website	
Maryland	Comptroller of Maryland 110 Carroll St. Annapolis, MD 21411 (410) 260-7980 or (800) MD-TAXES E-mail: taxprohelp@comp.state.md.us MD Comptroller's Website	
Massachusetts	Massachusetts Department of Revenue P.O. Box 7010 Boston, MA 02204 (617) 887-6367 or (800) 392-6089 (within MA) MA DOR Website	
Michigan	Michigan Department of Treasury Lansing, MI 48922 (517) 636-6925 E-mail: treasSUW@michigan.gov MI Dept. of Treasury Website	
Minnesota	Minnesota Department of Revenue 600 North Robert Street St. Paul, MN 55101 (651) 556-3000 MN DOR Website	
Mississippi	Mississippi Department of Revenue P.O. Box 1033 Jackson, MS 39215-1033 (601) 923-7000 MS DOR Website	
Missouri	Missouri Department of Revenue P.O. Box 3300 Jefferson City, MO 65105-3300 (573) 751-2836 E-mail: salesuse@dor.mo.gov MO DOR Website	
Nebraska	Nebraska Department of Revenue Nebraska State Office Building 301 Centennial Mall South P.O. Box 94818 Lincoln, NE 68509-4818 (402) 471-5729 or (800) 742-7474 (in NE & IA) NE DOR Website	
Nevada	Nevada Department of Taxation 1550 College Pkwy., Ste. 115 Carson City, NV 89706 (866) 962-3707 NV DOT Website	
New Jersey	New Jersey Division of Taxation P.O. Box 281 Trenton, NJ 08695-0281 (609) 292-6400 NJ DOT Website	

Jurisdiction	State Contacts	Comment
New Mexico	New Mexico Taxation and Revenue Department 1100 S. St. Francis Dr. Santa Fe, NM 87504-0630 (505) 827-0700 NM TRD Website	
New York	New York State Department of Taxation and Finance W.A. Harriman Campus Albany, NY 12227 (518) 485-2889 or (800) 698-2909 (in NY) DTF Website	
North Carolina	North Carolina Department of Revenue Sales and Use Tax Division P.O. Box 871 Raleigh, NC 27640-0640 (877) 252-3052 NC DOR Website	
North Dakota	North Dakota Office of State Tax Commissioner 600 E. Boulevard Ave. Bismarck, ND 58505-0599 (701) 328-7088 ND Tax Dept. Website	
Ohio	Ohio Department of Taxation Sales and Use Tax Division 4485 Northland Ridge Blvd. Columbus, OH 43229 (888) 405-4039 Fax: (206) 339-9305 OH Dept. of Taxation Website	
Oklahoma	Oklahoma Tax Commission 2501 North Lincoln Boulevard Oklahoma City, OK 73194 (405) 521-3160 OK Tax Commission Website	
Pennsylvania	Pennsylvania Department of Revenue P.O. Box 280905 Harrisburg, PA 17128-0905 (717) 787-1064 PA DOR Website	
Rhode Island	Rhode Island Division of Taxation One Capitol Hill Providence, RI 02908 (401) 222-2950 DOT Website	
South Carolina	South Carolina Department of Revenue 300A Outlet Pointe Boulevard PO Box 125 Columbia, SC 29214 Phone: 803-898-5000 DOR Website	

Jurisdiction	State Contacts	Comment
South Dakota	South Dakota Department of Revenue and Regulation Attn: Business Tax Division 445 East Capitol Ave. Pierre, SD 57501 (605) 773-3311 or (800) 829-9188 Fax: (605) 773-6729 Email: bustax@state.sd.us SD DRR Website	
Tennessee	Tennessee Department of Revenue Andrew Jackson Building, Room 1200 500 Deaderick St. Nashville, TN 37242-1099 (615) 253-0600 or (800) 342-1003 (within TN) E-mail: TN.Revenue@tn.gov TN DOR Website	
Texas	Texas Comptroller of Public Accounts P.O. Box 13528, Capitol Station Austin, TX 78711-3528 (800) 252-5555 (Sales and Use Tax) or (877) 662-8375 (Customer Service) E-mail: tax.help@cpa.state.tx.us; ombudsman@cpa.state.tx.us TX Comptroller Website	
Utah	Utah State Tax Commission 210 North 1950 West Salt Lake City, UT 84134 Phone: (801) 297-2200 or (800) 662-4335 TDD: (801) 297-2020 UT State Tax Commission Website	
Vermont	Vermont Department of Taxes 133 State St. Montpelier, VT 05633 (802) 828-5787 VT DOT Website	
Virginia	Virginia Department of Taxation P.O. Box 1115 Richmond, VA 23218-1115 (804) 367-8037 VA DOT Website	
Washington	Washington State Department of Revenue Taxpayer Account Administration P.O. Box 47476 Olympia, WA 98504-7476 Phone: (800) 647-7706 WA DOR Website	
West Virginia	West Virginia State Tax Department 1206 Quarrier St. Charleston, WV 25301 Phone: (304) 558-3333 or (800) WVA-TAXS (982-8297) WV Tax Dept. Website	
Wisconsin	Wisconsin Department of Revenue 2135 Rimrock Road Madison, WI 53713 (608) 266-2772 WI DOR Website	

Jurisdiction	State Contacts	Comment
Wyoming	Wyoming Department of Revenue Excise Tax Division 122 W. 25th St. Herschler Bldg., 2nd Floor West Cheyenne, WY 82002-0110 (307) 777-5200 or (307) 777-3745 E-Mail: dor@wy.gov WY DOR Website	

Taxpayer Representation

State policies vary as to who is allowed to represent a taxpayer before the tax authority in administrative proceedings and receive confidential taxpayer information. Some states limit taxpayer representation to **licensed attorneys**, while others allow representation by **CPAs or other accountants**. Some states also allow representation by **persons other than attorneys or accountants**, such as enrolled agents (before the IRS) or state recognized agents. Some states allow representation by any person with a valid power of attorney. Most states require a specific form to be filed. Others do not specify a particular form that must be filed, but provide for information that must be included in an authorization. Finally, some states are silent on the issue of a form or required information.

The chart below only reflects taxpayer representation before the taxing authority and administrative proceedings. Representation in judicial proceedings is governed by the laws and rules regulating the practice of law.

Jurisdiction	Taxpayer Representation	Comment
Alabama	Attorney Accountant Other	Form 2848A
Alaska	Attorney Accountant Other	Form 775
Arizona	Attorney Accountant Other (if amount less than $25,000)	Form 285/285 I
Arkansas	Attorney Accountant Other	IRS 2848
California	Attorney (representative authorized but not defined) Accountant (representative authorized but not defined) Other (representative authorized but not defined)	Form FTB 3520/BOE-392
Colorado	Attorney Accountant Other	Form DR 0145
Connecticut	Attorney Accountant Other	Form LGL-001
Delaware	Attorney Accountant Other	IRS 2848/IRS 8821
District of Columbia	Attorney Accountant Other	Form D-2848
Florida	Attorney Accountant Other	Form DR-835

Jurisdiction	Taxpayer Representation	Comment
Georgia	Attorney Accountant Other	Form RD-1061
Hawaii	Attorney Accountant Other	Form N-848
Idaho	Attorney Accountant Other	Document EFO00104
Illinois	Attorney Accountant (may assist in preparation of case for hearing) Other (may assist in preparation of case for hearing)	Form IL-2848
Indiana	Attorney (anyone with a power of attorney may represent) Accountant (anyone with a power of attorney may represent) Other (anyone with a power of attorney may represent)	Form POA-1
Iowa	Attorney (anyone with a power of attorney may represent) Accountant (anyone with a power of attorney may represent) Other (anyone with a power of attorney may represent)	Form IA 2848 (14-101)
Kansas	Attorney (informal proceedings only) Accountant (informal proceedings only) Other (informal proceedings only)	Form DO-10
Kentucky	Attorney Accountant Other	Form 20A110
Louisiana	Attorney Accountant Other	R-7006
Maine	Attorney (informal proceedings only) Accountant (informal proceedings only) Other (informal proceedings only)	Form 2848-ME
Maryland	Attorney Accountant (enrolled agents only) Other (enrolled agents only)	Form not specified
Massachusetts	Attorney Accountant Other	Form M-2848
Michigan	Attorney Accountant Other	Form 151
Minnesota	Attorney Accountant Other	Form REV-184
Mississippi	Attorney	Form 21-002-13

Jurisdiction	Taxpayer Representation	Comment
Missouri	Attorney Accountant Other	Form 2827
Montana	Attorney Accountant Other	Form not specified.
Nebraska	Attorney Accountant Other	Form 33
Nevada	Attorney Accountant Other	Form not specified.
New Hampshire	Attorney Accountant Other	Form DP-2848
New Jersey	Attorney Accountant	Form M-5008
New Mexico	Attorney Accountant Other	No form necessary for state-licensed attorneys or accountants and some enrolled agents; for all others, Form ACD-31102.
New York	Attorney Accountant Other (authorized for certain proceedings only)	Form POA-1
North Carolina	Attorney Accountant (enrolled agents only) Other (enrolled agents only)	Form 58
North Dakota	Attorney Accountant Other	Form 500
Ohio	Attorney Accountant Other	Form TBOR-1
Oklahoma	Attorney Accountant Other	Form BT-129
Oregon	Attorney Accountant Other	Form 150-800-005
Pennsylvania	Attorney Accountant Other	Form REV-677
Rhode Island	Attorney Accountant Other (any person approved by the IRS)	Form RI-2848
South Carolina	Attorney Accountant Other	Form SC 2848

Jurisdiction	Taxpayer Representation	Comment
South Dakota	Attorney Other (certain S corporation property tax appeals)	Form not specified
Tennessee	Attorney (informal proceedings only) Accountant (informal proceedings only) Other (informal proceedings only)	Form RV-2052
Texas	Attorney Accountant Other	Form 01-137
Utah	Attorney Accountant Other	TC-737
Vermont	Attorney Accountant Other	Form PA-1
Virginia	Attorney Accountant Other	Form PAR 101
Washington	Attorney Accountant Other	Form not specified
West Virginia	Attorney Accountant Other	Form WV-2848
Wisconsin	Attorney Accountant Other	Form A-222
Wyoming	Attorney Accountant Other	ETS Form 150

Whole Dollar Reporting

The chart below indicates the states that require whole dollar reporting for corporate and/or personal income taxes, as well as the states that allow the taxpayer the option to use whole dollar reporting. For states in which whole dollar reporting is optional, if the option is chosen, it must be used for all applicable amounts.

Jurisdiction	Whole Dollar Reporting	Comment
Alabama	Required	
Alaska	State does not indicate whether whole dollar reporting is allowed.	Corporate income only; no personal income tax.
Arizona	Required	
Arkansas	Required	
California	Required for FTB; elective for BOE.	
Colorado	Required	
Connecticut	Required	
Delaware	Required	
District of Columbia	Required	
Florida	Required	Corporate income only; no personal income tax.
Georgia	Required	
Hawaii	Required	
Idaho	Required	
Illinois	Required	
Indiana	Required	
Iowa	Required	
Kansas	Required	Required for personal income (silent as to corporate income).
Kentucky	Required	Required for personal income, optional for corporate income.
Louisiana	Required	
Maine	Required	
Maryland	Optional	
Massachusetts	Optional	
Michigan	Required	
Minnesota	Required	
Mississippi	Required	
Missouri	Required	

Jurisdiction	Whole Dollar Reporting	Comment
Montana	Optional	
Nebraska	Required	
Nevada	N/A	State imposes neither a corporate nor a personal income tax.
New Hampshire	Optional	
New Jersey	Optional	
New Mexico	Required	Required for personal income, optional for corporate income.
New York	Optional	
North Carolina	Required	
North Dakota	Required	
Ohio	Optional	
Oklahoma	Required	
Oregon	Required	
Pennsylvania	Required	
Rhode Island	Optional	
South Carolina	Optional	
South Dakota	N/A	State imposes neither a corporate nor a personal income tax.
Tennessee	Required	
Texas	Optional	Corporate income only; no personal income tax.
Utah	Required	
Vermont	Required	
Virginia	Required	
Washington	Optional.	Rounding permitted on Combined Excise Tax Return (business and occupation tax). State imposes neither a corporate nor a personal income tax.
West Virginia	Required	
Wisconsin	Optional	
Wyoming	N/A	State imposes neither a corporate nor a personal income tax.